App

Available

The ARRL Repeater Directory® is powered by **RFinder—the Worldwide Repeater Directory**. Why wait for updates? Get an annual subscription to **RFinder**, and you'll have the latest repeater listings at your fingertips. Always updated! Get access to listings for 55,000+ repeaters in 175+ countries.

RFinder is integrated with EchoLink® on Android™ and iOS. An annual subscription includes access to the directory in the Apps, RT Systems, CHIRP, **web.rfinder.net,** **routes.rfinder.net**, and a growing list of third party applications that use repeater data!

Screenshot of **RFinder** on the RFinder Android Radio.

To get the app:

- Go to **Subscribe.RFinder.net** on your phone's browser.

- Click the Google Play™ or Apple®® App Store logo [in most cases it detects the device and redirects to the app store]. Purchasing on Apple includes your firstyearsubscription, or adds a year if you are already subscribed.

- If you do not have an Android or Apple device, just subscribe on that webpage!

Only $14.99* Annual Subscription. Visit **Subscribe.RFinder.net** for additional subscription options and pricing.
*Price subject to change without notice.

The ARRL
Repeater Directory®
2023 Edition

Repeater Directory® is a registered trademark
of the American Radio Relay League, Inc.

W5SWL Electronics

Premium Quality

RF Connectors
Order Direct!

———— **Wide Selection of Connectors** ————

- UHF & N
- BNC & SMA
- Mini-UHF & FME
- TNC & C
- MC MCX & MMCX
- QMA SMB & SMC
- DIN & Low PIM
- Reverse Polarity
- RF Adapters
- Bulkheads

———— **And Much More!** ————

- Dave's Hobby Shop by W5SWL
- Ham Radio Gadgets
- RF & Technical Parts
- New & Surplus Materials

Order at www.W5SWL.com

Ships Fast From The Arkansas River Valley

TABLE OF CONTENTS

Repeater Listings

United States

Canada

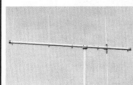

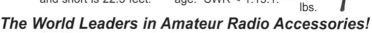

$\overset{\circ}{\text{ICOM}}$®

Handheld

NEW

IC-T10
2M / 70CM / FM

IC-V86
2M / FM

IC-V80 Sport
2M / FM

Analog

IC-2730A
2M / 70CM / FM

IC-2300H
2M / FM

For the love of **ham radio.**

Mobile

IC-V3500
2M / FM

ID-5100A
2M / 70CM / FM / D-STAR

D-STAR ready

IC-7100
HF / 6M / 2M / 70CM Multimode

D-STAR ready

www.icomamerica.com
insidesales@icomamerica.com

Labels and Abbreviations Used in Repeater *Directory* Listings

Location	The nearest city or geographic landmark
Mode	The repeater operating mode
	• ATV – Amateur Television
	• DMR – Digital Mobile Radio
	• DMR/BM – DMR repeaters linked through the BrandMeister network
	• DMR/MARC – DMR repeaters linked through the DMR-MARC network
	• D-STAR® – Digital Smart Technologies for Amateur Radio
	• FM – Analog FM
	• FUSION – Yaesu System Fusion® C4FM digital and analog FM
	• NXDN – An NXDN repeater system
	• P25 – APCO 25
Call Sign	The call sign of the repeater
Output	The repeater output frequency in MHz
Offset	Input frequency separation, plus or minus, in MHz. For example, –0.60000 equals minus 0.6 MHz or 600 kHz

When a listing shows "+" or "-", these common offsets typically apply:

Band *(MHz)*	Offset
50	500 kHz
144	600 kHz
222	1.6 MHz
430	5 MHz
1200	12 MHz

Access	The access method used by the repeater
	• A frequency (such as 100 Hz) indicates analog CTCSS access
	• "CC" followed by a number (such as CC25) is a DMR Color Code
Coordinator	The frequency coordination group that coordinated the repeater

CTCSS and DCS Information

The purpose of CTCSS (PL)™ is to reduce co-channel interference during band openings. CTCSS (PL)™ equipped repeaters respond only to signals having the sub-audible CTCSS tone required for that repeater. These repeaters do not retransmit distant signals without the required tone, and congestion is minimized.

The standard Electronic Industries Association (EIA) tones, in hertz, with their Motorola alphanumeric designators, are as follows:

67.0	- XZ	97.4	- ZB	141.3	- 4A	210.7	- M2
69.3	- WZ	100.0	- 1Z	146.2	- 4B	218.1	- M3
71.9	- XA	103.5	- 1A	151.4	- 5Z	225.7	- M4
74.4	- WA	107.2	- 1B	156.7	- 5A	233.6	- M5
77.0	- XB	110.9	- 2Z	162.2	- 5B	241.8	- M6
79.7	- WB	114.8	- 2A	167.9	- 6Z	250.3	- M7
82.5	- YZ	118.8	- 2B	173.8	- 6A		
85.4	- YA	123.0	- 3Z	179.9	- 6B		
88.5	- YB	127.3	- 3A	186.2	- 7Z		
91.5	- ZZ	131.8	- 3B	192.8	- 7A		
94.8	- ZA	136.5	- 4Z	203.5	- M1		

Some systems use tones not listed in the EIA standard. Motorola designators have been assigned to the most commonly used of these tones: 206.5 (8Z), 229.1 (9Z), and 254.1 (0Z). Some newer amateur transceivers support additional tones of 159.8, 165.5, 171.3, 177.3, 183.5, 189.9, 196.6, and 199.5 hertz.

Some newer amateur gear supports Digital Code Squelch (DCS), a similar form of access control less susceptible to false triggering than CTCSS. DCS codes are designated by three-digit numbers and are enabled in a manner similar to CTCSS tones.

Those wishing to use a CTCSS or DCS equipped system should check equipment specifications prior to purchase to ensure capability for the specified tone(s) or code(s).

About *The ARRL Repeater Directory*®

For decades, *The ARRL Repeater Directory*® has served radio amateurs with an annual "snapshot" of repeater listings. With the *Repeater Directory*, you are only fingertips away from finding repeaters and the users who operate and support the repeaters for their community. Some repeaters are networked with other repeaters, extending your ability to contact radio amateurs across the world. Take the *Repeater Directory* with you when you're traveling for vacation and business. Keep a copy in your automobile glovebox and emergency go-kit. You'll never be out of touch!

In recent years, a proliferation of digital repeaters and related communities maintaining lists of active repeaters has introduced new challenges to producing the annual *Repeater Directory*. Repeater users increasingly turn to online services such as RFinder for more regularly updated sources of repeater listings, and where listings are contributed and maintained by frequency coordinators, digital network databases, repeater owners, and users.

Submit Corrections Online

Since 2017, the listings included in *The Repeater Repeater Directory* have been supplied by RFinder. RFinder offers an online subscription service to its worldwide repeater database (sold separately). ARRL does not curate the listings included in the *Repeater Directory*. We encourage frequency coordinators and repeater owners to review listings published in the annual *Repeater Directory*, and to submit corrections directly to RFinder.

• If you believe an analog repeater is missing from *The ARRL Directory*, please add it at **http://add.rfinder.net** (or in the RFinder app on Android or iOS devices). You do not need to be a registered user to add analog machines.

• If you are a registered RFinder user (or have the trial Android version), you can submit corrections to current analog repeater listings. Just log in at **https://www.rfinder.net/websearch.html**, search for the repeater in question, and then click the pencil icon that appears to the left of the call sign. If you are using the RFinder app, just click on a repeater and press "Submit Update," or request delete at the top of the "Repeater Detail" screen.

• RFinder does not accept corrections or additions for digital repeaters. Instead, RFinder obtains its digital repeater listings from network databases that support DMR, Yaesu System Fusion, D-STAR, Phoenix, UKRepeaters, etc. That information is supplied to the databases directly by the repeater owners, and any corrections must be made by those owners. RFinder updates its digital listings automatically every day, starting at 0500 UTC and typically ending by 0900 UTC.

Subscribe to RFinder by installing the app on iOS or Android. Just search "RFinder" in Google Play or the App Store on Apple devices. You can renew your subscription at **http://subscribe.rfinder.net**.

Need More Help?

Go to **www.arrl.org/repeaters**

Frequency Coordinators

This book includes a listing of groups or individuals for the United States and Canada who are active in frequency coordination. Frequency coordinators are volunteers. The FCC Rules of the Amateur Radio Service define the frequency coordinator as "An entity, recognized in a local or regional area by amateur operators whose stations are eligible to be auxiliary or repeater stations, that recommends transmit/receive channels and associated operating and technical parameters for such stations in order to avoid or minimize potential interference" §97.3(a)(22).

A frequency coordinator will recommend frequencies for a proposed repeater in order to minimize interference with other repeaters and simplex operations. Therefore, anyone considering the installation of a repeater should check with the local frequency coordinator prior to such installation. The FCC Rules include the following provision: "Where the transmissions of a repeater cause harmful interference to another repeater, the two station licensees are equally and fully responsible for resolving the interference unless the operation of one station is recommended by a frequency coordinator and the operation of the other station is not. In that case, the licensee of the non-coordinated repeater has primary responsibility to resolve the interference" § 97.205(c).

Frequency coordinators keep extensive records of repeater input, output, and control frequencies, including those not published in directories (at the owner's request). The frequency listings in this book are supplied by RFinder, the creator of an online directory of amateur radio repeaters worldwide. We encourage frequency coordinators and repeater owners to review listings published in the annual *Repeater Directory*, and to submit corrections to RFinder.

ARRL is not a frequency coordinator, nor does ARRL organize or "certify" coordinators. Publication in the Repeater Directory *does not constitute nor imply endorsement or recognition of the authority of such coordinators, as coordinators derive their authority from the voluntary participation of the entire amateur community in the areas they serve.*

ALABAMA
Alabama Repeater Council
www.alabamarepeatercouncil.org

ALASKA
Alaska Amateur Radio Repeaters
www.alaskarepeaters.kl7.net

ARIZONA
Amateur Radio Council of Arizona
www.azfreqcoord.org

ARKANSAS
Arkansas Repeater Council
www.arkansasrepeatercouncil.org

CALIFORNIA
Northern
Northern Amateur Relay Council of California
www.narcc.org

Southern
(10 meters, 6 meters, 70 centimeters and above)
Southern California Repeater and Remote Base Association
www.scrrba.org

(2 meters only)
Two-Meter Area Spectrum Management Association
www.tasma.org

(222 MHz only)
220 MHz Spectrum Management Association
www.220sma.org

COLORADO
Colorado Council of Amateur Radio Clubs
www.ccarc.net

CONNECTICUT
Connecticut Spectrum Management
www.ctspectrum.com

DELAWARE
The Mid-Atlantic Repeater Council
www.tmarc.org

DISTRICT OF COLUMBIA
The Mid-Atlantic Repeater Council
www.tmarc.org

FLORIDA
Florida Amateur Spectrum Management Association
www.fasma.org

GEORGIA
Southeastern Repeater Association
www.sera.org

HAWAII
Hawaii State Repeater Advisory Council
www.hawaiirepeaters.net

IDAHO
Panhandle
Ken Rau, K7YR
kenr@nwi.net

Southeast
Bill Wheeler, W7RUG
w7rug@arrl.net

Southwest
Larry Smith, W7ZRQ
smith_larry@hotmail.com

ILLINOIS
Illinois Repeater Association
www.ilra.net

INDIANA
Indiana Repeater Council
www.ircinc.org

IOWA
Iowa Repeater Council
www.iowarepeater.org

KANSAS
Kansas Amateur Repeater Council
www.ksrepeater.com

KENTUCKY
Southeastern Repeater Association
www.sera.org

LOUISIANA
Roger Farbe, N5NXL
n5nxl@bellsouth.net

MAINE
New England Spectrum Management Council
www.nesmc.org

MARYLAND
The Mid-Atlantic Repeater Council
www.tmarc.org

MASSACHUSETTS
New England Spectrum Management Council
www.nesmc.org

MICHIGAN

Lower Peninsula
Michigan Area Repeater Council
www.miarc.com

Upper Peninsula
Upper Peninsula Amateur Radio Repeater
Association
www.uparra.org

MINNESOTA
Minnesota Repeater Council
www.mrc.gen.mn.us

MISSISSIPPI
Southeastern Repeater Association
www.sera.org

MISSOURI
Missouri Repeater Council
www.missourirepeater.org

MONTANA
Don Heide, W7MRI
w7mri@arrl.net

NEBRASKA
John Gebuhr, WBØCMC
wb0cmc@arrl.net

NEVADA—SOUTHERN
Southern Nevada Repeater Council
www.snrc.us

NEVADA—NORTHERN
Combined Amateur Relay Council of Nevada
www.carcon.org

NEW HAMPSHIRE
New England Spectrum Management Council
www.nesmc.org

NEW JERSEY
(All counties except Bergen, Essex, Hudson,
Middlesex, Monmouth, Morris, Passaic,
Somerset, and Union.)
Area Repeater Coordination Council
www.arcc-inc.org

NEW JERSEY
(Only Bergen, Essex, Hudson, Middlesex,
Monmouth, Morris, Passaic, Somerset, and
Union counties.)
Metropolitan Coordination Association
www.metrocor.net

NEW MEXICO
New Mexico Frequency Coordination
Committee
www.qsl.net/nmfcc

NEW YORK

Eastern and Central Upstate
Upper New York Repeater Council
www.unyrepco.org

NYC and Long Island
Metropolitan Coordination Association
www.metrocor.net

Northeast
Saint Lawrence Valley Repeater Council
www.slvrc.org

NORTH CAROLINA
Southeastern Repeater Association
www.sera.org

NORTH DAKOTA
Joseph Ferrasa, N7IV
ferrara@srt.com

OHIO
Ohio Repeater Council
www.oarc.com

OKLAHOMA
Oklahoma Repeater Society
www.oklahomarepeatersociety.org

OREGON
Oregon Region Relay Council
www.orrc.org

PENNSYLVANIA

Eastern
Area Repeater Coordination Council
www.arcc-inc.org

Western
Western Pennsylvania Repeater Council
www.wprcinfo.org

PUERTO RICO
Puerto Rico and Virgin Islands Volunteer
Frequency Coordinator
prvi-vfc.org

RHODE ISLAND
New England Spectrum Management
Council
www.nesmc.org

SOUTH CAROLINA
Southeastern Repeater Association
www.sera.org

SOUTH DAKOTA
Richard Neish, W0SIR
neish@itctel.com

TENNESSEE
Southeastern Repeater Association
www.sera.org

TEXAS
Texas VHF/FM Society
www.txvhffm.org

UTAH
Utah VHF Society
utahvhfs.org/frqcoord.html

VERMONT
Vermont Independent Repeater
Coordination Committee
www.ranv.org

VIRGINIA

South of the 38th Parallel and US Highway 33
Southeastern Repeater Association
www.sera.org

North of the 38th Parallel and US Highway 33
The Mid-Atlantic Repeater Council
www.tmarc.org

WASHINGTON

Eastern
Ken Rau, K7YR
krau@nwi.net

Western
Western Washington Amateur Relay
Association
www.wwara.org

WEST VIRGINIA

Eastern Panhandle
The Mid-Atlantic Repeater Council
www.tmarc.org

All Other Areas
Southeastern Repeater Association
www.sera.org

WISCONSIN
Wisconsin Association of Repeaters
www.wi-repeaters.org

WYOMING
Wyoming Repeater Coordinator Group
www.wyoham.com

CANADA

ALBERTA
Ken Oelke, VE6AFO
ve6afo@arrl.net

BRITISH COLUMBIA
British Columbia Amateur Radio
Coordination Council
www.bcarcc.org

MANITOBA
Manitoba Amateur Repeater Coordination
Council
www.winnipegarc.org/marcc/

MARITIME PROVINCES
Ron MacKay, VE1AIC
www.ve1cra.net

NEWFOUNDLAND AND LABRADOR
Ken Whalen, VO1ST
ken.vo1st@gmail.com

ONTARIO

Eastern and Northern
Saint Lawrence Valley Repeater Council
www.slvrc.org

Southwest
Western New York and Southern Ontario
Repeater Council
wnysorc.net

QUEBEC
Radio Amateurs du Quebec
http://ccfq.ca/

SASKATCHEWAN
Saskatchewan Amateur Radio League
www.sarl.ca

Band Plans

Although the FCC rules set aside portions of some bands for specific modes, there's still a need to further organize our space among user groups by "gentlemen's agreements." These agreements, or band plans, usually emerge by consensus of the band occupants, and are sanctioned by a national body like ARRL. For further information on band planning, please contact your ARRL Division Director (see page 15 of any issue of *QST*).

VHF-UHF Band Plans

When considering frequencies for use in conjunction with a proposed repeater, be certain that both the input and output fall within subbands authorized for repeater use, and do not extend past the subband edges. FCC regulation 97.205(b) defines frequencies that are currently available for repeater use.

For example, a 2-meter repeater on exactly 145.50 MHz would be "out of band," as the deviation will put the signal outside of the authorized band segment.

Packet-radio operations under automatic control should be guided by Section 97.109(d) of the FCC Rules.

Regional Frequency Coordination

ARRL encourages regional frequency coordination efforts by amateur groups. Band plans published in *The ARRL Repeater Directory* are recommendations based on a consensus as to good amateur operating practice on a nation-wide basis. In some cases, however, local conditions may dictate a variation from the national band plan. In these cases, the written determination of the regional frequency coordinating body shall prevail and be considered good amateur operating practice in that region.

28.000-29.700 MHz

Please note that this band plan is a general recommendation. Spectrum usage can be different depending upon local and regional coordination differences. Please check with your Frequency Coordinator for information.

28.000-28.070	CW
28.070-28.150	Data/CW
28.120-28.189	Packet/Data/CW
28.190-28.225	Foreign CW beacons
28.200-28.300	Domestic CW beacons (*)
28.300-29.300	Phone
28.680	SSTV
29.300-29.510	Satellites
29.510-29.590	Repeater inputs
29.600	National FM Simplex Frequency
29.610-29.690	Repeater outputs

*User note: In the United States, automatically controlled beacons may only operate on 28.2-28.3 MHz [97.203(d)].

In 1980, the ARRL Board of Directors adopted the following recommendations for CTCSS tones to be voluntarily incorporated by 10-meter repeaters:

Call Area	Tones	Call Area	Tones
W1	131.8/91.5	W7	162.2/110.9
W2	136.5/94.8	W8	167.9/114.8
W3	141.3/97.4	W9	173.8/118.8
W4	146.2/100.0	W0	179.9/123.0
W5	151.4/103.5	VE	127.3/88.5
W6	156.7/107.2	KP4	183.5/85.4
		KV4	186.2/82.5

The following band plan for 6 meters was adopted by the ARRL Board of Directors at its July 1991 meeting.

50-54 MHz

Please note that this band plan is a general recommendation. Spectrum usage can be different depending on location and regional coordination differences. Please check with your Frequency Coordinator for information.

50.0-50.1	CW, beacons
50.060-50.080	beacon subband
50.1-50.3	SSB,CW
50.10-50.125	DX window
50.125	SSB calling
50.3-50.6	All modes
50.4	AM calling frequency
50.6-50.8	Nonvoice communications
50.62	Digital (packet) calling
50.8-51.0	Radio remote control (20-kHz channels)

NOTE: Activities above 51.10 MHz are set on 20-kHz-spaced "even channels"

51.0-51.1	Pacific DX window
51.5-51.6	Simplex (6 channels)
51.12-51.48	Repeater inputs (19 channels)
51.12-51.18	Digital repeater inputs
51.62-51.98	Repeater outputs (19 channels)
51.62-51.68	Digital repeater outputs
52.0-52.48	Repeater inputs (except as noted; 23 channels)
52.02, 52.04	FM simplex
52.2	TEST PAIR (input)
52.5-52.98	Repeater output (except as noted; 23 channels)
52.525	Primary FM simplex
52.54	Secondary FM simplex
52.7	TEST PAIR (output)
53.0-53.48	Repeater inputs (except as noted; 9 channels)
53.0	Base FM simplex
53.02	Simplex
53.1, 53.2	Radio remote control
53.3, 53.4	
53.5-53.98	Repeater outputs (except as noted; 19 channels)
53.5, 53.6	Radio remote control
53.7, 53.8	
53.52-53.9	Simplex

Notes: The following packet radio frequency recommendations were adopted by the ARRL Board of Directors in July 1987.

Duplex pairs to consider for local coordination for uses such as repeaters and meteor scatter:

50.62-51.62	50.68-51.68	50.76-51.76
50.64-51.64	50.72-51.72	50.78-51.78
50.66-51.66	50.74-51.74	

Where duplex packet radio stations are to be co-existed with voice repeaters, use high-in, low-out to provide maximum frequency separation from low-in, high-out voice repeaters.

144-148 MHz

Please note that this band plan is a general recommendation. Spectrum usage can be different depending on location and regional coordination differences. Please check with your Frequency Coordinator for information.

144.00-144.05	EME (CW)
144.05-144.10	General CW and weak signals
144.10-144.20	EME and weak-signal SSB
144.200	SSB calling frequency
144.20-144.275	General SSB operation
144.275-144.300	Propagation beacons
144.30-144.50	OSCAR subband
144.50-144.60	Linear translator inputs
144.60-144.90	FM repeater inputs
144.90-145.10	Weak signal and FM simplex (145.01, 03, 05, 07, 09 are widely used for packet radio)
145.10-145.20	Linear translator outputs
145.20-145.50	FM repeater outputs
145.50-145.80	Miscellaneous and experimental modes
145.80-146.00	OSCAR subband
146.01-146.37	Repeater inputs
146.40-146.58	Simplex (*)
146.52	National Simplex Calling Frequency
146.61-147.39	Repeater outputs
147.42-147.57	Simplex (*)
147.60-147.99	Repeater inputs

NOTES: (*) Due to differences in regional coordination plans the simplex frequencies listed may be repeater inputs/outputs as well. Please check with local coordinators for further information.

1) Automatic/unattended operations should be conducted on 145.01, 145.03, 145.05, 145.07 and 145.09 MHz.

a) 145.01 should be reserved for inter-LAN use.

b) Use of the remaining frequencies should be determined by local user groups.

2) Additional frequencies within the 2-meter band may be designated for packet radio use by local coordinators.

Notes:

Specific VHF/UHF channels recommended above may not be available in all areas of the US.

Prior to regular packet radio use of any VHF/UHF channel, it is advisable to check with the local frequency coordinator. The decision as to how the available channels are to be used should be based on coordination between local packet radio users.

Some areas use 146.40-146.60 and 147.40-147.60 MHz for either simplex or repeater inputs and outputs.

States use differing channel spacings on the 146-148 MHz band. For further information on which states are currently utilizing which spacing structure, see the Offset Map immediately following.

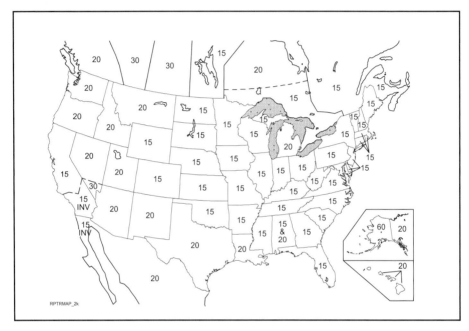

RPTRMAP_2k

Note: This map shows channel spacing in the US and southern Canada. Spacing is in kHz unless otherwise specified. Please check with your Regional Frequency Coordinator for further information.

The following band plan for 222-225 MHz was adopted by the ARRL Board of Directors in July 1991.

222-225 MHz

222.00-222.15	Weak signal modes (No repeater operating)
222.00-222.025	EME
222.05-222.060	Propagation beacons
222.1	SSB & CW calling
222.10-222.150	Weak signal CW & SSB
222.15-222.25	Local coordinator's option: weak signal, ACSB, repeater inputs and control
222.25-223.38	FM repeater inputs only
223.40-223.52	FM simplex
223.50	Simplex calling
223.52-223.64	Digital, packet
223.64-223.70	Links, control
223.71-223.85	Local coordinator's option; FM simplex, packet, repeater outputs
223.85-224.98	Repeater outputs only

Notes: Candidate packet simplex channels shared with FM voice simplex. Check with your local frequency coordinator prior to use. Those channels are:

223.42	223.46
223.44	223.48

Notes:

Specific VHF/UHF channels recommended above may not be available in all areas of the US.

Prior to regular packet radio use of any VHF/UHF channel, it is advisable to check with the local frequency coordinator. The decision as to how the available channels are to be used should be based on coordination between local packet radio users.

420-450 MHz

Please note that this band plan is a general recommendation. Spectrum usage can be different depending on location and regional coordination differences. Please check with your Frequency Coordinator for information.

420.00-426.00	ATV repeater or simplex with 421.25 MHz video carrier, control links and experimental
426.00-432.00	ATV simplex with 427.25 MHz video carrier frequency
432.00-432.07	EME
432.07-432.10	Weak signal CW
432.10	Calling frequency
432.10-432.30	Mixed-mode and weak-signal work
432.30-432.40	Propagation beacons
432.40-433.00	Mixed-mode and weak-signal work
433.00-435.00	Auxiliary/repeater links
435.00-438.00	Satellite only (internationally)
438.00-444.00	ATV repeater input with 439.250-MHz video carrier frequency and repeater links
442.00-445.00	Repeater inputs and outputs (local option)
445.00-447.00	Shared by auxiliary and control links, repeaters and simplex (local option)
446.00	National Simplex Callling Frequency
447.00-450.00	Repeater inputs and outputs (local option)

The following packet radio frequency recommendations were adopted by the ARRL Board of Directors in January 1988.

1) 100-kHz bandwidth channels

430.05	430.35	430.65
430.15	430.45	430.85
430.25	430.55	430.95

2) 25-kHz bandwidth channels

431.025	441.000	441.050
440.975	441.025	441.075

Notes:

Specific VHF/UHF channels recommended above may not be available in all areas of the US.

Prior to regular packet radio use of any VHF/UHF channel, it is advisable to check with the local frequency coordinator. The decision as to how the available channels are to be used should be based on coordination between local packet radio users.

902-928 MHz

Please note that this band plan is a general recommendation. Spectrum usage can be different depending on location and regional coordination differences. Please check with your Frequency Coordinator for information.

The following band plan was adopted by the ARRL Board of Directors in January 1991.

Frequency Range	Mode	Functional Use	Comments
902.000-902.075	FMVother including DV Or CW/SSB	Repeater inputs 25 MHz split paired with those in 927.000-927.075 or Weak signal	12.5 kHz channel spacing Note 2)
902.075-902.100	CW/SSB	Weak signal	
902.100	CW/SSB	Weak signal calling	Regional option
902.100-902.125	CW/SSB	Weak signal	
902.125-903.000	FM/other including DV	Repeater inputs 25 MHz split paired with those in 927.1250-928.0000	12.5 kHz channel spacing
903.000-903.100	CW/SSB	Beacons and weak signal	
903.100	CW/SSB	Weak signal calling	Regional option
903.100-903.400	CW/SSB	Weak signal	
903.400-909.000	Mixed modes	Mixed operations including control links	
909.000-915.000	Analog/digital	Broadband multimedia including ATV, DATV and SS	Notes 3) 4)
915.000-921.000	Analog/digital	Broadband multimedia including ATV, DATV and SS	Notes 3) 4)
921.000-927.000	Analog/digital	Broadband multimedia including ATV, DATV and SS	Notes 3) 4)
927.000-927.075	FM/other including DV	Repeater outputs 25 MHz split paired with those in 902.0000-902.0750	12.5 kHz channel spacing
927.075-927.125	FM/other including DV	Simplex	
927.125-928.000	FM/other including DV	Repeater outputs 25 MHz split paired with those in 902.125-903.000	12.5 kHz channel spacing Notes 5) 6)

Note 1: Significant regional variations in both current band utilization and the intensity and frequency distribution of noise sources preclude one plan that is suitable for all parts of the country. These variations will require many regional frequency coordinators to maintain band plans that differ in some respects from any national plan. As with all band plans, locally coordinated plans always take precedence over any general recommendations such as a national band plan.
Note 2: May be used for either repeater inputs or weak-signal as regional needs dictate
Note 3: Division into channels and/or separation of uses within these segments may be done regionally based on needs and usage, such as for 2 MHz-wide digital TV.
Note 4: These segments may also be designated regionally to accommodate alternative repeater splits.
Note 5: Simplex FM calling frequency 927.500 or regionally selected alternative.
Note 6: Additional FM simplex frequencies may be designated regionally.

1240-1300 MHz

Please note that this band plan is a general recommendation. Spectrum usage can be different depending on location and regional coordination differences. Please check with your Frequency Coordinator for information.

Frequency Range	Suggested Emission Types	Functional Use
1240.000-1246.000	ATV	ATV Channel #1
1246.000-1248.000	FM, digital	Point-to-point links paired with 1258.000-1260.000
1248.000-1252.000	Digital	
1252.000-1258.000	ATV	ATV Channel #2
1258.000-1260.000	FM, digital	Point-to-point links paired with 1246.000-1248.000
1240.000-1260.000	FM ATV	Regional option
1260.000-1270.000	Various	Satellite uplinks, Experimental, Simplex ATV
1270.000-1276.000	FM, digital	Repeater inputs, 25 kHz channel spacing, paired with 1282.000-1288.000
1270.000-1274.000	FM, digital	Repeater inputs, 25 kHz channel spacing, paired with 1290.000-1294.000 (Regional option)
1276.000-1282.000	ATV	ATV Channel #3
1282.000-1288.000	FM, digital	Repeater outputs, 25 kHz channel spacing, paired with 1270.000-1276.000
1288.000-1294.000	Various	Broadband Experimental, Simplex ATV
1290.000-1294.000	FM, digital	Repeater outputs, 25 kHz channel spacing, paired with 1270.000-1274.000 (Regional option)
1294.000-1295.000	FM	FM simplex
	FM	National FM simplex calling frequency 1294.500
1295.000-1297.000		Narrow Band Segment
1295.000-1295.800	Various	Narrow Band Image, Experimental
1295.800-1296.080	CW, SSB, digital	EME
1296.080-1296.200	CW, SSB	Weak Signal
	CW, SSB	CW, SSB calling frequency 1296.100
1296.200-1296.400	CW, digital	Beacons
1296.400-1297.000	Various	General Narrow Band
1297.000-1300.000	Digital	

Note: The need to avoid harmful interference to FAA radars may limit amateur use of certain frequencies in the vicinity of the radars.

2300-2310 and 2390-2450 MHz

Please note that this band plan is a general recommendation. Spectrum usage can be different depending on location and regional coordination differences. Please check with your Frequency Coordinator for information.

Frequency Range	Emission Bandwidth	Functional Use
2300.000-2303.000	0.05 - 1.0 MHz	Analog & Digital, including full duplex; paired with 2390-2393
2303.000-2303.750	< 50 kHz	Analog & Digital; paired with 2393-2393.750
2303.75-2304.000		SSB, CW, digital weak-signal
2304.000-2304.100	3 kHz or less	Weak Signal EME Band
2304.10-2304.300	3 kHz or less	SSB, CW, digital weak-signal (Note 1)
2304.300-2304.400	3 kHz or less	Beacons
2304.400-2304.750	6 kHz or less	SSB, CW, digital weak-signal & NBFM
2304.750-2305.000	< 50 kHz	Analog & Digital; paired with 2394.750-2395
2305.000-2310.000	0.05 - 1.0 MHz	Analog & Digital, paired with 2395-2400 (Note 2)
2310.000-2390.000	**NON-AMATEUR**	
2390.000-2393.000	0.05 - 1.0 MHz	Analog & Digital, including full duplex; paired with 2300-2303
2393.000-2393.750	< 50 kHz	Analog & Digital; paired with 2303-2303.750
2393.750-2394.750		Experimental
2394.750-2395.000	< 50 kHz	Analog & Digital; paired with 2304.750-2305
2395.000-2400.000	0.05 - 1.0 MHz	Analog & Digital, including full duplex; paired with 2305-2310
2400.000-2410.000	6 kHz or less	Amateur Satellite Communications
2410.000-2450.000	22 MHz max.	Broadband Modes (Notes 3, 4)

Note 1: 2304.100 is the National Weak-Signal Calling Frequency
Note 2: 2305 - 2310 is allocated on a primary basis to Wireless Communications Services (Part 27). Amateur operations in this segment, which are secondary, may not be possible in all areas.
Note 3: Broadband segment may be used for any combination of high-speed data (e.g. 802.11 protocols), Amateur Television and other high-bandwidth activities. Division into channels and/or separation of uses within this segment may be done regionally based on needs and usage.
Note 4: 2424.100 is the Japanese EME transmit frequency

3300-3500 MHz

Frequency (MHz)	Emission	Emission Bandwidth (Note 1)	Functional Use
3300.000-3309.000	Analog, Digital	0.1-1.0 MHz	Paired with 3430.0-3439.0; 130 MHz Split
3309.000-3310.000			Experimental
3310.000-3330.000	Analog, Digital	>1.0 MHz	Paired with 3410.0-3430.0; 100 MHz Split
3330.000-3332.000			Experimental
3332.000-3339.000	**Radio Astronomy – Protected (Note 4)**		
3339.000-3345.800	Analog, Digital	0.1-1.0 MHz	Paired with 3439.0-3445.8; 100 MHz Split
3345.800-3352.500	**Radio Astronomy – Protected (Note 4)**		
3352.500-3355.000	Analog, Digital	0.05-0.2 MHz	Paired with 3452.5-3455.0; 100 MHz Split
3355.000-3357.000			Experimental
3357.000-3360.000	Analog, Digital	50 kHz or less	Paired with 3457.0-3460.0
3360.000-3400.000	OFDM, others	22 MHz max.	Broadband Modes (Note 3)
3360.000-3380.000	ATV	20 MHz	Television
3400.000-3410.000		CW, SSB, NBFM	6 kHz or less Amateur Satellite Communications
3400.000-3400.300	CW, SSB, Digital	3 kHz or less	Weak Signal EME
3400.300-3401.000	CW, SSB, Digital	3 kHz or less	Terrestrial Weak Signal Band - Future (Note 2)
3400.100	CW, SSB, Digital		EME Calling Frequency
3410.000-3430.000	Analog, Digital	>1.0 MHz	Paired with 3310.0-3330.0; 100 MHz Split
3430.000-3439.000	Analog, Digital	0.1-1.0 MHz	Paired with 3300.0-3309.0; 130 MHz Split
3439.000-3445.800	Analog, Digital	0.1-1.0 MHz	Paired with 3339.0-3345.8; 100 MHz Split
3445.800-3452.500			Experimental
3452.500-3455.000	Analog, Digital	0.05-0.2 MHz	Paired with 3352.5-3355.0; 100 MHz Split
3455.000-3455.500		100 kHz or less	Crossband linear translator (input or output)
3455.500-3457.000		CW, SSB, FM, Dig	6 kHz or less Terrestrial Weak Signal Band - Legacy (Note 2)
3456.100		6 kHz or less	Weak Signal Terrestrial Calling Frequency

Frequency (MHz)	Emission	Emission Bandwidth (Note 1)	Functional Use
3456.300-3457.000		CW, Digital	1 kHz or less Propagation Beacons
3457.000-3460.000	Analog, Digital	50 kHz or less	Paired with 3357.0-3360.0; 100 MHz Split
3460.000-3500.000		OFDM, others	22 MHz max. Broadband Modes (Note 3)
3460.000-3480.000	20.0	ATV	Amateur Television

Note 1: Includes all other emission modes authorized in the 9 cm amateur band whose necessary bandwidth does not exceed the suggested bandwidths listed.

Note 2: Weak Signal Terrestrial legacy users are encouraged to move to 3400.3 to 3401.0 MHz as time and resources permit.

Note 3: Broadband segments may be used for any combination of high-speed data (e.g. 802.11 protocols), Amateur Television and other high-bandwidth activities. Division into channels and/or separation of uses within these segments may be done regionally based on need and usage.

Note 4: Per ITU RR 5.149 from WRC-07, these band segments are also used for Radio Astronomy. Amateur use of these frequencies should be first coordinated with the National Science Foundation (**esm@nsf.gov**).

5650-5925 MHz

Frequency Range (MHz)	Emission Bandwidth	Functional Use
5650.0-5670.0		Amateur Satellite; Uplink Only
5650.0-5675.0	0.05 - 1.0 MHz	Experimental
5675.0-5750.0	>= 1.0 MHz	Analog & Digital; paired with 5850-5925 MHz (Note 2)
5750.0-5756.0	>= 25 kHz and <1 MHz	Analog & Digital; paired with 5820-5826 MHz
5756.0-5759.0	<= 50 kHz	Analog & Digital; paired with 5826-5829 MHz
5759.0-5760.0	< 6 kHz	SSB, CW, Digital Weak-Signal
5760.0-5760.1	< 3kHz	EME
5760.1-5760.3	< 6 KHz	SSB, CW, Digital Weak-Signal (Note 1)
5760.3-5760.4	< 3 KHz	Beacons
5760.4-5761.0	< 6 KHz	SSB, CW, Digital Weak-Signal
5761.0-5775.0	<=50 kHz	Experimental
5775.0-5800.0	>=100 kHz	Experimental
5800.0-5820.0		Experimental
5820.0-5826.0	>=25 kHz and <1 MHz	Analog & Digital; paired with 5750-5756 MHz
5826.0-5829.0	<=50 kHz	Analog & Digital; paired with 5756-5759 MHz

Frequency Range (MHz)	Emission Bandwidth	Functional Use
5829.0-5850.0	0.05-1.0 MHz	Experimental
5830.0-5850.0		Amateur Satellite; Downlink Only
5850.0-5925.0	>=1.0 MHz	Analog & Digital; paired with 5675-5750 MHz (Note 2)

Note 1: 5760.1 is the National Weak-Signal Calling Frequency.

Note 2: Broadband segment may be used for any combination of high-speed data (eg: 802.11 protocols), Amateur Television and other high-bandwidth activities. Division into channels and/or separation of uses within this segment may be done regionally based on needs and usage.

10.000-10.500 GHz

Frequency Range (MHz)	Emission Bandwidth	Functional Use
10000.00-10050.000		Experimental
10050.000-10100.000	<=100 kHz	Analog & Digital; paired with 10300-10350
10100.000-10115.000	>=25 kHz and <1 MHz	Analog & Digital; paired with 10350-10365
10115.000-10117.000	<=50 kHz	Analog & Digital; paired with 10365-10367
10117.000-10120.000		Experimental
10120.000-10125.000	<=50 kHz	Analog & Digital; paired with 10370-10375
10125.000-10200.000	>=1 MHz	Analog & Digital; paired with 10375-10450 (Note 2)
10200.000-10300.000		Wideband Gunnplexers
10300.000-10350.000	<=100 kHz	Analog & Digital; paired with 10050-10100
10350.000-10365.000	>=25 kHz and <1 MHz	Analog & Digital; paired with 10100-10115
10365.000-10367.000	<=50 kHz	Analog & Digital; paired with 10115-10117
10367.000-10368.300	6 kHz or less	SSB, CW, Digital Weak-Signal & NBFM (Note 1)
10368.300-10368.400	6 kHz or less	Beacons
10368.400-10370.000	6 kHz or less	SSB, CW, Digital Weak-Signal & NBFM
10370.000-10375.000	<=50 kHz	Analog & Digital; paired with 10120-10125
10375.000-10450.000	>=1 MHz	Analog & Digital; paired with 10125-10200 (Note 2)
10450.000-10500.000		Space, Earth & Telecommand Stations

Note 1: 10368.100 is the National Weak-Signal Calling Frequency

Note 2: Broadband segment may be used for any combination of high-speed data (eg: 802.11 protocols), Amateur Television and other high-bandwidth activities. Division into channels and/or separation of uses within this segment may be done regionally based on needs and usage.

Repeater Lingo / Hints

This section explains many of the terms heard on your local repeater.

Autopatch – A device that interfaces the repeater system with the telephone system to extend ham communications over the telephone communications network.

Breaker – A ham who interjects his call sign during a contact in an attempt to get a chance to communicate over a repeater.

Channel – The pair of frequencies (input and output) a repeater operates on.

Closed Repeater – A repeater whose use is limited to certain individuals. These are completely legal under FCC rules.

Control Operator – An individual ham designated to "control" the repeater, as required by FCC regulations.

COR – Carrier-Operated-Relay, a device that, upon sensing a received signal, turns on the repeater's transmitter to repeat the received signal.

Courtesy Tone – A short tone sounded after each repeater transmission to permit other stations to gain access to the repeater before the tone sounds.

Coverage – The geographical area in which the repeater may be used for communications.

CTCSS – Continuous Tone Coded Squelch System, a sub-audible tone system which operates the squelch (COR) of a repeater when the corresponding sub-audible tone is present on a transmitted signal. The squelch on a repeater that uses CTCSS will not activate if the improper CTCSS tone, or no tone, is transmitted.

Crossband – Communications to another frequency band by means of a link interfaced with the repeater.

Desense – Degradation of receiver sensitivity caused by strong unwanted signals reaching the receiver front end.

Duplexer – A device that permits the use of one antenna for both transmitting and receiving, with minimal degradation to either the incoming or outgoing signals.

Frequency Synthesis – A scheme of frequency generation in modern transceivers using digital techniques.

Full Quieting – Signal strength in excess of amount required to mask ambient noise.

Handheld – A portable FM transceiver that is small enough to use and carry in one hand.

Input – The frequency the repeater receiver is tuned to: the frequency that a repeater user transmits on.

Intermod – Interference caused by spurious signals generated by intermodulation distortion in a receiver front end or transmitter power amplifier stage.

Key-Up – Turning on a repeater by transmitting on its input frequency.

LiTZ – Long Tone Zero (LiTZ) Alerting system. Send DTMF zero (0) for at least 3 seconds to request emergency/urgent assistance.

Machine – The complete repeater system.

Mag-Mount – A mobile antenna with a magnetic base that permits quick installation and removal from a motor vehicle.

Offset – The spacing between a repeater's input and output.

Omnidirectional – An antenna system that radiates equally in all directions.

Output – The frequency the repeater transmits on; the frequency that a repeater user receives on.

Picket-Fencing – Rapid flutter on a mobile signal as it travels past an obstruction.

Polarization – The plane an antenna system operates in; most repeaters are vertically polarized.

Reverse Autopatch – A device that interfaces the repeater with the telephone system and permits users of the phone system to call the repeater and converse with on-the-air repeater users.

Reverse Split – A split-channel repeater operating in the opposite direction of the standard.

RPT/R – Abbreviation used after repeater call signs to indicate that the call sign is being used for repeater operation.

Simplex – Communication on one frequency, not via a repeater.

Splinter Frequency – 2-meter repeater channel 15 kHz above or below the formerly standard 30 kHz-spaced channel.

Split Sites – The use of two locations for repeater operation (the receiver is at one site and the transmitter at another), and the two are linked by telephone or radio.

Squelch Tail – The noise burst that follows the short, unmodulated carrier following each repeater transmission.

Time-Out Timer – A device that limits the length of a single repeater transmission (usually 3 minutes).

Tone Pad – A device that generates the standard telephone system tones used for controlling various repeater functions.

About Emergencies

Regardless of the band, mode, or your license class, FCC rules specify that, in case of emergency, the normal rules can be suspended. If you hear an emergency call for help, you should do whatever you can to establish contact with the station needing assistance, and immediately pass the information to the proper authorities. If you are talking with another station and you hear an emergency call for help, stop immediately and take the emergency call.

Location	Mode	Call sign	Output	Input	Access	Coordinator
ALABAMA						
Alabaster	DMR/BM	N4FIV	444.75000	+	CC1	
	DSTAR	N4RON C	145.44000	-		
	DSTAR	N4RON B	442.07500	+		
	DSTAR	N4RON D	1248.60000			
	DSTAR	N4RON A	1293.00000	1273.00000		
	FM	N4PHP	444.55000	+	100.0 Hz	
Albertville	DMR/BM	KO4ATF	147.06000	+	CC5	
Alexander City	DMR/BM	K4YWE	145.33000	-	CC1	
Andalusia	FM	WC4M	147.26000	+	100.0 Hz	
Anniston	DSTAR	KJ4JGK C	145.28000	-		
	DSTAR	WB4GNA C	145.30000	-		
	DSTAR	WB4GNA	442.42500	+		
	DSTAR	WB4GNA B	442.42500	+		
	DSTAR	KJ4JGK B	443.35000	+		
	DSTAR	KJ4JGK	443.35000	+		
	DSTAR	WB4GNA D	1251.00000			
	DSTAR	WB4GNA A	1285.00000	-		
	DSTAR	WB4GNA	1285.00000	1265.00000		
	FM	WB4GNA	147.09000	+	131.8 Hz	
	FM	KF4RGR	444.05000	+	131.8 Hz	
	FM	WB4GNA	444.75000	+	131.8 Hz	
Arab	FM	AK4OV	443.22500	+	77.0 Hz	
Ashland	DMR/BM	N4KYO	444.90000	+	CC1	
	FM	KI4PSG	147.25500	+	131.8 Hz	
Athens	FM	AB4BT	145.15000	-	100.0 Hz	
	FM	KD4NTK	442.85000	+		
	FUSION	AG4OS	438.40000			
	FUSION	AG4OS	439.80000			
	FUSION	AB4BT	441.87500			
Athens Elkmont	DMR/MARC	WV4K	146.86000	-	CC1	
	DMR/MARC	WV4K	442.60000	+	CC1	
	DMR/MARC	WV4K	443.45000	+	CC1	
Auburn	DMR/BM	N4NQV	444.77500	+	CC1	
	FM	KA4Y	147.06000	+	123.0 Hz	
	FM	K4RY	147.24000	+	156.7 Hz	
	FM	W4HOD	147.30000	+	123.0 Hz	
	FM	KM4OKU	442.42000	+	100.0 Hz	
	FM	W4LEE	444.12500	+		
	FM	K4RY	444.80000	+	156.7 Hz	
Battle Ground	FM	W4CFI	147.41500	146.41500	123.0 Hz	
Bay Minette	FM	WB4EMA	147.04500	+	123.0 Hz	
Bessemer		KK4PTC-L	443.00000			
	FM	KA4KUN	444.62000	+	100.0 Hz	
	FUSION	N4WXI	147.50000			
Birmingham	DMR/BM	KC0EQQ	444.45000	+	CC1	
	DMR/BM	KA5GET	444.65000	+	CC1	
	DMR/MARC	W4RKZ	443.67500	+	CC1	
	DMR/MARC	KK4YOE	444.85000	+	CC1	
	DSTAR	KI4SBB C	144.96000	147.46000		
	DSTAR	K4DSO C	145.41000	-		
	DSTAR	KO4TM	442.07500	+		
	DSTAR	KO4TM B	442.07500	+		
	DSTAR	K4DSO	443.20000	+		
	DSTAR	K4DSO B	443.20000	+		
	DSTAR	KI4SBB	443.97500	+		
	DSTAR	KI4SBB B	443.97500	+		
	DSTAR	K4DSO D	1250.00000			
	DSTAR	KI4SBB D	1251.00000			
	DSTAR	KI4SBB A	1282.50000	-		

Location	Mode	Call sign	Output	Input	Access	Coordinator
Birmingham	DSTAR	KI4SBB	1282.50000	1262.50000		
	DSTAR	K4DSO	1283.40000	1263.40000		
	DSTAR	K4DSO A	1283.40000	-		
	DSTAR	KI4SBB	1285.50000	1270.50000		
	FM	W4CUE	146.88000	-	88.5 Hz	Birmingham ARC
	FM	W4TPA	147.28000	+	100.0 Hz	
	FM	N4VSU	443.12500	+	146.2 Hz	
	FM	KK4BSK	443.17500	+		
	FM	KK4BSK	443.45000	+	131.8 Hz	
	FM	KK4BSK	443.70000	+	131.8 Hz	
	FM	KE4ADV	444.42500	+	131.8 Hz	
	FM	AG4ZV	444.82500	+	131.8 Hz	
	FM	W4TPA	444.87500	+	85.4 Hz	
Boaz	FM	KN4UPN	444.20000	+	114.8 Hz	
Brewton	FUSION	WB4ARU	146.97000	-	103.5 Hz	
	FUSION	KI4GGH-R	444.65000	+		
Brilliant	FM	KT4JW	147.04000	+	192.8 Hz	
Brockton	DSTAR	KB1YAC B	449.27500	-		
Buhl	DMR/MARC	K4HDC	443.77500	+	CC1	
Camden	FM	N5GEB	147.13000	+	123.0 Hz	
Cayey	DMR/BM	KP4MSR	447.55000	-	CC1	
Cedar Bluff	FM	WA4OHM	444.40000	+	100.0 Hz	
Chelsea	DMR/BM	KV4S	432.20000	+	CC1	
Citronelle	FM	W4FRG	147.22500	+	203.5 Hz	
Clanton	DSTAR	W4AEC C	145.18000	-		
	DSTAR	W4AEC B	444.37500	+		
	DSTAR	W4AEC	444.37500	+		
	DSTAR	KF4LQK	1285.50000	1265.50000		
	FM	WB4UQT	147.10500	+	123.0 Hz	
	FM	KF4LQK	443.50000	+		
Columbiana	DMR/BM	WA4CYA	444.70000	+	CC1	
	FM	WA4CYA	147.14000	+	156.7 Hz	
	FM	KC4EUA	444.60000	+	156.7 Hz	
Cullman		AK4B-R	145.31000			
	DMR/BM	N4UAI	444.90000	+	CC1	
Curry	FM	KI4GEA	441.80000	+		
Dadeville	DMR/BM	WA4TAL	145.27000	-	CC1	
	DMR/BM	KN4WJC	146.70000	-	CC1	
	DMR/BM	WA4KIK	146.96000	-	CC1	
	DMR/BM	WA4TAL	444.52500	+	CC1	
	FM	KB4MDD	224.24000	-	146.2 Hz	
Daphne	FUSION	WB4CNL	145.56250			
Decatur	FM	W9KOP	442.35000	+		
	FM	W9KOP	442.67500	+		
	FM	W4ATD	443.85000	+		
	FUSION	KN4PHS	145.56250			
	FUSION	WB6IPQ	440.95000			
	FUSION	WB6IPQ	440.97500			
Delta	FM	WX4ZAC	224.38000	-		
	FM	KF4RGR	443.67500	+	203.5 Hz	
Dixons Mills	FM	W4WTG	147.08000	+	210.7 Hz	
Dothan	FM	KC4JBF	147.14000	+	186.2 Hz	
	FM	N4RNU	147.34000	+		
	FM	WB4ZPI	444.77500	+	186.2 Hz	
	FM	WA4MZL	444.90000	+		
Elba	DMR/BM	W4NQ	146.78000	-	CC1	
Enterprise	DSTAR	KJ4OTP C	145.13000	-		
	DSTAR	KJ4OTP B	442.65000	+		
	FM	WD4ROJ	147.24000	+	100.0 Hz	
	FM	KJ4OTP	442.65000	+		
	FUSION	W3STK	145.65000			
Eufaula	FM	WB4MIO	444.92500	+	151.4 Hz	

Location	Mode	Call sign	Output	Input	Access	Coordinator
Falkville	FM	WR4JW	444.32500	+	107.2 Hz	
Fayette	DMR/BM	KK4QXJ	443.07500	+	CC2	
	DSTAR	KK4QXJ C	145.40000	-		
	FM	W4GLE	147.20000	+	110.9 Hz	
	FM	N4GRX	444.85000	+		
Florence	DSTAR	AA1KK B	447.37500	-		
	FM	KF4GZI	147.32000	+	100.0 Hz	
	FM	KF4GZI	444.00000	+	100.0 Hz	
	FM	KF4GZI	444.15000	+	100.0 Hz	
	FM	KQ4RA	444.65000	+	131.8 Hz	
Foley	FM	WA4MZE	147.24000	+		
	FUSION	N4CMM	145.12500			
Forestdale	FM	W4YMW	444.72500	+		
Fort Payne	DSTAR	KI4SAY C	145.44000	-		
	DSTAR	KI4SAY B	443.32500	+		
	DSTAR	KI4SAY D	1253.50000			
	DSTAR	KI4SAY A	1282.50000	-		
	FM	W4DGH	147.27000	+	100.0 Hz	
	FM	W4OZK	444.62500	+	141.3 Hz	
	FM	KF4FWX	444.80000	+	100.0 Hz	
	FUSION	KM4NDU	441.25000	+		
Friendship	FM	KE4LTT	147.20000	+	107.2 Hz	
	FM	KE4LTT	444.57500	+	100.0 Hz	
Gadsden	DSTAR	K4RBC C	145.49000	-		
	DSTAR	K4RBC B	444.77500	+		
	FM	K4VMV	444.67500	+	100.0 Hz	
	FUSION	N4EXO	446.25000			
Gayles	DSTAR	W4CCA B	443.82500	+		
Gaylesville	FM	W4CCA	147.32000	+	100.0 Hz	
Geneva	DSTAR	W4GEN C	145.16000	-		
	FM	W4GEN	145.27000	-	103.5 Hz	
Gold Hill	DMR/BM	KK4ICE	442.17500	+	CC1	
Greenville	DSTAR	K4TNS C	145.19000	-		
	DSTAR	K3WRB C	145.43000	-		
	DSTAR	K4TNS B	442.22500	+		
	DSTAR	K4TNS	442.22500	447.32500		
Grove Hill	FM	AB4BR	147.28000	+	210.7 Hz	
Guntersville	DSTAR	KI4RYX C	145.14000	-		
Gurley	FM	K4DED	442.97500	+	100.0 Hz	
Haleyville	FM	W4ZZA	442.22500	447.32500	203.5 Hz	
Hamilton	FM	KJ4I	147.02000	+	123.0 Hz	
Hanover	FM	K4GR-R	444.22500	+		
Harvest	FM	W4END	146.80500	-	97.4 Hz	AFCRAS
	FM	W4END	224.24000	-		AFCRAS
	FM	W4END	440.77500	+		
	FM	W4END	927.28750	902.28750	97.4 Hz	AFCRAS
	FUSION	W4END	444.52500	+		
Heflin	FM	N4THM	444.17500	+		
Helena	DMR/BM	KC4SIG	442.70000	+	CC1	
	DMR/BM	KC4SIG	444.92500	+	CC1	
	FM	W4SHL	147.32000	+	88.5 Hz	
	FUSION	W4MRL	444.27500	+		
Helicon	FM	W4FSH	442.72500	+	71.9 Hz	
Holtville	DSTAR	K4IZN	444.95000	+	88.5 Hz	
Homer	FM	KL2T	447.20000	-	100.0 Hz	
Hoover		KC4SIG-R	147.43500			
	DMR/MARC	W4RKZ	444.80000	+	CC1	
	FM	KE4CAA	927.28750	902.28750	151.4 Hz	
	FUSION	KG4SLK	146.55000			
Hope Hull	DMR/BM	KN4YCD	433.80000	+	CC1	
Huntsville		W4HSV-R	146.94000			
	DMR/BM	W4FMX	442.27500	+	CC1	

Location	Mode	Call sign	Output	Input	Access	Coordinator
Huntsville	DSTAR	W4WBC C	145.36000	-		
	DSTAR	KI4PPF C	145.43000	-		
	DSTAR	KI4PPF	443.37500	+		
	DSTAR	KI4PPF B	443.37500	+		
	DSTAR	W4WBC B	443.42500	+		
	DSTAR	W4WBC	443.42500	+		
	DSTAR	N4DTC	444.22500	+		
	DSTAR	W4WBC D	1251.00000			
	DSTAR	KI4PPF D	1251.80000			
	DSTAR	W4WBC	1282.50000	1262.50000		
	DSTAR	KI4PPF	1284.00000	1264.00000		
	DSTAR	KI4PPF A	1284.00000	-		
	DSTAR	W4WBC A	1285.00000	-		
	FM	W4HSV	145.33000	-	100.0 Hz	
	FM	N4HSV	146.94000	-	100.0 Hz	
	FM	W4VM	147.10000	+	103.5 Hz	
	FM	WD4CPF	147.18000	+	100.0 Hz	
	FM	W4HMC	147.22000	+	136.5 Hz	
	FM	KB4CRG	147.24000	+	82.5 Hz	
	FM	W4QB	147.30000	+	103.5 Hz	
	FM	W4TCL	147.50500	146.50500	123.0 Hz	
	FM	N4HSV	224.94000	-	100.0 Hz	
	FM	KE4BLC	442.00000	+	203.5 Hz	
	FM	WB4UEE	442.37500	+	156.7 Hz	
	FM	KB4CRG	442.77500	+	107.2 Hz	
	FM	WA4NPL	443.00000	+		
	FM	WA1TDH	443.12500	+	107.2 Hz	
	FM	W4DYN	443.15000	+	103.5 Hz	
	FM	KE4LRX	443.25000	+	103.5 Hz	
	FM	W4VM	443.47500	+	103.5 Hz	
	FM	W4HSV	443.50000	+	110.9 Hz	
	FM	W4XE	443.62500	+	127.3 Hz	
	FM	W4LDX	443.75000	+	186.2 Hz	
	FM	N4WGY-R	443.80000	+	110.9 Hz	
	FM	KD4TFV	444.17500	+	151.4 Hz	
	FM	W4XE	444.30000	+	103.5 Hz	
	FM	W4TCL	444.35000	+		
	FM	W4XE	444.37500	+	100.0 Hz	
	FM	WB4LTT	444.50000	+		
	FM	W4WLD	444.52500	+		
	FM	N4WGY-L	444.75000	+	131.8 Hz	
	FUSION	KE4ROC	147.52000			
	FUSION	KK5H	434.00000			
	FUSION	KN4UIL	441.22500			
Ider	FM	N2EMA	147.04500	+	100.0 Hz	
Jacksonville	DMR/BM	KG4YRU	440.70000	+	CC2	
Jasper	DMR/MARC	N4MYI	443.92500	+	CC1	
	FM	KI4GEA	147.26000	+		
	FM	W4WCA	147.39000	+	110.9 Hz	
	FM	N4MYI	444.05000	+	123.0 Hz	
Jemison	FM	WB4UQT	444.47500	+	100.0 Hz	
Killen	FM	AB4RC	442.47500	+	131.8 Hz	
	FM	KS4QF	444.42500	+	203.5 Hz	
Lagrange	FM	KI4ZP	444.67500	+	156.7 Hz	
Leighton	FM	AC4EG	147.34000	+	100.0 Hz	
Lineville	FM	WB4VBA	444.00000	+		
Madison	DMR/BM	KJ4NYH	443.02500	+	CC2	
	FUSION	N4GV	145.60000			
	FUSION	KN4UIM	441.16250			
Magnolia Springs	DSTAR	KI4SAZ C	145.31000	-		
	DSTAR	KI4SAZ B	444.30000	+		
	DSTAR	KI4SAZ	444.30000	+		

Location	Mode	Call sign	Output	Input	Access	Coordinator
Magnolia Springs	DSTAR	KI4SAZ D	1251.00000			
	DSTAR	KI4SAZ A	1285.00000	-		
	DSTAR	KI4SAZ	1285.00000	1265.00000		
Marion	FM	KD4EXS	147.37500	+	123.0 Hz	
McCalla	DMR/MARC	W4RKZ	443.02500	+	CC1	
Mentone	DSTAR	KI4SAY	443.32500	+		
	DSTAR	KI4SAY	1285.00000	1265.00000		
	FM	W4OZK	224.72000	-	114.8 Hz	
Millport	DSTAR	KN4BOF C	145.24000	-		
Millry	FM	KF4ZLK	147.18000	+	114.8 Hz	
Mobile	DMR/BM	N4FIV	444.78750	+	CC1	
	DMR/BM	N4TAE	444.98750	+	CC1	
	DSTAR	W4IAX C	145.39000	-		
	DSTAR	W4IAX B	444.90000	+		
	FM	N4RGJ	147.01500	+		
	FM	WB4BXM	147.15000	+	103.5 Hz	
	FM	W4IAX	147.30000	+	203.5 Hz	
	FM	WX4MOB	444.52500	+	123.0 Hz	
	FM	W4IAX	444.90000	+		
	FUSION	KF4CLO	145.60000			
Monroeville	FM	WB4UFT	147.16000	+	167.9 Hz	
	FM	K8IDX	444.77500	+	123.0 Hz	
Montgomery	DMR/BM	KK4AXA	443.97500	+	CC1	
	DMR/BM	KG4RCK	444.00000	+	CC1	
	DMR/BM	K4DJL	444.97500	+	CC1	
	DSTAR	W4AP C	146.92000	-		
	DSTAR	W4AP B	443.97500	+		
	DSTAR	W4AP D	1251.00000			
	DSTAR	W4AP A	1284.00000	-		
	FM	W4AP	147.18000	+	123.0 Hz	
	FM	W4AP	444.50000	+	100.0 Hz	
	FM	W4OZK	444.62500	+	141.3 Hz	
Moody	DMR/MARC	KE4CAA	440.56250	+	CC1	
Moulton	FM	N4IDX	442.42500	+	107.2 Hz	
	FM	N4IDX	444.77500	+	107.2 Hz	
Moundville	FM	K4CR	147.22000	+	77.0 Hz	
Muscle Shoals	FM	K4VFO	444.40000	+	79.7 Hz	
Nectar	DMR/BM	W4PCI	147.44500	146.44500	CC1	
	FM	N3AST	443.87500	+	123.0 Hz	
New Market	FM	W4TCL	442.17500	+	100.0 Hz	
NOAA Anniston	WX	KIH58	162.47500			
NOAA Arab	WX	WNG642	162.52500			
NOAA Auburn	WX	WWF54	162.52500			
NOAA Brewton	WX	WNG646	162.47500			
NOAA Columbus	WX	WXM32	162.40000			
NOAA Cullman	WX	WWF66	162.45000			
NOAA Demopolis	WX	WXL72	162.47500			
NOAA Dozier	WX	KIH59	162.55000			
NOAA Florence	WX	KIH57	162.47500			
NOAA Greenville	WX	WNG607	162.42500			
NOAA Henagar	WX	WWF44	162.50000			
NOAA Huntsville	WX	KIH20	162.40000			
NOAA Jackson	WX	WWF55	162.50000			
NOAA Louisville	WX	KIH56	162.47500			
NOAA Mobile	WX	KEC61	162.55000			
NOAA Montgomery						
	WX	KIH55	162.40000			
NOAA Oneonta	WX	WNG606	162.42500			
NOAA Selma	WX	WNG635	162.45000			
NOAA Tuscaloosa						
	WX	KIH60	162.40000			
NOAA Winfield	WX	WWF53	162.52500			

Location	Mode	Call sign	Output	Input	Access	Coordinator
Northport	DMR/MARC	KD9Q	444.17500	+	CC1	
Northwood		AK4B-R	146.31000			
Odenville	NXDN	W4TCT	442.92500	+	162.2 Hz	
Oneonta	DMR/BM	KD4NJA	145.26000	-	CC1	
Opelika	DSTAR	W4LEE C	147.37500	+		
	DSTAR	W4LEE	147.37500	+		
	FM	W4LEE	147.12000	+	123.0 Hz	
	FM	WX4LEE	147.15000	+	123.0 Hz	
Opp	FM	N4SYB	147.21000	+	100.0 Hz	
Parrish	FM	W4WCA	442.30000	+	110.9 Hz	
	FM	WR4Y	443.27500	+	123.0 Hz	
Pelham	FM	W4TPA	444.15000	+		
Pell City	DMR/BM	N4KYO	444.40000	+	CC2	
	FM	N4BRC	444.72500	+	156.7 Hz	
Phenix City	FM	WA4QHN	444.20000	+	123.0 Hz	
	FUSION	KO4CCE	144.40000			
Pinson	FM	KA5GET	442.65000	+	131.8 Hz	
Pointe South Mobile Estates						
		N3FU-R	444.02500			
Powelldale	FM	WD4JRB	444.45000	+		
Quinton	FM	W4AI	444.20000	+	179.9 Hz	
Rainsville	FM	KF4BCR	442.55000	+	100.0 Hz	
Roanoke	DSTAR	KJ4JNX C	145.40000	-		
	DSTAR	KJ4JNX B	444.90000	+		
	DSTAR	KJ4JNX D	1251.60000			
	DSTAR	KJ4JNX A	1283.00000	1303.00000		
	DSTAR	KJ4JNX	1283.00000	1263.00000		
	FM	WD4KTY	147.04000	+		
	FM	KA4KBX	147.27000	+	141.3 Hz	
	FM	KA4KBX	224.92000	-		
	FM	KA4KBX	444.27500	+	141.3 Hz	
	FM	KJ4JNX	444.90000	+		
Robertsdale	FM	WB4EMA	147.09000	+	82.5 Hz	
	FUSION	WD4EGF	146.79000	-		
	FUSION	WD4EGF	147.42500			
Rocky Brook	FM	WB4BYQ	147.06000	+		
Rogersville	FM	KF4GZI	442.02500	+	203.5 Hz	
	FM	KJ4LEL	442.50000	+		
Roxana	FM	W4KEN	224.84000	-		
Russellville	FM	WX4FC	147.21000	+	103.5 Hz	
	FM	WX4FC	147.36000	+	103.5 Hz	
	FM	NV4B	224.34000	-		
	FM	WX4FC	444.67500	+		
Saginaw	FM	NR4J	224.50000	-	100.0 Hz	
Salem	FM	WA4QHN	444.10000	+	123.0 Hz	
Santuck	FM	W4KEN	224.88000	-	103.5 Hz	
Scottsboro	FM	K4NHA	224.58000	-		
Section	FM	K4SCO	147.36000	+	123.0 Hz	
Selma	FM	N4KTX	442.02500	+	100.0 Hz	
Sheffield	DMR/BM	N4GLE	146.88000	-	CC3	
	FM	N4GLE	444.05000	+	103.5 Hz	
Shelby	FM	N4PHP	442.00000	+	100.0 Hz	
	FM	WB4CCQ	444.35000	+		
Shorter	FM	KK4ICE	53.01000	52.01000	123.0 Hz	
	FM	KK4ICE	442.07500	+	123.0 Hz	
Skipperville	FM	KD4KRP	147.03000	+	71.9 Hz	
Somerville	DMR/BM	WR4JW	440.61250	+	CC1	
	DMR/BM	WR4JW	444.70000	+	CC1	
Spanish Fort	DMR/BM	N4FIV	444.98750	+	CC1	
	FM	N4FIV	444.60000	+	203.5 Hz	
Springville	FM	KA5GET	443.65000	+	131.8 Hz	
Stag Run	FM	KB4CRG	444.57500	+		

Location	Mode	Call sign	Output	Input	Access	Coordinator
Sweet Water		KK4QAM-L	445.25000			
Talladega	DSTAR	N4WNL C	145.16000	-		
	FM	W4PIG	224.22000	-	100.0 Hz	
	FM	WD4NOF	927.75000	902.75000	100.0 Hz	
Theodore	DMR/BM	WY5Y	443.50000	+	CC1	
Toney	FUSION	KV4AN	446.02500			
Trafford	FM	W3NH	147.07500	+	67.0 Hz	
Trinity	FM	W4CFI	444.27500	+		
Troy	DMR/MARC	W4NQ	147.07500	+	CC1	
	DMR/MARC	W4DBG	443.00000	+	CC1	
	FM	KT4ROY	145.51000			
Trussville	DMR/BM	KK4YOE	145.04000	146.44000	CC1	
	DMR/BM	KK4YOE	442.10000	+	CC1	
	DSTAR	KK4YOE C	145.04000	146.44000		
	DSTAR	KK4YOE B	442.10000	+		
Tuscaloosa	DMR/BM	W4XI	443.82500	+	CC1	
	DMR/MARC	K4CR	442.37500	+	CC1	
	DMR/MARC	KD9Q	444.90000	+	CC1	
	DSTAR	W4KCQ C	146.60500	-		
	DSTAR	W4TTR B	442.90000	+		
	DSTAR	W4TTR	442.90000	+		
	DSTAR	W4KCQ B	444.07500	+		
	DSTAR	W4KCQ	444.07500	+		
	DSTAR	W4KCQ D	1249.00000			
	DSTAR	W4KCQ A	1284.40000	-		
	DSTAR	W4KCQ	1284.40000	1264.40000		
	FM	KF4IZY	144.98000	147.48000	233.6 Hz	
	FM	KX4I	145.35000	-	91.5 Hz	
	FM	KX4I	145.47000	-	203.5 Hz	
	FM	W4XI	146.82000	-	118.8 Hz	
	FM	KX4I	147.06000	-	179.9 Hz	
	FM	KR4ET	147.24000	+	186.2 Hz	
	FM	W4WYN	147.30000	+	131.8 Hz	
	FM	W4MD	442.15000	+		
	FM	KX4I	442.55000	+	173.8 Hz	
	FM	W4MD	442.95000	+		
	FM	WS4I	443.30000	+	131.8 Hz	
	FM	KX4I	443.57500	+	192.8 Hz	
	FM	KX4I	444.02500	+	203.5 Hz	
	FM	KD9Q	444.57500	+	210.7 Hz	
	FM	N9YAY	444.90000	+		
	FUSION	KN4VZR	145.55000			
Tuscumbia	FM	W4ZZK	145.13000	454.87000	131.8 Hz	
	FM	W4ZZK	443.72500	+	131.8 Hz	
	FM	W4ZZK	444.87500	+	131.8 Hz	
Tuskegee	FM	N4LTX	444.87500	+	123.0 Hz	
Union Hill	FM	W5MEI	442.80000	+	162.2 Hz	
Valley	FUSION	KK4KSN	144.00000			
Valley Head	FUSION	N4GBN	146.55000			
Vernon	DMR/BM	KC4UG	444.50000	+	CC1	
	DSTAR	KC4UG C	145.21000	+		
	DSTAR	KC4UG B	444.50000	+		
	FM	KC4UG	444.40000	+	110.9 Hz	
Vincent	FM	KK4OWL	224.40000	-	218.1 Hz	
Warrior	DMR/MARC	KD4CIF	442.82500	+	CC1	
	DMR/MARC	N4UKE	443.55000	+	CC1	
	FM	KD4CIF	147.12000	+	100.0 Hz	
	FM	W4GQF	224.12000	-		
	FM	KD4CIF	224.44000	-		
	FUSION	KD4CIF	442.57500	+		
Waterloo	FM	KF4GZI	442.12500	+	100.0 Hz	
Wetumpka	DMR/MARC	W4TXM	438.80000	+	CC1	

Location	Mode	Call sign	Output	Input	Access	Coordinator
Wetumpka	FUSION	W4JFF	145.00000			
	FUSION	W4TXM	146.55000			
Windham Springs	FM	KX4I	145.35000	-	91.5 Hz	

ALASKA

Location	Mode	Call sign	Output	Input	Access	Coordinator
Anchorage	DMR/BM	KL7AA	444.20000	+	CC1	
	DMR/BM	KL4NE	448.90000	-	CC1	
	FM	WL7CWE	29.66000	-	110.9 Hz	
	FM	WL7CWE	51.65000	50.65000	103.5 Hz	
	FM	KL7AIR	146.67000	-	103.5 Hz	
	FM	WL7CWA	146.79000	-	100.0 Hz	
	FM	KL7AA	146.94000	-	100.0 Hz	
	FM	KL3K	147.21000	+	123.0 Hz	
	FM	KL7ION	147.30000	+	141.3 Hz	
	FM	KL7AA	224.94000	-		
	FM	WL7CWE	444.85000	+	103.5 Hz	
	FUSION	KL4AN	144.71000	+		
	FUSION	WL4DX	444.00000			
Bethel	FM	AL7YK	146.10000	+	114.8 Hz	
	FM	AL7YK	444.10000	+	100.0 Hz	
Central	FM	AL7FQ	146.82000	-	103.5 Hz	
Chicken	FM	KL7B	147.09000	+		
Delta Junction	DMR/MARC	KL2AV	444.80000	+	CC1	ARC
	FM	KL2AV	146.76000	-	103.5 Hz	
	FM	KL7KC	146.82000	-	103.5 Hz	
	FM	KL2AV	444.70000	+	103.5 Hz	
	FM	KL2AV	449.60000	-	103.5 Hz	
	FM	KL2AV	927.01250	902.01250	114.8 Hz	
Denali Natl Park	FM	KL7KC	146.76000	-	103.5 Hz	
Dot Lake	FM	KL7KC	146.82000	-		
	FM	KL7KC	146.88000	-	103.5 Hz	
Fairbanks	DMR/BM	KL7ET	434.30000	+	CC1	
	DMR/BM	KL7ET	443.30000	+	CC1	
	FM	KL7GNG	146.67000	-	103.5 Hz	
	FM	KL7KC	146.70000	-	103.5 Hz	
	FM	KL7XO	146.79000	-	103.5 Hz	
	FM	KL7KC	146.88000	-	103.5 Hz	
	FM	KL7KC	146.94000	-	103.5 Hz	
	FM	KL7KC	147.12000	+	103.5 Hz	
	FM	KL7EDK	147.30000	+	103.5 Hz	
	FM	KL3K	147.55000	+	123.0 Hz	
	FM	AL7FG	224.88000	-	103.5 Hz	
	FM	KL4BR	448.80000	-		
	FUSION	KL7LK	144.44000			
	FUSION	KL7TC	147.20000			
	FUSION	KL7ET	433.90000			
Fort Richardson	FM	KL7GG	147.39000	+	100.0 Hz	
	FM	KL7GG	444.50000	+	100.0 Hz	
Fox	FM	KL1AC	147.18000	+	123.0 Hz	
Galena	FM	AL2J	146.79000	-	103.5 Hz	
Healy	FM	KL3K	443.30000	+	103.5 Hz	
Homer	DMR/MARC	KL4GR	443.40000	+	CC1	
	FM	WL7PM	146.91000	-		
Houston	FM	KL3K	147.09000	+	123.0 Hz	
Juneau		KL7JVD-L	146.49000			
	DMR/BM	N6YMZ	447.70000	-	CC1	
	FM	WA6AXO	146.88000	-	100.0 Hz	
	FM	KL7PF	147.00000	-		
	FM	KL2ZZ	147.12000	+	123.0 Hz	
	FM	KL7PF	224.04000	-		
	FM	WA6AXO	444.70000	+	141.3 Hz	
Ketchikan	DMR/BM	KL0RG	442.20000	+	CC1	

Location	Mode	Call sign	Output	Input	Access	Coordinator
Ketchikan	DSTAR	KL7FF	147.38000	+		
	FM	KL0RG	146.67000	-		
	FM	KL7GIH	146.79000	-		
	FM	WL7N	444.50000	+		
Kodiak	DMR/BM	KL1KE	441.87500	+	CC1	ARC
	FM	WL7CWZ	146.88000	-	141.3 Hz	
	FM	WL7AML	444.55000	+	136.5 Hz	
	FM	AL7LQ	444.85000	+	141.3 Hz	
Manley Hot Springs						
	FM	KL7KC	147.03000	+	103.5 Hz	
Mendenhall	FM	KL7IWC	147.30000	+		
Nenana	FM	WL7BDO	147.06000	+	103.5 Hz	
Ninilchik	FM	AL7Q	145.79000	+	91.5 Hz	
	FM	AL7Q	443.27500	+	91.5 Hz	
NOAA Althorp Peak						
	WX	KZZ86	162.42500			
NOAA Anchorage	WX	KEC43	162.55000			
NOAA Barrow	WX	KZZ53	162.55000			
NOAA Bede Mountain						
	WX	WNG528	162.45000			
NOAA Bethel	WX	WNG675	162.55000			
NOAA Cape Fanshaw						
	WX	KZZ88	162.42500			
NOAA Cape Gull	WX	WNG529	162.50000			
NOAA Cape Hinchinbrook						
	WX	WNG532	162.52500			
NOAA Cold Bay	WX	KJY87	162.42500			
NOAA Cordova	WX	WXJ79	162.40000			
NOAA Dillingham	WX	WNG681	162.50000			
NOAA Duke Island						
	WX	KZZ92	162.45000			
NOAA East Point	WX	WNG530	162.50000			
NOAA Fairbanks	WX	WXJ81	162.55000			
NOAA Glennallen	WX	KPS503	162.55000			
NOAA Gravina Island						
	WX	KZZ96	162.52500			
NOAA Haines	WX	WXM97	162.40000			
NOAA Homer	WX	WXJ24	162.40000			
NOAA Ketchikan	WX	WXJ26	162.55000			
NOAA Kodiak	WX	WXJ78	162.55000			
NOAA Kotzebue	WX	KWN30	162.55000			
NOAA Manleyville	WX	KAD96	162.50000			
NOAA Marmot Island						
	WX	WNG716	162.50000			
NOAA Mount McArthur						
	WX	KZZ95	162.52500			
NOAA Mount Robert Baron						
	WX	KZZ87	162.45000			
NOAA Nenana	WX	KPS504	162.40000			
NOAA Ninilchik	WX	KZZ97	162.55000			
NOAA Nome	WX	WXJ62	162.55000			
NOAA Pillar Mountain						
	WX	WNG531	162.52500			
NOAA Point Pigot	WX	KZZ93	162.45000			
NOAA Raspberry Island						
	WX	KZZ90	162.42500			
NOAA Rugged Island						
	WX	WNG526	162.42500			
NOAA Sand Point	WX	WNG714	162.55000			
NOAA Seward	WX	KEC81	162.55000			
NOAA Sitka	WX	WXJ80	162.55000			

Location	Mode	Call sign	Output	Input	Access	Coordinator
NOAA Sitkinak Dome						
	WX	WNG718	162.45000			
NOAA Soldotna	WX	WWG39	162.47500			
NOAA Tripod Hill	WX	WNG715	162.45000			
NOAA Tuklung Mountain						
	WX	WNG525	162.42500			
NOAA Valdez	WX	WXJ63	162.55000			
NOAA Wasilla	WX	KZZ98	162.40000			
NOAA Whittier	WX	KXI29	162.47500			
NOAA Yakutat	WX	WXK69	162.40000			
NOAA Zarembo Island						
	WX	KZZ91	162.45000			
Nome	FM	AL7X	144.64000	148.04000	103.5 Hz	
	FM	KL0EF	145.00000	+		
	FM	KL0EF	146.94000	-		
	FM	KL0EF	147.15000	144.55000		
	FM	KL0EF	147.21000	144.51000		
	FM	KL0EF	147.27000	144.57000		
	FM	KL7RAM	147.36000	+	103.5 Hz	
North Pole	FM	WL7TY	146.70000	-		
	FM	WL7LP	147.25000	+	123.0 Hz	
Northway	FM	KL7KC	146.82000	-	103.5 Hz	
Palmer	FM	KL3K	146.61000	-	123.0 Hz	
	FM	WL7CVG	147.33000	+	103.5 Hz	
	FM	WL7CVG	443.90000	+	103.5 Hz	
	FM	KL3K	444.30000	+	123.0 Hz	
	FM	KL7CC	447.57000	147.57000	103.5 Hz	
Petersburg	FM	KD7WN	444.50000	+		
Seward	FM	KL3K	146.76000	-	123.0 Hz	
Sitka	FM	KL7SRK	146.08000	+	114.8 Hz	
	FM	KL7SRK	146.82000	-	114.8 Hz	
	FM	KL7SRK	444.00000	+	114.8 Hz	
	FM	KL7SRK	446.00000	-	114.8 Hz	
Soldotna	FM	AL7LE	146.88000	-		
Teller	FM	KL7RAM	146.73000	-	103.5 Hz	
Unalakleet	FM	KL7RAM	444.90000	+	103.5 Hz	
Valdez	FM	NL7R	146.94000	-		
Wasilla	DMR/BM	WL7DN	443.45000	+	CC15	
	DMR/BM	KL7JFU	443.80000	+	CC1	
	DSTAR	WL7CWI	147.00000	+		
	DSTAR	WL7CWI	442.00000	+		
	FM	KL7JFU	146.85000	-	103.5 Hz	
	FM	KL7DJE	147.09000	+	100.0 Hz	
	FM	NL7S	147.15000	+	107.2 Hz	
	FM	KL7JFU	444.60000	+	103.5 Hz	
	FUSION	KL2S	145.30000	-		
	FUSION	KL7RW	145.35000	-		
Willow	FM	KL7DOB	146.64000	-		

ARIZONA

Location	Mode	Call sign	Output	Input	Access	Coordinator
Aguila	FM	K7LKL	146.68000	-	162.2 Hz	
	FM	W7ARA	443.77500	+	100.0 Hz	
Ajo	FM	W7AJO	145.31000	-	100.0 Hz	
	FM	KL7DSI	448.10000	-	100.0 Hz	
Alpine	FM	K7EAR	145.27000	-	141.3 Hz	
	FM	N5IA	448.72500	+		
Anthem	FUSION	KJ7RIX	431.07500			
Arizona City	FM	AE7RR	440.75000	+		
Barkerville	FM	W7AI-R	444.10000	+	156.7 Hz	
Benson	FM	K7SPV	145.37000	-	131.8 Hz	
	FM	WA7PIQ	448.82500	-	107.2 Hz	
Bisbee	FM	K7RDG	146.76000	-	162.2 Hz	

Location	Mode	Call sign	Output	Input	Access	Coordinator
Bisbee	FM	K7RDG	147.02000	+	162.2 Hz	
	FM	K7EAR	147.08000	+	141.3 Hz	
	FM	K7RDG	449.52500	-	100.0 Hz	
Black Canyon City						
	FUSION	AE7JG	449.97500	-		
Blythe	FM	KR7AZ	147.06000	+	203.5 Hz	
Buckeye	DMR/BM	KE7CIU	446.57500	-	CC1	
Bullhead City	FM	K3MK	146.64000	-	123.0 Hz	
	FM	K7PFK	448.95000	-	123.0 Hz	
	FM	N7URK	449.50000	-		
	FUSION	W7GAA	145.17000	-		
Camp Verde	DMR/MARC	KF7LRD	445.53750	-	CC1	
	FM	W7EI	147.10000	+	131.8 Hz	
	FM	K6DLP	447.70000	-		
Casa Grande	FM	KA7TUR	446.82500	-	100.0 Hz	
	FM	N7ULY	447.72500	-	100.0 Hz	
Casa Grande, Sacaton PK						
	FM	K7PNX	448.02500	-	136.5 Hz	
Cave Creek	DMR/MARC	KJ7PLR	444.07500	+	CC1	
	FUSION	KB6JWK	144.56000			
	FUSION	KB6JWK	145.56250			
Chandler	DMR/BM	N4SMG	436.00000		CC1	
	DMR/BM	K7RTM	446.02500		CC1	
	DMR/MARC	KJ7CMR	438.80000	-	CC1	
	DMR/MARC	N7YF	445.30000	-	CC1	
	FM	WW7CPU	145.45000	-	162.2 Hz	
	FM	KE7JVX	224.92000	-	156.7 Hz	
	FM	W7MOT	442.97500	+	100.0 Hz	
	FM	KE7JVX	444.27500	+	100.0 Hz	
	FM	WB5DYG	447.50000	-	100.0 Hz	
	FM	WW7CPU	448.95000	-	100.0 Hz	
	FM	W7MOT	927.43750	902.43750	151.4 Hz	
	FUSION	W7AJC	144.00000			
	FUSION	N1QKD	145.10000			
	FUSION	KE7OHK	145.56250			
	FUSION	W7AJC	147.50000			
	FUSION	WF7D	434.50000			
Chino Valley	FM	K7POF-R	449.25000	-		
Clemenceau	FM	K9FUN-R	441.77500	+		
College Park	FM	KC7GHT-R	447.57500	-		
Concho AZ	DMR/BM	NX7R	449.62500	-	CC1	
Cottonwood	FM	K7YCA	145.29000	-	127.3 Hz	
	FM	W7ARA	146.82000	-	162.2 Hz	
	FM	K7MRG	147.00000	+	162.2 Hz	
	FM	KI6FH	224.08000	-	156.7 Hz	
	FM	W7ARA	448.50000	-	100.0 Hz	
	FM	WA6LSE	449.42500	-	141.3 Hz	
	FM	N7CI	449.70000	-		
	FM	WA7JC	449.72500	-	110.9 Hz	
	FM	WB7BYV	927.11250	902.11250		
	FUSION	KI6FH	446.87500			
Crown King	FM	W7WHP	447.30000	-	88.5 Hz	
	FM	WA7ZZT	447.62500	-		
	FM	WB7EVI	448.57500	-	100.0 Hz	
	FM	K7STA	449.00000	-		
	FM	KF7EZ	927.28750	902.28750	151.4 Hz	
Crown King, TOWERS MT						
	FM	WB7EVI	449.17500	-	100.0 Hz	
Crown King, Wildflower MTN						
	FM	WA7MKS	145.35000	-	162.2 Hz	
Dateland	FM	N7ACS	147.22000	+	100.0 Hz	

Location	Mode	Call sign	Output	Input	Access	Coordinator
Desert Hills, Daisy MT Fire ST						
	FM	KE7KMI	448.37500	-	100.0 Hz	ARCA
Eagar	FM	W7EH	145.31000	-	110.9 Hz	
	FM	K7EAR	146.70000	-	141.3 Hz	
	FM	W7ARA	448.37500	-	100.0 Hz	
	FM	N7QVU	449.35000	-	100.0 Hz	
	FM	W7ARA	927.16250	902.16250	151.4 Hz	
Flagstaff	DMR/MARC	KF7LRD	445.73750	-	CC1	
	FM	KD7IC	145.27000	-	162.2 Hz	
	FM	NO7AZ	145.45000	-	103.5 Hz	
	FM	W7ARA	147.14000	+	162.2 Hz	
	FM	K6DLP	223.84000	-	107.2 Hz	
	FM	N6IME	224.56000	-	67.0 Hz	
	FM	W7ARA	448.47500	-	100.0 Hz	
	FM	N7MK	448.62500	-		
	FM	W7ARA	448.87500	-	100.0 Hz	
	FM	NO7AZ	449.32500	-	103.5 Hz	
	FM	KD7IC	449.60000	-	162.2 Hz	
	FUSION	KE6GYD	145.78500			
	FUSION	KF6TTT	446.42500	-		
Fort Mohave	FM	KC6YLK	224.72000	-		
	FM	KC6YLK	446.12500			
	FUSION	AE7RZ	146.55000			
	FUSION	KC6YLK	432.40000			
	FUSION	AE7RZ	446.55000			
Fountain Hills	FM	N7MK	447.77500	-	110.9 Hz	
	FUSION	K0UC	440.40000			
Gila Bend	FM	K7PO	145.29000	-	103.5 Hz	
Gilbert	FUSION	K7XWZ	144.60000			
	FUSION	K7HAM	433.70000			
Glendale	FM	K7CAE	446.60000	-	103.5 Hz	
	FM	KD7HJN	447.40000	-	100.0 Hz	
	FUSION	K7LGF	144.50500			
	FUSION	KD7NHM	145.00000			
Globe	DMR/MARC	N7CI	445.86250	-	CC0	
	FM	K7EAR	145.41000	-	141.3 Hz	
	FM	WR7GC	146.74000	-	162.2 Hz	
	FM	W7ARA	147.20000	+	162.2 Hz	
	FM	N7MK	224.10000	-	156.7 Hz	
	FM	N2QWF	445.86250	-		
	FM	N7TWW	448.42500	-	103.5 Hz	
	FM	W7ARA	448.47500	-	100.0 Hz	
	FM	WA7KUM	448.65000	-		
	FM	WR7GC	449.65000	-	100.0 Hz	
	FM	W7ARA	927.41250	902.41250	151.4 Hz	
	FM	N7TWW	927.83750	902.83750	151.4 Hz	
	FM	N7TWW	1283.65000	1263.65000	100.0 Hz	
Globe Pinal	DMR/MARC	N7CI	445.86250	-	CC0	
Golden Valley	FM	N7FK	448.40000	-	123.0 Hz	
Goodyear		SM5OEM-L	434.35000			
	DSTAR	KG7HBZ B	440.73750	+		
Goodyear(Arizona)						
	FUSION	KJ7FME	147.30000			
Green Acres Trailer Court						
	FM	N7OKN-R	440.67500	+		
Green Valley	DMR/BM	AA7RP	449.22500	-	CC1	
	DMR/BM	N7GV	449.37500	-	CC1	
	FM	WE7GV	145.27000	-	107.2 Hz	
	FM	WE7GV	145.29000	-	107.2 Hz	
	FM	WB6TYP	145.43000	-		
	FM	KC0LL	444.87500	+	100.0 Hz	
	FM	AA7RP	449.37500	-	107.2 Hz	

Location	Mode	Call sign	Output	Input	Access	Coordinator
Guadalupe	FM	KJ6KW	224.88000	-	156.7 Hz	
Heber-Overgaard	FM	N7QVU-R	146.62000	-		
	FM	W7RIM-R	146.80000	-		
Holbrook	FM	KA7ARZ	146.68000	-		
Huachuca City	FM	N7MUE	147.56000			
	FUSION	N7MUE	442.00000	+		
Jacob Lake	FM	N7YSE	147.30000	+	100.0 Hz	
Kingman	DMR/BM	N6JFO	449.20000	-	CC15	
	DSTAR	W7KDS	145.13500	-		
	DSTAR	W7KDS C	145.13500	-		
	DSTAR	KR7MC C	145.14500	-		
	DSTAR	W7KDS B	445.90000	-		
	DSTAR	KR7MC B	445.95000	-		
	DSTAR	W7KDS	1284.00000	1264.00000		
	DSTAR	W7KDS A	1284.00000	-		
	DSTAR	W7KDS	1299.00000			
	DSTAR	W7KDS D	1299.00000			
	FM	KA6NLS	51.94000	-	100.0 Hz	
	FM	WB6RER	145.19000	+	131.8 Hz	
	FM	KD7HVE	145.21000	-	123.0 Hz	
	FM	K7RLW	146.62000	-		
	FM	N7DPS	146.80000	-	100.0 Hz	ARCA
	FM	K7RLW	146.94000	-		
	FM	KD7HVE	147.12000	+	123.0 Hz	
	FM	K7MPR	147.24000	+	123.0 Hz	
	FM	KD7MIA	147.36000	+	123.0 Hz	
	FM	KD7MIA	224.96000	-	123.0 Hz	ARCA
	FM	KJ6ZD	441.05000			
	FM	K7RLW	446.22500	-		
	FM	KA6NLS	447.10000	-	100.0 Hz	
	FM	K6DLP	448.10000	-		
	FM	N7SKO	448.25000	-	131.8 Hz	
	FM	K7MPR	448.55000	-	123.0 Hz	
	FM	W6PNM	448.68000	-		
	FM	K7RLW	449.47500	-	94.8 Hz	
	FM	KD7HVE	449.95000	-		
	FM	WB6TNP	927.47500	902.47500		
	FM	K7RLW	927.61250	902.61250		
	FUSION	KJ6ZD	433.45000			
Lake Havasu	DMR/MARC	W7DXJ	448.45000	-	CC1	
Lake Havasu City	DMR/BM	N6PL	444.07500	+	CC1	
	FM	K7RLW	146.72000	-	123.0 Hz	
	FM	W7LHC	146.90000	-	100.0 Hz	ARCA
	FM	W7DXJ	146.96000	-	162.2 Hz	
	FM	KE7ZIW	147.50000			
	FM	KF7X	224.24000	-	156.7 Hz	
	FM	W7LHC	446.10000	-	100.0 Hz	ARCA
	FM	W7LHC	446.25000	-	100.0 Hz	ARCA
	FM	WR7RAM	448.02000	-		
	FM	K7MPR	448.60000	-	123.0 Hz	
	FM	K6PNG	449.12500	-	67.0 Hz	
	FM	W7DXJ	449.95000	-	141.3 Hz	
	FUSION	N0VAO	433.80000			
	FUSION	KX7P	448.35000	-		
	FUSION	AD6NM	449.95000	-		
Lampliter Village Mobile Home						
	FM	W6NSA-R	443.90000	+		
Laughlin	DMR/BM	N6JFO	449.30000	-	CC15	
Laveen	FM	KC7QKS	449.25000	-	192.8 Hz	
	FUSION	K7SID	433.25000			
Lukachukai	FM	KB5ITS	145.25000	-	100.0 Hz	
Marana	FM	KC7CPB	448.00000	-	100.0 Hz	

Location	Mode	Call sign	Output	Input	Access	Coordinator
Maricopa	FM	KE7JVX	224.92000	-	156.7 Hz	ARCA
	FM	WY7H	449.12500	-	136.5 Hz	
	FM	KE7JVX	927.02500	902.02500	151.4 Hz	
	FUSION	KC7KF	146.78000	-		
	FUSION	W8RH	441.30000	+		
Maryvale Terrace		KF7SXJ-L	146.44500			
McNary	FM	W7ARA	146.72000	-	162.2 Hz	
Mesa	DMR/BM	KE7TR	440.72500	+	CC1	
	DMR/BM	K7EVR	440.75000	+	CC7	
	DMR/BM	K7DMK	441.75000	+	CC1	
	DMR/BM	K5EDJ	442.05000	+	CC3	
	DMR/BM	K7EVR	446.25000	-	CC7	
	DMR/MARC	KE7JFH	445.83750	-	CC1	
	DMR/MARC	N7DJZ	445.96250	-	CC1	
	DSTAR	KE7JFH C	145.12500	-		
	DSTAR	KE7JFH	145.12500	-		
	DSTAR	KE7JFH B	445.97500	-		
	DSTAR	KE7JFH	445.97500	-		
	DSTAR	KE7JFH	1285.65000	1265.65000		
	DSTAR	KE7JFH A	1285.65000	-		
	DSTAR	KE7JFH D	1297.50000			
	FM	WB7TUJ	145.33000	-	114.8 Hz	
	FM	KE7JFH	145.47000	-	79.7 Hz	
	FM	WB7TUJ	146.66000	-	162.2 Hz	
	FM	K7DAD	146.72000	-	100.0 Hz	
	FM	W7ARA	146.86000	-	162.2 Hz	
	FM	W7BSA	147.02000	+	162.2 Hz	
	FM	WB7TJD	147.12000	+	162.2 Hz	
	FM	N7TWW	224.02000	-	151.4 Hz	
	FM	W7ARA	224.68000	-	156.7 Hz	
	FM	KF7EUO	440.42500	+		
	FM	KE7JFH	448.72500	-		
	FM	N7DJZ	448.97500	-		
	FM	K7DAD	449.37500	-	100.0 Hz	
	FM	KA7ZEM	449.55000	-	100.0 Hz	
	FM	WB7TJD	449.60000	-	100.0 Hz	
	FM	W7ARA	449.62500	-	100.0 Hz	
	FM	W5WVI	449.85000	-		
	FM	N7MK	927.46250	902.46250		
	FUSION	KK7ABD	146.50000			
	FUSION	W7KLV	147.50000			
	FUSION	WB7TJD	448.27500	-		
Mesa, Usery Pass	FM	W7BSA	448.80000	-	100.0 Hz	
	FM	W7ARA	449.10000	-	100.0 Hz	
Mesquite Creek		AE7RZ-R	145.17000			
Mohave County	DMR/BM	K7RLW	440.11250	+	CC5	
	DMR/BM	K7RLW	442.11250	+	CC12	
	DMR/BM	K7RLW	448.00000	-	CC12	
	DMR/BM	K7RLW	448.11250	-	CC12	
	DMR/BM	K7RLW	448.21250	-	CC10	
	DMR/BM	K7RLW	449.00000	-	CC12	
	DMR/BM	K7RLW	449.13750	-	CC12	
	DMR/BM	K7RLW	449.33750	-	CC12	
	DMR/BM	K7RLW	449.68750	-	CC12	
Morenci	FM	N5IA	448.97500	-		
Mt Lemmon	DMR/MARC	N7HND	447.87500	-	CC1	
NOAA Flagstaff	WX	WXK76	162.40000			
NOAA Globe	WX	WWG42	162.50000			
NOAA Grand Canyon						
	WX	WWF52	162.47500			
NOAA Greer	WX	KXI23	162.52500			
NOAA Kingman	WX	KXI83	162.42500			

Location	Mode	Call sign	Output	Input	Access	Coordinator
NOAA Lake Havasu						
	WX	KXI84	162.40000			
NOAA Nogales	WX	WNG703	162.50000			
NOAA Payson	WX	WWG41	162.42500			
NOAA Phoenix	WX	KEC94	162.55000			
NOAA Prescott	WX	WWF98	162.52500			
NOAA Safford	WX	KXI24	162.55000			
NOAA Show Low	WX	WNG548	162.40000			
NOAA Tucson	WX	WXL30	162.40000			
NOAA Window Rock						
	WX	WWF99	162.55000			
Oracle	FM	WA7ELN	448.70000	-		
Oro Valley	DMR/BM	WD7ARC	445.53750	-	CC1	
	DMR/BM	WD7ARC	445.80000	-	CC1	
	DSTAR	W0HF B	445.80000	-		
	FM	WB7NUY	447.42500	-	107.2 Hz	
Overgaard	DMR/BM	N7QVU	439.97500	449.97500	CC13	
Parker	FM	WA7RAT	146.85000	-	162.2 Hz	
	FM	K7ZEU	224.00000	-	100.0 Hz	
	FM	K6DLP	448.27500	-		
	FM	K7AY	448.65000	-		
Patagonia	FM	W7JPI	146.64000	-	127.3 Hz	
Paulden	FM	W7BNW-R	446.55000	-		
Payson	DMR/BM	K7MWD	145.11000	-	CC1	
	DMR/BM	N7TAR	448.77500	-	CC1	
	DMR/MARC	KE7TR	449.30000	-	CC1	
	FM	WR7GC	146.96000	-	141.3 Hz	
	FM	N7TAR	147.39000	+	100.0 Hz	
	FM	W7NAZ	447.47500	-	88.5 Hz	
	FM	W7MOT	927.43750	902.43750	151.4 Hz	
Peoria	FM	WA7CBB	145.60000		162.2 Hz	
	FM	W7DGL	446.57500	-	127.3 Hz	
Phoenix		KG7NNB-L	147.58000			
	DMR/BM	WA6PNP	444.20000	+	CC1	
	DMR/BM	N0NKI	447.60000	-	CC1	
	DMR/BM	KM6VLB	449.20000	-	CC15	
	DMR/MARC	KD4IML	442.35000	+	CC1	
	DMR/MARC	N8NQP	445.25000	-	CC1	
	DMR/MARC	KF6FM	447.87500	-	CC1	
	DSTAR	W7MOT	145.13500	-		
	DSTAR	W7MOT C	145.13500	-		
	DSTAR	W7MOT	440.81250	+		
	DSTAR	W7MOT B	440.81250	+		
	DSTAR	K7PNX	1283.85000	1263.85000		
	DSTAR	W7MOT	1283.90000	1263.90000		
	DSTAR	W7MOT A	1283.90000	-		
	DSTAR	K7PNX	1298.00000			
	DSTAR	W7MOT	1299.50000			
	DSTAR	W7MOT D	1299.50000			
	FM	W7ATV	145.19000	-	162.2 Hz	
	FM	N7SKT	145.43000	-	100.0 Hz	
	FM	K7JAX	146.84000	453.16000	123.0 Hz	
	FM	W7UXZ	147.06000	+	162.2 Hz	
	FM	W7ARA	147.24000	+	162.2 Hz	
	FM	WA7UID	147.28000	+	162.2 Hz	
	FM	K5VT	147.32000	+		
	FM	N7ULY	147.38000	+	79.7 Hz	
	FM	W7DGL	223.98000	-	156.7 Hz	
	FM	KD7TKT	224.60000	-	156.7 Hz	
	FM	KE7JVX	224.84000	-	156.7 Hz	
	FM	W7ARA	224.90000	-	156.7 Hz	
	FM	KA7RVV	440.77500	+		

Location	Mode	Call sign	Output	Input	Access	Coordinator
Phoenix	FM	KB7CGA	441.20000	+	77.0 Hz	
	FM	WA7ZZT	442.00000	+		
	FM	W7MOT	442.05000	+	100.0 Hz	
	FM	N7AUW	442.12500	+	100.0 Hz	
	FM	K7PNX	442.20000	+	136.5 Hz	
	FM	W1OQ	442.27500	+	100.0 Hz	
	FM	WA7ZZT	442.55000	+	100.0 Hz	
	FM	N1KQ	442.60000	+	100.0 Hz	
	FM	WW7B	442.67500	+	123.0 Hz	
	FM	WW7B	442.70000	+	123.0 Hz	
	FM	W7ARA	442.85000	+	100.0 Hz	
	FM	N7SKT	442.92500	+	100.0 Hz	
	FM	W7ARA	444.30000	+	100.0 Hz	
	FM	AJ7T	444.82500	+	100.0 Hz	
	FM	W2MIX	445.27500	-		
	FM	K7PNX	447.10000	-	136.5 Hz	
	FM	WA6LSE	447.17500	-		
	FM	KB7OBJ	447.32500	-		
	FM	N7TWB	447.95000	-	100.0 Hz	
	FM	WA7ZZT	448.77500	-		
	FM	WA7GBL	449.15000	-		
	FM	N7ULY	449.35000	-		
	FM	K7PNX	449.45000	-		
	FM	W7MOT	927.21250	902.21250	151.4 Hz	
	FM	W7ARA	927.33750	902.33750	151.4 Hz	
	FM	KF7EZ	927.53750	902.53750	151.4 Hz	
	P25	N9VJW	440.17500	+	100.0 Hz	
	FUSION	KJ7PJD	145.60000			
	FUSION	N9BI	146.40000			
	FUSION	KD7JVP	146.54000			
	FUSION	K7WER	147.00000	+		
	FUSION	K7NZ	147.50000			
	FUSION	K7NZ	434.10000			
	FUSION	K7LRH	441.02500			
	FUSION	AE7JG	442.90000	+		
Phoenix ShawButte						
	DMR/MARC	KE7JFH	440.03750	+	CC0	
Phoenix Whitetanks						
	DMR/MARC	WA7KUM	440.10000	+	CC0	
Phoenix, Chase Building						
	FM	W7ARA	146.64000	-	162.2 Hz	
Phoenix, Far N MT.						
	FM	K7PNX	448.85000	-	136.5 Hz	
Phoenix, N MTN HOSPITAL						
	FM	W7TBC	146.70000	-	162.2 Hz	
Phoenix, North MT						
	FM	K7PNX	449.02500	-	136.5 Hz	
Phoenix, SHAW BUTTE						
	FM	W7ARA	449.52500	-	100.0 Hz	
Phoenix, South Mt						
	FM	W7BSA	147.02000	+	162.2 Hz	ARCA
	FM	W7MOT	443.05000	+	100.0 Hz	
Phoenix, White Tanks						
	FM	W7TBC	147.04000	+	162.2 Hz	
	FM	W7EX	441.72500	+	100.0 Hz	
	FM	W7TBC	446.15000	-	100.0 Hz	
Phoenix, White Tanks MTN						
	FM	W7EX	146.94000	-	162.2 Hz	
Pinal Mountain	DSTAR	N7CI B	445.85000	-		
Pinedale	FM	KB7ZIH	145.23000	-	110.9 Hz	
Pinetop	FM	AD7W	146.76000	-	162.2 Hz	
Pinetop-Lakeside	DMR/MARC	AD7W	449.05000	-	CC0	

Location	Mode	Call sign	Output	Input	Access	Coordinator
Point Of Rocks	FM	WY7H-R	145.21000	-		
Potato Patch	FM	WB6TNP	447.60000	-	141.3 Hz	
	FM	K6DLP	448.10000	-		
	FM	W6PNM	448.68000	-		ARCA
	FM	K7RLW	927.61250	902.61250		ARCA
Prescott	DMR/BM	K7DJF	445.70000	-	CC1	
	DMR/MARC	KB6BOB	447.87500	-	CC1	
	DMR/MARC	WB7BYV	449.67500	-	CC1	
	DMR/MARC	KF7LRD	449.87500	-	CC1	
	FM	N7NGM	52.56000	-	100.0 Hz	
	FM	K7YCA	145.37000	-	127.3 Hz	
	FM	W7YRC	146.88000	-	100.0 Hz	
	FM	K7YCA	147.26000	+	103.5 Hz	
	FM	K7QDX	440.45000	+	103.5 Hz	ARCA
	FM	K7MRG	442.15000	+	100.0 Hz	
	FM	WB7BYV	927.12500	902.12500	103.5 Hz	
	FM	WB7BYV	927.38750	902.38750	151.4 Hz	
	FM	WB7BYV	927.58750	902.58750	131.8 Hz	
	FUSION	KC6PHV	444.47500	+		
	FUSION	N7YMM	444.65000			
	FUSION	K6VVR	447.15000			
	FUSION	N7YMM	449.65000	-	100.0 Hz	
Prescott Valley	FM	W6PAT	442.52500	+	114.8 Hz	
	FUSION	KJ7UHL	440.75000			
Quartsite	DMR/MARC	WD6AML	448.95000	-	CC1	
Quartzsite	DMR/MARC	WD7FM	448.90000	-	CC1	
	DSTAR	KJ7LFN B	445.20000	-		
	FM	KG7HYF	145.19000	-	103.5 Hz	
	FM	WB7FIK	145.31000	-	107.2 Hz	
	FM	KJ6KW	224.88000	-	156.7 Hz	
	FM	W7AZQ	447.00000	-	123.0 Hz	
	FM	WD6FM	448.90000	-		
	FM	WB7FIK	448.97500	-		
Quartzsite, Guadalupe Pk						
	FM	K6TQM	147.36000	+	107.2 Hz	
Queen Creek	FM	AH6OD	147.48000		100.0 Hz	
	FUSION	N9NTH	448.27500	-		
Quivero-Williams	DMR/BM	N6TKA	440.76250	+	CC1	
Red Rock	FM	NM5SJ	146.82000	-	100.0 Hz	
Rio Rico	ATV	WA7JBG	147.38000	+	127.3 Hz	
	FM	KG7DNO	147.06000	+	127.3 Hz	
Sacaton Flats	FM	KE7JVX-R	927.65000	902.65000		
Safford	DMR/MARC	K7EAR	440.75000	+	CC1	
	FM	K7EAR	146.86000	-	141.3 Hz	
	FM	K7EAR	146.90000	-	141.3 Hz	
	FM	K7EAR	147.28000	+	141.3 Hz	
	FM	K7EAR	440.70000	+	141.3 Hz	
	FM	K7EAR	447.82500	-	100.0 Hz	
	FM	K7JEM	448.67500	-	100.0 Hz	
Saint Johns	DMR/BM	KE6GVK	446.52500	-	CC1	
	FM	KE6GVK	145.23000	-		
San Tan Valley	FM	N7DJZ	449.32500	-	100.0 Hz	
	FUSION	AC7KN	146.42000			
Santiago Rodeo Villas Mobile H						
		AE7RZ-L	145.17000			
Scottsdale	DMR/MARC	KF7CUF	445.20000	-	CC1	
	DSTAR	KF7CUF B	445.95000	-		
	DSTAR	KF7CUF A	1285.00000	-		
	FM	KB6POQ	145.31000	-	91.5 Hz	
	FM	W7ARA	146.76000	-	162.2 Hz	
	FM	W7UF	147.18000	+	162.2 Hz	
	FM	W7MOT	147.34000	+	162.2 Hz	

Location	Mode	Call sign	Output	Input	Access	Coordinator
Scottsdale	FM	W7UF	440.00000	+	100.0 Hz	
	FM	W0NWA	441.10000	+	103.5 Hz	
	FM	W7ARA	441.62500	+	100.0 Hz	
	FM	W7MOT	442.02500	+	100.0 Hz	
	FM	W7MOT	443.15000	+	100.0 Hz	
	FM	KB6POQ	445.90000	-	91.5 Hz	
	FM	KC7WVE	446.67500	-	146.2 Hz	
	FM	KG7UN	448.82500	-	100.0 Hz	
	FM	WA7VEI	448.90000	-		
	FM	N7KEG	449.65000	-		
	FM	K0NL	927.06250	902.06250	151.4 Hz	
	FM	W7ARA	927.16250	902.16250	151.4 Hz	
	FM	KF7EUO	927.23750	902.23750	151.4 Hz	
	FM	W7MOT	927.38750	902.38750	151.4 Hz	
	FUSION	KA7EMT	439.92500			
	FUSION	K7PY	446.07500			
	FUSION	N9EIV	448.10000	-		
Scottsdale, THOMPSON PK						
	FM	KG7UN	147.08000	+	162.2 Hz	
Seligman	DMR/BM	WA6GDF	449.82500	-	CC1	
	FM	WA6GDF	147.12000	+	192.8 Hz	
Serape		KM3N-L	145.61000			
Show Low	DMR/BM	W2MRA	446.57500	-	CC1	
	DMR/BM	N7OEI	448.85000	-	CC1	
	FM	W7EH	449.15000	-	110.9 Hz	
Sierra Vista	DMR/MARC	KA3IDN	445.85000	-	CC1	
	DSTAR	K7RDG C	145.12500	-		
	FM	N0NBH	224.96000	-	100.0 Hz	
	FM	K7LTN	442.45000	+	100.0 Hz	
	FM	K7RDG	447.95000	-	100.0 Hz	
	FM	N0NBH	449.82500	-	100.0 Hz	
	FM	N0NBH	927.91250	902.91250	100.0 Hz	
	FM	N0NBH	1282.50000	1262.50000	100.0 Hz	
	FUSION	KI7VHE	145.55000			
	FUSION	K2AK	434.75000			
	FUSION	K7LTN	441.20000	+		
Sierra Vista Estates						
	FM	N0NBH-R	147.36000	+		
Solomon	DMR/MARC	K7EAR	440.07500	+	CC1	
St Johns	FM	NR7G	449.62500	-	136.5 Hz	
Sun City	DMR/BM	N6TKA	440.76250	+	CC1	
	FM	NY7S	147.30000	+	162.2 Hz	
	FM	KA7G	442.45000	+	91.5 Hz	
	FM	W7JHQ	449.80000	-	100.0 Hz	
	FUSION	KD7DFV	145.65000			
	FUSION	W7JHQ	449.80000	-		
Sun Lakes	FUSION	K7GEL	445.75000			
Sunflower	FM	W7ARA	146.92000	-	162.2 Hz	
	FM	W7ARA	147.36000	+	162.2 Hz	
Sunflower, MT ORD						
	FM	W7ARA	444.50000	+	100.0 Hz	
Surprise	FUSION	KI7VWP	145.56250			
	FUSION	W7DJS	433.12500			
	FUSION	AF7JD	439.72500			
	FUSION	KF7EZ	447.22500	-		
Tanque Verde	FM	WD7F-R	146.94000	-		
	FM	N1DHS/R2	448.35000	-		
Tempe	DMR/MARC	K7TMP	442.37500	+	CC1	
	FM	WA2DFI	145.27000	-	162.2 Hz	
	FM	WA2DFI	224.20000	-		
	FM	KE7EJF	927.03750	902.03750		
Tolleson	FM	AJ9Y	448.07500	-	100.0 Hz	

Location	Mode	Call sign	Output	Input	Access	Coordinator
Tombstone	FM	NM2J	145.19000	-	88.5 Hz	
	FUSION	AB7CQ	146.92000	-		
Tucson	DMR/BM	KG7GWN	440.76250	+	CC1	
	DMR/BM	W7NFL	444.75000	+	CC1	
	DMR/BM	KG7PJV	445.13750	-	CC1	
	DMR/BM	N5SN	445.53750	-	CC1	
	DMR/BM	W7AI	445.80000	-	CC1	
	DMR/BM	KM7KK	447.50000	-	CC1	
	DMR/BM	WN0EHE	449.50000	-	CC1	
	DMR/MARC	N7HND	444.25000	+	CC1	
	DMR/MARC	N7HND	445.87500	-	CC1	
	DMR/MARC	N7HND	449.20000	-	CC1	
	DSTAR	K7RST	145.11500	-		
	DSTAR	K7RST C	147.41000	146.41000		
	DSTAR	W7NFL B	445.73750			
	DSTAR	K7RST B	445.90000	-		
	DSTAR	KR7ST	445.95000	-		
	DSTAR	K7RST A	1284.25000	-		
	DSTAR	K7RST D	1298.25000			
	FM	K7RST	29.64000	-	110.9 Hz	
	FM	K6PYP	51.86000	-	100.0 Hz	
	FM	K6PYP	53.04000	52.04000	141.3 Hz	
	FM	KA7LFX	53.72000	52.72000	136.5 Hz	
	FM	K6PPT	145.17000	-		
	FM	KA7LVX	145.33000	-	127.3 Hz	
	FM	W7AI	146.62000	-	156.7 Hz	
	FM	W7GV	146.66000	-	110.9 Hz	
	FM	K7RST	146.80000	-		
	FM	AG7H	146.85000	-		
	FM	N7OEM	146.88000	-	110.9 Hz	
	FM	N7HND	147.00000	+	110.9 Hz	
	FM	KC0LL	147.14000	+	100.0 Hz	
	FM	K7EAR	147.16000	+	141.3 Hz	
	FM	N7OEM	147.30000	+	110.9 Hz	
	FM	W7SA	147.34000	+	179.9 Hz	
	FM	KA3IDN	147.36000	+		
	FM	KA7LFX	224.06000	-	156.7 Hz	
	FM	K6PYP	224.50000	-	156.7 Hz	
	FM	W7SA	224.70000	-	179.9 Hz	
	FM	KC0LL	444.97500	+	100.0 Hz	
	FM	W7ATN	445.22500	-	103.5 Hz	
	FM	K6PPT	446.57500	-	156.7 Hz	
	FM	N7XJQ	447.50000	-	136.5 Hz	
	FM	KB7RFI	447.87500	-	88.5 Hz	
	FM	W7RAP	448.30000	-		
	FM	N1DHS	448.35000	-	107.2 Hz	
	FM	N7OEM	448.55000	-	110.9 Hz	
	FM	W7SA	448.77500	-	179.9 Hz	
	FM	KG7KV	448.90000	-		
	FM	N7CK	448.97500	-		
	FM	K7RST	449.30000	-	156.7 Hz	
	FM	N7DQP	449.47500	-	107.2 Hz	
	FM	KW7RF	449.67500	-	77.0 Hz	
	FM	N7HND	927.05000	902.05000		
	FM	KA3IDN	927.07500	902.07500	218.1 Hz	
	FM	K6PYP	927.11250	902.11250		
	FM	K6PYP	927.13750	902.13750		
	FM	N7OEM	927.97500	902.97500		
	FM	K7SPV	1282.75000	-	131.8 Hz	
	FUSION	AG7PL	146.80000	-		
	FUSION	KG7TPE	432.75000			
	FUSION	K1WAZ	445.55000	-		

Location	Mode	Call sign	Output	Input	Access	Coordinator
Tucson	FUSION	W9PDC	446.42000			
Vail	FM	KB7ZZY	444.92500	+		
	FM	KE7ULC	446.55000	-	100.0 Hz	
	FM	K7RST	448.32500	-	156.7 Hz	
	FM	K7LHR	449.55000	-	107.2 Hz	
	FUSION	W9MT	145.53000			
Verde		AB9U-L	147.46000			
Waddell	DMR/MARC	KE7JVX	927.02500	902.02500	CC1	
Wickenburg	FUSION	N0DAJ	449.93750			
	FUSION	N0DAJ	449.97500			
Wikieup		BD6JN-R	439.60000			
Wilcox	FM	K7EAR	145.35000	-	141.3 Hz	
Williams	DMR/BM	N6TKA	440.76250	+	CC1	
	DMR/MARC	KF7LRD	448.30000	-	CC1	
	DSTAR	K7NAZ	145.11500	-		
	DSTAR	K7NAZ C	145.11500	-		
	DSTAR	K7NAZ	445.78750	-		
	DSTAR	K7NAZ B	445.78750	-		
	DSTAR	K7NAZ	1284.60000	1264.60000		
	FM	K7NAZ	146.78000	-	91.5 Hz	
	FM	K6JSI	449.75000	-	123.0 Hz	
	FM	WB7BYV	927.07500	902.07500	218.1 Hz	
Wintersburg	FM	WT9S-R	442.07500	+		
Yarnell	FM	N7LOQ	146.62000	-	162.2 Hz	
Young	FUSION	K7AWW	145.11000	-		
Yuma	DMR/BM	KC6QLS	449.46250	-	CC1	
	DMR/MARC	KG7ARQ	440.95000	+	CC0	
	DMR/MARC	N7ADR	446.60000	-	CC1	
	FM	N7ACS	146.62000	-	103.5 Hz	
	FM	N7ACS	146.78000	-	103.5 Hz	
	FM	N7ACS	146.80000	-	162.2 Hz	
	FM	KJ7DLK	146.84000	-	88.5 Hz	
	FM	N7ACS	224.72000	-	103.5 Hz	
	FM	KJ6IZQ	448.00000	-	100.0 Hz	
	FM	N0RHZ	448.62500	-		
	FM	W7DIN	449.07500	-	88.5 Hz	ARCA
	FM	KC7EQW	927.46250	902.46250	88.5 Hz	
	FUSION	WA7LRL	433.40000			
	FUSION	N1OB	434.50000			
	FUSION	K7YUM	449.92500	-		

ARKANSAS

Location	Mode	Call sign	Output	Input	Access	Coordinator
Adona	FM	W5SRE	447.15000	-	100.0 Hz	
Alexander	FM	N5YLE	145.29000	-	131.8 Hz	
Alpine	FM	KD5ARC	147.22500	+	114.8 Hz	
Arkadelphia	FM	W5RHS	444.67500	+	114.8 Hz	
	FM	KB5ILY	444.87500	+	114.8 Hz	
Ashdown	FM	KB5SSW	147.38000	+	100.0 Hz	
Athens	FM	KD5NUP	146.92500	-	100.0 Hz	
	FM	N5THS	444.97500	+	88.5 Hz	
Batesville	FM	N5TSC	224.50000	-	107.2 Hz	
	FM	K5NES	444.25000	+		
Bauxite	FM	AD5EO	146.80500	-	131.8 Hz	
	FM	KJ5ZT-R	443.82500	+		
Bearden	FM	N5IOZ	147.33000	+	100.0 Hz	
	FM	N5IOZ	444.77500	+	100.0 Hz	
Benton	DMR/BM	N5CG	443.60000	+	CC1	
	FM	W5RHS	147.12000	+	131.8 Hz	
	FM	AD5EO	442.97500	+	151.4 Hz	
	FM	W5RHS	444.80000	+	131.8 Hz	
Bentonville	FM	N5UFO	442.95000	+	97.4 Hz	
Berryville	FM	N6WI	443.80000	+	91.5 Hz	

Location	Mode	Call sign	Output	Input	Access	Coordinator
Bismarck	FM	W5DI	147.27000	+	114.8 Hz	
Blytheville	DMR/BM	KG5A	444.17500	+	CC1	
	FM	W5ENL	146.67000	-	107.2 Hz	
Bodcaw	FM	W5UBS	444.75000	+	77.0 Hz	
Bradford	FM	W5BTM	146.74500	-	107.2 Hz	
Bryant	FM	N5TKG	444.30000	+	131.8 Hz	
Buffalolick (historical)						
	FM	K5TW-R	146.83500	-		
Cabot	DMR/BM	W5STR	447.47500	-	CC1	
	DSTAR	W5STR B	442.47500	+		
	FM	AI5Z	53.75000	52.05000		
	FM	W5STR-R	145.41000	-		
Caddo Valley	FM	KD5ARC	145.11000	-	88.5 Hz	
	FM	KD5ARC	444.95000	+	114.8 Hz	
Camden	FM	WA5OWG	146.91000	-	167.9 Hz	
Carryville	DSTAR	KK4VQG C	145.02000	146.42000		
Cash	FM	W5BE	443.87500	+	94.8 Hz	
Cherokee Village	FM	KG5ICO	146.64000	-	94.8 Hz	
	FUSION	KI5DSR	145.55000			
Clarkridge	DMR/BM	N5EWC	443.22500	+	CC1	
Clarksville	FM	W5OI	147.28500	+	114.8 Hz	
Clinton	FM	W5DI	145.37000	-	114.8 Hz	
	FM	N5UFC	146.91000	-	114.8 Hz	
	FM	N5YU	442.00000	+	82.5 Hz	
	FM	NE9DX	444.12500	+	114.8 Hz	
Conway	DMR/BM	W5AUU	145.21000	-	CC1	
	DMR/BM	W5AUU	443.75000	+	CC1	
	FM	W5AUU	53.21000	51.51000	114.8 Hz	
	FM	W5AUU	146.97000	-	114.8 Hz	
	FM	W5AUU	147.03000	+	114.8 Hz	
	FM	W5AUU	443.80000	+	114.8 Hz	
	FM	W5AUU	443.95000	+	114.8 Hz	
	FM	W5AUU	444.10000	+	114.8 Hz	
Coy	FM	W5STR	147.15000	+		
Crawfordsville	FM	KI5GEU	147.15000	+	107.2 Hz	
Crossett	DMR/BM	N5SEA	444.97500	+	CC1	
	FUSION	W5GIF	146.61000	-		
Dardanelle	FM	WD5B	146.68500	-	141.3 Hz	
	FM	K5PXP	146.82000	-	131.8 Hz	
	FM	K5PXP	443.40000	+	131.8 Hz	
Decatur	FM	N5UXE	51.92500	52.92500	114.8 Hz	
	FM	N5UXE	146.92500	-	114.8 Hz	
	FM	N5UXE	442.85000	+	123.0 Hz	
	FM	N5UXE	443.92500	+	114.8 Hz	
Dell	FM	W5ENL	444.65000	+	186.2 Hz	
Dequeen	FM	N5THR	145.13000	-	100.0 Hz	
	FM	WA5LTA	147.07500	+	100.0 Hz	
	FM	N5THR	147.31500	+	100.0 Hz	
	FM	WA5LTA	444.80000	+	88.5 Hz	
Edgemont	FM	W1ZM	145.18000	-		
El Dorado	FM	KC5AUP	146.74500	-		
Elkins	FM	WC5AR	146.70000	-	110.9 Hz	
Emerson	FM	N5PNB	146.95500	-		
Eureka Springs	DMR/BM	KG5JPK	443.42500	+	CC1	
	FM	N5UFO	146.86500	-	97.4 Hz	
	FM	K5AA	444.25000	+	100.0 Hz	
	FM	K5SRS	444.47500	+	110.9 Hz	
Fayetteville	DMR/BM	W5KMP	443.12500	+	CC1	
	FM	WC5AR	147.03000	+	110.9 Hz	
	FM	K5DVT	147.31500	+	97.4 Hz	
	FM	W5KMP	442.00000	+	97.4 Hz	
	FM	WC5AR	442.05000	+	110.9 Hz	

Location	Mode	Call sign	Output	Input	Access	Coordinator
Fayetteville	FM	K5SRS	444.92500	+	88.5 Hz	
	FUSION	W5XH	145.56250			
Forrest City	FM	KD5DF	146.76000	-	100.0 Hz	
	FUSION	WB5YUY	146.80500	-		
Fort Smith	FM	W5ANR	146.94000	-	88.5 Hz	
	FM	W5ANR	444.30000	+		
Fox	IDAS	N5QT	145.11000	-	110.9 Hz	
Garfield	FM	KD5DMT	443.02500	+	110.9 Hz	
Gentry	FM	K5SRS	146.67000	-	110.9 Hz	
Glenwood	FM	K5JSC	146.83500	-	114.8 Hz	
Green Forest	FM	K5DVT	145.31000	-	97.4 Hz	
	FM	KJ6TQ	146.73000	-	136.5 Hz	
	FM	N5UFO	442.70000	+	97.4 Hz	
Greenbrier	FM	W5AUU	146.62500	-	114.8 Hz	
Greers Ferry	FM	W5GFC	147.33000	+		
	FM	W5RHL	443.65000	+	88.5 Hz	
Gurdon	FM	KD5ARC	145.37000	-	88.5 Hz	
Hamburg	FUSION	W5GIF	147.77500			
Harrisburg	DMR/BM	NI5A	444.60000	+	CC1	
	FM	K5TW	444.52500	+	94.8 Hz	
Harrison	DMR/BM	W5NWA	442.90000	+	CC1	
	FM	WB5CYX	53.15000	51.45000		
	FM	WB5CYX	147.00000	-	103.5 Hz	
	FM	W5NWA	147.45000		103.5 Hz	
	FM	WX5T/R	444.35000	+	123.0 Hz	
	FM	W5NWA	446.22500	-	103.5 Hz	
	WX	WX5T	446.25000		88.5 Hz	
Hartford	FM	KC5JBX	146.89500	-	141.3 Hz	
	FM	WD5MHZ	442.42500	+	88.5 Hz	
	FM	WD5MHZ	442.82500	+	88.5 Hz	
Heber Springs	FM	N5XUN	145.23000	-		
	FM	W5HSC	145.43000	-	94.8 Hz	
	FM	W5HSC	443.37500	+	91.5 Hz	
Helena	FM	N5KGA	146.68500	-	100.0 Hz	
	FM	N5MIG	146.80500	-	91.5 Hz	
	FUSION	N5MIG	444.87500	+		
Hickory Ridge	FM	KI5BGC	145.31000	-	107.2 Hz	
Holiday Island	FM	K5AA	146.83500	-	100.0 Hz	
Hollis	FM	K5KM	146.74500	-		
Hollywood Beach	FM	WD5B-L	443.87500	+		
Hope	FM	N5OXP	146.68500	-	114.8 Hz	
Hot Springs	DMR/BM	WB5SPA	442.35000	+	CC2	
	DMR/BM	WX5HOT	444.27500	+	CC3	
	FM	KF5AF	145.27000	-	114.8 Hz	
	FM	W5LVB	146.88000	-	114.8 Hz	
	FM	W5HSV	147.01500	+	114.8 Hz	
	FM	WB5SPA	147.18000	+	114.8 Hz	
	FM	W5YTR	224.16000	-		
	FM	WB5PIB	444.00000	+		
	FM	W5LVB	444.60000	+	114.8 Hz	
	FM	W5HSV	444.72500	+	114.8 Hz	
Huntsville	FM	K5DVT	145.31000	-	103.5 Hz	
	FM	KG5OQF	443.62500	+	97.4 Hz	
Imboden	DMR/BM	W5WRA	442.40000	+	CC1	
Jasper	FM	WB5CYX	146.61000	-	103.5 Hz	
Jonesboro	DMR/BM	K5NEA	442.21250	+	CC0	
	DSTAR	KG5NAU	443.93750	+		
	FM	W5JBR	146.61000	-	107.2 Hz	
	FM	NI5A	147.24000	+	107.2 Hz	
	FM	K5NEA	443.15000	+	107.2 Hz	
	FM	KF5OTW	444.15000	+	94.8 Hz	
Kingsland	FUSION	K5DCX	147.47000			

Location	Mode	Call sign	Output	Input	Access	Coordinator
Knoxville Junction	FM	KE5SQC-R	442.12500	+		
Ladelle	FM	N5SEA	444.57500	+	127.3 Hz	
Lake City	FM	KC5TEL	444.32500	+	107.2 Hz	
Lepanto	FM	W5MLH	443.32500	+	107.2 Hz	
Little Rock		W6ABC-R	145.00000			
		KP3AMG-R	147.44000			
		AB8E-R	442.10000			
		KB5NUR-L	444.87500			
		KC2ABV	441.10000			
	DMR/BM	K5NSX	145.17000	-	CC1	
	DMR/BM	K5NSX	442.65000	+	CC1	
	DMR/BM	AC5XV	443.12500	+	CC2	
	DMR/BM	K5BRM	443.92500	+	CC1	
	DMR/MARC	N5QM	438.45000	430.85000	CC1	
	DSTAR	K5NSX C	145.17000	-		
	DSTAR	N5DSD	147.48000	144.98000		
	DSTAR	N5DSD C	147.48000	144.98000		
	DSTAR	N5DSD	444.01250	+		
	DSTAR	N5DSD B	444.01250	+		
	FM	N5AT	145.13000	-	114.8 Hz	
	FM	N5CG	145.49000	-	114.8 Hz	
	FM	WA5PGB	146.73000	-	114.8 Hz	
	FM	N5CG	146.77500	-	162.2 Hz	
	FM	WA5LRU	146.85000	-		
	FM	W5DI	146.94000	-		
	FM	W5DI	147.06000	+	114.8 Hz	
	FM	W5DI	147.13500	+	114.8 Hz	
	FM	W5DI	147.30000	+	114.8 Hz	
	FM	NT5LA	442.32500	+	85.4 Hz	
	FM	N5CG	443.00000	+	100.0 Hz	
	FM	N5CG	443.20000	+	114.8 Hz	
	FM	KG5DPK	443.47500	+	156.7 Hz	
	FM	W5DI	444.20000	+	114.8 Hz	
	FM	WA5OOY	444.40000	+	114.8 Hz	
	FM	W5FD	444.45000	+	123.0 Hz	
	FM	W5RXU	444.65000	+	114.8 Hz	
	FM	N5CG	444.70000	+	114.8 Hz	
Lowell	FM	K5SRS	147.22500	+	103.5 Hz	
Lynn	DSTAR	K5CWR	444.80000	+		
Magazine	FM	N5XMZ	53.11000	51.41000	131.8 Hz	
	FM	N5XMZ	145.35000	-	151.4 Hz	
	FM	W5MAG	147.09000	+	151.4 Hz	
	FM	N5XMZ	443.25000	+	123.0 Hz	
Magnolia	FM	KC5OAS	147.10500	+	100.0 Hz	
Malvern	DMR/BM	KI5ENC	145.27000	-	CC1	
	DMR/BM	K9EAG	442.42500	+	CC1	
	DMR/BM	K9EAG	443.05000	+	CC1	
	DMR/BM	W5DSD	444.52500	+	CC1	
	DMR/BM	WD5JPG	444.55000	+	CC1	
	DMR/BM	K9EAG	444.92500	+	CC1	
	FM	KJ5YJ	145.31000	-	88.5 Hz	
	FM	W5BXJ	147.39000	+	136.5 Hz	
	FM	K5SZM	443.10000	+		
	FM	W5BXJ	443.50000	+	136.5 Hz	
Marianna	DMR/BM	K5WMS	444.37500	+	CC6	
Marion	FUSION	K3JRB	147.75000	-		
Marshall	FM	W5NWA	443.05000	+	103.5 Hz	
Maumelle	DMR/MARC	N5QM	442.30000	+	CC1	
Mena	DMR/BM	KB5JBS	442.95000	+	CC1	
	DMR/BM	KC5MMW	444.92500	+	CC1	
	FM	W5HUM	146.79000	-	100.0 Hz	
	FM	K5PS	444.67500	+		

Location	Mode	Call sign	Output	Input	Access	Coordinator
Monticello	FM	N5SEA	146.83500	-		
	FM	W5GIF	444.82500	+	127.3 Hz	
Morrilton	FM	N5CG	145.33000	-	114.8 Hz	
	FM	KE5FSY	146.68500	-	141.3 Hz	
	FM	KE5FSY	443.87500	+	79.7 Hz	
Mount Ida	FM	KA5WPC	52.91000	51.21000	100.0 Hz	
	FM	KA5WPC	146.71500	-	127.3 Hz	
	FM	KA5WPC	444.47500	+	114.8 Hz	
Mountain Home		K5FOY-L	145.55500			
	DMR/BM	NA1MH	147.30000	+	CC1	
	FM	K5OZK	146.88000	-	103.5 Hz	
	FM	KC5RBO	147.07500	+		
	FM	K5OZK	442.30000	+	103.5 Hz	
	FM	K5BAX	442.55000	+		
	FM	WB5NFC	444.00000	+	100.0 Hz	
	FM	WB5NFC	444.97500	+	100.0 Hz	
Mountain View	DMR/BM	KA0JTI	443.60000	+	CC1	
	DMR/MARC	KA0JTI	442.70000	+	CC1	
	DSTAR	KF5BZP	442.63750	+		
	FM	W5PEB	147.47500		123.0 Hz	
	FM	K5GNT	224.40000	-		
	FM	KF5BZP	442.85000	+	97.4 Hz	
	FUSION	KA0JTI	146.70000	-		
	FUSION	W5PEB	433.15000			
Mt. Nebo	DMR/BM	K5CS	442.07500	+	CC1	
Nashville	FM	N5THS	147.04500	+		
	FM	N5BAB	444.35000	+	88.5 Hz	
	FM	N5THS	444.97500	+	88.5 Hz	
NOAA Cherokee Village						
	WX	WNG639	162.47500			
NOAA El Dorado	WX	WNG725	162.52500			
NOAA Fayetteville						
	WX	WXJ52	162.47500			
NOAA Fort Smith	WX	WXJ50	162.55000			
NOAA Fountain Hill						
	WX	KGG86	162.47500			
NOAA Gurdon	WX	WXJ48	162.47500			
NOAA Harrison	WX	WXN92	162.52500			
NOAA Jonesboro	WX	WXJ51	162.55000			
NOAA Little Rock	WX	WXJ55	162.55000			
NOAA Marvell	WX	WNG643	162.52500			
NOAA Mena	WX	KXI97	162.40000			
NOAA Morrilton	WX	KXI91	162.47500			
NOAA Mount Ida	WX	KXI92	162.42500			
NOAA Mountain View						
	WX	WXL66	162.45000			
NOAA Russell	WX	KXI96	162.40000			
NOAA Russellville	WX	WWF96	162.52500			
NOAA Springdale	WX	WNG694	162.40000			
NOAA Star City	WX	WXJ54	162.40000			
NOAA Yellville	WX	WWG54	162.50000			
Ola	FM	WA5YHN	147.21000	+		
	FM	WA5YHN	444.55000	+		
Omaha	FM	KD5DLJ	444.72500	+	103.5 Hz	
	FM	KD5DLJ	446.10000	-	88.5 Hz	
Ozone	FM	K5OO	147.04500	+		
	FM	KC5LVW	442.62500	+		
Paragould	FM	W5BJR	145.47000	-		
Paron	FUSION	K5WRS	146.50000			
Pea Ridge	FM	K5SRS	146.95500	-	110.9 Hz	
Perla	FM	W5BXJ-R	147.36000	+		
Pine Bluff	FM	K5DAK	146.70000	-	82.5 Hz	

Location	Mode	Call sign	Output	Input	Access	Coordinator
Pine Bluff	FM	W5RHS	442.42500	+	114.8 Hz	
Pocahontas	FUSION	N5WWW	145.20000			
	FUSION	N5WWW	145.60000			
Pottsville	DMR/MARC	KI5AAC	443.57500	+	CC1	
	FUSION	WB5NFC	449.57500	-		
Prairie Grove	FM	WC5AR	146.76000	-	110.9 Hz	
Prattsville	FM	KD5RTO	145.19000	-	114.8 Hz	
	FM	KD5RTO	442.87500	+	85.4 Hz	
Providence	FM	KG5S	146.92500	-	94.8 Hz	
Quitman	FM	KC5PLA	444.05000	+	127.3 Hz	
Redfield	FM	N5KWH	147.19500	+		
Ridgeway	DMR/BM	W5NWA	444.15000	+	CC1	
Rocky Comfort (historical)						
		K5ITM-L	147.54000			
Rogers	DSTAR	KG5JPJ B	442.52500	+		
	FM	N5UFO	443.17500	+	97.4 Hz	
Rose Bud	FM	W4GXI	444.42500	+		
Royal	DMR/BM	KG5QYM	145.23000	-	CC2	
	DMR/BM	KG5QYM	442.10000	+	CC1	
	DMR/BM	WX5HOT	444.27500	+	CC3	
Rudy	FM	KD5ZMO	147.16500	+	123.0 Hz	
	FM	KD5ZMO	443.72500	+	123.0 Hz	
Russell	FM	WA5OOY	147.31500	+	114.8 Hz	
Russellville	DMR/BM	K5CS	442.36250	+	CC1	
Salem	DMR/BM	W5JDW	145.17000	145.11000	CC1	
	DMR/BM	W5JDW	443.00000	+	CC1	
Searcy	DMR/BM	N5QZ	442.20000	+	CC1	
	DMR/BM	N5QI	444.00000	+	CC1	
	DMR/BM	W1ZM	444.87500	+	CC1	
	FM	AB5ER	146.65500	-	94.8 Hz	
	FM	W1ZM	146.89500	-	85.4 Hz	
	FM	AC5AV	147.39000	+	94.8 Hz	
	FM	N5LKE	442.10000	+		
	FM	N5QS	444.50000	+	192.8 Hz	
Sheridan	FM	K5BTM	146.98500	-		
	FM	K5BTM	444.90000	+	88.5 Hz	
Sherwood	DMR/BM	N5QLC	146.64000	-	CC1	
	DMR/BM	K5NSX	443.90000	+	CC1	
	FM	N1RQ	147.25500	+	114.8 Hz	
	FUSION	KD5JVV	439.15000			
	FUSION	KD5JVV	443.21000			
Siloam Springs	FM	WX5SLG	443.57500	+	114.8 Hz	
	FM	N5YEI	444.32500	+	114.8 Hz	
Springdale	DMR/BM	NW5AR	439.12500	432.55000	CC1	
	DMR/BM	KE5LXK	442.45000	+	CC1	
	FM	K5DVT	53.03000	51.33000	97.4 Hz	
	FM	N5UFO	442.20000	+	97.4 Hz	
	FM	KE5LXK	443.65000	+	97.4 Hz	
	IDAS	K5SRS	443.20000	+		
Star City	FM	W5DI	146.67000	-	114.8 Hz	
Stuttgart	FM	KB5LN	147.00000	-	114.8 Hz	
Summers	DMR/MARC	KI5DWB	442.02500	+	CC1	
Texarkana	FM	N5LQV-R	147.28500	+		
Trumann	FM	NI5A	146.95500	-	107.2 Hz	
	FM	NI5A	443.50000	+	94.8 Hz	
Van Buren	FM	KC5YQB	145.19000	-	141.3 Hz	
	FUSION	KA5PZR	146.55500			
	FUSION	KA5PZR	432.30000			
Vanndale	FM	WA5CC	147.37500	+	107.2 Hz	
Vilonia	FM	N5EWC	145.27000	-	100.0 Hz	
	FM	N5EWC	146.49000		100.0 Hz	
	FM	W5AMI	444.82500	+	85.4 Hz	

Location	Mode	Call sign	Output	Input	Access	Coordinator
West Memphis	FM	AB5BC	147.15000	+	107.2 Hz	
	FM	KI5GEU	442.40000	+	107.2 Hz	
White Hall	DMR/BM	KC5MN01	442.17500	+	CC1	
	FM	K5DAK	147.24000	+		
	FM	N5RN	147.45000			
	FM	KJ5PE	442.17500	+	82.5 Hz	
	FM	AF5AR	443.70000	+		
Willisville	FM	N5ZAY	146.65500	-	100.0 Hz	
	FM	N5ZAY	444.92500	+		
Winslow	DSTAR	KG5JPI B	442.61250	+		
	FM	K5SRS	444.77500	+	103.5 Hz	
Wynne	FM	WY5AR	146.86500	-	107.2 Hz	
Y City	FM	W5AWX	442.50000	+	79.7 Hz	
Yellville	FM	W5DHH	147.24000	+	103.5 Hz	

CALIFORNIA

Location	Mode	Call sign	Output	Input	Access	Coordinator
Acton	FM	K6ECS	147.70500	-	103.5 Hz	
Agoura	FM	KE6HGO	447.50000	-		
	FM	N6IGG	1284.25000	-		
Ahwahnee	FM	WB6NIL	224.40000	-	123.0 Hz	
Alameda	DMR/BM	KG7NBL	442.30000	+	CC1	
	DMR/BM	KA7QQV	443.50000	+	CC1	
	FM	KF6ALA	147.82500	-	88.5 Hz	
	FM	K6QLF	444.57500	+	88.5 Hz	
Alamo	FUSION	KD6KWV	441.05000	+		
Alhambra	FM	KM6EON	445.06000	-	186.2 Hz	
Aliso Viejo	FM	KI6DB	445.10000	-	100.0 Hz	
Alleghany	FM	WR6ASF	444.92500	+	88.5 Hz	
Alpine	DMR/MARC	WD6AML	447.90000	-	CC1	
	FM	N6LZR	441.55000	+		
	FM	K6KTA	447.58000	-	107.2 Hz	
	FM	N6LVR	449.30000	-	88.5 Hz	
Altadena	FM	N6LXX	53.62000	-	107.2 Hz	
	FM	K6CPT	145.30000	-	100.0 Hz	
	FM	K6VGP	147.36000	+	100.0 Hz	
	FM	K6CPT	224.30000	-	100.0 Hz	
	FM	K6VGP	224.56000	-	114.8 Hz	
	FM	WA6DVG	224.94000	-	94.8 Hz	
	FM	W6TOI	445.64000	-	156.7 Hz	
	FM	WA6IBL	445.80000	-		
	FM	K6VGP	446.24000	-		
	FM	WA6LWW	446.78000	-	107.2 Hz	
	FM	WA6VLD	448.50000	-		
	FM	W6JYP	448.88000	-		
	FM	N6CIZ	449.70000	-	131.8 Hz	
	FM	WA6TTL	449.72000	-		
	FM	K6VGP	1283.25000	-		
	FM	K6CPT	1285.30000	-	100.0 Hz	
	FUSION	KM6KAQ	437.95000			
Altaville		AE6LA-R	145.17000			
Alturas	FM	WB6HMD	146.97000	-	100.0 Hz	
	FM	N6KMR	147.36000	+	100.0 Hz	
	FM	K6PRN	441.22500	+	100.0 Hz	
	FM	WB6HMD	442.35000	+	85.4 Hz	
	FM	N6KMR	444.25000	+	100.0 Hz	
Amboy	DMR/MARC	KF6FM	448.31250	-	CC1	
American Canyon	FM	K6ZRX	927.40000	902.40000	192.8 Hz	
Anaheim	DMR/BM	WI6Y	449.46250	-	CC3	
	DSTAR	W6HRO C	147.57000	145.01500		
	DSTAR	W6HRO	147.57000	144.97000		
	DSTAR	W6HRO B	449.84000	-		
	DSTAR	W6HRO	449.84000	-		

Location	Mode	Call sign	Output	Input	Access	Coordinator
Anaheim	DSTAR	W6HRO A	1287.82500	-		
	FM	KE6FUZ	146.94000	-	131.8 Hz	
	FM	WI6Y	445.22000	-		
	FUSION	N6DXA	442.27000			
Anchor Bay	FM	WA6RQX	147.27000	+	114.8 Hz	
Angels Camp	FM	NC6R	441.12500	+	156.7 Hz	
	FM	N6LZR	444.85000	+	103.5 Hz	
Angwin	DMR/BM	K6LO	147.85500	-	CC1	
	DMR/BM	K6LO	440.07500	+	CC1	
Antioch	FM	KC6WYA	440.65000	+	127.3 Hz	
Anza	FM	W6YQY	224.10000	-		
	FM	WB6RHQ	224.18000	-	156.7 Hz	
	FM	WV6H	1284.85000	-		
Anza, Toro Pk	FM	WD6FZA	446.38000	-	156.7 Hz	
Apple Valley	FM	KB6BZZ	445.68000	-	141.3 Hz	
Aptos	DMR/BM	K6LNK	145.01250	147.51250	CC10	
Arbuckle	FM	N6NHI	147.12000	+	118.8 Hz	
	FM	N6NHI	224.54000	-	118.8 Hz	
Arcadia	FM	N6AH	145.20000	-	103.5 Hz	
	FM	WA6CGR	224.28000	-	107.2 Hz	
	FM	K6TEM	445.48000	-	131.8 Hz	
	FM	N6EX	445.50000	-	85.4 Hz	
	FM	K6JSI	447.58000	-	100.0 Hz	
	FM	WA6SBH	449.40000	-		
	FM	KD6WLY	927.17500	902.17500	103.5 Hz	
	FM	W6VHU	1283.30000	-		
	FM	WA6CGR	1283.90000	-		
Arnold	FM	KD6GIY	441.72500	+	162.2 Hz	
Arroyo Fairways Mobile Home Cl						
	FM	N7OD-R	145.42000	-	88.5 Hz	
Arroyo Grande	FM	WB6FMC	146.70000	-	127.3 Hz	
	FM	W6SLO	146.94000	-	127.3 Hz	
	FM	N6CAV	147.03000	+	127.3 Hz	
	FM	W6YDZ	443.97500	+	127.3 Hz	
Atascadero	DMR/MARC	W6FM	441.02500	+	CC1	
Auberry	FM	KG6IBA	444.27500	+	127.3 Hz	
	P25	N6LYE	443.60000	+		
Auburn	DMR/BM	NG6D	442.96250	+	CC1	
	DSTAR	K6IOK	444.50000	+		
	DSTAR	K6IOK B	444.50000	+		
	FM	N6JSL	29.62000	-	156.7 Hz	
	FM	K6IOK	145.13000	-	114.8 Hz	
	FM	W6SAR	145.27000	-	156.7 Hz	
	FM	W6EK-R	145.43000	-		
	FM	N6JSL	146.76000	-	136.5 Hz	
	FM	N6NMZ	147.31500	+	77.0 Hz	
	FM	WB6ALS	223.82000	-	131.8 Hz	
	FM	W6EK	223.86000	-	110.9 Hz	
	FM	N6NMZ	223.90000	-	100.0 Hz	
	FM	W7FAT	224.02000	-	100.0 Hz	
	FM	W4WIL	224.58000	-	167.9 Hz	
	FM	K6IOK	444.47500	+	94.8 Hz	
	FM	N6NMZ	444.60000	+	192.8 Hz	
	FM	K6JSI	444.95000	+	100.0 Hz	
	FM	N6NMZ	927.15000	902.15000		
	FM	KI6SSF	927.36250	902.36250		
	FM	N6NMZ	927.77500	902.77500	77.0 Hz	
	P25	N6LYE	443.60000	+		
	FUSION	W6EK	440.57500	+		
Aukum	FM	W6HMT-R	52.64000	-		
Avalon	FM	AA6DP	446.14000	-	110.9 Hz	
	FM	N6SCI	446.86000	-	141.3 Hz	

Location	Mode	Call sign	Output	Input	Access	Coordinator
Baker	DMR/MARC	KF6FM	448.16250	-	CC2	
	FM	N6BKL	53.94000	-	82.5 Hz	
	FM	K6DK	147.15000	+	131.8 Hz	
	FM	WR6TM	446.38000	-	136.5 Hz	
	FM	WD6DIH	446.96000	-	136.5 Hz	
	FM	W7DOD	448.16000	-	141.3 Hz	
Bakersfield	DMR/BM	WX6D	440.00000	+	CC1	
	DMR/BM	K6RET	442.67500	+	CC1	
	DMR/BM	K6RET	443.00000	+	CC1	
	DMR/BM	K6RET	444.92500	+	CC1	
	DMR/MARC	WX6D	440.95000	+	CC1	NARCC
	FM	W6LIE-R	145.15000	-	100.0 Hz	
	FM	KF6JOQ	145.21000	-	100.0 Hz	
	FM	W6LI	145.41000	-	103.5 Hz	
	FM	W6LIE	146.91000	-	100.0 Hz	
	FM	KG6KKV	147.15000	+	100.0 Hz	
	FM	KC6EOC	147.21000	+	100.0 Hz	
	FM	K6RET	147.27000	+	94.8 Hz	
	FM	W6LIE	224.06000	-	100.0 Hz	
	FM	W6PVG	224.42000	-	156.7 Hz	
	FM	KG6KKV	224.52000	-	100.0 Hz	
	FM	N7BJD	443.27500	+	141.3 Hz	
	FM	W6LIE	443.90000	+	100.0 Hz	
	FM	KG6KKV	444.42500	+	100.0 Hz	
	FM	N6SMU	444.75000	+	141.3 Hz	
	FM	K6JSI	447.64000	-	100.0 Hz	
	FM	K6RET	927.12500	902.12500		
	FM	W6LIE	1285.45000	-	100.0 Hz	
	P25	KE6YJC	440.97500	+		
	FUSION	WM7C	433.00000			
	FUSION	WM7C	438.80000			
	FUSION	N6SMU	447.04000	-		
Banning	DMR/MARC	KF6FM	448.16250	-	CC3	
	FM	W6CDF	147.91500	-	123.0 Hz	
	FM	W6CTR	445.16000	-	67.0 Hz	
	FM	KE6PCV	445.26000	-	100.0 Hz	
	FM	N6AJB	448.40000	-		
	FM	WB6TZC	448.66000	-		
	FM	AF6HP	449.60000	-	100.0 Hz	
Barstow	DMR/BM	KC6NKK	147.91500	-	CC1	
	DMR/MARC	K6DEW	447.90000	-	CC1	
	FM	N6SLD	145.22000	-	114.8 Hz	
	FM	WA6TST	146.97000	-	151.4 Hz	
	FM	WA6TST	147.18000	+	151.4 Hz	
	FM	W6SCE	224.32000	-	100.0 Hz	
	FM	KE6JZS	447.58000	-	107.2 Hz	
	FM	W6ATN	448.42000	-		
	FM	WR6OM	449.78000	-	136.5 Hz	
	FM	KC6NKK	927.55000	902.55000	100.0 Hz	
Bayshore		KA6TGI-R	144.00000			
Bear Mountain	DMR/BM	K6GTA	442.22500	-	CC1	
	DMR/BM	K6GTA	447.12000	-	CC1	
Bear Valley Springs						
	FM	W6SLZ	146.70000	-	123.0 Hz	
Bell	FM	N6WZK	445.02000	-	167.9 Hz	
	FM	N6WZK	448.40000	-	151.4 Hz	
Bellota	FM	N6QDY-R	441.10000	+		
Belmont	FM	WB6CKT	147.09000	+	100.0 Hz	
	FM	KR6WP	440.07500	+	114.8 Hz	
Ben Lomond	FM	WR6AOK	147.12000	+	94.8 Hz	
Benbow		KB6VSE-L	146.55500			
Benicia	FM	KR6BEN	441.25000	+	100.0 Hz	

Location	Mode	Call sign	Output	Input	Access	Coordinator
Benicia	FM	KR6BEN	442.75000	+	100.0 Hz	
Berkeley	FM	KB6LED	145.29000	-	131.8 Hz	
	FM	K6GOD	223.78000	-	110.9 Hz	
	FM	KB6LED	224.34000	-	100.0 Hz	
	FM	N6BRK	224.90000	-	131.8 Hz	
	FM	K6GOD	440.17500	+	131.8 Hz	
	FM	WB6WTM	440.40000	+	127.3 Hz	
	FM	WB6IXH	440.82500	+		
	FM	WA2UNP	440.90000	+	131.8 Hz	
	FM	WA6ZTY	442.27500	+	100.0 Hz	
	FM	WB6UZX	442.67500	+		
	FM	K6DJR	442.72500	+		
	FM	KK6PH	1285.30000	-	88.5 Hz	
	FM	WA2UNP	1285.55000	-	114.8 Hz	
Big Bear City	FM	KK6MOS	224.92000	-		
	FM	WA6ITC	446.40000	-	162.2 Hz	
	FM	WA6ITC	446.42000	-	162.2 Hz	
	FM	W6RRN	448.74000	-		
Big Bear Lake	FM	K6BB	446.20000	-	103.5 Hz	
Big Bear Onyx Peak						
	DMR/BM	KB6CRE	449.34000	-	CC1	
Big Bear, Onyx Pk						
	FM	N6LXX	446.88000	-	110.9 Hz	
Bijou Park	FM	W6SUV-L	146.11500	+		
Bishop	FM	N6OV	146.94000	-	103.5 Hz	
	FM	W6SCE	224.76000	-		
Black Mountain	FM	WA6LAW	146.88000	-	162.2 Hz	
	FM	WM6Z	147.12000	+	103.5 Hz	
Blossom Valley	FM	KH6N-R	440.87500	+		
Blueridge	DSTAR	W6CPAR C	145.58500	-		
	DSTAR	WB6IRC C	147.54000	144.98500		
	DSTAR	W6CPAR B	446.87000	-		
	DSTAR	WB6IRC B	446.88000	-		
Blythe	DMR/BM	N6YMZ	447.70000	-	CC1	
	FM	W6CDF	147.09000	+	123.0 Hz	
	FM	W6SCE	224.32000	-		
	FM	K6JRM	446.05000	-	88.5 Hz	
Bodega Bay	DMR/BM	KJ6QBM	440.32500	+	CC1	
Bonny Doon	DMR/BM	WB6ECE	440.58750	+	CC2	
	FM	N6NAC	224.06000	-	110.9 Hz	
Borrego Springs	FM	K6VGP	445.28000	-	114.8 Hz	SCRRBA
Boulder City	FM	W6SCE	446.92000	-	127.3 Hz	
Boulder Creek	FM	KI6YDR	145.35000	-	94.8 Hz	
Boulder Park	FM	K6CLX-R	147.00000	+		
Brawley	FM	N6LVR	146.67000	-	103.5 Hz	
Brea	FM	WB6DNX	446.54000	-	192.8 Hz	
Brentwood		KK6KFV-R	446.35000			
	DMR/BM	W6APX	444.37500	+	CC1	
Brisbane	FM	K6CV	440.70000	+	123.0 Hz	
Buena Park	DMR/BM	W6EMS	439.65000	-	CC1	
	FM	K6KBF	445.52000	-	85.4 Hz	
Burbank	DMR/BM	KE6ZRP	439.42000		CC1	
	FM	WA6PPS	147.30000	+	110.9 Hz	
	FM	N6MQS	224.20000	-	123.0 Hz	
	FM	KA6AZB	1283.95000	-		
Burney	FM	KE6CHO	444.65000	+	94.8 Hz	
Cactus City	DMR/MARC	K6TMD	446.06250	-	CC1	
	FM	NR6P	146.02500	+	107.2 Hz	
	FM	W6SCE	224.32000	-		
	FM	W6CDF	445.02000	-	186.2 Hz	
Cadenasso	FM	KE6YUV-R	146.97000	-		
Cajon Heights	FM	W6HDC-R	447.52000	-		

Location	Mode	Call sign	Output	Input	Access	Coordinator
Calexico	DMR/BM	N2IX	438.80000		CC1	
	DMR/BM	K6CLX	449.70000	-	CC1	
Calistoga	FM	K6ZRX	52.62000	-	114.8 Hz	
	FM	N6PMF	444.15000	+		
	FM	N6TKW	444.17500	+	151.4 Hz	
	FM	K6IRC	444.47500	+		
	FM	WZ6X	1283.90000	-	88.5 Hz	
Calsbad	DMR/MARC	N6ZEK	449.90000	-	CC4	
Camarillo	FM	K6BBK	147.61500	-		
	FM	K6ERN	147.91500	-	127.3 Hz	
	FM	WD6EBY	445.60000	-	141.3 Hz	
	FM	K6ERN	447.00000	-	103.5 Hz	
Cambria	FM	KC6TOX	147.27000	+	127.3 Hz	
	FM	WB6JWB	224.68000	-		NARCC
Cameron Park		KD6CQ-L	145.37000			
	FM	N6RDE	147.03000	+	77.0 Hz	
	FM	N6RDE	440.12500	+		
	FM	WA6NHC	441.00000	+	100.0 Hz	
Camino	FM	AG6AU	147.82500	-	82.5 Hz	
	FM	W6MPD	224.06000	-		
Campbell	FM	NO1PC	438.97500			
	FM	K9GVF	442.17500	+	100.0 Hz	
	FM	K6KMT	1284.85000	-	100.0 Hz	
	FUSION	KN6BJC	433.60000			
Canyon Country	FM	KC6TKA	445.90000	-	107.2 Hz	
	FM	KI6JL	1282.00000	-		
	FM	KI6JL	1284.30000	-		
Canyon Crest Mobile Home Park						
		AC6F-L	146.59500			
Canyon Lake	FM	KI6IGR	147.91500	-	100.0 Hz	
Carlsbad	DMR/BM	AI6BX	445.34000	-	CC3	
	DMR/BM	WB6YES	447.26000	-	CC3	
	DMR/BM	WB6YES	447.30000	-	CC3	
	DMR/BM	W6THC	447.60000	-	CC7	
	DMR/BM	AA4CD	449.38000	-	CC11	
	FM	W6THC	147.91500	-		
	FM	K6VST	446.86000	-	103.5 Hz	
	FUSION	KF6TTT	146.49000			
Carmichael	FM	KJ6JD	224.88000	-	162.2 Hz	
Carson	FM	KK6BE	1285.37500	-		
Casas Jara	FM	N6UG-R	442.00000	+		
Casmalia	FM	WA6VPL	52.60000	-	82.5 Hz	
Castaic	FUSION	W6PWM	447.20000	-		
Castro Valley		K6KBL-L	441.00000			
Catalina	DMR/BM	AA6DP	147.09000	+	CC1	
	FM	AA6DP	224.42000	-	110.9 Hz	
	FM	KR6AL	927.93750	902.93750		
Catalina Island	FM	N6KNW	51.86000	-	82.5 Hz	
Cathedral City	FM	WD6RAT	146.94000	-	107.2 Hz	
	FM	K6JR	449.24000	-	131.8 Hz	
Cazadero	FM	K6ACS	147.97500	-	88.5 Hz	
Cedar Pines Park	FM	W6CDF	224.26000	-	110.9 Hz	
	FM	W6CDF	445.02000	-	107.2 Hz	
Centerville	FM	KE6CHO-R	145.11000	-		
Cerritos	FUSION	KN6NUH	437.95000			
Chatsworth	DMR/MARC	KF6FM	447.52000	-	CC2	
	FM	K6LRB	53.76000	-	82.5 Hz	
	FM	WD6EBY	145.24000	-	127.3 Hz	
	FM	KB6C	147.73500	-	100.0 Hz	
	FM	KF6JWT	147.94500	-	136.5 Hz	
	FM	WD6FZA	224.40000	-		
	FM	WA6DVG	224.58000	-	156.7 Hz	

Location	Mode	Call sign	Output	Input	Access	Coordinator
Chatsworth	FM	K6LRB	224.62000	-	82.5 Hz	
	FM	W6SCE	224.74000	-		
	FM	WD6AWP	445.10000	-	82.5 Hz	
	FM	K6LAM	445.46000	-		
	FM	W6RRN	445.80000	-		
	FM	WD6EBY	445.84000	-	141.3 Hz	
	FM	K7FY	445.88000	-		
	FM	W6XC	446.38000	-		
	FM	WA6TTL	446.66000	-		
	FM	WA6LWW	446.68000	-		
	FM	N6LXX	446.80000	-	103.5 Hz	
	FM	WA6TTL	447.16000	-		
	FM	WB6LST	447.56000	-	136.5 Hz	
	FM	KE6PGN	447.82000	-	67.0 Hz	
	FM	N6LXX	927.58750	902.58750	131.8 Hz	
Cherry Valley	FM	KD6DDM-R	146.61000	-		
Chester	FM	N6TZG	441.37500	+		
	FM	KF6CCP	444.50000	+	103.5 Hz	
Chico	DMR/BM	KI6ND	440.40000	+	CC1	
	DSTAR	K6CHO C	146.89500	-		
	DSTAR	K6CHO A	1286.52500	-		
	DSTAR	K6CHO D	1299.35000			
	FM	KI6ND	145.49000	-	110.9 Hz	
	FM	W6RHC	146.85000	-	110.9 Hz	
	FM	W6ECE	146.94000	-	123.0 Hz	
	FM	K6NP	147.30000	+	141.3 Hz	
	FM	N6TZG	147.97500	-	110.9 Hz	
	FM	WA6UHF	224.28000	-	110.9 Hz	
	FM	K6JSI	224.44000	-	100.0 Hz	
	FM	KI6ND	224.62000	-	88.5 Hz	
	FM	KI6PNB	440.00000	+	100.0 Hz	
	FM	WA6UHF	440.50000	+		
	FM	WB6RHC	440.55000	+		
	FM	W6RHC	440.65000	+	110.9 Hz	
	FM	N6EJX	440.67500	+		
	FM	WB6RHC	441.40000	+	110.9 Hz	
	FM	W6ECE	442.37500	+	100.0 Hz	
	FM	KI6ND	444.40000	+	110.9 Hz	
	FM	KI6ND	927.07500	902.07500	88.5 Hz	
Chino	DMR/BM	KN6CBZ	449.96000	-	CC1	
	FM	K6OPJ	445.56000	-	136.5 Hz	
	FM	K0JPK	447.50000	-		
Chino Hills	FM	W6AJP	445.84000	-		
	FUSION	KN6HHX	144.15000			
	FUSION	W6DSL	145.50000			
	FUSION	K5LFE	448.88000	-		
	FUSION	K5LFE	449.32000	-		
Chorro	FM	W6FM-R	444.52500	+		
Chuckwalla Pk	DMR/MARC	WD6AML	447.90000	-	CC1	
Chula Vista	FM	KK6KD	145.26000	-	107.2 Hz	
	FM	KK6KD	224.94000	-	107.2 Hz	
	FUSION	WE6CW	435.70500			
	FUSION	AI6MH	443.32500			
Cimarron	FM	N6BEN-L	442.02500	+		
Cisco Grove	FM	N6MVT	443.47500	+	100.0 Hz	
Citrus Heights	FM	KA6FTY	444.72500	+		
Claremont	DMR/BM	WB6YES	449.36000	-	CC1	
	FM	WA1IRS	224.90000	-	103.5 Hz	
	FM	N6LXX	446.10000	-	100.0 Hz	
	FM	N6SIM	446.30000	-	127.3 Hz	
	FM	K4ELE	446.48000	-		
	FM	N6DKA	447.72000	-		

Location	Mode	Call sign	Output	Input	Access	Coordinator
Claremont	FM	W7BF	448.36000	-		
	FM	N6ENL	448.52000	-		
	FM	W6RRN	448.76000	-		
	FM	WH6NZ	448.78000	-		
	FM	WB6TZA	449.00000	-		
	FM	W6OY	449.14000	-	100.0 Hz	
	FM	K6UFX	449.52000	-	100.0 Hz	
	FM	N6LXX	927.55000	902.05000	123.0 Hz	
Clayton	DMR/BM	W6CX	144.92500	147.42500	CC1	
	FM	N6AMG	927.11250	902.11250		
Clearlake	FM	WR6COP	442.82500	+		
Cloverdale	DMR/BM	KG6NLW	440.10000	+	CC1	
	FM	KI6B	146.97000	-	103.5 Hz	
	FM	WB6QAZ	449.70000	-	88.5 Hz	
Clovis	DMR/MARC	WX6D	145.45000	-	CC1	
	DMR/MARC	WX6D	440.05000	+	CC1	NARCC
	FM	K6ARP	147.67500	-	141.3 Hz	
	FM	N6JXL	224.38000	-	141.3 Hz	
	FM	K6ARP	440.05000	+	123.0 Hz	
	FM	NI6M	440.35000	+	141.3 Hz	
	FM	N6IB	443.82500	+	141.3 Hz	
	FM	K6ARP	444.72500	+	141.3 Hz	
	FUSION	W6KKO	147.70500	-		
Coalinga	DMR/BM	N6VYT	145.02500	147.50000	CC1	NARCC
	DMR/MARC	WX6D	442.00000	+	CC1	
	DMR/MARC	KF6FM	442.42500	-	CC1	
	FM	W6VFZ	224.44000	-	100.0 Hz	
	FM	N6LEX	440.52500	+	146.2 Hz	
	FM	W6EMS	440.67500	+	146.2 Hz	
	FM	K6JKL	440.75000	+	114.8 Hz	
	FM	K6JSI	441.67500	+	100.0 Hz	
	FM	N6OA	441.90000	+	100.0 Hz	
	FM	NC9RS	927.66250	902.66250	146.2 Hz	
	P25	K6NOX	443.72500	+	107.2 Hz	
Coarsegold	FM	W6HMH	146.64000	-	127.3 Hz	
	FM	W6HMH	442.90000	+	127.3 Hz	
	FM	K6MXZ	444.37500	+	123.0 Hz	
	FM	KE6YMW	444.40000	+	82.5 Hz	
	FM	WB6NIL	444.50000	+	131.8 Hz	
Cohasset	FM	N6YCK	224.36000	-	110.9 Hz	
	FM	KH8AF	444.12500	+		
Colton		KD6MHS-L	147.48000			
Columbia	FM	W6FEJ	147.94500	-	100.0 Hz	
	FM	K6DEL	440.85000	+	146.2 Hz	
	FM	K6TUO	440.97500	+	103.5 Hz	
	FM	K6NOX	927.40000	902.40000	107.2 Hz	
Concord		AA1FD-L	147.55500			
	DSTAR	W6CX C	145.00000	147.50000		
	DSTAR	W6CX	145.00000	147.50000		
	FM	K6POU	145.33000	-	100.0 Hz	
	FM	AB6CR	145.35000	-	88.5 Hz	
	FM	W6CX	147.06000	+	100.0 Hz	
	FM	WA6HAM	147.73500	-	107.2 Hz	
	FM	W6YOP	223.98000	-	85.4 Hz	
	FM	W6CX	224.78000	-	77.0 Hz	
	FM	W6YOP	224.92000	-	85.4 Hz	
	FM	WB6FRM	440.32500	+	127.3 Hz	
	FM	N6BLA	440.77500	+		
	FM	WA6HAM	440.87500	+		
	FM	W6CX	441.32500	+	100.0 Hz	
	FM	W6YOP	441.75000	+	127.3 Hz	
	FM	WB6BDD	441.82500	+	114.8 Hz	

Location	Mode	Call sign	Output	Input	Access	Coordinator
Concord	FM	WA6ZTY	442.65000	+	100.0 Hz	
	FM	K6JJC	443.50000	+		
	FM	K6IRC	443.57500	+		
	FM	K6POU	443.80000	+	100.0 Hz	
	FM	K6FJ	444.87500	+	123.0 Hz	
	FM	N6OLD	927.55000	902.55000	141.3 Hz	
	FUSION	KD6KWV	431.40000			
	FUSION	N6CMB	441.06250	+		
Contractors Point	FM	KC6JAR	445.34000	-	103.5 Hz	
Copperopolis	FM	KG6TXA	29.66000	-	141.3 Hz	
	FM	N6GKJ	147.01500	+	114.8 Hz	
	FM	KB6RYU	224.34000	-	141.3 Hz	
	FM	KD6FVA	441.65000	+	156.7 Hz	
	FM	N6MAC	442.37500	+	186.2 Hz	
Cordelia	FM	WZ6X	1282.40000	-	88.5 Hz	
Corning	DMR/BM	N6YCK	147.97500	-	CC1	
	FM	NC9RS	927.63750	902.63750	123.0 Hz	
Corona		KG6ERK-L	449.53700			
	DMR/BM	KE6PCV	445.22000	-	CC1	
	DSTAR	WB6BA B	446.36000	-		
	FM	KI6ITV	146.76000	-	136.5 Hz	
	FM	W6PWT	147.06000	+	162.2 Hz	
	FM	W6CPD	147.22500	+	156.7 Hz	
	FM	W6NUT	147.45000	146.45000	127.3 Hz	
	FM	W6CPD	147.88500	-	88.5 Hz	
	FM	W6KRW	223.76000	-	110.9 Hz	
	FM	W7BF	224.80000	-		
	FM	W6CTR	445.94000	-	151.4 Hz	
	FM	WB6ORK	447.10000	-	136.5 Hz	
	FM	K6ARN	448.28000	-	107.2 Hz	
	FM	W7BF	448.36000	-		
	FM	W6KRW	1282.27500	-	88.5 Hz	
	FUSION	KO6TX	445.74000	-		
	FUSION	KO6TX	447.74000	-		
	FUSION	KO6TX	449.60000	-		
Corona Del Mar	FM	N6ACG	448.90000	-	110.9 Hz	
Coronado	DSTAR	W6MLI B	447.20000	-		
	DSTAR	W6SH	447.20000	-		
	FM	W6RDF	145.38000	-	107.2 Hz	
	FM	W6SH	147.18000	+	110.9 Hz	
Corralitos	FM	KJ6FFP	146.70000	-	94.8 Hz	
Costa Mesa	FM	WB6HRO	147.06000	+	100.0 Hz	
	FM	AD6HK	224.32000	-	151.4 Hz	
Cottonwood	FM	K6JSI	147.30000	+	123.0 Hz	
Covelo	FM	WB6TCS	147.21000	+	103.5 Hz	
Covina	DMR/BM	K9KAO	145.36000	-	CC1	
	DMR/BM	N7YMM	449.68000	-	CC1	
	FM	WA6NJJ	223.84000	-	151.4 Hz	
	FUSION	N7YMM	444.65000	+		
	FUSION	KN6DFR	446.76000	-		
Crescent City	FM	W6HY	146.88000	-	136.5 Hz	
	FM	K6JSI	147.06000	+	100.0 Hz	
	FM	W6HY	147.39000	+	136.5 Hz	
	FM	KA7PRR	224.62000	-	91.5 Hz	
	FM	KA7PRR	224.72000	-	103.5 Hz	
	FM	KA7PRR	442.52500	+		
	FM	KD6GDZ	443.05000	+	100.0 Hz	
Crestline	FM	W6JBT	146.85000	-	146.2 Hz	
	FM	N6QCU	224.20000	-		
	FM	W6JBT	224.86000	-	77.0 Hz	
	FM	W6JJR	445.36000	-		
	FM	WB6LOT	446.33500	-		

Location	Mode	Call sign	Output	Input	Access	Coordinator
Crestline	FM	WB6LOT	446.37500	-	123.0 Hz	
	FM	K6IOJ	448.42000	-		
	FM	K6JTH	448.70000	-		
	FM	K6DLP	449.86000	-	107.2 Hz	
	FM	K6DLP	449.92000	-		
	FM	W6ATN	1253.25000	-		
Culver City	DMR/MARC	KJ6YQW	446.43000	-	CC1	
	FM	WA6TFD	146.92500	-	114.8 Hz	
	FM	WA6MDJ	445.32000	-	88.5 Hz	
Cupertino	FM	KA2FND	224.62000	-	110.9 Hz	
	FM	W6AMT	440.12500	+		
	FM	W6TDM	440.15000	+	100.0 Hz	
	FM	W6VB	441.55000	+		
	FM	N6MBB	1284.00000	-	100.0 Hz	
	FM	W6MOW	1285.65000	-	110.9 Hz	
Cypress	DMR/BM	N0CSW	444.50000	+	CC1	
	DSTAR	N6CYP	144.89500	+		
	FUSION	W6DXC	145.70000			
	FUSION	W6DXC	431.52500			
Daly City	DMR/MARC	W6BUR	442.75000	+	CC0	
	DMR/MARC	N6DOZ	443.52500	+	CC7	
	DSTAR	KN6CDC	144.95000	147.45000		
	DSTAR	KN6CDC C	144.95000	147.45000		
	FM	WD6INC	146.83500	-	123.0 Hz	
	FM	KC6IAU	146.95500	-	146.2 Hz	
	FM	KA6TGI	434.15000			
	FM	K6TEA	440.67500	+		
	FM	KC6PGV	442.37500	+	156.7 Hz	
	FUSION	KC6IAU	146.95500	-		
Dana Point	FM	N6OCS	927.17500	902.17500	123.0 Hz	
Danville	DMR/BM	N6TRB	440.65000	+	CC1	
Davis	FM	K6JRB	145.45000	-	203.5 Hz	
Del Mar	DMR/BM	WB9COY	449.46250	-	CC1	
Desert Center	FM	KA6GBJ	147.03000	+	107.2 Hz	
	FM	WC6MRA	224.04000	-		
	FM	W6YQY	224.70000	-		
	FM	W6SCE	224.76000	-		
Desert Center, Chuckwalla Mt						
	FM	W6DRA	145.38000	-	100.0 Hz	
Devon	FM	W6AB-R	145.36000	-		
Diamond Bar	FM	W7BF	146.64000	-	167.9 Hz	
	FM	N6XPG	147.03000	+	100.0 Hz	
	FM	WR6JPL	224.70000	-	114.8 Hz	
	FM	NO6B-R	445.08000	-		
	FM	NO6B	446.28000	-		
	FM	WA6TTL	447.14000	-		
Diamond Springs	FM	WA6EUZ	444.07500	+		
Dillon Beach	FM	KI6SUD	146.86500	-	88.5 Hz	
Dinsmore	FM	K6FWR	146.98000	-	103.5 Hz	
Dinuba	FM	N6SGW	147.30000	+	94.8 Hz	
	FM	N6SGW	444.82500	+	141.3 Hz	
Dixon	FM	K6JWN	441.88750	+	94.8 Hz	
Dobbins	FM	N6NMZ	147.04500	+	77.0 Hz	
	FM	N6ICW	444.30000	+		
Downey	FUSION	AA6DB	145.50000			
	FUSION	KN6GNG	438.56000			
	FUSION	N6TEB	438.90000			
Duarte	FM	KA6AMR	146.08500	+	110.9 Hz	
Dublin	FM	KQ6RC	224.40000	-		
Dunnigan	FM	NA6DF	224.72000	-	77.0 Hz	
Dunsmuir	FM	W7PRA	146.67000	-	136.5 Hz	
	FM	K6SIS	146.82000	-	100.0 Hz	

Location	Mode	Call sign	Output	Input	Access	Coordinator
Eastvale	FM	KG6YGC	144.33500		100.0 Hz	
	FUSION	KK6DSB	433.30000			
Edgewood	FM	KJ6RA	444.35000	+	100.0 Hz	
El Cajon	DMR/BM	KF6YB	449.90000	-	CC1	
	DMR/MARC	W6HDC	446.06250	-	CC1	
	FM	W6SS	146.26500	+	107.2 Hz	
	FM	KN6NA	146.35500	+	123.0 Hz	
	FM	WA6BGS	147.42000	146.52000	107.2 Hz	
	FM	K6JCC	223.80000	-		
	FM	WV6H	223.94000	-	141.3 Hz	
	FM	WA6BGS	224.08000	-	107.2 Hz	
	FM	WA6BGS	445.90000	-	107.2 Hz	
	FUSION	N6SIX	448.94000	-	141.3 Hz	
El Cerrito	DMR/MARC	AH6KD	441.87500	+	CC0	
	FM	N6GVI	444.70000	+	100.0 Hz	
El Dorado	FM	W6OIU	52.56000	-	107.2 Hz	
	FM	WA6JQV	927.02500	902.02500		
	FM	WA6JQV	927.47500	902.47500		
El Dorado Hills	DMR/BM	W6JMP	145.01250	147.51250	CC1	
	FM	W7CCE	52.82000	-	110.9 Hz	
	FM	NC9RS	927.01250	902.01250	100.0 Hz	
El Dorado Hills.	DMR/BM	KA6ZRJ	442.70000	+	CC1	
El Mirage	FM	AA7SQ	147.99000	-		
El Monte	DMR/BM	W1REI	443.72500	+	CC1	
El Segundo	FM	WB6VMV	445.24000	-	88.5 Hz	
	FM	W6HA	445.62000	-	127.3 Hz	
Elk Creek	FM	N6YCK	147.10500	+	110.9 Hz	
Ellis Place	FM	N6BYH-L	146.76000	-		
Elsinore Peak	DMR/BM	WB6YES	445.72000	-	CC1	
Elverta	DMR/BM	K9WWV	441.85000	+	CC1	
	FM	N6ICW	927.95000	902.95000		
Engineer Springs	FM	K6GAO	145.28000	-	107.2 Hz	
Escondido	DMR/BM	AA6TU	449.46250	-	CC1	
	DMR/MARC	W6PSA	446.14000	-	CC1	
	DSTAR	KI6MGN	147.57000	144.97000		
	DSTAR	KI6MGN	1282.67500	-		
	FM	W6JLL	51.72000	-	82.5 Hz	
	FM	W6NWG	52.68000	-	107.2 Hz	
	FM	W6ZN	145.28000	-	74.4 Hz	
	FM	N6NIK	145.44000	-	186.2 Hz	
	FM	W6NWG	146.70000	-		
	FM	K6RIF	147.03000	+	103.5 Hz	
	FM	W6NWG	147.07500	+	107.2 Hz	
	FM	W6NWG	147.13000	+	107.2 Hz	
	FM	K6JCC	147.19500	+	203.5 Hz	
	FM	KK6KD	224.38000	-	107.2 Hz	
	FM	WD6HFR	224.90000	-	107.2 Hz	
	FM	K6RIF	447.80000	-	88.5 Hz	
	FM	K6JXY	448.54000	-	103.5 Hz	
	FM	KE6VK	448.96000	-	131.8 Hz	
	FM	K6JSI	449.08000	-	123.0 Hz	
	FM	WA6TTL	449.72000	-		
	FM	W6YJ	927.11250	902.11250		
	FUSION	W6ZAR	145.67500			
	FUSION	K9EQ	445.54000	-		
Esparto	FM	NC6R	441.12500	+	127.3 Hz	
Eureka	FM	W6ZZK	145.47000	-	103.5 Hz	
	FM	K6FWR	146.70000	-	103.5 Hz	
	FM	WB6HII	147.44500	-	103.5 Hz	
	FM	AE6R	442.00000	+	100.0 Hz	
	FM	WA6RQX	442.22500	+		
	FM	WA6RQX	444.75000	+	100.0 Hz	

Location	Mode	Call sign	Output	Input	Access	Coordinator
Fair Oaks	FM	W6HIR	146.79000	-	100.0 Hz	
Fairbanks Ranch	DMR/MARC	K6RYA	449.90000	-	CC0	
Fairfield		WZ6X-R	441.45000			
	DMR/BM	KK6X	443.40000	+	CC1	
	FM	W6ER	224.38000	-	77.0 Hz	
	FM	K6SOL	441.15000	+	77.0 Hz	
	FM	KC6UJM	442.77500	+	77.0 Hz	
	FM	WL3DZ	443.40000	+		
	FM	KE3RQ	444.12500	+		
	FUSION	AA6GF	145.01000			
	FUSION	KJ6DLF	146.41500			
Fallbrook	DMR/BM	KU6E	442.72500	+	CC1	
	DMR/MARC	WD6AML	446.06250	-	CC1	
	FM	N6FQ	146.17500	+	107.2 Hz	
	FM	KF6ATL	445.22000	-		
	FM	N6FQ	445.60000	-	107.2 Hz	
	FM	KG6HSQ-R	446.80000	-		
	FUSION	KD6CWI	436.71000			
Felton	FM	W6JWS	146.74500	-	94.8 Hz	
Fiddletown	FM	NC6R	146.88000	-	156.7 Hz	
	FM	W6SF	147.16500	+	107.2 Hz	
	FM	KG6TXA	224.86000	-	141.3 Hz	
	FM	W6SF	442.25000	+	107.2 Hz	
	FM	K6SZQ	443.87500	+	156.7 Hz	
Folsom	DSTAR	KS6HRP C	147.67500	-		
	DSTAR	KS6HRP	147.67500	-		
	FM	KS6HRP	146.61000	-	136.5 Hz	
	FM	KS6HRP	224.72000	-	136.5 Hz	
	FM	AB6LI	440.35000	+	156.7 Hz	
	FM	KS6HRP	442.35000	+	136.5 Hz	
	FM	K6IOK	442.52500	+	77.0 Hz	
	FM	W6YDD	1283.75000	-	88.5 Hz	
Fontana	FM	KA6GRF	447.32000	-	136.5 Hz	
Foothill Farms		KP4MD-L	145.51000			
Foresthill	FM	W6YDD	146.35500	+	94.8 Hz	
	FM	W6SAR	146.74500	-	156.7 Hz	
	FM	W6SAR	223.76000	-	100.0 Hz	
	FM	KA6ZRJ	442.70000	+	114.8 Hz	
	FM	KA6EBR	442.87500	+	131.8 Hz	
Fort Bragg	FM	K6MHE	147.03000	+	103.5 Hz	
Fort Jones	FM	KK6OAH	146.92000	-		
Fortuna	FM	KA6ROM	147.09000	+	103.5 Hz	
	FUSION	KM6RSD	144.45000			
Fountain Valley	FM	WA6FV	145.26000	-	136.5 Hz	
	FM	WA6FV	447.32000	-	94.8 Hz	
Fouts Springs	DMR/BM	K6LNK	927.17500	902.17500	CC6	
Frazier Park	DMR/MARC	WD6FM	448.16250	-	CC1	
	FM	N6BKL	52.56000	-	82.5 Hz	
	FM	K6SS	147.76500	-	123.0 Hz	
	FM	N6XKI	224.72000	-	156.7 Hz	
	FM	K6NYB	445.64000	-	67.0 Hz	
	FM	WB6TZH	448.68000	-		
	FM	W6HWW	448.86000	-		
	FM	N6ENL	449.12000	-		
Fremont	DMR/MARC	KI6KGN	440.02500	+	CC12	
	DMR/MARC	KI6KGN	440.88750	+	CC13	
	FM	K6GOD	223.78000	-	110.9 Hz	
	FM	KU6V	224.18000	-	94.8 Hz	
	FM	NT6S	224.66000	-	110.9 Hz	
	FM	WA6GG	224.84000	-	127.3 Hz	
	FM	WA6FSP	440.00000	+	110.9 Hz	
	FM	K6GOD	440.17500	+	131.8 Hz	

Location	Mode	Call sign	Output	Input	Access	Coordinator
Fremont	FM	KI6KGN	440.90000	+	141.3 Hz	
	FM	KC6WXO	441.12500	+	100.0 Hz	
	FM	WB6ECE	441.30000	+	110.9 Hz	
	FM	WA6PWW	442.60000	+	107.2 Hz	
	FM	N6IGF	443.40000	+		
	FM	K6JJC	443.70000	+	136.5 Hz	
	FM	N6HWI	443.72500	+	127.3 Hz	
Fresno	DMR/MARC	WX6D	435.10000		CC1	
	DMR/MARC	WX6D	440.06250	+	CC1	
	DMR/MARC	WX6D	442.23750	+	CC1	NARCC
	DMR/MARC	W6EDX	442.80000	+	CC1	
	DSTAR	WX6D B	442.31250	+		
	DSTAR	WD6SJV D	1250.00000			
	DSTAR	WD6SJV A	1285.30000	-		
	FM	WR6VHF	51.82000	-	162.2 Hz	
	FM	WA6IPZ	52.84000	-	82.5 Hz	
	FM	W6FSC	145.23000	-	141.3 Hz	
	FM	K6WGJ	145.43000	-	141.3 Hz	
	FM	W7POR	145.47000	+	141.3 Hz	
	FM	KE6JZ	146.82000	-	141.3 Hz	
	FM	WQ6CWA	146.85000	-	141.3 Hz	
	FM	N6HEW	147.15000	+	141.3 Hz	
	FM	N6VRC	147.16500	+	141.3 Hz	
	FM	W6DXW	147.30000	+	94.8 Hz	
	FM	KE6JZ	224.70000	-	156.7 Hz	
	FM	KJ6HUP	224.74000	-	156.7 Hz	
	FM	N6VRC	440.00250	+	141.3 Hz	
	FM	KF6FGL	440.12500	+	110.9 Hz	
	FM	N6AMG	440.37500	+		
	FM	N6LYE	441.80000	+		
	FM	N6IB	442.52500	+	141.3 Hz	
	FM	WQ6CWA	443.25000	+	107.2 Hz	
	FM	N6LYE	443.30000	+	107.2 Hz	NARCC
	FM	KE6JZ	443.37500	+	123.0 Hz	
	FM	NA6MM	443.40000	+	141.3 Hz	
	FM	W6WYT	443.42500	+	141.3 Hz	
	FM	W6FSC	443.60000	+	141.3 Hz	
	FM	KE6SHK	443.65000	+	141.3 Hz	
	FM	K6SRA	443.97500	+		
	FM	W6NIF	444.10000	+	100.0 Hz	
	FM	W6TO	444.20000	+	141.3 Hz	
	FM	KJ6HUP	927.03750	902.03750	146.2 Hz	
	FM	N6VRC	927.05000	902.05000	141.3 Hz	
	FM	K6VAU	927.06250	902.06250	141.3 Hz	
	FM	W6YEP	1283.45000	-	100.0 Hz	
	P25	KF6FGL	443.77500	+		
	P25	KF6FGL	443.87500	+		
	FUSION	KN6SGP	144.85000			
	FUSION	KB6GFD	146.55000			
Frink	FM	W6SCE	224.32000	-		
Fullerton	FM	N6ME	145.40000	-	103.5 Hz	
	FM	K6QEH	146.97000	-	136.5 Hz	
	FM	N6ME	224.18000	-	103.5 Hz	
	FM	KK6HS	445.12000	-	100.0 Hz	
	FM	K6QEH	446.44000	-	114.8 Hz	
Galt	FM	K6SAL	443.45000	+	107.2 Hz	
Garberville	FM	N6VA	146.61000	-	103.5 Hz	
	FM	W6CLG	146.79000	-	103.5 Hz	
	FM	KA6ROM	147.15000	+	103.5 Hz	
Gardena	DMR/MARC	K6YO	451.81250	+	CC10	
Gasquet	FM	W6HY	147.18000	+	136.5 Hz	
Georgetown	FM	AG6AU	52.78000	-	107.2 Hz	

Location	Mode	Call sign	Output	Input	Access	Coordinator
Georgetown	FM	W6YDD	146.62500	-	123.0 Hz	
	FM	W6HIR	224.84000	-	100.0 Hz	
	FM	K6IRC	441.57500	+		
	FM	K6IRC	443.17500	+		
	FM	K6SRA	443.55000	+		
	FM	WA6APX	443.85000	+		
	FM	K6JJC	444.02500	+	107.2 Hz	
	FM	KA6GWY	444.98750	+	156.7 Hz	
	FM	K6YC	927.85000	902.85000	123.0 Hz	
Geyserville	FM	WA6OYK	442.05000	+	100.0 Hz	
Gibraltar	FM	WB9KMO	224.86000	-	131.8 Hz	
Gilroy	DMR/BM	K6SIA	440.13750	+	CC3	NARCC
	DMR/MARC	KJ6WZS	443.52500	+	CC0	
Glendale	DMR/MARC	N6JLY	445.68000	-	CC1	
	FM	W6AM	145.48000	-	100.0 Hz	
	FM	WB6ZTY	146.02500	+	136.5 Hz	
	FM	KD6AFA	146.67000	-	192.8 Hz	
	FM	AA6TL	147.49500	146.49000	186.2 Hz	
	FM	W6CPA	223.90000	-	136.5 Hz	
	FM	WA6TTL	224.04000	-		
	FM	N6ENL	224.78000	-	151.4 Hz	
	FM	WB6FYR	224.92000	-	94.8 Hz	
	FM	K6VGP	445.26000	-	100.0 Hz	
	FM	K6CCC	445.38000	-		
	FM	KI6QK	446.22000	-	123.0 Hz	
	FM	W6EL	446.86000	-	100.0 Hz	
	FM	WA6DYX	447.06000	-		
	FM	WA6UZS	447.24000	-	100.0 Hz	
	FM	WR6TWE	448.02000	-	100.0 Hz	
	FM	K6UHF	448.20000	-		
	FM	KC6ZQR	448.54000	-	136.5 Hz	
	FM	WA6ZRB	448.56000	-		
	FM	KF6JBN	448.58000	-	118.8 Hz	
	FM	WB6LVZ	448.62000	-		
	FM	WB6YMH	449.22000	-	131.8 Hz	
	FM	N6CIZ	449.26000	-		
	FM	WA6DPB	449.80000	-		
	FM	KO6TD	1282.07500	-	100.0 Hz	
	FM	WA6DPB	1282.47500	-	77.0 Hz	
	FM	KB6SUA	1284.12500	-		
	FM	AA6TL	1285.33000	-		
	FM	AB6BX	1285.60000	-		
	FM	KC6MQP	1286.32500	-		
Glendora	FM	KK6JYT-R	446.86000	-		
Glennville	FM	W6SCE	224.32000	-		
Gold Run	FM	WB6OHV	440.95000	+	192.8 Hz	
	FUSION	KA6SUB	146.92500	-		
	FUSION	KA6SUB	444.10000			
Goleta	FM	N6HYM	224.00000	-	156.7 Hz	
Gorman	FM	N6SMU	447.04000	-	136.5 Hz	
	FM	WB6ORK	447.10000	-	203.5 Hz	
	FM	WR6FM	447.36000	-		
	FM	KK6AC	447.86000	-	141.3 Hz	
	FM	KF6BXW	448.66000	-		
	FM	W6RRN	448.72000	-		
	FM	W6RLW	1282.97500	-	88.5 Hz	
	FM	WA6RLW	1285.15000	-		
Grand Terrace	FM	AE6TV	147.88500	-		
	FM	AE6TV	432.87500		100.0 Hz	
	FM	AE6TV	444.56000	+	127.3 Hz	
	FM	AE6TV	449.46000	-	77.0 Hz	
Grass Valley	FM	N1OES	52.72000	-	100.0 Hz	

Location	Mode	Call sign	Output	Input	Access	Coordinator
Grass Valley	FM	KF6GLZ	52.76000	-	131.8 Hz	
	FM	W6YDD	146.62500	-	151.4 Hz	
	FM	W6DD	147.01500	+	136.5 Hz	
	FM	W6DD	147.28500	+	151.4 Hz	
	FM	KD6GVO	224.90000	-	151.4 Hz	
	FM	KO6CW	440.10000	+	151.4 Hz	
	FM	KB6LCS	440.52500	+	192.8 Hz	
	FM	W6RCA	441.02500	+	151.4 Hz	
	FM	KF6GLZ	442.42500	+		
	FM	W6AI	442.62500	+		
	FM	N6VYQ	442.95000	+	107.2 Hz	
	FM	WA6WER	443.02500	+	114.8 Hz	
	FM	KG6BAJ	443.65000	+	114.8 Hz	
	FM	K6NP	444.05000	+		
	FM	K6RTL	444.75000	+	167.9 Hz	
	FM	WB4YJT	927.05000	902.05000		
	FM	N6NMZ	927.13750	902.13750	77.0 Hz	
Green Valley	FM	KI6BKN	147.64500	-		
	FUSION	KK6KEA	147.52500			
Greenacres		WA6ALB-L	145.15000			
Gualala	DMR/BM	K6LNK	442.07500	+	CC1	
	FM	W6ABR	147.82500	-	103.5 Hz	
Guerneville	FM	KM6XU	51.80000	-	114.8 Hz	
	FM	K6CDF	145.19000	-	88.5 Hz	
Half Moon Bay	FM	WR6HMB	147.28500	+	114.8 Hz	
	FM	N6IMS	927.70000	902.70000		
Hamilton Branch	FM	K6PLU	145.37000	-	123.0 Hz	
Hanford		KK6DOI-R	449.66000			
	DMR/MARC	WX6D	442.53750	+	CC1	
	FM	N6CVC	145.11000	-	100.0 Hz	
	FM	N6VRC	147.28500	+	141.3 Hz	
	FM	W6FBW-R	444.66000	+		
	FM	N6CVC	444.95000	+	100.0 Hz	
Happy Camp	FM	K6SIS	146.91000	-	100.0 Hz	
Harbor City	DMR/BM	N9QE	449.46000	-	CC15	
Hartley	DMR/BM	K6LNK	440.21250	+	CC7	
Haterstyle	FM	W6RGG	444.20000	+	107.2 Hz	
Hawthorne	FM	AC6FB	1283.72500	-		
	FUSION	NB6I	431.47500			
Hayward	DMR/BM	KQ6RC	147.31500	+	CC5	
	DMR/BM	KB6LED	442.25000	+	CC1	
	DMR/BM	KQ6RC	442.65000	+	CC4	
	DMR/BM	KB6LED	444.37500	+	CC1	
	DMR/BM	KB6LED	444.85000	+	CC1	
	DMR/BM	KQ6RC	444.87500	+	CC3	
	FM	K6EAG	52.76000	-	114.8 Hz	
	FM	K6EAG	145.13000	-	127.3 Hz	
	FM	KQ6YG	440.05000	+	156.7 Hz	
	FM	KB6LED	440.95000	+	100.0 Hz	
	FM	K6DDR	442.87500	+	100.0 Hz	
Healdsburg	FM	NN6J	224.36000	-	88.5 Hz	
Hemet	FM	W6COH	144.50500	+	100.0 Hz	
	FM	W6COH	224.12000	-	97.4 Hz	
	FM	K6JRM	446.86000	-	100.0 Hz	
	FM	KB6JAG-R	446.88000	-		
	FUSION	W6WDS	438.80000			
	FUSION	KJ6COI	446.42000	-		
Herald	DMR/BM	N6RXT	439.10000	-	CC1	
Hesperia	FM	W6ECS	146.02500	+		
	FM	WA6AV	146.17500	+	97.4 Hz	
High Lakes	FM	K6FHL	146.70000	-	110.9 Hz	
High Pass	FM	W6JAM	147.99000	-		

Location	Mode	Call sign	Output	Input	Access	Coordinator
Hollister	FM	W6KRK	145.11000	-	94.8 Hz	
	FM	N6SBC-R	147.31500	+		
	FM	W6MOW	441.90000	+	110.9 Hz	
	FM	W6MOW	443.60000	+	110.9 Hz	
	FM	W6MOW	1286.22500	-	110.9 Hz	
Hollywood	FM	WB6BJM	147.00000	+		
	FM	WB6BJM	147.03000	+		
	FM	KD6JTD	147.07500	+	100.0 Hz	
	FM	WB6BJM	446.28000	-		
	FM	WD8CIK	446.56000	-	127.3 Hz	
	FM	KB6IBB	449.62000	-		
Hopland	FM	WA6RQX	145.47000	-	103.5 Hz	
Horseshoe Bend	DMR/BM	W6ELL	446.26000	-	CC1	
Huntington Beach		K6MJH-L	146.43000			
	DMR/MARC	WD6AWP	439.86000	430.33000	CC1	
	DMR/MARC	W6LDS	446.88000	-	CC1	
	DMR/MARC	WA6IAJ	448.30000	-	CC1	
	FM	W6VLD	147.46500	146.46500	103.5 Hz	
	FM	W6VLD	445.58000	-	94.8 Hz	
	FM	W6BRP	447.94000	-	100.0 Hz	
	FUSION	KJ6WXD	433.52500			
	FUSION	WT6F	445.36000	-		
Idyllwild	FM	KD6OI	146.89500	-	118.8 Hz	
Imperial Beach	FM	KH2FI	433.00000		100.0 Hz	
	FM	KH2FI	444.00000	+	100.0 Hz	
Independence	FM	W6TD	146.76000	-	103.5 Hz	
	P25	WA6BAI	146.88000	-	103.5 Hz	
Indian Wells	FM	KF6FM	146.08500	+	141.3 Hz	
Indio	DMR/MARC	KF6FM	448.81250	-	CC1	
	FM	WA6MDJ	51.92000	-	82.5 Hz	
	FM	N6BKL	52.90000	52.50000	82.5 Hz	
	FM	W6KSN	447.58000	-	100.0 Hz	
Inglewood	FM	W6LMU	147.85500	-	127.3 Hz	
	FM	WS6C	224.46000	-	131.8 Hz	
Inverness	FM	KI6B	145.17000	-	88.5 Hz	
Inyokern	DMR/MARC	WD6BVD	440.37500	+	CC2	
Ione	FM	K6KBE	224.00000	-	107.2 Hz	
Irvine	DMR/MARC	WB6SRC	448.13750	-	CC1	
	FM	N6FFI	52.80000	-	82.5 Hz	
	FM	N6OCS	927.18750	902.18750	103.5 Hz	
	FM	W6KRW	1282.52500	-	88.5 Hz	
	FUSION	KE6GYD	145.78500			
	FUSION	N6PAK	447.62000	-		
Johnson Valley	DMR/MARC	KF6FM	448.13750	-	CC2	
Juniper Hills	FM	KD6KTQ	145.20000	-	114.8 Hz	
	FM	WA6GDF	449.50000	-	192.8 Hz	
Kelseyville	FM	N1PPP	146.77500	-	103.5 Hz	
	FM	KG6UFR	441.35000	+	100.0 Hz	
	FM	N6GJM	441.42500	+	100.0 Hz	
Kensington	DMR/MARC	AH6KD	441.88750	+	CC1	
King City	FM	N6SPD	145.37000	-	94.8 Hz	
	FM	K6TAZ	443.97500	+	131.8 Hz	
	FM	WA6VPL	444.27500	+		
	FM	W6FM	444.55000	+		
Kingsburg	FM	KB6RHD	444.60000	+	141.3 Hz	
	FM	KB6RHD	444.97500	+	100.0 Hz	
Klamath	FM	KA7PRR	224.86000	-		
La Canada	FM	WR6JPL	147.15000	+	103.5 Hz	
	FM	W6ATN	448.42000	-		
La Conchita	FM	W6SCE	224.76000	-		
La Crescenta	FM	NW6B	447.96000	-		
La Honda	FM	W6SCF	146.73000	-	114.8 Hz	

Location	Mode	Call sign	Output	Input	Access	Coordinator
La Honda	FM	KC6ULT	146.80500	-	114.8 Hz	
	FM	WA6DQP	440.10000	+	114.8 Hz	
La Jolla	FM	KK6UC	927.46250	902.46250	100.0 Hz	
La Mesa	DMR/BM	KF6YB	446.88000	-	CC1	
	DMR/BM	KM6VLB	448.26000	-	CC15	
	FM	WA6HYQ	145.24000	-	123.0 Hz	
	FM	N6QWD	146.67000	-	156.7 Hz	
	FM	WA6HYQ	223.88000	-	107.2 Hz	
	FM	WA6ZFT	446.88000	-	131.8 Hz	
La Palma	FUSION	AD6WI	446.50000			
La Presa	FM	W6HDC	145.12000	-	123.0 Hz	
La Quinta	FM	WA6HYQ	223.88000	-	110.9 Hz	
Laguna	DMR/MARC	KF6FM	430.96250	439.96250	CC1	
Laguna Beach	DSTAR	K6SOA	146.11500	+		
	DSTAR	K6SOA C	146.11500	+		
	DSTAR	K6SOA	445.70500	-		
	DSTAR	K6SOA B	445.70500	-		
	DSTAR	K6SOA	1282.30000	-		
	DSTAR	K6SOA A	1282.60000	-		
	DSTAR	K6SOA D	1299.90000			
	FM	K6SOA	224.10000	-	110.9 Hz	
	FM	K6SOA	445.66000	-	110.9 Hz	
Laguna Hills	FUSION	W6BIK	431.45000			
Laguna Niguel	DSTAR	K6LLL C	145.61500			
	DSTAR	K6VO C	145.61500			
	FM	AJ6EE	437.00000			
	FUSION	AJ6EE	431.00000			
Laguna Seca	FM	W6JSO	927.28250	902.08250		
Lake Arrowhead	FM	WW6Y	445.10000	-	179.9 Hz	
	FM	NO6B	445.46000	-		
	FM	K6ZXZ	447.08000	-	136.5 Hz	
	FM	WB6TZU	448.18000	-		
	FM	W6YJ	449.66000	-		
	FM	WA6RQD	449.68000	-	156.7 Hz	
Lake Elsinore	FM	W6CDW	144.89500	+	156.7 Hz	
	FM	W6CDW	445.62000	-	173.8 Hz	
	FUSION	KF6FYI	439.02500			
Lake Forest	ATV	W6ATN	1253.25000	2441.55000		SCRRBA
	DMR/BM	AF6FB	446.86000	-	CC11	
	FM	W6KRW	29.64000	-	107.2 Hz	
	FM	W6KRW	52.62000	-	103.5 Hz	
	FM	KA6EEK	145.16000	-	136.5 Hz	
	FM	N6SLD	145.22000	-	103.5 Hz	
	FM	K6MWT	147.43500	146.43500	103.5 Hz	
	FM	WA6SVT	223.82000	-		
	FM	K6SOA	224.64000	-	151.4 Hz	
	FM	W6SCE	224.76000	-		
	FM	K8BUW	224.82000	-	156.7 Hz	
	FM	KB6TRD	224.88000	-	107.2 Hz	
	FM	WB6MIE	446.12000	-		
	FM	KI6QK	446.22000	-		
	FM	N6SIM	446.30000	-	127.3 Hz	
	FM	AA4CD	446.32000	-		
	FM	KF6PHX	446.64000	-	77.0 Hz	
	FM	WD6DIH	446.90000	-	110.9 Hz	
	FM	KG6GI	447.18000	-	131.8 Hz	
	FM	W6YJ	447.38000	-		
	FM	K6UHF	447.68000	-	118.8 Hz	
	FM	W6YQY	447.70000	-		
	FM	K6JSI	448.06000	-	100.0 Hz	
	FM	KD6ZLZ	448.08000	-	162.2 Hz	
	FM	KA6JRG	448.12000	-		

Location	Mode	Call sign	Output	Input	Access	Coordinator
Lake Forest	FM	WB6SRC	448.14000	-	131.8 Hz	
	FM	W6KRW	448.32000	-	141.3 Hz	
	FM	W6ZOJ	448.82000	-		
	FM	N6SLD	448.92000	-	91.5 Hz	
	FM	WA6SBH	449.40000	-		
	FM	WA6TTL	449.74000	-		
	FM	WB6BWU	449.80000	-	110.9 Hz	
	FM	WR6SGO	449.94000	-		
	FM	KB6SUA	1184.27500	-		
	FM	W6KRW	1282.02500	-	88.5 Hz	
	FM	WA6MDJ	1282.15000	-	114.8 Hz	
	FM	K6ARN	1282.62500	-	82.5 Hz	
	FM	W6KRW	1282.72500	-	88.5 Hz	
	FM	KB6KZA	1284.17500	-		
	FM	WA6SVT	1286.15000	-		
	P25	N6OCS	927.12500	902.12500		
Lake Forrest	DMR/BM	WB6YES	446.82000	-	CC1	
Lake Hughes	FM	K6DK	147.15000	+	131.8 Hz	
Lake Isabella	FM	WB6RHQ	224.64000	-	156.7 Hz	
Lakehead	FM	N0ASA	440.32500	+	100.0 Hz	
	FM	KH8AF	442.17500	+		
Lakeside		KX9KX-L	147.42000			
Lakside	DMR/BM	KJ6KHI	147.22500	146.44500	CC1	
Lancaster	FM	WB6RSM	146.67000	-		
	FM	WA6YVL	223.92000	-	100.0 Hz	
	FM	KI6CHH	445.22000	-		
Landers	FM	WB6CDF	447.58000	-	173.8 Hz	
	FUSION	N6GIW	145.56250			
Larkmead		KA7AID-L	147.18000			
Lathrop	FUSION	KC6WPK	434.67500	+		
	FUSION	AF6JP	438.80000			
Laytonville	FM	WA6RQX	145.43000	-	103.5 Hz	
	FM	K7BUG	146.65500	-	103.5 Hz	
	FM	K6JSI	443.00000	+	100.0 Hz	
	FM	WA6RQX	444.80000	+		
Leisure Village		K6WMD-R	145.77000			
Lemon Grove	FM	W6YEC	223.98000	-	107.2 Hz	
Lemoore	FM	W6BY	145.27000	-	88.5 Hz	
	FM	KM6OU	145.33000	-	146.2 Hz	
	FM	KM6OU	146.80500	-	118.8 Hz	
Leona Valley	FM	AF6TG	445.84000	-	100.0 Hz	
Lewiston	FM	K6SDD	145.11000	-	85.4 Hz	
Lincoln	FM	K6PAC	147.33000	+	123.0 Hz	
	FM	KU6V	224.04000	-	123.0 Hz	
	FM	W6LHR	443.22500	+	167.9 Hz	
Littlerock	FM	K6SRT	145.38000	-	151.4 Hz	
	FM	KN6RW	147.07500	+	100.0 Hz	
Live Oak	FM	K6BJ-R	146.79000	-		
Livermore	DMR/BM	KB6FEC	147.15000	+	CC1	
	DMR/BM	K6LRG	441.82500	+	CC1	
	FM	KO6PW	145.43000	-	100.0 Hz	
	FM	W6LLL	146.77500	-	100.0 Hz	
	FM	KO6PW	224.74000	-	100.0 Hz	
	FM	K6LRG	224.88000	-		
	FM	WA6JQV	927.02500	902.02500		
	FM	WA6JQV	927.43750	902.43750		
	FM	WA6JQV	927.47500	902.47500		
	FM	W6RLW	1282.22500	-	88.5 Hz	
Lodi	DMR/BM	N6GKJ	444.22500	+	CC1	
	FM	WB6ASU	147.09000	+	114.8 Hz	
	FM	WB6ASU	444.25000	+	114.8 Hz	
	FM	WB6ASU	927.07500	902.07500	100.0 Hz	

Location	Mode	Call sign	Output	Input	Access	Coordinator
Lodi	FM	N6GKJ	927.08750	902.08750	100.0 Hz	
	FM	N6GKJ	927.10000	902.10000	100.0 Hz	
Lokoya	DSTAR	W6CO-R	440.05000	+		
Loma Linda	FM	K6LLU	445.60000	-	118.8 Hz	
Lomita	FM	WA6TTL	447.16000	-	136.5 Hz	
	FM	N6CA	927.65000	902.65000		
Lompoc	DMR/BM	WA6VPL	145.12000	-	CC1	
	DMR/BM	WA6VPL	440.57500	+	CC1	
	DMR/BM	K7AZ	443.27500	+	CC3	
	DMR/BM	K7AZ	443.35000	+	CC7	
	DMR/BM	K7AZ	443.42500	+	CC1	
	FM	WA6VPL	147.12000	+	131.8 Hz	
	FM	W6AB	224.50000	-	131.8 Hz	
	FM	K7AZ/R	443.27500	+	91.5 Hz	
	FM	WA6VPL	444.27500	+	88.5 Hz	
	FM	WA6VPL	444.80000	+		
	FM	W6AB	449.14000	-	131.8 Hz	
Lone Pine	FM	N6BKL	52.90000	-	100.0 Hz	
	FM	W6TNT	145.49000	-	123.0 Hz	
	FM	W6PH	147.21000	+	103.5 Hz	
	FM	N6AZY	447.70000	-	100.0 Hz	
Long Beach	FM	K6SYU	146.79000	-	103.5 Hz	
	FM	KE6HE	146.80500	-		
	FM	K6SYU	224.50000	-	156.7 Hz	
	FM	KD6CIX	1283.97500	-		
	FUSION	N6UTC	431.52500			
	FUSION	N6UTC	431.67500			
	FUSION	AA6PA	446.96000	-		
Loomis	FM	N6ZN	927.21250	902.21250		
Loop Canyon	FM	KB6DWO	146.65000	-	131.8 Hz	
	FM	WA6WLZ	446.98000	-		
Los Alamitos	FUSION	N6NAV	439.00000			
	FUSION	KK6ZTV	439.50000			
Los Altos	FM	W6LAH	146.74500	-	110.9 Hz	
	FM	K6AIR	146.94000	-	123.0 Hz	
	FM	WB6WTM	441.25000	+		
	FM	K6AIR	441.52500	+	123.0 Hz	
	FM	K6MSR	443.67500	+		
	FM	W6BUG	443.85000	+		
	FM	KE6JTK	444.22500	+	131.8 Hz	
	FM	K6AIR	1282.60000	-	100.0 Hz	
	FM	W6SRI	1283.15000	-	100.0 Hz	
Los Angeles	DMR/BM	W6DVI	438.00000	-	CC1	
	DMR/BM	K6PUW	447.20000	-	CC1	
	DMR/BM	W6DVI	449.46250	-	CC1	
	DMR/BM	N6YN	449.48000	-	CC1	
	DMR/MARC	WD6AWP	430.50000	439.50000	CC1	
	DMR/MARC	KI6KQU	449.38000	-	CC1	
	DSTAR	WA6IRC C	147.56000	145.00500		
	DSTAR	WA6IRC B	447.04000	-		
	DSTAR	KI6JKA B	447.83500	-		
	DSTAR	KE6LE B	449.82000	-		
	DSTAR	WA6IRC A	1286.10000	-		
	DSTAR	WA6IRC D	1299.70000			
	FM	W6NUT	147.45000	146.45000	127.3 Hz	
	FM	W6JUN	224.04000	-		
	FM	WR6JPL	224.70000	-	114.8 Hz	
	FM	K6VGP	446.94000	-	100.0 Hz	
	FM	N6LXX	927.47500	901.97500	110.9 Hz	
	FM	K6PYP	1282.57500	-	103.5 Hz	
	FM	KK6QY	1285.02500	-		
	FUSION	KE6NFO	145.56250			

Location	Mode	Call sign	Output	Input	Access	Coordinator
Los Banos	FM	K6TJS	146.92500	-	123.0 Hz	
	FM	K6TJS	147.21000	+	123.0 Hz	
	FM	K6TJS	444.00000	+	123.0 Hz	
Los Gatos	DMR/BM	AD1U	443.95000	+	CC1	
	DMR/MARC	N6DOZ	443.30000	+	CC7	
	FM	KU6V	51.92000	-	114.8 Hz	
	FM	K6FB	145.45000	-	100.0 Hz	
	FM	KB6LCS	223.82000	-	156.7 Hz	
	FM	K6FB	223.88000	-	100.0 Hz	
	FM	K6INC	224.48000	-		
	FM	WB6KHP	224.54000	-	100.0 Hz	
	FM	NU6P	224.80000	-	118.8 Hz	
	FM	N6DVC	224.88000	-	88.5 Hz	
	FM	KC6TYG	440.65000	+	94.8 Hz	
	FM	W6RCA	441.62500	+	100.0 Hz	
	FM	K6UB	441.70000	+	127.3 Hz	
	FM	WA6ABB	443.02500	+		
	FM	K9GVF	443.75000	+	100.0 Hz	
	FM	WB6LPZ	444.12500	+		
	FM	KB6LCS	444.92500	+	151.4 Hz	
	FM	WB6KHP	444.97500	+	127.3 Hz	
	FM	WA6JQV	927.02500	902.02500		
	FM	N6NMZ	927.15000	902.15000	156.7 Hz	
	FM	K6INC	927.25000	902.25000	114.8 Hz	
	FM	WA6JQV	927.46250	902.46250		
	FM	WA6JQV	927.47500	902.47500		
	FM	K6DND	927.91250	902.91250	167.9 Hz	
	P25	KI6KGN	440.52500	+		
Los Molinos	FM	KI6PNB	145.39000	-	110.9 Hz	
Los Osos	FM	W6SLO	146.86000	-	127.3 Hz	
	FM	W6SLO	444.97500	+	127.3 Hz	
Lotus	FM	AG6AU	441.72500	+	82.5 Hz	
Loyalton	FM	N5TEN	440.10000	+		
Lucerne Valley	FM	KC6JTN	145.18000	-	123.0 Hz	
	FM	K6DLP	224.52000	-		
Ludlow	FM	WA6TST	147.88500	-	151.4 Hz	
Madera	P25	N6LYE	443.31250	+		
Magalia	DMR/MARC	KB6FEC	147.15000	+	CC0	
	FM	KC6USM	51.94000	-	114.8 Hz	
Malibu	DSTAR	KJ6BWR B	445.85500	-		
	DSTAR	KJ6BWR A	1286.80000	-		
	DSTAR	KJ6BWR D	1298.90000			
	FM	N6FDR	145.26000	-	100.0 Hz	
	FM	K6DCS	147.22500	+	94.8 Hz	
	FM	K6VGP	224.98000	-		
	FM	WB6ZTR	445.18000	-		
	FM	K6VGP	445.82000	-	100.0 Hz	
	FM	N6CIZ	446.26000	-		
	FM	W6YJ	446.42000	-		
	FM	WA6ZPS	448.24000	-		
	FM	WR6BRN	448.70000	-		
	FM	W6XC	449.74000	-		
Mammoth	FM	KB6DWO	146.88000	-	131.8 Hz	
Mammoth Lakes	FM	NW6C	146.73000	-	100.0 Hz	
	FM	WA6TTL	444.72500	+		
Manteca		K6PKL-L	441.00000			
	DMR/BM	KM6IRY	443.02500	+	CC14	
	FM	K6MAN	146.98500	-	100.0 Hz	
	FM	K6MAN	146.98500	-	100.0 Hz	
	FM	KM6IRY	440.87500	+	100.0 Hz	
Maricopa	FM	KK6PHE	145.29000	-	94.8 Hz	
	FM	KC6WRD	224.98000	-	94.8 Hz	

Location	Mode	Call sign	Output	Input	Access	Coordinator
Maricopa	FM	KC6WRD	443.07500	+	94.8 Hz	
Marigold	FM	AI6BX-R	447.00000	446.40000	123.0 Hz	
Marina Del Rey	FM	K6CYC	147.03000	+	127.3 Hz	
Mariposa	DMR/MARC	WX6D	442.28750	+	CC1	
	DMR/MARC	AB6BP	442.70000	+	CC1	NARCC
	DSTAR	W6HHD	1284.10000	-		
	FM	W6HHD	145.13000	-		
	FM	W6PPM	146.74500	-	146.2 Hz	
	FM	W6BXN	147.03000	+	100.0 Hz	
	FM	W6MPA	147.25500	+	146.2 Hz	
	FM	KF6CLR	224.16000	-	74.4 Hz	
	FM	KF6CLR	224.30000	-	74.4 Hz	
	FM	W6BRB	224.50000	-	123.0 Hz	
	FM	N6LYE	440.83750	+		
	FM	K6SIX	441.35000	+	107.2 Hz	
	FM	KF6CLR	441.42500	+	74.4 Hz	
	FM	N6IB	442.35000	+	141.3 Hz	
	FM	KI6HHU	442.67500	+	107.2 Hz	
	FM	K6IXA	443.07500	+	107.2 Hz	
	FM	W6BXN	444.70000	+	107.2 Hz	
	FM	W6HHD	444.80000	+		
	FM	K6RDJ	927.15000	902.15000	100.0 Hz	
	FM	W6BXN	1284.30000	-	88.5 Hz	
	P25	N6LYE	440.80000	+	114.8 Hz	
Markleeville	DMR/BM	K6LNK	145.01250	147.51250	CC8	
Martinez	FM	KF6HTE	444.45000	+	107.2 Hz	
Maxwell	FM	N6NMZ	147.04500	+	156.7 Hz	
	FM	N6NMZ	442.27500	+	100.0 Hz	
McFarland	FM	N6RDN	443.27500	+	141.3 Hz	
Meadow Lakes		KD6FW-L	146.70000			
	FM	KJ6CE	145.25000	-	141.3 Hz	
	FM	WA6OIB	146.61000	-	141.3 Hz	
	FM	K6JSI	146.79000	-	100.0 Hz	
	FM	W6TO	146.94000	-	141.3 Hz	
	FM	N6VQL	147.09000	+		
	FM	N6IB	147.39000	+	141.3 Hz	
	FM	K6TVI	441.40000	+	107.2 Hz	
	FM	K6JSI	444.25000	+	100.0 Hz	
	FM	W6BJ	444.97500	+	136.5 Hz	
	P25	N6VQL	147.31500	+		
Meadow Lakes CA						
	DMR/MARC	KF6FGL	440.03750	+	CC1	
Mendocino	FM	WD6HDY	146.82000	-	103.5 Hz	
Menifee	DMR/MARC	W6ERF	433.25000	+	CC1	
	FUSION	KN6SOJ	145.56250			
Menlo Park	DMR/BM	W6FBK	440.90000	+	CC11	
	DSTAR	W6OTX	1284.15000	-		
	FM	KB7IP	51.78000	-	114.8 Hz	
	FM	W6FBK	441.65000	+	162.2 Hz	
	FM	W6OTX	1272.15000	-		
Merced	DMR/BM	AB6BP	145.37000	-	CC1	NARCC
	DMR/MARC	KF6FM	442.40000	-	CC1	
	FM	N6WEB	441.60000	+		
	FM	W6TCD	444.52500	+	107.2 Hz	
Merritt	DMR/BM	K6LNK	145.01250	147.51250	CC9	
Meyers	ATV	NC9RS	927.67500	902.67500	156.7 Hz	
Middletown	DMR/BM	K6LO	440.10000	+	CC2	
	FM	AC6VJ	29.64000	-	156.7 Hz	
	FM	WA6JQV	927.02500	902.02500		
	FM	WA6JQV	927.48750	902.48750		
	FM	WA6JQV	927.93750	902.93750		
Mill Valley	FM	K6GWE	443.25000	+	179.9 Hz	

Location	Mode	Call sign	Output	Input	Access	Coordinator
Mill Valley	FM	KJ6RA	444.67500	+	100.0 Hz	
	FM	W6GHZ	1285.05000	-	88.5 Hz	
Millbrae	FM	K6HSV	442.10000	+	107.2 Hz	
Milpitas	DMR/BM	WA6KPX	443.40000	+	CC1	
	FM	W6ZN	145.42000	-	74.4 Hz	
	FM	W6MLP	145.43000	-	85.4 Hz	
	FM	N6QDY	147.94500	-	77.0 Hz	
	FM	W6MLP	224.72000	-	100.0 Hz	
	FM	W6KCS	442.02500	+	162.2 Hz	
	FM	K6GOD	442.35000	+	100.0 Hz	
	FM	K6EXE	443.02500	+		
	FM	K6GOD	444.72500	+	162.2 Hz	
	FM	K6ATF	927.06250	902.06250	100.0 Hz	
	FM	WB6PHE	927.16250	902.16250	127.3 Hz	
Miramar	FM	K6ARN	51.80000	-	127.3 Hz	
Mission Hills	FM	WD6APP	145.32000	-	107.2 Hz	
	FM	WD6APP	223.80000	-		
	FM	KJ6HVS	446.88000	-	123.0 Hz	
Mission Viejo	FM	KA6TBF	146.16000	+	107.2 Hz	
	FM	K6MWT	927.40000	902.40000	103.5 Hz	
Moccasin	FM	K6DPB	145.29000	-	100.0 Hz	
Modesto	DMR/BM	K6ACR	442.17500	+	CC1	
	FM	K6GTO	51.94000	-	114.8 Hz	
	FM	WD6EJF	145.11000	-	136.5 Hz	
	FM	WD6EJF	145.39000	-	136.5 Hz	
	FM	WA6OYF	146.35500	+	156.7 Hz	
	FM	N5FDL	146.89500	-	114.8 Hz	
	FM	N6OGN	147.85000	+	100.0 Hz	
	FM	WD6EJF	224.14000	-	136.5 Hz	
	FM	WD6EJF	440.22500	+	136.5 Hz	
	FM	K6RDJ	441.27500	+	77.0 Hz	
	FM	N6QOP	442.07500	+	123.0 Hz	
	FM	N6APB	442.55000	+		
	FM	K6JJC	443.17500	+	107.2 Hz	
	FM	N6LYE	443.30000	+	107.2 Hz	NARCC
	FM	K6JSI	443.52500	+	107.2 Hz	
	FM	K6TJS	444.00000	+	123.0 Hz	
	FM	WA6JQV	927.02500	902.02500		
	FM	WA6JQV	927.03750	902.03750		
	P25	N6LYE	440.80000	+		
Moffett Field	DMR/BM	W6CMU	443.82500	+	CC1	NARCC
	DMR/MARC	NA6MF	443.60000	+	CC10	
Monrovia	DMR/BM	W9WDX	446.88000	-	CC1	
	FM	WA6DVG	224.58000	-	100.0 Hz	
Montclair	DMR/MARC	WA6FM	446.03750	-	CC1	
Monterey		W6BGL-R	444.27500			
	FM	WE6R	51.76000	-	114.8 Hz	
	FM	WE6R	146.08500	+		
	FM	N6FNP	147.67500	-		
	FM	WA6YBD	224.90000	-	107.2 Hz	
	FM	WB6ECE	441.30000	+	136.5 Hz	
	FM	WE6R	441.32500	+		
	FM	WH6KA	442.22500	447.32500		
	FM	N6SPD	444.27500	+	123.0 Hz	
	FM	N6AMO	444.47500	+	110.9 Hz	
	FM	W6JSO	927.28750	902.28750		
	FM	WE6R	927.97500	902.97500		
	P25	N6AMO	443.65000	+	110.9 Hz	
Monterey Park	FM	KF6YLB	146.35500	+	71.9 Hz	
Moraga	FM	KI6O	442.45000	+		
	FM	KB7IP	443.42500	+		
	FM	K6SJH	927.32500	902.32500	100.0 Hz	

Location	Mode	Call sign	Output	Input	Access	Coordinator
Moreno Valley	DMR/MARC	W6OY	447.04000	-	CC1	
	FM	KC6VMB	145.25000	-	123.0 Hz	
	FM	WA6HYQ	146.67000	-	123.0 Hz	
	FM	K6AFN	223.96000	-	100.0 Hz	
	FM	KJ6QFS	445.18000	-		
	FM	KI6REC	449.30000	-	103.5 Hz	
	FUSION	AB6MV	146.65500	-		
	FUSION	W7DTH	439.00000			
Morgan Hill	DMR/BM	KC6WTF	444.10000	+	CC1	
	FM	KJ6VRC	147.30000	+	107.2 Hz	
	FM	K7DAA-R	147.33000	+		
	FM	W6GGF	147.82500	-	100.0 Hz	
	FM	WA6YBD	223.80000	-	107.2 Hz	
	FM	K6GOD	440.47500	+		
	FM	KA6ZRJ	440.57500	+	114.8 Hz	
	FM	K7DAA-L	442.97500	+		
	FM	KJ6VRC	443.50000	+		
Mount Shasta	DMR/MARC	W6BML	441.27500	+	CC1	
	DMR/MARC	NR6J	442.27500	+	CC1	
	DSTAR	W6BML B	441.27500	+		
Mountain Ranch	FM	N6GVI	440.90000	+		
Mountain View	DMR/MARC	K6HLE	442.51250	+	CC0	
	FM	W6ASH	145.27000	-	100.0 Hz	
	FM	K6CBR	146.55000		110.9 Hz	
	FM	W6ASH	224.14000	-	88.5 Hz	
	FM	W6ASH	440.80000	+	100.0 Hz	
	FM	N6SGI	1284.25000	-	88.5 Hz	
Mt Diablo	DMR/BM	K6MDD	144.97500	147.47500	CC1	
Mt San Bruno	DMR/BM	N6AMG	440.50000	+	CC1	
Mt Shasta City	FM	W6BML	146.88000	-	123.0 Hz	
	FM	KI6WJP	440.27500	+	118.8 Hz	
	FM	AB7BS	444.47500	+	141.3 Hz	
	FM	AB6MF	444.82500	+	100.0 Hz	
Mt Woodson / Ramona						
	FUSION	N6SIX	449.78000	-	141.3 Hz	
Mt. Allison	DMR/BM	W6TCP	144.98750	147.48750	CC1	
	DMR/BM	W6TCP	440.12500	+	CC3	
Mt. Bullion	DMR/BM	W6BXN	144.93750	147.43750	CC1	
	DMR/BM	W6BXN	444.78750	+	CC1	
	DSTAR	W6HHD C	145.13000	-		
	DSTAR	W6HHD B	444.80000	+		
	DSTAR	W6HHD D	1249.22500			
	DSTAR	W6HHD A	1284.10000	-		
Mt. Disappointment						
	FM	K6VGP	224.56000	-	114.8 Hz	
Mt. Laguna	FM	K6KTA	446.42000	-	107.2 Hz	
Mt. Oso	DMR/BM	W6BXN	440.18750	+	CC1	
Mt. Pinos	FM	K6NYB	147.37500	149.87500	67.0 Hz	
	FM	K6NYB	445.07500	-	67.0 Hz	
Mt. Shasta City	FM	W6PRN	52.72000	-	110.9 Hz	
	FM	W6PRN	444.35000	+	100.0 Hz	
Mt. Wilson	DMR/BM	N6CIZ	449.20000	-	CC7	
	FM	K6JTH	448.10000	-		
	FUSION	WD6ABC	445.54000	-		
Murrieta	DMR/BM	KM6AYR	441.02500		CC1	
	DMR/BM	KE6UPI	447.40000	-	CC2	
Napa	DMR/BM	KE6O	442.48750	+	CC2	
	DSTAR	W6CO B	440.05000	+	114.8 Hz	
	FM	N6TKW	51.72000	-	114.8 Hz	
	FM	WR6VHF	51.82000	-	151.4 Hz	
	FM	N6TKW	146.11500	+	123.0 Hz	
	FM	N6TKW	146.65500	-	88.5 Hz	

Location	Mode	Call sign	Output	Input	Access	Coordinator
Napa	FM	W6BYS	146.82000	-	151.4 Hz	
	FM	W6CO	147.18000	+	151.4 Hz	
	FM	N6NAR	440.85000	+	173.8 Hz	
	FM	W6CO	441.80000	+	151.4 Hz	
	FM	W6CO	441.90000	+	151.4 Hz	
	FM	N6TKW	442.25000	+	151.4 Hz	
	FM	K6ZRX	444.52500	+	151.4 Hz	
	FM	K6ZRX	927.52500	902.52500	173.8 Hz	
	FM	W6FMG	1285.70000	+	173.8 Hz	
National City	FUSION	KK6NDM	145.72000			
	FUSION	KN6OGZ	446.40000			
Needles	DMR/BM	AI6BX	445.30000	-	CC3	
	DMR/BM	WA6GDF	445.60000	-	CC1	
Nevada City	FM	KG6TZT	145.31000	-	151.4 Hz	
	FM	W6JP	444.95000	+	100.0 Hz	
Newberry Springs	FM	WA6MTZ	146.70000	-		
Newbury Park	FM	N6JMI	146.67000	-	127.3 Hz	
	FM	N6JMI	147.88500	-	127.3 Hz	
	FM	N6CFC	223.96000	-	141.3 Hz	
	FM	W6RRN	448.60000	-		
Newhall	FM	WB6DZO	223.98000	-	110.9 Hz	
Newport Beach	DMR/BM	KC6AGL	447.40000	-	CC1	
	FM	K6NBR	145.42000	-	136.5 Hz	
	FM	K6NBR	445.22000	-		
	FM	WB6TZD	448.64000	-	100.0 Hz	
	FM	N6IPD	449.58000	-	88.5 Hz	
	FM	N6EX	927.13750	902.13750		
Nipomo	DMR/BM	K9ALN	444.75000	+	CC1	
	DMR/MARC	K6DOA	444.65000	+	CC4	
	FM	WA6VPL	52.58000	-	82.5 Hz	
	FM	WB6MIA	147.99000	-	127.3 Hz	
	FM	KB6Q	444.70000	+	100.0 Hz	
NOAA Avalon	WX	WNG584	162.52500			
NOAA Bakersfield	WX	WXL89	162.55000			
NOAA Big Rock Ridge						
	WX	KDX54	162.50000			
NOAA Coachella	WX	KIG78	162.40000			
NOAA Coachella Spanish						
	WX	WNG712	162.52500			
NOAA Contra Costa County						
	WX	WNG655	162.42500			
NOAA Conway Summit						
	WX	WNG595	162.52500			
NOAA El Paso Peaks						
	WX	WNG659	162.42500			
NOAA Eureka	WX	KEC82	162.40000			
NOAA Fresno	WX	KIH62	162.40000			
NOAA Grass Valley						
	WX	WWF67	162.40000			
NOAA Los Angeles						
	WX	KWO37	162.55000			
NOAA Monterey	WX	KEC49	162.55000			
NOAA Monterey Marine						
	WX	WWF64	162.45000			
NOAA Point Arena						
	WX	KIH30	162.55000			
NOAA Redding	WX	WXL88	162.55000			
NOAA Sacramento						
	WX	KEC57	162.55000			
NOAA San Diego	WX	KEC62	162.40000			
NOAA San Diego Marine						
	WX	WNG637	162.42500			

Location	Mode	Call sign	Output	Input	Access	Coordinator
NOAA San Francisco						
	WX	KHB49	162.40000			
NOAA San Luis Obispo						
	WX	KIH31	162.55000			
NOAA San Simeon						
	WX	WNG592	162.52500			
NOAA Sandberg	WX	WZ2505	162.40000			
NOAA Santa Ana	WX	WWG21	162.45000			
NOAA Santa Barbara						
	WX	KIH34	162.40000			
NOAA Santa Barbara Marine						
	WX	WWF62	162.47500			
NOAA Sonoma County						
	WX	WZ2504	162.47500			
NOAA Ukiah	WX	WNG720	162.52500			
NOAA Victorville	WX	WXM66	162.50000			
NOAA Yosemite	WX	KAD94	162.45000			
NOAA Yuma	WX	WXL87	162.55000			
North Hills	DSTAR	K6PUW B	447.20000	-		
	FUSION	N6MIB	145.67500			
	FUSION	KM6TNQ	446.35000			
Northam (historical)						
		W7JZP-L	146.42000			
		W7JZP-L	146.44500			
Northridge	FM	WA6AQQ	146.26500	+	103.5 Hz	
	FUSION	N7EAL	145.60000			
Novato	DMR/BM	KG6MZV	440.65000	+	CC2	
	FM	K6GWE	146.70000	-	203.5 Hz	
	FM	N6GVI	440.25000	+		
	FM	KI6B	443.60000	+		
	FM	KM6PA	927.35000	902.35000	131.8 Hz	
	FUSION	KG6MZV	440.65000	+		
Oak Flat	FM	KK6AC	145.19000	-	141.3 Hz	
Oak Glen	FM	N6LIZ	53.56000	-	107.2 Hz	
	FM	N6AJB	927.37500	902.37500		
Oakhurst	FM	W6PPM	146.74500	-	123.0 Hz	
	FM	W6WGZ	147.18000	+	146.2 Hz	
	FM	WB6BRU	224.90000	-	156.7 Hz	
	FM	W6WGZ	441.17500	+	146.2 Hz	
Oakland	DMR/BM	W6UUU	144.95000	147.45000	CC1	
	DMR/BM	AC6OT	443.35000	+	CC1	
	DMR/BM	K6LNK	443.50000	+	CC1	
	DMR/BM	K6LNK	927.17500	902.17500	CC5	
	DMR/MARC	N6DOZ	440.92500	+	CC7	
	DMR/MARC	KB6FEC	443.82500	+	CC0	
	FM	W6MTF	52.62000	-	114.8 Hz	
	FM	W6EBW	53.72000	-	118.8 Hz	
	FM	W6MTF	146.62500	-		
	FM	W6BUR	146.67000	-	85.4 Hz	
	FM	K6LNK	146.85000	-	162.2 Hz	
	FM	WB6NDJ	146.88000	-	77.0 Hz	
	FM	W6JMX	224.00000	-	123.0 Hz	
	FM	KC6LHL	224.16000	-	156.7 Hz	
	FM	W6MTF	224.68000	-	114.8 Hz	
	FM	W6YOP	224.76000	-	85.4 Hz	
	FM	W6WOP	224.92000	-	100.0 Hz	
	FM	KM6EF	440.35000	+	123.0 Hz	
	FM	W6EBW	440.57500	+	118.8 Hz	
	FM	W6RCA	441.22500	+	100.0 Hz	
	FM	W6MTF	441.42500	+	156.7 Hz	
	FM	W6YOP	441.47500	+	127.3 Hz	
	FM	KH8AF	442.20000	+		

Location	Mode	Call sign	Output	Input	Access	Coordinator
Oakland	FM	WB6NDJ	442.40000	+	77.0 Hz	
	FM	KQ6YG	442.87500	+	114.8 Hz	
	FM	N6GVI	443.20000	+		
	FM	WB6SHU	443.37500	+	114.8 Hz	
	FM	W6MTF	443.87500	+		
	FM	WW6BAY	443.97500	+	100.0 Hz	
	FM	WB6TCS	444.25000	+	100.0 Hz	
	FM	W6PUE	444.65000	+		
	FM	W6YOP	444.77500	+	127.3 Hz	
	FM	KD6GLT	444.80000	+	110.9 Hz	
	FM	WA6JQV	927.03750	902.03750		
	FM	WA6JQV	927.42500	902.42500		
	FM	N6SSB	927.57500	902.57500	100.0 Hz	
	FM	NC9RS	927.65000	902.65000	131.8 Hz	
	FM	WA6JQV	927.93750	902.93750		
	FM	KD6GLT	1284.45000	-		
Oat Mountain	DMR/BM	KB6CRE	447.56000	-	CC1	
Oceanside	DMR/BM	K6JSI	448.80000	-	CC1	
	FUSION	N6JO	147.97500	-		
	FUSION	W6BJB	445.20000	-		
Oildale	FM	KG6KKV	51.88000	-	114.8 Hz	
Ojai	DMR/BM	N6BMW	445.72000	-	CC3	
	DMR/MARC	K6VCD	445.70000	-	CC1	
	DSTAR	K6OJI C	147.55000	144.99500		
	DSTAR	K6OJI B	445.70000	-		
	FM	WD6EBY	145.20000	-	127.3 Hz	
	FM	N6FL	145.40000	-	114.8 Hz	
	FM	WD6EBY	445.56000	-	141.3 Hz	
Olympia Glade		KG6BAJ-R	52.72000			
Onyx	FM	N6LXX	53.82000	-	107.2 Hz	
Orange	DMR/MARC	KF6FM	448.15000	-	CC3	
	FM	K6COV	147.91500	-	136.5 Hz	
	FM	KB6CJZ	446.14000	-	94.8 Hz	
	FM	KB6CJZ	1283.15000	-	85.4 Hz	
Orange Cove	FM	KC6QIT	146.89500	-	100.0 Hz	
Orcutt	FM	W6AB	145.14000	-	131.8 Hz	
	FM	KA6BFB-L	146.17500	+		
	FM	WB9STH	927.42500	902.42500	82.5 Hz	
Orinda	DMR/BM	K6LNK	144.93750	147.43750	CC5	
	DMR/BM	K6LNK	927.17500	902.17500	CC5	
	FM	K6CHA	52.68000	-	162.2 Hz	
	FM	WA6HAM	145.49000	-	107.2 Hz	
	FM	WA6HAM	440.62500	+		
	FM	W6CBS	441.97500	+	100.0 Hz	
	FM	N6QOP	443.05000	+	114.8 Hz	
	FM	K6JJC	443.82500	+	136.5 Hz	
	FM	KE6PTT	444.00000	+	100.0 Hz	
Orland	DMR/BM	W6GRC	144.96250	147.46250	CC1	
Orland Low Level	DMR/BM	W6GRC	144.98750	147.48750	CC1	
Oroville	DSTAR	KJ6LVV B	444.27500	+		
	DSTAR	KJ6LVV	444.27500	+		
	FM	W6AF	146.65500	-	136.5 Hz	
	FM	WA6UHF	224.50000	-	110.9 Hz	
	FM	W6YOP	441.47500	+	114.8 Hz	NARCC
	FM	WA6CAL	442.17500	+	123.0 Hz	
	FM	WA6UHF	442.35000	+	110.9 Hz	
Otay Mesa	DMR/MARC	KF6FM	448.15000	-	CC1	
Oxnard	FM	W6XC	51.90000	-	82.5 Hz	
	FM	W6XC	146.73000	-		
	FM	KJ6HCX	146.80500	-	127.3 Hz	
	FM	WB6YQN	146.97000	-	127.3 Hz	
	FM	K6BBK	147.85500	-		

Location	Mode	Call sign	Output	Input	Access	Coordinator
Oxnard	FM	W6XC	448.34000	-	141.3 Hz	
	FM	K6BBK	448.80000	-	131.8 Hz	
Pacific Grove	FM	K6CQX	444.60000	+	151.4 Hz	
Pacific Palisades	FM	K6BDE	445.52000	-	123.0 Hz	
Pacifica	DMR/MARC	K6HN	440.67500	+	CC1	
	FM	WA6TOW	146.92500	-	114.8 Hz	
	FM	WA6AFT	440.72500	+		
	FM	WA6TOW	441.07500	+	114.8 Hz	
	FM	K6HN	441.72500	+		
Pacines	FM	W6KRK	442.85000	447.95000	100.0 Hz	
Pahrump	FM	WR7NV	223.52000	-	100.0 Hz	
Paicines	FM	N6SBC	145.41000	-	118.8 Hz	
	FM	N6SBC	146.62500	-	94.8 Hz	
Palm Desert	FM	N6MRN	145.34000	-	107.2 Hz	
	FM	W6DRA	447.32000	-	107.2 Hz	
Palm Springs	DMR/BM	WB6YES	445.41000	-	CC3	
	DMR/BM	W6THC	446.58000	-	CC1	
	DSTAR	K6IFR B	447.14000	-		
	FM	KD6QLT	144.93000	147.63000	107.2 Hz	
	FM	W6DRA	145.48000	-	107.2 Hz	
	FM	KD6QLT	146.76000	-	107.2 Hz	
	FM	K6IFR	445.64000	-	107.2 Hz	
Palm Springs Tram						
	FM	W6DRA	145.20000	-	131.8 Hz	
Palmdale	DMR/BM	KC6ZQR	445.92000	+	CC1	
	FM	WA6YVL	52.66000	-	82.5 Hz	
	FM	W6CLA	146.73000	-	100.0 Hz	
	FM	WB6BFN	147.27000	+	156.7 Hz	
	FM	N6ND	445.48000	-	77.0 Hz	
	FM	K6LMA	445.52000	-	162.2 Hz	
	FM	KJ6W	445.60000	-	100.0 Hz	
	FM	K6VGP	446.74000	-	107.2 Hz	
	FM	WB6FYR	927.37500	902.37500	114.8 Hz	
Palo Alto	DMR/BM	W6EI	441.60000	+	CC1	
	DMR/BM	K6OTR	441.85000	+	CC1	
	DMR/BM	WW6BAY	444.35000	+	CC1	
	DSTAR	WW6BAY	444.07500	+		
	FM	WA6FUL	52.64000	-	114.8 Hz	
	FM	N6NFI	145.23000	-	100.0 Hz	
	FM	WW6BAY	145.39000	-	100.0 Hz	
	FM	W6TI	147.36000	+	110.9 Hz	
	FM	N6BDE	440.20000	+	123.0 Hz	
	FM	K6IRC	441.57500	+		
	FM	WW6HP	442.00000	+	151.4 Hz	
	FM	W6PMI	442.12500	+	162.2 Hz	
	FM	KJ6VU	442.45000	449.35000		
	FM	K6FB	442.57500	+	100.0 Hz	
	FM	K6OTR	442.80000	+	114.8 Hz	
	FM	W6OOL	443.00000	+		
	FM	WW6BAY	443.22500	+	100.0 Hz	
	FM	KK6KPQ	443.60000	+		
	FM	WB6NNY	443.75000	+	100.0 Hz	
	FM	KB6LED	444.95000	+	162.2 Hz	
	FM	WA6FUL	927.13750	902.13750		
	FM	KJ6VU	927.86250	902.86250		
	FM	W6YX	1282.50000	-	88.5 Hz	
	FM	K6BAM	1284.95000	-	88.5 Hz	
	FM	W6RLW	1285.15000	-	88.5 Hz	
	FUSION	WW6BAY	444.42500	+		
Palomar Mountain	DMR/BM	K6VZK	446.04000	-	CC1	
Palomar Mtn	DMR/BM	WB6YES	445.86000	-	CC1	
Palomar Mtn.	DSTAR	KI6MGN C	147.57000	145.01500		

Location	Mode	Call sign	Output	Input	Access	Coordinator
Palomar Mtn.	DSTAR	KI6MGN B	445.86500	-		
	DSTAR	KI6MGN A	1282.67500	-		
	DSTAR	KI6MGN D	1299.50000			
Palos Verdes	DMR/MARC	K6EH	446.06000	-	CC1	
	FM	K6VGP	445.28000	-		
	FM	WD6FZA	446.70000	-	127.3 Hz	
	FM	W6RRN	448.60000	-	131.8 Hz	
Palos Verdes Estates						
	FM	W6PVE	447.80000	-	131.8 Hz	
Panorama City	FM	K6ARN	51.74000	-	146.2 Hz	
Paradise		K6PBT-L	147.52500			
	FM	K6JSI	147.33000	+	123.0 Hz	
	FM	KJ6ZEB	445.60000	-	114.8 Hz	
	FM	WD6EBY	445.64000	-	141.3 Hz	
Park View Commons						
		KI6RYE-L	147.48000			
Pasadena	FM	N6LIZ	29.66000	-	107.2 Hz	
	FM	W6MPH	145.18000	-	156.7 Hz	
	FM	WR6JPL	224.08000	-	156.7 Hz	
	FM	WR6JPL	445.20000	-	103.5 Hz	
	FM	W6UE	445.44000	-		
	FM	N6EX	927.15000	902.15000		
Paso Robles	DMR/BM	AG6VS	446.85000	-	CC15	
	FM	W6HD	51.82000	-	100.0 Hz	
	FM	KK6ATA	146.98000	-	127.3 Hz	
	FM	WB6JWB	224.68000	-	91.5 Hz	
	FM	WB6JWB	441.05000	+		
Patterson	FM	NC6R	146.77500	-	156.7 Hz	
	FM	KK6AT	927.62500	902.62500	100.0 Hz	
Pebble Beach	FM	K6LY	146.97000	-	94.8 Hz	
	FM	K6LY	444.70000	+	123.0 Hz	
Pescadero	FM	KE6MNJ	146.62500	-	114.8 Hz	
	FM	N6QZH	442.32500	+		
Petaluma	FM	WB6TMS	146.91000	-	88.5 Hz	
	FM	NI6B	444.22500	+		
	FM	W6GHZ	1286.25000	-	88.5 Hz	
Phelan	FM	N6RPG	445.90000	-	146.2 Hz	
	FM	WA6KXK	448.98000	-		
	FM	K6UHF	449.02000	-		
	FM	N6LXX	927.47500	902.47500		
Pine Cove	DMR/MARC	K6TMD	446.06250	-	CC1	
Pine Grove	FM	K6ARC	146.83500	-	100.0 Hz	
	FM	K6ARC	441.52500	+	100.0 Hz	
Pine Valley	FM	N6JAM	147.99000	-	156.7 Hz	
Pinecrest	FM	K6TUO	147.97500	-	100.0 Hz	
Pioneer	FM	KJ6BJL	146.55000			
	FM	K6MSR	443.62500	+		
Pismo Beach	DMR/BM	KB6BF	444.60000	+	CC2	
Pittsburg	DMR/BM	K6PIT	144.52000	147.99000	CC1	
	DMR/BM	K6PIT	440.13750	+	CC2	
	DMR/BM	K6BIV	440.60000	+	CC1	
	DMR/BM	AA4JK	441.06250	+	CC2	
	FUSION	K6MDD	145.52000			
	FUSION	WH6SL	436.35000			
	FUSION	K6BIV	441.92500	+		
Place Hoilder	DMR/MARC	WX6D	442.32500	+	CC2	
Place Holder	DMR/MARC	WX6D	438.00000	-	CC1	
	DMR/MARC	WX6D	443.43750	+	CC1	
	DMR/MARC	WX6D	446.00000	+	CC1	
Placentia	DMR/BM	N6MIK	446.54000	-	CC10	
	FM	WA6YNT	147.85500	-	100.0 Hz	
Placerville	FM	KA6GWY	146.80500	-	123.0 Hz	

Location	Mode	Call sign	Output	Input	Access	Coordinator
Placerville	FM	N6QDY	147.25500	+	123.0 Hz	
	FM	WA6BTH	440.70000	+	123.0 Hz	
	FM	N6UUI	441.05000	+	127.3 Hz	
	FM	W6LOA	441.25000	+	94.8 Hz	
	FM	W6RCA	441.62500	+		
	FM	WA6BTH	442.47500	+	110.9 Hz	
	FM	N6QDY	443.92500	+	180.0 Hz	
Pleasant Hil	FUSION	KN6GST	441.05000	+		
Pleasanton	DMR/BM	N6LDJ	443.51250	+	CC1	
	DMR/BM	N6LDJ	444.27500	+	CC1	
	DMR/BM	N6LDJ	444.58750	+	CC1	
	FM	W6SRR	29.68000	-	94.8 Hz	
	FM	W6SRR	147.04500	+	94.8 Hz	
	FM	W6SRR	442.62500	+	94.8 Hz	
	FM	W6RGG	442.92500	+		
	FM	K6TEA	443.65000	+		
	FM	W6SRR	927.18750	902.18750	94.8 Hz	
	FM	N6QL	927.37500	902.37500	88.5 Hz	
	FM	N6AKK	1283.55000	-	88.5 Hz	
	FM	N6QL	1284.72500	-	88.5 Hz	
	FM	N6QL	1284.75000	-	88.5 Hz	
Point Arena	FM	W6ABR	146.61000	-	88.5 Hz	
Point Sur	FM	KI6PAU	146.94000	-	94.8 Hz	
Pollock Pines	FM	WB6DAX	52.98000	-	141.3 Hz	
	FM	WA6BTH	146.86500	-	146.2 Hz	
Pomona	DMR/MARC	N6DOZ	446.00000	-	CC7	
	DSTAR	KC6ACS	446.16000	-		
	DSTAR	KM6KUO B	446.16000	-		
	DSTAR	KC6ACS B	446.16000	-		
	FM	N6USO	145.44000	-	136.5 Hz	
	FM	WB6RSK	146.02500	+	103.5 Hz	
	FM	K4ELE	146.70000	-		
	FM	KC6FMX	147.07500	+	110.9 Hz	
	FM	K6JSI	147.21000	+	100.0 Hz	
	FM	K6JSI	224.16000	-	71.9 Hz	
	FM	KF6FM	446.04000	-	131.8 Hz	
	FM	W6GAE	447.52000	-		
	FM	N6DD	447.62000	-		
	FM	N6XPG	447.92000	-		
	FM	K9KAO	449.50000	-	100.0 Hz	
	FM	K6TEM	449.88000	-	146.2 Hz	
	FM	K6DLP	927.61250	902.61250	100.0 Hz	
	FM	K6TEM	1282.82500	-	88.5 Hz	
	FM	KB6MQQ	1284.05000	-		
	FM	KM6NP	1284.37500	-		
	FM	WH6NZ	1285.27500	-		
	FUSION	K6RDH	145.46000	-		
	FUSION	K6RDH	440.00000			
Pomona Islander Mobile Home Pa						
	FM	K6CPP-R	445.58000	-		
Porterville	FM	KE6WDX	145.31000	-	100.0 Hz	
	FM	KE6WDX	146.65500	-	123.0 Hz	
	FM	AB6MJ	440.25000	+	186.2 Hz	
	FM	W6XC	440.82500	+		
	FM	WC6HP	441.52500	+	67.0 Hz	
	FM	KE6WDX	443.05000	+	123.0 Hz	
Portola Valley	DMR/BM	WB5NVN	145.00000	147.55000	CC1	
	FM	WB5NVN	146.08500	+	100.0 Hz	
	FM	K6TSR	440.25000	+	107.2 Hz	
	FM	K6TSR	440.70000	+	107.2 Hz	
	FM	KC6ULT	440.97500	+	114.8 Hz	
Portuguese Bend	FM	KE6TZG-R	146.38500	+	142.6 Hz	

Location	Mode	Call sign	Output	Input	Access	Coordinator
Poway		K6SSN-L	145.67500			
	DMR/MARC	W6SRC	446.03750	-	CC2	
	DMR/MARC	W6CRC	446.05000	-	CC2	
	FM	K6KTA	145.18000	-	107.0 Hz	
	FM	K6JCC	147.19500	+	110.9 Hz	
Pozo	FM	W6SLO	146.83500	-	127.3 Hz	
Prunedale	FM	W6OPI	146.91000	-	94.8 Hz	
	FM	KC6UDC	441.12500	+	123.0 Hz	
	FM	W6DXW	442.77500	+	110.9 Hz	
Quartz Hill	FM	KG6SLC	445.56000	-	110.9 Hz	
	FM	KD6PXZ	446.40000	-	100.0 Hz	
Queen City	FM	KD6CQ-R	145.37000	-		
Quincy	FM	W7OWC	51.90000	-	103.5 Hz	
	FM	AF6AP	147.94500	-	123.0 Hz	
	FM	W6RCA	441.62500	+	100.0 Hz	
Quintette	FM	AG6AU	927.27500	902.27500	127.3 Hz	
Ramona	DMR/BM	WB6YES	445.96000	-	CC1	
	FM	KD6RSQ	145.30000	-	88.5 Hz	
	FM	KD6RSQ	445.76000	-	88.5 Hz	
Rancho Bernardo	FM	NG6ST	146.79000	-	107.2 Hz	
Rancho Cordova	FM	W6AK	224.10000	-	100.0 Hz	
Rancho Cucamonga						
	FM	K6ONT	447.20000	-	114.8 Hz	
	FUSION	K6FED	434.70000			
Rancho Mirage	FUSION	KJ6JEP	445.11000			
Rancho Palos Verdes						
	DMR/BM	N6RPV	445.72000	-	CC1	
	DMR/BM	K6PV	447.12000	-	CC1	
	DMR/MARC	N6RPV	445.72000	-	CC1	
	FM	WA6LA	145.38000	-	100.0 Hz	
	FM	KA6TSA	146.23500	+	127.3 Hz	
	FM	K6VGP	147.36000	-	97.4 Hz	
	FM	AA6RJ	147.42000	146.52000	131.8 Hz	
	FM	WA6LA	223.78000	-	100.0 Hz	
	FM	W6SBA	224.38000	-	192.8 Hz	
	FM	K6VGP	224.98000	-	114.8 Hz	
	FM	WZ6A	445.98000	-	107.2 Hz	
	FM	K6VGP	446.74000	-	100.0 Hz	
	FM	W6TRW	447.00000	-	100.0 Hz	
	FM	KE6LE	449.82000	-		
	FM	K6IUM	449.98000	-	173.8 Hz	
	FM	WA6DPB	1282.47500	-	131.8 Hz	
	FM	N6YKE	1283.32500	-		
	FM	N6UL	1283.55000	-		
	FM	K6MOZ	1284.50000	-		
	FM	KV6D	1285.15000	-		
Rancho Santa Margarita						
	FUSION	AD6SS	147.56000			
Randsburg	FM	N6BKL	52.68000	-	82.5 Hz	
Red Bluff	FM	KF6KDD	145.45000	-	88.5 Hz	
	FM	KH8AF	444.15000	+		
Redding	DMR/BM	W6GRC	145.00000	147.50000	CC1	
	DMR/BM	KD6MTU	440.05000	+	CC1	
	DMR/BM	WA6IO	443.70000	+	CC1	
	FM	WR6TV	52.66000	-	107.2 Hz	
	FM	W6STA	146.64000	-	88.5 Hz	
	FM	WB6CAN	146.76000	-	107.2 Hz	
	FM	N4SMF	146.92500	-	85.4 Hz	
	FM	NC6I	147.09000	+	88.5 Hz	
	FM	KK6JP	147.36000	+	162.2 Hz	
	FM	NA0SA	440.05000	+		
	FM	NA0SA	440.17500	+		

Location	Mode	Call sign	Output	Input	Access	Coordinator
Redding	FM	AB7BS	444.32500	+	100.0 Hz	
	FM	NC6SV	444.55000	+	100.0 Hz	
	FM	WR6TV	927.12500	902.12500	107.2 Hz	
	FM	KE6CHO	927.22500	902.22500		
Redlands	DMR/BM	AI6BX	445.30000	-	CC3	
	DMR/BM	N6LKA	446.88000	-	CC10	
	DMR/BM	AD5MT	449.08000	-	CC7	
	DMR/BM	N6LKA	449.64000	-	CC10	
	FM	AI6BX	147.18000	+	88.5 Hz	
	FM	AI6BX	445.34000	-	88.5 Hz	
	FM	N6AJB	447.02000	-	123.0 Hz	
Redondo Beach	DMR/MARC	W6TRW	449.46250	-	CC2	
	FM	W6TRW	145.32000	-	114.8 Hz	
	FUSION	KM6HRD	446.12500			
Redwood City	DMR/BM	W6BSD	440.17000	5440.17000	CC1	
	FM	K6MPN	53.68000	-	114.8 Hz	
	FM	KC6ULT	146.86500	-	114.8 Hz	
	FM	WD6GGW	441.40000	+	114.8 Hz	
	FM	K6MPN	444.50000	+	100.0 Hz	
	FM	WI6H	927.88750	902.88750	192.8 Hz	
	FM	WD6GGW	1284.70000	-	114.8 Hz	
	FM	KE6UIE	1285.25000	-	88.5 Hz	
Reedley	FM	K6NOX	927.40000	902.40000	114.8 Hz	
Rescue	FM	AG6AU	224.06000	-	127.3 Hz	
	FM	AG6AU	927.23750	902.23750	127.3 Hz	
Rialto	FM	K6RIA	147.64500	-	127.3 Hz	
Richmond	FM	K6LOU	440.97500	+		
	FM	WA6DUR	442.15000	+	100.0 Hz	
Ridgecrest	FM	WA6YBN	145.34000	-	100.0 Hz	
	FM	WA6YBN	147.00000	+	107.2 Hz	
	FM	K6RFO	147.21000	+		
	FM	WI6RE	147.97500	-	100.0 Hz	
	FM	W5WH	224.90000	-		
	FM	W5HMV	447.02000	-	123.0 Hz	
	FM	WI6RE	448.80000	-	100.0 Hz	
	FM	NC9RS	927.01250	902.01250	88.5 Hz	
Rio Linda	DMR/BM	K9WWV	441.61250	+	CC1	
	FUSION	K6FNX	446.50000			
Riverside	DMR/BM	KC9GKA	145.23000	-	CC1	
	DMR/BM	KC7NP	449.46250	-	CC1	
	DMR/MARC	KF6FM	446.03750	-	CC3	
	DMR/MARC	KF6FM	446.05000	-	CC1	
	DMR/MARC	KF6FM	448.15000	-	CC1	
	FM	KB6OZX	445.06000	-	162.2 Hz	
	FUSION	KK6BXJ	146.11500	+		
Robinson Ranch	FM	WR6AAC-R	224.22000	-		
Rock Haven	FM	W6LY	147.61500	-		
Rockland		W7VN-L	145.70000			
Rocklin	DMR/BM	K6IOK	442.52500	+	CC1	
	DMR/BM	KI6SSF	444.97500	+	CC1	
Rohnert Park	FM	WD6FTB	223.90000	-	88.5 Hz	
Rolling Hills	DMR/BM	K6RH	445.30000	-	CC1	
Rosamond	FM	KK6KU	224.66000	-	110.9 Hz	
	FM	WA6CAM	444.57500	+		
Rosemead	FM	KB6MRC	445.90000	-	123.0 Hz	
Roseville	FM	W6SAR	146.64000	-	156.7 Hz	
	FM	KA6OIJ	1282.65000	-	100.0 Hz	
	FUSION	KA6UAI	145.19000			
Rowland Heights	FM	NO6B	446.28000	-		
	FUSION	KN6TXN	147.03000	+		
Running Springs	DMR/BM	KE6TZG	146.38500	-	CC1	
	DMR/MARC	KF6FM	447.52000	-	CC1	

Location	Mode	Call sign	Output	Input	Access	Coordinator
Running Springs	DSTAR	KI6WZX	147.55000	144.95000		
	DSTAR	KI6WZX	446.34000	-		
	FM	WA6ISG	145.12000	-	131.8 Hz	
	FM	KI6JVF	147.61500	-	186.2 Hz	
	FM	K6ECS	147.70500	-	167.9 Hz	
	FM	WA6MTN	224.00000	-		
	FM	WA6DVG	224.06000	-	94.8 Hz	
	FM	K6AMS	445.70000	-	151.4 Hz	
	FM	WR6HP	447.28000	-	136.5 Hz	
	FM	KE6PCV	447.74000	-		
	FM	KV6D	447.98000	-		
	FM	WA6VAW	448.86000	-		
	FM	N6CIZ	449.76000	-		
	FM	KA6MEP	449.98000	-	151.4 Hz	
	FM	AA6QO	1285.07500	-		
	FM	KA6RWW	1286.00000	-		
Saco	FM	KG6FOS-R	444.67500	+		
Sacramento	DMR/MARC	K6INC	443.15000	+	CC1	
	FM	KC6MHT	145.23000	-	162.2 Hz	
	FM	N6NA	145.25000	-	162.2 Hz	
	FM	K6INC	146.70000	-		
	FM	KF6SQL	147.12000	+	162.2 Hz	
	FM	K6NP	147.30000	+	179.9 Hz	
	FM	KC6MHT	224.22000	-	123.0 Hz	
	FM	WA6ZZK	224.56000	-	94.8 Hz	
	FM	AA6IP	224.70000	-	107.2 Hz	
	FM	KJ6JD	224.82000	-	77.0 Hz	
	FM	KU6P	440.20000	+	131.8 Hz	
	FM	KJ6KO	441.45000	+		
	FM	NA6DF	441.85000	+	77.0 Hz	
	FM	K6YC	441.95000	+	114.8 Hz	
	FM	KF6BIK	442.32500	+		
	FM	WB6GWZ	442.40000	+		
	FM	WA6ZZK	442.50000	+	151.4 Hz	
	FM	K6NP	442.90000	+	136.5 Hz	
	FM	KJ6JD	443.27500	+	127.3 Hz	
	FM	N0RM	443.45000	+		
	FM	W6YDD	443.90000	+	136.5 Hz	
	FM	W6PRN	444.42500	+	100.0 Hz	
	FM	K7QDX	927.10000	902.10000	103.5 Hz	
	FM	K6YC	927.20000	902.20000	100.0 Hz	
	FM	N6ICW	927.96250	902.96250		
	FM	KD6GFZ	1284.85000	-	88.5 Hz	
Sacramento, Folsom Lake						
	FM	K6IS	145.19000	-	162.2 Hz	
	FM	K6IS	224.40000	-	162.2 Hz	
Sacramento, KOVR/KXTV Tower						
	FM	K6DTV	147.39000	+	146.2 Hz	
Salinas	DMR/BM	W6JSO	444.52500	+	CC1	
	FM	W6CER	145.41000	-		
	FM	N6SPD	145.43000	-	94.8 Hz	
	FM	KC6UDC	146.08500	+	100.0 Hz	
	FM	WB6ECE	147.27000	+	94.8 Hz	
	FM	N6LEX	224.32000	-	146.2 Hz	
	FM	N6LEX	442.02500	+	146.2 Hz	
	FM	KG6UYZ	442.60000	+	110.9 Hz	
	FM	KG6UYZ	927.95000	902.95000		
Salinas, Fremont Pk						
	FM	K6JE	145.47000	-	94.8 Hz	
	FM	K6JE	441.45000	+	123.0 Hz	
San Andreas	FM	W6ALL	441.70000	+		
	FM	NC6R	443.35000	+	156.7 Hz	

Location	Mode	Call sign	Output	Input	Access	Coordinator
San Andreas	FM	N6GKJ	927.07500	902.07500	100.0 Hz	
San Anselmo	FM	K6BW	146.77500	-	127.3 Hz	
	FM	W6RV	440.55000	+	100.0 Hz	
San Antonio Heights						
		K4ELE-L	927.23700			
	FM	K6PQN-R	445.86000	-		
	FM	KD6AFA-R	445.92000	-		
San Ardo	FM	WR6VHF	51.82000	-	136.5 Hz	
	FM	W6RTF-L	145.49000	-		
San Ardo, Williams Hill						
	FM	W6FM	146.73000	-	127.3 Hz	
San Bernardino	DMR/BM	AE6TV	448.90000	-	CC1	
	DMR/BM	AE6TV	449.16000	-	CC1	
	DSTAR	KI6WZX C	147.55000	144.99500		
	DSTAR	KI6WZX B	446.34000	-		
	DSTAR	KI6WZX A	1285.20000	-		
	FM	N6LXX	224.44000	-	94.8 Hz	
	FM	WA6JBD	927.95000	902.95000		
San Bernardino, Twin Peaks						
	FM	WA6TJQ	224.56000	-	100.0 Hz	
San Bruno	DMR/MARC	AH6KD	145.01250	147.51250	CC0	
	DMR/MARC	N6DOZ	441.90000	+	CC1	
	FM	W6JMX	224.24000	-	141.3 Hz	
	FM	KM6EF	1286.05000	-	123.0 Hz	
San Carlos	FM	W6CBS	441.61250	+	100.0 Hz	
San Clemente	DMR/MARC	KK6TTJ	144.65000	147.55000	CC1	
	FM	K6SOA	146.02500	+	110.9 Hz	
	FM	W6KRW	146.89500	-	136.5 Hz	
	FM	W6KRW	1282.77500	-	88.5 Hz	
San Diego	DMR/BM	K6RRR	145.49370	147.66000	CC1	
	DMR/BM	W6RDX	444.46250	+	CC9	
	DMR/BM	AF6YU	445.20000	-	CC1	
	DMR/BM	N6RVI	445.31250	-	CC3	
	DMR/BM	KK6KD	448.46000	-	CC1	
	DMR/BM	K6RRR	449.10000	-	CC1	
	DMR/BM	K6RRR	449.22000	-	CC1	
	DMR/BM	N6VVY	449.36000	-	CC1	
	DMR/BM	N7OEI	449.85000	-	CC1	
	DMR/MARC	WA6NVL	445.62000	-	CC0	
	DMR/MARC	KI6MGN	445.86000	-	CC1	
	DMR/MARC	W6SS	448.16000	-	CC1	
	DMR/MARC	KI6KQU	448.52000	-	CC1	
	DMR/MARC	WA6YVX	449.00000	-	CC1	
	DMR/MARC	AI6DZ	449.46250	-	CC6	
	DMR/MARC	W6SS	449.60000	-	CC1	
	DMR/MARC	WA6YVX	449.86250	-	CC1	
	DSTAR	KJ6FCH B	446.56500	-		
	DSTAR	KW6HRO B	446.98000	-		
	DSTAR	KJ6LKA B	447.19000	-		
	DSTAR	KI6KQU B	447.84500	-		
	DSTAR	KW6HRO A	1283.77500	-		
	FM	K6JCC	52.60000	-	107.2 Hz	
	FM	N6LXX	53.58000	-	103.5 Hz	
	FM	W6HDC	145.12000	-	107.2 Hz	
	FM	W6XC	145.34000	0.00000		
	FM	WR7NV	145.36000	-	100.0 Hz	
	FM	K6AIL	147.88500	-	107.2 Hz	
	FM	N6WYF	147.94500	-	107.2 Hz	
	FM	WA6HYQ	224.16000	-	107.2 Hz	
	FM	WD6FZA	224.40000	-	103.5 Hz	
	FM	N6LXX	224.72000	-	94.8 Hz	
	FM	W6GIC	224.74000	-	107.2 Hz	

Location	Mode	Call sign	Output	Input	Access	Coordinator
San Diego	FM	K6ERN	445.58000	-	100.0 Hz	
	FM	N6LXX	446.10000	-	123.0 Hz	
	FM	K6VGP	447.44000	-	107.2 Hz	
	FM	K6JSI	447.64000	-	100.0 Hz	
	FM	KE6VK	448.94000	-		
	FM	KJ6GRS	449.00000	-		
	FM	N6VCM	449.14000	-		
	FM	K6KTA	449.58000	-	107.2 Hz	
	FM	W6XC	449.74000	-		
	FM	K6RIF	449.98000	-	88.5 Hz	
	FUSION	KK6BAD-M	144.54500			
	FUSION	W6BVI	145.00000			
	FUSION	KD6CYY	433.00000			
	FUSION	KN6GXQ	438.80000			
	FUSION	KK6BAD/RFM	441.50000	+		
	FUSION	N6DCR	445.68000	-		
San Diego / San Miguel						
	DMR/BM	KB6PLH	449.84000	-	CC1	
San Diego, Kearney Mesa						
	FM	W6UUS	447.32000	-	107.2 Hz	
San Diego, Mount Laguna						
	FM	WB6WLV	147.15000	+	107.2 Hz	
	FM	KA6DAC	446.75000	-	107.2 Hz	
San Diego, Mt. Otay						
	FM	K6XI	223.84000	-	107.2 Hz	
	FM	WR6BLU	448.52000	-		
	FM	KF6BYB	448.98000	-		
	FM	K6XI	449.12000	-	100.0 Hz	
	FM	K6XI	449.44000	-	107.2 Hz	
	FM	N6JOJ	449.82000	-	136.5 Hz	
San Diego, Mt. Soledad						
	P25	KI6KHB	447.28000	-	91.5 Hz	
San Diego, Mt. Woodson						
	FM	WA6JAF	448.72000	-		
San Diego, Old Town						
	FM	KM6RPT	448.28000	-	82.5 Hz	
San Diego, Otay Mountain						
	FM	WB6WLV	146.64000	-	107.2 Hz	
	FM	N6VVY	147.21000	+	91.5 Hz	
	FM	N6VVZ	224.26000	-	107.2 Hz	
	FM	WR6MO	448.02000	-	91.5 Hz	
	FM	K6RRR	449.06000	-	88.5 Hz	
	FM	WB6CYT	449.22000	-	91.5 Hz	
	FM	KW6HRO	449.38000	-	100.0 Hz	
	FM	WB6DTR	449.78000	-	123.0 Hz	
	FM	WB6WLV	1282.30000	-	107.2 Hz	
San Diego, Otay Mtn						
	FM	KK6BAD	447.04000	-	123.0 Hz	
	FM	WA6OSB	449.70000	-	151.4 Hz	
San Diego, Paradise Hills						
	FM	W6JVA	145.48000	-	127.3 Hz	
San Diego, Rattlesnake Peak						
	FM	AA6WS	147.76500	-	79.7 Hz	
	FM	N6JOJ	446.18000	-		
San Diego, San Miguel Mountain						
	FM	KR6FM	53.66000	-	103.5 Hz	
San Dimas	DMR/MARC	WD6AML	447.90000	-	CC1	
	FM	K6VGP	224.84000	-	114.8 Hz	
	FM	K6VGP	447.62000	-	114.8 Hz	
San Dimas, Johnstone Peak						
	FM	W6FNO	146.82000	-		
	FM	W6NRY	223.98000	-	103.5 Hz	

Location	Mode	Call sign	Output	Input	Access	Coordinator
San Dimas, Johnstone Peak						
	FM	W6FNO	446.02000	-		
	FM	WA6FZH	446.40000	-	103.5 Hz	
	FM	KM6RW	446.80000	-	131.8 Hz	
	FM	W6NRY	447.30000	-		
	FM	K6OES	448.34000	-	114.8 Hz	
	FM	K6MVH	448.84000	-		
San Fernando	DMR/BM	WB6YES	447.26000	-	CC1	
	FM	N6BKL	51.80000	-	82.5 Hz	
	FM	W6IN	146.91000	-	136.5 Hz	
	FM	WA6TTL	446.62000	-		
San Francisco	DMR/BM	KC6IAU	444.00000	+	CC1	
	DMR/MARC	KC6YDH	443.60000	+	CC8	
	DSTAR	W6PW C	147.10500	+		
	DSTAR	W6PW B	444.16250	+		
	FM	W6TP	146.79000	-	114.8 Hz	
	FM	W6WNG	147.13000	+	107.2 Hz	
	FM	KJ7EEP-L	147.55500			
	FM	WA6GG	224.22000	-	100.0 Hz	
	FM	W6TP	224.50000	-	114.8 Hz	
	FM	KA6TGI	224.52000	-	67.0 Hz	
	FM	N6MVT	442.07500	+	100.0 Hz	
	FM	W6TP	443.10000	+		
	FM	K6MSR	443.67500	+		
	FM	KB6LCS	444.92500	+	136.5 Hz	
	FM	KA6TGI	1284.90000	-	67.0 Hz	
	FUSION	N6DOZ	433.00000			
San Francisco, Twin Peaks						
	FM	WA6GG	442.05000	+	127.3 Hz	
San Francsico	DMR/BM	W6PW	444.22500	+	CC1	
San Jacinto	DMR/BM	AI6BX	445.26000	-	CC3	
San Jose	DMR/BM	W6OTX	144.96250	147.46250	CC3	
	DMR/BM	KC6IAU	147.70500	-	CC1	
	DMR/BM	N6BWJ	433.50000	+	CC5	
	DMR/BM	WX6PD	441.21250	+	CC1	
	DMR/BM	W6TCP	441.66250	+	CC1	
	DMR/BM	WA6YCZ	442.53750	+	CC1	
	DMR/BM	WX6INC	443.95000	+	CC1	
	DMR/BM	WX6INC	443.96250	+	CC1	
	DMR/BM	K6HLE	444.02500	+	CC1	
	DMR/BM	K6HLE	444.03750	+	CC1	
	DMR/BM	W6OTX	444.47500	+	CC1	
	DMR/BM	AD1U	465.02500	+	CC1	
	DMR/MARC	W6YYY	440.03750	+	CC1	
	DMR/MARC	K6LLC	440.22500	+	CC1	
	DMR/MARC	AD1U	441.82500	+	CC1	
	DMR/MARC	N6JET	441.87500	+	CC1	
	DMR/MARC	AD1U	443.30000	+	CC1	
	DSTAR	W6IOS B	440.30000	+		
	DSTAR	WW6BAY B	444.07500	+		
	DSTAR	WW6BAY D	1251.00000			
	DSTAR	K6HLE A	1286.52500	-		
	DSTAR	K6HLE D	1299.35000			
	FM	W6PIY	52.58000	-	151.4 Hz	
	FM	KD6AOG	52.66000	-	127.3 Hz	
	FM	KG6HAT	52.94000	-	100.0 Hz	
	FM	WA2IBM	145.19000	-	151.4 Hz	
	FM	KB6FEC	145.31000	-	162.2 Hz	
	FM	KE6MON	146.35500	+	123.0 Hz	
	FM	K6INC	146.82000	-	123.0 Hz	
	FM	KB6FEC	146.89500	-	110.9 Hz	
	FM	AD1U	146.97000	-		

Location	Mode	Call sign	Output	Input	Access	Coordinator
San Jose	FM	W6UU	146.98500	-	114.8 Hz	
	FM	WB6KHP	147.03000	+	107.2 Hz	
	FM	KB6FEC	147.16500	+	100.0 Hz	
	FM	W6PIY	147.39000	+	151.4 Hz	
	FM	KI0GU	147.51000		100.0 Hz	
	FM	K6GOD	223.86000	-	107.2 Hz	
	FM	W6PIY	223.96000	-	156.7 Hz	
	FM	KU6V	224.04000	-	100.0 Hz	
	FM	WB6KHP	224.68000	-	107.2 Hz	
	FM	NT6S	224.98000	-	110.9 Hz	
	FM	W6IOS	430.30000	+		
	FM	W6SMQ	440.10000	+	127.3 Hz	
	FM	WA6YOP	440.27500	+	127.3 Hz	
	FM	N6TNR	440.37500	+		
	FM	K6GOD	441.10000	+	203.5 Hz	
	FM	KC6BJO	441.15000	+	100.0 Hz	
	FM	KF6FWO	441.17500	+	103.5 Hz	
	FM	K6BEN	441.27500	+		
	FM	WB6ECE	441.30000	+	146.2 Hz	
	FM	W6PIY	441.35000	+	88.5 Hz	
	FM	WA6QDP	441.72500	+		
	FM	KG6KCL	441.85000	+		
	FM	N1UFD	442.17500	+		
	FM	K6INC	442.30000	+	114.8 Hz	
	FM	WB6KHP	442.45000	+	100.0 Hz	
	FM	WB6ZVW	442.50000	+	100.0 Hz	
	FM	N6MNV	442.70000	+	100.0 Hz	
	FM	KU6V	442.77500	+	131.8 Hz	
	FM	WR6COP	442.82500	+		
	FM	K6JSI	442.90000	+	162.2 Hz	
	FM	K6YZS	442.95000	+	85.4 Hz	
	FM	N6MVT	443.07500	+	123.0 Hz	
	FM	W6AMT	443.27500	+	107.2 Hz	
	FM	KB5JR	443.30000	+	136.5 Hz	
	FM	K6MF	443.45000	+		
	FM	K6LNK	443.47500	+	123.0 Hz	
	FM	K6TAZ	443.55000	+		
	FM	K6MSR	443.62500	+		
	FM	WA6GFY	443.77500	+	100.0 Hz	
	FM	W6YL	443.90000	+	100.0 Hz	
	FM	K6JJC	444.02500	+	136.5 Hz	
	FM	KD6CUC	444.05000	+		
	FM	N6TLQ	444.10000	+		
	FM	KE6JTK	444.22500	+	131.8 Hz	
	FM	WB6RNH	444.30000	+	162.2 Hz	
	FM	WA6INC	444.32500	+	114.8 Hz	
	FM	AD1U	444.32500	+	114.8 Hz	
	FM	WB6OQS	444.60000	+	141.3 Hz	
	FM	N6NAC	444.62500	+	110.9 Hz	
	FM	WB6KHP	444.70000	+	127.3 Hz	
	FM	WA6GEL	444.80000	+		
	FM	W6RLW	1282.00000	-	88.5 Hz	
	FM	W6RLW	1282.20000	-	88.5 Hz	
	FM	N6AKK	1283.10000	-	88.5 Hz	
	FM	N6EEZ	1283.40000	-	94.8 Hz	
	FM	WA6GFY	1283.70000	-	100.0 Hz	
	FM	N6AKB	1284.30000	-	100.0 Hz	
	FM	W6RLW	1285.00000	-	88.5 Hz	
	FM	KD6AOG	1285.80000	-	127.3 Hz	
	FM	KU6V	1285.95000	-	100.0 Hz	
	FM	N6NAC	1286.00000	-	110.9 Hz	
	FM	WB6OCD	1286.07500	-	88.5 Hz	

Location	Mode	Call sign	Output	Input	Access	Coordinator
San Jose	FM	KD6AOG	1286.15000	-	127.3 Hz	
	FM	W6PIY	1286.20000	-	100.0 Hz	
	P25	KE6STH	443.57500	+		
	FUSION	WB6PFJ	145.77000			
	FUSION	KG6KZZ	146.55000			
	FUSION	KI0GU	433.01250			
	FUSION	AD1U	443.95000	+		
San Jose, Loma Prieta						
	FM	WR6ABD	146.64000	-	162.2 Hz	
	FM	WB6OQS	146.76000	-	151.4 Hz	
	FM	WB6OQS	224.26000	-	123.0 Hz	
San Jose, Mt Hamilton						
	FM	KB6ABM	224.60000	-	156.7 Hz	
San Jose, Mt Umunhum						
	FM	WA6YCZ	147.15000	+	110.9 Hz	
San Jose, Regional Medical Cen						
	FM	W6UU	442.42500	+	107.2 Hz	
San Jose, Santa Cruz Mountains						
	FM	KU6V	444.90000	+	110.9 Hz	
San Jose, Santa Cruz Mts.						
	FM	N6NAC	224.64000	-	110.9 Hz	
San Leandro	DSTAR	AC6SO B	440.02500	+		
	DSTAR	AC6SO A	1282.70000	-		
	DSTAR	AC6SO D	1299.50000			
	FM	W6RGG	147.24000	+	107.2 Hz	
	FM	KB6NCL	442.77500	+		
	FM	K6KBL	443.37500	+	156.7 Hz	
San Lorenzo	FM	KQ6YG	224.70000	-	156.7 Hz	
	FM	KM6HJA	441.45000	+	162.2 Hz	
	FM	KF6REK-R	442.47500	+		
San Lorzenzo	FM	KM6HJA	147.20000	+	103.5 Hz	
San Luis Obispo	DMR/BM	K7AZ	443.30000	+	CC3	NARCC
	DMR/BM	KK6DJ	444.93750	+	CC1	
	DMR/MARC	WX6D	443.43750	+	CC1	
	FM	KC6WRD	145.29000	-		
	FM	W6SLO	146.62000	-	127.3 Hz	
	FM	W6SLO	146.67000	-	127.3 Hz	
	FM	W6SLO	146.80000	-	127.3 Hz	
	FM	WB6JWB	441.07500	+	94.8 Hz	
	FM	W6BHZ	442.30000	+	127.3 Hz	
	FM	W6SLO	442.70000	+	127.3 Hz	
	FM	WB6FMC	442.87500	+		
	FM	K7AZ/R	443.30000	+	91.5 Hz	
	FM	W6FM	443.57500	+		
	FM	N6HYM	443.80000	+		
	FM	W6SLO	444.10000	+	127.3 Hz	
	FM	KC6WRD	444.90000	+	127.3 Hz	
San Luis Obispo, Black Butte						
	FM	WB6NYS	224.58000	-	151.4 Hz	
San Luis Obispo, Mt Lowe						
	FM	W6FM	147.36000	+	127.3 Hz	
San Marcos	DMR/BM	WB6YES	445.88000	-	CC3	
	DMR/BM	WB6YES	446.08000	-	CC1	
	FM	WD6FZA	446.58000	-	156.7 Hz	
	FM	K6VGP	447.36000	-	91.5 Hz	
San Martin	FM	KU6V	223.92000	-	100.0 Hz	
San Mateo	DMR/BM	KG6TN	443.92500	+	CC1	
	FM	N6MPX	147.30000	+	100.0 Hz	
	P25	K7CBL	440.05000	+	100.0 Hz	
San Miguel	DMR/BM	KB6CIO	444.17500	+	CC1	
San Pablo	FM	WA6KQB	145.11000	-	82.5 Hz	
	FM	WA6KQB	224.30000	-	82.5 Hz	

Location	Mode	Call sign	Output	Input	Access	Coordinator
San Pablo	FM	WA6JQV	927.02500	902.02500		
	FM	WA6JQV	927.45000	902.45000		
	FM	WA6JQV	927.47500	902.47500		
San Rafael	FM	K6GWE	147.33000	+	173.8 Hz	
	FM	KH8AF	440.92500	+		
	FM	KH8AF	442.17500	+		
	FM	K6GWE	443.52500	+	82.5 Hz	
San Ramon	FM	WA6HAM	440.42500	+	79.7 Hz	
San Simeon	FM	W6SLO	444.10000	+	127.3 Hz	
Santa Ana	DMR/BM	WA6LIF	446.82000	-	CC1	
	FUSION	WD6ABC	445.76000	-		
Santa Barbara		K6LCM-L	147.48000			
	DMR/BM	K6TZ	445.48000	-	CC1	
	DMR/BM	WB6OBB	449.30000	-	CC3	
	DMR/MARC	KA6SOX	445.38000	-	CC1	
	DMR/MARC	KK6GFX	446.98000	-	CC1	
	FM	K6TZ	51.82000	-	82.5 Hz	
	FM	AF6VU	147.07500	+	131.8 Hz	
	FM	WC6MRA	224.04000	-		
	FM	K6TZ	224.08000	-	131.8 Hz	
	FM	K6TZ	224.16000	-	131.8 Hz	
	FM	WA6TTL	446.20000	-		
	FM	W6XC	447.16000	-		
	FM	W6RRN	448.76000	-		
	FM	K6JSI	448.90000	-	123.0 Hz	
	FM	K6VGP	448.92000	-	100.0 Hz	
Santa Barbara, Gibraltar Peak						
	FM	K6RCL	224.04000	-		
	FM	K6RCL	1286.20000	-		
Santa Barbara, Gibralter Peak						
	FM	KD6OVS	146.70000	-	131.8 Hz	
Santa Barbara, Santa Ynez Peak						
	FM	WB6BBE	449.56000	-		
	FM	K6RCL	1284.05000	-		
Santa Barbara, UCSB						
	FM	KG6MNB	927.46250	902.46250	131.8 Hz	
Santa Barbara, UCSB - Storke T						
	FM	W6RFU	145.48000	-	136.5 Hz	
Santa Clara	DMR/MARC	W6RNR	444.87500	-	CC2	
	FM	K6SNC	442.02500	+		
	FM	K6SNC	927.73750	902.73750	100.0 Hz	
	FM	N6MEF	927.83750	902.83750	100.0 Hz	
Santa Clarita	FM	N6KNW	51.86000	-	82.5 Hz	
	FM	KI6AIT	145.20000	-		
	FM	N6NMC	448.34000	-	67.0 Hz	
	FM	KB6C	448.48000	-		
	FUSION	KC6ESW	430.30000			
	FUSION	KJ6EO	431.55000			
Santa Clarita, Duck Mountain						
	FM	W6MEP	147.24000	+	67.0 Hz	
Santa Clarita, Mad Mountain						
	FM	W6JW	146.79000	-	123.0 Hz	
	FM	W6JW	445.30000	-	100.0 Hz	
Santa Clarita, Oat Mtn.						
	FM	WA6EQU	448.22000	-		
	FM	WA6TXY	449.24000	-		
Santa Cruz		AF6JP-L	146.98500			
	DSTAR	K6DRI C	145.00000	147.50000		
	DSTAR	K6DRI	145.00000	147.50000		
	FM	K6HJU	29.66000	-	156.7 Hz	
	FM	KE6IEL	52.68000	-	94.8 Hz	
	FM	W6SLG	145.31000	-	94.8 Hz	

Location	Mode	Call sign	Output	Input	Access	Coordinator
Santa Cruz	FM	KA6TGI	224.52000	-	136.5 Hz	
	FM	W6JWS	440.85000	+	94.8 Hz	
	FM	N7WG	441.67500	+	123.0 Hz	
	FM	WA6FUL	442.55000	+		
	FM	WB6PHE	443.47500	+	127.3 Hz	
Santa Cruz Island	FM	K6TZ	223.92000	-	131.8 Hz	
	FM	W6XC	446.60000	-		
	P25	W6XC	146.65500	-		
Santa Cruz, Empire Grade						
	FM	W6WLS	147.18000	+		
	P25	W6DXW	442.75000	+	110.9 Hz	
Santa Cruz, Loma Prieta						
	FM	AE6KE	146.83500	-	94.8 Hz	
Santa Maria	DMR/BM	K7AZ	440.42500	+	CC2	
	FM	N6UE	146.64000	-		
	FM	W6AB	147.30000	+	131.8 Hz	
	FM	W6NO	147.91500	-	103.5 Hz	
Santa Monica	FM	K6FCC	145.28000	-	127.3 Hz	
	FM	WA6TTL	224.34000	-		
	FM	WD6FZA	445.42000	-	127.3 Hz	
	FM	K6VGP	445.82000	-		
	FM	W6XC	447.78000	-		
Santa Monica, Brentwood / San						
	FM	K6CYC	147.03000	+	127.3 Hz	
Santa Monica, Saddle Pk						
	FM	WA6JQB	447.84000	-		
	FM	WR6SP	447.86000	-		
Santa Paula	DMR/MARC	K6VCD	447.36000	-	CC1	
	FM	K6ERN	51.84000	-	103.5 Hz	
Santa Paula, South Mountain						
	FM	WA6ZSN	146.38500	+	127.3 Hz	
	FM	WA6ZSN	224.10000	-	127.3 Hz	
Santa Rosa	DMR/BM	AA6RH	440.27500	+	CC1	
	DMR/BM	AA6RH	441.00000	+	CC1	
	DMR/BM	K6ACS	442.11250	+	CC1	
	DMR/BM	AA6RH	443.38750	+	CC1	
	DSTAR	K6ACS C	145.04000	144.64000		
	DSTAR	K6ACS	145.04000	-		
	FM	WA6YGD	145.35000	-	88.5 Hz	
	FM	K6ACS	146.73000	-	88.5 Hz	
	FM	KE6EAQ	146.83500	-	88.5 Hz	
	FM	KE6N	223.76000	-	85.4 Hz	
	FM	K6ACS	224.82000	-	103.5 Hz	
	FM	KD6CJQ	440.20000	+	88.5 Hz	
	FM	K6EAR	440.45000	+	88.5 Hz	
	FM	KD6RC	441.30000	+	88.5 Hz	
	FM	WB7ABP	443.82500	+	100.0 Hz	
	FM	WB6RUT	444.37500	+		
	FM	WA6RQX	444.75000	+	123.0 Hz	
	FM	KC6REK	1283.20000	-	88.5 Hz	
	FUSION	K6SON	441.37500	+		
Santa Ynez	DMR/BM	WB6YES	446.98000	-	CC1	
	DMR/BM	N6JFO	447.70000	-	CC15	
	DSTAR	KK6GFX	447.84000	-		
	DSTAR	KK6GFX B	447.84000	-		
	FM	K6TZ	145.16000	-	127.3 Hz	
	FM	K6TZ	224.12000	-	131.8 Hz	
Santa Ynez, Broadcast Peak						
	FM	WB6OBB	147.00000	+	131.8 Hz	
Santa Ynez, Santa Ynez Peak						
	FM	K6TZ	145.18000	-	131.8 Hz	
	FM	K6BVA	145.44000	-		

Location	Mode	Call sign	Output	Input	Access	Coordinator
Santa Ynez, Santa Ynez Peak						
	FM	WA6TZE	449.00000	-		
Santee	FM	WA6OSB	147.91500	-	151.4 Hz	
Santee, Kearney Mesa						
	FM	KD6GNB	224.92000	-	107.2 Hz	
Santiago Peak	DMR/BM	KB6CRE	447.54000	-	CC1	
	DMR/BM	K6IRF	448.26000	-	CC1	
	DSTAR	KJ6GRS B	446.56000	-		
Saratoga	DMR/BM	KK6USZ	441.95000	+	CC1	NARCC
	DMR/MARC	NU6P	440.43750	+	CC1	
	FM	K6SA	146.65500	-	114.8 Hz	
	FM	K6BEN	224.46000	-		
	FM	K6BEN	443.12500	+		
	FM	W6RLW	1283.00000	-	88.5 Hz	
Saugus	FUSION	KN6JCP	446.58000	-	127.3 Hz	
Sausalito, Wolfback Rdg						
	FM	K6ER	442.52500	+	114.8 Hz	
Scotia	FM	N7HQZ	29.60000	-	156.7 Hz	
	FM	N7HQZ	50.30000	-	114.8 Hz	
	FM	N7HQZ	51.84000	-	114.8 Hz	
	FM	WB6TMS	145.17000	-	103.5 Hz	
	FM	WB6TMS	145.47000	-	88.5 Hz	
	FM	N7HQZ	223.50000	-	103.5 Hz	
	FM	K6FWR	443.25000	+	103.5 Hz	
Scotia, Monument Peak						
	FM	K6FWR	146.76000	-	103.5 Hz	
Sea Ranch	FM	W6ABR	147.94500	-	88.5 Hz	
Seal Beach	FM	K6NX	445.36000	-	100.0 Hz	
	FM	WA6FZH	446.40000	-	88.5 Hz	
	FM	KC6YNQ	449.30000	-	141.3 Hz	
Sebastopol	DMR/BM	W6SON	443.10000	+	CC1	
	DMR/BM	WA6TIP	444.82500	+	CC1	
	DMR/BM	KC6SOT	444.98750	+	CC1	
	FM	WA6FUL	52.64000	-	114.8 Hz	
	FM	WA6FUL	440.47500	+	97.4 Hz	
	FM	WA6FUL	440.95000	+	123.0 Hz	
	FM	WA6FUL	443.42500	+	88.5 Hz	
Sebastopol, English Hill						
	FM	W6SON	147.31500	+	88.5 Hz	
	FM	W6SON	224.48000	-	88.5 Hz	
Seigler	FM	KI6QCU	145.15000	-	103.5 Hz	
Sequoia	FM	KK6AC	442.95000	+	141.3 Hz	
Shasta Lake	FM	K7JKL	442.07500	+	114.8 Hz	
Sherman Oaks	FM	NK6S	145.24000	-	91.5 Hz	
Shingle Springs	FM	KG6HAT	52.90000	-	100.0 Hz	
	FM	N6NA	145.25000	-	162.2 Hz	
	FM	WO3B	146.94000	-	136.5 Hz	
	FM	N6NA	441.30000	+	127.3 Hz	
Shingle Springs, Mt Aukum						
	FM	NC6R	146.67000	-	156.7 Hz	
	FM	NC6R	442.05000	+	156.7 Hz	
Shingletown	FM	WO6P	147.03000	+	88.5 Hz	
	FM	WO6P	147.16500	+	88.5 Hz	
Sierra City	FM	W7FEH	145.17000	-	114.8 Hz	
Sierra Madre, Santa Anita Ridg						
	FM	W6QFK	147.76500	-	131.8 Hz	
Sierra Vista Trailer Park						
		KJ6ZD-R	445.00000			
Signal Hill	FM	K6CHE	146.14500	+	156.7 Hz	
	FM	K6CHE	223.80000	-	156.7 Hz	
	FM	K6CHE	449.78000	-	131.8 Hz	
	FM	K6CHE	1286.30000	-	156.7 Hz	

Location	Mode	Call sign	Output	Input	Access	Coordinator
Silicon Valley	FM	KA6DWN	443.75000	+	100.0 Hz	
Silverado	DMR/MARC	N6DOZ	447.80000	-	CC7	
	DMR/MARC	KA6P	449.03750	-	CC1	
Simi Valley	FM	WA6TTL	145.34000	-		
	FM	WA6FGK	146.64000	-	127.3 Hz	
	FM	K6ERN	146.80500	-	100.0 Hz	
	FM	AD6SV	224.06000	-	156.7 Hz	
	FM	N6XPG	224.44000	-	100.0 Hz	
	FM	K6ERN	445.58000	-	100.0 Hz	
	FUSION	KM6VGG	147.48000			
Smith River	FM	K6SLS	443.10000	+	100.0 Hz	
Soledad	FM	N6HU	145.21000	-		
	FM	WA6RQX	444.37500	+	100.0 Hz	
Solvang	FM	K6SYV	146.89500	-	131.8 Hz	
Sonoma	DMR/BM	W6AJF	440.01250	+	CC1	
Sonora	DMR/BM	KJ6NRO	442.97500	+	CC1	
	FM	WB6PHE	441.47500	+	110.9 Hz	
	FM	K6LNK	443.47500	+	103.5 Hz	
	FM	K6KVA	444.65000	+	114.8 Hz	
	FM	NC9RS	927.61250	902.61250	107.2 Hz	
Soquel	DMR/MARC	WX6D	442.53750	+	CC1	
Soulsbyville	FM	N6HUH	146.11500	+	100.0 Hz	
South Lake Tahoe						
	DMR/BM	WA6EWV	442.47500	+	CC3	CARCON
	FM	W6SUV	144.89500	-		
	FM	N6ICW	145.15000	-	123.0 Hz	
	FM	KA6GWY	145.35000	-	110.9 Hz	
	FM	WA6EWV	146.85000	-	123.0 Hz	
	FM	NR7A	224.02000	-		
	FM	N3KD	1285.00000	-	88.5 Hz	
South Lake Tahoe, East Peak						
	FM	NR7A	147.24000	+	123.0 Hz	
South Lake Tahoe, Heavenly Val						
	FM	W6SUV	442.82500	+	88.5 Hz	
South San Francisco						
	DMR/BM	KK4PHN	443.30000	+	CC7	
	DMR/MARC	N6DOZ	441.45000	+	CC7	
	FM	K6HN	440.60000	+		
	FM	K6DNA	441.25000	+	141.3 Hz	
	FM	N6MNV	442.70000	+	173.8 Hz	
Spring Valley	FUSION	N6RVI	445.34000	-		
Springville	FM	KE6WDX	441.97500	+	100.0 Hz	
St. Helena	DMR/BM	K6LO	440.10000	+	CC1	
Stallion Meadow Mobile Home Pa						
		AD6TG-L	145.60000			
Stockton	FM	N5FDL	147.21000	+	114.8 Hz	
	FM	WA6TCG	224.62000	-	192.8 Hz	
	FM	KE6DXF	440.07500	+	131.8 Hz	
	FM	K6GTO	442.27500	+	103.5 Hz	
	FM	N6GVI	443.10000	+		
	FM	KI6KGN	443.12500	+	107.2 Hz	
	FM	KI6KGN	444.22500	+	107.2 Hz	
	FM	K6KJQ	444.32500	+	94.8 Hz	
	FM	K6TRK	444.50000	+	114.8 Hz	
	FM	KI6KGN	444.87500	+	107.2 Hz	
	FM	K6NOX	927.41250	902.41250	107.2 Hz	
Stonyford	FM	K6LNK	146.11500	-	123.0 Hz	
	FM	N6MVT	443.07500	+	114.8 Hz	
	FM	K6BIQ	443.87500	+	100.0 Hz	
Sugarpine	FM	W6MAG	443.05000	+	71.9 Hz	
Sun City	FM	KB6SSB	146.70000	-	103.5 Hz	
	FUSION	N6PB	146.22500	-		

Location	Mode	Call sign	Output	Input	Access	Coordinator
Sun Valley	FM	KC6HUR	445.22000	-	110.9 Hz	
Sunnyvale	FM	K6SNY	145.17000	-	94.8 Hz	
	FM	NA6MF	145.25000	-	123.0 Hz	
	FM	WA6DY	147.10500	+	100.0 Hz	
Sunol	DMR/MARC	W6SRR	443.51250	+	CC1	
Sunset Peak	DMR/BM	WB6YES	449.36000	-	CC1	
Sunset Ridge	DMR/BM	WB6YES	449.36000	-	CC0	
Susanville	DMR/MARC	KE6NDG	444.57500	+	CC1	
	DMR/MARC	KE6NDG	444.77500	+	CC1	
	DMR/MARC	KE6NDG	444.87500	+	CC1	
Susanville, Fredonyer Peak						
	FM	K6LRC	146.91000	-	91.5 Hz	
Susanville, Hamilton Mountain						
	FM	K6LRC	146.83500	-	91.5 Hz	
Susanville, Shaffer Mountain						
	FM	K6LRC	146.88000	-	91.5 Hz	
Swingle	DMR/BM	K6LNK	927.28750	902.28750	CC3	
Sylmar	FM	WA6TTL	224.36000	-		
	FM	W6CTR	445.16000	-	100.0 Hz	
	FM	K6VGP	449.64000	-	114.8 Hz	
	FM	K6LRB	927.48750	902.48750		
	FM	W6CPA	1285.90000	-	123.0 Hz	
Sylmar, Contractors Point						
	DSTAR	WA6IRC	147.56000	144.96000		
	DSTAR	WA6IRC	447.04000	-		
	DSTAR	WA6IRC	1286.10000	-		
	FM	KC6PXL	145.12000	-	103.5 Hz	
	FM	W6WAX	224.24000	-	162.2 Hz	
	FM	KC6PXL	224.52000	-	103.5 Hz	
	FM	KC6JAR	445.34000	-	71.9 Hz	
Sylmar, Contractors Pt						
	FM	KF6HKM	224.26000	-	103.5 Hz	
	FM	KC6PXL	447.22000	-		
	FM	W6FRT	447.34000	-	162.2 Hz	
Taft	DMR/MARC	K6KGE	441.27500	+	CC1	
	FM	KC6KGE	927.08750	902.08750	100.0 Hz	
	FUSION	K6KGE	441.57500	+		
	FUSION	K6KGE	441.60000	+		
Tahoe City	FM	WA6FJS	146.94000	-	100.0 Hz	
	FM	W6AV	224.76000	-	123.0 Hz	
	FM	K1BMW	440.27500	+	114.8 Hz	
	FM	KH8AF	440.92500	+		
	FM	N7VXB	441.17500	+	107.2 Hz	
	FM	KH8AF	442.17500	+		
	FM	WA6FJS	442.95000	+	131.8 Hz	
	FM	K6SRA	443.97500	+		
	FM	W6PUE	444.95000	+		
Tancred	FM	N6QDY	147.25500	+	123.0 Hz	
Tassajara	DMR/MARC	W6FM	444.47500	+	CC1	NARCC
Tassajera Peak	DMR/MARC	K6DOA	444.35000	+	CC6	
Tehachapi	FM	W6PVG	147.06000	+		
	FM	KF6MXK	224.00000	-	151.4 Hz	
	FM	K6RET	224.78000	-	100.0 Hz	
	FM	WB6FYR	224.92000	-	94.8 Hz	
	FM	W6SLZ	440.62500	+	100.0 Hz	
	FM	KI6HHU	442.92500	+	141.3 Hz	
	FM	KI6HHU	446.32000	-	141.3 Hz	
	FM	KI6HHU	447.92000	-	141.3 Hz	
	FM	WA6CAM	927.02500	902.02500	146.2 Hz	
	FM	WA6CGR	927.72500	902.72500		
Temecula	FM	KE6UPI	445.08000	-	82.5 Hz	

Location	Mode	Call sign	Output	Input	Access	Coordinator
Temecula Ranchos						
		AG6IF-R	146.20500			
Templeton	FM	W6YDZ	146.88000	-	127.3 Hz	
The Homestead	FM	KD6ITH-R	223.94000	-		
Thousand Oaks	DMR/BM	KF6GOI	445.56000	-	CC1	
	FM	K0AKS	147.15000	+	127.3 Hz	
	FM	WB6RHQ	223.94000	-	156.7 Hz	
	FM	KC6IJM	447.02000	-	127.3 Hz	
	FM	K6JSI	448.94000	-	100.0 Hz	
	FM	WA6TTL	449.10000	-		
Thousand Oaks, Grissom Pk						
	FM	N6EVC	146.85000	-	94.8 Hz	
	FM	K6HB	224.70000	-	156.7 Hz	
Thousand Oaks, Rasnow Peak						
	FM	W6AMG	449.44000	-	131.8 Hz	
Thousand Oks	DMR/BM	WB6YES	446.36000	-	CC5	
Thousand Palms	FM	KA6GBJ	447.20000	-	107.2 Hz	
Thousand Palms, Indio Hills						
	FM	KA6GBJ	51.84000	-	107.2 Hz	
Tiki Mobile Village		W6YJ-L	449.32000			
Timber Cove	FM	K6CHG	444.03750	+		
Topanga Canyon	FM	W6DRT	146.11500	+		
Torrance	DMR/BM	K6DAN	448.26000	-	CC1	
	FM	K6TPD	223.86000	-	100.0 Hz	
	FM	KE6LDM	1284.07500	-		
	FUSION	N3CE	432.77500			
	FUSION	AB6UI	445.62000	-		
Trabuco Canyon	FM	K6SOA	145.24000	-	110.9 Hz	
Tracy	DMR/BM	K7FED	442.20000	+	CC3	
	FM	W6LLL	146.65500	-	100.0 Hz	
	FM	KB6LED	224.34000	-	141.3 Hz	
Tracy, Mt Delux	FM	WA6SEK	145.21000	-	100.0 Hz	
Tranquillion Peak VAFB						
	DMR/BM	K7AZ	440.50000	+	CC3	
Trevarno	FM	K7FED-R	444.12500	+		
Trona	FM	K6YYJ	146.97000	-	123.0 Hz	
Truckee	DMR/BM	K6BIB	440.85000	+	CC1	
	DMR/BM	K1BMW	441.47500	+	CC1	
	DMR/BM	K1BMW	446.01250	-	CC1	
	FM	K1BMW	441.75000	+	123.0 Hz	
	FM	WA6JQV	444.27500	+		
Truckee, Donner Peak						
	FM	W6SAR	146.64000	-	131.8 Hz	
	FM	W6SAR	223.82000	-	100.0 Hz	
	FM	W6SAR	440.70000	+	131.8 Hz	
Tujunga	DMR/BM	WB6YES	449.38000	-	CC1	
	FM	W7JAM	146.16000	+	146.2 Hz	
	FM	NW6B	447.98000	-		
	FM	NW6B	1285.25000	-		
Tulare	DMR/MARC	WX6D	442.47500	+	CC2	NARCC
Tuolumne	DMR/BM	KJ6NRO	144.96250	147.46250	CC2	
	DMR/BM	KJ6NRO	442.47500	+	CC1	
Turlock		KK6IMI-R	446.50000			
	DMR/BM	W6BXN	444.35000	+	CC2	
	FM	WB6PBN	442.17500	+	110.9 Hz	
Tustin	FM	W6KRW	146.89500	-	136.5 Hz	
	FM	W6KRW	449.10000	-		
Twain Harte	DMR/BM	K6CV	444.65000	+	CC1	
	FM	KE6KUA	440.55000	+	114.8 Hz	
	FM	W6YOP	441.92500	+	123.0 Hz	
Twentynine Palms						
	DSTAR	KJ6KTV	147.57000	144.97000		

Location	Mode	Call sign	Output	Input	Access	Coordinator
Twentynine Palms						
	DSTAR	KJ6KTV C	147.57000	145.01500		
	FM	W6BA	147.06000	+	136.5 Hz	
Ukiah	FM	WA6RQZ	440.02500	+	141.3 Hz	
Union City	FUSION	KM6EF	146.61000	-		
Upland	DMR/BM	K6DLP	446.30000	-	CC9	
	FM	WB6QHB	147.30000	+	123.0 Hz	
	FM	K6PQN	224.58000	-	88.5 Hz	
	FM	K6PQN	927.32500	902.32500	114.8 Hz	
Vacaville	DMR/BM	K6LNK	144.95000	147.45000	CC7	
	DMR/BM	K6LNK	927.17500	902.17500	CC3	
	DMR/BM	WA6JQV	927.38750	902.38750	CC1	
	FM	WR6VHF	51.82000	-	141.3 Hz	
	FM	WA6CAX	51.98000	-	114.8 Hz	
	FM	N6NMZ	52.86000	-	136.5 Hz	
	FM	W6YDD	146.62500	-	100.0 Hz	
	FM	KM6KW	223.92000	-	85.4 Hz	
	FM	KJ6MB	224.12000	-	141.3 Hz	
	FM	WV6F	224.20000	-	127.3 Hz	
	FM	KB6SJG	224.24000	-	136.5 Hz	
	FM	N6NMZ	224.42000	-	100.0 Hz	
	FM	WV6F	440.02500	+	127.3 Hz	
	FM	KB6LCS	440.52500	+	136.5 Hz	
	FM	K6LNK	440.75000	+	173.8 Hz	
	FM	KH8AF	440.92500	+		
	FM	W6RCA	441.60000	+	100.0 Hz	
	FM	W6RCA	441.97500	+	94.8 Hz	
	FM	W6KCS	442.02500	+	179.9 Hz	
	FM	KH8AF	442.22500	447.32500		
	FM	W6NQJ	442.30000	+		
	FM	N6APB	442.55000	+		
	FM	AB6CQ	442.85000	+	146.2 Hz	
	FM	K6JJC	442.97500	+	136.5 Hz	
	FM	WA6KBP	443.75000	+		
	FM	WA6RTL	444.75000	+	107.2 Hz	
	FM	W6PUE	444.85000	+		
	FM	WA6JQV	927.02500	902.02500		
	FM	WA6JQV	927.03750	902.03750		
	FM	N6ICW	927.05000	902.05000	77.0 Hz	
	FM	WV6F	927.08750	902.08750	127.3 Hz	
	FM	W6NQJ	927.12500	902.12500	131.8 Hz	
	FM	KI6SSF	927.26250	902.26250		
	FM	KI6SSF	927.33750	902.33750	162.2 Hz	
	FM	WA6JQV	927.37850	902.37850		
	FM	WA6JQV	927.47500	902.47500		
	FM	WA6JQV	927.93750	902.93750		
	FM	N6ICW	927.97500	902.97500		
	FM	K6HEW	1282.90000	-	88.5 Hz	
	FM	W6YDD	1285.85000	-	100.0 Hz	
	FM	KD6ZNG	1285.90000	-	156.7 Hz	
Vacaville, Mt Vaca						
	FM	W6VVR	145.47000	-	127.3 Hz	
	FM	W6SAR	146.74500	-		
	FM	K6MVR	147.00000	-	136.5 Hz	
	FM	N6ICW	147.19500	+	123.0 Hz	
	FM	W6AEX	147.27000	+	77.0 Hz	
	FM	KB6ABM	223.84000	-	141.3 Hz	
	FM	N6ICW	441.77500	+		
	FM	K6MVR	443.95000	+	136.5 Hz	
	FM	WA6EUZ	444.57500	+		
	FM	W6KCS	927.06250	902.06250	167.9 Hz	
Vallejo	DMR/BM	K6LI	145.31000	+	CC3	

Location	Mode	Call sign	Output	Input	Access	Coordinator
Vallejo	FM	K6LI	442.42500	+	88.5 Hz	
	FM	KC6PGV	1284.35000	-	131.8 Hz	
	FUSION	K6HT	146.40000			
Valley Center	DMR/BM	N6VCC	449.92000	-	CC1	
	FUSION	W9EN	146.67000	-		
Valley Center , Paradise Mtn						
	FM	N6VCC	146.23500	+		
Valley Springs	FM	KC6TTZ	146.92500	-	94.8 Hz	
	FM	W6EBW	441.07500	+	114.8 Hz	
Valyermo, Blue Ridge						
	FM	N6GMS	1285.12500	-		
Ventura	DMR/BM	K6VCD	446.32500	-	CC2	
	FM	K6ERN	52.98000	-	82.5 Hz	
	FM	N6VUY	147.97500	-		
	FM	AF6GD	222.13000	-	186.2 Hz	
	FM	KI6HHU	445.76000	-	141.3 Hz	
	FM	WA6TTL	447.14000	-		
	FM	K6ERN	448.18000	-	100.0 Hz	
	FM	K6ERN	927.87500	902.87500	103.5 Hz	
	FM	KO6TD	1282.10000	-	127.3 Hz	
Ventura, South Mtn						
	FM	WA6ZSN	447.32000	-	100.0 Hz	
Vernalis	DMR/BM	K6LNK	927.17500	902.17500	CC8	
Victorville	DMR/MARC	N6GGS	446.06000	-	CC2	
	DMR/MARC	KF6FM	448.15000	-	CC2	
	FM	AA7SQ	147.39000	+	100.0 Hz	
	FUSION	KC6ZGG	146.02500	+		
Victorville, Blue Ridge						
	FM	W6NVY	51.96000	-	82.5 Hz	
Victorville, Fairgrounds						
	FM	K7GIL	146.11500	+	91.5 Hz	
Victorville, Quartzite Mountai						
	FM	W6NVY	147.19500	+	141.3 Hz	
	FM	W6NVY	147.85500	-	186.2 Hz	
	FM	K7GIL	223.84000	-	156.7 Hz	
	FM	WR6QZ	446.10000	-	136.5 Hz	
	FM	K6PNG	448.90000	-	67.0 Hz	
	FM	KK6SVL	449.20000	-	146.2 Hz	
	FM	W6NVY	449.70000	-	141.3 Hz	
Victorville, Quartzite Mtn.						
	FM	K7GIL	147.12000	+	91.5 Hz	
Visalia	DMR/BM	N6VQL	144.95000	147.45000	CC2	
	DMR/BM	N0JKR	442.30000	+	CC1	
	DSTAR	K6VIS	145.01250	147.51250		
	DSTAR	K6VIS	145.45000	-		
	DSTAR	K6VIS	442.30000	+		
	DSTAR	K6VIS	1286.32500	-		
	DSTAR	WX6D	1286.35000	+		
	FM	KE6WDX	146.97000	-	100.0 Hz	
	FM	WA6BAI	223.88000	-	103.5 Hz	
	FM	WA6BAI	440.40000	+	103.5 Hz	
	FM	N6BYH	440.45000	+	141.3 Hz	
	FM	WA6BLB	443.02500	+	88.5 Hz	
	FM	WA6MSN	444.45000	+	127.3 Hz	
	FM	WA6BAI	1286.30000	-	103.5 Hz	
	P25	N6VQL	147.39000	+	127.3 Hz	
	P25	WA6YLB	443.35000	+	141.3 Hz	
	P25	N6IB	927.02500	902.02500	141.3 Hz	
Visalia, Blue Ridge						
	FM	KM6OR	146.73000	-	141.3 Hz	
	FM	KM6OR	443.20000	+	141.3 Hz	
Vista	DMR/MARC	KA3AJM	447.90000	-	CC0	

Location	Mode	Call sign	Output	Input	Access	Coordinator
Vista	FM	KI6AZQ	146.67000	-	156.7 Hz	
	FM	KA3AJM	146.97000	-	107.2 Hz	
	FM	WB6FMT	446.14000	-	123.0 Hz	
	FM	KA3AJM	446.30000	-		
	FM	WI6RE	448.80000	-	100.0 Hz	
	FM	WB0BMY	927.50000	902.50000	151.4 Hz	
	FUSION	K0CFI	446.50000			
Volcano	FM	W6KAP	440.45000	+	127.3 Hz	
	FM	N3CKF	446.50000	-	100.0 Hz	
	FM	W6KAP	927.90000	902.90000	127.3 Hz	
W.Warwick	DSTAR	W1HDN C	147.04500	+		
Walnut Creek	DMR/BM	K6LNK	440.21250	+	CC1	
	DMR/BM	WB6PQM	442.65000	+	CC1	
	DMR/BM	WB6PQM	444.15000	+	CC1	
	DMR/BM	WB6PQM	927.50000	902.50000	CC3	
	DMR/MARC	W6CX	145.00000	147.50000	CC1	
	FM	N6MVT	443.47500	+	114.8 Hz	
	FM	KK6BSN	443.82500	+	167.9 Hz	
	FM	K6NOX	927.71250	902.71250		
	FUSION	W6JIM	145.58000			
	FUSION	KM6ZUO	431.66250			
Walnut Grove	DMR/BM	K6DTV	147.39000	+	CC1	
	FM	WA6JIV	443.70000	+		
	FM	K6YC	927.30000	902.30000	100.0 Hz	
Watsonville	FM	W6UNI	145.17000	-	131.8 Hz	
	FM	W6TUW	145.29000	-	94.8 Hz	
	FM	W6DNC	145.33000	-	123.0 Hz	
	FM	KB6MET	146.77500	-	123.0 Hz	
	FM	W6NAD	146.95500	-		
	FM	KI6EH	147.94500	-	94.8 Hz	
	FM	KB6MET	224.38000	-		
	FM	KB6MET	224.84000	-	156.7 Hz	
	FM	KB6MET	443.35000	+	123.0 Hz	
	FM	N6NAC	1286.20000	-	110.9 Hz	
Watsonville, Hospital						
	FM	K6RMW	147.00000	+	94.8 Hz	
Watsonville, Watsonville Commu						
	FM	K6RMW	443.05000	+	94.8 Hz	
Weaverville	FUSION	KM6RNZ	445.00000			
Weaverville, Hayfork Bally						
	FM	N6TKY	146.73000	-	85.4 Hz	
Wedekind		KA7ZAU-R	147.42000			
Weott	FM	KM6TE	147.33000	+	103.5 Hz	
West Covina	DMR/BM	K6KWB	449.66000	-	CC1	
	DMR/MARC	KE6YEP	431.55000	+	CC1	
	DMR/MARC	KE6YEP	433.55000	+	CC1	
	DMR/MARC	KE6YEP	433.80000	+	CC1	
	FM	WB6QZK	1282.87500	-		
West Los Angeles	FM	N6GLA	447.32000	-	103.5 Hz	
West Point	FM	WB6LZV	441.37500	+	123.0 Hz	
West Sacramento	FM	W6AK	146.91000	-	162.2 Hz	
Westley	FM	K6ACR	147.12000	+	77.0 Hz	
	FM	K6MSR	443.62500	+		
	FM	WA6RQX	444.17500	+	141.3 Hz	
	FM	K6RDJ	1282.80000	-		
Westley, Mt Oso	FM	K6JJC	443.82500	+	107.2 Hz	
Westminster	FUSION	KM6DZQ	144.32000			
Westwood	FM	W6YRA	448.54000	-	82.5 Hz	
Whitmore/Redding						
	DMR/BM	KD6MTU	145.07500	147.57500	CC1	
Whittier		KE6CIA-R	220.00000			
	FM	KA6VHA	1283.05000	-		

Location	Mode	Call sign	Output	Input	Access	Coordinator
Whittier	FUSION	KD6IOW	445.76000	-		
Whittier, Rio Hondo Peak						
	FM	K0JPK	146.73000	-	103.5 Hz	
Whittier, Whittier Hills						
	FM	N6CRG	224.12000	-	151.4 Hz	
Wildomar		W5RLA-L	144.00000			
	FM	KI6ITV	145.40000	144.60000	146.2 Hz	
Williams	FM	N6NMZ	146.76000	-	131.8 Hz	
	FM	N6NMZ	224.26000	-	100.0 Hz	
Willits	FM	WA6RQX	147.39000	+	103.5 Hz	
	FM	WA6RQX	440.07500	+		
Willits, Laughlin Ridge						
	FM	K7WWA	51.74000	-	114.8 Hz	
	FM	K7WWA	147.12000	+	103.5 Hz	
	FM	K7WWA	444.92500	+	100.0 Hz	
	P25	K7WWA	442.10000	+		
Willow Creek, Horse Mountain						
	FM	K6FWR	147.00000	+	103.5 Hz	
Willow River	FM	N6WZK	449.56000	-		
Wilson	FM	K6JP	1284.10000	-		
Wilton	DMR/BM	K6JWN	433.75000	+	CC9	
	DMR/BM	K6JWN	444.52500	+	CC9	
Winchester	FM	WR6AAC	224.36000	-	151.4 Hz	
Windsor	FM	W6IBC	146.98500	-	88.5 Hz	
Winterhaven, Black Mountain						
	FM	K6CKS	1284.60000	-		
Winters	DMR/BM	N6UTX	144.93750	147.43750	CC2	
Wofford Heights	FM	KB6DJT	224.54000	-	77.0 Hz	
Woodside	DMR/BM	W6JMX	442.10000	+	CC1	
	FM	W6MTF	52.62000	-	192.8 Hz	
	FM	KC6ZIS	224.44000	-	107.2 Hz	
	FM	KB6LED	224.56000	-	107.2 Hz	
	FM	WB6ECE	441.30000	+	123.0 Hz	
	FM	KF6JEE	446.28000	-	131.8 Hz	
Wrightwood	DMR/BM	K6UHF	449.74000	-	CC7	
	DMR/MARC	KA6P	449.03750	-	CC2	
	DSTAR	W6CPA	147.54000	144.94000		
	DSTAR	W6CPA	446.87000	-		
	DSTAR	KJ6LJZ B	447.83500	-		
	FM	N6LXX	53.58000	-	107.2 Hz	
	FM	KW6WW	147.24000	+	91.5 Hz	
	FM	N6LXX	224.14000	-	94.8 Hz	
	FM	KW6WW	224.40000	-	91.5 Hz	
	FM	KD6AFA	224.74000	-	186.2 Hz	
	FM	KW6WW	445.24000	-	127.3 Hz	
	FM	N6LXX	446.86000	-	110.9 Hz	
	FM	KB6BZZ	927.22500	902.22500		
Wrightwood, Blue Ridge						
	FM	KC6JAR	224.02000	-	110.9 Hz	
	FM	KD6OFD	447.44000	-		
	FM	WB6SLR	449.74000	-		
Wrightwood, Table Mountain						
	FM	WR6AZN	145.28000	-	131.8 Hz	
	FM	WR6AZN	223.96000	-	156.7 Hz	
Yermo	FM	N6LXX	53.84000	-	107.2 Hz	
	FM	N6LXX	446.80000	-	110.9 Hz	
	FM	KF6FM	448.14000	-	123.0 Hz	
Yermo, Mount Rodman						
	FM	WB6TNP	448.26000	-		
Yorba Linda	DMR/BM	WD6DIH	449.44000	-	CC1	
	DMR/BM	W6ELL	449.46000	-	CC1	
Yosemite	FM	W6BXN	147.00000	+	100.0 Hz	

Location	Mode	Call sign	Output	Input	Access	Coordinator
Yountville, Mt Veeder						
	FM	N6TKW	444.72500	+	151.4 Hz	
Yreka	FM	K6SIS	146.79000	-	100.0 Hz	
	FM	AB7BS	147.12000	+	136.5 Hz	
	FM	K6SIS	443.75000	+	100.0 Hz	
	FM	W6PRN	444.42500	+	100.0 Hz	
Yuba City	FM	N6IQY	145.21000	-	127.3 Hz	
	FM	W6GNO	224.96000	-	100.0 Hz	
Yuba City, Sutter Butte						
	FM	WD6AXM	146.08500	+	127.3 Hz	
Yuba City, Sutter Buttes						
	FM	KN6TED	927.73750	902.03750	127.3 Hz	
Yucaipa	FM	N6RXL	145.71000		103.5 Hz	
	FM	W7DOD	448.16000	-	131.8 Hz	
Yucaipa, Little San Gorgonio P						
	FM	W6DXX	445.14000	-		
Yucca Valley	DMR/MARC	WB6CDF	447.00000	-	CC10	
	FM	WB6CDF	145.12000	-		
	FM	W6BA	146.79000	-	136.5 Hz	
Yuma, Quartz Peak						
	FM	WB6YFG	224.96000	-		
Zamora	FM	W6OF	440.15000	+		
COLORADO						
Acres Green	FM	W0SKY-L	449.00000			
Akron	DMR/MARC	W0FT	448.17500	-	CC7	CCARC
	FM	KB0VJJ	145.40000	-	88.5 Hz	
	FM	N0STY	446.22500	-	141.3 Hz	
Allenspark	FM	KI0HG	147.03000	+	100.0 Hz	
Almagre	DMR/MARC	K7PFJ	446.95000	-	CC1	
Aspen	FM	K0VQ-L	447.15000	-		
Aspen, Aspen Mountain						
	FM	KD0NU	447.05000	-	179.9 Hz	CCARC
Aurora		W5CP-R	145.65500			
	DMR/BM	AA0FK	224.42000	-	CC7	
	DMR/BM	K0PWO	438.25000	-	CC7	
	FM	AJ2E	446.35000	-	100.0 Hz	
	FM	W0BG	448.27500	-	156.7 Hz	CCARC
	FM	N0ZUQ	448.40000	-	94.8 Hz	CCARC
	FM	WA0RES	449.27500	-	141.3 Hz	
	FM	W9SL	449.95000	-	77.0 Hz	CCARC
	FUSION	AA0FK	447.40000	-		
Aurora, Smokey Hill						
	FM	KB0UDD	448.50000	-	100.0 Hz	CCARC
Aurora, Smoky Hill						
	FM	KB0UDD	145.40000	-	100.0 Hz	
Bailey, Dick Mountain						
	FM	AB0PC	146.89500	-	100.0 Hz	
Blue Valley		N0PQV-R	145.34000			
	FM	W0CRA-L	447.57500	-		CCARC
	FM	W0TX-R	449.35000	-		CCARC
Boulder	DSTAR	KC0DS C	145.38500	-		
	DSTAR	KC0DS	145.38750	-		
	DSTAR	KC0DS	446.86250	-		CCARC
	DSTAR	KC0DS B	446.86250	-		
	DSTAR	KC0DS	1283.86250	1263.86250		CCARC
	DSTAR	KC0DS A	1283.86250	-		
	DSTAR	KC0DS D	1299.50000			
	DSTAR	W0DK	1299.50000	1279.50000		CCARC
	FM	W0DK	146.61000	-	100.0 Hz	
Boulder North	DMR/MARC	N0SZ	445.05000	-	CC1	
Boulder South	DMR/MARC	K7PFJ	446.98750	-	CC1	CCARC

Location	Mode	Call sign	Output	Input	Access	Coordinator
Boulder, Blue Mountain						
	FM	KE0SJ	145.47500	-	100.0 Hz	
Boulder, Eldorado Mountain						
	FM	W0CRA	145.46000	-	107.2 Hz	
	FM	W0CRA	447.97500	-	107.2 Hz	CCARC
Boulder, Gunbarrel Hill						
	FM	W0IA	146.76000	-	100.0 Hz	
Boulder, Lee Hill	FM	W0IA	224.02000	-		
	FM	N0SZ	446.98750	-		
	FM	N0SZ	447.75000	-	141.3 Hz	CCARC
Boulder, Table Mesa						
	FM	W0DK	448.90000	-	100.0 Hz	CCARC
Boulder, Table Mountain						
	FM	W0DK	146.70000	-	100.0 Hz	
Boulder, Thorodin Mountain						
	FM	KB0VJJ	145.31000	-	88.5 Hz	
Breckenridge	DMR/MARC	N0SZ	445.08750	-	CC7	
	FM	WB0QMR	146.70000	-	107.2 Hz	
Breckenridge, Bald Mountain						
	FM	KB0VJJ	147.39000	+	88.5 Hz	
Brighton	FUSION	G7LWN	146.42000			
Broken Arrow Acres						
	FM	W0CRA	147.22500	+	103.5 Hz	CCARC
Broomfield	FM	N0PSO	445.90000		127.3 Hz	
	WX	W0WYX	449.82500	-	103.5 Hz	CCARC
Burlington	DMR/MARC	N0SZ	445.05000	-	CC6	
Canon City	DMR/BM	K0JSC	449.50000	-	CC1	
	DMR/MARC	N0SZ	438.00000	-	CC15	
	DMR/MARC	K0JSC	446.73750	-	CC1	
	DMR/MARC	K0JSC	449.50000	-	CC15	
	FM	WD0EKR	224.66000	-	71.9 Hz	
	FM	K0JSC	447.25000	-	100.0 Hz	CCARC
	FM	K0JSC	447.97500	-	100.0 Hz	CCARC
	FM	WD0EKR	927.77500	902.77500		
Canon City, Eightmile Mountain						
	FM	WB0WDF	449.00000	-	67.0 Hz	CCARC
Canon City, Fremont Peak						
	FM	WB0WDF	53.03000	51.33000	88.5 Hz	
	FM	WD0EKR	145.49000	-	103.5 Hz	
	FM	WD0EKR	223.96000	-	103.5 Hz	
	FM	WD0EKR	447.75000	-	103.5 Hz	CCARC
	FM	KB0TUC	927.70000	902.70000		CCARC
Carbondale, Four Mile Ridge						
	FM	K0SNO	147.39000	+	107.2 Hz	
	FM	K0ELK	449.72500	-	179.9 Hz	CCARC
Cascade		KC5EVE-L	443.63500			
Castle Rock		AD0BQ-R	144.00000			
	DMR/BM	N0XLF	434.55000	446.30000	CC10	
	DMR/BM	WA0DE	446.82500	-	CC1	
	FM	K0HYT	448.05000	-		
Cattle Creek		K0RV-R	146.88000			
Cedar Point	FM	K0UPS	449.25000	-	123.0 Hz	CCARC
Cedaredge	FM	W0ALC	147.36000	+	100.0 Hz	
	FM	W0ALC	449.82500	-	100.0 Hz	CCARC
Cedaredge, Cedar Mesa						
	FM	KC0QXX	147.19500	+	107.2 Hz	
Centennial	DMR/MARC	K0PWO	448.45000	-	CC7	
	FM	K0PWO	448.05000	-	179.9 Hz	
	FUSION	KC0RF	146.56500			
Centennial, Warren Mountain						
	FM	N0PUF	146.88000	-	100.0 Hz	
	FM	N0PUF	449.60000	-	100.0 Hz	CCARC

Location	Mode	Call sign	Output	Input	Access	Coordinator
Center	FM	N0KM	447.10000	-	77.0 Hz	
Colorado Springs	DMR/BM	K0HYT	440.00000	+	CC1	
	DMR/BM	N0SZ	445.06250	+	CC1	
	DMR/MARC	N0SZ	145.23500	-	CC1	
	DMR/MARC	N0PKT	442.20000	+	CC3	
	DMR/MARC	KF4TNP	445.28750	-	CC7	
	DSTAR	KC0CVU C	145.38500	-		
	DSTAR	KE0VUW B	446.88750	-		
	DSTAR	KC0CVU B	446.91250	-		
	DSTAR	KC0CVU A	1287.91250	-		
	DSTAR	KC0CVU D	1299.70000			
	FM	AD0TP	146.85000	-	156.7 Hz	
	FM	K0IRP	146.91000	-	151.4 Hz	
	FM	AA0L	147.13500	+	100.0 Hz	
	FM	W0MOG	147.39000	+	103.5 Hz	
	FM	WA9WWS	147.48000			
	FM	KB0SRJ	224.06000	-		
	FM	W0MOG	224.72000	-	103.5 Hz	
	FM	K0IRP	447.35000	-	151.4 Hz	CCARC
	FM	NX0G	447.47500	-	107.2 Hz	CCARC
	FM	WA6IFI	447.55000	-	123.0 Hz	CCARC
	FM	AA0L	448.30000	-	100.0 Hz	CCARC
	FM	W0MOG	448.60000	-	114.8 Hz	CCARC
	FM	KB0SRJ	448.80000	-	100.0 Hz	CCARC
	FM	W0MOG	927.80000	902.80000		CCARC
	WX	KB0SRJ	146.97000	-	100.0 Hz	CCARC
	WX	KB0SRJ	448.45000	-		CCARC
	FUSION	AD5J	445.72500			
Colorado Springs, Almagre Moun						
	FM	AA0SP	147.18000	+	100.0 Hz	
	FM	WA6IFI	927.72500	902.02500		CCARC
Colorado Springs, Cheyenne Mou						
	DSTAR	KC0CVU	145.38500	-		
	FM	KC0CVU	146.76000	-	107.2 Hz	
	FM	KC0CVU	147.34500	+	107.2 Hz	
	FM	KC0CVU	448.00000	-	107.2 Hz	CCARC
	FM	KC0CVU	448.10000	-	107.2 Hz	CCARC
	FM	KC0CVU	927.85000	902.85000		CCARC
Colorado Springs, Fillmore Hil						
	FM	KA0TTF	448.72500	-	123.0 Hz	CCARC
Conifer	DMR/MARC	N9GDM	147.25500	+	CC7	
Conifer, Critchell Mountain						
	FM	N0OWY	447.50000	-	88.5 Hz	CCARC
Cortez	FM	KD5LWU	146.79000	-	127.3 Hz	
	FM	KE0GGG	223.50000	-		
Craig	FM	WD0HAM	145.26500	-	107.2 Hz	
	FM	KB0VJJ	146.97000	-	88.5 Hz	
Cripple Creek	FM	WB0WDF	145.46000	-	67.0 Hz	
	FM	NX0G	147.01500	+	107.2 Hz	
	FM	WB0WDF	224.94000	-	67.0 Hz	
	FM	WB0WDF	447.40000	-	67.0 Hz	CCARC
	FM	WB0WDF	1287.70000	1267.70000	67.0 Hz	CCARC
Critchell, Critchell Mountain						
	FM	N0ARA	147.12000	+	88.5 Hz	
Deckers	WX	N0ESQ	447.52500	-	146.2 Hz	CCARC
Deer Trail	FM	N6LXX	447.87500	-	107.2 Hz	
Delta	FM	KB0YNA	449.40000	-	131.8 Hz	CCARC
Denver		K0GUR-L	448.32500			
	DMR/BM	W0SKY	420.42000	427.32000	CC2	
	DMR/BM	KF4TNP	445.23750	-	CC7	
	DMR/BM	WR0AEN	449.00000	-	CC1	CCARC
	DMR/BM	WR0AEN	449.15000	-	CC1	

Location	Mode	Call sign	Output	Input	Access	Coordinator
Denver	DMR/BM	K0GUR	449.27500	-	CC1	
	DMR/BM	WR0AEN	449.65000	-	CC1	CCARC
	DMR/BM	WR0AEN	449.67500	-	CC1	CCARC
	DMR/MARC	N0SZ	145.17500	-	CC1	
	DMR/MARC	N0SZ	145.37000	-	CC7	
	DMR/MARC	KD0NQA	146.92500	-	CC1	
	DMR/MARC	W0TX	446.78750	-	CC1	
	DMR/MARC	N0SZ	446.80000	-	CC7	CCARC
	DMR/MARC	WA2YZT	446.83750	-	CC1	CCARC
	DMR/MARC	N0SZ	446.93750	-	CC7	CCARC
	DSTAR	W0CDS C	145.25000	-		
	DSTAR	W0CDS B	446.96250	-		
	DSTAR	W0CDS A	1283.96250	-		
	DSTAR	W0CDS D	1299.90000			
	FM	N0JXN	146.71500	-	123.0 Hz	
	FM	K0FEZ	447.92500	-	100.0 Hz	CCARC
	FM	N5EHP	448.07500	-	123.0 Hz	CCARC
	FM	KF0GCR	449.62500			
	WX	WB5YOE	449.45000	-	103.5 Hz	CCARC
	FUSION	KF0GCR	146.41000			
	FUSION	KC8I	445.75000			
	FUSION	WD0CIV	447.56250	-		
Denver, Green Valley Ranch						
	FM	WE0FUN	448.15000	-	141.3 Hz	CCARC
Denver, Thorodin Mountain						
	FM	N0SZ	449.22500	-	141.3 Hz	CCARC
Deployable QRV2	DMR/MARC	N0SZ	146.83500	-	CC7	
	DMR/MARC	N0SZ	438.22500	-	CC7	
Devils Head	DMR/MARC	N0ESQ	446.92500	-	CC1	CCARC
Dolores	FM	KB5ITS	145.19000	-	100.0 Hz	
	FM	KB5ITS	447.27500	-	100.0 Hz	
	FUSION	KD2RPX	144.91250			
Dotsero		K0AMA-L	146.88000			
Durango	DMR/MARC	N0SZ	445.13750	-	CC7	
	FM	KB5ITS	147.13500	+	100.0 Hz	
	FM	KC5EVE	448.62500	-	131.8 Hz	CCARC
	FM	K0EP	449.85000	-	100.0 Hz	CCARC
Durango, Eagle Pass						
	FM	K0EP	146.67000	-	100.0 Hz	
Durango, Missionary Ridge						
	FM	K0EP	146.70000	-	100.0 Hz	
	FM	KB0VJJ	147.34500	+	88.5 Hz	
Elizabeth	FM	KB0BS	448.77500	-	141.3 Hz	
Englewood	DMR/MARC	N0SZ	438.22500	-	CC7	
Estes Park	DMR/BM	N0WAR	147.24000	+	CC2	
	FM	N0FH	449.80000	-	123.0 Hz	CCARC
Evans	DMR/BM	WD0HDR	445.57500	-	CC2	
	DMR/BM	WD0HDR	448.92500	-	CC1	
	FUSION	WD0HDR	430.22000			
Evergreen	DMR/MARC	W0VG	445.10000	-	CC7	
	FM	KE4GUQ	145.34000	-	103.5 Hz	
Evergreen, Squaw Mountain						
	FM	N0PYY	147.30000	+	103.5 Hz	
Fairplay	DMR/MARC	K7PFJ	446.76250	-	CC7	
Fairplay, Sacramento Mountain						
	FM	AA0BF	447.12500	-	103.5 Hz	CCARC
Falcon, Black Forest						
	FM	KD0MDP	447.62500	-	100.0 Hz	
Firestone	DMR/MARC	N0SZ	445.01250	+	CC1	
	DMR/MARC	K7PFJ	445.06250	-	CC7	
First View	FUSION	KD0OXW	447.60000	-	103.5 Hz	
Five Points	FM	W0JRL-R	447.17500	-		CCARC

Location	Mode	Call sign	Output	Input	Access	Coordinator
Fort Collins	DMR/BM	W1VAN	145.32500	-	CC2	
	DMR/BM	N7VDR	445.02500	-	CC1	
	DMR/BM	W1VAN	446.77500	-	CC2	
	DMR/MARC	KT0L	145.20500	-	CC10	
	DMR/MARC	W0DMR	147.39000	+	CC2	
	DMR/MARC	N0AOL	446.73750	-	CC2	
	DMR/MARC	K7PFJ	446.75000	-	CC1	
	DMR/MARC	W0DMR	446.77500	-	CC2	
	DSTAR	W0QEY	446.81250	-		CCARC
	FM	W0QEY	147.36000	+	100.0 Hz	
	FM	W7RF	447.72500	-	131.8 Hz	CCARC
	FM	W0QEY	449.85000	-	100.0 Hz	CCARC
	FM	W0QEY	927.95000	902.95000	100.0 Hz	CCARC
	FM	K1TJ	1283.55000	1263.55000	100.0 Hz	CCARC
	WX	W0UPS	447.70000	-	100.0 Hz	CCARC
	WX	W0UPS	448.02500	-	100.0 Hz	CCARC
Fort Collins, Buckhorn Mountai						
	FM	W0UPS	146.62500	-	100.0 Hz	
Fort Morgan	DMR/MARC	W0FT	448.20000	-	CC1	CCARC
Franktown	DSTAR	K0PRA	446.85000	-		CCARC
Friendly Village		K0GUR-R	448.15000			
Ft Collins	DMR/MARC	KB0VGD	145.26500	-	CC2	
Gateway	DMR/BM	WJ0NF	433.55000	+	CC0	
Genoa	FM	KE0AE	147.06000	+	103.5 Hz	
Glenwood Springs						
	FM	KI0G	224.02000	-		
	FM	KI0G	447.60000	-		CCARC
Glenwood Springs, Lookout Moun						
	FM	WA4HND	449.85000	-	131.8 Hz	CCARC
Glenwood Springs, Sunlight Pea						
	FM	KB0VJJ	146.85000	-	88.5 Hz	
	FM	KI0G	146.88000	-	107.2 Hz	
	FM	N0XLI	449.60000	-	107.2 Hz	CCARC
Gold Hill	FM	W0JZ	146.91000	+	123.0 Hz	
Golden	DMR/BM	KI0GO	449.75000	-	CC1	
	DMR/MARC	KB0VGD	446.97500	-	CC2	
	FM	N0PYY	448.12500	-	107.2 Hz	CCARC
	FM	W0GV	448.97500	-	123.0 Hz	CCARC
	FM	N0PYY	927.78750	902.78750	156.7 Hz	
Golden, Centennial Cone						
	FM	KE0SJ	145.28000	-	100.0 Hz	
	FM	WB0TUB	146.64000	-	100.0 Hz	
	FM	K0FEZ	146.98500	-	100.0 Hz	
	FM	W0TX	448.62500	-	100.0 Hz	CCARC
	FM	KE0SJ	449.52500	-		CCARC
	FM	KI0HC	927.83750	902.03750		CCARC
Golden, Guy Hill	FM	W0CBI	147.15000	+	100.0 Hz	
	FM	N0MHU	224.00000	-	103.5 Hz	
	FM	N0POH	224.74000	-	88.5 Hz	
	FM	K0IBM	448.85000	-	88.5 Hz	CCARC
	P25	WT0C	145.22000	-	103.5 Hz	
Golden, Lookout Mountain						
	DSTAR	W0CDS	145.25000	-		
	DSTAR	W0CDS	446.96250	-		CCARC
	DSTAR	W0CDS	1283.96250	1263.96250		CCARC
	DSTAR	W0CDS	1299.90000			
	FM	N0SZ	145.37000	-		
	FM	KE0VH	449.62500	-	141.3 Hz	CCARC
	FM	W0SKY	927.97500	902.07500	67.0 Hz	
Granby	FM	KA0YDW	146.82000	-	123.0 Hz	
Grand Junction	DMR/BM	KB0YNA	445.72500	-	CC1	
	DMR/BM	W0BX	446.91250	-	CC1	

Location	Mode	Call sign	Output	Input	Access	Coordinator
Grand Junction	DMR/MARC	N0SZ	445.05000	-	CC6	
	DSTAR	KD0RED	446.77500	-		
	DSTAR	KD0RED B	446.77500	-		
	FM	W0RRZ	145.17500	-	107.2 Hz	
	FM	KE0TY	145.22000	-	107.2 Hz	
	FM	W0GJT	146.82000	-	107.2 Hz	
	FM	K0SSI	147.10500	+		
	FM	KE0TY	147.39000	+	107.2 Hz	
	FM	KC0ARV	447.50000	-	114.8 Hz	CCARC
	FM	W0GJT	448.15000	-	100.0 Hz	CCARC
	FM	KB0SW	449.00000	-		CCARC
	FM	KB0YNA	449.65000	-	151.4 Hz	CCARC
	FM	KD0SMZ	449.77500	-	173.8 Hz	CCARC
Grand Junction, Black Ridge						
	FM	W0RRZ	146.94000	-	107.2 Hz	
	FM	WA4HND	449.57500	-	131.8 Hz	CCARC
Grand Junction, Grand Mesa						
	FM	KB0VJJ	145.35500	-	88.5 Hz	
	FM	KB0VJJ	147.35500	-	88.5 Hz	
	FM	WA4HND	449.30000	-	107.2 Hz	CCARC
Grand Lake	FM	WC3W	449.42500	-	103.5 Hz	
Greeley	DMR/BM	KB0VGD	445.13750	-	CC2	
	DMR/BM	K0AEN	449.32500	-	CC1	
	FM	W0UPS	146.85000	-	100.0 Hz	CCARC
	FM	KC0KWD	448.47500	-	100.0 Hz	CCARC
	FM	WR0AEN	449.32500	-		CCARC
Green Mountain Falls						
	FM	AC0V	147.55500		88.5 Hz	
Greenwood Village						
	FUSION	KC0SKC	448.25000	-		
Gunnison	FM	W0VTL	147.12000	+		
	FM	KB0YNA	447.65000	-	151.4 Hz	CCARC
	FM	K5GF	449.95000	-		CCARC
Hesperus	FM	KB0VIU	145.37000	-	100.0 Hz	
Highlands Ranch	DMR/BM	WA0DE	445.08750	-	CC1	
	FUSION	W0MCB	147.55500			
Holyoke	DMR/BM	N0FON	445.16250	-	CC1	
Horsetooth Heights						
	FM	KC0RBT-R	447.45000	-	123.0 Hz	CCARC
	WX	W0UPS-R	447.27500	-	100.0 Hz	CCARC
Hudson	FM	K0EB	449.92500	-	114.8 Hz	CCARC
Hugo	FUSION	KC0VJD	447.15000	-		
Idaho Springs	DSTAR	K0PRA B	446.85000	-		
Idaho Springs, Centennial Cone						
	FM	W0TX	145.49000	-	100.0 Hz	
Idaho Springs, Squaw Mountain						
	FM	KB0UDD	146.67000	-	100.0 Hz	
	FM	W0WYX	146.94000	-	103.5 Hz	
	FM	N0SZ	448.22500	-	141.3 Hz	CCARC
	FM	W0CFI	448.67500	-	100.0 Hz	CCARC
	FM	WG0N	449.05000	-	107.2 Hz	CCARC
	FM	K1DUN	449.45000	-	103.5 Hz	CCARC
Ignacio	FM	KB5ITS	147.15000	+	100.0 Hz	
Indian Hills, Chief Mtn						
	FM	KI0HC	927.93750	902.03750		CCARC
Kremmling, Santoy Peak						
	FM	KB0VJJ	147.07500	+	88.5 Hz	
La Veta	FM	N0JPX	145.35500	-	100.0 Hz	
La Veta, Cordova Pass						
	FM	N0ZSN	449.75000	-	100.0 Hz	CCARC
Lake City	FM	KB5ITS	147.13500	-	123.0 Hz	
Lake George	FM	WZ0N	448.57500	-	103.5 Hz	CCARC

Location	Mode	Call sign	Output	Input	Access	Coordinator
Lake George, Badger Mountain						
	FM	NX0G	146.68500	-	107.2 Hz	
	FM	KC0CVU	147.36000	+	107.2 Hz	
Lakewood		KC0IHA-L	146.55000			
Lakewood, Green Mountain						
	FM	W0TX	147.33000	+	100.0 Hz	
	FM	W0TX	224.38000	-	100.0 Hz	
Lakewood, Green Mtn						
	FM	W0TX	449.77500	-		CCARC
Lakewood, Moffat Treatment Pla						
	FM	KD0SSP	147.21000	+	100.0 Hz	
Lakewood, St Anthony Medical C						
	FM	W0TX	447.82500	-		CCARC
Lamar	DMR/BM	W0CTS	147.15000	+	CC1	
	DMR/BM	W0CTS	449.20000	-	CC1	
	FM	N0LAR	146.61000	-	123.0 Hz	
	FM	KC0HH	449.50000	-	123.0 Hz	CCARC
Larkspur	FM	K0JSC	449.97500	-	100.0 Hz	CCARC
Larkspur, Westcreek						
	FM	W0CRA	448.42500	-	107.2 Hz	
Leadville	DMR/MARC	N0SZ	445.05000	-	CC7	
	FM	KB0VJJ	145.44500	-	123.0 Hz	CCARC
Leadville, Quail Mountain						
	FM	N0ZSN	147.24000	+	156.7 Hz	
Limon	DMR/MARC	K0RTS	446.73750	-	CC8	
	FUSION	KD0OXW	442.65000	+		
Littleton	FUSION	KE0NCQ	449.60000	-		
Lochbuie	FM	KE0SJ	447.62500	-	100.0 Hz	
Loma, Baxter Pass						
	FM	KB0SW	447.00000	-	107.2 Hz	CCARC
Lone Tree	FUSION	W0SUN	145.56000			
Longmont	FM	W0ENO-R	147.27000	+		
	FM	N0EPA	448.52500	-	151.4 Hz	CCARC
	FM	W0ENO	448.80000	-	88.5 Hz	CCARC
Louisville	DMR/BM	W0RMT	441.60000	+	CC1	
	DMR/BM	W0RMT	445.70000	-	CC7	
Loveland, Namaqua Hill						
	FM	W0LRA	147.19500	+	100.0 Hz	
	FM	W0LRA	449.57500	-	100.0 Hz	CCARC
Mancos	DMR/MARC	N5UBJ	446.73750	-	CC6	
	FM	KB5ITS	145.32500	-	100.0 Hz	
	FM	KB5ITS	442.37500	+	100.0 Hz	
Maryvale	FM	WA4CCC-R	447.45000	-		CCARC
Montrose	FM	KD5OPD	146.79000	-	107.2 Hz	
	FM	KC0UUX	146.91000	-	107.2 Hz	
	FM	KB0YNA	448.65000	-	151.4 Hz	CCARC
Montrose, Waterdog Peak						
	FM	WA4HND	447.20000	-	107.2 Hz	CCARC
Monument	FUSION	KE0YAK	145.56000			
	FUSION	WD0AJG	439.50000			
Monument, Monument Hill						
	FM	K0NR	447.72500	-	100.0 Hz	CCARC
Morrison	FM	N6LXX	447.87500	-	107.2 Hz	CCARC
Nathrop	FM	W0LSD	146.74500	-	100.0 Hz	
New Castle	FUSION	N0SWE	448.50000			
NOAA Alamosa	WX	WXM54	162.42500			
NOAA Anton	WX	KJY84	162.45000			
NOAA Bethune	WX	WWF77	162.52500			
NOAA Boyero	WX	WWH32	162.45000			
NOAA Canon City	WX	KJY81	162.50000			
NOAA Colorado Springs						
	WX	WXM56	162.47500			

Location	Mode	Call sign	Output	Input	Access	Coordinator
NOAA Deer Trail	WX	WXJ45	162.50000			
NOAA Denver	WX	KEC76	162.55000			
NOAA Dillon	WX	WNG737	162.40000			
NOAA Durango	WX	KWN54	162.42500			
NOAA Fort Collins / Ault						
	WX	WXM92	162.45000			
NOAA Fort Morgan						
	WX	KWN40	162.52500			
NOAA Fowler	WX	WWG44	162.42500			
NOAA Franktown	WX	WNG550	162.45000			
NOAA Glenwood Springs						
	WX	WWG43	162.50000			
NOAA Grand Junction						
	WX	WXM55	162.55000			
NOAA Greeley	WX	WXM50	162.40000			
NOAA La Junta	WX	WWG23	162.50000			
NOAA Lamar	WX	KWN60	162.52500			
NOAA Mead / Longmont						
	WX	WXM51	162.47500			
NOAA Montrose	WX	KXI90	162.45000			
NOAA Pueblo	WX	WXM52	162.40000			
NOAA Springfield	WX	WNG664	162.40000			
NOAA Steamboat Springs						
	WX	KWN56	162.52500			
NOAA Sterling	WX	WXM53	162.40000			
NOAA Walsenburg						
	WX	WNG579	162.45000			
NOAA Wray	WX	WXM87	162.47500			
Northglenn	FM	K0ML	147.04500	+	123.0 Hz	
Ouray	FM	KB5ITS	147.27000	+	127.3 Hz	
Pagosa Springs	WX	N0JSP	146.61000	-	123.0 Hz	CCARC
Palmer Divide	FM	N0PWZ	449.72500	-	100.0 Hz	CCARC
Palmer Lake, Monument Hill						
	FM	N0XLF	145.19000	-	131.8 Hz	
Paonia	FM	KI0MR	147.33000	+	107.2 Hz	
Parker	DMR/BM	N0KEG	439.35000	-	CC1	
	DMR/BM	N0KEG	447.30000	-	CC1	
	DMR/MARC	W1FLO	437.30000	+	CC4	
	DMR/MARC	W9CN	440.01250	+	CC7	
	DMR/MARC	W9CN	442.00000	+	CC7	
	DMR/MARC	K0PRA	445.07500	-	CC1	
	FM	K0CTS	147.54000			
	FM	WQ8M	448.70000	-	146.2 Hz	
	P25	KI0HC	927.83750	902.03750		CCARC
	FUSION	K0CTS	147.57500			
	FUSION	K0CHK	446.50000			
	FUSION	K0PRA	447.22500	-		
Parker, Hess Reservoir						
	FM	N0AUX	447.52500	-	203.5 Hz	CCARC
Perry Park	FM	N0OBA-R	145.19000	-		
Peyton	FUSION	N0MBM	444.00000			
Pinewood Springs	FM	N0FH-R	146.68500	-		
Powars	FM	AC0KC-R	447.30000	-		CCARC
Pueblo	DMR/MARC	KF0KR	446.86250	-	CC1	
	DMR/MARC	W0VG	446.96250	-	CC8	
	DMR/MARC	K0JSC	446.98750	-	CC1	
	DMR/MARC	KF0KR	447.70000	-	CC1	
	FM	K0ST	146.65500	-	123.0 Hz	
	FM	NE0Z	147.00000	+		
	FM	K0JSC	447.27500	-	100.0 Hz	CCARC
	FM	K0JSC	448.97500	-	100.0 Hz	CCARC
	FM	K0JSC	449.97500	-	100.0 Hz	CCARC

Location	Mode	Call sign	Output	Input	Access	Coordinator
Pueblo	WX	ND0Q	146.79000	-	88.5 Hz	CCARC
Pueblo West	FUSION	NE0DA	144.00000			
	FUSION	KD0SBN	442.90000	+		
	FUSION	NE0DA	446.22500			
	FUSION	KD0SBN	447.70000	-		
Pueblo West, Liberty Point						
	FM	NA0PW	447.45000	-	123.0 Hz	
Pueblo, Baculite Mesa						
	FM	W0PHC	146.79000	-	88.5 Hz	
Pueblo, Deer Peak						
	FM	KC0CVU	449.62500	-	107.2 Hz	CCARC
Punkin Center	FM	N1FSX	449.90000	-	107.2 Hz	CCARC
Quail Hill		K0RCW-L	147.41000			
Rangely	DMR/MARC	N0SZ	445.26250	-	CC7	
	DMR/MARC	N0SZ	445.27500	-	CC7	
Red Feather Lakes						
	DMR/BM	W1VAN	447.60000	-	CC2	
Ridgway	DMR/BM	AD0RM	447.80000	-	CC1	
Rollinsville	FM	W0RM	224.60000	-	100.0 Hz	
Sableridge		AG0S-L	446.47500			
Salida	DMR/MARC	N0SZ	446.81250	-	CC7	
	DSTAR	KD0QPG B	446.97500	-		
	FM	K0JSC	449.97500	-	100.0 Hz	CCARC
Salida, Methodist Mountain						
	DSTAR	KD0QPG	446.97500	-		CCARC
	FM	KC0CVU	145.29500	-	107.2 Hz	
	FM	KB0VJJ	147.28500	+	88.5 Hz	
	FM	KC0CVU	449.65000	-	107.2 Hz	CCARC
	FM	WZ0N	449.92500	-	103.5 Hz	CCARC
Sevenmile Plaza	FM	N0KM-L	146.64000	-		
Severance, Cactus Hill						
	FM	K0FNL	447.20000	-	82.5 Hz	CCARC
Silverton	FM	KB5ITS	145.32500	-	127.3 Hz	
	FM	KB5ITS	147.37500	+	156.7 Hz	
	FM	KB5ITS	444.00000	+	67.0 Hz	
	FM	KB5ITS	447.52500	-	127.3 Hz	CCARC
Silverton, Engineer Mountain						
	FM	KB5ITT	147.27000	+	127.3 Hz	
Simla	DMR/BM	WD0ESY	445.11250	-	CC10	
	FM	WA0DE	147.10500	+	107.2 Hz	
Snowmass Village						
	FM	K0CL	146.67000	-	107.2 Hz	
Springfield	FM	KZ0DEM	147.09000	+	118.8 Hz	
	WX	KZ0DEM	147.33000	+	118.8 Hz	CCARC
	WX	KZ0DEM	449.20000	-	118.8 Hz	CCARC
Squaw Mountain	FM	K1DUN	449.45000	-	103.5 Hz	
Squaw Mtn	FM	WOCRA	145.14500	-	107.2 Hz	
Steamboat Springs						
	FM	KB0VJJ	147.16500	+	88.5 Hz	
	FM	KB0VJJ	449.62500	-	123.0 Hz	
	WX	KD0H	147.21000	+	107.2 Hz	CCARC
Sterling	FM	WA0JTB	145.29500	-		
Stratton	FM	KE0AE	146.89500	-	103.5 Hz	
	FUSION	K0MC	145.56000			
Sunnyside		N0PKT-R	449.52500			
Sunshine	FM	W0IA-R	449.55000	-		CCARC
Superior		KU0HP-L	145.52000			
Telluride	DMR/BM	KF0R	446.80000	-	CC1	
Thornton	FUSION	KB0PAK	146.56500			
Trinidad	FUSION	K6TDX	449.82500	-		
Trinidad, Raton Pass						
	FM	WA6IFI	145.43000	-	107.2 Hz	

Location	Mode	Call sign	Output	Input	Access	Coordinator
Vail	DMR/MARC	N0SZ	445.07500	-	CC7	
	FM	KB0VJJ	147.34500	+	88.5 Hz	
Vail, Bald Mountain						
	FM	K0RV	146.61000	-	107.2 Hz	
Walsenburg, N Rattlesnake Butt						
	FM	W0PHC	146.73000	-	88.5 Hz	
Walsh	DMR/BM	KZ0DEM	445.12500	-	CC1	
	DMR/BM	KC0YWX	446.76250	-	CC7	
Wellington	FM	WB7UPS	448.32500	-	110.9 Hz	CCARC
Westcliffe	FM	KB0TUC	147.06000	+	77.0 Hz	
	FM	KB0TUC	448.15000	-	103.5 Hz	CCARC
	FM	K0JSC	448.32500	-	100.0 Hz	
	FM	KB0TUC	927.77500	902.77500		CCARC
Westcreek	DMR/MARC	N0SZ	446.87500	-	CC6	CCARC
Westminster	ATV	W0ATV	1253.25000	1257.25000		
	FM	N1UPS	449.30000	-	100.0 Hz	CCARC
Weston	FUSION	KD0SBN	446.07500			
	FUSION	KD0SBN	447.70000	-		
Whitepine	DMR/BM	K7JEO	438.50000	145.50000	CC1	
Winter Park, Winter Park						
	FM	KB0VJJ	147.28500	+	88.5 Hz	
Woodland Park	FM	KA0WUC	145.41500	-	179.9 Hz	
	FM	KA0WUC	447.67500	-	179.9 Hz	CCARC
	FM	NX0G	448.65000	-	107.2 Hz	CCARC
	FM	KA0WUC	449.02500	-	141.3 Hz	CCARC
	FM	KA4EPS	449.32500	-	103.5 Hz	CCARC
	FM	KA0WUC	927.90000	902.90000		CCARC

CONNECTICUT

Location	Mode	Call sign	Output	Input	Access	Coordinator
Ansonia	DMR/BM	AC1KV	444.85000	+	CC2	
	DMR/MARC	K1EIR	444.35000	+	CC2	CSMA
	FM	WK1M	145.19000	-	77.0 Hz	CSMA
Arrl Headquarters	DMR/MARC	W1AW	442.10000	+	CC1	
Avon	DMR/MARC	W1HDN	442.05000	+	CC1	
	FM	W1JNR	224.94000	-		CSMA
	FM	N1KBY	449.30000	-	218.1 Hz	
Backus Corner		KA1CQR-R	146.73000			
Baltic	FUSION	W1OOW	435.50000			
Barkhamsted	FM	W1RWC	147.27000	+	151.4 Hz	CSMA
Bethel	FM	KA1KD	147.03000	+	100.0 Hz	CSMA
Bloomfied	DMR/MARC	W1SP	446.43750	-	CC1	CSMA
Bloomfield	DMR/BM	N1AJW	425.00000	-	CC1	
	DMR/BM	N1AJW	449.80000	-	CC1	
	FM	W1CWA	146.82000	-		CSMA
	FM	W1SP	449.12500	-		
Branford	DMR/MARC	N1HUI	449.32500	-	CC1	CSMA
	FM	N1HUI	927.81250	902.81250		CSMA
Bridgeport	DMR/MARC	N1TGE	440.76250	+	CC1	CSMA
	DMR/MARC	AG2K	442.20000	+	CC1	
	FM	WA1RJI	146.44500	147.44500	77.0 Hz	
	FM	N1MUC	146.89500	-	77.0 Hz	CSMA
	FM	N1LXV	224.96000	-	77.0 Hz	CSMA
	FM	KA1HCX	449.40000	-	110.9 Hz	CSMA
Bristol	DMR/MARC	W1IXU	448.87500	-	CC1	
	DSTAR	W1IXU C	145.14000	-		
	DSTAR	W1IXU B	448.37500	-		
	FM	KB1CDI	29.64000	-	88.5 Hz	CSMA
	FM	WA1IXU	53.05000	52.05000	162.2 Hz	CSMA
	FM	KB1CDI	53.39000	52.39000	88.5 Hz	
	FM	K1DII	145.31000	-	110.9 Hz	
	FM	K1IFF	146.59250	147.59250		
	FM	W1DHT	146.68500	-	77.0 Hz	CSMA

Location	Mode	Call sign	Output	Input	Access	Coordinator
Bristol	FM	K1CRC	146.88000	-	77.0 Hz	CSMA
	FM	KB1AEV	224.16000	-	77.0 Hz	CSMA
	FM	WA1IXU	224.22000	-	118.8 Hz	CSMA
	FM	KB1CDI	224.82000	-	88.5 Hz	
	FM	K1CRC	442.85000	+	77.0 Hz	CSMA
	FM	KB1AEV	444.65000	+	151.4 Hz	CSMA
	FM	WE1SPN	448.72500	-	77.0 Hz	
Bristol, South Mountain						
	DSTAR	W1IXU	145.14000	-		CSMA
	DSTAR	W1IXU	448.37500	-		
Brooklyn	DMR/MARC	KB1NTA	445.73750	-	CC3	CSMA
Burlington	FM	K1CRC	147.15000	+	77.0 Hz	
Colchester	DMR/MARC	K1JCL	440.80000	+	CC1	
	DMR/MARC	WH6SW	445.98750	-	CC1	CSMA
	DSTAR	KB1YPL	442.95000	+		CSMA
Cornwall	DMR/MARC	W1SP	444.35000	+	CC1	CSMA
Coventry	DMR/MARC	K1JCL	449.87500	-	CC1	CSMA
CT Portable Rptr	DMR/MARC	W1SP	442.00000	+	CC3	
	DMR/MARC	K1IIG	444.90000	+	CC1	
Cuttyhunk	FM	W1WPD-R	442.50000	+		
Danbury		KC1CBL-L	146.56500			
	DMR/MARC	KX1EOC	445.73750	-	CC1	CSMA
	FM	W1HDN	147.12000	+	141.3 Hz	
	FM	W1HDN	443.65000	+	114.8 Hz	CSMA
Durham	DSTAR	KB1UHS	444.55000	+		
	FM	KB1MMR	927.83750	902.83750		
Durham/Middlefield						
	FM	KB1MMR	446.92500	-		CSMA
East Haddam	FM	K1IKE	147.01500	+	110.9 Hz	CSMA
East Hampton	DSTAR	KB1CDI	147.13500	+	88.5 Hz	CSMA
	FM	KB1CDI	53.11000	52.11000	88.5 Hz	
	FM	KC1AJR	444.32500	+	77.0 Hz	
East Hartford	FM	W1EHC	443.25000	+	141.3 Hz	CSMA
	FUSION	K1AJD	147.57000			
East Hartland	FM	W1XOJ	53.19000	52.19000	162.2 Hz	CSMA
	FM	K1YON	145.23000	-		CSMA
East Haven	DMR/MARC	AA1VE	147.25500	-	CC1	
	DMR/MARC	KA1MJ	449.82500	-	CC1	CSMA
Elliotville (historical)						
		KA1JRL-L	146.48000			
Enfield	DMR/BM	N1XDN	448.07500	-	CC1	
	DSTAR	K1CDG B	444.10000	+		
	FM	N1XDN	146.43000	+		
	FM	K1ENF	442.40000	+	94.8 Hz	
Fairfield	DMR/MARC	KA1HCX	442.75000	+	CC3	
	FM	WB1CQO	146.62500	-	100.0 Hz	CSMA
	FM	N3AQJ	224.10000	-	77.0 Hz	CSMA
	FM	W1GHW	434.00000		100.0 Hz	
	FM	N3AQJ	440.00000	-	88.5 Hz	
	FM	N1ZU	440.45000	447.45000		
	FM	N1LXV	441.50000	+	77.0 Hz	CSMA
	FM	N3AQJ	446.82500	-	110.9 Hz	CSMA
Farmington	FM	N1GCN	442.70000	+	173.8 Hz	CSMA
	FM	WA1ARC	448.57500	-	146.2 Hz	
Glastonbury	DMR/BM	KA1VSC	449.82500	-	CC1	NESMC
	DMR/MARC	W1EDH	449.12500	-	CC1	
	FM	W1EDH	147.09000	+	110.9 Hz	CSMA
	FM	W1EDH	449.62500	-	110.9 Hz	CSMA
Goshen	FM	KU1Q	440.25000	+	123.0 Hz	CSMA
Groton	FM	W1NLC	146.67000	-	156.7 Hz	CSMA
	FM	W1CGA	146.86500	-	156.7 Hz	
	FM	KB1CJP	448.42500	-	127.3 Hz	

Location	Mode	Call sign	Output	Input	Access	Coordinator
Guilford	DMR/MARC	W1SP	441.26250	+	CC1	CSMA
	FM	NI1U	53.75000	52.75000	110.9 Hz	
Haddam	DSTAR	KB1UHS B	444.55000	+		
Hamden	FM	N1GTL	444.45000	+	100.0 Hz	
	FM	WA1MIK	927.41250	902.41250		CSMA
Hartford	DMR/MARC	W1SP	447.97500	-	CC1	CSMA
	FM	W1HDN	146.64000	-	141.3 Hz	CSMA
	FM	N1ABL	443.10000	+	114.8 Hz	CSMA
Hartland	FM	W1OBQ	448.00000	-	162.2 Hz	CSMA
Hebron	FM	N1CBD	224.70000	-	156.7 Hz	CSMA
	FM	K1PTI	449.37500	-		CSMA
Killingly	DMR/MARC	K1JCL	444.85000	+	CC1	
	DSTAR	N1GAU	444.10000	+		CSMA
	DSTAR	N1GAU B	444.10000	+		
Killingworth	FM	W1BCG	145.29000	-	110.9 Hz	CSMA
	FM	KB1MMR	146.41500	+		
Lebanon	FM	NA1RC	147.30000	+	77.0 Hz	
Ledyard	DMR/MARC	W1SP	449.27500	-	CC1	CSMA
	FM	W1DX	145.39000	-	156.7 Hz	CSMA
	FM	W1DX	224.38000	-	103.5 Hz	CSMA
Manchester	FM	WA1VOA	145.33000	-	88.5 Hz	CSMA
	FM	N1SPI	147.04500	+	88.5 Hz	CSMA
	FM	WA1YQB	449.22500	-	77.0 Hz	CSMA
Meriden	DSTAR	W1ECV C	145.49000	-		
	DSTAR	W1ECV	145.49000	-		CSMA
	DSTAR	W1ECV	444.25000	+		CSMA
	FM	K1HSN	224.80000	-	77.0 Hz	CSMA
	FM	N1SZM	442.45000	+		
	FM	KB1AEV	444.20000	+	151.4 Hz	
	FM	W1OBQ	448.00000	-	162.2 Hz	CSMA
Middlebury	DMR/MARC	W1SP	445.83750		CC2	
Middletown	FM	N1SFE	446.32500	-	203.5 Hz	
	FM	K1IKE	446.87500	-	156.7 Hz	CSMA
Milford	DMR/BM	N1EG	445.92500	-	CC1	
	FM	KA1OYS	53.27000	52.27000	77.0 Hz	CSMA
	FM	KA1FAI-R	146.92500	-		
	FM	N1JKA	223.88000	-		CSMA
	FM	N1LUF	443.55000	+	77.0 Hz	CSMA
	FM	KA1FAI	446.60000	-	136.5 Hz	
Mobile	DMR/MARC	N1RHN	444.35000	+	CC2	
Monroe	DMR/MARC	KA1HCX	444.40000	+	CC3	CSMA
Montville	FM	K1IKE	53.41000	52.41000	156.7 Hz	CSMA
	FM	WA1IXU	224.82000	-	110.9 Hz	CSMA
Morris	FM	KB1TIF	146.95500	-	100.0 Hz	
	FM	KB1CDI	224.32000	-	88.5 Hz	CSMA
Multiple	DMR/MARC	AG2K	442.20000	+	CC1	
Mystic	DSTAR	KB1TMO C	146.67000	-		
	DSTAR	KB1TMO	448.97500	-		
	DSTAR	KB1TMO B	448.97500	-		
	FM	KB1CJP	147.27000	+	127.3 Hz	
	FM	KB1JCP	446.57500	-	127.3 Hz	CSMA
Natchaug (historical)						
	FM	K1MUJ-R	147.22500	+		CSMA
Naugatuck	FM	WA1NQP	224.46000	-		CSMA
New Britain	FM	WA1VRP	446.72500	-	123.0 Hz	
New Canaan	FM	N1LLL	146.77500	-	100.0 Hz	CSMA
	FUSION	N1LLL	447.27500	-	123.0 Hz	CSMA
New Haven	DMR/MARC	KB1TTN	441.46250	+	CC1	CSMA
	FM	KB1CDI	224.08000	-		
	FM	WA1UFC	224.18000	-		CSMA
New London	FM	W1NLC	224.26000	-	156.7 Hz	CSMA
New Milford	DMR/MARC	NA1RA	440.96250	+	CC1	CSMA

Location	Mode	Call sign	Output	Input	Access	Coordinator
New Milford	FM	KA1RFM	224.72000	-		CSMA
	FUSION	KC1OGS	146.55000			
	FUSION	KC1OGS	441.15000	+		
Newfield	FM	N1KGN-R	441.70000	+		CSMA
Newington	DMR/MARC	W1AW	145.45000	-	CC0	CSMA
	DSTAR	W1HQ C	147.39000	+		
	DSTAR	W1HQ B	442.10000	+		
	DSTAR	W1HQ A	1284.12500	-		
	DSTAR	W1HQ	1284.12500	1264.12500		
	DSTAR	W1HQ D	1299.05000			
	FM	W1HQ	147.39000	+		
	FM	N1OGB	224.02000	-	100.0 Hz	CSMA
	FM	W1AW	224.84000	-	127.3 Hz	CSMA
	FM	W1OKY	443.05000	+	100.0 Hz	CSMA
	FM	WA1UTQ	449.57500	-	79.7 Hz	CSMA
	FM	WA1UTQ	1292.15000	1272.15000	88.5 Hz	CSMA
Newtown	FM	WA1SOV	145.23000	-		CSMA
NOAA Cornwall	WX	WWH33	162.50000			
NOAA Hartford	WX	WXJ41	162.47500			
NOAA Meriden	WX	WXJ42	162.40000			
NOAA New London						
	WX	KHB47	162.55000			
North Guilford, Bluff Head						
	FM	NI1U	927.48750	902.48750		CSMA
Northford	DMR/MARC	N1OFJ	449.47500	-	CC1	
Norwalk		K2IDZ-R	224.08000			
	DMR/MARC	W1NLK	448.07500	-	CC1	CSMA
	DSTAR	W1NLK	441.60000	+		
	DSTAR	W1NLK B	441.60000	+		
	FM	W1NLK	146.47500	147.47500	123.0 Hz	CSMA
	FUSION	KB1O	147.52000			
	FUSION	KW1Y	147.56000			
Norwich	FM	N1NW	449.72500	-	156.7 Hz	CSMA
	FM	N1NW	927.43750	902.43750	156.7 Hz	CSMA
Norwich, Plain Hill	FM	N1NW	146.73000	-	156.7 Hz	CSMA
Orange	FM	KC1LVB	447.67500	-		CSMA
	FUSION	KC1OGG	145.56250			
Plainville	FM	AA1WU	447.07500	-	110.9 Hz	CSMA
	FUSION	N1JGR	442.85000	+		
Portable	DMR/MARC	KB1TTN	145.43000	-	CC1	
	DMR/MARC	K1IIG	446.42500	-	CC1	
	DMR/MARC	KA1HCX	448.62500	-	CC1	
Portable 2	DMR/MARC	K1IIG	449.27500	-	CC1	
Portland	FM	W1EDH	147.03000	+	110.9 Hz	CSMA
	FM	N1JML	147.19500	+	71.9 Hz	CSMA
	FM	N1JML	443.45000	+	100.0 Hz	
Prospect	DMR/MARC	W1LAS	448.17500	-	CC1	
	FM	W1LAS	146.83500	-	100.0 Hz	
	FM	W1HDN	147.18000	+	141.3 Hz	
Ridgefield	FM	KR1COM	145.47000	-	100.0 Hz	CSMA
Rocky Hill	DMR/MARC	W1VLA	444.15000	+	CC3	CSMA
	DSTAR	W1VLA	145.27000	-		CSMA
	DSTAR	KB1CDI	444.40000	+	88.5 Hz	
	FM	N1OTW	145.19000	-	71.9 Hz	
	FM	KB1CDI	147.37500	+	88.5 Hz	CSMA
	FM	KB1CDI	224.30000	-	88.5 Hz	CSMA
	FM	N1JBS	224.68000	-	123.0 Hz	
	FM	KB1CDI	224.78000	-	88.5 Hz	CSMA
	FM	N1OTW	444.75000	+	71.9 Hz	
Salem	DSTAR	KD1STR B	443.40000	+		
	DSTAR	KD1STR	443.40000	+		
	FM	W1DX	224.14000	-	103.5 Hz	CSMA

Location	Mode	Call sign	Output	Input	Access	Coordinator
Saugatuck		W1NLK-R	146.52000			
Seymour	DMR/BM	W0JAY	444.50000	+	CC1	
	DMR/MARC	KA1HCX	442.90000	+	CC1	
	DMR/MARC	W0JAY	444.50000	+	CC1	
	FM	W0JAY-L	146.41500		114.8 Hz	
Sharon	FM	W1BAA	147.28500	+	77.0 Hz	CSMA
Shelton	DSTAR	WD1CRS C	145.55000			
	FM	W1VAR	146.98500	-	141.3 Hz	
	FM	W1VAR	446.97500	-	77.0 Hz	
Somers	DMR/MARC	W1SP	445.88750	-	CC1	CSMA
	FM	N1TUP	441.80000	+	77.0 Hz	CSMA
Southington	DSTAR	WD1STR	446.45000	-		
	FM	W1ECV	145.17000	-	77.0 Hz	CSMA
Stamford	FM	W1EE-R	146.65500	-	100.0 Hz	CSMA
	FUSION	KB1O	147.52000			
Sterling	DMR/MARC	N1CLV	445.83750	-	CC1	CSMA
Storrs	DMR/MARC	W1JLZ	441.46250	+	CC2	CSMA
Straitsville		WA1SSB-L	53.55000			
Stratford	DSTAR	K1TMW C	145.57000			
Terryville	FM	KB1CDI	147.31500	+	88.5 Hz	CSMA
	FM	K1MKY	224.30000	-	88.5 Hz	
	FM	KB1CDI	442.30000	+	88.5 Hz	
Thompson	FUSION	KC1PAU	147.44000			
Tolland	FM	N1PAH	53.29000	52.29000	127.3 Hz	CSMA
Torrington	DMR/MARC	W1HDN	441.55000	+	CC1	CSMA
	DSTAR	N1GAU	444.10000	+		
	FM	W1RWC	145.37000	-	151.4 Hz	CSMA
	FM	W1HDN	146.85000	-	141.3 Hz	CSMA
	FM	W1RWC	147.24000	+	151.4 Hz	CSMA
	FM	W1HDN	443.60000	+	82.5 Hz	CSMA
	FM	KB1AEV	447.22500	-	151.4 Hz	CSMA
	FM	K1KGQ	449.77500	-		CSMA
	FUSION	WV1M	146.55000			
Uncasville	FUSION	W1LCJ	146.55000			
Union	DMR/MARC	KB1NTA	443.80000	+	CC1	CSMA
Various	DMR/BM	AA1HD	442.00000	+	CC1	
Vernon	DMR/MARC	AA1HD	440.86250	+	CC1	
	DMR/MARC	W1HDN	443.95000	+	CC1	CSMA
	DMR/MARC	K1IIG	444.95000	+	CC1	
	DSTAR	AA1HD C	145.26000	-		
	DSTAR	AA1HD	145.26000			CSMA
	DSTAR	AA1HD B	442.15000	+		
	DSTAR	AA1HD	442.15000	+		CSMA
	FM	W1HDN	53.45000	52.45000	82.5 Hz	CSMA
	FM	W1HDN	145.41000	-	141.3 Hz	CSMA
	FM	W1HDN-R	146.79000	-	82.5 Hz	CSMA
	FM	KB1AEV	147.34500	+	151.4 Hz	CSMA
	FM	W1HDN	224.12000	-	82.5 Hz	CSMA
	FM	KB1AEV	224.36000	-	77.0 Hz	CSMA
	FM	K1WMS	224.60000	-	123.0 Hz	CSMA
	FM	KB1AEV	442.60000	+	151.4 Hz	CSMA
	FM	W1HDN	443.30000	+	114.8 Hz	CSMA
	FM	W1BRS	443.75000	+	77.0 Hz	CSMA
	FM	K1IIG	449.95000	-		
	FUSION	KB1AEV	442.55000	+		
Vernon, Box Mountain						
	FM	W1BRS	145.11000	-	77.0 Hz	CSMA
Wallingford	DMR/MARC	K1IIG	447.92500	-	CC1	
	DMR/MARC	K1IIG	448.62500	-	CC1	
	FM	W1NRG	147.36000	+	162.2 Hz	
Warren	FM	NA1RA	53.97000	52.97000	151.4 Hz	
Washington	FM	NA1RA	441.85000	+	151.4 Hz	CSMA

Location	Mode	Call sign	Output	Input	Access	Coordinator
Waterbury	FM	KB1EPA	442.45000	+	88.5 Hz	
	FM	K1IFF	449.98750	-		
Waterford	DMR/MARC	W1NLC	448.97500	-	CC1	CSMA
	FM	W1NLC	146.97000	-		CSMA
Watertown	DSTAR	KB1AEV	441.65000	+	151.4 Hz	CSMA
	FM	KB1ALU	224.04000	-	151.4 Hz	CSMA
West Hartford	FM	N1XLU	146.70000	-	162.2 Hz	
	FM	W1HDN	146.74500	-	141.3 Hz	CSMA
	FM	N1XLU	224.28000	-	114.8 Hz	CSMA
	FM	N1CRS	449.37500	-		
West Haven	DMR/BM	KC1JFN	433.50000	+	CC1	
	DMR/MARC	KB1TTN	449.92500	-	CC1	
	FM	W1GB	146.61000	-	110.9 Hz	CSMA
	FM	K1SOX	224.50000	-	77.0 Hz	CSMA
	FUSION	KC1JFN	442.00000			
Westbrook	DMR/MARC	WB1EOC	445.73750	-	CC2	
	DSTAR	W1BCG B	444.00000	+		
	DSTAR	W1BCG	444.00000	+		
	FM	W1BCG	146.77500	-	110.9 Hz	CSMA
Wethersfield	FM	KA1BQO	145.35000	-		CSMA
	FM	KA1DFH	224.68000	-		CSMA
Wilton	DMR/MARC	W1SP	440.75000	+	CC1	
Winsted	FM	N1ZCW	146.80500	-	100.0 Hz	
	FM	W1EOO	147.33000	+	141.3 Hz	CSMA
	FM	W1ECR	447.47500	-	100.0 Hz	
Wolcott	DMR/MARC	KB1TTN	440.81250	+	CC1	
	DMR/MARC	W1HDN	442.55000	+	CC1	
Woodbridge	FM	K1SOX-R	147.50500	146.50500		
Woodbury	FM	NA1RA	444.80000	+	151.4 Hz	

DELAWARE
Careys Estate Mobile Home Park

Location	Mode	Call sign	Output	Input	Access	Coordinator
		W3MLK-L	146.46000			
Claymont	FM	KC3AM	146.95500	-	131.8 Hz	
Dagsboro	DMR/MARC	N3YMS	443.10000	+	CC1	T-MARC
Delaware City	FM	N3JLH	448.82500	-	131.8 Hz	T-MARC
Dover	DMR/MARC	N3YMS	146.79000	-	CC1	T-MARC
	DMR/MARC	N3YMS	449.07500	-	CC1	T-MARC
	FM	KC3ARC	146.97000	-	123.0 Hz	T-MARC
	FM	N3IOC	444.50000	-	114.8 Hz	T-MARC
	FUSION	K3REW	144.90000			
	FUSION	W2PB	445.91250			
Felton	FUSION	W4ADZ	147.43500			
Frederica	DMR/MARC	N3YMS	449.72500	-	CC1	
Greenwood	FM	W3WMD	224.44000	-		T-MARC
Harrington	FM	KB3IWV	442.45000	+	127.3 Hz	T-MARC
Hazlettville	DMR/MARC	N3YMS	448.07500	-	CC2	
	FM	N3YMS	147.30000	+	77.0 Hz	T-MARC
Laurel	FM	N3KNT	146.71500	-	156.7 Hz	
	FUSION	W3TBG	145.21000	-		
Lewes	FM	W3LRS	147.33000	+	156.7 Hz	T-MARC
Lewesr	FM	W4ALT	443.55000	+	156.7 Hz	T-MARC
Middletown		WV8PC-L	145.09500			
	FM	W3CER	442.50000	+	100.0 Hz	T-MARC
	FUSION	KC3WSR	438.60000			
	FUSION	W1LVY	439.97500			
Milford	FUSION	KB2KBD	145.56250			
	FUSION	KB2KBD	446.06250			
Millsboro	FM	WS3ARA-R	147.09000	+	156.7 Hz	T-MARC
	FM	WS3ARA	224.84000	-	156.7 Hz	T-MARC
	FM	WS3ARA	449.82500	-	156.7 Hz	T-MARC
	FUSION	KC3QNY	145.04500			

Location	Mode	Call sign	Output	Input	Access	Coordinator
New Castle	DMR/BM	KA3WOW	224.40000	-	CC1	
	FUSION	K3HRO	144.95000			
Newark	DSTAR	W3CER	145.11000	-		T-MARC
	FM	W3UD	145.31000	+	141.3 Hz	
	FM	KB3MEC	224.00000		100.0 Hz	T-MARC
	FM	N3JCR	224.72000	-		T-MARC
	FM	W3CER	444.95000	+	100.0 Hz	T-MARC
Newark (Mobile-MCU37)						
	DSTAR	W3MCU B	447.87500	-		
Newark, Windy Hills Water Towe						
	FM	W3DRA	146.70000	-	131.8 Hz	T-MARC
	FM	W3DRA	449.02500	-	131.8 Hz	T-MARC
NOAA Salisbury	WX	KEC92	162.47500			
Rehoboth Beach	DMR/MARC	N3QEM	145.12000	-	CC1	
	DMR/MARC	N3QEM	443.06250	+	CC2	
Roxana	DMR/MARC	W3BXW	448.72500	-	CC1	T-MARC
Sand Hill		KB3PML-L	146.50500			
Seaford	DMR/MARC	N3YMS	442.81250	+	CC1	
	FM	W3TBG	145.21000	-	156.7 Hz	T-MARC
	FM	N3KNT	146.71500	-	156.7 Hz	T-MARC
	FUSION	N3SVB	147.51000			
Selbyville	FM	WS3ARA	147.01500	+	156.7 Hz	T-MARC
Smyrna	FM	K3CRK	146.65500	-	146.2 Hz	T-MARC
	FM	K3CRK	443.05000	+	156.7 Hz	T-MARC
	FUSION	WB3JUV	147.60000			
	FUSION	WB3JUV	445.60000			
Thomas Landing		K3MOT-L	144.00000			
Vhf Test	DMR/MARC	N3YMS	147.30000	+	CC7	
Wilmington	DMR/MARC	WR3IRS	448.42500	-	CC1	T-MARC
	FM	W3DRA	146.73000	-	131.8 Hz	T-MARC
	FM	WA3UYJ	146.95500	-	131.8 Hz	T-MARC
	FM	W3DRA	224.52000	-	131.8 Hz	T-MARC
	FM	N3KZ	442.00000	+	131.8 Hz	
	FM	W3CER	444.40000	+	100.0 Hz	T-MARC
	FM	W3DRA	448.37500	-	131.8 Hz	T-MARC
	FUSION	N3GJB	144.12500			
Woodside	FM	KC3ARC	146.91000	-	77.0 Hz	T-MARC
Wyoming	FM	N3IOC	449.77500	-	114.8 Hz	T-MARC

DISTRICT OF COLUMBIA

Location	Mode	Call sign	Output	Input	Access	Coordinator
NW Washington	DMR/MARC	N3JLT	145.11000	-	CC1	
Washington	DMR/MARC	W3AGB	147.36000	+	CC1	
	DMR/MARC	W3AGB	444.16250	+	CC1	

FLORIDA

Location	Mode	Call sign	Output	Input	Access	Coordinator
Altamonte Springs						
	FM	N1FL	147.09000	+	103.5 Hz	FASMA
	FM	N4EH	147.28500	+	107.2 Hz	FASMA
	FM	N1FL	442.75000	+	103.5 Hz	FASMA
	FM	N4EH	442.97500	+	103.5 Hz	FASMA
Andytown	FM	N0LO-SAR	442.82500	+	110.9 Hz	
Anthony	FM	KA4WJA	146.97000	-		
	FM	KA4WJA	224.10000	-	103.5 Hz	FASMA
	FM	KA2MBE	444.32500	+	123.0 Hz	FASMA
	FUSION	K2ADA	147.21000	+		
Arcadia	FM	W4MIN	147.07500	+	100.0 Hz	
	FM	W4MIN	147.18000	+	100.0 Hz	FASMA
	FM	W4MIN	444.20000	+	100.0 Hz	
Auburndale	DMR/MARC	NP2OL	441.60000	+	CC1	
Ave Maria	FM	N4DJJ	444.07500	+	103.5 Hz	
Aventura	FM	K4PAL	147.21000	+	103.5 Hz	FASMA
	FM	K4PAL	442.25000	+	114.8 Hz	FASMA

Location	Mode	Call sign	Output	Input	Access	Coordinator
Aventura	FM	K4PAL	443.82500	+	114.8 Hz	FASMA
Avon Park	FM	N4EMH	145.29000	-	127.3 Hz	FASMA
	FM	W4HEM	145.33000	-	100.0 Hz	FASMA
	FM	W4HCA	442.35000	+		FASMA
	FM	W4HEM	444.82500	+	100.0 Hz	FASMA
Babson Park	DMR/MARC	KJ4SHL	444.68750	+	CC1	
Bartow	FM	NI4CE	442.82500	+	100.0 Hz	
Bell	FM	KE4HDG	147.28500	+	123.0 Hz	
Belle Glade	FM	AB4BE	147.12000	+		FASMA
Belleair Bluffs	FM	KK4EQF-R	145.47000	-		
Beverly Hills	FUSION	N8DA	446.20000			
	FUSION	K4OW	446.42500			
Big Pine Key	FM	KC2CWC	145.23000	-	94.8 Hz	FASMA
	FM	NQ2Z	442.37500	+		FASMA
Bithlo	FM	N4FL	145.23000	-	103.5 Hz	FASMA
	FM	N4FL	442.62500	+	103.5 Hz	
Boca Raton	DMR/BM	N4BRF	442.87500	+	CC1	FASMA
	DMR/MARC	N4DES	442.00000	+	CC8	
	FL-DMR	AC4XQ	443.93750	+		FASMA
	FM	W4BUG	146.82000	-	110.9 Hz	FASMA
	FM	KC4GH	444.70000	+	123.0 Hz	
	FM	KF4LZA	444.75000	+	110.9 Hz	
	FM	KI4LJM	927.62500	902.62500	100.0 Hz	FASMA
	FM	KF4LZA	927.72500	902.72500	110.9 Hz	
	OpenDMR	KF4LZA	444.10000	+		
	P25	N4DES	147.39000	+		
Bonifay	FM	N4LMI	145.11000	-	100.0 Hz	FASMA
	FM	KF4KQE	146.91000	-	100.0 Hz	FASMA
Bonita Springs	DMR/BM	W9LP	442.67500	+	CC1	
	DMR/BM	NP2DL	443.60000	+	CC1	
	FM	KM4OWA	444.75000	+		
Boynton Beach	DMR/BM	WX3C	147.25000	-	CC7	
	DMR/BM	WX3C	442.30000	+	CC7	FASMA
	DMR/BM	WX3C	444.25000	+	CC7	FASMA
	DMR/BM	WX3C	902.98750	927.98750	CC7	
	FM	NR4P	147.22500	+	107.2 Hz	FASMA
	FM	NR4P	444.65000	+	127.3 Hz	FASMA
	P25	WX3C	442.12500	+		
	FUSION	WB2APB	446.50000			
Bradenton	FM	K4GG	146.82000	-	100.0 Hz	FASMA
	FM	KF4MBN	147.19500	+	103.5 Hz	FASMA
	FM	K4CVL	224.62000	-		
	FM	KF4MBN	442.12500	+	100.0 Hz	FASMA
	FM	K4MPX	444.27500	+		FASMA
	FM	K4TAP	444.87500	+	82.5 Hz	
	FUSION	KA3ZAI	439.42000			
	FUSION	WA4CSS	446.05000			
Brandon	FM	W4HSO	146.61000	-	141.3 Hz	FASMA
	FM	K4TN	147.16500	+	136.5 Hz	FASMA
	P25	WA6KDW	444.37500	+		
	P25	WA6KDW	927.60000	902.60000		
	FUSION	KB4DW	439.83750			
	FUSION	N4DLW	443.50000	+		
Bristol	FM	KG4ITD	146.71500	-	94.8 Hz	FASMA
Brooksville	DMR/BM	K4WZV	222.22200	222.82200	CC1	
	FM	K4BKV	146.71500	-		FASMA
	FM	K4BKV	442.12500	+		FASMA
	FM	W4RPT	443.82500	+	103.5 Hz	FASMA
	P25	W4RPT	147.07500	+		FASMA
	FUSION	WA0FQV	145.05000			
	FUSION	W4LBY	146.55000			
Bryceville	FM	W4NAS	146.83500	-	127.3 Hz	FASMA

Location	Mode	Call sign	Output	Input	Access	Coordinator
Buena Vista		K4ZPZ-R	443.10000			
Bunnell	DMR/MARC	KC2CWT	444.97500	+	CC1	
	FM	KB4JDE	145.45000	-	88.5 Hz	FASMA
	FM	KB4JDE	224.02000	-		FASMA
	FM	KB4JDE	444.00000	+	123.0 Hz	FASMA
	FUSION	ND1C	144.79000	+		
	FUSION	ND1C	145.39000	-		
	FUSION	ND1C	145.56250			
Bushnell	FM	KI4DYE	145.49000	-	123.0 Hz	
Callahan	FM	W4NAS	145.31000	-		
	FM	W4NAS-R	147.00000	-	127.3 Hz	FASMA
Cantonment	FUSION	KQ4QC	439.80000			
Cape Coral	DMR/MARC	KN4EOF	443.80000	+	CC1	
	FM	KN2R	444.72500	+	136.5 Hz	
	FUSION	WB2IWC	145.70000			
Carolina	DMR/MARC	WP3JJ	447.97500	-	CC1	
Chattahoochee	DMR/MARC	NX4DN	442.13750	+	CC1	
	FM	K4GFD-SAR	444.97500	+	94.8 Hz	
Chiefland	FM	KG4WKX	145.51000			
	FM	W4DAK	147.39000	+	123.0 Hz	FASMA
	FUSION	KG4WKX	145.56250			
	FUSION	KG4WKX	445.93750			
Chipley	FM	N4PTW	146.62500	-	100.0 Hz	FASMA
	FM	WA4MN-SAR	444.75000	+	100.0 Hz	FASMA
Chuluota	FM	N1FL	147.16500	+	103.5 Hz	FASMA
Clearwater	DMR/BM	KD4YAL	441.95000	+	CC1	
	DMR/MARC	KN4GVY	443.37500	+	CC1	
	DSTAR	KA9RIX	147.28500	+		
	FM	WD4SCD	147.03000	+	156.7 Hz	
	FM	WD0DIA	443.05000	+	141.3 Hz	
	FM	KA9RIX	444.46750	+		
Clermont	DMR/MARC	W4VCO	442.45000	+	CC1	
	FM	WA2UPK	146.49000		103.5 Hz	
	FM	WA2UPK	147.49000		103.5 Hz	
	FM	KA0OXH	223.94000	-		FASMA
	FM	KR4Q	224.82000	-		
	FM	KG4RPH	442.45000	+	103.5 Hz	FASMA
	FM	K4VJ	442.47500	+	103.5 Hz	FASMA
	FM	WA2UPK	442.60000	+	103.5 Hz	FASMA
	FM	KA0OXH-SAR	444.97500	+	103.5 Hz	FASMA
Clewiston	DMR/BM	WB4TWQ	444.67500	+	CC1	
	FM	WB4TWQ	145.35000	-	127.3 Hz	
	FM	WA4PAM	146.76000	-	97.4 Hz	
	FM	N4PAZ	442.37500	+		
	FUSION	WB4TWQ	145.14000	-		
	FUSION	N4PAZ	447.37500	-		
	FUSION	WB4TWQ	449.40000	-		
Club Manor	FM	W4KPR-R	145.45000	-		FASMA
Cocoa	ATV	K4ATV	427.25000	428.25000		FASMA
	DMR/BM	K4DJN	444.57500	+	CC3	FASMA
	DSTAR	KJ4OXT C	147.03000	+		
	FM	AJ4IR	224.12000	-	123.0 Hz	FASMA
	FM	W4NLX-SAR	444.65000	+	107.2 Hz	FASMA
	FUSION	W4LOV	144.98750			
Cocoa Beach	FM	AA4CD	444.40000	+	103.5 Hz	FASMA
Coral Gables	FM	KD4BBM	146.76000	-		FASMA
	FM	K4AG	147.15000	+	94.8 Hz	FASMA
Coral Springs	FM	WR4AYC	145.27000	-	110.9 Hz	
	FM	N4RQY	146.65500	-	131.8 Hz	FASMA
	FM	WR4AYC	443.85000	+		
Crawfordville	FM	K4WAK	145.45000	-	94.8 Hz	FASMA
	FM	KN4NN	147.25500	+	94.8 Hz	FASMA

Location	Mode	Call sign	Output	Input	Access	Coordinator
Crawfordville	FM	K4TLH	442.85000	+	94.8 Hz	FASMA
	FM	K4WAK	444.45000	+	94.8 Hz	FASMA
Crescent City	FM	KJ4UOP	145.19000	-	127.3 Hz	
Cresent City	FM	KJ4UOP	53.73000	52.73000		
Crestview	DMR/MARC	KB4LSL	443.00000	+	CC1	
	DSTAR	KO4EOC C	145.15000	-		
	DSTAR	KO4EOC	145.15000	-		
	DSTAR	KO4EOC	444.60000	+		
	DSTAR	KO4EOC B	444.60000	+		
	DSTAR	KO4EOC D	1251.30000			
	DSTAR	KO4EOC A	1291.30000	1271.30000		
	DSTAR	KO4EOC	1291.30000	1271.30000		
	FM	W4AAZ	147.36000	+	100.0 Hz	FASMA
	FM	KC4YBZ-SAR	444.90000	+	100.0 Hz	
	FM	N4NID	444.95000	+		FASMA
	FM	KB4LSL	927.76250	902.76250	100.0 Hz	
Crystal River	DMR/MARC	KN4GVY	444.37500	+	CC1	
Cudjoe Key	DMR/BM	K4HG	441.52500	+	CC8	
	DMR/MARC	K4ECT	444.32500	+	CC8	
	FM	AK3ML-R	147.06000	+		FASMA
Cutler Bay	DMR/MARC	KD4NYC	442.12500	+	CC1	
	OpenDMR	KF4LZA	442.41250	+		
	FUSION	W7HU	446.90000			
Cypress Lake		W9BS-L	446.95000			
Dade City	DMR/MARC	N3OS	442.37500	+	CC1	
	DMR/MARC	W3LR	443.68750	+	CC1	
	FM	K4EX/R	146.88000	-	146.2 Hz	
	FM	WX4PEM	147.13500	+	146.2 Hz	FASMA
	FUSION	K4EX/R	145.56250			
Dania Beach	FM	W6BXQ	146.64000	-	103.5 Hz	
	FM	KG4UGK	441.52500	+	77.0 Hz	FASMA
Davenport	FM	WC4PEM	444.62500	+	127.3 Hz	
Davie	DMR/BM	NA4DC	443.25000	+	CC1	
	DMR/BM	K9PSL	444.87500	+	CC1	
Daytona	DMR/MARC	W2BFD	443.21250	+	CC1	
Daytona Beach	DMR/MARC	NY4Z	442.12500	+	CC1	
	DSTAR	KJ4RYH C	145.38000	-		
	FM	K4BV	147.15000	+	127.3 Hz	FASMA
	FM	N4ZKF	147.37500	+	103.5 Hz	FASMA
	FM	W4TAM	444.85000	+		
	FM	KE4NZG	927.65000	902.65000	107.2 Hz	FASMA
	FUSION	K4EAE	145.56250			
	FUSION	KG4WKX	445.93750			
Deerfield Beach	FM	N4ZUW	444.42500	+	110.9 Hz	FASMA
	FM	KA4EPS	444.92500	+	110.9 Hz	
	FUSION	N4IFP	439.60000			
DeFuniak Springs	DSTAR	N4EMA C	146.96250	-		
	DSTAR	N4EMA B	443.10000	+		
	FM	WF4X	147.28500	+	100.0 Hz	
	FM	KJ4JAH	147.37500	+	100.0 Hz	FASMA
Deland	DMR/BM	KN4EHC	442.22500	+	CC1	
	FM	KV4EOC	147.24000	+	123.0 Hz	FASMA
	FM	K4HEK	444.15000	+	103.5 Hz	
Dellwood	FM	W4BKD-R	144.67000	-		
Delray Beach	DMR/MARC	W2GGI	443.30000	+	CC1	
Deltona	FM	AF4FX-L	145.53000		103.5 Hz	
	FM	NP4ND	146.95500	-	107.2 Hz	
	FM	NP4ND	444.25000	+	103.5 Hz	FASMA
Destin	FM	N4NID	145.29000	-		FASMA
	FM	W4RH	147.00000	+	100.0 Hz	FASMA
Doral	FUSION	KI4DK	445.45000			
Drew Park	DMR/BM	KJ4SHL	442.61250	+	CC15	

Location	Mode	Call sign	Output	Input	Access	Coordinator
Duke Field	FM	W4ZBB	147.22500	+	100.0 Hz	FASMA
Dundee	FM	WC4PEM	146.98500	-	127.3 Hz	FASMA
	FM	K4LKW	442.42500	+	127.3 Hz	FASMA
Dunedin	DMR/MARC	KN4GVY	145.11000	-	CC1	
	DMR/MARC	KN4GVY	444.35000	+	CC1	
	FM	K4LK	145.23000	-	146.2 Hz	FASMA
	FM	KE4EMC	146.70000	-	146.2 Hz	FASMA
	FM	K4JMH	444.15000	+	146.2 Hz	FASMA
	FM	KE4EMC	444.97500	+	100.0 Hz	FASMA
	FM	KJ4JBO	1285.50000	1265.50000	103.5 Hz	FASMA
Dupree Gardens	FM	K4EX-R	146.88000	-	146.2 Hz	FASMA
Durbin	FM	KK4BD	146.80500	-	127.3 Hz	FASMA
Eglin AFB	FM	W4NN	147.12000	+	100.0 Hz	FASMA
	FM	W4NN	444.80000	+	100.0 Hz	FASMA
Englewood	DMR/BM	W4AC	444.10000	+	CC1	
	FM	K0DGF	146.77500	-	77.0 Hz	
	FM	W4AC	146.80500	-	100.0 Hz	
	FM	K0DGF	444.62500	+	77.0 Hz	FASMA
	FUSION	AA4FB	145.25000	-		FASMA
Espanola	DMR/MARC	KG4IDD	443.40000	-	CC1	
	FM	KD4QOF	146.74500	-	123.0 Hz	FASMA
Estero	FM	N5ICT	442.12500	+		FASMA
Estero ,Fl	FM	W2PAX	147.28500	+	136.5 Hz	
Eustis	DMR/MARC	W4ALR	444.55000	+	CC1	
	DSTAR	KK4KYK	443.02500	+		
	FM	KD4MBN	53.23000	52.23000	103.5 Hz	FASMA
	FM	W4ALR	146.89500	-	103.5 Hz	FASMA
	FM	KD4MBN	147.18000	+	103.5 Hz	FASMA
	FM	K4AUS	444.55000	+		FASMA
	FM	N4ZSN	444.87500	+	103.5 Hz	FASMA
Everglades City	DMR/BM	WD2E	444.75000	+	CC1	
	FM	WD2E	145.09000			
	FUSION	WD2E	144.99000			
Fanning Springs	FM	KB8BSO	53.17000	52.17000	107.2 Hz	FASMA
Flagler Beach	FUSION	WA3QCV	145.72500			
Flagler County	DMR/MARC	W2BFD	441.18750	+	CC1	
Fleming Island	FM	KI4UWC-R	146.92500	-	156.7 Hz	FASMA
Fll	DMR/MARC	KK4ZMG	145.40000	-	CC1	
Florahome	DMR/BM	WO5CID	145.37000	-	CC1	
Florida City	FM	SAR-FLC	442.05000	889.10000	114.8 Hz	
Fort Lauderdale	DMR/BM	N4MOT	442.42500	+	CC1	
	DMR/BM	K4ABB	442.77500	+	CC7	
	DMR/MARC	KK4ZMG	440.00000	+	CC1	
	DSTAR	W4BUG	442.20000	+	110.9 Hz	FASMA
	DSTAR	W4AB	442.45000	+		
	DSTAR	W4AB B	442.45000	+		
	FM	N4THW	146.73000	-	103.5 Hz	
	FM	W4AB	146.91000	-	110.9 Hz	
	FM	K4FK	147.33000	+	103.5 Hz	FASMA
	FM	KF4LZA	224.40000	-	110.9 Hz	
	FM	W4BEN	224.76000	-	110.9 Hz	
	FM	W4AB-SAR	442.85000	+	110.9 Hz	
	FM	KD4CPG	443.80000	+	131.8 Hz	
	FM	W4AB	444.82500	+	110.9 Hz	
	FM	KF4LZA	927.05000	902.05000	110.9 Hz	
	FM	KB2TZ	927.67500	902.67500		FASMA
	FM	KF4LZA	927.70000	902.70000	110.9 Hz	
	P25	N4MOT	146.79000	-	88.5 Hz	
	FUSION	N4POA	145.34000	-		
	FUSION	KM4DY	442.10000	+		
Fort Meyers	DMR/BM	W4LCO	443.45000	+	CC1	
Fort Myers	DMR/MARC	KF5IW	442.17500	+	CC1	

Location	Mode	Call sign	Output	Input	Access	Coordinator
Fort Myers	DMR/MARC	NQ6U	442.50000	+	CC9	
	DSTAR	W4LCO B	443.45000	+		
	FL-DMR	AC4XQ	443.13750	+		
	FM	KY1U	147.52500		100.0 Hz	
	FM	KD4NFS	445.52500	-		
	FM	AA4JS	445.92500	-	136.5 Hz	
	FUSION	W4LCO	145.17000	-		
	FUSION	WU8C	440.00000			
	FUSION	AA4JS	444.67500	+		
Fort Pierce	DMR/MARC	K4SRN	927.70000	902.70000	CC1	
	DSTAR	W4AKH B	444.50000	+		
	FM	W4AKH-R	147.34500	+		
	FUSION	KO4MAX	145.78000			
Fort White	DMR/BM	AI4UI	440.52500	+	CC1	
Frostproof	FM	WC4PEM	444.95000	+	127.3 Hz	FASMA
Ft Lauderdale	DMR/MARC	W2GGI	443.62500	+	CC1	
	DSTAR	W4BUG C	145.34000	-		
	DSTAR	W4BUG B	442.20000	+		
	DSTAR	W4BUG A	1291.60000	1271.60000		
	FM	KF4LZA	53.75000	52.75000	110.9 Hz	
	FM	KF4LZA	443.75000	+	110.9 Hz	
	OpenDMR	KF4LZA	443.58750	+		
Ft McCoy	FM	N4STP	147.16500	+	123.0 Hz	
	FM	N4STP	444.37500	+	123.0 Hz	
Ft Myers	DSTAR	W4LCO B	443.45000	+		
	FM	KM4OWA	145.17000	-	136.5 Hz	
	FM	K4QCW	145.39000	-	136.5 Hz	
	FM	AC4TM	146.82000	-	136.5 Hz	
	FM	W4LCO	147.16500	+	127.3 Hz	
	FM	KJ4WPV	147.34500	+	136.5 Hz	
	FM	W2PAX	224.52000	-	136.5 Hz	
	FM	NX4Y-SAR	444.22500	+	136.5 Hz	FASMA
	FM	WB4FOW	444.45000	+	77.0 Hz	
	FM	W4WJN	444.67500	+		
	FM	WX4L	444.77500	+	136.5 Hz	
Ft Myers, North Ft Myers						
	FM	KI4ODC	146.88000	-	136.5 Hz	
Ft Pierce	DSTAR	W4AKH	444.50000	+		
	FM	W4SLC	147.24000	+	107.2 Hz	
	FM	W4SLC	444.60000	+	107.2 Hz	
	FM	K4NRG	927.60000	902.60000	100.0 Hz	FASMA
	FM	K4NRG	927.61250	902.61250	100.0 Hz	FASMA
	OpenDMR	KF4LZA	444.98750	+		
Ft Walton Beach	FM	W4ZBB	146.79000	-		
	FM	K4FWB	444.45000	+	100.0 Hz	
Ft. Lauderdale	DMR/MARC	N4MOT	147.10500	+	CC1	
	DMR/MARC	N4MOT	443.00000	+	CC1	
Ft. Pierce	DMR/MARC	W4AKH	444.80000	+	CC1	
	DMR/MARC	KC4DEA	927.61250	902.61250	CC1	
Gainesville	DMR/BM	KC4MHH	146.64000	-	CC1	
	DMR/BM	K4GNV	146.68500	-	CC1	
	DMR/BM	KC4MHH	444.83750	+	CC1	
	DMR/MARC	W4DFU	444.81250	+	CC1	FASMA
	FM	K4GNV	146.82000	-	123.0 Hz	
	FM	KC4MHH	146.85000	-	123.0 Hz	FASMA
	FM	W4DFU	146.91000	-	123.0 Hz	FASMA
	FM	K4GNV	146.98500	-	123.0 Hz	
	FM	KD4MGR	147.27000	+	123.0 Hz	
	FM	K4GNV	444.92500	+	123.0 Hz	
	FM	KC4MHH	444.98750	+	123.0 Hz	
	FM	KC4MHH	444.98750	+	123.0 Hz	
Gasden	FM	W4EAF	147.16500	+	94.8 Hz	FASMA

Location	Mode	Call sign	Output	Input	Access	Coordinator
Grand Island Mobile Home Park						
		KD4WOV-L	440.05000			
Grant-Valkaria		NN4BJ-L	441.40000			
Green Cove Springs						
	FM	K4BT	146.67000	-	127.3 Hz	
Greensboro	DMR/MARC	NX4DN	444.98750	+	CC1	
	FM	NX4DN	147.39000	+	94.8 Hz	
	FM	NX4DN	444.12500	+	94.8 Hz	
Groveland	DMR/MARC	K4AUS	444.05000	+	CC1	FASMA
	FM	KD4MBN	147.34500	+	103.5 Hz	FASMA
Gulf Hammock	FM	K4NCA	147.33000	+	123.0 Hz	
Hawthorne	FM	K3YAN	147.10500	+		FASMA
Hernando	FUSION	N4ZBO	446.10000			
Hialea	FUSION	KJ4NQA	444.46250	+		
Hialeah	DMR/MARC	W4PHR	441.85000	+	CC4	FASMA
	FM	KC2CWC	145.23000	-	110.9 Hz	FASMA
	FM	AE4EQ	145.25000	-	110.9 Hz	FASMA
	FM	KB4AIL	145.33000	-		FASMA
	FM	KF4ZCL	145.43000	-		FASMA
	FM	KC2CWC	146.70000	-	156.7 Hz	FASMA
	FM	N2GKG	442.37500	+	103.5 Hz	FASMA
	FM	WD4DPS	442.92500	+	110.9 Hz	
	FM	WB4ESB	444.00000	+	110.9 Hz	
	FM	KA4EPS	444.35000	+	103.5 Hz	FASMA
	FM	K4ABB	446.02500	-	88.5 Hz	
	FUSION	N4PSL	145.08500			
	FUSION	HP8EFF	147.06000	+		
Hickory Flat	FM	KD4Z	442.25000	+		
High Springs	FM	KB4MS	145.47000	-	123.0 Hz	
Hines	FM	K4PRY	146.74500	-	94.8 Hz	FASMA
Hobe Sound	FM	W4JUP	146.62500	-	110.9 Hz	FASMA
Holiday	FM	KP4PC	145.15000	-	146.2 Hz	FASMA
Hollister	FM	KF4CWI	147.06000	+	123.0 Hz	FASMA
	FUSION	KD4BEE	443.90000	+	94.8 Hz	FASMA
Holly Hill	FM	KI4RF	29.66000	-	100.0 Hz	FASMA
	FM	KI4RF	53.05000	52.05000	100.0 Hz	FASMA
	FM	KI4RF	146.65500	-	103.5 Hz	
	FM	KI4RF	223.85000	-	131.8 Hz	FASMA
Hollywood		WD4CLZ-L	146.79000			
	DMR/BM	K4ABB	442.90000	+	CC7	
	FM	AC4XQ	145.21000	-	107.2 Hz	FASMA
	FM	W4RCC	147.03000	+	103.5 Hz	FASMA
	FM	WF2C	147.18000	+	91.5 Hz	
	FM	KO4WYZ	147.37500	+	94.8 Hz	
	FM	WF2C	444.15000	+	88.5 Hz	
	FM	AC4XQ	444.17500	+	107.2 Hz	FASMA
	FM	KC4MNI	444.55000	+	88.5 Hz	FASMA
	FM	KF4LZA	1291.75000	1271.75000	110.9 Hz	
	FUSION	KO4WYZ	443.15000			
Homestead	DMR/BM	N4ODB	443.07500	+	CC14	
	DSTAR	KN4HYG	145.40000	-		
	FM	W4MBU	147.00000	-		
	FM	W4MBU	224.00000	-		
	FM	W4MBU	444.00000	+	103.5 Hz	
	FUSION	KN4HYG	443.77500	+		
Hudson	DMR/BM	KD4ACG	447.58750	-	CC1	
	FUSION	KD4ACG	145.80000			
Huntington		KA2MBE-R	145.43000			
Hypoluxo	FM	K9EE-L	445.52500	-		
Interlachen	FUSION	KD4BEE	443.90000	+		
Inverness	FM	KC4EOC	442.05000	+	103.5 Hz	FASMA
Islamarada	FM	SAR-ISL	442.85000	890.70000	114.8 Hz	

Location	Mode	Call sign	Output	Input	Access	Coordinator
Jacksonville	DMR/BM	KF4EOK	147.36000	+	CC2	
	DMR/BM	K7BEN	442.00000	+	CC1	
	DMR/BM	K4ABB	442.57500	+	CC7	
	DMR/BM	KF4EOK	444.55000	+	CC1	
	DMR/MARC	KM4SM	444.11500	+	CC2	
	DMR/MARC	K4QHR	444.27500	+	CC7	FASMA
	DMR/MARC	N2XDA	444.42500	+	CC7	FASMA
	DMR/MARC	W4COJ	444.78750	+	CC7	
	DSTAR	KJ4RYF C	145.36000	-		
	DSTAR	W4RNG C	146.88000	-		
	FM	N4GIH	145.29000	-	127.3 Hz	
	FM	W4IZ	146.70000	-	127.3 Hz	FASMA
	FM	W4RNG	146.76000	-	127.3 Hz	FASMA
	FM	WJ4EOC	146.95500	-	127.3 Hz	FASMA
	FM	W4EMN	147.13500	+	127.3 Hz	FASMA
	FM	W4RNG	147.31500	+	127.3 Hz	FASMA
	FM	W4FZM	224.78000	-	103.5 Hz	
	FM	K4QHR	444.20000	+		FASMA
	FM	W4IZ	444.40000	+	127.3 Hz	FASMA
	FM	W4RNG	444.67500	+	127.3 Hz	
	FM	SAR-JAC	444.70000	+	127.3 Hz	
	FM	N4GIH	444.92500	+	127.3 Hz	
	FUSION	NP4TR	145.13500			
Jacksonville Beach						
	DMR/MARC	KM4CTB	442.42500	+	CC1	FASMA
	DSTAR	KJ4RYG B	444.97500	+		
	FM	K2LSF	147.39000	+	127.3 Hz	
	FM	KB4ARS	444.87500	+		FASMA
Jay	FUSION	KE4JEA	145.12000	-	103.5 Hz	
Jupiter	DMR/MARC	KD4SJF	442.60000	+	CC10	
	FM	AG4BV	145.17000	-	110.9 Hz	FASMA
	FM	KA4EPS	443.82500	+	110.9 Hz	FASMA
	OpenDMR	KF4LZA	444.93750	+		
Kathleen	FM	WC4PEM	443.90000	+	127.3 Hz	FASMA
Kendale Lakes		AE4SR-L	446.27500			
Kendall	FM	KC2CWC	145.17000	-	141.3 Hz	FASMA
	FM	KA4EPS	444.12500	+	94.8 Hz	FASMA
	FM	KJ4OBN	444.62500	+	97.4 Hz	FASMA
Kendall Lake	FM	KI4BCO	145.45000	-	94.8 Hz	FASMA
Key Largo	FM	WX4SFL	146.61000	-	94.8 Hz	FASMA
	FM	KC4SFA	147.16500	+	94.8 Hz	FASMA
	FUSION	W4TFF	449.45000	-		
Key West	DMR/BM	K1ST	444.05000	+	CC8	
	FM	N2GKG	145.17000	-		FASMA
	FM	KA4EPS	146.55000		94.8 Hz	
	OpenDMR	KF4LZA	442.13750	+		
Keystone Heights	FM	WB4EN	145.13000	-		
	FM	KI4UWC	147.22500	+	156.7 Hz	FASMA
Kings Point	FM	W4KPR	927.01250	952.01250	162.2 Hz	
Kissimmee	DMR/MARC	N4GUS	444.97500	+	CC1	
	DSTAR	N4ARG C	147.21000	+		
	DSTAR	N4ARG B	444.45000	+		
	FM	N4ARG	147.21000	+		FASMA
	FM	N4OTC	442.10000	+	103.5 Hz	FASMA
	FM	NO9S	444.45000	+		FASMA
LaBelle	FM	WA4PAM	145.47000	-	97.4 Hz	
Lady Lake	DMR/BM	KF4CQ	442.55000	+	CC1	
Lake Buena Vista	DMR/MARC	WD4WDW	444.00000	+	CC3	FASMA
	FM	WD4WDW-R	147.30000	+	103.5 Hz	FASMA
Lake City	DMR/BM	KN4YGT	442.42500	+	CC6	
	DMR/BM	KN4YGT	444.37500		CC1	
	DSTAR	KN4YGT B	439.90000			

Location	Mode	Call sign	Output	Input	Access	Coordinator
Lake City	FM	N4SVC	53.39000	52.39000		
	FM	NF4CQ	145.49000	-		FASMA
	FM	WA4ZFQ	146.94000	-	123.0 Hz	
	FM	NF4CQ	147.15000	+	110.9 Hz	FASMA
	FM	NF4CQ-SAR	444.90000	+	110.9 Hz	FASMA
Lake Placid	FM	W4HEM	145.21000	-	100.0 Hz	FASMA
	FM	W4HCA	147.04500	+	100.0 Hz	FASMA
	FM	NI4CE	443.95000	+	100.0 Hz	FASMA
Lake Wales	FM	K4LKW	147.33000	+	127.3 Hz	FASMA
	FUSION	KD8IOK	144.56500			
Lake Worth	DMR/BM	WX3C	443.37000	+	CC7	
	DMR/MARC	KG4GOQ	444.45000	+	CC10	
	FM	KA4EPS	444.85000	+	110.9 Hz	FASMA
	FUSION	N1JIW	445.00000			
Lakeland	DMR/MARC	W4CLL	146.65500	-	CC6	
	DMR/MARC	W4CLL	442.02500	+	CC1	FASMA
	DMR/MARC	W4CLL	442.97500	+	CC1	
	DMR/MARC	KD4EFM	444.66250	+	CC1	
	DMR/MARC	KN4GVY	444.77500	+	CC1	
	DMR/MARC	W4VCO	444.85000	+	CC1	
	DSTAR	KJ4ACN	1293.00000	1273.00000		FASMA
	FM	WP3BC	145.27000	-	127.3 Hz	FASMA
	FM	K4LKL	146.68500	-	127.3 Hz	FASMA
	FM	KD4EFM	442.27500	+	82.5 Hz	FASMA
	P25	N4KEG	146.65500	-	127.3 Hz	
	P25	W4CLL	147.37500	+	127.3 Hz	
	P25	WP3BC	444.30000	+	127.3 Hz	FASMA
Lakewood Ranch	FM	NI4MX	443.87500	+	100.0 Hz	FASMA
Land O Lakes	DMR/BM	KM4ZRT	441.85000	442.35000	CC1	
	FM	WA4GDN	145.33000	-	146.2 Hz	FASMA
Lantana	FM	WV4I	147.04500	+	110.9 Hz	FASMA
	FM	WV4I	443.97500	+	110.9 Hz	FASMA
Largo	DMR/MARC	KN4GVY	444.37500	+	CC1	
	FM	KJ4RUS	442.92500	+	146.2 Hz	FASMA
Laurel	DMR/BM	N4SER	444.70000	+	CC1	
Lecanto	FM	W4CIT	146.77500	-	146.2 Hz	FASMA
	FM	W1XJ	146.95500	-	103.5 Hz	FASMA
Lee	FM	W1JXG	145.11000	-	123.0 Hz	
	FM	W4FAO	145.19000	-	123.0 Hz	FASMA
Leesburg	DSTAR	KJ4TJD	444.50000	+		FASMA
	FM	K4FC	147.00000	+	103.5 Hz	FASMA
	FM	N4GOZ	441.82500	+	146.2 Hz	
Lehigh Acres	DMR/BM	W4BIY	145.15000	-	CC4	
	DMR/BM	W4BIY	442.80000	+	CC1	
	FM	N2FSU	147.71500	-	74.4 Hz	
	FM	KA2SEY	444.10000	+		
	FM	WB4TWQ	444.50000	+	67.0 Hz	
Lithia	P25	WA6KDW	927.10000	902.10000		
Little Torch Key	FM	K4CIO	146.64000	-	94.8 Hz	FASMA
	FM	K4CIO	444.77500	+	94.8 Hz	FASMA
Live Oak	DMR/BM	KC4GOL	443.60000	+	CC7	
	FM	N4SVC	145.41000	-	100.0 Hz	
	FM	N4SVC	442.92500	+	127.3 Hz	FASMA
	FM	SAR-LIO	443.70000	+	110.9 Hz	
Long Key	FUSION	W4TFF	438.50000	+		
Longwood	DMR/MARC	KE4GLA	444.00000	893.00000	CC1	
Loxahatche	DMR/MARC	KK4ZMG	444.70000	+	CC7	
Loxahatchee	DMR/BM	N4KVL	443.72500	+	CC1	
	FM	KA4EPS	444.30000	+	110.9 Hz	
	FM	WB2SNN	444.35000	+	110.9 Hz	
	P25	AK4JQ	147.36000	+		FASMA
Macclenny	DMR/BM	W4DNQ	442.87500	+	CC1	

Location	Mode	Call sign	Output	Input	Access	Coordinator
Macclenny	FM	AB4GE	147.09000	+	100.0 Hz	
	FM	AB4GE	444.07500	+	100.0 Hz	FASMA
Madeira Beach	DSTAR	KA9RIX	444.46250	+		
	DSTAR	KA9RIX B	444.50000	+		
Madison	DMR/BM	W4FAO	442.00000	+	CC1	
	FM	K4NRD-SAR	444.30000	+	94.8 Hz	FASMA
Magonia Park	FM	W4ESA	146.94000	-	91.5 Hz	
	P25	AG4BV	444.32500	+	110.9 Hz	FASMA
Maitland	FM	AG4YD	442.80000	+	103.5 Hz	FASMA
	FUSION	NM2V	436.10000			
Marathon	DMR/BM	K1ST	444.78750	+	CC8	
	FM	KF4LZA	442.18750	+		
	FM	KA4EPS	444.02500	+	94.8 Hz	FASMA
	FM	W1FXX	444.32500	+		
Marco Island	DMR/MARC	K5MI	444.81250	+	CC1	
	DSTAR	K5MI	146.98500	-		FASMA
	FM	K5MI	146.85000	-	141.3 Hz	
Margate	FM	KD6YTS	441.90000	+	107.2 Hz	
	FM	KA4EPS	444.02500	+	107.2 Hz	FASMA
Marianna	FM	W4BKD	444.95000	+	123.0 Hz	
Martin County West						
	DMR/BM	N4PSK	443.90000	+	CC1	
Mas Verde Mobile Home Estates						
	FM	W2SDB-R	145.37000	-		
McGregor		KA0GYF-L	445.07500			
Melbourne	DMR/BM	K4MRG	444.82500	+	CC1	
	DMR/MARC	AC4XQ	443.33750	+	CC9	
	DSTAR	K4RPT	442.02500	+		
	FM	K4HRS	145.47000	-	107.2 Hz	FASMA
	FM	W4MLB	146.61000	-	107.2 Hz	FASMA
	FM	AF4Z	146.68500	-		FASMA
	FM	K4YWC	147.00000	-	167.9 Hz	FASMA
	FM	KI4SWB	147.48000		107.2 Hz	
	FM	K4DCS	444.32500	+	107.2 Hz	
	FM	W4MLB	444.42500	+	107.2 Hz	FASMA
	IDAS	KI4SWB	444.90000	+	118.8 Hz	FASMA
	FUSION	AB4TL	446.15000			
Merritt Island	DMR/BM	KC2UFO	444.77500	+	CC1	
	FM	KC2UFO	444.87500	+	107.2 Hz	FASMA
Miami	DMR/BM	WD4EHU	147.12000	-	CC1	
	DMR/BM	WD4EHU	442.95000	+	CC1	
	DMR/BM	AC4VK	443.41000	+	CC1	
	DMR/BM	WO9C	443.45000	+	CC1	
	DMR/BM	WD4EHU	443.60000	+	CC1	
	DMR/BM	WD4EHU	443.95000	+	CC1	
	DMR/BM	WO9C	444.90000	+	CC1	
	DMR/MARC	K7HJE	441.10000	+	CC1	
	DMR/MARC	KC2CWT	442.22500	+	CC1	
	DMR/MARC	W2GGI	444.98750	+	CC1	
	DSTAR	WD4ARC C	145.28900	-		
	DSTAR	W4NVU D	1292.00000			
	FM	AC4XQ	53.03000	52.03000	107.2 Hz	FASMA
	FM	W4HN	53.25000	52.25000	110.9 Hz	FASMA
	FM	KB4AIL	145.28000	-		FASMA
	FM	KI4IJQ	146.70000	-	156.7 Hz	FASMA
	FM	AE4EQ	146.80500	-	110.9 Hz	FASMA
	FM	K4PAL	146.85000	-	91.5 Hz	
	FM	AE4WE	146.89500	-	100.0 Hz	FASMA
	FM	KF4ACN	146.92500	-	103.5 Hz	FASMA
	FM	W4NR	146.95500	-	110.9 Hz	FASMA
	FM	KB4MBU	147.06000	+	103.5 Hz	FASMA
	FM	KR4DQ	147.30000	+	88.5 Hz	FASMA

Location	Mode	Call sign	Output	Input	Access	Coordinator
Miami	FM	K4AG	147.36000	+	94.8 Hz	FASMA
	FM	K4AG	442.15000	+	94.8 Hz	FASMA
	FM	KI4IJQ	442.32500	+	156.7 Hz	FASMA
	FM	KR4DQ	442.52500	+	88.5 Hz	FASMA
	FM	KB4ELI	442.65000	+	94.8 Hz	FASMA
	FM	KC4MND	442.72500	+		FASMA
	FM	N4CR	443.05000	+		FASMA
	FM	KN4OIP	443.52500	+		
	FM	AE4EQ	443.92500	+	110.9 Hz	FASMA
	FM	KA4HLO	444.20000	+	94.8 Hz	FASMA
	FM	K4PCS	444.27500	+	94.8 Hz	FASMA
	FM	KI4ZYV	444.32500	+	156.7 Hz	
	FM	KC4MNE	444.37500	+	94.8 Hz	FASMA
	FM	KC2CWC	444.50000	+	127.3 Hz	FASMA
	FM	KD4IMM	444.52500	+	114.8 Hz	FASMA
	FM	K4AG-SAR	444.60000	+	94.8 Hz	FASMA
	FM	KS4WF	444.77500	+		FASMA
	FM	KF4LZA	444.80000	+	94.8 Hz	
	OpenDMR	KF4LZA	442.66250	+		
	FUSION	KO4KDB	144.94500			
	FUSION	KN4ITN	145.52500	-		
	FUSION	KD4WET	146.86500	-		
	FUSION	KN4OIP	439.00000			
	FUSION	KB4AIL	442.65000	+		
	FUSION	KN4OIP	442.80000	+		
	FUSION	KB4EC	447.20000			
	FUSION	KO4SJB	448.02500	-		
	FUSION	WD4EHU	448.42500	-		
	FUSION	KB4EC	448.90000	-		
	FUSION	KJ4NQA	449.42500	-		
	FUSION	KN4OIP	449.67500	-		
Miami Gardens	OpenDMR	KF4LZA	442.75000	+		
Middleburg	DMR/BM	AF4JC	442.60000	+	CC1	
Milton	DMR/BM	K4LWC	444.40000	+	CC1	
	DSTAR	KI4WZA C	147.33000	+		
	DSTAR	KI4WZA	147.33000	+		
	DSTAR	KI4WZA	444.92500	+		
	DSTAR	KI4WZA B	444.92500	+		
	FM	N3CMH	145.25000	-	100.0 Hz	FASMA
	FM	W4VIY	145.49000	-	100.0 Hz	FASMA
	FM	WA5HC	146.44000		100.0 Hz	
	FM	K4SRC	146.70000	-	100.0 Hz	FASMA
	FM	SAR-MIL	444.72500	+	100.0 Hz	
Mims	FM	KE4NUZ	146.62500	-	100.0 Hz	FASMA
	FM	K4KSC	146.77500	-	100.0 Hz	
Minneola	FM	W4ALR	147.22500	+	103.5 Hz	FASMA
Miramar	OpenDMR	KF4LZA	444.97500	+		
Monet	FM	W4JUP	444.22500	+		
Monticello	DMR/BM	KM4TTS	145.43000	-	CC4	
Moore Haven	FM	KJ4FJD	147.30000	+	100.0 Hz	FASMA
Murdock		K1UTI-L	145.60000			
		AJ4AN-L	146.45000			
	FM	N4FOB-R	442.70000	+		
	FM	N9OJ	444.60000	+	82.5 Hz	
Naples	DMR/MARC	AB4NP	438.38750	430.78750	CC1	
	DMR/MARC	KC4RPP	443.10000	+	CC0	
	DSTAR	AB4NP	145.27000	-		
	DSTAR	AA4PP	145.49000	-		FASMA
	DSTAR	AA4PP C	145.49000	-		
	DSTAR	AA4PP	441.50000	+		
	DSTAR	AA4PP B	441.50000	+		
	DSTAR	AC4FL B	443.27500	+		

Location	Mode	Call sign	Output	Input	Access	Coordinator
Naples	DSTAR	AB4FL B	448.80000	-		
	FM	WB2QLP-R	146.67000	-	136.5 Hz	
	FM	K4YHB	147.03000	+		FASMA
	FM	KC1AR	224.38000	-	67.0 Hz	FASMA
	FM	KC1AR	442.75000	+		
	FM	KF4YEN	443.60000	+	114.8 Hz	
	FM	N5ICT	443.90000	+	67.0 Hz	
	FM	AB4NP	444.72500	+		
	FM	KC4SSD	444.87500	+	67.0 Hz	
	FM	WA1QDP	444.90000	+	67.0 Hz	
	FM	SAR-NAP	444.95000	+	103.5 Hz	
	FUSION	AG0X	444.48750	+		
Nassauville	FM	W4NAS	444.47500	+	127.3 Hz	
Navarre	FM	KC4ERT	444.20000	+	100.0 Hz	FASMA
New Port Richey	DMR/MARC	KN4GVY	444.20000	+	CC1	FASMA
	FM	WA4T	145.35000	-		
	FM	KK4ONE	449.50000	-	100.0 Hz	
	FUSION	WA4GDN	146.67000	-	146.2 Hz	FASMA
	FUSION	KC3CJU	445.00000			
New Smyrna	FM	K4BO	145.33000	-	127.3 Hz	
NOAA Belle Glade						
	WX	WXM58	162.40000			
NOAA Bethlehem	WX	WWH20	162.45000			
NOAA Daytona Beach						
	WX	KIH26	162.40000			
NOAA East Point	WX	WWF86	162.50000			
NOAA Fort Myers	WX	WXK83	162.47500			
NOAA Fort Pierce	WX	WWF69	162.42500			
NOAA Gainesville	WX	WXJ60	162.47500			
NOAA Inverness	WX	WWF38	162.40000			
NOAA Jacksonville						
	WX	KHB39	162.55000			
NOAA Key West	WX	WXJ95	162.40000			
NOAA Lake City	WX	KEB97	162.40000			
NOAA Largo	WX	KEC38	162.45000			
NOAA Melbourne	WX	WXJ70	162.55000			
NOAA Miami	WX	KHB34	162.55000			
NOAA Morriston	WX	KWN38	162.55000			
NOAA Naples	WX	WWG92	162.52500			
NOAA Ocala	WX	WWF85	162.52500			
NOAA Orlando	WX	KIH63	162.47500			
NOAA Palatka	WX	WNG522	162.42500			
NOAA Panama City						
	WX	KGG67	162.55000			
NOAA Pensacola	WX	KEC86	162.40000			
NOAA Princeton	WX	WNG663	162.42500			
NOAA Salem	WX	WWF88	162.42500			
NOAA Sebring	WX	WXK83A	162.50000			
NOAA Sneads	WX	WNG633	162.42500			
NOAA Sumterville	WX	KPS505	162.50000			
NOAA Tallahassee						
	WX	KIH24	162.40000			
NOAA Tampa Bay						
	WX	KHB32	162.55000			
NOAA Venice	WX	WWG59	162.40000			
NOAA West Palm Beach						
	WX	KEC50	162.47500			
North Bay County	FM	KE4FD	146.94000	-	100.0 Hz	
North Dade	DMR/MARC	AC4XQ	443.12500	+	CC10	FASMA
	FL-DMR	AC4XQ	443.17500			
North Key Largo	DMR/BM	K1ST	443.28750	+	CC8	

Location	Mode	Call sign	Output	Input	Access	Coordinator
North Meadowbrook Terrace						
	FM	AJ4FR-R	444.57500	+		FASMA
North Miami Beach						
	FM	K4PAL	147.37500	+	118.8 Hz	FASMA
North Naples	DMR/MARC	AB4L	443.80000	+	CC1	
	DSTAR	AB4FL B	448.80000	-		
North Port	FM	W8YNY	145.23000	-	107.2 Hz	
	FM	K4NPT	147.12000	+	136.5 Hz	FASMA
	FM	KA2LAL	442.15000	+	94.8 Hz	
	FUSION	W8YNY	145.23000	-		
Ocala	DMR/BM	NA4DA	442.77500	+	CC1	
	DSTAR	KG4NXO	145.17000	-	123.0 Hz	FASMA
	DSTAR	KG4NXO C	145.17000	-		
	DSTAR	KK4DFC	146.79000	-		FASMA
	DSTAR	KK4DFC C	146.79000	-		
	DSTAR	KK4DFC	147.19500	+		
	DSTAR	KG4NXO B	443.87500	+		
	FM	KA2MBE	29.68000	-		FASMA
	FM	WA3YOX	145.27000	-	123.0 Hz	FASMA
	FM	KD4GME	145.43000	-	141.3 Hz	
	FM	K4GSO	146.61000	-	123.0 Hz	FASMA
	FM	NX4Y	444.02500	+	123.0 Hz	
	FUSION	N4AXX	146.50500			
	FUSION	K2ADA	147.21000	+	123.0 Hz	FASMA
	FUSION	W3HH	430.45000			
	FUSION	WA1PMA	443.75000			
	FUSION	WA1PMA	446.05000			
Ocalla	DMR/MARC	KN4GVY	444.10000	+	CC1	
Okeechobee	FM	K4OKE	147.09000	+	100.0 Hz	FASMA
	FM	K4OKE	147.19500	+	100.0 Hz	
	FUSION	K4IIA	146.50000			
Oramge Park	FUSION	WH2AAT	145.56250			
Orange City	DMR/BM	N2NEI	442.47500		CC1	
Orange Mountain		KB4JKL-L	445.00000			
Orange Park	DMR/MARC	KK4ECR	443.08750	+	CC1	
	FM	K4SIX	53.19000	52.19000		
	FM	W4NEK	147.25500	+	103.5 Hz	FASMA
	FM	K4BT	444.50000	+	127.3 Hz	FASMA
Orlando	DMR/BM	KD2TCQ	441.02500		CC1	
	DMR/BM	W4MCO	443.16250	+	CC11	
	DMR/MARC	KJ4OVA	443.13750	+	CC1	
	DSTAR	K1XC	146.82000	-		FASMA
	DSTAR	K1XC C	146.82000	-		
	DSTAR	WD4WDW	442.00000	+		
	DSTAR	WD4WDW B	442.00000	+		
	DSTAR	K1XC B	443.27500	+		
	DSTAR	KN4DCI B	443.32500	+		
	DSTAR	W4AES B	443.62500	+		
	DSTAR	K1XC D	1255.00000			
	DSTAR	K1XC	1285.00000	1265.00000		FASMA
	DSTAR	K1XC A	1285.00000	-		
	FM	AC0Y	145.13000	-	103.5 Hz	FASMA
	FM	W4MCO	146.73000	-	103.5 Hz	FASMA
	FM	WD4MRR	147.06000	+	103.5 Hz	FASMA
	FM	N4LGH	147.12000	+	103.5 Hz	FASMA
	FM	W4LOV	442.07500	+	103.5 Hz	FASMA
	FM	NN4TT	442.37500	+	103.5 Hz	FASMA
	FM	W4MCO	442.70000	+		FASMA
	FM	W4MCO	443.05000	+	103.5 Hz	FASMA
	FM	NW4GT	443.65000	+	103.5 Hz	
	FM	N4ATS	443.85000	+	103.5 Hz	FASMA
	FM	KR4KZ	443.97500	+	103.5 Hz	FASMA

Location	Mode	Call sign	Output	Input	Access	Coordinator
Orlando	FM	NX4Y SAR	444.07500	+	103.5 Hz	
	FM	W4AES	444.12500	+	103.5 Hz	FASMA
	FM	K4HEK	444.15000	+	88.5 Hz	FASMA
	FM	K4HEK	444.80000	+	88.5 Hz	FASMA
	FM	WA2UPK	444.80000	+	103.5 Hz	
	FUSION	KB4UT	147.01500	+		
	FUSION	KP4WR	433.15000			
	FUSION	KJ4YOB	445.54000			
Ormond Beach	FM	KA2AYR	145.27000	-	156.7 Hz	FASMA
	FM	N4GOA	146.86500	-	127.3 Hz	FASMA
	FM	N4GOA	147.27000	+	127.3 Hz	FASMA
	FM	N4JRF	442.40000	+		
	FM	KA2AYR	442.65000	+	127.3 Hz	FASMA
	FM	KE4NZG	443.82500	+	118.8 Hz	FASMA
	FM	N4GOA	443.87500	+	127.3 Hz	FASMA
Osceola Mobile Park						
		N4ARG-R	224.00000			
Oviedo	DMR/BM	KD4JQX	448.12500	-	CC5	
	FM	WD4DSV	442.95000	+	103.5 Hz	FASMA
Ozello		N8DA-L	146.43000			
Palatka	FM	KF4PXZ	145.37000	-		
	FUSION	N6OA	146.55000			
	FUSION	KN4ZGY	147.47000			
	FUSION	KN4ZGY	445.00000	+		
Palm Bay	DMR/BM	KM4OP	444.95000	+	CC1	
	DSTAR	N4OTC	444.47500	+		
	DSTAR	N4OTC B	444.47500	+		
	FM	WW4AL	145.25000	-	82.5 Hz	
	FM	W4MLB	146.85000	-	107.2 Hz	FASMA
	FM	K4EOC	146.89500	-		FASMA
	FM	K4DCS	147.25500	+	107.2 Hz	FASMA
	FM	K4MER	927.60000	902.60000	100.0 Hz	
	FUSION	K4DCS/R	147.25500	+		
	FUSION	KN4ZGM	147.56000			
Palm Beach	DSTAR	K4WPB C	145.32000	-		
	FM	FL SARNET	444.32500	+	110.9 Hz	
Palm Beach Gardens						
	DMR/MARC	KD4SJF	442.10000	+	CC10	FASMA
	P25	AG4BV	444.40000	+		FASMA
Palm City	DMR/MARC	N4IRS	438.35000	430.75000	CC1	
	DMR/MARC	N4IRS	927.62500	902.62500	CC1	
Palm Coast	DMR/BM	KF4I	443.30000	+	CC1	
	DMR/MARC	KG4IDD	442.20000	+	CC1	
	DSTAR	W4SRT	442.32500	+		
	DSTAR	KG4TCC B	442.32500	+		
	DSTAR	KG4TCC	1293.40000	1313.40000		
	DSTAR	KG4TCC A	1293.40000	1273.40000		
	FM	KG4IDD	145.47000	-	123.0 Hz	FASMA
	FM	WA3QCV	147.07500	+	123.0 Hz	FASMA
	FUSION	KO4PDI	145.56250			
	FUSION	K3SRE	146.01250			
	FUSION	AK4FZ	146.55500			
	FUSION	WA3QCV	146.71500	-	123.0 Hz	
	FUSION	KO4PDI	147.47000			
	FUSION	WB0AOD	445.00000			
Palm Harbor	DMR/MARC	WD9BBE	443.95625	+	CC15	
	DMR/MARC	KN4GVY	444.57500	+	CC1	
	DSTAR	W4AFC	442.50000	+		FASMA
	DSTAR	W4AFC B	442.50000	+		
	FM	W4AFC	147.12000	+	100.0 Hz	
	FM	W4AFC	442.70000	+		
Palm Spring	FUSION	KN4QFD	144.00000			

Location	Mode	Call sign	Output	Input	Access	Coordinator
Palma Sola Park		KM4BGQ-L	29.60000			
Panama	DSTAR	KI4VKC C	145.61000	144.31000		
	DSTAR	KI4VKC B	444.52500	+		
Panama City	FM	AC4QB	53.05000	52.05000		
	FM	W4RYZ	145.21000	-		FASMA
	FM	KV4ATV	145.25000	-	100.0 Hz	
	FM	AC4QB	145.33000	-	100.0 Hz	FASMA
	FM	KF4JMM	146.74500	-		
	FM	KM4OAR	147.06000	+		FASMA
	FM	KV4ATV	224.25000	-	100.0 Hz	
	FM	SAR-PAN	441.17500	+	100.0 Hz	
	FM	KB9PTP	443.02500	+	103.5 Hz	
	FM	N1HQ	444.10000	+		FASMA
	FM	KV4ATV	444.25000	+	100.0 Hz	
	FM	KF4JMM	444.50000	+	103.5 Hz	
	FM	KP3AMG	445.10000	-	123.0 Hz	
	FM	KV4ATV	919.25000			
Parkland	FM	WR4AYC	145.11000	-	110.9 Hz	
Pembroke Pines	FM	K4BRY	147.58500			
	FM	KF4LZA	224.40000	-	110.9 Hz	
	FM	K2HXC	441.90000	+		FASMA
	FM	K4BRY	443.32500	554.22500	110.9 Hz	
	FUSION	KC4MNI	444.55000	+		
	FUSION	KC4MNI	449.46250	-		
Pensacola	DMR/BM	WB4OQF	443.70000	+	CC1	
	FM	W4UAC	146.76000	-	100.0 Hz	
	FM	WB4OQF	146.85000	-	100.0 Hz	
	FUSION	W4UC	145.45000	-	100.0 Hz	
	FUSION	W4UC	146.76000	-	100.0 Hz	FASMA
	FUSION	W4UC	443.85000	+	100.0 Hz	FASMA
Pensacola Beach	FM	N3CMH-R	443.97500	+		FASMA
Perry	FM	K4PRY	145.35000	-	123.0 Hz	FASMA
	FM	K4PRY	146.97000	-	123.0 Hz	
	FM	SAR-PER	443.10000	+	94.8 Hz	
	FM	K4III	444.10000	+	94.8 Hz	FASMA
Pinellas	FM	SAR-PIN	442.25000	+	146.2 Hz	
Pinellas Park	DMR/MARC	KN4GVY	443.82500	+	CC1	
Plant City	DMR/MARC	W4CLL	442.67500	+	CC1	
	DSTAR	N4CLL C	147.20000	+		
	DSTAR	N4CLL B	442.02500	+		
	DSTAR	N4CLL D	1251.40000			
	DSTAR	N4CLL A	1292.10000	-		
Plantation	DMR/MARC	W4MOT	442.40000	+	CC1	
	FM	N4MOT	146.79000	-	88.5 Hz	
	FM	K4GET-L	147.48000		110.9 Hz	
	FM	N4RQY	224.18000	-	131.8 Hz	FASMA
	FM	K4GET	441.42500	+	103.5 Hz	FASMA
Plantation Key	DMR/BM	K1ST	444.36250	+	CC8	
Poinciana	FM	K9YCG	146.71500	-	103.5 Hz	FASMA
Polk City	DMR/MARC	W4VCO	444.27500	+	CC1	
Pompano Beach	DMR/BM	W4BUG	443.35000	+	CC11	
	FM	W4BUG	146.61000	-	110.9 Hz	FASMA
	FM	KM4HJJ	441.80000	+	110.9 Hz	
	FM	W4BUG	442.50000	+	110.9 Hz	
	FM	KF4LZA	927.71250	902.71250		
Ponte Vedra	FM	KX4EOC	147.01500	+	127.3 Hz	FASMA
Port Charlotte	FM	KB0EVM	147.01500	+	136.5 Hz	FASMA
Port Everglades	DMR/MARC	N4MOT	147.10500	+	CC1	
Port Orange	FUSION	K4BO/R	145.33000	-		
	FUSION	KM4WHO	145.56250			
Port Richey	DMR/BM	WB8VTW	443.07500	+	CC1	
	DMR/BM	KJ4FPA	443.93750	+	CC1	

Location	Mode	Call sign	Output	Input	Access	Coordinator
Port Richey	DMR/MARC	KJ4LXT	444.93750	+	CC1	
	DSTAR	KJ4BYI B	442.76250	+		
	FM	KG4YZY	442.65000	+		FASMA
	FUSION	KM4ZLV	145.55000			
	FUSION	WB4CL	146.83500	-		
Port Salerno	DMR/MARC	N4IRS	444.97500	+	CC1	
Port St Joe	FM	W4WEB	147.30000	+	103.5 Hz	
Port St Lucie	DMR/MARC	K2DMR	440.85000	+	CC1	
	FM	K4PSL	146.95500	-	107.2 Hz	FASMA
	FM	W4SLC	147.01500	+	107.2 Hz	FASMA
	FM	K4NRG	444.00000	+		FASMA
	FM	K4NRG	927.66250	902.66250	100.0 Hz	FASMA
Port St. Lucie	DMR/MARC	W4SLC	442.02500	+	CC1	
	FM	W4SLC	442.00000	+	107.2 Hz	
Port St.Lucie	DMR/MARC	K4SRN	444.00000	+	CC1	
Princeton	FM	KF4ACN	146.83500	-	94.8 Hz	FASMA
	FM	KF4ACN	442.35000	+	103.5 Hz	FASMA
	FM	KF4ACN	442.68750	+		FASMA
Punta Gorda	DMR/BM	N4ADI	444.65000	+	CC1	
	DMR/MARC	W4DUX	442.92500	+	CC1	FASMA
	FM	KF4QWC	146.68500	-	136.5 Hz	FASMA
	FM	WX4E	146.74500	-	136.5 Hz	FASMA
	FM	W4DUX-R	147.25500	+	136.5 Hz	FASMA
	FUSION	KB9NDJ	146.52000			
	FUSION	WX8P	147.55500			
Ravenwood Estates						
		KB1NCJ-L	147.52500			
River Park		KB2VUQ-L	146.49000			
Riverview	DSTAR	NI4CE B	444.42500	+		
	FM	K4SIP	441.90000	+	146.2 Hz	
	FM	NI4CE	442.55000	+	100.0 Hz	
	NXDN	NI4CE	444.42500	+		FASMA
Riviera Beach	FM	AK4JQ	146.88000	-	110.9 Hz	FASMA
	FM	KF4ACN	443.92500	+		FASMA
	FM	KF4ACN	927.52500	902.52500		FASMA
Rockledge	FM	W4NLX	146.88000	-	107.2 Hz	FASMA
	FM	K4GCC	146.94000	-	107.2 Hz	FASMA
	FM	K4EOC	147.13500	+	107.2 Hz	FASMA
	FM	K4EOC	444.52500	+	103.5 Hz	FASMA
Ross Prairie	FM	KI4LOB-R	147.36000	+		FASMA
Safety Harbor	DSTAR	KJ4ARB	1292.00000	1272.00000		FASMA
Saint Augustine	DMR/BM	N4AUG	442.87500	+	CC1	
Saint Lucie	DMR/MARC	K2DMR	440.75000	+	CC10	
Saint Petersburg	DMR/MARC	W4ILD	440.00000	+	CC0	
Samsula	FM	KB4GW	147.21000	+		
Sandalfoot Cove	FM	N4BRF	145.29000	-		FASMA
Sanford	DSTAR	W4PLB C	145.16000	-		
	DSTAR	W4PLB	145.16000	-		FASMA
	DSTAR	W4PLB	442.30000	+		
	DSTAR	W4PLB B	442.30000	+		
	DSTAR	KJ4NHF B	448.65000	+		
	DSTAR	KK4CQQ	1291.30000	1271.30000		
	FM	N4EH	146.80500	-	103.5 Hz	FASMA
	FUSION	KK4LTF	433.65000			
Sanibel Island	FM	W4SBL	146.79000	-	136.5 Hz	
Sarasota	FM	W4IE	146.91000	-	100.0 Hz	FASMA
	FM	N4SER	147.39000	+	100.0 Hz	FASMA
	FM	SAR-SAR	444.80000	+	100.0 Hz	
	FM	W4IE	444.92500	+	100.0 Hz	FASMA
	P25	NX4Y	444.80000	+		
Sebastain	DMR/BM	W4JEA	444.32500	+	CC1	
	DMR/BM	W4JEA	444.35000	+	CC1	

Location	Mode	Call sign	Output	Input	Access	Coordinator
Sebastian	DSTAR	W4OT C	145.27000	-		
	DSTAR	W4OT B	443.80000	+		
	FM	SAR-SEB	444.37500	+	107.2 Hz	
Sebring	DMR/BM	N8MI	433.80000	+	CC1	
	FM	W4HEM	147.27000	+	100.0 Hz	FASMA
	FUSION	KW4G	442.73750	+		
Seminole	FM	KA4CNP	444.40000	+	192.8 Hz	FASMA
Shell Point Village	FM	KN2R-R	146.61000	-		
Silver Springs	FUSION	KE8LTL	439.45000			
South Miami	FM	KF4LZA	927.75000	902.75000	94.8 Hz	
South Vero Beach	FM	AB4AZ	145.13000	-	107.2 Hz	FASMA
Southgate		WB9AYD-L	145.37000			
Southwest Ranches						
	DMR/BM	W4RCC	442.57500	+	CC7	
	FM	KK4GUB	145.52500		88.5 Hz	
Spring Hill	DMR/MARC	K2DLJ	442.76250	+	CC1	
	FM	KC4MTS	146.76000	-	123.0 Hz	FASMA
	FM	KF4IXU	146.80500	-		FASMA
St Augustine	DMR/BM	KE4LF	447.70000	-	CC13	
	FM	AB4EY	145.17000	-	107.2 Hz	FASMA
	FM	KX4EOC	145.21000	-	127.3 Hz	
	FM	KF4MX	146.62500	-		
	FM	KC5LPA	442.80000	+	127.3 Hz	FASMA
St Cloud	FM	KG4EOC	145.35000	-	103.5 Hz	
	FM	W4SIE	146.79000	-	103.5 Hz	
	FM	KG4EOC	444.10000	+	123.0 Hz	
St Petersburg	FM	KA9RIX	145.39000	-	141.3 Hz	
	FM	W4ORM	146.85000	-	146.2 Hz	
	FM	W4GAC	147.06000	+		
	FM	N4BSA	147.31500	+		FASMA
	FM	W4MRA	147.36000	+	127.3 Hz	FASMA
	FM	WA4AKH	224.66000	-		
	FM	AG4UU	442.25000	+	146.2 Hz	FASMA
	FM	W4ABC	443.92500	+		FASMA
	FM	N3FU	444.02500	+	146.2 Hz	
St. Augustine	DSTAR	W4SRT B	442.32500	+		
	DSTAR	W4SRT A	1293.40000	1273.40000		
	FM	SAR-STA	442.80000	+	127.3 Hz	
St. Petersburg	DMR/MARC	KN4GVY	443.97500	+	CC1	
	DMR/MARC	KN4GVY	444.62500	+	CC1	
	DMR/MARC	KJ4SHL	444.96250	+	CC1	FASMA
	IDAS	KJ4SHL	443.76250	+		
St.Petersburg	DMR/BM	W4ICY	442.75000	+	CC1	
Starke	DSTAR	KJ4RYI C	145.38000	+		
	FUSION	K4BAR	145.15000	-		
Stuart	DMR/BM	N4PSK	443.90000	+	CC1	
	DMR/BM	WX4MC	444.90000	+	CC7	
	DSTAR	KB4DD C	145.44000	-		
	FM	WX4MC	145.15000	-	107.2 Hz	
	FM	K4ZK	147.06000	+	107.2 Hz	
	FM	KA3COZ-SAR	144.15000	+	107.2 Hz	
	OpenDMR	KF4LZA	444.96250	+		
Summerfield	FM	K4HOG	147.03000	+	123.0 Hz	FASMA
Sumterville	FM	KS4EOC	146.92500	-	123.0 Hz	FASMA
Sun City Center	DMR/BM	WD1SCC	442.45000	+	CC5	
	DMR/BM	WA4EMN	446.04000	446.54000	CC6	
	DSTAR	W1SCC C	147.26250	+		
	DSTAR	W1SCC	147.26250	+		FASMA
	DSTAR	W1SCC	442.22500	447.32500		FASMA
	DSTAR	W1SCC B	442.22500	+		
	FM	KE4ZIP-R	147.22500	+		
	FM	W4KPR	440.10000	+	162.2 Hz	

Location	Mode	Call sign	Output	Input	Access	Coordinator
Sun City Center	FM	W4KPR	442.45000	+		FASMA
	FM	KE4ZIP	443.25000	+	146.2 Hz	
	P25	W4KPR	927.01250	902.01250	162.2 Hz	FASMA
Sunrise	DMR/BM	KK4ZMG	444.70000	+	CC7	
	FM	K4BRY	443.05000	+	110.9 Hz	FASMA
Sunset Beach	FM	W3YT-R	146.86500	-		
Tall	DMR/MARC	NX4DN	444.13750	+	CC1	
Tallahassee	DMR/BM	W4JMF	441.82500	+	CC1	
	DMR/MARC	NX4DN	443.13750	+	CC1	
	DSTAR	NF4DG C	146.83500	-		
	DSTAR	NF4DG B	443.45000	+		
	DSTAR	NF4DG D	1253.00000			
	DSTAR	NF4DG A	1293.00000	1273.00000		
	FM	K4TLH	29.66000	-	94.8 Hz	FASMA
	FM	N4PG	146.61000	-	203.5 Hz	
	FM	AE4S	146.65500	-	94.8 Hz	
	FM	K4TLH	146.91000	-	94.8 Hz	
	FM	K4TLH	147.03000	+	94.8 Hz	
	FM	KA4EOC	147.28500	+	94.8 Hz	FASMA
	FM	K4TLH-SAR	442.10000	+	94.8 Hz	FASMA
	FM	AE4S	443.95000	+	94.8 Hz	
	FM	KD4MOJ	444.00000	+	94.8 Hz	FASMA
	FM	N4NKV	444.40000	+	131.8 Hz	FASMA
	FM	K4TLH	444.80000	+		FASMA
	FUSION	WC2F	446.50000			
Tamarac	OpenDMR	KF4LZA	443.71250	+		
Tampa	DMR/MARC	W4CLL	145.41000	-	CC5	FASMA
	DMR/MARC	W4CLL	443.11250	+	CC1	
	DMR/MARC	KP4CJ	443.35000	+	CC1	
	DMR/MARC	W4CLL	443.77500	+	CC1	
	DSTAR	KJ4ARB	147.01000	+		FASMA
	DSTAR	KJ4ARB C	147.01000	+		
	DSTAR	KJ4ARB	443.98750	+		FASMA
	DSTAR	KJ4ARB B	444.67500	+		
	DSTAR	W4RNT B	444.81250	+		
	DSTAR	W4RNT	444.81250	+		FASMA
	DSTAR	KJ4ARB D	1253.00000			
	DSTAR	KJ4ARB A	1293.00000	1273.00000		
	FM	W4EFK	145.49000	-	88.5 Hz	FASMA
	FM	W4BCI	146.79000	-	146.2 Hz	
	FM	KC4LSQ	146.83500	-	131.8 Hz	FASMA
	FM	NI4M	146.94000	-	146.2 Hz	FASMA
	FM	W4AQR	147.00000	+	107.2 Hz	FASMA
	FM	N4TP	147.10500	+	146.2 Hz	FASMA
	FM	KD4HVC	147.24000	+	88.5 Hz	FASMA
	FM	KK4AFB	147.34500	+	146.2 Hz	FASMA
	FM	W9CR	224.28000	-	146.2 Hz	
	FM	W4RNT	224.74000	-		
	FM	W4RNT	442.72500	+	146.2 Hz	
	FM	NX4Y-SAR	442.85000	+		FASMA
	FM	N4TP	443.02500	+	146.2 Hz	FASMA
	FM	W4BCI	444.22500	+	146.2 Hz	FASMA
	FM	W4RNT	444.25000	+	146.2 Hz	
	FM	KB4ABE	444.52500	+	141.3 Hz	FASMA
	FM	W4EFK	444.60000	+	88.5 Hz	FASMA
	FM	W4AQR	444.67500	+	103.5 Hz	FASMA
	FM	N4TP	444.75000	+	146.2 Hz	FASMA
	FM	W4HSO	444.90000	+	141.3 Hz	FASMA
	FM	W9CR	927.05000	902.05000		
	FM	N1CDO	927.31250	902.31250	162.2 Hz	
	P25	N1CDO	440.10000	+		FASMA
	P25	WA6KDW	927.20000	902.20000		

Location	Mode	Call sign	Output	Input	Access	Coordinator
Tampa	FUSION	KP4PC	144.55000	+		
	FUSION	N4TP	145.57000			
	FUSION	KP4CJ	147.40000			
	FUSION	KP4PC	443.35000			
	FUSION	W4HSO	449.90000	-		
Tampa Airport	DMR/MARC	KJ4SHL	442.60000	+	CC1	FASMA
Tarpon Springs	FM	K4JMH	444.45000	+	146.2 Hz	FASMA
Tavares	DMR/MARC	K4LAK	444.61250	+	CC1	
	DSTAR	KK4KYK B	443.02500	+		
	DSTAR	KJ4TJD B	444.50000	+		
	FM	N4FLA	147.25500	+	103.5 Hz	FASMA
	FM	K4AUS	147.39000	+	103.5 Hz	FASMA
	FM	K4FC	442.90000	+	103.5 Hz	FASMA
Tavernier	OpenDMR	KF4LZA	442.21250	+		
The Villages		K4LFK-R	443.15000			
	FM	K4LFK	145.21000	-	110.9 Hz	FASMA
	FM	K4LFK	146.67000	-	103.5 Hz	
	FM	K4VRC	443.15000	+	103.5 Hz	
	FM	WA1UTQ	444.25000	+	110.9 Hz	FASMA
	FM	WA1UTQ	1292.15000	1272.15000	91.5 Hz	FASMA
	P25	WN4AMO	146.85000	-	103.5 Hz	FASMA
	FUSION	KZ4JON	144.97000			
	FUSION	WA1UTQ	146.94000	-		
	FUSION	WA1UTQ	444.57500	+		
Titusville	DMR/BM	KD4WLE	439.41250	+	CC1	
	DMR/BM	K4DJN	444.67500	+	CC3	FASMA
	DMR/MARC	K2JO	444.15000	+	CC1	
	FM	WN3DHI	145.49000	-		
	FM	KJ4VEH	145.60000		107.2 Hz	
	FM	K4KSC	146.97000	-	107.2 Hz	FASMA
	FM	K4EOC	147.07500	+	107.2 Hz	FASMA
	FM	K4NBR	147.33000	+	107.2 Hz	FASMA
	FM	N4TDX	147.36000	+	107.2 Hz	FASMA
	FM	N4TDX	444.75000	+	156.7 Hz	FASMA
	FM	N1KSC	444.92500	+	131.8 Hz	FASMA
	FM	KJ4VEH	445.60000	-	107.2 Hz	
	FUSION	N4TDX	442.85000	+		
Trenton	FM	N4TSV	921.20000	-		FASMA
Turkey Foot	FM	NX4Y	444.95000	+	100.0 Hz	
Valkaria	FM	K4HV	444.70000	+		FASMA
Valparaiso	FM	K4DTV	146.73000	-		FASMA
Valrico	DSTAR	NI4M C	145.19000	-		
	DSTAR	NI4M B	443.00000	+		
Venice	FM	N4SER	145.13000	-	100.0 Hz	FASMA
	FM	KB2WVY	442.05000	+	100.0 Hz	
Verna	FM	NI4CE	145.43000	-	100.0 Hz	FASMA
	FM	NI4CE	442.95000	+		FASMA
	FM	NI4CE	444.31250	+		FASMA
Vero Beach	DMR/BM	KB1YBB	442.60000	+	CC1	
	DMR/BM	W4CJA	444.40000	+	CC1	
	DSTAR	WA4TCD C	145.40000	-		
	DSTAR	WA4TCD B	444.87500	+		
	FM	W4IRC	145.31000	-	107.2 Hz	
	FM	W4PHJ	146.64000	-	107.2 Hz	FASMA
	FM	K4CPJ	444.72500	+	107.2 Hz	FASMA
	FM	KA4EPS	444.85000	+	107.2 Hz	FASMA
	FM	N4IRS	927.48750	902.48750	123.0 Hz	
	FUSION	AB4AZ	145.13000	-		
Villas		NG2F-L	443.05000			
Wacissa	FM	K4TLH	53.03000	52.03000	94.8 Hz	FASMA
	FM	K4TLH	147.00000	+	94.8 Hz	FASMA
Wakulla	FM	SAR-WAK	443.50000	+	94.8 Hz	

Location	Mode	Call sign	Output	Input	Access	Coordinator
Walsingham	FM	KO4CR-R	224.22000	-		
Wauchula	FM	N4EMH	146.62500	-	127.3 Hz	
Weeki Wachee	DSTAR	KK4ONE	445.44500	-		
	FM	KF4CIK	53.13000	52.13000	100.0 Hz	FASMA
	FM	KB4SYU	147.04500	+		FASMA
Welcome	DMR/MARC	W4VCO	443.81250	+	CC1	FASMA
Wellborn	FM	W1QBI	145.27000	-	123.0 Hz	FASMA
Wellington	DMR/BM	WX3C	443.32500	+	CC7	
	DMR/MARC	K4PKT	442.93750	+	CC1	
	FM	K4WRC	147.28500	+	103.5 Hz	FASMA
	FM	K4WRC	442.05000	+	103.5 Hz	
	FUSION	K4WRC	447.05000	-		
Wesley Chapel	DSTAR	W4SRT	1293.40000	1273.40000		
West Palm Beach	DMR/BM	W2WDW	444.07500	+	CC0	
	DMR/MARC	N4KYS	440.14500	+	CC2	
	DMR/MARC	W2GGI	444.91250	+	CC1	
	DSTAR	K4WPB	145.32000	-		FASMA
	FL-DMR	AC4XQ	443.63750	+		FASMA
	FM	KC4UDZ	53.21000	52.21000		
	FM	AK4JQ	145.39000	-	110.9 Hz	FASMA
	FM	WR4AKX	146.67000	-	110.9 Hz	FASMA
	FM	W4JUP	146.71500	-	110.9 Hz	FASMA
	FM	K4LJP	146.97000	-	162.2 Hz	
	FM	AK4JQ	147.36000	+	110.9 Hz	
	FM	KS4EC	442.90000	+	110.9 Hz	
	FM	KA4EPS	444.12500	+	107.2 Hz	
	OpenDMR	KF4LZA	444.87500	+		
	P25	W2WDW	927.01250	902.01250		
Westly Chapel	DMR/MARC	KN4GVY	444.77500	+	CC1	
Wewahitchka	FM	W4FFC	146.86500	-	100.0 Hz	FASMA
Wildwood	FM	WA1UTQ	224.98000	-	91.5 Hz	FASMA
	FM	K4VRC	443.22500	+	103.5 Hz	
	FUSION	WA1UTQ	146.94000	-	91.5 Hz	
Winter Haven	FUSION	W4JLQ	438.80000			
Winter Park	P25	W4MCO	442.52500	+	103.5 Hz	FASMA
	FUSION	N2QGV	434.31250	433.31250		
Winter Springs	FUSION	KN4JHG	147.17000			
Woodland Acres		KP4TR-R	446.30000			
Youngstown	FUSION	N4RJJ	447.30000			
Yulee	FM	KC5LPA	145.23000	-	127.3 Hz	FASMA
	FM	KC5LPA-SAR	442.90000	+	127.3 Hz	FASMA
Zephyrhills	FM	NI4M	145.19000	-	146.2 Hz	FASMA
	FM	W1PB	146.91000	-	146.2 Hz	FASMA
GEORGIA						
Acworth	FM	KC4YNF	441.80000	+	77.0 Hz	
	FUSION	AI4AK	444.62500	+		
	FUSION	AI4RJ	445.30000			
Adairsville	FM	WB4AEG	443.72500	+	167.9 Hz	
Albany	DSTAR	W4MM	144.96000	+		
	DSTAR	W4MM	440.70000	+		
	FM	W4MM	146.73000	-		
	FM	W4MM	146.82000	-	110.9 Hz	
	FM	W4MM	444.50000	+		
Allenhurst	FM	KF4ZUR	147.27000	+	162.2 Hz	
Alma	FM	KM4EYX	145.25000	-	141.3 Hz	
Alpharetta	FM	K9RFA	224.58000	-	100.0 Hz	
Americus	FM	W4VIR	147.27000	+	131.8 Hz	
Appling	FM	K4KNS	145.19000	-	71.9 Hz	SERA
	FM	K4KNS	442.90000	+	71.9 Hz	SERA
Ashburn	FM	N4OME	145.35000	-	141.3 Hz	SERA
Athens	DMR/BM	KZ4FOX	440.66250	+	CC5	

Location	Mode	Call sign	Output	Input	Access	Coordinator
Athens	DMR/BM	KZ4FOX	442.37500	+	CC2	
	DSTAR	KJ4PXY	144.98000	+		
	DSTAR	KJ4PXY C	144.98000	147.48000		
	DSTAR	KJ4PXY	440.63250	+		
	DSTAR	KJ4PXY B	440.63250	+		
	DSTAR	KJ4PXY D	1298.75000			
	FM	KD4QHB	146.74500	-	123.0 Hz	
	FM	KD4AOZ	146.95500	-	123.0 Hz	
	FM	K4TQU	147.37500	+	127.3 Hz	
	FUSION	KU4SD	146.53500			
Atlanta	DMR/BM	NI4Y	440.61250	+	CC1	
	DMR/BM	W4KIP	444.93750	+	CC1	
	DMR/BM	NI4Y	927.57500	902.57500	CC1	
	DMR/MARC	W4JEW	440.52500	+	CC3	
	DMR/MARC	W4JEW	440.92500	+	CC1	
	DMR/MARC	W7QO	442.45000	+	CC1	
	DMR/MARC	W7QO	443.02500	+	CC1	SERA
	DMR/MARC	W4KST	443.27500	+	CC7	
	DMR/MARC	W7QO	444.02500	+	CC1	
	DMR/MARC	KC6OVD	444.12500	+	CC0	
	DMR/MARC	K1DMR	444.43750	+	CC1	
	DMR/MARC	W4DOC	444.82500	+	CC10	SERA
	DSTAR	KJ4PYB C	145.06000	146.46000		
	DSTAR	W4DOC C	145.35000	-		
	DSTAR	W4DOC	145.35000	-		
	DSTAR	KJ4PYB B	440.56250	+		
	DSTAR	W4DOC B	440.60000	+		
	DSTAR	WX4ATL B	444.56700	+		
	DSTAR	WX4ATL	444.56700	+		
	DSTAR	W4DOC A	1282.60000	-		
	DSTAR	W4DOC	1282.60000	1262.60000		
	DSTAR	W4DOC D	1297.62500			
	FM	W4DOC	146.82000	-	146.2 Hz	
	FM	K4CLJ	146.97000	-	100.0 Hz	SERA
	FM	WA4GBT	147.03000	+		
	FM	N4NFP	224.12000	-	151.4 Hz	
	FM	N4MTA	224.32000	-	123.0 Hz	
	FM	W4DOC	224.34000	-	146.2 Hz	
	FM	N4NEQ	224.44000	-	151.4 Hz	
	FM	N4MTA	224.50000	-	123.0 Hz	
	FM	K4RFL	224.96000	-	100.0 Hz	
	FM	W4CML	442.02500	+	127.3 Hz	SERA
	FM	W4CML	443.65000	+	123.0 Hz	
	FM	N4NEQ	444.05000	+	151.4 Hz	
	FM	W4PME	444.15000	+	100.0 Hz	
	FM	N4NEQ	444.77500	+	151.4 Hz	
	FM	WA4NNO	444.92500	+		
	FM	K5TEX	927.11250	902.11250		
	FM	KD4GPI	927.51250	902.51250		
	FM	KB4KIN	1292.00000	1272.00000		
	FUSION	WB4HRO	442.15000	+		
	FUSION	KE5JWF	442.57500	+		
	FUSION	W4LRA	445.85000			
Atlanta, Buckhead	FM	WB4RTH	147.10500	+	110.9 Hz	SERA
Atlanta, Georgia Tech						
	FM	W4AQL	145.15000	-	167.9 Hz	SERA
Augusta	FM	K4KNS	53.03000	52.03000		
	FM	W4DV	145.11000	-	71.9 Hz	SERA
	FM	W4DV	145.29000	-	71.9 Hz	
	FM	W4QK	145.41000	-	71.9 Hz	
	FM	KT4N	146.94000	-	146.2 Hz	
	FM	W4DV	147.18000	+	71.9 Hz	

Location	Mode	Call sign	Output	Input	Access	Coordinator
Augusta	FM	K4KNS	444.67500	+	71.9 Hz	SERA
	FM	W4DV	444.95000	+	71.9 Hz	
Austell	FM	WA4YUR	442.82500	+		SERA
Bachlott	FM	N4RSW-L	146.46000			
Bainbridge	FM	W4DXX	443.00000	+	100.0 Hz	
Baldwin	FM	WD4NHW	147.18000	+		
	FM	WD4NHW	442.35000	+		SERA
Ball Ground	DMR/BM	KD4APP	442.48750	+	CC1	
Ballground	DSTAR	KJ4DWC A	1284.50000	-		
	DSTAR	KJ4DWC D	1298.50000			
Barnesville	FM	W8JI	147.22500	+	131.8 Hz	SERA
	FM	N4GWO	443.67500	+		
Baxley	DMR/MARC	KK4GXP	443.11250	+	CC1	
	FUSION	K4VD	144.60000			
Between	DMR/MARC	N4TAW	443.73750	+	CC3	
	FM	WC4RG	147.27000	+		SERA
Blackshear	FM	KI4LDE	145.37000	-	141.3 Hz	
Blacksville	FM	KI4FVI-R	146.71500	-		SERA
Blairsville	FM	KF4SKT	442.20000	+		
	FM	W6IZT	444.60000	-	100.0 Hz	
Blairsville, Rocky Top Mtn						
	FM	K5PRE	146.95500	-	100.0 Hz	
Blueridge	FM	KD4GRU	442.12500	+	146.2 Hz	
Bogart	FM	W4EEE	147.00000	+	85.4 Hz	
	FM	WW4GA	443.30000	+		
	FM	W4EEE	443.47500	+		
Bolingbroke	FM	WB4NFG	146.83500	-	77.0 Hz	
Boston	FM	W4UCJ	147.24000	+	141.3 Hz	
Braselton	DSTAR	WJ4FD B	440.58750	+		
	FM	WX4TC	146.62500	-	127.3 Hz	
Brent	FM	KJ4ZZF-L	146.50000			
Brewer (historical)	FM	KT4J-R	146.98500	-		
Broom Hall		AB4KN-L	435.00000			
Brunswick	DMR/BM	KG4PXG	442.20000	+	CC7	
	DSTAR	K3RCB B	440.56250	+		
Brunswick , Sidney Lanier Brid						
	FM	WX4BWK	145.33000	-	131.8 Hz	
Buckhead	FM	WB4RTH	444.97500	+	100.0 Hz	SERA
	FM	K5TEX	927.06250	902.06250	151.4 Hz	
Buford	DSTAR	KJ4BDF B	440.72500	+		
	FM	N4GJF	927.62500	902.62500		
Butler	FM	KC4TVY	145.31000	-		
Byron	FM	WX4PCH	145.29000	-	82.5 Hz	SERA
Calhoun	FM	K4WOC	146.74500	-	100.0 Hz	
Canton	DMR/BM	KO4PQJ	433.55000	434.15000	CC3	
	DMR/MARC	KD4KHO	434.40000	+	CC1	
	FM	WA4EOC	443.07500	+	107.2 Hz	SERA
	FUSION	N9NWS	434.25000			
Carnesville	DMR/BM	W4PFT	444.11250	+	CC1	
	FM	N4VNI	146.89500	-	100.0 Hz	
Carrollton	FM	W4FWD	146.64000	-	131.8 Hz	
	FM	WR4VR	442.77500	+	127.3 Hz	SERA
Cartersville, Pine Mt.						
	FM	W4CLM	443.17500	+	100.0 Hz	SERA
Cedar Grove	FM	WA4FRI	147.15000	+	123.0 Hz	
Cedar Grove, Biskey Mtn						
	FM	KC4JNN	53.05000	52.05000	100.0 Hz	
Cedartown	FM	W4CMA	147.12000	+		SERA
Chatsworth	FM	N4YYD	224.24000	-	71.9 Hz	
	FM	KJ4SPI	443.80000	+	141.3 Hz	
	FM	N4DMX	444.85000	+	141.3 Hz	
	FM	NS4U	927.61250	902.61250		SERA

Location	Mode	Call sign	Output	Input	Access	Coordinator
Chatsworth, Fort Mountain						
	FM	W4DRC	145.23000	-	141.3 Hz	
	FM	W4DRC	443.00000	+		
Chatsworth/Ft. Mtn						
	DSTAR	KJ4KLF C	145.08000	146.48000		
	DSTAR	KJ4KLF B	440.65000	+		
	DSTAR	KJ4KLF D	1299.50000			
Chickamauga	DMR/BM	K4KR	438.00000	+	CC1	
	DMR/BM	K4KR	448.00000	-	CC1	
Claxton	FM	W4CLA	147.07500	+	123.0 Hz	
Clayton	FM	N4TS	147.12000	+	67.0 Hz	
	FM	W1CP	442.82500	+	162.2 Hz	
Clayton, Rainey Mountain						
	FM	KK4BSA	444.50000	+		
Clermont	DMR/MARC	KA3JIJ	444.81250	+	CC0	
Cleveland	DSTAR	K4GAR	440.51250	+		
	DSTAR	K4GAR B	440.51250	+		
	DSTAR	K4GAR D	1299.00000			
	FM	K4GAR-R	146.91000	-		
	FM	K4VJM	442.62500	+	100.0 Hz	
Cleveland, Long Mountain						
	FM	K4GAR	443.55000	+		
Cochran	DMR/MARC	KE4PMP	440.65000	+	CC1	
	FM	W4MAZ	53.01000	52.01000	77.0 Hz	
Colbert	FM	N4ALE	147.30000	+	123.0 Hz	
College Park	DMR/MARC	KK4EQB	442.92500	+	CC4	
Columbus	FM	KB9LFZ	145.65000		127.3 Hz	
	FM	WX4RUS	146.74500	-	123.0 Hz	
	FM	W4CVY	146.88000	-	123.0 Hz	
	FM	W4CVY	442.10000	+	123.0 Hz	
	FM	W4CVY	442.20000	+		
	FM	KB9LFZ	443.20000	+	127.3 Hz	
Commerce	FUSION	W4CMB	443.20000	+		
Concord	DMR/MARC	WB4GWA	442.31250	+	CC1	
	FM	WB4GWA	145.25000	-	110.9 Hz	
	FM	WB4GWA	224.46000	-	110.9 Hz	
	FM	WB4GWA	443.40000	+	110.9 Hz	
Conley	FM	N4MNA	53.65000	52.65000	100.0 Hz	
	FM	N4MNA	224.28000	-		
Conyers	FM	WB4JEH	51.55000	50.55000	151.4 Hz	
	FM	WB4JEH	53.55000	52.55000	151.4 Hz	
	FM	K1KC	146.61000	-	103.5 Hz	SERA
	FM	KF4GHF	147.21000	+	162.2 Hz	
	FM	WB4JEH	442.55000	+	151.4 Hz	
	FM	WX4RCA	444.30000	+	131.8 Hz	
	FM	K1KC	444.55000	+	103.5 Hz	SERA
	FM	KC4ELV	444.75000	+	162.2 Hz	
	FM	WX4RCA	449.30000	-	131.8 Hz	SERA
	FUSION	K4SID	145.75000			
	FUSION	K1KC/R	146.61000	-		
	FUSION	K1KC	446.07500			
Cornelia	FM	WB4VAK	444.27500	+	100.0 Hz	
Country Ridge		KI4RDO-L	147.53500			
Covington	DMR/BM	WA4ASI	146.92500	-	CC2	
	DMR/BM	WA4ASI	444.80000	+	CC2	SERA
	FM	WA4ASI	443.35000	+	88.5 Hz	SERA
Crawford	FM	KD4FVI	53.33000	52.33000	88.5 Hz	
Cumming	DMR/MARC	W4OO	440.52500	+	CC1	
	DMR/MARC	W9SH	444.12500	+	CC2	
	DMR/MARC	W4CBA	444.62500	+	CC1	
	DSTAR	KI4SBA C	145.20000	-		
	DSTAR	KI4SBA B	444.35000	+		

Location	Mode	Call sign	Output	Input	Access	Coordinator
Cumming	DSTAR	KI4SBA D	1250.00000			
	DSTAR	KI4SBA A	1284.40000	-		
	FUSION	AA4PW	145.05000			
Cumming, Sawnee Mountain						
	FM	WB4GQX	147.15000	+	141.3 Hz	SERA
	FM	WB4GQX	441.90000	+	141.3 Hz	SERA
Dacula	DMR/BM	KN4OAJ	443.92500	+	CC5	SERA
	FUSION	W4OG	146.42500			
	FUSION	K8LIN	433.80000			
	FUSION	KD4YDD	444.52500	+		
Dahlonega	FM	N4KHQ-R	146.83500	+	100.0 Hz	SERA
	FUSION	K4BS	431.13750			
Dahlonega, Black Mountain						
	FM	N4KHQ	443.10000	ı	100.0 Hz	
Dahlonega, High House						
	FM	N4KHQ	224.48000	-	100.0 Hz	
Dallas	DMR/BM	K4CGA	442.67500	+	CC1	
	DMR/MARC	KJ4KKB	442.95000	+	CC3	
	DMR/MARC	KJ4KKB	443.80000	+	CC3	
	DSTAR	WX4PCA C	145.34900	-		
	DSTAR	WX4PCA B	440.57500	+		
	FM	N4YDX	224.18000	-	71.9 Hz	
	FM	N4YEA	224.54000	-		
	FUSION	W4UEM	147.54000			
Dalton	DSTAR	KA4RVT C	145.33000	-		
	DSTAR	KA4RVT B	444.50000	+		
	FM	N4BZJ	147.13500	+	141.3 Hz	
	FM	N4BZJ	224.46000	-	141.3 Hz	
	FM	N4BZJ	224.68000	-	141.3 Hz	
	FM	N4KVC	224.74000	-	141.3 Hz	
	FUSION	WI4L	448.00000	-		
Dalton, Dug Gap Mountain						
	DSTAR	KA4RVT	145.33000	-		
	DSTAR	KA4RVT	444.50000	+		
Decatur	DMR/BM	N4MPC	440.77500	+	CC1	
	DMR/BM	N4MPC	444.90000	+	CC1	
Decatur, Exchange Park						
	FM	W4BOC	145.45000	-	107.2 Hz	
	FM	W4BOC	224.76000	-		
	FM	W4BOC	444.25000	+	131.8 Hz	SERA
Devereux	DMR/BM	KC4YAP	444.05000	+	CC4	
Doerun	FM	KG4ABK	147.22500	+		
Don (historical)	FM	WB4QOJ-R	146.95500	-		SERA
Doraville	DSTAR	WB4HRO	440.71250	+		
	FM	WB4HRO	1284.45000	1264.45000		
Doraville (Atlanta)	DSTAR	WB4HRO B	440.71250	+		
	DSTAR	WB4HRO A	1284.45000	-		
	DSTAR	WB4HRO D	1297.87500			
Douglas	DMR/MARC	KM4EYX	443.13750	+	CC3	
	FM	KE4ZRT	147.04500	+	141.3 Hz	
	FM	W4JSF	147.16500	+	141.3 Hz	SERA
	FM	AD4EQ	147.31500	+	141.3 Hz	
	FM	KE4ZRT	443.00000	+	141.3 Hz	
Douglasville	FM	K4NRC	145.11000	-	88.5 Hz	SERA
Dover Bluff	FM	KG4PXG	53.11000	52.11000	100.0 Hz	
Dry Branch	FM	KC4TVY	444.65000	+	77.0 Hz	
Dublin	DMR/BM	KD4IEZ	147.33000	+	CC1	
	DMR/MARC	KD4IEZ	444.78750	+	CC1	
	DSTAR	KJ4PYD C	145.04000	146.24000		
	DSTAR	KJ4YNR	145.18000	-		
	DSTAR	KJ4YNR C	145.18000	-		
	DSTAR	KJ4YNR B	440.52500	+		

Location	Mode	Call sign	Output	Input	Access	Coordinator
Dublin	DSTAR	KJ4PYD B	444.48750	+		
	DSTAR	KJ4YNR A	1282.85000	-		
	DSTAR	KJ4YNR D	1299.50000			
Eastman	FM	KC4YNB	145.21000	-	103.5 Hz	
	FM	KB4MQ	444.85000	+		
Eatonton	DMR/BM	K4EGA	444.42500	+	CC1	
	FM	NZ2X	53.19000	52.19000	156.7 Hz	
	FM	K4EGA	146.65500	-	186.2 Hz	
	FM	K4PAR	443.17500	+	186.2 Hz	
Eden	FM	K4VYX	145.19000	-		
Elberton	FM	KI4CCZ	145.21000	-	118.8 Hz	SERA
	FM	KI4CCZ	444.70000	+	118.8 Hz	SERA
Ellerslie	DMR/BM	WB4ULK	444.61250	+	CC1	
	FM	WB4ULJ	224.66000	-	110.9 Hz	
Ellijay	DSTAR	W4HHH B	443.98750	+		
	FM	W4HHH-R	145.17000	-	100.0 Hz	SERA
	FM	KC4ZGN	146.98500	-	77.0 Hz	SERA
	FM	KC4ZGN	442.70000	+	77.0 Hz	SERA
Ellijay, Coosawattee River Res						
	DSTAR	W4HHH	443.98750	+		SERA
Emerson	FM	N4RSW	443.30000	+		
	FM	AE4JO	443.42500	+	103.5 Hz	
Emerson, Lake Point						
	FM	N4RSW	446.17500	-		
Evans	FM	K4KNS	146.98500	-	71.9 Hz	
	FM	W4QK	444.90000	+	71.9 Hz	
	FUSION	KB3ZAX	446.77500			
Fairmount	FM	AB4LZ	146.68500	-	167.9 Hz	
Fayetteville	DMR/BM	W0WHS	442.50000	+	CC1	
	DMR/BM	KN4RQL	446.00000		CC15	
	DSTAR	KK4GQ	442.56200	+		
	DSTAR	KK4GQ B	442.56250	+		
	DSTAR	KK4GQ	444.43750	+		
	FM	KK4GQ	145.21000	-	131.8 Hz	
	FM	KK4GQ	146.68500	-	131.8 Hz	
	FM	AG4ZR	224.56000	-	131.8 Hz	
	FM	W4PSZ	444.60000	+	77.0 Hz	
Folkston	DMR/BM	AB4KK	436.00000	+	CC1	
	DMR/BM	AB4KK	442.10000	+	CC1	
	DMR/BM	AB4KK	444.00000	+	CC1	
	FM	AB4KK	146.79000	-	141.3 Hz	
Forsyth	DMR/BM	KK4JPG	444.97500	+	CC1	
	DSTAR	KK4JPG	146.48000	145.08000		
	FM	KK4JPG	449.75000	-	100.0 Hz	
Free Home	DMR/BM	N5FL	428.97500	-	CC1	
	DMR/BM	K5TEX	927.95050	902.95050	CC1	
Gainesville	DMR/BM	KA3JIJ	145.31000	-	CC1	SERA
	DMR/MARC	KA3JIJ	444.95000	+	CC1	SERA
	DSTAR	KJ4ZLL C	145.12000	-		
	DSTAR	KJ4ZLL B	441.86250	+		
	FM	AA4BA	145.08000	146.48000		
	FUSION	KJ4LY	145.52500			
	FUSION	KJ4LY	441.82500	+		
Gainesville, Wauka Mountain						
	FM	W4ABP	146.67000	-	131.8 Hz	SERA
Gray	FM	WB4JOE	145.37000	-	88.5 Hz	
	FM	N5BI	443.70000	+	100.0 Hz	SERA
Gray, Round Oak	FM	WB4JOE	145.37000	-	88.5 Hz	
Grayson	FM	W4GR	224.58000	-	100.0 Hz	
Graysville	FM	N4YAV	444.52500	+	131.8 Hz	
Greensboro	FM	K4EGA	147.09000	+	186.2 Hz	
Griffin	DSTAR	W4AMI C	145.48000	-		

Location	Mode	Call sign	Output	Input	Access	Coordinator
Griffin	FM	WB4GWA	145.39000	-	110.9 Hz	
	FM	W4AMI	145.48000	-		
	FM	K4HYB	146.91000	-	88.5 Hz	
	FM	NQ4AE	443.55000	+		SERA
Guyton	DMR/MARC	K4VYX	442.35000	+	CC8	
	FM	W4ECA	146.74500	-	97.4 Hz	
Hahira	DMR/BM	WP3NIS	147.97500	-	CC1	
Hannah's Mill	FM	K4NRC	147.36000	+	88.5 Hz	SERA
Hannahsb Mill	FM	W4OHH-R	147.39000	+		
Hawkinsville	FM	WR4MG	224.82000	-	107.2 Hz	
Helen	FM	K4PE	444.42500	+	127.3 Hz	
Hiawassee, Bell Mtn						
	FM	KI4ENN	146.86500	+	151.4 Hz	
High Point	FM	KB4VAK	443.45000	+	77.0 Hz	
Hinesville	DSTAR	KG4OGC	444.85000	+		
	FM	KG4OGC	147.01500	+		
Hiram	FM	W4TIY	224.70000	-	100.0 Hz	
Howardville	FM	W4CLM-R	147.24000	+		
Irwington	FM	WB4NFG	443.27500	+	77.0 Hz	SERA
Irwinton	FM	WB4NFG	147.24000	+	77.0 Hz	
	FM	WB4NFG	444.92500	+	77.0 Hz	
Jackson	FM	WX4BCA	147.28500	+	131.8 Hz	
	FM	WX4BCA	443.32500	+	131.8 Hz	
Jasper	DMR/MARC	N8WHG	145.37000	-	CC3	
	DMR/MARC	N8WHG	444.37500	+	CC3	
	DSTAR	KJ4PYC	145.08000	146.48000		
	DSTAR	KJ4PYC C	145.08000	146.48000		
	DSTAR	KJ4PYC	440.66250	+		
	FM	KB4IZF	145.37000	-	103.5 Hz	
	FM	K4UFO	146.70000	-	123.0 Hz	
	FM	KC4AQS	224.40000	-	100.0 Hz	
	FM	KC4AQS	224.60000	-	100.0 Hz	SERA
	FM	KC4AQS	443.37500	+	100.0 Hz	
	FM	KB4IZF	444.37500	+		
Jasper, Biskey Mountain						
	FM	KC4JNN	224.16000	-	100.0 Hz	SERA
	FM	KC4AQS	443.50000	+	100.0 Hz	
Jasper, Burnt Mountain						
	FM	W4RRG	224.98000	-		
Jasper, Little Hendricks Mount						
	FM	N3DAB	147.19500	+	77.0 Hz	
Jasper, Mount Oglethorpe						
	P25	K4SJR	441.67500	+	100.0 Hz	SERA
	P25	W3CP	927.02500	902.02500		SERA
Jasper, Mt. Oglethorpe						
	FM	KC4AQS	146.80500	+	100.0 Hz	
Jasper, Sassafras Mtn						
	FM	KB3KHP	443.95000	+	131.8 Hz	
Jersey	DSTAR	WC4RG C	145.30000	-		
	DSTAR	WC4RG B	443.00000	+		
Jesup		KD4GGY-L	147.57000			
	DMR/BM	AB4KK	438.80000		CC3	
	DMR/BM	AB4KK	439.00000	+	CC1	
	DMR/MARC	KD4GGY	440.92500		CC1	
	DMR/MARC	KD4GGY	441.81250	+	CC1	
	FM	N4ZON	146.86500	-	141.3 Hz	
	FM	N4PJR	146.92500	-	141.3 Hz	
	FM	KE4ZFR	441.67500	+	131.8 Hz	
	FM	N4PJR	444.92500	+	141.3 Hz	
Kathleen	DMR/BM	WY4EMA	440.57500	+	CC1	
	DMR/BM	AF1G	443.51250	+	CC3	
Kingsland	DMR/BM	N9USN	442.85000	+	CC3	

Location	Mode	Call sign	Output	Input	Access	Coordinator
Kingsland	DMR/MARC	K4QHR	442.11250	+	CC7	
	DMR/MARC	W1KFR	444.62500	+	CC3	SERA
	DMR/MARC	W1KFR	444.83750	+	CC7	
	DSTAR	KN4EMQ C	146.88000	-		
	FM	W4ULB	146.50000			
	FM	W4NAS	146.83500	-	127.3 Hz	
	FM	K4QHR	146.89500	-	127.3 Hz	SERA
	FM	N6EMA	147.19500	+	118.8 Hz	SERA
Kingston	FM	AF4PX	444.12500	+		
Knotts Landing	FM	NF4GA-R	145.47000	-	100.0 Hz	
Lagrange	DMR/BM	AB4KE	146.70000	453.30000	CC1	
	DMR/BM	WB4BXO	147.33000	747.33000	CC1	
	DMR/BM	WB4BXO	440.51250	+	CC1	
	DSTAR	KJ4PJE D	1252.60000			
	DSTAR	KJ4PJE A	1285.00000	1305.00000		
Lake Park	FM	WR4SG	147.13500	+	141.3 Hz	
Lakemont	FM	W4WCR	443.15000	+	127.3 Hz	
	FM	N4ZRF	444.75000	+		
Lavonia	FM	K4NVG	146.71500	-	100.0 Hz	
	FM	K4NVG	442.47500	+	203.5 Hz	
	FM	N4VNI	443.20000	+	151.4 Hz	SERA
Lawrenceville		K4GTA-R	147.07500			
	DMR/BM	AI1U	442.70000	+	CC1	
	DMR/BM	N5JMD	442.90000	+	CC1	
	DMR/MARC	AI1U	442.53750	+	CC7	
	DSTAR	WD4STR	145.06000	+		
	DSTAR	WD4STR	440.55000	+		
	DSTAR	WD4STR	1282.55000	1262.55000		
	FM	WB4HJG	442.85000	+	82.5 Hz	
	FM	K4HQV	444.20000	+	100.0 Hz	
Lawrenceville, Georgia Gwinnet						
	FM	W4GGC	442.22500	447.32500		
Lilburn	FUSION	W4MAA	144.00000			
Loganville	FUSION	WC4FM	145.55500			
	FUSION	WC4FM	146.57000			
	FUSION	WC4FM	433.80000			
	FUSION	WC4FM	442.07500	+		
Lookout Mountain	DMR/BM	N4LMC	441.87500		CC1	
	DMR/BM	N4LMC	442.72500	+	CC1	
	DMR/BM	N4LMC	444.71250	+	CC1	
	DMR/MARC	N4LMC	145.35000		CC1	
	DMR/MARC	KO4GVX	441.87500	+	CC1	
	DMR/MARC	N4LMC	442.65000		CC1	
	FUSION	W4EDP	432.20000			
	FUSION	N4LMC	442.65000	+		
	FUSION	N4LMC	442.72500	+		
Lookout Mountain, Lookout Moun						
	FM	W4GTA	145.35000	-	100.0 Hz	SERA
Lookout Mountain, Lookout Mt						
	FM	N4LMC	224.56000	-	146.2 Hz	SERA
Mableton	FM	W4JLG	442.32500	+		
Macon	DMR/MARC	WX4EMA	443.07500	+	CC7	
	DSTAR	WX4EMA	145.34000	-		
	DSTAR	WX4EMA C	145.34000	-		
	DSTAR	WX4EMA B	440.62500	+		
	DSTAR	WX4EMA D	1297.37500			
	FM	AA4RI	145.43000	-	88.5 Hz	
	FM	WA4DDI	146.77500	-		
	FM	K4PDQ	146.80500	-	77.0 Hz	SERA
	FM	KD4UTQ	146.89500	-	88.5 Hz	
	FM	WX4EMA	147.01500	+	88.5 Hz	SERA
	FM	WA4DDI	147.06000	+	141.3 Hz	

Location	Mode	Call sign	Output	Input	Access	Coordinator
Macon	FM	WA4DDI	224.64000	-	88.5 Hz	
	FM	WA4DDI	442.27500	+	123.0 Hz	
	FM	W4OCL	444.27500	+	123.0 Hz	
	FM	WA4DDI	444.70000	+	103.5 Hz	
Macon, Round Oak						
	FM	AA4RI	53.43000	52.43000	88.5 Hz	SERA
Madison	FM	WB4DKY	146.86500	-	179.9 Hz	
	FM	WR4MC	443.75000	+	118.8 Hz	
Madras / Newnan	FM	K4NRC	147.16500	+	131.8 Hz	SERA
	FM	K4NRC	442.25000	+		SERA
Mansfield, White Pine Ln						
	FM	K4IO	145.23000	-	151.4 Hz	SERA
Maretts		KM4CBA-L	147.57000			
Marietta	DMR/BM	W4KIP	146.73000	-	CC1	
	DMR/BM	N4IRR	441.37500	+	CC1	
	DMR/BM	W4KIP	444.77500	+	CC1	
	DMR/MARC	KD4Z	442.97500	+	CC1	SERA
	DMR/MARC	N4IRR	927.70000	902.70000	CC1	
	DSTAR	W4BTI B	440.68750	+		
	DSTAR	W4BTI D	1298.50000			
	FM	WC4RAV	147.53500	146.63500	103.5 Hz	SERA
	FM	KE4QFG	224.26000	-	110.9 Hz	
	FM	WK4E	442.42500	+	107.2 Hz	
	FM	WC4RAV	443.45000	+	103.5 Hz	SERA
	FUSION	K8MDM	443.21250			
Marietta, Sweat Mountain						
	DSTAR	W4BTI	440.68750	+		
	FM	W4BTI	146.88000	-		
Marietta, Sweat Mtn						
	FM	W4PME	224.62000	-	100.0 Hz	SERA
Martinez	FM	WE4GW	441.90000	+	123.0 Hz	
McDonough	DMR/BM	WX4BCA	443.32500	+	CC1	
	DMR/BM	KE4UAS	444.87500	+	CC1	SERA
	FM	W4NOC	927.13750	902.13750	103.5 Hz	SERA
	FUSION	KN4FRK	146.55000			
McIntyre	FM	KC4TVY	53.73000	52.73000	77.0 Hz	
Metcalf	DMR/MARC	NX4DN	444.13750	+	CC1	
	FM	W4UCJ	147.19500	+	141.3 Hz	
Midland	FM	WB4ULK	224.44000	-		SERA
	FM	KM4OKU	442.00000	+	88.5 Hz	
Milledgeville	FM	W4PCF	146.70000	-	67.0 Hz	SERA
	FM	W4PCF	147.13500	+	123.0 Hz	SERA
Milton	FM	K5TEX	927.65000	902.65000		
Monroe	FM	WC4RG	442.05000	+	88.5 Hz	
	FUSION	K4HQV	447.07500	-		
Montezuma	FM	KI4BEO	146.64000	-	97.4 Hz	
Morganton	DSTAR	KM4MAD C	145.40000	-		
Morganton, Brawley Mountain						
	DSTAR	KM4MAD	145.40000	-		
Morganton, Brawley Mtn						
	FM	W4HBS	443.22500	+	100.0 Hz	
Moultrie	DMR/BM	K4KV	444.50000	+	CC1	
	FM	WD4KOW	146.79000	-	141.3 Hz	
	FM	N4JMD	443.32500	+	114.8 Hz	
	FM	N4JMD	927.01250	902.01250	100.0 Hz	SERA
Mt Zion	DSTAR	WX4LDS C	145.40000	+		
Murrayville	FUSION	KS4GD	145.56250			
Newnan	DMR/MARC	WX4SKY	442.25000	+	CC1	
	FM	K4NRC	145.13000	-	156.7 Hz	SERA
	FUSION	WA4TAW	145.56250			
Nicholls	DMR/BM	W4JSF	444.41250	+	CC3	
NOAA Americus	WX	WXJ30	162.42500			

Location	Mode	Call sign	Output	Input	Access	Coordinator
NOAA Ashburn	WX	KWN50	162.45000			
NOAA Athens	WX	WXK56	162.40000			
NOAA Atlanta	WX	KEC80	162.55000			
NOAA Augusta	WX	WXK54	162.55000			
NOAA Baxley	WX	WXM65	162.52500			
NOAA Blakely	WX	KZZ70	162.52500			
NOAA Blue Ridge	WX	KXI75	162.47500			
NOAA Brasstown Bald						
	WX	KXI22	162.50000			
NOAA Brunswick	WX	WWH39	162.42500			
NOAA Buchanan	WX	WWH23	162.42500			
NOAA Chatsworth						
	WX	WXK52	162.40000			
NOAA Clayton	WX	KXI81	162.45000			
NOAA Cleveland	WX	WXJ53	162.52500			
NOAA Eastman	WX	KXI77	162.40000			
NOAA Eatonton	WX	KXI89	162.52500			
NOAA Jesup	WX	WXJ28	162.45000			
NOAA La Grange	WX	KXI76	162.45000			
NOAA Macon	WX	WXK71	162.47500			
NOAA Metter	WX	WWH25	162.42500			
NOAA Pelham	WX	WXK53	162.55000			
NOAA Sandersville						
	WX	KXI28	162.45000			
NOAA Summerville						
	WX	WXJ72	162.45000			
NOAA Thomaston	WX	WXJ31	162.50000			
NOAA Toccoa	WX	WWH24	162.42500			
NOAA Valdosta	WX	WWH31	162.50000			
NOAA Washington						
	WX	KPS506	162.50000			
NOAA Waycross	WX	WXK75	162.47500			
NOAA Waynesboro						
	WX	WXM88	162.42500			
Norcross	FM	W4GR	442.10000	+	100.0 Hz	SERA
Oak Bluff	FM	KG4PXG-R	146.68500	-		
Ola	FM	K1KC	444.55000	+	103.5 Hz	
Omaha	FM	KI4VDP	443.72500	+	77.0 Hz	
Parrot	DMR/MARC	KE4PMP	444.48750	+	CC1	
Parrott	FM	WG4JOE	147.36000	+	173.8 Hz	
Peach County	DSTAR	KG4BMS B	443.35000	+		
Peachtree City	FM	W4PSZ	442.50000	+	77.0 Hz	
Pelham	DMR/MARC	KE4PMP	441.81250	+	CC1	
Pembroke	DSTAR	KJ4GGV	145.28000	-		SERA
	DSTAR	KJ4GGV C	145.28000	-		
	DSTAR	KJ4GGV	440.70000	+		SERA
	DSTAR	KJ4GGV B	440.70000	+		
	DSTAR	KJ4GGV	1282.70000	1302.70000		SERA
	DSTAR	KJ4GGV A	1282.70000	-		
	DSTAR	KJ4GGV D	1298.50000			
	FM	KF4DG	147.10500	+		SERA
Perry	FM	WR4MG	146.95500	-	107.2 Hz	SERA
Pine Mountain	DSTAR	KJ4KLE	144.92000	147.42000		
	FM	WB4ULJ	145.19000	-	110.9 Hz	
Powder Springs	DMR/MARC	N8WHG	440.80000	+	CC3	
Pyne	FM	WB4BXO-R	224.72000	-		
Quitman	FM	WA4NKL	146.88000	-		
	FM	WA4NKL	444.60000	+	141.3 Hz	
Ray City	FM	WR4SG	224.22000	-	141.3 Hz	
Reno	FM	KE4URL	145.17000	-	141.3 Hz	
Riceboro	FM	KG4OGC	145.47000	-		
Ringgold	FM	W4ABZ	146.71500	-	67.0 Hz	

Location	Mode	Call sign	Output	Input	Access	Coordinator
Ringgold	FM	KK4LPW	442.35000	+		SERA
	FM	W4BAB	443.92500	+		
River Ridge	FM	W4VO-R	146.94000	-		
Riverdale	FUSION	WA4GBT	147.03000	+		
	FUSION	WA4GBT	147.19500	+		
	FUSION	WA4GBT	442.57500	+		
Rockmart	FM	WX4PCA	443.47500	+	77.0 Hz	SERA
Rome	DMR/BM	WA4OKJ	442.23750	+	CC1	
	DSTAR	W4VO C	145.38000	-		
	DSTAR	W4VO B	440.62500	+		
	FM	WA4OKJ	146.92500	146.34000	88.5 Hz	
	FM	N4EBY	147.30000	+	100.0 Hz	
	FM	WB4LRA	224.64000	-	141.3 Hz	
	FM	W4VO	441.92500	+		
	FUSION	WA4OKJ	147.39000	+		
	FUSION	W4VO	441.92500	+		
Rome, Mt. Alto	DSTAR	W4VO	145.38000	-		
	DSTAR	W4VO	440.62500	+		SERA
	FM	WA4OKJ	443.20000	+	100.0 Hz	
Roswell	FM	NF4GA	147.06000	+	100.0 Hz	SERA
	FM	W4PME	443.15000	+	100.0 Hz	
	FUSION	K5TXS	145.70000			
Sandersville	DSTAR	W4SAN C	145.32000	-		
	FM	K4GK	145.27000	-	77.0 Hz	
Sandy Springs	DMR/MARC	KE4OKD	441.95000	+	CC0	SERA
Sardis Estates	FM	W4GR-R	147.07500	+	82.5 Hz	SERA
Savannah	DMR/MARC	K4VYX	442.81250	+	CC3	
	DSTAR	KK4SGC C	144.94000	147.44000		
	DSTAR	KK4SGC B	440.58750	+		
	DSTAR	KK4SGC A	1282.74000	-		
	DSTAR	KK4SGC D	1298.00000			
	FM	K3SRC	146.85000	-	100.0 Hz	
	FM	W4HBB	146.97000	-	123.0 Hz	
	FM	W4LHS	147.21000	+		
	FM	W4LHS	147.33000	+	203.5 Hz	
	FM	W4LHS-R	442.70000	+		
	FM	WD4AFY	444.00000	+		
Sawnee Mountain	DMR/MARC	NG4RF	442.11250	+	CC1	
Sharpsburg	FM	AG4ZR	29.64000	-	146.2 Hz	
Snellville	DMR/MARC	W8RED	442.60000	+	CC3	
	FM	W4GR	147.25500	+	107.2 Hz	
	FM	W4CSX	224.92000	-	100.0 Hz	
	FM	W4GR	444.52500	+	82.5 Hz	
Snellville, Lanier Mountain						
	FM	W4CML	444.02500	+	127.3 Hz	
Sparta	DMR/BM	KC4YAP	147.19500	+	CC4	
Split Silk	FM	KD4HLV	444.10000	+	77.0 Hz	
St Simons Isl	DMR/BM	K8GI	443.06250	+	CC10	
Statesboro	FM	KF4DG	147.39000	+	100.0 Hz	
Statham	DMR/BM	W4EEE	147.00000	-	CC0	
	FM	W4EEE/R	449.95000			
	FUSION	W4EEE/R	147.44000			
Statham, Hwy 53/Hebron Church						
	FM	WW4T	442.30000	-		
Stockbridge	DMR/MARC	KJ4KPX	443.22500	+	CC1	
	FUSION	NX1Q	145.56250			
Stockbridge, Piedmont Henry Ho						
	FM	KJ4KPY	443.22500	+	146.2 Hz	SERA
Stockbridge, Piedmont Henry Me						
	FM	KJ4KPY	145.17000	-	146.2 Hz	SERA
Stone Mountain	DMR/MARC	W4BOC	441.81250	+	CC1	
	DSTAR	WX4GPB C	144.96000	147.46000		

Location	Mode	Call sign	Output	Input	Access	Coordinator
Stone Mountain	DSTAR	WX4GPB B	440.70000	+		
	DSTAR	WX4GPB A	1282.70000	-		
	DSTAR	WX4GPB D	1297.12500			
	FM	W4BOC-R	146.76000	-	107.2 Hz	
	FM	KG4LMT	927.71250	902.71250		
Stone Mountain, Stone Mountain						
	DSTAR	WX4GPB	145.35000	-		
	DSTAR	WX4GPB	440.60000	+		
Sugar Hill	FM	KI4UNI	146.59500			
Summerville	FM	K4PS	53.75000	52.75000	127.3 Hz	
	FM	W4RLP	147.22500	+	100.0 Hz	
Sumner	FM	W4PVW	147.28500	+	141.3 Hz	SERA
	FM	W4CCS	444.90000	+	141.3 Hz	
Swainsboro	FM	K4VYX	146.79000	-		
Sycamore	FM	KF4BI	444.92500	+	141.3 Hz	
Sylvania	FUSION	KG4ERR	442.40000	+		
Thomaston	FM	W4OHH	444.45000	+	131.8 Hz	
	FUSION	KT4YP	436.05000			
	FUSION	KT4YP	444.45000	+		
Thomasville	DSTAR	KJ4PYB	440.65000	+		
	DSTAR	KJ4PYB	1248.75000	1268.75000		
	FM	W4UCJ	145.37000	-	141.3 Hz	SERA
	FM	W4UCJ	147.06000	+		
	FM	WR4SG	224.32000	-	141.3 Hz	
	FM	W4UCJ	442.60000	+	141.3 Hz	SERA
Tifton	DMR/MARC	KE4RJI	444.87500	+	CC1	
	DSTAR	W4PVW	145.12000	-		SERA
	DSTAR	W4PVW C	145.12000	-		
	DSTAR	W4PVW B	444.56250	+		
	DSTAR	W4PVW	1282.65000	1262.65000		SERA
	DSTAR	W4PVW A	1282.65000	-		
	DSTAR	W4PVW D	1299.00000			
	FM	W4PVW	444.56250	+		
Toccoa	FM	K4TRS	145.25000	-	71.9 Hz	
	FM	KR4CW	147.33000	+	127.3 Hz	
	FM	W4BNG	442.50000	+	88.5 Hz	
Trenton	FM	K4SOD	146.76000	-		SERA
	FM	K4GC	441.85000	+		
Twin City	DMR/MARC	N4SFU	443.56250	+	CC1	
	FM	N4SFU	146.71500	-	88.5 Hz	
	FM	N4SFU	146.77500	-	156.7 Hz	
	FM	N4SFU	147.00000	+	156.7 Hz	SERA
	FM	N4SFU	443.60000	+	94.8 Hz	
	FM	N4SFU	444.25000	+	94.8 Hz	
Union	FM	WD4LUQ	224.88000	-	77.0 Hz	
Valdosta	DMR/BM	K4VLD	147.07500	+	CC1	
	DMR/BM	WR4SG	442.71250	+	CC1	
	DSTAR	W4VLD C	145.14000	-		
	DSTAR	W4VLD	145.15000	-		
	DSTAR	W4VLD B	443.71250	+		
	DSTAR	W4VLD A	1282.82500	-		
	DSTAR	W4VLD D	1282.82500			
	DSTAR	W4VLD	1282.82500	1262.82500		
	FM	W4VLD	146.76000	-	141.3 Hz	SERA
	FM	WR4SG	224.46000	-	141.3 Hz	
	FM	W4VLD	443.71250	+		
	FM	W4VLD	444.70000	+	141.3 Hz	
Vidalia	DMR/BM	KE4PMP	146.62500	-	CC1	
	DMR/BM	KE4PMP	147.30000	+	CC1	
	DMR/MARC	KE4UHF	444.57500	+	CC1	
	DMR/MARC	KG4BKO	444.98750	+	CC1	
	FM	K4HAO	146.62500	-	88.5 Hz	SERA

Location	Mode	Call sign	Output	Input	Access	Coordinator
Vienna	FM	K4WDN	147.37500	+	131.8 Hz	
Villa Rica	DSTAR	WR4VR	145.24000	-		SERA
	FM	WR4VR	147.18000	+	127.3 Hz	SERA
	FM	WR4VR	224.30000	-	127.3 Hz	SERA
Villanow	FM	N2YYP	443.52500	+		SERA
Waleska	DMR/BM	W4KIP	444.05000	+	CC1	SERA
	FM	KD4ALC	224.14000	-		
	FM	KR4FN	224.20000	-	100.0 Hz	SERA
	FM	KD4DXR	441.35000	+		
Waleska, Pine Log Mountain						
	FM	K4PLM	53.29000	52.29000	192.8 Hz	
	FM	WD4OVN	53.45000	52.45000		
	FM	KG4VUB	145.27000	-	100.0 Hz	SERA
	FM	K4AIS	224.52000	-		
	FM	KJ4JJX	224.94000	-		
	FM	K4PLM	443.85000	+	192.8 Hz	
Waleska, Pine Log Mtn						
	DSTAR	KI4GOM	145.02000	146.42000		
Waleska, Pine Log Mtn.						
	FM	KK4YLX	147.01500	+	100.0 Hz	SERA
Warm Springs	DSTAR	KJ4KLE C	144.92000	147.42000		
	DSTAR	KJ4KLE B	440.67500	+		
	DSTAR	KJ4KLE D	1298.25000			
	FM	KD4BDB	53.23000	52.23000	97.4 Hz	
	FM	N4UER	146.98500	-		
	FM	N4UER	442.40000	+		
Warner Robins	FM	WR4MG	29.66000	-		
	FM	WR4MG	53.79000	52.79000		
	FM	WM4B-R	146.67000	-	82.5 Hz	SERA
	FM	WA4ORT	146.85000	-		SERA
	FM	WB4BDP	147.18000	+	107.2 Hz	
	FM	WR4MG	442.90000	+	107.2 Hz	
Warner Robins, Houston County						
	FM	WR4MG	147.30000	+	107.2 Hz	SERA
Watkinsville	FM	KD4AOZ	53.57000	52.57000	123.0 Hz	
	FM	KD4AOZ	53.71000	52.71000		
	FM	KD4AOZ	147.04500	+	123.0 Hz	
	FM	KD4AOZ	224.42000	-	123.0 Hz	
	FM	KD4AOZ	444.72500	+	123.0 Hz	
Waycross	DMR/MARC	KM4DND	444.02500	+	CC3	SERA
	FM	AE4PO	53.41000	52.41000	141.3 Hz	
	FM	KM4DND	145.27000	-	141.3 Hz	
	FM	KF4SUY	146.64000	-	141.3 Hz	
	FM	KM4DND	146.82000	-		
Waynesboro	DSTAR	K4BRK	145.23000	-	71.9 Hz	SERA
	DSTAR	K4BRK	444.10000	+	71.9 Hz	SERA
	FM	K4BRK	146.64000	-	71.9 Hz	SERA
	FM	K4BRK	442.80000	+		SERA
Willow Wind	FM	W4FLQ-L	443.32500	+		
Wilmington Island		W4LHS-R	146.55000			
Wilmington Park	FM	KA4CID-R	443.30000	+		SERA
Winder	FM	WR4BC	145.13000	-	100.0 Hz	
	FM	W4WYI	443.52500	+	100.0 Hz	SERA
Woodbury	FM	WB4GWA	443.80000	+	110.9 Hz	
Woodstock	FM	KF4RMB	442.27500	+	67.0 Hz	
	FM	KE4SJO	444.22500	+		
Wrens	DMR/MARC	KD4IEZ	444.17500	+	CC1	
	FM	KT4N	147.12000	+	71.9 Hz	
Wrightsville	FM	WA4RVB	146.94000	-		
	FM	WA4RVB	443.02500	+	156.7 Hz	
Young Harris	FM	W4NGT	147.21000	+	100.0 Hz	
	FM	NP2Y	224.66000	-	100.0 Hz	

Location	Mode	Call sign	Output	Input	Access	Coordinator
GUAM						
Asan	FM	AH2G	146.94000	-		
Barragada Heights						
	FM	AH2G	146.91000	-		
HAWAII						
Aiea		KH6BB-L	146.78000			
	FM	WH6PD	147.16000	+	103.5 Hz	
	FM	WH6Q	442.97500	+	103.5 Hz	
Central	DMR/MARC	KH6C	444.95000	+	CC3	
Ewa	FM	WH6PD	146.60000	-	103.5 Hz	HSRAC
	FM	WH6MK	147.38000	+		
	FM	WH6PD	224.50000	-	103.5 Hz	
	FM	WH6PD	442.02500	+		
	FM	KH6CY	443.10000	+	103.5 Hz	
Glenwood	FM	AH6GG	52.20000	51.20000	141.3 Hz	HSRAC
	FM	AH6GG	147.00000	+	141.3 Hz	HSRAC
	FM	AH6GG	442.02500	+	156.7 Hz	
Hakalau	FM	AF7DX	443.20000	+	100.0 Hz	
Haleakala	DMR/BM	AH6GR	442.85000	+	CC1	
	DMR/MARC	KH6C	443.15000	+	CC3	HSRAC
	FM	KH6COM	146.94000	-	110.9 Hz	HSRAC
	FM	KH6H	147.02000	+	103.5 Hz	HSRAC
	FM	NH6XO	147.08000	+	123.0 Hz	HSRAC
	FM	N6HPQ	147.26000	+		
	FM	AH6GR	442.10000	+	136.5 Hz	HSRAC
	FM	AH6GR	444.22500	+	110.9 Hz	HSRAC
Haleiwa	FM	KH6LJ	146.90000	-		
	FM	KH6LJ	224.02000	-		
Hanalei, Waimea Canyon						
	FM	NH6HF	147.10000	+	100.0 Hz	
Hanamaulu	FM	KH6BFU	223.98000	-		
Hilo	DMR/BM	KH6EJ	442.57500	+	CC10	
	DMR/MARC	KH6HPZ	147.04000	+	CC1	
	DMR/MARC	KH6KL	444.12500	+	CC1	
	DMR/MARC	AH6JA	444.17500	+	CC4	
	DMR/MARC	WH6FM	444.90000	+	CC4	HSRAC
	FM	KH6QAI	145.35000	-		HSRAC
	FM	AH6JA	146.40000		100.0 Hz	
	FM	AH6GG	146.66000	-	141.3 Hz	
	FM	WH6HQ	147.10000	+		HSRAC
	FM	AF7DX	147.28000	+		
	FM	AH6JA	444.15000	+		HSRAC
	FM	WH6FM	444.72500	+		HSRAC
	FM	AH6JA	444.75000	+		HSRAC
	FM	WH6FM	444.77500	+	123.0 Hz	
	FM	KH6KL	444.92500	+		HSRAC
	FUSION	K0BAD	444.60000	+		
Holualoa	DMR/BM	KH7MS	444.40000	+	CC1	
Honaunau	DMR/BM	KH7MS	444.95000	+	CC1	
Honolulu	DMR/BM	NH6NN	442.65000	+	CC1	
	DMR/BM	AH6OO	443.20000	+	CC1	
	DMR/BM	WH6CZB	444.10000	+	CC4	
	DMR/BM	WH6CZB	444.50000	+	CC5	HSRAC
	DMR/MARC	KH6OCD	146.86000	-	CC1	
	DMR/MARC	KH6HPZ	147.06000	+	CC1	
	DMR/MARC	AH6CP	147.30000	+	CC5	HSRAC
	DMR/MARC	KH7EC	443.00000	+	CC1	
	DMR/MARC	KH6FV	443.42500	+	CC2	
	DMR/MARC	KH6FV	443.82500	+	CC1	
	DMR/MARC	AH6KD	444.20000	+	CC0	

Location	Mode	Call sign	Output	Input	Access	Coordinator
Honolulu	DMR/MARC	AH6CP	444.30000	+	CC0	
	DMR/MARC	AH6CP	444.40000	+	CC0	
	DMR/MARC	AH6HI	444.42500	+	CC0	HSRAC
	DMR/MARC	AH6Q	444.57500	+	CC1	
	DMR/MARC	AH6CP	444.90000	+	CC0	HSRAC
	FM	WH6F	53.03000	52.03000		HSRAC
	FM	KH7EC	145.19000	-		
	FM	AH7HI	145.21000	-		
	FM	WH6CZP	145.39000	-		
	FM	WH6F	145.47000	-		HSRAC
	FM	KH6JUU	146.84000	-		HSRAC
	FM	WH6CZB	146.88000	-	88.5 Hz	HSRAC
	FM	WH6DIG	146.92000	-		HSRAC
	FM	WH6CZB	146.98000	-	88.5 Hz	HSRAC
	FM	WH6DIG	147.18000	+		HSRAC
	FM	KH6ICX	147.22000	+		HSRAC
	FM	NH6WP	147.28000	+		HSRAC
	FM	WH7MN	147.34000	+		HSRAC
	FM	KH6OJ	223.94000	-		HSRAC
	FM	NH7ZD	224.74000	-		HSRAC
	FM	KH7NM	224.94000	-		
	FM	KH6XP	442.30000	+	103.5 Hz	
	FM	KH6AZ	442.80000	+		HSRAC
	FM	KH7EC	443.02500	+		
	FM	KH7TX	443.20000	+		
	FM	KH6FV	443.25000	+	114.8 Hz	
	FM	KH6OJ	443.45000	+	103.5 Hz	
	FM	WH6HR	443.62500	+		
	FM	WH6UG	443.67500	+		HSRAC
	FM	KH7TK	443.95000	+	118.8 Hz	HSRAC
	FM	NH6WP	444.00000	+		HSRAC
	FM	KH6OCD	444.05000	+		HSRAC
	FM	WH6CZB	444.20000	+		HSRAC
	FM	WH6FM	444.72500	+	123.0 Hz	HSRAC
	FM	AH7HI	444.82500	+		HSRAC
	FM	KH6MP	444.87500	+		HSRAC
	FM	WH6DIG	444.92500	+		HSRAC
	FM	AH6CP	925.60000	922.00000		HSRAC
Honolulu, Diamond Head						
	FM	AH6RH	147.06000	+	103.5 Hz	HSRAC
	FM	WR6AVM	147.26000	+		HSRAC
Honolulu, Round Top						
	FM	KH6HFD	443.42500	+	114.8 Hz	HSRAC
	FM	KH6HFD	443.82500	+	114.8 Hz	HSRAC
	FM	KH6MEI	444.70000	+	100.0 Hz	HSRAC
	FM	KH6HFD	444.85000	+	114.8 Hz	
Ka'u	FM	WH6FC	145.29000	-	100.0 Hz	HSRAC
Kaaawa	DMR/MARC	KH7HO	443.47500	+	CC0	
Kaala	FM	NH6XO	146.68000	-	123.0 Hz	HSRAC
	FM	NH6XO	147.36000	+		
	FM	NH6XO	444.77500	+	123.0 Hz	HSRAC
Kaanapali	DMR/BM	AH6GR	442.50000	+	CC1	
Kahalui	FM	AH6GR	147.18000	+		HSRAC
Kahanamoku	DMR/MARC	AH6CP	444.52500	+	CC0	
Kahua	FM	AH6GR	442.27500	+	136.5 Hz	HSRAC
Kahuku	DMR/MARC	KH7HO	443.72500	+	CC0	
Kailua	DMR/MARC	KH7EC	442.90000	+	CC2	
	DMR/MARC	KH7HO	443.97500	+	CC0	
	FM	WH6CZB	146.66000	-	88.5 Hz	HSRAC
	FM	WR6AVM	147.00000	+		HSRAC
	FM	WH6CZB	444.15000	+		HSRAC
Kailua Kona	DMR/BM	KH6BFD	444.67500	+	CC1	

Location	Mode	Call sign	Output	Input	Access	Coordinator
Kailua Kona	DMR/BM	KH6BFD	927.11250	902.11250	CC15	
	FM	WB6EGR	927.13750	902.13750		HSRAC
Kailua Kona, Koloko Peak						
	FM	KH6BFD	443.65000	+	100.0 Hz	HSRAC
Kailua-Kona	DMR/BM	WH6DEW	444.20000	+	CC1	
	FM	KH7AX	445.55000	-	100.0 Hz	
Kaimuki, Diamond Head						
	FM	WH6ARC	147.36000	+		HSRAC
Kalaheo	DMR/BM	NH6HI	442.22500	+	CC1	
Kalaheo, Mt. Kahili						
	FM	KH6E	146.92000	-	100.0 Hz	
Kalaoa	FM	KH7MS	145.41000	-		HSRAC
Kalaoa, Hualalai	FM	WH6DEW	147.16000	+		HSRAC
Kamuela	FM	WH6FEE	145.21000	-	110.9 Hz	
Kaneohe	DMR/MARC	KH7HO	444.60000	+	CC0	
	FM	WH6CZP	145.35000	-		
	FM	KH6BFZ	147.20000	+		
	FUSION	WH6GPZ	146.68000	-		
Kapaa	DMR/MARC	WH7J	442.45000	+	CC1	
	DMR/MARC	WH6TF	444.30000	+	CC0	
	FM	NH6JC	147.08000	+	100.0 Hz	
	FM	KH6KWS	147.34000	+	100.0 Hz	HSRAC
Kapalua	DMR/MARC	KH6C	444.92500	+	CC0	
	FM	KH6RS	442.00000	+	110.9 Hz	HSRAC
Kapolei	DMR/MARC	KH6FV	443.47500	+	CC1	
	FM	KH6WOW	446.52500	-		
Kau	FM	KH6EJ	146.92000	-		HSRAC
	FM	KH6EJ	444.60000	+		HSRAC
Kaumana	DMR/BM	KH7MS	444.95000	+	CC1	
Kaunakakai Molokai						
	DMR/BM	AH6GR	442.30000	+	CC1	
Kea'au	FM	KH6EJ	146.68000	-		HSRAC
Keaau	FM	NH6WT	146.80000	-	100.0 Hz	
	FM	NH6HT	147.28000	+		HSRAC
	FM	KH6EJ	442.50000	+		HSRAC
	FM	NH6HT	442.57500	+		
Keaau, Kaumana	FM	K2FFT	146.64000	-	100.0 Hz	HSRAC
Keanae	FM	AH6GR	146.90000	-	110.9 Hz	HSRAC
Kilauea	FM	KH6E	146.70000	-		HSRAC
Kohala	FM	KH6EJ	444.45000	+	88.5 Hz	HSRAC
Kona	DMR/MARC	KH6FV	444.55000	+	CC4	
	FM	WB6EGR	927.21250	902.21250		HSRAC
Kona South Estates						
	FM	AH6DX-R	145.49000	-		
Kualapuu	FM	W6KAG	145.37000	-		HSRAC
	FM	WH6IT	146.40000		100.0 Hz	
Kukuilono	DMR/MARC	AH6CP	444.35000	+	CC1	HSRAC
Kula	DMR/MARC	KH6HPZ	147.02000	+	CC1	
Kulani	FM	KH6EJ	146.76000	-		HSRAC
	FM	WH6ECW	442.15000	+		
Kunia	DMR/MARC	KH7EC	443.85000	+	CC1	
Kurtistown	FM	K1ENT	146.84000	-	100.0 Hz	HSRAC
Lahaina	FM	AL4A	146.64000	-	136.5 Hz	HSRAC
	FM	WH6YF	147.45000		100.0 Hz	
Laie	FM	KH6BYU	145.29000	-	123.0 Hz	HSRAC
	FM	K7OJL	147.49500		100.0 Hz	
Lanai	DMR/BM	AH6GR	442.07500	+	CC1	
Lanai City	FM	KH6CED	146.60000		100.0 Hz	
	FM	KH6HC	146.74000	+		HSRAC
	FM	KH6RS	442.22500	447.32500	110.9 Hz	HSRAC
Leeward	DSTAR	WH6DHT	145.45000	-		HSRAC
	DSTAR	WH6DHT	442.70000	-		

Location	Mode	Call sign	Output	Input	Access	Coordinator
Leeward	DSTAR	WH6DHT	1293.00000	1273.00000		HSRAC
	FM	KH6AZ	145.13000	-		HSRAC
	FM	KH7TK	145.43000	-	77.0 Hz	
	FM	KH7INC	145.49000	-		HSRAC
	FM	AH6IH	147.32000	+		HSRAC
	FM	NH7QH	224.92000	-		HSRAC
	FM	KH6NYC	442.60000	+		
Lihue	DMR/MARC	KH6HPZ	147.04000	+	CC1	
	DMR/MARC	NH7YS	444.32500	+	CC0	
	FM	KH6S	442.25000	+		
	FM	KH6CVJ	444.67500	+	100.0 Hz	HSRAC
Manawahua	FM	KH6HFD	443.47500	+	114.8 Hz	HSRAC
	FM	KH6HFD	443.55000	+	114.8 Hz	HSRAC
Mauna Kapu, Palihua Ridge						
	FM	KH6OCD	147.12000	+	88.5 Hz	HSRAC
Mauna Kea	DMR/MARC	KH6FV	444.37500	+	CC3	
Mauna Loa	FM	WH6FM	146.82000	-	100.0 Hz	
	FM	AH6JA	147.04000	+		
Mililani	DMR/BM	WH6CZB	442.30000	+	CC1	
Moana Loa	DMR/MARC	AH6CP	444.75000	+	CC1	
Mokuleia	DMR/MARC	KH6FV	443.60000	+	CC0	
Mokuleia, Peacock Flats						
	FM	KH6FV	146.76000	-	114.8 Hz	HSRAC
Mountain View	FM	KH6QAJ	444.35000	+		HSRAC
Mt. Halekala	DMR/MARC	KH6FV	444.85000	+	CC0	HSRAC
Na'alehu	FM	KH6VFD	145.41000	-		HSRAC
Naalehu	DMR/BM	KH7MS	444.95000	+	CC1	
NOAA Hawaii Kai	WX	WWF39	162.40000			
NOAA Honolulu	WX	KBA99	162.55000			
NOAA Kauai	WX	WWG74	162.40000			
NOAA Kulani Cone						
	WX	WWG76	162.55000			
NOAA Maui	WX	WWG75	162.40000			
NOAA South Point						
	WX	WWG27	162.55000			
North Shore	DMR/MARC	KH7HO	442.62500	+	CC0	
	FM	WR6AVM	147.00000	-		HSRAC
Oahu	FM	AH6GR	442.27500	+	136.5 Hz	
Ocean View	DMR/BM	KH7MS	145.41000	-	CC1	
	DMR/BM	KH7MS	444.95000	+	CC1	
Paauilo	FM	KH6EJ	146.72000	-		HSRAC
Pahala	DMR/BM	KH7MS	444.95000	+	CC1	
Pahoa	FM	WH6DYN	147.12000	+		
	FM	NH6P	147.14000	+		
	FM	NH6P	442.25000	+	114.8 Hz	HSRAC
Pearl City	DMR/MARC	KH7EC	443.02500	+	CC1	
Pepeekeo	DMR/BM	KH7MS	444.95000	+	CC1	
	FM	KH6EJ	146.88000	-		HSRAC
Portable	DMR/MARC	KH6FV	444.65000	+	CC5	
Puu Hoku	FM	AH6GR	442.12500	+	110.9 Hz	HSRAC
Puu Kilea	FM	KH6RS	442.07500	+	110.9 Hz	HSRAC
Puu Mahoe	FM	KH6RS	442.05000	+	136.5 Hz	HSRAC
Salt Lake	FM	KH6IB	147.10000	+	123.0 Hz	
	FM	KH6MEI	442.17500	+	103.5 Hz	HSRAC
Test Repeater	DMR/BM	KH7MS	444.95000	+	CC1	
Upper Ocean View						
	DMR/BM	KH7MS	443.40000	+	CC1	
Volcano	DMR/BM	KH7MS	443.40000	+	CC1	
Waiakea		AH6JA-L	145.31000			
Waialua	DMR/MARC	KH7EC	442.42500	+	CC1	
Waianae	DMR/MARC	KH7EC	442.90000	+	CC1	
	FM	WH6CZB	146.80000	-		HSRAC

Location	Mode	Call sign	Output	Input	Access	Coordinator
Waianae, Mauna Kapu						
	FM	KH7O	146.62000	-	103.5 Hz	HSRAC
	FM	KH7O	442.40000	+		
	FM	WR6AVM	442.47500	+		HSRAC
Waikiki	DMR/MARC	WB6EGR	443.65000	+	CC0	
Waikiki Beach	DSTAR	WH6DWF	444.70000	+		
	FM	WH6DWF	442.27500	+	118.8 Hz	
Waikoloa	FM	NH6EE	147.24000	+	100.0 Hz	HSRAC
	FM	NH6EE	444.97500	+		HSRAC
Wailuku	DMR/BM	WH6AV	442.72500	+	CC1	
	DMR/BM	AH6GR	442.75000	+	CC1	
	FM	KH6DT	146.76000	-	100.0 Hz	HSRAC
	FM	AH6GR	443.22500	+	110.9 Hz	HSRAC
Waimanalo	DMR/MARC	KH6FV	443.60000	+	CC0	
	FM	WH6CXI	145.23000	-		
	FM	KH6HFD	443.40000	+	114.8 Hz	
	FM	KH6HFD	443.60000	+	100.0 Hz	HSRAC
	FM	KH6CB	444.02500	+		HSRAC
	FM	AH6CP	444.32500	+	103.5 Hz	HSRAC
	FM	KH6HFD	444.37500	+	114.8 Hz	HSRAC
Waimea	FM	NH7HI	147.32000	+	100.0 Hz	HSRAC
	FM	KH7T	147.38000	+		HSRAC
Waimea, Mauna Kea						
	FM	WB6EGR	443.62500	+	100.0 Hz	
West Maui	DMR/MARC	KH6C	444.82500	+	CC0	
Whitmore Village	DMR/BM	WH6CZB	443.25000	+	CC6	
Windward	FM	KH6BS	147.14000	+		HSRAC

IDAHO

Location	Mode	Call sign	Output	Input	Access	Coordinator
Blackfoot	FM	WB6EVM	447.95000	-		
Blacks Creek	FM	K7ZZL	443.25000	+	110.9 Hz	UVHFS
Blanchard, Hoodoo Mt						
	FM	K7JEP	145.49000	-	136.5 Hz	IACC
Boise	DMR/MARC	WA7GSK	444.07500	+	CC1	
	DSTAR	W7VOI C	145.50000	-		
	DSTAR	W7VOI	444.35000	+		W7ZRQ
	DSTAR	W7VOI B	444.35000	+		
	FM	WA7FDR	145.13000	-	100.0 Hz	
	FM	KD0PTX	146.55000			
	FM	W7VWR	146.78000	-	100.0 Hz	
	FM	AB7HP	147.26000	+	100.0 Hz	UVHFS
	FM	N7DJX	147.30000	+	100.0 Hz	
	FM	N7FYZ	147.32000	+	100.0 Hz	UVHFS
	FM	KG6GCQ	147.50000		107.2 Hz	
	FM	KB7ZD	223.94000	-	100.0 Hz	UVHFS
	FM	KA7EWN	224.50000	-	100.0 Hz	UVHFS
	FM	NU7L	433.15000			
	FM	N7DJX	443.80000	+	100.0 Hz	W7ZRQ
	FM	W7VWR	444.72500	+	100.0 Hz	W7ZRQ
	FUSION	KC7USQ	145.55000			
	FUSION	KD0PTX	147.54000			
	FUSION	KJ7OOB	432.05000			
	FUSION	N7MKY	438.90000			
	FUSION	KB7VVD	441.28750			
	FUSION	N7MKY	443.87500	+		
	FUSION	WV7I	449.85000	-		
Boise City		KC3EOL-L	147.18000			
Boise, Blacks Creek						
	FM	K3ZFF	145.25000	-	100.0 Hz	W7ZRQ
Boise, Boise Bench						
	FM	W7VOI	145.29000	-	100.0 Hz	W7ZRQ
Boise, Deer Point	FM	KE7YD	444.47500	+		W7ZRQ

Location	Mode	Call sign	Output	Input	Access	Coordinator
Boise, Downtown	FM	W7VWR	444.27500	+		
Boise, Seaman's Gulch						
	FM	N7BOI	147.38000	+		W7ZRQ
Boise, Shafer Butte						
	FM	N7BOI	145.15000	-		W7ZRQ
Boise, Wilderness Ridge						
	FM	WA9WSJ	52.62000	51.62000	110.9 Hz	UVHFS
	FM	KA7EWN	444.65000	+	110.9 Hz	UVHFS
Bonners Ferry	FM	W7BFI	147.04000	+	100.0 Hz	IACC
	FM	KL3EZ	147.10000	+		IACC
	FM	W7BFI	443.02500	+	100.0 Hz	IACC
Bonners Ferry, Black Mountain						
	FM	W7BFI	146.96000	-	123.0 Hz	IACC
Buhl	DMR/BM	W6RNK	447.70000	-	CC1	
Burley	ATV	K6ZVA	434.00000	1253.30000		
	FM	WA7FDR	145.27000	-	100.0 Hz	UVHFS
Burley, Mt Harrison						
	FM	K7ACA	145.33000	-	123.0 Hz	W7ZRQ
	FM	KC7SNN	147.00000	-	100.0 Hz	UVHFS
	FM	KC7SNN	449.20000	-		UVHFS
Caldwell		K9TVR-L	446.68700			
	FUSION	K7OD	443.70000	+		
	FUSION	K7OD	444.15000	+		
Cascade	DMR/BM	W7CIA	146.64000	-	CC2	
	DMR/BM	W7CIA	146.96000	-	CC1	UVHFS
	FM	K7ZZL	443.30000	+	110.9 Hz	UVHFS
	FM	NB7C	927.16250	902.16250	151.4 Hz	W7ZRQ
Cascade, Snowbank Mountain						
	FM	W7VOI	146.62000	-	100.0 Hz	W7ZRQ
Centerville	DMR/BM	KA7ERV	443.67500	+	CC2	
Challis, Grouse Peak						
	FM	AA7WG	146.78000	-	110.9 Hz	
Cleft	FM	KD7RMB	145.41000	-	114.8 Hz	
Cocolalla	FM	K7ZOX	53.09000	51.39000	100.0 Hz	IACC
	FM	K7ID	146.68000	-	127.3 Hz	IACC
	FM	K7ZOX	442.00000	+	110.9 Hz	IACC
Coeur D' Alene	FM	NV2Z	443.27500	+	127.3 Hz	IACC
	FM	N7LNA	444.77500	+	127.3 Hz	IACC
Coeur D'Alene	FM	KB6UMY	53.39000	51.69000	100.0 Hz	IACC
	FUSION	KE7BXZ	145.56250			
Coeur D'Alene, Canfield Mounta						
	FM	K7ID	443.97500	+	136.5 Hz	IACC
Coeur DAlene	DMR/MARC	WA7DMR	440.92500	+	CC1	
Coolin	FM	K7KAM	145.41000	-	77.0 Hz	IACC
	FM	KC6CSC	444.85000	+		IACC
Coolin, Priest Lake						
	FM	N7KAM	145.41000	-	77.0 Hz	
Cottonwood	FM	K7EI	444.72500	+	100.0 Hz	IACC
Cottonwood, Cottonwood Butte						
	FM	K7EI	444.95000	+	100.0 Hz	UVHFS
Couer D Alene	DMR/MARC	NO7RF	440.92500	+	CC1	
Council, Council Mtn						
	FM	W7KAU	145.37000	-	100.0 Hz	
Deary	FM	N7WEE	145.35000	-	114.8 Hz	UVHFS
Donnelly	FUSION	W7BOB	144.95000			
Driggs	DMR/BM	W7RAC	449.80000	-	CC1	
Driggs, Relay Ridge						
	FM	K7ENE	146.94000	-	123.0 Hz	UVHFS
	FM	W7RAC	147.14000	+	123.0 Hz	
	FM	KB7ITU	447.87500	-		
Eagle	FM	WV7I	449.85000	-		UVHFS

Location	Mode	Call sign	Output	Input	Access	Coordinator
Elk River, Elk Butte						
	FM	KF7WOR	145.19000	-	67.0 Hz	IACC
Emida	FM	KB7SIJ	145.31000	-	88.5 Hz	IACC
Emmett	FM	N7UBO	147.22000	+		
	FM	K7WIR	224.88000	-	100.0 Hz	UVHFS
Emmett, Squaw Butte						
	FM	K7WIR	147.20000	+	100.0 Hz	UVHFS
Filer	FM	KB7SQS	444.60000	+		W7ZRQ
Fruitland	FM	KC7BSA	443.65000	+	100.0 Hz	UVHFS
Grace, Sedgwick Peak						
	FM	AE7TA	146.80000	-	88.5 Hz	UVHFS
	FM	AE7T	449.37500	-	88.5 Hz	UVHFS
Grangeville	FM	KC7MGR	146.68000	-	100.0 Hz	UVHFS
Hailey	FUSION	KJ7GUI	146.42000			
Howe	FM	WA7FDR	146.85000	-	100.0 Hz	UVHFS
Howe, Jumpoff Peak						
	FM	W7RUG	447.62000	-	88.5 Hz	
Idaho City	FM	NB7C	927.11250	902.11250		UVHFS
Idaho City, Grimes Creek						
	FM	K7WIR	443.35000	+		
Idaho City, Schaefer Butte						
	FM	WI7ATV	145.47000	-	100.0 Hz	W7ZRQ
Idaho City, Shafer Butte						
	FM	W7VOI	146.84000	-	100.0 Hz	W7ZRQ
	FM	K7BSE	146.94000	-	100.0 Hz	UVHFS
	FM	WR7ID	444.50000	+	100.0 Hz	
	FM	W7VOI	444.90000	+	100.0 Hz	W7ZRQ
Idaho Falls	DMR/BM	W7RUG	449.50000	-	CC2	
	DSTAR	KG7WZG B	448.90000	-		
	DSTAR	KG7WZG	448.90000	-		
	FM	WA4VRV	443.00000	+	100.0 Hz	UVHFS
Idaho Falls, Peterson Hill						
	FM	K7EFZ	146.74000	-		UVHFS
Iona, Iona Hill	FM	K7EFZ	146.64000	-		UVHFS
	FM	KD7SUF	448.17500	-	100.0 Hz	UVHFS
Island Park	FM	WA7FDR	145.23000	-	100.0 Hz	UVHFS
Jerome	DSTAR	KF7VTM	444.80000	+		W7ZRQ
	DSTAR	KF7VTM B	444.80000	+		
Jerome, Flat Top Butte						
	FM	K7MVA	146.66000	-	100.0 Hz	UVHFS
	FM	K7MVA	442.30000	+	100.0 Hz	
Josephson		KG7ALS-L	146.54000			
Kaimah	FM	KC5MSQ	146.70000	-	88.5 Hz	IACC
Kamiah	FM	KC7MSQ	147.12000	+	88.5 Hz	IACC
	FM	KD6MNA	443.92500	+	100.0 Hz	IACC
Kellogg	FM	N7SZY	52.81000	51.11000	136.5 Hz	IACC
Kellogg, Wardner Peak						
	FM	N7SZY	146.94000	-	127.3 Hz	IACC
	FM	N7SZY	444.00000	+	127.3 Hz	
Ketchum	FUSION	N7XTR	444.30000	+		
Ketchum, Bald Mountain						
	FM	WX7XX	147.18000	+	100.0 Hz	W7ZRQ
Kimberly, Hansen Butte						
	FM	K7MVA	146.76000	-	100.0 Hz	UVHFS
	FM	K7MVA	147.10000	+	100.0 Hz	
Kooskia	FM	KK3ARC	146.62000	-	88.5 Hz	IACC
Kootenai	FM	KD7WPQ	443.67500	+	100.0 Hz	
Lewiston	DMR/MARC	KB7SIJ	442.10000	+	CC1	
	FM	KB7RKY	223.96000	-		UVHFS
	FM	W7TRO	444.40000	+	162.2 Hz	UVHFS
	FM	K7EI	444.85000	+	100.0 Hz	IACC
	FM	K7EI	444.92500	+	100.0 Hz	UVHFS

Location	Mode	Call sign	Output	Input	Access	Coordinator
Lewiston	FUSION	W7KMM	433.45000			
Lewiston, Craig Mountain						
	FM	K7EI	53.35000	51.65000	100.0 Hz	UVHFS
	FM	K7EI	146.92000	-	110.9 Hz	UVHFS
	FM	K7EI	442.10000	+	103.5 Hz	UVHFS
Lewiston, Lewiston Hill						
	FM	KK6RYR	145.21000	-	203.5 Hz	IACC
	FM	K7EI	444.90000	+	100.0 Hz	UVHFS
Lowman, Pilot Peak						
	FM	KA7ERV	145.31000	-	100.0 Hz	
Malad City	DMR/MARC	KI7WQR	447.98750	-	CC1	
Marsing	DMR/BM	AK7DX	442.30000	+	CC7	
	FM	K7ZZL	146.88000	-	100.0 Hz	W7ZRQ
	FM	K7ZZL	443.55000	+	100.0 Hz	W7ZRQ
Marsing, French John Hill						
	FM	K7TRH	147.36000	+	100.0 Hz	UVHFS
	FM	K7TRH	442.90000	+	100.0 Hz	W7ZRQ
Mc Call	DMR/BM	N7IBC	444.12500	+	CC2	
Mccall	DMR/BM	W7ELE	146.64000	-	CC1	
	DMR/BM	N7IBC	441.92500	+	CC1	
	DMR/BM	N7IBC	444.12500	+	CC1	W7ZRQ
McCall, Brundage Mtn						
	FM	KC7MCC	146.90000	-	123.0 Hz	
McCall, No Business Montain						
	FM	KC7MCC	147.02000	+	100.0 Hz	UVHFS
Melba, Hat Butte	FM	K7LCD	145.35000	-		W7ZRQ
	FM	K7LCD	444.17500	+		W7ZRQ
Menan, Menan Buttes						
	FM	K7ENE	146.88000	-	100.0 Hz	UVHFS
Meridian	FM	KG7CHH	145.47000			
	FM	KC9CJ	147.08000	+	100.0 Hz	W7ZRQ
	FM	KC7LHV	442.60000	+		W7ZRQ
	FUSION	N7LGN	443.87500	+		
	FUSION	K7OZD	446.25000			
Middleton	FM	K6LOR	146.50000			
	FM	K6LOR	444.27500	+		
Montpelier	FM	AG7BL	147.12000	+	123.0 Hz	UVHFS
	FM	AC7TJ	147.38000	+	88.5 Hz	UVHFS
	FUSION	KE7LVI	447.65000	-		
Moore	FM	N7GJV	146.96000	-	100.0 Hz	
Moscow	FM	KC7RSN	145.13000	-	123.0 Hz	IACC
	FM	K9GRZ	443.00000	+	88.5 Hz	IACC
	FM	KI7LAC	444.00000	+	103.5 Hz	IACC
Moscow, Moscow Mountain						
	FM	WA7HWD	146.82000	-	127.3 Hz	UVHFS
	FM	K7EI	444.97500	+	100.0 Hz	UVHFS
Moscow, Moscow Mtn						
	FM	KA7FVV	147.32000	+	103.5 Hz	
Mountain Home	FM	K7ECI	145.19000	-	110.9 Hz	
	FM	K7ECI	442.82500	+	110.9 Hz	
	FM	K7ECI	444.70000	+	110.9 Hz	
Mountain Home, Rattlesnake But						
	FM	K7ECI	147.34000	+	100.0 Hz	W7ZRQ
Moyie Springs	DSTAR	KF7MJA	145.12500	-		IACC
	DSTAR	KF7MJA C	145.12500	-		
	FM	AF7LJ	145.45000	-	88.5 Hz	
Nampa	FM	KC7LHV	442.67500	+	100.0 Hz	
	FM	NF7T	444.02500	+	100.0 Hz	
	FM	NG7O	444.10000	+	156.7 Hz	W7ZRQ
	FM	NF7T	444.17500	+	100.0 Hz	
	FUSION	K7JBC	443.70000	+		
Nampa, Hat Butte	FM	K7OVG	927.18750	902.18750		W7ZRQ

Location	Mode	Call sign	Output	Input	Access	Coordinator
Naples, Peterson Hill						
	FM	NK7I	147.32000	+	167.9 Hz	
New Meadows	DMR/BM	KC7MCC	442.50000	+	CC1	
NOAA Boise	WX	WXK68	162.55000			
NOAA Bonners Ferry						
	WX	WWG99	162.50000			
NOAA Burley	WX	WNG605	162.47500			
NOAA Driggs	WX	KJY57	162.45000			
NOAA Grangeville						
	WX	KXI82	162.45000			
NOAA Lewiston	WX	WXK98	162.55000			
NOAA McCall	WX	WWF58	162.47500			
NOAA Payette	WX	WXK88	162.40000			
NOAA Pocatello	WX	WXL33	162.55000			
NOAA Salmon	WX	KPS509	162.50000			
NOAA Sedgwick Peak						
	WX	KZZ72	162.42500			
NOAA Sun Valley	WX	WZ2520	162.45000			
NOAA Twin Falls	WX	WXL35	162.40000			
Orofino	FM	KD7ALJ	145.27000	-	100.0 Hz	UVHFS
	FM	KC7VBT	145.49000	-		UVHFS
	FM	K7EI	444.87500	+	100.0 Hz	UVHFS
Orofino, Wells Bench						
	FM	K7NDX	146.76000	-	131.8 Hz	UVHFS
Payette	FM	NB7C	443.05000	+	114.8 Hz	UVHFS
	FM	NB7C	927.11250	902.11250		
	FM	NB7C	927.12500	902.12500	103.5 Hz	UVHFS
Peck	FM	AH6I	145.35000	-	131.8 Hz	IACC
Peck, Teakean Butte						
	FM	KK6RYR	145.21000	-	206.5 Hz	IACC
Plano		KB7ITU-L	146.70000			
Pocatello		N7TZK-L	146.41500			
	FM	AD7UI	146.82000	-	100.0 Hz	UVHFS
	FM	KA7MLM	147.30000	+		
	FM	K9GP	147.34000	+		UVHFS
	FM	KF7FY	147.52000		123.0 Hz	
	FM	WB6EVM	449.12500	-		
Pocatello, Kinport Peak						
	FM	N7PI	147.36000	+	100.0 Hz	UVHFS
Pocatello, Scout Montain						
	FM	N7PI	147.06000	+	100.0 Hz	UVHFS
Post Falls	FM	KB6UMY	442.97500	+	100.0 Hz	IACC
	FM	N7ISP	445.92500	-		
	FUSION	N7BRB	146.60500			
Post Falls, Idaho Mica Peak						
	FM	K7ID	443.27500	+		
Post Falls, Mica Peak						
	FM	K7ID	146.98000	-	127.3 Hz	IACC
	FM	KC7ODP	147.08000	+	100.0 Hz	IACC
Preston	DMR/BM	KE7TJB	448.75000	-	CC1	
Rexburg	FM	K7BYI-R	145.41000	-		W7ZRQ
	FM	N7UNY	146.70000	-	100.0 Hz	UVHFS
	FM	K7WIP	448.60000	-	100.0 Hz	W7ZRQ
Roberts	FM	KE7JFA	448.80000	-	100.0 Hz	
Saint Maries	DMR/MARC	KB7SIJ	443.75000	+	CC1	
Salmon, Baldy Mountain						
	FM	AA7WG	442.10000	+	100.0 Hz	
	FM	AA7WG	442.22500	447.32500	100.0 Hz	
Salmon, Baldy Summit						
	FM	AA7WG	146.98000	-	100.0 Hz	
Salmon, Old Dump Hill Above Sa						
	FM	AA7WG	147.03000	+	100.0 Hz	

Location	Mode	Call sign	Output	Input	Access	Coordinator
Sandpoint	FM	K7LNA	147.00000	+	123.0 Hz	IACC
	FM	K7BNR	442.50000	+	131.8 Hz	
	FM	N7JCT	446.02500	-		
	FM	K7JEP	448.37500	+		
Sawtooth City, Galena Peak						
	FM	AE6DX	147.14000	+	100.0 Hz	UVHFS
Shafer Butte	FM	N7KNL	444.67500	+	156.7 Hz	
Silver City, War Eagle						
	FM	KJ7GGR	147.04000	+	123.0 Hz	
	FM	W7VOI	147.24000	+	100.0 Hz	
Spirit Lake	FM	K7ZOX	442.00000	+	110.9 Hz	IACC
St. Marie's, St. Joe Baldy						
	FM	KB7SIJ	147.26000	+	88.5 Hz	IACC
St. Maries	DMR/MARC	KB7SIJ	443.75000	+	CC0	IACC
Stanley	FM	KJ7GUI	444.60000	+	100.0 Hz	
Twin Falls	FM	W7CTH	442.60000	+	100.0 Hz	
	FUSION	KB7SQS	145.17000	-		
	FUSION	KJ7RBS	145.55000			
	FUSION	KB7DFP	147.47500			
	FUSION	KB7DFP	442.00000	+		
	FUSION	K7MVA	442.30000	+		
	FUSION	K6UDA	444.50000	+		
	FUSION	KB7SQS	444.60000	+		
	FUSION	KB7SQS	444.70000	+		
	FUSION	KB7SQS	448.75000	-		
	FUSION	KB7SQS	449.20000	-		
Twin Falls, Mt Harrison						
	ATV	K6ZVA	1253.25000	426.25000		W7ZRQ
Wallace, Goose Peak						
	FM	KB7BYR	147.18000	+	118.8 Hz	
	FM	KB7BTU	224.76000	-	100.0 Hz	IACC
Weiser, Sheep Creek						
	FM	K7OJI	145.39000	-		
	FM	K7OJI	147.12000	+		UVHFS
Wendell	FUSION	K8MPW	443.95000	+		
Wolf Lodge	FM	KB6UMY-R	147.28000	+		IACC

ILLINOIS

Location	Mode	Call sign	Output	Input	Access	Coordinator
Aledo	FM	KC9HDD	145.31000	-	100.0 Hz	IRA
	FM	KC9HDD	443.25000	+	100.0 Hz	IRA
	FM	N1USA	444.25000	444.85000		
Algonquin	DMR/MARC	WD9BBE	443.95625	+	CC15	IRA
	FM	N9IVM	444.02500	+	103.5 Hz	IRA
Allerton	FM	K9LOF	147.28500	+	146.2 Hz	IRA
Alton	FM	K9HAM	224.64000	-	123.0 Hz	
	FM	K9HAM	442.22500	+	123.0 Hz	IRA
	FM	K9HAM	442.90000	+	123.0 Hz	IRA
	FM	K9HAM	927.01250	902.01250	123.0 Hz	
	FM	KB9GPF	927.60000	902.60000	79.7 Hz	IRA
Anna	FM	KD9EVL	145.25000	-		IRA
	FM	WA9LM	442.85000	+	88.5 Hz	IRA
Antioch	FM	KA9VZD	145.29000	-	107.2 Hz	IRA
	FM	N9EMS	927.65000	902.65000	192.8 Hz	IRA
Arboretum Estates						
	FM	W9YRC-R	442.87500	+		IRA
Arcola	FM	WA9WOB	444.37500	+	192.8 Hz	IRA
Arlington Heights	FM	N9IVM	444.02500	+	100.0 Hz	IRA
	FUSION	W9GIL	441.32500	+		
Athens	FM	W9DUA	147.04500	+	103.5 Hz	IRA
Aurora	DMR/MARC	W9LSL	443.42500	+	CC1	IRA
Ava	FM	W9RNM	147.09000	+	88.5 Hz	IRA
Aviston	FM	KT9TR	147.21000	+	79.7 Hz	IRA

Location	Mode	Call sign	Output	Input	Access	Coordinator
Aviston	FM	KT9TR	443.17500	+	79.7 Hz	IRA
Batavia	DMR/MARC	WB9PHK	443.08125	+	CC1	
	DSTAR	W9CEQ	147.22500	+		IRA
	DSTAR	W9CEQ C	147.22500	+		
	DSTAR	W9CEQ	442.10625	+		IRA
	DSTAR	W9CEQ B	442.10625	+		
	DSTAR	W9NE D	1241.90000			
	DSTAR	W9NE A	1291.90000	1271.90000		
	FM	W9ZGP	147.06000	+	103.5 Hz	IRA
	FM	W9XA	224.40000	-	110.9 Hz	IRA
	FM	KA9LFU	444.10000	+	100.0 Hz	IRA
	FM	WB9IKJ	444.22500	+	114.8 Hz	IRA
	FM	W9CEQ	444.30000	+	114.8 Hz	IRA
	FM	W9XA	1292.00000	1272.00000	88.5 Hz	IRA
	FUSION	W9AUV	147.22500	+		
	FUSION	W9AUV	442.12500	+		
Beardstown	FM	W9ACU	443.95000	+	103.5 Hz	IRA
Belleville, Turkey Hill						
	FM	K9GXU	147.12000	+		IRA
	FM	K9GXU	224.12000	-	127.3 Hz	IRA
	FM	K9GXU	444.62500	+	127.3 Hz	IRA
Bellwood	FM	KC9ZI	444.57500	+	114.8 Hz	IRA
Belvidere	DMR/MARC	K9VO	442.75000	+	CC10	IRA
	FM	K9ORU	147.37500	+	100.0 Hz	IRA
	FM	N9KUX	442.82500	+	114.8 Hz	IRA
Berwyn	FM	WA9HIR	444.15000	+	146.2 Hz	IRA
Bethalto	FM	K9HAM	145.13000	-	123.0 Hz	IRA
Bleachery		KP4KWB-R	223.32500			
Bloomingdale	FM	K9NB	224.22000	-	110.9 Hz	IRA
Bloomington		N8IQT-L	446.77500			
	DMR/BM	WX9WX	444.23750	+	CC12	
	DSTAR	KJ9P	444.58125	+		IRA
	FM	W9AML	146.04000	+	156.7 Hz	IRA
	FM	WD9HRU	146.79000	-	103.5 Hz	
	FM	N9BXI	147.01500	+	156.7 Hz	IRA
	FM	W9AML	444.95000	+	97.4 Hz	IRA
Bloomington, BMI	FM	K9MBS	224.46000	-	107.2 Hz	IRA
Blue Island	FM	W9SRC	442.67500	+	131.8 Hz	IRA
Bolingbrook	DMR/MARC	K9BAR	443.70000	+	CC1	IRA
	FM	K9BAR	147.33000	+	107.2 Hz	IRA
	FM	K9BAR	224.54000	-	110.9 Hz	IRA
	FM	K9BAR	443.52500	+	114.8 Hz	IRA
Bridgeview	FM	KB9EPL	224.48000	-	110.9 Hz	IRA
Brookfield	FM	K9SAD	224.16000	-	110.9 Hz	IRA
Buffalo Grove	FM	KC9IL	145.65000		156.7 Hz	
	FM	WB9TAL	224.58000	-	110.9 Hz	IRA
	FUSION	KC9IL	145.65000			
Burnt Prairie	FM	W9KXP	147.33000	+		IRA
Cadwell	DSTAR	W9BIL	145.19500	-		IRA
	DSTAR	W9BIL C	145.19500	-		
	DSTAR	W9BIL	440.64375	+		IRA
	DSTAR	W9BIL B	440.64375	+		
Campbell Hill		KC9FIQ-L	146.85000			
Canton	DMR/BM	K9ILS	444.72500	+	CC12	
	FM	K9ILS	147.28500	+	103.5 Hz	IRA
Cantrall	DMR/BM	WX9DX	444.50000	+	CC1	
Carbondale	DMR/BM	KE6IOC	444.77500	+	CC0	
	DSTAR	W9UIH B	442.12500	+		
	DSTAR	W9UIH	442.65625	+		
	FM	W9UIH	442.02500	+	88.5 Hz	IRA
Carlinville	FM	N9OWS	443.27500	+	100.0 Hz	IRA
Carol Stream	FUSION	WB9SGD	433.80000			

Location	Mode	Call sign	Output	Input	Access	Coordinator
Carterville	FUSION	AC1MC	145.27500			
Carthage	DMR/MARC	KC9LMF	147.10500	+	CC7	
Cary	DSTAR	KO9H	224.96000	-		IRA
Champaign	DSTAR	W9YR B	443.48125	+		
	DSTAR	W9YR	443.48125	+		IRA
	FM	K9SI	444.10000	+	162.2 Hz	IRA
	FM	W9YH	444.52500	+	162.2 Hz	
Chana	P25	N9ST	147.16500	+	146.2 Hz	
Channahon	FUSION	W9CHI	444.60000	+		
Charleston	FM	KC9KRA	443.87500	+	162.2 Hz	
Cherry Valley	FM	W9FT	442.62500	+	123.0 Hz	IRA
Chicago		KB9NTX-L	224.52000			
		W9DIG-L	440.50000			
	DMR/BM	KB9NTX	442.45000	+	CC15	
	DMR/BM	KB9PTI	443.97500	+	CC1	
	DMR/MARC	N9OZR	440.20000	+	CC1	
	DMR/MARC	W9BMK	440.30000	+	CC1	IRA
	DMR/MARC	KC9MNL	440.40000	445.00000	CC1	
	DMR/MARC	W9DIG	440.85625	+	CC1	IRA
	DMR/MARC	K9QI	440.90000	+	CC1	
	DMR/MARC	AA9VI	441.21875	+	CC1	
	DMR/MARC	K9TOW	441.33125	+	CC4	
	DMR/MARC	WD9BBE	442.97500	+	CC4	
	DMR/MARC	K9VO	443.92500	+	CC1	
	DMR/MARC	KC9DTO	444.12500	5444.12500	CC10	
	DSTAR	WA9ORC B	441.90625	+		
	DSTAR	NS9RC	442.09375	+		IRA
	DSTAR	NS9RC B	442.09375	+		
	DSTAR	NS9RC D	1242.20000			
	DSTAR	NS9RC	1292.20000	1272.20000		IRA
	DSTAR	NS9RC A	1292.20000	1272.20000		
	FM	AA9RA	145.76000		100.0 Hz	
	FM	W9SRO	147.15000	+	107.2 Hz	IRA
	FM	KC9EBB	223.88000	-	110.9 Hz	IRA
	FM	W9TMC	224.02000	-	103.5 Hz	IRA
	FM	WD9GEH	224.06000	-	110.9 Hz	IRA
	FM	WA9ORC	224.10000	-	110.9 Hz	IRA
	FM	W9RA	224.34000	-	103.5 Hz	IRA
	FM	AB9OV	442.17500	+	114.8 Hz	IRA
	FM	K9NBC	442.40000	+	114.8 Hz	IRA
	FM	N9OZG	442.57500	+	131.8 Hz	IRA
	FM	K9QKW	443.37500	+	114.8 Hz	IRA
	FM	KC9DFK	443.67500	+		IRA
	FM	WA9ORC	443.75000	+	114.8 Hz	IRA
	FM	K9SAD	443.80000	+	114.8 Hz	IRA
	FM	K9GFY	444.37500	+	114.8 Hz	IRA
	FM	N9SHB	444.62500	+	110.9 Hz	IRA
	FM	NS9RC	444.72500	+	114.8 Hz	IRA
	FM	WA9ORC	1291.10000	1271.10000	114.8 Hz	IRA
	FUSION	WA9NNN	147.34500	+		
	FUSION	WA9NNN	432.20000			
	FUSION	W9DIG	442.65000	+		
Clinton	FM	KA9KEI	442.37500	+	91.5 Hz	IRA
	FUSION	N9IUA	147.44000			
Collinsville	FM	K9HAM	442.77500	+	123.0 Hz	
	FUSION	KD6TVP	442.17500	+		
Congerville	FM	KE9HB	443.32500	+	107.2 Hz	IRA
Country Club Hills	FM	N9ZD-R	443.27500	+		IRA
Crescent City	FM	AD9L	147.03000	+	103.5 Hz	IRA
Crystal Lake	DMR/MARC	K9QI	439.22500	431.62500	CC6	
	DMR/MARC	K9VI	444.80625	+	CC4	IRA
	FM	K9VI	224.70000	-	100.0 Hz	IRA

Location	Mode	Call sign	Output	Input	Access	Coordinator
Crystal Lake	FM	N9EAO	443.20000	+	131.8 Hz	IRA
	FM	N9HEP	443.47500	+	114.8 Hz	IRA
Cuba	FUSION	N9ATF	446.25000			
Dakota	FM	N9WSQ	147.30000	+	88.5 Hz	IRA
Dallas City	FM	KA9JNG	444.92500	+	123.0 Hz	IRA
Danville	DMR/BM	NE9RD	443.72500	+	CC1	IRA
	DMR/MARC	N9WEW	443.82500	+	CC1	
	FM	W9MJW	29.66000	-	100.0 Hz	IRA
	FM	NU9R	52.97000	51.27000	88.5 Hz	IRA
	FM	W9MJW	927.62500	902.62500	100.0 Hz	IRA
	FUSION	N9NVU	146.55000			
Darien	FM	W9ANL	145.19000	-	114.8 Hz	IRA
	FUSION	KA9CUT	433.45000			
Decatur	DSTAR	KC9YFX	147.24000	+		IRA
	DSTAR	KC9YFX C	147.24000	+		
	DSTAR	KC9YFX B	442.64375	+		
	DSTAR	KC9YFX	442.64375	+		
	FM	K9HGX	29.62000	-	103.5 Hz	IRA
	FM	K9HGX	53.23000	51.53000	103.5 Hz	IRA
	FM	WA9RTI	147.10500	+	103.5 Hz	IRA
	FM	WA9RTI	442.25000	+	103.5 Hz	IRA
	FM	K9HGX	443.80000	+	123.0 Hz	IRA
	FM	K9MCA	444.17500	+	100.0 Hz	IRA
Deer Park	FM	KP4EOP	444.00000	+		IRA
Deerfield	FM	KA9REN	224.24000	-	110.9 Hz	IRA
Dekalb	FM	KB9FMU	444.45000	+	114.8 Hz	IRA
Denmark (historical)						
		WA9EIC-L	145.73000			
Dixon	FM	W9DXN	444.80000	+	114.8 Hz	IRA
	NXDN	N9JWI	146.97000	-	82.5 Hz	
Downers Grove	FM	W9DUP	224.68000	-	110.9 Hz	IRA
	FM	KC9WPR	442.25000	+		
	FM	W9DUP	442.55000	+	114.8 Hz	IRA
	FM	N9ATO	443.90000	+	114.8 Hz	IRA
	FM	W9CCU	444.47500	+	114.8 Hz	IRA
	FUSION	N9MDK	147.52500			
	FUSION	W9YRC	442.25000	+		
Dunlap	FM	N9BBO	224.08000	-	156.7 Hz	IRA
	FM	N9BBO	443.12500	+	156.7 Hz	IRA
DuPage County	DSTAR	KC9PWC B	440.10620	+		
Eagleton	FM	W9IMP	224.84000	-	82.5 Hz	IRA
	FM	KB2MAU	443.40000	+		
East Dundee	P25	W9DWP	927.62500	902.62500	151.4 Hz	IRA
Edwardsville	FM	W9AIU	224.06000	-	127.3 Hz	IRA
	FM	W9AIU	442.40000	+	127.3 Hz	IRA
	FUSION	W9LRM	147.40500			
Effingham	DMR/BM	N9BIG	441.50000	+	CC7	
	FM	K9UXZ	444.12500	+	110.9 Hz	IRA
El Paso		N9DOA-R	444.35000			
Elburn	DMR/MARC	W9XA	443.64375	+	CC6	IRA
	FM	W9DWP	145.27000	-		IRA
	FM	W9CEQ	147.21000	+	103.5 Hz	IRA
	FUSION	AC9JD	146.41000			
	FUSION	W9DWP	443.02500	+		
Eldorado	FUSION	KB9BNM	147.44500			
Elgin	FM	WR9ABQ	52.95000	51.95000	114.8 Hz	IRA
	FM	K9EL-R	224.56000	-		IRA
	FM	WR9ABQ	444.95000	+	114.8 Hz	IRA
Elizabeth	FM	W9SBA	147.33000	+	250.3 Hz	IRA
Elk Grove Village		N9GM-L	146.54500			
	FUSION	KB9L	147.01500	+		
Elmhurst	DMR/MARC	KB9UUU	440.85000	448.85000	CC0	

Location	Mode	Call sign	Output	Input	Access	Coordinator
Fairfield	FM	KC9TON	145.13000	-	88.5 Hz	IRA
	FM	N9BRG	444.82500	+		IRA
Fairview Heights	FM	KA9HNT	145.27000	-	123.0 Hz	
	FUSION	KA9HNT	144.67000	+		
Forest City	FM	WI9MP	223.94000	-	110.9 Hz	IRA
Frankfort	FM	WD9HSY	443.32500	+	114.8 Hz	IRA
	FM	W9WIL	444.55000	+	114.8 Hz	IRA
Freeport	FM	KB9RNT	147.39000	+	114.8 Hz	IRA
	FM	W9FN	224.92000	-	74.4 Hz	IRA
	FM	W9SBA	442.00000	+	146.2 Hz	IRA
	FM	KB9RNT	443.27500	+	114.8 Hz	IRA
Galesburg	FM	W9GFD	147.00000	-	103.5 Hz	IRA
	FM	KA9QMT	147.21000	+	107.2 Hz	IRA
	FUSION	W9GFD	444.45000	+		
Galva	FM	WA9BA	443.30000	+	103.5 Hz	IRA
	FM	W9YPS	443.35000	+	225.7 Hz	IRA
Geff	FM	KC9GMX	444.40000	+		IRA
Geneseo	FM	W9MVG	444.87500	+	136.5 Hz	IRA
Gillespie	FM	K9MCE	444.25000	+	103.5 Hz	IRA
Glendale Heights	DSTAR	KC9PWC	440.10625	+		IRA
	FM	K9XD	444.87500	+	114.8 Hz	IRA
	FM	KD9AUP	927.55000	902.55000	151.4 Hz	IRA
	FUSION	WA9E	444.05000	+		
Glenview	FM	W9AP	224.60000	-	110.9 Hz	IRA
Godfrey	FUSION	KB9BPF	445.02500			
Grant Park	FM	WA9WLN	441.30000	+	114.8 Hz	IRA
Greenup	FM	W9GWF	147.03000	+	107.2 Hz	IRA
Greenville	DMR/MARC	K7QLL	443.43125	+	CC7	IRA
	FM	AD9OV	442.92500	+	103.5 Hz	IRA
Gridley	FM	KE9HB	444.35000	+	107.2 Hz	IRA
Groveland	DSTAR	W9PIA	145.10500	-		IRA
	FM	W9UVI	147.07500	+	156.7 Hz	IRA
Gurnee	FM	N9OZB	443.15000	+	114.8 Hz	IRA
Hainesville	FUSION	KD9QZO	430.25000	+		
Hardin	FM	ND2D	147.30000	+		IRA
Harrisburg	FUSION	KD9GSX	146.44500			
Hawthorne Woods						
	FM	W9AP	147.09000	+	107.2 Hz	IRA
Herald	FM	W9KXP	147.30000	+		IRA
Herod, Williams Hill						
	FM	KB9JNO	145.13000	-		
	FM	K9OWU	444.80000	+	88.5 Hz	IRA
Heyworth	DMR/BM	KD9AKF	444.87500	+	CC12	
	FM	KG9DW	442.82500	+	141.3 Hz	IRA
Hickory Hills	DMR/BM	KC9POS	440.20000	+	CC1	
Highland Park	FUSION	NS9RC	147.34500	+		
Hinsdale	FM	KB9OYP	444.20000	+	114.8 Hz	IRA
Hoffman Estates	FM	K9IIK-R	145.23000	-	107.2 Hz	IRA
	FM	N9RJV	444.12500	+		
Homer Glen	DMR/MARC	WB9PHK	423.30625	420.30625	CC3	
	DMR/MARC	KC9NCS	442.83125	+	CC3	IRA
Homewood	FM	WA9WLN	442.37500	+	114.8 Hz	IRA
Hoopeston	FM	KB9YZI	444.82500	+	127.3 Hz	IRA
Huntley	DMR/MARC	W9IV	440.04375	+	CC1	IRA
	FM	KC9ONA	441.62500	+		IRA
	FM	AB9OU	927.72500	902.72500	114.8 Hz	IRA
Ina	FM	W9RLC	145.19000	-	71.9 Hz	IRA
Indian Head Park		K9ONA-R	146.97000			
Ingleside		K9RUF-L	146.41500			
	FM	K5TAR	440.81875	+	114.8 Hz	IRA
	FUSION	K9RUF	147.84000	-		
Inverness	DMR/MARC	K9ORD	147.39000	+	CC1	

Location	Mode	Call sign	Output	Input	Access	Coordinator
Inverness	DMR/MARC	K9ORD	441.05000	+	CC1	
	DMR/MARC	K9ORD	441.95625	+	CC1	IRA
	DSTAR	WX9NC	147.39000	+		
Jacksonville	FM	K9JX	444.67500	+	103.5 Hz	IRA
Joliet	FM	KC9PLK	145.25000	-	156.7 Hz	IRA
	FM	WD9AZK	147.30000	+	94.8 Hz	IRA
	FM	W9OFR	223.82000	-		IRA
	FM	W9OFR	442.30000	+	114.8 Hz	IRA
	FM	WA9VGI	442.95000	+		IRA
	FM	N9WYS	927.52500	902.52500	151.4 Hz	IRA
	FUSION	AB9LY	144.93000			
	FUSION	K9QA	433.90000			
Jonesboro	FM	WA9LM	443.57500	+	192.8 Hz	
Kankakee	FM	WD9HSY	147.16500	+	107.2 Hz	IRA
	FM	W9AZ	444.80000	+	100.0 Hz	IRA
Kansas	FM	W9COD	53.29000	51.59000	162.2 Hz	IRA
	FM	W9COD	147.37500	+	162.2 Hz	IRA
	FM	W9COD	443.62500	+	162.2 Hz	IRA
Kendall Hill	FM	K9HAM-R	145.23000	-		IRA
Kenwood		K9CU-R	146.76000			
Kewanee	FM	N9ZK	442.17500	+	225.7 Hz	IRA
Kickapoo	FM	K9WRA	444.20000	+	103.5 Hz	IRA
La Grange Park	FM	K9ONA	443.30000	+	114.8 Hz	IRA
Lake Zurich	DSTAR	K9SA B	441.23125	+		
Lake In The Hills	FM	KC9ONA	144.98500			
	FM	KC9ONA	146.40000			
	FM	KC9ONA	146.41500			
Lake Villa	FM	WB9RKD	147.03000	+	107.2 Hz	IRA
	FM	N9FJS	442.32500	+	107.2 Hz	IRA
	FUSION	KD9NXG	434.20000			
	FUSION	WB9RKD	444.40000	+		
Lake Zurich	DMR/BM	KD9LZ	443.85000	+	CC1	
	DSTAR	KC9OKW	441.23125	+		IRA
	FM	K9SA	223.84000	-	110.9 Hz	IRA
	FM	W9SRO	224.86000	-	110.9 Hz	IRA
	FM	K9SA	443.25000	+	114.8 Hz	IRA
	FM	W9JEM	927.68750	902.68750	151.4 Hz	IRA
Libertyville	FM	K9IQP	147.18000	+	127.3 Hz	IRA
	FM	N9KTW	441.12500	+	114.8 Hz	IRA
	FM	K9IQP	442.52500	+	114.8 Hz	IRA
Lincoln	FM	K9ZM	147.34500	+	103.5 Hz	IRA
Lincoln, ALMH	FM	KC9WMV	442.80000	+	203.5 Hz	IRA
Lisle	DSTAR	W9AUX	440.26880	+		IRA
	FM	W9AEK	224.62000	-	110.9 Hz	IRA
	FM	W9AUX	442.05000	+		
	FM	WA9WSL	442.22500	+	114.8 Hz	IRA
	FM	W9AEK	442.70000	+	203.5 Hz	IRA
	FM	W9AEK	1293.10000	1273.10000	114.8 Hz	IRA
Litchfield	FM	W9BXR	444.45000	+	94.8 Hz	IRA
	FUSION	KD9EFO	433.30000			
Lockport	DMR/MARC	N2BJ	443.22500	+	CC2	IRA
	FM	W9SBE	146.55500			
	FM	W9SBE	223.42000	-	136.5 Hz	
	FM	N2BJ	224.94000	-	114.8 Hz	IRA
	FM	NC9T	442.02500	+	100.0 Hz	IRA
	FM	W9SBE	446.20000	-	136.5 Hz	
	FM	W9SBE	446.60000	-		
	FM	N9OWR	927.58750	902.58750		IRA
Loda	FM	K9UXC	442.42500	+	179.9 Hz	IRA
Loves Park	FM	K9RFD	147.19500	+	114.8 Hz	IRA
Lovington	FM	KR9X	223.86000	-	103.5 Hz	IRA
	FM	WC9V	444.27500	+	103.5 Hz	IRA

Location	Mode	Call sign	Output	Input	Access	Coordinator
Macomb	FM	W9SSP	147.06000	+	103.5 Hz	IRA
	FM	WB9TEA	444.30000	+	103.5 Hz	IRA
Markham	FM	W9YPC	147.13500	+		IRA
Marseilles	DMR/MARC	KA9FER	146.74500	-	CC1	
	DMR/MARC	KA9FER	442.60000	+	CC1	
Maryville	FM	KG9OV	224.70000	-	151.4 Hz	IRA
	FM	KB9KLD	443.20000	+	103.5 Hz	IRA
McCook	DMR/MARC	N9CWM	440.75625	+	CC1	
McHenry	FM	WA9VGI	442.92500	+	114.8 Hz	
	FM	KB9I	444.07500	+	88.5 Hz	IRA
Melrose Park	FM	W9FT	442.62500	+	114.8 Hz	IRA
	FM	K9VMP	443.87500	+	114.8 Hz	IRA
Mendon	FUSION	NR9Q	443.90000	+		
Metamora	DMR/BM	KC9GQR	444.00000	+	CC1	
Mobile Repeater	DMR/BM	KB9YVN	442.22500	+	CC12	
Monee	FM	KB9VR	441.87500	+	114.8 Hz	
Monmouth	FM	KD9J	444.32500	+	173.8 Hz	IRA
Monticello	IDAS	KB9ZAM	442.72500	+	103.5 Hz	IRA
Morris	DMR/MARC	KC9KKO	146.71500	-	CC1	
	DMR/MARC	KC9KKO	441.50000	+	CC1	
	DMR/MARC	KC9KKO	442.00000	+	CC1	
	DMR/MARC	KB9SZK	442.32500	+	CC0	IRA
	FM	KB9SZK-R	147.27000	+	107.2 Hz	IRA
Mount Carmel	FM	KC9MAK	147.25500	+	151.4 Hz	IRA
	FM	W9KTL	442.15000	+	203.5 Hz	
	FM	AI9H	442.32500	+	114.8 Hz	IRA
	FM	KC9MAK	443.87500	+	151.4 Hz	IRA
	FM	AI9H	444.77500	+	114.8 Hz	IRA
Mount Pulaski	DMR/MARC	N9NWI	443.82500	+	CC3	
Mount Vernon	DMR/BM	N9BIG	443.05000	+	CC7	
	FM	KB9KDE	147.13500	+	88.5 Hz	IRA
Mt. Pulaski	FM	N9NWI	223.90000	-	94.8 Hz	
	FUSION	N9NWI	446.05000			
Mulberry Grove	FM	W9KXQ	224.14000	-	103.5 Hz	IRA
Mundelein	DMR/MARC	WB9PHK	423.29375	420.29375	CC2	
Murphysboro	FUSION	K9LRE	438.00000			
Naperville	FM	WA9WSL	145.17000	-	103.5 Hz	IRA
	FM	W9NPD	224.20000	-	110.9 Hz	IRA
	FM	NE9MA	443.05000	+	114.8 Hz	IRA
New Lenox	DMR/MARC	N2BJ	145.18000	-	CC2	
	DMR/MARC	N2BJ	444.40000	+	CC2	IRA
	FM	WB9IRL	145.21000	-	107.2 Hz	IRA
Niles	FM	W9FO	147.31500	+	107.2 Hz	IRA
NOAA Bloomington						
	WX	KZZ65	162.52500			
NOAA Champaign						
	WX	WXJ76	162.55000			
NOAA Chester	WX	KXI42	162.45000			
NOAA Chicago	WX	KWO39	162.55000			
NOAA Crescent City						
	WX	KXI86	162.50000			
NOAA Crystal Lake						
	WX	KXI41	162.50000			
NOAA DeKalb	WX	WNG536	162.55000			
NOAA Dixon	WX	KZZ55	162.52500			
NOAA Freeport	WX	KZZ56	162.45000			
NOAA Galesburg	WX	KZZ66	162.40000			
NOAA Hillsboro	WX	KXI79	162.42500			
NOAA Jacksonville						
	WX	WXM90	162.52500			
NOAA Jerseyville	WX	KXI70	162.45000			
NOAA Kankakee	WX	KZZ58	162.52500			

Location	Mode	Call sign	Output	Input	Access	Coordinator
NOAA Lockport	WX	KZZ81	162.42500			
NOAA Macomb	WX	WXJ92	162.50000			
NOAA Marion	WX	WXM49	162.42500			
NOAA McLeansboro						
	WX	KXI52	162.40000			
NOAA Newton	WX	KXI48	162.45000			
NOAA Odell	WX	WXK24	162.45000			
NOAA Paris	WX	KXI47	162.52500			
NOAA Peoria	WX	WXJ71	162.47500			
NOAA Plano	WX	KXI58	162.40000			
NOAA Princeton	WX	WXL22	162.42500			
NOAA Quad Cities						
	WX	WXJ73	162.55000			
NOAA Rockford	WX	KZZ57	162.47500			
NOAA Salem	WX	KXI49	162.47500			
NOAA Shelbyville	WX	KXI46	162.50000			
NOAA Springfield	WX	WXJ75	162.40000			
Noble	FM	KC9RHH	442.37500	+		
Normal	FM	WB9UUS-R	442.70000	+		IRA
North Riverside	FM	K9ONA	224.82000	-	110.9 Hz	IRA
	FUSION	N9SRY	146.35000			
Northbrook	FM	NS9RC	224.32000	-	110.9 Hz	IRA
O Fallon	DMR/BM	WF1RES	440.52500	+	CC3	
	FM	K9AIR	443.10000	+	127.3 Hz	IRA
O'Fallon	FUSION	N9PBD	444.30000	+		
Oak Brook	FM	N9XKY	443.12500	+		IRA
Oak Forest	DMR/BM	N9ZD	443.27500	+	CC1	
Oak Lawn	FM	W9OAR	444.90000	+	114.8 Hz	IRA
Oak Park	DMR/BM	AC9CO	441.50000	+	CC4	
Oblong	DMR/MARC	W9DJF	444.87500	+	CC1	IRA
	FUSION	W9DJF	146.61000	-	169.7 Hz	
Old Mill Grove	FM	KD9GY-R	443.85000	+		IRA
Old Ripley	FM	AD9OV-R	147.16500	+		IRA
Olive Branch	FM	K9IM	147.25500	+	118.8 Hz	IRA
Olney	DMR/BM	KC9ZHV	442.52500	+	CC8	
	FM	KC9ZHV/R	147.22500	+	141.3 Hz	
Oregon	P25	N9ST	147.16500	+	146.2 Hz	IRA
	FUSION	WB2FZC	145.70000			
Orland Park	FM	WA9PAC	444.77500	+	114.8 Hz	IRA
	FM	WD9HGO-R	444.85000	+		IRA
Oswego	FM	NK9M	224.92000	-	110.9 Hz	IRA
	FUSION	K9ISO	433.00000			
Palatine	FM	KA9ORD	443.00000	+	114.8 Hz	IRA
	FUSION	WA9PEB	441.50000	+		
Palos Heights	FUSION	KF4TIM	442.70000			
Pana	DMR/BM	KB9TZQ	444.72500	+	CC1	IRA
	FM	KB9TZQ	145.15000	-	94.8 Hz	IRA
Park Forest	FM	WB9UAR	223.96000	-	110.9 Hz	IRA
Park Ridge	DSTAR	WA9ORC	441.90625	+		
	FM	WA9ZMY	224.78000	-		IRA
Pawnee	FM	N9RYR	442.60000	+	94.8 Hz	IRA
Pekin	FM	W9FED	147.39000	+	110.9 Hz	
Peoria	DMR/BM	WX9PIA	442.50000	+	CC12	IRA
	DSTAR	W9PIA C	145.10500	-		
	DSTAR	W9PIA B	443.46875	+		
	FM	WX9PIA	147.33000	+	103.5 Hz	IRA
	FM	K9WRA	443.17500	+	156.7 Hz	IRA
	FM	W9UVI	443.87500	+	156.7 Hz	IRA
	FM	N9BBO	444.37500	+	156.7 Hz	IRA
	FM	W9JWC	444.47500	+	103.5 Hz	IRA
Peotone	DMR/BM	W9AJI	441.27500	+	CC9	
Plano	DMR/MARC	W9XA	443.65625	+	CC6	IRA

Location	Mode	Call sign	Output	Input	Access	Coordinator
Plato Center	DMR/MARC	WR9ABQ	444.97500	+	CC1	
	FM	W8ZS	223.92000	-	114.8 Hz	IRA
	FM	W9ZS	444.97500	+		IRA
Princeton, 911 Tower						
	FM	KD9ABX	444.92500	+	118.8 Hz	IRA
Quincy	DSTAR	W9AWE	147.19500	+		IRA
	DSTAR	W9AWE C	147.19500	+		
	DSTAR	W9AWE	441.89375	+		
	DSTAR	W9AWE B	441.89375	+		
	FM	W9AWE	147.03000	+	103.5 Hz	IRA
	FM	W9AWE	443.90000	+	103.5 Hz	IRA
	FUSION	W9WJO	146.43000			
	FUSION	AA9CT	146.55000			
	FUSION	W9WJO	445.50000			
Ramsey	FUSION	KB9TZQ	445.07500			
River Grove	DMR/MARC	K9SA	443.35000	+	CC1	
Roanoke	FM	K9WRA	444.75000	+		IRA
	FUSION	K9WRA	449.75000			
Robinson	FM	WA9ISV	147.36000	+	107.2 Hz	IRA
	FM	WA9ISV	442.80000	+	107.2 Hz	IRA
Rock Island	DSTAR	W9QCR B	440.83125	+		
	DSTAR	W9QCR	440.83125	+		IRA
	FM	W9QCR	444.90000	+	100.0 Hz	IRA
	FUSION	AB9QZ	145.56500			
Rockford	DMR/MARC	NN9P	443.32500	+	CC1	IRA
	DMR/MARC	WX9MCS	443.45000	+	CC1	
	FM	W9AXD	147.00000	+	114.8 Hz	IRA
	FM	K9RFD	442.65000	+	192.8 Hz	IRA
	FM	WW9P	442.77500	+	118.8 Hz	IRA
	FUSION	W9SBA	145.56250			
Rockton	FM	N9JTA	440.87500	+	88.5 Hz	IRA
Rolling Meadows	DSTAR	KC9RBB B	442.80000	+		
	FM	N9EW	444.92500	+	114.8 Hz	
Roselle		W9SBE-L	145.50500			
	FUSION	K9KQX	440.97500			
Round Lake	FM	W9GWP	444.60000	+	114.8 Hz	IRA
Round Lake Beach						
	FM	N9VUD	443.10000	+	114.8 Hz	
	FM	N9JSF	443.77500	+		IRA
	FUSION	KC9NSA	440.57500	+		
Salem	FM	W9CWA-R	147.27000	+		IRA
	FM	W9CWA	442.20000	+	103.5 Hz	IRA
Sandoval	DSTAR	KC9URF C	145.63750			
Sandwich	FM	N9EF-R	443.50000	+		IRA
	FM	KA9QPN	444.42500	+	131.8 Hz	IRA
Savanna	FM	N9FID	147.13500	+	107.2 Hz	IRA
Schaumburg	DMR/MARC	WB9PHK	146.70000	-	CC1	
	DMR/MARC	K9PW	439.87500	430.47500	CC1	
	DMR/MARC	WB9PHK	443.06875	+	CC0	IRA
	DMR/MARC	WB9PHK	443.08125	+	CC1	IRA
	DMR/MARC	K9MOT	443.57500	+	CC1	IRA
	DMR/MARC	K9MOT	444.79375	+	CC1	IRA
	DMR/MARC	WB9PHK	927.66250	902.66250	CC0	IRA
	FM	N9CXQ	147.28500	+	107.2 Hz	IRA
	FM	WB9YBM	224.66000	-		IRA
	FM	N9CXQ	224.76000	-	110.9 Hz	IRA
	FM	KB2MAU	224.88000	-	110.9 Hz	IRA
	FM	K9MOT	442.17500	+		
	FM	WB9PHK	443.10000	+	114.8 Hz	IRA
	FM	N9CXQ	443.62500	+	114.8 Hz	IRA
	FM	N9KNS	443.72500	+		IRA
	FM	K9PW	444.50000	+	114.8 Hz	IRA

Location	Mode	Call sign	Output	Input	Access	Coordinator
Schaumburg	FM	KB2MAU	444.80000	+	203.5 Hz	IRA
	FUSION	K9IIK	442.27500	+		
	FUSION	N9AWQ	443.94375	+		
Schiller Park	DMR/MARC	K9TOW	441.33750	+	CC4	IRA
	FM	WB9AET	224.98000	-	110.9 Hz	IRA
Seward	FM	W9TMW-R	442.35000	+		IRA
Shiloh	DMR/BM	WS9IDG	444.30000	+	CC7	IRA
	FM	AA9RT	145.11000	-		IRA
Skokie	DMR/BM	KB9JRC	440.45000	+	CC1	
	FM	KB9TAP	443.17500	+	127.3 Hz	IRA
Skokie Highlands		AA9VI-R	441.21900			
South Beloit	FUSION	N2RON	445.00000			
Springfield	DMR/BM	N9BIG	441.50000	+	CC1	
	DMR/BM	KD9KOO	442.12500	+	CC5	
	DMR/BM	KD9KOO	442.75000	+	CC5	
	DMR/BM	W9DUA	443.70625	+	CC5	
	DMR/BM	KD9KOO	444.40000	+	CC5	
	DSTAR	W9DUA	443.78125	+		IRA
	DSTAR	W9DUA B	443.78125	+		
	FM	W9DUA	443.00000	+	94.8 Hz	IRA
	FM	WA9KRL	443.37500	+	94.8 Hz	IRA
	FM	K9CZ	444.32500	+		IRA
	FM	KB9TZS	444.40000	+	103.5 Hz	IRA
	FUSION	KF9TA	432.55000			
St. Charles	FUSION	N9NLE	444.52500	+		
Sterling	FM	N9JWI	444.02500	+	82.5 Hz	
	FUSION	K9HKS	147.80000			
Stockton	FM	N9NIX	443.97500	+	127.3 Hz	IRA
Stone Park	FM	W9BZW-R	147.36000	+		IRA
Streamwood	FUSION	NA9PL	440.25000	+		
Sugar Grove	DMR/MARC	K9NRO	442.42500	+	CC1	IRA
	FM	KA9HPL	442.47500	+	103.5 Hz	IRA
Swansea	DSTAR	KC9WKE-R	444.17500	+		IRA
Tallula	FM	W9DUA	442.67500	+	151.4 Hz	IRA
	FM	W9DUA	444.90000	+	151.4 Hz	IRA
Taylorville	DMR/BM	N9OGL	146.83500	-	CC1	
	FM	N9FU	442.05000	+	79.7 Hz	IRA
Tinley Park	FM	W9IC	441.80000	+	107.2 Hz	IRA
Tonti		WD9EON-L	147.27000			
Toulon	FUSION	AD9Z	147.42500			
Towerhill, Williamsburg Hill						
	FM	WB9QPM	147.39000	+	203.5 Hz	IRA
Tremont	DMR/BM	W6PC	444.97500	+	CC12	
	FM	W9TAZ	444.55000	+		IRA
Tremont / Peoria	DMR/MARC	W6PC	444.15000	+	CC1	
Trivoli	DMR/BM	KT9Y	442.10000	+	CC12	
Troy	FM	KT9R	442.65000	+	79.7 Hz	IRA
Tunnel Hill	FM	W9WG	147.34500	+	88.5 Hz	IRA
	FM	WB9F	224.86000	-	88.5 Hz	IRA
Unknown	DMR/MARC	KB9SAR	440.00000	+	CC0	
Urbana	FM	KD9FDD	147.06000	+	162.2 Hz	IRA
Utica	FM	KC9CFU	145.29000	-	103.5 Hz	IRA
Vernon Hills	FUSION	KC9KJY	446.20000			
Versailles	FM	KB9JVU	29.68000	-	103.5 Hz	IRA
	FM	KB9JVU	443.92500	+	88.5 Hz	
Virden	DMR/BM	N9BIG	443.05000	+	CC7	
Warrenville	DMR/MARC	AA9AZ	442.12500	+	CC14	
	FM	WA9WSL-R	224.36000	-		IRA
Washington		K9SOI-L	147.57000			
Washington / Morton						
	DMR/BM	KB9YVN	442.20000	+	CC12	
Waterloo	FM	KC0TPS	147.25500	+		IRA

Location	Mode	Call sign	Output	Input	Access	Coordinator
Waterloo	FM	N9OMD	444.70000	+	127.3 Hz	IRA
Watseka	FM	AD9L	444.62500	+	103.5 Hz	IRA
Wauconda	DMR/MARC	N9CWM	441.75625	+	CC1	
	FM	K9SGR	442.50000	+	114.8 Hz	IRA
Waukegan		KD9CWS-L	146.46000			
	FM	N9IJ	441.17500	+	88.5 Hz	
	FM	AA9RA	442.17500	+		IRA
Wayne	DSTAR	W9AUX	1292.60000	1272.60000		IRA
West Chicago	DMR/MARC	WD9BBE	442.96250	+	CC5	
	FM	N9XP	224.64000	-	110.9 Hz	IRA
	FM	N9XP	441.85000	+	114.8 Hz	
	FM	W9DMW	927.70000	902.70000	114.8 Hz	IRA
	FUSION	N9XP	446.85000	-		
West Dundee	DMR/MARC	N9NLE	444.52500	+	CC15	IRA
	FUSION	N9NLE	144.90000			
	FUSION	N9NLE	440.92500			
West Frankfort	FM	AB9ST	147.04500	+	97.4 Hz	IRA
Western Dunning		AB9OV-L	147.53500			
Westmont	FM	N9TO	223.86000	-	110.9 Hz	IRA
Westville	DMR/BM	W9MJW	443.08750	+	CC1	
Wheaton	FM	W9CCU	224.14000	-	110.9 Hz	IRA
	FM	KA9KDC	444.27500	+	114.8 Hz	IRA
	FUSION	WA9WSL	145.17000	-		
	FUSION	WA9WSL	442.22500	+		
Wheeling	FM	WB9OUF	444.32500	+	114.8 Hz	IRA
Williamsburg		AA9VI-L	444.50000			
Willow Springs	FUSION	W9WOX	147.42000			
Winnebago	DMR/MARC	W9TMW	440.05625	+	CC3	IRA
Woodson	DMR/BM	KD9KOO	442.75000	+	CC5	
Worth	FM	WA9ORC	224.18000	-	110.9 Hz	IRA
Yorkville	FM	WX9KRC	145.15000	-	103.5 Hz	IRA
	FM	WA9BSA	443.55000	+	114.8 Hz	IRA
	FUSION	KD9FA	440.72500	+		
Zion	FM	KA9VMV	444.82500	+	74.4 Hz	IRA
INDIANA						
Anderson	FM	W9VCF	145.39000	-	151.4 Hz	
	FM	W9OBH	146.82000	-	110.9 Hz	
	FM	KC9JWO	223.86000	-	151.4 Hz	IRC
	FM	WA9CWE	443.35000	+	110.9 Hz	IRC
	FM	WA9EOC	444.67500	+		IRC
Angola	FM	W9LKI	53.05000	-	123.0 Hz	
	FM	W9LKI	147.10500	+	131.8 Hz	IRC
	FM	W9LKI	147.18000	+	131.8 Hz	IRC
	FM	K9HD	147.21000	+	97.4 Hz	
	FM	KC9QDO	444.35000	+	131.8 Hz	
	FM	W9LKI	444.60000	+	131.8 Hz	IRC
Atlanta	DMR/BM	KB9PFM	442.47500	+	CC1	
Attica	DMR/MARC	W9ABH	442.97500	+	CC1	IRC
	FM	WB9ARC	145.19000	-	88.5 Hz	IRC
	FM	WB9ARC	927.51250	902.51250	88.5 Hz	IRC
Auburn	FM	W9OU	147.01500	+		IRC
	FM	KA9LCF	442.45000	+	131.8 Hz	
	FUSION	KD9QDL	145.36000	-		
	FUSION	K9RYN	444.30000	+		
	FUSION	N9XOR	444.45000	+		
Augusta	FM	W9ICE	442.65000	+	77.0 Hz	IRC
Avon	FUSION	W9YZU	439.17500			
Bean Blossom	FUSION	W9DBA	446.35000			
Bedford	DMR/BM	W9QYQ	444.05000	+	CC1	IRC
	DMR/MARC	N9UMJ	147.34500	+	CC1	IRC
	DMR/MARC	N9UMJ	442.47500	+	CC1	

Location	Mode	Call sign	Output	Input	Access	Coordinator
Bedford	FM	N9UMJ	29.68000	-	136.5 Hz	IRC
	FM	W9QYQ	145.31000	-	107.2 Hz	IRC
	FM	AA9WR	145.49000	-	136.5 Hz	IRC
Belleville	FM	N9HC/R	147.01500	+	88.5 Hz	
Bloomfield	FM	W9HD	147.24000	+	103.5 Hz	IRC
Bloomington	DMR/BM	K9IU	146.94000	-	CC1	
	DMR/BM	K9IU	147.18000	+	CC1	IRC
	DMR/MARC	K9IU	444.90000	+	CC1	IRC
	FM	KD9HQT	146.45000			
	FM	WB9TLH	146.64000	-	136.5 Hz	IRC
	FM	K7JOE	441.22500	+	136.5 Hz	
	FM	K9IU	442.82500	+		IRC
	FM	K9SOU	442.92500	+	107.2 Hz	IRC
	FM	KB9SGN	443.77500	+	136.5 Hz	IRC
Bluffton	FM	AB9HP	145.42000	-		
	FM	W9SR	147.06000	+		
Boonville	FM	KC9SOC	147.07500	+	88.5 Hz	IRC
Bremen	FM	W9LRT	145.19000	-		
Bristow	FUSION	KD9LUU	145.56250			
Brockton Manor	FM	KB9RRN-R	443.32500	+		IRC
Brookville	DMR/BM	KD9COF	441.93120	+	CC1	
	FM	N9HHM	224.28000	-		IRC
Brownsburg	FUSION	WA9FDO	442.77500	+		
Brownstown		KC9ZXM-R	145.43000			
	FM	KC9JOY	441.55000	+	103.5 Hz	IRC
Carlisle	FM	W9AZM	444.22500	+	107.2 Hz	IRC
Cedar Lake	FM	WB9VRG	146.83500	-	131.8 Hz	IRC
Center Point	FM	N9CCA	145.42000	-	151.4 Hz	
Centerville	FM	KB9SJZ-R	147.18000	+		
Chalmers	FM	KC9PQA	147.25500	+	131.8 Hz	IRC
Chapel Hill	FM	W9RCA-R	146.88000	-	88.5 Hz	IRC
Chrisney	FM	KC9FTG	146.91000	-		
Clarksville	FM	KJ4ZMV	144.25500			
	FUSION	KJ4ZMV	440.10000			
Clinton	FM	W9COD	146.71500	-	151.4 Hz	
	FM	W9COD	442.17500	+	151.4 Hz	IRC
Cloverdale	DMR/BM	N9NDS	441.81250	+	CC1	IRC
	FM	KB9SGN	444.47500	+	136.5 Hz	IRC
Coatesville	FM	K9ERV	444.07500	+	151.4 Hz	IRC
Columbia City	DMR/MARC	N9MTF	442.80000	+	CC1	IRC
	FM	N9WNH	53.27000	-	141.3 Hz	IRC
	FM	WC9AR	145.27000	-	141.3 Hz	IRC
	FM	K9BLU	146.71500	-	141.3 Hz	IRC
	FM	K9BLU	223.90000	-	141.3 Hz	IRC
	FM	N9FGN	224.86000	-		IRC
	FM	N9WNH	442.55000	+	141.3 Hz	IRC
	FM	WC9AR	444.55000	+	141.3 Hz	IRC
Columbus	DMR/BM	KV9Q	438.80000	-	CC0	
	FM	W9ALQ	146.79000	-	103.5 Hz	IRC
Columbus, Carr Hill						
	FM	WB9AEP	443.07500	+	103.5 Hz	
Connersville	DMR/BM	KB9JDB	441.27500	+	CC1	IRC
	DMR/BM	W2NAP	441.97500	+	CC1	
	FM	KB9JDB	145.12000	-	127.3 Hz	IRC
	FM	KB9RVR	146.74500	-		
	FM	N9TU	442.05000	+		IRC
Corydon	FM	WD9HMH	146.77500	-	103.5 Hz	IRC
Covington	DMR/BM	W9MJW	443.08750	+	CC1	
	DMR/MARC	W9ABH	443.98750	+	CC1	IRC
	FM	WB9ARC	145.49000	-	88.5 Hz	IRC
	FM	W9ABH	224.30000	-	88.5 Hz	
Crawfordsville	FM	KB9GPB	146.86500	-	77.0 Hz	IRC

Location	Mode	Call sign	Output	Input	Access	Coordinator
Crawfordsville	FM	KC9ZED	147.22500	+	88.5 Hz	IRC
	FM	KC9QKL	147.27000	+		
Crown Point	DMR/MARC	N9IAA	444.35000	+	CC1	IRC
	FM	W9EMA	146.70000	-	131.8 Hz	IRC
	FM	W9EMA	443.45000	+	131.8 Hz	IRC
Culver	DMR/BM	N9GPY	441.21250	+	CC1	
	DMR/MARC	N9GPY	443.92500	+	CC1	
	FM	K9ZLQ	146.67000	-	131.8 Hz	
Danville	DMR/BM	WX9HC	145.13000	-	CC1	IRC
	DMR/MARC	WX9HC	444.57500	+	CC1	IRC
	FM	KD9EST	145.36000	-	151.4 Hz	
	FM	K9LMK	147.16500	+		
	FM	KD9EST	224.22000	-	88.5 Hz	
	FM	KD9EST	442.02500	+	151.4 Hz	IRC
Darlington	FM	KB9HRS	53.11000	52.11000	88.5 Hz	
Decatur	FM	KB9KYM	145.47000	-	97.4 Hz	IRC
	FM	KB9KYM	224.36000	-	97.4 Hz	IRC
	FM	K9OMW	444.32500	+	97.4 Hz	IRC
	FM	K9OMW	927.86250	902.86250	97.4 Hz	IRC
Demotte	FUSION	K9CRS	144.20000			
Dugger	FM	KC9AK	146.77500	-	136.5 Hz	IRC
Duneland Beach		KB9ND-L	147.04500			
Eaton	FM	K9NZF	444.10000	+	127.3 Hz	
Edinburgh	DMR/MARC	AF9H	441.91250	+	CC1	
Elizabethtown	FUSION	N9LGO	144.90000			
Elkhart	DMR/MARC	K9DEW	444.05000	+	CC1	IRC
	FM	KC9GMH	145.25000	-	141.3 Hz	
	FM	K9DEW	145.43000	-	141.3 Hz	IRC
	FM	N8AES	146.74500	-		
	FM	N8AES	223.94000	-	131.8 Hz	IRC
	FM	KC9GMH	224.08000	-	141.3 Hz	
	FM	K9DEW	224.90000	-	131.8 Hz	IRC
	FM	KC9GMH	442.37500	+	131.8 Hz	IRC
	FM	N8AES	442.60000	+	131.8 Hz	IRC
	FM	KC9GMH	927.21250	902.21250	131.8 Hz	IRC
	FM	N8AES	927.97500	902.97500	131.8 Hz	
Evansville	DMR/MARC	W9OG	442.18750	+	CC1	
	FM	W9KXP	53.55000	-	162.2 Hz	
	FM	AB9JT	145.11000	-	107.2 Hz	
	FM	W9OG	146.79000	-	88.5 Hz	IRC
	FM	W9KXP	146.83500	-		
	FM	W9MAR	147.10500	+	94.8 Hz	IRC
	FM	W9OG	147.15000	+	107.2 Hz	IRC
	FM	KC9ZAR	443.35000	+	107.2 Hz	IRC
	FM	K9RVB	443.55000	+		IRC
	FM	W9MAR	444.50000	+	167.9 Hz	IRC
	FM	N9WYN	444.95000	+		IRC
Ferdinand	DMR/MARC	KC9CFM	444.17500	+	CC1	
Flora	FM	W9RJB	444.65000	+	131.8 Hz	IRC
Florence	DMR/BM	K9PVC	443.20000	+	CC1	
Floyds Knobs	DMR/MARC	AF9H	441.87500	+	CC0	IRC
	FM	W9BGW	224.82000	-		IRC
	FM	WD9ANK	927.52500	902.52500	67.0 Hz	IRC
	IDAS	WB9GNA	442.30000	+	146.2 Hz	IRC
Fort Branch	FM	KB9SGN	145.15000	-	136.5 Hz	IRC
Fort Wayne	DMR/MARC	N9MTF	442.63750	+	CC1	
	DSTAR	W9TE	442.99375	+		IRC
	FM	W9FEZ	53.33000	-	141.3 Hz	
	FM	W9TE	146.76000	-		IRC
	FM	W9INX	146.88000	-		IRC
	FM	W9TE	146.94000	-	141.3 Hz	IRC
	FM	W9INX	147.25500	+		

Location	Mode	Call sign	Output	Input	Access	Coordinator
Fort Wayne	FM	W9FEZ	224.78000	-	141.3 Hz	IRC
	FM	N9MTF	442.60000	+		IRC
	FM	W9INX	443.80000	+		IRC
	FM	W9AVW	444.25000	+	141.3 Hz	IRC
	FM	W9FEZ	444.80000	+	141.3 Hz	IRC
	P25	K9MMQ	443.27500	+		IRC
	FUSION	N9MR	145.65000			
	FUSION	WB9UBF	444.00000			
Foster	FM	N9UWE	443.45000	+	88.5 Hz	IRC
Fountaintown	FUSION	W9TLW	445.00000			
Frankfort	DMR/MARC	W9SMJ	441.37500	+	CC1	
	FM	W9SMJ	147.04500	+	173.8 Hz	IRC
	FM	W9SMJ	224.88000	-	173.8 Hz	
	FM	W9SMJ	442.57500	+	173.8 Hz	IRC
Franklin	FM	KC9LGZ	223.96000	-	151.4 Hz	IRC
Freetown	DMR/BM	NA9VY	145.78500		CC1	
	DMR/MARC	NA9VY	441.73750	+	CC1	
Fremont	FM	KC9QDO	146.77500	-	141.3 Hz	IRC
Frenchtown	FM	W9BGW	146.82000	-	103.5 Hz	IRC
	FM	WB9GNA	224.70000	-	103.5 Hz	IRC
	IDAS	WB9GNA	442.30000	+	146.2 Hz	IRC
Ft. Wayne	DMR/MARC	K9MMQ	443.10000	+	CC1	IRC
Fulton	FM	WD8IEJ	442.70000	+		IRC
Galena	FM	N9CVA-L	444.20000	+		IRC
Galveston	DMR/MARC	W9SMJ	441.85000	+	CC1	IRC
	FM	W9SMJ	146.95500	-	131.8 Hz	
Gary	DMR/MARC	W9CTO	146.91000	-	CC1	IRC
	DMR/MARC	W9CTO	442.75000	+	CC1	
	FM	W9CTO	224.46000	-	131.8 Hz	IRC
Gas City	DMR/BM	KB9CRA	443.82500	+	CC1	
Georgetown		K9LXH-L	223.46000			
Glen Eden	FM	KC9QDO-R	442.87500	+		IRC
Glenwood	FM	WB9SBI	53.43000	-	131.8 Hz	
	FM	WB9SBI	146.68500	-	131.8 Hz	IRC
Gosport	FM	KB9SGN	146.89500	-	136.5 Hz	IRC
Greencastle	FM	WB9EOC	442.22500	+		IRC
	IDAS	WB9EOC	147.33000	+		
Greendale	FM	W9TE-R	146.91000	-		
	FM	K9GPS-R	443.87500	+		
Greenfield	FM	W9ATG	145.33000	-	88.5 Hz	
	FM	W9ATG	444.45000	+	88.5 Hz	IRC
Greens Fork	FM	K9APR	29.66000	-	110.9 Hz	IRC
Greensburg	FM	N9LQP	146.95500	-	146.2 Hz	IRC
	FM	N9LQP	224.78000	-	100.0 Hz	IRC
Greentown	FM	N9ZEZ	442.11250	+	173.8 Hz	IRC
Greenwood	DMR/MARC	W9AMT	442.11250	+	CC1	
	FM	W9MID	146.83500	-	151.4 Hz	IRC
	FM	KB9RRN	446.03750	448.33750		
Hammond		N9SES-L	146.57000			
	FM	KA9QJG	147.04500	+	131.8 Hz	IRC
	FM	W9FXT	147.19500	+	131.8 Hz	IRC
	FM	W9FXT	224.00000	-	131.8 Hz	IRC
	FM	KA9QJG	224.74000	-	131.8 Hz	IRC
	FM	W9FXT	442.20000	+	131.8 Hz	IRC
Hartford CITY	FM	WB9HLA-R	146.92500	-		IRC
	FM	WB9HLA	443.57500	+		IRC
	FUSION	WB9HLA	448.57500	-		
Hartford City, IN	FM	K9VND	146.65500	-	141.3 Hz	IRC
Hebron	FM	N9TAX	442.35000	+	131.8 Hz	IRC
Hobart	P25	KA9QJG	444.75000	+		IRC
Huntertown	FUSION	K9WJM	145.61000			
Huntington	FM	KB9UMI	145.15000	-	141.3 Hz	IRC

Location	Mode	Call sign	Output	Input	Access	Coordinator
Huntington	FM	K9HC	146.68500	-	141.3 Hz	IRC
	FM	KC9GX	443.97500	+	131.8 Hz	IRC
Huron	IDAS	N9UMJ-R	442.25000	+	136.5 Hz	IRC
Imperial Hills		KD9AKX-L	144.00000			
Indianapolis	DMR/BM	N9ALD	145.41000	-	CC1	IRC
	DMR/BM	N9ALD	441.20000	+	CC1	IRC
	DMR/MARC	NF9K	442.45000	+	CC1	
	DMR/MARC	W9AMT	927.93750	902.93750	CC1	IRC
	DSTAR	W9ICE	444.12500	+		IRC
	FM	K9IPL	52.70000	-	136.5 Hz	IRC
	FM	K9TNW	53.01000	-		
	FM	NE9T	145.21000	-	100.0 Hz	IRC
	FM	W9IRA	146.62500	-	88.5 Hz	IRC
	FM	K9IPL	146.67000	-		
	FM	W9IRA	146.70000	-		
	FM	K9LPW	146.76000	-	151.4 Hz	IRC
	FM	W9ICE	146.97000	-	107.2 Hz	IRC
	FM	W9IRA	147.12000	+		
	FM	K9DC	147.31500	+	94.8 Hz	IRC
	FM	KC9COP	224.50000	-		IRC
	FM	W9ICE	441.35000	+	77.0 Hz	IRC
	FM	W9CRC	441.87500	+		
	FM	KA9GIX	442.00000	+		IRC
	FM	K9DC	442.37500	+		IRC
	FM	W9EMO	442.50000	+		
	FM	W9SEM	442.72500	+	88.5 Hz	
	FM	KB9RBF	442.95000	+		IRC
	FM	WB9PGW	443.00000	+	100.0 Hz	IRC
	FM	KM9E	443.25000	+	100.0 Hz	IRC
	FM	K9IP	443.42500	+	94.8 Hz	IRC
	FM	K9LPW	443.75000	+		
	FM	KC9COP	443.80000	+		IRC
	FM	W9IRA	443.85000	+	88.5 Hz	IRC
	FM	NE9T	444.00000	+	100.0 Hz	IRC
	FM	KB9SGN	444.32500	+	136.5 Hz	IRC
	FM	KA9GIX	444.87500	+		IRC
	FM	W9ICE	927.48750	902.48750	131.8 Hz	IRC
	FM	W9ICE	927.98750	902.98750	77.0 Hz	
	FM	W9ICE	1293.50000	1273.50000	77.0 Hz	IRC
	FUSION	W9NMM	145.56250			
	FUSION	N9GZK	443.75000	+		
Indianapolis City (balance)						
		AF9A-R	146.88000			
Inverness	FM	KC9TIK-R	927.70000	902.70000		IRC
Jasonville	FM	KC9AK	53.31000	-	88.5 Hz	
Jasper	FM	KB9LHX	147.19500	+	107.2 Hz	
	FM	N9MZF	444.67500	+	107.2 Hz	IRC
Jonesboro	FM	N9PKL	443.82500	+	141.3 Hz	IRC
Kendallville	FM	K9NDU	443.60000	-	97.4 Hz	IRC
Kirksville	DMR/BM	WB9TLH	443.05000	+	CC1	IRC
Knox	FM	KN9OX	145.41000	-	131.8 Hz	IRC
	FM	W9QN	442.95000	+	131.8 Hz	IRC
Kokomo	DMR/MARC	KB9TTX	442.40000	+	CC1	
	DMR/MARC	W9SMJ	444.60000	+	CC1	IRC
	FM	W9SMJ	53.39000	-	131.8 Hz	IRC
	FM	W9SMJ	145.35000	-	131.8 Hz	IRC
	FM	W9KRC	146.91000	-	173.8 Hz	IRC
	FM	W9KRC	147.24000	+	173.8 Hz	IRC
	FM	W9KRC-R	147.37500	+		IRC
	FM	W9SMJ	224.14000	-	131.8 Hz	IRC
	FM	W9KRC	442.30000	+	173.8 Hz	IRC
	FM	KA9GFS	443.30000	+		IRC

Location	Mode	Call sign	Output	Input	Access	Coordinator
Kokomo	P25	W9SMJ	927.12500	902.12500		IRC
	FUSION	WH6CDU	146.45000			
	FUSION	W9KRC	147.37500	+		
La Porte		KD9EOE-L	146.49000			
	DMR/MARC	N9IAA	444.67500	+	CC1	
	FM	K9JSI	146.61000	-	131.8 Hz	IRC
	FUSION	AC9HO	445.56250			
	FUSION	N4SV	446.55000			
Ladoga	FUSION	N9DBJ	437.10000			
Lafayette	DSTAR	W9ARP C	146.73000	-		
	DSTAR	W9ARP B	444.30000	+		
	FUSION	KE9CK	145.56250			
LaGrange	DMR/MARC	NT9M	443.67500	+	CC1	
Lake Village	FUSION	KD9JYA	442.92500	+		
Laotto	FM	KB9VTK	927.46250	902.46250	141.3 Hz	IRC
Laporte	FM	W9SAL	444.95000	+	131.8 Hz	IRC
	FUSION	W9LY	441.95000	+		
Lawrenceburg	FM	KB9GYO	147.28500	+	146.2 Hz	IRC
	FM	KB9GYO	443.87500	+	146.2 Hz	IRC
Leavenworth	FM	KC9OLF	443.30000	+	103.5 Hz	IRC
Leopold	FM	KC9OBN	145.19000	-	107.2 Hz	
Ligonier	FM	N9BCP	147.15000	+	97.4 Hz	IRC
Linton	FM	KA9JOK	145.17000	-	100.0 Hz	IRC
	FM	W9GCR	145.39000	-	118.8 Hz	IRC
	FM	KC9ZAR	444.42500	+	100.0 Hz	IRC
Linwood	FM	KB9VE	147.09000	+	110.9 Hz	IRC
Logansport	FM	W9VMW	443.65000	+		
Logansport, EMA Building						
	FM	W9VMW	145.23000	-	173.8 Hz	IRC
	FM	W9VMW	147.18000	+	173.8 Hz	IRC
Loogootee	FM	N9NGA	147.28500	+	107.2 Hz	IRC
Louisville	FM	N9GTO	147.09000	+		
Lowell	FM	KA9OOI	443.95000	+	131.8 Hz	IRC
Lynn	DMR/MARC	N9CZV	441.17500	+	CC1	
	DMR/MARC	K9NZF	441.51250	+	CC1	
	FM	K9NZF	927.01250	902.01250	131.8 Hz	IRC
	FM	K9NZF	927.57500	902.57500	131.8 Hz	IRC
Madison	FM	W9EFU	145.17000	-	103.5 Hz	
	FUSION	K9URT	146.54000			
Marion	DMR/BM	KB9CRA	442.75000	+	CC1	IRC
	DSTAR	W9EBN B	443.40000	+		
	DSTAR	W9EBN	443.40000	+		IRC
	FM	WB9UCF	145.31000			IRC
	FM	W9EBN	146.79000	-	141.3 Hz	IRC
	FM	W9EBN	147.19500	+	141.3 Hz	IRC
	FM	K9MMQ	444.75000	+	141.3 Hz	IRC
Martinsville	FM	K9PYI	147.06000	+	88.5 Hz	IRC
	FM	W9ZSK	147.25500	+	88.5 Hz	
	FM	K9PYI	224.66000	-		IRC
	FM	W9ZSK	444.25000	+	100.0 Hz	IRC
	FM	K9PYI	444.95000	+	100.0 Hz	IRC
	FUSION	K9JTV	145.00000			
	FUSION	K9JTV	434.00000			
	FUSION	N9AWU	444.25000	+		
Meridian Hills		AF9A-L	146.88000			
Merrillville	FM	W9LJ	147.00000	+	131.8 Hz	IRC
	FM	W9LJ	442.07500	+	131.8 Hz	IRC
Michigan City	FM	W9LY-R	146.97000	-		IRC
	FM	W9LY	441.95000	+	131.8 Hz	IRC
Middlebury	FM	K9DEW	146.64000	-	141.3 Hz	
Mishawaka	DMR/MARC	K9DEW	442.05000	+	CC1	
	FM	N9GVU	147.09000	+	131.8 Hz	

Location	Mode	Call sign	Output	Input	Access	Coordinator
Mishawaka	FM	K9DEW	147.33000	+	131.8 Hz	IRC
Mitchell	DMR/MARC	N9UMJ	147.34500	-	CC1	
	FM	W9QYQ	146.73000	-	107.2 Hz	IRC
	FUSION	KD9LFH/ND	443.17500	+		
Modoc	FM	K9NZF-R	443.32500	+		IRC
Monrovia	DMR/BM	K9DKC	441.78750	+	CC1	
	DMR/MARC	K9DKC	442.75000	+	CC1	
	DMR/MARC	NF9K	443.47500	+	CC1	
Montpelier	DMR/MARC	N9CZV	441.47500	+	CC1	
Mooresville	FM	W9WWV	145.11000	-	88.5 Hz	
	FM	KB9DJA	444.70000	+		IRC
	FM	N9AWM	444.77500	+		
Morgantown	DMR/MARC	KC9TKJ	443.16250	+	CC1	IRC
Morocco	FM	KD9JYA	145.33000	-	131.8 Hz	
	FM	KD9JYA	442.92500	+	131.8 Hz	IRC
Mount Vernon	FM	KD9ABT	442.75000	+	107.2 Hz	IRC
Muncie	DMR/MARC	W9AMT	441.28750	+	CC1	IRC
	DMR/MARC	N9CZV	441.30000	+	CC1	IRC
	DSTAR	W9DUK	443.40000	+		
	FM	WB9HXG	146.73000	-	127.3 Hz	IRC
	FM	K9NZF	146.85000	-	127.3 Hz	IRC
	FM	WB9HXG	223.92000	-		IRC
	FM	WD9HQH	224.70000	-		IRC
	FM	K9NZF	441.90000	+	127.3 Hz	IRC
	FM	WB9HXG	444.37500	+	127.3 Hz	IRC
	P25	N9CZV	441.82500	+		IRC
	FUSION	W9DSW	146.48000			
	FUSION	W9DSW	147.96000			
	FUSION	KD9SZA	444.35000	+		
Napoleon	FM	KC9MBX	146.80500	-		
Nashville	DMR/MARC	AF9H	443.58750	+	CC1	IRC
	FM	KD9KQS	147.30000	+	136.5 Hz	IRC
	FM	KD9KQS	443.27500	+	136.5 Hz	IRC
New Albany	FM	WD9HMH	146.74500	-	151.4 Hz	IRC
	FM	KC9UMH	146.85000	-		
	FM	N9VQ	441.95000	146.95000		
New Castle		KC9QEW-L	147.51000			
	DMR/MARC	N9CZV	441.56750	+	CC1	
	DMR/MARC	K9NZF	441.95500	+	CC1	
	FM	N9JDP	145.45000	-		
	FM	N9WB	147.36000	+		
	FM	K9TDX	441.40000	+		
	FM	N9JDP	444.27500	+	131.8 Hz	IRC
New Haven	DSTAR	W9TE B	442.99375	+		
Newburgh	FM	KA9VKO	145.43000	-		
	FM	KC9DPD	442.12500	+	136.5 Hz	IRC
Newport	DMR/BM	W9MJW	443.08750	+	CC1	
	DSTAR	KC9YGI C	145.14500	+		
NOAA Angola	WX	KXI94	162.42500			
NOAA Bloomington						
	WX	WXM78	162.45000			
NOAA Edwardsport						
	WX	WWG83	162.42500			
NOAA Evansville	WX	KIG76	162.55000			
NOAA Fort Wayne						
	WX	WXJ58	162.55000			
NOAA Georgia	WX	WWG72	162.50000			
NOAA Hebron	WX	WNG689	162.45000			
NOAA Indianapolis						
	WX	KEC74	162.55000			
NOAA Marion	WX	WXM98	162.45000			

Location	Mode	Call sign	Output	Input	Access	Coordinator
NOAA Michigan City						
	WX	KJY62	162.50000			
NOAA Monticello / Lafayette						
	WX	WXK74	162.47500			
NOAA Muncie	WX	KJY93	162.42500			
NOAA New Albany						
	WX	KIH43	162.47500			
NOAA Newport	WX	KZZ27	162.42500			
NOAA North Webster						
	WX	WWG45	162.50000			
NOAA Putnamville						
	WX	WXK72	162.40000			
NOAA Richmond	WX	KHB52	162.50000			
NOAA Seymour	WX	WWG73	162.52500			
NOAA South Bend						
	WX	WXJ57	162.40000			
Noblesville	DMR/MARC	NF9K	441.57500	+	CC5	
	DMR/MARC	NF9K	443.10000	+	CC1	
	DMR/MARC	K3HTK	444.41250	+	CC1	
	FM	N9EOC	145.17000	-	77.0 Hz	
	FM	N9EOC	443.55000	+	77.0 Hz	IRC
	FM	W9ICE	443.90000	+	77.0 Hz	IRC
	FM	K3HTK	927.08750	902.08750	131.8 Hz	IRC
	P25	NF9K	927.53750	902.53750		IRC
	FUSION	W9KD	433.55000			
	FUSION	N9EOC	443.95000	+		
North Vernon	FUSION	KD9RWN	144.87000			
Osgood	DMR/BM	N9ICV	145.38000	-	CC2	
	DMR/MARC	KM4COM	434.30000		CC1	
Otterbein	FM	W9CBA	927.56250	902.56250	82.5 Hz	IRC
Paoli	FM	WB9FHP	53.63000	-		
	FM	KB9OHY-R	147.04500	+		IRC
	FM	KB9OHY	444.02500	+	103.5 Hz	IRC
Parker City	FM	K9EKP	224.04000	-	127.3 Hz	IRC
Paxton	FM	KC9ZAR	146.92500	-	107.2 Hz	IRC
Pennville	FM	WA9BFF	145.21000	-	97.4 Hz	
Peru	DMR/MARC	W9SMJ	441.26250	+	CC1	
	FM	K9ZEV	443.17500	+	131.8 Hz	IRC
	FUSION	KC9USW	144.30000			
Petersburg	FM	WA9FGT	145.45000	-		
	FM	W9UL	147.00000	+	107.2 Hz	IRC
	FM	KB9EDT	444.00000	+	107.2 Hz	IRC
Plainfield	DMR/BM	N9ALD	441.21250	+	CC1	
Pleasant Lake	FM	K9CWM	445.02500	-		
	FM	K9CWM	445.90000	-	107.2 Hz	
Plymouth	DMR/MARC	N9GPY	444.92500	+	CC1	IRC
Portable	DMR/BM	N9ALD	441.21250	+	CC1	
Portland	FM	WA9JAY	146.89500	-	97.4 Hz	IRC
	FM	W9JKL	443.47500	+	97.4 Hz	IRC
Princeton	FM	KB9NEJ	145.41000	-	136.5 Hz	IRC
	FM	W9KXP	147.39000	+	131.8 Hz	IRC
	FM	KC9MEW	442.05000	+	210.7 Hz	IRC
Reynolds	DMR/MARC	KC9PQA	441.95625	+	CC1	
	FM	WA9RAY	442.15000	+	131.8 Hz	IRC
Richmond	DMR/MARC	N9CZV	444.60000	+	CC1	
	FM	W1IDX	147.27000	+	131.8 Hz	IRC
	FM	KC9ITT	147.46500	146.56500	131.8 Hz	
	FM	W1IDX	444.35000	+	127.3 Hz	
	FM	W1IDX	444.98000	+	131.8 Hz	
Ridgeport	FM	KB9SIP	145.47000	-	136.5 Hz	IRC
Ridgeview	FM	K9ZEV-R	147.34500	+	131.8 Hz	IRC
Roanoke	DMR/MARC	K9MMQ	442.92500	+	CC1	IRC

Location	Mode	Call sign	Output	Input	Access	Coordinator
Roanoke	DMR/MARC	K9MMQ	444.15000	+	CC1	IRC
	FM	K9MMQ	146.62500	-	141.3 Hz	IRC
	FM	K9MMQ	224.40000	-	141.3 Hz	IRC
	FM	WD9JFC	441.37500	+	141.3 Hz	IRC
	P25	K9MMQ	927.02500	902.02500		IRC
Rochester	FM	KB9WSL	146.80500	-		
Rockville	FUSION	W9GMW	147.50000			
	FUSION	W9GMW	445.40000			
Rossville	FM	WI9RES	145.37000	-	131.8 Hz	IRC
	FM	WI9RES	443.50000	+	131.8 Hz	IRC
Rushville	FM	W9NTP	147.00000	+	127.3 Hz	IRC
	FM	W9NTP	442.60000	+	127.3 Hz	IRC
Russiaville	FM	W9SMJ	224.26000	-	131.8 Hz	IRC
	FM	W9SMJ	441.67500	+		IRC
	FM	W9SMJ	442.52500	+	131.8 Hz	IRC
	FM	W9SMJ	927.05000	902.05000	131.8 Hz	IRC
	P25	W9SMJ	444.02500	+		IRC
Saint John	FM	W9LJ	147.24000	+	131.8 Hz	
Saint Paul	DMR/MARC	KD9GUD	441.98125	+	CC1	
Salem	FM	KB9KPG	146.65500	-	103.5 Hz	IRC
	FM	KB9SGN	444.92500	+	136.5 Hz	IRC
Scipio	DMR/MARC	AF9H	441.31250	+	CC1	
	FM	KC9PIE	145.25000	-		IRC
	FM	KC9TME	442.97500	+	103.5 Hz	IRC
	FM	N9JWR	443.02500	+	103.5 Hz	IRC
Scottsburg	FM	WR9G	146.61000	-	103.5 Hz	IRC
	FUSION	KD9RWO	145.00000			
	FUSION	KD9GUV	445.00000			
Sellersburg	FUSION	KD9IQO	145.56250			
	FUSION	KD9IQO	145.78750			
Seymour	FM	KC9JOY	145.43000	-	103.5 Hz	IRC
	FM	KI9G	147.13500	+	103.5 Hz	IRC
	FM	N9PUG	224.86000	-	218.1 Hz	IRC
Sharpsville	FM	K9TRC	443.70000	+	131.8 Hz	IRC
Shelbyville	DMR/MARC	W9NTP	441.48750	+	CC1	
	DMR/MARC	W9NTP	441.84375	+	CC1	
	DSTAR	W9NTP	442.18750	+		IRC
	DSTAR	W9NTP B	442.18750	+		
	FM	W9NTP	145.48000	-	88.5 Hz	IRC
	FM	W9NTP	224.44000	-		IRC
	FM	W9NTP	444.97500	+		IRC
Shoals	FM	KA9PSX	145.21000	-	107.2 Hz	
Snacks	FM	NF9K-R	442.85000	+		IRC
South Bend	DMR/MARC	N9IAA	443.42500	+	CC1	
	FM	N9JHQ	53.85000	-		
	FM	N9OCB	145.29000	-	131.8 Hz	
	FM	N9YOU	145.39000	-	131.8 Hz	
	FM	N9ABN	145.41000	-	173.8 Hz	
	FM	W9AB	147.22500	+	131.8 Hz	IRC
	FM	WB9AGX	147.39000	+	131.8 Hz	IRC
	FM	WB9YPA	223.98000	-	131.8 Hz	IRC
	FM	WB9AGX	442.10000	+	131.8 Hz	IRC
	FM	KC9MEC	442.65000	+	131.8 Hz	IRC
	FM	ND1U	443.35000	+	131.8 Hz	IRC
	FM	KA9LAW	444.17500	+	131.8 Hz	IRC
	FM	K9SIQ	444.97500	+	107.2 Hz	IRC
Speedway	FUSION	N9NIC	439.40000			
Spencer	FM	K9QZX	146.98500	-	136.5 Hz	IRC
Spencerville	FM	W9QR	147.36000	+	141.3 Hz	IRC
Springville	FM	N9HXU	223.80000	-	107.2 Hz	IRC
Stilesville	FM	AB9D	145.29000	-	88.5 Hz	IRC

Location	Mode	Call sign	Output	Input	Access	Coordinator
Sunnybrook Acres						
		KB9IBW-L	145.59500			
Terre Haute		KC9VFQ-L	146.80500			
	DMR/BM	K9IKQ	442.08750	+	CC1	
	FM	W9SKI	145.23000	-		
	FM	NC9U	145.35000	-		
	FM	K9IKQ	146.68500	-	151.4 Hz	
	FM	KC9SJJ	146.80500	-		
	FM	W0DQJ	147.09000	+		IRC
	FM	W9SKI	444.35000	+		IRC
	FM	W0THI	444.60000	+		IRC
	FM	K9ITK	444.75000	+	151.4 Hz	IRC
	FM	K9EDP	444.85000	+	151.4 Hz	IRC
Tipton	FM	K9TRC	443.12500	+		IRC
Upland	DMR/MARC	KB9TTX	442.40000	+	CC1	
Valparaiso	DMR/BM	N9IAA	147.10500	+	CC1	
	DMR/MARC	N9IAA	441.57500	+	CC1	IRC
	FM	N9IAA	53.57000	52.57000	173.8 Hz	IRC
	FM	N9IAA	146.68500	-	173.8 Hz	IRC
	FM	K9PC	146.77500	-	131.8 Hz	IRC
	FM	KC9YNM	224.28000	-	131.8 Hz	IRC
	FM	K9PC	442.25000	+	131.8 Hz	IRC
Versailes	FM	KC9MBX	224.46000	-		IRC
Versailles	FM	KC9MBX	146.80500	-		
	FM	WY9L	441.77500	+		IRC
Vevay	DMR/BM	KD9OKY	145.65000		CC0	
Vicksburg	FM	KB9SIP	442.42500	+	118.8 Hz	IRC
Vincennes	FM	W9EOC	146.67000	-	91.5 Hz	IRC
	FM	KC9ZAR	147.12000	+	107.2 Hz	IRC
	FM	KC9ZAR	224.60000	-	94.8 Hz	IRC
	FM	W9EOC	443.67500	+	91.5 Hz	
	FM	KC9ZAR	443.92500	+	107.2 Hz	IRC
	FUSION	KD9VCW	145.00000			
Wabash	FM	KB9LDZ	147.03000	+	131.8 Hz	IRC
	FM	N9MNU	441.50000	+	97.4 Hz	
Warsaw	FM	K9DEW	146.98500	-	141.3 Hz	IRC
	FM	K9DEW	443.05000	+		IRC
	FM	K9CWD	444.20000	+		IRC
Washington	FM	WA9IN	147.31500	+	107.2 Hz	IRC
	FM	KB9LOW	442.70000	+	107.2 Hz	IRC
	FM	KC9ZAR	443.22500	+	107.2 Hz	IRC
West Lafayette	DMR/MARC	W9YB	443.60000	+	CC1	IRC
	DSTAR	W9ARP	146.73000	-		IRC
	DSTAR	W9ARP	444.30000	+		IRC
	FM	W9YB	53.19000	-	131.8 Hz	
	FM	W9YB	146.76000	-	131.8 Hz	IRC
	FM	WI9RES	147.13500	+	131.8 Hz	IRC
	FM	KB9KHM	421.25000	439.25000		
	FM	KA9VXS	441.52500	+	131.8 Hz	IRC
	FM	W9YB	444.16250	+		IRC
	FM	W9YB	444.50000	+	131.8 Hz	IRC
Williamsburg	FM	W1IDX-L	145.78500	145.38500		
Williamsport	FM	WB9ARC	443.67500	+	156.7 Hz	IRC
Winchester	DMR/MARC	N9CZV	441.80000	+	CC1	
	FM	N9CZV	53.41000	-	110.9 Hz	
	FM	K5VOM	224.90000	-	127.3 Hz	
Yorktown	FM	W9YFD	441.70000	+	127.3 Hz	IRC
IOWA						
Ackley	DMR/BM	WB0EMJ	448.05000	-	CC1	
	FM	WB0EMJ	145.11000	-		IRC
	FM	WB0EMJ	147.25500	+	136.5 Hz	IRC

Location	Mode	Call sign	Output	Input	Access	Coordinator
Ackley	FM	WB0EMJ	223.85000	-	136.5 Hz	
	FM	KB0EMJ	443.75000	+	136.5 Hz	
Adel	DMR/BM	N0GIK	444.52500	+	CC1	
Afton	FM	AC0IK	442.40000	+	151.4 Hz	IRC
Algona	DMR/BM	K0HU	444.82500	+	CC2	
	FM	KC0MWG	147.21000	+	110.9 Hz	IRC
	FM	K0HTF	438.10000		100.0 Hz	
	FM	K0HTF	440.20000	+		
	FM	KC0MWG	444.82500	+	110.9 Hz	IRC
Alleman	FM	W0DM	145.31000	-	114.8 Hz	IRC
Ames	DMR/BM	N0CF	441.98750	+	CC1	
	DMR/BM	W0YR	443.97500	+	CC1	
	FM	W0YL	147.24000	+	114.8 Hz	IRC
	FM	KI0Q	443.25000	+	114.8 Hz	IRC
	FM	W0ISU	443.37500	+	114.8 Hz	IRC
	FM	W0DP	444.25000	+		IRC
Ames, ISU	FM	W0ISU	147.37500	+	114.8 Hz	IRC
Anamosa	DMR/BM	K7PEM	444.63750	+	CC1	
	FM	W0CWP	145.39000	-	77.0 Hz	IRC
Aredale	FUSION	KA0AQG	444.80000			
Atlantic	FM	N0DYB	147.15000	+	151.4 Hz	IRC
Audubon	FM	WA0GUD	147.12000	+		IRC
Avoca	FM	N0DYB	147.25500	+	151.4 Hz	IRC
	FM	N0DYB	443.95000	+	151.4 Hz	IRC
Bartlett	FM	WB0YLA-R	145.39000	-		IRC
Baxter	DMR/BM	N0VPR	444.60000	+	CC1	
	FM	KC0NFA	444.22500	+	151.4 Hz	IRC
Bedford	DMR/BM	KA0RDE	442.25000	+	CC1	
	FM	KA0RDE	147.13500	+	127.3 Hz	IRC
	FM	KA0RDE	443.70000	+	136.5 Hz	
	FM	KA0RDE	443.75000	+	136.5 Hz	IRC
Bettendorf		KD0UHN-L	145.76500			
Bondurant	DMR/BM	N0MB	443.83750	+	CC1	
Boone	DMR/BM	N0ISU	443.07500	+	CC1	
	FM	KB0TLM	146.85000	-		IRC
	FM	KB0TLM	443.90000	+		IRC
Breda	FM	N0NAF	147.28500	+	110.9 Hz	IRC
Bridgewater	DMR/MARC	WD0FIA	443.80000	+	CC10	IRC
	FM	WD0FIA	145.23000	-	136.5 Hz	IRC
	FM	WD0FIA	224.82000	-	136.5 Hz	IRC
Brooklyn	FM	K0TSK	442.65000	+		
Brunsville	FM	KD0XD	444.22500	+	110.9 Hz	IRC
Burlington	FM	W0LAC	146.79000	-	100.0 Hz	IRC
Calrinda	FM	N0NHB	145.35000	-		IRC
Carroll	FM	KC0UIO	146.80500	-	110.9 Hz	IRC
Castana	FM	K0BVC	145.47000	-	136.5 Hz	IRC
Cedar Falls	DMR/BM	N0CF	441.98750	+	CC1	
	DMR/BM	N0CF	927.08750	902.08750	CC1	
	FM	NK0T	224.90000	-	136.5 Hz	IRC
Cedar Rapids	DMR/BM	W0GQ	443.66000	+	CC1	IRC
	DMR/BM	K0LVB	444.82500	+	CC1	
	DSTAR	N0CXX	147.40500	146.40500		
	DSTAR	N0CXX C	147.40500	146.41500		
	DSTAR	N0CXX B	442.05000	+		
	DSTAR	N0CXX	442.05000	+		
	FM	W0WSV	145.15000	-	192.8 Hz	
	FM	N0DX	145.19000	-	192.8 Hz	
	FM	W0GQ	146.74500	-	192.8 Hz	IRC
	FM	W0WSV	147.09000	+	192.8 Hz	IRC
	FM	W0WSV	224.94000	-	192.8 Hz	IRC
	FM	W0VCK	443.00000	+	192.8 Hz	
	FM	N0MA	443.80000	+	192.8 Hz	

Location	Mode	Call sign	Output	Input	Access	Coordinator
Cedar Rapids	FM	NN0V	444.30000	+	192.8 Hz	
	FM	W0IY	927.11250	902.11250		
	FUSION	WM1KE	145.00000			
	FUSION	WM1KE	145.56250			
	FUSION	W0VFK	146.55000			
Center Point	FM	W0IY	927.50000	902.50000	192.8 Hz	
Chariton	FM	KB0AJ	146.83500	-	146.2 Hz	IRC
	FUSION	N0EHQ	145.60000			
Chelsea	FM	WD0GAT	442.12500	+	151.4 Hz	IRC
Clarinda	FM	K0SKU	146.97000	-	136.5 Hz	
Clear Lake	DMR/BM	KK6RQ	147.30000	144.30000	CC1	
Clinton	DMR/MARC	KD0WY	147.31500	+	CC23	
	FM	W0CS	145.43000	-	100.0 Hz	
	FM	KN0BS	224.18000	-	136.5 Hz	IRC
	FUSION	KE0FIS	433.02500			
	FUSION	KD0WY	444.22500			
Coralville	FM	W0FDA	147.15000	+	192.8 Hz	IRC
	FM	K0GH	444.75000	+	151.4 Hz	IRC
Council Bluffs		K0NHV-L	446.50000			
	FM	K0SWI	146.82000	-		IRC
	FUSION	KB0TDW	433.10000			
	FUSION	K0SWI	442.22500	+		
	FUSION	KD0YTI	447.60000	-		
Cresco, Hawkeye Tri County REC						
	FM	W0CYY	146.92500	-	103.5 Hz	IRC
Creston	DMR/BM	K0CSQ	443.12500	+	CC1	
	FM	N0GMH	146.79000	-	136.5 Hz	IRC
	FUSION	KB0NBE	146.42000			
Davenport, KWQC						
	FM	W0BXR	146.70000	-		IRC
Davenport, Saint Ambrose Unive						
	FM	W0BXR	146.94000	-		
Denison		K0FZZ-L	147.42000			
	FM	K0CNM	147.09000	+		IRC
	FM	KC0LGI	147.33000	+		IRC
	FM	KC0LGI	444.00000	+		IRC
Des Moines	DMR/BM	W0RAY	146.75500	-	CC1	
	DMR/BM	N0VPR	443.10000	+	CC1	
	DMR/BM	W0KWM	443.50000	+	CC1	
	DMR/BM	W0RAY	449.87500	-	CC1	
	DSTAR	KD0IAN	147.10500	-		IRC
	DSTAR	KD0IAN C	147.10500	+		
	DSTAR	KD0IAN B	443.17500	+		
	FM	W0AK	145.13000	-	114.8 Hz	IRC
	FM	W0AK	146.94000	-	114.8 Hz	IRC
	FM	W0AK	146.98500	-	114.8 Hz	IRC
	FM	WA0QBP	147.30000	+	114.8 Hz	IRC
	FM	WA0QBP	444.62500	+	151.4 Hz	
	FM	K0SXY	444.67500	+	114.8 Hz	IRC
	FM	N9MXX	446.87500	-	100.0 Hz	
	FUSION	W0DM	145.31000	-		
	FUSION	W0DM	146.53500			
	FUSION	WX7UTE	432.45000			
	FUSION	W0DM	444.67500	+		
Des Moines, Alleman						
	FM	W0KWM	444.57500	+	151.4 Hz	
Des Moines, Broadlawn's Hospit						
	FM	K0DSM	444.05000	+	151.4 Hz	
Des Moines, Lucas State Office						
	FM	W0KWM	146.82000	-	203.5 Hz	IRC
	FM	WD0FIA	224.98000	-	114.8 Hz	IRC

Location	Mode	Call sign	Output	Input	Access	Coordinator
Des Moines, Methodist Hospital						
	FM	K0DSM	444.10000	+	151.4 Hz	IRC
Des Moines, Sherman Hills						
	FM	KD0WPK	29.67000	-	103.5 Hz	IRC
Dubuque	DMR/BM	KD9HAE	443.20000	+	CC1	
	DMR/BM	KD9HAE	444.05000	+	CC0	
Dumont	FM	N0RJJ	145.43000	-	136.5 Hz	IRC
Early	FM	W0DOG-R	146.61000	-		IRC
Eldridge	FM	W0BXR	146.88000	-	77.0 Hz	IRC
Estherville, Airport	FM	W0MDM	146.70000	-		IRC
Fairport	FM	N2AM	444.95000	+	100.0 Hz	
Fayette	DMR/BM	W0OEL	443.95000	+	CC1	IRC
	FM	W0OEL	147.34500	+	103.5 Hz	IRC
Forest City	FM	WB0URC	147.27000	+	103.5 Hz	IRC
Fort Dodge	FM	K0RJV	146.68500	-	110.9 Hz	IRC
Fort Madison	FM	WF0RT	146.86500	-	100.0 Hz	IRC
Frankville	FM	K0RTF	146.67000	-	103.5 Hz	IRC
	FM	K0RTF	444.10000	+	103.5 Hz	IRC
Garrison	FM	K0DKS	145.23000	-	141.3 Hz	IRC
Gilman	DMR/BM	NF0T	444.15000	+	CC1	
	FM	NF0T	53.03000	51.33000	151.4 Hz	IRC
Glenwood	FM	N0WKF	145.29000	-		IRC
	FM	N0WKF	444.32500	+		IRC
Greenfield	DMR/BM	N0BKB	444.70000	+	CC1	IRC
	DMR/MARC	N0BKB	444.55000	+	CC1	
	FM	N0BKB	146.86500	-	146.2 Hz	IRC
Grimes	DMR/BM	N0INX	444.72500	+	CC1	IRC
	DSTAR	KD0IAN	443.17500	+		IRC
	FM	N0INX	53.25000	51.55000	110.9 Hz	IRC
	FM	N0INX	146.61000	-	114.8 Hz	IRC
	FM	N0INX	224.54000	-	114.8 Hz	IRC
	FM	N0INX	443.40000	+	151.4 Hz	IRC
	FM	N0INX	927.02500	902.02500	156.7 Hz	IRC
	FM	N0INX	927.43500	902.43500		
Grundy Center	DMR/MARC	W0RBK	443.87500	+	CC1	
	FM	N0MXK	444.32500	+	110.9 Hz	IRC
Grundy Center, High School						
	FM	W0RBK	146.65500	-	136.5 Hz	IRC
Hamburg	FUSION	KE0YMN	434.80000			
Herndon	FM	N2RDP	444.27500	+		IRC
Holy Cross	DMR/BM	KE0OSQ	433.02000	432.42000	CC1	
Homestead	FM	WC0C	442.42500	+	151.4 Hz	IRC
Honey Creek	FM	AB0VX	145.41000	-	97.4 Hz	IRC
	FM	AB0VX	444.80000	+	97.4 Hz	IRC
Humboldt	DMR/BM	K0HU	145.50000	-	CC3	
	DMR/BM	K0HU	442.40000	+	CC3	IRC
	DMR/MARC	K0HU	147.18000	+	CC1	
	DMR/MARC	K0HU	147.39000	+	CC4	
Independence	DMR/BM	KC0RMS	442.90000	+	CC1	IRC
	FM	KC0RMS	145.33000	-	103.5 Hz	IRC
Indianola	FM	KD0FGV-R	146.64000	-		IRC
Iowa City	DMR/BM	KD0MVJ	443.47500	+	CC1	
	DMR/BM	K0GH	443.77500	+	CC1	
	FM	KE0BX	145.47000	-	100.0 Hz	
	FM	W0JV	146.85000	-	192.8 Hz	IRC
Johnston	DMR/BM	N0VPR	442.50000	+	CC1	
	DMR/BM	N0VPR	442.57500	+	CC1	
	FM	KC0MTI	147.16500	+	114.8 Hz	IRC
	FM	KC0MTI	442.80000	+	151.4 Hz	IRC
Johnston, Camp Dodge						
	FM	KC0MTI	146.70000	-	114.8 Hz	IRC
Kelly	FM	KC0MTI	444.42500	+	151.4 Hz	IRC

Location	Mode	Call sign	Output	Input	Access	Coordinator
Kingsley	DMR/BM	KD0QQL	439.55000	+	CC12	
Larchwood	FM	N0DCA-R	443.75000	+		WB0CMC
Laurel	FM	WC0C	444.80000	+	151.4 Hz	IRC
Le Mars	DMR/BM	KI0EO	444.25000	+	CC1	
	FM	KD0PMM	147.19500	+	110.9 Hz	IRC
	FM	KI0EO	444.67500	+	110.9 Hz	IRC
	FM	KD0VYD	446.12500	-	110.9 Hz	
LeClaire	FUSION	K0IS	147.56000			
LeMars	DMR/BM	KD0PMM	444.92500	+	CC1	
	FM	KD0PMM	147.19500	+	110.9 Hz	
Lenox	DMR/BM	K9ADL	444.95000	+	CC1	
	FM	KD0TWE	146.88000	-	136.5 Hz	IRC
Leon	FM	K0FFX	444.97500	+	114.8 Hz	
Logansport	FM	N0AN-L	438.50000			IRC
Madrid	FM	N0QIX	145.25000	-	114.8 Hz	IRC
	FM	N0SFF	442.60000	+	151.4 Hz	IRC
	FM	KC0MTE	443.85000	+	151.4 Hz	IRC
Magnolia	DMR/MARC	WB0QQK	444.65000	+	CC1	
Manchester	FM	W0II	147.30000	+		IRC
	FUSION	AD0AM	145.55500			
Manilla	FM	N0JRX	147.22500	+	151.4 Hz	IRC
Marion	DMR/BM	K0LVB	146.68500	-	CC1	
Marshalltown	DMR/BM	K0MIW	444.52500	+	CC2	
	FM	NF0T	147.13500	+	141.3 Hz	IRC
	FM	N0MXK	443.32500	+	110.9 Hz	IRC
	FM	NF0T	927.82500	902.82500	151.4 Hz	IRC
Mason City	FM	KE0POU	442.27500	+	100.0 Hz	
	FUSION	WA0SPF	443.35000	+		
Mason City, Interstate Grain E						
	FM	W0MCW	146.76000	-	103.5 Hz	IRC
Mason City, Red & White Tower						
	FM	KB0JBF	147.31500	+	103.5 Hz	IRC
Mediapolis	FM	N0GES	443.10000	+	151.4 Hz	
Menlo	DMR/BM	W0RAY	444.55000	+	CC1	
	FM	N0BKB	147.04500	+	127.3 Hz	IRC
Minden	FUSION	N0GR	449.07500	-		
Mineola	FM	N0WKF	442.02500	+		IRC
	FM	N0WKF	444.02500	+		IRC
Missouri Valley	DMR/BM	N0ZHX	444.07500	+	CC1	
Mondamin	FM	K0BVC	53.39000	51.69000	136.5 Hz	IRC
	FM	K0BVC	145.13000	-	136.5 Hz	IRC
	FM	K0BVC	444.92500	-	136.5 Hz	IRC
Monona	DMR/BM	N0CKR	443.65000	+	CC1	
Moravia	DMR/BM	W0ALO	146.32500	-	CC1	
	DMR/MARC	W0ALO	444.47500	+	CC1	IRC
	FM	W0ALO	146.92500	-	146.2 Hz	IRC
	FM	W0ALO	927.33750	902.33750	136.5 Hz	IRC
Morningside	FM	KS0F-R	443.57500	+		
Mount Pleasant	DMR/BM	KE0IHD	443.62500	+	CC1	
	DSTAR	KD0NJC	444.35000	+		
	FM	KE0IHD	146.45000		100.0 Hz	
	FM	W0MME	147.16500	+	156.7 Hz	
	FM	W0MME	147.39000	+		IRC
Mount Pleasant, Iowa						
	FM	KE0IHD	444.62500	+	100.0 Hz	
Mount Vernon	DMR/BM	K0LVB	147.27000	+	CC1	
Mt Pleasant	DMR/BM	WB0VHB	444.35000	+	CC1	
Mt. Ayr	FM	KA0RDE	443.30000	+	136.5 Hz	IRC
Mt. Pleasant	DMR/BM	WB0VHB	444.52500	+	CC1	
	DSTAR	KD0NJC C	145.67000			
	DSTAR	KD0NJC A	147.57500			
	DSTAR	KD0NJC B	444.35000	+		

Location	Mode	Call sign	Output	Input	Access	Coordinator
Muscatine	DMR/BM	AC0EC	444.12500	+	CC2	
	DMR/BM	KC0WWV	444.40000	+	CC1	
	FM	KC0AQS	146.91000	-	192.8 Hz	IRC
	FM	WA0VUS	444.27500	+	192.8 Hz	IRC
	FUSION	KB0VK	432.30000			
New Boston	FM	KC0TPI-R	147.30000	+		IRC
Newton	FM	W0WML	147.03000	+	114.8 Hz	IRC
	FM	KC0NFA	442.30000	+	151.4 Hz	IRC
NOAA Burlington	WX	WXN83	162.52500			
NOAA Carroll	WX	KZZ51	162.42500			
NOAA Cedar Rapids						
	WX	WXL61	162.47500			
NOAA Decorah	WX	KXI60	162.52500			
NOAA Denison	WX	WNG668	162.55000			
NOAA Des Moines						
	WX	WXL57	162.55000			
NOAA Essex	WX	KZZ50	162.55000			
NOAA Fairfield	WX	WXN85	162.40000			
NOAA Forest City	WX	KJY63	162.50000			
NOAA Fort Dodge	WX	WXK84	162.40000			
NOAA Hancock / Pottawattam						
	WX	KZZ52	162.52500			
NOAA Iowa Falls	WX	WNG666	162.52500			
NOAA Lake Rathbun						
	WX	WXN91	162.42500			
NOAA Lenox	WX	KXI65	162.45000			
NOAA Manchester						
	WX	KJY64	162.45000			
NOAA Maquoketa	WX	KZZ83	162.42500			
NOAA Marshalltown						
	WX	KXI98	162.50000			
NOAA Milford	WX	KZZ80	162.55000			
NOAA Montezuma						
	WX	KXI62	162.45000			
NOAA Ottumwa	WX	WNG730	162.50000			
NOAA Ringsted	WX	WNG688	162.47500			
NOAA Sanborn	WX	KWN48	162.52500			
NOAA Sioux City	WX	WXL62	162.47500			
NOAA St. Ansgar	WX	KXI68	162.45000			
NOAA Storm Lake						
	WX	KWN47	162.45000			
NOAA Van Wert	WX	KZZ68	162.47500			
NOAA Waterloo	WX	WXL94	162.55000			
Ogden	FM	N0AN	144.39000			
	FUSION	N0AN	438.50000			
Osceola	FM	KC0UNH	147.21000	+	136.5 Hz	
Oskaloosa	FM	KB0VXL	145.49000	-	146.2 Hz	IRC
Otho	DMR/MARC	K0HU	443.57500	+	CC5	
Ottumwa		KE0BX-R	145.41000			
	DMR/BM	WA0DX	443.97500	+	CC1	
	DMR/BM	KE0BX	444.85000	+	CC1	
	FM	KE0BX-R	146.97000	-		
Overland Mobile Home Park						
		KB0TDW-L	224.40000			
Pacific Junction	FM	N0WKF	443.02500	+		IRC
Paullina	FM	N0OYK	147.13500	+	110.9 Hz	IRC
Pella	FM	KE0SQA	145.17000	-	114.8 Hz	IRC
Perry	FM	KD0NEB	145.19000	-	114.8 Hz	IRC
	FM	KD0NEB	444.37500	+	151.4 Hz	IRC
Portsmouth	FM	K0BVC	146.74500	-	136.5 Hz	IRC
Prescott	FM	N0DTS	145.15000	-	127.3 Hz	IRC
Primghar	FM	KC0TQU	444.87500	+		

Location	Mode	Call sign	Output	Input	Access	Coordinator
Red Oak	FM	N0NHB	146.65500	-	146.2 Hz	IRC
Reinbeck	DMR/BM	W0RBK	444.60000	+	CC1	
Richfield		N0VTZ-L	144.00000			
Rock Rapids		AD0HZ-R	147.30000			
Rock Valley	FM	W0VHQ	147.30000	+	110.9 Hz	IRC
Rockwell City	FM	K0FBP	145.49000	-	110.9 Hz	IRC
Sac City	FM	WD0CLO	146.92500	-		IRC
Saint Ansgar	FM	KC0VII-R	147.19500	+		IRC
Sanborn	FM	W0VHQ	145.31000	-	110.9 Hz	IRC
	FM	W0VHQ	443.90000	+		
Saylor Township, Saylor FD						
	FM	KD0QED	145.39000	-	114.8 Hz	IRC
Saylorville	FM	KB0NFF	443.67500	+		
Saylorville, East Mixmaster						
	FM	KB0NFF	444.50000	+		
Saylorville, Fire Dept Comm Ct						
	FM	KB0NFF	444.17500	+		IRC
Saylorville, I-35 & I-80 Cross						
	FM	KB0NFF	146.89500	-	114.8 Hz	IRC
Scotch Grove	FUSION	K0ELY	436.00000			
Scranton	DMR/BM	N0VPR	444.30000	+	CC1	
Sheldahl	FM	N0QFK	53.09000	51.39000		IRC
	FM	W0QFK	147.07500	+	114.8 Hz	IRC
Shenandoah	FM	KB0NUR	145.21000	-		IRC
Sioux City	DMR/BM	KI0KO	444.40000	+	CC1	
	DMR/BM	KI0EO	444.62500	+	CC1	
	FM	K0AAR	146.91000	-	110.9 Hz	IRC
	FM	K0TFT	146.97000	-	110.9 Hz	IRC
	FM	K0TFT	147.06000	+	110.9 Hz	IRC
	FM	KC0DXD	147.27000	+	110.9 Hz	IRC
	FM	K0NH	444.72500	+	110.9 Hz	IRC
Spencer	DMR/BM	KG0CK	146.82000	-	CC1	IRC
	DMR/BM	KG0CK	444.70000	+	CC1	IRC
	FM	WA0DOY	444.97500	+	110.9 Hz	IRC
Springbrook	FM	W0DBQ	147.06000	+	114.8 Hz	
Storm Lake	DMR/BM	WB0FNA	444.52500	+	CC1	
	FM	WB0FNA	444.75000	+		
Stratford	FM	K0KQT	146.62500	-		IRC
Thurman	DMR/BM	WB0YLA	444.50000	+	CC1	IRC
Tipton	DMR/BM	K0WLC	444.07500	+	CC2	
Truro	FM	W0AK	146.98500	-	114.8 Hz	
Twin Lakes	FM	K0FBP	442.50000	+		IRC
Urbandale	FM	N2RDP	444.27500	+	151.4 Hz	
Van Meter	FM	N0XD	443.10000	+	151.4 Hz	IRC
Victor	DMR/BM	K0TSK	444.95000	+	CC1	
Vinton	DMR/BM	NO3R	442.00000	+	CC1	
Vista Estates Mobile Home Park						
		WA0UZI-R	146.77500			
Wapello	FM	KC0AQS	146.98500	-	192.8 Hz	
Washington	FM	W0ARC	147.04500	+	146.2 Hz	
	FM	W0ARC	443.70000	+	146.2 Hz	IRC
Waterloo	DMR/BM	W0GEN	442.40000	+	CC3	
	DMR/BM	W0GEN	442.82500	+	CC1	
	DMR/BM	W0GEN	443.72500	+	CC1	
	DMR/BM	W0EL	444.70000	+	CC1	
	DMR/MARC	W0ALO	444.90000	+	CC1	IRC
	FM	W0ALO	146.82000	-	136.5 Hz	
	FM	W0MG	444.97500	+	136.5 Hz	IRC
	P25	W0ALO	444.92500	+	136.5 Hz	IRC
Waterloo, Cedar Valley TechWor						
	FM	KB0VGG	444.55000	+	103.5 Hz	IRC

Location	Mode	Call sign	Output	Input	Access	Coordinator
Waterloo, Kimball Ridge Center						
	FM	N0CF	927.06250	902.06250		IRC
Waterloo, Water Tower						
	FM	W0MG	146.94000	-	136.5 Hz	IRC
Webster	FM	N0PSF	146.91000	-		IRC
Webster City	FM	K0KWO	147.01500	+	103.5 Hz	IRC
West Bend	FM	N0DOB	145.17000	-	110.9 Hz	IRC
	FM	N0QQS	444.77500	+	110.9 Hz	IRC
West Des Moines	FM	KB0SL	927.90000	902.90000		IRC
Williams	FM	W0MCW	444.50000	+	151.4 Hz	IRC
Wilton	DMR/BM	N0MRZ	444.07500	+	CC2	
Winterset	FM	WA0O	147.27000	+	114.8 Hz	IRC
	FUSION	W0WXZ	446.60000			
Woodbine	FM	K0BVC	444.35000	+	136.5 Hz	IRC

KANSAS

Location	Mode	Call sign	Output	Input	Access	Coordinator
Alma, K-Link	FM	W0KHP	444.52500	+	162.2 Hz	Kansas RC
Arkansas City	FM	WA0JBW	147.00000	+	97.4 Hz	Kansas RC
Basehor	DMR/MARC	K0USY	444.75000	+	CC1	
	FM	K0HAM	145.39000	-	88.5 Hz	Kansas RC
	FM	N0GRQ	443.55000	+	151.4 Hz	Kansas RC
Beaumont	FM	KS0KE	145.13000	-	156.7 Hz	Kansas RC
	FM	KD5IMA	443.52500	+	156.7 Hz	Kansas RC
Beloit, K-Link	FM	K0KSN	442.80000	+		Kansas RC
Carbondale	FM	KB0WTH	147.30000	+	88.5 Hz	Kansas RC
	FM	WB0PTD	443.12500	+		Kansas RC
Chanute	FM	KZ0V	147.10500	+	91.5 Hz	Kansas RC
Chanute, Walnut	FM	AI0E	146.74500	-	91.5 Hz	Kansas RC
Clay Center		KD7QAS-L	145.15000			
	DMR/MARC	N0XRM	442.75000	+	CC1	Kansas RC
	FM	N0XRM	147.16500	+	162.2 Hz	Kansas RC
Coffeyville	FM	WR0CV	146.61000	-	91.5 Hz	Kansas RC
	FM	NU0B	147.30000	+	91.5 Hz	Kansas RC
	FM	N0TAP	224.52000	-	91.5 Hz	Kansas RC
	FM	WR0MG	442.87500	+	91.5 Hz	
	FM	N0TAP	444.55000	+	91.5 Hz	Kansas RC
Colby	DMR/MARC	NV8Q	444.75000	+	CC1	Kansas RC
	DSTAR	NW0K B	444.65000	+		
	FM	NW0K	146.82000	-	156.7 Hz	Kansas RC
	FUSION	NW0K	449.65000	-		
Colwich	DMR/BM	WA0RJE	444.00000	+	CC1	
Concordia	FM	K0KSN	146.86500	-		Kansas RC
De Soto	FUSION	W1AC	439.00000			
Derby	FM	W0UUS	146.85000	-	156.7 Hz	Kansas RC
Dodge City	FM	K0ECT	147.03000	+	123.0 Hz	
	FM	K0ECT	442.37500	+	123.0 Hz	Kansas RC
	FM	KY0J	443.35000	+	123.0 Hz	Kansas RC
	FM	K0ECT	444.55000	+	141.3 Hz	Kansas RC
	FUSION	KF0CZN	431.00000	+		
	FUSION	KF0CZN	433.00000	+		
Dodge City, K-Link						
	FM	K0HAM	443.67500	+	162.2 Hz	Kansas RC
Eastborough	FM	N0EQS-R	444.57500	+		Kansas RC
Edgerton	FM	WB0OUE	224.82000	-	151.4 Hz	Kansas RC
Effingham	FM	K0DXY	146.61000	-	100.0 Hz	
El Dorado	DMR/MARC	K0JWH	441.97500	+	CC1	
	DMR/MARC	K0USY	444.98750	+	CC1	
	FM	KB0VAC	147.15000	+		Kansas RC
Elkader	FM	K0ECT	444.30000	+	141.3 Hz	Kansas RC
Ellsworth, K-Link	FM	K0HAM	444.77500	+	162.2 Hz	Kansas RC
Emporia	DMR/BM	K0ESU	443.00000	+	CC1	Kansas RC
	FM	N0OFG	145.31000	-	103.5 Hz	Kansas RC

Location	Mode	Call sign	Output	Input	Access	Coordinator
Emporia	FM	K0HAM	146.98500	-	88.5 Hz	Kansas RC
Flush	DMR/MARC	K0USY	444.80000	+	CC1	
Fort Scott	FM	K0EFJ	146.71500	-	91.5 Hz	Kansas RC
	FM	K0EFJ	444.17500	+	88.5 Hz	Kansas RC
Garden City	FM	WA0OQA	52.87000	51.17000	141.3 Hz	Kansas RC
	FM	WA0OQA	146.91000	-	141.3 Hz	Kansas RC
Garden City, Tennis						
	FM	K0ECT	442.50000	+	141.3 Hz	Kansas RC
Garden Plain	FM	W0VFW-R	145.27000	-		Kansas RC
Gardner		KD0KKV-L	446.15000			
	FM	K0NK	224.78000	-		Kansas RC
Gas	FM	WI0LA	147.37500	+	179.9 Hz	Kansas RC
Girard	FM	K0SEK	147.24000	+	91.5 Hz	Kansas RC
Great Bend	DMR/BM	KE0PTS	442.07500	+	CC1	
	FM	KI0NN	146.76000	-	103.5 Hz	Kansas RC
	FM	KE0PTS	444.10000	+	100.0 Hz	Kansas RC
Hays	DMR/BM	N7JYS	147.04500	+	CC7	Kansas RC
	DMR/MARC	K0USY	444.75000	+	CC1	
	DMR/MARC	K0USY	444.80000	+	CC1	
	DMR/MARC	K0USY	444.82500	+	CC1	MACC-KARC
	DMR/MARC	K0USY	444.98750	+	CC1	
	FM	N7JYS	52.52500	51.52500		
	FM	KE0KIY	147.18000	+	100.0 Hz	Kansas RC
	FM	N7JYS	443.57500	+	131.8 Hz	
	FM	N0ECQ	444.82500	+	114.8 Hz	Kansas RC
	FUSION	KA0FCT	435.30000			
	FUSION	K0HYS	443.60000	+		
Hays, K-Link	FM	N7JYS	442.45000	+	162.2 Hz	Kansas RC
Haysville	FM	KA0RT	147.10500	+	151.4 Hz	Kansas RC
	FM	W0SY-R	444.97500	+		Kansas RC
Hiawatha	DMR/BM	K1CCN	442.70000	+	CC1	
	FM	WA0W	147.18000	+	88.5 Hz	Kansas RC
Hill City, K-Link	FM	N0NM	443.70000	+	162.2 Hz	Kansas RC
Hillsboro	FM	WX0RG	442.50000	+	162.2 Hz	Kansas RC
Hoisington	DMR/MARC	K0HAM	147.13500	+	CC1	Kansas RC
	FM	N7JYS	224.00000	-	131.8 Hz	
Hoisington, Beaver						
	FM	KE0PTS	444.92500	+	100.0 Hz	Kansas RC
Holton, Courthouse						
	FM	AA0MM	146.77500	-		Kansas RC
Hometown Santa Barbara Mobile						
	FM	K0ECS-R	145.47000	-		
Hopkins	FM	K0JWH-R	443.10000	+		Kansas RC
Hoyt	FM	W0CET	145.27000	-	88.5 Hz	
	FM	K0HAM	444.72500	+	88.5 Hz	Kansas RC
Hutchinson	DMR/MARC	NV8Q	444.47500	+	CC1	
	FM	W0WR	147.12000	+	103.5 Hz	Kansas RC
	FM	KA0HN	443.72500	+		Kansas RC
Hutchinson, KWCH-12						
	FM	W0UUS	146.82000	-	103.5 Hz	Kansas RC
Hutchinson, Partridge						
	FM	W0WR	146.67000	-		Kansas RC
Independence	FM	N0ID	147.01500	+	91.5 Hz	Kansas RC
	FM	KW0I	442.65000	+	91.5 Hz	Kansas RC
	FUSION	W0HLK	447.30000			
Independence, Elk City State L						
	FM	N0ID	145.49000	-	91.5 Hz	Kansas RC
Iola	FM	KS0AL	444.82500	+	91.5 Hz	Kansas RC
	FUSION	KC5VKG	145.00000			
Isabel	FM	K0HPO	442.02500	+	103.5 Hz	Kansas RC
	FM	W5ALZ	442.40000	+	103.5 Hz	Kansas RC
Itinerant	DMR/MARC	WA0EDA	444.98750	+	CC1	

Location	Mode	Call sign	Output	Input	Access	Coordinator
Joplin	FM	N0CSW	444.62500	+	91.5 Hz	MRC
Junction City	FM	N0VGY	146.88000	-		Kansas RC
	FUSION	N0OER	440.50000			
Junction City, K-Link						
	FM	KS1EMS	147.31500	+	162.2 Hz	Kansas RC
Kansas City		KD0VXJ-L	146.45000			
	DMR/BM	WD0GQA	442.85000	+	CC1	Kansas RC
	DMR/BM	WD0GQA	443.85000	+	CC1	Kansas RC
	FM	WB0NSQ	53.85000	52.15000		Kansas RC
	FM	WA0NQA	145.13000	-	151.4 Hz	Kansas RC
	FM	K0HAM	146.94000	-	88.5 Hz	Kansas RC
	FM	W0LB	147.15000	+	151.4 Hz	Kansas RC
Kansas City, Foxridge Towers						
	FM	WB0NSQ	444.85000	+	151.4 Hz	Kansas RC
Kansas City, KU Med						
	FM	KU0MED	442.32500	+		Kansas RC
Kansas City, Providence Medica						
	FM	W0KCK	147.21000	+	151.4 Hz	
Kingman	FM	KD0SLE	442.12500	+	103.5 Hz	Kansas RC
Lakin	FM	N0OMC	146.98500	-	156.7 Hz	Kansas RC
Lansing	FUSION	K0AVN	438.87500			
Lawrence	DMR/BM	KU0JHK	444.50000	+	CC7	Kansas RC
	DMR/MARC	K0USY	444.37500	+	CC1	
	FM	W0UK	146.76000	-	88.5 Hz	Kansas RC
	FM	KE0QNS	147.03000	+	88.5 Hz	Kansas RC
	FM	K0HAM	444.90000	+	88.5 Hz	MACC-KARC
Leavenworth	DMR/BM	WA0SLL	442.57500	+	CC1	
	FM	N0KOA	145.33000	-	151.4 Hz	Kansas RC
	FM	KS0LV	147.00000	+	151.4 Hz	Kansas RC
Leavenworth, St. John Hospital						
	FM	W0ROO	444.80000	+	151.4 Hz	Kansas RC
Leawood	DMR/BM	WI0JIM	442.30000	+	CC1	
Lecompton	DMR/MARC	K0USY	444.47500	+	CC1	
Lenexa		KB0MZF-L	147.50000			
Lenora, K-Link	FM	N0KOM	146.88000	-	162.2 Hz	Kansas RC
Liberal	FM	W0KKS	146.80500	-	103.5 Hz	Kansas RC
	FM	K0ECT	443.10000	+	141.3 Hz	Kansas RC
Logan	DMR/MARC	N0KOM	444.47500	+	CC1	Kansas RC
Louisburg	DSTAR	K0HAM C	145.12000	-		
	DSTAR	K0HAM B	442.12500	+		
	DSTAR	K0HAM D	1257.00000			
	DSTAR	K0HAM A	1287.00000	-		
	FM	K0HAM	53.13000	52.13000	88.5 Hz	MACC-KARC
	FM	K0HAM	145.41000	-		Kansas RC
	FM	K0HAM	147.31500	+	88.5 Hz	MACC-KARC
	FM	K0HAM	442.12500	+		Kansas RC
Manhattan	DMR/MARC	K0USY	444.37500	+	CC1	
	FM	W0QQQ	145.41000	-	151.4 Hz	Kansas RC
	FM	KS0MAN	147.25500	+	88.5 Hz	Kansas RC
	FM	KS0MAN	442.00000	+	88.5 Hz	Kansas RC
	FM	W0QQQ	444.17500	+	88.5 Hz	
Matfield Green	DMR/MARC	K0USY	444.37500	+	CC1	
Matfield Green, K-Link						
	FM	K0HAM	147.04500	+	88.5 Hz	Kansas RC
McPherson	DMR/MARC	N5NIQ	444.80000	+	CC1	Kansas RC
	FM	W0TWU	147.33000	+	162.2 Hz	Kansas RC
McPherson, K-Link						
	FM	N0SGK	444.60000	+	162.2 Hz	Kansas RC
Medicine Lodge, Gyp Hills						
	FM	K0UO	146.88000	-	103.5 Hz	Kansas RC
Merriam	DMR/BM	KC0DMR	442.87500	+	CC1	

Location	Mode	Call sign	Output	Input	Access	Coordinator
Merriam, Shawnee Mission Medic						
	FM	K0KN	927.71250	902.71250	151.4 Hz	Kansas RC
Middleton	FM	KD7QAS-R	145.15000	-		Kansas RC
Minneapolis	DMR/MARC	NV8Q	147.22500	+	CC1	Kansas RC
	DMR/MARC	N7KLR	444.75000	+	CC1	Kansas RC
Mission	DMR/BM	WB0KIA	147.16500	+	CC1	Kansas RC
	DMR/BM	WB0YRG	442.10000	+	CC1	
	DMR/BM	WB0YRG	443.10000	+	CC1	
	DMR/BM	WB0YRG	927.58750	902.58750	CC1	Kansas RC
	FM	WB0KIA	224.10000	-		Kansas RC
Montezuma	FM	K0ECT	444.25000	+	141.3 Hz	Kansas RC
Mound City	FM	WA0PPN	147.28500	+	91.5 Hz	Kansas RC
	FM	W0PT	444.42500	+		Kansas RC
Mulvane	FM	N0KTA	146.71500	-	100.0 Hz	Kansas RC
	FM	N0KTA	443.55000	+		Kansas RC
Neodesha	FM	KC0QYD	146.77500	-	91.5 Hz	Kansas RC
	FM	KC0QYD	442.20000	+	146.2 Hz	Kansas RC
Newton	FM	W0BZN	146.61000	-	103.5 Hz	Kansas RC
Norway, K-Link	FM	K0KSN	146.92500	-	162.2 Hz	Kansas RC
Oberlin	FM	KB0DZB	145.19000	-		Kansas RC
Olathe	DMR/BM	KD0JWD	145.23000	-	CC1	Kansas RC
	DSTAR	WA0RC B	442.52500	+		
	FM	N0CRD	52.97000	51.27000	91.5 Hz	Kansas RC
	FM	K0KN-L	146.40000			
	FM	W0QQ	224.94000	-		
	FM	K0HAM	444.25000	+	88.5 Hz	Kansas RC
	FM	K0HCV	444.40000	+		
	FM	K0KN	446.90000	-	151.4 Hz	
	FM	KD0JWD	927.03750	902.03750	151.4 Hz	Kansas RC
	FUSION	KC0KW	145.11000	-		
	FUSION	K0HCV	145.66500			
	FUSION	KC0KW	146.91000	-		
	FUSION	KC0PLA	147.20000	+		
	FUSION	KC0KW	147.31500	+		
	FUSION	KC0KW	442.82500	+		
	FUSION	KC0KW	444.25000	+		
	FUSION	KC0KW	444.72500	+		
Olathe, Garmin Building						
	DSTAR	WA0RC	442.52500	+		Kansas RC
Olathe, I-35 And 135th St.						
	FM	KE5BR	442.20000	+	151.4 Hz	Kansas RC
Olathe, Sheridan Bridge						
	FM	N0CRD	442.62500	+	91.5 Hz	Kansas RC
Osawatomie	FM	AA0X	145.25000	-	151.4 Hz	Kansas RC
	FM	N0SWP	442.05000	+	151.4 Hz	Kansas RC
Osborne, K-Link	FM	NZ0M	147.37500	+	162.2 Hz	Kansas RC
Ottawa	DMR/BM	W0QW	147.39000	+	CC1	Kansas RC
Overland Park		K0KN-R	927.71200			
	DMR/MARC	W0WJB	146.83500	-	CC1	Kansas RC
	FM	W0ERH	145.29000	-	151.4 Hz	Kansas RC
	FM	K0HAM	146.91000	-		Kansas RC
	FM	W0LHK	442.15000	+	82.5 Hz	Kansas RC
	FUSION	W0ERH	443.72500	+		
Paola	FM	WS0WA	147.36000	+	151.4 Hz	Kansas RC
Paola, K-Link	FM	N0SWP	442.47500	+	151.4 Hz	Kansas RC
Parsons	FM	AA0PK	146.68500	-	91.5 Hz	Kansas RC
Pawnee Rock	DMR/BM	KE0PTS	444.32500	+	CC1	
	FM	KE0PTS	146.83500	-	100.0 Hz	Kansas RC
Phillipsburg	FM	AA0HJ	443.27500	+	100.0 Hz	Kansas RC
Pittsburg	DMR/MARC	K0PRO	146.94000	-	CC1	Kansas RC
	DMR/MARC	K0PRO	444.80000	+	CC1	Kansas RC
	FM	K0SEK	442.67500	+	91.5 Hz	Kansas RC

Location	Mode	Call sign	Output	Input	Access	Coordinator
Pittsburg	FUSION	WB0HKE	145.74000			
Plains	FM	WK0DX	147.18000	+		Kansas RC
	FM	WK0DX	443.50000	+	141.3 Hz	Kansas RC
Ransom, K-Link	FM	K0HAM	443.57500	+	162.2 Hz	Kansas RC
Riley, K-Link	FM	KS1EMS	146.68500	-	162.2 Hz	Kansas RC
Russell	DMR/BM	KB0SJR	442.00000	+	CC1	
	DMR/BM	N7JYS	442.47500	+	CC7	Kansas RC
	FM	AB0UO	147.28500	+	162.2 Hz	Kansas RC
	FM	KC0HFA	442.85000	+	141.3 Hz	Kansas RC
Russell, K-Link	FM	AB0UO	444.95000	+	162.2 Hz	Kansas RC
Saint Marys	FM	K0HAM	146.95500	-	88.5 Hz	Kansas RC
Salina	DMR/MARC	NV8Q	444.37500	+	CC1	
	FM	W0CY	147.03000	+		Kansas RC
	FM	N0KSC	147.27000	+	118.8 Hz	Kansas RC
	FM	W0CY	443.90000	+	118.8 Hz	Kansas RC
Salina, K-Link	FM	N0KSC	442.20000	+	162.2 Hz	Kansas RC
Scott City		KD0EZS-R	444.90000			
	DSTAR	W0MI B	443.22500	+		
	FM	WA0OQA	52.87000	51.17000		MACC-KARC
	FM	WA0OQA	146.70000	-	141.3 Hz	Kansas RC
Sedan	FM	WX0EK	146.95500	-	100.0 Hz	
Shawnee	FM	WB0HAC	145.21000	-	151.4 Hz	Kansas RC
	FM	W0ERH	223.94000	-	151.4 Hz	Kansas RC
	FM	W0ERH	442.60000	+		Kansas RC
	FUSION	K0GBW	442.00000	+		
Shawnee Mission	FM	K0GXL	443.52500	+	167.9 Hz	Kansas RC
Smith Center	FM	N0LL	146.61000	-		Kansas RC
Smolan	FM	WD0GAH	146.62500	-		Kansas RC
St. John	FM	W5ALZ	146.70000	-	103.5 Hz	Kansas RC
Sterling, K-Link	FM	WB0LUN	444.45000	+	162.2 Hz	Kansas RC
Syracuse	FM	KB0CKE	146.77500	-		Kansas RC
	FM	K0ECT	444.00000	+	141.3 Hz	Kansas RC
Tescott	FM	KS0LNK-R	444.85000	+		Kansas RC
Topeka	DMR/MARC	WV0S	146.80500	-	CC1	Kansas RC
	DMR/MARC	K0USY	444.98750	+	CC1	
	FM	K0HAM	52.91000	51.21000	88.5 Hz	Kansas RC
	FM	W0CET	145.45000	-	88.5 Hz	Kansas RC
	FM	WA0VRS	146.67000	-	88.5 Hz	Kansas RC
	FM	WA0VRS	224.84000	-	88.5 Hz	
	FM	W0SIK	442.02500	+		Kansas RC
	FM	W0CET	442.42500	+	88.5 Hz	Kansas RC
	FM	WA0VRS	443.92500	+	88.5 Hz	Kansas RC
	FM	N0CBG	444.40000	+	88.5 Hz	
Topeka, NEKSUN	FM	K0HAM	444.90000	+	88.5 Hz	Kansas RC
Tribune	FM	K0WPM	442.17500	+	156.7 Hz	
Udall	FM	KD0HNA	147.16500	+	97.4 Hz	
	FM	KD0HNA	444.30000	+	97.4 Hz	Kansas RC
Ulysses	FM	K0ECT	147.06000	+		Kansas RC
Ulysses, Wagon Bed Springs						
	FM	K0ECT	444.52500	+	141.3 Hz	Kansas RC
Wallace	FM	WA0VJR	444.60000	+	146.2 Hz	
Wichita	ATV	W0SOE	442.52500	+		Kansas RC
	DMR/BM	W0SOE	145.17000	-	CC3	Kansas RC
	DMR/BM	W0SOE	442.17500	+	CC3	Kansas RC
	FM	KC0AHN	146.89500	-		Kansas RC
	FUSION	W0SOE	442.25000	+		
Wichita, Colwich	FM	WA0RJE	146.94000	-	103.5 Hz	Kansas RC
	FM	WA0RJE	444.00000	+		Kansas RC
Wichita, K-Link	FM	W0VFW	443.32500	+	162.2 Hz	Kansas RC
Wichita, WMC	FM	W0SOE	146.79000	-	103.5 Hz	Kansas RC
	FM	W0SOE	442.25000	+		Kansas RC
	FM	W0SOE	442.32500	+	103.5 Hz	

Location	Mode	Call sign	Output	Input	Access	Coordinator
Wilson	FM	K0BHN	146.97000	-	118.8 Hz	Kansas RC
	FUSION	K0BHN	145.79000			
Winfield		K0EMA-L	445.85000			
	FM	WA0JBW	145.19000	-	97.4 Hz	Kansas RC
	FM	N5API-R	442.10000	+		Kansas RC
	FM	WA0JBW	444.02500	+	97.4 Hz	Kansas RC
Yates Center	FM	KF5WPV	146.96000	-	85.4 Hz	

KENTUCKY

Location	Mode	Call sign	Output	Input	Access	Coordinator
Agnes	FM	W4RRA	145.45000	-	77.0 Hz	
Albany	FUSION	KN4SZW	146.46500			
Ashland	DMR/MARC	KY4TVS	145.41000	-	CC1	
	DMR/MARC	KY4ECC	440.61250	+	CC1	
	FM	KC4QK	147.24000	+	107.2 Hz	
	FM	KC4QK	223.94000	-	107.2 Hz	
Audubon Park	FM	W4CN-R	147.18000	+		
Bardstown	FM	KB4KY	145.47000	-	151.4 Hz	
	FM	W4CMY	442.05000	+	91.5 Hz	SERA
	FUSION	KN4RFJ	145.47000	-		
	FUSION	K4LTZ	146.55000			
	FUSION	KN4RFJ	433.10000			
Barren River Lake	FUSION	K4UOJ	146.49000			
Baskett		KD4PQF-L	444.90000			
Beaver Dam	FM	KI4HEC	145.17000	-	136.5 Hz	SERA
Berea	FM	KF4OFT	146.71500	-	100.0 Hz	
Big Hill, Big Hill Mountain						
	FM	AJ4AJ	224.36000	-	77.0 Hz	
Blackey	DMR/BM	AF4Y	446.50000	+	CC1	
Bonnieville	FM	KY4X	146.89500	-	114.8 Hz	
	FM	KY4X	444.85000	+	114.8 Hz	SERA
Bowling Green	DMR/BM	W4WSM	146.62500	-	CC11	
	DMR/BM	W4WSM	444.37500	+	CC1	
	DMR/BM	W4WSM	444.70000	+	CC1	
	DMR/BM	N4UPC	446.30000	446.90000	CC2	
	FM	W4WSM	147.16500	+		SERA
	FM	KY4BG	147.33000	+	107.2 Hz	
	FM	W4WSM	444.10000	+	100.0 Hz	SERA
Brooks	DMR/BM	W4FAO	444.35000	+	CC1	
Brooks, WAMZ Tower						
	FM	KY4KY	146.70000	-	79.7 Hz	SERA
Buckhorn Lake	FM	K4XYZ	147.37500	+	103.5 Hz	
Buffalo	DMR/BM	N1DTA	147.03000	-	CC1	
	DMR/BM	N1DTA	440.61250	+	CC1	
Burkesville	FM	KI4NTU	147.37500	+	100.0 Hz	
Burlington	FUSION	KA3MTT	446.50000			
Burnside, Alien Grave Mountain						
	ATV	KY6MTR	53.03000	52.03000		
Buttonsberry	FM	KY4MA	146.73000	-	82.5 Hz	
Campbellsville	DSTAR	WA4UXJ	146.81000	-		
Cane Valley, WGRB TV						
	FM	WA4UXJ	146.64000	-	107.2 Hz	
Carrollton	FM	KI4CER	146.71500	-		
Catlettsburg	DMR/BM	KG4DVE	444.31250	+	CC7	
Cave Run	FM	KJ4VF	145.13000	-	100.0 Hz	
Cecilia	DMR/BM	K4KTR	443.11250	+	CC1	
Cerulean	FM	KY4KEN	147.19500	+	136.5 Hz	
	FUSION	WD4INS	449.65000	-		
Christy	FM	KY4HS-R	146.91000	-	123.0 Hz	
Columbia	FUSION	NM4P	147.19500	+		
	FUSION	K4SGK	442.65000	+		
Concord	FM	W4NJA-R	147.06000	+		
Corbin	DSTAR	KK4RQX	442.11250	+		

Location	Mode	Call sign	Output	Input	Access	Coordinator
Corbin	FM	WD4KWV	146.61000	-	100.0 Hz	
	FM	WB4IVB	444.90000	+	100.0 Hz	
Crestwood	FM	KY4OC	147.39000	+	151.4 Hz	SERA
Cumberland, Kindom Come State						
	FM	KK4WH	146.76000	-	103.5 Hz	SERA
Danville	DSTAR	KM4OON	444.23750	+		
	DSTAR	KM4OON B	444.23750	+		
Danville, Locklin Lane						
	FM	W4CDA	440.80000	+		
Danville, Persimmon Knob						
	FM	W4CDA	145.31000	-		SERA
Dawson Springs	FM	KF4CWK	146.77500	-		
	FM	W4WKY	147.31500	+		
	FUSION	KF4WLQ	145.95000			
	FUSION	KY4LR	446.50000			
Delafield		K4WKU-L	147.16500			
Dewdrop	FM	KD4DZE	147.03000	+	107.2 Hz	
Dixon	FM	AJ4SI	145.35000	-	71.9 Hz	
Dorton	DMR/BM	W4VJE	440.60000	+	CC1	
Dorton, Flatwoods	FM	KD4KZT	442.15000	+	167.9 Hz	
Dorton, Flatwoods Mountain						
	FM	KS4XL	224.52000	-		SERA
Drakesboro	FM	KF4DKJ	146.82000	-	107.2 Hz	
East Bernstadt	DMR/BM	KE4GJG	442.30000	+	CC1	
Edgewood	DMR/MARC	K4TCD	440.60000	+	CC1	
	FM	K4CO	146.89500	-	123.0 Hz	
	FM	K4CO	147.25500	+	123.0 Hz	
Edgewood, St. Elizabeth Hospit						
	FM	K8SCH	146.62500	-	123.0 Hz	
Elizabethtown	DMR/BM	N1DTA	440.72500	+	CC1	
	DMR/BM	K4KTR	444.76250	+	CC1	
	DMR/BM	KG4LHQ	444.91250	+	CC1	
	FM	WX4HC	145.35000	-	103.5 Hz	SERA
	FM	W4BEJ	146.98000	-		SERA
	FM	W4BEJ	444.80000	+		
Eminence	FM	NG0O	443.42500	+	203.5 Hz	
Eubank	FUSION	WA4SKU	146.54000			
Fairdale	FM	KK4CZ	53.41000	52.41000	100.0 Hz	SERA
	FM	KK4CZ	145.41000	-		SERA
	FM	KK4CZ	444.41000	+		
	FUSION	KR4XG	146.50000			
Fairdealing	FM	KI4HUS-R	145.39000	-		
Five Points	FM	K4MSU-R	443.80000	+		
Flemingsburg	FM	KF4BRO	146.95500	-	107.2 Hz	
Frankfort	FM	K4TG	147.10500	+	107.2 Hz	SERA
	FM	K4TG	147.24000	+	100.0 Hz	SERA
	FUSION	N4HZX	443.55000	+		
Franklin	FM	KE4SZK	147.13500	+	136.5 Hz	
Fredonia	FUSION	KO4KRI/WESI	45.37000	-		
	FUSION	KO4KRI/WESI	46.62000			
Georgetown	DMR/BM	W4VJE	440.51250	+	CC1	
	FM	NE4ST	146.68500	-	141.3 Hz	SERA
	FM	NE4ST	443.62500	+		
	FUSION	KN4DZP	145.70000			
Glasgow	FM	KY4X	146.94000	-	114.8 Hz	
	FM	KY4X	444.92500	+		
	FUSION	KY4X	146.85000			
Goshen	FM	KC4ZMZ	145.28000	-	77.0 Hz	
	FUSION	KC4ZMZ	442.85000	+		
Graefenburg	FUSION	N4HZX	443.55000	+	123.0 Hz	SERA
Gravel Switch	DMR/BM	N1DTA	146.85000	-	CC1	
	DMR/BM	N1DTA	444.65000	+	CC1	

Location	Mode	Call sign	Output	Input	Access	Coordinator
Grayson	FM	KD4DZE	146.70000	-	107.2 Hz	
Halls Gap	FM	AG4TY	146.79000	-	79.7 Hz	
Hamlin	FM	W4GZ	147.24000	+	91.5 Hz	
Hardinsburg	FM	KG4LHQ	443.32500	+	107.2 Hz	SERA
	FUSION	WI4B	146.46000			
Harlan	FM	KK4KCQ	147.10500	+	103.5 Hz	
Harrodsburg	DMR/BM	KK4FJO	440.53750	+	CC1	SERA
	IDAS	KK4FJO	145.39000	-	107.2 Hz	SERA
Hawesville	FM	KY4HC	146.71500	-	136.5 Hz	SERA
Hazard	DMR/BM	KY4MT	444.82500	+	CC1	
	FM	K4TDO	146.85000	-	77.0 Hz	SERA
	FM	WR4AMS	224.72000	-	203.5 Hz	
Hazard, Buffalo Mountain						
	FM	KY4MT	146.67000	-	103.5 Hz	SERA
Henderson	FM	W4KVK	145.49000	-	103.5 Hz	
	FM	WA4GDU	146.97000	-	82.5 Hz	SERA
	FUSION	WA4GDU	145.49000	-		
Henderson, WEHT TV Tower						
	FM	WA4GDU	444.72500	+	82.5 Hz	
Highland Heights	DSTAR	K4CO C	145.42000	-		
	FM	AD4CC	53.33000	52.33000	123.0 Hz	
	FM	W4YWH	146.79000	-	123.0 Hz	
Hopkinsville	FM	WD9HIK	224.78000	-	179.9 Hz	
	FM	N1YKT	442.45000	-	192.8 Hz	
	FUSION	WQ1X	442.50000	+		
Hopkinsville, Trace Industries						
	FM	K4ULE	147.03000	+	103.5 Hz	SERA
	FUSION	KG4CKR	442.50000	+	103.5 Hz	
Horse Cave	FUSION	W4RRK	446.20000			
Hueysville	FM	K4NLT	145.47000	-	79.7 Hz	
Inez	DMR/BM	W4VJE	440.55000	+	CC3	
	FM	N4KJU	145.27000	-	127.3 Hz	
Ingle	FM	AC4DM	29.68000	-	146.2 Hz	
Irvine	FM	W4CMR	146.82000	-	192.8 Hz	
	FM	AD4RT	147.01500	+	100.0 Hz	
	FM	AD4RT	224.94000	-		
	FM	AD4RT	444.00000	+	100.0 Hz	
	FUSION	KK4JW	441.50000			
Irvine, Sandhill Road Irvine						
	FM	KA4PND	443.47500	+		
Irvington	DMR/BM	KG4LHQ	444.51250	+	CC1	
Jonathan Creek	FM	N4SEI	146.98500	-	123.0 Hz	
LaGrange	DMR/BM	WF1RES	440.52500	+	CC3	
Lancer	FM	KB8QEU	53.41000	52.41000	127.3 Hz	SERA
Lawrenceburg	DMR/BM	KG4LHQ	444.81250	+	CC1	
	FM	K4TG	145.11000	-	107.2 Hz	
	FM	K4TG	146.83500	-	107.2 Hz	
	FM	K4TG	444.37500	+	107.2 Hz	SERA
	FM	K4TG	444.50000	+	107.2 Hz	
Lebanon	DMR/BM	N1DTA	145.21000	-	CC1	
	DMR/BM	N1DTA	444.57500	+	CC1	
	FM	KN4HWX	145.21000	-	146.2 Hz	
Lebanon, Marion/Taylor County						
	FM	N1DTA	145.21000	-	146.2 Hz	
Leitchfield	FM	KY4RFE	147.22500	+	179.9 Hz	
Lexington	DMR/MARC	KA4OBT	442.76250	+	CC1	
	DSTAR	W4DSI C	145.46000	-		
	DSTAR	W4DSI B	441.81250	+		
	DSTAR	W4DSI D	1253.00000			
	FM	AD4YJ	145.25000	-	110.9 Hz	
	FM	K4KJQ	147.16500	+		
	FM	AD4YJ	444.72500	+		

Location	Mode	Call sign	Output	Input	Access	Coordinator
Lexington	FM	KK4PQU	444.95000	+	88.5 Hz	SERA
	FUSION	KO4ZJU	432.46250			
	FUSION	KK4FWU	444.12500	+		
Lexington, Lexington Financial						
	DSTAR	W4DSI	145.46000	-		
	DSTAR	W4DSI	441.81250	+		
	FM	KY4K	146.94000	-	88.5 Hz	SERA
	FUSION	KY4K	444.12500	+		
Lexington, UK Hospital						
	FM	K4UKH	147.12000	+	141.3 Hz	
Lexington, WKYT Tower						
	FM	K4KJQ	146.76000	-		
Liberty	FM	AG4TY	442.97500	+		
London	DMR/BM	KE4GJG	443.20000	+	CC1	
	DMR/MARC	KE4GJG	442.30000	+	CC1	
	FM	KE4GJG-R	147.18000	+	74.4 Hz	
	FM	KI4FRJ	442.90000	+	77.0 Hz	
London, Cold Hill	FM	KI4FRJ	147.28500	+		
Louisa	DMR/BM	KJ4GRJ	440.65000	+	CC1	
	FM	WA4SWF	147.39000	+	127.3 Hz	
Louisville	DMR/BM	KK4JPB	441.90000	+	CC1	
	DMR/BM	K4KTR	443.00000	+	CC1	
	DMR/BM	KE6IOC	444.77500	+	CC0	
	DMR/MARC	KK4PGE	147.46000	144.96000	CC1	SERA
	DMR/MARC	KK4JPB	443.10000	+	CC1	
	DMR/MARC	KM4SGI	444.70000	+	CC1	
	DSTAR	KK4PGE C	147.46000	144.96000		
	DSTAR	KM4SGI B	444.70000	+		
	FM	N7BBW	53.43000	52.43000	167.9 Hz	
	FM	KE4JVM	145.23000	-		SERA
	FM	W4PF	146.88000	-	100.0 Hz	
	FM	WB4EJK	147.03000	+	151.4 Hz	
	FM	WB4EJK	147.27000	+	151.4 Hz	
	FM	KQ9Z	147.36000	+		
	FM	KA4MKT	224.30000	-		
	FM	KK4CZ	441.35000	+		SERA
	FM	N4ORL	442.00000	+	146.2 Hz	
	FM	N4MRM	444.60000	+	151.4 Hz	
	FM	W4PF	444.90000	+	100.0 Hz	
	FUSION	KA4NPN	145.62500			
	FUSION	KC4ZMZ	147.18000	+		
	FUSION	KE4JVM	442.62500	+		
	FUSION	N4KWT	443.87500			
Louisville, Bardstown Rd., Fer						
	FM	WB4UMR	444.42500	+		
Lynch	DSTAR	KK4BSG C	145.40000	-		
	DSTAR	KK4BSG	145.40000	-		
	DSTAR	KK4BSG	444.46250	+		
	DSTAR	KK4BSG B	444.46250	+		
	DSTAR	KK4BSG A	1284.50000	-		
Lynch, Black Mountain						
	FM	K4BKR	147.21000	+	103.5 Hz	
	FM	WB4IVB	442.35000	+	100.0 Hz	
Madisonville	DMR/BM	KK4RYS	927.70000	902.70000	CC1	
	FM	KC4FRA	146.61000	-	100.0 Hz	
	FM	WB4JRO	147.27000	+	77.0 Hz	
	FM	KK4RYS	442.42500	+	82.5 Hz	
	FM	KC4FIE	442.77500	+	82.5 Hz	
Magnolia	FM	WA4FOB	146.67000	-	77.0 Hz	
	FM	WA4FOB	443.67500	+	77.0 Hz	
	FUSION	KN4KOP	438.80000			
Manchester	FM	WR4AMS	224.98000	-	100.0 Hz	

Location	Mode	Call sign	Output	Input	Access	Coordinator
Manchester	FM	KD4GMH	444.50000	+		
Manchester, Pilot Mountain						
	FM	KG4LKY	146.92500	-	79.7 Hz	SERA
Manitou	FUSION	KK4RYS	442.42500	+		
Mayfield	FM	WA6LDV	145.11000	-		SERA
	FM	WA6LDV	224.82000	-	179.9 Hz	
	FM	WA6LDV	441.87500	+	179.9 Hz	
Maysville	FM	KF4BRO	145.47000	-		
Meta	FM	WR4AMS	224.38000	-		SERA
Middlesboro	DSTAR	WA4YZY C	145.30000	-		
	DSTAR	AJ4G	145.30000	-		
	DSTAR	WA4YZY B	443.46250	+		
	DSTAR	AJ4G	443.46250	+		
	DSTAR	WA4YZY D	1254.00000			
	DSTAR	AJ4G	1282.40000	1262.40000		
	DSTAR	WA4YZY A	1282.40000	-		
	FM	KA4OAK	146.77500	-	79.7 Hz	SERA
	FM	AJ4G	224.12000	-	100.0 Hz	
Middlesboro, White Oak Spur						
	FM	AJ4G	442.32500	+	100.0 Hz	
Monticello	FM	AC4DM	145.15000	-	100.0 Hz	
	FUSION	WB9SHH	449.75000	-		
Morgantown	DMR/BM	W4WSM	444.37500	+	CC1	
Morgantown, County Courthouse						
	FM	W4WSM	146.65500	-	100.0 Hz	SERA
Mount Sterling, Montgomery Co.						
	FM	KD4ADJ	147.31500	+	100.0 Hz	SERA
	FM	KD4ADJ	442.05000	+		SERA
Murray	DMR/BM	KA4WWS	442.87500	+	CC1	
	FUSION	WB8SKP	147.55500			
Murray, Price Doyle Fine Arts						
	FM	K4MSU	146.94000	-	91.5 Hz	
Nancy	DSTAR	NN4H	444.23750	+		
	FM	AC4DM	53.27000	52.27000	100.0 Hz	
	FM	AC4DM	224.10000	-	100.0 Hz	
	FM	AC4DM	443.60000	+	100.0 Hz	
Nicholasville	FM	K4HH	145.49000	-		
	FM	K4HH	444.97500	+		
NOAA Ashland	WX	KIH39	162.55000			
NOAA Beattyville	WX	WWG67	162.50000			
NOAA Bowling Green						
	WX	KIH45	162.40000			
NOAA Burkesville	WX	KZZ62	162.47500			
NOAA Campbellsville						
	WX	KZZ63	162.52500			
NOAA East Madison County						
	WX	WWF82A	162.52500			
NOAA Ekron	WX	KZZ64	162.45000			
NOAA Elizabethtown						
	WX	KIH43A	162.55000			
NOAA Frankfort	WX	WZ2523	162.50000			
NOAA Frenchburg						
	WX	WWG63	162.47500			
NOAA Harlan	WX	WWG68	162.45000			
NOAA Hazard	WX	KIH40	162.47500			
NOAA Hopkinsville						
	WX	KXI26	162.45000			
NOAA Horse Cave						
	WX	WNG570	162.50000			
NOAA Irvine	WX	WNG727	162.47500			
NOAA Jackson	WX	WWG26	162.42500			
NOAA Lexington	WX	KIH41	162.40000			

Location	Mode	Call sign	Output	Input	Access	Coordinator
NOAA London	WX	WWG65	162.47500			
NOAA Madison County						
	WX	WWF82C	162.52500			
NOAA Madisonville						
	WX	WXJ91	162.52500			
NOAA Manchester						
	WX	WWG66	162.40000			
NOAA Mayfield	WX	KIH46	162.47500			
NOAA Maysville	WX	KZZ49	162.42500			
NOAA McKee	WX	WWG64	162.45000			
NOAA Monticello	WX	WWG80	162.42500			
NOAA Morehead	WX	WWG71	162.42500			
NOAA Mount Vernon						
	WX	WWG70	162.42500			
NOAA Owenton	WX	KZZ48	162.45000			
NOAA Paintsville	WX	WWG28	162.52500			
NOAA Phelps	WX	WWG81	162.50000			
NOAA Pikeville	WX	WWG69	162.40000			
NOAA Pineville	WX	WWG62	162.52500			
NOAA Somerset	WX	KIH44	162.55000			
NOAA Stanton	WX	WWG61	162.55000			
NOAA West Liberty						
	WX	WWG79	162.45000			
NOAA West Madison County						
	WX	WWF82B	162.52500			
NOAA Whitesville	WX	KZZ61	162.47500			
NOAA Williamsburg						
	WX	WWG78	162.50000			
Nortonville	DMR/BM	KM4RWG	441.95000	+	CC1	
Oak Ridge		K4TCD-L	147.25500			
Oakland	FUSION	KY4UE	433.33000			
Ono		NN4H-L	144.46000			
Oven Fork	FM	KK4WH-R	444.25000	+		SERA
Owensboro	DMR/BM	KG4LHQ	444.96250	+	CC1	SERA
	DSTAR	N4WJS	443.65000	+	110.9 Hz	
	FM	N4WJS	146.69000	-	110.9 Hz	
	FM	WA4GDU	146.86500	-	82.5 Hz	
	FM	K4HY	147.21000	+	146.2 Hz	
	FM	KI4JXN	444.55000	+	103.5 Hz	
	FUSION	W4NHO	433.50000			
Owensboro, Greenwood Cemetery						
	FM	K4HY	145.33000	-	103.5 Hz	
Owingsville	FM	N4EWW-R	147.07500	+		
	FM	W4WOO	442.00000	+	100.0 Hz	SERA
Paducah	FM	KY4OEM	146.76000	-	179.9 Hz	
	FM	KD4DVI	147.12000	+	179.9 Hz	
	FM	KD4DVI	443.00000	+	179.9 Hz	
	FUSION	K4KMW	147.12000	+		
Paintsville	DMR/MARC	W4VJE	145.48000	-	CC1	SERA
	FM	N4KJU	441.52500	+	127.3 Hz	
Paintsville, Starfire Hill						
	FM	KY4ARC	147.22500	+	127.3 Hz	SERA
Payneville	FM	K4ULW	146.62500	-	151.4 Hz	
Phelps	DMR/BM	W4VJE	440.62500	+	CC4	
Phelps, Dick's Knob						
	FM	N4MWA	147.09000	+	100.0 Hz	
Pikeville	DMR/BM	W4VJE	440.70000	+	CC2	
	DMR/BM	KN4TRV	443.65000	+	CC7	
	FM	K4PDM	145.15000	-	127.3 Hz	
	FM	AD4BI	444.47500	+		
Pikeville, Poor Farm Ridge						
	FM	KD4DAR	224.62000	-		SERA

Location	Mode	Call sign	Output	Input	Access	Coordinator
Pineville, Chained Rock						
	FM	WA4YZY	146.83500	+	100.0 Hz	SERA
Pleasure Ridge Park						
	FM	N4MRM	147.37500	+	151.4 Hz	
Prestonburg, Abbott Hill						
	FM	KY4ARC	145.31000	-	127.3 Hz	
Prestonsburg	DMR/BM	K4KBR	444.47500	+	CC1	
	FM	WR4AMS	224.72000	-	203.5 Hz	
Princeton	FM	W4KBL	145.23000	-	179.9 Hz	
	FM	W4KBL	444.17500	+		SERA
Providence	FM	AG4BT	147.25500	+		
Radcliff	FM	W4BEJ	146.92500	-		SERA
	FM	WX4HC	147.15000	+	103.5 Hz	
Reeds Crossing	FM	KF4REN-R	146.86500	-	192.8 Hz	
Richmond	DSTAR	KE4YVD B	442.81250	+		
	DSTAR	KE4YVD	442.81250	+		SERA
	FM	KE4YVD	145.37000	-	192.8 Hz	
	FM	KM4EOC	146.86500	-	192.8 Hz	
	FM	KE4ISW	444.62500	+	192.8 Hz	SERA
Rockport	FM	KD4BOH	444.07500	+	77.0 Hz	
Russell Springs	FM	KV4D	444.40000	+	179.9 Hz	
Russell Springs, Lake Cumberla						
	FM	N4SQV	146.95500	-	100.0 Hz	
Sadieville	FUSION	WY4LD	438.35000			
Salvisa	FM	KC4UPE	444.87500	+	167.9 Hz	
Salyersville	FM	KY4CM	146.62500	-	127.3 Hz	
Sandy Hook	FM	KD4DZE	147.13500	+	107.2 Hz	
Shelbyville	FM	KE4LR	147.00000	+	173.8 Hz	SERA
	FM	KB4PTJ	444.05000	+	91.5 Hz	SERA
Shepherdsville	DMR/BM	KY4KY	443.70000	+	CC2	
Sidell	FM	KF4IFC-R	444.27500	+		
Slaughters	FUSION	KN4MC	145.05000			
Somerset	FM	AC4DM	146.88000	-	77.0 Hz	SERA
	FM	N4AI	224.30000	-		
	FM	N4AI	224.88000	-		
	FM	KY4TB	443.40000	+	136.5 Hz	
	FUSION	N4DFQ	147.55500			
Stamping Ground	FUSION	W4IOD	433.12500			
	FUSION	W4IOD	442.10000	+		
Stanton	FM	KC4TUK	145.29000	-		
	FM	KC4TUK	442.07500	+		
Taylor Mill	FM	WB8CRS	147.03000	+	123.0 Hz	SERA
Taylorsville	FM	KX4DN	443.82500	+		
Tompkinsville	FM	KJ4OG	146.77500	-	151.4 Hz	
Union	DSTAR	WW4KY C	147.39000	+		
	DSTAR	WW4KY	147.39000	+		SERA
	FM	AD4CC	441.80000	+	179.9 Hz	
Uniontown	FM	KJ4HNC	145.29000	-	77.0 Hz	SERA
Versailles		KY4WC-R	145.33000			
	DMR/BM	KY4DMR	440.58750	+	CC1	
	FM	KY4WC	224.22000	-	107.2 Hz	SERA
	FM	AD4CR	444.25000	+	107.2 Hz	
Versailles, United Bank Buildi						
	FM	KY4WC	443.77500	+	107.2 Hz	SERA
Vine Grove	DMR/BM	KM4LNN	444.91250	+	CC1	
	DSTAR	KM4LNN	145.12000	-		
	DSTAR	KM4LNN C	145.12000	-		
	DSTAR	KM4LNN B	444.91250	+		
Walton	FM	K4CO	147.37500	+	123.0 Hz	
Waverly Hills	FM	N4KWT-R	443.97500	+		
Waynesburg	FM	AC4DM	53.39000	52.39000	100.0 Hz	
Westview	FM	KY3O	147.06000	+	136.5 Hz	SERA

Location	Mode	Call sign	Output	Input	Access	Coordinator
Whitesburg	DMR/BM	KK4WH	444.66250	+	CC1	
Whitesburg, Little Shephard Tr						
	FM	KK4WH	224.96000	-	203.5 Hz	SERA
Whitesburg, Pine Mtn						
	FM	KM4IAL	145.35000	-	186.2 Hz	SERA
Williamsburg	FM	KB4PTJ	444.05000	+	100.0 Hz	
	FUSION	KB4PTJ	146.70000	-		
Williamstown	FM	K4KPN	444.42500	+	107.2 Hz	
Winchester	FM	W4PRC	145.43000	-	203.5 Hz	SERA
	FM	W4PRC	441.90000	+	203.5 Hz	
LOUISIANA						
Abbeville	FM	KD5QYV	147.06000	+	103.5 Hz	LCARC
Abita Springs	FUSION	N5YHM	434.60000			
Alexandria	DSTAR	KC5ZJY	145.15000	-		LCARC
	DSTAR	KF5PIE	147.21000	+		LCARC
	DSTAR	KF5PIE C	147.21000	+		
	FM	KC5ZJY	145.47000	-	173.8 Hz	LCARC
	FM	KC5ZJY	444.97500	+	173.8 Hz	LCARC
Alexandria, Downtown						
	FM	KC5ZJY	53.23000	52.23000	173.8 Hz	LCARC
Alexandria, I-49 South						
	FM	KC5ZJY	147.33000	+	173.8 Hz	LCARC
	FM	KC5ZJY	443.30000	+	173.8 Hz	LCARC
Amelia	FM	W5BMC	146.74500	-		LCARC
Amite	FM	WB5NET-R	147.00000	-	107.2 Hz	LCARC
	FM	W5TEO	444.32500	+	107.2 Hz	LCARC
Bastrop	FM	N5EXS	146.92500	-	127.3 Hz	LCARC
Baton Rouge	DMR/BM	W5SJL	145.45000	454.55000	CC1	
	DMR/BM	W5RAR	443.10000	+	CC1	LCARC
	DMR/BM	W5SJL	444.45000	+	CC1	
	DSTAR	KD5CQB C	146.88000	-		
	DSTAR	KD5CQB	146.88000	-		LCARC
	DSTAR	KD5CQB B	442.92500	+		
	DSTAR	KD5CQB	442.92500	+		LCARC
	FM	W5GQ	145.23000	-	107.2 Hz	
	FM	WA5TQA	145.45000	-	107.2 Hz	LCARC
	FM	W5GIX	146.79000	-	107.2 Hz	LCARC
	FM	KD5QZD	443.37500	+		LCARC
	FM	W5DJA	443.45000	+		
	FM	W5GIX	444.40000	+	107.2 Hz	LCARC
	FM	WB5LHS	444.62500	+	156.7 Hz	LCARC
	FM	KC5BMA	444.85000	+	107.2 Hz	LCARC
	FM	KE5QJQ	444.95000	+	107.2 Hz	LCARC
	FUSION	AC5H	145.23000	-		
	FUSION	AC5H	145.49000	-		
	FUSION	AC5H	446.50000			
Baton Rouge, Downtown						
	FM	KD5CQB	443.92500	+	107.2 Hz	LCARC
Baton Rouge, LSU						
	FM	K5LSU	442.80000	+		LCARC
Bayou L'Ourse	FM	W5MCC	147.01500	+	103.5 Hz	
	FM	WB5MC	148.00000	-	103.5 Hz	
Belle Chasse	FM	KA5EZQ	444.17500	+	114.8 Hz	
Belle Chasse, Near Bridge/Tunn						
	FM	KA5EZQ	146.89500	-	114.8 Hz	LCARC
Belle Chasse, Port Sulphur Fir						
	FM	KA5EZQ	444.17500	+	114.8 Hz	LCARC
Bernice	FM	W5JC	147.07500	+	127.3 Hz	LCARC
	FM	W5JC	444.07500	+		LCARC
Bogalusa		KB5YJX-L	145.75000			
Bossier	FUSION	K5BMO	147.15000	+	186.2 Hz	LCARC

Location	Mode	Call sign	Output	Input	Access	Coordinator
Bossier City	DMR/BM	AF6BZ	442.02500	+	CC1	LCARC
	FM	N5FJ	444.30000	+	186.2 Hz	LCARC
Brittany	FM	K5ARC-R	147.22500	+		LCARC
Bryceland	FM	N5RD	147.30000	+	186.2 Hz	LCARC
Bush	FUSION	WI5ARD	439.00000			
	FUSION	WI5ARD	443.40000	+		
Calhoun, Portable Tower						
	FM	W5KGT	145.17000	-		LCARC
	FM	W5KGT	444.10000	+		LCARC
Carencro	DSTAR	W5NB C	147.00000	+		
	DSTAR	WD5TR	444.90000	+		LCARC
	DSTAR	WD5TR B	444.90000	+		
	FM	W5NB	145.29000	-	103.5 Hz	LCARC
	FM	W5NB	443.80000	+	103.5 Hz	LCARC
Centerville	DMR/BM	W5TGK	442.02500	+	CC1	
Central	FM	KD5CQB	146.94000	-	107.2 Hz	LCARC
	FM	WB5BTR	442.40000	+	156.7 Hz	LCARC
	FM	KD5CQB	443.55000	+	107.2 Hz	LCARC
Chalmette	FM	W5MCC	146.86000	-	114.8 Hz	LCARC
	FM	W5MCC	444.80000	+	114.8 Hz	LCARC
Convent	DMR/BM	W5RAR	442.07500	+	CC1	LCARC
	FM	WB5BTR	442.50000	+		LCARC
	FM	K5ARC	443.27500	+	107.2 Hz	LCARC
Convent, Sunshine Bridge						
	FM	K5ARC	146.98500	-	107.2 Hz	LCARC
Coushatta	FM	K5EYG	145.27000	-	186.2 Hz	LCARC
Covington	DMR/BM	KD5KNZ	444.87500	+	CC5	
Crowley, Falcon Rice Mill						
	FM	N9QO	145.19000	-	103.5 Hz	LCARC
Cynthia Park	FM	K5SAR	146.76000	-		LCARC
Delhi	DSTAR	KF5PID C	147.19500	+		
	FUSION	KI5ANX	446.50000			
DeRidder	FM	KE5PFA	146.85000	-		LCARC
	FUSION	K5LJO	147.24000	+		
Des Allemands	FM	WX5RLT	442.10000	+	114.8 Hz	LCARC
Farmerville	FM	KC5DR	145.23000	-		LCARC
Folsom	FM	W5NJJ	146.71500	-	114.8 Hz	LCARC
	FM	W5NJJ	147.37500	+	114.8 Hz	LCARC
	FM	W5NJJ	444.05000	+	114.8 Hz	LCARC
Franklin	FM	W5BMC	147.12000	+	103.5 Hz	LCARC
Franklinton	DSTAR	KF5BSZ C	147.44000	144.94000		
	DSTAR	KF5BSZ B	444.58750	+		
	DSTAR	KF5BSZ D	1253.00000			
	DSTAR	KF5BSZ A	1293.00000	-		
	FM	W5LMS	145.75000			
Gonzales	FUSION	KJ5MD	445.02500			
Gonzales, Praireville						
	FM	K5ARC	145.31000	-	107.2 Hz	LCARC
Gray	FM	W5YL	147.39000	+	114.8 Hz	LCARC
Greensburg	FM	WB5BTR	442.27500	+	156.7 Hz	LCARC
Gretna	DSTAR	KF5SKU	145.25000	-		LCARC
	DSTAR	KF5SKU	444.47500	+		LCARC
	DSTAR	KF5SKU	1295.30000	1275.30000		LCARC
	FM	W5MCC	147.07500	+	114.8 Hz	
	FM	W5UK	444.20000	+	114.8 Hz	LCARC
Hammond, North Oaks Medical Ce						
	FM	WB5NET	145.13000	-	107.2 Hz	LCARC
	FM	WB5NET	444.25000	+	107.2 Hz	LCARC
Haughton	DSTAR	W5SLY C	147.24000	+		
	FM	W5JLH	53.05000	52.05000	186.2 Hz	LCARC
	FM	N5RD	145.43000	-	186.2 Hz	LCARC
	FM	WN5AIA	147.03000	+	186.2 Hz	LCARC

Location	Mode	Call sign	Output	Input	Access	Coordinator
Holden	FM	W5LRS	146.73000	-	107.2 Hz	LCARC
Hornbeck	FM	KE5RRA	146.62500	-	173.8 Hz	LCARC
Houma	FM	W5YL	147.33000	+	114.8 Hz	
Houma, Bayou Cane						
	FM	W5YL	444.50000	+	114.8 Hz	LCARC
Jackson	FM	KD5UZA	53.83000	52.83000	107.2 Hz	LCARC
	FM	KD5UZA	146.83500	-	114.8 Hz	
	FM	WB5BTR	443.62500	+	156.7 Hz	LCARC
	FUSION	KB5YSC	147.28500	+		
Jefferson	DSTAR	W5GAD	146.92500	-		LCARC
	DSTAR	W5GAD	444.92500	+		LCARC
	DSTAR	W5GAD	1285.00000	1265.00000		LCARC
Jonesboro	FM	WB5NIN	444.80000	+		LCARC
Jonesboro, Water Tower						
	FM	WB5NIN	146.79000	-		LCARC
Jonesville	FM	N5TZH	146.96000	-	127.3 Hz	
	FM	N5TZH	444.57500	+	127.3 Hz	
Kentwood, Lewiston Water Tank						
	FM	WB5ERM	442.05000	+	107.2 Hz	LCARC
Kinder	FM	W5ELM-R	146.92500	-		LCARC
LaCombe	DMR/BM	W5SLA	147.27000	+	CC1	
	DMR/BM	W5SLA	444.10000	+	CC1	LCARC
	FM	W5MCC	146.62000	-	114.8 Hz	LCARC
	FM	N5UK	146.64000	-	114.8 Hz	LCARC
Lafayette		KF5VH-R	145.37000			
		KA9TWO-R	445.00000			
	DMR/BM	N5WE	444.01000	+	CC1	
	FM	WA5TNK	145.37000	-	103.5 Hz	LCARC
	FM	W5DDL-R	146.82000	-		LCARC
	FM	W5DDL	443.00000	+	103.5 Hz	LCARC
	FM	KF5VH	445.55000	-	103.5 Hz	
Lake Charles	DMR/BM	W5BII	145.21000	-	CC10	
	DMR/BM	KC5JMJ	224.20000	+	CC10	
	DMR/BM	KC5JMJ	443.22500	+	CC10	
	DMR/BM	KC5JMJ	444.22500	+	CC10	
	DSTAR	W5SUL C	147.36000	+		
	FM	W5BII	146.73000	-	173.8 Hz	LCARC
	FM	KC5JMJ	147.10500	+	103.5 Hz	
	FM	W5BII	444.30000	+	88.5 Hz	LCARC
LaPlace	DMR/BM	W5RAR	442.67500	+	CC1	LCARC
	FM	W5RAR	53.73000	52.73000	114.8 Hz	LCARC
	FM	W5RAR	146.80500	-	114.8 Hz	LCARC
	FM	W5RAR	443.82500	+	114.8 Hz	LCARC
	FM	W5RAR	444.67500	+	114.8 Hz	LCARC
Leesville	DSTAR	KF5QAR C	146.80000			
	DSTAR	KE5PFA C	147.34500	+		
	DSTAR	KE5PFA	147.34500	+		LCARC
	DSTAR	KF5PWS C	147.52000			
	DSTAR	KE5PFA	442.05000	+		LCARC
	DSTAR	KE5PFA B	442.05000	+		
	FM	W5TMP	147.39000	+	203.5 Hz	LCARC
	FM	KE5PFA	442.62500	+	203.5 Hz	LCARC
	FM	W5LSV	444.70000	+	118.8 Hz	LCARC
	FUSION	W5TMP	147.99000	-		
Livingston	FM	W5GQ	145.23000	-	107.2 Hz	LCARC
	FM	WB5LIV	147.16500	+	107.2 Hz	LCARC
	FM	WB5BTR	147.25500	+		LCARC
	FM	WB5LIV	442.35000	+	156.7 Hz	LCARC
	FM	WB5BTR	444.35000	+	156.7 Hz	LCARC
Lockport	DMR/BM	W5XTR	443.32500	+	CC1	
	DMR/BM	W5LPG	444.40000	+	CC1	
	FM	W5XTR	147.19500	+	114.8 Hz	LCARC

Location	Mode	Call sign	Output	Input	Access	Coordinator
Loranger	FM	K5WDH	443.87500	+	107.2 Hz	LCARC
Lydia	FM	K5BLV	145.41000	-		
Madisonville	FM	W5NJJ	224.14000	-	114.8 Hz	LCARC
Many	DSTAR	N5MNY	146.80500	-		LCARC
	DSTAR	N5MNY C	146.80500	-		
	FM	K5MNY	444.20000	+	173.8 Hz	LCARC
Marrero	DMR/BM	W5MCC	443.57500	+	CC1	
	DMR/BM	NO5LA	444.55000	+	CC1	
	FUSION	KB5OZE	146.77500	-		
	FUSION	KB5OZE	444.80000	+		
Mathews	DMR/BM	W5LPG	442.62500	+	CC2	
Metairie	DMR/BM	AE5BZ	442.65000	+	CC5	
	FM	W5GAD	444.00000	+		LCARC
	FM	AE5BZ	444.62500	+	114.8 Hz	LCARC
	FUSION	W5GAD	147.24000	+		
Minden	DSTAR	N5MAD	144.92000	147.42000		LCARC
	DSTAR	N5MAD C	144.92000	147.42000		
	DSTAR	N5MAD	442.51250	+		LCARC
	DSTAR	N5MAD B	442.51250	+		
Monroe	FM	N5DMX	146.85000	-		LCARC
Morgan City		W5BMC	146.91000	-		
	DMR/BM	K5MOB	144.98000	147.48000	CC7	
	FM	W5BMC	443.75000	+	103.5 Hz	LCARC
Morgan City, Bayou L'Ourse						
	FM	W5MCC	147.01500	+	103.5 Hz	LCARC
Morgan City, Rig Museum						
	FM	WA5MC	444.62500	+		LCARC
Natchitoches	FM	KC5ZJY	146.88000	-	173.8 Hz	LCARC
New Iberia	FM	K5BLV	145.41000	-	123.0 Hz	LCARC
	FM	K5ARA	146.68000	-	103.5 Hz	LCARC
	FUSION	WR5U	442.02500	+		
	FUSION	WR5U	443.20000	+		
New Orleans	DMR/BM	K5LZP	146.77500	-	CC1	
	DMR/BM	N5UXT	444.22500	+	CC5	
	DMR/BM	WB5ITT	444.60000	+	CC1	
	DMR/BM	N5OZG	444.77500	+	CC10	
	DMR/BM	KB5OZE	444.82500	+	CC1	
	DSTAR	KF5SKU C	145.25000	-		
	DSTAR	W5GAD C	146.92500	-		
	DSTAR	KF5SKU B	444.47500	+		
	DSTAR	W5GAD B	444.92500	+		
	DSTAR	W5GAD D	1251.00000			
	DSTAR	W5GAD A	1285.00000	-		
	FM	N5OZG	146.82000	-	114.8 Hz	
	FM	W4NDF	147.12000	+	114.8 Hz	LCARC
	FM	W5RU	147.36000	+		
	FM	KB5AVY	444.15000	+	114.8 Hz	LCARC
	FM	N5OZG	444.57500	+	114.8 Hz	LCARC
	FM	W5MCC	444.70000	+	114.8 Hz	LCARC
	FM	N5UXT-R	444.95000	+		LCARC
New Orleans, LA	FM	W5MCC	224.12000	-	114.8 Hz	LCARC
NOAA Alexandria	WX	WXK78	162.47500			
NOAA Baton Rouge						
	WX	KHB46	162.40000			
NOAA Bogalusa	WX	WNG521	162.52500			
NOAA Buras	WX	WXL41	162.47500			
NOAA Lafayette	WX	WXK80	162.55000			
NOAA Lake Charles						
	WX	KHB42	162.40000			
NOAA Monroe	WX	WXJ96	162.55000			
NOAA Morgan City						
	WX	KIH23	162.47500			

Location	Mode	Call sign	Output	Input	Access	Coordinator
NOAA Natchitoches						
	WX	WXN87	162.50000			
NOAA New Orleans						
	WX	KHB43	162.55000			
NOAA Shreveport	WX	WXJ97	162.40000			
Opelousas	FM	N5TBU	444.87500	+	103.5 Hz	LCARC
Otis	FM	KG5POW	442.00000	+	173.8 Hz	
Parks	FM	WR5U	443.20000	+	103.5 Hz	LCARC
Paulina	FM	WB5GCL	443.67500	+	114.8 Hz	LCARC
Pineville	DSTAR	KC5ZJY C	145.15000	-		
	FM	KD5DFL	446.10000	-	173.8 Hz	
Pineville, Red River						
	FM	KC5ZJY	147.37500	+	173.8 Hz	LCARC
Port Fourchon	DMR/BM	W5XTR	442.00000	+	CC5	
Port Sulphur	FM	KA5EZQ	444.07500	+	114.8 Hz	LCARC
Port Sulphur, Port Sulpher Fir						
	FM	KA5EZQ	146.65500	-	114.8 Hz	LCARC
Prairieville	FUSION	N5EKF	439.25000			
Rayville	FM	KF5OVT	144.60000			
	FM	WA5KNV	145.49000	-	100.0 Hz	LCARC
	FM	WA5KNV	444.95000	+	100.0 Hz	LCARC
Ruston	DSTAR	N5APB	145.14000	-		LCARC
	DSTAR	N5APB C	145.14000	-		
	FM	WC5K	147.12000	+	94.8 Hz	LCARC
	FM	W5MCH	444.35000	+	94.8 Hz	LCARC
Sheridan	DSTAR	KF5BSZ	147.44000	144.94000		LCARC
	DSTAR	KF5BSZ	444.58750	+		LCARC
	DSTAR	KF5BSZ	1293.00000	1273.00000		LCARC
	FM	WB5BTR	442.42500	+	156.7 Hz	
Sheridan, WP 911 Center						
	FM	WA5ARC	145.43000	-	107.2 Hz	LCARC
Shreveport	DMR/BM	KG5RWA	444.65000	+	CC10	
	DSTAR	W5SHV	147.36000	+		LCARC
	DSTAR	W5SHV C	147.36000	+		
	DSTAR	W5SHV	442.00000	+		LCARC
	DSTAR	W5SHV B	442.00000	+		
	DSTAR	W5SHV D	1253.00000			
	DSTAR	W5SHV A	1293.00000	1273.00000		
	FM	K5SAR	145.11000	-	186.2 Hz	LCARC
	FM	K5EMU	145.60000			
	FM	K5SAR	146.67000	-	186.2 Hz	
	FM	K5SAR	146.82000	-	186.2 Hz	LCARC
	FM	N5SYV	224.26000	-	100.0 Hz	LCARC
Shreveport Louisiana						
	DMR/BM	KD0KMT	444.77500	+	CC10	
Shreveport, Downtown						
	FM	WB5QFM	147.09000	+	186.2 Hz	LCARC
Shreveport, Schumpert Hospital						
	FM	K5SAR	444.90000	+	186.2 Hz	LCARC
Shreveport, VA Hospital						
	FM	K5SAR	146.70000	-	186.2 Hz	
Slaughter	DMR/BM	K5LLY	442.20000	+	CC1	
Slidell	FUSION	KG5CEN	145.01000			
	FUSION	W5SLA	442.12500	+		
Slidell, Water Tower On Front						
	FM	W5SLA	444.42500	+	114.8 Hz	
Springhill	DMR/BM	W5KJN	443.75000	+	CC1	
	FM	W5KJN	146.73000	-		
	FM	AF5P	147.16500	+		LCARC
St Martinville	DSTAR	KF5ZUZ	147.00000	+		LCARC
	DSTAR	KF5ZUZ	443.85000	+		LCARC
	DSTAR	KF5ZUZ	1292.10000	1272.10000		LCARC

Location	Mode	Call sign	Output	Input	Access	Coordinator
St. Martinville	DSTAR	KF5ZUZ C	147.00000	+		
	DSTAR	KF5ZUZ B	443.85000	+		
	DSTAR	KF5ZUZ D	1253.00000			
	DSTAR	KF5ZUZ A	1292.10000	1272.10000		
Stanley	FM	WI5M	146.92500	-	186.2 Hz	LCARC
Storyville		KB5AVY-R	444.97500			
Sulphur	FM	W5BII	145.35000	-	103.5 Hz	LCARC
Tallulah	FM	KC5GIB	147.24000	+	94.8 Hz	
Thibodaux	DMR/BM	W5XTR	442.10000	+	CC3	
	DMR/MARC	KK5CM	444.37500	+	CC1	
	FM	W5XTR	442.00000	+	114.8 Hz	
Thibodeaux Mobile Home Park						
	FM	W5EXI-R	147.04000	+		LCARC
Tickfaw	FUSION	N5NIB	444.25000	+		
University Terrace		K5LSU-L	146.58000			
Walker	FM	W5LRS	444.52500	+	107.2 Hz	LCARC
	FUSION	KC5AD	440.80000			
West Monroe	DMR/MARC	KC5DR	443.70000	+	CC3	
	FM	WB5SOT	146.97000	-		LCARC
	FM	KC5DR	147.13500	+		LCARC
	FM	WB5SOT	444.30000	+		LCARC
	FUSION	KC5DR	444.70000	+		
Westlake	DMR/MARC	WA5LRC	444.97500	+	CC10	
Wilmer	FM	KE5ILT	147.34500	+		LCARC
Winnfield, Red Hill						
	FM	WB5NIN	147.06000	+	173.8 Hz	LCARC
Winnsboro, LA	FM	KC5DR	146.70000	-	127.3 Hz	LCARC
MAINE						
Alfred	FM	WJ1L	448.72500	-	103.5 Hz	NESMC
	FM	KB1PRG	449.82500	-	103.5 Hz	NESMC
Alfred, Brackett Hill						
	FM	WJ1L	145.41000	-	103.5 Hz	NESMC
Alfred, York County EMA EOC						
	FM	W1BHR	147.34500	+	123.0 Hz	
Allagash, Rocky Mountain						
	FM	N1SJV	146.71500	-	100.0 Hz	
Arundel, Arundel Hill						
	FM	W6BZ	146.92500	-	103.5 Hz	NESMC
Auburn	FM	KA1SHU	146.95500	-	107.2 Hz	NESMC
Auburn, Goff Hill	FM	W1NPP	146.61000	-	88.5 Hz	NESMC
Augusta	DMR/MARC	KQ1L	145.17000	-	CC12	
	DMR/MARC	KQ1L	145.30000	-	CC12	
	FM	KA1SHU	146.95500	-	100.0 Hz	NESMC
	FM	KQ1L	224.72000	-		
Augusta, Sand Hill						
	FM	KQ1L	146.67000	-	100.0 Hz	NESMC
Bar Harbor, Ireson Hill						
	FM	W1TU	147.03000	+	100.0 Hz	NESMC
Bath	DMR/MARC	N1XBM	449.77500	-	CC1	
Belfast, Waldo Co EMA						
	FM	W1EMA	147.16500	+		
Belgrade Lakes	FM	W1PIG	449.27500	-	88.5 Hz	
Biddeford	DMR/BM	KC1ALA	147.15000	+	CC1	
	DMR/BM	KC1ALA	443.05000	+	CC1	
	DMR/BM	KC1ALA	444.50000	+	CC1	
	DMR/BM	KC1ALA	448.05000	+	CC1	
	DMR/BM	KC1ALA	449.50000	-	CC1	
Brownville	FUSION	W1QT	448.72500	-		
Brownville, Stickney Hill						
	FM	N1BUG	147.10500	+	103.5 Hz	NESMC
Brunswick	DSTAR	KS1R B	447.57500	-		

Location	Mode	Call sign	Output	Input	Access	Coordinator
Brunswick, Growston Hill						
	FM	WZ1J	147.13500	+	103.5 Hz	NESMC
Brunswick, Oak Hill						
	FM	K1MNW	1284.00000	1264.00000	88.5 Hz	NESMC
Brunswick, Woodward Cove						
	FM	K0LDO	147.33000	+	100.0 Hz	NESMC
Buckfield	DMR/MARC	K1YFY	145.32000	-	CC12	
	DMR/MARC	K1YFY	146.88000	-	CC12	
Calais	DMR/MARC	W1LH	147.04500	+	CC1	
Calais, Magurrewock Mtn						
	FM	K1QA	145.15000	-	100.0 Hz	NESMC
Camden	DMR/MARC	K1XI	145.37000	-	CC12	
Camden, Ragged Mtn						
	FM	KQ1L	146.82000	-	100.0 Hz	NESMC
Caribou	FM	N1RTX	444.40000	+	241.8 Hz	NESMC
Carrabasset, Sugarloaf Mountai						
	FM	KQ1L	146.97000	-	100.0 Hz	NESMC
Cooper	WX	W1LH	146.98500	-	179.9 Hz	NESMC
	WX	W1LH	147.33000	+	118.8 Hz	NESMC
Cooper, Cooper Hill						
	FM	W1LH	444.30000	+	100.0 Hz	NESMC
Corinna	FM	KB1UAS	224.84000	-	103.5 Hz	
	FM	N1GNN	449.72500	-	103.5 Hz	
Cornish, Hessian Hill						
	FM	N1KMA	145.21000	-	156.7 Hz	NESMC
Dedham, Bald Mtn						
	FM	KC1FRJ	146.80500	-	82.5 Hz	NESMC
	FM	KC1FRJ	224.90000	-	103.5 Hz	
	FM	KC1FRJ	444.00000	+	100.0 Hz	
Dexter	DMR/MARC	KB1UAS	145.22000	-	CC0	
Dixmont, Mt Harrison						
	FM	KQ1L	146.85000	-	100.0 Hz	NESMC
Dresden	DMR/MARC	N1UGR	145.43000	-	CC12	
Durham	FUSION	K1PN	146.43000			
Ellsworth, Beckwith Hill						
	FM	KB1NEB	146.91000	-	151.4 Hz	NESMC
Exeter	FM	AA1PN	224.24000	-	103.5 Hz	
Falmouth	DMR/MARC	N1XBM	448.82500	-	CC1	
Falmouth, Blackstrap Hill						
	FM	W1QUI	147.09000	+	100.0 Hz	NESMC
Falmouth, Blackstrap Hill (PAW						
	FM	W1KVI	146.73000	-	100.0 Hz	NESMC
Farmington	DMR/MARC	W1BHR	442.40000	+	CC11	
	FM	KY1C	147.18000	+	123.0 Hz	NESMC
	FM	W1IMD	449.07500	-	114.8 Hz	
	FM	W1BHR	449.92500	-		
Five Points		KA1JWM-R	147.15000			
Fort Kent	DMR/MARC	KC1FRJ	145.20000	-	CC12	
	FM	N1SJV	146.64000	-	100.0 Hz	
Franklin , Martins Ridge						
	FM	WB5NKJ	146.61000	-	107.2 Hz	NESMC
Franklin, Martins Ridge						
	FM	N1DP	444.80000	+		
Frenchville	FM	N1CHF	224.18000	-		
Gardiner, Libby Hill						
	FM	KB1RAI	147.25500	+	114.8 Hz	NESMC
Gouldsboro	DMR/MARC	KC1FRJ	145.21000	-	CC12	
Gray, NWS Forecast Office						
	FM	K1MV	147.04500	+	103.5 Hz	NESMC
Hampden	FM	W1GEE	147.30000	+	100.0 Hz	NESMC
Harrison	FUSION	W1BKW	146.62500	-		
Hebron	FM	W1IF	224.62000	-	103.5 Hz	

Location	Mode	Call sign	Output	Input	Access	Coordinator
Higgins Corner	FM	W1PIG-R	145.39000	-		NESMC
Hiram	DMR/BM	W1IMD	448.57500	+	CC2	
	FM	K1AAM	53.37000	52.37000	136.5 Hz	
	FM	W6BZ	442.20000	+	82.5 Hz	
Hiram, Peaked Pass Mtn						
	FM	K1AAM	147.01500	+	103.5 Hz	NESMC
Holden	DMR/MARC	N1ME	145.31000	-	CC10	
	FM	N1ME	146.94000	-	136.5 Hz	
Holden, Riders Bluff						
	FM	N1ME	444.40000	+		
Hope	FM	WA1ZDA	224.00000	-		
Hope, Hatchet Mtn						
	FM	WA1ZDA	147.24000	+	110.9 Hz	NESMC
	FM	K1EHO	449.52500	-	110.9 Hz	
Houlton	WX	W1BC	146.79000	-	100.0 Hz	NESMC
Island Falls	FM	KB1JVQ	145.17000	-	123.0 Hz	
Kents Hill	FM	W1PIG	147.00000	+	100.0 Hz	NESMC
Kibby Township	DMR/MARC	W1FCA	145.12000		CC11	
Knox	DMR/MARC	W1EMA	145.42000	-	CC12	NESMC
Knox, Aborn Hill	FM	W1EMA	147.27000	+	136.5 Hz	NESMC
	FM	KD1KE	443.50000	+	103.5 Hz	
Levant, Pember Ridge						
	FM	W1DLO	147.36000	+	77.0 Hz	NESMC
Lincoln	DMR/MARC	KC1FRJ	145.35000	-	CC12	
	FM	K1AQ	449.27500	-		
Lincoln , Bagley Mtn						
	FM	KQ1L	147.00000	+	100.0 Hz	NESMC
Litchfield	DMR/MARC	N1ITR	146.70000	-	CC12	
	FM	K1AAM	53.05000	52.05000	136.5 Hz	
Livermore Falls, Moose Hill						
	FM	W1BHR	147.22500	+	123.0 Hz	
Long A Township, Lincoln Ridge						
	FM	KA1EKS	146.74500	-	100.0 Hz	NESMC
Machias	DMR/BM	W1BSB	444.50000	+	CC1	
Madawaska	FM	W1ACP	449.82500	-		
	FUSION	W1ACP	441.82500	449.82500		
	FUSION	N1HYP	449.42500			
Madison	FM	KA1C	449.62500	-	91.5 Hz	
Madison, Blackwell Hill						
	FM	KA1C	146.73000	-	91.5 Hz	NESMC
Manks Corner		KB1DBL-R	147.06000			
Marshfield	FM	K1HF	146.77500	-		NESMC
Mechanic Falls	FUSION	N1YDP	147.45000			
Millinocket, South Twin Lake						
	FM	KA1EKS	145.25000	-	100.0 Hz	NESMC
Milo, Sargent Hill	FM	KB1ZQY	147.15000	+	123.0 Hz	NESMC
Naples	FM	K1AAM	146.83500	-	103.5 Hz	NESMC
New Sharon	DMR/MARC	W1BHR	145.14000	-	CC11	
New Sharon, York Hill						
	FM	N1UGR	147.37500	-	131.8 Hz	
Newport	FUSION	KC1DLN	147.01500	+		
NOAA Caribou	WX	WXM77	162.52500			
NOAA Dresden	WX	WSM60	162.47500			
NOAA Falmouth	WX	KDO95	162.55000			
NOAA Frenchville	WX	KHB55	162.47500			
NOAA Greenville	WX	WNG542	162.42500			
NOAA Jonesboro	WX	WNG543	162.45000			
NOAA Meddybemps						
	WX	KHC47	162.42500			
NOAA Milo	WX	KHB54	162.55000			
NOAA Springfield	WX	WXN28	162.50000			

Location	Mode	Call sign	Output	Input	Access	Coordinator
NOAA Sugarloaf Mountain						
	WX	WNG547	162.45000			
Nobleboro	FM	W1AUX	224.32000	-	103.5 Hz	
North Wade, Near Presque Isle						
	FM	K1FS	146.73000	-		
Norway, Pike Hill	FM	W1OCA	147.12000	+		
Old Orchard Beach						
	FUSION	W1OOB	145.55500			
	FUSION	N1BIM	147.09000	+		
Palermo, Marden Hill						
	FM	K1XI	145.27000	-	100.0 Hz	NESMC
Phippsburg	DSTAR	KS1R	447.57500	-		
	FM	KS1R	147.21000	+	100.0 Hz	NESMC
Plymouth	FM	N1YMM	442.00000	+		
	FUSION	N1YMM	447.00000	-		
Poland Spring, White Oak Hill						
	FM	W1NPP	147.31500	+	103.5 Hz	NESMC
Portland	DMR/MARC	W1IMD	145.34000	-	CC12	
	FM	KA1SHU	146.76000	-	100.0 Hz	NESMC
Portland, Mitchell Hill						
	FM	K1SA	147.36000	+	100.0 Hz	NESMC
Presque Isle	DMR/MARC	KC1FRJ	145.18000	-	CC12	
Rangeley Saddleback Mtn						
	DMR/MARC	K1XI	145.20000	-	CC12	
Raymond	DMR/BM	N1XBM	448.42500	-	CC1	
Rumford, Black Mtn						
	FM	N1BBK	146.91000	-	100.0 Hz	
Sanford	FM	N1ROA	146.80500	-	103.5 Hz	
	FM	N1KMA	223.82000	-		
	FM	W1LO	441.60000	+	203.5 Hz	
Sanford, Mt Hope	FM	KQ1L	147.18000	+	131.8 Hz	NESMC
Shapleigh	DMR/MARC	K1DQ	145.11000	-	CC4	
Sherman	FUSION	W1NOC	448.20000	-		
Sidney	DMR/MARC	KQ1L	145.24000	-	CC12	
	FUSION	N1UB	146.62500	-		
Skowhegan, Bigelow Hill						
	FM	KA1ZGC	147.34500	+		NESMC
Smyrna	DMR/MARC	KC1FRJ	147.09000	+	CC12	
Springfield, Almanac Mtn						
	FM	WA1ZJL	147.37500	+	100.0 Hz	NESMC
Topsfield, Musquash Mtn						
	FM	W1LH	146.67000	-	100.0 Hz	NESMC
Topsham	DMR/MARC	N1IPA	145.19000	-	CC13	
	FM	KS1R	444.40000	+	88.5 Hz	
	FUSION	NG1P	147.57000			
Trenton	FM	AA1PI	146.71500	-		NESMC
Turner	DMR/BM	N1DOT	442.70000	+	CC1	
	FM	N1DOT	446.50000		100.0 Hz	
Veazie	FUSION	N1AFS	146.51500			
Waldoboro	FM	N1PS	224.78000	-	107.2 Hz	
Waldoboro, RW Glidden Auto Bod						
	FM	K1NYY	147.39000	+	179.9 Hz	NESMC
Wales, Oak Hill	FM	W1PIG	145.29000	-	100.0 Hz	NESMC
Warren	FM	WA1ZDA	224.10000	-		
Washington	FM	KC1CG	53.55000	52.55000	91.5 Hz	
	FM	KC1CG	224.28000	-	91.5 Hz	NESMC
	FM	WZ1J	444.90000	+	91.5 Hz	
Washington, Benner Hill						
	FM	W1PBR	147.06000	+	91.5 Hz	NESMC
Washington, Lenfest Mountain						
	FM	KC1CG	145.49000	-	91.5 Hz	NESMC
Waterville	DMR/MARC	KQ1L	146.92500	-	CC12	

Location	Mode	Call sign	Output	Input	Access	Coordinator
Wells	DMR/MARC	KY1C	442.40000	+	CC11	
West Bath	DMR/BM	N1XBM	449.77500	-	CC1	
Westbrook	FM	N1ULM	444.25000	+	82.5 Hz	
	FM	W1CKD	444.60000	+	82.5 Hz	
Westbrook, Rocky Hill						
	FM	W1CKD	147.27000	+	103.5 Hz	NESMC
Windham Hill	FM	N1FCU	29.68000	-	173.8 Hz	NESMC
Winslow	FM	KD1MM	146.76000	-	103.5 Hz	NESMC
Winterport	FUSION	KC1DXD	147.48000			
Wiscasset, Blinn Hill						
	FM	K1LX	146.98500	-	136.5 Hz	
Woodstock	FM	W1IMD	53.09000	52.09000	71.9 Hz	
	FM	W1IMD	223.94000	-	103.5 Hz	
	FM	W1IMD	449.02500	-	82.5 Hz	
Yarmouth	FM	K1JW	146.94000	-		
York	FM	W1XOJ	448.00000	-	173.8 Hz	

MARYLAND

Location	Mode	Call sign	Output	Input	Access	Coordinator
Accokeek	FM	W3TOM	444.50000	+	127.3 Hz	T-MARC
Adelphi	FM	W3ARL	145.37000	-		T-MARC
	FM	N3TUK	147.48000		103.5 Hz	
Annapolis	DMR/MARC	W4ATN	443.78750	+	CC3	T-MARC
Annapolis, Broad Creek Park						
	FM	KB3CMA	442.30000	+	107.2 Hz	T-MARC
Anywhere	DMR/MARC	N3LHD	447.87500	-	CC6	
Ashton	DMR/MARC	K3UCB	442.23750	+	CC1	T-MARC
	FM	N3AGB	53.25000	52.25000	100.0 Hz	T-MARC
	FM	K3WX	224.54000	-	156.7 Hz	T-MARC
	FM	K3WX	443.15000	+		T-MARC
	FM	K3WX	927.72500	902.72500	156.7 Hz	T-MARC
Baltimore	DMR/MARC	N3CDY	927.06250	902.06250	CC1	
	FM	WB3DZO	147.03000	+		T-MARC
	FM	N3HIA	224.48000	-		T-MARC
	FM	KS3L	224.68000	-		T-MARC
	FM	WA3KOK	442.25000	+	107.2 Hz	T-MARC
	FM	K3CUJ	448.27500	-	156.7 Hz	T-MARC
	FM	W3PGA	449.57500	-	123.0 Hz	T-MARC
	FM	N3ST	449.67500	-	167.9 Hz	T-MARC
	FUSION	AC3EO	145.55500			
	FUSION	KC3TRJ	449.47500	-		
Baltimore, Kenwood High School						
	FM	W3PGA	147.24000	+	123.0 Hz	T-MARC
Barstow	FM	KA3GRW	443.70000	+	179.9 Hz	T-MARC
Bel Air	DMR/MARC	KB3WHR	449.61250	-	CC1	T-MARC
	DSTAR	KC3FHC	145.12000	-		T-MARC
	DSTAR	KC3FHC	447.98750	-		T-MARC
	DSTAR	KC3FHC	1282.30000	1262.30000		T-MARC
	FM	KC3FHC	146.77500	-	146.2 Hz	T-MARC
	FM	N3EKQ	147.12000	+		T-MARC
	FM	N3EKQ	223.96000	-		T-MARC
	FM	KC3FHC	449.77500	-	162.2 Hz	T-MARC
Belair	DMR/BM	KO3L	147.12000	+	CC1	
Berlin	FUSION	KC3NDI	144.10000			
Boonsboro	FM	KD3SU	442.65000	+	79.7 Hz	
	FM	KD3SU	442.95000	+	94.8 Hz	T-MARC
Bowie	FM	W3XJ	442.15000	+		T-MARC
Brandywine	DMR/MARC	N3LHD	444.65000	+	CC6	
	FM	W3SMR	147.15000	+	114.8 Hz	T-MARC
Branton Manor		W3APL-L	147.58500			
Burtonsville	FM	WA3KOK	444.05000	+		T-MARC
Calverton	FM	WB3GXW-R	147.22500	+		T-MARC

Location	Mode	Call sign	Output	Input	Access	Coordinator
Carroll Woods Estates						
		KB3BVW-L	146.48000			
Centerville	FM	KE3AO	146.94000	-	107.2 Hz	T-MARC
Centreville	FM	N8ADN	448.22500	-	107.2 Hz	T-MARC
Charles Town	FM	KD8DWU	927.58750	902.58750	123.0 Hz	
Charlestown	FM	N3RCN	145.47000	-	94.8 Hz	T-MARC
Charlestown, Water Tower						
	FM	N3RCN	442.95000	+	103.5 Hz	T-MARC
Charlotte Hall	DMR/MARC	K3OCM	443.18750	+	CC6	T-MARC
Chesapeake Beach						
	DMR/BM	WG3K	444.35000	+	CC1	
Chestertown	DMR/MARC	N3YMS	441.66250	+	CC1	
Chingville		K3KLC-L	147.42000			
Clear Spring	FM	K3MAD	147.34500	+	123.0 Hz	T-MARC
	FM	N3UHD-R	442.65000	+		T-MARC
Clear Spring, Fairview Mountai						
	FM	W3CWC	146.94000	-	100.0 Hz	T-MARC
Cockeysville	FM	K3NXU	145.19000	-	110.9 Hz	T-MARC
College Park, UMD						
	FM	W3EAX	145.49000	-		T-MARC
Columbia	FM	K3CUJ	147.13500	+	156.7 Hz	T-MARC
	FM	W3CAM	224.86000	-		T-MARC
	FM	K3CUJ	449.47500	-	156.7 Hz	T-MARC
Cooksville	FM	K3CUJ	147.39000	+		
Crisfield	DMR/MARC	KC3DVC	145.13000	-	CC1	
Cumberland	FM	AB3FE	442.30000	+	167.9 Hz	T-MARC
	FM	KK3L	444.00000	+	123.0 Hz	T-MARC
	FUSION	N3ZBL	444.56250			
Curtis Bay	FM	W3VPR	147.07500	+	107.2 Hz	T-MARC
Damascus	DMR/MARC	KB3LYL	442.21250	+	CC1	
	FM	N3VNG	145.25000	-	146.2 Hz	T-MARC
	FM	KB3LYL	441.88750	+		T-MARC
Darnestown		N3PPD-L	147.42000			
Davidsonville	FM	W3VPR	147.10500	+	107.2 Hz	T-MARC
	FM	W3VPR	223.88000	-	107.2 Hz	T-MARC
	FM	W3VPR	444.40000	+	107.2 Hz	T-MARC
Dayton	FM	W3YVV	443.95000	+		T-MARC
	FM	W3YVV	927.53750	902.53750	156.7 Hz	T-MARC
District Heights	FM	K3ERA	145.23000	-	110.9 Hz	T-MARC
Dundalk	FM	AC3CZ	446.10000			
Dundalk, Key Bridge						
	FM	KC3APF	448.67500	-	91.5 Hz	T-MARC
Easton	FUSION	KC3HMA	442.20000	+		
Easton, UM/Shore Regional Medi						
	FM	K3EMD	442.20000	+	156.7 Hz	T-MARC
Elkton	DMR/BM	K3DRF	145.25000	-	CC1	
	FM	KX3B	448.77500	-	131.8 Hz	
Ellicott City	FM	N3EZD	224.32000	-		T-MARC
Essex	DMR/BM	K3LPV	449.20000		CC1	
	DMR/BM	K3LPV	449.90000		CC1	
Fallstaff		KB3JQQ-L	445.42500			
Fallston	DMR/BM	N3CNJ	145.27000	-	CC1	
Federalsburg	DMR/MARC	N3KNT	442.05000	+	CC1	
Fishers Hollow	FM	W3ICF	146.73000	-	141.3 Hz	T-MARC
Flintstone	FM	KB3VJO	147.31500	+		T-MARC
	FM	KB3VJO	443.90000	+		T-MARC
Forest Hill	DSTAR	KB3TOG C	145.12000	-		
	DSTAR	KB3TOG B	447.98750	-		
	DSTAR	KB3TOG D	1248.10000			
	DSTAR	KB3TOG A	1282.30000	-		
Four Corners		K2KSB-L	446.52500			
Frederick	DMR/BM	K3DO	441.96250	+	CC1	

Location	Mode	Call sign	Output	Input	Access	Coordinator
Frederick	DSTAR	W3FDK C	145.17000	-		
	DSTAR	W3FDK B	444.80000	+		
	FM	N3KTX	53.47000	52.47000	107.2 Hz	
	FM	N3IGM	53.75000	52.75000	100.0 Hz	T-MARC
	FM	K3ERM	146.64000	-	156.7 Hz	T-MARC
	FM	K3MAD	147.06000	+	146.2 Hz	T-MARC
	FM	K3MAD	224.20000	-	123.0 Hz	T-MARC
	FM	WA3KOK	443.40000	+	136.5 Hz	T-MARC
	FM	N3ST	444.10000	+	167.9 Hz	T-MARC
	P25	N3ITA	442.80000	+		T-MARC
	P25	K3MAD	448.12500	-		T-MARC
	FUSION	N3ZBL	444.10000			
Frederick, Braddock Mountain						
	FM	W3ARK	444.35000	+	100.0 Hz	T-MARC
Frederick, Gambril Mountain						
	FUSION	K3ERM	448.42500	-	100.0 Hz	T-MARC
Frederick, Gambrill Mountain						
	DSTAR	W3FDK	444.80000	+		T-MARC
Frederick, Gambrill State Park						
	DSTAR	KB3YBH	145.17000	-		T-MARC
Frederick, Gambrils State Park						
	FM	N3KTX	53.47000	52.47000	107.2 Hz	T-MARC
Frostburg	DMR/MARC	K3YDA	147.10500	+	CC1	
	DMR/MARC	N3IVK	444.07500	+	CC1	
Gaithersburg	FM	KV3B	53.27000	52.27000	156.7 Hz	T-MARC
Galena	FM	KB3MEC	224.00000	-	131.8 Hz	T-MARC
Gambrills	FM	N3SCP	442.55000	+	107.2 Hz	
Germantown	DSTAR	KV3B	444.20000	+		T-MARC
	DSTAR	KV3B B	444.20000	+		
	FM	WA3KOK	147.27000	+	156.7 Hz	T-MARC
Glen Burnie	FM	N3MIR	224.60000	-		T-MARC
	FM	N3MIR	442.60000	+	127.3 Hz	T-MARC
Great Falls		KJ4DGE-L	147.59000			
Greenbelt	FM	W3GMR	146.88000	-		T-MARC
Hagerstown	FM	K3UMV	147.37500	+		T-MARC
	FM	W3ARK	447.12500	-	123.0 Hz	T-MARC
Havre De Grace	DMR/MARC	WR3IRS	443.65000	+	CC1	
	FM	N3KZ	444.15000	+	131.8 Hz	T-MARC
Hillendale		KA2JAI-R	442.30000			
Hollywood	DSTAR	N3PX	147.19500	+		T-MARC
	DSTAR	N3PX C	147.19500	+		
Horse Shoe Farms Estates						
		K3BOA-L	443.17500			
Hughesville	FM	W3ZO	145.39000	-	186.2 Hz	T-MARC
Hyattsville	DMR/MARC	N3LHD	444.65000	+	CC6	T-MARC
Jarrettsville	FM	N3UR	53.93000	52.93000		T-MARC
Jefferson	FM	K3LMS	443.30000	+	100.0 Hz	T-MARC
Jessup	DMR/MARC	KA3LAO	442.71250	+	CC1	
	FM	WA3DZD	146.76000	-	107.2 Hz	T-MARC
	FM	WA3DZD	444.00000	+	107.2 Hz	T-MARC
Joppa	DMR/MARC	N3CNJ	145.23000	-	CC1	
Kentfield	FM	K3ARS-R	147.37500	+		T-MARC
Knoxville	DMR/BM	W3FDK	441.96250	+	CC1	
Lake Shore		K3BAY-L	145.54000			
Land-O-Lakes		KB3UUN-L	145.35000			
Landover Park		K3BEQ-L	147.57000			
Lanham, Doctors Community Hosp						
	FM	K3ERA	447.32500	-	110.9 Hz	
Laurel	DMR/BM	W3SQN	442.90000	+	CC1	
	FM	W3LRC	442.50000	+	156.7 Hz	T-MARC
	FM	WA3GPC	444.70000	+	167.9 Hz	T-MARC
	FM	K3UQQ	923.25000	1265.25000		T-MARC

Location	Mode	Call sign	Output	Input	Access	Coordinator
Leedstown	FM	K3WX-R	147.00000	+		T-MARC
Leonardtown	FUSION	N3JTN	441.00000			
Lexington Park	FM	K3HKI	146.64000	-	146.2 Hz	T-MARC
	FM	WA3UMY	443.05000	+		T-MARC
	FUSION	KB2SKP	440.25000	+		
Littlestown	FM	N3ST	449.67500	-	167.9 Hz	
Madonna Hills	FM	N3UR-R	448.47500	-		T-MARC
Manchester	FM	N3KZS	146.89500	-		
Mechanicsville	DMR/MARC	N3PPH	441.78750	+	CC1	
Middle River	DMR/BM	KB3WYD	145.17000	-	CC1	
	DMR/BM	KB3WYD	447.37500	-	CC1	
Middle-River	DSTAR	KC3MDK B	442.42500			
Midland	FM	WX3M	147.10500	+	192.8 Hz	T-MARC
	FM	AB3FE	442.75000	+	167.9 Hz	T-MARC
Midland, Dan's Mountain						
	FM	W3YMW	146.88000	-	123.0 Hz	T-MARC
Midland, Dans Mountain						
	FM	KK3L	147.24000	+		T-MARC
Midland, Dans Rock						
	FM	W3YMW	444.50000	+	118.8 Hz	T-MARC
Millersville	DMR/BM	KP4IP	442.40000	+	CC1	T-MARC
	DMR/BM	KP4IP	447.40000	-	CC1	
	FM	W3CU	146.80500	-	107.2 Hz	T-MARC
	FM	W3VPR	224.56000	-	107.2 Hz	T-MARC
	FM	W3CU	449.12500	-	107.2 Hz	T-MARC
Mount Airy		KC3FMP-L	146.44500			
New Windsor	FUSION	N3CHW	438.60000			
NOAA Baltimore	WX	KEC83	162.40000			
NOAA Frostburg	WX	WXM43	162.42500			
NOAA Hagerstown						
	WX	WXM42	162.47500			
NOAA Sudlersville						
	WX	WXK97	162.50000			
Oakland		KC3LL-L	147.58500			
	FM	KB3AVZ	146.70000	-	173.8 Hz	T-MARC
	FM	KB8NUF	146.80500	-	123.0 Hz	T-MARC
	FM	KB3AVZ	444.27500	+	110.9 Hz	T-MARC
	FUSION	K3WJ	145.60000			
Ocean City	DMR/MARC	K3ORB	444.01250	+	CC1	T-MARC
	FM	K3ORB-R	443.45000	+	151.4 Hz	
Ocean Pines	FM	NW2M	146.95500	-		
Oldtown, Warrior Mountain WMA						
	FM	W3YMW	145.45000	-	123.0 Hz	T-MARC
Olney	DMR/MARC	K3UCB	442.90000	+	CC1	
	FUSION	K3UCB	446.10000			
Owings Mills	DMR/MARC	N3CDY	449.07500	-	CC1	
	FM	N3CDY	449.62500	-	107.2 Hz	
	FM	N3CDY	927.51250	902.51250	156.7 Hz	T-MARC
Parkton	FUSION	AK3B	144.42500			
Parkville	FUSION	KC3FBM	145.72500			
Parsonsburg	FUSION	W3ZY	444.05000	+		
Pasadena	FUSION	N3HUG	145.60000	-		
Pen Mar, High Rock						
	FM	W3CWC	147.09000	+	100.0 Hz	T-MARC
	FUSION	W3CWC	447.97500	-	100.0 Hz	T-MARC
Perry Hall	FM	W3JEH	223.84000	-		T-MARC
Pittsville	FUSION	WS3ARA	449.82500	-		
Port Deposit	FM	WA3SFJ	53.83000	52.83000	94.8 Hz	T-MARC
	FM	WA3SFJ-R	146.85000	-	107.2 Hz	T-MARC
	FM	WA3SFJ	449.82500	-	167.9 Hz	T-MARC
Prince Frederick	FM	W3PQS	53.17000	52.17000	100.0 Hz	T-MARC

Location	Mode	Call sign	Output	Input	Access	Coordinator
Prince Frederick, Barstow						
	FM	N3PX	145.35000	-	156.7 Hz	T-MARC
	FM	W3SMD	223.90000	-		T-MARC
Princess Anne	DMR/MARC	N3YMS	441.88750	+	CC2	T-MARC
	DMR/MARC	N3NRL	442.03750	+	CC1	
	FM	KA3MRX	146.62500	-	156.7 Hz	T-MARC
Rockville	DMR/MARC	N3JFW	442.48750	+	CC1	
	FM	KV3B	146.95500	-		T-MARC
	FM	K3ATV	224.94000	-	156.7 Hz	T-MARC
	FM	KV3B	442.75000	+	156.7 Hz	T-MARC
Rockville, Mongomery County Ex						
	FM	WA3YOO	443.90000	+	156.7 Hz	T-MARC
Rogers Heights	FM	K3GMR-R	146.61000	-		T-MARC
Salisbury	DMR/MARC	K3OCM	442.65000	+	CC6	
	DSTAR	W3PRO	145.28000	-		T-MARC
	DSTAR	W3PRO C	145.28000	-		
	DSTAR	W3PRO B	444.20000	+		
	DSTAR	W3PRO	444.20000	+		T-MARC
	FM	W3PRO	146.92500	-	156.7 Hz	T-MARC
	FM	N3HQJ	442.65000	+	156.7 Hz	T-MARC
	FM	K3RIC	444.05000	+		
Salisbury, WMDT Tower						
	FM	K3DRC	146.82000	-	156.7 Hz	T-MARC
Severn	FUSION	KB7ICI	147.44500			
Shawsville	FM	K3HT	145.33000	-		T-MARC
	FM	N3UR	224.92000	-		T-MARC
	FM	W3EHT	449.37500	-		T-MARC
Silver Spring	FM	N3AUY	29.66000	-	141.3 Hz	T-MARC
	FM	KA3LAO	147.18000	+		T-MARC
	FM	WB3GXW	444.25000	+	156.7 Hz	T-MARC
South Glen		KB3MKJ-L	446.95000			
South Kensington		K0TIN-L	446.10000			
Starr	FM	WA3NAN-R	146.83000	-		
Suitland	FM	N3ST	448.92500	-	167.9 Hz	T-MARC
Sunderland	DMR/MARC	N3PPH	441.63750	+	CC1	
	FM	K3CAL	146.98500	-	156.7 Hz	T-MARC
Swanton	DMR/BM	N6IO	439.40000	-	CC4	
Sykesville	FM	K3PZN	147.28500	+	107.2 Hz	
Test	DMR/MARC	KA3LAO	441.88750	+	CC1	
Thurmont	FM	K3KMA	448.02500	-	103.5 Hz	T-MARC
Thurmont VHF	DMR/MARC	N3EJT	147.19500	+	CC1	T-MARC
Towson	DMR/MARC	WR3IRS	441.40000	+	CC1	T-MARC
	DMR/MARC	K3OCM	443.85000	+	CC6	T-MARC
	DSTAR	W3DHS	145.14000	-		T-MARC
	DSTAR	W3DHS C	145.14000	-		
	DSTAR	W3DHS	442.11250	+		T-MARC
	DSTAR	W3DHS B	442.11250	+		
	DSTAR	W3DHS D	1248.30000			
	DSTAR	W3DHS A	1282.70000	-		
	DSTAR	W3DHS	1282.70000	1262.70000		T-MARC
	FM	W3FT	146.67000	-	107.2 Hz	T-MARC
	FM	N3CDY	449.27500	-	107.2 Hz	T-MARC
	FM	N3CDY	927.48750	902.48750	156.7 Hz	T-MARC
Trappe	DMR/MARC	N3YMS	442.53750	+	CC1	
	FM	K3EMD	147.04500	+	156.7 Hz	T-MARC
Tyaskin VHF	DMR/MARC	N3HQJ	146.86500	-	CC1	
Upper Marlboro	DMR/MARC	N3LHD	444.65000	+	CC6	
	FUSION	KB3IIE	145.43000	-		
West Laurel	FM	K3WS	447.92500	-	123.0 Hz	T-MARC
Westminster	FM	K3PZN	53.09000	52.09000	107.2 Hz	T-MARC
	FM	K3PZN	145.41000	-	114.8 Hz	T-MARC
	FM	K3PZN	449.87500	-	127.3 Hz	T-MARC

Location	Mode	Call sign	Output	Input	Access	Coordinator
White Oak		WB3GXW-L	147.18000			
	FM	N3HF-R	443.45000	+		T-MARC
Woodbine	DMR/MARC	KA3LAO	442.46250	+	CC1	T-MARC
Worton	DMR/BM	K3ARS	447.73750	-	CC1	
Wye Mills	DMR/MARC	N3YMS	441.91250	+	CC1	

MASSACHUSETTS

Location	Mode	Call sign	Output	Input	Access	Coordinator
Abington	DMR/BM	W1EHT	927.62500	902.06250	CC1	
	FM	WG1U	927.45000	902.45000		
Acton	DMR/MARC	NO1A	146.42000	144.92000	CC1	
	DMR/MARC	NO1A	442.35000	+	CC1	
Adams	FUSION	K1FFK	146.91000	-		
Adams, Mount Greylock						
	FM	K1FFK	53.23000	52.23000	162.2 Hz	NESMC
Adams, Mt Greylock						
	FM	KB1EXR	145.21000	-	77.0 Hz	
	FM	K1FFK	927.87500	902.87500	100.0 Hz	NESMC
Agawam	DSTAR	W1KK	449.17500	-		
	FM	KA1JJM	449.77500	-		
	FM	W1KK	927.80000	902.80000		
Agawam Town	DSTAR	AA1KK B	447.37500	-		
Agawam, Provin Mtn						
	FM	W1TOM	146.67000	-	127.3 Hz	
Andover	FM	N1LHP	146.83500	-	77.0 Hz	NESMC
Ashland	FM	N3HFK	927.88750	902.88750	131.8 Hz	
Assonet	IDAS	N1KIM	145.43750	-		
	IDAS	WG1U	449.99695	-		
Attleboro	WX	K1SMH-R	147.19500	+		NESMC
Auburn	FM	K1WPO	443.90000	+	100.0 Hz	
	FM	K1WPO	448.12500	-	88.5 Hz	
Barnstable	FM	N1YHS	53.01000	52.01000	173.8 Hz	
	FM	W1SGL-R	146.73000	-	67.0 Hz	NESMC
	FM	W1SGL	927.82500	902.02500	82.5 Hz	NESMC
Belchertown	FM	N1SIF	443.70000	+	71.9 Hz	
Belmont	FM	KC1CLA	145.43000	-	146.2 Hz	NESMC
	FM	KB1FX	223.86000	-	100.0 Hz	
Beverly	FM	WA1PNW	147.39000	+		
	FM	WA1PNW	442.85000	+	103.5 Hz	
Billerica	FM	W1DC	147.12000	+	103.5 Hz	
Bliss Corner	FM	W1AEC-R	147.00000	+	67.0 Hz	
	FM	W1AEC-L	224.80000	-		
Boston	DMR/MARC	N1PA	146.49000	144.99000	CC1	
	DMR/MARC	KB1VKI	442.05000	+	CC2	
	DMR/MARC	W1DSR	447.07500	-	CC1	
	DMR/MARC	W1BOS	449.17500	-	CC1	
	FM	KB1BEM	145.21000	-		
	FM	W1BOS	145.23000	-	88.5 Hz	
	FM	W1KBN	145.31000	-	123.0 Hz	
	FM	K1BOS	146.82000	-	127.3 Hz	NESMC
	FM	W1KRU	444.70000	+		NESMC
	FM	K1RJZ	927.06250	902.06250		NESMC
Bourne	DMR/MARC	K1RK	145.20000	-	CC10	
	FM	N1YHS	224.22000	-	100.0 Hz	
Braintree	FM	K1GUG	53.03000	52.03000		
	FM	AE1TH	53.39000	52.39000	71.9 Hz	
	FM	AE1TH	442.50000	+	118.8 Hz	
Bridgewater	FM	W1MV	444.55000	+	88.5 Hz	
	FM	W1WCF	927.42500	902.42500	131.8 Hz	
	WX	W1MV-R	147.18000	+		NESMC
Brookline	DMR/MARC	NN1PA	146.49000	144.99000	CC1	
	DSTAR	K1MRA C	145.16000	-		
	DSTAR	K1MRA	145.16000	-		

Location	Mode	Call sign	Output	Input	Access	Coordinator
Brookline	FM	K1DVD	146.98500	-	88.5 Hz	
	FM	W1CLA	446.32500	-	146.2 Hz	
Burlington	FM	W1DYJ	446.77500	-	88.5 Hz	
	FM	W1CLA	447.02500	-	146.2 Hz	
Cambridge, Green Building						
	FM	W1XM	449.72500	-	114.8 Hz	NESMC
Canton	FM	K1BFD	146.74500	-	146.2 Hz	
	FM	K1BFD	449.42500	-	88.5 Hz	
Chatham	FM	WA1WCC	145.40000	-	146.2 Hz	
Chelmsford	DMR/MARC	N1IW	145.18000	-	CC2	
Clinton	FM	N1ZUZ	146.65500	-	74.4 Hz	
	FM	N1KUB	442.30000	+	74.4 Hz	
Concord	FM	N1CON	447.57500	-	110.9 Hz	
Concord, Annursnac Hill						
	FM	N1CON	145.11000	-	110.9 Hz	
Dalton	FM	N1FZH	224.40000	-		
Danvers	DMR/MARC	NS1RA	442.80000	+	CC4	
	FM	N1UEC	53.85000	52.85000	71.9 Hz	
	FM	NS1RA	145.47000	-	136.5 Hz	
	FM	NS1RA	223.88000	-	136.5 Hz	
Dartmouth	DSTAR	NN1D	145.29000	-		
	FM	W1AEC	927.83750	902.03750	77.0 Hz	
Deerfield	FM	AB1RS	145.13000	-		
	FM	AB1RS	443.45000	+	173.8 Hz	
Dennis	DMR/MARC	W1MLL	146.47000	144.97000	CC11	
	FM	W1MA	146.95500	-	88.5 Hz	
Dixmont, Peaked Mt						
	FUSION	KC1DLN	147.01500	+		
Dogtown Commons						
	FM	W1GLO-R	145.13000	-		
Dorchester	DMR/MARC	KC1AVD	442.40000	+	CC1	
Dorothy Manor	FM	N1EKO-R	224.48000	-		
Dukes Co.	DMR/MARC	K1MVY	145.18000	-	CC10	
East Littleton	FM	WB1GOF-R	146.95500	-	74.4 Hz	NESMC
Eastham	DMR/MARC	W1MLL	145.36000	-	CC10	
Egremont	FM	WB2BQW	145.25000	-	100.0 Hz	
Fall River	DSTAR	K1RFI	145.42000	-		
	DSTAR	K1RFI C	145.42000	-		
	DSTAR	K1RFI	449.52500	-		
	DSTAR	K1RFI B	449.52500	-		
	FM	NN1D	146.80500	-	67.0 Hz	
	FM	WB0YLE	224.54000	-	141.3 Hz	
	FM	NN1D	927.03750	-		
	FM	N1JBC	927.65000	902.65000	91.5 Hz	
Falmouth	DSTAR	KB1ZEG	145.21000	-		
	DSTAR	KB1ZEG C	145.21000	-		
	FM	N1YHS	147.37500	+	110.9 Hz	
	FM	K1RK	927.85000	902.05000	88.5 Hz	
Falmouth, Hospital						
	FM	K1RK	146.65500	-	88.5 Hz	
Feeding Hills	DSTAR	W1KK	145.15000	-		
	DSTAR	W1KK C	145.15000	-		
	DSTAR	W1KK B	449.17500	-		
	DSTAR	W1KK D	1248.50000			
	DSTAR	W1KK	1282.50000	1262.50000		
	DSTAR	W1KK A	1282.50000	-		
Fitchburg	FM	WB1EWS	53.83000	52.83000	71.9 Hz	
	FM	W1GZ-R	145.45000	-	74.4 Hz	
	FM	WB1EWS	147.31500	+	100.0 Hz	
	FM	WB1EWS	442.95000	+	88.5 Hz	
Flint Village	FM	WA1DGW-R	145.15000	-	123.0 Hz	
Florence	FM	AA1AK	53.35000	52.35000	71.9 Hz	

Location	Mode	Call sign	Output	Input	Access	Coordinator
Framingham	DMR/BM	WA1NVC	441.45000	+	CC9	
	FM	W1FRS	53.27000	52.27000	71.9 Hz	
	FM	W1FY-R	147.15000	+	100.0 Hz	
	FM	WB1CTO	224.24000	-	103.5 Hz	NESMC
	FM	N1OMJ	444.75000	+	88.5 Hz	
	FM	W1FRS	448.17500	-	88.5 Hz	
	FM	W1FRS	927.01250	902.01250	131.8 Hz	
Freetown	DSTAR	KB1WUW	146.41000	144.91000		
	DSTAR	KB1WUW	147.57500	-		
	DSTAR	KB1WUW	449.77500	-		
Gardner	DMR/MARC	N1WW	145.34000	-	CC3	
	FM	W1GCD	145.37000	-	136.5 Hz	
	FM	W1GCD	442.10000	+	88.5 Hz	
	WX	W1SEX	145.37000	-	136.5 Hz	NESMC
	WX	W1SEX	442.10000	+	88.5 Hz	NESMC
Gloucester	FM	W1GLO	224.90000	-		
	FM	W1GLO	443.70000	+	107.2 Hz	
	FM	W1RAB	447.52500	-	114.8 Hz	
	FUSION	W1TAT	446.50000			
Granville	DMR/MARC	KB1AEV	442.75000	+	CC1	
	WX	W1TOM	147.00000	+	127.3 Hz	NESMC
Great Barrington	FM	KC1AJX	146.71500	-	77.0 Hz	
Great Barrington, Monument Mou						
	FM	KC1GLK	442.65000	+	162.2 Hz	NESMC
Great Barrington, Ski Butternu						
	IDAS	KA1OA	145.27000	-		
Greenfield	FM	KB1BSS	448.27500	-	136.5 Hz	
Hancock	FM	N1ARO	146.83500	-	110.9 Hz	
Harvard	FM	W1DVC	145.41000	-	74.4 Hz	
Harwich	FM	K1KEK	224.34000	-	100.0 Hz	NESMC
Harwich Port	FM	WA1YFV	145.27000	-	67.0 Hz	
Haverhill	FM	KT1S	145.35000	-	136.5 Hz	
	FM	N1IRS	224.12000	-	103.5 Hz	
Hingham	DMR/MARC	K1GAS	146.43000	144.93000	CC1	
Holliston	DMR/MARC	W1DSR	145.14000	-	CC1	NESMC
	DSTAR	W1DSR B	447.07500	-		
	FM	KB3ZOO	449.57500	-	88.5 Hz	
Holyoke	DSTAR	AA1KK	447.37500	-		
	FM	K1ZJH	146.71500	-	100.0 Hz	NESMC
	FM	W1TOM	443.20000	+	127.3 Hz	
	FM	AA1KK	927.83750	902.83750		
Holyoke, Mt Tom	FM	W1TOM	146.94000	-	127.3 Hz	
Hopkinton	FM	K1KWP	223.94000	-	103.5 Hz	
	FM	W1BRI	449.57500	-	88.5 Hz	NESMC
Ipswich	FUSION	K1MDA	144.62000			
Lawrence	DMR/BM	KB1SFG	441.37500	+	CC1	
	DMR/BM	KB1SFG	446.37500	-	CC1	
	FM	N1EXC	146.65500	-	107.2 Hz	
	FM	N1EXC	224.30000	-		
	FM	N1EXC	447.62500	-	88.5 Hz	
Leominster	FM	AA1JD	224.76000	-	85.4 Hz	
Leyden	FM	KB1BSS	146.98500	-	136.5 Hz	
Littleton	FM	K1PRE	927.43750	902.43750	131.8 Hz	NESMC
Lowell	FM	K1LVF	442.25000	+	88.5 Hz	NESMC
	FM	KB2KWB	444.96250	+	179.9 Hz	
Lynn	FM	W1DVG	147.01500	+	88.5 Hz	
Malden		K1LVA-L	145.77000			
Mansfield	FM	KB1CYO	147.01500	+	67.0 Hz	
	FM	KB1JJE	446.92500	-	100.0 Hz	
	FM	N1UEC	449.67500	-	146.2 Hz	
Marblehead	DMR/MARC	K1XML	145.37000	-	CC0	
	DMR/MARC	K1XML	445.87500	-	CC1	

Location	Mode	Call sign	Output	Input	Access	Coordinator
Marions Camp	FM	KA1AQP-R	444.90000	+		
Marlborough	DSTAR	W1MRA B	448.22500	-		
	FM	W1MRA	29.68000	-	131.8 Hz	
	FM	W1BRI	53.81000	52.81000	71.9 Hz	NESMC
	FM	WA1NPN	147.24000	+	71.9 Hz	
	FM	W1MRA	147.27000	+	146.2 Hz	NESMC
	FM	W1MRA	224.88000	+	103.5 Hz	NESMC
	FM	N1EM	446.67500	-	88.5 Hz	
	FM	K1IW	447.87500	-	136.5 Hz	
	FM	W1MRA	927.70000	902.70000		NESMC
Marshfield	DMR/BM	W1ATD	145.39000	-	CC9	
Marshfield, WATD-FM Tower						
	P25	W1ATD	927.47500	902.07500	131.8 Hz	NESMC
Medfield	FM	N1KUE	441.50000	+	88.5 Hz	
Medford	DMR/MARC	W1DSR	146.94000	-	CC1	
Medway	FM	W1KG	147.06000	+		
	FM	W1KG	224.66000	-		
	FUSION	K1NDG	146.61000	-		
Mendon	FM	K1KWP	146.61000	-	146.2 Hz	NESMC
Methuen	DMR/MARC	N1EXC	147.01500	747.01500	CC1	
	FM	WB1CXB	223.92000	-	141.3 Hz	
	FM	N1LHP	224.68000	-	88.5 Hz	
	FM	N1WPN	448.32500	-	88.5 Hz	
	FUSION	W1ACB	146.43000			
Milford	FM	WA1QGU	446.82500	-	100.0 Hz	NESMC
	FM	W1NAU	448.72500	-		
Milton	FM	N1MV	224.36000	-		
Mt. Greylock	FM	K1FFK	224.10000	+	162.2 Hz	
N Oxford	DMR/BM	KC1ACI	447.27500	-	CC1	
Nantucket	FM	W1TUK	146.79000	-	107.2 Hz	NESMC
Natick	FM	W1STR	449.12500	-	146.2 Hz	
Natick, Police Station						
	FM	KB1DFN	447.67500	-	203.5 Hz	
New Bedford	FM	W1RJC	145.11000	-	67.0 Hz	NESMC
Newton	FM	W1TKZ	147.03000	+	123.0 Hz	
	FM	W1LJO	147.36000	+	67.0 Hz	
	FM	WA1GPO	442.75000	+	141.3 Hz	
	FM	W1TKZ	444.60000	+	88.5 Hz	
NOAA Boston	WX	KHB35	162.47500			
NOAA Bourne / Hyannis						
	WX	KEC73	162.55000			
NOAA Mount Greylock						
	WX	WWF48	162.52500			
NOAA Worcester	WX	WXL93	162.55000			
North Adams	FM	KC1EB	145.49000	-	100.0 Hz	
North Andover	FM	N1LHP	444.10000	+		
North Attleboro	DMR/BM	NA1HS	447.97500	-	CC3	
North Dartmouth	FM	W1SMA-R	145.49000	-	67.0 Hz	
North Oxford	DSTAR	KC1ACI B	447.27500	-		
North Reading, Tower						
	FM	KC1US	146.71500	-	146.2 Hz	
North Saugus	P25	W1MHL-R	146.64000	-		
Northampton	DMR/MARC	KA1QFE	145.18000	-	CC1	
	DMR/MARC	KA1OAN	449.52500	-	CC1	
Northborough	FM	K1WPO	441.60000	+	88.5 Hz	
Norton	FUSION	K1JWP	438.50000			
	FUSION	KD1HF	448.65000	-		
Norwell	DMR/BM	AC1M	145.25000	-	CC5	
	DMR/BM	AJ1L	224.06000	-	CC6	NESMC
	FM	KC1HO	53.33000	52.33000	71.9 Hz	
Norwood	FM	W1JLI	147.21000	+	100.0 Hz	
Oakham	FM	KA1OXQ	53.67000	52.67000	123.0 Hz	

Location	Mode	Call sign	Output	Input	Access	Coordinator
Orange	DMR/BM	W1WWX	447.15000	446.65000	CC1	
	FM	NA1P	146.62500	-	110.9 Hz	
Otis	DMR/BM	N1ATP	447.93750	-	CC1	
	DMR/BM	N1ATP	448.93750	-	CC1	
	DMR/BM	N1ATP	449.93750	-	CC1	
Oxford	FM	K1AOI	147.25500	+	88.5 Hz	
Paxton	FM	W1BIM	146.97000	-	114.8 Hz	
	FM	WR1O	224.38000	-		
	FM	W1XOJ	447.98750	-	136.5 Hz	
Pelham	FM	N1PAH	53.09000	52.09000	162.2 Hz	
	FM	WA1VEI	224.74000	-	88.5 Hz	
Pepperell	FM	N1MNX	145.07000			
	FM	N1MNX	147.34500	+	100.0 Hz	
	FM	WA1VVH	224.64000	-		
	FM	N1MNX	442.90000	+	100.0 Hz	
	FM	WA1VVH	446.52500	-		
	FM	WA1VVH	927.46250	902.46250	88.5 Hz	
Pepperrell	FM	N1MNX	53.89000	52.89000	100.0 Hz	
Pittsfield	FM	KD2NSA	146.70000	-	69.3 Hz	
	FM	K1FFK	147.03000	+		
Plymouth	FM	N1ZIZ	146.68500	-	131.8 Hz	
	FM	WG1U	147.31500	+	67.0 Hz	
Princeton	WX	W3DEC	448.62500	-	88.5 Hz	NESMC
Princeton, Mount Wachusett						
	FM	WC1MA	53.31000	52.31000	71.9 Hz	
Quincy	DSTAR	WA1JIM B	432.55000			
	FM	W1BRI	146.67000	-	146.2 Hz	NESMC
	FM	N1KUG	224.40000	-	103.5 Hz	NESMC
	FUSION	KC1HHK	147.57000			
Randolph	FUSION	KC1JHH	145.25000	-		
Raynham	FUSION	K1BAD	146.56500			
Reading	FM	WA1RHN	446.52500	-	151.4 Hz	
Rockport	FUSION	K1SCD	449.50000			
Salem	FM	NS1RA	146.88000	-	118.8 Hz	
	FM	NS1RA	446.62500	-	88.5 Hz	
	FM	NS1RA	927.75000	902.75000	131.8 Hz	
Savoy	DSTAR	KA1SUN B	434.30000			
	FM	K1FFK	449.42500	-	162.2 Hz	
Sharon	FM	K1CNX	146.86500	-	103.5 Hz	
South Deerfield	FM	N1PMA	147.16500	+	118.8 Hz	
South Orleans	FM	N5API-L	145.67000			
South Swansea	FM	KB1NYT-R	224.18000	-		
Southboro	DMR/MARC	AE1C	145.27000	-	CC7	
	DMR/MARC	AE1C	448.37500	-	CC1	NESMC
Spencer	FM	N1VOR	224.54000	-		
Stanley		K3RQ-R	144.00000			
Stoneham	FM	WA1HUD	53.25000	52.25000	71.9 Hz	NESMC
	FUSION	WO1VES	147.07500	+		
Sudbury	DMR/MARC	K1IR	146.47000	144.97000	CC0	
Sutton	DMR/BM	KC1AZZ	442.85000	+	CC1	NESMC
Swansea	FM	KC1JET	145.32000	-		
Taunton	FM	KA1GG	147.13500	+	67.0 Hz	
	FM	N1UMJ-R	927.57500	902.57500		
Topsfield	FM	W1VYI	147.28500	+	100.0 Hz	
Truro Station (historical)						
	FM	WA1YFV-R	147.25500	+	67.0 Hz	
Uxbridge	FM	KB1MH	53.43000	52.43000	118.8 Hz	NESMC
	FM	KB1MH	147.39000	+		
	FM	W1WNS	447.32500	-		
	FM	KB1MH	447.47500	-	118.8 Hz	
	FUSION	W1MVP	145.63000			
Wakefield	FM	WA1RHN	147.07500	+	151.4 Hz	

Location	Mode	Call sign	Output	Input	Access	Coordinator
Wakefield	FM	WA1RHN	223.80000	-		
	FM	WA1WYA	224.26000	-	67.0 Hz	
Walpole	DMR/MARC	W1JFR	145.38000	-	CC12	
	DSTAR	WA1PLE	446.43750	-		
	DSTAR	WA1PLE B	446.43750	-		
	FM	W1ZSA	224.32000	-	118.8 Hz	
	FM	W1ZSA	448.97500	-	141.3 Hz	
	WX	K1HRV	146.89500	-	123.0 Hz	NESMC
Waltham	FM	W1MHL	146.64000	-	136.5 Hz	
	FM	W1MHL	224.94000	-		
	FM	W1MHL	449.07500	-	88.5 Hz	
	FM	W1MHL	927.13750	902.13750	131.8 Hz	
Warren	FM	K1QVR	147.21000	+	88.5 Hz	
Webster	DMR/MARC	N1PFC	446.00000	-	CC0	
West Bridgewater	DMR/BM	KA1GG	449.98750	-	CC4	
	IDAS	WG1U	145.28000	-		
West Bridgwater	FM	NA1R	146.77500	-		
West Millbury 01586						
	FUSION	KA1AQP	449.90000	-		
West Newbury	FM	K1KKM	146.62500	-	131.8 Hz	
West Tisbury	FM	KB1QL	147.34500	+	88.5 Hz	
West Village	FM	W1MRA-R	449.92500	-		NESMC
Westborough	FM	W1WNS	448.77500	-		
Westfield	FM	W1JWN	147.07500	+	88.5 Hz	
	FM	W1MBT	446.77500	-	77.0 Hz	
	FM	N1PAH	449.82500	-	110.9 Hz	NESMC
Westford	DMR/BM	KB1SBJ	145.33000	143.83000	CC1	
	DMR/BM	WB1GOF	146.45000	144.95000	CC1	
	DMR/BM	WB1GOF	443.25000	+	CC1	
	DMR/MARC	N1PA	146.45000	144.95000	CC1	
	DSTAR	WB1GOF C	145.33000	-		
	DSTAR	WB1GOF B	442.45000	+		
	FM	WB1GOF	442.45000	+		NESMC
Westford, Prospect Hill Water						
	FM	WB1GOF	145.33000	-		
Weston	FM	N1BE	146.79000	-	146.2 Hz	
	FM	N1NOM	224.70000	-	103.5 Hz	
	FM	W1MRA	442.70000	+	88.5 Hz	
Weymouth	FM	N1BGT	147.30000	+		
Weymouth, South Shore Hospital						
	FM	W1SSH	147.34500	+	110.9 Hz	NESMC
Whitinsville	FUSION	W1MEK	146.97000	-		
Whitman	FM	WA1NPO-R	147.22500	+	67.0 Hz	
	P25	KC1EFG	927.68750	902.68750		NESMC
Wilbraham	FM	W1XOJ	147.10500	+	162.2 Hz	
Wilmington	DMR/BM	N1QIG	441.46250	+	CC9	
	DMR/MARC	K1KZP	146.47000	144.97000	CC10	
	FM	K1KZP	224.16000	-	67.0 Hz	
	FM	K1KZP	441.90000	+	88.5 Hz	
Winchendon	FM	AA1JD	224.44000	-		
	FM	WC1P	447.20000	-	88.5 Hz	
Woburn	FM	N1LHP	449.82500	-	136.5 Hz	
Worcester	DMR/MARC	W1DSR	147.37500	+	CC1	
	DMR/MARC	N1PFC	442.20000	+	CC1	
	FM	N1OHZ	443.30000	+	100.0 Hz	
	FM	W1WPI	449.02500	-	88.5 Hz	
	FM	WE1CT	927.73750	902.73750		
	P25	WE1CT	146.48000	144.98000	107.2 Hz	NESMC
	P25	W1YK	146.92500	-	100.0 Hz	
	P25	N1PFC	449.87500	-		NESMC
Worcester, WPI	FM	W1WPI	145.31000	-	100.0 Hz	
Wrentham	FM	K1LBG	147.09000	+	146.2 Hz	

Location	Mode	Call sign	Output	Input	Access	Coordinator
Wrentham	FM	N1UEC	224.78000	-		
	FM	K1LBG	444.45000	+	127.3 Hz	
	FM	K1LBG	448.57500	-	88.5 Hz	
	FM	N1UEC	927.48750	902.48750	131.8 Hz	NESMC
Wyoma		W1SWR-L	147.07500			

MICHIGAN

Location	Mode	Call sign	Output	Input	Access	Coordinator
Ada	DMR/BM	K8SN	444.16250	+	CC1	
Adrian	FM	W8TQE	145.37000	-	85.4 Hz	MiARC
	FM	K8ADM	443.37500	+	107.2 Hz	MiARC
Albion	DMR/BM	K4KWQ	442.11250	+	CC1	
Allegan	FM	AC8RC	147.24000	+	94.8 Hz	MiARC
Alma, Alma College						
	FM	KC8MUV	145.37000	-	100.0 Hz	MiARC
Alpena		K8QBZ-R	146.16000			
	FM	K8PA	146.76000	-	88.5 Hz	
	FM	N8BIT	442.47500	+	100.0 Hz	
Alpena, Manning Hill						
	FM	K8PA	146.76000	-	88.5 Hz	MiARC
Ann Arbor	DMR/BM	W8RP	443.50000	+	CC1	
	DMR/MARC	N8LBV	443.05000	+	CC1	
	FM	N8DUY	145.15000	-	100.0 Hz	MiARC
	FM	W8UM-R	145.23000	-	100.0 Hz	MiARC
	FM	WB8TKL	146.96000	-	100.0 Hz	MiARC
	FM	W8PGW	224.38000	-		MiARC
	FUSION	KE8LLL	438.70000			
Athens	FUSION	AB8WD	442.72500	+		
Auburn Hills	FUSION	W8MJC	432.50000			
Aurelius	FM	KC8LMI	443.87500	+	136.5 Hz	MiARC
Avoca, Greenwood Energy Center						
	FM	K8DD	147.30000	+	192.8 Hz	MiARC
Bad Axe	DMR/MARC	KA8WYN	442.03750	+	CC2	
	FM	N8LFR	145.47000	-	110.9 Hz	MiARC
	FM	KA8PZP	146.88000	-		MiARC
Baker Village Mobile Home Park						
	FM	W8DF-R	224.24000	-		MiARC
Baldwin, Wolf Lake						
	FM	AF8U	146.90000	-	94.8 Hz	MiARC
Bancroft	DMR/MARC	W8FSM	443.31250	+	CC1	
Bangor	FM	K8BRC	147.36000	+	94.8 Hz	MiARC
Barton City	FM	WB8ZIR	145.49000	-	100.0 Hz	
Battle Creek	DSTAR	W8DF	146.79000	-		MiARC
	DSTAR	W8DF C	146.79000	-		
	DSTAR	W8DF	442.76250	+		MiARC
	DSTAR	W8DF B	442.76250	+		
	FM	W8IRA	145.15000	-	94.8 Hz	MiARC
	FM	W8DF	146.66000	-	94.8 Hz	MiARC
	FM	KD8PVK	147.12000	+	186.2 Hz	MiARC
	FM	W8DF	443.95000	+	94.8 Hz	MiARC
Bay City	DMR/MARC	W8CMN	146.50000	-	CC1	
	DMR/MARC	KC8ELQ	443.81250	+	CC1	
	FM	N8BBR	147.36000	+	131.8 Hz	MiARC
	FM	KB8YUR	444.50000	+	123.0 Hz	MiARC
Belle River - East China						
	FM	KD8GRU	147.32000	+	167.9 Hz	
Benzonia	FUSION	W8BNZ	442.60000	+		
Bessemer	DMR/MARC	W9RCG	443.12500	+	CC8	
Bessemer, Blackjack Mountain S						
	FM	K8ATX	146.76000	-		UPARRA
Beulah	FUSION	W8BNZ	147.04000	+		
Beverly Hills	FM	W8HP	443.22500	+	107.2 Hz	MiARC
Big Rapids	FM	W8IRA	145.29000	-	94.8 Hz	MiARC

Location	Mode	Call sign	Output	Input	Access	Coordinator
Big Rapids, Ferris State Unive						
	FM	KB8QOI	443.90000	+		MiARC
Big Rapids, WDEE Tower						
	FM	KB8QOI	146.74000	-		MiARC
Blissfield		N8TAT-L	146.43000			
	FUSION	N8TAT	445.92500			
Bloomfield Township						
	FUSION	AA8GK	443.82500	+		
Breckenridge	FM	W8QPO	442.65000	+	100.0 Hz	MiARC
Bridgeport	FM	KC8BXI	443.40000	+		MiARC
Bridgman	FM	W8MAI	442.77500	+	88.5 Hz	MiARC
Britton	DMR/BM	W8ATE	444.05000	+	CC1	
Brooklyn	DMR/BM	N8GY	443.90000	+	CC1	
Brooklyn, Clark Lake						
	FM	N8URX	443.75000	+	146.2 Hz	
Brownstown	FM	K8JTT	444.12500			
	FUSION	K8JTT	147.35000			
Buchanan	FM	N8NIT	443.65000	+		MiARC
Burnside	DMR/MARC	W8CMN	443.11250	+	CC1	
Burt	FM	KC8ELQ	442.20000	+	103.5 Hz	MiARC
Burton	FM	N8NE	147.38000	+	88.5 Hz	MiARC
	FM	W8JDE	224.72000	-		MiARC
Byron Center	DMR/BM	KD8RXD	442.92500	+	CC2	
	DMR/MARC	KD8RXD	444.62500	+	CC1	MiARC
Cadillac	FM	K8CAD	146.98000	-		
Calumet, Mount Horace Greeley						
	FM	K8MDH	147.31500	+	100.0 Hz	UPARRA
Calumet, Old Calumet Air Base						
	FM	K8MDH	443.15000	+	100.0 Hz	UPARRA
Canton	FUSION	KD8DXQ	446.50000			
Caro	FM	KC8CNN	146.66000	-	100.0 Hz	MiARC
	FM	WA8CKT	146.82000	-	100.0 Hz	MiARC
	FM	KC8CNN	442.55000	+	103.5 Hz	MiARC
Cassopolis	DMR/MARC	KD8UJM	443.55000	+	CC1	
Cedar Springs	FM	NW8J	52.72000	-	136.5 Hz	MiARC
	FM	NW8J	146.88000	-	141.3 Hz	MiARC
	FM	NW8J	224.14000	-		MiARC
	FM	NW8J	443.07500	+	94.8 Hz	MiARC
	FM	AB8DT	443.47500	+	100.0 Hz	
	FUSION	AB8DT	146.88000	-		
	FUSION	AB8DT	443.07500	+		
	FUSION	AB8DT	445.50000	-	100.0 Hz	
	FUSION	AB8DT	445.82500			
	FUSION	AB8DT	445.95000			
Central Lake	DMR/BM	W8VPC	443.22500	+	CC1	
Centreville, Glen Oaks Communi						
	FM	K8SJC	145.31000	-	123.0 Hz	MiARC
	FM	KC8BRO	442.15000	+	94.8 Hz	MiARC
Charlotte	DMR/BM	N8HEE	442.26250	+	CC1	MiARC
	FM	K8CHR	147.08000	+	103.5 Hz	MiARC
	FM	N8HEE	443.62500	+	100.0 Hz	MiARC
Charlotte, County EOC						
	DSTAR	K8ETN	145.20000	-		MiARC
	DSTAR	K8ETN	443.43750	+		MiARC
Cheboygan	DMR/BM	W8CCE	444.13750	+	CC1	
	FM	W8IPQ	146.74000	-	103.5 Hz	MiARC
	FM	WB8DEL	444.85000	+	100.0 Hz	MiARC
Chelsea	DMR/BM	KB8POO	444.75000	+	CC1	
	FM	WD8IEL	145.45000	-	100.0 Hz	MiARC
	FM	KC8LMI	443.57500	+	100.0 Hz	MiARC
Chelsea, Sylvan Township Water						
	FM	KC8LMI	145.31000	-	136.5 Hz	

Location	Mode	Call sign	Output	Input	Access	Coordinator
Clarkston	DMR/MARC	KD8VIV	444.83750	+	CC2	
	FM	W8JWB	146.84000	-	100.0 Hz	MiARC
Clinton Township	DMR/BM	N8PBX	443.67500	+	CC2	
Clio	FM	KB5TOJ	443.40000	+	156.7 Hz	MiARC
	FM	W8JDE	444.37500	+		MiARC
Clyde	DMR/BM	KE8JOT	146.92000	-	CC2	
Coldwater	DSTAR	WD8KAF B	442.96250	+		
	DSTAR	KD8JGF	442.96250	+		MiARC
	FM	WD8KAF	147.30000	+	100.0 Hz	MiARC
	FM	WD8KAF	443.30000	+	123.0 Hz	MiARC
Commerce Township						
	DMR/BM	N4KCD	442.97500	+	CC1	
Commerce Twp	DMR/MARC	WB8SFY	444.93750	+	CC1	
Commerce Twp.	DMR/MARC	WB8SFY	446.50000	-	CC5	
Comstock Park	FUSION	N8NIJ	145.23000	-		
Cooks	FM	WA8WG	146.70000	-	110.9 Hz	UPARRA
Crystal Falls	DMR/BM	KD9LUJ	434.35000	+	CC9	
	FM	WA8OOM	145.23000	-	107.2 Hz	
Dansville	DMR/MARC	N8OBU	444.70000	+	CC1	
	FM	N8OBU	444.57500	+	107.2 Hz	MiARC
Davisburg	DMR/MARC	N8UE	444.83750	+	CC2	MiARC
Dearborn	FM	K8UTT	145.27000	-		MiARC
	FM	WR8DAR	147.16000	-	100.0 Hz	MiARC
	FM	K8UTT	224.52000	-	100.0 Hz	MiARC
	FM	WR8DAR	442.80000	+	107.2 Hz	MiARC
	FM	K8UTT	443.42500	+	107.2 Hz	MiARC
Decatur	FM	KF8ZF	52.94000	-	94.8 Hz	MiARC
Detroit	DMR/MARC	K9DPD	442.53750	+	CC1	
	DMR/MARC	W8FSM	444.00000	+	CC1	
	DMR/MARC	W8CMC	444.67500	+	CC2	MiARC
	FM	K8PLW	51.84000	-	100.0 Hz	MiARC
	FM	W8DET	145.11000	-	100.0 Hz	MiARC
	FM	WR8DAR	145.33000	-	100.0 Hz	MiARC
	FM	KC8LTS	147.33000	+		MiARC
	FM	KC8LTS	224.36000	-	103.5 Hz	MiARC
	FM	K8PLW	442.10000	+	107.2 Hz	MiARC
	FM	KC8LTS	442.17500	+	123.0 Hz	MiARC
	FM	KD8IFI	443.02500	+	107.2 Hz	MiARC
	FM	WW8GM-R	443.07500	+	123.0 Hz	MiARC
	FM	WR8DAR	443.47500	+	88.5 Hz	MiARC
	FUSION	KG8ZH	146.55000			
	FUSION	KC8LTS	443.02500	+		
Detroit, AT&T Michigan Headqua						
	FM	KE8HR	146.76000	-	100.0 Hz	MiARC
Dexter	FM	W8SRC	446.15000	-	100.0 Hz	MiARC
Dimondale	FM	N9UV	442.05000	+	100.0 Hz	MiARC
Dorr	FUSION	WB8SQJ	445.90000			
Dowagiac	FM	KU8Y	145.21000	-	94.8 Hz	MiARC
	FM	W6GVS	146.50000	147.50000	94.8 Hz	
Dowagiac, Building						
	FM	N9QID	927.68750	902.68750	94.8 Hz	
Dundee	FM	K8RPT	442.82500	+	100.0 Hz	MiARC
Dunken	FM	W8CDZ	146.67000	-	100.0 Hz	UPARRA
Durand	FM	N8IES	145.29000	-	100.0 Hz	MiARC
	FM	N8IES	224.86000	-	100.0 Hz	MiARC
	FM	N8IES	442.62500	+	100.0 Hz	MiARC
Eagle	DMR/BM	KB8SXK	444.71250	+	CC2	
	FM	K8VEB-R	443.35000	+		MiARC
Eagle/Portland	FM	K8VEB	224.66000	-	100.0 Hz	MiARC
East Jordan	FM	W8COL	147.28000	+	103.5 Hz	MiARC
East Lansing	FM	W9WSW	446.27500	-	100.0 Hz	
	FM	W9WSW	446.50000	-	107.2 Hz	

Location	Mode	Call sign	Output	Input	Access	Coordinator
Eastmont	FM	K8SN-L	442.17500	+		MiARC
Eckerman		N8XYR-L	446.25000			
Edmore	FM	WB8VWK	146.80000	-	103.5 Hz	MiARC
	FM	KC8LEQ	444.70000	+	103.5 Hz	MiARC
Elk Rapids	FUSION	WT8BZ	442.85000			
Elmira	DSTAR	NM8ES	145.32000	-		MiARC
	DSTAR	NM8ES C	145.32000	-		
	DSTAR	NM8ES	444.11250	+		MiARC
	DSTAR	NM8ES B	444.11250	+		
Engadine	DSTAR	W8NBY B	444.03750	+		
Erie	FUSION	KD8AAK	145.54000			
Escanaba	FM	KB9BQX	145.13000	-		UPARRA
	FM	N8JWT	147.15000	+	123.0 Hz	
	FM	N8JWT	147.24000	+	123.0 Hz	
	FM	W8JRT	442.40000	+		
	FM	WD8RTH	444.30000	+		UPARRA
Farmington Hills	FM	WA8SEL	442.70000	+	100.0 Hz	MiARC
Fenton	DMR/MARC	W8FSM	443.20000	+	CC2	
	DMR/MARC	W8FSM	443.92500	+	CC1	
	FM	W8CMN	146.78000	-	151.4 Hz	MiARC
	FM	KC8YGT-R	443.20000	+	151.4 Hz	MiARC
	FM	N8VDS	927.53750	902.53750	131.8 Hz	MiARC
Fenton Oaks Mobile Home Commun						
	FM	KB8PGF-R	443.97500	+		MiARC
Fivemile Corner		K8BMZ-L	434.25000			
Flint	DMR/BM	W8CMN	443.80000	+	CC1	MiARC
	DSTAR	N8UMW	442.00000	+	100.0 Hz	MiARC
	FM	KC8KGZ	147.10000	+	100.0 Hz	MiARC
	FM	W8ACW	147.34000	+	100.0 Hz	MiARC
	FM	KC8KGZ	224.48000	-	100.0 Hz	MiARC
	FM	W8ACW	444.20000	+	107.2 Hz	MiARC
	FM	W8JDE	444.60000	+		MiARC
Fort Gratiot	FM	KG8OU	146.80000	-	100.0 Hz	MiARC
Frankenmuth	DMR/BM	KB8SWR	444.72500	+	CC1	
	DMR/MARC	W8FSM	444.25000	+	CC1	
	FM	KB8SWR	444.02500	+	100.0 Hz	MiARC
Frankfort	FM	KE8OOD	145.41000	-	110.9 Hz	
	FM	W8BNZ	442.20000	+	114.8 Hz	MiARC
Fraser	FUSION	W8IR	443.60000			
Fremont	DMR/MARC	KC8MSE	442.01250	+	CC1	
	FM	KC8MSE	146.92000	-	94.8 Hz	MiARC
Gaastra	FUSION	W8YNY	145.17000	-		
Garden City	DSTAR	N8RTS B	442.12500	+		
	DSTAR	N8RTS	442.12500	+		MiARC
	FM	KK8GC	146.86000	-	100.0 Hz	MiARC
Gaylord	DSTAR	KD8QCC	444.03750	+		
	FUSION	W1WRS	147.12000	+		
Gladwin	FM	W8GDW	147.18000	+	173.8 Hz	MiARC
	FM	K8EO	442.45000	+		
Gladwin, Lake Lancer						
	FUSION	W8CSX	145.25000	-	103.5 Hz	
Glen Arbor	FM	WI0OK	52.92000	-	146.2 Hz	MiARC
	FM	WI0OK	444.72500	+	114.8 Hz	MiARC
Glendale	FM	W8GDS	224.84000	-	94.8 Hz	MiARC
Glenwood	FM	W8GDS	224.84000	-	94.8 Hz	
Grand Haven	FM	W8CSO	145.49000	-	94.8 Hz	MiARC
	FM	W8CSO	443.77500	+	94.8 Hz	MiARC
Grand Marais	FM	KC8BAN	147.19500	+	100.0 Hz	UPARRA
Grand Rapids	DMR/BM	K8SN	444.98750	+	CC1	
	DMR/BM	KD8RXD	446.50000	-	CC2	
	DMR/MARC	KD8RXD	444.25000	+	CC1	
	DSTAR	WX8GRR C	147.29000	+		

Location	Mode	Call sign	Output	Input	Access	Coordinator
Grand Rapids	DSTAR	WX8GRR	147.29000	+		MiARC
	DSTAR	WX8GRR B	442.55000	+		
	DSTAR	WX8GRR	442.55000	+		MiARC
	DSTAR	WX8GRR A	1284.50000	-		
	DSTAR	WX8GRR D	1298.50000			
	FM	NW8J	145.11000	-	94.8 Hz	MiARC
	FM	K8WM	145.41000	-	94.8 Hz	MiARC
	FM	W8DC	147.26000	+	94.8 Hz	MiARC
	FM	K8DMR	421.25000	439.25000		MiARC
	FM	K8EFK	442.00000	+	141.3 Hz	MiARC
	FM	KA8YSM	443.80000	+	94.8 Hz	MiARC
	FM	N8NET	444.10000	+		MiARC
	FM	N8WKN	444.32500	+	82.5 Hz	MiARC
	FM	W8DC	444.40000	+	94.8 Hz	MiARC
	FM	W8USA	444.45000	+	94.8 Hz	
	FM	K8WM	444.77500	+	94.8 Hz	MiARC
	FM	N8WKM	927.26250	902.26250		MiARC
	FUSION	WA8EBM	144.75000			
	FUSION	W8DC	146.76000	-		
	FUSION	K8ENT	430.17500			
Grass Lake	DMR/MARC	W8CMN	443.81250	+	CC1	
	FM	KC8LMI	224.16000	-	100.0 Hz	MiARC
Grayling	FM	N8AHZ	145.13000	-	107.2 Hz	MiARC
Green Lake		K8SN-R	442.17500			
	FM	N8JPR-R	223.92000	-		
Greenville	DMR/BM	KD8RXD	442.47500	+	CC2	
	DMR/MARC	KD8RXD	443.38750	+	CC1	
	DSTAR	WX8GRN B	444.65000	+		
	FM	KB8ZGL	927.48750	902.48750	131.8 Hz	MiARC
Greilickville	DSTAR	WI0OK	145.36000	-		MiARC
Grosse Ile	FM	N8ZPJ	444.90000	+	107.2 Hz	MiARC
Grosse Pointe Farms						
	FM	N8XN	444.22500	+	107.2 Hz	MiARC
Gwinn	FM	K8LOD	146.64000	-	100.0 Hz	UPARRA
Hamilton	DMR/MARC	W8FSM	443.92500	+	CC1	
Hanover	FM	K8WBG	52.62000	-	123.0 Hz	MiARC
Harrison	FM	KA8DCJ	147.20000	+	103.5 Hz	MiARC
Harrisville	FM	W8HUF	147.04000	+	123.0 Hz	MiARC
Hart	FM	N8UKH	146.64000	-	94.8 Hz	MiARC
	FM	W8VTM	443.67500	+	94.8 Hz	MiARC
Hastings	FM	K8YPW	146.84000	-	94.8 Hz	
	FUSION	AC8AZ	146.56000			
	FUSION	AC8AZ	442.72500	+		
Heather Hill Estates Mobile Ho						
	FM	KC8KGZ-R	147.26000	+	100.0 Hz	MiARC
Hell	DSTAR	K8LCD C	147.21000	+		
	DSTAR	K8LCD	147.21000	+		MiARC
	DSTAR	K8LCD	444.06250	+		MiARC
	DSTAR	K8LCD B	444.06250	+		
	DSTAR	K8LCD D	1254.48000			
	DSTAR	K8LCD	1294.48000	-		MiARC
	DSTAR	K8LCD A	1294.48000	1274.48000		
Hemlock	FM	N8ERL	145.33000	-	88.5 Hz	MiARC
Hillsdale	FM	W9LKI	445.90000	-	107.2 Hz	
Holland	DMR/BM	K8DAA	443.88750	+	CC4	
	FM	K8DAA	146.50000	147.50000	94.8 Hz	MiARC
	FM	K8DAA	147.06000	+	94.8 Hz	MiARC
	FM	K8DAA	443.82500	+	94.8 Hz	MiARC
	FUSION	N8XPQ	444.80000	+		
Holly	FM	W8FSM	224.62000	-	100.0 Hz	MiARC
	FM	W8FSM	442.35000	+	107.2 Hz	MiARC

Location	Mode	Call sign	Output	Input	Access	Coordinator
Holton, M-120 Highway						
	FM	WD8MKG	147.32000	+	91.5 Hz	MiARC
Hopkins	FUSION	N8JMY	146.43000			
	FUSION	K1HI	146.46000			
Houghton	DMR/MARC	N8WAV	147.12000	+	CC1	
	DMR/MARC	N8WAV	435.00000	+	CC1	
	DMR/MARC	W8YY	444.50000	+	CC1	
	FM	N8WAV	147.39000	+	100.0 Hz	UPARRA
Houghton, Wadsworth Hall						
	FM	W8YY	444.65000	+	100.0 Hz	UPARRA
Howell	DMR/BM	W8LRK	442.57500	+	CC1	
	DMR/BM	W8LRK	444.52500	+	CC1	
	DSTAR	W8LIV C	145.32000	-		
	DSTAR	W8LIV	145.32000	-		MiARC
	DSTAR	W8LIV	444.03750	+		MiARC
	DSTAR	W8LIV B	444.03750	+		
	FM	K8JBA	145.41000	-	162.2 Hz	
	FM	W8LRK	146.68000	-	162.2 Hz	MiARC
	FM	N8AR	147.04000	+	110.9 Hz	
	FM	N8AR	147.58000			
	FM	N8AR	446.02500	-		
Hudsonville	FM	K8TB	442.25000	+	94.8 Hz	MiARC
	FM	K8IHY	444.90000	+	94.8 Hz	MiARC
	FUSION	K8TB	447.25000	-		
Ida	FM	K8RPT	146.72000	-	100.0 Hz	MiARC
	FM	K8RPT	442.65000	+	100.0 Hz	MiARC
Indian Ridge Estates						
	FM	K7IOU-R	224.74000	-		
Iron Mountain	FM	WA8FXQ	146.85000	-	100.0 Hz	UPARRA
	FM	WA8FXQ	444.85000	+	100.0 Hz	UPARRA
	FUSION	N7SWX	144.00000			
	FUSION	N7SWX	147.28500	+	100.0 Hz	
	FUSION	N7SWX	442.10000	+	100.0 Hz	
Iron River, Ski Brule Moutain						
	FM	N8LVQ	145.17000	-	107.2 Hz	UPARRA
Ironwood		WA1MAR-L	146.55000			
		KD8UDD-L	147.25500			
	DMR/BM	WX8NWS	146.58000	+	CC1	
	DMR/BM	N6NWS	147.07500	+	CC1	
	DMR/BM	KC8NWS	442.55000	+	CC1	
	DMR/BM	N6NWS	443.97500	+	CC1	
	DMR/BM	WX8NWS	444.02500	+	CC1	
	FM	N8JJB	146.80500	-	141.3 Hz	UPARRA
	FM	W8MAR	147.37500	+	141.3 Hz	
	FM	WA1MAR	441.43750	+	107.2 Hz	
Ishpeming, Cliffs Shaft Museum						
	FM	K8LOD	146.91000	-		UPARRA
Ithaca	DSTAR	KD8IEK C	147.15000	+		
	DSTAR	KD8IEK	147.15000	+		MiARC
	DSTAR	KD8IEK	443.13750	+		MiARC
	DSTAR	KD8IEK B	443.13750	+		
Jackson	DMR/BM	N8URW	442.50000	+	CC1	
	FM	W8IRA	145.47000	-	114.8 Hz	MiARC
	FM	W8JXN	146.88000	-	100.0 Hz	MiARC
	FM	KA8HDY	147.36000	+	100.0 Hz	MiARC
	FM	WD8EEQ	443.17500	+	77.0 Hz	MiARC
	FM	KA8YRL	444.17500	+	100.0 Hz	MiARC
James Twp.	DMR/MARC	N8VDS	443.60000	+	CC1	MiARC
Jerome	FM	KC8QVX	444.82500	+	107.2 Hz	MiARC
Jonesville	FM	KC8QVX	147.06000	+	179.9 Hz	MiARC
Kalamazoo	DMR/BM	KE8EVF	442.67500	+	CC1	
	DMR/BM	KM8CC	443.40000	+	CC1	

Location	Mode	Call sign	Output	Input	Access	Coordinator
Kalamazoo	DSTAR	NK8X B	444.50000	+		
	FM	K8KZO	51.72000	-	94.8 Hz	MiARC
	FM	N8FYZ	145.17000	-	94.8 Hz	MiARC
	FM	W8VY	147.00000	+	94.8 Hz	MiARC
	FM	K8KZO	147.04000	+	94.8 Hz	MiARC
	FM	W8VY	444.65000	+	131.8 Hz	MiARC
	FM	K8KZO	444.87500	+	94.8 Hz	MiARC
	FUSION	K8KZ0	449.87500	-		
Kalamazoo, Borgess Hospital						
	DSTAR	NK8X	444.50000	+		
Kalkaska	FM	W8KAL	52.82000	-		MiARC
Kent City	DMR/MARC	KD8RXD	442.21250	+	CC1	MiARC
Kincheloe	FM	W8EUP	444.90000	+	107.2 Hz	
	FUSION	W8DDB	440.75000			
La Salle	FM	K8RPT	224.78000	-	100.0 Hz	MiARC
Lake Angelus	FM	NE9Y	53.94000	-	131.8 Hz	MiARC
Lake City	FM	KG8QY	145.21000	-		MiARC
	FM	KA8ABM	444.52500	+	100.0 Hz	MiARC
Lake Leelanau	FM	N8JKV	146.92000	-	114.8 Hz	MiARC
Lake Orion	DSTAR	K8DXA	145.13000	-		MiARC
	DSTAR	K8DXA C	145.13000	-		
	DSTAR	K8DXA B	444.26250	+		
	DSTAR	K8DXA	444.26250	+		MiARC
Lake Orion, Great Lakes Shoppi						
	FM	WW8GM	145.61000		123.0 Hz	
Lakeport	FUSION	N8JJO	146.72000	-		
Lansing	DMR/BM	KB8SXK	444.78750	+	CC2	MiARC
	DMR/MARC	KB8SXK	442.08750	+	CC1	MiARC
	DMR/MARC	W8JTT	446.50000		CC1	
	FM	KD8PA	52.96000	-	100.0 Hz	MiARC
	FM	KB8LCY	147.28000	+	100.0 Hz	MiARC
	FM	KD8IFI	443.00000	+	107.2 Hz	MiARC
	FM	KD8PA	927.97500	902.97500		MiARC
Lansing, Ingham Regional Medic						
	FM	W8BCI	146.70000	-	107.2 Hz	MiARC
	FM	W8BCI	146.94000	-	100.0 Hz	MiARC
	FM	W8BCI	224.98000	-	100.0 Hz	MiARC
Lapeer	DSTAR	W8LAP	442.75000	+		MiARC
	DSTAR	W8LAP B	442.75000	+		
	FM	W8LAP-R	146.62000	-	100.0 Hz	MiARC
Leland	FM	W8SGR	145.39000	-	103.5 Hz	
Lewiston	FM	N8SCY	145.19000	-		MiARC
Life O'Riley Mobile Home Park						
	FM	KD8PA-L	442.42500	+		MiARC
Lincoln	DMR/MARC	W8JJR	442.01250	+	CC1	MiARC
Little Point Sable	FM	W8LRC-R	145.27000	-		MiARC
Livonia		WJ8I-L	446.02500			
	DSTAR	K8UNS B	444.87500	+		
	FM	K8PLW	224.84000	-	100.0 Hz	MiARC
	FM	K8UNS	444.87500	+	123.0 Hz	MiARC
	FUSION	N8PVL	434.95000			
Lowell	DMR/BM	KD8RXD	443.65000	+	CC2	
	DMR/MARC	KD8RXD	443.11250	+	CC1	MiARC
	FM	AA8JR	443.85000	+	94.8 Hz	MiARC
	FUSION	W8LRC	442.80000	+		
Ludington	FM	W8IRA	145.31000	-	94.8 Hz	MiARC
	FM	K8DXF	145.47000	-	103.5 Hz	MiARC
	FM	WB8ERN	146.62000	-	94.8 Hz	MiARC
Lupton	FM	N8RSH	147.08000	+		MiARC
Mackinaw City	DMR/BM	W8CCE	443.37500	+	CC1	
	DMR/BM	W8AGB	444.37500	+	CC1	
	FM	W8AGB	145.11000	-	103.5 Hz	

Location	Mode	Call sign	Output	Input	Access	Coordinator
Mancelona	FM	K8WQK	51.98000	-		MiARC
	FM	K8WQK	147.38000	+	107.2 Hz	
Manchester	DMR/BM	KB8POO	146.61000	-	CC1	
	DMR/BM	KB8POO	444.47500	+	CC1	
	DMR/BM	KB8POO	927.60000	902.60000	CC1	
Manistee	FM	W8GJX	146.78000	-	94.8 Hz	MiARC
	FM	KB8BIT	224.12000	-	100.0 Hz	MiARC
	FUSION	N8OVA	145.55000			
Marcellus	FM	KD8UJM	442.22500	+	94.8 Hz	MiARC
Marquette	DMR/BM	KB0P	442.20000	+	CC1	
	FM	KE8IL-R	146.97000	-		UPARRA
	FM	K8LOD	147.27000	+	100.0 Hz	UPARRA
	FM	K8LOD	443.45000	+	100.0 Hz	UPARRA
Mason	FM	WB8RJY	51.70000	-	192.8 Hz	MiARC
	FM	WB8RJY	443.70000	+		MiARC
Mattawan	FUSION	KE8SZX	146.40000			
Mayville	DMR/MARC	KB8SWR	443.85000	+	CC1	MiARC
	FM	KB8ZUZ	51.82000	-	131.8 Hz	MiARC
	FM	KB8ZUZ	443.77500	+	100.0 Hz	MiARC
Mecosta	FUSION	N8KDR	144.85000	+		
	FUSION	N8KDR	145.75000			
Menominee	FM	AB9PJ	53.11000	51.41000	114.8 Hz	UPARRA
	FM	W8PIF-R	147.00000	+		UPARRA
	FUSION	W8PIF	444.07500	+	107.2 Hz	UPARRA
Midland	DMR/BM	KE8MSP	448.22550	147.78750	CC1	
	DSTAR	KC8ARJ B	444.35000	+		
	FM	W8KEA	147.00000	+	103.5 Hz	MiARC
Milan	DMR/MARC	W2PUT	443.11250	+	CC1	MiARC
	FM	W2PUT	146.50000	147.50000	88.5 Hz	
	FM	W2PUT	444.10000	+	82.5 Hz	MiARC
	FM	W2PUT	927.52500	902.52500	131.8 Hz	
Milford	FM	WR8DAR	444.42500	+	118.8 Hz	MiARC
	FUSION	N8KPE	145.52500			
Millington	DSTAR	KC8KGZ	444.65000	+	100.0 Hz	MiARC
Mio	FM	WT8G	145.35000	-		MiARC
Mobile	DMR/MARC	KB8SWR	444.70000	+	CC1	
Moline	DMR/BM	K8SN	442.26250	+	CC1	
	FUSION	K8SN	443.22500	+		
Monroe, Downtown						
	FM	W8OTC	446.07500	-		MiARC
Moorestown	FM	KA8ABM	146.96000	-	103.5 Hz	MiARC
Morley	FM	K8SN	442.07500	+	103.5 Hz	
Mount Clemens	FM	WA8MAC	147.20000	+	100.0 Hz	MiARC
	FUSION	N8ZA	147.42000			
	FUSION	K8UO	444.77500	+		
Mount Pleasant	FM	KC8RTU	442.82500	+	100.0 Hz	MiARC
Mt Clemens	DMR/MARC	K9DPD	443.95000	+	CC1	
Mt. Clemens	FM	KC8UMP	443.62500	+	151.4 Hz	MiARC
	FM	W8FSM	927.25000	902.25000	131.8 Hz	MiARC
Munith	DMR/BM	N8URW	443.89000	+	CC1	
Muskegon	DMR/MARC	K8WNJ	444.95000	+	CC1	MiARC
	DSTAR	WD8MKG	145.36000	-		MiARC
	DSTAR	K8WNJ C	145.36000	-		
	DSTAR	WD8MKG	444.01250	+		MiARC
	DSTAR	K8WNJ B	444.01250	+		
	FM	K8COP	52.80000	-	94.8 Hz	MiARC
	FM	W8IRA	145.33000	-	94.8 Hz	MiARC
	FM	K8WNJ	146.82000	-	94.8 Hz	MiARC
	FM	W8ZHO	146.94000	-	94.8 Hz	MiARC
	FM	KE8LZ	147.38000	+		MiARC
	FM	N8KQQ	224.70000	-	94.8 Hz	MiARC
	FM	N8UKF	442.30000	+		MiARC

Location	Mode	Call sign	Output	Input	Access	Coordinator
Muskegon	FM	N8KQQ	442.95000	+	94.8 Hz	MiARC
	FM	W8ZHO	444.55000	+	94.8 Hz	MiARC
	FUSION	KC8LLN	446.07500			
National City	FUSION	N8EK	144.00000			
New Haven	FUSION	N8SA	145.55000			
New Hudson	FM	N8BK-R	442.77500	+		MiARC
Newberry	FM	W8NBY	146.61000	-	114.8 Hz	UPARRA
Niles	DSTAR	KE8GVB C	145.14000	-		
	DSTAR	KE8GVB B	442.82500	+		
	FM	KC8BRS	147.18000	+	94.8 Hz	MiARC
	FM	WB9YPA	224.50000	-	94.8 Hz	
	FM	WB9WYR	444.12500	+	94.8 Hz	MiARC
NOAA Adrian / Petersburg						
	WX	WNG647	162.45000			
NOAA Alpena	WX	KIG83	162.55000			
NOAA Bad Axe	WX	WNG701	162.52500			
NOAA Copper Harbor						
	WX	WZ2513	162.50000			
NOAA Crystal Falls						
	WX	KJY76	162.47500			
NOAA Detroit	WX	KEC63	162.55000			
NOAA Emmet County						
	WX	WNG572	162.47500			
NOAA Escanaba	WX	KZZ35	162.50000			
NOAA Flint	WX	KIH29	162.47500			
NOAA Gaylord	WX	WWF70	162.50000			
NOAA Grand Marais						
	WX	WZ2515	162.42500			
NOAA Grand Rapids						
	WX	KIG63	162.55000			
NOAA Hesperia	WX	WWF36	162.47500			
NOAA Houghton	WX	WXK73	162.40000			
NOAA Manistique	WX	WNG684	162.52500			
NOAA Marquette	WX	KIG66	162.55000			
NOAA Mount Marenisco						
	WX	WNG683	162.55000			
NOAA Mount Pleasant						
	WX	KZZ33	162.52500			
NOAA Munising	WX	WZ2514	162.47500			
NOAA Newberry	WX	WNG576	162.45000			
NOAA Onondaga	WX	WXK81	162.40000			
NOAA Plainwell	WX	WWF34	162.47500			
NOAA Sandusky	WX	WNG582	162.45000			
NOAA Sault Ste. Marie						
	WX	KIG74	162.55000			
NOAA Traverse City						
	WX	KIH22	162.40000			
NOAA West Branch						
	WX	KXI33	162.45000			
NOAA West Olive	WX	WXN99	162.42500			
NOAA Wolf Lake	WX	WNG672	162.42500			
Norrie		W8MAR-L	146.55000			
North Branch	FM	KG8ID	443.45000	+	100.0 Hz	MiARC
Northville	FM	WR8DAR	443.10000	+	82.5 Hz	MiARC
Norton Shores	FM	N8UKF	443.20000	+		MiARC
	FUSION	W8AEG	145.75000			
	FUSION	N8UKF	147.38000	+		
Novi	DMR/MARC	KC8LTS	442.21250	+	CC1	MiARC
	FM	N8OVI	444.80000	+	110.9 Hz	MiARC
Oak Park	FM	W8HP	146.64000	-	100.0 Hz	MiARC
Oaklawn Beechwood						
	FUSION	N8XPQ-R	444.80000	+		MiARC

Location	Mode	Call sign	Output	Input	Access	Coordinator
Onsted	DMR/BM	N8URW	442.51250	+	CC1	
Orion Township	FUSION	WW8GM	432.50000			
Oshtemo	DMR/BM	KM8CC	444.57500	+	CC1	
Ovid	FM	N8TSK	51.92000	-	203.5 Hz	MiARC
	FM	N8TSK	444.00000	+	225.7 Hz	MiARC
	FM	KD8AGP	445.50000	-	94.8 Hz	MiARC
Owosso	DSTAR	W8SHI C	145.24000	-		
	DSTAR	W8SHI	145.24000	-		MiARC
	DSTAR	W8SHI B	444.30000	+		
	DSTAR	W8SHI	444.30000	+		MiARC
	FM	N8DVH	147.02000	+	100.0 Hz	MiARC
	FM	N8DVH	442.40000	+	100.0 Hz	MiARC
Oxford	FM	KA8CSH	443.00000	+		MiARC
Paavola		K6IPC-R	146.88000			
Paw Paw	DSTAR	W8VY C	145.34000	-		
	DSTAR	W8VY	145.34000	-		
	DSTAR	W8VY	444.07500	+		MiARC
	DSTAR	W8VY B	444.07500	+		
	FM	W8GDS	147.20000	+	94.8 Hz	MiARC
Pellston	FM	WA8EFE	444.95000	+	103.5 Hz	MiARC
Phoenix	DMR/MARC	W8YY	444.75000	+	CC1	UPARRA
Pickford	FM	W8EUP	146.64000	-	107.2 Hz	UPARRA
Pinckney	FM	W2GLD	224.50000	-	100.0 Hz	
	FUSION	W2GLD	442.67500	+		
Pleasant Lake	FM	KC8LMI	224.18000	-	88.5 Hz	MiARC
	FM	KC8LMI	446.80000	-	136.5 Hz	
Pleasant Lk.	DMR/MARC	KC8LMI	442.51250	+	CC1	
Plymouth	FUSION	K8AGY	445.87500			
Pointe Aux Peaux		HS9KRG-R	145.73700			
Pontiac	DMR/MARC	W8OAK	444.46250	+	CC1	
	FM	W8OAK	146.90000	-	100.0 Hz	MiARC
	FM	WN8G	443.82500	+		MiARC
	FM	KB9WIS	927.45000	902.45000		MiARC
Port Huron		KE8BIT-L	145.00000			
	FM	AA8K	146.72000	-	186.2 Hz	MiARC
	FM	N8YTV	443.70000	+	100.0 Hz	MiARC
	FM	KE8JOT	444.90000	+	131.8 Hz	
Portland	FM	N8ZMT	145.13000	-	94.8 Hz	MiARC
Potterville	FM	W8BCI	145.39000	-	100.0 Hz	MiARC
	FM	N8JI	442.02500	+	173.8 Hz	MiARC
Prescott	FUSION	W8SKB	144.30000			
Quanicassee	FM	N8BBR	145.31000	-	131.8 Hz	MiARC
Republic	FM	K8LOD	146.82000	-	100.0 Hz	UPARRA
Riverview	FM	KC8LTS	927.48750	902.48750	131.8 Hz	MiARC
Rochester	FUSION	KC8P	145.70000			
Rochester Hills	FUSION	WC8D	433.50000			
	FUSION	K8RO	442.92500	+		
Rockford		KD8VHV-R	927.10000			
	FM	W8AGT	927.68750	902.68750	131.8 Hz	MiARC
Rogers City	FM	WB8TQZ	147.02000	+	103.5 Hz	MiARC
	FUSION	W8WLC	145.17000	-		
Romeo	P25	K8FBI	442.07500	+	123.0 Hz	MiARC
Romulus	FM	W8TX	442.27500	+	107.2 Hz	MiARC
Roscommon	DSTAR	WD7ROS C	147.23000	+		
	DSTAR	WD7ROS B	443.36250	+		
	FM	N8QOP	52.64000	-		MiARC
	FM	N8QOP	145.45000	-	141.3 Hz	MiARC
	FM	N8QOP	443.10000	+	146.2 Hz	MiARC
Rose City	FM	W8DMI	145.11000	-	131.8 Hz	MiARC
	FUSION	W8COP	146.55000			
Roseville	FM	N8EDV	147.22000	+	100.0 Hz	MiARC
	FM	N8EDV	224.46000	-	100.0 Hz	MiARC

Location	Mode	Call sign	Output	Input	Access	Coordinator
Rust	FM	NM8RC-R	146.82000	-		MiARC
Saginaw	DSTAR	K8DAC B	442.06250	+		
	FM	K8DAC-R	147.24000	+	103.5 Hz	MiARC
Saint Johns	FM	W8CLI	443.52500	+	100.0 Hz	MiARC
Saint Joseph	FM	KB8VIM	146.72000	-	131.8 Hz	MiARC
Sandusky	FM	W8AX	146.86000	-		MiARC
Saranac, Saranac Bus Garage						
	FM	WA8RRA	444.72500	+	94.8 Hz	MiARC
Saugatuck	FM	AC8GN	146.96000	-	94.8 Hz	MiARC
	FM	AC8GN	442.70000	+		MiARC
Sault Sainte Marie						
	DMR/BM	KE8FJW	444.13750	+	CC1	
Sault St Marie	FM	W8EUP	147.21000	+	107.2 Hz	UPARRA
Sault Ste Marie	FM	KE8FJW	145.43000	-	107.2 Hz	
Sharon Hollow	FM	WD8IEL-R	146.98000	-		MiARC
Sherman	FM	W8QPO	147.10000	+	104.5 Hz	MiARC
Sister Lakes	FM	W8MAI	146.82000	-	88.5 Hz	MiARC
South Lyon	FM	N8AR	146.04000	+	110.9 Hz	
	FUSION	N8BHT/R	147.04000	+		
	FUSION	N8JS	433.52500			
	FUSION	W8ELD	434.12500			
Southfield	FM	W8HD	52.68000	-		MiARC
Southgate	DMR/MARC	KC8LTS	443.32500	+	CC1	MiARC
Sparta	FM	W8USA	145.23000	-	94.8 Hz	MiARC
Spring Valley Mobile Home Park						
		W8AGT-R	927.68800			
Springfield	FM	KB0NHX	444.87500	+	162.2 Hz	
St Johns	DSTAR	KD8IEI	145.44000	-		MiARC
	DSTAR	KD8IEI	442.93750	+		MiARC
St. Clair Shores	FUSION	W8SOX	147.43500			
	FUSION	N8PYN	442.45000	+		
	FUSION	W8SOX	444.22500	+		
St. Johns	DSTAR	KD8IEI C	145.44000	-		
	DSTAR	KD8IEI B	442.93750	+		
St. Joseph	DSTAR	W8MAI B	442.27500	+		
	DSTAR	W8MAI	442.27500	+		MiARC
Sterling	FM	K8WBR	147.06000	+	103.5 Hz	MiARC
Sterling Heights	DMR/MARC	K9DPD	444.87500	+	CC1	
	FM	N8LC	442.92500	+		MiARC
	FM	KD8EYF	927.28750	902.28750		
Strongs	FM	W8ARS	147.33000	+	107.2 Hz	UPARRA
Stutsmanville	DMR/MARC	W8FSM	442.08750	+	CC1	
	DSTAR	W8CCE	443.37500	+		MiARC
	FM	W8GQN	146.68000	-	110.9 Hz	MiARC
	FM	WB8DEL	224.56000	-	100.0 Hz	MiARC
Suburban Estates Mobile Home P						
	FM	W8TVC-R	145.27000	-		MiARC
Sumnerville	DSTAR	KE8GVB	145.14000	-		MiARC
	DSTAR	KE8GVB	442.82500	+		MiARC
Sylvan Glen Mobile Estates						
		N8NQN-L	146.52000			
Tawas	FM	W8ICC	146.64000	-	103.5 Hz	
Tecumseh	DMR/BM	K8JAD	449.50000	442.50000	CC1	
	FM	W8MSU-L	442.90000	+		MiARC
Temperance	FM	K8RPT	444.55000	+	100.0 Hz	MiARC
Thompsonville, Crystal Mountai						
	FM	W8BNZ	147.04000	+	114.8 Hz	MiARC
Town And Country Mobile Villag						
	FM	N8CN-L	444.40000	+		
Traverse City	DMR/BM	W8TCM	442.50000	+	CC1	
	DMR/BM	KD8OXV	443.31250	+	CC1	
	DMR/BM	N8DMH	444.35000	+	CC1	

Location	Mode	Call sign	Output	Input	Access	Coordinator
Traverse City	DMR/BM	WB2LHP	445.50000	-	CC1	
	DMR/MARC	N8OUZ	442.87500	+	CC1	
	DSTAR	WI0OK C	145.36000	-		
	DSTAR	KD8OXV B	443.31250	+		
	FM	W8IRA	145.15000	-	114.8 Hz	MiARC
	FM	W8TCM	146.86000	-	114.8 Hz	
	FM	W8QPO	147.10000	+	100.0 Hz	
	FM	W8QPO	442.90000	+	114.8 Hz	MiARC
	FM	KJ4KFJ	443.00000	+	114.8 Hz	MiARC
	FUSION	KJ4KFJ	147.04000	+		
	FUSION	N8DMH	442.28750	+		
Trenary	FM	W8FYZ	147.03000	+	100.0 Hz	UPARRA
Troy	FM	N8KD	147.14000	+	100.0 Hz	MiARC
	FUSION	W5TH	444.62500	+		
Ubly	FM	KC8KOD	442.32500	+	103.5 Hz	MiARC
Utica	FM	K8UO	147.18000	+	100.0 Hz	MiARC
Vanderbilt	FM	W8IRA	145.29000	-	103.5 Hz	MiARC
Village Of Grosse Pointe Shore						
		N8BNA-R	146.74000			
Walkerville	FM	NW8J	145.43000	-	94.8 Hz	MiARC
Wallace	FM	KS8O	444.65000	+		UPARRA
Warren	DMR/BM	K8FBI	444.48750	+	CC2	
	DMR/MARC	KA8WYN	442.03750	+	CC3	
	DMR/MARC	KA8WYN	443.55000	+	CC3	
	DSTAR	WA8BRO B	442.03750	+		
	DSTAR	WA8BRO	442.03750	+		MiARC
Waterford	DMR/MARC	N8QQS	442.83750	+	CC1	
Waterloo State Recreation						
	DMR/BM	KB8POO	147.31000	+	CC1	
Watrousville	FM	N8UT	147.32000	+	110.9 Hz	MiARC
	FM	N8UT	442.50000	+	91.5 Hz	MiARC
West Bloomfield	FM	WB8ARC	442.50000	+	107.2 Hz	
West Branch	DMR/MARC	W8FSM	443.95000	+	CC1	
	FM	W8YUC	145.41000	-	91.5 Hz	MiARC
West Branch, Pointer Hill Park						
	FM	K8OAR	146.94000	-	103.5 Hz	MiARC
	FM	K8OAR	444.97500	+	103.5 Hz	MiARC
West Branch, WBMI Tower						
	FM	KD8NCN	444.22500	+	107.2 Hz	MiARC
West Olive	DMR/MARC	K8OEC	443.57500	+	CC1	MiARC
Westland	DSTAR	W8DTW C	145.17000	-		
	DSTAR	W8DTW	145.17000	-		MiARC
	DSTAR	W8DTW B	444.72500	+		
	DSTAR	W8DTW	444.72500	+		MiARC
	DSTAR	W8DTW A	1284.40000	1264.40000		
	DSTAR	W8DTW	1284.40000	-		MiARC
	DSTAR	W8DTW D	1298.40000			
	DSTAR	W8DTW	1298.40000			MiARC
	FM	K8WX	443.15000	+	107.2 Hz	MiARC
	FM	N8ISK	443.27500	+	107.2 Hz	MiARC
Wetmore	FM	KC8BAN	145.41000	-	100.0 Hz	UPARRA
Wetmore, Michigan, Holiday Gas						
	FM	WB8Q	446.10000	-	100.0 Hz	
White Cloud	FUSION	KB8IFE	444.97500	+		
White Cloud, Maike Fire Lookou						
	FM	KB8IFE	145.45000	-		MiARC
	FM	KB8IFE	444.97500	+		MiARC
White Lake	DMR/BM	N8JY	444.65000	+	CC10	
	FM	N8BIT	145.49000	-	67.0 Hz	MiARC
White Pine	FM	AA8YF	147.30000	+	100.0 Hz	UPARRA
Whitehall	DMR/MARC	K8COP	443.25000	+	CC1	MiARC
	FM	K8COP	146.68000	-	94.8 Hz	MiARC

Location	Mode	Call sign	Output	Input	Access	Coordinator
Winona	FM	W8UXG	146.73000	-		UPARRA
Wixom	FM	AC8IL	145.25000	-	100.0 Hz	
Wolverine Lake	FUSION	N8PWM	431.10000			
Wyandotte	FM	WY8DOT-R	147.24000	+	100.0 Hz	MiARC
Yale	FM	N8ERV	443.30000	+	100.0 Hz	MiARC
Ypsilanti, St. Joseph Mercy Ho						
	FM	W8FSA	146.92000	-	100.0 Hz	MiARC
Zeeland		N8XPQ-L	444.80000			

MINNESOTA

Location	Mode	Call sign	Output	Input	Access	Coordinator
Aitkin	FM	KC0QXC-R	146.80500	+	127.3 Hz	Minnesota RC
	FM	N0BZZ	147.36000	+	203.5 Hz	Minnesota RC
Albert Lea	FM	WA0RAX	443.52500	+	100.0 Hz	Minnesota RC
Alexandria	FM	W0ALX	146.79000	-	146.2 Hz	Minnesota RC
	FM	W0ALX	442.02500	+	146.2 Hz	Minnesota RC
Anoka	DMR/BM	N0NKI	442.10620	+	CC1	
Arden Hills	FM	KA0PQW	223.94000	-	100.0 Hz	Minnesota RC
	FM	WI9WIN	442.07500	+	110.9 Hz	Minnesota RC
Askov	FM	W0MDT	146.95500	-	146.2 Hz	
Aurora	FM	N0BZZ	147.24000	+	156.7 Hz	Minnesota RC
Austin	FM	W0AZR	145.47000	-	100.0 Hz	Minnesota RC
	FM	W0AZR	146.73000	-	100.0 Hz	Minnesota RC
	FM	N0RZO	443.50000	+		Minnesota RC
Avon	FM	K0STC	147.10500	+	85.4 Hz	Minnesota RC
	FM	K0VSC	443.50000	+		
Balaton	DMR/BM	WA0CQG	442.15000	+	CC1	
Barnesville	FM	KC0SD	147.06000	+	123.0 Hz	Minnesota RC
Becker	FM	KD0YLG	147.34500	+		Minnesota RC
	FM	KD0YLG	443.47500	+		Minnesota RC
Belle Plaine		KA0KMJ-R	444.92500			
Bemidji	DMR/BM	KC0OQR	145.39000	-	CC13	
	DMR/BM	KC0FTV	443.22500	+	CC6	
	DSTAR	W0BJI C	145.24500	-		
	FM	KB0MM	145.45000	-		Minnesota RC
	FM	W0BJI	146.73000	-		Minnesota RC
	FM	WA0IUJ	147.18000	147.68000	82.5 Hz	Minnesota RC
	FM	W0BJI	444.02500	+	71.9 Hz	Minnesota RC
	FM	NI0K	444.95000	+	123.0 Hz	Minnesota RC
Bertha, Water Tower						
	FM	N0WN	147.12000	+	123.0 Hz	Minnesota RC
	FM	N0WN	444.75000	+		Minnesota RC
Big Falls	FM	N0NKC	146.91000	-	103.5 Hz	Minnesota RC
Big Lake	FM	K0SCA	145.49000	-	146.2 Hz	Minnesota RC
	FM	N0JDH	443.60000	+	114.8 Hz	Minnesota RC
Blaine	FM	W0YFZ	146.67000	-	114.8 Hz	Minnesota RC
Bloomington	DMR/BM	N0NKI	443.10000	+	CC1	Minnesota RC
	DSTAR	WT0O	442.90000	+		
	FM	KD0CL	147.09000	+	100.0 Hz	Minnesota RC
	FM	KF0B	442.20000	+		
	FUSION	W0REE	146.40000	-		
Blue Earth	FM	N0PBA	147.00000	+	136.5 Hz	
	FM	KE0RTF	443.02500	+	114.8 Hz	
	FUSION	KC0UWG	145.56250			
	FUSION	KC0UWG	432.45000			
Brainerd	FM	W0UJ	53.11000	52.11000	123.0 Hz	Minnesota RC
	FM	W0UJ	146.70000	-	141.3 Hz	Minnesota RC
Brooklyn Park	DMR/MARC	KA0KMJ	445.42500	-	CC1	
Buck Hill-Burnsville						
	DMR/MARC	N0AGI	443.12500	+	CC1	Minnesota RC
Buffalo	FM	N0FWG	444.37500	+	156.7 Hz	Minnesota RC
Burnsvile	FM	W0BU	224.54000	-	100.0 Hz	Minnesota RC
Burnsville	FM	W0BU	53.37000	52.37000	100.0 Hz	Minnesota RC

Location	Mode	Call sign	Output	Input	Access	Coordinator
Burnsville	FM	W0BU	147.21000	+	100.0 Hz	Minnesota RC
	FUSION	W0BU	444.30000	+		
Burntside	FM	K0VRC-R	147.19500	+		Minnesota RC
Carlton	FM	KC0RTX	146.79000	-	103.5 Hz	Minnesota RC
Carver	FM	KB0FXK	443.92500	+		
Carver, Carver Water Tower						
	FM	WB0RMK	147.16500	+		Minnesota RC
Centervill	DMR/MARC	K0GOI	443.67500	+	CC11	
Centerville	FUSION	N0MQL	441.75000			
Chaska	DMR/BM	N0NKI	443.95000	+	CC1	
	DSTAR	KD0JOS	53.27000	52.27000	114.8 Hz	Minnesota RC
	DSTAR	KD0JOS C	147.27000	+		
	DSTAR	KD0JOS	147.27000	+		Minnesota RC
	DSTAR	KD0JOS B	442.12500	+		
	DSTAR	KD0JOT	1282.50000	1262.50000		
	DSTAR	KD0JOT A	1282.50000	-		
	DSTAR	KD0JOS	1283.50000	1263.50000		Minnesota RC
	DSTAR	KD0JOS A	1283.50000	-		
	DSTAR	KD0JOT D	1298.50000			
	DSTAR	KD0JOS D	1299.50000			
	FM	N0BVE	53.45000	52.45000		Minnesota RC
	FM	N0BVE	145.23000	-	114.8 Hz	
	FM	KD0JOS	442.12500	+		Minnesota RC
Clara City	DMR/BM	K0WPD	443.35000	+	CC3	
Cloquet	FM	WA0GWI	146.67000	-		Minnesota RC
	FM	KB0YHX	443.10000	+		
Cohasset	FM	KB0CIM	146.98500	-	118.8 Hz	Minnesota RC
	FM	KB0CIM	444.15000	+	114.8 Hz	Minnesota RC
Coleraine	FM	KB0QYC	147.16500	+	114.8 Hz	Minnesota RC
Collegeville	FM	W0SV	147.01500	+	100.0 Hz	Minnesota RC
	FM	W0SV	442.22500	+		
Cologne	FM	N0KP	444.60000	+		Minnesota RC
Columbia Heights		KD0LVH-L	144.00000			
	FM	K0FCC	224.50000	-	114.8 Hz	Minnesota RC
	FM	K0FCC	224.66000	-	114.8 Hz	Minnesota RC
	FM	K0FCC	444.75000	+	114.8 Hz	Minnesota RC
Cook	FM	N0BZZ	147.36000	+	162.2 Hz	Minnesota RC
Coon Rapids	P25	KD0ORH	444.40000	+		Minnesota RC
Cooper	DSTAR	W1SCV C	146.98500	-		
Cottage Grove	FM	W0CGM	147.18000	+	74.4 Hz	Minnesota RC
Crookston	FM	KB0BSJ	147.12000	+	123.0 Hz	
Crosby	FM	W0UJ	147.22500	+	141.3 Hz	Minnesota RC
	FM	W0UJ	444.92500	+		Minnesota RC
Crosslake	FM	W0UJ	147.03000	+	141.3 Hz	Minnesota RC
Crown	FM	N0GEF	145.21000	-	114.8 Hz	Minnesota RC
Dalton	FM	KB0JPT	224.08000	-	225.7 Hz	Minnesota RC
Darwin	FM	W0CRC	146.68500	-	146.2 Hz	Minnesota RC
Dayton	DMR/MARC	KA0KMJ	442.85000	+	CC1	
	FM	W0MDT	443.25000	+		Minnesota RC
Deer Creek, Water Tower						
	FM	N0WN	146.92500	-		Minnesota RC
Deer River	FM	KD0JFI	146.62500	-	103.5 Hz	Minnesota RC
Detroit Lakes	FM	W0EMZ	147.19500	+		Minnesota RC
Dilworth	FUSION	W0JPJ	442.50000	+		
Duluth		K0DSL-L	445.95000			
	DMR/BM	N0NKI	443.30000	+	CC1	
	DMR/BM	K0OE	444.90000	+	CC1	
	DSTAR	N0EO	147.37500	+		Minnesota RC
	DSTAR	N0EO B	442.20000	+		
	DSTAR	N0EO	442.20000	+		Minnesota RC
	FM	KB0QYC	53.13000	52.13000	103.5 Hz	Minnesota RC
	FM	N0EO	145.31000	-	110.9 Hz	Minnesota RC

Location	Mode	Call sign	Output	Input	Access	Coordinator
Duluth	FM	KC0HXC	145.41000	-	100.0 Hz	Minnesota RC
	FM	KC0RTX	145.45000	-	103.5 Hz	Minnesota RC
	FM	W0GKP	146.94000	-	103.5 Hz	Minnesota RC
	FM	KA0TMW	147.18000	+	103.5 Hz	Minnesota RC
	FM	K0DSL	147.52500		186.2 Hz	
	FM	KB0QYC	442.80000	+		Minnesota RC
	FM	W0GKP	444.10000	+		Minnesota RC
	FM	KC0RTX	444.20000	+	103.5 Hz	Minnesota RC
	FM	N0EO	444.30000	+	103.5 Hz	
	FM	KB0QYC	927.48750	902.48750	103.5 Hz	Minnesota RC
	FM	KB0QYC	927.60000	902.60000	114.8 Hz	Minnesota RC
Duxbury	FM	KE0ACL	146.91000	-	146.2 Hz	Minnesota RC
East Grand Forks	FM	WA0VFY	147.39000	+		
Eastview Mobile Home Park						
		W0EQO-R	145.47000			
Eden Prairie	FM	KD0ZIM-R	146.88000	-		Minnesota RC
Eden Prairie, MN Hwy 5 And Del						
	FM	W5RTQ	444.35000	+	114.8 Hz	Minnesota RC
Edina	FM	WC0HC	145.43000	-	127.3 Hz	Minnesota RC
	FM	WC0HC	444.20000	+	127.3 Hz	Minnesota RC
	FM	KG0BP	444.85000	+	114.8 Hz	Minnesota RC
Elk River	FM	K0CJD	146.97000	-	146.2 Hz	Minnesota RC
	FM	K0SCA	147.28500	+	131.8 Hz	Minnesota RC
Ellendale	DMR/MARC	KD0TGF	442.02500	+	CC1	Minnesota RC
	DMR/MARC	KD0TGF	442.07500	+	CC10	
	FM	KA0PQW-R	224.64000	-		
	FM	KA0PQW	442.92500	+	114.8 Hz	Minnesota RC
Ely	FM	N0OIW	146.64000	-	151.4 Hz	Minnesota RC
	FM	K0VRC/R	147.19500	+	151.4 Hz	
Emmaville, Camp Wilderness Boy						
	FM	K0NLC	147.39000	+		Minnesota RC
Fairmont	DSTAR	K6ZC C	146.97000	-		
	DSTAR	K6ZC B	443.92500	+		
	DSTAR	K6ZC D	1249.00000			
	DSTAR	K6ZC A	1284.50000	-		
	FM	K0SXR	146.64000	-		Minnesota RC
	FM	N0PBA	444.35000	+	136.5 Hz	Minnesota RC
Falcon Heights	FM	W0YC	53.15000	147.15000		Minnesota RC
Falcon Heights, U Of M, St. Pa						
	FM	W0YC	147.15000	+	114.8 Hz	Minnesota RC
Falcon Heights, UMSP						
	FM	W0YC	444.42500	+	114.8 Hz	Minnesota RC
Faribault		KA0PQW-L	443.00000			
	DMR/MARC	KD0YRF	442.17500	+	CC1	
	DMR/MARC	N0PQK	444.57500	+	CC1	Minnesota RC
	DSTAR	KD0ZSA B	444.62500	+		
	DSTAR	KD0ZSA	444.62500	+		Minnesota RC
	FM	N0ZR	145.19000	-	100.0 Hz	Minnesota RC
	FM	KD0ZSA	146.79000	-	100.0 Hz	Minnesota RC
	FM	KB0IOA	444.70000	+		
	FUSION	W0IRX	145.55500			
Fergus Falls	FM	K0QIK	146.64000	-		Minnesota RC
	FM	K0QIK	147.28500	+	91.5 Hz	Minnesota RC
	FM	K0QIK	444.20000	+	151.4 Hz	Minnesota RC
Finland	FM	N0BZZ	145.41000	-	114.8 Hz	Minnesota RC
Fisher	FM	KC0SD	146.70000	-		Minnesota RC
Foley	FM	KD0NRL	147.07500	+	85.4 Hz	
Forest Lake	FM	N0VOW-R	146.89500	-		
Foreston	FM	N0GOI	146.74500	-	107.2 Hz	Minnesota RC
	FM	N0GOI	443.67500	+	114.8 Hz	Minnesota RC
Fredenberg		K0EKL-L	445.45000			
Fulda	FM	W0DRK	147.36000	+	141.3 Hz	

Location	Mode	Call sign	Output	Input	Access	Coordinator
Fulda	FM	W0DRK	444.25000	+	141.3 Hz	
	FUSION	W0DRK/R	146.79000	-		
Gaylord	FM	KC0QNA	146.80500	-	141.3 Hz	Minnesota RC
Gem Lake	DSTAR	KA0JSW B	444.00000	+		
	DSTAR	KA0JSW A	1285.50000	1305.50000		
	FM	K0LAV	224.10000	-		Minnesota RC
	FM	K0LAV	444.95000	+	114.8 Hz	Minnesota RC
Giese	FM	KB0QYC	146.86500	-	146.2 Hz	Minnesota RC
Gilbert	FM	KB0QYC	443.50000	+	141.3 Hz	Minnesota RC
Gilbert, Water Tower						
	FM	NT0B	147.15000	+		
Glenville	FM	WA0RAX	146.88000	-	100.0 Hz	Minnesota RC
	FM	WA0YCT	444.97500	+	100.0 Hz	
Golden Valley	DSTAR	KD0JOV C	145.15000	-		
	DSTAR	KD0JOV	145.15000	-		
	DSTAR	KD0JOV B	442.90000	+		
	FM	W0PZT	146.82000	-	127.3 Hz	Minnesota RC
	FM	WC0HC	444.17500	+	127.3 Hz	
Gordonsville	FM	NX0P-R	146.68500	-		Minnesota RC
Grand Marais	FM	W0BBN	444.25000	+	151.4 Hz	Minnesota RC
	FM	N0LCR	444.60000	+	103.5 Hz	
Grand Marais, Gunflint Lake						
	FM	W0BBN	146.73000	-	151.4 Hz	Minnesota RC
Grand Marais, Maple Hill						
	FM	W0BBN	146.89500	-	151.4 Hz	Minnesota RC
Grand Portage	FM	W0BBN	146.65500	-	151.4 Hz	Minnesota RC
Grand Rapids	FM	KB0CIM	53.29000	52.29000	146.2 Hz	Minnesota RC
	FM	K0GPZ	444.55000	+	123.0 Hz	Minnesota RC
Grand Rapids, Coleraine						
	FM	K0GPZ	146.88000	-		Minnesota RC
Granite Falls	FM	W0YMC	147.22500	+	141.3 Hz	
Green Isle	FM	KC0QNA	443.82500	+	141.3 Hz	
Ham Lake	DSTAR	W0ANA	145.40500	-		Minnesota RC
	DSTAR	W0ANA	443.77500	+		Minnesota RC
	DSTAR	W0ANA	1287.00000	1267.00000		Minnesota RC
	FM	W0YC	224.94000	-	100.0 Hz	
	FM	K9EQ	444.02500	+		Minnesota RC
	FUSION	K9EQ	439.35000			
	FUSION	K9EQ	444.52500	+		
Hampton	FM	K0JTA-R	146.36000	+		Minnesota RC
Harris	DSTAR	WB0VGI B	438.80000	+		
Hastings	FM	W0CGM	146.98500	-		Minnesota RC
	FUSION	N0FKU	146.52000			
Hennepin	FM	W0RRC	145.39000	-		
Hibbing	FM	N0AGX	147.12000	+		
Hilltop	FM	K0FCC-R	145.29000	-	114.8 Hz	Minnesota RC
Hoffman	FUSION	N0QXM	146.79000	-		
	FUSION	N0QXM	442.02500	+		
Hopkins	FM	N0BVE-R	145.45000	-		Minnesota RC
Hugo	FM	N0SBU	443.05000	+	118.8 Hz	Minnesota RC
Hutchinson	FM	KB0WJP	147.37500	+	146.2 Hz	Minnesota RC
Isabella	FM	KB0QYC	147.30000	+	114.8 Hz	Minnesota RC
Isanti	DSTAR	KE0KKN	442.27500	+		Minnesota RC
	FM	N0JOL	146.64000	-	146.2 Hz	Minnesota RC
Isle, Mille Lacs Lake						
	FM	W0REA	146.61000	-	141.3 Hz	Minnesota RC
Janesville	DMR/MARC	KD0TGF	442.50000	+	CC1	
Karlstad	DMR/BM	KB0ISW	443.97500	+	CC6	Minnesota RC
	FM	KA0NWV	145.47000	-	123.0 Hz	
	FUSION	KB0ISW	146.65500	-		
	FUSION	KB0ISW	147.87000			
Kelliher	DMR/BM	KC0OQR	147.00000	+	CC13	

Location	Mode	Call sign	Output	Input	Access	Coordinator
Knife River	FM	KC0RTX	147.13500	+	103.5 Hz	
	FM	NA0RC	444.40000	+	103.5 Hz	
La Crescent	FM	WR9ARC	146.97000	-	131.8 Hz	Minnesota RC
Lakeville	FUSION	KB0MDQ	147.43500			
Le Center	FM	KC0LSR	444.22500	+	136.5 Hz	
Le Sueur	FM	WB0ERN	146.61000	-	136.5 Hz	Minnesota RC
Lengby	FM	W0BJI	147.27000	+		Minnesota RC
Lino Lakes	FUSION	AD0MI	445.54000	-		
Litchfield	DMR/BM	KC0CAP	443.80000	+	CC3	
	FM	AE0GD	146.62500	-	146.2 Hz	Minnesota RC
	FM	K0MCR	147.30000	+	146.2 Hz	Minnesota RC
	FUSION	KC0CAP	145.25000	-		
Little Falls	DSTAR	W0REA B	444.00000	+		
	DSTAR	W0REA	444.00000	+		Minnesota RC
	FM	KA0JSW	443.12500	+	123.0 Hz	Minnesota RC
	FUSION	N0BJN	434.22500			
	FUSION	N0RND	443.07500	+		
	FUSION	N0BJN	443.65000	+		
Little Falls, Little Falls AT&						
	FM	W0REA	147.13500	+	123.0 Hz	Minnesota RC
Littlefork	FM	KA0WRT	444.90000	+	103.5 Hz	Minnesota RC
Long Prairie	FM	KC0TAF	146.65500	-		Minnesota RC
Madison	FM	NY0I	444.90000	+		Minnesota RC
Mahnomen	FM	W0BJI	444.50000	+		Minnesota RC
Mahtowa	FM	KB0TNB	53.17000	52.17000	103.5 Hz	Minnesota RC
	FM	W0GKP	147.00000	-	103.5 Hz	Minnesota RC
Mankato	FM	W0WCL	147.04500	+	136.5 Hz	Minnesota RC
	FM	W0WCL	147.24000	+	136.5 Hz	Minnesota RC
	FM	WA2OFZ	442.82500	+	136.5 Hz	Minnesota RC
	FM	W0WCL	444.67500	+	100.0 Hz	Minnesota RC
	P25	K2KLN	443.65000	+	114.8 Hz	Minnesota RC
Mankato , Good Counsel Hill						
	FM	K0JCR	442.52500	+	136.5 Hz	
Maple Grove	FM	K0LTC	443.55000	+	114.8 Hz	Minnesota RC
Maple Plain	FM	K0LTC	147.00000	+	114.8 Hz	Minnesota RC
Maplewood	DSTAR	KC0TQJ A	1285.10000	1305.10000		
	FM	W0MR	147.12000	+		Minnesota RC
	FM	K0AGF	442.45000	+		Minnesota RC
	FM	KC0MQW	442.60000	+	156.7 Hz	Minnesota RC
	FM	W0MR	444.82500	+		Minnesota RC
	FM	W0MR	1285.00000	1265.00000		
Marcell	FM	K0GPZ	147.07500	+		Minnesota RC
Marshall		K0APR-L	146.58000			
	DMR/BM	N0NKI	443.70000	+	CC1	
	FM	W0WX	146.95500	-	141.3 Hz	Minnesota RC
Medford	DMR/MARC	KD0TGF	442.05000	+	CC1	
Medina	DMR/MARC	W0PZT	443.20000	+	CC11	
Mendota	FM	N0BVE-L	444.32500	+		Minnesota RC
Milaca	FM	KD0JOU	145.35000	-	141.3 Hz	Minnesota RC
Minneapolis	DMR/BM	NH7CY	442.42500	+	CC1	Minnesota RC
	DMR/BM	N0NKI	443.30000	+	CC1	
	DMR/BM	W0PZT	444.72500	+	CC11	
	DMR/MARC	N0BVE	442.65000	+	CC2	Minnesota RC
	DSTAR	KD0JOU	145.11000	-		
	DSTAR	KD0JOU C	145.11000	-		
	DSTAR	W1AFV B	442.95000	+		
	DSTAR	W1AFV	442.95000	+		
	DSTAR	W0YC B	443.42500	+		
	DSTAR	KD0JOU B	444.87500	+		
	DSTAR	KD0JOU	444.87500	+		Minnesota RC
	DSTAR	KE8TX D	1251.00000			
	DSTAR	KD0JOU	1283.30000	1263.30000		Minnesota RC

Location	Mode	Call sign	Output	Input	Access	Coordinator
Minneapolis	DSTAR	KD0JOU A	1283.30000	-		
	DSTAR	WD0HWT D	1298.00000			
	DSTAR	KD0JOU D	1299.30000			
	FM	K0MSP	145.37000	-	107.2 Hz	Minnesota RC
	FM	KD0JOU	147.03000	+	114.8 Hz	Minnesota RC
	FM	WB0ZKB	147.27000	+	114.8 Hz	Minnesota RC
	FM	KB0FJB	443.80000	+	114.8 Hz	Minnesota RC
	FM	N0BVE	444.65000	+	114.8 Hz	Minnesota RC
Minneapolis, U Of Minn						
	FM	KA0KMJ	444.42500	+	114.8 Hz	Minnesota RC
Minnetonka	DMR/BM	N0BVE	442.67500	+	CC2	
	FM	KA0KMJ	443.00000	+	100.0 Hz	Minnesota RC
Montevideo	FM	NY0I	147.12000	+	146.2 Hz	Minnesota RC
Moorhead	DMR/BM	W0JPJ	145.15000	-	CC6	
	FM	W0ILO	145.35000	-	123.0 Hz	Minnesota RC
	FM	W0ILO	444.87500	+	123.0 Hz	Minnesota RC
	FUSION	W0JPJ	442.50000	+		
Moorhead, Clay County Social S						
	FM	W0JPJ	145.15000	-		Minnesota RC
Morris	FM	NG0W	444.40000	+	103.5 Hz	Minnesota RC
Mounds View		N0KFB-L	223.70000			
	DSTAR	W0ANA C	145.40500	-		
	DSTAR	W0ANA B	443.77500	+		
	DSTAR	W0ANA A	1287.00000	-		
	DSTAR	W0ANA D	1295.50000			
	FM	W0MDT	444.52500	+		Minnesota RC
Mounds View, Medtronic CRDM Ca						
	FM	K9EQ	444.07500	+	100.0 Hz	Minnesota RC
MSP-Airport	DMR/MARC	N0BVE	444.92500	+	CC11	
New Prague		AC0UK-L	147.57000			
New Richland	FM	N0RPJ	145.33000	-	100.0 Hz	Minnesota RC
Nisswa, WJJY Tower						
	FM	W0UJ	443.92500	+	110.9 Hz	Minnesota RC
NOAA Aitkin	WX	KZZ84	162.45000			
NOAA Appleton	WX	KXI32	162.55000			
NOAA Bemidji	WX	WXM99	162.42500			
NOAA Clearwater	WX	WNG676	162.50000			
NOAA Coleraine	WX	KZZ29	162.40000			
NOAA Detroit Lakes						
	WX	WXM64	162.40000			
NOAA Duluth	WX	KIG64	162.55000			
NOAA Elephant Lake						
	WX	KZZ44	162.45000			
NOAA Ely	WX	KXI44	162.50000			
NOAA Fergus Falls						
	WX	WNG680	162.50000			
NOAA Finland	WX	WNG630	162.42500			
NOAA Fulda	WX	WNG702	162.42500			
NOAA Grand Marais						
	WX	KXI43	162.45000			
NOAA Gun Flint Lake						
	WX	KXI45	162.52500			
NOAA International Falls						
	WX	WXK45	162.55000			
NOAA Jeffers	WX	KXI31	162.45000			
NOAA Kensington	WX	WNG707	162.40000			
NOAA La Crescent						
	WX	WXJ86	162.55000			
NOAA Lake Bronson						
	WX	WNG583	162.52500			
NOAA Leader	WX	WXJ64	162.55000			

Location	Mode	Call sign	Output	Input	Access	Coordinator
NOAA Long Prairie						
	WX	WNG673	162.52500			
NOAA Mankato	WX	WXK40	162.40000			
NOAA Minneapolis / St. Paul						
	WX	KEC65	162.55000			
NOAA New Ulm	WX	KXI39	162.52500			
NOAA Norwood	WX	WNG685	162.42500			
NOAA Olivia	WX	WNG711	162.40000			
NOAA Park Rapids						
	WX	WWG98	162.47500			
NOAA Pine City	WX	WNG678	162.42500			
NOAA Red Wing	WX	KJY80	162.45000			
NOAA Rochester	WX	WXK41	162.47500			
NOAA Roosevelt	WX	WWF45	162.45000			
NOAA Russell	WX	KXI50	162.50000			
NOAA St. Cloud	WX	WXL65	162.40000			
NOAA Thief River Falls						
	WX	WXK43	162.55000			
NOAA Virginia	WX	KZZ45	162.47500			
NOAA Waubun	WX	WNG610	162.45000			
NOAA Willmar	WX	WXK44	162.47500			
North Branch	FM	K0GOI	147.31500	+	91.5 Hz	Minnesota RC
Northfield	FM	N0OTL	146.65500	-	136.5 Hz	Minnesota RC
	FUSION	KE0NAO	147.52500			
Northwest Angle	FM	N0MHO	147.21000	+	123.0 Hz	Minnesota RC
Oak Grove	DMR/BM	KE0ABR	444.72500	+	CC11	
Oak Knoll	FM	W0EF-R	146.76000	-	114.8 Hz	Minnesota RC
Oakdale	DMR/MARC	N0YNT	443.42500	+	CC1	
	FM	WD0HWT	146.85000	-		
	FUSION	N0XOC	146.95500	-		
Ogilvie	FM	KD0CI	147.24000	+	146.2 Hz	Minnesota RC
Ortonville	FM	NY0I	444.50000	+	146.2 Hz	Minnesota RC
Outing	FM	WR0G	145.43000	-	127.3 Hz	Minnesota RC
Owatonna	FM	K0HNY	145.49000	-	100.0 Hz	
	FM	WB0VAJ	147.10500	+	100.0 Hz	Minnesota RC
	FM	WB0VAK	444.45000	+	100.0 Hz	Minnesota RC
Park Rapids	FM	K0GUV	147.30000	+		Minnesota RC
Paynesville	FM	WD0DEH	145.27000	-		Minnesota RC
	FM	KD0YLG	224.80000	-		Minnesota RC
	FM	N0ANC	444.62500	+		Minnesota RC
Pequot Lakes, Maple Hill						
	FM	W0REA	147.09000	+	123.0 Hz	Minnesota RC
Perham	FM	K0QIK	147.15000	+		
Pine Island	FUSION	KE0YJJ	443.87500	+		
Pine River	FUSION	W0YJC	440.15000	+		
Pinewood	DMR/BM	KC0FTV	443.50000	+	CC6	
	FM	KC0FTV	442.22500	447.32500	118.8 Hz	Minnesota RC
Pipestone	FM	W0DRK	147.07500	+	141.3 Hz	
Plymouth	FM	WC0HC	146.70000	-	127.3 Hz	Minnesota RC
	FM	N0FWG	444.37500	+	114.8 Hz	Minnesota RC
	FM	W0PZT	444.50000	+	127.3 Hz	Minnesota RC
Porter	FUSION	KA0KAE	446.20000			
Princeton	DMR/BM	W9YZI	442.50000	+	CC3	
	FM	KD0YEQ	146.77500	-	146.2 Hz	Minnesota RC
	FM	K0SCA	444.70000	+	146.2 Hz	Minnesota RC
Prior Lake	DMR/MARC	N0AGI	443.07500	+	CC1	Minnesota RC
Proctor	FM	N0BZZ	147.33000	+	151.4 Hz	Minnesota RC
Ramsey	DSTAR	KE0MVE	442.52500	+		Minnesota RC
	DSTAR	KE0MVE	1287.10000	1267.10000		Minnesota RC
	FM	K0MSP	444.97500	+	114.8 Hz	Minnesota RC
Red Wing	DMR/BM	N0BVE	442.47500	+	CC2	
	FM	AA0RW	147.30000	+	136.5 Hz	Minnesota RC

Location	Mode	Call sign	Output	Input	Access	Coordinator
Red Wing	FUSION	AA0RW	442.25000	+		
Redwood Falls	FM	KB0CGJ	146.86500	-	141.3 Hz	Minnesota RC
Richfield		KC0TJ-L	144.50000			
		KB0GTF-L	446.02500			
	FM	W0RRC	145.39000	-		Minnesota RC
	FM	W0RRC	444.47500	+	118.8 Hz	Minnesota RC
Riverside Mobile Home Court						
	FM	K0HKZ-R	146.97000	-		Minnesota RC
Robbinsdale	FM	K0YTH	444.77500	+	114.8 Hz	Minnesota RC
Rochester	DMR/MARC	KD0YRF	443.97500	+	CC2	Minnesota RC
	DSTAR	W0MXW B	443.85000	+		
	FM	W0MXW	146.82000	-	100.0 Hz	Minnesota RC
	FM	W0EAS	147.25500	+	100.0 Hz	Minnesota RC
	FM	KD0EBO	147.85500	146.95500	100.0 Hz	
	FUSION	N7EXL	433.10000			
	FUSION	AB0BW	449.95000	-		
Rochester, Mayo Clinic						
	DSTAR	W0MXW	443.85000	+		Minnesota RC
	FM	W0MXW	146.62500	-	100.0 Hz	Minnesota RC
Roosevelt	FM	N0MHO	147.00000	-	123.0 Hz	
Rosemount	FM	W0EIB	224.94000	-		Minnesota RC
Roseville	DMR/MARC	N0NMZ	443.52500	+	CC11	Minnesota RC
Rush City	FM	K0ECM	145.33000	-	146.2 Hz	Minnesota RC
Sabin, Water Tower						
	FM	WB0BIN	146.89500	-	100.0 Hz	
Saint Paul	DMR/MARC	K0GOI	442.02500	+	CC11	
Saint Anna	FM	KG0CV-L	443.65000	+		Minnesota RC
Saint Anthony	FM	KD0WIL-R	443.57500	+		Minnesota RC
Saint Bonifacius	DMR/MARC	N0VZC	442.10000	+	CC5	
	DMR/MARC	N0VZC	919.00000	-	CC5	
Saint Cloud	DMR/MARC	KC0ARX	442.22500	+	CC3	
	FUSION	KE0EMB	443.47500	+		
Saint Paul	DMR/BM	NH7CY	442.41250	+	CC11	
	DMR/MARC	N0YNT	443.00000	+	CC11	
Saint Peter	FUSION	WQ0A	145.23000	-		
	FUSION	WQ0A	442.52500	+		
	FUSION	W0JRG	444.15000	+		
Sauk Centre	FM	W0ALX	147.25500	+		Minnesota RC
Sauk Rapids, Water Tower On To						
	FM	W0SV	146.94000	-	100.0 Hz	Minnesota RC
Sebeka, Water Tower						
	FM	N0WN	147.33000	+		Minnesota RC
Shakopee	DMR/BM	KC0NPA	444.72500	+	CC4	
Shoreview	FUSION	NY9D	449.27500	-		
Silver Bay	FM	N0LCR	444.60000	+	103.5 Hz	
Silver Lake	FM	KB0WJP	443.40000	+	146.2 Hz	
Slayton, DOT On HWY 59						
	FM	W0DRK	146.79000	-	141.3 Hz	Minnesota RC
South St. Paul	FUSION	AB0XE	146.55000			
Spring Lake Park	FUSION	KD0ZPF	145.52000			
Spring Valley	FM	N0ZOD	147.01500	+	110.9 Hz	Minnesota RC
St Cloud	DMR/BM	WJ0U	442.22500	+	CC3	
St Paul	DSTAR	W8WRR B	443.35000	+		
	DSTAR	W8WRR D	1249.00000			
St. Bonifacius	DMR/MARC	N0VZC	444.72500	+	CC2	
St. Charles		AD0KY-L	146.50500			
St. Cloud	DSTAR	KD0YLG	443.85000	+		Minnesota RC
	DSTAR	KD0YLG B	443.85000	+		
	FM	N0OYQ	146.83500	-	85.4 Hz	Minnesota RC
	FM	K0VSC	443.45000	+	123.0 Hz	Minnesota RC
St. Cloud, St. Cloud Hospital						
	FM	N0ANC	145.19000	-	146.2 Hz	Minnesota RC

Location	Mode	Call sign	Output	Input	Access	Coordinator
St. Cloud, St. Cloud Hospital						
	FM	N0ANC	442.15000	+		Minnesota RC
St. Louis Park	FM	W0EF	444.10000	+	114.8 Hz	Minnesota RC
St. Paul	DMR/BM	K9MLS	442.37500	+	CC4	
	DSTAR	W8WRR	444.32500	+		
	FM	W0BU	53.37000	52.37000	100.0 Hz	
	FM	K0GOI	53.47000	52.47000		Minnesota RC
	FM	K0GOI	145.17000	-	100.0 Hz	Minnesota RC
	FM	KE0NA	223.90000	-	100.0 Hz	Minnesota RC
	FM	W0BU	224.54000	-	100.0 Hz	
	FM	N0GOI	444.05000	+		
	FM	WD0HWT	444.80000	+	114.8 Hz	Minnesota RC
St. Paul, Univ. Of St. Thomas						
	FM	K0AGF	145.31000	-	114.8 Hz	Minnesota RC
St. Peter	FM	N0KP	224.52000	+		Minnesota RC
	FM	WQ0A	444.15000	+		Minnesota RC
	WX	WQ0A	147.13500	+	100.0 Hz	Minnesota RC
	FUSION	W0TJW	435.00000			
Stewartville	FM	N0ZQB	444.25000	+	136.5 Hz	Minnesota RC
Stillwater	FUSION	W0JH	147.06000	+		
Tamarack	FM	N0BZZ	443.20000	+	114.8 Hz	Minnesota RC
Thief River Falls	DMR/BM	WB0WTI	147.36000	+	CC6	
	DMR/BM	WB0WTI	444.80000	+	CC6	
	FM	WB0WTI	146.85000	-	123.0 Hz	Minnesota RC
Tofte, Lutsen	FM	W0BBN	146.86500	-	151.4 Hz	Minnesota RC
Tracy	FM	W0DRK	147.15000	+	141.3 Hz	
Two Harbors	FM	KB0TNB	53.02000	52.02000	103.5 Hz	Minnesota RC
	FM	WB0DGK	147.27000	+	103.5 Hz	
	FM	N0LCR	444.50000	+	103.5 Hz	
Tyler	FM	WB6AMY	145.11000	-	146.2 Hz	Minnesota RC
	FM	W0ZZY	145.35000	-	156.7 Hz	Minnesota RC
	FUSION	KB0NLY	444.67500	+		
Ulen	FM	W0QQK	146.68500	-		Minnesota RC
Virginia	FM	KB0QYC	53.15000	52.15000	103.5 Hz	Minnesota RC
Wabasha	FM	WA0UNB	146.74500	-	136.5 Hz	Minnesota RC
	FM	WA0UNB	421.25000	439.25000		Minnesota RC
Wabasso	DMR/BM	KB0CGJ	444.52500	+	CC10	
Walker	FM	NA0RC	146.79000	-	103.5 Hz	Minnesota RC
Wanda	DSTAR	KD0IAI B	444.02500	+		
	DSTAR	KD0IAI	444.02500	+		Minnesota RC
Wannaska	FM	KC0IGT	147.09000	+	123.0 Hz	Minnesota RC
Warroad	DMR/BM	N0MHO	443.00000	+	CC1	
Waseca	FM	KB0UJL	146.71500	-	141.3 Hz	Minnesota RC
	FM	KB0UJL	442.30000	+	141.3 Hz	Minnesota RC
Waseca, Water Tower						
	FM	WA0CJU	146.94000	-		Minnesota RC
White Bear Lake	DMR/MARC	W0REA	147.39000	+	CC11	Minnesota RC
	DMR/MARC	K0LTZ	443.15000	+	CC8	
	DSTAR	KA0JSW	444.00000	+		Minnesota RC
	DSTAR	KA0JSW	1285.50000	1265.50000		Minnesota RC
	FM	WD0HWT	444.25000	+	100.0 Hz	Minnesota RC
WhiteBearTownship/Be						
	DMR/BM	N0NKI	443.95000	+	CC1	
Willmar	FM	W0SW	146.91000	-		Minnesota RC
	FM	W0SW	147.03000	-		Minnesota RC
	FM	KB0MNU	444.80000	+	146.2 Hz	Minnesota RC
Wilton		AB0RE-L	147.55500			
Windom	FM	W0DRK	147.25500	+	141.3 Hz	Minnesota RC
Winona	FM	W0NE	146.64000	-	100.0 Hz	Minnesota RC
	FM	W0NE	146.83500	-	131.8 Hz	
	FM	N0PDD	147.28500	+	100.0 Hz	Minnesota RC
	FUSION	N0QK	145.55500			

Location	Mode	Call sign	Output	Input	Access	Coordinator
Winona	FUSION	N0QK	147.55500			
	FUSION	W0NE	442.15000	+		
	FUSION	AD0UU	445.00000			
Woodbury	DMR/MARC	K0GOI	442.82500	+	CC11	
	FUSION	W0GAU	145.07500			
Woodbury, Woodwinds Hospital						
	FM	N0GOI	442.82500	+		Minnesota RC
Woodland Mobile Home Park						
		K0DMF-L	146.73000			
Worthington	FM	K0QBI	146.67000	-	141.3 Hz	Minnesota RC
	FM	W0DRK	444.85000	+	141.3 Hz	
Wyoming	DMR/BM	N0DZQ	444.23120	+	CC3	
Zimmerman	FM	KE0ATF	444.45000	+		Minnesota RC

MISSISSIPPI

Location	Mode	Call sign	Output	Input	Access	Coordinator
Abbeville	FM	WB5VYH	145.47000	-	107.2 Hz	SERA
Aberdeen	FM	WB5TZN	147.27000	+	210.7 Hz	
	FM	WB5TZN	444.45000	+	210.7 Hz	SERA
Ackerman, ETV Tower						
	FM	NO5N	147.12000	+	136.5 Hz	SERA
Amory	DMR/BM	AD5T	443.20000	+	CC1	SERA
	FM	KB5DWX	146.94000	-	192.8 Hz	SERA
Bay Springs	FM	W5NRU	145.49000	-		SERA
Bay St Louis	FM	WO5V	444.75000	+	179.9 Hz	SERA
Biloxi, Cableone Tower						
	FM	W5SGL	146.73000	-	136.5 Hz	SERA
Booneville	FM	WX5F	147.15000	+	110.9 Hz	SERA
	FM	WX5F	441.85000	+	118.8 Hz	
	FM	KG5UYK	442.97500	+	203.5 Hz	
Boonville	DSTAR	W5NEM	146.83500	-		
Brandon	DSTAR	K5RKN C	145.17000	-		
	DSTAR	K5RKN B	444.82500	+		
	FM	K5RKN	147.34500	+	100.0 Hz	SERA
Brookhaven, Water Tower						
	FM	W5WQ	146.85000	-	103.5 Hz	SERA
Byrd Heights	FUSION	W5PFR-R	444.00000	+	77.0 Hz	SERA
Carrollton	FM	KE5ATI	147.28500	+	107.2 Hz	
Clinton		W5PFC-R	444.00000			
	DSTAR	W5PFR	441.81250	+		SERA
	FUSION	W5DRA	147.38000	+		
	FUSION	W5PFR	444.00000	+		
	FUSION	W5PFR	444.60000	+		
Coldwater	DMR/MARC	KG5IRU	146.44000	145.04000	CC1	
	DMR/MARC	KB5DMT	441.92500	+	CC1	
	DMR/MARC	KG5IRU	442.92500	+	CC1	
	DMR/MARC	KG5IRU	443.92500	+	CC1	
	DMR/MARC	W5GWD	444.92500	+	CC1	
Collins	FM	W5NRU	146.95500	-	179.9 Hz	
Columbia	FM	N5LJC	147.28500	+	123.0 Hz	SERA
	FM	N5LJC	444.80000	+		
	FUSION	AF5NG	146.58000			
Columbus	DSTAR	KC5ULN	444.92500	+		SERA
	DSTAR	KC5ULN B	444.92500	+		
	FM	KC5ULN	146.62500	-	136.5 Hz	
Coonwood (historical)						
	FM	N5EYM-R	146.97000	-		
Corinth	DMR/MARC	K5WHB	147.28500	+	CC1	
	DMR/MARC	K5WHB	444.60000	+	CC1	
	FM	WF5D	145.39000	-	100.0 Hz	
	FM	W5AWP	146.92500	-	107.2 Hz	
	FM	KC5CO	147.34500	+	123.0 Hz	
	FM	W5AWP	441.80000	+	107.2 Hz	SERA

Location	Mode	Call sign	Output	Input	Access	Coordinator
Corinth	FM	KJ5CO	443.90000	+	123.0 Hz	SERA
Corinth, LakeHill Motors						
	FM	K5WHB	53.07000	52.07000	203.5 Hz	
Corinth, Pine Mountain						
	FM	KB5YNM	147.00000	-	203.5 Hz	
Diamondhead, Near Diamondhead						
	FM	KA5EPR	444.45000	+	136.5 Hz	
Edinburg	FM	W5PPB	145.33000	-	77.0 Hz	SERA
Ellisville	DMR/BM	W5NRU	442.17500	+	CC1	
	DMR/BM	N5EKR	443.87500	+	CC1	
	DMR/BM	NE5L	444.86250	+	CC1	
	DSTAR	W5NRU C	145.48000	-		
	DSTAR	W5NRU B	441.81250	+		
	FM	W5NRU	145.23000	-		SERA
	FM	W5NRU	224.88000	-	179.9 Hz	
	FM	W5NRU	442.25000	+	136.5 Hz	SERA
	FM	W5NRU	443.60000	+	179.9 Hz	SERA
	FM	W5NRU	443.65000	+	77.0 Hz	SERA
	FUSION	W5NRU	442.30000	+	179.9 Hz	SERA
Ellisville, South, YSF Auto/Au						
	FM	W5NRU	442.90000	+	179.9 Hz	SERA
Forest	FUSION	KF5SEB	145.24000	-	100.0 Hz	SERA
Fulton	FM	WX5P	145.45000	-	192.8 Hz	SERA
Gloster	FM	KX5E	145.43000	-	136.5 Hz	SERA
	FM	N5ZNS	443.82500	+		SERA
Greenwood	FM	KE5ATI	147.28500	+	107.2 Hz	
Grenada	FM	W5LV	146.70000	-		SERA
	FM	AD5IT	444.70000	+	107.2 Hz	SERA
	FUSION	AD5IT	147.00000	-		
Gulfport	FM	WD5BJT	444.15000	+	77.0 Hz	SERA
	FUSION	N5DDZ	146.10000			
Guntown	FM	WJ5D	145.15000	-	156.7 Hz	
Hattiesburg	DMR/BM	W5NRU	442.70000	+	CC1	SERA
	FM	KD5MIS	147.31500	+	136.5 Hz	SERA
	FUSION	KK4TXB	145.54000			
	FUSION	W5CJR/DG	147.36000	+		
Hattiesburg, Hburg-Laurel Airp						
	FM	K5IJX	444.77500	+	136.5 Hz	SERA
Hattiesburg, Richburg Hill						
	FM	N5LRQ	442.72500	+	167.9 Hz	SERA
Heidelberg	FM	W5NRU	147.57000		179.9 Hz	
	FM	KC5RC	444.30000	+	100.0 Hz	SERA
Hernando	FM	N5PYQ	145.37000	-	107.2 Hz	
	FM	W5GWD	146.91000	-	107.2 Hz	
	FM	N5PYQ	444.92500	+	107.2 Hz	SERA
Holly Springs	FM	KD5VMV	147.22500	+	107.2 Hz	
Horn Lake	DMR/BM	W5AV	442.01250	+	CC1	
	DSTAR	W5AV	144.96000	+		SERA
	DSTAR	W5AV	145.55000	-		
	FM	N5NBG	145.27000	-	107.2 Hz	SERA
	FM	N5NBG	444.65000	+		SERA
Houston	FM	KD5YBU	146.89500	-	141.3 Hz	SERA
Hurley	FUSION	KB5SAT	147.52500			
Indianola	FM	AB5DU	444.85000	+	136.5 Hz	SERA
Iuka	FM	W5TCR	146.85000	-	141.3 Hz	SERA
Jackson	FM	W5PFC	146.76000	-	77.0 Hz	SERA
	FM	KA5SBK	146.94000	-	100.0 Hz	
	FM	NC5Y	444.70000	+	77.0 Hz	SERA
Jackson, St. Dominic's Hospita						
	FM	W5PFC	146.88000	-	77.0 Hz	
Kosciusko	FM	KB5ZEA	146.85000	-	79.7 Hz	SERA
Laurel	FM	KC5PIA	53.45000	52.45000	136.5 Hz	

Location	Mode	Call sign	Output	Input	Access	Coordinator
Laurel	FM	W5NRU	146.61000	-	136.5 Hz	SERA
	FM	WV5D	147.03000	-	136.5 Hz	SERA
	FM	W5FSJ	147.06000	+	146.2 Hz	SERA
	FM	W5NRU	147.13500	+		SERA
	FM	WV5D	442.37500	+	136.5 Hz	SERA
	FM	KC5PIA	444.97500	+	136.5 Hz	SERA
Leakesville	FM	KE5WGF	147.00000	+	136.5 Hz	SERA
	FM	KE5WGF	444.22500	+	136.5 Hz	SERA
Long Beach	FM	K5XXV	145.33000	-	136.5 Hz	SERA
Love Station	DMR/MARC	KB5DMT	431.92500	446.92500	CC1	
Lucedale	DMR/BM	KD4VVZ	444.20000	+	CC1	
	FUSION	KD4VVZ	147.12000	+	136.5 Hz	
Madison	FM	K5XU	146.64000	-	77.0 Hz	SERA
McComb	FM	W5WQ	444.87500	+	100.0 Hz	SERA
Mccomb, SW MS Reg Med Ctr						
	FM	W5WQ	146.94000	-	103.5 Hz	SERA
McDonald	FM	W5NRU-R	146.98500	-		SERA
McHenry	DSTAR	KI4TMJ	145.17000	-		SERA
	DSTAR	KI4TMJ C	145.17000	-		
	DSTAR	KI4TMJ	444.47500	+		
	DSTAR	KI4TMJ B	444.47500	+		
	DSTAR	KI4TMJ	1250.00000			SERA
	DSTAR	KI4TMJ D	1250.00000			
	DSTAR	KI4TMJ A	1284.00000	-		
	DSTAR	KI4TMJ	1284.00000	1264.00000		SERA
	FM	KA5VFU	147.37500	+	136.5 Hz	SERA
McVille	FM	KG5EVY	444.20000	+	103.5 Hz	
Meridian	FM	W5LRG	145.41000	-	97.4 Hz	
	FM	W5FQ	146.70000	-	100.0 Hz	
	FM	NO5C	146.97000	-	100.0 Hz	
	FM	W5LRG	444.50000	+	107.2 Hz	SERA
Monticello, 379 Firetower Road						
	FM	N5JHK	147.01500	+		SERA
Moselle, Hattiesburg-Laurel Re						
	FM	K5IJX	145.37000	-	136.5 Hz	
Mount Zion	FM	K5YVY-R	146.74500	-		SERA
Natchez	DSTAR	N5TAM C	145.25000	-		
	DSTAR	N5TAM B	447.41250	-		
	FM	K5OCM	146.91000	-	91.5 Hz	SERA
	FM	K5SVC	147.36000	+	100.0 Hz	
	FUSION	KD5BIG	441.80000	+		
New Albany, Union County Fairg						
	FM	NA5MS	146.67000	-	131.8 Hz	
NOAA Ackerman	WX	KIH51	162.47500			
NOAA Booneville	WX	KIH53	162.40000			
NOAA Bude	WX	KIH48	162.55000			
NOAA Carthage	WX	KJY83	162.50000			
NOAA Columbia	WX	WXL21	162.40000			
NOAA Gulfport	WX	KIH21	162.40000			
NOAA Hattiesburg						
	WX	KIH47	162.47500			
NOAA Inverness	WX	KIH50	162.55000			
NOAA Jackson	WX	KIH38	162.40000			
NOAA Kosciusko	WX	WWG38	162.42500			
NOAA Leakesville	WX	WNG640	162.42500			
NOAA Meridian	WX	KIH49	162.55000			
NOAA Oxford	WX	KIH52	162.55000			
NOAA Parchman	WX	WWG37	162.50000			
Oak Forrest		K5TLL-L	146.67000			
Ocean Springs	FM	KB5CSQ	444.25000	+	77.0 Hz	SERA
Olive Branch		K5OLV-L	147.25500			
	FUSION	KD5BS	443.70000	+	107.2 Hz	

Location	Mode	Call sign	Output	Input	Access	Coordinator
Olive Branch, Lewisburg Water						
	FM	W5OBM	444.70000	+	107.2 Hz	SERA
Olive Branch, Water Tower Hwy						
	FM	W5OBM	147.25500	+	79.7 Hz	SERA
Oxford	DMR/BM	KC5KLW	145.47000	290.34000	CC1	
	DMR/BM	KC5KLW	145.47000	-	CC1	
	DMR/BM	KC5KLW	444.98750	894.97450	CC1	
	FM	W5LAF	147.33000	+	107.2 Hz	SERA
	FM	W5LAF	444.35000	+	107.2 Hz	SERA
Pascagoula	FM	KC5LCW	443.45000	+	123.0 Hz	SERA
Pelahatchie	FM	W5PPB	145.39000	-	77.0 Hz	SERA
Perkinston	FM	K5GVR	147.16500	+	136.5 Hz	SERA
	FM	K5GVR	442.47500	+	136.5 Hz	SERA
Petal	FM	W5CJR	145.19000	-	136.5 Hz	SERA
	FM	N5YH	443.15000	+	136.5 Hz	
	FUSION	AG5IL	145.20000			
Petal, PHS Football Pressbox						
	FM	N5QXX	444.82500	+	114.8 Hz	
Philadelphia	FM	N5EPP	147.33000	+		SERA
	FM	WB5YGI	444.95000	+		SERA
Picayune	FM	KE5LT	443.72500	+	179.9 Hz	SERA
Pontotoc, Silo	FM	AF5FM	444.50000	+	131.8 Hz	
Poplarville	FM	K5PRC	145.15000	-	136.5 Hz	
	FM	W5PMS	145.21000	-	136.5 Hz	SERA
Poplarville, Hillsdale						
	FM	W5NRU	145.41000	-	136.5 Hz	SERA
Port Gibson	DMR/BM	AF5OQ	146.62500	-	CC3	
Purvis	FM	K5IJX	146.67000	-	136.5 Hz	
Quitman		KF5MWE-L	147.55000			
	FM	KF5MWE-R	147.39000	+		SERA
Raymond	DSTAR	W5DRA	147.38000	+	77.0 Hz	SERA
	FUSION	W5PFR	444.00000	+		
Richton	FUSION	NI5I	441.16250			
Ridgeland	FM	N5WDG	443.70000	+	77.0 Hz	SERA
Robinsonville, Horseshoe Casin						
	FM	W5GWD	443.30000	+	107.2 Hz	
Rolling Fork Estates						
	FM	KC5ULN-R	147.00000	+		
Saltillo	DMR/BM	KI5CMA	444.42500	+	CC1	
	DMR/BM	KI5CMA	444.87500	+	CC1	
	DSTAR	K5LLO B	442.57500	+		
Senatobia	FM	KG5IRU	439.50000		114.8 Hz	
Sharon	FM	W5PPB-R	145.45000	-	77.0 Hz	SERA
Shiloh	FM	KF5SEB	147.04500	+	100.0 Hz	SERA
Slidell, Stennis Space Center						
	FM	N5GJB	147.21000	+	136.5 Hz	SERA
Soso	FM	WV5D	444.27500	+	136.5 Hz	SERA
Southaven	FM	W5GWD	145.35000	-	107.2 Hz	
Starkville	DMR/BM	AD5HM	440.55000	+	CC1	
	FM	K5DY	146.73000	-	210.7 Hz	SERA
	FM	W5YD	146.80500	-		
	FM	K5DY	444.75000	+	136.5 Hz	SERA
Sumner	FM	W5JWW	147.09000	+		SERA
Sumrall	FM	K5PN	443.35000	+	136.5 Hz	SERA
Synagogue	FM	KE5HYT-R	444.90000	+		SERA
Taylorsville	FM	W5NRU	224.48000	-	179.9 Hz	SERA
Tupelo	DMR/BM	AB5OR	145.49000	-	CC1	
	DMR/BM	N5VGK	444.95000	+	CC1	
	DSTAR	KE5LUX	146.64000	-		
	DSTAR	KE5LUX B	444.95000	+		
	FM	N5VGK	145.49000	-	141.3 Hz	
	FM	W5NEM	147.07500	+	103.5 Hz	

Location	Mode	Call sign	Output	Input	Access	Coordinator
Tupelo	FM	N5VGK	444.82500	+	141.3 Hz	
	FUSION	WP3JM	449.95000			
Tupelo, Tupelo Airport						
	FM	K5TUP	147.24000	+	100.0 Hz	
Union	FM	K5SZN	147.24000	+	103.5 Hz	SERA
Vancleave	FM	W5WA	145.11000	-	123.0 Hz	SERA
	FUSION	WV5Q	146.26500	+		
	FM	W5WAF	145.41000	-	100.0 Hz	SERA
Vicksburg	FM	W5WAF	145.41000	-	100.0 Hz	SERA
	FM	K5ZRO	147.27000	+	100.0 Hz	SERA
	FM	K5ZRO	444.85000	+	100.0 Hz	SERA
	FUSION	WB5TGF	146.55000			
Water Valley	DMR/BM	KD5NDU	147.27000	+	CC1	
Waynesboro	DMR/BM	N5IDX	450.00000	+	CC1	
	FM	KG5NUB	147.10500	+	136.5 Hz	SERA
West	FUSION	N5XXM	449.40000	-		
West Point	FM	KD5RZQ	147.18000	+		SERA
	FM	N5WXD	443.45000	+		SERA
Wiggins	FM	N5UDK	145.27000	-	136.5 Hz	SERA
	FM	N5UDK	443.30000	+	167.9 Hz	SERA
Yazoo City	FM	KE5YES	147.22500	+	77.0 Hz	

MISSOURI

Location	Mode	Call sign	Output	Input	Access	Coordinator
Amity	FM	KB0ALL	51.13000	52.83000	146.2 Hz	MRC
	FM	KB0ALL	147.39000	+	146.2 Hz	MRC
	FM	KB0ALL	443.12500	+	146.2 Hz	MRC
Appleton City	FM	K0KRB	146.67000	-		MRC
	FM	WA9QME	146.85000	-	107.2 Hz	MRC
Arcadia	FM	KA0CUU	146.95500	-	100.0 Hz	
Arnold	DMR/BM	KD0BQS	442.45000	+	CC2	MRC
Ash Grove		KE0DJP-L	146.50000			
Ashland	FM	KB0IRV	52.89000	51.19000	127.3 Hz	MRC
	FM	KD0SAF	444.17500	+	107.2 Hz	MRC
Ava	FM	N0RFI	146.62500	-	110.9 Hz	MRC
	FM	K0DCA	442.75000	+		MRC
Barnhart	FM	K0AMC	50.50000	50.40000		
	FM	K0AMC	443.72500	+	192.8 Hz	MRC
Belle	DMR/BM	N0NOE	442.60000	+	CC2	MRC
Bethany	DMR/BM	WB0OKX	443.07500	+	CC7	
Bloomfield, MSHP Tower						
	FM	KM0HP	147.33000	+	100.0 Hz	MRC
Blue Branch		KD0CNC-R	146.92500			
Blue Springs	FM	KB0EPY	146.70000	-	107.2 Hz	
	FM	KB0VBN	147.01500	+	151.4 Hz	MRC
	FM	KB0VBN	444.95000	+	107.2 Hz	MRC
	FUSION	KB0EPY	445.92500			
	FUSION	KU0S	446.00000			
	FUSION	KB0EPY	446.50000			
Bolivar	DMR/BM	K0NXA	145.29000	-	CC5	
	DMR/BM	K0NXA	443.67500	+	CC5	MRC
	FM	K0NXA	147.06000	+	162.2 Hz	MRC
Bonne Terre, Bonne Terre Airpo						
	FM	W0EMM	442.32500	+	151.4 Hz	MRC
Boonville	FM	W0BRC	147.36000	+		MRC
	FM	KA0GFC-R	442.70000	+		MRC
	FM	KA0GFC	444.70000	+	77.0 Hz	MRC
Bourbon	FM	AA0GB	146.98500	-	141.3 Hz	
Branson	DMR/BM	KC0M	147.15000	+	CC5	MRC
	DMR/BM	K0NXA	444.45000	+	CC5	MRC
	FM	KJ6TQ	147.10500	+	136.5 Hz	MRC
	FM	KC0M	147.19500	+	162.2 Hz	MRC
	FM	KJ6TQ	224.10000	-	162.2 Hz	MRC
	FM	KJ6TQ-R	443.55000	+		MRC

Location	Mode	Call sign	Output	Input	Access	Coordinator
Branson, Water Tower - Near Ti						
	P25	K0NXA	146.65500	-	91.5 Hz	MRC
Bridgeton, SSM De Paul Hospita						
	FM	W0KE	146.73000	-	141.3 Hz	MRC
	FM	W0KE	443.45000	+		MRC
Brinktown	FM	N0GYE	146.89500	-		MRC
Brookfield	FM	W0CIT	147.34500	+		MRC
Bunker	FM	KD0IM	147.27000	+	156.7 Hz	
Butler	FM	KD0PVP	147.22500	+	91.5 Hz	MRC
Calm	FM	N0IQM	442.52500	+		MRC
Calwood	FM	KS0B	444.95000	+	127.3 Hz	MRC
Cape Girardeau	FM	KE0UWK	444.45000	+	100.0 Hz	
	FUSION	AD0BY	147.09000	+		
Cape Girardeau, River Radio Tr						
	FM	W0QMF	146.68500	-	100.0 Hz	MRC
	FM	W0RMS	444.20000	+		MRC
Carrollton	FM	N0SAX-R	146.65500	-	94.8 Hz	MRC
Carthage	FM	W0LF	146.88000	-		MRC
	FM	W0LF	442.32500	+	103.5 Hz	MRC
Cedar Rapids	P25	N0ERH	444.60000	+	210.7 Hz	
Centralia	DMR/BM	AA0RC	443.02500	+	CC3	
Cherryville	FM	N0BJM	146.64000	-	110.9 Hz	MRC
Chillicothe	DMR/BM	KB0YAS	444.40000	+	CC7	MRC
	FM	K0MPT	147.22500	+		MRC
	FUSION	K0ION	446.22500			
Clayton	FM	W0SRC	146.94000	-	141.3 Hz	MRC
	FM	W0SRC	442.10000	+	141.3 Hz	MRC
Clever	FM	K0NXA	224.28000	-	162.2 Hz	MRC
	FM	K0NXA	442.42500	+	162.2 Hz	MRC
Cole Camp	DMR/BM	KE0CYW	145.11000	-	CC3	
Columbia	DMR/BM	K0SI	444.42500	+	CC3	MRC
	DSTAR	WX0BC B	442.32500	+		
	FM	WX0BC	146.61000	-	127.3 Hz	MRC
	FM	K0SI	146.76000	-	127.3 Hz	MRC
	FM	WX0BC	442.32500	+		MRC
Columbus Square	FM	W9AIU-R	146.76000	-		MRC
Concordia	FM	KE0PKD	147.10500	+	156.7 Hz	MRC
Conway	DMR/BM	K0NXA	145.47000	-	CC12	MRC
	FM	K0LH	146.70000	-	88.5 Hz	MRC
Crane, Water Tower						
	FM	KB0NHX	927.11250	902.11250	162.2 Hz	MRC
Crystal City, Buck Nob						
	FM	KD0RIS	146.77500	-	100.0 Hz	MRC
Cuba	FM	KD0JOX	147.34500	+	110.9 Hz	MRC
De Soto	FM	K0MGU	442.85000	+		MRC
Deepwater	DMR/BM	KM0HP	443.30000	+	CC4	
Deering Junction	FM	KB0UFL	145.45000	-	100.0 Hz	MRC
Defiance	DMR/BM	N0KQG	146.49000	147.49000	CC2	
Des Peres, West County Mall						
	FM	W0SRC	146.91000	-	141.3 Hz	MRC
Dexter	FM	N0GK	147.00000	-	100.0 Hz	MRC
	FM	N0DAN	443.90000	+	100.0 Hz	MRC
Dexter, Hospital	FM	N0DAN	147.15000	+	100.0 Hz	MRC
Dixon	FM	W0GS	146.79000	-	88.5 Hz	MRC
East Independence						
		KA0YIW-L	146.40000			
Eastvale		K6FN-L	144.65000			
Edgerton	FUSION	WA0QFJ	147.33000	+		
	FUSION	WA0QFJ	444.55000	+		
El Dorado Springs	DMR/BM	KB8VLL	443.88750	+	CC5	
	DMR/MARC	KB8VLL	443.25000	+	CC5	

Location	Mode	Call sign	Output	Input	Access	Coordinator
El Dorado Springs, Cedar Sprin						
	FM	W0BRN	146.67000	-		MRC
Eldon	FM	KC0KWL	53.05000	51.35000	127.3 Hz	MRC
	FM	AA0NC	146.62500	-	131.8 Hz	MRC
	FM	N0QVO	147.27000	+	123.0 Hz	MRC
	FM	N0GYE	224.58000	-		MRC
Eldridge	FM	K0LH	146.70000	-	88.5 Hz	MRC
Eminence	FM	KN0D	145.31000	-	100.0 Hz	MRC
Eolia	FM	KA0EJQ	145.19000	-		MRC
Excelsior Springs	DMR/BM	K0BSJ	145.19000	-	CC4	MRC
	DMR/BM	K0AMJ	443.32500	+	CC4	
	FM	W0MRM	53.29000	51.59000	146.2 Hz	
	FM	K0ESM	147.37500	+	156.7 Hz	MRC
	FM	K0ESM	444.65000	+	156.7 Hz	MRC
Fairport	FM	N0AAP-R	444.35000	+		MRC
Farmington	DMR/BM	KC9SDU	442.52500	+	CC2	
	WX	K0EOR	147.03000	+	100.0 Hz	MRC
Festus, Hwy CC	FM	W0KLX	443.95000	+	71.9 Hz	MRC
Fordland	FM	N0NWS-R	145.49000	-	136.5 Hz	MRC
Fulton	DMR/BM	WB8SQS	442.95000	+	CC1	
	DMR/BM	AC0WZ	444.95000	+	CC1	
	FM	KC0MV	147.31500	+	127.3 Hz	
Gabriels Mills		KC0RDO-R	147.30000			
Gainesville	FM	WB0JJJ	147.39000	+	110.9 Hz	MRC
	FM	WB0JJJ	444.35000	+	110.9 Hz	MRC
Gladstone, Gladstone Water Tan						
	FM	W0MB	145.43000	-		MRC
Granby, MSHP Tower						
	FM	KM0HP	145.39000	-	91.5 Hz	MRC
Grandview	DMR/BM	K0XM	146.47000	147.47000	CC4	
	DMR/BM	K0XM	442.00000	+	CC4	
	DMR/BM	K0XM	927.23750	902.23750	CC1	
Grant City	FM	W0BYU	147.06000	+	94.8 Hz	
Gravois Mills	FM	AA0IY-R	442.92500	+		MRC
Greenville	FM	KD0MRV	145.23000	-	123.0 Hz	MRC
Hamilton	FM	WD0BBR	146.74500	-	141.3 Hz	MRC
Hannibal	FM	W0KEM	146.62500	-	103.5 Hz	MRC
Hannibal, Grape Street Hill						
	FM	W0KEM	146.88000	-	103.5 Hz	MRC
Harrisonville	FM	W0JD	443.70000	+		MRC
Hayti, Pemiscot-Dunklin Co-op						
	FM	KB0UFL	146.98500	-	100.0 Hz	MRC
Hermitage	DMR/BM	AC0HA	146.83500	-	CC3	MRC
Higginsville	FM	KC0HJG	442.95000	+	94.8 Hz	
High Hill	DMR/BM	AD0JA	444.02500	+	CC2	
High Ridge	FM	K0AMC	146.92500	-	192.8 Hz	MRC
	FM	K0AMC	444.55000	+	192.8 Hz	
	FM	K0AMC	444.75000	+	192.8 Hz	MRC
	FM	K0AMC	444.85000	+		MRC
Hillsboro	FM	KB0TLL	147.07500	+	141.3 Hz	MRC
Holden	FM	W0AU	53.55000	51.85000		MRC
	FM	W0AU	224.88000	-		MRC
	FM	KM0HP	444.52500	+	107.2 Hz	
	FUSION	W0AU	442.50000	+		
Holliday	FM	KM0HP	145.29000	-	127.3 Hz	MRC
Holts Summit	FM	KD0SAF	443.80000	+		MRC
	FM	KB4VSP-R	444.87500	+		MRC
Hoover	FM	KA0FKL	442.07500	+	151.4 Hz	MRC
Houston	FM	KB0MPO	147.13500	+	100.0 Hz	MRC
Houston Lake	FUSION	WE0Z	446.50000			
Iconium	DMR/BM	WB0YRG	447.55000	-	CC4	
Imperial	FM	N0DSS	144.93000			

Location	Mode	Call sign	Output	Input	Access	Coordinator
Imperial	FM	N0NSP	147.44500			
	FUSION	N0DSS	144.93000			
	FUSION	KB0TLL	147.10500	+		
Independence	FM	N0OEV	146.68500	-		MRC
	FM	W0SHQ-R	146.73000	-		MRC
Independence, Bank Of America						
	FM	W0TOJ	147.09000	+		MRC
Independence, I-435 And 23rd S						
	FM	K0GQ	442.40000	+	151.4 Hz	MRC
Independence, IFD Station #1						
	FM	K0EJC	145.31000	-		MRC
Jackson	FM	W0QMF	146.61000	-		MRC
Jacksonville	DMR/BM	WB6PQM	442.65000	+	CC1	
Jane, Walmart	FM	K5QBX	147.25500	+	162.2 Hz	ARC
Jefferson City	DMR/BM	KB4VSP	146.86500	-	CC3	MRC
	DMR/BM	KM0HP	443.00000	+	CC3	
	DSTAR	KB4VSP C	146.86500	+		
	FM	K0ETY	147.00000	-	127.3 Hz	MRC
	FM	KB4VSP	443.17500	+	127.3 Hz	MRC
Jefferson City, Capitol						
	FM	K0ETY	442.15000	+	127.3 Hz	MRC
Joplin	DMR/BM	W0IN	444.50000	+	CC5	
	DMR/BM	N0ZSG	444.62500	+	CC1	
	DSTAR	N0ARM C	147.45000	148.45000		
	DSTAR	N0ARM B	444.62500	+		
	FM	N0NWS	145.35000	-	91.5 Hz	MRC
	FM	WB0IYC	147.00000	+		MRC
	FM	W0IN	147.21000	+		MRC
	FM	WB0UPB	443.47500	+		MRC
	FM	N0NWS	444.05000	+	77.0 Hz	MRC
	FM	N0ARM	444.62500	+	91.5 Hz	
Joplin, Mercy Hospital						
	FM	W0IN	145.19000	-	91.5 Hz	MRC
Kansas City	DMR/BM	WA0QFJ	444.05000	+	CC4	
	DMR/BM	WB0YRG	927.01250	902.01250	CC1	MRC
	DMR/BM	WB0YRG	927.11250	902.11250	CC1	MRC
	DMR/BM	WB0YRG	927.48750	902.48750	CC1	
	DMR/MARC	W0WJB	443.45000	+	CC1	
	DMR/MARC	K0USY	444.47500	+	CC1	
	DSTAR	W0CW B	443.40000	+		
	DSTAR	W0CW D	1253.05000			
	DSTAR	W0CW A	1285.05000	-		
	FM	K0HAM	53.13000	51.43000	88.5 Hz	MRC
	FM	K0GXL	53.19000	51.49000		MRC
	FM	W0TE	146.79000	-	107.2 Hz	MRC
	FM	W0WJB	146.97000	-		MRC
	FM	WA0SMG	147.27000	+		MRC
	FM	N0EQW	443.05000	+		MRC
	FM	W0WJB	443.17500	+		
	FM	WV0T	443.35000	+		MRC
	FM	WA0NQA	443.77500	+	110.9 Hz	MRC
	FM	N0NKX	444.12500	+	123.0 Hz	MRC
	FM	W0CW	1285.05000	1265.05000		MRC
	FUSION	N0EIR	145.05000			
	FUSION	N0EIR	147.06000	+		
Kansas City - Booth						
	DMR/BM	WB0YRG	444.97500	+	CC1	MRC
Kansas City - Midtown						
	DMR/BM	WB0YRG	442.55000	+	CC4	
Kansas City - Test Repeater						
	DMR/BM	WB0YRG	442.10000	+	CC4	

Location	Mode	Call sign	Output	Input	Access	Coordinator
Kansas City - The Facility						
	DMR/BM	W0NQX	420.20000	433.20000	CC4	
Kansas City -Trimble						
	DMR/BM	WB0YRG	444.46250	+	CC4	MRC
Kansas City, Booth						
	FM	WB0KIA	224.20000	-		
Kansas City, City Hall						
	FM	W0OEM	443.25000	+	131.8 Hz	MRC
Kansas City, NWS Central Regio						
	FM	WA0QFJ	147.33000	+	151.4 Hz	MRC
Kansas City, Plaza/Midtown						
	FM	N0WW	443.27500	+	151.4 Hz	MRC
Kansas City, Top Of KCMO City						
	FM	K0HAM	146.82000	-	151.4 Hz	MRC
Kansas City, VA Hospital						
	FM	KC0VA	443.50000	+	151.4 Hz	
Kearney	FM	N0TIX	147.04500	+		MRC
	FM	KB0EQV	443.90000	+	127.3 Hz	MRC
Kennet	FM	KC0LAT	147.19500	+		MRC
Kennett	FM	KC0LAT	444.57500	+	107.2 Hz	MRC
Kimberling City	FM	K0EI	147.34500	+	162.2 Hz	MRC
	FM	K0EI	444.30000	+	162.2 Hz	MRC
Kingston	FM	W0BYU	443.37500	+	192.8 Hz	
	FM	KC0GP	444.67500	+	107.2 Hz	MRC
Kingston, 3.5mi West - State R						
	FM	W0BYU	443.37500	+	192.8 Hz	MRC
Kirksville, KTVO Studio Link T						
	FM	W0CBL	145.13000	-		MRC
Kirkwood, Near Kirkwood Train						
	FM	K0ATT	147.15000	+	141.3 Hz	MRC
Lamar	FM	K0KWC	442.97500	+	91.5 Hz	
Landrum		KE0DJP-R	147.33000			
Lathrop	DMR/BM	KC0DMR	442.35000	+	CC1	Kansas RC
Laurie	FM	KA0RFO	146.95500	-	192.8 Hz	MRC
Lawson	FM	KZ0G	443.82500	+	151.4 Hz	MRC
Lebanon	DMR/BM	N0GW	443.50000	+	CC12	
Lee's Summit	FM	K0HAM	147.31500	+		MRC
	FM	K0MRR	444.30000	+	131.8 Hz	MRC
Lee's Summit, Missouri State H						
	FM	KC0SKY	146.70000	-	107.2 Hz	MRC
	FM	KM0HP	444.77500	+	151.4 Hz	MRC
Lees Summit	DMR/BM	K0MGS	443.60000	+	CC4	MRC
	FUSION	W0FH	438.80000			
Liberty	FM	N0ELK	145.11000	-		MRC
	FM	K0KMO	444.20000	+	94.8 Hz	
	FUSION	W0BYU	443.37500	+		
	FUSION	KF0FPF	449.27500	-		
Licking	FM	N0KBC	146.85000	-		MRC
Linn, MSHP Tower						
	FM	KM0HP	145.39000	-	127.3 Hz	MRC
Macomb	FM	N0NWS	146.74500	-	136.5 Hz	MRC
Macon	FM	N0PR	146.80500	-	156.7 Hz	MRC
Madison	FM	N0SYL	146.98500	-	110.9 Hz	MRC
Marceline	FM	KD0ETV	145.35000	-	110.9 Hz	
	FM	KD0ETV	443.15000	+	110.9 Hz	
Marshall	FM	WB0WMM	147.16500	+	127.3 Hz	MRC
	FUSION	AA0KM	146.46000			
	FUSION	AA0KM	446.10000			
Marshall Junction, MSHP Tower						
	FM	KM0HP	442.17500	+	127.3 Hz	MRC
Marshfield	FM	K0NI	146.86500	-	156.7 Hz	MRC
Maryville	DMR/BM	N0GGU	444.47500	+	CC7	MRC

Location	Mode	Call sign	Output	Input	Access	Coordinator
Maryville	FM	W0BYU	146.68500	-		MRC
Mexico, KWWR Backup Tower						
	FM	AA0RC	147.25500	+	127.3 Hz	MRC
	FM	AA0RC	443.42500	+		MRC
Mexico, SSM Audrain						
	FM	AA0RC	444.82500	+	127.3 Hz	MRC
Milan	FM	AC0OK	147.18000	+	103.5 Hz	MRC
Milano	FM	K0GOB	443.55000	+		MRC
Mineral Point	FM	AB0TL	146.83500	-	100.0 Hz	MRC
Moberly	FM	K0MOB	147.09000	+	127.3 Hz	MRC
	FM	K0MOB	443.97500	+		
Monett	FM	W0OAR	146.97000	-	162.2 Hz	MRC
	FM	K0SQS	147.30000	+		MRC
	FM	K0SQS	444.65000	+		MRC
Monroe City	FM	KA0EJQ	146.70000	-		MRC
	FM	KA0EJQ	444.20000	+	141.3 Hz	MRC
Mosby	FM	K0MRR	444.30000	+	131.8 Hz	MRC
Mount Vernon	FUSION	AF0SS	443.60000	+		
	FUSION	K5TUX	446.57500	-		
Mountain Grove	FM	KG0LF	147.28500	+		MRC
N Kansas City	DMR/BM	KF0EKR	444.50000	+	CC1	
Neosho	DMR/BM	KC0NQE	444.52500	+	CC5	
	FM	KC0FDQ	146.80500	-	127.3 Hz	MRC
	FUSION	KB0DXS	434.50000			
Nevada	DMR/BM	W0HL	443.97500	+	CC5	
	FM	W0HL	145.45000	-	91.5 Hz	MRC
	FM	WB0NYD	147.13500	+		
	FM	K0CB	444.00000	+		MRC
	FM	W0HL	444.22500	+	91.5 Hz	MRC
New Madrid	FM	KB0UFL	146.92500	-		MRC
Nixa	FM	N0SAP	147.18000	+		MRC
	FUSION	WZ0T	145.40000			
	FUSION	W0RS	145.79000			
Nixa, Water Tower						
	FM	K0NXA	145.27000	-	162.2 Hz	MRC
Norwood	FM	K0DCA	147.16500	+	162.2 Hz	MRC
O'Fallon	FM	W0ECA	145.49000	-	141.3 Hz	MRC
	FM	KA0EJQ	224.54000	-		MRC
	FM	KA0EJQ	444.20000	+		MRC
	FM	W0ECA	444.47500	+	141.3 Hz	MRC
	FUSION	KC0LKV	145.00000			
O'Fallon, Water Tower						
	FM	WB0HSI	146.67000	-		MRC
Oak Grove	FM	KB0THQ	444.27500	+	123.0 Hz	MRC
Odessa	FUSION	N0YSQ	442.37500			
Odin	FM	KC0ROS	147.09000	+	162.2 Hz	MRC
OFallon	DMR/BM	K0RBR	444.27500	+	CC2	
Olivette, Lindbergh And Olive						
	FM	W0SRC	146.85000	-	141.3 Hz	MRC
	FM	W0SRC	224.52000	-	141.3 Hz	MRC
	FM	W0SRC	443.07500	+		MRC
Ongo	FM	K0DCA	145.15000	-	162.2 Hz	MRC
	FM	K0DCA	443.92500	+		MRC
Osage Beach	DMR/MARC	KB8KGU	442.20000	+	CC1	
	FM	N0QVO	444.50000	+	127.3 Hz	MRC
Osborn	FM	WD0SKY	145.15000	-	107.2 Hz	MRC
	FM	N0SWP	442.67500	+	127.3 Hz	
Owensville		N0NOE-R	144.80500			
		N0NOE-L	444.30000			
	DMR/BM	N0NOE	442.65000	+	CC2	
	FM	N0NOE	146.50000			
Ozark	DMR/BM	K0NXA	146.77500	-	CC5	MRC

Location	Mode	Call sign	Output	Input	Access	Coordinator
Pacific	DSTAR	KD0ZEA	146.45000	147.45000		
	DSTAR	KD0ZEA C	146.45000	147.45000		
	DSTAR	KD0ZEA B	442.30000	+		
Pacific, Nike Missile Base Con						
	FM	WA0FYA	224.94000	-	141.3 Hz	MRC
	FM	KD0ZEA	442.30000	+		MRC
Paris	FM	N0SYL	146.83500	-		MRC
Peculiar	DMR/BM	K0LW	443.87500	+	CC1	
	DMR/BM	WB0YRG	444.02500	+	CC1	MRC
	DSTAR	WB0YRG B	442.97500	+		
	FM	W0MCJ	146.86500	-	186.2 Hz	MRC
	FM	WB0YRG	444.32500	+	151.4 Hz	MRC
Piedmont	FM	K0WCR	147.37500	+	100.0 Hz	MRC
Pineville	FM	WB6ARF	147.05000	+	162.2 Hz	MRC
Platte City	FM	W0USI	444.15000	+	88.5 Hz	MRC
	FUSION	AB0GD	444.55000	+		
	FUSION	KC0YSY	446.70000			
Plattsburg	DMR/BM	KC0QLU	146.89500	-	CC7	
Pleasant Hill	DMR/BM	WB0YRG	146.45000	147.45000	CC4	
	DMR/BM	WB0YRG	443.40000	+	CC4	
PleasantValley	FUSION	N0EWQ	145.56250			
Polk, KRBK-TV Tower						
	FM	N0NWS	147.18000	+	136.5 Hz	MRC
Poplar Bluff	FM	AB0JW	444.92500	+	179.9 Hz	MRC
Poplar Bluff, MSHP Station, No						
	FM	KM0HP	146.91000	-	100.0 Hz	MRC
Poplar Bluff, R-1 School Maint						
	FM	AB0JW	145.35000	-	100.0 Hz	MRC
Potosi	FM	N0WNC	147.19500	+	141.3 Hz	MRC
	FM	N0WNC	444.40000	+	100.0 Hz	MRC
Prescott	FM	N0KBC	146.85000	-	114.8 Hz	MRC
Raymore	DMR/MARC	K0DAN	443.47500	+	CC1	MRC
	FM	WB0YRG	146.86500	-	151.4 Hz	
Raytown	FUSION	N0DPR	146.50000			
Red Oak	FM	N0NHB	145.35000	-	146.2 Hz	MRC
Renick	FM	KM0HP	145.29000	-	127.3 Hz	MRC
Republic	FM	K0NXA	53.27000	51.57000	162.2 Hz	MRC
	FM	K0EAR	146.82000	-	162.2 Hz	MRC
	FM	W6OQS	444.60000	+	77.0 Hz	MRC
Richmond	FM	AC0JR	442.02500	+		MRC
Riverside	DMR/MARC	W0OES	448.45000	-	CC5	
	DMR/MARC	W0OES	448.70000	-	CC4	
Rock Creek		N0DSS-L	144.93000			
Rockport	DMR/BM	WB0OKX	444.77500	+	CC7	
Rolla		WB9KHR-R	443.60000			
	DMR/BM	W0EEE	442.67500	+	CC12	
	DSTAR	W0CMD B	444.00000	+		
	DSTAR	W0EEE B	448.82500	-		
	FM	W0EEE-R	145.45000	-		MRC
	FM	W0GS	147.21000	+	88.5 Hz	MRC
Rolla, Phelps Health Medical O						
	DSTAR	W0CMD	444.00000	+		MRC
Saint Charles	DMR/BM	WB0HSI	444.65000	+	CC2	MRC
Saint Joseph	DMR/BM	WB0OKX	443.42500	+	CC7	
	DMR/BM	WA0HBX	444.92500	+	CC7	MRC
	FM	W0NH/R	146.74500	-	141.3 Hz	
	FM	WA0HBX	443.95000	+	100.0 Hz	
	FUSION	N0RFF	146.50000			
Saint Joseph, KQ2 TV Tower						
	FM	W0NH	146.85000	-	100.0 Hz	MRC
Saint Louis	FUSION	K0QS	433.20000	+		
Saint Peters	FUSION	N0IQM	145.10000			

Location	Mode	Call sign	Output	Input	Access	Coordinator
Saint Peters	FUSION	N0IQM	145.17000			
Salem	FM	WB0NRP	146.65500	-		MRC
	FM	K0GGM	146.97000	-	110.9 Hz	MRC
Scopus, KMHM Tower						
	FM	W0QMF	146.82000	-		MRC
Scott City	FM	WB0TYV	146.94000	-		MRC
Sedalia	FM	WA0SDO	147.03000	-	179.9 Hz	MRC
	FM	WB0LRX	224.44000	-	107.2 Hz	MRC
Settletown		KC0LKV-L	146.21000			
Seymour	FM	K0DCA	145.37000	-		MRC
Seymour, Highway 60 And Route						
	FM	W9IQ	145.19000	-	123.0 Hz	MRC
Shell Knob, Fire Lookout Tower						
	FM	AC0JK	145.21000	-	162.2 Hz	MRC
Sikeston	DMR/MARC	KE0MQF	147.21000	+	CC1	
	FM	KB0ZAW	147.07500	+	100.0 Hz	MRC
Smithville	DMR/BM	WB0YRG	146.64000	-	CC4	
	FM	N0NKX	224.46000	-	151.4 Hz	MRC
Springfield	DMR/BM	K0NXA	146.68500	-	CC5	MRC
	DMR/BM	W0PM	442.37500	+	CC2	
	DMR/BM	K0NXA	443.40000	+	CC5	MRC
	DMR/BM	KG0PE	444.67500	+	CC5	MRC
	DMR/MARC	W0PM	442.37500	+	CC1	
	FM	K0AAJ	145.05000		100.0 Hz	
	FM	KA0FKF	145.43000	-	107.2 Hz	MRC
	FM	K0NXA	147.01500	+	162.2 Hz	MRC
	FM	K0AAJ	440.44000	+	107.2 Hz	
	FM	WX0OEM	443.57500	+	162.2 Hz	MRC
	FM	W0EBE	444.40000	+	162.2 Hz	MRC
	FM	W0YKE	444.72500	+	136.5 Hz	MRC
	FM	K0NXA	927.01250	902.01250	162.2 Hz	MRC
	FUSION	KC0QA	146.91000	-		
	FUSION	N0FB	446.60000			
Springfield / Branson						
	DSTAR	W0OMD C	146.77500	-		
Springfield, Cox South Hospita						
	FM	KC0DBU	145.33000	-	156.7 Hz	MRC
Springfield, Hammons Tower						
	FM	W0EBE	146.91000	-	162.2 Hz	MRC
Springfield, Rayfield Communic						
	FM	W0PM	147.22500	+	162.2 Hz	
Springfield, Troop D MSHP HQ						
	FM	W0EBE	146.64000	-	162.2 Hz	MRC
St Charles	DMR/BM	N0KQG	443.25000	+	CC2	
	DMR/BM	K0RBR	444.27500	+	CC2	
	FUSION	KJ0A	145.37000	-		
St Charles, Water Tower - Lind						
	FM	KO0A	145.33000	-		MRC
St Genevieve	FM	K0QOD	146.62500	-	100.0 Hz	MRC
St Louis	DMR/MARC	K0MDG	443.55000	+	CC2	MRC
	DSTAR	K0MDG C	147.01500	+		
	DSTAR	K0MDG B	442.57500	+		
	DSTAR	K0MDG D	1251.00000			
	DSTAR	K0MDG A	1285.00000	-		
	FM	N0ARS	442.37500	+	141.3 Hz	
	FM	K0MDG	1285.00000	-		MRC
	FUSION	K0ATT	147.15000	+		
	FUSION	N9ES	443.77500	+		
St Peters	FUSION	N0OQL	144.95000			
St. Charles	FUSION	N0SO	434.14000			
St. Joseph	FUSION	KB0LSM	145.56250			
	FUSION	KB0LSM	147.39000	+		

Location	Mode	Call sign	Output	Input	Access	Coordinator
St. Joseph	FUSION	KB0LSM	442.75000	+		
	FUSION	KB0LSM	444.00000	+		
St. Louis	FM	WB0QXW	145.21000	-	123.0 Hz	MRC
	FM	N0FLC	443.15000	+		MRC
	FM	W9AIU	443.32500	+	141.3 Hz	MRC
	FM	WB0QXW	444.15000	+	146.2 Hz	MRC
	FUSION	W0SRC	443.07500	+		
St. Louis, Bates And Virginia						
	FM	KC0TPS	146.61000	-		MRC
St. Louis, Dorchester Apartmen						
	FM	W0SRC	146.97000	-	141.3 Hz	MRC
St. Louis, Forest Park						
	FM	K0KYZ	145.17000	-		
	FM	K0GFM	442.82500	+	127.3 Hz	MRC
St. Louis, I-270 And McDonnell						
	FM	W0MA	147.06000	+	141.3 Hz	MRC
	FM	W0MA	442.87500	+	141.3 Hz	MRC
St. Louis, Mercy Hospital						
	FM	W0SLW	147.39000	+	100.0 Hz	MRC
St. Louis, Pine Street And Tuc						
	FM	N9ES	443.77500	+	141.3 Hz	MRC
St. Louis, Red Cross - Lindber						
	FM	W0MDG	147.36000	+		MRC
	FM	K0GOB	224.98000	-		MRC
	FM	K0MDG	442.57500	+		MRC
	FM	K0GOB	442.70000	+		MRC
	FM	W0MDG	442.97500	+	141.3 Hz	
St. Louis, SLU Hospital						
	FM	WD0EFP	443.47500	+	77.0 Hz	MRC
St. Louis, Tilles Park						
	FM	N0ARS	145.35000	-	123.0 Hz	MRC
St. Paul	FM	N0EEA	224.66000	-		MRC
St.Joseph	FUSION	KB0LSM	146.95000	-		
Stockton Lake	FM	K0NXA	444.97500	+	162.2 Hz	MRC
Stover	FM	KB0QWQ	147.39000	+	127.3 Hz	MRC
	FM	KB0QWQ	444.92500	+	127.3 Hz	MRC
Sullivan	DMR/BM	N0NOE	444.60000	+	CC2	MRC
	FM	K0CSM	145.15000	-		MRC
Sullivan, West Sullivan Water						
	FM	KC0DBS	146.80500	-	110.9 Hz	MRC
Sunrise Beach	FM	N0ZS	146.73000	-	127.3 Hz	MRC
Ten Brook		KE0BKQ-L	144.46000			
Thayer	FM	W0WZR	146.80500	-	110.9 Hz	MRC
Trenton, Courthouse						
	FM	KB0RPJ	146.95500	-	156.7 Hz	MRC
Turney	DMR/BM	N0MIJ	440.00000	+	CC7	
Unionville	FM	KD0IZE	145.11000	-	103.5 Hz	MRC
Van Buren	FM	N0IBV	146.86500	-	100.0 Hz	MRC
Viburnum	FM	KD0KIB	147.30000	+	100.0 Hz	MRC
	FM	KD0KIB	442.05000	+	100.0 Hz	MRC
Walnut Grove	FM	AK0C	147.33000	+	162.2 Hz	MRC
Warrensburg	DMR/MARC	KU0G	442.82500	+	CC1	
	FM	W0AU	146.88000	-	107.2 Hz	MRC
	FM	W0APR	146.94000	-	107.2 Hz	
	FM	W0AU	443.20000	+	107.2 Hz	MRC
Warrenton	DMR/BM	KD0VKG	444.91250	+	CC2	
	FM	KA0CWU	147.04500	+	141.3 Hz	MRC
Warrenton, MSHP Tower West Of						
	FM	WA0EMA	147.33000	+	123.0 Hz	MRC
Warsaw	DMR/MARC	KF0KR	442.77500	+	CC3	
	FM	WB0EM	146.92500	-	107.2 Hz	MRC
	FM	KD0CNC	147.30000	+		MRC

Location	Mode	Call sign	Output	Input	Access	Coordinator
Warsaw, MSHP Tower						
	FM	KM0HP	147.07500	+	127.3 Hz	MRC
Washburn	FM	KE0CZQ	444.85000	+	123.0 Hz	MRC
Washington	DMR/BM	K0FDG	442.62500	+	CC2	
	DMR/BM	KO0OOL	443.90000	+	CC2	
	DMR/BM	K0FDG	444.10000	+	CC2	
	FM	WA0FYA	147.24000	+	141.3 Hz	MRC
	FM	WA0FYA	444.35000	+	141.3 Hz	MRC
Washington, Indian Prairie Sch						
	FM	WA0FYA	147.18000	+	79.7 Hz	
West Lebanon		NR0Q-L	446.00000			
West Plains	FM	KD0AIZ	145.25000	-	110.9 Hz	MRC
	FM	W0HCA	146.94000	-	110.9 Hz	MRC
Willow Springs	DMR/BM	K0NXA	146.67000		CC12	
Windsor	DMR/BM	N0TLE	443.87500	+	CC3	MRC
	FM	K0UG	147.19500	+	107.2 Hz	MRC
Wright City	DMR/BM	AD0JA	443.85000	+	CC2	
	DMR/BM	AD0JA	444.52500	+	CC2	
	P25	AD0JA	146.47000	147.47000	173.8 Hz	MRC

MONTANA

Location	Mode	Call sign	Output	Input	Access	Coordinator
Anaconda	FM	KB7IQN	53.03000	52.03000	131.8 Hz	
	FM	KB7IQO	147.02000	+		
	FM	K0PP	147.08000	+	107.2 Hz	
	FM	KA7NBR	446.80000	-		
Baker	DMR/BM	KJ7QMT	448.00000	-	CC1	
Belgrade	FM	WB7USV	448.85000	-	100.0 Hz	
Big Sky	DMR/BM	KL7JGS	444.70000	-	CC1	
	FM	W7LR	146.82000	-	82.5 Hz	MRCC
Big Timber	FM	NU7Q	146.64000	-	100.0 Hz	MRCC
Bigfork	DMR/BM	NE7AL	444.15000	+	CC1	
	DMR/BM	NE7AL	444.32500	+	CC1	
	FM	KA5LXG	146.62000	-	100.0 Hz	
	FM	KA5LXG	442.07500	+	88.5 Hz	
Billings	DMR/BM	WR7HLN	147.10000	+	CC2	
	DMR/BM	N7YHE	448.65000	-	CC1	
	DSTAR	K7EFA B	449.00000	-		
	DSTAR	K7EFA	449.00000	-		MRCC
	FM	KE7JUX	146.55000			
	FM	WR7MT	147.08000	+		
	FM	N7YHE	147.10000	+	100.0 Hz	MRCC
	FM	K7EFA	147.24000	+		
	FM	K7EFA	147.30000	+	100.0 Hz	
	FM	W7JDX	449.25000	-	100.0 Hz	
	FM	N7VR	449.75000	-		
	FUSION	KE7JUX	145.56250			
	FUSION	KW7EET	443.12500			
	FUSION	W7JDX	446.10000			
	FUSION	KC7AX	447.00000	-		
Billings Central	DMR/BM	KC7NP	449.46250	-	CC1	
Billings East	DMR/BM	KC7NP	448.25000	-	CC1	
Billings West	DMR/BM	KC7NP	448.25000	-	CC1	
Billings, Red Lodge Mountain						
	FM	K7EFA	147.36000	+	100.0 Hz	
Blacktail Mountain	FM	K7LYY	147.18000	+	100.0 Hz	
Boulder	DMR/BM	NW7RG	443.62500	+	CC1	
	DMR/BM	NW7RG	444.85000	+	CC1	
	FUSION	KC7MRQ	441.00000	444.00000		
Boulder, Depot Hill						
	FM	KC7MRQ	146.70000	-	162.2 Hz	MRCC
Boulder-Boulder Hill						
	DMR/BM	WR7HLN	449.20000	-	CC1	

Location	Mode	Call sign	Output	Input	Access	Coordinator
Bozeman	DMR/BM	WA7U	447.95000	-	CC1	
	DMR/BM	KL7JGS	448.35000	-	CC1	
	DMR/BM	KL7JGS	449.50000	-	CC1	
	DMR/BM	KL7JGS	449.90000	-	CC1	
	FM	KD7TQM	145.01000			
	FM	WR7MT	147.18000	+	100.0 Hz	
	FM	KB7KB	448.35000	-	100.0 Hz	
Bozeman, Bridger Bowl						
	FM	W7YB	146.88000	-	100.0 Hz	
Bozeman, MSU	FM	KI7XF	447.70000	-	77.0 Hz	
Butte	DMR/BM	AE7NZ	444.00000	+	CC1	
	FM	W7ROE	146.94000	-	100.0 Hz	
	FM	W7VNE	147.02000	+	107.2 Hz	
Clear Creek Terrace Trailer Co						
		AE7SM-R	447.12500			
Colstrip, Little Wolf Mountain						
	FM	KC7KCF	146.90000	-		
Columbia Falls	DMR/BM	K6KUS	146.90000	-	CC1	
	DMR/BM	K6KUS	444.75000	+	CC1	
	DMR/BM	W7YP	447.50000	-	CC1	
Countryside Village						
	FM	W7GMC-R	147.36000	+		MRCC
Dillon	FM	N7AFS	146.76000	-	107.2 Hz	
Dillon (Badger Pass)						
	DMR/BM	WR7HLN	444.10000	-	CC2	
Dixon	FM	K7KTR	444.55000	+		
East Glacier, Mt Baldy						
	FM	K7HR	146.70000	-	103.5 Hz	
Eldridge (historical)						
		AF7HG-R	146.88000			
		AF7HG-L	446.10000			
Eureka, Pinkham Mountain						
	FM	KC7CUE	147.34000	+	100.0 Hz	
	FM	WR7DW	444.25000	+		
Eureka, Sams Hill	FM	KC7CUE	145.43000	-	100.0 Hz	MRCC
Eureka, Virginia Hill						
	FM	WR7DW	145.39000	-	100.0 Hz	MRCC
	FM	WR7DW	443.80000	+	100.0 Hz	MRCC
Fairfield	FM	W7ECA	147.26000	+	100.0 Hz	MRCC
Forsyth	FM	KC7BOB	147.20000	+	100.0 Hz	MRCC
Glasgow	FM	WX7GGW	146.84000	-	100.0 Hz	
Glendive	FM	W7DXQ	146.76000	-	100.0 Hz	
Great Falls	DMR/BM	K7GDM	146.80000	-	CC2	
	DMR/BM	K7GDM	442.80000	+	CC2	
	FM	AA7GS	146.68000	-	100.0 Hz	
	FM	AA7GS	147.84000		100.0 Hz	
	FM	W7ECA	444.35000	+		
	FUSION	AA7GS	147.84000	-		
	FUSION	N7YO	449.50000	-		
Great Falls (Black Horse Ridge						
	DMR/BM	WR7HLN	449.20000	-	CC2	
Great Falls, 1708 6 St NW						
	FM	AG7AD	145.23000	-	123.0 Hz	
Great Falls, Gore Hill						
	FM	W7ECA	147.30000	+	100.0 Hz	
Great Falls, Highwood Baldy Mo						
	FM	W7ECA	146.74000	-	100.0 Hz	MRCC
Great Falls, Porphyry Peak						
	FM	W7ECA	147.12000	+		
Greycliff	FM	WR7MT	147.28000	+	100.0 Hz	MRCC
Hamilton	DMR/BM	AE7OD	448.30000	-	CC1	
	DMR/BM	AE7OD	449.50000	-	CC1	

Location	Mode	Call sign	Output	Input	Access	Coordinator
Hamilton	DMR/MARC	KG6MQE	422.02500	429.02500	CC11	
	FM	W7FTX	146.72000	-	203.5 Hz	MRCC
Havre	FM	KC7NV	146.91000	-	100.0 Hz	
	FM	W7HAV	444.70000	+	100.0 Hz	
Havre, Havre Air Base						
	FM	W7HAV	146.98000	-	100.0 Hz	
Helen-North Hills	DMR/BM	WR7HLN	448.90000	-	CC1	
Helena (MacDonald Pass)						
	DMR/BM	WR7HLN	147.10000	+	CC1	MRCC
Helena Valley Northeast						
		W7MRI-R	448.90000			
Helena, Hogback Mountain						
	FM	W7MRI	145.45000	-	100.0 Hz	
Helena, Mount Belmont						
	FM	N7RB	147.22000	+	100.0 Hz	
Helena-MacDonald Pass						
	DMR/BM	WR7HLN	444.10000	+	CC1	
Hot Springs	FM	W1KGK	147.12000	+	103.5 Hz	
Jefferson City	DMR/BM	WR7HLN	444.10000	+	CC2	
Kalispell	FM	N7LT	448.45000	-	67.0 Hz	
Kalispell, Blacktail Mtn						
	FM	N7LT	147.36000	+	100.0 Hz	
Kellogg	FM	KB7ARA	147.02000	+	103.5 Hz	IACC
Lakeside, Blacktail Mountain						
	FM	K7LYY	146.76000	-	100.0 Hz	
Lewistown	FM	K7VH	442.00000	+	100.0 Hz	
Lewistown, Judith Peak.						
	FM	K7VH	146.96000	-	100.0 Hz	
Libby	FM	KB7SQE	53.15000	52.15000		
	FM	KB7SQE	444.35000	+		MRCC
	FM	KB7SQE	444.82500	+	100.0 Hz	
Libby, Blue Mountain						
	FM	W3YAK	444.22500	+	88.5 Hz	
Libby, King Mountain						
	FM	K7LBY	146.84000	-	100.0 Hz	MRCC
Libby, Meadow Peak						
	FM	AG7FF	145.31000	-	100.0 Hz	MRCC
Miles City	FM	K7HWK	146.92000	-		
	FM	K7RNS	444.95000	+		
Missoula	DMR/BM	W1KGK	147.12000	+	CC1	
Missoula (University Mountain)						
	DMR/BM	WR7HLN	448.90000	-	CC1	
Missoula, Point Six						
	FM	W7PX	146.90000	-	88.5 Hz	
	FM	W7PX	147.04000	+		
	FM	W7PX	444.80000	+	88.5 Hz	
Missoula, University Mountain						
	FM	NZ7S	147.00000	+		
NOAA Baker	WX	WXK57	162.55000			
NOAA Belgian Hill	WX	WWG84	162.50000			
NOAA Billings	WX	WXL27	162.55000			
NOAA Bozeman	WX	KGG97	162.50000			
NOAA Broadus	WX	WNG567	162.42500			
NOAA Browning	WX	WNG533	162.52500			
NOAA Butte	WX	WXL79	162.55000			
NOAA Circle	WX	KHC26	162.55000			
NOAA Dillon	WX	WNG638	162.47500			
NOAA Forsyth	WX	WNG719	162.52500			
NOAA Glasgow	WX	WXL32	162.40000			
NOAA Glendive	WX	WWF93	162.47500			
NOAA Glentana	WX	KPS507	162.52500			
NOAA Great Falls	WX	WXJ43	162.55000			

Location	Mode	Call sign	Output	Input	Access	Coordinator
NOAA Hardin	WX	WNG724	162.45000			
NOAA Havre	WX	WXL53	162.40000			
NOAA Helena	WX	WXK66	162.40000			
NOAA Jordan	WX	KHB53	162.50000			
NOAA Kalispell	WX	WXL82	162.55000			
NOAA Lewistown	WX	KZZ54	162.50000			
NOAA Livingston	WX	WNG682	162.52500			
NOAA Malta	WX	WWG85	162.47500			
NOAA Miles City	WX	WXL54	162.40000			
NOAA Missoula	WX	WXL25	162.40000			
NOAA Plentywood						
	WX	WWF50	162.47500			
NOAA Poplar	WX	KGG94	162.42500			
NOAA Ryegate	WX	KAD95	162.45000			
NOAA Scobey	WX	WWF92	162.45000			
NOAA Winnett	WX	WNG670	162.40000			
Noxon, Green Mountain						
	FM	KD7OCP	145.33000	-	123.0 Hz	
Olney, Werner Peak						
	FM	WR7DW	444.65000	+	100.0 Hz	
Plains	DMR/BM	W1KGK	146.64000	-	CC1	
	DMR/BM	W1KGK	449.00000	-	CC2	
	DMR/BM	W1KGK	449.12500	-	CC2	
	DSTAR	W1KGK C	146.88000	+		
Polson	FM	W7CMA	145.35000	-	100.0 Hz	
Pompeys Pillar	FM	KF7FW	147.18000	+	123.0 Hz	MRCC
Red Lodge, Grizzly Peak Mtn						
	FM	WB7RIS	147.00000	+	100.0 Hz	MRCC
Red Lodge, Palisades Peak, Rad						
	FM	KE7FEL	449.90000	-		
Rexford	DMR/BM	W7JFO	444.72500	+	CC6	
	FUSION	W7JFO	443.80000	+		
Ronan	FM	KC7MRQ	146.70000	-	162.2 Hz	
Round Butte	FM	K7KTR-R	147.14000	+		
Roundup	FM	KF7ELT	146.72000	-	100.0 Hz	
Roundup, Bull Mountain						
	FM	K7EFA	145.41000	-	100.0 Hz	
Saltese (Lookout Pass)						
	DMR/BM	WR7HLN	444.20000	+	CC2	MRCC
Saltese, Lookout Pass						
	FM	K7HPT	147.02000	+		
Scobey	FM	N0PL	443.50000	+		
Shepherd	FM	KD0CST	146.40000	+	118.8 Hz	
Sidney	FM	W7DXQ	147.38000	+		
	FM	W7DXQ	444.50000	+		
Spion Kop	FM	N7YO-L	146.74000	-	100.0 Hz	
St Ignatius	FM	KD7YAC	145.43000	-		
St. Mary, Hudson Bay Divide						
	FM	K7JAQ	146.82000	-	100.0 Hz	
	FM	K7JAQ	441.20000	+		
Stevensville	DMR/BM	KD7HP	449.42500	-	CC1	
	FM	W7FTX	447.50000	-	203.5 Hz	
	FM	KD7HP	927.75000	902.75000	114.8 Hz	
	FUSION	K7PTL	146.54000			
Superior, Thompson Peek						
	FM	W7PX	146.96000	-	88.5 Hz	
Thompson Falls, Clarks Peak So						
	FM	W1KGK	146.68000	-	100.0 Hz	
Three Forks	FM	KL7JGS	224.72000	-		
	FM	KB7KB	448.35000	-		
Three Forks, Round Spring						
	FM	WR7MT	147.38000	+	100.0 Hz	MRCC

Location	Mode	Call sign	Output	Input	Access	Coordinator
Toston (Lombard Mountain)						
	DMR/BM	WR7HLN	449.30000	-	CC1	MRCC
Victor	FM	N6MGM	440.34000	+	71.9 Hz	
West Glacier, West Entrance To						
	FM	W7YP	447.50000	-		
West Yellowstone	DMR/BM	KL7JGS	449.90000	-	CC1	
Whitefish, Big Mountain						
	FM	KO8N	145.27000	-	100.0 Hz	
Whitefish, Sandy Hill						
	FM	K7LYY	147.38000	+		
Yegen	FM	N7YHE-R	147.20000	+		
Zortman	FM	N7ARA	146.79000	-		
	FM	W7ECA	147.26000	+	100.0 Hz	

NEBRASKA

Location	Mode	Call sign	Output	Input	Access	Coordinator
Ainsworth	FUSION	WM0L	147.36000	+		
Albion	FM	KB0TLX	147.37500	+		
Alliance	FM	N0NEB	146.71500	-	103.5 Hz	
Alma	FM	KA0RCZ	145.20500	-		WB0CMC
Ashland, KUON-TV Tower						
	FM	K0ASH	145.31000	-		WB0CMC
Auburn		KA0FWC-L	445.75000			
Aurora	FM	W0CUO	147.18000	+	123.0 Hz	
Axtell, NTV Studio	FM	KA0RCZ	444.62500	+		WB0CMC
Battle Creek	FUSION	W0TDL	432.55000			
Beatrice	DMR/MARC	KC0MLT	443.17500	+	CC1	
	DMR/MARC	KC0SWG	443.47500	+	CC1	
	FM	KC0MLT	145.34000	-	100.0 Hz	WB0CMC
	FUSION	KC0SWG	145.22000	-	131.8 Hz	WB0CMC
Beatrice, Homestead Monument						
	FM	K0ORU	146.79000	-		WB0CMC
Bellevue	DMR/BM	KB0ZZT	443.65000	+	CC2	WB0CMC
	DMR/MARC	KB0ZZT	442.27500	+	CC1	WB0CMC
	FM	WB0QQK	145.11500	-	179.9 Hz	
	FM	WB0EMU	147.06000	+	131.8 Hz	
	FM	W0WYV	147.39000	+	131.8 Hz	
	FM	WB0QQK	443.35000	+	179.9 Hz	
	FM	W0JJK	443.82500	+	179.9 Hz	
	FM	WB0QQK	444.87500	+	179.9 Hz	
Broken Bow	FM	KR0A	147.06000	+		
Brownville, Indian Cave State						
	FM	K0TIK	444.22500	+		WB0CMC
Burwell	FM	W0EJL	147.09000	+		WB0CMC
Campbell, Mid-Rivers E911 Disp						
	FM	W0WWV	444.47500	+	136.5 Hz	WB0CMC
Cedar Bluffs	DMR/BM	KD0EFC	443.27500	+	CC1	
Chadron	FM	W0FLO	145.62000		100.0 Hz	
Chadron, Nebraska National For						
	FM	W0FLO	147.36000	+	123.0 Hz	WB0CMC
Columbus	DSTAR	WA0COL C	146.95500	-		
	DSTAR	WA0COL	146.95500	-		WB0CMC
	DSTAR	WA0COL B	442.17500	+		
	DSTAR	WA0COL	442.17500	+		
	FM	WA0COL	146.64000	-		
	FM	N0RHM	146.77500	-	131.8 Hz	
	FM	WA0COL	442.05000	+	167.9 Hz	
Edison	FM	KD0AN	146.74500	-		WB0CMC
Elba	FM	W0CUO	147.24000	+	123.0 Hz	
Fairbury	FM	WB0RMO	147.12000	+		
Falls City	DSTAR	KD0TLM C	147.31500	+		
Fremont	DMR/MARC	KC0HYI	444.85000	+	CC1	
	FM	W0UVQ	444.17500	+		

Location	Mode	Call sign	Output	Input	Access	Coordinator
Grand Island	DSTAR	KD0PBV C	146.65500	-		
	FM	W0CUO	53.35000	51.65000		
	FM	W0CUO	146.94000	-	123.0 Hz	
	FM	NI0P	443.95000	+	123.0 Hz	WB0CMC
	FUSION	KD0ENX	147.34500	+		
Grand Island, Heartland Event						
	FM	KD0ENX	444.75000	+		WB0CMC
Grand Island, Nebraska State F						
	FM	W0CUO	145.41500	-	123.0 Hz	WB0CMC
Green Meadows		KB0TDW-R	224.76000			
Gretna	FM	W0MAO	444.90000	+		WB0CMC
Harrisburg	FM	N0NEB	147.00000	-	103.5 Hz	
Hastings	FM	KC0EQA	147.52500			
Hastings, Hastings Dog-Walk Pa						
	FM	W0WWV	443.20000	+	82.5 Hz	WB0CMC
Hastings, KCNT Tower						
	FM	W0WWV	145.13000	-	123.0 Hz	WB0CMC
Heartwell, KGIN TV Tower						
	FM	W0WWV	146.82000	-	123.0 Hz	
Humboldt		KB0DVW-R	147.07500			
	DMR/MARC	NV8Q	443.57500	+	CC1	
Huntington	FM	W2LRC	448.42500	-	114.8 Hz	
Jackson	FUSION	N0DCA	146.79000	-		
Jackson, KFHC Radio Tower						
	FM	N0DCA	146.79000	-	110.9 Hz	WB0CMC
Julian	FM	W0MAO	444.62500	+		
Kearney	DSTAR	KD0PBV C	147.03000	+		
	FM	W0KY	146.62500	-	123.0 Hz	WB0CMC
	FM	KA0RCZ	147.31500	+	123.0 Hz	
	FM	KA0DBK	147.39000	+	123.0 Hz	
	FM	KA0RCZ	444.85000	+	74.4 Hz	WB0CMC
Kearney, County Courthouse						
	DSTAR	KD0PBW	147.03000	+		
Kearney, Kearney Water Tower						
	FM	KC0WZL	147.00000	-	123.0 Hz	
Lexington	FM	N0VL	146.85000	-	123.0 Hz	WB0CMC
Lincoln	DMR/MARC	WB0QQK	442.42500	+	CC1	WB0CMC
	DSTAR	W0MAO C	145.25000	-		
	DSTAR	W0MAO B	442.15000	+		
	FM	N0FER	145.19000	-		
	FM	N0UNL	145.32500	-		
	FM	WB0KBK	146.62500	-	100.0 Hz	
	FM	K0KKV	146.76000	-	100.0 Hz	WB0CMC
	FM	N0FER	147.04500	+		
	FM	K0SIL	147.19500	+		
	FM	N0FER	147.24000	+		
	FM	W0MAO	147.33000	+		WB0CMC
	FM	N0FER	224.98000	-		
	FM	K0KKV	442.70000	+	146.2 Hz	
	FM	N0FER	443.00000	+		
	FM	N0FER	443.50000	+	162.2 Hz	
	FM	W0DMS	444.10000	+		
	FUSION	K0RPT	147.19500	+		
Lincoln, Capitol	DSTAR	W0MAO	145.25000	-		
	DSTAR	W0MAO	442.15000	+		
Loomis	FM	K0PCA	146.89500	-	123.0 Hz	WB0CMC
McCook	FM	K0TAJ	147.27000	+		
	FM	N7UVW	444.50000	+	151.4 Hz	
	FM	N7UVW	444.80000	+	162.2 Hz	
Mitchell	FM	WD0BQM	445.10000	-	100.0 Hz	
Murray	FM	KA0IJY-R	147.21000	+		
	FM	KA0IJY	442.57500	+	100.0 Hz	

Location	Mode	Call sign	Output	Input	Access	Coordinator
Nebraska City	DMR/MARC	WA0RJR	442.80000	+	CC1	
	FM	K0TIK	146.70000	-		
	FM	K0TIK	442.10000	+		
Nehawka	FM	K0LNE-R	146.85000	-		WB0CMC
Neligh	FM	KB0TRU	146.83500	-		WB0CMC
Nelson	FM	W0WWV	147.21000	+	123.0 Hz	WB0CMC
NOAA Albion	WX	WNG645	162.50000			
NOAA Bassett	WX	WXL73	162.47500			
NOAA Beatrice	WX	KZZ69	162.45000			
NOAA Cambridge	WX	KEC39	162.52500			
NOAA Chadron	WX	KXI20	162.52500			
NOAA Columbus	WX	WNG549	162.45000			
NOAA Grand Island						
	WX	WXL74	162.40000			
NOAA Holdrege	WX	WXL75	162.47500			
NOAA Lexington	WX	KGG99	162.42500			
NOAA Lincoln	WX	WXM20	162.47500			
NOAA Merna	WX	WXN72	162.50000			
NOAA Merriman	WX	WXL76	162.40000			
NOAA Mullen	WX	KPS502	162.42500			
NOAA Norfolk	WX	WXL77	162.55000			
NOAA North Platte						
	WX	WXL68	162.55000			
NOAA Omaha	WX	KIH61	162.40000			
NOAA Ord	WX	KWN62	162.52500			
NOAA Oshkosh	WX	KHA55	162.52500			
NOAA Scottsbluff	WX	WXL67	162.47500			
NOAA Shubert	WX	KWN41	162.50000			
NOAA Sidney	WX	WXN61	162.50000			
NOAA Superior	WX	WNG578	162.52500			
NOAA Trenton	WX	WNG524	162.50000			
NOAA Valentine	WX	WXN82	162.45000			
NOAA Yankton	WX	KXI21	162.50000			
Norfolk	FM	W0OFK	146.73000	-	131.8 Hz	
	FUSION	K0FJW	441.15000			
	FUSION	W0OFK	444.25000	+		
North Platte	FM	K0KDC	146.83500	-		
	FM	N0UGO	146.94000	-	123.0 Hz	WB0CMC
	FM	N0IQ	147.33000	+	123.0 Hz	
	FM	N0IQ	444.40000	+	123.0 Hz	
O'Neill	FM	KB0GRP	444.87500	+	146.2 Hz	
Oakhurst	FM	W2GSA	145.04500		67.0 Hz	
Oceanview	DSTAR	NJ2CM B	440.09375	+		
Ogallala	FM	N0UGO	146.76000	-	123.0 Hz	
Omaha	DMR/BM	K0OQL	442.00000	+	CC1	
	DMR/BM	KW1RKY	442.32500	+	CC1	
	DMR/BM	KW1RKY	442.95000	+	CC1	
	DMR/BM	KW1RKY	443.97500	+	CC1	
	DMR/MARC	K0BOY	442.65000	+	CC1	WB0CMC
	DMR/MARC	WB0QQK	442.82500	+	CC1	WB0CMC
	DMR/MARC	KI0PY	444.97500	+	CC1	WB0CMC
	DSTAR	KD0CGR	145.17500	-		
	DSTAR	KD0CGR C	145.17500	-		
	DSTAR	KD0CGR B	442.12500	+		
	DSTAR	KD0CGR	442.12500	+		WB0CMC
	FM	K0BOY	145.45000	-	131.8 Hz	WB0CMC
	FM	WB0CMC	147.00000	+		
	FM	WA0WTL	147.30000	+		WB0CMC
	FM	WB0YLA	224.76000	-	146.2 Hz	WB0CMC
	FM	K0SWI	442.22500	+	136.5 Hz	WB0CMC
	FM	KA0IJY	442.47500	+	100.0 Hz	WB0CMC
	FM	KC0YUR	442.95000	+	146.2 Hz	

Location	Mode	Call sign	Output	Input	Access	Coordinator
Omaha	FM	KB0SMX	443.45000	+	100.0 Hz	
	FM	KF6SWL	443.72500	+	100.0 Hz	
	FM	WB0WXS	444.05000	+		WB0CMC
	FUSION	K0OQL	444.42500	+		
Omaha, CHI Immanuel Hospital						
	FM	N0YMJ	145.37000	-		WB0CMC
Omaha, Douglas County Communic						
	FM	K0BOY	147.36000	+		
Omaha, KETV Tower (Crown Point						
	FM	K0USA	146.94000	-		WB0CMC
Omaha, KPTM	FM	WB0CMC	444.95000	+		
Omaha, KPTM/KXVO TV Tower						
	FM	W0EQU	443.77500	+		WB0CMC
ONeill	DMR/BM	KB0GRP	146.61000	-	CC1	
Papillion	FM	WB0EMU	145.23500	-	131.8 Hz	
	FM	WB0EMU	146.71500	-		
Papillion, Sarpy County Courth						
	FM	WB0EMU	442.72500	+	131.8 Hz	WB0CMC
Papillon	FUSION	KF0FBO	145.14000	-		
Pilger	FM	KG0S	444.12500	+	131.8 Hz	
Ralston	FM	KG0S-R	443.92500	+		
Rushville	FUSION	KB0JWR	446.15000			
Scottsbluff	DMR/BM	N0NEB	444.25000	+	CC1	
	FM	WD0BQM	145.47500	-		
	FM	AG0N	146.44500		88.5 Hz	
	FM	N0NEB	147.07500	+		
	FM	W0KAV	444.82500	+		
Scottsbluff, Stage Hill						
	FM	WB7GR	444.12500	+	114.8 Hz	
Scribner	FM	KE0IBU	147.10500	+		WB0CMC
So. Plainfield	FM	W2LPC	445.27500	-	141.3 Hz	
South Sioux City	FM	K9NHP	147.47000			
	FM	N0DCA	443.75000	+	110.9 Hz	
	FUSION	W0MEG	144.75500	+		
	FUSION	K9NHP	147.47000			
South Sioux City, Law Enforcem						
	FM	W0MEG	145.35500	-		WB0CMC
Spencer	FM	KC0HMN	147.33000	+	131.8 Hz	WB0CMC
St Libory, Microwave Tower						
	FM	NI0P	444.92500	+	100.0 Hz	WB0CMC
Stanton	FUSION	NA0W	146.35000			
Telbasta	FM	KD0EFC-R	146.67000	-		WB0CMC
Trailerville Court	FM	N2VHZ-R	147.01500	+		
Valley	FM	KD0PGV	145.26500	-		WB0CMC
Wahoo	DMR/MARC	KB0ZZT	443.60000	+	CC1	WB0CMC
Wayne	FM	N0ZQR	147.03000	+		
Weeping Water	DMR/MARC	KC0HYI	442.77500	+	CC1	WB0CMC
Wilber	FM	KD0VKC	146.98500	-	100.0 Hz	WB0CMC
Winslow	FM	WB0IEN	147.16500	+		WB0CMC
	FM	KD0PGV	444.37500	+	100.0 Hz	WB0CMC
Wood River	DMR/BM	KE0HZX	444.70000	+	CC1	
	FM	KE0HZX	440.00000	+		
York	FM	WA0HOU	147.27000	+		WB0CMC
	FM	WA0HOU	444.20000	+		
Yorktown Heights	FM	K2HR	146.94000	-	127.3 Hz	
NEVADA						
Amargosa Valley	FM	NV7AV	146.76000	-	123.0 Hz	
Angel Peak	DMR/MARC	N6DOZ	449.80000	-	CC15	
Battle Mountain, Mount Lewis						
	FM	WA6TLW	52.52500	51.52500		CARCON
	FM	WA6TLW	146.79000	-		

Location	Mode	Call sign	Output	Input	Access	Coordinator
Battle Mountain, Mount Lewis						
	FM	W7LKO	443.90000	+		
Battle Mountain, Mt Lewis						
	FM	W7LKO	146.91000	-	100.0 Hz	
	FM	WA6TLW	444.85000	+	94.8 Hz	
Beatty	FM	W7NYE	145.64000		100.0 Hz	
	FM	K6DLP	449.86000	-		
Beatty, Sawtooth Mtn						
	FM	WB6TNP	449.22500	-	141.3 Hz	SNRC
Bijou Park		K6SUV-R	444.17500			
BLK MTN Henderson NV						
	DMR/BM	NX7R	448.62500	-	CC15	
Boulder City	DMR/MARC	WB6TNP	449.05000	-	CC15	
	FM	W6SCE	224.70000	-	100.0 Hz	
Boulder City, Opal Mountain						
	FM	WB6TNP	448.80000	-	141.3 Hz	SNRC
	FM	WB6TNP	927.31250	902.31250		SNRC
Buffalo	FM	N2DOG	146.41500			
Bullhead City	DSTAR	K7RLW	446.22500	-		SNRC
	FM	N7SKO	145.27000	-	131.8 Hz	SNRC
	FM	WR7NV	224.98000	-	100.0 Hz	SNRC
Bullhead City, Spirit Mountain						
	FM	K7GIL	446.37500	-		SNRC
	FM	WR7RED	448.20000	-	156.7 Hz	SNRC
	FM	WB6TNP	448.70000	-	141.3 Hz	SNRC
	FM	N6JFO	449.30000	-	131.8 Hz	SNRC
	FM	KI7D	449.32500	-		SNRC
	FM	WB6TNP	927.88750	902.88750		SNRC
Cannery N.LV NV	DMR/BM	NX7R	445.62500	-	CC15	SNRC
Carlin	FM	W7LKO	146.85000	-	100.0 Hz	
	FM	W7LKO	147.09000	+	100.0 Hz	CARCON
	FM	W7LKO	441.97500	+	186.2 Hz	CARCON
	FUSION	KC7ARS	443.85000	+		
Carson City	DMR/BM	KD7FPK	444.37500	+	CC4	
	DMR/MARC	W7TA	442.05000	+	CC1	
	FM	K5BLS	145.41000	-	156.7 Hz	
	FM	WA7DG	146.82000	-	123.0 Hz	
	FM	K6LNK	443.32500	+		CARCON
	FM	WA6JQV	444.32500	+	127.3 Hz	
	FM	WA6JQV	927.50000	902.50000	127.3 Hz	
	FUSION	N7BUZ	437.95000			
	FUSION	W7DEM	441.25000			
	FUSION	K5BLS	442.12500			
Carson City, McClellan						
	FM	KB7MF	145.24000	-		CARCON
Carson City, McClellan Peak						
	FM	WA6JQV	444.55000	+	127.3 Hz	
Carson City, Nevada DEM Buildi						
	FM	W7DEM	442.90000	+	156.7 Hz	CARCON
Cold Springs, QTH						
	FM	KE7DZZ	448.62500	-	100.0 Hz	
Dayton	DMR/BM	NH7M	443.45000	+	CC1	
Eastland Heights		WR7NV-R	145.35000			
Elko	DMR/BM	KB7SJZ	442.40000	+	CC1	
	DMR/BM	N7NNV	442.62500	+	CC7	
	FM	W7LKO	145.49000	-	100.0 Hz	CARCON
	FM	WB7BTS	146.94000	-	100.0 Hz	
	FM	KE7LKO	147.33000	+	100.0 Hz	
	FM	K9VX	147.39000	+		
	FM	KI6V	440.32500	+		
	FM	W7LKO	442.05000	+	100.0 Hz	
	FM	W7LKO	442.50000	+	186.2 Hz	CARCON

Location	Mode	Call sign	Output	Input	Access	Coordinator
Elko	FM	W7LKO	444.80000	+		CARCON
	FM	W7LKO	444.95000	+	100.0 Hz	
	FM	W7LKO	449.75000	-		
Elko, Adobe	FM	KE7LKO	53.01000	52.01000	100.0 Hz	CARCON
Elko, Adobe Summit						
	FM	W7LKO	444.70000	+		
Elko, Grindstone Mountain						
	FM	W7LKO	53.25000	52.25000	100.0 Hz	CARCON
Elko, Lamoille Summit						
	FM	W7LKO	147.21000	+	100.0 Hz	
Elko, Swales Mountain						
	FM	KE7LKO	29.68000	-	100.0 Hz	CARCON
Ely	DMR/BM	N6FIR	443.40000	+	CC10	
	DMR/BM	N7ELY	444.65000	+	CC1	
	DMR/BM	N7ELY	444.75000	+	CC1	
Ely, Kimberly Mountain						
	FM	N7ELY	147.18000	+	114.8 Hz	CARCON
Ely, Squaw Peak	FM	N7ELY	146.88000	-	114.8 Hz	CARCON
	FM	N7ELY	442.10000	+		
Fallon	FM	K5BLS	147.34500	+		
	FM	K5BLS-R	442.12500	+		CARCON
	FM	K5BLS	442.22500	+	156.7 Hz	CARCON
	FM	WA6KDW	444.37500	+	100.0 Hz	
	FUSION	N7AER	442.22500	+		
Fallon, Fairview Peak						
	FM	KE6QK	145.35000	-	123.0 Hz	CARCON
Fernley	DMR/BM	K7WBY	446.35000	-	CC1	
	DMR/MARC	W7TA	441.95000	+	CC1	CARCON
	FM	W7JA	443.25000	+	192.8 Hz	
	FM	K7UI	443.90000	+	103.5 Hz	
	FM	WA6JQV	444.45000	+		
	FM	WA6TLW	444.75000	+		
	FM	N7TR	444.90000	+	123.0 Hz	
	FM	N7RMK	446.87500	-		
Fernley, Eagle Ridge						
	FM	N7PLQ	147.36000	+	123.0 Hz	
	FM	N7PLQ	443.50000	+	100.0 Hz	
	FM	WA6TLW	444.70000	+	94.8 Hz	
Gardnerville	DMR/BM	KD7FPK	442.15000	+	CC4	CARCON
	DMR/BM	KD7FPK	443.97500	+	CC4	
Genoa	FM	NH7M	443.77500	+		CARCON
	FM	WA6JQV	444.00000	+		
Gerlach	FM	K1C	147.03000	+	100.0 Hz	
Gerlach, Fox Mountain						
	FM	K7UI	441.70000	+	146.2 Hz	
Gerlach, Granite Ridge						
	FM	KD7YIM	145.23000	-	123.0 Hz	CARCON
Glenbrook	FM	N3KD	146.70000	-		
Glendale	FM	W7MVR	146.58000		100.0 Hz	
Glendale, Beacon Hill						
	FM	N7SGV	145.30000	-		SNRC
Goldfield	FM	WB7WTS	223.70000	-		
Goldfield, Montezuma Peak						
	FM	WB7WTS	146.64000	-		CARCON
	FM	WA6TLW	444.85000	+	94.8 Hz	
Goodsprings	FM	WB6TNP-L	449.25000	-		SNRC
Hawthorne	FM	K6LNK	440.72500	+		CARCON
Hawthorne, Corey Peak						
	FM	WA6TLW	146.79000	-		CARCON
	FM	WA6BXP	1284.97500	1264.97500		
Hawthorne, Montgomery Pass						
	FM	KE6VVB	146.67000	-		

Location	Mode	Call sign	Output	Input	Access	Coordinator
Hawthorne, Montgomery Pass						
	FM	KE6VVB	444.20000	+		
Henderson		KF7TBH-L	145.59000			
	DMR/BM	K7IZA	447.80000	-	CC1	
	DMR/BM	N6YFN	447.92500	-	CC1	
	DMR/BM	K7IZA	448.90000	+	CC1	
	FM	KH7R	447.37500	-		SNRC
	FM	KE7OPJ	447.65000	-	123.0 Hz	
	FM	N8HC	447.72500	-	114.8 Hz	
	FM	N6YFN	927.08750	902.08750		
Henderson, Black Mountain						
	FM	NK2V	145.39000	-	100.0 Hz	SNRC
	FM	N7OK	147.09000	+	100.0 Hz	SNRC
	FM	NX7R	1293.62500	1273.62500	114.8 Hz	SNRC
Henderson, CSN Henderson						
	P25	N4NJJ	420.85000	+		
Henderson, Sun City Anthem						
	FM	WA7SCA	445.68000	-	123.0 Hz	SNRC
Henderson, Sun City Anthem, In						
	FM	WA7SCA	145.28000	-	123.0 Hz	SNRC
Incline	FM	K6LNK	441.55000	+	127.3 Hz	CARCON
Incline Village	DMR/MARC	W7TA	443.95000	+	CC1	CARCON
	FM	N7VXB	441.20000	+	100.0 Hz	
Incline Village, Relay Peak, M						
	FM	W7TA	147.15000	+	123.0 Hz	CARCON
Jackpot	FM	W7GK	147.27000	+	100.0 Hz	
Jarbridge, Deer Mountain						
	FM	KA7CVV	147.16000	+		
Lake Tahoe / Truckee						
	DMR/MARC	W7TA	443.92500	+	CC1	
Lancaster	FUSION	KC7ARS	443.67500	+		
Las Vegas		K7DHS-R	441.37500			
	DMR/BM	KB6XN	146.79000	-	CC15	SNRC
	DMR/BM	KB6XN	146.97000	-	CC15	SNRC
	DMR/BM	N5VAE	147.36000	+	CC1	
	DMR/BM	K7STI	441.85000		CC1	
	DMR/BM	K7STI	441.87500		CC1	
	DMR/BM	KB6XN	445.80000	-	CC15	
	DMR/BM	KB6XN	445.82500	-	CC15	
	DMR/BM	KB6XN	445.85000	-	CC15	
	DMR/BM	KB6XN	445.87500	-	CC15	
	DMR/BM	W6OLI	446.03750	-	CC1	
	DMR/BM	N7ARR	446.45000	-	CC1	SNRC
	DMR/BM	N7Y0R	446.62500	-	CC15	
	DMR/BM	N7YOR	446.62500	-	CC15	
	DMR/BM	N5VAE	446.95000	-	CC1	
	DMR/BM	KG7SS	447.35000	-	CC15	
	DMR/BM	K7IZA	447.80000	+	CC1	
	DMR/BM	N6JFO	449.32500	-	CC15	
	DMR/BM	WB6PHE	449.70000	-	CC1	
	DMR/BM	N6JFO	449.80000	-	CC15	
	DMR/BM	KB6XN	449.97500	-	CC15	SNRC
	DMR/BM	KB6XN	927.91250	902.91250	CC15	
	DMR/BM	KB6XN	927.92000	902.92000	CC15	
	DMR/BM	KB6XN	927.93750	902.93750	CC15	
	DMR/MARC	KB6XN	146.73000	-	CC2	
	DMR/MARC	KB6XN	147.43500	146.43500	CC2	
	DMR/MARC	WB6EGR	445.01250	-	CC15	SNRC
	DMR/MARC	KB6XN	445.70000	+	CC2	SNRC
	DMR/MARC	KB6XN	445.72500	-	CC2	
	DMR/MARC	KB6XN	445.75000	-	CC2	
	DMR/MARC	KG7SS	447.27500	-	CC15	

Location	Mode	Call sign	Output	Input	Access	Coordinator
Las Vegas	DMR/MARC	KG7SS	447.30000	-	CC15	
	DMR/MARC	KF6FM	448.27500	-	CC1	
	DMR/MARC	KG6DTL	448.32500	-	CC15	
	DMR/MARC	WB9STH	448.45000	-	CC15	SNRC
	DMR/MARC	WB6TNP	448.92500	-	CC15	
	DMR/MARC	WB9STH	448.97500	-	CC15	
	DSTAR	N7ARR C	145.17500	-		
	DSTAR	N7ARR	145.17500	-		SNRC
	DSTAR	W7AES C	147.97500	-		
	DSTAR	W7AES	147.97500	-		SNRC
	DSTAR	N7ARR	446.80000	-		SNRC
	DSTAR	N7ARR B	446.80000	-		
	DSTAR	W7HEN B	446.97500	-		
	DSTAR	W7AES B	449.57500	-		
	DSTAR	W7AES	449.57500	-		SNRC
	DSTAR	N7ARR D	1251.00000			
	DSTAR	W7AES A	1282.39000	-		
	DSTAR	W7AES	1282.39000	1262.39000		SNRC
	DSTAR	N7ARR A	1293.90000	1271.90000		
	DSTAR	W7AES D	1299.39000			
	FM	KE6DV	145.16000	-		SNRC
	FM	K6JSI	145.25000	-	100.0 Hz	SNRC
	FM	K7OAC	145.72500		151.4 Hz	
	FM	K7OAC	145.79000		100.0 Hz	
	FM	K7OAC	146.41000		100.0 Hz	
	FM	N7ARR	147.00000	-	123.0 Hz	SNRC
	FM	KB7VLX	147.10500	+		SNRC
	FM	K7OAC	147.46000			
	FM	W7EB	223.58000	-		SNRC
	FM	WR7NV	224.98000	-	100.0 Hz	
	FM	NO7BS	429.98750	+		
	FM	N7VGK	433.82500			
	FM	KF7QIB	438.00000			
	FM	K7OAC	445.10000	-	100.0 Hz	
	FM	WB6EGR	445.12500	-		
	FM	N2DOG	445.37500	-		
	FM	W7JCA	445.87500	-	100.0 Hz	SNRC
	FM	WB6MIE	446.12500	-	131.8 Hz	
	FM	W7HEN	446.47500	-	156.7 Hz	
	FM	KG7OKC	446.57500	-	199.5 Hz	SNRC
	FM	N7ARR	446.70000	-	118.8 Hz	SNRC
	FM	WB6MIE	446.87500	-	100.0 Hz	
	FM	N6LXX	447.22500	-	110.9 Hz	
	FM	WB6ORK	447.90000	-	156.7 Hz	SNRC
	FM	K6JSI	447.95000	-	100.0 Hz	SNRC
	FM	KF6QYX	448.05000	-	123.0 Hz	
	FM	KE7KD	448.30000	-	118.8 Hz	SNRC
	FM	NO7BS	448.47500	-	100.0 Hz	SNRC
	FM	N8DBM	448.67500	-	77.0 Hz	SNRC
	FM	N6DD	449.00000	-	131.8 Hz	SNRC
	FM	WA7HXO	449.15000	-	136.5 Hz	
	FM	WB7RAA	449.35000	-		SNRC
	FM	KK7AV	449.47500	-	114.8 Hz	
	FM	WA7GIC	449.52500	-		SNRC
	FM	KE7CCH	449.60000	-	107.2 Hz	SNRC
	FM	WB6TNP	927.03750	902.03750		
	FM	N6JFO	927.66200	902.66200	123.0 Hz	CARCON
	FM	K7RRC	927.71250	902.71250	127.3 Hz	SNRC
	P25	KG7SS	927.05000	902.05000		
	FUSION	N9BAT	145.00000			
	FUSION	KD9Z	146.50000			
	FUSION	K6JET	431.08000			

Location	Mode	Call sign	Output	Input	Access	Coordinator
Las Vegas	FUSION	N7VGK	433.82500			
	FUSION	KJ7NDZ	439.55000			
	FUSION	K6RRS	446.52500			
	FUSION	N6JFO	448.45000	-		
	FUSION	AK7RF	448.82500	-		
Las Vegas, Angel Peak						
	FM	N9CZV	53.19000	52.19000	110.9 Hz	SNRC
	FM	N7ARR	145.37000	-	123.0 Hz	SNRC
	FM	N7SGV	147.30000	+	127.3 Hz	SNRC
	FM	WB6TNP	224.50000	-	131.8 Hz	SNRC
	FM	N7OK	447.47500	-	110.9 Hz	SNRC
	FM	WB6TNP	448.57500	-	141.3 Hz	SNRC
	FM	WR7WHT	449.02500	-	156.7 Hz	SNRC
	FM	KI7D	449.20000	-	114.8 Hz	SNRC
	FM	N7TND	449.50000	-	146.2 Hz	SNRC
	FM	KI7D	449.85000	-		SNRC
	FM	WB6TNP	927.25000	902.25000	114.8 Hz	SNRC
Las Vegas, Angel Pk						
	FM	N7SGV	147.18000	+		SNRC
Las Vegas, Apex	FM	KG7SS	927.05000	902.05000		SNRC
Las Vegas, Apex Mountain						
	FM	KC7TMC	147.06000	+	100.0 Hz	SNRC
	FM	KD5MSS	447.85000	-	127.3 Hz	SNRC
	FM	KC7TMC	449.87500	-	127.3 Hz	SNRC
Las Vegas, Blue Diamond Hill						
	FM	W7HTL	446.20000	-	77.0 Hz	SNRC
	FM	W7HTL	446.22500	-	85.4 Hz	SNRC
	FM	W7HTL	447.97500	-	82.5 Hz	SNRC
Las Vegas, Blue Diamond Mounta						
	FM	N7ARR	447.00000	-	123.0 Hz	SNRC
Las Vegas, CSN Henderson						
	FM	N4NJJ	445.37500	-	107.2 Hz	SNRC
Las Vegas, Fitzgerald Hotel						
	FM	WN9ANF	448.07500	-	127.3 Hz	SNRC
Las Vegas, Frenchman Mountain						
	FM	N3TOY	927.11250	902.11250		SNRC
	FM	N7OK	927.28750	902.28750	151.4 Hz	SNRC
Las Vegas, Hi Potosi Mountain						
	FM	WA7HXO	146.88000	-	100.0 Hz	SNRC
	FM	WA6TLW	447.17500	-		SNRC
	FM	WA7HXO	449.17500	-	136.5 Hz	SNRC
Las Vegas, Lo Potosi Mountain						
	FM	W7EB	224.48000	-	110.9 Hz	SNRC
	FM	WR7BLU	448.52500	-	156.7 Hz	SNRC
	FM	KG6ALU	448.82500	-	146.2 Hz	SNRC
	FM	W7OQF	449.40000	-	136.5 Hz	SNRC
	FM	WB9STH	449.42500	-		SNRC
	FM	WB6TNP	927.03750	902.03750	141.3 Hz	SNRC
	FM	WB9STH	927.42500	902.42500		SNRC
	FM	KB6XN	1290.00000	1270.00000	100.0 Hz	SNRC
Las Vegas, MGM Grand						
	FM	N7RMB	145.30000	-	100.0 Hz	SNRC
Las Vegas, Red Mountain						
	FM	WA7LAT	449.10000	-	136.5 Hz	SNRC
Las Vegas, Southern Hills Hosp						
	FM	K7UGE	448.50000	-	100.0 Hz	SNRC
Las Vegas, Summerlin						
	FM	WB6TNP	927.67500	902.67500	82.5 Hz	SNRC
Las Vegas, Suncoast Casino						
	FM	WB6TNP	449.22500	-	141.3 Hz	SNRC
Las Vegas, Sunrise Hospital						
	FM	KC7DB	147.27000	+		SNRC

Location	Mode	Call sign	Output	Input	Access	Coordinator
Las Vegas, Sunrise Mountain						
	FM	W7AOR	449.72500	-	97.4 Hz	SNRC
	FM	N7OK	927.18750	902.18750	151.4 Hz	SNRC
Las Vegas, Westgate Hotel And						
	P25	K7UGE	146.94000	-	100.0 Hz	SNRC
Laughlin	DMR/MARC	KF6FM	447.52500	-	CC1	
	DMR/MARC	N6DOZ	449.30000	-	CC15	
	FM	K7MPR	146.82000	-	123.0 Hz	SNRC
Lincoln, Highland Peak						
	FM	WA7HXO	145.22000	-	100.0 Hz	SNRC
Logandale	FM	K7YWF	147.58000			
Logandale, Beacon Hill						
	FM	W7MVR	147.39000	+		SNRC
Lovelock	FUSION	N7AER	442.22500	+		
	FUSION	N7AER	444.20000			
Lovelock, Tia's Hill						
	FM	KE7INV	145.31000	-		CARCON
Lovelock, Toulon Peak						
	FM	W7TA	146.92500	-	123.0 Hz	CARCON
McCoy		BH1ULD-L	438.02500			
Mesquite	FM	WA7HXO	448.02000	-	136.5 Hz	SNRC
	FM	N7ARR	449.82500	-	123.0 Hz	SNRC
Middlegate, Fairview Peak						
	FM	NV7CC	444.50000	+	123.0 Hz	
Minden	DMR/BM	KB7DWO	444.10000	+	CC1	
	FM	W7DI	147.27000	+		
	FM	W7DI	443.75000	+	123.0 Hz	
	FUSION	KC7ARS	442.30000	+		
Minden, Leviathan Peak						
	FM	NV7CV	147.33000	+	123.0 Hz	
Mission Hills Hend						
	DMR/BM	NX7R	447.62500	-	CC15	
Mountains Edge LV						
	DMR/BM	NX7R	420.62500	+	CC15	
Mustang Ranch		KE6LRO-L	146.80500			
Needles	FM	N6CRS	147.30000	+	156.7 Hz	
New Washoe City	FM	NH7M	53.00000	103.50000	103.5 Hz	CARCON
	FM	NH7M	145.41000	-	97.4 Hz	CARCON
	FM	NH7M	440.37500	+	97.4 Hz	
New Washoe City, McClellan Pea						
	FM	W7RHC	145.31000	-	110.9 Hz	CARCON
Nixon	FUSION	KC7MSX	445.25000			
NOAA Bullhead City						
	WX	KQC45	162.50000			
NOAA Elko	WX	WXL28	162.55000			
NOAA Ely	WX	WXL69	162.40000			
NOAA Eureka	WX	WWF81	162.55000			
NOAA Fernley	WX	WWG20	162.45000			
NOAA Hawthorne	WX	WWF59	162.47500			
NOAA Jackpot	WX	WNG700	162.50000			
NOAA Las Vegas	WX	WXL36	162.55000			
NOAA Owyhee	WX	WNG731	162.45000			
NOAA Pahrump	WX	WNG634	162.40000			
NOAA Reno	WX	WXK58	162.55000			
NOAA Tonopah	WX	WZ2519	162.40000			
NOAA Winnemucca						
	WX	WXL29	162.40000			
North Las Vegas	DMR/BM	W1PAA	149.77000	-	CC1	
	DMR/BM	W1PAA	444.77000	+	CC1	
	DMR/BM	W7XM	445.30000	+	CC15	
	DMR/BM	W7XM	446.07500	-	CC1	
	DMR/BM	W1PAA	447.77000		CC1	

Location	Mode	Call sign	Output	Input	Access	Coordinator
North Las Vegas	DMR/BM	W1PAA	449.77000	-	CC15	
	FM	KE7ZHN	145.46000	-	100.0 Hz	SNRC
	FM	WH6CYB	146.56000		110.9 Hz	
	FM	WA7CYC	146.67000	-	136.5 Hz	SNRC
	FM	W7NLV	146.90000	-	100.0 Hz	
	FM	WH6CYB	448.77500	-		SNRC
	FUSION	W7DEM	449.55000	-		
North Las Vegas , Nellis AFB						
	FM	KP4UZ	447.77500	-	114.8 Hz	SNRC
North Las Vegas, Apex Mountain						
	FM	W7HEN	449.92500	-	131.8 Hz	
Overton	DMR/BM	AA4Z	445.52500	-	CC15	
Overton, Overton	FM	KG7OUI	447.05000	-	114.8 Hz	SNRC
Pahrump	DMR/BM	KW7MMK	146.64000	-	CC15	
	DMR/BM	N6JFO	445.02500	-	CC15	
	DMR/BM	WB7DRJ	449.27500	-	CC15	
	DMR/MARC	N6DOZ	445.02500	-	CC15	
	DSTAR	KJ7OIR C	147.36000	+		
	DSTAR	KJ7OIR B	446.85000	-		
	DSTAR	KJ7OIR A	1284.50000	1264.50000		
	DSTAR	KJ7OIR D	1299.50000			
	FM	W7NYE-R	145.13000	-		SNRC
	FM	W7NYE	145.49000	-	100.0 Hz	SNRC
	FM	W6NYK	147.03000	+	100.0 Hz	SNRC
	FM	AD7DP	147.12000	+	94.8 Hz	
	FM	ND7M	147.36000	+		
	FM	N7HYV	223.84000	-		SNRC
	FM	KF7DXU	446.32500	-	141.3 Hz	SNRC
	FM	K6JSI	447.40000	-	100.0 Hz	
	FM	WB6TNP	448.72500	-	131.8 Hz	SNRC
	FM	N7HYV	448.85000	-	127.3 Hz	
	FM	N7ARR	449.75000	-	123.0 Hz	SNRC
	FM	WB6AMT	449.85000	-	156.7 Hz	
Pahrump, Desert View Reg Med C						
	FM	W7NYE	447.70000	-	123.0 Hz	
Pequop, Pequop Summit						
	FM	WA6TLW	444.85000	+	94.8 Hz	
Pioche	FUSION	KC7ARS	449.37500	-		
Pronto	FM	WO7I	146.73000	-	88.5 Hz	CARCON
	FM	WO7I	442.82500	+	141.3 Hz	CARCON
Red Mtn Boulder City Nv						
	DMR/BM	NX7R	449.62500	-	CC15	
Reno	DMR/BM	W7NV	443.11250	+	CC4	
	DMR/BM	W7NV	443.86250	+	CC6	
	DMR/BM	WU7ANG	444.40000	+	CC1	
	DMR/MARC	K6JR	444.05000	+	CC1	
	DMR/MARC	W7TA	444.92500	+	CC1	CARCON
	DSTAR	N7NDS B	444.62500	+		
	FM	WA6TLW	52.61000	51.61000		
	FM	KD7DTN	145.15000	-	123.0 Hz	CARCON
	FM	N7PLQ	147.06000	+	123.0 Hz	
	FM	KK7RON	223.92000	-		
	FM	K7IY	224.06000	-	123.0 Hz	
	FM	W7UIZ	224.10000	-		
	FM	WA7RPS	224.42000	-	88.5 Hz	
	FM	KH6UG	440.00000	+	110.9 Hz	
	FM	WA6CBA	440.10000	+	123.0 Hz	
	FM	WA7RPS	440.12500	+		
	FM	KD7DTN	440.72500	+	123.0 Hz	CARCON
	FM	K6LNK	440.75000	+		
	FM	KD7DTN	441.30000	+	114.8 Hz	
	FM	WA6TLW	442.17500	+	127.3 Hz	

Location	Mode	Call sign	Output	Input	Access	Coordinator
Reno	FM	W7NIK	442.55000	+	110.9 Hz	
	FM	N7TGB	443.17500	+	123.0 Hz	
	FM	K7VI	443.60000	+	103.5 Hz	
	FM	K7VI	443.70000	+	103.5 Hz	
	FM	WA7RPS	444.02500	+		CARCON
	FM	KR7EK	444.42500	+		
	FM	KE7KD	444.50000	+	114.8 Hz	
	FM	N7PLQ	444.52500	+	146.2 Hz	
	FM	W7NIK	445.00000	-	123.0 Hz	
	FM	K7PTT	445.50000	-	77.0 Hz	
Reno, Airport	FM	W7NIK	442.37500	+		
Reno, Chimney Peak						
	FM	N7PLQ	146.55000			CARCON
Reno, Grand Sierra Resort Hote						
	FM	W7TA	147.30000	+	123.0 Hz	CARCON
Reno, Lemon Valley						
	FM	KB6TDJ	52.90000	51.90000	107.2 Hz	CARCON
	FM	KB6TDJ	440.20000	+	107.2 Hz	
Reno, Lower Peavine Peak						
	IDAS	NT7Q	442.25000	+	141.3 Hz	CARCON
Reno, McClellen Peak						
	FM	KR7EK	444.25000	+	146.2 Hz	
Reno, Mt. Rose Relay Station						
	FM	AE7I	224.58000	-		CARCON
Reno, Northern Nevada Hosp						
	FM	KE7R	444.35000	+	123.0 Hz	
Reno, Olinghouse	FM	W7NV	51.80000	50.80000	110.9 Hz	CARCON
Reno, Ophir	FM	W7TA	147.39000	+	123.0 Hz	CARCON
Reno, Ophir Hill	FM	W7TA	146.61000	-	123.0 Hz	CARCON
	FM	W7TA	146.67000	-		
	FM	W7TA	147.00000	+		
	FM	N7PLQ	443.05000	+	123.0 Hz	
	FM	W7TA	443.07500	+	123.0 Hz	
Reno, Peavine Lookout						
	FM	W7UIZ	145.39000	-		CARCON
Reno, Peavine Peak						
	FM	W7OFT	146.73000	-	123.0 Hz	
	FM	K7AN	146.76000	-	123.0 Hz	
	FM	W7TA	147.21000	+	100.0 Hz	CARCON
	FM	AE7I	224.54000	-		CARCON
	FM	N7TUA	440.07500	+		
	FM	N7ARR	441.65000	+	123.0 Hz	
	FM	W7TA	444.12500	+	123.0 Hz	CARCON
	FM	N7PLQ	444.80000	+	123.0 Hz	
	FM	N7PLQ	444.97500	+	146.2 Hz	CARCON
Reno, Pond Peak	FM	K7AN	145.45000	-	123.0 Hz	CARCON
	FM	K7AN	444.40000	+	118.8 Hz	
Reno, QTH	FM	W9CI	444.60000	+		
Reno, Red Peak	FM	W7UNR	145.29000	-	123.0 Hz	CARCON
	FM	N7PLQ	440.02500	+	123.0 Hz	
	FM	WA7NHJ	443.12500	+	136.5 Hz	
Reno, RHC	FM	W7RHC	145.21000	-		CARCON
Reno, Slide Mountain						
	FM	N7VXB	146.94000	-	123.0 Hz	
	FM	WA7NHJ	440.15000	+	110.9 Hz	
	FM	W6KCS	442.02500	+	156.7 Hz	
	FM	WA6TLW	444.65000	+	94.8 Hz	
	FM	WA6TLW	905.90000	930.90000		
	FM	W6CYX	1282.00000	1262.00000		
Reno, VA Hosp	FM	KE7R	147.12000	+	123.0 Hz	
Reno, Virginia City						
	FM	W7TA	147.39000	+	100.0 Hz	CARCON

Location	Mode	Call sign	Output	Input	Access	Coordinator
Reno, Virginia Peak						
	FM	WA7WOP	147.18000	+		
	FM	WA6TLW	444.85000	+	94.8 Hz	
Reno, Windy Hill	FM	W7UIZ	145.37000	-		
Schurz, Bald Mountain						
	FM	K7UI	441.90000	+	123.0 Hz	
Shores	FM	KA7CVV	146.70000	-	100.0 Hz	CARCON
	FM	KA7CVV	146.76000	-	100.0 Hz	CARCON
Silver Springs	FM	KE6QK-R	441.87500	441.27500		CARCON
	FM	K7WBY	446.35000	-	156.7 Hz	
So Lake Tahoe	FM	W6SUV	442.82500	+	88.5 Hz	CARCON
South Lake Tahoe						
	FM	K5BLS	442.30000	+	156.7 Hz	CARCON
Spanish Springs	FM	W7TA	147.03000	+	123.0 Hz	CARCON
Sparks	DMR/MARC	NV7RP	440.97500	+	CC15	
	FM	N7KP	52.80000	51.80000	123.0 Hz	CARCON
	FM	KK7RON	146.86500	-		
	FM	N7VN	147.09000	+	127.3 Hz	
	FM	K1SER	147.36000	+	100.0 Hz	
	FM	KK7RON	443.40000	+	103.5 Hz	
	FM	N7KP	443.62500	+	103.5 Hz	
	FM	N7KP	443.80000	+	123.0 Hz	
	FM	KD7DTN	444.22500	+		
	FM	N7PLQ	444.80000	+	123.0 Hz	
	FM	N7KP	927.35000	902.35000	114.8 Hz	
Sparks / Fernley	DMR/MARC	W7TA	442.87500	+	CC1	
Sparks, Liberty Hill						
	FM	N7KP	145.23000	-		CARCON
Spring Valley	FM	WB9STH	447.42500	-	173.8 Hz	SNRC
Sun Valley	FM	KC7STW	440.30000	+	141.3 Hz	
Sun Valley, McCellan Peak						
	FM	KC7STW	145.27000	-	141.3 Hz	CARCON
Tonopah	FM	N7ARR	146.64000	-	123.0 Hz	SNRC
	FM	KB7PPG	147.12000	+	114.8 Hz	
Touplon	FM	K6ALT	445.55000	-		
Tuscarora	FM	KD7CWA	147.30000	+	100.0 Hz	
	FM	W7LKO	444.50000	+	100.0 Hz	
	FM	WA6TLW	444.65000	+	94.8 Hz	
Upper Potosi	DMR/BM	KB6CRE	449.95000	-	CC1	SNRC
Vacaville	FM	W6KCS	927.06250	902.06250	100.0 Hz	CARCON
VC Highlands, Comstock Memoria						
	FM	K7RC	146.86500	-	123.0 Hz	CARCON
	FM	K7RC	441.62500	+	114.8 Hz	
Victory Village		K7RSW-L	448.87500			
Virginia City	DMR/MARC	W7TA	444.82500	+	CC1	CARCON
	FM	WA7UEK	145.47000	-	123.0 Hz	CARCON
Virginia City, McClellan Peak						
	FM	W6JA	145.49000	-	123.0 Hz	
Virginia City, Ophir Hill						
	FM	KC7ARS	444.37500	+	156.7 Hz	CARCON
Walker	FM	N7TR	443.27500	+		
Warm Springs, Warm Springs Sum						
	FM	WB7WTS	146.85000	-		
Washoe Valley	DMR/BM	KM6CQ	440.27500	+	CC1	
	FM	W7RHC	440.55000	+		CCARC
Wellington	FUSION	KD7NHC	440.05000	+		
Wellington, Lobdell Peak						
	FM	KD7NHC	146.88000	-	123.0 Hz	
	FM	KD7NHC	440.05000	+		
Wells	DMR/BM	N6FIR	443.62500	+	CC10	
	FM	W7LKO	146.96000	-	100.0 Hz	
	FM	W7LKO	444.90000	+		

Location	Mode	Call sign	Output	Input	Access	Coordinator
Winnemucca	DSTAR	KJ7OSQ C	147.36000	+		
	DSTAR	KJ7OSQ B	442.82500	+		
	DSTAR	KJ7OSQ A	1285.50000	-		
	FM	W7TA	146.67000	-	123.0 Hz	CARCON
	FUSION	N7AER	444.22500	+		
Yerington	FM	WA6JQV	444.30000	+		
Yerington, Lobdell Summit						
	FM	W7DED	444.87500	+	100.0 Hz	CARCON

NEW HAMPSHIRE

Location	Mode	Call sign	Output	Input	Access	Coordinator
Acworth	DMR/BM	WX1NH	446.42500	-	CC5	
Alton	FM	K1JEK	146.86500	-		
	FM	K1JEK	444.05000	+	88.5 Hz	
Amherst	FM	K1ZQ	224.02000	-	136.5 Hz	
Barrington	WX	K1FDP	147.19500	+	136.5 Hz	NESMC
Bedford	DMR/BM	W3UA	442.75000	+	CC7	
	FM	N1QC	146.68500	-	100.0 Hz	
Belmont	FUSION	K2WBB	146.60000			
	FUSION	N1KWH	434.50000			
Berlin, Cates Hill	FM	W1COS	145.68500	+	100.0 Hz	
Bethlehem	WX	W1COS	147.10500	+	100.0 Hz	NESMC
Bethlehem, Mt Agassiz						
	FM	N1PCE	442.95000	+		
Bow	DMR/MARC	K1OX	145.17000	-	CC8	
	FM	KB1QV	53.15000	52.15000	71.9 Hz	
Bow, Quimby Mountain						
	FM	KA1SU	447.32500	-	88.5 Hz	
Brattleboro, Schofield Mtn						
	FM	WR1VT	146.86500	-	100.0 Hz	NESMC
Brookline	FM	N1IMO	53.41000	52.41000	88.5 Hz	
Campton	DMR/MARC	KC1KAM	145.18000	-	CC6	
Center Barnstead	FM	K1DED	446.47500	-	88.5 Hz	NESMC
Charlestown	FM	NX1DX	146.92500	-	118.8 Hz	
Chester	DMR/MARC	K1OX	145.19000	-	CC9	
	FM	K1OX	224.20000	-		
	FM	N1IMO	224.50000	-	88.5 Hz	
	FM	K1JC	442.55000	+	88.5 Hz	
Chesterfield	FM	KK1CW	223.98000	-	100.0 Hz	
Claremont	DMR/BM	WX1NH	446.32500	-	CC7	
	FM	WX1NH	53.07000	52.07000	97.4 Hz	
	FM	KU1R	147.28500	+	103.5 Hz	
	FM	KU1R	443.95000	+	103.5 Hz	
Clarksville	DMR/MARC	W1COS	145.25000	-	CC0	NESMC
Clarksville, Ben Young Hill						
	FM	KB1IZU	146.71500	-	100.0 Hz	
Colebrook	FM	W1HJF	147.30000	+	110.9 Hz	
Concord	DMR/BM	NE1DS	145.48000	-	CC1	
	DMR/MARC	KB1CFL	145.42000	-	CC7	
Concord NH	FUSION	K1NRO	146.94000	-		
Crotched Mtn	DMR/MARC	WA1ZYX	446.97500	-	CC10	
Deerfield, Saddleback Mountain						
	FM	W1SRA	147.00000	-	100.0 Hz	
Deerfield, WENH Tower						
	FM	WA1ZYX	449.45000	-	123.0 Hz	
Derry	DMR/MARC	K1QVC	145.31000	-	CC1	
	DSTAR	NN1PA B	447.22500	-		
	DSTAR	K1QVC	447.37500	-	85.4 Hz	
	FM	K1LVA	145.71000		100.0 Hz	
	FM	K1CA	146.85000	-	85.4 Hz	
	FM	KC2LT	147.21000	+	107.2 Hz	
	FM	KC2LT	441.30000	+	107.2 Hz	
	FM	W1AJI	441.55000	+	127.3 Hz	

Location	Mode	Call sign	Output	Input	Access	Coordinator
Derry	FM	N1VQQ	447.82500	-	88.5 Hz	
	FM	K1CA	449.62500	-	85.4 Hz	
	FUSION	N1YXE	447.97500	-		
Derry, Warner Hill	DSTAR	NN1PA	447.22500	-		
Dover	DMR/BM	KC1AWV	441.47500	+	CC1	
Dublin, Snow Hill	FM	WQ2H	441.70000	+	100.0 Hz	NESMC
East Derry	FM	NM1D-R	146.74500	-		
East Kingston	DSTAR	KB1TIX C	145.40000	-		
	FM	KC1EWP	441.35000	+	88.5 Hz	
Enfield	DMR/BM	WX1NH	447.07500	-	CC7	
	FM	KA1UAG	444.90000	+	131.8 Hz	
Epsom	FUSION	N1LIB	438.80000			
Epsom, Fort Mountain						
	P25	W1ASS	443.85000	+		
Exeter	FM	K1KN	224.22000	-	67.0 Hz	
Farmington	FUSION	N1EDU	147.24000	+		
Francestown	FM	KA1BBG	147.06000	+	123.0 Hz	
Franconia	DMR/BM	K1EME	145.43000	-	CC1	NESMC
Franklin	DMR/BM	W1JY	145.46000	-	CC1	
Franklin, Veterans Memorial Sk						
	DSTAR	NE1DS	145.48000	-		
	FM	W1JY	147.30000	+	88.5 Hz	NESMC
Gilford	DMR/MARC	K1RE	449.42500	-	CC3	NESMC
	WX	K1RJZ	53.77000	52.77000	71.9 Hz	NESMC
Gilford, Gunstock Mountain						
	DSTAR	W1CNH	447.77500	-		
Gilsum	FM	KA1BBG	147.36000	+	123.0 Hz	
Goffstown	DMR/MARC	NN1PA	145.20000	-	CC10	
	DMR/MARC	KM3T	145.22000	-	CC11	
	DMR/MARC	KM3T	444.30000	+	CC10	NESMC
	DSTAR	NE1DV	446.57500	-		
	DSTAR	NE1DV B	446.57500	-		
	FM	W1ASS	927.71250	902.71250	100.0 Hz	
	FUSION	KX1B	446.52500	-		
Goffstown, Mt Uncanoonic						
	FM	NN1PA	444.20000	+	186.2 Hz	
Gorham, Mount Washington						
	FM	W1NH	146.65500	-	100.0 Hz	NESMC
Greenfield	FM	KA1BBG	448.52500	-	123.0 Hz	
Greenland	DSTAR	KB1UVE B	446.72500	+		
Gunstock Mtn	DMR/MARC	K1RE	145.36000	-	CC3	
	DMR/MARC	K1RJZ	447.87500	-	CC9	
Hampton	DSTAR	K1HBR C	145.44000	-		
	DSTAR	K1HBR B	449.47500	-		
Hampton Beach	DSTAR	K1HBR	145.44000	-		
	DSTAR	K1HBR	449.47500	-		
Hanover	FM	W1FN	443.55000	+	136.5 Hz	
	FM	W1ET	444.95000	+	88.5 Hz	
Hanover, Moose Mountain						
	FM	W1FN	145.33000	-	100.0 Hz	
Henniker, Pats Peak						
	FM	K1BKE	146.89500	-	100.0 Hz	NESMC
Hillsboro	FUSION	N1FDR	146.89500	-		
Hollis	FM	N1IMO	146.73000	-	88.5 Hz	
	FM	N1IMO	443.50000	+	88.5 Hz	
	FM	N1VQQ	444.25000	+	107.2 Hz	
Hooksett	DMR/MARC	K1DED	446.47500	-	CC1	
Hubbard		K1QVC-L	145.19000			
Hudson	DMR/BM	KB1UAP	449.97500	-	CC1	
	DMR/MARC	K1MOT	145.26000	-	CC5	
	DMR/MARC	NE1B	147.10500	+	CC0	
	DMR/MARC	K1MOT	447.72500	-	CC1	

Location	Mode	Call sign	Output	Input	Access	Coordinator
Hudson	FM	N1VQQ	53.97000	52.97000	100.0 Hz	
	FM	KC2LT	448.27500	-	107.2 Hz	
	FUSION	N1SFT	145.51000			
	FUSION	N1SFT	446.87500	-		
Keene	DMR/MARC	WA1ZYX	444.65000	+	CC1	
	FM	WA1ZYX	53.73000	52.73000	141.3 Hz	
	FUSION	K1PH	147.03000	+		
Kensington	DSTAR	KB1TIX	145.40000	144.60000		
	FM	W1WQM	145.15000	-	127.3 Hz	
	FM	W1WQM	444.40000	+	100.0 Hz	
Kensington, Waymouth Hill						
	FM	KB1VTL	443.45000	+	88.5 Hz	
Kezer Seminary		K1PDY-R	146.89500			
Lancaster	DMR/BM	W1FVB	444.40000	+	CC1	
	FM	KC1SR	444.85000	+		NESMC
Lincoln, Cannon Mtn						
	FM	K1EME	224.08000	-	114.8 Hz	
Littleton	FM	K1EME	147.34500	+	114.8 Hz	
	FM	N1PCE	445.95000	-	91.5 Hz	
Londonderry	FM	K1DED	442.00000	+	100.0 Hz	
Loudon	FM	W1FKF	449.32500	-	88.5 Hz	
Madbury	DSTAR	N1HIT C	145.38000	-		
	DSTAR	N1HIT B	448.87500	-		
	DSTAR	N1HIT D	1248.50000			
	DSTAR	N1HIT A	1285.00000	-		
	FM	N1HIT	448.87500	-		NESMC
Manchester	DSTAR	K1COM B	441.80000	+		
	FM	N1SM	147.33000	+	141.3 Hz	
	FUSION	KA1PAT	146.54000			
Mason	FM	K1TLV	443.75000	+		
Milford	FM	K3RQ	146.44500	147.44500	123.0 Hz	
Mont Vernon	FM	WA1HCO	447.12500	-	88.5 Hz	
	FM	K3RQ	448.42500	-	88.5 Hz	
Moose Mountain	DMR/MARC	W1UWS	146.64000	-	CC7	
Moultonborough	FM	N1TZE	145.31000	-	88.5 Hz	
	FM	N1EMS	147.25500	+	156.7 Hz	
Moultonborough, Red Hill						
	FM	W1JY	147.39000	+	123.0 Hz	
Mountain Base	FM	W1AKS-R	147.13500	+		
Mt. Washington	DMR/MARC	W1IMD	448.97500	-	CC2	
	FM	WA1PBJ	448.22500	-	88.5 Hz	NESMC
Nashua	DMR/BM	N1DAS	446.42500	-	CC5	
	DMR/MARC	KB1URC	449.97500	-	CC5	
	FM	WW1Y	147.04500	+	100.0 Hz	
	FM	N1KXT	444.80000	+	131.8 Hz	
	FM	N1IMO	448.82500	-	88.5 Hz	
	FUSION	KC1NPN	144.90000			
	FUSION	N1MJS	147.57000			
New Boston	FUSION	KB1ESM	147.57000			
	FUSION	N1YEI	445.02500			
	FUSION	KB1ESM	445.47500			
New Boston, Chestnut Hill						
	FM	W1VTP	147.37500	+	88.5 Hz	
New Ipswich	FM	N3LEE	443.15000	+	71.9 Hz	
New London	FM	W1VN	145.25000	-	88.5 Hz	
NOAA Clarksville	WX	WNG544	162.40000			
NOAA Concord	WX	WXJ40	162.40000			
NOAA Deerfield	WX	KZZ40	162.45000			
NOAA Hanover	WX	WNG546	162.52500			
NOAA Holderness						
	WX	WNG545	162.55000			

Location	Mode	Call sign	Output	Input	Access	Coordinator
NOAA Mount Washington						
	WX	KZZ47	162.50000			
NOAA Pack Monadnock						
	WX	WNG575	162.52500			
North Conway	DMR/MARC	W1MWV	448.77500	-	CC2	
North Hampton	DMR/MARC	W1IF	449.47500	-	CC1	
Northwood	FM	K1JEK	146.70000	-	88.5 Hz	
Ossipee	FM	W1BST	51.64000	-	131.8 Hz	
	FM	W1BST	147.03000	+	88.5 Hz	
	FM	W1WU	224.60000	-	123.0 Hz	
Pack Monadnock	FM	KA1OKQ	443.35000	+	110.9 Hz	
	FM	W1XOJ	448.00000	-	203.5 Hz	
	FM	N1IMO	449.37500	-	88.5 Hz	
Pelham	DMR/MARC	W1STT	146.50000	145.00000	CC5	
Pembroke	FM	W1ALE	146.94000	-	114.8 Hz	NESMC
	FM	KA1OKQ	147.22500	+	100.0 Hz	
	FM	N1KXT	443.65000	+	131.8 Hz	
Peppermint Corner						
		KB1XI-L	145.71000			
Peterborough	FM	N1IMO	147.19500	+	88.5 Hz	
Peterborough, Temple Mountain						
	FM	WA1ZYX	447.42500	-	141.3 Hz	
Pittsfield		K1JEK-R	147.00000			
	FM	N1IMO	146.79000	-	88.5 Hz	
	FM	N1AKE	224.54000	-	103.5 Hz	
Portsmouth	FM	KB1ZDR	441.95000	+		
Puckershire	FM	WX1NH-L	446.52500	444.92500		
Quint		KB1EZJ-R	145.45000			
Rindge	FM	WA1UNN	146.77500	-	123.0 Hz	NESMC
	FM	WA1HOG	223.92000	-	100.0 Hz	
Rochester	DMR/MARC	K1LTM	145.24000	-	CC3	
Salem	DSTAR	K1HRO C	145.32000	-		
	DSTAR	K1HRO	145.32000	-		
	DSTAR	K1HRO	444.35000	+		NESMC
	DSTAR	K1HRO B	444.35000	+		
	DSTAR	K1HRO	1293.00000	1273.00000		
	FM	NY1Z	147.16500	+	136.5 Hz	
	FM	NY1Z	449.77500	-		
Sanbornton, Steele Hill Resort						
	DSTAR	W1VN	449.67500	-		NESMC
	FM	W1JY	146.67000	-	123.0 Hz	
Seabrook	FM	WA1NH	146.61000	-	141.3 Hz	NESMC
Somersworth	DMR/MARC	W1WNS	145.18000	-	CC5	
Stratford	FM	KC1FZQ	443.95000	+	91.5 Hz	
Sunapee	FM	K1JY	442.35000	+	88.5 Hz	
Surry	FM	KB1HPK	224.98000	-	123.0 Hz	NESMC
Unity	FM	KA1BBG	147.18000	+	123.0 Hz	
Wakefield	DMR/MARC	K1LTM	145.28000	-	CC7	
Walpole	FM	WA1ZYX	443.80000	+	141.3 Hz	
Walpole, WEKW Tower						
	FM	K1PH	147.03000	+		
Wendell		AA1TT-L	223.44000			
		WX1NH-R	224.06000			
West Lebanon	FM	KA1UAG	443.50000	+	131.8 Hz	NESMC
West Ossipee	DMR/MARC	K1LTM	147.07500	+	CC6	
Westmoreland	FM	K1TQY	146.80500	-	100.0 Hz	
Whitefield		W1FVB-L	445.47500			
	DMR/BM	N1PCE	442.30000	+	CC1	
	FM	N1PCE	145.37000	-		NESMC
	FM	N1PCE	449.82500	-	82.5 Hz	NESMC
Windham Depot		K1LVA-R	445.10000			
Yale Estates	FM	W1JY-R	146.98500	-		

Location	Mode	Call sign	Output	Input	Access	Coordinator
NEW JERSEY						
Absecon	FM	N2HQX	147.21000	+	123.0 Hz	ARCC
Allenwood	DMR/BM	W2NJR	448.12500	-	CC1	
	FM	N2MO	145.11000	-	127.3 Hz	MetroCor
Alpine	FM	W2VH	224.98000	-	107.2 Hz	MetroCor
	FM	K2FJ	442.90000	+		MetroCor
	FM	WB2ZZO	444.20000	+	136.5 Hz	
Alpine, Armstrong Tower						
	FM	W2MR	442.70000	+	97.4 Hz	MetroCor
Arrowhead Village		N2QKV-R	224.76000			
Asbury Park	DMR/BM	W2NJR	448.82500	-	CC1	
Atco	FUSION	K2AA	145.29000	-		
	FUSION	K2AA	146.86500	-		
Atlantic City	DMR/MARC	K2ACY	445.23125	-	CC1	ARCC
	FM	AG2NJ	53.39000	52.39000		
	FM	KC2GUM-R	146.44500	147.44500		
	FM	AG2NJ	224.24000	-	100.0 Hz	
	FM	AA2BP	444.35000	+	107.2 Hz	ARCC
Atlantic County	DSTAR	KC2VAC B	442.01250	+		
Avon	FM	KB2MMR	442.15000	+	141.3 Hz	
Barnegat	DMR/MARC	N2MRH	440.90000	+	CC1	
	FM	N2NF	224.28000	-		ARCC
	FM	N2AYM	927.83750	902.83750	162.2 Hz	ARCC
Bayonne	DMR/MARC	AA2QD	446.62500	-	CC1	
	FM	W2ODV	145.43000	-	123.0 Hz	
	FM	W2CTL	446.62500	-	141.3 Hz	
Bayville	FM	N2IXU	448.47500	-	74.4 Hz	
Beach Haven	FM	WA2NEW	448.57500	-	141.3 Hz	ARCC
Beachwood	FM	N2MDX	441.50000	+		
Belle Mead	FM	KD2ARB	442.40000	-	123.0 Hz	
Belle Meade	FM	KB2EAR	224.04000	-	151.4 Hz	
	FM	KB2EAR	927.36250	902.36250	141.3 Hz	
Bergenfield	DSTAR	K9GTM	145.42000	-		
Bloomsbury	FM	N3MSK	449.57500	-	151.4 Hz	ARCC
	FM	N3MSK	449.58000	-	151.4 Hz	
Blue Anchor	FM	KB2AYS	445.12500	-	91.5 Hz	
Boonton	DMR/MARC	N2WH	449.67500	+	CC1	
	DMR/MARC	N2WH	449.77500	-	CC1	
Boonton, Sheep Hill						
	FM	W2TW	147.03000	+	151.4 Hz	MetroCor
Brick	DMR/BM	W2NJR	146.49000	147.49000	CC1	
	DMR/MARC	WB2HHH	442.20000	+	CC1	
	FUSION	N2AJO	146.37500			
Bricktown	FM	K2RFI	146.49000	147.49000	141.3 Hz	
Bridgeton	DSTAR	KC2TXB B	445.31875	-		
	DSTAR	KC2TXB D	1299.80000			
	FM	N2YIR	440.75000	+	131.8 Hz	
	FUSION	KD2DVW	147.59000			
Bridgewater	FM	WA2OCN	444.95000	+	141.3 Hz	ARCC
Brigantine	DMR/MARC	K2ACY	444.65625	+	CC1	
	DSTAR	KC2TGB B	447.52500	-		
	FM	K2ACY-R	447.57500	-	156.7 Hz	ARCC
Brown Mills	DMR/BM	K2JZO	449.02500	-	CC1	ARCC
Browns Mills	FM	WA2JWR-R	146.65500	-		
	FM	K2JZO	224.86000	-	131.8 Hz	ARCC
	FM	K2JZO	449.67500	-	141.3 Hz	ARCC
Brunswick	DSTAR	KS1R B	447.57500	-		
Budd Lake	DMR/BM	K2SRT	441.22500	+	CC1	
	DMR/MARC	K2DMR	440.80000	+	CC1	
	FM	WR2M	223.86000	-	136.5 Hz	
	FM	WS2P	448.67500	-		MetroCor

Location	Mode	Call sign	Output	Input	Access	Coordinator
Camden	FM	N3KZ	145.43000	-	79.7 Hz	
	FM	N2KDV	442.15000	+	156.7 Hz	ARCC
	FM	WB3EHB	444.30000	+	131.8 Hz	ARCC
	FM	N2HQX	448.02500	-	131.8 Hz	ARCC
Cape May	DMR/BM	N2ICV	443.05000	+	CC2	
	FM	KI2Y	147.00000	+	110.9 Hz	
	FM	KC2JPP	449.87500	-	146.2 Hz	ARCC
	FUSION	AD2CM	144.90000			
	FUSION	KI2Y	144.91000			
	FUSION	KI2Y	441.07500			
Cape May Court House						
	FM	W2CMC	147.24000	+	146.2 Hz	ARCC
	FM	W2CMC	442.00000	+	146.2 Hz	
	FM	W2CMC	443.60000	+	146.2 Hz	
	FM	NJ2DS	447.47500	-		ARCC
Cape May Courthouse						
	DMR/MARC	N3JCS	447.76250	-	CC1	
	DSTAR	NJ2DS C	146.77500	-		
	DSTAR	NJ2DS B	447.47500	-		
	DSTAR	NJ2DS A	1255.30000	+		
	DSTAR	NJ2DS D	1297.30000			
Carteret	FM	K2ZV	447.67500	-	136.5 Hz	MetroCor
Cedar Grove	DSTAR	W2DGL C	146.44500	147.44500		
	DSTAR	W2DGL	146.44500	147.44500		
	DSTAR	W2DGL A	1293.05000	1273.05000		
Chatsworth	FM	KC2QVT	145.47000	-	127.3 Hz	ARCC
	FUSION	KC3KLW	145.56250			
Cherry Hill	DMR/BM	KB3MMJ	432.10000		CC1	
	FM	NJ2CH	145.37000	-	91.5 Hz	ARCC
Cherryville	FM	N3MSK	53.25000	52.25000	146.2 Hz	ARCC
	FM	WB2NQV	147.37500	+	151.4 Hz	ARCC
	FM	K2PM	224.60000	-	203.5 Hz	ARCC
	FM	W2CRA	444.85000	+	141.3 Hz	ARCC
Cinnaminson	FM	K2CPD	445.62500	-	127.3 Hz	ARCC
Clark	FM	NJ5R	444.70000	+	88.5 Hz	MetroCor
Cliffside Park	DMR/MARC	N2AZT	447.32500	-	CC13	
	FM	N2OFY	445.77500	-	141.3 Hz	
	FM	KB2OOJ	447.42500	-	127.3 Hz	MetroCor
	FM	WA2YYX	447.57500	-		
Clifton, Bohn Hall MSU						
	FM	KB2N	224.36000	-	141.3 Hz	MetroCor
Collings Lakes	FM	N3YYZ	444.85000	+	91.5 Hz	
Columbia, Hainesburg						
	FM	WB2NMI	146.47500	147.47500	110.9 Hz	
Congers	FM	KB2ULG	147.59500		100.0 Hz	
Corbin City	DMR/MARC	WR3IRS	440.40000	+	CC1	ARCC
	FM	W2FLY	440.75000	+		ARCC
	FM	N3KZ	441.35000	447.35000	131.8 Hz	ARCC
Denville	FM	KD2EKH	449.37500	-	141.3 Hz	ARCC
Denville, St Clares Hospital						
	FM	KC2DEQ	442.05000	+	123.0 Hz	
Dover	FM	N4TCT	224.72000	-	82.5 Hz	ARCC
Eagleswood Township						
	FM	KA2PFL	442.75000	+	131.8 Hz	ARCC
Egg Harbor	FM	K2BR-R	146.74500	-	146.2 Hz	ARCC
Egg Harbor City	FM	W3BXW	53.91000	52.91000	131.8 Hz	ARCC
	FM	W3BXW	146.64000	-	131.8 Hz	ARCC
	FM	AG2NJ	147.16500	+	91.5 Hz	
Egg Harbor Township						
	DMR/BM	WX2Q	449.97500	-	CC2	
	FM	K2BR	448.77500	-	118.8 Hz	ARCC
	FM	KD2KVZ	448.97500	-	123.0 Hz	ARCC

Location	Mode	Call sign	Output	Input	Access	Coordinator
Elizabeth	DMR/BM	KB2OOJ	448.52500	-	CC1	
	DMR/MARC	K2ZZ	449.77500	-	CC3	
	FM	W2JDS	145.41000	-	107.2 Hz	MetroCor
	FM	K2ETS	443.15000	+	141.3 Hz	ARCC
Elizabeth , Trinitas Regional						
	FM	WB2CMN	442.40000	+	141.3 Hz	
Ellisdale	FM	K2NI	224.16000	-	131.8 Hz	MetroCor
	FM	K2NI	447.53000	-	123.0 Hz	MetroCor
Elmer	FUSION	W2SDR	145.61500			
	FUSION	W2SDR	434.10000			
Fair Lawn	DSTAR	W2KBF	145.68000			
	FM	W2NPT	145.47000	-	167.9 Hz	
Fairview	FM	KC2DUX-R	147.12000	+		
Fishing Creek	FM	N2CSA	442.00000	530.50000	88.5 Hz	
Flemington	DMR/BM	NJ2HN	445.51875	-	CC1	
Forked River	DMR/MARC	KA2DMR	446.14500	-	CC1	
Fort Lee	FM	W2MPX-R	145.45000	-		
	FM	W2QAQ	224.24000	-	107.2 Hz	
	FM	K2QW	442.95000	+	141.3 Hz	
Franklin Lakes	FM	W2IP	441.30000	+	114.8 Hz	
Franklinville	FUSION	KD2ANM	145.51000			
	FUSION	K2ZA	440.10625	+		
Freehold	DMR/BM	W2NJR	449.52500	-	CC1	
Frenchtown	FM	K2PM	448.12500	-	151.4 Hz	ARCC
Galloway	DMR/MARC	AG2NJ	446.02500	-	CC1	
	FM	KC2TGB	444.65000	+		
Glassboro	DSTAR	KC2TXX B	440.10625	+		
	DSTAR	KC2TXX D	1299.80000			
Glassboro, Rowan University						
	FM	KD2LNB	440.10625	+		
Glen Gardner	DMR/BM	KD2DMU	446.50000	+	CC1	
	DMR/MARC	WR3IRS	445.53125	-	CC1	
Glen Gardner, Mt Kipp						
	FM	WB2NQV	147.01500	+		
	FM	K2PM	224.12000	-		ARCC
	FM	W2CRA	446.47500	-	141.3 Hz	
Gloucester City	FM	NJ2GC	447.77500	-	146.2 Hz	ARCC
Green Brook	FM	WB2BQW	145.25000	-	100.0 Hz	MetroCor
	FM	N2NSV	444.50000	+	131.8 Hz	MetroCor
Greenbrook	FM	W2FUV	224.24000	-	141.3 Hz	
Greenwich	FM	N3KZ	443.70000	+	131.8 Hz	
Guttenberg	DMR/MARC	N2DXZ	444.83750	+	CC1	
Hackensack	FM	W2AKR	444.10000	+	141.3 Hz	
Hackettstown	FUSION	W2MHL	146.52000			
Hackettstown, Strand Theater/H						
	FM	WW2BSA	448.07500	-	141.3 Hz	ARCC
Haddonfield	FUSION	WB2WEK	448.22500	-		
Haledon	FM	WB2CKD	442.30000	+	141.3 Hz	ARCC
Hamburg, Hamburg Mt						
	FM	N2BEI	446.32500	-	151.4 Hz	
Hampton	FUSION	KB2FUM	145.56250			
Hardyston	FM	W2VER	51.72000	50.72000	136.5 Hz	ARCC
	FM	W2VER	449.08000	-	141.3 Hz	ARCC
Harrington Park, Oradell Reser						
	DSTAR	K2MCI	145.55000			
	FM	K2MCI	439.92500			
Hasbrouck Heights						
	FM	K2OMP	442.50000	+	141.3 Hz	ARCC
Hawthorne	FM	WA2CAI	444.90000	+	114.8 Hz	ARCC
Hillsborough	FM	K2NJ	147.13500	+	151.4 Hz	MetroCor
Hoboken	DMR/BM	WK2M	446.52500	-	CC8	
	FM	K2XDX	223.88000	-	250.3 Hz	

Location	Mode	Call sign	Output	Input	Access	Coordinator
Holland Township	FM	WA2GWA	146.85000	-	151.4 Hz	ARCC
Hopatcong	DMR/MARC	K2DMR	446.77500	-	CC1	
	DMR/MARC	N2VUG	449.45000	-	CC1	
	FM	N2QJN	224.28000	-	88.5 Hz	ARCC
	FM	N2OZO	448.17850	-	141.3 Hz	
Hopatcong Borough						
	FM	K2SRT	446.77500	-		
	FM	N2OZO	448.17500	-		ARCC
Hopewell	DMR/MARC	N2VVL	442.20000	+	CC1	
Howell	DMR/MARC	KB2RF	440.30000	+	CC1	MetroCor
Hudson	P25	KC2GOW	146.88000	-		
Jackson	DMR/BM	W2NJR	440.10000	+	CC1	
	DMR/MARC	K2NYX	443.61250	+	CC6	
	FM	N2RDM	224.30000	-	127.3 Hz	ARCC
Jefferson	DMR/MARC	K2DMR	448.62500	-	CC1	
	FM	WR2M	53.39000	52.39000	146.2 Hz	
	FM	WR2M	440.85000	+	94.8 Hz	MetroCor
	FM	K2WMA	444.95000	+	131.8 Hz	
Jersey City	FM	NY4Z	440.62500	+	74.4 Hz	MetroCor
Jersey City, Christ Hospital						
	FM	N2DCS	441.20000	+		MetroCor
Kearny	FM	N2NSS-R	446.12500	-		MetroCor
Kendall Park		KB2EAR-R	444.91300			
	DMR/BM	KB2EAR	440.76250	+	CC1	
	FM	KB2EAR	444.91250	+	141.3 Hz	
Keyport	FM	KB2SEY	224.96000	-		ARCC
Lake Hopatcong	DMR/MARC	KB2UNV	442.30000	+	CC1	
	DSTAR	NJ2MC C	145.18000	-		
	DSTAR	NJ2MC	145.18000	-		MetroCor
	DSTAR	NJ2MC B	441.60000	+		
	DSTAR	NJ2MC	441.60000	+		MetroCor
	FM	KC2DEQ	51.70000	-	123.0 Hz	
	FM	WR2M	53.39000	52.39000		ARCC
	FM	WA2EPI	224.62000	-	107.2 Hz	MetroCor
Lakehurst	FM	W2DOR	443.35000	+	141.3 Hz	
	FM	W3BXW	447.22500	-	131.8 Hz	ARCC
	FM	NJ2AR	927.32500	902.32500		
Lakewood	FM	W2RAP	146.95500	-	103.5 Hz	
	FM	N2AYM	223.82000	-	162.2 Hz	ARCC
	FM	NE2E	449.37500	-	141.3 Hz	ARCC
	FM	NE2E	449.38000	-	123.0 Hz	
	FM	N2AYM	1295.00000	1275.00000	127.3 Hz	ARCC
Landing	DMR/BM	KE2GKB	438.80000	-	CC1	
Lawrenceville, Ch.52 WNJT TOWE						
	FM	N2RE	146.46000	147.46000	131.8 Hz	ARCC
Leesburg	FM	WT2Y	147.00000	+	110.9 Hz	ARCC
Lindenwold	DSTAR	K2EOC B	440.24375	+		
	DSTAR	K2EOC D	1297.10000			
	FM	K2EOC	440.24375	+		
Little Falls	FM	W2XTV	443.05000	+		MetroCor
Little Falls, Monclair State U						
	FM	WO2X	443.45000	+		ARCC
Little Ferry	FM	W2NIW	441.85000	+	136.5 Hz	
Little Rock	FM	W2GCM-R	441.50000	+		MetroCor
Livingston	FM	NE2S	146.59500	147.59500	100.0 Hz	MetroCor
Mahwah	DMR/BM	KB2SHJ	449.50000	-	CC1	
	P25	KD2IBK	442.22500	+	141.3 Hz	
Manahawkin	DMR/BM	W2NJR	449.47500	-	CC1	
	DMR/MARC	K2HR	445.42500	-	CC3	
	DMR/MARC	WA3BXW	448.07500	-	CC1	ARCC
	FM	N2OO	146.83500	-	127.3 Hz	
Manalapan	DMR/BM	KB2RF	446.10000	-	CC1	

Location	Mode	Call sign	Output	Input	Access	Coordinator
Manasquan	FM	N2IXU	445.67500	-	94.8 Hz	
Manchester, Manchester Water T						
	FM	WA2RES	145.17000	-	131.8 Hz	ARCC
Mantua	FM	W2FHO	449.97500	-	131.8 Hz	ARCC
Margate	FM	KD2FVV	147.44000		91.5 Hz	
Martinsville	DMR/BM	W2NJR	147.28500	+	CC1	
	DMR/MARC	K1DO	447.07500	-	CC1	MetroCor
	DSTAR	NJ2DG	145.14000	-		
	DSTAR	NJ2DG C	145.14000	-		
	DSTAR	NJ2DG B	441.65000	+		
	DSTAR	NJ2DG	441.65000	+		MetroCor
	DSTAR	NJ2DG	1250.50000			
	DSTAR	NJ2DG D	1250.50000			
	DSTAR	NJ2DG	1284.00000	1264.00000		MetroCor
	DSTAR	NJ2DG A	1284.00000	-		
	FM	N2ZAV	224.64000	-	151.4 Hz	MetroCor
	FM	WX3K	224.88000	-	103.5 Hz	MetroCor
	FM	N3MSK	445.72500	-	136.5 Hz	
	FM	WA2OCN	448.18000	-	141.3 Hz	MetroCor
	FUSION	NJ2DG	441.40000	+		
Medford	FM	K2AA	145.29000	-	91.5 Hz	ARCC
Middletown	FM	AA2OW	145.48500	-	151.4 Hz	ARCC
	FM	N2DR	448.72500	-	151.4 Hz	MetroCor
Milltown	DMR/MARC	N2SRT	449.27500	-	CC0	
	FM	KC2OMU	146.40000			
	FUSION	KC2OMU	144.35000			
Millville	FM	W2SCR	449.62500	-	123.0 Hz	ARCC
Minotola	FM	KE2CK	146.80500	-	118.8 Hz	ARCC
	FM	KE2CK	448.92500	-	192.8 Hz	
Monroe Township	FM	KA2CAF	53.71000	52.71000		
	FM	K2DX	145.39000	-	91.5 Hz	
Monroe Township, Englishtown S						
	FM	KA2CAF	224.50000	-	131.8 Hz	
Montague	FM	N2KMB	144.62000	+	192.8 Hz	
	FM	N2KMB	147.90000	-	131.8 Hz	
	FM	N2KMB	147.91250	-	192.8 Hz	
	FM	K2KMB	441.00000	+	131.8 Hz	
	FM	N2KMB	441.35000	+	192.8 Hz	
	FM	K2KMB	447.90000	-	131.8 Hz	
Montana	FM	W2SJT-R	146.82000	-		ARCC
Montana Mt	DMR/MARC	WB3EHB	444.29375	+	CC1	
Montvale	FM	K2ZD	446.97500	-	141.3 Hz	MetroCor
Morristown	FM	WS2Q-R	145.37000	-		
	FM	WS2Q	224.94000	-	107.2 Hz	
	FM	WS2Q	443.25000	+	141.3 Hz	
Mount Arlington	FM	WB2SLJ	224.72000	-	141.3 Hz	ARCC
Mount Laurel	DSTAR	KC2QVT B	445.33125	-		
	DSTAR	KC2QVT D	1299.00000			
Mount Laurel, BCC						
	DSTAR	KC2QVT	445.33125	-		
Mountain View	DMR/MARC	N2WH	439.78750	-	CC1	
Murray Hill	DMR/BM	W2NJR	147.25500	+	CC1	
	DMR/BM	W2NJR	449.97500	-	CC1	
	FM	W2LI	147.25500	+	141.3 Hz	MetroCor
	FM	W2LI	449.97500	-	141.3 Hz	MetroCor
Mystic Island	FM	KA2PFL	449.47500	-	131.8 Hz	ARCC
New Brunswick	FM	NE2E	440.45000	+	123.0 Hz	
Newark	DMR/BM	W2RLA	440.25000	+	CC2	
	DMR/MARC	N2DMJ	145.12000	-	CC1	
	DMR/MARC	N2DMJ	443.09000	+	CC1	
	FM	KD2HQY	145.12000	-	91.5 Hz	
	FM	K2MFF-R	147.22500	+		MetroCor

Location	Mode	Call sign	Output	Input	Access	Coordinator
Newark	FM	WB2MFC	147.28500	+		MetroCor
	FM	W2KB	224.28000	-	123.0 Hz	
	FM	N2BEI	446.90000	-	141.3 Hz	MetroCor
Newton	FM	W2LV	147.21000	+	151.4 Hz	
	FM	W2LV	147.30000	+	151.4 Hz	
	FM	W2LV	147.33000	+	151.4 Hz	
	FM	W2LV	443.00000	+	103.5 Hz	
Newton, Kittatiny Mountain						
	FM	W2LV	224.50000	-	141.3 Hz	
NOAA Hardyston	WX	KZZ31	162.50000			
NOAA Southard	WX	WXM60	162.45000			
North Caldwell	FM	W2JT	147.18000	+	156.7 Hz	
North Stelton		KB2YMD-L	147.55000			
Northfield	DMR/BM	KC2VAC	445.16875	-	CC1	
Nutley	FM	N2SMI	441.75000	+		
	FM	W2FOY	446.33000	-	151.4 Hz	
Oak Island Junction						
		K2CDP-R	145.64500			
		K2CDP-L	145.69500			
	FM	W2RLA-R	145.35000	-		MetroCor
Oakhurst	FUSION	N2MO/R	145.11000	-		
	FUSION	KG2CM	446.02500			
Oakland	DMR/MARC	N2JTI	446.16250	-	CC1	
Ocean	FUSION	K2CYS	144.42000			
Ocean City	FM	W3PS	147.28500	+	91.5 Hz	
	FM	WA3UNG	448.62500	-	131.8 Hz	ARCC
Ocean County	DMR/BM	W2NJR	440.00000	-	CC1	
	DMR/BM	AC2DW	440.90000	+	CC1	
Ocean Township	FM	WW2ARC	443.00000	+	127.3 Hz	
Ocean View	DSTAR	NJ2CM	440.09375	+		
Oceanview	DSTAR	NJ2CM B	440.09375	+		
	DSTAR	NJ2CM D	1299.30000			
Old Bridge	FM	WB2HKK	444.05000	+	141.3 Hz	
Paramus	DMR/MARC	KM4WUD	444.15000	+	CC0	MetroCor
	FM	W2AKR	146.79000	-	141.3 Hz	MetroCor
	FM	KA2MRK	441.95000	+	114.8 Hz	
	IDAS	KM4WUD	448.88750	-		MetroCor
Paramus, Bergen Toll Plaza						
	FM	WB2MAZ	53.49000	52.49000	136.5 Hz	
Parin	FM	W2CJA	53.67000	52.67000		MetroCor
Parlin	FM	W2CJA	147.12000	+		MetroCor
	FM	W2CJA	446.17500	-	114.8 Hz	MetroCor
Parsippany	FM	WB2JTE	440.10000	+	141.3 Hz	
Pennsville	FM	N2YIR	449.12500	-	131.8 Hz	
Perth Amboy	DMR/MARC	K2JZD	440.75000	+	CC9	
Philadelphia	FM	N3OOU	445.97500	-	91.5 Hz	
Phillipsburg	FUSION	KA2ING	445.44000	+		
Phillipsburg, St. Luke's Hospi						
	FM	W2MCC	447.92500	-		
Pilesgrove	FM	N2SRQ	445.03125	-		
Pine Hill	FM	K2UK	146.86500	-	131.8 Hz	ARCC
	FM	K2UK	442.35000	+	131.8 Hz	ARCC
Pitman	FM	W2MMD	147.18000	+	131.8 Hz	ARCC
	FM	W2MMD	442.10000	+	131.8 Hz	ARCC
	FM	W2MMD	1284.40000	1264.40000		ARCC
Port Murray	FUSION	W4MII	144.50000			
Portable	DMR/MARC	W2ITG	446.56250	-	CC1	
Pottersville	FUSION	KD2VXO	145.55000			
Powell Park		N2FVB-L	146.58500			
Princeton	FM	KD2ARB	223.40000	-	100.0 Hz	
	FM	N3KZ	442.85000	+	131.8 Hz	ARCC
Quinton	FM	N2KEJ	53.71000	52.71000	74.4 Hz	ARCC

Location	Mode	Call sign	Output	Input	Access	Coordinator
Riverdale	DMR/BM	KM2C	441.75000	+	CC1	
Rockaway	DSTAR	WK3SS B	446.62500	-		
Roselle, Firehouse						
	FM	N2PSU	445.92500	-	141.3 Hz	ARCC
Rosenhayn	FM	KC2TXB	147.25500	+	179.9 Hz	
	FM	KC2TXB	445.31875	-		
	FM	KE2CK	448.12500	-	192.8 Hz	ARCC
Roxbury	DMR/MARC	N2VUG	448.92500	-	CC1	
Roxbury, Mooney Mountain Meado						
	FM	N2XP	146.98500	-	131.8 Hz	
Saddle Brook	FM	WB2IZC	224.42000	-	88.5 Hz	MetroCor
Salem	FM	N2KEJ	224.46000	-	74.4 Hz	ARCC
Sayervlle	FM	K2MID	440.80000	+	141.3 Hz	
Sayreville	FM	K2GE	145.05000			
	FM	K2GE	146.76000	-	156.7 Hz	
	FM	K2MID	224.56000	-	141.3 Hz	
	FM	K2GE	443.20000	+	141.3 Hz	
Secaucus, Impreveduto Towers						
	FM	KC2IES	441.55000	+	88.5 Hz	
Sewell	FUSION	N2JXG	445.52500			
Shongum	FM	WS2Q	146.89500	-	151.4 Hz	MetroCor
South Amboy	DMR/BM	WB2FYF	440.25000	+	CC1	
South Brunswick	FM	KA2RLM	443.40000	+	141.3 Hz	
	FM	KC2CWP	449.28000	-	151.4 Hz	
South Plainfield	FM	W2LPC	445.27500	-	141.3 Hz	
South Plainfield, Police Stati						
	FM	NJ2SP	146.97000	-	97.4 Hz	
South River		KA2OON-R	927.11200			
	DMR/BM	KA2OON	449.42500	-	CC1	
	FM	NE2E	224.78000	-	123.0 Hz	
	FM	NE2E	444.25000	+	123.0 Hz	
	FM	NE2E	1291.20000	1271.20000		
Sparta	DSTAR	KC2QZE C	145.60000			
	FUSION	N2DRB	434.20000			
Springfield	DMR/BM	W2FCC	146.68500	-	CC1	
	DMR/BM	W2NJR	449.42500	-	CC1	
	FM	WA2BAT	147.50500	146.50500	123.0 Hz	MetroCor
	FM	W2FCC	224.14000	-	123.0 Hz	
Succasunna	FM	N2XP	447.77500	-	136.5 Hz	
	FM	WT2S	447.78000	-	136.5 Hz	
Summit	DMR/BM	W2NJR	445.02500	-	CC1	
Swedesboro	FUSION	K2SLB	145.51500			
	FUSION	K2SLB	147.55500			
	FUSION	K2SLB	433.10000			
	FUSION	K2SLB	434.10000			
TEST Anywhere NJ						
	DMR/MARC	WB3EHB	444.30625	+	CC1	
Tinton Falls	FUSION	W2GSA	147.04500	+		
Toms River	DMR/BM	W2NJR	146.65500	-	CC1	
	DMR/BM	AC2DW	447.51870	-	CC2	
	DMR/MARC	N2IXU	441.90000	+	CC1	
	DMR/MARC	WA2JWR	445.77500	-	CC3	
	FM	W2DOR	223.92000	-		
	FM	KE2HC	224.70000	-		ARCC
	FM	WA2OTP	444.00000	+	141.3 Hz	ARCC
	FUSION	NJ2AR	448.62500	-		
Toms River, The Bennett Bubble						
	FM	W2DOR	146.91000	-	127.3 Hz	
Trenton	DMR/MARC	WR3IRS	443.65000	+	CC2	
Tuckerton		KI4KWR-L	146.44000			
	FM	N2NF	146.70000	-	192.8 Hz	ARCC
Union	DMR/BM	W2NJR	449.47500	-	CC1	

Location	Mode	Call sign	Output	Input	Access	Coordinator
Union	FM	W2FCC	446.37500	-	141.3 Hz	MetroCor
Union City	FM	KD2VN	224.20000	-	131.8 Hz	MetroCor
Vernon	DSTAR	W1JDC B	433.00000	+		
	FM	W2VER	146.92500	-	141.3 Hz	ARCC
	FM	W2VER	449.07500	-	141.3 Hz	ARCC
	FM	W2VER	918.07500	893.07500	141.3 Hz	ARCC
	FM	W2VER	927.33750	902.33750	141.3 Hz	ARCC
Verona	FM	W2UHF	448.87500	-	151.4 Hz	MetroCor
Villas	FM	KC2DOK	447.82500	-	162.2 Hz	ARCC
Vineland	DSTAR	K2GOD	446.62500	-		
	DSTAR	K2GOD B	446.62500	-		
	FM	WA2WUN	145.49000	-	179.9 Hz	ARCC
	FM	WB3EHB	224.62000	-	131.8 Hz	
	FUSION	WA2JCT	147.46500			
Voorhees	FM	K2EOC	146.89500	-	192.8 Hz	
Wall Township	DMR/BM	W2NJR	146.77500	-	CC1	
	DMR/BM	W2NJR	444.35000	+	CC1	
Wall Twp	FM	N2CTD	146.77500	-	103.5 Hz	MetroCor
	FM	WB2ANM	444.35000	+	141.3 Hz	
Wanaque	FM	WA2SNA	146.49000	147.49000	107.2 Hz	MetroCor
	FM	WA2SNA	446.17500	-	107.2 Hz	MetroCor
Warren	DMR/MARC	WR3IRS	440.28750	+	CC1	
	FM	K2ETS	223.96000	-	110.9 Hz	MetroCor
Warrensville	FM	K2PM	224.00000	-	151.4 Hz	
Warrenville	FM	W2QW-R	146.62500	-	141.3 Hz	
Washington		KD2ARB-L	223.42000			
	FM	WC2EM	223.78000	-	110.9 Hz	
	FM	W2SJT	443.85000	+	110.9 Hz	ARCC
Watchung	DMR/BM	W2NJR	440.05000	+	CC1	
	FM	K2ETS	146.94000	-	141.3 Hz	MetroCor
Waterford Works	DMR/MARC	WR3IRS	443.30000	+	CC1	ARCC
	FM	KA2PFL	52.60000	52.80000	131.8 Hz	ARCC
	FM	W2FLY	145.21000	-		ARCC
	FM	WA3BXW	147.34500	+	127.3 Hz	ARCC
	FM	W2MX	224.62000	-		ARCC
	FM	KA2PFL	442.30000	+	131.8 Hz	ARCC
	FM	N3KZ	442.70000	+	131.8 Hz	ARCC
	FM	W2FLY	444.45000	+		ARCC
Wayne	FM	KD2KWT	224.06000	-	79.7 Hz	
	FM	WA2SQQ	442.00000	+		
Wayne, St Josephs Hospital						
	FM	KD2KWT	444.80000	+	79.7 Hz	MetroCor
Wayne, St. Josephs Hospital						
	FM	KD2KWT	145.21000	-	79.7 Hz	MetroCor
Wertheins Corner	FM	K2EPD-R	448.92500	-		MetroCor
West Atlantic City	FM	W2HRW	146.98500	-	146.2 Hz	ARCC
	FM	W2HRW	443.25000	+	146.2 Hz	ARCC
West Orange	DMR/BM	W2NJR	440.05000	+	CC1	
	DMR/BM	N2MH	442.60000	+	CC1	
	DMR/MARC	KC2NFB	446.22500	-	CC1	
	FM	WA2JSB	146.41500	147.41500	85.4 Hz	MetroCor
	FM	WA2JSB	447.87500	-	156.7 Hz	
West Trenton	FM	W2ZQ	146.67000	-	131.8 Hz	ARCC
	FM	NJ2EM	224.32000	-	67.0 Hz	
	FUSION	W2ZQ	442.65000	+		
West Windsor	FM	W2MER	147.10500	+		
Westampton	DMR/MARC	KB2RF	448.32500	-	CC1	
	FM	KC2QVT	147.15000	+	127.3 Hz	ARCC
Wildwood	FM	WA2WUN	146.67000	-		
Wileys Corners	FM	W2GSA-R	147.04500	+	67.0 Hz	MetroCor
Willingboro	FM	WB2YGO	146.92500	-	131.8 Hz	ARCC
	FM	WB2YGO	223.88000	-	118.8 Hz	ARCC

Location	Mode	Call sign	Output	Input	Access	Coordinator
Willingboro	FM	WB2YGO	442.05000	+	118.8 Hz	ARCC
Winslow	FM	K2AX	145.15000	-	91.5 Hz	ARCC
Wood-Ridge	FM	W2RN-R	443.75000	+		
Woodbine	FM	N2CMC	146.61000	-	88.5 Hz	ARCC
Woodland Park, Rifle Camp Park						
	FM	NJ2BS	146.61000	-	141.3 Hz	
Woodstown	DSTAR	NJ2SC B	445.03125	-		
	DSTAR	NJ2SC D	1298.50000			

NEW MEXICO

Location	Mode	Call sign	Output	Input	Access	Coordinator
Alamogordo	DMR/BM	KE5MIQ	147.22000	+	CC1	NMFCC
	DMR/BM	N6CID	433.50000	+	CC5	
	DMR/BM	N6CID	442.95000	+	CC1	
	DMR/MARC	KD5OH	442.65000	+	CC1	
	DSTAR	W6DHS C	144.96000	144.56000		
	FM	KA5BYL	53.41000	52.41000		NMFCC
	FM	K5LRW	146.80000	-	127.3 Hz	
	FM	KC5OWL	146.90000	-	77.0 Hz	NMFCC
	FM	K5LRW	224.04000	-	100.0 Hz	
	FM	KA5BYL	224.60000	-		NMFCC
	FM	KF5LGO	444.97500	+	100.0 Hz	
	FUSION	N7SGT	146.55000			
Alamogordo, La Luz						
	DSTAR	W6DHS	144.96000	144.56000		
Alamogordo, Long Ridge						
	FM	WA5IHL	145.35000	-	88.5 Hz	
Albquerque	DMR/MARC	WA5IHL	442.25000	+	CC1	NMFCC
Albuquerque	DMR/BM	NM5SH	443.65000	+	CC1	NMFCC
	DMR/BM	N5GU	444.60000	+	CC1	
	DMR/MARC	KA8JMW	442.90000	+	CC7	NMFCC
	DSTAR	K5URR C	146.86000	-		
	DSTAR	K5URR B	449.45000	-		
	FM	W5LMM	146.40000			
	FM	KF5ERC	146.92000	-	67.0 Hz	
	FM	K5URR	146.94000	-	100.0 Hz	
	FM	K5LXP	147.32000	+	100.0 Hz	NMFCC
	FM	N5GU	147.38000	+		NMFCC
	FM	KB5UGU	223.90000	-		
	FM	KA5BIW	224.38000	-	100.0 Hz	
	FM	KH6JTM	224.58000	-	100.0 Hz	NMFCC
	FM	KE5XE	443.50000	-	123.0 Hz	
	FM	KC0QIZ	443.85000	+	103.5 Hz	NMFCC
	FUSION	K9POL	441.70000			
	FUSION	K5EJN	446.57500			
Albuquerque - Sandia Crest						
	DMR/BM	WR7HLN	443.30000	+	CC1	
Albuquerque - West Mesa						
	DMR/BM	WR7HLN	443.30000	+	CC1	
Albuquerque, BCFD Fire Station						
	FM	NM5BC	145.13000	-	100.0 Hz	NMFCC
Albuquerque, NE Heights						
	FM	W7FED	442.60000	+	100.0 Hz	NMFCC
Albuquerque, Northeast Heights						
	FM	K6LIE	224.48000	-	100.0 Hz	NMFCC
Albuquerque, Northern Sandia M						
	FM	K5FIQ	442.45000	+	67.0 Hz	
Albuquerque, Op Center						
	DSTAR	W5URR	449.45000	-		NMFCC
Albuquerque, Op Ctr						
	FM	K5FIQ	146.90000	-	67.0 Hz	NMFCC
	FM	K5FIQ	449.55000	-	71.9 Hz	NMFCC
	FM	K5FIQ	449.80000	-	67.0 Hz	NMFCC

Location	Mode	Call sign	Output	Input	Access	Coordinator
Albuquerque, Sandia Crest						
	DSTAR	W5MPZ B	443.80000	+		
	DSTAR	W5MPZ	443.80000	+		NMFCC
	DSTAR	W5MPZ A	1283.96250	-		
	DSTAR	W5MPZ D	1299.90000			
	FM	W5SCA	145.01000			
	FM	NM5ML	145.29000	-	100.0 Hz	NMFCC
	FM	W5CSY	145.33000	-	100.0 Hz	NMFCC
	FM	KB5GAS	442.10000	+	162.2 Hz	
	FM	W5CSY	444.00000	+	100.0 Hz	NMFCC
Albuquerque, Sandia Mnts						
	FM	WA5IHL	145.29000	-	100.0 Hz	
Albuquerque, Southeast						
	FM	KC5ZXW	444.10000	+	100.0 Hz	NMFCC
Albuquerque, UNM Campus						
	FM	K5PRN	442.52500	+	100.0 Hz	NMFCC
Albuquerque, West Mesa						
	FM	K5BIQ	442.05000	+	100.0 Hz	NMFCC
Alto	DMR/BM	W5JXT	444.40000	+	CC1	
Angel Fire, Agua Fria Peak						
	FM	N5LEM	147.34000	+	100.0 Hz	NMFCC
Antelope Springs	FM	KB5VPZ-R	447.27500	-		
Artesia	FM	KU5J	442.00000	+		NMFCC
	FM	K5CNM	442.45000	+	162.2 Hz	NMFCC
	FM	W5COW	444.97500	+	156.7 Hz	NMFCC
Aztec	DMR/MARC	N5UBJ	442.25000	+	CC1	NMFCC
	DSTAR	KF5VBE	1291.10000	1271.10000		NMFCC
	FM	NM5SJ	146.74000	-	100.0 Hz	NMFCC
	FM	KB5ITS	146.88000	-	100.0 Hz	NMFCC
	FM	KB5ITS	447.45000	-	107.2 Hz	NMFCC
Belen	FM	KC5OUR	146.70000	-	100.0 Hz	
Bloomfield	FM	K5WXI	146.92000	-	100.0 Hz	NMFCC
	FM	KB5ITS	448.65000	-	127.3 Hz	NMFCC
Bloomfield, Harris Mesa						
	DSTAR	KF5VBD	1292.30000	1272.30000		NMFCC
	FM	NM5ML	147.28000	+	67.0 Hz	NMFCC
Caballo	DMR/MARC	NM5C	448.50000	-	CC1	NMFCC
	FM	K7EAR	145.47000	-	141.3 Hz	
Caballo (Truth Or Consequences						
	FM	NM5EM	145.13000	-	141.3 Hz	
Capitan	FM	KC5QVN	146.61000	-	100.0 Hz	NMFCC
Caprock, Caudill Ranch						
	FM	NM5EM	145.25000	-	141.3 Hz	
Carlsbad	FM	KD6WJG	53.08000	52.08000	127.3 Hz	NMFCC
	FM	KG5BOM	145.39000	-	100.0 Hz	
	FM	KD6WJG	146.76000	-	127.3 Hz	NMFCC
	FM	N5CNM	146.88000	-	88.5 Hz	NMFCC
	FM	K5CNM	147.28000	+	123.0 Hz	NMFCC
	FM	N5MJ	224.46000	-	127.3 Hz	NMFCC
Chama, Overlook Mtn						
	FM	W5SF	147.08000	+	162.2 Hz	NMFCC
Cimarron	FM	N5GDR	145.21000	-	110.9 Hz	NMFCC
Clines Corners, Tapia Mesa						
	FM	K5FIQ	147.06000	+	67.0 Hz	NMFCC
Cloudcroft, Benson Ridge						
	FM	K5BEN	145.23000	-	123.0 Hz	NMFCC
	FM	NM5EM	145.37000	-	156.7 Hz	NMFCC
Cloudcroft, James Ridge						
	FM	KE5MIQ	147.34000	+	151.4 Hz	NMFCC
Clovis	DMR/MARC	K4USD	442.17500	+	CC1	
	DMR/MARC	K5NEC	442.32500	+	CC1	
	FM	KA5B	147.24000	+	67.0 Hz	NMFCC

Location	Mode	Call sign	Output	Input	Access	Coordinator
Clovis	FM	WS5D	147.32000	+	71.9 Hz	NMFCC
	FM	NM5ML	442.52500	+	67.0 Hz	NMFCC
	FM	KA5B	443.45000	+	131.8 Hz	NMFCC
	FM	WS5D	444.45000	+	88.5 Hz	
Clovis, Claud	FM	NM5EM	145.37000	-	141.3 Hz	NMFCC
Columbus	FM	W5DAR	145.43000	-	88.5 Hz	NMFCC
Conchas Dam, Mesa Rica						
	FM	NM5ML	147.36000	+	100.0 Hz	NMFCC
Corona, Gallinas Peak						
	FM	NM5EM	145.51500	-	141.3 Hz	
	FM	NM5ML	147.28000	+	100.0 Hz	NMFCC
Corrales	DMR/BM	N5QD	443.20000	+	CC1	
Cuba	FM	NM5SC	443.10000	+		
Cuba, Eureka Mesa						
	FM	NM5ML	147.24000	+	67.0 Hz	NMFCC
Datil, Davenport Lookout						
	FM	NM5ML	147.04000	+	100.0 Hz	NMFCC
Datil, Luera Peak	FM	NM5ML	147.14000	+	100.0 Hz	NMFCC
Datil, Madre Mtn.	FM	NM5EM	147.32000	+	141.3 Hz	NMFCC
Deming	FM	N5IA	147.04000	+		NMFCC
	FM	K7EAR	147.06000	+	141.3 Hz	NMFCC
	FM	W5JX	147.08000	+		NMFCC
	FM	NM2J	147.12000	+	88.5 Hz	NMFCC
	FM	WA6RT	449.47500	-	77.0 Hz	NMFCC
	FM	N5WSB	449.85000	-	100.0 Hz	NMFCC
Deming, Little Florida Mtn						
	FM	W5DAR	146.82000	-	88.5 Hz	NMFCC
	FM	NM5ML	147.02000	+	100.0 Hz	NMFCC
Des Moines, Sierra Grande						
	FM	NM5EM	147.17500	+	141.3 Hz	NMFCC
Dixon, Cerro Abajo						
	FM	KD5PX	147.18000	+	100.0 Hz	NMFCC
Dona Ana	FM	KC5SJQ	224.34000	-		NMFCC
Dulce	FM	NM5SJ	145.43000	-	136.5 Hz	NMFCC
Eagle Nest, Iron Mountain						
	FM	NM5ML	444.35000	+	100.0 Hz	NMFCC
Eagle Nest, Touch Me Not						
	FM	NM5EM	147.04000	+	141.3 Hz	NMFCC
Farmington		KG5KTT-L	144.90000			
	DMR/MARC	N5UBJ	440.30000	+	CC6	
	DMR/MARC	N5UBJ	442.32500	+	CC1	NMFCC
	DSTAR	KF5VBE	145.11500	-		
	DSTAR	KF5VBD C	145.11500	-		
	DSTAR	KF5VBF B	444.15000	+		
	DSTAR	KF5VBF	444.15000	+		
	DSTAR	KF5VBE D	1248.00000			
	DSTAR	KF5VBF D	1248.60000			
	DSTAR	KF5VBD D	1249.20000			
	DSTAR	KF5VBE A	1291.10000	1271.10000		
	DSTAR	KF5VBF A	1291.70000	1271.70000		
	DSTAR	KF5VBD A	1292.30000	1272.30000		
	FM	KB5ITS	53.01000	52.01000	131.8 Hz	NMFCC
	FM	KB5ITS	146.76000	-	100.0 Hz	NMFCC
	FM	K5WXI	146.85000	-	100.0 Hz	NMFCC
	FM	KB5ITS	147.00000	+	100.0 Hz	NMFCC
	FM	K5WY	449.00000	-	100.0 Hz	NMFCC
Farmington, Farmington Bluffs						
	DSTAR	KF5VBF	1291.70000	1271.70000		NMFCC
Fort Sumner	FM	KB5ZFA	147.14000	+	100.0 Hz	NMFCC
Frontier Post	FM	N5MJ-R	444.45000	+		NMFCC
Fruitvale (historical)						
		K5HDL-L	146.54000			

Location	Mode	Call sign	Output	Input	Access	Coordinator
Gallup	FM	KC5WDV-R	449.75000	-		NMFCC
Gallup, Deza Bluff	FM	KC5WDV	448.20000	-		
Gallup, Deza Bluffs						
	FM	NM5ML	147.22000	+	67.0 Hz	NMFCC
	FM	KC5WDV	448.20000	-	100.0 Hz	NMFCC
Gallup, Gibson Peak						
	FM	KC5WDV	147.26000	+	100.0 Hz	NMFCC
Glenwood, Brushy Mountain						
	FM	WY5G	448.77500	-	103.5 Hz	NMFCC
Grants	DMR/BM	KE5FYL	441.32500	+	CC1	
	DMR/BM	KE5FYL	444.65000	+	CC1	
	DSTAR	KE5FYL B	444.65000	+		
	FUSION	KE5FYL	147.18000	+		
Grants - La Mosca Peak						
	DMR/BM	WR7HLN	443.35000	+	CC1	NMFCC
Grants, 515 West High Street						
	FM	K5EMO	444.97500	+	67.0 Hz	NMFCC
Grants, La Mosca	FM	NM5ML	444.80000	+	67.0 Hz	NMFCC
Grants, La Mosca Peak						
	FM	KE5FYL	444.95000	+	100.0 Hz	NMFCC
Grants, Microwave Ridge						
	FM	NM5ML	146.66000	-	100.0 Hz	NMFCC
Grants, Mt Taylor	FM	K5URR	146.94000	-	100.0 Hz	
	FM	NM5EM	146.98000	-	141.3 Hz	
Grants, MW Ridge						
	FM	K5URR	146.64000	-	67.0 Hz	NMFCC
High Rolls		K6CBL-L	144.44000			
	FM	W5AKU	442.80000	-	100.0 Hz	NMFCC
High Rolls, Cloudcroft/ Alamog						
	FM	KF5MQH	147.00000	+	100.0 Hz	
Hobbs	FM	N5LEA	444.15000	+	162.2 Hz	NMFCC
Hobbs, Professional Communicat						
	FM	AH2AZ	444.27500	+	162.2 Hz	
Hope	FM	K5CNM	147.38000	+	123.0 Hz	NMFCC
Hurley, Murray Tank						
	FM	WD5EZC	147.06000	+		NMFCC
Jal	FM	N5SVI	147.10000	+		NMFCC
	FM	N5LEA	444.25000	+	100.0 Hz	
Johns Place	FM	KD5MHQ-R	146.74000	-		NMFCC
Kenton	FM	WB5NJU	147.39000	+	88.5 Hz	
La Cueva	FM	N9PGQ	146.84000	-	107.2 Hz	NMFCC
	FM	N9PGQ	442.12500	+	107.2 Hz	NMFCC
La Loma		K5AZI-L	147.52500			
La Luz	DMR/BM	W6DHS	440.60000	+	CC1	
Las Cruces	DMR/BM	KA5ECS	449.75000	-	CC1	
	DSTAR	W5GB	146.84000	-		NMFCC
	DSTAR	W5GB C	146.84000	-		
	FM	N5BL	146.64000	-	100.0 Hz	NMFCC
	FM	KA5ECS	146.94000	-		NMFCC
	FM	NM5ML	147.18000	+	100.0 Hz	NMFCC
	FM	W7DXX	147.38000	+	100.0 Hz	NMFCC
	FM	N5IAC	223.94000	-		NMFCC
	FM	N5IAC	447.50000	-		NMFCC
	FM	KC5EVR	449.57500	-	100.0 Hz	
	FM	KC5IEC	449.80000	-	100.0 Hz	NMFCC
	FM	WA8FBN	449.90000	-		NMFCC
Las Cruces, Twin Peaks						
	FM	N5BL	448.20000	-	100.0 Hz	NMFCC
Las Vegas, Elk Mountain						
	FM	W5SF	147.30000	+	162.2 Hz	NMFCC
Las Vegas, Mesa Apache						
	FM	WA5IHL	444.37500	+	100.0 Hz	NMFCC

Location	Mode	Call sign	Output	Input	Access	Coordinator
Little Florida	FM	WB5QHS	448.72500	-	100.0 Hz	
	FM	W5DAR	449.47500	-	77.0 Hz	NMFCC
	FM	W5CF	449.85000	-	127.3 Hz	
Logan, Ute Lake	FM	K5DST	147.34000	+	131.8 Hz	NMFCC
Lordsburg	DMR/MARC	N5IA	440.82500	+	CC1	NMFCC
	FM	N5IA	145.17000	-	100.0 Hz	NMFCC
	FM	WB5QHS	145.25000	-	88.5 Hz	NMFCC
	FM	N5IA	449.00000	-	100.0 Hz	
Lordsburg, Jacks Peak						
	FM	NM5EM	145.14500	-	141.3 Hz	
Los Alamos	DMR/MARC	NM5BB	442.22500	+	CC7	NMFCC
	DSTAR	NM5WR B	442.42500	+		
	DSTAR	NM5WR	442.42500	+		
	FM	KA5BIW-R	224.04000	-		NMFCC
	FM	WD9CMS	927.90000	902.90000		NMFCC
Los Alamos, Barranca Mesa						
	FM	W5PDO	146.88000	-		NMFCC
Los Alamos, Pajarito Mountain						
	DSTAR	NM5EC	145.19000	-		
	FM	KB5RX	223.94000	-		NMFCC
Los Lunas	FM	WA5TSV	444.12500	+	100.0 Hz	NMFCC
Loving	FM	K5CNM	147.36000	+	123.0 Hz	NMFCC
Lybrook	FM	NM5SJ	145.49000	-	100.0 Hz	NMFCC
Maljamar	FM	NM5ML	147.14000	+	67.0 Hz	NMFCC
	FM	N5LEA	444.35000	+	162.2 Hz	
Melrose	FM	NM5ML	147.28000	+	67.0 Hz	NMFCC
Mesa Village	FM	W5MHG-L	144.00000			
Midway (Portales)	FM	KE5RUE	147.00000	+	67.0 Hz	
Mountainair - Capilla Peak						
	DMR/BM	WR7HLN	443.25000	+	CC1	
Mountainair, Capilla Peak						
	FM	W5NES	444.07500	+	100.0 Hz	NMFCC
Navajo		N0SRF-R	144.59000			
Navajo Dam	FM	KB5ITS	147.36000	+	100.0 Hz	NMFCC
Nebo	FM	NM5SJ	147.06000	+	100.0 Hz	NMFCC
NOAA Albuquerque						
	WX	WXJ34	162.40000			
NOAA Artesia	WX	WXN24	162.42500			
NOAA Carlsbad	WX	WWF37	162.47500			
NOAA Clovis	WX	WXJ35	162.47500			
NOAA Des Moines						
	WX	WXL90	162.55000			
NOAA Farmington						
	WX	WXJ37	162.47500			
NOAA Hobbs	WX	WXJ36	162.40000			
NOAA Las Cruces						
	WX	WXL91	162.40000			
NOAA Roswell	WX	WWG36	162.45000			
NOAA Ruidoso	WX	WXJ38	162.55000			
NOAA Santa Fe	WX	WXJ33	162.55000			
NOAA Silver City	WX	WZ2516	162.42500			
Ora Vista	FM	W5TWY	147.30000	+	100.0 Hz	NMFCC
Organ	FM	KC5SJQ	1293.90000	1273.90000	127.3 Hz	NMFCC
Organ, San Augustin Peak						
	FM	N5IAC	146.78000	-	100.0 Hz	NMFCC
Pecos, Elk Mountain						
	FM	NM5ML	147.26000	+	67.0 Hz	NMFCC
Pinos Altos	FM	NM5ML	145.11500	-	67.0 Hz	NMFCC
	FM	WB5QHS	448.30000	-	100.0 Hz	
Placitas, La Madera						
	FM	NM5SC	147.08000	+	100.0 Hz	NMFCC

Location	Mode	Call sign	Output	Input	Access	Coordinator
Placitas, Sandia Peak						
	FM	NM5SV	443.40000	+	100.0 Hz	NMFCC
Ponderosa Pine	FM	K5CQH-R	146.72000	-		NMFCC
Portable Repeater	DMR/MARC	K4USD	434.97500	-	CC1	
Portales	DMR/MARC	W5OMU	443.75000	+	CC3	
	FM	KE5RUE	146.82000	-	67.0 Hz	NMFCC
Portales, Eastern New Mexico U						
	DSTAR	KE5RUE	443.80000	+		NMFCC
Portales, ENMU Greyhound Stadi						
	FM	W5OMU	147.00000	+	67.0 Hz	
Queen, Queen Fire Station						
	FM	K5CNM	147.30000	+	123.0 Hz	NMFCC
Quemado, Fox Mtn						
	FM	WB7EGF	448.05000	-	103.5 Hz	
Raton	DSTAR	KD0RDI B	446.77500	-		
Raton, Raton Pass						
	DSTAR	KD0RDI	446.77500	-		NMFCC
Raton, Sierra Grande						
	FM	NM5ML	147.28000	+	100.0 Hz	NMFCC
Red River, Valle Vidal						
	FM	KF5PFO	145.25000	-	123.0 Hz	NMFCC
Redlake	FM	KE5RUE	146.84000	-	67.0 Hz	NMFCC
	FM	KE5RUE	442.25000	+	67.0 Hz	NMFCC
Reserve, Frisco	FM	NM5EM	147.34000	+	141.3 Hz	NMFCC
Reserve, Frisco Divide						
	FM	NM5ML	147.36000	+	67.0 Hz	NMFCC
Rio Rancho	FM	NM5HD	145.37000	-	162.2 Hz	
	FM	WA5OLD	442.35000	+	100.0 Hz	NMFCC
	FM	KC5IPK-R	442.75000	+		NMFCC
	FM	NM5RR-R	443.00000	+		NMFCC
	FM	NM5F-R	443.70000	+		NMFCC
	FUSION	W5SLG	446.12500			
Rio Rancho, Intel Corp						
	FM	K5CPU	444.70000	+	100.0 Hz	NMFCC
Rio Rancho, Rainbow						
	FM	NM5RR	147.10000	+	100.0 Hz	NMFCC
Roswell	DMR/BM	W5JXT	444.40000	+	CC1	
	DMR/BM	W5JXT	444.95000	+	CC1	NMFCC
	DMR/MARC	KJ5UFO	444.30000	+	CC1	
	DSTAR	W5ZU B	444.42500	+		
	FM	W5GNB	52.94000	-	100.0 Hz	
	FM	NM5ML	147.26000	+	100.0 Hz	NMFCC
	FM	W5GNB	147.32000	+	146.2 Hz	NMFCC
	FM	W5GNB	444.95000	+	179.9 Hz	
Roswell, Capitan Peak						
	FM	WA5IHL	146.66000	-	67.0 Hz	NMFCC
Roswell, Comanche Hill						
	DSTAR	W5ZU	444.42500	+		NMFCC
	FM	W5GNB	52.94000	-	100.0 Hz	NMFCC
	FM	N5IMJ	444.00000	+	100.0 Hz	NMFCC
	FM	W5GNB	444.55000	+	162.2 Hz	NMFCC
Roswell, Nmmi	FM	N5MMI	146.64000	-	100.0 Hz	NMFCC
Ruidoso	FM	N5SN	443.60000	+	85.4 Hz	
Ruidoso, Alto Crest						
	FM	KR5NM	146.92000	-	100.0 Hz	NMFCC
Ruidoso, Buck Mountain						
	FM	NM5ML	444.37500	+	67.0 Hz	NMFCC
Ruidoso, Buck Mtn						
	FM	K5RIC	443.92500	+	100.0 Hz	NMFCC
San Luis, Cabezon						
	FM	K5YEJ	443.00000	+	100.0 Hz	NMFCC

Location	Mode	Call sign	Output	Input	Access	Coordinator
San Ysidro, Pajarito Peak						
	FM	NM5SC	443.10000	+	100.0 Hz	NMFCC
Sandia Knolls	FM	W5AOX-L	444.15000	+		NMFCC
Santa Fe	DMR/BM	W6EZY	432.55000		CC1	
	DMR/BM	KE5ZBG	442.40000	+	CC4	
	DMR/BM	WR7HLN	443.15000	+	CC1	
	DSTAR	W5SF C	145.21000	+		
	DSTAR	W5SF	145.21000	-		
	DSTAR	W5SF B	444.57500	+		
	DSTAR	W5SF	444.57500	+		
	FM	KF5SGT	447.77500	-	100.0 Hz	
	FM	K9GAJ	449.27500	-	146.2 Hz	
	FUSION	W6EZY	432.50000			
Santa Fe, St Vincent Hospital						
	FM	W5SF	147.20000	+	162.2 Hz	NMFCC
Santa Fe, Tesuque Peak						
	FM	W5SF	146.82000	-	162.2 Hz	NMFCC
	FM	NM5EM	147.02000	+	141.3 Hz	NMFCC
	FM	KB5ZQE	442.82500	+	131.8 Hz	NMFCC
Santa Rosa, Moon Ranch						
	FM	NM5EM	147.04000	+	141.3 Hz	NMFCC
Silver City	FM	WY5G	448.80000	-	100.0 Hz	NMFCC
	FM	WA7ACA	448.87500	-	100.0 Hz	NMFCC
Silver City, Black Peak						
	FM	K5GAR	146.98000	-	103.5 Hz	NMFCC
Socorro	DSTAR	W5AQA B	444.50000	+		
Socorro, M Mountain						
	DSTAR	W5AQA	444.50000	+		
	FM	W5AQA	146.68000	-	100.0 Hz	NMFCC
Socorro, Socorro Peak						
	FM	NM5EM	145.17500	-	141.3 Hz	NMFCC
	FM	NM5ML	147.24000	+	100.0 Hz	NMFCC
Socorro, West Peak						
	FM	KC5ORO	442.12500	+	123.0 Hz	NMFCC
T Or C, Caballo Peak						
	FM	NM5ML	147.26000	+	100.0 Hz	NMFCC
T Or C, Caballo Pk						
	FM	N5BL	146.76000	-	100.0 Hz	NMFCC
	FM	WB5QHS	448.17500	-	100.0 Hz	
	FM	WB5QHS	448.97500	-	114.8 Hz	NMFCC
Tank Mountain	FM	KB5ITS	146.88000	-	100.0 Hz	
Taos	DMR/BM	KF5PFO	146.76000	-	CC5	
	DMR/MARC	KF5PFO	442.17500	+	CC5	
Taos, Picuris Peak						
	FM	KF5PFO	51.50000	-	100.0 Hz	
	FM	KF5PFO	147.12000	+	67.0 Hz	NMFCC
	FM	KF5PFO	224.40000	-	225.7 Hz	NMFCC
Taos, Ski Valley	FM	NM5ML	147.14000	+	67.0 Hz	
Taos, Wheeler Peak						
	FM	N5TSV	444.97500	+	123.0 Hz	NMFCC
Tijeras, Cedro Peak						
	FM	NM5BC	145.15000	-	100.0 Hz	NMFCC
	FM	NM5ML	147.34000	+	67.0 Hz	NMFCC
Timberon	FM	KF5MQH	146.86000	-	100.0 Hz	NMFCC
Tres Piedras	DSTAR	KF5PFO B	442.07500	+		
Tres Piedras, San Antonio Moun						
	FM	NM5ML	147.22000	+	100.0 Hz	NMFCC
Tucumcari	FM	WA5EMA	146.88000	-		NMFCC
	FM	WA5EMA	224.98000	-		NMFCC
	FM	WA5EMA	443.75000	+	100.0 Hz	NMFCC
Tucumcari, Tucumcari Mountain						
	FM	NM5ML	147.22000	+	100.0 Hz	NMFCC

Location	Mode	Call sign	Output	Input	Access	Coordinator
Tularosa	FM	W5TYW	443.90000	+	100.0 Hz	NMFCC
Wagon Mound, Turkey Mountain						
	FM	NM5ML	147.20000	+	67.0 Hz	
Weed, Weed Lookout						
	FM	KE5MIQ	146.96000	-	151.4 Hz	NMFCC
Zuni	FM	KD5SAR	145.43000	-	162.2 Hz	NMFCC

NEW YORK

Location	Mode	Call sign	Output	Input	Access	Coordinator
Albany	DMR/MARC	KM4WUD	444.00000	+	CC0	
	DMR/MARC	WB2ERS	444.75000	+	CC1	MetroCor
	DSTAR	KJ4KLD C	144.96000	147.46000		
	DSTAR	KJ4KLD B	440.70000	+		
	DSTAR	WA2UMX B	443.30000	+		
	DSTAR	KJ4KLD D	1249.25000			
	FM	W2GBO	53.41000	52.41000	100.0 Hz	UNYREPCO
	FM	KA2QYE	147.37500	+	100.0 Hz	UNYREPCO
	FM	K2AD	444.00000	+	100.0 Hz	UNYREPCO
	FM	KB2SIY	444.70000	+	94.8 Hz	UNYREPCO
Albany, Blue Hill	FM	WA2MMX	927.21250	902.21250	114.8 Hz	UNYREPCO
Albany, Helderberg Mtn						
	FM	K2CT	145.19000	-	103.5 Hz	UNYREPCO
Albany, St. Peter's Hospital						
	FM	K2ALB	146.64000	-	100.0 Hz	
Albion Center		KD2HLB-L	146.41000			
Alfred	FM	K2BVD	146.95500	-	127.3 Hz	UNYREPCO
Alma, Alma Hill	FM	KA2AJH	147.21000	+	123.0 Hz	WNYSORC
	FM	KA2AJH	444.10000	+	107.2 Hz	
Amherst	FUSION	K2EAG	434.77500			
Amherst - North	DMR/MARC	N2CID	442.18750	+	CC1	
Arcade	FUSION	KC2PES	442.27500	+		
Arcadia, Brantling Ski						
	DSTAR	WA2EMO	444.75000	+		UNYREPCO
	FM	WA2EMO	146.68500	-	71.9 Hz	UNYREPCO
Arkport	FM	KC2FSW	147.04500	+	110.9 Hz	UNYREPCO
Arkwright	FM	K2XZ	146.67000	-	88.5 Hz	WNYSORC
Arlington		W2RTV-L	146.55500			
Armonk, Kensico Reservoir						
	FM	W2TWY	224.30000	-	114.8 Hz	MetroCor
Astoria	DMR/MARC	N2YGI	439.56250	-	CC1	
	DMR/MARC	KC2EFN	447.32500	-	CC1	
Athens	DMR/MARC	KM4WUD	442.57500	+	CC0	
	DSTAR	K2MCI	145.55000			
Auburn	FM	K2INH	53.05000	52.05000	71.9 Hz	UNYREPCO
	FM	W2QYT	145.23000	-	103.5 Hz	UNYREPCO
	FM	W2QYT	147.00000	+	71.9 Hz	UNYREPCO
	FM	K2RSY	147.27000	+	71.9 Hz	UNYREPCO
Austerlitz	DMR/MARC	N2JTI	445.18750	-	CC1	
	FM	KQ2H	442.75000	+		
	FM	N2ACF	445.12500	-	114.8 Hz	UNYREPCO
Austerlitz, Austerlitz Mountai						
	FM	WA2ZPX	442.85000	+	156.7 Hz	UNYREPCO
Averill Park	FM	W1GRM	449.35000	-	71.9 Hz	
Avon	FM	WR2AHL	146.94000	-	162.2 Hz	
Babylon	DSTAR	W2TOB B	440.25000	+		
Bainbridge		W2KWO-L	446.30000			
Bald Mountain	FM	KT2D	927.88750	902.88750	100.0 Hz	
Baldwinsville	FM	WA2DAD	444.90000	+	131.8 Hz	UNYREPCO
	FUSION	KD2UCR	145.31000			
Barkersville, Lake Nancy						
	FM	K2DLL	147.24000	+	91.5 Hz	
Batavia	FM	W2SO	147.28500	+	141.3 Hz	WNYSORC

Location	Mode	Call sign	Output	Input	Access	Coordinator
Batavia, NY State School For T						
	FM	W2SO	444.27500	+		
Bath	FM	N2AAR	145.19000	-	110.9 Hz	UNYREPCO
	FM	KS2ARR	146.80500	-	100.0 Hz	UNYREPCO
Bayside	DMR/MARC	K2JRC	438.58750	-	CC3	MetroCor
Beacon	DMR/MARC	K2HR	145.39625	-	CC5	
	DMR/MARC	NY4Z	441.45000	+	CC7	
	DMR/MARC	K2HR	443.15625	+	CC9	
Beacon, Mt Beacon						
	FM	K2ROB	53.31000	52.31000	114.8 Hz	UNYREPCO
	FM	WR2ABB	146.97000	-	100.0 Hz	
	FM	W2GIO	223.92000	-	100.0 Hz	UNYREPCO
	FM	KC2OUR	443.55000	+	156.7 Hz	UNYREPCO
	FM	WA2GZW	449.57500	-	100.0 Hz	UNYREPCO
	FM	KC2VTJ	927.48750	902.48750	136.5 Hz	
Bear Mountain	FM	N2ACF	447.80000	-	114.8 Hz	
Bemus Point	FM	WA2LPB	145.29000	-	127.3 Hz	WNYSORC
	FUSION	KB2OBF	144.30000			
Bethany	FM	WA1W	146.36000	+	123.0 Hz	
Bethpage	FM	K2ATT	449.30000	-	156.7 Hz	MetroCor
Binghamton	FM	N2YOW	444.30000	+		
	FM	AA2EQ	444.55000	+		
Binghamton Township						
	FM	W2EWM	145.47000	-		UNYREPCO
Binghamton, Airport						
	FM	WA2QEL	146.86500	-	146.2 Hz	UNYREPCO
Binghamton, Ingraham Hill						
	FM	K2TDV	146.73000	-	100.0 Hz	UNYREPCO
Binghamton, Trim Street						
	FM	K2VQ	147.07500	+		
Binghamton/Endicott						
	FM	AC2YS	442.80000	+	100.0 Hz	
Blodgett Mills	FM	KB2FAF-R	147.22500	+		UNYREPCO
Blue Mountain Lake						
	FM	W2CJS	146.86500	-	162.2 Hz	UNYREPCO
Bohemia	FM	N2HBA	444.60000	+	136.5 Hz	MetroCor
Boonville	FM	WD2ADX	146.65500	-		UNYREPCO
Boston	DMR/BM	W2BRW	442.15000	+	CC1	
	FM	WB2JQK	29.68000	-	107.2 Hz	
	FM	N2ZDU	224.82000	-	107.2 Hz	
Branchport	FM	N2LSJ	442.60000	+	110.9 Hz	UNYREPCO
Brewster	FM	WA2ZPX	147.39000	+	151.4 Hz	UNYREPCO
Briarcliff Manor	DMR/MARC	K2HR	443.60000	+	CC1	
Bristol	FM	W2IMT	224.68000	-	110.9 Hz	UNYREPCO
Bristol, Worden Hill						
	FM	WR2AHL	145.11000	-	110.9 Hz	UNYREPCO
Brockport	FM	N2HJD	147.22500	+	110.9 Hz	UNYREPCO
Bronx	DMR/MARC	N2NSA	440.36750	+	CC1	
	DMR/MARC	N2NSA	443.30000	+	CC1	MetroCor
	DMR/MARC	N2NSA	443.35000	+	CC1	MetroCor
	DMR/MARC	KC2IVF	445.42500	-	CC2	
	DMR/MARC	K2HR	446.43750	+	CC7	
	FM	KC2ARE	146.55500	-		
	FM	WB2KVO	224.58000	-		MetroCor
	FM	KB2NGU	440.20000	+	88.5 Hz	MetroCor
	FM	W2MGF	441.20000	+		
	FM	N2YN	442.75000	+	173.8 Hz	
	FM	N2HBA	447.62500	-	136.5 Hz	MetroCor
	FUSION	K2CSX	145.67000			
	FUSION	K2HZE	145.70000			
	FUSION	KD2SPF	440.35000	+		
	FUSION	N2YN	440.80000	+		

Location	Mode	Call sign	Output	Input	Access	Coordinator
Bronx , New York	FM	K2CSX	145.67000			
Brookhaven	FM	W2OFD	444.85000	+	123.0 Hz	
Brooklyn	DMR/BM	KB2RNI	146.61000	-	CC1	
	DMR/BM	KB2RNI	441.15000	+	CC1	
	DMR/MARC	WB2ZEX	438.27500	-	CC1	
	DMR/MARC	N2AZT	439.61250	-	CC1	
	DMR/MARC	K2QQJ	440.50000	+	CC1	
	DMR/MARC	NY4Z	442.09375	+	CC1	
	FM	WB2HWW	29.66000	-	114.8 Hz	SLVRC
	FM	KB2RQE	145.31000	-	100.0 Hz	UNYREPCO
	FM	KC2RA	146.43000	147.43000	136.5 Hz	MetroCor
	FM	NB2A	146.74500	-	136.5 Hz	MetroCor
	FM	KB2NGU	147.30000	+	146.2 Hz	MetroCor
	FM	W2SN	224.60000	-	100.0 Hz	MetroCor
	FM	KA2VJD	224.60000	-	100.0 Hz	
	FM	NN2N	224.74000	-	123.0 Hz	MetroCor
	FM	KB2NGU	439.50000	-		
	FM	N2UOL	446.17500	-	136.5 Hz	MetroCor
	FM	WA2JNF	446.67500	-	114.8 Hz	MetroCor
	FM	KB2NGU	448.37500	-	162.2 Hz	
	FM	KB2PRV	448.97500	-	136.5 Hz	MetroCor
	FM	K2MAK	449.77500	-		MetroCor
	FM	N2HBA	927.88750	902.88750	151.4 Hz	MetroCor
	FUSION	W2DEA	144.91000			
	FUSION	KA2BNY	144.95000			
	FUSION	KC2NJC	145.60000			
	FUSION	N1UFO	147.56250			
	FUSION	KC2NJC	432.70000			
	FUSION	KD2OVM	432.80000			
	FUSION	KB2NGU	445.67500	-		
	FUSION	K2RMX	446.82500	-		
Brooklyn (New York City)						
	DSTAR	WG2MSK B	445.47500	-		
Brooklyn Heights	FM	W2CMA	145.23000	-	114.8 Hz	UNYREPCO
Brooklyn, Downtown						
	DSTAR	WG2MSK	445.47500	-		MetroCor
Brownville	FM	AC2GE-R	147.03000	+		
Brunswick, Bald Mountain						
	FM	W2GBO	146.94000	-		
	FM	WA2MMX	927.21250	902.21250	114.8 Hz	
Bufallo	FM	W2ERD	927.22500	902.22500	88.5 Hz	
Buffalo	DMR/BM	W2BRW	444.92500	+	CC1	
	DMR/BM	N4NJJ	445.97500	+	CC2	SNRC
	DSTAR	KC2ZCE C	146.88500	-		
	FM	AB2UK	29.68000	-	107.2 Hz	SLVRC
	FM	N4NJJ	146.41500			
	FM	WB2ECR	146.86500	+	151.4 Hz	WNYSORC
	FM	WB2ECR	224.76000	-	107.2 Hz	
	FM	WB2ECR	443.52500	+		
	FM	WB2ECR	443.97500	+	141.3 Hz	
	FM	WA2HKS	444.00000	+		WNYSORC
	FM	N2LYJ	927.32500	902.32500	88.5 Hz	WNYSORC
	FM	WA2WWK	927.47500	902.47500	131.8 Hz	
Buffalo - South	DMR/MARC	N2CID	442.18750	+	CC1	
Buffalo, UB Kimball Tower						
	FM	WA2HKS	444.06250	+		
Burlington	FM	W2EES	146.71500	-	167.9 Hz	UNYREPCO
Cairo	FM	KB2DYB	146.74500	-	210.7 Hz	UNYREPCO
	FM	N2SQW	147.09000	+		UNYREPCO
Camillus	FM	N2PYK	146.62500	-	103.5 Hz	
Campbell	FUSION	N9RIM	147.27000	+		
	FUSION	N9RIM	442.75000	+		

Location	Mode	Call sign	Output	Input	Access	Coordinator
Canadice, Bald Hill						
	FM	W2XRX	145.29000	-	110.9 Hz	UNYREPCO
	FM	WR2AHL	444.95000	+	110.9 Hz	
Canandaigua	FM	K2BWK	146.82000	-	110.9 Hz	UNYREPCO
Candor, Candor Hill						
	FM	K2OQ	147.30000	+	91.5 Hz	UNYREPCO
Carle Place	FM	N2YXZ-R	445.97500	-		MetroCor
Carlisle Gardens		K2MJ-L	224.36000			
Carmel	DMR/MARC	KC2CWT	438.36250	430.76250	CC1	
	DMR/MARC	KC2CWT	443.50000		CC1	
	DMR/MARC	KC2CWT	446.00000	+	CC1	
	DMR/MARC	KC2CWT	446.18750	-	CC1	
	DSTAR	K2PUT B	445.87500	-		
	FM	KC2CWT	224.02000	-	136.5 Hz	UNYREPCO
Carmel, Mt. Ninham						
	DSTAR	K2PUT	445.87500	-		UNYREPCO
	FM	K2PUT	145.13000	-	136.5 Hz	UNYREPCO
Cazenovia	FM	N2LZI	147.07500	+	97.4 Hz	UNYREPCO
Cazenovia, Route 92						
	FM	W2CM	147.21000	+	103.5 Hz	UNYREPCO
Cedarhurst	DSTAR	N2XPM	445.52500	-		
Central Islip	FM	WB2ROL	147.03000	+	136.5 Hz	ASMA
	FM	WB2GLW	927.85000	902.85000	146.2 Hz	
Cheektowaga	FUSION	KD4HLV	438.55000			
	FUSION	N2DJS	446.30000			
Chemung	DMR/MARC	N2NUO	443.75000	+	CC1	
Cherry Valley	FM	NC2C	145.35000	-	167.9 Hz	
	FM	WA2IJE	224.98000	-		UNYREPCO
Chili	FM	WR2AHL	146.76000	-	110.9 Hz	
Churchville	DMR/BM	KB2CHM	433.50000	+	CC1	
	DMR/BM	KB2CHM	443.90000	+	CC1	
	FM	KB2CHM	443.10000	+	110.9 Hz	
Clarence	DMR/MARC	KD2QPO	446.37500	-	CC1	
	FM	AG2AA	147.36000	+	107.2 Hz	
Clay	FM	KD2CDY	146.64000	-	131.8 Hz	UNYREPCO
	FM	WA2DAD	444.25000	+	131.8 Hz	UNYREPCO
Clinton	FUSION	WB2VSL	146.83500	-		
Clyde	DMR/BM	KA2NDW	443.07500	+	CC3	UNYREPCO
	FM	KA2NDW	53.47000	52.47000	82.5 Hz	UNYREPCO
	FM	KA2NDW	145.47000	-	82.5 Hz	UNYREPCO
	FM	KA2NDW	224.47000	-	82.5 Hz	UNYREPCO
	FM	KA2NDW	449.07500	-	82.5 Hz	
Cobleskill	FM	WA2ZWM	146.61000	-	123.0 Hz	UNYREPCO
Cohoes	DMR/BM	WA2CW	442.40000	+	CC1	
Colden	DMR/BM	W2BRW	442.15000	+	CC1	
	FM	W2IVB	53.57000	52.57000	88.5 Hz	WNYSORC
	FM	W2IVB	145.31000	-	88.5 Hz	WNYSORC
	FM	W2IVB	442.10000	+	88.5 Hz	WNYSORC
	FM	WB2JPQ	444.10000	+	88.5 Hz	
Colden, WIVB Tower						
	FM	WB2ELW	147.09000	+	107.2 Hz	WNYSORC
Colesville	FM	WA2QEL	146.82000	-	146.2 Hz	UNYREPCO
Cooperstown	FM	NC2C	146.64000	-		UNYREPCO
Corinth	FM	K2DLL	448.22500	-	91.5 Hz	
Corinth, Spruce Mountian						
	FM	K2DLL	147.00000	+	91.5 Hz	UNYREPCO
Corning	FM	N2IED	147.01500	+	123.0 Hz	
Corona, Hall Of Science						
	FM	KC2PXT	145.27000	-	136.5 Hz	MetroCor
Cortland	FM	KB2LUV	145.49000	-	71.9 Hz	UNYREPCO
	FM	KB2FAF	147.03000	+	71.9 Hz	UNYREPCO
	FUSION	K2HEI	434.85000			

Location	Mode	Call sign	Output	Input	Access	Coordinator
Coxsackie	DMR/MARC	N2LEN	445.02500	-	CC1	
	FM	N2LEN	147.09000	+		
Cragsmoor	DMR/MARC	N2LEN	443.40000	+	CC1	
	FM	WB2BQW	29.69000	-	100.0 Hz	UNYREPCO
	FM	WB2BQW	53.33000	52.33000	100.0 Hz	UNYREPCO
Cranberry Lake	DMR/MARC	K2WW	444.75000	+	CC1	
Cronomer Valley		K2ATY-L	145.59500			
Dannemora		AD2Z-L	145.72000			
Dansville	DMR/BM	KC2REY	434.46250	446.46250	CC1	
	DMR/BM	KC2REY	434.93750	446.93750	CC1	
Deer Park	DMR/BM	N2GQ	440.50000	+	CC1	
Deerfield	FM	W2JIT	146.76000	-		
Deerfield, Smith Hill						
	FM	WA2CAV	224.66000	-		UNYREPCO
Defreestville	FM	K2CWW	444.30000	+	100.0 Hz	
Delevan	DMR/MARC	N2CID	444.20000	+	CC1	
	FM	WB2JPQ	51.62000	50.62000	88.5 Hz	WNYSORC
	FM	K2XZ	145.39000	-		WNYSORC
	FM	K2XZ	444.17500	+	88.5 Hz	
Dexter	FM	KD2CPX	443.15000	+	151.4 Hz	
Dix Hills	DMR/MARC	W2RGM	147.07500	+	CC1	MetroCor
	DMR/MARC	W2RGM	448.47500	-	CC1	
	DMR/MARC	W2RGM	448.52500	-	CC1	MetroCor
	FM	W2RGM	53.85000	52.85000	114.8 Hz	ASMA
	FM	W2RGM	224.56000	-	136.5 Hz	
Dobbs Ferry	FM	K2UTB	442.85000	+	118.8 Hz	MetroCor
	FUSION	KD2D	445.13500			
Dundee	FM	KD2NOL	146.98500	-	82.5 Hz	
Dunkirk	FUSION	KD2WBC	146.52000			
East Bay Park	FM	K2RRA-R	146.88000	-		
East Fishkill	FM	N2SPF	53.61000	52.61000	100.0 Hz	UNYREPCO
East Flatbush		KB2NGU-R	445.67500			
East Galway	FM	K2DLL	147.36000	+		
East Grafton	FM	K1FFK-R	146.91000	-		NESMC
East Hampton	FM	W2HLI	224.60000	-		MetroCor
East Meadow	DMR/MARC	KC2NFB	443.40000	+	CC1	
	FM	K2CX	443.32500	+	141.3 Hz	MetroCor
	FM	KB2BWV	443.52500	+	114.8 Hz	MetroCor
	FM	AA2UC	443.80000	+	141.3 Hz	MetroCor
	FM	NC2PD	444.88700	+	179.9 Hz	MetroCor
	FUSION	WB2CYN	147.13500	+	136.5 Hz	
East Rockaway	FM	WA2YUD	224.54000	-	136.5 Hz	MetroCor
Eastern Long Island						
	DMR/MARC	K1IMD	449.62500	-	CC1	
Eden	DMR/MARC	N2CID	442.18750	+	CC1	
	FM	WB2JPQ	146.83500	-	88.5 Hz	WNYSORC
	FM	WB2JPQ	444.20000	+	88.5 Hz	
	FUSION	K2CRM	441.20000			
Ellenville	FM	KQ2H	53.73000	52.73000	146.2 Hz	UNYREPCO
Elmira	DMR/BM	N2NUO	443.87500	+	CC1	
	DMR/BM	N2NUO	444.60000	+	CC1	
	DMR/MARC	KC2EQ	443.00000	+	CC3	
	FM	W2ZJ	146.70000	-	100.0 Hz	UNYREPCO
	FM	N3AQ	147.36000	+		UNYREPCO
	FM	NR2P	223.98000	-	100.0 Hz	UNYREPCO
	FM	KA3EVQ	444.20000	+	100.0 Hz	UNYREPCO
	FM	N3AQ	444.90000	+		
	FUSION	KC2EQ	146.55000			
	FUSION	N2EUS	448.75000	-		
Endicott	FM	N2YR	145.39000	-	123.0 Hz	UNYREPCO
	FM	WA2VCS	147.25500	-	100.0 Hz	UNYREPCO
Esopus	FM	N2ACF	439.12500	+	118.8 Hz	

Location	Mode	Call sign	Output	Input	Access	Coordinator
Esopus	FM	N2ACF	447.80000	-	114.8 Hz	
Fairport	DSTAR	KB2VZS	444.80000	+		UNYREPCO
	DSTAR	KB2VZS B	444.80000	+		
Falconer	DSTAR	KD2LWX	444.97500	+	127.3 Hz	WNYSORC
Farmingdale	FM	W2YMM	147.53500		110.9 Hz	
	FM	W2YMM	449.67500	-	110.9 Hz	
	FUSION	N2CLJ	446.77500	-		
Farmingville	FM	WB2BQW	145.25000	-	100.0 Hz	ASMA
	FM	K2SPD-R	145.31000	-		ASMA
	FM	WA2UMD	146.71500	-	136.5 Hz	MetroCor
	FM	WA2LIR	224.86000	-	107.2 Hz	ASMA
	FM	WR2UHF-R	444.70000	+	114.8 Hz	MetroCor
	FM	K2LI	445.72500	-	91.5 Hz	MetroCor
	FM	K2SPD	446.51250	-	118.8 Hz	UNYREPCO
Farmingville, Telescope Hill						
	FM	WA2DCI	446.32500	-	127.3 Hz	
Fayetteville	FUSION	KD2ULR	146.55000			
Fenner	DMR/BM	N2ADK	449.47500	-	CC1	
Finchville	FM	WA2VDX	146.76000	-	100.0 Hz	UNYREPCO
	FM	WA2ZPX	147.39000	+	156.7 Hz	UNYREPCO
	FM	WA2VDX	449.52500	-	123.0 Hz	UNYREPCO
Fine	FM	WA2NAN-R	147.13500	+		SLVRC
Fine, Adirondack Foothills						
	FM	WA2NAN	442.02500	+		
Fleischmanns	FM	WA2SEI	53.47000	52.47000	107.2 Hz	UNYREPCO
Flushing	DSTAR	K2HAM	147.09000	+	114.8 Hz	MetroCor
	FM	KB2HRA	444.95000	+	114.8 Hz	MetroCor
Flushing, Queens College						
	FM	WB2HWW	53.47000	52.47000		
	FM	WB2HWW	440.70000	+	114.8 Hz	MetroCor
Fort Plain	FUSION	KB2RSK	146.50000			
Fredonia	DMR/BM	KD2MNA	147.19500	+	CC1	WNYSORC
	FM	W2SB	146.62500	-	127.3 Hz	WNYSORC
Fresh Meadows	DMR/MARC	W2KTU	449.72500	-	CC1	
Frewsburg	FM	W2DRZ	146.79000	-	127.3 Hz	WNYSORC
Fulton	FM	K2QQY	146.85000	-	123.0 Hz	UNYREPCO
	FM	WN8Z	444.35000	+	103.5 Hz	UNYREPCO
	FUSION	WN8Z	147.39000	+		
Ga	DMR/MARC	KC2CWT	443.50000		CC1	
Gainesville	FM	WB2JPQ	145.49000	-	88.5 Hz	WNYSORC
Garden City South						
		KD2AVU-L	446.17500			
Gasport	DMR/MARC	KD2WA	443.45000	+	CC11	
	DSTAR	KD2STR B	443.68750	+		
	FUSION	KD2WA	443.58750	+		
Gates	DMR/MARC	KD2EHW	443.05000	+	CC1	
Geneva	FM	W2ONT	147.09000	+	110.9 Hz	UNYREPCO
Ghent	FM	K2RVW-R	147.21000	+		UNYREPCO
	FUSION	WA2UET	146.54000			
Glen	FM	K2JJI	146.97000	-		
	FM	N2MNT	147.19500	+	156.7 Hz	UNYREPCO
Glen Oaks	DMR/MARC	WB2WAK	438.51250	-	CC1	MetroCor
	DMR/MARC	K2JRC	438.61250	-	CC3	
	FM	K2CJP	145.41000	-	114.8 Hz	MetroCor
	FM	W2VL	146.85000	-	136.5 Hz	MetroCor
	FM	W2KPQ	224.82000	-	136.5 Hz	MetroCor
	FM	KB2EKX	440.75000	+	162.2 Hz	MetroCor
	FM	K2CJP	445.37500	-	114.8 Hz	MetroCor
	FM	WB2VTJ	448.77500	-	114.8 Hz	MetroCor
	FUSION	WB2WAK	447.02500	-		
Glen Spey	FM	N2ACF	446.12500	-	114.8 Hz	
Glenmont	FM	K2QY	147.12000	+	100.0 Hz	

Location	Mode	Call sign	Output	Input	Access	Coordinator
Glens Falls North	FM	W2WCR-R	443.45000	+		
Glenville	FM	W2IR	146.79000	-	100.0 Hz	UNYREPCO
Gloversville	FM	W8NUD	53.13000	51.13000		
	FM	K2JJI	224.70000	-		UNYREPCO
	FM	K1YMI	443.70000	+	100.0 Hz	UNYREPCO
Goshen, Orange County Emergenc						
	FM	KC2OUR	449.67500	-	162.2 Hz	UNYREPCO
Grafton	FM	K2CBA	145.31000	-		UNYREPCO
	FM	K2REN	147.18000	+	100.0 Hz	UNYREPCO
	FM	WB2HZT	147.33000	+	146.2 Hz	UNYREPCO
Greene & Columbia Countie						
	DSTAR	KD2HCQ C	147.05000	+		
	DSTAR	KD2HCQ B	445.02500	-		
Greenfield Center	FUSION	KC2TVJ	147.52500			
Greenport	FM	W2AMC	440.05000	+	107.2 Hz	MetroCor
Greenwich	DMR/MARC	N2LEN	447.27500	-	CC1	
Groveland	FM	AA2GV	147.03000	-	110.9 Hz	UNYREPCO
Grymes Hill	P25	KC2LEB-R	440.55000	+		MetroCor
Half Moon	FM	W2GBO	448.87500	-	203.5 Hz	
Hamburg	DMR/BM	KB2FX	442.46250	+	CC1	
	DMR/MARC	N2GSF	442.18750	+	CC1	
	DMR/MARC	N2CID	442.36250	+	CC1	
Hampton Bays	FM	WA2UEG	147.19500	+	136.5 Hz	
Harriman	DMR/MARC	N2JTI	443.80000	+	CC1	
	FM	W2AEE	53.17000	52.17000	136.5 Hz	UNYREPCO
	FM	W2AEE	223.80000	-	107.2 Hz	UNYREPCO
	FM	N2ACF	439.87500	+	118.8 Hz	
Hartsdale	FUSION	KF2FK	146.86500	-		
Hasbrouck		W2FLA-R	146.62500			
Hauppague	FM	WB2ROL	442.85000	+	151.4 Hz	
Hauppauge	DSTAR	WD2NY	444.23750	+		
	FM	WA2LQO	145.33000	-	136.5 Hz	ASMA
	FM	W2LRC	145.43000	-	136.5 Hz	ASMA
	FM	WB2ERS	444.75000	+	110.9 Hz	
	FUSION	WR2ABA	448.67500	-	114.8 Hz	MetroCor
Hemlock	DSTAR	K2BWK	147.37500	+		UNYREPCO
	DSTAR	K2BWK C	147.37500	+		
	DSTAR	K2BWK	443.50000	+		UNYREPCO
	DSTAR	K2BWK B	443.50000	+		
Henrietta	DMR/BM	W2JSB	442.12500	+	CC1	
Herkimer	FM	N2ZWO	147.09000	+		UNYREPCO
Highbridge	FM	K2CSX	438.10000			
Highland	DMR/MARC	KC2OBW	440.31250	+	CC11	
Highland, Illinois Mountain						
	FM	N2OXV	147.04500	+	100.0 Hz	UNYREPCO
Highland, WRWD	FM	KC2OBW	927.65000	902.65000	136.5 Hz	
Holland	DMR/MARC	N2CID	442.36250	+	CC1	
Hollis	FUSION	N2OWR	145.72500			
Holtsville	FM	WB2MOT	146.94000	-	136.5 Hz	ASMA
	FM	AG2I	442.05000	+	114.8 Hz	ASMA
	FM	W2SBL	449.17500	-	114.8 Hz	MetroCor
Hoosick Falls, Hoosick Falls						
	FM	K2FCR	146.65500	-	100.0 Hz	
Hornell	DMR/MARC	KD2WA	443.45000	+	CC12	
	FM	KD2WA	51.66000	-	110.9 Hz	UNYREPCO
Horseheads	FUSION	N2OJM	442.75000	+		
Hudson	FM	N2LEN	147.15000	+	114.8 Hz	
Hudson Falls		N1NDN-L	224.96000			
Hunter	FM	WB2UYR	145.15000	-		UNYREPCO
Huntington	DMR/MARC	W2RGM	448.47500	-	CC1	
	FM	WR2ABA	147.21000	+	136.5 Hz	
	FM	KC2QHN	448.22500	-		

Location	Mode	Call sign	Output	Input	Access	Coordinator
Huntington Station						
	DMR/BM	N2YGI	438.46000	-	CC1	
	DMR/BM	N2YGI	439.65000	-	CC13	
Huntington, Huntington Hospita						
	FM	KF2GV	448.22500	-	69.3 Hz	MetroCor
Hunts Point		K2CSX-L	145.67000			
Ilion	FM	N2ZWO	145.11000	-	167.9 Hz	UNYREPCO
	FM	N3SQ	146.80500	-		UNYREPCO
Inlet	DMR/MARC	N2LBT	147.43750	144.93750	CC1	
	DMR/MARC	N2LBT	449.52500	-	CC1	
Islip	FM	K2IRG	147.34500	+	100.0 Hz	ASMA
Islip Terrace	FM	WA2UMD	447.77500	-	114.8 Hz	MetroCor
Ithaca	DSTAR	AF2A B	449.02500	-		
	DSTAR	AF2A	449.02500	-		
	FM	K2ZG	146.89500	-	107.2 Hz	UNYREPCO
Ithaca, Connecticut Hill						
	FM	AF2A	146.97000	-	103.5 Hz	UNYREPCO
Ithaca, Cornell Univ						
	FM	W2CXM	146.61000	-	103.5 Hz	UNYREPCO
Ithaca, Hungerford Hill						
	FM	AF2A	146.94000	-	103.5 Hz	UNYREPCO
Jamestown	FM	KS2D	145.33000	-	127.3 Hz	WNYSORC
	FM	W2BBI	146.43000			
	FM	K2LUC	146.94000	-	127.3 Hz	WNYSORC
Jasper	FM	KC2JLQ	147.33000	+	110.9 Hz	UNYREPCO
Jeffereson Valley	DMR/MARC	NY4Z	448.92500	-	CC1	
Jewett	FM	W1EQX	145.45000	-		SLVRC
Johnsburg	FM	W2CDY	146.46000		114.8 Hz	
Kenmore	FM	K2LED	147.00000	+	107.2 Hz	
Kerhonkson	FUSION	KB2RWW	145.75000			
Kew Gardens	FM	N2XBA	224.46000	-	141.3 Hz	
	FM	NB2A	927.28750	902.58750		MetroCor
Kingston	DMR/BM	N2MCI	441.56250	+	CC1	
	DMR/BM	N2MCI	448.62500	-	CC1	
	FM	WA2MJM	146.80500	-	103.5 Hz	
	FM	WA2MJM	147.25500	+	103.5 Hz	UNYREPCO
	FM	WA2MJM	448.62500	-	77.0 Hz	UNYREPCO
Kirkland	FM	K1DCC	147.24000	+	71.9 Hz	
	FM	KA2FWN	443.85000	+	103.5 Hz	
Knapp Creek	FM	W3VG	146.85000	-	127.3 Hz	WNYSORC
Krumville	FM	KC2BYY	146.74500	-	123.0 Hz	UNYREPCO
Lake George	DMR/MARC	W2WCR	443.25000	+	CC1	
	FM	N2ACF	444.45000	+	114.8 Hz	
Lake George, Prospect Mountain						
	FM	W2WCR	224.78000	-		UNYREPCO
Lake Luzerne	DMR/BM	N2YQT	445.00000	-	CC1	
Lake Peekskill	FM	W2NYW	146.67000	-	156.7 Hz	UNYREPCO
	FM	KB2CQE	449.92500	-	179.9 Hz	UNYREPCO
Lake Placid	DMR/MARC	N2NGK	446.67500	-	CC1	
	DMR/MARC	N2NGK	446.97500	-	CC1	
	DMR/MARC	N2NGK	449.67500	-	CC1	
	FM	N2NGK	147.30000	+	100.0 Hz	VIRCC
Lake Placid, Blue Mountain						
	FM	N2JKG	442.75000	+	123.0 Hz	VIRCC
Lancaster	DMR/BM	W2BRW	444.08750	+	CC1	
	FM	W2SO	53.17000	52.17000	107.2 Hz	WNYSORC
	FM	W2SO	147.25500	+	107.2 Hz	WNYSORC
	FM	W2SO	224.64000	+		
	FM	W2SO	443.85000	+		
Latham	FM	KT2D	927.21250	902.21250	114.8 Hz	
Liberty	FM	KC2AXO	147.13500	+	94.8 Hz	UNYREPCO
	FM	N2ACF	441.95000	+	114.8 Hz	UNYREPCO

Serving The Amateur Radio Community Since 1965

Our 58th Year

LIMARC

Long Island Mobile Amateur Radio Club

The **Long Island Mobile Amateur Radio Club** is an ARRL Affiliated Special Service Club serving the Amateur Radio community since 1965. LIMARC, one of the largest Amateur Radio clubs in the USA, is a nonprofit organization, dedicated to the advancement of Amateur Radio, public service and assistance to fellow amateurs.

LIMARC operates nine club repeaters, all using a 136.5 PL. (except DMR)

Repeater Frequencies: Our two 2m repeaters are linked.
W2VL 146.850 [-] (Glen Oaks)
ECHOLINK W2VL-R, Node 487981

W2KPQ 147.375 [+] (Selden)
ECHOLINK W2KPQ-R, Node 503075

IRLP via Reflector Node 9126

Allstar, Node 576290

WA2LQO 146.745 [-] Fusion (Plainview)

W2VL 1288.00 [-] (Glen Oaks)

W2KPQ 449.125 [-] IRLP Node 4969,
ECHOLINK W2KPQ-L, Node 500940

W2KPQ 224.820 [-] (Glen Oaks)

449.075 (-) Middle Island

Weekly Nets
Technical Net: Sunday @ 8:00 PM
Club Info Net: Monday @ 8:30 PM followed by the **Swap & Shop Net**
Other Regularly Scheduled Nets
Computer Net: 3rd and 4th Wednesday at 8:30 PM
Nostalgia/Trivia Net: @ 8:30 PM on the fifth Wednesday of those months where one occurs.
Note: All Nets are linked between the 146.850 and 147.375 Repeaters

DMR -CC1 W2KPQ) 449,375 (-) (Plainview), W2KPQ 449.3625 [-] (Selden), Packet Node W2KPQ and BBS W2KPQ-4 on 145.07MHz

Repeater Trustees: W2VL, W2QZ; **W2KPQ**, WB2WAK

Special Events Callsign WV2LI: Trustee N2GA

Some of LIMARC's regular activities are

General Meetings: 2nd Wednesday (except July and August) at Levittown Hall, Hicksville, NY @ 8:00 PM

VE Tests: 2nd Saturday in odd numbered months at Levittown Hall — check our web-site for additional information

License Classes and Field Day
Co- SPONSOR OF THE SCHOOL CLUB ROUNDUP
2023 Events
Hamfests-February, June, and November
Special Event Stations K2CAM, (Cradle of Aviation Museum)
May - Lindbergh Flight, July - Apollo 11

For more information on current LIMARC events:
Access LIMARC on the World Wide Web:
https://www.limarc.org or e-mail us at: **limarc@limarc.org**
Write: **LIMARC, P.O. Box 392, Levittown, NY 11756**
Phone 516-450-5153

Location	Mode	Call sign	Output	Input	Access	Coordinator
Limestone	FM	W3VG	53.31000	52.31000	127.3 Hz	WNYSORC
Liverpool	DMR/MARC	WB2WGH	443.80000	+	CC1	
Lockport	DMR/MARC	KC2WBX	443.71250	+	CC1	
	DMR/MARC	W2OM	444.62500	+	CC1	
	DSTAR	K2MJ	144.46500			
	FM	KC2WBX	445.92500			
	FUSION	K2MJ	145.65000			
	FUSION	KC2WBX	443.71250	+		
Lockport, Niagara County EOC						
	FM	W2RUI	146.82000	-	107.2 Hz	WNYSORC
Long Island	FM	N2HBA	927.96250	902.96250	151.4 Hz	UNYREPCO
Long Island-NYC	DMR/MARC	WB2ERS	444.75000	+	CC1	
Long Lake	FM	KD2BAD	146.64000	-	162.2 Hz	UNYREPCO
	FM	KD2BAD	443.85000	+	162.2 Hz	UNYREPCO
Lowville	FM	W2RHM	146.95500	-	156.7 Hz	UNYREPCO
Lyon Mountain	FM	W2UXC	147.28500	+	123.0 Hz	VIRCC
	FM	WA2LRE	224.02000	-	123.0 Hz	VIRCC
Macedon	FM	W1YX	147.18000	+		
	FM	N2HJD	442.92500	+	110.9 Hz	
	FUSION	KA1CNF	147.52500			
	FUSION	KA1CNF	444.77500	+		
	FUSION	KA1CNF	446.70000			
Mahattan, Lincoln Center						
	FM	N2BEI	147.19500	+		
Mahopac	DMR/MARC	NY4Z	145.39000	-	CC1	
	DMR/MARC	K2HR	146.91000	-	CC5	
	DMR/MARC	NY4Z	440.61875	+	CC3	
	DMR/MARC	NY4Z	446.27500	-	CC10	
	DMR/MARC	NY4Z	448.12500	-	CC9	
	FM	K2HR	29.66000	-	74.4 Hz	SLVRC
	FM	K2HR	224.00000	-	79.7 Hz	UNYREPCO
	FM	NY4Z	224.70000	-	79.7 Hz	UNYREPCO
Malone	FM	WB2RYB	53.15000	52.15000	123.0 Hz	SLVRC
	FM	NG2C	147.09000	+		SLVRC
	FM	WB2RYB	147.22500	+	100.0 Hz	
	FM	NG2C	444.75000	+		SLVRC
Malverne	DMR/MARC	WB2WAK	446.42500	-	CC1	MetroCor
	FUSION	WB2WAK	147.13500	+		
	FUSION	WB2WAK	447.02500	-		
	FUSION	WB2WAK	447.97500	-		
Mamaroneck	DMR/MARC	KF2C	442.15000	+	CC1	
Manhattan	DMR/MARC	KD2LS	433.40000	+	CC1	
	DMR/MARC	K2HR	440.60000	+	CC1	
	DMR/MARC	NY4Z	442.05000	+	CC7	MetroCor
	DSTAR	K2DIG	445.27500	-		MetroCor
	FM	KQ2H	29.62000	-	146.2 Hz	SLVRC
	FM	K2HR	145.29000	-	94.8 Hz	MetroCor
	FM	WR2MSN	145.57000	146.57000	192.8 Hz	MetroCor
	FM	WB2ZSE	147.00000	-	136.5 Hz	MetroCor
	FM	W2ABC	147.27000	+	141.3 Hz	
	FM	WR2MSN	223.76000	-	192.8 Hz	MetroCor
	FM	KB2TM	223.90000	-	141.3 Hz	MetroCor
	FM	WA2HDE	224.66000	-	127.3 Hz	MetroCor
	FM	KQ2H	224.80000	-	141.3 Hz	
	FM	WR2MSN	440.42500	+	156.7 Hz	MetroCor
	FM	NY4Z	440.60000	+	141.3 Hz	MetroCor
	FM	NE2E	441.45000	+	123.0 Hz	MetroCor
	FM	KB2RQE	442.45000	+	179.9 Hz	MetroCor
	FM	N2YN	443.65000	+	77.0 Hz	
	FM	WA2CBS	445.07500	-	114.8 Hz	MetroCor
	FM	K2NYR	445.22500	-	74.4 Hz	MetroCor
	FM	KF2GV	446.92500	-	69.3 Hz	MetroCor

Location	Mode	Call sign	Output	Input	Access	Coordinator
Manhattan	FM	WB2ZTH	447.17500	-	141.3 Hz	MetroCor
	FM	KE2EJ	447.20000	-	100.0 Hz	MetroCor
	FM	KC2IMB	448.43000	-	107.2 Hz	MetroCor
	FM	N2JDW	449.02500	-	123.0 Hz	MetroCor
	FM	WB2ZSE	449.80000	-	114.8 Hz	MetroCor
	FUSION	KC2ECR	145.31000	-		
Manhattan , Bowling Green						
	FM	K2IRT	441.70000	+	100.0 Hz	
Manhattan NYC	DMR/MARC	K2JRC	438.56250	-	CC2	MetroCor
Manhattan West Side						
	DMR/MARC	K2JRC	443.70000	+	CC3	
Manhattan, Empire State Buildi						
	FM	KQ2H	449.22500	-	82.5 Hz	MetroCor
Manhattan, Lincoln Center - Up						
	FM	N2BEI	449.32500	-	136.5 Hz	MetroCor
Manhattan, Rockefeller Center						
	FM	WA2ZLB	147.36000	+	107.2 Hz	MetroCor
	FM	WA2ZLB	223.94000	-	107.2 Hz	MetroCor
	FM	WA2ZLB	447.82500	-	107.2 Hz	MetroCor
Manhattan, Sheraton Hotel						
	FM	WB2SEB	449.62500	-	179.9 Hz	MetroCor
Manhattan, Washington Heights						
	FM	N2JDW	147.15000	+	136.5 Hz	MetroCor
Manorville	FM	N2NFI	145.37000	-	136.5 Hz	UNYREPCO
Martindale, Forest Lake						
	FM	K2RVW	224.28000	-		
	FM	K2RVW	449.92500	-	110.9 Hz	
Maryland	DMR/BM	KD2FRD	443.60000	+	CC1	
Mattituck	DMR/MARC	K1IMD	449.67500	-	CC1	
Mayville	FM	WB2EDV	444.45000	+		
Mayville, Emergency Operations						
	DSTAR	KD2LYO	146.76000	-	127.3 Hz	
Melville	FM	WB2CIK	53.11000	51.31000	107.2 Hz	MetroCor
	FM	KB2AKH	147.28500	+	97.4 Hz	MetroCor
	FM	WB2CIK	442.95000	+	114.8 Hz	MetroCor
Merrick	DMR/BM	KJ2CAT	433.65000	+	CC1	
Middle Grove	FM	WB2BGI	145.43000	-	156.7 Hz	UNYREPCO
Middle Island	FM	W2OQI	146.82000	-	136.5 Hz	MetroCor
Middletown	FM	WR2MSN	224.54000	-	156.7 Hz	UNYREPCO
Middletown, Scotchtown Ave						
	DSTAR	K9CEO	145.60000			
Milan	DMR/BM	K2JLV	449.50000	-	CC4	
Millbrook	FM	N2EYH	146.89500	-	100.0 Hz	
Mineola	FM	W2EJ	146.64000	-	100.0 Hz	MetroCor
	FM	KC2DVQ	443.25000	+	123.0 Hz	MetroCor
Mineville	FM	WA2LRE	53.35000	52.35000	123.0 Hz	VIRCC
	FM	WA2LRE	147.25500	+	123.0 Hz	VIRCC
Mohawk	DMR/BM	KA2FWN	449.42500	-	CC1	
Montauk	DMR/MARC	WZ2Y	443.20000	+	CC1	
	FM	WZ2Y	145.27000	-	136.5 Hz	MetroCor
Monticello, Sackett Lake						
	DSTAR	K2ASS	147.55000			
Morrisville	FM	WA2DTN	444.60000	+	162.2 Hz	UNYREPCO
Mount Vernon	FM	K2UQT	145.49500	-		MetroCor
Mt. Beacon	DMR/MARC	K2ATY	441.01875	+	CC10	
Munnsville	DMR/BM	N2ADK	443.00000	+	CC1	
Nanuet	FM	WR2I	443.35000	+	114.8 Hz	UNYREPCO
Napanoch	FM	KC2FBI	147.53500	145.53500	100.0 Hz	
Naples	FM	NO2W	146.92000	-		UNYREPCO
Naples-Gannet Hill						
	FM	W2ONT	442.20000	+	110.9 Hz	UNYREPCO

Location	Mode	Call sign	Output	Input	Access	Coordinator
Naples-Gannett Hill						
	FM	W2ONT	145.45000	-	110.9 Hz	UNYREPCO
Nassau	DMR/MARC	WW2FD	145.41000	-	CC1	
New Baltimore	DMR/BM	N2LEN	145.45000	-	CC1	
	DMR/MARC	N2LEN	449.02500	-	CC1	
New Hartford	DMR/BM	N2USB	147.01500	+	CC1	
	DMR/MARC	N2USB	446.37500	-	CC2	
New Oregon	FM	WB2JPQ	444.37500	+	88.5 Hz	
New Paltz	FUSION	K2MTB	447.92500			
New Rochelle		N2YGI-R	145.08500			
	DMR/MARC	NY1FD	145.49500	-	CC1	
	DMR/MARC	KC2TOM	147.04000	+	CC1	
	DMR/MARC	N2YGI	439.58750	-	CC1	
	DMR/MARC	NY4Z	446.28125	-	CC1	
	FM	N2YGI	147.58500	145.08500	88.5 Hz	
	FM	NY4Z	446.72500	-	192.8 Hz	
New Scotland	FM	K2CWW	145.33000	-		UNYREPCO
New Windsor	FM	KB2MTA	145.20000			
	FM	KD2ANX	146.48500	-	88.5 Hz	
New York		W2MGF-L	145.69000			
		KB2EAR-L	224.84000			
		N2QLW-L	446.05000			
	DMR/MARC	KC2NFB	439.97500	-	CC1	
	DMR/MARC	K2ZZ	448.27500	-	CC3	
	DSTAR	K2DIG B	445.27500	-		
	DSTAR	K2DIG D	1253.00000			
	DSTAR	K2DIG A	1293.00000	1273.00000		
	FM	N2MCC	448.42500	-		
	FUSION	KG2KB	442.43500			
New York City	DMR/MARC	N2NSA	443.88750	+	CC1	MetroCor
Newark	DMR/MARC	N2MKT	443.25000	+	CC1	UNYREPCO
Newark, Water Tower						
	FM	KA2NDW	927.21250	902.21250	82.5 Hz	
Newark, Water Tower Hill						
	FM	WA2AAZ	224.90000	-	110.9 Hz	UNYREPCO
Newburgh	FM	N2HEP	449.47500	-	71.9 Hz	UNYREPCO
Newburgh, Cronomer Hill						
	FM	N2HEP	146.43000	147.43000	71.9 Hz	UNYREPCO
Newport		KA2ENE-L	443.55000			
Niagara Falls	DSTAR	KD2GBR C	146.73000	-		
	DSTAR	KD2GBR B	444.83750	+		
	FUSION	KD2MFW	145.02500			
NOAA Albany	WX	WXL34	162.55000			
NOAA Binghamton						
	WX	WXL38	162.47500			
NOAA Buffalo	WX	KEB98	162.55000			
NOAA Call Hill	WX	WXN29	162.42500			
NOAA Cattaraugus						
	WX	WWG32	162.42500			
NOAA Cooperstown						
	WX	WWH35	162.45000			
NOAA Egremont	WX	WXM82	162.45000			
NOAA Elmira	WX	WXM31	162.40000			
NOAA Frewsburg	WX	WNG541	162.52500			
NOAA Gore Mountain						
	WX	KSC43	162.45000			
NOAA Highland	WX	WXL37	162.47500			
NOAA Ithaca	WX	WXN59	162.50000			
NOAA Middleville	WX	WXM45	162.42500			
NOAA Mount Washington						
	WX	WXN55	162.45000			

Location	Mode	Call sign	Output	Input	Access	Coordinator
NOAA New York City						
	WX	KWO35	162.55000			
NOAA Norwich	WX	KHC49	162.52500			
NOAA Riverhead	WX	WXM80	162.47500			
NOAA Rochester	WX	KHA53	162.40000			
NOAA Spencerport						
	WX	WNG539	162.52500			
NOAA Stamford	WX	WWF43	162.40000			
NOAA Syracuse	WX	WXL31	162.55000			
NOAA Walton	WX	WWH34	162.42500			
NOAA Watertown	WX	WXN68	162.47500			
NOAA Whites Hill	WX	KBS508	162.52500			
North Babylon	FM	KB2UR	224.12000	-	131.8 Hz	MetroCor
North Babylon, Babylon Town Ha						
	FM	KB2UR	147.25500	+		
	FM	KB2UR	446.77500	-	110.9 Hz	
North Chatham	FM	W2JWR	449.12500	-	100.0 Hz	
	FM	W2JWR	927.12500	902.12500	100.0 Hz	
North Chili	FM	W2XRX	444.82500	+		
	P25	KD2AWT	146.70000	-		
North Creek	DMR/MARC	W2WCR	442.25000	+	CC1	
North Creek, Gore Mountain						
	FM	W2WCR	147.12000	+	123.0 Hz	UNYREPCO
North Hebron	DMR/MARC	N2ZTC	442.30000	+	CC7	
North Lindenhurst	DSTAR	W2TOB	440.25000	+		MetroCor
	FM	W2GSB	146.68500	-	110.9 Hz	
North Tonawanda	DMR/BM	W2BRW	442.48750	+	CC1	
	FM	W2SEX	146.95500	-	151.4 Hz	WNYSORC
	FM	N2WUT	443.60000	+	67.0 Hz	
Norway	FM	N2ZWO	147.04500	+	167.9 Hz	UNYREPCO
Norwich	FM	W2RME	146.68500	-	110.9 Hz	UNYREPCO
Nyack	FM	N2ACF	29.64000	-	114.8 Hz	SLVRC
Nyack, Tappan Zee Bridge						
	FM	WR2I	449.42500	-	114.8 Hz	UNYREPCO
Oceanside	DMR/MARC	N2ION	447.92500	447.42500	CC7	
	DMR/MARC	N2ION	449.07500	-	CC7	
Ogdensburg		KC2KVE-R	146.47500			
	DMR/BM	KC2KVE	146.79000	147.79000	CC1	
	DMR/MARC	W2SLV	442.85000	442.35000	CC4	
	FM	W2EX	147.16500	+	151.4 Hz	
Olean	FM	K2XZ	444.85000	+	88.5 Hz	WNYSORC
Oneida	DMR/BM	KA2FWN	444.80000	+	CC1	
	FM	W2MO	145.17000	-		UNYREPCO
	FM	W2MO	443.65000	+	103.5 Hz	
Oneonta	DMR/MARC	N2ZNH	448.17500	-	CC1	
	FM	KI6VPH	146.44000		123.0 Hz	
	FM	W2SEU	146.85000	-	167.9 Hz	
Ontario	FUSION	K2AS	446.25000			
Orange County RACES						
	FM	N2TMT	147.28500	+	118.8 Hz	
Orangeburg	DMR/MARC	N2JTI	444.00000	+	CC1	UNYREPCO
Orangetown	FM	N2ACF	53.37000	52.37000	114.8 Hz	UNYREPCO
	FM	WB2RRA	147.16500	+	114.8 Hz	UNYREPCO
	FM	WA2MLG	224.38000	-	114.8 Hz	UNYREPCO
	FM	N2ACF	443.85000	+	114.8 Hz	UNYREPCO
	FM	N2ACF	927.85000	902.05000	114.8 Hz	UNYREPCO
Oriskany	FM	KD2MCI	146.23500	+	71.9 Hz	
Oriskany, Oneida County Sherif						
	FM	KD2MCI	146.83500	-	71.9 Hz	UNYREPCO
Oswegatchie	DMR/BM	WA2NAN	442.17500	+	CC1	SLVRC
Oswego	FM	W2OSC	147.15000	+	103.5 Hz	UNYREPCO
	FUSION	N1JUX	446.17500			

Location	Mode	Call sign	Output	Input	Access	Coordinator
Otisville	DSTAR	KC2YYF	145.63000			
	DSTAR	KC2YYF C	145.63000			
	DSTAR	K9RRD B	448.57500	-		
Otisville, Goshen Turnpike						
	DSTAR	K9RRD	448.57500	-		UNYREPCO
Otisville, Graham Hill						
	FM	KC2OUR	448.32500	-	123.0 Hz	
Owego	FM	W2VDX	146.76000	-		
	FM	K2OQ	147.39000	+	91.5 Hz	UNYREPCO
	FUSION	W2FJH	433.50000	+		
Palmyra	FUSION	KB2NHY	147.37500	+		
Parishville	DMR/MARC	K2WW	147.07500	+	CC1	
	DMR/MARC	W2SLV	442.30000	+	CC1	
	FM	W2LCA	444.85000	+	151.4 Hz	SLVRC
Patchogue	DMR/BM	WD2NY	147.03000	+	CC1	
Patterson	FM	K2CQS	224.88000	-		UNYREPCO
Pearl River	FM	NJ2BS	146.83500	-	151.4 Hz	UNYREPCO
Peconic	DMR/MARC	K1IMD	449.97500	-	CC1	
Perinton, Baker Hill						
	FM	KB2VZS	146.71500	-	110.9 Hz	
Perrysburg	FM	KC2DKP	444.90000	+	107.2 Hz	WNYSORC
Peru	DMR/MARC	NV2M	442.28750	+	CC1	VIRCC
	FM	NV2M	224.02000	-	123.0 Hz	
Peru, Terry Mountain						
	FM	WA2LRE	145.49000	-	123.0 Hz	VIRCC
Piffard	DMR/BM	N2YSG	147.19500	+	CC1	
	DMR/BM	N2YSG	147.38750	+	CC1	
	DMR/BM	N2YSG	442.83750	+	CC1	
	FUSION	KD2OWU	145.64000			
Pine Bush	FM	AA2XX	443.70000	+	141.3 Hz	
Pine Hill	FM	KQ2H	444.05000	+		
Pittsford	DMR/BM	W2RDK	434.00000	+	CC1	
Plainview	DMR/MARC	W2KPQ	449.37500	-	CC1	
	DMR/MARC	K2LIE	449.41250	-	CC5	
	FM	WA2LQO	146.74500	-	136.5 Hz	MetroCor
	FM	WB2WAK	146.80500	-	136.5 Hz	MetroCor
	FM	WA2UZE	147.33000	+	136.5 Hz	MetroCor
	FM	KC2AOY	441.40000	+	151.4 Hz	MetroCor
	FM	WB2WAK	446.47500	-	136.5 Hz	MetroCor
	FM	N2FLF	447.35000	-	114.8 Hz	MetroCor
	FM	W2KPQ	449.12500	-	136.5 Hz	MetroCor
Plattsburgh	DMR/MARC	KD2MAJ	145.07000	147.44500	CC1	
	FM	WA2LRE	53.59000	52.59000	123.0 Hz	VIRCC
	FM	W2UXC	147.15000	+	123.0 Hz	VIRCC
	FM	NV2M	447.57500	-	123.0 Hz	VIRCC
	FM	WA2LRE	448.07500	-	123.0 Hz	
Poland	FM	N2CNY	145.21000	-	167.9 Hz	
Pomfret, Concord Drive						
	FM	W2SB	444.35000	+	88.5 Hz	WNYSORC
Pomona	FM	N2ACF	145.17000	-	114.8 Hz	
	FM	KQ2H	146.46000	147.46000	77.0 Hz	UNYREPCO
	FM	N2ACF	223.82000	-	114.8 Hz	UNYREPCO
	FM	N2ACF	444.45000	+	114.8 Hz	UNYREPCO
Pompey Hill	FM	KD2AYD	144.39000			
Pompey, Pompey Hill						
	FM	W2CNY	146.77500	-	151.4 Hz	UNYREPCO
	FM	W2CM	146.91000	-	103.5 Hz	UNYREPCO
Port Jefferson	FM	W2RC	449.52500	-	114.8 Hz	MetroCor
Port Jefferson, St. Charles Ho						
	FM	W2RC	145.15000	-	136.5 Hz	UNYREPCO
Port Jervis	DSTAR	W2TAO B	441.35000	+		
	FM	N2ACF	449.12500	-	114.8 Hz	

Location	Mode	Call sign	Output	Input	Access	Coordinator
Portable Repeat	DMR/MARC	NY4Z	440.60000	+	CC3	
Potsdam	DMR/BM	K2CC	146.89500	-	CC1	
	DMR/BM	K2CC	443.35000	+	CC1	SLVRC
Poughquag	DMR/MARC	K2HR	447.07500	-	CC3	
Putnam CTY	DMR/MARC	NY4Z	446.27500	+	CC2	
Putnam Valley	FM	N2CBH	448.72500	-	107.2 Hz	UNYREPCO
Queens	DMR/MARC	KC2CQR	449.72500	-	CC1	
	DSTAR	KB2NYC	224.18000	-	114.8 Hz	
	DSTAR	WB2CYN B	449.72500	-		
	FM	KB2NYC	446.38750	-	114.8 Hz	
	FM	KC2LAI	446.81250	-	71.9 Hz	MetroCor
Queens Village	FUSION	WB2QBP	442.65000	+	141.3 Hz	MetroCor
Queensbury, NY	DSTAR	W2CDY	145.55000			
Rand Hill	DMR/MARC	WA2LRE	145.07000	147.44500	CC1	
Remsen	FM	KB2AUJ	145.33000	-	71.9 Hz	UNYREPCO
Richmond		WA2IAF-R	447.37500	-		MetroCor
Richmond Hill	FM	NB2A	445.17500	-	141.3 Hz	MetroCor
Ripley	FM	K2OAD	145.47000	-	127.3 Hz	WNYSORC
Riverhead	DMR/MARC	N2NFI	442.30000	+	CC1	UNYREPCO
	FUSION	K2RPF	434.10000			
Rochester	DMR/BM	W2RIT	442.07500	+	CC1	
	DMR/BM	KD2EHW	443.05000	+	CC1	
	DMR/BM	KD2FRD	443.30000	+	CC1	
	DMR/BM	KD2FRD	443.60000	+	CC1	
	DMR/BM	WB2KAO	444.85000	+	CC1	
	FM	N2HJD	29.68000	-	123.0 Hz	SLVRC
	FM	N2HJD	53.33000	52.33000	123.0 Hz	
	FM	K2OI	145.29000	-	110.9 Hz	
	FM	N2HJD	146.92500	-	110.9 Hz	UNYREPCO
	FM	N2HJD	224.58000	-	110.9 Hz	
	FM	N2HJD	442.80000	+	110.9 Hz	UNYREPCO
	FM	W2RFC	444.40000	+	110.9 Hz	UNYREPCO
	FM	WR2AHL	444.95000	+		
Rochester , Cobbs Hill						
	FM	N2MPE	444.45000	+		
Rochester, Cobbs Hill						
	FM	N2MPE	146.61000	-	110.9 Hz	
Rochester, Highland Hospital						
	FM	WR2ROC	146.79000	-	110.9 Hz	
Rochester, Seneca Towers						
	FM	N2HJD	444.70000	+	110.9 Hz	UNYREPCO
Rochester, URMC	FM	WR2ROC	147.31500	+	110.9 Hz	UNYREPCO
Rockaway Park	DMR/BM	KE4DYI	438.40000	-	CC0	
Rocky Point	FM	N2FXE	146.59500	+	136.5 Hz	MetroCor
	FM	N2FXE	443.90000	+	123.0 Hz	
Rosedale	FM	K2EAR	145.35000	-	114.8 Hz	MetroCor
Royalton	FM	KD2WA	29.66000	-	107.2 Hz	SLVRC
	FM	KD2WA	443.45000	+	107.2 Hz	
	FM	KD2WA	927.45000	902.45000		
Rush	DMR/BM	N2CHP	444.22500	+	CC1	
Rush/East Avon, Watts Electron						
	FM	N2YCK	29.64000	-	110.9 Hz	UNYREPCO
	FM	N2YCK	53.37000	52.37000	110.9 Hz	UNYREPCO
	FM	N2YCK	145.35000	-	110.9 Hz	UNYREPCO
	FM	N2YCK	224.02000	-	110.9 Hz	UNYREPCO
	FM	N2YCK	443.75000	+	110.9 Hz	UNYREPCO
	FM	N2YCK	927.85000	902.85000	110.9 Hz	UNYREPCO
Russell	DMR/MARC	W2SLV	442.35000	+	CC1	
Russell, Kimball Hill						
	FM	KA2JXI	146.92500	-	151.4 Hz	SLVRC
Rye Brook	FM	KB2GTE	444.65000	+	114.8 Hz	MetroCor

Location	Mode	Call sign	Output	Input	Access	Coordinator
S. Bristol , Bristol Mountain						
	FM	W2SIX	53.63000	52.63000	110.9 Hz	
S. Bristol, Bristol Mountain S						
	FM	WR2AHL	444.55000	+	110.9 Hz	
S. Bristol, Mees Observatory						
	FM	WR2ROC	146.65500	-	110.9 Hz	
Sag Harbor	FM	K2GLP	449.98000	-	94.8 Hz	ASMA
Sams Point, New York						
	FM	KC2OUR	53.55000	52.55000	156.7 Hz	
Saranac Lake	FM	W2TLR	145.31000	-	127.3 Hz	SLVRC
	FM	W2WIZ	147.03000	+	123.0 Hz	VIRCC
Schenectady	DMR/BM	N2LEN	448.27500	-	CC1	
	DMR/MARC	N2LEN	147.30000	+	CC1	
	FM	K2AE	444.20000	+		
Schenectady, Crawford Hill						
	FM	K2AE	147.06000	+		
Schenevus	FM	KC2AWM	223.96000	-	100.0 Hz	UNYREPCO
Selden	DMR/BM	WD5TAR	444.70000	+	CC1	
	DMR/MARC	WA2VNV	448.82500	-	CC1	
	DMR/MARC	W2KPQ	449.36250	-	CC1	
	DSTAR	WD5TAR B	444.70000	+		
	DSTAR	WD2NY B	445.72500	-		
	FM	WA2VNV	146.76000	-	136.5 Hz	
	FM	W2KPQ	147.37500	+	136.5 Hz	MetroCor
	FM	WA2UMD	447.52500	-		MetroCor
	FM	WA2UMD	447.80000	-	114.8 Hz	MetroCor
Selden, NY	FM	W2KPQ	147.37500	+	136.5 Hz	
Sentinel Heights	FM	KD2SL-R	146.67000	-		UNYREPCO
Setauket	FM	K2YBW	147.04500	+	136.5 Hz	WNYSORC
Shadigee	FM	K2SRV-R	442.87500	+		UNYREPCO
Shakers	FM	N2TY-R	145.17000	-		UNYREPCO
Sherburne	FM	KD2HKB	443.05000	+	179.9 Hz	
Sherman	FM	WB2EDV	53.61000	52.61000	127.3 Hz	WNYSORC
	FM	WB2EDV	442.75000	+		
Shirley	DMR/BM	KC2WCB	443.52500	+	CC1	
Sidney	FM	AC2KP	146.95500	-		
Sloatsburg	FM	N2ACF	444.85000	+	114.8 Hz	UNYREPCO
Smithtown	FM	W2LRC	224.62000	-		MetroCor
South Blooming Grove						
	FM	N2OKB	449.62500	-	136.5 Hz	
South Bristol	FM	NR2M	224.46000	-	110.9 Hz	UNYREPCO
South Vestal	FM	KD2HNW-R	446.02500	-		
South Wales	DMR/BM	N2WLS	442.28750	+	CC1	
Southampton	FM	WA2UEG	147.19500	+	136.5 Hz	UNYREPCO
Southold	FM	W2OQI	448.32500	-	107.2 Hz	MetroCor
Speculator	FM	KA2VHF	147.16500	+		
Spencerport	DMR/BM	KD2TWM	442.72500	+	CC1	
	DMR/BM	K2SA	443.70000	+	CC1	
Stamford	FM	K2NK	53.27000	52.27000	107.2 Hz	UNYREPCO
	FM	KQ2H	449.22500	-	82.5 Hz	
Stanley	DMR/BM	KD2HVC	444.30000	+	CC3	
	FM	W2ACC	224.26000	-	110.9 Hz	
Staten Island	DMR/BM	KB2EA	447.72500	-	CC1	
	DMR/MARC	W2RJR	440.65000	+	CC1	
	DMR/MARC	KC2RQR	442.30000	+	CC3	
	FM	WA2IAF	146.88000	-	141.3 Hz	MetroCor
	FM	KA2PBT	445.82500	-	156.7 Hz	MetroCor
	FM	N2BBO	445.87500	-	136.5 Hz	
	FM	N2IXU	448.47500	-	74.4 Hz	MetroCor
	FM	KC2GOW	927.43750	902.43750	100.0 Hz	MetroCor
	FUSION	N2UFM	145.50000			

Location	Mode	Call sign	Output	Input	Access	Coordinator
Staten Island, Grymes Hill						
	FM	KC2GOW	224.10000	-	141.3 Hz	MetroCor
Staten Island, North Shore						
	FM	N2EHN	445.57500	-	141.3 Hz	MetroCor
Staten Island, Todt Hill						
	FM	KC2GOW	53.83000	52.83000	136.5 Hz	MetroCor
	FM	KC2GOW	147.31500	+		MetroCor
	FM	KC2GOW	927.70000	902.00000	100.0 Hz	MetroCor
Stockton	FM	K2HE	146.88000	-	127.3 Hz	
Suitcase	DMR/MARC	K1IMD	449.97500	-	CC1	
Sunset Park	FM	K2RMX-R	446.82500	-	141.3 Hz	MetroCor
Sycaway	FM	W2SZ-R	146.82000	-		
Syosset	FM	N2HBA	448.02500	-	136.5 Hz	MetroCor
	FUSION	WB2CYN	447.97500	-	136.5 Hz	MetroCor
Syracuse	DMR/MARC	W2CM	443.30000	+	CC1	UNYREPCO
	FM	KD2SL	53.67000	52.67000	103.5 Hz	UNYREPCO
	FM	KC2VER	145.31000	-		
	FM	WA2AUL	443.10000	+	103.5 Hz	UNYREPCO
Syracuse, Museum Of Science An						
	FM	K2MST	443.15000	+	71.9 Hz	
Syracuse, Onondaga Community C						
	FM	K2OCR	147.30000	+	67.0 Hz	
Syracuse, Sentinal Heights						
	FM	KD2SL	444.00000	+	103.5 Hz	
Syracuse, Sentinel Heights						
	FM	KD2SL	145.15000	-	123.0 Hz	
Test Box	DMR/MARC	K2HR	442.15000	+	CC1	
Test System	DMR/MARC	K1IMD	433.65000	+	CC1	
Thiells	DMR/BM	KD2EQY	441.80000	+	CC1	
	DMR/MARC	W2LGB	443.20000	+	CC1	
	DMR/MARC	W2LGB	447.87500	-	CC1	
	DMR/MARC	KD2EQY	449.18750	-	CC1	
	DSTAR	W2LGB B	449.67500	-		
	FM	W2LGB	449.77500	-		
Thiells, Rosman Center						
	FM	W2LGB	441.58750	+		
	FUSION	W2LGB	442.18750	+		
	FUSION	W2LGB	449.18750	-	114.8 Hz	UNYREPCO
Todt Hill, Staten Island						
	FM	W2RJR-R	224.84000	-	141.3 Hz	
Tomaselli Estates		WX2U-L	145.54500			
Troy	FM	K2REN	146.76000	-	103.5 Hz	UNYREPCO
	FM	W2SZ	224.42000	-		UNYREPCO
	FM	KB2HPW	224.64000	-		UNYREPCO
	FM	W2SZ	443.00000	+		
	FM	N2TY	447.07500	-	127.3 Hz	UNYREPCO
	FM	W2GBO	448.42500	-		
	FUSION	N2UIF	146.40000			
	FUSION	N2WMZ	146.45000			
Tupper Lake	DMR/MARC	W2TUP	446.02500	-	CC1	
	FM	W2TUP	147.33000	+	100.0 Hz	UNYREPCO
Tupper Lake, Big Tupper Ski Ar						
	FM	W2TUP	444.70000	+	110.9 Hz	UNYREPCO
Turner	DSTAR	KB1VFA C	147.43000			
Tuxedo Park	DSTAR	K9GOD	145.67000			
Upton	FM	K2BNL	442.40000	+	114.8 Hz	MetroCor
Usa-link	DMR/MARC	W2HVL	446.18750	445.68750	CC1	
Utica	DMR/MARC	KA2FWN	449.32500	-	CC1	
Valhalla	DMR/BM	W2ECA	438.71250	-	CC14	MetroCor
	DSTAR	W2ECA B	448.18750	-		
	DSTAR	W2ECA	448.18750	-		
	FM	WB2ZII	224.40000	-	114.8 Hz	MetroCor

Location	Mode	Call sign	Output	Input	Access	Coordinator
Valhalla	FM	K2XD	440.65000	+	114.8 Hz	MetroCor
Valhalla, Grasslands Tower						
	FM	WB2ZII	927.98750	902.98750	114.8 Hz	MetroCor
Valley Stream	FM	WB2IIQ	444.65000	+	103.5 Hz	MetroCor
	FM	N2ZEI	448.62500	-	136.5 Hz	MetroCor
Verona	DMR/BM	K1DCC	442.25000	+	CC1	
	FM	K1DCC	146.94000	-	71.9 Hz	
Vestal	FM	N2VFD	145.47000	-	100.0 Hz	
	FM	AA2EQ	224.48000	-	88.5 Hz	UNYREPCO
	FM	KD2HNW	444.30000	+		
Victor, Baker Hill	FM	N2HJD	145.41000	-	110.9 Hz	UNYREPCO
	FM	N2HJD	442.90000	+	110.9 Hz	
Virgil	FM	K2IWR-R	147.18000	+		UNYREPCO
Voorheesville	DSTAR	WA2UMX	443.30000	+		
Wading River	DMR/BM	W2CYK	433.00000	+	CC1	
	DMR/BM	W2CYK	442.12500	+	CC1	
	DMR/BM	W2CYK	445.75000	441.75000	CC1	
Walden	FM	KC2OUR	146.62500	147.92500	127.3 Hz	UNYREPCO
Walton	FM	K2NK	29.66000	-	107.2 Hz	SLVRC
Warrensburg	DMR/MARC	N2LEN	442.05000	+	CC1	
Warsaw	DMR/BM	N2FQN	147.10500	+	CC1	
Warwick	FM	N2ACF	448.22500	-	114.8 Hz	
Warwick, Mt Peter	FM	N2IXA	147.63000	-	107.2 Hz	
Washingtonville	DSTAR	N2KI C	145.31000			
	DSTAR	N2KI B	445.01500			
	FM	N2ACF	443.80000	+	114.8 Hz	
	FM	KQ2H	445.90000	-	82.5 Hz	
Washingtonville, Schunnemunk M						
	FM	WB2BQW	145.25000	-	100.0 Hz	UNYREPCO
Waterloo	FM	W2ACC	145.13000	-	110.9 Hz	UNYREPCO
	FM	W2ACC	442.22500	447.32500	82.5 Hz	UNYREPCO
Watertown	DMR/BM	W2BRW	443.52500	+	CC1	
	FM	WB2OOY	146.70000	-	151.4 Hz	
	FM	KA2QJO	147.25500	+	151.4 Hz	
Waterville	DMR/BM	KA2FWN	449.32500	-	CC1	
Watkins Glen	FM	KA2IFE	147.16500	+		UNYREPCO
	FM	WR2M	224.96000	-	88.5 Hz	UNYREPCO
Waverly	DMR/BM	N2NUO	444.50000	+	CC1	
	DMR/BM	N2NUO	444.65000	+	CC1	
	DMR/MARC	N2NUO	443.50000	+	CC1	
Webster	FUSION	KA2Y	431.55000			
Wellsville, Madison Hill						
	FM	WB2MOD	444.47500	+		
West Babylon	FUSION	KB2UR/R	446.77500	-		
West Canadice Corners						
		AE2EA-L	446.90000			
West Islip	FM	W2GSB	223.86000	-	110.9 Hz	MetroCor
	FM	W2GSB	440.85000	+	110.9 Hz	MetroCor
	FM	W2YMM	927.31250	902.31250		
West Nyack	FM	KC2EHA-R	147.53500	145.53500		UNYREPCO
West Point	FM	W2KGY	145.27000	-		
West Shokan, Ashokan Reservoir						
	FM	N2NCP	51.76000	-	103.5 Hz	UNYREPCO
Westbury	DMR/MARC	N2AZT	438.46000	-	CC1	
	DSTAR	NC2EC	146.67000	-		
	DSTAR	NC2EC C	146.67000	-		
	DSTAR	NC2EC	448.57500	-		
	DSTAR	NC2EC B	448.57500	-		
Westerlea		KB2ERJ-L	446.90000			
Westside Mobile Home Park						
	FM	WA2DQL-R	145.27000	-		WNYSORC
Wethersfield	FM	K2ISO	145.17000	-	110.9 Hz	WNYSORC

Location	Mode	Call sign	Output	Input	Access	Coordinator
Wethersfield	FM	K2XZ	146.64000	-		WNYSORC
	FM	N2FQN	147.10500	+	141.3 Hz	WNYSORC
	FM	KC2QNX	147.31500	+	141.3 Hz	WNYSORC
White Plains	DMR/MARC	NY4Z	442.10625	+	CC3	
Whiteface, Whiteface Mountain						
	FM	N2JKG	447.77500	-	123.0 Hz	VIRCC
Whitestone, Whitestone Bridge						
	FM	W2BAT	444.90000	+	225.7 Hz	MetroCor
Williamsville	FUSION	N2RKK	443.57500			
Willowbrook	FM	KC2GOW-R	445.12500	-		MetroCor
Wilmington, Whiteface Mountain						
	FM	N2JKG	145.11000	-	123.0 Hz	VIRCC
Wilton-McGregor	DMR/MARC	N1NDN	145.37000	-	CC1	
	DMR/MARC	WB2ERS	444.65000	+	CC1	
Woodstock	FM	N2WCY	53.11000	52.11000	77.0 Hz	UNYREPCO
Wurtsboro	FM	KQ2H	447.52500	-	82.5 Hz	UNYREPCO
	FM	N2ACF	449.87500	-	114.8 Hz	UNYREPCO
Wurtsburo, Catskill Mountains						
	FM	KQ2H	29.62000	-	146.2 Hz	SLVRC
Yaleville	FM	W2OFQ-R	146.88000	-		
Yaphank	FM	KA2RGI	53.79000	52.79000	156.7 Hz	ASMA
	FM	W2DQ	145.21000	-	136.5 Hz	ASMA
	FM	W2DQ	446.62500	-	110.9 Hz	ASMA
Yonkers	FM	W2YRC	146.86500	-	110.9 Hz	MetroCor
	FM	K2JQB	146.91000	-	114.8 Hz	MetroCor
	FM	N2PAL	224.08000	-	114.8 Hz	
	FM	W2YRC	224.94000	-	88.5 Hz	MetroCor
	FM	WP4LYI	433.07500		100.0 Hz	
	FM	WP4LYI	443.17500	+		
	FM	N2QNB	445.42500	-	136.5 Hz	MetroCor
	FUSION	W2YRC	440.15000	+		
York Town Hts	DMR/BM	KB2LFH	441.56250	+	CC3	
Yorktown	FM	WB2IXR	147.01500	-	114.8 Hz	MetroCor
Yorktown Heights	DMR/BM	K2HPS	446.56250	-	CC3	
	DMR/MARC	NY4Z	443.15000	+	CC1	
	FM	WA2TOW	146.94000	-	162.2 Hz	MetroCor
	FM	AF2C	443.15000	+	88.5 Hz	MetroCor
Yorktown Hts	DMR/MARC	K2HPS	446.56250	-	CC3	
NORTH CAROLINA						
Aberdeen	FM	KW1B	147.30000	+	100.0 Hz	SERA
Ahoskie	DMR/MARC	WB4YNF	444.33750	+	CC1	
	FM	WB4YNF	145.13000	-	131.8 Hz	SERA
	FM	KG4GEJ	146.91000	-	131.8 Hz	
	FM	WB4YNF	224.12000	-	131.8 Hz	
Albemarle	DMR/BM	K4DVA	144.92000	147.42000	CC1	
	DMR/BM	K4DVA	440.68750	+	CC1	
	DMR/MARC	K4DVA	440.56250	+	CC1	
	FM	K4OGB	146.98500	-	77.0 Hz	SERA
	FM	N4HRS	444.90000	+	110.9 Hz	
Albemarle, Morrow Mountain Sta						
	FM	K4DVA	443.52500	+	77.0 Hz	
Alexander	FM	KG4LGY	53.19000	52.19000	100.0 Hz	
Andrews		KG4LVO-L	146.57500			
	FM	K4AIH	224.88000	-		
	FM	K4AIH	443.65000	+	151.4 Hz	
Andrews, Joanna Bald						
	FM	WD4NWV	442.60000	+	151.4 Hz	SERA
Andrews, Joanna Mtn						
	FM	K4AIH	147.04500	-	151.4 Hz	
Angier	FM	KA0GMY	147.01500	+	110.9 Hz	SERA
Angier 900MHZ	DMR/MARC	NC4RA	927.62500	902.62500	CC1	

Location	Mode	Call sign	Output	Input	Access	Coordinator
Apex	DMR/MARC	KI4EMS	147.07500	-	CC1	
Arabia		K4FX-L	147.53000			
Archers Lodge	FM	K4JDR	444.00000	+	100.0 Hz	SERA
Asheville	DMR/BM	K4HCU	440.62500	+	CC1	
	DMR/MARC	WA4TOG	442.55000	+	CC1	
	DMR/MARC	WA4TOG	927.72500	902.72500	CC1	
	FM	KI4DNY	224.60000	-	94.8 Hz	
	FM	KE4MU	442.15000	+	94.8 Hz	
	FM	AC4JK	442.42500	+		
Asheville, Mount Mitchell						
	FM	N2GE	224.54000	-		
Asheville, Oteen / Azalea						
	FM	W4DCD	444.56250	+		SERA
Asheville, Spivey Mountain						
	FM	W4MOE	146.91000	-	91.5 Hz	
	FM	K4HCU	442.65000	+	100.0 Hz	
Asheville, Stradley Mountain						
	FM	W4MOE	224.52000	-	91.5 Hz	
Auburn	DSTAR	K4ITL	442.21250	+		
	FM	AK4H	147.27000	+		
	FM	K4ITL	224.16000	-	91.5 Hz	
Auburn, WRAL Tower						
	FM	K4ITL	145.21000	-	82.5 Hz	
Bakersville	FM	W4LNZ	222.12000	-		
	FM	W4LNZ	444.87500	+		
Bakersville, Locust Knob						
	FM	KK4MAR	145.31000	-	123.0 Hz	
Banner Elk, Sugartop						
	FM	KX4CZ	442.17500	+	123.0 Hz	SERA
Bath	FM	NC4ES	442.55000	+	82.5 Hz	SERA
Bearwallow Mountain						
	DSTAR	NC4BS	442.96250	+		SERA
Beech Mtn	FM	WA4NC	444.57500	+	151.4 Hz	
Benson	FM	K4JDR	444.02500	+	100.0 Hz	
Bethel	FM	KD4EAD	147.37500	+	151.4 Hz	
Bolivia	FM	K4PPD	145.37000	-	88.5 Hz	
	FM	K4PPD	147.31500	+	118.8 Hz	
	FM	N4GM-R	444.60000	+	88.5 Hz	SERA
Boone	DMR/MARC	WA4NC	440.75000	+	CC1	
	DMR/MARC	WA4NC	443.03750	+	CC1	SERA
Boone, Rich Mountain						
	FM	WA4J	147.36000	+	103.5 Hz	
Brevard, Rich Mountain						
	FM	AG4AZ	442.85000	+		
Broadway	FM	K4ITL	147.10500	+	82.5 Hz	
Browns Summit	FM	N2DMR	146.76000	-	156.7 Hz	SERA
Bryson City	FM	N0SU	443.40000	+	151.4 Hz	
Bunn	FM	KC4WDI	444.25000	+	100.0 Hz	
Burgaw	FM	N4JDW	442.02500	+	88.5 Hz	
Burlington	DSTAR	AK4EG C	145.32000	-		
	DSTAR	AK4EG B	444.88750	+		
	DSTAR	AK4EG A	1284.40000	1264.40000		
	DSTAR	AK4EG D	1299.40000			
	FM	K4EG	443.60000	+	123.0 Hz	SERA
Burnsville	FM	KF4LCG	146.95500	-		
	FM	KD4GER	441.92500	+		
	FM	KF4LCG	443.65000	+		
Burnsville, Phillips Knob						
	FM	KD4WAR	147.37500	+	123.0 Hz	SERA
Butner	FM	WA4IZG	146.94000	-	100.0 Hz	SERA
	FM	KC4WDI	443.20000	+	100.0 Hz	SERA
Buxton	DMR/BM	K4OBX	146.62500	-	CC1	SERA

Location	Mode	Call sign	Output	Input	Access	Coordinator
Buxton	DMR/MARC	K4OBX	444.06250	+	CC1	SERA
	FM	K4OBX	53.01000	52.01000	131.8 Hz	SERA
	FM	K4OBX	145.15000	-	131.8 Hz	SERA
	FM	K4OBX	442.42500	+	100.0 Hz	
Calabash	FM	N4DBM	145.33000	-	162.2 Hz	SERA
	FM	KD4GHL	444.75000	+	118.8 Hz	SERA
Canton	FM	KI4GMA	444.85000	+	100.0 Hz	
Canton, Mount Pisgah						
	FM	N2GE	146.76000	-		SERA
	FM	N2GE	224.26000	-		
Carthage	FM	NC4ML	147.24000	+	91.5 Hz	SERA
	FM	N1RIK	442.85000	+	107.2 Hz	SERA
Cary		KE4IFE-L	446.17500			
	DMR/BM	W1CKD	441.36250	+	CC1	
	DMR/BM	N1FTE	441.78750	+	CC1	
	DMR/MARC	KB4CTS	443.78750	+	CC1	
	FM	K4JDR	444.77500	+	100.0 Hz	SERA
Cashiers	DMR/MARC	W3WDD	444.55000	+	CC1	SERA
	DMR/MARC	KD4CED	444.60000	+	CC1	
Castalia, Water Tower						
	FM	N4JEH	444.95000	+	107.2 Hz	
Chalybeate Springs						
	FM	W4RLH	443.10000	+	100.0 Hz	
Chambers (historical)						
	FM	KC4QPR-R	146.74500	-		
Chapel Hill	DSTAR	KR4RDU	442.53750	+		
	DSTAR	KR4RDU B	442.53750	+		
	FM	W4UNC	53.45000	52.45000	107.2 Hz	SERA
	FM	K4ITL	147.13500	+	82.5 Hz	SERA
	FM	W4UNC	442.15000	+	131.8 Hz	SERA
Charlotte	DMR/BM	NC1L	443.98750	+	CC1	
	DMR/MARC	KC4YPB	440.80000	+	CC1	
	DMR/MARC	W4ZO	442.41250	+	CC1	SERA
	DMR/MARC	WG8E	443.22500	+	CC4	
	DMR/MARC	KM4BRM	443.43750	+	CC1	
	DMR/MARC	KI4WXS	443.86250	+	CC1	
	DMR/MARC	N4HRS	444.22500	+	CC3	
	DMR/MARC	KA4YMY	927.01250	902.01250	CC1	
	DSTAR	KI4WXS C	145.14000	-		
	DSTAR	KI4WXS B	444.02500	+		
	DSTAR	KA4YMZ A	1292.00000	1272.00000		
	FM	W4BFB	145.29000	-	118.8 Hz	
	FM	W4BFB	146.94000	-	118.8 Hz	
	FM	WB4ETF	147.06000	-		
	FM	W4BFB	224.40000	-		
	FM	KD4ADL	442.72500	+	110.9 Hz	
	FM	K4CBA	444.05000	+	136.5 Hz	
	FM	K4KAY	444.35000	+	151.4 Hz	
	FM	W4BFB	444.60000	+	118.8 Hz	
	FM	K4KAY	927.61250	902.61250	118.8 Hz	
	FUSION	KI4WXS	443.10000	+		
Charlotte, UNC Charlotte						
	FM	W0UNC	442.65000	+	88.5 Hz	
Cherry Mountain, Rutherfordton						
	FM	KG4JIA	442.50000	+	94.8 Hz	
Cherryville	FM	N4DWP	224.96000	-		
China Grove	FM	N4UH	145.41000	-	136.5 Hz	
	FM	N4UH	443.25000	+	136.5 Hz	SERA
Chocowinity, WLGT-FM Tower						
	FM	K4BCH	147.25500	+	131.8 Hz	
Clayton	FM	N4TCP	443.67500	+		SERA
	FM	NI4J	446.07500	-	100.0 Hz	

Location	Mode	Call sign	Output	Input	Access	Coordinator
Clemmons	FM	WB9SZL	224.70000	-	100.0 Hz	SERA
Cleveland	FM	N4YR	53.25000	52.25000	100.0 Hz	SERA
Cleveland , Young Mountain						
	FM	KU4PT	146.73000	-	94.8 Hz	
Cleveland, Young Mountain						
	FM	K4CH	443.70000	+	127.3 Hz	
Clinton	FM	W4TLP	146.79000	-	88.5 Hz	
	FM	W4TLP	224.28000	-	91.5 Hz	
Clinton, Taylors Bridge						
	FM	N4JDW	443.07500	+	100.0 Hz	
Coats	FM	K4JDR	444.55000	+	100.0 Hz	SERA
Columbia	DMR/MARC	KX4NC	440.58750	+	CC1	
Columbia, WUND-TV Tower						
	FM	KX4NC	146.83500	-	131.8 Hz	SERA
	FM	KX4NC	443.30000	+	131.8 Hz	SERA
Concord	FM	KD4ADL	147.21000	+	110.9 Hz	
	FM	N2QJI	442.52500	+	94.8 Hz	
	FM	W4ZO	444.25000	+		
	FM	KD4ADL	444.77500	+	110.9 Hz	
Concord, Cabarrus Sheriff's Of						
	FM	K4WC	443.35000	+	136.5 Hz	
Connelly Springs, South Mounta						
	FM	NA4CC	442.57500	+	82.5 Hz	SERA
Conover	FUSION	N4LED	446.10000			
Corolla	DMR/MARC	K4OBX	444.33750	+	CC1	
Cowee Mountain	FM	KF4RC-R	145.49000	-	167.9 Hz	
Creedmoor	FM	N4MEC	146.98500	-	100.0 Hz	SERA
Crowders Mt	FUSION	KK4JDH	443.43750	+		
Cullowhee	DMR/MARC	W3WDD	444.97500	+	CC1	
Dallas	FM	W4CQ	444.45000	+	82.5 Hz	
Dallas, TV Tower	FM	KA4YMZ	224.02000	-	82.5 Hz	SERA
Delco, UNC-TV Tower Delco						
	FM	AD4DN	224.50000	-	88.5 Hz	
Denton	FM	KD4LHP	442.75000	+	118.8 Hz	SERA
Dobson	FM	W4DCA	53.97000	52.97000	100.0 Hz	
	FM	N4DAJ	146.92500	-	100.0 Hz	SERA
	FUSION	W4DCA	441.16250			
Duck	DMR/MARC	K4OBX	442.63750	+	CC1	
Dunn	FM	W4PEQ	146.70000	-	82.5 Hz	
Durham	DMR/BM	W4BAD	444.85000	+	CC1	
	DMR/MARC	W4BAD	147.36000	+	CC1	SERA
	DMR/MARC	KI4EMS	441.97500	+	CC2	
	FM	K4WCV	53.63000	52.63000	88.5 Hz	SERA
	FM	WR4AGC-R	145.45000	-	82.0 Hz	
	FM	WR4AGC	444.10000	+	82.5 Hz	SERA
	FM	WR4AGC	444.45000	+	100.0 Hz	SERA
	FM	K4JDR	444.92500	+	94.8 Hz	SERA
	FUSION	W4BAD	145.37000	-	100.0 Hz	SERA
Durham, TV Hill	FM	NC4TV	421.25000	434.05000		
Eagle Chase		KB4RGC-L	441.30000			
Eastover	FM	KN4ZZ	443.90000	+	100.0 Hz	
Edenton	FM	W4UUU	443.32500	+	123.0 Hz	
Elizabeth City	DMR/MARC	WA4VTX	440.56250	+	CC1	
	FM	WA4VTX	146.65500	-	131.8 Hz	SERA
Elizabethtown	FM	N4DBM	146.98500	-	162.2 Hz	SERA
	FM	N4DBM	224.38000	-	91.5 Hz	SERA
Elk Park	FM	KX4CZ	443.40000	+	123.0 Hz	
Elm City	FM	K2IMO	442.32500	+	88.5 Hz	
Engelhard	FM	K4OBX	146.71500	-	131.8 Hz	SERA
Engelhard	DMR/MARC	WB4YNF	442.46250	+	CC1	SERA
Erwin Heights		WW4DC-R	147.00000			
Fargo	DSTAR	KD0SWQ B	444.00000	+		

Location	Mode	Call sign	Output	Input	Access	Coordinator
Farmville	FUSION	KN4VJR	147.42000			
Fayetteville	FM	W4EBM	53.81000	52.81000		
	FM	K4MN	146.91000	-	100.0 Hz	
	FM	K4MN	444.40000	+	100.0 Hz	
Fayetteville, WAMC						
	FM	WA4FLR	147.33000	+	100.0 Hz	
Flat Rock, Sauratown Mountain						
	FM	KQ1E	443.05000	+	136.5 Hz	
Fletcher	DSTAR	NC4BS B	442.96250	+		
Forest City	FM	K4OI	146.67000	-	114.8 Hz	
	FM	AI4M	442.00000	+	114.8 Hz	
Forest City, Cherry Mountain						
	FM	AI4M	443.30000	+	123.0 Hz	
Fountain	FM	N4HAJ	444.42500	+	88.5 Hz	
Franklin	DMR/MARC	W3WDD	444.20000	+	CC1	SERA
	DMR/MARC	N4DTR	444.37500	+	CC1	
	DMR/MARC	N4DTR	927.76250	902.76250	CC1	
	FM	W4GHZ	147.24000	+	151.4 Hz	
Fraziers Crossroads						
	FM	WB4YNF-R	444.20000	+		
Galax, VA	FM	N4VL	145.13000	-	103.5 Hz	
Garner	FM	KD4PBS	442.07500	+	114.8 Hz	
	FM	NE4Y	443.30000	+	100.0 Hz	
Gastonia	DMR/BM	N4GAS	445.72500	-	CC1	
	DMR/MARC	KA4YMZ	443.91250	+	CC1	SERA
	DSTAR	KK4JDH B	443.86250	+		
	DSTAR	NC1L B	443.98750	+		
	FUSION	W7CSA	147.17000	+		
Gastonia, Crowder's Mtn						
	FM	K4CBA	442.05000	+		
Gastonia, Crowders Mountain						
	DSTAR	KK4JDH	443.86250	+		SERA
	FM	K4GNC	146.80500	-	100.0 Hz	
	FM	KC4IRA	224.62000	-	127.3 Hz	
	FM	KC4IRA	442.70000	+	100.0 Hz	
	FM	KA4YMZ	443.43750	+		SERA
	FM	KC4IRA	927.03750	902.03750	94.8 Hz	
Gastonia, Spencer Mountain						
	FM	KA4YMZ	927.01250	902.01250		
	IDAS	KA4YMY	444.70000	+		SERA
Georgetown		WX4CMA-L	443.90000			
Goldsboro	DMR/MARC	KB4CTS	442.36250	+	CC1	
	DMR/MARC	KD2HUY	444.40000	+	CC1	
	FM	K4JDR	145.33000	-	100.0 Hz	SERA
	FM	K4CYP	146.85000	-	88.5 Hz	
	FM	WA4DAN	224.46000	-	91.5 Hz	
	FM	K4CYP	443.00000	+	88.5 Hz	SERA
Graham	DMR/MARC	N2DMR	443.72500	+	CC1	SERA
Grants Mobile Home Park						
	FM	NI4SR-R	145.41000	-		
Grantsboro	FM	KR4LO	444.35000	+		
Grantsboro, WMGV Tower						
	FM	KF4IXW	145.23000	-	85.4 Hz	SERA
	FM	KF4IXW	444.87500	+	85.4 Hz	
Greensboro	DMR/BM	ND4L	441.92500	+	CC1	
	DMR/BM	W4ADC	442.38750	+	CC7	
	DMR/BM	W4GSO	442.86250	+	CC1	
	DMR/MARC	N4DUB	441.86250	+	CC11	SERA
	DMR/MARC	NC4RA	442.88750	+	CC1	
	DMR/MARC	W4GG	444.22500	+	CC1	SERA
	DSTAR	W4GSO B	442.86250	+		
	FM	W4GSO	145.15000	-	100.0 Hz	SERA

Location	Mode	Call sign	Output	Input	Access	Coordinator
Greensboro	FM	W4ADC	443.62500	+	123.0 Hz	
Greenville	DMR/BM	WD4JPQ	145.35000	-	CC1	
	DMR/BM	NC4ES	444.62500	+	CC1	
	DMR/BM	NC4ES	902.55000	927.55000	CC1	
	DMR/MARC	WB4PMQ	444.80000	+	CC1	SERA
	DMR/MARC	NC4ES	445.53750	+	CC1	
	FM	W4GDF	147.09000	+	131.8 Hz	SERA
	FM	N4HAJ	444.72500	+	91.5 Hz	
	FUSION	KE4TZN	145.35000	-		
Grifton	FM	W4NBR	146.68500	-	88.5 Hz	
	FM	WA4DAN	224.84000	-	91.5 Hz	
Hampstead, Topsail Fire Tower						
	FM	NC4PC	443.55000	+	100.0 Hz	SERA
Hamstead	FM	N4JDW	146.94000	-	88.5 Hz	
Haw River	FM	KD4JFN	224.62000	-	107.2 Hz	
Hayesville	DMR/MARC	K1DMR	443.03750	+	CC1	
	FM	KC4CBQ	444.67500	+	186.2 Hz	SERA
Hays	FUSION	KK4YWI	146.41500			
Hazelwood	DMR/MARC	KK4FFE	927.58750	902.58750	CC1	
Henderson	FM	K4JDR	444.37500	+	100.0 Hz	SERA
Hendersonville	DMR/MARC	W4FOT	441.88750	+	CC1	
	DMR/MARC	WA4TOG	442.45000	+	CC1	
	DMR/MARC	WA4TOG	927.55000	902.55000	CC1	SERA
	DSTAR	KJ4JAL C	147.25500	+		
	DSTAR	KJ4JAL	147.25500	+		
	DSTAR	KJ4JAL B	442.02500	+		
	FM	W4FOT	53.13000	52.13000	100.0 Hz	
	FM	WB4YAO	146.64000	-	91.5 Hz	
	FM	WA4KNI	147.10500	+	91.5 Hz	SERA
	FM	WA4KNI	224.24000	-		
	FM	N4KOX	927.56250	902.56250	127.3 Hz	
Hendersonville, Bearwallow Mou						
	FM	WA4KNI	145.27000	-	91.5 Hz	
Hendersonville, Bearwallow Mtn						
	FM	WA4KNI	444.25000	+	91.5 Hz	
Hendersonville, Pinnacle Mount						
	DSTAR	KJ4JAL	442.02500	+		
Hertford	DMR/MARC	WB4YNF	442.16250	+	CC1	
	FM	WA4VTX	147.33000	+	131.8 Hz	SERA
	FM	WA4VTX	444.30000	+	131.8 Hz	SERA
Hickory	FM	WA4PXV	53.05000	52.05000	151.4 Hz	
	FM	WA4PXV	146.85000	-		SERA
Hickory, Barretts Mountain						
	FM	WA4PXV	442.37500	+	131.8 Hz	SERA
High Point	DSTAR	W4GSO1 C	146.36000	-		
	DSTAR	W4GSO1 B	442.88750	+		
	FM	NC4AR	145.29000	-	88.5 Hz	
	FM	W4UA	147.16500	+	67.0 Hz	SERA
	FM	KF4OVA	442.97500	+	107.2 Hz	
	FM	KF4OVA	444.62500	+	107.2 Hz	SERA
	FM	N2DMR	444.97500	+	107.2 Hz	SERA
Highlands, Big Bearpen Mtn						
	FM	WD4NFT	444.65000	+	167.9 Hz	
Hillsborough	DMR/BM	W4BAD	146.97000	-	CC1	
	DMR/MARC	WR4AGC	443.13750	+	CC1	
	FM	WR4AGC	147.22500	+	82.5 Hz	SERA
	FM	WR4AGC	224.26000	-		
	FUSION	W4BAD	145.37000	-		
Holly Springs	FM	KF4AUF	444.32500	+	100.0 Hz	SERA
Hope Mills, Water Tower						
	FM	W4KMU	146.83500	+		
Hubert	FM	KE4FHH	443.31250	+		SERA

Location	Mode	Call sign	Output	Input	Access	Coordinator
Jaars		K4WBT-R	146.86500			
Jackson	FM	KB4CTS	444.32500	+	107.2 Hz	
Jacksonville	DMR/BM	NC4ES	440.70000	+	CC1	
	DMR/MARC	KE4FHH	441.83750	+	CC1	SERA
Jefferson, Phoenix Mountain						
	FM	W4YSB	147.30000	+	103.5 Hz	
	FM	W4JWO	224.22000	-	88.5 Hz	
	FM	W4JWO	443.07500	+	94.8 Hz	
Kelly	FM	WA4DAN	224.54000	-	91.5 Hz	
Kenansville	FM	N4HAJ	444.12500	+	91.5 Hz	
Kernersville	FM	KF4OVA	53.01000	52.01000	88.5 Hz	SERA
	FM	KF4OVA	146.86500	+	88.5 Hz	SERA
	FM	KF4OEV	224.24000	-	107.2 Hz	
	FM	KF4OVA	224.34000	-	88.5 Hz	SERA
Kilby Gap	FM	WA4PXV	443.57500	+	173.8 Hz	SERA
King	DMR/BM	W4SNA	442.63750	+	CC2	
	DMR/MARC	W4SNA	442.68750	+	CC1	
	FM	K4GW	146.31500	+	100.0 Hz	
	FM	K4GW	444.12500	+	100.0 Hz	SERA
	FM	KE4QEA	444.20000	+	107.2 Hz	
King, Sauratown Mountain						
	FM	W4SNA	53.95000	52.95000	100.0 Hz	
	FM	W4NC	145.47000	-	100.0 Hz	SERA
	FM	K4GW	147.31500	+	100.0 Hz	SERA
	FM	W4SNA	444.75000	+	100.0 Hz	SERA
King, Sauratown Mtn						
	FM	W4WAU	224.72000	-	114.8 Hz	SERA
Kings Mountain	DSTAR	W4NYR	145.08000	146.48000		SERA
	DSTAR	W4NYR C	145.08000	146.48000		
	DSTAR	W4NYR	444.18750	+		
	DSTAR	W4NYR B	444.18750	+		
Kinston	DMR/BM	N4DEA	440.51250	+	CC1	
	DMR/BM	N4DEA	443.93750	+	CC1	
	FM	W4OIX	145.47000	-	88.5 Hz	
	FM	N4HAJ	442.00000	+	88.5 Hz	
Lake Norman Of Catawba						
		KF4LLF-L	442.72500			
Lansing	FM	WB4ZCP	224.84000	-	103.5 Hz	
Lansing, Phoenix Mountain						
	FM	W4MLN	444.30000	+	103.5 Hz	
Laurinburg	FM	KI4RR	146.62500	-		
Leland	FM	N4JDW	145.17000	-	88.5 Hz	
Lennon Crossroads						
	FM	KE4TUD-R	444.70000	+		
Lenoir	DMR/MARC	KG4BCC	443.18750	+	CC1	
	FM	N4LNR	146.62500	-	94.8 Hz	SERA
Lenoir, Hibriten Mountain						
	FM	KG4BCC	147.33000	+	141.3 Hz	
Lexington	DMR/BM	W2PP	440.60000	+	CC1	
	DMR/MARC	N4TZD	441.93750	+	CC1	
	FM	N4LEX	145.31000	-	107.2 Hz	
	FM	W4PAR	146.91000	-	107.2 Hz	
	FM	K4AE	441.90000	+	127.3 Hz	SERA
	FM	KO0NTZ	442.27500	+	146.2 Hz	
	FM	W4PAR	444.50000	+	146.2 Hz	SERA
Lincolnton	FM	NC4LC	147.01500	+	141.3 Hz	
	FM	WA4YGD	442.35000	+	141.3 Hz	
Locust	FM	W4DEX	147.39000	+	77.0 Hz	SERA
	FM	W4DEX	224.48000	-		SERA
Louisburg	FM	AA4RV	146.80500	-	118.8 Hz	SERA
	FM	KD4CPV	224.22000	-		
Lumberton	FM	W4LBT	147.36000	+	82.5 Hz	

Location	Mode	Call sign	Output	Input	Access	Coordinator
Madison	FM	N4IV	147.34500	+	103.5 Hz	SERA
Maiden	FM	KT4NC	145.17000	-	88.5 Hz	
	FM	W4FTK	444.65000	+		
Malmo	FM	N4ILM	147.06000	+	88.5 Hz	
Mamie	DMR/BM	W4PCN	147.06000	+	CC1	
	DMR/MARC	W4PCN	442.85000	+	CC1	
Mamie, Powells Point						
	FM	W4PCN	146.94000	-	131.8 Hz	SERA
Margarettsville	DMR/MARC	W4BSB	442.35000	+	CC1	
Marion		W4HOG-R	146.98500			
	DMR/MARC	WD4PVE	444.85000	+	CC1	
	FM	WD4PVE-R	146.98500	-		
Mars Hill, Wolf Ridge						
	FM	N2GE	224.66000	-		SERA
Mars Hill, Wolf Ridge Ski Area						
	FM	KI4DNY	442.72500	+	100.0 Hz	SERA
Marshall, Duckett Top Mountain						
	FM	K4HCU	224.36000	-	79.7 Hz	SERA
Matthews	FUSION	AE4WS	444.42500	+		
McCain	FM	N1RIK	146.80500	-	107.2 Hz	
	FM	N1RIK	442.25000	+	107.2 Hz	SERA
	FM	N1RIK	927.13750	902.13750	131.8 Hz	SERA
Millers Creek	FM	N4GGN	146.71500	-	94.8 Hz	
Mocksville	DMR/BM	NG8M	444.80000	+	CC8	
Monroe	FM	NC4UC	145.39000	-	94.8 Hz	
	FM	W4ZO	444.30000	+	100.0 Hz	
	FM	NC4UC	444.42500	+	94.8 Hz	
	FUSION	WB4U	145.55500			
Mooresville	FM	WG8E	443.82500	+	110.9 Hz	
Moravian Falls	DMR/MARC	NI4L	442.13750	+	CC1	
	FM	KK4OVN	53.77000	52.77000	100.0 Hz	SERA
	FM	N1KKD	147.22500	+	162.2 Hz	
	FM	KA2NAX	224.12000	-	123.0 Hz	
	FM	KA2NAX	442.67500	+	88.5 Hz	
Morehead City	DMR/MARC	W4YMI	444.97500	+	CC1	
	FM	KF4IXW	53.09000	52.09000	162.2 Hz	
Morganton	DMR/MARC	KC4QPR	442.30000	+	CC1	
Morganton, High Peak						
	FM	KM4VIQ	147.15000	+	94.8 Hz	SERA
Morganton, High Peak Mountain						
	FM	K4OLC	145.21000	-	94.8 Hz	
Morganton, Jonas Ridge						
	FM	N4HRS	444.62500	+	110.9 Hz	
Morrisville, Cisco Campus, Bui						
	FM	KC4SCO	444.07500	+	100.0 Hz	
Mount Airy	FM	KF4UY	444.82500	+	100.0 Hz	
Mount Airy, Fisher Peak						
	FM	KD4ADL	443.42500	+	110.9 Hz	
Mount Gilead	FM	KI4DH	147.09000	+	100.0 Hz	
	FM	KI4DH	442.20000	+	100.0 Hz	
Mount Mitchell	FM	N4YR	53.63000	52.63000	100.0 Hz	
Mount Sterling		KM4IXK-L	146.45000			
Moyock	FM	W4NV	443.02500	+		
Mt Mitchell	FM	N4YR	442.22500	+	107.2 Hz	
Mt. Airy	DSTAR	KJ4HFV B	444.56250	+		
Mt. Mitchell	FM	N2GE-R	145.19000	-		SERA
Murphy	DMR/MARC	N4DTR	444.10000	+	CC1	
	FM	KE4EST	444.75000	+	100.0 Hz	
Nags Head	DMR/MARC	K4OBX	444.98750	+	CC1	
Nashville	DMR/MARC	KB4CTS	442.61250	+	CC1	SERA
Needmore	FM	KT4WO	444.55000	+	88.5 Hz	
New Bern	FM	WO3F	442.07500	+	100.0 Hz	

Location	Mode	Call sign	Output	Input	Access	Coordinator
Newell	FM	WT4IX	442.12500	+	156.7 Hz	
Newport	DMR/MARC	WO3F	444.82500	+	CC1	
	FM	K4GRW	29.66000	-		
	FM	K4GRW	145.45000	-	100.0 Hz	
Newton	FM	K4CCR	147.07500	+	88.5 Hz	
NOAA Asheville	WX	WXL56	162.40000			
NOAA Buck Mountain						
	WX	WWF60	162.50000			
NOAA Cape Hatteras						
	WX	KIG77	162.47500			
NOAA Chapel Hill	WX	WXL58	162.55000			
NOAA Charlotte	WX	WXL70	162.47500			
NOAA Ellerbe	WX	WNG597	162.40000			
NOAA Fayetteville						
	WX	WXL50	162.47500			
NOAA Garner	WX	WNG706	162.45000			
NOAA Henderson	WX	WNG586	162.50000			
NOAA Linville	WX	WNG538	162.45000			
NOAA Mamie	WX	WWH26	162.42500			
NOAA Margaretsville						
	WX	WWG33	162.45000			
NOAA Mooresville						
	WX	KJY85	162.52500			
NOAA Mount Jefferson						
	WX	WNG588	162.50000			
NOAA New Bern	WX	KEC84	162.40000			
NOAA Robbinsville						
	WX	WWG82	162.52500			
NOAA Rocky Mount						
	WX	WXL59	162.47500			
NOAA Warsaw	WX	KXI95	162.42500			
NOAA Wilmington	WX	KHB31	162.55000			
NOAA Windsor	WX	WNG537	162.52500			
NOAA Winston-Salem						
	WX	WXL42	162.40000			
North Wilkesboro	FM	N4VL	145.13000	-	103.5 Hz	
Northmont		KA3KDL-L	144.94500			
Oak Island	FM	N2MH	442.60000	+		
	FUSION	N4GM	145.37000	-		
Oriental	FM	W4SLH	147.21000	+	151.4 Hz	
Oxford	FM	W4BAD	145.17000	-	100.0 Hz	
	FM	NO4EL	444.60000	+	100.0 Hz	
Palmer		N4JDL-L	145.75000			
Petersburg		K4RIT-L	147.51000			
Pikeville	FM	KI4RK	444.47500	+		SERA
Pine Bluff	FM	N4VLZ	147.18000	+	67.0 Hz	
Pinebluff	FM	N4VLZ	443.97500	+	67.0 Hz	
Pinehurst	FM	N1RIK	145.27000	-	107.2 Hz	SERA
	FM	N1RIK	444.70000	+	107.2 Hz	SERA
Polkville	FM	N4DWP	444.97500	+		
Pollocksville	FM	W4EWN	146.61000	-	100.0 Hz	
Portable Repeater	DMR/MARC	KM4BRM	440.80000	+	CC1	
Purlear	FM	W4NCG	442.25000	+	127.3 Hz	
Raleigh	DMR/MARC	K4JDR	441.72500	+	CC0	
	DMR/MARC	K4ITL	442.51250	+	CC1	
	DMR/MARC	K4ITL	443.33750	+	CC1	SERA
	DSTAR	K4SWR C	146.73000	-		
	DSTAR	W4RNC B	442.21250	+		
	FM	K4ITL	53.03000	52.03000		
	FM	K4GWH	145.19000	-	156.7 Hz	
	FM	W4DW	146.64000	-		
	FM	KD4RAA	146.77500	-	88.5 Hz	

Location	Mode	Call sign	Output	Input	Access	Coordinator
Raleigh	FM	WB4TQD	146.88000	-	82.5 Hz	SERA
	FM	KA0GMY	147.01500	+	110.9 Hz	
	FM	KC4WDI	441.60000	+	77.0 Hz	
	FM	K4ITL	442.57500	+	79.7 Hz	
	FM	W4ATC	442.67500	+	100.0 Hz	
	FM	W4RNC	444.52500	+	82.5 Hz	
	FM	K4GWH	444.82500	+	146.2 Hz	
	FUSION	W4EIP	441.10000			
	FUSION	N2HJK	446.25000			
Raleigh, Downtown						
	FM	W4BAD	443.17500	+	100.0 Hz	
Randleman	FM	K4ITL	147.25500	+	82.5 Hz	
	FM	N2DMR	147.37500	+	114.8 Hz	SERA
	FM	K4ITL	442.82500	+	82.5 Hz	
Ranlo, Spencer Mountain						
	FM	W4BFB	145.23000	-	118.8 Hz	
	FM	N4GAS	147.12000	+	100.0 Hz	SERA
	FM	N4GAS	224.86000	-		
	FM	N4GAS	444.55000	+	100.0 Hz	SERA
Redwood		K4WCV-R	53.45000			
Reidsville	FM	N4IV	442.47500	+	103.5 Hz	SERA
Research Triangle Park						
	FM	W4DW	145.13000	-	82.5 Hz	
Richlands	DMR/MARC	KK4VBH	443.97500	+	CC1	
Roanoke Rapids		AJ4RC-R	146.74500			
	FUSION	KI4TPI	145.01000			
	FUSION	N4UED	147.48000			
Roaring Gap	FM	WA4PXV	53.05000	52.05000	151.4 Hz	
Robbinsville	FM	N4GSM	145.11000	-	151.4 Hz	
	FM	K4KVE	442.37500	+	103.5 Hz	
Robbinsville, Joanna Bald Moun						
	FM	K4KVE	53.31000	52.31000	167.9 Hz	SERA
Rockfish, Rockfish Watertank						
	FM	KG4HDV	442.10000	+	100.0 Hz	
Rockingham	FM	K4RNC	146.95500	-	88.5 Hz	SERA
	FM	KF4DBW	442.58750	+		SERA
Rocky Mount	FM	N4JEH	29.66000	-		
	FM	WR4RM	147.12000	+	131.8 Hz	
	FM	K4ITL	147.18000	+	82.5 Hz	
	FM	KR4AA	224.58000	-	91.5 Hz	
	FM	NC4ES	444.70000	+	107.2 Hz	SERA
	FM	WN4Z	444.85000	+	131.8 Hz	
Rolesville	FM	AA4RV	444.95000	+	88.5 Hz	
Rosebud	FM	WA4AEC-R	444.90000	+		
Rosman	FM	W4TWX	444.87500	+		
Rougemont	FM	NC4CD	443.27500	+	100.0 Hz	
Roxboro	FM	W4BAD	441.67500	+	100.0 Hz	
	FUSION	KO4WIV	444.30000	+		
Royal Valley Mobile Home Park						
	FM	KE4FHH-R	147.00000	-		SERA
Salisbury	FM	KU4PT	224.76000	-		
	FUSION	W4KMC	146.25000	+		
Sanford	DMR/MARC	K4ITL	442.33750	+	CC1	SERA
	DSTAR	KE4DSU	147.50500	146.50500		
	FM	KB4HG	441.95000	+	136.5 Hz	
	P25	W0SMT	146.61000	-		
Scotland Neck	FM	NC4FM	444.07500	+	203.5 Hz	
Selma	FM	K4JDR	444.15000	+	100.0 Hz	SERA
Shallotte	FUSION	WA1DYR	431.30000			
Shannon	FM	N4DBM	444.57500	+	77.0 Hz	SERA
Shelby	FM	W4NYR	147.34500	+		
	FM	W4NYR	224.06000	-		

Location	Mode	Call sign	Output	Input	Access	Coordinator
Shelby	FM	N4DWP	224.46000	-		
	FM	AE6JI	444.27500	+	127.3 Hz	
Snow Camp	DSTAR	AK4EG	1284.40000	1264.40000		
Sophia	DMR/MARC	K4NWJ	440.71250	+	CC1	
	FM	WR4BEG	224.14000	-		
	FM	WR4BEG	443.07500	+		
Sorrento Skies		KB4W-R	443.52500			
Southern Pines	DMR/MARC	KF4DBW	443.76250	+	CC1	
Southport	FUSION	K5EK	145.37000	-		
	FUSION	W3GP	147.50625			
	FUSION	K4OSG	444.95000	+		
Sparta	FM	W4DCA	53.97000	52.97000	100.0 Hz	
	FM	W4DCA	443.95000	+	100.0 Hz	
	FM	N1RIK	927.02500	902.02500	107.2 Hz	SERA
Sparta, Air Bellows Gap						
	FM	WA4PXV	29.67000	-	151.4 Hz	
	FM	WA4PXV	442.15000	+	192.8 Hz	SERA
	FM	WA4PXV	442.60000	+	94.8 Hz	SERA
Sparta, Green Mountain						
	FM	K4ITL	145.43000	-		
Sparta, Roaring Gap						
	FM	WA4PXV	443.57500	+	173.8 Hz	
Spruce Pine	DMR/MARC	KC4TVO	443.38750	+	CC1	
Spruce Pine, Iowa Hill						
	FM	KK4MAR	147.21000	+	123.0 Hz	SERA
Spruce Pine, Woodys Knob						
	FM	KK4MAR	443.92500	+	123.0 Hz	
St Pauls	FM	W4LBT	147.04500	+		SERA
Stacy	FM	KD4KTO	444.00000	+	131.8 Hz	
Stanfield	FM	W4DEX	443.20000	+	77.0 Hz	
Star	FUSION	KN4MYF	441.67500			
Statesville	FM	KK4OVN	443.77500	+	118.8 Hz	SERA
	FM	N4SZF	443.85000	+		
Statesville, WSIC Tower						
	FM	W4SNC	146.68500	-	77.0 Hz	SERA
Sugar Mountain	DMR/MARC	WA4NC	442.08750	+	CC1	
Summerfield		KJ6ZTK-L	441.45000			
Sunny Point	FM	K4CTE-R	147.31500	+		
Sunset Beach	FUSION	AB4D	441.15000			
Sunshine, Cherry Mountain						
	FM	KG4JIA	147.24000	+	131.8 Hz	
	FM	KG4JIA	224.64000	-	71.9 Hz	
Swansboro, Swansboro Water Tow						
	FM	KE4FHH	146.76000	-	88.5 Hz	
Swepsonville	FM	K4EG	146.67000	-		SERA
Sylva	DMR/MARC	W3WDD	442.97500	+	CC1	SERA
	FM	KJ4VKD	444.15000	+		
Sylva, Kings Mountain						
	FM	KF4DTL	147.34500	+	151.4 Hz	SERA
Tarboro	DMR/BM	NC4ES	444.92500	+	CC1	
	FM	NC4ES	444.50000	+	100.0 Hz	SERA
Taylorsville	FM	W4ERT	147.19500	+	94.8 Hz	
	FM	W4ERT	441.62500	+	123.0 Hz	
Thomasville	FM	W4TNC	441.80000	+	127.3 Hz	
	FM	WW4DC	443.32500	+	88.5 Hz	
Thompson	FM	K4JDR	441.72500	+		SERA
Tobaccoville	DMR/MARC	W4SNA	441.93750	+	CC1	
	FM	KK4GAF-R	447.40000	-		
Tryon	DSTAR	KK4LVF	442.87500	+		
	DSTAR	KK4LVF B	442.87500	+		
	FM	KF4JVI	145.33000	-	91.5 Hz	
	FM	KJ4SPF	442.55000	+	107.2 Hz	

Location	Mode	Call sign	Output	Input	Access	Coordinator
Tryon	FM	K4SV	442.87500	+	123.0 Hz	
Tryon, White Oak Mountain						
	FM	W4RCW	147.28500	+		
Wadesboro	FM	W4USH	147.31500	+	74.4 Hz	
Wake Forest	DMR/BM	KD2LH	444.30000	+	CC1	
Walkertown	FM	W4GG	145.25000	-	97.4 Hz	SERA
Washington	DMR/BM	NC4ES	440.52500	+	CC1	
Waves	FM	K4OBX	444.32500	+	131.8 Hz	
Waxhaw	FM	K4WBT	444.52500	+	94.8 Hz	
Waynesville	DMR/MARC	K4KGB	443.85000	+	CC1	
	DMR/MARC	N4DTR	444.45000	+	CC1	SERA
	DMR/MARC	N4DTR	927.48750	902.48750	CC1	
	DMR/MARC	N4DTR	927.66250	902.66250	CC1	
Waynesville, Chambers Mountain						
	FM	N4DTR	147.39000	+	94.8 Hz	SERA
Waynesville, Sylva						
	FM	K4RCC	444.87500	+	131.8 Hz	SERA
Wendel	FM	KD4RAA	444.87500	+	100.0 Hz	SERA
West Bend	FM	W4NC-R	146.64000	-		SERA
West Concord	FM	WA1WXL-R	146.00000	-		
West Jefferson	DMR/MARC	W4MLN	444.73750	+	CC1	
Wilkesboro	DMR/MARC	W4FAR	440.53750	+	CC1	
	FM	W4MIS	145.04000	-	100.0 Hz	
	FM	WB4PZA	146.82000	-	94.8 Hz	SERA
Wilkesboro, Pores Knob						
	FM	W4FAR	145.37000	-	94.8 Hz	
Williamston	DMR/BM	K4SER	442.38750	+	CC1	
	FM	K4SER	53.31000	52.31000	131.8 Hz	SERA
	FM	K4SER	145.41000	-	131.8 Hz	SERA
	FM	K4SER	444.25000	+	131.8 Hz	SERA
Willow Spring	DMR/MARC	K4ZXX	146.73000	-	CC1	
Willowmere		W4PFI-L	446.15000			
Wilmington	DMR/MARC	K4ITL	444.23750	+	CC1	
	FM	N4ILM	29.66000	-	88.5 Hz	
	FM	N4JDW	53.33000	52.33000	88.5 Hz	
	FM	AD4DN	53.43000	52.43000	88.5 Hz	
	FM	AD4DN	146.67000	-	88.5 Hz	SERA
	FM	AC4RC	147.18000	+	88.5 Hz	
	FM	WA4US	224.20000	-		
	FM	KD4MEA	224.68000	-	91.5 Hz	
	FM	WA4US	442.17500	+		
	FM	WA4US	442.20000	+		
	FM	AC4RC	442.50000	+	88.5 Hz	
	FM	KB4FXC	442.75000	+	67.0 Hz	
	FM	AD4DN	443.40000	+	88.5 Hz	
	FM	WA4US	443.85000	+		
	FM	WA4US	443.95000	+		
	FM	WA4US	444.20000	+		
	FM	WA4US	444.45000	+		
	FM	KB4FXC	444.50000	+	67.0 Hz	
	FM	WA4US	444.65000	+		
	FM	N4PLY	444.77500	+	131.8 Hz	
Wilmington, Porter's Neck						
	FM	N4ILM	146.73000	-	88.5 Hz	
Wilson	DMR/MARC	NE4J	440.10000	+	CC1	
	FM	WA4WAR	146.76000	-	131.8 Hz	
Wingate	DMR/MARC	W4ZO	444.38750	+	CC1	
	DSTAR	W4FAN	444.86250	+		
	DSTAR	W4FAN　B	444.86250	+		
	FM	N4HRS	443.95000	+	110.9 Hz	SERA
Winnabow	FM	N4ILM	146.82000	-	88.5 Hz	SERA
	FM	K4ITL	147.34500	+	88.5 Hz	

Location	Mode	Call sign	Output	Input	Access	Coordinator
Winnabow	FM	N4ILM	444.85000	+	88.5 Hz	
Winston-Salem	FM	N4YR	224.60000	-	107.2 Hz	
	FM	KD4MMP	444.72500	+	107.2 Hz	
Winston-Salem, NC Baptist Hosp						
	FM	W4NC	444.27500	+	100.0 Hz	SERA
Wolf Ridge, Ski Area						
	FM	K4MFD	147.18000	+	94.8 Hz	
Yadkinville	FM	KM4MHZ	146.61000	-	85.4 Hz	SERA
	FM	N4YSB	147.01500	-	100.0 Hz	
	FM	KD4KMK	442.02500	+	100.0 Hz	
	FM	N4AAD	442.80000	+	100.0 Hz	SERA
Youngsville	FM	WB4TQD	145.39000	-	82.5 Hz	
	FM	N4TAB	442.17500	+	82.5 Hz	
	FM	WB4IUY	442.30000	+	100.0 Hz	
Zebulon	FM	WB4IUY	224.80000	-	88.5 Hz	

NORTH DAKOTA

Location	Mode	Call sign	Output	Input	Access	Coordinator
Albuquerque, Capilla Peak						
	DSTAR	W5URD B	444.52500	+		
Bismarck	FM	W0ZRT	146.85000	-	107.2 Hz	
	FM	KC0AHL	444.65000	+	107.2 Hz	
Boise / Cinnabar Mtn						
	DSTAR	KF7VTN B	443.37500	+		
Bowman, Twin Buttes						
	FM	KB0DYA	145.31000	-		
Carrington, Big Chief						
	FM	K0BND	147.58500		100.0 Hz	
Cathay	FUSION	ND0B/RPT	444.40000	+		
Cavalier	FM	N0CAV-R	147.15000	+		
Cleveland	FM	W0FX	53.01000	52.01000		
	FM	W0FX	147.18000	+		
Fargo	DMR/BM	W0HSC	147.09000	+	CC1	
	DMR/BM	KC0LOK	443.00000	891.00000	CC3	
	DMR/BM	K0RQ	443.40000	+	CC1	
	FM	K0EED	145.49000	-	82.5 Hz	
	FM	W0RRW	146.97000	-		
	FUSION	K0RQ	147.09000	+		
Fargo, Multiband Tower						
	FM	K0EED	145.49000	-	82.5 Hz	
Fargo, NDSU	FM	W0HSC	147.09000	+		
	FM	KD0SWQ	444.00000	+		
Forbes	FM	KC5ZCH	145.33000	-	136.5 Hz	
Glen Ullin	FM	KD7RDD	147.30000	+	162.2 Hz	
Grand Forks	FM	N0LAC	147.93000		123.0 Hz	
	FUSION	N0LAC	147.33000	+		
Grandin	FM	W0ILO	146.76000	-	123.0 Hz	
Granville	FUSION	KD0ASL	438.77000			
Hannover	FM	W0ZRT	145.43000	-		
Harlow	FM	KF0HR	147.01500	+	123.0 Hz	
Horace	FUSION	N0RF	433.60000			
Jamestown	FM	WB0TWN	444.92500	+		NDFC
	FUSION	KC0GCJ	147.72000	-		
Killdeer	FM	K0ND	146.64000	-		
Lisbon	FM	N0BQY	147.00000	-		
Maddock	FM	KF0HR	147.24000	+	141.3 Hz	
	FM	K0AJW	449.80000	-	67.0 Hz	
Mandan	FM	W0ZRT	146.94000	-		
Mandan, Old Red Trail						
	FM	N0FAZ	444.20000	+	103.5 Hz	
Minot	FM	K0AJW	146.97000	-	77.0 Hz	
	FM	W0ND	444.50000	+	67.0 Hz	
	FM	K0AJW	444.80000	+		

Location	Mode	Call sign	Output	Input	Access	Coordinator
Minot	FUSION	K0BKO	448.40000	-		
	FUSION	W0ND	449.50000	-		
Rugby	FM	WB0ATB	147.06000	+		
Sentinal Butte	FM	K0ND	146.73000	-		NDFC
St. Anthony	FM	W0ZRT	146.85000	-	123.0 Hz	NDFC
Stanley	FM	K0WSN	146.61000	-	100.0 Hz	
	FM	K0PHH	146.79000	-		
	FM	K0PHH	443.25000	+		
	FUSION	N0ATN	145.51000			
Turtle Lake		KD0RMF-L	145.52000			
Valley City	FUSION	KE0ARE	146.55000			
Wahpeton	FUSION	W0END	443.80000	+		
Wahpeton, College						
	FM	W0END	147.37500	+		
	FM	W0END	443.80000	+		
West Fargo	DMR/BM	KD0IOE	444.62500	+	CC1	
Williston	FM	AB0JX	147.21000	+	100.0 Hz	
	FM	K0WSN	443.85000	+		

OHIO

Location	Mode	Call sign	Output	Input	Access	Coordinator
Akron	DMR/BM	KD8ASA	440.50000	+	CC1	
	DMR/BM	W8UPD	443.11250	+	CC1	OARC
	DMR/BM	KD8YCF	443.58750	+	CC1	
	DMR/BM	WB8AVD	444.51250	+	CC7	
	FM	N8XPK	53.17000	52.17000	107.2 Hz	OARC
	FM	W8UPD	145.17000	-		OARC
	FM	WB8HHP	146.95500	-	110.9 Hz	OARC
	FM	N8XPK	1292.20000	1272.20000		
	WX	W8ODJ	444.55000	+	131.8 Hz	OARC
Akron, Spring Hill Apartments						
	FM	N8XPK	147.13500	+	110.9 Hz	OARC
Alliance	FM	W8LKY	442.35000	+	131.8 Hz	
Amelia	DMR/BM	N8EMA	442.20000	+	CC1	
Amherst	DMR/MARC	N1TVI	444.33750	+	CC1	
	WX	WD8OCS	146.62500	-		OARC
Andover	DMR/BM	W8VFD	444.96250	+	CC2	
	DMR/MARC	N8OHU	444.25000	+	CC1	
	DSTAR	W8TEN C	146.41500			
	DSTAR	W8TEN B	442.12500	+		
Archbold	FM	N8RLD	145.41000	-	107.2 Hz	OARC
Ashland	DMR/BM	N8IHI	444.03750	+	CC7	
	FUSION	WX8ASH	443.22500			
Ashley	FM	KC8BVF	444.62500	+		OARC
Athens	FM	KC8AAV	147.15000	+		OARC
	FUSION	W8UKE	145.15000	-		OARC
	FUSION	N8VZ	147.52500			
Attica	FM	N0CZV	443.67500	+	131.8 Hz	OARC
Atwater	DMR/BM	W8FAA	435.00000		CC7	
	DMR/BM	W8FAA	443.97500	+	CC7	
	FM	WA8LCA	224.14000	-		
Avon	FM	N8SIW	443.70000	+		
Avon Lake	DMR/BM	K8CMI	443.01250	+	CC2	
Bainbridge	DMR/MARC	KD8SPV	443.58750	+	CC7	
	FM	W8BAP	146.92500	-	74.4 Hz	OARC
	FM	WR8ANN	147.06000	+	110.9 Hz	OARC
	FM	KD8GRN	443.62500	+		
Barberton	FM	WB8OVQ	147.09000	+	110.9 Hz	OARC
Barnesville	FM	WB8WJT	146.64000	-	100.0 Hz	OARC
Bascom	FM	KB8EOC	145.15000	-		
	FM	KB8EOC	442.30000	+		
	WX	W8ID	145.45000	-	107.2 Hz	OARC
	WX	N8VWZ	146.68500	-		OARC

Location	Mode	Call sign	Output	Input	Access	Coordinator
Batavia	WX	N8NKS	444.32500	+		OARC
	FUSION	W8VI	147.48000			
Batavia, WOBO Tower						
	FM	K8YOJ	224.00000	-	123.0 Hz	OARC
Bay View	DMR/BM	KD8AVO	443.57500	+	CC7	
Beavercreek	FM	N8NPT	53.73000	52.73000		OARC
	FM	N8DCP	224.58000	-		OARC
Bedford Hts	FUSION	KB8ZXI	439.50000			
Bellbrook	DMR/BM	N8NQH	444.43750	+	CC11	
	DMR/BM	N8NQH	444.87500	+	CC13	
	FM	W8GCA	146.91000	-		OARC
	FM	W8DGN	147.04500	+	118.8 Hz	OARC
	FUSION	W8DGN	443.67500	+		
Bellefontaine	DMR/BM	N8AGJ	443.93750	+	CC5	
Bellefontaine, Campbell Hill						
	FM	W8FTV	147.00000	+	100.0 Hz	OARC
	FM	W8FTV	443.82500	+	186.2 Hz	OARC
Bellevue	WX	NF8E	442.62500	+	110.9 Hz	OARC
Belpre	FM	N8NBL	146.97000	-	91.5 Hz	OARC
	FM	KI8JK	147.31500	+	103.5 Hz	
Berlin Hts	FM	WB8LLY	146.80500	-	110.9 Hz	OARC
Bevan		K8KHW-R	444.12500			
Birmingham	FM	K8KXA	443.52500	+		OARC
Blanchester	FM	KB8CWC	145.25000	-	162.2 Hz	OARC
	FM	KB8CWC	442.02500	+		OARC
Bloomfield	DMR/BM	KD8MST	442.05000	+	CC2	
Boardman	FM	KD8ODF	444.52500	+	110.9 Hz	
Bowling Green	DMR/BM	WD8LEI	443.91250	+	CC1	
	FM	KD8BTI	146.79000	-	103.5 Hz	OARC
	FM	K8TIH	147.18000	+	67.0 Hz	OARC
	FM	K8TIH	442.12500	+	67.0 Hz	OARC
	FM	KD8BTI	443.51250	+	103.5 Hz	OARC
	FM	K8TIH	444.47500	+	67.0 Hz	OARC
	FUSION	W8PSK	446.00000			
Brecksville	FM	K8IIU	442.65000	+	131.8 Hz	OARC
Broadwell		W8JTW-R	443.05000			
Brunswick	FM	N8OVW	53.19000	52.19000		OARC
	FM	K8SCI	145.29000	-	110.9 Hz	OARC
	FM	K8VMC	147.00000	+	123.0 Hz	
	FM	N8OVW	443.02500	+	131.8 Hz	
	FM	W8WIN	444.65000	+	131.8 Hz	
	FM	W8WIN	444.67500	+	131.8 Hz	
	FM	KB8DTC	446.22500	-	136.5 Hz	
	FM	KB8DTC	446.62500	-	136.5 Hz	
	FM	KB8DTC	449.95000	-	173.8 Hz	
Bryan	FM	KA8OFE	146.82000	-		OARC
Bucyrus	DMR/MARC	KD8NCL	443.87500	+	CC1	OARC
	WX	W8DZN	147.16500	+	88.5 Hz	OARC
Cable	FM	WB8UCD	224.86000	-	100.0 Hz	OARC
Cadiz	FM	WB8FPN	146.65500	-	114.8 Hz	OARC
Calcutta	WX	K8BLP-R	146.70000	-		OARC
Caldwell	FM	NC8OH	147.28500	+	91.5 Hz	OARC
Cambridge	FM	W8VP	146.85000	-	91.5 Hz	OARC
	FM	KB8ZMI	147.00000	+	91.5 Hz	OARC
	FM	KB8ZMI	444.37500	+	91.5 Hz	OARC
Canal Winchester	FM	KA8ZNY	224.38000	-		
Canfield	FM	KD8DWV	145.27000	-	110.9 Hz	OARC
	FM	KC8WY	442.75000	+	131.8 Hz	OARC
Canton	DMR/BM	W8NP	444.78750	+	CC7	
	FM	KB8MIB	53.57000	52.57000	110.9 Hz	OARC
	FM	W8AL	146.79000	-	141.3 Hz	OARC
	FM	W8TUY	443.85000	+		OARC

Location	Mode	Call sign	Output	Input	Access	Coordinator
Canton, Mercy Medical Center						
	FM	N8ATZ	147.12000	+	110.9 Hz	OARC
Cardington	FUSION	KB8BKA	147.26500	+		
Carrollton	FM	K8VPJ	51.86000	50.86000		
	FM	K8VPJ	442.40000	+		OARC
	FM	N8RQU	442.58750	+		OARC
	FM	K8VPJ	442.62500	+		OARC
Celina	WX	KC8KVO	443.07500	+	107.2 Hz	OARC
Centerville	DMR/MARC	WB8SCT	147.13500	+	CC1	
	FM	WB8ART	145.43000	-	88.5 Hz	OARC
	FM	KC8QGP	444.60000	+		OARC
Chagrin Falls	FM	KF8YK	444.22500	+	131.8 Hz	
Chardon	FM	W8DES	146.94000	-	110.9 Hz	OARC
	FM	KF8YK	927.56250	902.56250	131.8 Hz	OARC
	P25	KF8YK	444.81250	+		OARC
Cherry Fork	FM	K8GE	147.00000	+	94.8 Hz	
Chesapeake	FUSION	KC8GYP	144.62000			
Chesterland	FM	K9IC	224.40000	-	141.3 Hz	
	FM	K9IC	444.60000	+	131.8 Hz	OARC
Chillicothe	DMR/MARC	KD8SPV	444.35000	+	CC7	OARC
	DMR/MARC	KD8SPV	444.42500	+	CC7	
	DSTAR	W8BAP C	147.01500	+		
	DSTAR	W8BAP B	444.42500	+		
Chillicothe, Scioto Trail Stat						
	DSTAR	W8BAP	147.01500	+		OARC
	FM	KA8WWI	53.23000	52.23000		OARC
	FM	W8BAP	146.85000	-	74.4 Hz	OARC
Cincinnati	DMR/BM	W8SAI	444.95000	+	CC1	
	DMR/MARC	WB8FXJ	442.17500	+	CC1	
	DMR/MARC	WB8CRS	443.40000	+	CC1	
	DMR/MARC	K8BIG	443.90000	+	CC1	
	DSTAR	K8BIG	145.35000	-		OARC
	DSTAR	K8BIG C	145.35000	-		
	FM	KD8TE	53.19000	52.19000	114.8 Hz	OARC
	FM	W8ESS	145.19000	-	123.0 Hz	
	FM	N8SIM	145.31000	-	123.0 Hz	OARC
	FM	K8YOJ	145.37000	-		OARC
	FM	K8SCH	146.67000	-	123.0 Hz	
	FM	WR8CRA	146.76000	-	162.2 Hz	OARC
	FM	K8YOJ	146.85000	-	123.0 Hz	OARC
	FM	K8SCH	146.92500	-	123.0 Hz	OARC
	FM	K8BIG	147.09000	+	123.0 Hz	OARC
	FM	K8YOJ	224.06000	-	100.0 Hz	OARC
	FM	W8ESS	224.62000	-	110.9 Hz	OARC
	FM	N8JRX	442.20000	+	192.8 Hz	
	FM	W8NWS	443.70000	+		OARC
	FM	W8ESS	444.22500	+	123.0 Hz	OARC
	FM	N8TVU	444.30000	+	118.8 Hz	OARC
	FM	KB8BWE	444.75000	+		OARC
	FM	K8CF	444.92500	+		OARC
	FM	W8ESS	927.55000	902.55000	110.9 Hz	OARC
	P25	K8BIG	147.15000	+		OARC
	P25	K8BIG	444.00000	+	123.0 Hz	
	WX	WB8CRS	146.88000	-	123.0 Hz	OARC
	FUSION	W8CRO	147.52500			
Cincinnati, Star Tower						
	P25	K8BIG	927.02500	902.02500	123.0 Hz	
Circleville	DMR/BM	WA8PYR	442.70000	+	CC1	
	FM	KD8HIJ	147.18000	+	74.4 Hz	OARC
	FM	KD8HIJ	442.70000	+		OARC
Cleveland	DMR/MARC	AD8G	444.95000	+	CC1	
	DSTAR	WB8THD	145.35000	-		OARC

Location	Mode	Call sign	Output	Input	Access	Coordinator
Cleveland	DSTAR	WB8THD C	145.35000	-		
	DSTAR	WB8THD	442.32500	+		OARC
	DSTAR	WB8THD B	442.32500	-		
	FM	NA8SA	147.19500	+	110.9 Hz	OARC
	FM	N8OND	444.27500	+	131.8 Hz	OARC
	WX	WR8ABC	146.76000	-	110.9 Hz	OARC
	FUSION	W8MPX	145.50000			
	FUSION	W8KRF	145.56250			
Clyde	FM	NF8E	145.35000	-	110.9 Hz	OARC
Coldwater	WX	W8MCA	145.25000	-	107.2 Hz	OARC
Colerain Township						
	FM	K8CR	443.57500	+	123.0 Hz	OARC
Columbia Heights	FM	W8CCI-R	146.97000	-	118.8 Hz	
Columbus	ATV	WR8ATV	444.97500	+		OARC
	DMR/BM	KA8ZNY	224.38000	-	CC1	
	DMR/BM	N8RQJ	441.50000		CC1	
	DMR/BM	N8RQJ	443.42500	+	CC1	OARC
	DMR/BM	AC8GI	444.85000	+	CC7	OARC
	DMR/MARC	W8TRB	145.37000	-	CC1	
	DMR/MARC	W8TRB	224.28000	-	CC1	
	DMR/MARC	KE8SVT	443.15000	+	CC1	
	DMR/MARC	W8TRB	927.01250	902.01250	CC1	
	DMR/MARC	W8TRB	927.52500	902.52500	CC1	
	DSTAR	W8DIG C	145.39000	-		
	DSTAR	W8DIG	145.39000	-		OARC
	DSTAR	W8CMH	145.49000	-		OARC
	DSTAR	W8CMH C	145.49000	-		
	DSTAR	W8LT B	442.60000	+		
	DSTAR	W8DIG B	442.65000	+		
	DSTAR	W8DIG	442.65000	+		OARC
	DSTAR	W8CMH	444.00000	+		OARC
	DSTAR	W8CMH B	444.00000	+		
	DSTAR	W8DIG	1285.00000	1265.00000		OARC
	DSTAR	W8DIG A	1285.00000	-		
	DSTAR	W8DIG D	1298.00000			
	FM	WC8OH	145.11000	-	67.0 Hz	OARC
	FM	WB8MMR	145.23000	-		OARC
	FM	WA8PYR	145.27000	-	82.5 Hz	
	FM	N8PVC	145.43000	-	123.0 Hz	OARC
	FM	WB8LAP	146.80500	-		OARC
	FM	W8RRJ	146.97000	-	123.0 Hz	OARC
	FM	K8DDG	147.06000	+	94.8 Hz	OARC
	FM	W8CQK	147.15000	+		OARC
	FM	N8OIF	147.21000	+		OARC
	FM	K8DRE	147.24000	+		OARC
	FM	WR8ATV	427.25000	439.25000		OARC
	FM	K8NIO	442.80000	+	151.4 Hz	
	FM	WB8YOJ	443.57500	+		OARC
	FM	K8MK	443.81250	+		OARC
	FM	N8YMT	444.10000	+		OARC
	FM	K8ARW	444.12500	+		
	FM	WA8PYR	444.17500	+	82.5 Hz	
	FM	W8AIC	444.20000	+	151.4 Hz	OARC
	FM	WB8INY	444.27500	+	94.8 Hz	OARC
	FM	WB8YOJ	444.30000	+		OARC
	FM	WX8CMH	444.57500	+	141.3 Hz	
	FM	N8ADL	444.90000	+		OARC
	FM	N8VJF	446.68750	-	131.8 Hz	
	FM	W8RW	927.01250	902.01250	131.8 Hz	
	FM	KA8ZNY	927.48750	902.48750	131.8 Hz	OARC
	FM	WR8ATV	1250.00000	1280.00000		OARC
	FM	WR8ATV	1258.00000	1280.00000		OARC

Location	Mode	Call sign	Output	Input	Access	Coordinator
Columbus	P25	W8DIG	443.65000	+		OARC
	P25	W8DIG	927.03750	902.03750	131.8 Hz	
	WX	W8AIC	146.76000	-	123.0 Hz	OARC
	FUSION	KE8CLD	144.25000			
	FUSION	N8RQJ-RPT	443.42500	+		
	FUSION	KD8GRN	446.50000			
	FUSION	WJ8B	446.82500			
Columbus Grove	DMR/MARC	K8TEK	444.30000	+	CC1	
Columbus, Ohio State Universit						
	FM	W8LT	442.60000	+	114.8 Hz	OARC
Conneaut	FM	W8BHZ	147.39000	+		OARC
Constitution	WX	W8TAP	146.74500	-	114.8 Hz	OARC
Copley	FM	WD8BIW	147.24000	+		
Cortland	FM	N8GZE	147.10500	+	114.8 Hz	OARC
	FM	WA8ILI	443.87500	+		OARC
Coshocton	WX	KE8BDF	145.23000	-	71.9 Hz	OARC
	FUSION	AB8RR	446.10000			
Cuyahoga Falls	FM	W8VPV	147.27000	+	110.9 Hz	OARC
	FM	W8VPV	444.85000	+	110.9 Hz	OARC
CuyahogaFalls	WX	W8DFA	443.78750	+		OARC
Dayton	DMR/BM	NY1A	443.56250	+	CC5	
	DMR/MARC	WA8PLZ	147.36000	+	CC1	OARC
	DMR/MARC	W8AK	442.87500	+	CC1	
	DMR/MARC	WB8SCT	444.60000	+	CC1	OARC
	DSTAR	W8HEQ C	145.27000	-		
	DSTAR	W8RTL C	147.10500	+		
	DSTAR	W8RTL B	443.05000	+		
	DSTAR	W8HEQ B	444.08750	+		
	DSTAR	W8RTL D	1249.00000			
	DSTAR	W8RTL	1283.50000	1263.50000		OARC
	DSTAR	W8RTL A	1283.50000	-		
	FM	WC8OH	145.11000	-	67.0 Hz	OARC
	FM	WA8PLZ	146.82000	-	77.0 Hz	OARC
	FM	W8BI	146.94000	-	123.0 Hz	OARC
	FM	WF8M	146.98500	-	123.0 Hz	OARC
	FM	W8BI	223.94000	-		OARC
	FM	WC8OH	224.16000	-		OARC
	FM	KB8CSL	224.72000	-		
	FM	W8BI	442.10000	+	123.0 Hz	OARC
	FM	WB8VSU	442.30000	+	123.0 Hz	OARC
	FM	W6CDR	442.75000	+	94.8 Hz	OARC
	FM	KB8CSL	443.60000	+		OARC
	FM	WF8M	443.77500	+	131.8 Hz	OARC
	FM	W8KSE	444.25000	+	123.0 Hz	OARC
	FM	N8YFM	927.48750	902.48750		
	WX	K8MCA	146.64000	-	123.0 Hz	OARC
	FUSION	KD8GRN	443.22500	+		
Defiance	FM	KT8EMA	444.73750	+		
	WX	K8VON	442.57500	+	107.2 Hz	OARC
Delaware	DMR/BM	KC8BPE	442.13750	+	CC1	
	FM	W8SMK	145.17000	-	74.4 Hz	OARC
	FM	N8DCA	145.19000	-	123.0 Hz	OARC
	FM	KA8IWB	145.29000	-	123.0 Hz	
	FUSION	KE8O	443.55000	+		
Delphos	FM	W8YEK	147.12000	+		OARC
	FM	KB8UDX	443.15000	+	107.2 Hz	OARC
Delta	DMR/BM	KE8ITJ	433.00000	432.40000	CC2	
	FM	K8LI-R	147.28500	+	103.5 Hz	OARC
	FM	K8LI	444.45000	+	103.5 Hz	OARC
Deshler	FM	KC8QYH	444.93750	+	103.5 Hz	
Doylestown	DMR/BM	W8WKY	442.27500	+	CC1	OARC
	FM	W8WKY	147.39000	+	114.8 Hz	OARC

Location	Mode	Call sign	Output	Input	Access	Coordinator
Dublin	FUSION	N8ASH	445.85000			
East Crestline		KC8JFA-L	445.55500			
East Liverpool	FM	K8BLP	442.17500	+		OARC
East Palestine	FM	W8GMM	146.77500	-	162.2 Hz	OARC
Eaton	FM	K8YR	145.47000	-	100.0 Hz	OARC
	FM	W8VFR	444.02500	+	74.4 Hz	OARC
	FM	W8VFR	444.93750	+	97.4 Hz	OARC
Eaton, Preble County EMA Offic						
	FM	K8YR	442.90000	+	100.0 Hz	
Elyria	DMR/BM	NW8S	444.31250	+	CC1	
	DSTAR	WA8DIG	443.43750	+		OARC
	FM	W8HF	145.23000	-	110.9 Hz	OARC
	FM	K8KRG-R	146.70000	-		OARC
	FM	WD8CHL	224.04000	-	141.3 Hz	
	FM	KB8O	444.31250	+	131.8 Hz	OARC
	FM	K8KRG	444.80000	+	131.8 Hz	OARC
	WX	KA8VDW	443.98750	+	162.2 Hz	OARC
	FUSION	K8KRG/R	444.80000	+		
Elyria, Lorain County Communit						
	FM	KC8BED	444.17500	+	131.8 Hz	
Englewood	FM	KB8ZR	443.50000	+	103.5 Hz	OARC
Euclid	DMR/MARC	N8CXU	444.85000	+	CC1	
	DMR/MARC	N8CXU	449.85000	+	CC1	
Fairborn	FM	KI6SZ	51.66000	50.66000		OARC
	FM	K8FBN	145.41000	-	118.8 Hz	OARC
	FM	K8FBN	442.37500	-	118.8 Hz	OARC
	FM	N8QBS	442.57500	+	127.3 Hz	OARC
	FM	N8QBS	442.82500	+		OARC
	FM	KI6SZ	444.31250	+		OARC
Fairfield	FM	W8WRK	146.70000	-	123.0 Hz	OARC
	FM	W8KJ	443.57500	+		
	FUSION	N8WLY	438.80000			
Fairfield, Jungle Jim's						
	FM	KD8WDU	443.95000	+	123.0 Hz	
Fairlawn	FM	N8NOQ	443.75000	+	131.8 Hz	OARC
Fairport Hrbr	FM	N8JCV	224.08000	-	141.3 Hz	OARC
Fayette	FM	KB8GOM	442.07500	+	103.5 Hz	OARC
Findlay	DMR/BM	W8FT	443.70000	+	CC1	
	DMR/MARC	N8PC	147.04500	+	CC1	
	DMR/MARC	N8PC	442.87500	+	CC1	
	FM	W8FT	147.15000	+	88.5 Hz	OARC
	FM	W8JES	443.42500	+	91.5 Hz	
	FUSION	W8FT	444.15000	+		
Fort Recovery	FM	KB8SCR-R	442.67500	+		OARC
	FM	KB8SCR	444.81250	+	107.2 Hz	OARC
Franklin	FM	WB8ZVL	145.29000	-	118.8 Hz	OARC
	FM	WE8N	442.42500	+	77.0 Hz	OARC
	FM	WB8ZVL	443.15000	+	118.8 Hz	OARC
Fremont	DMR/BM	N8SCA	442.06250	+	CC7	
	DMR/BM	N8FIS	443.00000	+	CC7	OARC
	FM	W8NCK	145.25000	-	186.2 Hz	OARC
	FM	KC8EPF	443.45000	+		OARC
	WX	N8SCA	145.49000	-	107.2 Hz	OARC
Fresno	FM	KB9JSC	443.53750	+	162.2 Hz	OARC
Ft. Recovery	FM	KB8SCR	223.96000	-	107.2 Hz	
Gahanna	FM	KB8SXJ	442.50000	+	82.5 Hz	OARC
Galena	FM	W8RUT	224.66000	-		
Galion	FM	W8BAE	146.85000	-	71.9 Hz	OARC
Gallipolis	DMR/BM	KC8VJK	444.11250	+	CC7	
	DMR/MARC	KD8SPV	444.11250	+	CC7	
Gallipolis, Mound Hill						
	FM	KC8ZAB	442.27500	+	74.4 Hz	OARC

Location	Mode	Call sign	Output	Input	Access	Coordinator
Gallipolis, Warehime Hill						
	FM	K8ATG	146.73000	-	91.5 Hz	
Georgetown	FM	N1DJS	146.73000	-	162.2 Hz	OARC
Germantown	FM	WG8ARS	443.18750	+	123.0 Hz	
Gibsonburg	FM	K8KXA	444.76250	+	131.8 Hz	
Goshen	FM	K8DV	443.45000	+	123.0 Hz	OARC
	FUSION	W8MRC	448.45000	-		
Greenfield, WVNU Radio Tower						
	FM	K8HO	146.68500	-		OARC
	FM	K8HO	444.77500	+		OARC
Greenhills	FM	WB8CRS	146.88000	-	123.0 Hz	
Greenville	DMR/BM	W8FLH	443.68750	+	CC1	
	FM	N8OBE	444.17500	+		OARC
	WX	W8FLH	146.79000	-	94.8 Hz	OARC
Halliday Heights	FM	KC8ZAB-R	147.06000	+	74.4 Hz	OARC
Hamilton	DMR/MARC	KD8VLU	442.96250	+	CC1	
	DSTAR	W8RNL	145.15000	-		OARC
	DSTAR	W8RNL C	145.15000	-		
	DSTAR	W8RNL	442.62500	+		OARC
	DSTAR	W8RNL B	442.62500	+		
	DSTAR	KD8TUZ	442.65000	+		OARC
	DSTAR	W8RNL D	1253.00000			
	DSTAR	W8RNL	1293.00000	1273.00000		OARC
	DSTAR	W8RNL A	1293.00000	1273.00000		
	FM	W8WRK	147.00000	+	123.0 Hz	OARC
	FM	W8CCI	147.33000	+	118.8 Hz	OARC
	FM	WB8TCB	224.54000	-		
	FM	W8WRK	443.33750	+		OARC
	FM	KD8EYB	444.11250	+	118.8 Hz	OARC
	FM	K8KY	444.65000	+	123.0 Hz	OARC
	FUSION	KA8YRN	147.52500			
Hamilton, North C Street Hill						
	FM	W8AJT	224.88000	-		
Hannibal	FM	WB8CSW	147.24000	+		OARC
Hanover Township						
	FUSION	W8XJF	145.54000			
Hanoverton	FUSION	NN8B	433.75000			
Hanoverton, Guilford Lake Stat						
	FM	NN8B	444.91250	+		
Harrisburg		N8HHV-R	444.60000			
Hayesville	FM	N8IHI	147.10500	+	71.9 Hz	OARC
	FM	KD8BIW	223.04000	-	110.9 Hz	
	FM	KD8BIW-R	224.58000	-		OARC
Hebron	DMR/BM	K8MDM	443.21250	+	CC1	
Highland Hills	FM	WB8APD	444.95000	+		OARC
Highland Hils	WX	WX8CLE	442.12500	+	82.5 Hz	OARC
Hillsboro	DMR/BM	W8CTC	443.07500	+	CC1	
	WX	K8HO	147.21000	+	100.0 Hz	OARC
	FUSION	KB8DOT	145.50000			
Hillsboro, Rocky Fork State Pa						
	FM	K8HO	444.67500	+		OARC
Hinckley Twp	WX	W8WGD	443.42500	+	131.8 Hz	OARC
Holland	FM	W8AK	444.27500	+	107.2 Hz	OARC
Howard	DMR/BM	KD8EVR	441.00000	+	CC7	
Hubbard	FM	W8IZC	443.10000	+		OARC
Huber Heights	DMR/BM	K1CCN	443.26250	+	CC7	
	FM	NO8I	224.30000	-	123.0 Hz	OARC
	FM	W8AK	442.92500	+	123.0 Hz	OARC
	FM	NO8I-R	442.95000	+	118.8 Hz	
Huber Heights, W8BI Clubhouse						
	DSTAR	W8HEQ	145.27000	-		
	DSTAR	W8HEQ	444.08750	+		

Location	Mode	Call sign	Output	Input	Access	Coordinator
Hudson	DMR/BM	W8HD	444.08750	+	CC1	
	FM	K8KSW	145.25000	-		OARC
	FM	KD8FL	443.47500	+		OARC
Hunters Chase	FM	WB8ULC-R	444.92500	444.32500		OARC
Ironton	FM	W8SOE	444.62500	+	103.5 Hz	OARC
Jacksonville	FM	KC8QDQ	147.22500	+		OARC
Jersey	FM	W8RRJ	52.70000	52.90000	123.0 Hz	
	FM	KA8ZNY	927.58750	902.58750		
Johnstown	DMR/BM	KD8USF	145.47000	-	CC7	
	DMR/BM	KD8USF	443.28750	+	CC7	
Keene	FM	W8CCA	147.04500	+		OARC
Kent		N8JBT-L	146.49000			
	DMR/BM	N8ZPS	442.02500	+	CC7	
	DMR/BM	K8GI	443.06250	+	CC10	
	DMR/BM	N8BHU	444.30000	+	CC1	
	FM	N8ZPS	145.11000	-		
	FM	K8IV	146.89500	-	118.8 Hz	
	FM	N8BHU	224.02000	-	141.3 Hz	OARC
Kenton	FM	W8VMV	146.62500	-	85.4 Hz	OARC
Kettering	DMR/MARC	W8AK	443.75000	+	CC1	OARC
	FM	W8GUC	444.66250	+	123.0 Hz	OARC
Kingsville	FM	N8XUA	443.65000	+	103.5 Hz	OARC
Lakeside	FM	N8GCI	146.74000		100.0 Hz	
Lakewood	FM	WR8ABC	146.88000	-	110.9 Hz	OARC
	FM	WR8ABC	224.90000	-	141.3 Hz	OARC
	FUSION	WR8ABC	444.70000	+		OARC
Lancaster	DMR/MARC	KC8MLN	147.25500	+	CC9	
	DMR/MARC	KC8MLN	147.27500	+	CC9	
	DMR/MARC	KC8MLN	147.37500	+	CC8	
	DMR/MARC	KC8MLN	442.97500	+	CC9	
	DMR/MARC	KC8MLN	927.43750	902.43750	CC9	
	DMR/MARC	KC8MLN	927.86250	902.86250	CC8	
	FM	K8QIK	53.09000	52.09000	71.9 Hz	
	FM	K8QIK	443.87500	+	71.9 Hz	OARC
Lebanon	DSTAR	KE8AOQ	443.15000	+		
	DSTAR	KE8AOQ B	443.15000	+		
	FM	WC8EMA	444.18750	+	88.5 Hz	OARC
Lexington	FM	WD8Q	443.22500	+	146.2 Hz	OARC
	FUSION	N8YOA	147.01500	+		
Liberty Township	FUSION	KD8OFO	145.57500			
Liberty Twp	FUSION	WM6X	443.12500	+		
Lima	DSTAR	KT8APR B	443.62500	+		
	FM	WB8ULC	146.67000	-		
	FM	W8EQ	146.94000	-		OARC
	FM	K8TCF	147.03000	+		OARC
	FM	N8GCH	444.07500	+		OARC
	WX	W8AOH	146.74500	-	100.0 Hz	OARC
Lima, Husky Refinery Complex						
	FM	N8GCH	145.17000	-		OARC
Lima, WLIO Tower						
	DSTAR	KT8APR	443.62500	+		OARC
	FM	KT8APR	53.63000	52.63000	107.2 Hz	OARC
	FM	KT8APR	145.37000	-	107.2 Hz	OARC
Lisbon	DMR/BM	KD8XB	443.93750	+	CC10	
	FM	KC8PHW	421.25000	434.05000		OARC
	FM	KD8XB	442.52500	+	162.2 Hz	OARC
	WX	K8GQB	146.80500	-	162.2 Hz	OARC
	FUSION	WX8EMA	145.49000			
Lithopolis	FM	KB8WQ	145.21000	-	100.0 Hz	
Little Hocking	FUSION	W8LGZ	433.90000			
Logan	DMR/BM	KD8ORN	442.35000	+	CC1	
	FM	K8LGN	443.12500	+		OARC

Location	Mode	Call sign	Output	Input	Access	Coordinator
London	FM	KE8RV	147.28500	+	82.5 Hz	OARC
Lorain	FM	WA8CAE	443.60000	+	131.8 Hz	OARC
	FM	WD8CHL	444.12500	+	131.8 Hz	OARC
Loudonville	FM	W3YXS	146.74500	-	71.9 Hz	
Loveland	FM	WD8KPU	442.77500	+		OARC
	FM	WB8BFS	443.80000	+		OARC
	FM	WU8S	444.52500	+	100.0 Hz	OARC
	FUSION	KE8PBA	146.56000			
Macedonia	FM	WR8ABC	444.40000	+	131.8 Hz	OARC
Malvern	FM	K8VPJ	147.07500	+	131.8 Hz	OARC
Mansfield	DMR/BM	W8WE	444.70000	+	CC7	
	FM	W8NDB	145.33000	-	71.9 Hz	OARC
	WX	KA8VDW	443.07500	+	151.4 Hz	OARC
	FUSION	N8RGO	443.22500	+		
Mantua	DMR/MARC	KD8DRG	443.55000	+	CC7	
Maplewood	DSTAR	KD8YFZ B	442.35000	+		
	WX	K8ZUK	146.83500	-	156.7 Hz	OARC
Marietta	DMR/BM	N8OJ	442.47500	+	CC1	
	DMR/BM	N8OJ	442.72500	+	CC7	
	DMR/BM	W8JL	442.90000	+	CC7	
	DMR/MARC	N8OJ	443.05000	+	CC1	
	FM	KI8JK	146.80500	-		OARC
	FM	W8HH	146.88000	-	91.5 Hz	OARC
	FM	WO8G	147.52500		100.0 Hz	
	FM	W8HH	443.40000	+	91.5 Hz	OARC
Marion	DMR/MARC	KC8BPE	442.01250	+	CC1	
	FM	WW8MRN	146.89500	-	250.3 Hz	OARC
	FM	WW8MRN	147.30000	+	250.3 Hz	OARC
	FM	KC8BPE	444.98750	+	110.9 Hz	
	FM	WW8MRN	447.01250	-	123.0 Hz	
	FM	W8MRN	449.73750	-	123.0 Hz	
Martins Ferry	DMR/BM	KC8VLD	145.44000	-	CC0	
Marysville	DMR/BM	K8JWL	443.45000	+	CC7	OARC
	FM	N8YRF	147.39000	+		OARC
	WX	N8IG	145.35000	-	127.3 Hz	OARC
Mason	DMR/BM	WR7HLN	444.95000	+	CC1	
	FM	W8BRQ	145.13000	-		OARC
	FM	W8ESS	442.27500	+	110.9 Hz	OARC
	FM	WB8WFG	444.15000	+		OARC
	FM	W8SAI	444.95000	+	131.8 Hz	OARC
Massillon	DMR/BM	W8NP	442.11250	+	CC7	
	FM	WA8GXM	53.05000	52.05000	136.5 Hz	OARC
	FM	W8NP	147.18000	+	110.9 Hz	OARC
	FM	W8NP	442.85000	+	131.8 Hz	OARC
	FM	WA8GXM	443.67500	+		OARC
Maumee	FM	W8TER	444.70000	+	103.5 Hz	OARC
Maybee	FM	K8HF-R	147.36000	+		OARC
Mayfield Heights	FM	N8QBB	51.62000	-	107.2 Hz	OARC
McArthur	DSTAR	W8VCO	147.10500	+	88.5 Hz	OARC
McConnelsvill	FM	WB8VQV	147.19500	+		OARC
McDermott	FM	KB8RBT	443.32500	+		OARC
Medina	DMR/MARC	N8OND	443.32500	+	CC1	
	FM	W8EOC	147.03000	+	141.3 Hz	OARC
	FM	W8HN	147.28500	+	110.9 Hz	
	FM	W8EOC	224.86000	-		OARC
	FM	N8OND	927.68750	902.68750	131.8 Hz	OARC
Medway	FUSION	WT8W	145.31000	-		
	FUSION	WB8IXW	147.48000			
Mentor	FM	N9AGC	145.21000	-	110.9 Hz	OARC
	FM	N8BC	147.16500	+	110.9 Hz	OARC
	FM	WB8PHI	147.25500	+		OARC
	FM	N9AGC	444.47500	+	131.8 Hz	OARC

Location	Mode	Call sign	Output	Input	Access	Coordinator
Mentor, Tri-Point Hospital						
	FM	N8BC	224.50000	-	141.3 Hz	OARC
Mentor, Tripoint Hospital						
	FM	N8BC	147.21000	+	110.9 Hz	OARC
Miamisburg	FM	W6CDR	146.77500	-	77.0 Hz	OARC
	FM	W8NCI	147.01500	+	77.0 Hz	OARC
	FM	NV8E	442.45000	+	123.0 Hz	OARC
	FM	W8DYY	443.00000	+	88.5 Hz	OARC
Miamisburg, Sycamore Hospital						
	FM	W8DYY	145.33000	-		OARC
Middle Point	FM	W8FY	146.85000	-		OARC
Middlefield	FM	KC8IBR	442.25000	+		OARC
Middletown	DMR/MARC	W8BLV	444.36250	+	CC1	
	FM	W8BLV-R	146.61000	-	77.0 Hz	OARC
	FM	N8COZ	146.71500	-		OARC
	FM	W8MUM	443.53750	+	94.8 Hz	
	FM	AG8Y	444.47500	+	100.0 Hz	OARC
	FM	W8BLV	444.82500	+	77.0 Hz	OARC
	FUSION	KX8U	146.70000	-		
	FUSION	KD8EDT	442.03750	+		
Miller City	FM	NO8C	443.56250	+	107.2 Hz	OARC
Millersburg	FM	KD8QGQ	146.67000	-	71.9 Hz	OARC
	FM	KD8CJ	444.87500	+	131.8 Hz	OARC
Minerva	FM	KD8XB	442.95000	+	162.2 Hz	OARC
Minford	FM	KF8YO	224.92000	-	114.8 Hz	
Mogadore	FM	KC8MXW	444.48750	+		OARC
Monroe	FM	W8JEU	147.31500	+	77.0 Hz	OARC
	FM	WA8MU	442.55000	+	118.8 Hz	OARC
Montville	DMR/BM	KD8AVO	444.73750	+	CC7	
	DMR/MARC	KD8AVO	442.47500	442.97500	CC7	
	FM	N8XUA	145.33000	-		OARC
	FM	N8XUA	443.45000	+		OARC
Mount Airy	FM	W8VND-L	147.24000	+		OARC
Mount Gilead	DMR/BM	WN7C	444.91250	+	CC7	OARC
	FUSION	W8GBL	444.86250	+		
Mount Vernon	DMR/BM	KD8EVR	441.00000	+	CC7	
	FM	K8EEN	146.79000	-	71.9 Hz	
Mount Vrrnon	FM	K8EEN	444.60000	+	71.9 Hz	
Mt Eaton	FM	KB8PXM	53.33000	52.33000	100.0 Hz	OARC
Mt Gilead	DMR/BM	W8NL	444.86250	+	CC1	OARC
	FM	WY8G	224.94000	-	71.9 Hz	OARC
Mt Gilead, US 42	FM	W8NL	146.77500	-	107.2 Hz	OARC
Munroe Falls	FM	WB8CXO	147.33000	+	110.9 Hz	
Napoleon	FM	K8TII	147.22500	+		OARC
	FM	K8TII	147.31500	+		OARC
Nashport	DMR/MARC	K8QG	145.25000	-	CC1	
New Boston		WW8O-R	145.45000			
New Carlisle	FM	W8RMF	443.23750	+	141.3 Hz	
New Concord	DMR/BM	KD8USF	442.05000	+	CC2	
New Lexington	DMR/BM	KD8USF	442.07500	+	CC2	
New Springfield	DMR/BM	KD8XB	444.88750	+	CC10	
	FM	K8TKA	147.31500	+	156.7 Hz	
New Springfld	FM	KF8YF	443.52500	+	162.2 Hz	OARC
New Vienna	WX	WB8ZZR	444.57500	+	141.3 Hz	OARC
Newark	DMR/BM	KD4LPU	147.35000	+	CC7	
	FM	W8WRP	146.88000	-	141.3 Hz	OARC
	FM	WD8RVK	442.05000	+		OARC
	FM	W8AJL	443.60000	+	71.9 Hz	
	FM	W8WRP	444.50000	+	141.3 Hz	OARC
Newbury	FM	K8SGX	52.68000	52.88000	107.2 Hz	OARC
	FM	W8LYD	146.85000	-	110.9 Hz	OARC
	FM	WB8QGR	444.62500	+	131.8 Hz	OARC

Location	Mode	Call sign	Output	Input	Access	Coordinator
Newbury	FM	K8SGX	444.97500	+		OARC
Newport	DSTAR	W8ORG B	443.60000	+		
	FUSION	K8KHW	146.55000			
Newton Falls	WX	N8VPR	147.22500	+		OARC
NOAA Akron	WX	KDO94	162.40000			
NOAA Athens	WX	KZZ46	162.42500			
NOAA Bridgeport	WX	WWF35	162.52500			
NOAA Carey	WX	KZZ47	162.52500			
NOAA Chillicothe	WX	KJY68	162.50000			
NOAA Cleveland	WX	KHB59	162.55000			
NOAA Columbus	WX	KIG86	162.55000			
NOAA Covington	WX	KIH42	162.55000			
NOAA Dayton	WX	WXJ46	162.47500			
NOAA Grafton	WX	WNG698	162.50000			
NOAA High Hill	WX	WXJ47	162.47500			
NOAA Lima	WX	WXJ93	162.40000			
NOAA Mansfield	WX	WWG57	162.45000			
NOAA Marietta	WX	WNG734	162.40000			
NOAA New Philadelphia						
	WX	WNG735	162.42500			
NOAA Otway	WX	WXM69	162.52500			
NOAA Sandusky	WX	KHB97	162.40000			
NOAA Toledo	WX	WXL51	162.55000			
NOAA Youngstown						
	WX	WWG56	162.50000			
North Canton	FUSION	KN4FYR	449.40000	-		
North Ridgeville		KB8ZUN-L	445.00000			
	DMR/MARC	N8LXM	443.12500	443.62500	CC1	
	FM	K8IC	444.50000	+		OARC
North Royalton	FM	K8KRG	145.15000	-	110.9 Hz	OARC
	FM	K8SCI	224.76000	-		OARC
	FM	K8SCI	443.15000	+	131.8 Hz	OARC
	FM	WA8CEW	443.90000	+		OARC
	FM	K8YSE-R	444.07500	+		OARC
Northwood	FM	KB8YVY	442.42500	+	103.5 Hz	OARC
Norton	DMR/BM	KE8LDH	442.51250	+	CC1	OARC
	DMR/BM	KD8DRG	443.85000	+	CC7	
	DMR/MARC	KD8DRG	444.00000	+	CC7	
	DSTAR	KE8LDH B	442.51250	+		
	FM	WB8UTW	53.15000	52.15000		OARC
	FM	WA8DBW	146.68500	-	110.9 Hz	OARC
	FM	WB8UTW	224.06000	-		OARC
	FM	WD8KNL	444.00000	+		OARC
Norwalk	FM	KA8VDW	442.67500	+	162.2 Hz	OARC
Oak Harbor	FM	K8VXH	147.07500	+	100.0 Hz	OARC
	FM	K8VXH	442.25000	+	100.0 Hz	
Okeana	FUSION	NE8AL	145.67000			
Oregon	DSTAR	KD8QOF B	444.25000	+		
	FM	N8UAS	443.30000	+	103.5 Hz	OARC
	FM	W8MTU	444.92500	+	103.5 Hz	
	WX	W8RZM	147.37500	+		OARC
	FUSION	WJ8E	442.95000	+		
Orrville	FM	KD8SQ	146.71500	-		OARC
Orwell	FM	KF8YF	146.65500	-		OARC
	FM	KF8YF	444.25000	+		OARC
Ottawa	FM	W8ZRZ	443.88750	+	107.2 Hz	OARC
Ottawa, Putnam County Health D						
	FM	W8MCB	146.71500	-	107.2 Hz	OARC
Owensville	FM	W8MRC	147.34500	+	123.0 Hz	
Oxford	FM	W8CCI	145.21000	-	118.8 Hz	OARC
Painesville	DMR/MARC	N1TVI	443.33750	+	CC1	
Parma	DSTAR	W8QV B	444.45000	+		

Location	Mode	Call sign	Output	Input	Access	Coordinator
Parma	FM	WA8Q	145.31000	-	110.9 Hz	OARC
	FM	KB8WLW	145.41000	-	110.9 Hz	OARC
	FM	W8KDG-L	223.44000		141.3 Hz	
	FM	KB8WLW	224.48000	-	141.3 Hz	OARC
	FM	W8DRZ	442.05000	+	131.8 Hz	OARC
	FM	KB8WLW	442.22500	+	131.8 Hz	OARC
	FM	KB8WLW	442.45000	+		OARC
	FM	K8ZFR	443.82500	+	131.8 Hz	
	FM	WR8SS	444.77500	+	131.8 Hz	OARC
	FM	W8CJB	444.90000	+	131.8 Hz	OARC
	FM	KB8WLW	927.61250	902.61250	131.8 Hz	
	FUSION	W8NIN	145.60000			
	FUSION	N8JLK	446.32500			
Parma Heights	FUSION	K8CVM	443.35000			
	FUSION	K8CVM	446.40000			
Parma, WJW Tower						
	FM	W8DRZ	444.05000	+	131.8 Hz	OARC
Pataskala	FM	W8NBA	147.33000	+	123.0 Hz	OARC
Paulding	FM	KE8FJX	147.13500	+	141.3 Hz	
	FM	KE8FJX	442.27500	+	141.3 Hz	OARC
Peebles	FM	KJ8I	145.17000	-	77.0 Hz	OARC
	FM	KJ8I	442.67500	+	77.0 Hz	OARC
	FUSION	WD8LSN	444.02500	+		
Perrysburg	DSTAR	W8ODR B	444.51250	+		
Philo	FM	W8ZZV	146.61000	-	74.4 Hz	OARC
Pickerington	FUSION	W4JER	445.10000			
Piqua		N8VTU-L	446.07500			
	DMR/BM	N8BCM	444.46250	+	CC1	
	DMR/MARC	W8AK	444.83750	+	CC1	
	FM	N8OWV	442.12500	+	123.0 Hz	OARC
	FM	W8AK	444.72500	+	123.0 Hz	OARC
	FM	N8VTU	446.27500		123.0 Hz	
	FUSION	N8VTU	145.62500			
Piqua, Water Tower						
	FUSION	W8SWS	147.21000	+	67.0 Hz	
Polk	FM	N8SIW	145.13000	-	110.9 Hz	OARC
	FM	WA8TJC	442.15000	+	88.5 Hz	OARC
	FM	N8SIW	442.97500	+	131.8 Hz	OARC
	WX	KA8VDW	443.62500	+	162.2 Hz	OARC
Pomeroy	FM	KC8LOE	146.86500	-	88.5 Hz	OARC
	FM	K8ATG	443.70000	+	91.5 Hz	OARC
Port Clinton	FUSION	KE8OOE	146.55000			
	FUSION	KE8DZK	147.58500			
Portable	DMR/BM	KB8UDE	442.00000	+	CC15	
Portsmouth	FM	KC8BBU	147.36000	+	136.5 Hz	OARC
	FM	N8QA	444.60000	+		
Quail Highlands	FM	N8BC-R	444.65000	+		OARC
Quincy		KD8LMH-L	146.56000			
Ravenna	FM	KB8ZHP	145.39000	-		OARC
	FM	KB8ZHP	442.87500	+	100.0 Hz	OARC
	FM	K8IV	444.57500	+		
Ray	DMR/MARC	KD8SPV	146.89500	-	CC7	OARC
	DMR/MARC	KD8SPV	442.22500	+	CC7	OARC
	FM	W8YUL	146.79000	-		OARC
Rayland	FUSION	KX8DRA	146.94000	-		
Republic	FM	KC8RCI	147.25500	+	107.2 Hz	OARC
	FM	KC8RCI	444.43750	+	107.2 Hz	OARC
Reynoldsburg	FM	W8FEH	146.91000	-	71.9 Hz	OARC
	FM	W8LAD	443.95000	+		OARC
Richfield	FM	N8CPI	442.55000	+	131.8 Hz	OARC
	FM	KA8JOY	443.92500	+	131.8 Hz	OARC
Richmond	FUSION	AD8AT	147.52500			

Location	Mode	Call sign	Output	Input	Access	Coordinator
Rittman		KE8ABM-R	442.73800			
	DMR/BM	WW8TF	146.68500	+	CC1	
	DMR/BM	WW8TF	442.37500	+	CC1	OARC
	DMR/BM	KE8LDG	442.73750		CC1	OARC
	DMR/BM	N8OFP	443.73750	+	CC7	
Rosemount		KC4ECC-R	440.61200			
Roseville	FM	N8ROA	442.17500	+	91.5 Hz	OARC
Rossford	DMR/BM	KB8OTP	441.55000	+	CC12	
Rushsylvania	FUSION	KE8KHN	145.78000			
Salem	FM	KB8MFV	29.68000	-		
	FM	KB8MFV	146.86500	-	110.9 Hz	OARC
	FM	K8GQB	444.96250	+	162.2 Hz	
	WX	KB8MFV	53.03000	52.03000	88.5 Hz	OARC
	WX	KA8OEB	147.25500	+	156.7 Hz	OARC
	WX	KB8MFV-R	147.28500	+		OARC
	WX	KB8MFV	442.10000	+	88.5 Hz	OARC
	WX	KA8OEB	444.67500	+	156.7 Hz	OARC
Sandburr Corners	FM	K8TTE-R	444.21200	+		
Sandusky	DSTAR	K8RRG B	444.76250	+		
	FM	W8LBZ	444.37500	+	110.9 Hz	OARC
Sciotoville	FM	W8KKC	145.45000	-	114.8 Hz	
Seaman	FM	KC8FBG	444.51250	+		OARC
Seven Hills	FUSION	AC8TN	145.60000			
Shaffers (historical)						
	FM	W8LKY-R	145.37000	-		OARC
Shaker Heights		WX8CUY-R	53.11000			
		WX8CUY-L	146.47500			
	FM	KD8LDE	224.38000	-	131.8 Hz	
	FM	K8ZFR	444.75000	+	131.8 Hz	OARC
Shaker Heights, Shaker Towers						
	FM	KD8LDE	443.80000	+		OARC
Shelby	FM	W8DZN	442.52500	+	88.5 Hz	OARC
Shiloh		W8DLB-L	145.55000			
	DMR/BM	N8TWM	444.03000	+	CC7	
Sidney	DMR/MARC	N8YFM	443.90000	+	CC1	OARC
	FM	W8AK	147.34500	+	107.2 Hz	OARC
	FM	W8JSG	442.47500	+		OARC
	FM	KE8BCY	443.20000	+		OARC
	FM	N6JSX	444.88750	+	107.2 Hz	OARC
Simplex	FM	HAMVENTION	146.52000			
Smith Corners		KD8WOF-L	446.50000			
Solon	FM	KD8ZNQ	147.50500			
South Charleston	FM	KB8GJG	53.39000	52.39000		OARC
South Denmark		N8CT-L	146.71500			
South Euclid	FM	N8APU	146.79000	-	88.5 Hz	OARC
South Webster	FM	N8QA-R	145.39000	-		OARC
South Zanesville	DMR/BM	KD8USF	443.10000	+	CC2	
	DMR/BM	KD8USF	444.07500	+	CC7	
	DMR/BM	KD8MST	444.40000	+	CC2	
	DMR/BM	KD8MST	444.95000	+	CC2	
	FM	KD8MST	442.24000	+		
Springboro		W1FJI-L	147.52000			
	DMR/MARC	W8CYE	147.13500	+	CC1	
	FM	W8CYE	145.49000	-	77.0 Hz	OARC
	FM	K8DZ	223.82000	-	77.0 Hz	OARC
	FM	N8RXL	224.22000	-	100.0 Hz	OARC
Springfield	DMR/MARC	KC8NYH	442.51250	+	CC1	
	DMR/MARC	KC8NYH	443.41250	+	CC1	OARC
	FM	W8OG	145.31000	-	82.5 Hz	
	FM	W8OG	146.73000	-	77.0 Hz	OARC
	FM	KA8HMJ	147.22500	+	100.0 Hz	OARC
	FM	KA8HMJ	444.41250	+		OARC

Location	Mode	Call sign	Output	Input	Access	Coordinator
Springfield	FUSION	K8KVN	442.43750	+		
Springfield, Ohio Masonic Home						
	FM	W8BUZ	443.30000	+	146.2 Hz	OARC
Sprotts Corners		K8SRR-R	146.89500			
St Clairsville	FM	W8GBH	145.21000	-	103.5 Hz	OARC
St Marys	FM	W8GZ	146.80500	-	107.2 Hz	OARC
	FM	K8QYL	147.33000	+	107.2 Hz	OARC
St. Paris	FM	WB8UCD	224.60000	-	100.0 Hz	OARC
Steubenville	FM	WD8IIJ	147.06000	+	114.8 Hz	
Stockport	DMR/BM	KE8ANE	443.23900	442.63900	CC2	
Stone Creek	FM	W8ZX	444.82500	+	71.9 Hz	
Stonecreek	FM	W8ZX	146.73000	-	71.9 Hz	OARC
Stoutsville	DMR/MARC	KD8SPV	442.20000	+	CC7	
	FM	KD8GRN	443.06250	+		OARC
Stow	DSTAR	W8TWE B	444.45000	+		
	FM	AF1K	442.42500	+	131.8 Hz	OARC
Sugarcreek	FM	W8ZX	146.92500	-	71.9 Hz	OARC
Swanton	FM	N3VGX	442.36250	+	103.5 Hz	
Sylvania		KD8WCD-L	446.03700			
	FM	KC8GWH	443.77500	+	103.5 Hz	OARC
Tallmadge	DSTAR	N8DXE C	146.98500	-		
Taylor Station	FM	W8ZPF-L	146.67000	-		OARC
Thompson	DMR/MARC	N8NOD	443.47500	+	CC1	
	FM	WB5OD	443.70000	+		
	FM	KF8YK	444.56250	+	131.8 Hz	OARC
	WX	KB8FKM	224.96000	-	141.3 Hz	OARC
Thornville	DMR/BM	AC8GI	145.25000	-	CC7	OARC
	DMR/BM	AC8GI	442.45000	+	CC7	OARC
	FM	WW8JS	145.57000		91.5 Hz	
	FM	KB8ZMI	146.83500	-	91.5 Hz	OARC
	FM	AC8GI	445.45000	-		
Tiffin	DMR/BM	W3BWW	444.82500	+	CC1	OARC
	DSTAR	KB8EOC-C	147.50000			
	FM	WB8REI-L	146.45000			
	FM	K8EMR	443.80000	+	107.2 Hz	OARC
	FUSION	W8SPB	147.52500			
	FUSION	WB8REI	443.26250	+	107.2 Hz	
Tipp City	FM	N8RVS	444.53750	+		OARC
Toledo	DMR/BM	K8XG	444.65000	+	CC1	
	DMR/MARC	WB8WEA	444.16250	+	CC1	
	DMR/MARC	N8EFJ	444.85000	+	CC1	OARC
	DMR/MARC	KD8KCF	446.12500	-	CC1	
	DSTAR	W8HHF	442.75000	+		OARC
	DSTAR	W8HHF B	442.75000	+		
	DSTAR	KD8QOF	444.25000	+		
	FM	K8ALB	146.61000	-	103.5 Hz	OARC
	FM	WJ8E	147.34500	+	103.5 Hz	OARC
	FM	N8LPQ-R	444.95000	+	103.5 Hz	OARC
	FM	W8HHF	927.02500	902.02500	131.8 Hz	OARC
	FM	KD8KCF	927.91250	902.91250	131.8 Hz	
	FM	WJ8E	1285.00000	1265.00000	103.5 Hz	OARC
	FM	WJ8E	1287.00000	1267.00000		
	WX	WJ8E	442.95000	+	103.5 Hz	OARC
	FUSION	W8HHF	146.83500	-		
	FUSION	N8LPQ	443.97500	+		
	FUSION	KD8UOU	446.07500			
	FUSION	KD8BIN	446.50000			
Toledo, University Of Toledo						
	FM	W8HHF	224.14000	-	103.5 Hz	OARC
Toledo, University Of Toledo C						
	FM	W8HHF	147.27000	+	103.5 Hz	OARC
	FM	W8HHF	442.85000	+	103.5 Hz	OARC

Location	Mode	Call sign	Output	Input	Access	Coordinator
Traffic Bulletin Station						
	FM	HAMVENTION	145.52500			
Troy	DMR/BM	WI8DX	446.60000	-	CC1	
	FM	W8FW	145.23000	-	100.0 Hz	OARC
	FM	KD8KID	147.24000	+		OARC
	FM	N8OWV	223.98000	-		OARC
	FM	WD8CMD	442.97500	+		OARC
	FM	KB8MUV	443.63750	+		OARC
	FUSION	WB8PMG	147.33000	+		
Uhrichsville	FM	K8CQA	443.50000	+		OARC
Uniontown	FM	WD8BIW	53.25000	52.25000		OARC
	FM	WD8BIW	145.45000	-	110.9 Hz	OARC
Upper Sandusky	FM	KE8PX	147.21000	+	107.2 Hz	OARC
Urbana	FM	K8VOR	146.95500	-	100.0 Hz	OARC
	FM	K7GUN	147.22500	+		OARC
	FM	K7GUN	224.98000	-	100.0 Hz	OARC
	FM	WB8UCD	443.17500	+	123.0 Hz	OARC
	FM	K7DN	443.35000	+		OARC
	WX	WB8UCD	147.37500	+	100.0 Hz	OARC
Van Wert	DMR/BM	W8EJC	444.92500	+	CC1	
	FM	W8FY-R	146.70000	-		OARC
	FM	W8FY	434.00000	923.30000		OARC
	FM	W8FY	444.85000	+	136.5 Hz	OARC
	FM	N8IHP	446.02500	447.02500	156.7 Hz	
Vanceburg		KI4KQD-L	146.53500			
Vermilion	FM	W8DRZ	443.05000	+	131.8 Hz	OARC
Vermillion	WX	KA8VDW	53.29000	52.29000	107.2 Hz	OARC
Vienna	FM	N8NVI	147.04500	+		OARC
Vincent	FM	W8JTW-L	443.05000	+		OARC
	WX	KC8BED-R	147.15000	+		OARC
Wacker Heights	FM	K8QIK-L	146.70000	-		OARC
	FM	K8QIK-R	147.03000	+		OARC
Wadsworth	FM	KD8DRG	145.49000	-	110.9 Hz	OARC
	FM	WB8UTW	927.66250	902.66250		OARC
	WX	WA8DBW	444.42500	+	131.8 Hz	OARC
Wapakoneta	WX	KD8CQL	442.15000	+	107.2 Hz	OARC
Warren	FM	N8DOD	146.83500	-	131.8 Hz	OARC
	FM	N8DOD	224.16000	-	131.8 Hz	OARC
	FM	KA9YTS	442.82500	+	131.8 Hz	OARC
	FM	W8VTD	443.00000	+		OARC
	FM	N8DOD	443.72500	+	131.8 Hz	OARC
	FM	WA8ILI	444.83750	+		OARC
	WX	W8VTD	146.97000	-	100.0 Hz	OARC
	WX	N8NVI	442.82500	+	131.8 Hz	OARC
Warrensville Heights						
	DMR/MARC	N8NOD	442.08750	+	CC1	OARC
Washington Court House						
	FM	N8EMZ	147.27000	+		OARC
	FM	N8QLA	442.07500	+	77.0 Hz	OARC
	FM	N8EMZ	444.61250	+		OARC
Waterville	DMR/MARC	N8XLJ	443.75000	+	CC1	
Wauseon	FM	KB8MDF	53.41000	52.41000		OARC
	FM	K8BXQ	147.19500	+	103.5 Hz	OARC
Waynesburg	FM	KC8ONY	442.20000	+		OARC
Wellington	FM	K8TV	444.66250	+		OARC
Wellston	DMR/BM	N8OJ	147.37500	+	CC1	
	DMR/BM	N8OJ	443.25000	+	CC1	
West Carrollton	FM	K8ZQ	444.50000	+		OARC
West Chester	DMR/BM	W8SDR	443.73750	+	CC1	
	DMR/MARC	W8SDR	444.97500	+	CC1	
	FM	WC8RA	442.32500	+	123.0 Hz	OARC
	FM	W8VVL	442.70000	+	123.0 Hz	OARC

Location	Mode	Call sign	Output	Input	Access	Coordinator
West Chester, VOA Museum						
	FM	WC8VOA	443.65000	+		OARC
West Lafayette	FM	WX8OH	443.32500	+	71.9 Hz	OARC
West Milton	FM	N8EIO	444.56250	+		OARC
West Salem	FM	KE8X	53.27000	52.27000	107.2 Hz	OARC
	FM	KE8X	443.30000	+	131.8 Hz	OARC
Westlake	FUSION	KF8PM	146.44000			
Wickliffe	FM	WA8PKB	444.15000	+		OARC
	FM	WA8PKB	444.72500	+		OARC
Williamstown	FM	K8VON-R	147.09000	+		OARC
Willow Wood	DMR/MARC	KD8SPV	442.11250	+	CC7	
	FM	W8SOE	146.61000	-	103.5 Hz	OARC
Wilmington	DSTAR	W8GO C	145.16000	-		
	DSTAR	W8GO B	442.15000	+		
	FM	NOAA	162.47500			
	FM	K8IO	443.37500	+	123.0 Hz	OARC
Winchester		KD8QED-L	146.55500			
Wintersville, Blessed Sacramen						
	FM	WD8IIJ	443.77500	+		OARC
Wintersville, OH	FM	N8GD-R	147.06000	+	114.8 Hz	
Woodsfield	FM	WD8RED	147.27000	+		
Wooster	DMR/BM	W8WOO	443.17500	+	CC1	
	FM	W8WOO	147.21000	+	88.5 Hz	OARC
	FM	WB8VPG	147.34500	+	110.9 Hz	OARC
	FM	K8WAY	443.40000	+		OARC
	FM	KD8EU	444.25000	+	131.8 Hz	OARC
Wrightsville	FM	KF8RC	147.18000	+	118.8 Hz	OARC
Xenia	FM	W8XRN	147.16500	+	123.0 Hz	OARC
	FM	W8XRN	443.10000	+	123.0 Hz	OARC
Youngstown	DSTAR	K8WGR B	442.72500	+		
	FM	KC9WKE	144.91000			
	FM	W8QLY	146.74500	-	110.9 Hz	OARC
	FM	KB8N	147.00000	+		OARC
Youngstown, WHOT Tower						
	FM	W8IZC	146.91000	-	110.9 Hz	OARC
Zanesville	ATV	W8TJT	444.95000	+		OARC
	DMR/BM	KD8MST	444.10000	+	CC2	OARC
	FM	KB8ZMI	147.07500	+	91.5 Hz	OARC
	FM	KJ8N	224.94000	-		OARC
	FM	KB8ZMI	442.25000	+	91.5 Hz	OARC
OKLAHOMA						
Ada	DMR/BM	N7OKD	446.50000	-	CC15	
	FM	KE5GLC	145.27000	-	141.3 Hz	ORSI
	FM	WB5NBA	147.28500	+	114.8 Hz	ORSI
Alfalfa	FM	K5GSM	145.11000	-		ORSI
Altus	DMR/BM	WX5ASA	146.89500	-	CC1	
	DSTAR	AJ5Q	442.22500	447.32500		ORSI
	DSTAR	AJ5Q B	442.22500	+		
	FM	WX5ASA	147.28500	+	100.0 Hz	ORSI
	FM	WX5ASA	442.05000	+	100.0 Hz	ORSI
	FUSION	KA7NWT	147.52500			
Altus, Navajo Mountain						
	FM	WX5ASA	146.79000	-	100.0 Hz	ORSI
Altus, OK, Navajo Mountain						
	DSTAR	AJ5Q	432.20000			
Alva, Hardtner	FM	W5ALZ	444.90000	+	103.5 Hz	ORSI
Anadarko	FM	WX5LAW	147.27000	+		ORSI
Antlers	FM	KI5KC	145.49000	-		ORSI
	FM	KD5DAR	444.20000	+	88.5 Hz	ORSI
	FM	KI5KC	444.92500	+	114.8 Hz	ORSI
Ardmore	FM	W5BLW	146.97000	-		ORSI

Location	Mode	Call sign	Output	Input	Access	Coordinator
Ardmore	FM	KB5LLI	147.07500	+	123.0 Hz	ORSI
	FM	W5CVE	433.50000			
Bartlesville		N5XQK-L	147.09000			
	DMR/BM	W5RAB	442.18750	+	CC1	ORSI
	DMR/BM	W5RAB	442.35000	+	CC1	ORSI
	DMR/BM	W5IAS	442.47500	+	CC2	
	DMR/BM	W5RAB	443.65000	+	CC1	ORSI
	DMR/BM	W5RAB	443.82500	+	CC1	
	DMR/BM	WD5ETD	444.37500	+	CC1	
	DMR/BM	W5IAS	444.45000	+	CC1	ORSI
	DMR/BM	W5RAB	444.47500	+	CC2	
	DMR/BM	W5IAS	444.85000	+	CC1	
	FM	W5NS	146.65500	-	88.5 Hz	ORSI
	FM	W5NS	146.76000	-	88.5 Hz	ORSI
	FM	W5RAB	224.26000	-	88.5 Hz	ORSI
	FM	KD5IMA	443.12500	+	88.5 Hz	ORSI
	FM	W5RAB	927.65000	902.65000		ORSI
	IDAS	KD5IMA	145.15000	-	88.5 Hz	ORSI
	IDAS	KF5FWE	442.27500	+	100.0 Hz	ORSI
	IDAS	KF5FWE	444.25500	+	100.0 Hz	
	WX	W5IAS	444.42500	+	88.5 Hz	ORSI
	FUSION	N5XQK	145.27000	-		
Beggs	FUSION	K5DBW	147.50000			
Bennington		AB5CC-L	147.54000			
Bethany	FM	N5USR	224.96000	-	103.5 Hz	ORSI
	FM	N5USR	442.85000	+	103.5 Hz	ORSI
	FM	WA5CZN	444.05000	+	192.8 Hz	ORSI
Big Cabin, Big Cabin						
	FM	W5RAB	223.94000	-	88.5 Hz	
Big Cedar	FM	N5JMG	147.37500	+	123.0 Hz	ORSI
Bixby, Leonard Mountain						
	FM	W5RAB	224.18000	-	88.5 Hz	
Blackwell	FM	KD5MTT	145.31000	-		ORSI
Blackwell, Water Tower						
	FM	KD5MTT	444.95000	+		ORSI
Blanchard	DSTAR	KF5ZLE B	442.97500	+		
	DSTAR	KF5ZLE	442.97500	+		ORSI
	FM	W0DXA	442.00000	+	141.3 Hz	ORSI
	FM	W5LHG-R	444.62500	+		ORSI
Bridge Creek	FM	KS5B	145.47000	-	141.3 Hz	ORSI
	FM	W5PAA	146.85000	-	141.3 Hz	ORSI
	FM	W5PAA	444.85000	+	141.3 Hz	ORSI
Broken Arrow	DMR/BM	WX5OU	440.15000		CC1	
	FUSION	WX5OU	144.61000			
	FUSION	N5XET	433.00000			
	FUSION	W5WWA	445.90000			
Broken Arrow, Tiger Hill						
	FM	W5DRZ	146.91000	-	88.5 Hz	ORSI
	FM	W5DRZ	444.00000	+		ORSI
Broken Bow	FM	K7RM	53.03000	51.33000	100.0 Hz	ORSI
Broken Bow, Carter Mountain						
	FM	K5DYW	147.13500	+	67.0 Hz	ORSI
Buffalo	FM	W5HFZ	52.81000	51.11000	131.8 Hz	ORSI
	FM	W5HFZ	145.13000	-	131.8 Hz	ORSI
	FM	W5GPR	147.12000	+	203.5 Hz	ORSI
	FM	W5HFZ	442.07500	+	131.8 Hz	ORSI
Calumet	DMR/BM	AE5DN	444.32500	+	CC1	
	FM	WA5FLT	146.61000	-		ORSI
Cement	DMR/BM	W5PAA	444.40000	+	CC1	
	WX	WX5LAW	444.45000	+	123.0 Hz	ORSI
Chandler	FM	WB5BCR	147.36000	+	192.8 Hz	ORSI
Chickasha	FM	W5KS	145.23000	-	141.3 Hz	ORSI

Location	Mode	Call sign	Output	Input	Access	Coordinator
Choctaw	DMR/MARC	WW5ENZ	444.61500	445.11500	CC1	
	FM	K5CAR	147.09000	+	141.3 Hz	ORSI
Chouteau	FM	K5LEE	145.13000	-		ORSI
Claremore	WX	WX5RC	147.09000	+	88.5 Hz	ORSI
Claremore, Rogers State Univer						
	FM	WX5RC	444.35000	+		
Clarita	FM	KF5IUL	442.02500	+	114.8 Hz	ORSI
Clayton	FM	KM5VK	146.73000	-	114.8 Hz	ORSI
	FM	N5AVV	444.10000	+		
Cleora	DMR/BM	W5BIV	442.62500	+	CC1	
Clinton	FM	K5ODN	147.30000	+	127.3 Hz	ORSI
Clinton, At 200 Ft On Wright R						
	FM	KE5RRK	145.19000	-	88.5 Hz	ORSI
Coleman	FM	WG5B	147.16500	+	131.8 Hz	ORSI
College Hill		WW5LOV-R	147.13500			
Cyril	FM	KB5LLI	147.04500	+	123.0 Hz	ORSI
Cyrill	FM	KB5LLI	147.00000	+		ORSI
	WX	KB5LLI	442.27500	+	123.0 Hz	ORSI
Daisy	FM	W5CUQ	145.21000	-	114.8 Hz	ORSI
Davis	FM	KN6UG	146.86500	-	192.8 Hz	ORSI
Davis, Arbuckle Mountains						
	FM	WG5B	145.23000	-	179.9 Hz	
	FM	WG5B	147.15000	+	131.8 Hz	ORSI
	FM	WG5B	443.07500	+	107.2 Hz	ORSI
Del City		K5GLH-L	445.95000			
	FM	WN5J	443.10000	+	100.0 Hz	ORSI
Del City, Arvest Bank						
	FM	W5MWC	442.95000	+		
Duncan	FM	WD5IYF	146.73000	-	118.8 Hz	ORSI
	FM	WD5IYF	444.82500	+	118.8 Hz	ORSI
	WX	KB5LLI	147.30000	+	123.0 Hz	ORSI
	FUSION	AC5XJ	146.73000	-		
Durant	DMR/BM	AB5CC	444.12500	+	CC1	
	FM	K5CGE	147.25500	+	114.8 Hz	ORSI
	FM	K5KIE	147.39000	+	118.8 Hz	ORSI
	WX	K5BQG	146.98500	-	118.8 Hz	ORSI
Edmond	DMR/BM	W5RLW	442.32500	+	CC1	
	DMR/BM	KP4DJT	443.02500	+	CC7	
	DMR/BM	W5RLW	443.05000	+	CC1	ORSI
	FM	K5CPT	145.21000	-	131.8 Hz	ORSI
	FM	K5SBH	145.27000	-	100.0 Hz	ORSI
	FM	K5EOK	147.13500	+	79.7 Hz	ORSI
	FM	KD5SKS	442.20000	+	123.0 Hz	ORSI
	FM	K5CPT	442.22500	447.32500	131.8 Hz	ORSI
	FM	KC5GEP	443.15000	+	79.7 Hz	ORSI
	FM	K5EOK	443.42500	+	88.5 Hz	ORSI
	FM	KD5SKS	444.42500	+		ORSI
El Reno	FM	K5OL	442.25000	+	141.3 Hz	ORSI
	FM	W5ELR	444.25000	+		ORSI
Elk City	DMR/BM	N5CH	147.22500	+	CC1	
	DSTAR	K5ELK	146.68500	-		ORSI
	DSTAR	K5ELK C	146.68500	-		
	DSTAR	K5ELK	443.02500	+		ORSI
	DSTAR	K5ELK B	443.02500	+		
	DSTAR	K5ELK A	1290.00000	1270.00000		
	FM	WX5BSA	444.52500	+	88.5 Hz	ORSI
Elmore City	WX	KB5LLI	146.74500	-	141.3 Hz	ORSI
Enid	FM	W5HTK	145.29000	-	141.3 Hz	ORSI
	FM	W5HTK	147.15000	+	88.5 Hz	ORSI
	FM	N5LWT	147.37500	+		ORSI
	FM	WA5QYE	444.40000	+	141.3 Hz	ORSI
	FM	N5LWT	444.82500	+		ORSI

Location	Mode	Call sign	Output	Input	Access	Coordinator
Enterprise	FM	N5JMG	147.27000	+	141.3 Hz	ORSI
	FM	KA5HET	442.10000	+	123.0 Hz	ORSI
	FM	W5CUQ	444.62500	+	88.5 Hz	ORSI
Enterprise, Blue Mtn						
	FM	W5CUQ	147.10500	+	114.8 Hz	ORSI
Eufaula	DSTAR	KG5EEP B	443.05000	+		
Fairland	FM	W0GMM	147.28500	+	110.9 Hz	ORSI
Fairview	FM	WK5V	147.07500	+		ORSI
Forgan	FM	N5AKN	147.39000	+		ORSI
Fort Gibson	DMR/MARC	WA5VMS	442.12500	+	CC1	ORSI
	FM	WA5VMS	927.65000	902.65000		ORSI
Fort Smith, Cavanal Mountain						
	FM	W5ANR	146.64000	-	88.5 Hz	ORSI
	FM	W5ANR	444.50000	+	88.5 Hz	ORSI
Ft. Gibson	NXDN	WA5VMS	444.80000	+		ORSI
Garber		KE5ZHW-L	144.48500			
Goltry	FM	W5ALZ	443.20000	+	103.5 Hz	
Grandfield	FM	KB5LLI	147.25500	+	192.8 Hz	ORSI
	FM	WX5LAW	442.20000	+	123.0 Hz	ORSI
	FUSION	N5XTR	442.60000	+		
Granfield	FM	KD5BAK	147.07500	+	97.4 Hz	ORSI
Granite	DMR/MARC	K5XTL	442.07500	+	CC1	ORSI
	DSTAR	WX5ASA	147.34500	+		ORSI
	FM	KE5HRS	224.92000	-	151.4 Hz	ORSI
	FM	WX5ASA	432.17500			
	WX	KB5LLI	146.71500	-		ORSI
Granite, Walsh Mountain						
	DSTAR	WX5ASA	432.17500			
	FM	K5XTL	146.98500	-	156.7 Hz	ORSI
Guthrie	FM	W5KSU	147.10500	+		ORSI
	FM	W5IAS	443.92500	+	88.5 Hz	ORSI
	WX	W5IAS	443.25000	+	88.5 Hz	ORSI
Guymon	FM	N5DFQ	147.15000	+	88.5 Hz	ORSI
	FM	N5DFQ	444.97500	+	88.5 Hz	ORSI
Hartshorne	DMR/MARC	N5AVV	147.30000	+	CC1	ORSI
Headrick	FM	WX5LAW	443.30000	+	123.0 Hz	ORSI
Hugo	FM	KB5JTR	146.61000	-	114.8 Hz	ORSI
Ketchum	FM	W5RAB	444.87500	+	88.5 Hz	ORSI
Kingfisher	FM	W5GLD	146.64000	-	100.0 Hz	ORSI
	FM	W5GLD	444.97500	+	100.0 Hz	ORSI
Kingston	FM	N4SME	443.45000	+	127.3 Hz	ORSI
	FM	N5BCW	444.97500	+		
Lawton	DMR/BM	KB5SKY	145.25000	454.75000	CC4	
	DMR/BM	N4RDB	442.00000	+	CC1	
	DMR/BM	N7DOD	443.70000	+	CC1	
	DMR/MARC	WX5LAW	147.33000	+	CC4	
	DMR/MARC	N5PLV	443.60000	+	CC4	ORSI
	DSTAR	KG5ACV B	442.65000	+		
	FM	KC5AVY	145.17000	-		ORSI
	FM	K5VHF	145.43000	-		ORSI
	FM	N5PYD	146.80500	-		ORSI
	FM	W5KS	146.91000	-		ORSI
	FM	WX5LAW	147.18000	+	123.0 Hz	ORSI
	FM	W5KS	147.36000	+	173.8 Hz	ORSI
	FM	N4RDB-R	442.45000	+		ORSI
	FM	W5KS	443.85000	+		ORSI
	FM	KD5IAE	444.70000	+	141.3 Hz	ORSI
	FM	K5VHF	444.90000	+	118.8 Hz	ORSI
	WX	AB5J	147.39000	+	173.8 Hz	ORSI
	WX	WX5LAW	442.52500	+	123.0 Hz	ORSI
Liberty, Jerimah Mountain						
	ATV	W5JWT	145.11000	-	114.8 Hz	ORSI

Location	Mode	Call sign	Output	Input	Access	Coordinator
Lindsay	FM	N5RAK	444.87500	+	131.8 Hz	ORSI
Lone Grove	FM	W5BLW	146.79000	-		ORSI
Mangum, Navajo Mt.						
	FM	KF5CRF	442.10000	+	123.0 Hz	ORSI
Mannford	FM	W5IAS	147.04500	+	88.5 Hz	ORSI
	FM	W5IAS	442.80000	+	88.5 Hz	
Marietta	FM	N5KEY	146.83500	-	173.8 Hz	ORSI
Marlow	FM	K5UM	146.95500	-		ORSI
McAlester	FM	W5CUQ	145.37000	-	71.9 Hz	ORSI
	FM	W5CUQ	444.62500	+	88.5 Hz	ORSI
Medford, Salt Plains Lake						
	FM	KB0HH	147.30000	+	103.5 Hz	ORSI
Medicine Park	FM	WX5LAW	444.07500	+	123.0 Hz	ORSI
	WX	AF5Q	224.50000	-	123.0 Hz	ORSI
	WX	AF5Q	442.17500	+	123.0 Hz	ORSI
Miami	FM	KG5FJI	442.65000	+		ORSI
Midwest City	FM	W5MWC	444.00000	+	151.4 Hz	ORSI
Mooreland	DSTAR	W5OKT B	444.27500	+		
	FM	K5GUD	145.39000	-	88.5 Hz	ORSI
	FM	K5GUD	444.27500	+		ORSI
	WX	K5GUD	444.67500	+	103.5 Hz	ORSI
Mounds	FM	WB5NJU	147.39000	+	88.5 Hz	ORSI
	FM	W5IAS	444.60000	+	88.5 Hz	ORSI
Mt. Sycamore	WX	N5CST	145.41000	-	88.5 Hz	ORSI
Muskogee	FM	KK5I	146.74500	-	88.5 Hz	ORSI
	FM	KK5I	146.85000	-		
	FM	WA5VMS	147.33000	+	88.5 Hz	ORSI
	FM	KK5I	224.34000	-	88.5 Hz	ORSI
	WX	W5IAS	443.10000	+	88.5 Hz	ORSI
	FUSION	WA5VMS	443.57500	+		
	FUSION	KI5NEX	446.00000			
Nashoba, Cripple Creek Mountai						
	FM	KM5VK	145.29000	-	162.2 Hz	ORSI
	FM	KM5VK	145.33000	-	162.2 Hz	ORSI
	FM	KM5VK	224.56000	-	114.8 Hz	ORSI
	FM	KM5VK	442.90000	+	114.8 Hz	ORSI
Newalla	FM	K5UV	145.15000	-	114.8 Hz	ORSI
Newcastle	FM	KX5MOT	444.67500	+	192.8 Hz	ORSI
	FUSION	K0BFE	432.57500			
NOAA Altus	WX	WWG97	162.42500			
NOAA Antlers	WX	KJY77	162.40000			
NOAA Ardmore	WX	KXI57	162.52500			
NOAA Atoka	WX	KWN49	162.50000			
NOAA Bartlesville	WX	WNG644	162.42500			
NOAA Broken Bow						
	WX	WXJ65	162.45000			
NOAA Chickasha	WX	KJY94	162.45000			
NOAA Clinton	WX	WXK87	162.52500			
NOAA Enid	WX	WXL48	162.47500			
NOAA Grove	WX	WWH38	162.50000			
NOAA Guymon	WX	KJY96	162.50000			
NOAA Lawton	WX	WXK86	162.55000			
NOAA McAlester	WX	WXL49	162.47500			
NOAA Oklahoma City						
	WX	WXK85	162.40000			
NOAA Oktaha	WX	WNG632	162.52500			
NOAA Ponca City	WX	WWF42	162.45000			
NOAA Stillwater	WX	WNG654	162.50000			
NOAA Tulsa	WX	KIH27	162.55000			
NOAA Wewoka	WX	KJY95	162.55000			
NOAA Woodward	WX	WWG46	162.50000			
Norman	DMR/BM	N5MS	442.75000	+	CC1	

Location	Mode	Call sign	Output	Input	Access	Coordinator
Norman	DMR/MARC	N5MS	443.82500	+	CC1	
	DSTAR	W5TC B	444.75000	+		
	FM	K9KK	224.44000	-		ORSI
	FM	WA5LKS	442.12500	+	107.2 Hz	ORSI
	FM	N5KUK	444.35000	+	141.3 Hz	ORSI
Norman, County Tower						
	FM	W5NOR	147.06000	+	141.3 Hz	ORSI
	FM	W5NOR	443.70000	+	141.3 Hz	ORSI
Norman, National Weather Cente						
	DSTAR	W5TC	444.75000	+		ORSI
Norman, OU Physical Sciences C						
	FM	W5OU	146.88000	-		ORSI
Nowata	FM	N5ZZX	145.37000	-		ORSI
Octavia	DMR/MARC	N5LLH	443.07500	+	CC1	
Oklahoma City	DMR/BM	N5KNU	442.50000	+	CC1	ORSI
	DMR/BM	KB5KWV	443.17500	+	CC1	
	DMR/BM	AA5KD	444.57500	+	CC1	
	DMR/MARC	KB5KWV	443.17500	+	CC1	
	DMR/MARC	W5GDL	443.22500	+	CC1	ORSI
	DSTAR	WD5AII B	444.21250	+		
	FM	WN5J	145.33000	-		ORSI
	FM	KK5FM	145.37000	-	141.3 Hz	ORSI
	FM	KD5AHH	145.49000	-	131.8 Hz	ORSI
	FM	W5PAA	146.76000	-	141.3 Hz	ORSI
	FM	W5RLW	146.79000	-	100.0 Hz	
	FM	W5MEL	146.82000	-	151.4 Hz	ORSI
	FM	W5PAA	146.98500	-	141.3 Hz	ORSI
	FM	W5MEL	147.21000	+	141.3 Hz	ORSI
	FM	KE5DXI	147.85000		88.5 Hz	
	FM	W5PAA	224.10000	-		ORSI
	FM	NZ5W	224.30000	-	123.0 Hz	ORSI
	FM	WN5J	224.88000	-		ORSI
	FM	W5PAA	442.70000	+	141.3 Hz	ORSI
	FM	KK5FM	442.77500	+	141.3 Hz	ORSI
	FM	WX5OKC	444.25000	+	141.3 Hz	ORSI
	FM	W5MEL	444.30000	+	141.3 Hz	ORSI
	FM	W5PAA	927.91250	902.91250	123.0 Hz	
	FM	WN5J	1283.10000	1263.10000		ORSI
	WX	WX5OKC	145.41000	-	141.3 Hz	ORSI
	WX	WX5OKC	444.22500	+	141.3 Hz	ORSI
	FUSION	W5DEL	443.30000	+		
Oklahoma City NW						
	DMR/BM	AE5DN	442.62500	+	CC1	
Oklahoma City, KFOR Tower						
	FM	WD5AII	147.03000	+	167.9 Hz	ORSI
	FM	W5MWC	444.20000	+	167.9 Hz	ORSI
Oklahoma City, KFOR-TV Tower						
	FM	W5PAA	146.67000	-	151.4 Hz	ORSI
	FM	W5PAA	444.10000	+	141.3 Hz	ORSI
Oklahoma City, Sandbridge Buil						
	FM	W5GDL	444.21250	+	141.3 Hz	ORSI
Oklahoma City, Sandridge Build						
	FM	W5GDL	224.92000	-	141.3 Hz	ORSI
Owasso	FUSION	AF5XC	449.90000			
Owasso, Keetonville						
	FM	WD5ETD	224.48000	-	88.5 Hz	
Pawhuska	FM	KC5KLM	147.27000	+	88.5 Hz	ORSI
	FM	W5RAB	444.97500	+	167.9 Hz	ORSI
Pecola	FM	KB5SWA	444.02500	+		ORSI
Perry	FM	KL7MA	442.92500	+	141.3 Hz	ORSI
	WX	KF5RDI	146.86500	-	141.3 Hz	ORSI

Location	Mode	Call sign	Output	Input	Access	Coordinator
Pittsburgh, Tiger Mtn						
	FM	AD5MC	146.95500	-	151.4 Hz	ORSI
Ponca City	DMR/BM	K5BOX	444.75000	+	CC1	
	FM	W5HZZ	146.97000	-	88.5 Hz	ORSI
	FM	W5BE	442.67500	+	88.5 Hz	ORSI
	FM	AF5VB	443.50000	+	88.5 Hz	ORSI
	FM	W5RAB	444.60000	+	167.9 Hz	ORSI
	FM	W5HZZ	444.70000	+		ORSI
Ponca City, McCord Water Tower						
	FM	N5PC	146.73000	-	88.5 Hz	
Pond Creek	FM	KW5FAA	442.30000	+	141.3 Hz	ORSI
Porum	DMR/MARC	W4NFD	443.12500	+	CC1	
	FM	W4NFD	53.05000	52.05000	114.8 Hz	
	FM	W4NFD	444.52500	+	107.2 Hz	
Poteau	WX	K6CKS	444.55000	+	136.5 Hz	ORSI
Prague	FUSION	N0LOZ	447.00000	-	100.0 Hz	
Preston	FM	W5KO	145.33000	-	88.5 Hz	ORSI
	FM	WX5OKM	147.22500	+	88.5 Hz	ORSI
	FM	KD5FMU	444.17500	+	88.5 Hz	ORSI
Pryor	FM	WX5MC	444.67500	+	88.5 Hz	ORSI
	WX	WX5MC	147.06000	+	88.5 Hz	ORSI
Rose	FM	KC5DBH	146.98500	-	110.9 Hz	
Sapulpa	FUSION	KI5EGH/R	145.43000	-		
Seiling	FM	W5OKT	444.92500	+	103.5 Hz	ORSI
Seminole	FM	WJ5F	147.01500	+		ORSI
	FM	WJ5F	147.19500	+	141.3 Hz	ORSI
Seward	FM	KA5LSU	145.17000	-	100.0 Hz	ORSI
	FM	KA5LSU	442.07500	+		ORSI
	FM	KK5FM	444.77500	+	141.3 Hz	ORSI
Sharon	DSTAR	K5GUD	147.31500	+		ORSI
Shawnee	FM	W5SXA	145.39000	-	131.8 Hz	ORSI
Shawnee, Shawnee Twin Lakes						
	FM	KG5BGO	145.19000	-	131.8 Hz	
Skiatook, 3-10 Y Tower						
	FM	WA5LVT	444.72500	+		
Stillwater	DMR/BM	AE5DN	444.47500	+	CC1	
	FM	K5SRC	145.35000	-	107.2 Hz	ORSI
	FM	K5FVL	147.25500	+	107.2 Hz	ORSI
	FM	K5FVL	442.60000	+	103.5 Hz	ORSI
	FM	K5FVL	444.47500	+	100.0 Hz	ORSI
	WX	K5FVL	444.52500	+	88.5 Hz	ORSI
	WX	K5FVL	444.90000	+	141.3 Hz	ORSI
Stuart	FM	W5CUQ	146.89500	-	114.8 Hz	ORSI
	FM	W5CUQ	443.72500	+	127.3 Hz	
Tahlequah	FM	N5ROX	442.70000	+		
	WX	N5ROX	147.24000	+		ORSI
	WX	N5ROX	442.22500	+	88.5 Hz	ORSI
Tecumseh	DMR/BM	K5THS	443.37500	+	CC1	
	FM	KD5WAV	146.62500	-	131.8 Hz	ORSI
The Village	FM	KB5QND	443.40000	+	141.3 Hz	ORSI
Tishomingo	FM	W5JTB	145.31000	-	141.3 Hz	
Tulsa	DMR/BM	WD5ETD	441.97500	+	CC1	
	DSTAR	KN5V B	442.60000	+		
	DSTAR	N5XP B	443.02500	+		
	FM	W5IAS	145.11000	-	88.5 Hz	ORSI
	FM	WA5LVT	146.80500	-	88.5 Hz	ORSI
	FM	K5JME	147.00000	+	100.0 Hz	ORSI
	FM	AE5RH	224.86000	222.86000	88.5 Hz	
	FM	K5LAD	444.30000	+	100.0 Hz	ORSI
	WX	WA5LVT	146.88000	-	88.5 Hz	ORSI
	WX	W5IAS	443.85000	+	88.5 Hz	ORSI
	FUSION	W5DRZ	443.60000	+		

Location	Mode	Call sign	Output	Input	Access	Coordinator
Tulsa	FUSION	W5GGW	448.00000	-		
Tulsa South	DMR/BM	W5IAS	441.97500	+	CC1	
Tulsa, Asbury Methodist Church						
	DSTAR	KN5V	442.60000	+		
Tulsa, Channel 8 TV Studios						
	FM	W5IAS	443.75000	+	88.5 Hz	
Tulsa, CityPlex Towers						
	FM	WD5ETD	927.70000	902.70000		ORSI
Tulsa, Lookout Mountain						
	FM	W5IAS	443.00000	+		ORSI
Tulsa, Reservoir Hill						
	FM	WT5EOC	146.83500	-	103.5 Hz	ORSI
Tulsa, Sun Building						
	FM	WA5LVT	146.94000	-	88.5 Hz	ORSI
	FM	WA5LVT	444.95000	+	88.5 Hz	
Tuttle	DMR/BM	N5PTV	444.10000	+	CC1	
	FM	WA7WNM	224.68000	-		ORSI
	FM	K8TOR	443.90000	+		ORSI
Velma	FM	KC5JCO	444.95000	+		ORSI
Vian	DMR/BM	W5ACR	442.00000	+	CC1	
Vici	FM	N5WO	444.95000	+	88.5 Hz	ORSI
Vinita	DSTAR	NO5RA C	147.16500	+		
	DSTAR	NO5RA	147.16500	+		ORSI
	DSTAR	NO5RA B	443.07500	+		
	FM	KC5VVT	444.37500	+	88.5 Hz	ORSI
	FUSION	N5BYS	443.07500	+	88.5 Hz	ORSI
Walsh Mountain At Granite						
	DSTAR	WX5ASA C	147.34500	+		
	DSTAR	WX5ASA B	442.15000	+		
Watonga	FM	K5GSM	442.37500	+		ORSI
Waurika	FM	W5KS	145.29000	-	123.0 Hz	ORSI
Waynoka	FM	W5ALZ	443.45000	+	103.5 Hz	ORSI
Weatherford	FM	KB5TOO	147.07500	+		
Wewoka, Tate Mountain						
	FM	WJ5F	147.01500	+	141.3 Hz	ORSI
Wilburton	FM	KL7JW	146.62500	-	88.5 Hz	ORSI
Winchester	FM	N5LW	147.15000	+	88.5 Hz	ORSI
Woodward	DSTAR	WW5EM C	147.31500	+		
	DSTAR	WW5EM B	444.47500	+		
	FM	W5GPR	146.73000	-	203.5 Hz	ORSI
	FM	K5GSM	147.00000	+	103.5 Hz	ORSI
	FM	W5ALZ	442.05000	+	103.5 Hz	ORSI
	WX	W5OKT	145.39000	-	103.5 Hz	ORSI
	WX	K5GUD-R	444.87500	+		ORSI
Woodward, Airport						
	FM	W5GPR	146.73000	-	203.5 Hz	ORSI
Yukon	FUSION	N6YSC	433.02500			

"The Northwest's Largest Ham Convention"

SEA🔥PAC '23

SEA🔥PAC '24

June 2 - June 4, 2023

May 31 - June 2, 2024

ARRL Northwestern Division Convention

Seaside Convention Center, Seaside Oregon

Commercial Exhibits ● Giant Flea Market ● Banquet/Entertainment

Workshops ● Seminars ● Prizes ● VE Testing ● Special Event Station

Near the Beautiful Pacific Northwest Ocean Beach

General Info—info@seapac.org

Registration Info—registration@seapac.org

SEA-PAC
Post Office Box 7263
Aloha OR 97007-0963

Exhibitor Info—exhibitors@seapac.org

Flea Market Info—fleamarket@seapac.org

SEA-PAC on the Web: www.seapac.org

Location	Mode	Call sign	Output	Input	Access	Coordinator
OREGON						
Agness	FM	WA7JAW	147.04000	+	88.5 Hz	ORRC
Albany		K7IHS-R	147.49000			
	FM	KD6VLR	444.97500	+	100.0 Hz	ORRC
Aloha	FM	NM7B	443.35000	+	156.7 Hz	
Aloha, Cooper Mountain						
	FM	N7QQU	147.36000	+	107.2 Hz	ORRC
	FM	KA7OSM	442.52500	+	107.2 Hz	
Aloha, Oregon	FM	K7RPT	442.35000	+	100.0 Hz	
Alsea	FM	W6PRN	444.35000	+	173.8 Hz	
Amity	FM	K7RPT	444.12500	+	100.0 Hz	
Ashland	FM	W9PCI	146.62000	-	100.0 Hz	ORRC
	FM	W7PRA	146.70000	-	136.5 Hz	
	FM	WX7MFR	440.70000	+	162.2 Hz	ORRC
	FM	AB7BS	442.30000	+		ORRC
Ashland, Mount Ashland						
	FM	WX7MFR	147.26000	+	123.0 Hz	ORRC
Ashland, Soda Mountain						
	FM	WA6RHK	147.16000	+	136.5 Hz	ORRC
Astoria	FM	K7RPT	146.72000	-	114.8 Hz	
	FM	N7HQR	440.82500	+	118.8 Hz	ORRC
	FM	W7BU	444.85000	+	118.8 Hz	
Astoria, Nicolai Mountain						
	FM	W7BU	146.76000	-	118.8 Hz	ORRC
	FM	WA6TTR	444.50000	+	118.8 Hz	ORRC
Astoria, Wickiup Mountain						
	FM	KF7TCG	146.66000	-	118.8 Hz	
Astoria, Wickiup Mtn						
	FM	W7BU	442.50000	+	118.8 Hz	ORRC
Athena	DSTAR	K7LW	444.90000	+		
Athena, Weston Mountain						
	FM	W7NEO	147.04000	+		
Athena, Weston Mtn						
	FM	W7NEO	441.70000	+	131.8 Hz	
Baker City, Beaver Mountain						
	FM	W7NYW	145.27000	-	110.9 Hz	
Banks, Chrysler Rd						
	FM	KC7UQB	440.87500	+	103.5 Hz	ORRC
Barnes Heights	FM	K7QDX-R	927.12500	902.12500		ORRC
Beaver Homes	FM	K7RPT-R	147.38000	+		ORRC
Beavercreek, Highland Butte						
	FM	AH6LE	146.92000	-	107.2 Hz	
Beaverton	DMR/BM	KG7RFM	441.47500	+	CC2	
	FM	W7BVT	444.75000	+	123.0 Hz	ORRC
	FUSION	N7OZO	431.25000			
Beaverton, St Vincent Hosp						
	FM	W7PSV	444.85000	+	123.0 Hz	ORRC
Bend	DMR/BM	KC7DMF	147.26000	+	CC1	
	FM	W7DCO	442.55000	+	162.2 Hz	
	FM	KB7LNR	443.65000	+	162.2 Hz	ORRC
	FUSION	KJ7SGG	432.15000			
	FUSION	KB7FD	443.75000	+		
Bend, Long Butte	FM	W7JVO	146.94000	-	162.2 Hz	
Bend, Mt Bachelor						
	FM	W7DCO	145.45000	-	103.5 Hz	ORRC
Biggs Junction	DMR/MARC	N7LF	443.32500	+	CC1	
Blue River	FM	W7PRA	147.34000	+		
	FM	AB7BS	444.80000	+		
Blue River, Indian Ridge						
	FM	W7EUG	145.37000	-	100.0 Hz	ORRC

Location	Mode	Call sign	Output	Input	Access	Coordinator
Blue River, Mount Hagan						
	FM	W7EXH	145.11000	-	100.0 Hz	ORRC
	FM	K7SLA	443.10000	+	100.0 Hz	ORRC
Boardman	DMR/MARC	N7LF	443.37500	+	CC1	
	FUSION	K7ELJ	145.19000	-		
	FUSION	K7ELJ	147.32000	+		
Boardman, Coalfire Plant						
	FM	AI7HO	147.16000	+		
Boring, Fire Station						
	FM	KD7WGZ	441.77500	+	107.2 Hz	
Brookings	DMR/MARC	K6JR	443.80000	+	CC1	
Brookings, Bosley Butte						
	FM	N7UBQ	147.25000	+	88.5 Hz	ORRC
Brookings, Fire Station						
	FM	W7BKG	146.84000	-	88.5 Hz	ORRC
Brookings, Harbor	FM	KA7GNK	444.97500	+	100.0 Hz	ORRC
Brookings, Harbor Hill						
	FM	W7BKG	146.96000	-	88.5 Hz	ORRC
Brownsville	FM	W7WZA	147.30000	+	77.0 Hz	ORRC
Brownsville, Scott Mountain						
	FM	W7NK	147.26000	+		ORRC
Brownsville, Washburn Heights						
	FM	K7VFO	224.00000	-	100.0 Hz	ORRC
	FM	KB7KUB	442.60000	+		ORRC
Burns	FM	W7PRA	145.11000	-	136.5 Hz	
Burns, Radar Hill	FM	KF7HPT	146.76000	-	103.5 Hz	
Burns, Sharps Ridge						
	FM	W7JVO	147.30000	+	162.2 Hz	ORRC
Buxton-GREEN MTN						
	DMR/MARC	KB7APU	444.02500	+	CC9	
Camas Valley	FM	W7PRA	146.92000	-	136.5 Hz	ORRC
Canby	FM	K7CFD	224.76000	-	131.8 Hz	ORRC
	FM	K7CFD	444.45000	+	131.8 Hz	
Cannon Beach, Arch Cape						
	FM	W7BU	146.74000	-	118.8 Hz	ORRC
Canyon City, Eagle Peak						
	FM	N7LZM	146.64000	-		
Cape Meares	FM	KA7AHV	147.16000	+	118.8 Hz	ORRC
	FM	N7IS	442.97500	+	100.0 Hz	ORRC
Cascade Locks	DMR/MARC	N7LF	443.32500	+	CC1	
Cascade Locks, Mt Defiance						
	FM	KF7LN	927.16250	902.16250	151.4 Hz	ORRC
Cave Junction, $8 Mountain						
	FM	WB6YQP	145.49000	-	136.5 Hz	
Cedar Mill	FM	N7PRM	444.80000	+	107.2 Hz	
Central Point	FM	WA6RHK	440.82500	+	136.5 Hz	ORRC
	FM	WB7QAZ-R	442.90000	+		ORRC
	FM	W9PCI	444.10000	+	100.0 Hz	ORRC
	FUSION	KL7VK	147.38000	+		
Central Point, Johns Peak						
	FM	KB7SKB	147.10000	+	136.5 Hz	
Chemult	FM	WA7TYD	444.92500	+	100.0 Hz	ORRC
Chemult, Walker Mountain						
	FM	WA7TYD	145.47000	-	162.2 Hz	ORRC
Chiloquin, Train Mtn						
	FM	K7LNK	444.95000	+	136.5 Hz	ORRC
Clackamas	FM	KJ7IY	146.80000	-	107.2 Hz	ORRC
	FM	KB7WUK	1291.00000	1271.00000	107.2 Hz	ORRC
Clackamas, Mount Scott						
	FM	KR7IS	29.68000	-	162.2 Hz	ORRC
Clackamas, Mt Scott						
	FM	W7LT	147.18000	+		

Location	Mode	Call sign	Output	Input	Access	Coordinator
Clackamas, Mt Scott						
	FM	WB7QIW	147.28000	+	167.9 Hz	ORRC
	FM	KC7MZM	440.30000	+	167.9 Hz	
	FM	KJ7IY	443.15000	+	107.2 Hz	
	FM	WB7QIW	443.47500	+	167.9 Hz	ORRC
Coburg	FM	K7QT-R	441.12500	+		ORRC
Coburg, Buck Mountain						
	FM	W7EXH	224.70000	-	100.0 Hz	ORRC
Colton	FM	WB7DZG	442.92500	+	107.2 Hz	ORRC
Colton, Goat Mountain						
	FM	W7OTV	146.96000	-	127.3 Hz	ORRC
	FM	WB6EGS	441.40000	+	88.5 Hz	
	FM	N7PIR	443.70000	+	103.5 Hz	ORRC
Colton- GOAT MTN						
	DMR/MARC	KB7APU	442.75000	+	CC1	
Coos Bay	FM	W7OC	147.10000	+	110.9 Hz	ORRC
	FM	W7OC	441.72500	+	131.8 Hz	ORRC
	FUSION	K7REA	145.67000			
Coos Bay, Blossom Hill						
	FM	W7OC	147.28000	+	146.2 Hz	ORRC
	FM	WA7JAW	440.80000	+	103.5 Hz	ORRC
Coos Bay, Noah Butte						
	FM	K7TVL	146.88000	-	136.5 Hz	ORRC
Coquille	FUSION	KC7LHU	445.45000			
Coquille, Beaver Hill						
	FM	K7CCH	146.61000	-	110.9 Hz	ORRC
Corbett	DMR/MARC	N7LF	443.10000	+	CC1	
	FM	K7NE	145.41000	-	100.0 Hz	
	FM	N7LF	443.07500	+		
	FM	N7LF	443.32500	+		
Corbett- Testing	DMR/MARC	N7LF	444.00000	+	CC1	
Corvallis	DMR/BM	K7WVD	444.27500	+	CC1	
	DSTAR	KF7LDG B	434.91000	+		
	FUSION	N7TWP	145.50000			
Corvallis, Elmers	FM	W7OSU	443.05000	+	100.0 Hz	
Corvallis, Good Sam Hospital						
	FM	N8GFO	442.30000	+	162.2 Hz	ORRC
Corvallis, Mary's Peak						
	FM	K7LNK	440.42500	+		ORRC
Corvallis, Marys Peak						
	FM	WA7TUV	146.82000	-	100.0 Hz	
Corvallis, Vineyard Mountain						
	FM	W7OSU	147.16000	+	100.0 Hz	ORRC
Cottage Grove	FM	AB7BS	145.39000	-	146.2 Hz	ORRC
	FM	WB7LCS	440.87500	+		
	FM	K7SLA	443.02500	+	156.7 Hz	ORRC
Cottage Grove, Bear Mtn						
	FM	K7LNK	444.55000	+	100.0 Hz	
Cottage Grove, Fairview Peak						
	FM	W7SLA	145.23000	-	110.9 Hz	ORRC
Cottage Grove, Harness Mountai						
	FM	W7ZQE	146.66000	-	100.0 Hz	
Creswell	FM	N7NPA	440.10000	+	110.9 Hz	ORRC
Culver	DMR/BM	KC7DMF	147.24000	+	CC1	
	DMR/BM	KC7DMF	444.42500	+	CC1	
Deer Island	FM	N7EI	224.38000	-	114.8 Hz	ORRC
Deer Island, Meissner Lookout						
	FM	N7EI	146.88000	-	114.8 Hz	ORRC
Deschutes	FM	KB7LNR-R	147.36000	+		ORRC
Diamond Lake, Cinnamon Butte						
	FM	K7RBG	147.22000	+	67.0 Hz	
Dufur, Tygh Ridge	FM	WC7EC	147.26000	+	82.5 Hz	ORRC

Location	Mode	Call sign	Output	Input	Access	Coordinator
Elgin, Spout Springs Ski Resor						
	FM	WF7S	146.80000	-	123.0 Hz	ORRC
Estacada	FM	KD7DEG	440.85000	+	107.2 Hz	ORRC
Eugene		AI7BQ-R	432.22500			
	DMR/BM	W7OEC	442.42500	+	CC1	
	DMR/BM	KC7RJK	444.42500	+	CC1	
	P25	W7EXH	443.27500	+	100.0 Hz	ORRC
	FUSION	K7REA	442.70000	+		
Eugene, Blanton Heights						
	FM	W7ARD	145.45000	-	123.0 Hz	ORRC
	FM	K7TBL	146.88000	-	100.0 Hz	ORRC
	FM	W7NK	147.26000	+	100.0 Hz	ORRC
	FM	W7NK	147.36000	+	123.0 Hz	ORRC
	FM	W7DTV	442.80000	+	77.0 Hz	
	FM	W7NK	442.90000	+	110.9 Hz	ORRC
Eugene, Buck Mountain						
	FM	W7NK	145.17000	-	100.0 Hz	ORRC
Eugene, Coburg Ridge						
	FM	W7CQZ	147.08000	+	100.0 Hz	ORRC
	FM	K7UND	441.32500	+	100.0 Hz	
	FM	K7THO	442.12500	+		ORRC
Falls City, Laurel Mountain						
	FM	W7SRA	147.02000	+	186.2 Hz	ORRC
Florence	FUSION	KA8ZGM	442.57500	+		
Florence, Glenada Hill						
	FM	W7FLO	441.10000	+		ORRC
Florence, Herman Peak						
	FM	W7FLO	442.57500	+		ORRC
Forest Grove	DMR/MARC	K7RPT	440.81250	+	CC1	
	FM	K7RPT	442.32500	+	100.0 Hz	ORRC
Fossil	FM	KG7CXO	146.68000	-	162.2 Hz	
Fossil, Snowboard Ridge						
	FM	KG7CXO	146.68000	-	162.2 Hz	ORRC
Four Corners	FM	KL7VK	147.38000	+	136.8 Hz	ORRC
Frenchglen	FM	AB7BS	145.13000	-	136.5 Hz	
Gales Creek	FM	K7RPT-L	147.32000	+		ORRC
	FM	KJ7IY	927.11250	902.11250	107.2 Hz	ORRC
Gardenhome	FUSION	KF7MLE	431.07500			
Gates	FM	WA7ABU	145.19000	-	100.0 Hz	ORRC
Gearhart	FM	WA7VE-R	145.49000	-	118.8 Hz	ORRC
	FM	W7BU	146.80000	-	118.8 Hz	
Glendale	FM	AB7BS	146.86000	-	123.0 Hz	ORRC
Glide	FM	WB7RKR	444.87500	+	127.3 Hz	
Glide, Lane Mountain						
	FM	WA7BWT	147.24000	+	136.5 Hz	ORRC
Glide, Scott Mountain						
	FM	WA7BWT	145.43000	-	88.5 Hz	
	FM	WB7RKR	224.10000	-	114.8 Hz	ORRC
	FM	WB7RKR	444.62500	+	91.5 Hz	ORRC
Gold Beach, Grizzly Mountain						
	FM	K7SEG	146.74000	-	88.5 Hz	ORRC
Government Camp						
		AC7QE-R	147.12000			
	DMR/MARC	K7PN	444.15000	+	CC1	
	FM	KB7APU	224.78000	-	136.5 Hz	ORRC
	FM	KB7APU	444.10000	+		ORRC
Government Camp, Timberline Lo						
	FM	WB7DZG	52.97000	51.27000	107.2 Hz	ORRC
Government Camp--open Use						
	DMR/MARC	KB7APU	224.78000	-	CC1	
Government Camp-MT HOOD						
	DMR/MARC	KB7APU	442.98750	+	CC1	

Location	Mode	Call sign	Output	Input	Access	Coordinator
Grants Pass	DSTAR	KE7LKX	440.46250	+		
	DSTAR	KE7LKX B	440.46250	+		
	FM	WA6OTP	147.22000	+		ORRC
	FM	AB7BS	440.55000	+	173.8 Hz	ORRC
	FM	AB7BS	444.55000	+	173.8 Hz	ORRC
	FM	W6PRN	444.67500	+	100.0 Hz	
	FUSION	KJ7VZY	144.42000			
Grants Pass, Bluey Mountain						
	FM	WB6QYP	147.14000	+	162.2 Hz	
Grants Pass, Gilbert Peak						
	FM	K7LIX	146.64000	-		
	FM	K7LIX	147.30000	+	136.5 Hz	
Gresham	DMR/BM	N8VHM	443.80000	-	CC1	
	DMR/MARC	N7LF	443.07500	+	CC1	
	FM	N7DOD	446.27500	-	167.9 Hz	
Gresham, Walters Hill						
	FM	KE7AWR	441.62500	+	146.2 Hz	ORRC
Hammond	DMR/MARC	NA7Q	444.77500	+	CC1	
Hampton	FM	K7SQ	223.98000	-	103.5 Hz	
Hampton, Glass Butte						
	FM	W7JVO	147.20000	+	162.2 Hz	ORRC
Happy Valley	FUSION	N7FJC	431.87500			
Harrisburg	FM	W7PRA	444.82500	+		ORRC
Hebo, Mount Hebo						
	FM	N7QFT	147.26000	+	162.2 Hz	ORRC
Hebo, Mt Hebo	DSTAR	W7GC	147.39000	+		
	FM	W7LI	147.22000	+	100.0 Hz	ORRC
	FM	W7GC	440.90000	+	118.8 Hz	ORRC
	FM	W7LI	441.25000	+	118.8 Hz	
	FM	WB7QIW	443.07500	+	167.9 Hz	ORRC
Heceta Beach	FM	W7FLO-L	146.80000	-		ORRC
Heppner , Black Mountain						
	FM	KC7SOY	145.23000	-	67.0 Hz	
Heppner, Black Mountain						
	FM	KC7SOY	146.78000	-	67.0 Hz	
Hermiston	DSTAR	W7URG C	147.39000	+		
	DSTAR	W7URG B	441.95000	+		
	FM	WB7ILL	443.80000	+	123.0 Hz	
Hillsboro	DSTAR	N7QQU B	440.55000	+		
	DSTAR	N7QQU D	1294.40000			
	FM	KE7AWR	441.22500	+	100.0 Hz	ORRC
Hillsboro, Intel's Jones Farm						
	FM	K7CPU	444.97500	+	107.2 Hz	ORRC
Hillsboro, Synopsys						
	DSTAR	N7QQU	440.55000	+		ORRC
Hillsdale	FM	N7PIR-R	440.45000	+		ORRC
Hood River	DMR/MARC	N7LF	443.07500	+	CC1	
Hood River, Columbia River Gor						
	FM/YSF	AF7YV	440.60000	+	100.0 Hz	
Hood River, Middle Mountain						
	FM	KA7HRC	444.90000	+	100.0 Hz	
Hood River, Mount Defiance						
	FM	WA7ROB	145.15000	-	94.8 Hz	ORRC
	FM	KF7LN	147.10000	+	100.0 Hz	ORRC
Horton, Prairie Mountain						
	FM	W7NK	443.50000	+	103.5 Hz	ORRC
Horton, Prairie Mtn						
	FM	W7EUG	146.68000	-	100.0 Hz	
Huntington, Lime Hill						
	FM	K7OJI	147.12000	+	100.0 Hz	
	FM	K7OJI	444.15000	+	100.0 Hz	

Location	Mode	Call sign	Output	Input	Access	Coordinator
Indian Valley (historical)						
	FM	KF7GOR-R	444.92500	+		
Jackson	FM	W7UIV	440.95000	+		
Jacksonville	FM	W9PCI	444.20000	+	100.0 Hz	ORRC
	FM	W9PCI	444.30000	+	100.0 Hz	ORRC
John Day, Airport	FM	W7JVO	145.24000	-	162.2 Hz	
John Day, Fall Mountain						
	FM	N7LZM	147.22000	+	123.0 Hz	
Johnson Crossing	FM	AA7BG-L	146.50000	+		
Jordan Valley	FM	KC7GLR	444.80000	+		ORRC
Joseph	DMR/BM	KB7DZR	444.78750	+	CC1	
	FM	KB7DZR-R	147.00000	+		ORRC
Junction City	FM	W7PRA	145.13000	-		ORRC
	FM	AB7BS	443.57500	+		ORRC
	FM	W7LDN	445.47500	-	123.0 Hz	
	FUSION	W7CUL	146.55000			
Keizer	FM	KD7PFG	53.23000	51.53000	100.0 Hz	ORRC
	FM	KD7PFG	440.80000	+	156.7 Hz	ORRC
	FUSION	N7UVA	145.65000			
Keno	FM	KD7TNG	442.52500	+	118.8 Hz	ORRC
	FM	K6PRN	443.20000	+	100.0 Hz	
Keno, Chase Mountain						
	FM	WA6RHK	440.67500	+	173.8 Hz	ORRC
Keno, Hamaker Mountain						
	FM	N6MRX	147.18000	+	100.0 Hz	
Kibler		K7KLA-L	147.47000			
Klamath Falls	FM	W7PRA	147.20000	+	136.5 Hz	ORRC
Klamath Falls, Hamaker Mountai						
	FM	W7VW	146.85000	-	118.8 Hz	
Klamath Falls, Hogback Mountai						
	FM	W7VW	146.61000	-	118.8 Hz	
Klamath Falls, Hogsback Mtn						
	FM	W7VW	443.90000	+	118.8 Hz	
La Grande, Grande Ronde Hospit						
	FM	W7GRA	146.98000	-	100.0 Hz	ORRC
La Grande, Mount Fanny						
	FM	W7NYW	145.15000	-	110.9 Hz	
	FM	K7RPT	147.26000	+	103.5 Hz	ORRC
La Pine	FM	WA7TYD	145.49000	-	77.0 Hz	ORRC
Lake Oswego	FM	WA7LO	444.30000	+	82.5 Hz	
Lakeside	FM	W7PRA	147.14000	+	136.5 Hz	ORRC
Lakeview, Drake Peak						
	FM	KE7QP	145.31000	-	173.8 Hz	ORRC
Lakeview, Grizzly Peak						
	FM	KE7QP	147.34000	+	173.8 Hz	
Langlois, Stone Butte						
	FM	KA7GNK	145.21000	-	88.5 Hz	ORRC
Laurelwood, Bald Peak						
	FM	K7AUO	443.65000	+	100.0 Hz	ORRC
	FM	K7AUO	1291.50000	1271.50000		ORRC
Lime, Lime Hill	FM	W7NYW	145.17000	-	110.9 Hz	
Lincoln City	FM	W7VTW	147.04000	+	100.0 Hz	ORRC
Lyons , McCully Mtn						
	FM	W1ARK	147.06000	+	100.0 Hz	ORRC
Lyons, McCulley Mountain						
	FM	K7RTL	440.60000	+	100.0 Hz	ORRC
Madras, Eagle Butte						
	FM	K7RPT	442.22500	+	114.8 Hz	
Mapleton	FM	AB7BS	147.14000	+	136.5 Hz	ORRC
McMinnville	FM	W7RXJ-R	146.64000	-	100.0 Hz	ORRC
	FUSION	WA7IB	439.62500			

Location	Mode	Call sign	Output	Input	Access	Coordinator
McMinnville, Eola Hill						
	FM	W7YAM	441.80000	+	114.8 Hz	ORRC
Medford	DMR/BM	KD7MPA	442.80000	+	CC1	
	DSTAR	KG7FOJ	145.24000	-		ORRC
	DSTAR	KG7FOJ C	145.24000	-		
	DSTAR	KE7MVI B	443.77500	+		
	DSTAR	KG7FOJ B	444.36250	+		
	DSTAR	KG7FOJ	444.65000	+		
	DSTAR	KG7FOJ D	1248.50000			
	DSTAR	KG7FOJ	1293.12500	1313.12500		
	DSTAR	KG7FOJ A	1293.12500	1273.12500		
	FM	KG7FOJ	1248.50000	1228.50000		ORRC
Medford, Baldy	DSTAR	KE7MVI	443.77500	+		ORRC
	FM	K7JAX	146.84000	-	123.0 Hz	ORRC
Medford, Downtown						
	FM	K7RPT	147.02000	+	100.0 Hz	ORRC
Medford, Rogue Valley Manor						
	FM	K7RVM	147.00000	+	123.0 Hz	ORRC
Megler (Astoria)	DMR/MARC	NA7Q	147.43750	146.33750	CC1	
	DMR/MARC	NA7Q	440.96250	+	CC1	
Mill City-house Mtn-- Or Sar						
	DMR/MARC	K7MTW	442.97500	+	CC1	
Millican, Pine Mountain						
	FM	W7JVO	146.70000	-	162.2 Hz	
	FM	W7JVO	444.75000	+	156.7 Hz	ORRC
Milton-Freewater, Pikes Peak						
	FM	KD7DDQ	147.28000	+	103.5 Hz	
Milwaukie	FUSION	KC6RZW	145.65000			
Mitchell, Stephenson Mountain						
	FM	W7JVO	147.18000	+	162.2 Hz	ORRC
Molalla	DMR/MARC	WB7AWL	440.27500	+	CC1	
Molalla, Molalla Fire District						
	FM	W7DTV	440.70000	+	77.0 Hz	ORRC
Monmouth	FM	KE7AAJ	927.70000	902.70000	162.2 Hz	ORRC
Monroe, Prairie Peak						
	FM	W7ARD	53.03000	51.33000	100.0 Hz	ORRC
Mt Hebo--or Sar	DMR/MARC	KB7APU	442.81250	+	CC1	
Mt. Hebo	DSTAR	W7GC C	147.39000	+		
Myrtle Creek, Boomer Hill						
	FM	KC7UAV	147.12000	+	100.0 Hz	ORRC
Myrtle Creek, Sheep Hill						
	FM	WA6KHG	444.15000	+		
Myrtle Point	FM	W7OC	444.17500	+	146.2 Hz	ORRC
Myrtle Point, Bennett Butte						
	FM	W7OC	145.19000	-	146.2 Hz	
	FM	KD7IOP	444.52500	+	123.0 Hz	ORRC
Newberg	DMR/MARC	N7MAQ	444.48750	+	CC1	
	FM	KR7IS	52.83000	51.13000	107.2 Hz	ORRC
	FM	KR7IS	224.06000	-	107.2 Hz	ORRC
	FM	K7RPT	443.75000	+	100.0 Hz	ORRC
	FM	K7RPT	444.12500	+	100.0 Hz	
Newberg, Bald Peak						
	FM	K0INK	442.55000	+	114.8 Hz	ORRC
Newberg, Chehalem Mountain						
	FM	KB7PSM	145.11000	-	103.5 Hz	ORRC
	FM	K7WWG	146.90000	-	127.3 Hz	ORRC
	FM	KB7PSM	442.15000	+		ORRC
Newberg, Parrett Mountain						
	FM	AH6LE	442.67500	+	100.0 Hz	ORRC
Newport	FM	W7PRA	145.39000	-		ORRC
Newport, Cape Foulweather						
	FM	W7VTW	145.37000	-	167.9 Hz	

Location	Mode	Call sign	Output	Input	Access	Coordinator
Newport, Courthouse						
	FM	W7VTW	145.47000	-	167.9 Hz	ORRC
Newport, Otter Crest						
	FM	W7VTW	147.30000	+	156.7 Hz	ORRC
	FM	W7GC	444.75000	+	118.8 Hz	ORRC
NOAA Bend / Redmond						
	WX	WWF80	162.50000			
NOAA Brookings	WX	KIH37	162.55000			
NOAA Burns Butte						
	WX	KHB30	162.47500			
NOAA Cape Blanco						
	WX	WNG596	162.42500			
NOAA Coos Bay	WX	KIH32	162.40000			
NOAA Eugene	WX	KEC42	162.40000			
NOAA Florence	WX	WNG674	162.50000			
NOAA Fossil	WX	WNG559	162.55000			
NOAA Gleason	WX	WWH29	162.42500			
NOAA Heppner	WX	WWH28	162.42500			
NOAA John Day	WX	WNG560	162.50000			
NOAA Klamath Falls						
	WX	WXL97	162.55000			
NOAA Medford	WX	WXL85	162.40000			
NOAA Mount Ashland						
	WX	WWF97	162.47500			
NOAA Mount Hebo						
	WX	WNG697	162.52500			
NOAA Neahkahnie						
	WX	WWF94	162.42500			
NOAA Newport	WX	KIH33	162.55000			
NOAA Pendleton	WX	WNG708	162.42500			
NOAA Portland	WX	KIG98	162.55000			
NOAA Reedsport	WX	WZ2509	162.52500			
NOAA Roseburg	WX	WXL98	162.55000			
NOAA Salem	WX	WXL96	162.47500			
NOAA Spout Springs						
	WX	WXL95	162.40000		123.0 Hz	
NOAA Tillamook	WX	WWF95	162.47500			
NOAA Umatilla	WX	WWF57	162.50000			
North Bend	FM	WA7JAW	444.97500	+		ORRC
North Plains	FM	KE7DC	145.45000	-	136.5 Hz	ORRC
	FM	KE7DC	442.40000	+	136.5 Hz	ORRC
Oakridge	FM	W7PRA	441.67500	+	100.0 Hz	ORRC
Oakridge, Wolf Mountain						
	FM	W7ARD	53.07000	51.37000	100.0 Hz	ORRC
	FM	N7EXH	146.98000	-	100.0 Hz	ORRC
Ontario	FM	K7RHB	443.15000	+	100.0 Hz	
Ontario, Malheir	FM	W7NYW	145.17000	-	110.9 Hz	
Ontario, Malheur Butte						
	FM	K7OJI	147.10000	+	100.0 Hz	ORRC
Or Sar-portable Rptr						
	DMR/MARC	KB7APU	443.00000	+	CC1	
Oregon City	DMR/MARC	WB7AWL	145.25000	-	CC1	
	DMR/MARC	WB7AWL	444.88750	+	CC1	
	FM	K7RTL	145.21000	-	110.9 Hz	ORRC
Oregon City, Boynton Standpipe						
	FM	W7ZRS	442.07500	+	103.5 Hz	ORRC
Pendleton	FUSION	W7NEO	444.82500	+		
Pendleton, Cabbage Hill						
	FM	W7NEO	146.88000	-		
	FM	N7NKT	224.56000	-		
	FM	W7URG	444.97500	+	136.5 Hz	
	FM	N7ERT	927.50000	902.50000		

Location	Mode	Call sign	Output	Input	Access	Coordinator
Pendleton, Mission						
	FM	W7NEO	444.82500	+		
Phoenix	FM	K7RVM-R	444.45000	+		ORRC
Pleasant Valley	FM	KJ7IY-R	145.27000	-		ORRC
Port Orford	FM	K7POH	147.20000	+	118.8 Hz	ORRC
Port Orford, Cape Blanco						
	FM	KD7IOP	440.72500	+	114.8 Hz	ORRC
Portable Rpt	DMR/BM	AA7BG	440.27500	+	CC1	
Portland	DMR/BM	K7KSN	440.15000	+	CC5	
	DMR/MARC	W7OZM	440.30000	+	CC1	
	DMR/MARC	K7RPT	440.51250	+	CC1	
	DMR/MARC	KA7AGH	441.32500	+	CC7	ORRC
	DMR/MARC	WA7HAA	443.23750	+	CC7	
	DMR/MARC	WA7HAA	444.83750	+	CC7	
	DSTAR	WB7DZG C	146.62000	-		
	DSTAR	WB7DZG B	444.31250	+		
	DSTAR	WB7DZG D	1248.75000			
	DSTAR	KG7KOU D	1249.75000			
	DSTAR	WB7DZG A	1292.00000	1272.00000		
	DSTAR	KG7KOU A	1292.01250	1272.01250		
	FM	K7RPT	147.04000	+	100.0 Hz	ORRC
	FM	WB2QHS	426.25000	910.25000		ORRC
	FM	AB7BS	440.50000	+		
	FM	K7RPT	442.22500	+	103.5 Hz	
	FM	K6PRN	443.20000	+	173.8 Hz	
	FM	W7PMC	443.22500	+	107.2 Hz	ORRC
	FM	KB7OYI	443.85000	+	107.2 Hz	ORRC
	FM	KG7KOU	1249.75000	1229.75000		ORRC
	FM	W7AMQ	1257.00000	426.20000		ORRC
Portland - Testing	DMR/MARC	N7LF	444.00000	+	CC1	
Portland, Council Crest						
	FM	K7LJ	145.23000	-		ORRC
	FM	WB2QHS	440.67500	+	136.5 Hz	ORRC
	FM	K7LJ	442.65000	+	100.0 Hz	ORRC
	FM	K7NE	443.30000	+	100.0 Hz	
	FM	W7PGE	444.67500	+		ORRC
Portland, Emanuel Hospital						
	FM	K7LHS	440.82500	+	110.9 Hz	ORRC
Portland, Garden Home						
	FM	K7GDS	443.55000	+	100.0 Hz	
Portland, Healy Heights						
	FM	N7NLL	53.09000	51.39000	107.2 Hz	
Portland, KGW Tower						
	FM	N7EXH	146.98000	-		ORRC
Portland, KOIN Tower						
	FM	W7RAT	440.40000	+	123.0 Hz	ORRC
Portland, KPDX Tower						
	FM	W7PM	442.25000	+	100.0 Hz	ORRC
Portland, Mt Tabor						
	FM	K7LJ	145.39000	-	100.0 Hz	ORRC
Portland, OHSU	FM	K7LTA	442.70000	+	100.0 Hz	ORRC
	FM	K0HSU	444.00000	+	100.0 Hz	
Portland, Skyline	FM	N7EXH	145.31000	-	123.0 Hz	ORRC
	FM	W7AC	147.14000	+	107.2 Hz	ORRC
	FM	W7EXH	441.35000	+	100.0 Hz	
	FM	W7DTV	443.62500	+	77.0 Hz	ORRC
Portland, Stonehenge Tower						
	FM	KE7AWR	146.70000	-	100.0 Hz	ORRC
	FM	KB7OYI	440.35000	+	127.3 Hz	
	FM	WA7BND	443.05000	+		ORRC
Portland, VA Hospital						
	FM	KE7FBE	145.25000	-	136.5 Hz	

Location	Mode	Call sign	Output	Input	Access	Coordinator
Portland, West Hills						
	FM	N7NLL	442.02500	+	100.0 Hz	
Portland-WEST HILLS--OR SAR						
	DMR/MARC	KB7APU	440.62500	+	CC1	
Prineville	DMR/MARC	N7CCO	441.25000	+	CC1	
	FUSION	N7SHG	145.56250			
Prineville, Grizzly Mountain						
	FM	N7CCO	147.38000	+	162.2 Hz	ORRC
	FM	N7PIR	444.17500	+	103.5 Hz	ORRC
Prineville, Round Mtn						
	FM	N7CCO	145.21000	-	141.3 Hz	ORRC
Prineville-DT	DMR/MARC	N7CCO	441.25000	+	CC1	
Rainier, Rainier Hill						
	FM	NU7D	224.66000	-	114.8 Hz	ORRC
Redmond	FM	W7PRA	145.13000	-		ORRC
	FUSION	W7JVO	443.75000	+		
Redmond, Cinder Butte						
	FM	K7RPT	147.04000	+	114.8 Hz	ORRC
Redmond-GRAY BUTTE						
	DMR/MARC	KB7APU	442.95000	+	CC1	
Reedsport	FM	AB7BS	443.55000	+		ORRC
Reedsport, Winchester Hill						
	FM	W7OC	147.18000	+	146.2 Hz	ORRC
	FM	W7OC	444.40000	+		
Ripplebrook/Mt Hood National F						
	DMR/MARC	KB7APU	440.63750	+	CC9	
Rockaway Beach	FM	W7GC	442.75000	+	118.8 Hz	ORRC
Rogue River	FM	N7AGX	53.17000	51.47000		ORRC
	FM	AB7BS	440.85000	+	94.8 Hz	ORRC
Rogue River, Elk Mountain						
	FM	WA6HWW	145.27000	-	136.5 Hz	
Roseburg	DMR/BM	N2DME	449.25000	-	CC1	
	FM	W7PRA	145.21000	-	136.5 Hz	ORRC
	FM	W7PRA	146.70000	-	136.5 Hz	ORRC
	FM	AB7BS	441.85000	+		ORRC
	FM	WB6MFV	441.87500	+	88.5 Hz	ORRC
	FUSION	N2DME	446.50000			
Roseburg, Lane Mountain						
	FM	K7RBG	146.90000	-	100.0 Hz	
Ruch	FM	KL7VK	146.72000	-	131.8 Hz	ORRC
	FM	KA6FUB	441.57500	+	100.0 Hz	
Saginaw	FM	W7NK	444.85000	+		ORRC
Saginaw, Bear Mountain						
	FM	N7EXH	146.76000	-	123.0 Hz	ORRC
Saint Helens	FM	KJ7AXA	146.68000	-	114.8 Hz	
	FUSION	KJ7AXA	145.55000			
Salem		KG7ZBE-L	147.45000			
	DMR/MARC	K7LWV	145.35000	-	CC1	
	DMR/MARC	W7SRA	441.27500	+	CC1	ORRC
	DMR/MARC	N7MAQ	442.88750	+	CC1	
	FM	W7PRA	145.49000	-	136.5 Hz	ORRC
	FM	WB7RKR	224.24000	-	100.0 Hz	ORRC
	FM	KE7DLA	224.60000	-	100.0 Hz	ORRC
	FM	AC7RF	440.27500	+	107.2 Hz	ORRC
	FM	KB7PPM	440.72500	+		ORRC
	FM	AB7F	441.37500	+	123.0 Hz	ORRC
	FM	AB7BS	442.45000	+		
	FM	KE7DLA	442.50000	+	100.0 Hz	ORRC
	FM	KC7CFS	443.45000	+	123.0 Hz	ORRC
	FM	W6WHD	444.92500	+		
	FUSION	WA7CXG	145.65000			
	FUSION	W7OEM	147.43500			

Location	Mode	Call sign	Output	Input	Access	Coordinator
Salem	FUSION	WA7ABU	444.95000	+		
Salem, Bald Hill (Eagle Crest)						
	FM	N7PIR	440.07500	+	103.5 Hz	ORRC
	FM	W7NK	441.75000	+	123.0 Hz	
Salem, CCC	FM	AD7ET	443.17500	+	88.5 Hz	ORRC
Salem, Eagle Crest						
	FM	W7SRA	145.33000	-	186.2 Hz	ORRC
Salem, Popcorn Hill						
	FM	K7MRR	145.35000	-	186.2 Hz	ORRC
	FM	K7UN	441.70000	+	186.2 Hz	ORRC
Salem, Prospect Hill						
	FM	W7SRA	146.86000	-	186.2 Hz	ORRC
	FM	W7DTV	441.17500	+	77.0 Hz	
	FM	W7SRA	441.27500	+	100.0 Hz	ORRC
Salem, Salem Hills						
	FM	W6WHD	224.92000	-	136.5 Hz	ORRC
	FM	W6WHD	444.10000	+	136.5 Hz	ORRC
Salem, Silver Creek Falls						
	FM	WA7ABU	444.95000	+	100.0 Hz	ORRC
Sandy		KG7NLO-L	146.10000			
	FM	KJ7IY	53.35000	51.65000	107.2 Hz	ORRC
	FM	KJ7IY	145.43000	-	107.2 Hz	ORRC
	FM	KJ7IY	442.87500	+	107.2 Hz	ORRC
Scappoose	DMR/BM	AA7BG	441.86250	+	CC1	
	FUSION	AG7FU	145.50000			
Scio, Rodgers Mountain						
	FM	KA7ENW	146.61000	-	167.9 Hz	
	FM	KA7ENW	442.85000	+	167.9 Hz	ORRC
Seaside	DMR/MARC	NA7Q	444.90000	+	CC1	
	FM	WA7PIX	147.00000	+	118.8 Hz	
	FM	N7PIR-L	443.87500	+	100.0 Hz	ORRC
Seven Oaks	FM	W9PCI-R	145.33000	-		ORRC
Sheridan	FM	AC7ZQ	224.56000	-	100.0 Hz	ORRC
Sherwood	DSTAR	WB7DZG	146.62000	-		ORRC
	DSTAR	WB7DZG	444.31250	+		ORRC
	DSTAR	WB7DZG	1292.00000	1272.00000		ORRC
	FM	KR7IS	145.47000	-	107.2 Hz	ORRC
	FM	KJ7IY	442.27500	+	107.2 Hz	
	FM	KR7IS	443.42500	+	107.2 Hz	ORRC
	FUSION	N7LGK	432.50000			
Silverton, Silver Creek Falls						
	FM	WA7ABU	52.99000	51.29000	100.0 Hz	ORRC
Silverton, Silver Falls						
	FM	W7SAA	147.34000	+	77.0 Hz	
	FM	KE7DLA	224.16000	-	100.0 Hz	ORRC
	FM	W7SAA	444.25000	+	100.0 Hz	ORRC
Sisters	FM	W7EXH	147.34000	+	100.0 Hz	ORRC
	FM	W7PRA	441.62500	+	100.0 Hz	ORRC
Sisters, Fivemile Butte						
	FM	W7DUX	146.90000	-	123.0 Hz	ORRC
South Saddle	DMR/MARC	K7RPT	440.81250	+	CC1	
Springfield, Willamette Height						
	FM	WA7FQD	146.74000	-	100.0 Hz	ORRC
St Helens	FUSION	KI7HML	145.75500			
Stanfield	DMR/BM	N7NKT	444.95000	+	CC1	
Summer Lake, Dead Indian Mount						
	FM	KE7QP	146.80000	-	173.8 Hz	ORRC
Sunriver, Spring River Butte						
	FM	WA7TYD	146.64000	-	123.0 Hz	ORRC
Sunset Beach		K7LEN-L	144.36000			
Sweet Home	FUSION	KG7BZ	443.12500	+		

Location	Mode	Call sign	Output	Input	Access	Coordinator
Sweet Home, Marks Ridge						
	FM	KG7BZ	52.91000	51.21000	100.0 Hz	
	FM	K7ENW	147.20000	+	167.9 Hz	ORRC
	FM	KG7BZ	443.12500	+	77.0 Hz	ORRC
Terrebonne, Crooked River Ranc						
	FM	W7JVO	147.06000	+	162.2 Hz	ORRC
The Dalles	DMR/MARC	N7LF	443.10000	+	CC1	
	FM	KC7LDD	146.74000	-	100.0 Hz	ORRC
The Dalles, Stacker Butte						
	FM	KF7LN	146.52000	+	100.0 Hz	ORRC
Tigard	FM	KK7TJ	442.57500	+	107.2 Hz	ORRC
Tigard, QTH	FM	K7ICY	440.10000	+	162.2 Hz	
Tillamook, Triangulation Point						
	FM	W7EM	440.52500	+	77.0 Hz	ORRC
Timber	FM	KR7IS	52.85000	51.15000	107.2 Hz	ORRC
Timber, Hoffman Hill						
	FM	KJ7IY	441.82500	+	107.2 Hz	ORRC
Timberline	FM	K7RPT	147.12000	+	100.0 Hz	ORRC
	FM	K7RPT	444.22500	+	100.0 Hz	ORRC
Tualatin	FM	KK7WK	441.57500	+	103.5 Hz	
Ukiah, Carney Butte						
	FM	W7URG	444.95000	+	136.5 Hz	ORRC
Vale, Lime Hill	FM	K7OJI	444.15000	+	100.0 Hz	
Vernonia, Corey Hill						
	FM	W7VER	145.25000	-	114.8 Hz	
Waldport, Table Mountain						
	FM	W7VTW	147.00000	+	136.5 Hz	ORRC
Walton, Walker Point						
	FM	W7EXH	145.31000	-	100.0 Hz	ORRC
	FM	K7LNK	444.92500	+		
Warren	FM	W6WHD	224.92000	-	107.2 Hz	
Warren, McNulty Water Tower						
	FM	N7EI	146.68000	-	114.8 Hz	ORRC
	FM	N7EI	444.62500	+	107.2 Hz	ORRC
Warrenton		WA7WIW-R	145.45000			
	FUSION	KY7LE	146.46000			
West Linn	FUSION	WA7BND	443.05000	+		
Wilamina	FM	W7GRT	442.82500	+	123.0 Hz	
Wilhoit	FM	WA7ABU-R	145.29000	-		ORRC
Willamina	FM	W7GRT	146.66000	-	136.5 Hz	
Willaura Estates		K7AGE-L	446.00000			
Wolf Creek	FM	N7EXH	146.84000	-	74.4 Hz	ORRC
	FM	W7PRA	146.94000	-		ORRC
	FM	W6PRN	443.52500	+	173.8 Hz	
	FM	AB7BS	444.50000	+		ORRC
Wolf Creek, King Mountain						
	FM	WB6YQP	147.34000	+	136.5 Hz	
Woodburn	DMR/MARC	N7MAQ	441.32500	+	CC1	
Yoncalla	FM	AB7BS	444.90000	+		
Zigzag-or Sar	DMR/MARC	KB7APU	442.81250	+	CC1	
PENNSYLVANIA						
Abbottstown	FUSION	KS3M	147.51000			
	FUSION	KS3M	446.35000			
Abington	FM	WA3DSP-R	223.76000	-	131.8 Hz	ARCC
Abington Township, Abington Ho						
	FM	K3DN	441.15000	+	88.5 Hz	
Acme	FM	N3QZU	51.78000	-		
	FM	W3SDR	146.67000	-	131.8 Hz	
	FM	W3NBN	421.25000	439.25000		
Akron	FUSION	W3LAS	433.95000			
Albion	FM	WA3WYZ	53.55000	52.55000	186.2 Hz	

Location	Mode	Call sign	Output	Input	Access	Coordinator
Albion	FM	WA3USH	223.94000	-		
Allentown	DMR/MARC	KC2LHJ	441.40000	+	CC1	
	DMR/MARC	N3RPV	441.60000	+	CC0	
	DMR/MARC	WR3IRS	443.50000	+	CC1	
	DMR/MARC	N3RPV	448.71250	-	CC0	
	DSTAR	W3OI	147.16500	+		
	DSTAR	W3OI C	147.16500	+		
	DSTAR	W3OI	445.02500	-		
	DSTAR	W3OI B	445.02500	-		
	DSTAR	W3OI A	1291.00000	1271.00000		
	FM	W3OI	147.13500	+		ARCC
	FM	KA3NRJ	224.08000	-	203.5 Hz	
	FM	N3HES	443.50000	+	156.7 Hz	ARCC
	FM	N3KZ	444.15000	+	131.8 Hz	ARCC
	FM	N3MFT	448.77500	-	131.8 Hz	ARCC
	FM	N3RPV	927.06250	902.06250	131.8 Hz	
	FUSION	WA3VHL	147.22500	+		
Allentown, Lehigh Mountain						
	FM	W3OI	146.94000	-	71.9 Hz	ARCC
Allentown, Scholl Woodlands Pr						
	FM	N3XG	443.35000	+	100.0 Hz	
Allentown, South Mountain						
	FM	K4MTP	224.40000	-		
	FM	KA3NRJ	444.10000	+	151.4 Hz	ARCC
Almont	FM	K3MFI	53.23000	52.23000	146.2 Hz	ARCC
Altoona, Wopsy Ridge						
	FM	W3QZF	146.61000	-	123.0 Hz	WPRC
	FM	W3QW	146.82000	-	123.0 Hz	WPRC
Ambler	FM	WA3GM	145.58000		131.8 Hz	
Ambridge	DMR/BM	K3UKE	441.70000	+	CC1	
	FM	K3UKE	147.13500	+	131.8 Hz	
Apollo	FM	N1RS	29.68000	-	131.8 Hz	
	FM	N1RS	51.90000	-	141.3 Hz	
	FM	N1RS	146.97000	-	131.8 Hz	
	FM	N1RS	224.30000	-	131.8 Hz	
	FM	KB3UEM	224.64000	-	131.8 Hz	
Arnot	DMR/MARC	N3FE	444.85000	+	CC1	
Atlantic	DSTAR	K3AWS C	147.15000	+		
Bangor	DMR/MARC	N2DCE	445.21875	-	CC1	
	FM	WA3MDP	147.04500	+	131.8 Hz	
	FM	N2VIN	444.60000	+	110.9 Hz	
	FM	N3TXG	447.22500	-	131.8 Hz	ARCC
Barnesville	DMR/BM	KB2MXV	440.75000	+	CC5	
	DMR/BM	KB2MXV	441.10000	+	CC5	
Barnesville, Mountain Valley G						
	FM	W3TWA	449.77500	-	131.8 Hz	ARCC
Bear Creek	FM	N3SQ	147.76500	-	127.3 Hz	
Bear Creek Village						
		KC2CWN-R	146.50500			
Beaver	FM	KA3IRT	442.45000	+	100.0 Hz	
Beaver Falls	FM	W3SGJ	145.31000	-	131.8 Hz	
Beaver Mills	FM	W3PHB-R	146.43000	147.43000	173.8 Hz	WPRC
Beaver, Brighton Township Wate						
	FM	WW3AAA	146.85000	-	131.8 Hz	
	FM	N3TN	224.88000	-	131.8 Hz	
	FM	N3TN	444.25000	+	131.8 Hz	
Beaver, Heritage Valley						
	FM	N3TN	147.13500	+	131.8 Hz	
Bedford	FM	K3NQT	145.49000	-	123.0 Hz	
	FM	K3NQT	224.48000	-	123.0 Hz	WPRC
Bedford, Kinton Knob						
	FM	K3NQT	444.20000	+	123.0 Hz	

Location	Mode	Call sign	Output	Input	Access	Coordinator
Belle Valley	FM	N3APP-R	147.27000	+		WPRC
Bellefield	FM	W3YJ-R	443.45000	+		
Bellefonte	DMR/MARC	K3ARL	147.10500	+	CC1	
Bensalem	DMR/MARC	WB0YLE	445.05250	-	CC1	
	FM	W3BXW	444.20000	+	131.8 Hz	ARCC
	FUSION	W3SK	448.22500	-		
Bentleyville	FM	WA3QYV	224.58000	-		
Bentleyville,	FM	WB3CCN	147.27000	+		
Benton, Red Rock	FM	N3VTH	147.00000	+	77.0 Hz	
	FM	N3KZ	441.80000	+	131.8 Hz	
Berwick	FUSION	KC3NIH	146.83500	0.60000		
Bethel Park	FUSION	AI3J	446.15000			
Bethel, Booths Corner Farmers						
	FM	W3KG	224.22000	-	88.5 Hz	ARCC
Bethlehem	DMR/MARC	N3RPV	145.23000	-	CC1	
	DMR/MARC	K3IHI	444.37500	-	CC1	
	FM	K3LPR	146.77500	-	136.5 Hz	ARCC
	FM	KC2ABV	445.17500	-	100.0 Hz	
	FUSION	K3IHI	146.46500			
Biglerville	FM	W3KGN	443.10000	+	103.5 Hz	ARCC
Biglerville, Big Flat So Mt						
	FM	W3BD	443.05000	+	151.4 Hz	ARCC
Birdsboro	DMR/BM	N3GAR	442.85000	+	CC1	
Blairsville	FM	W3BMD	146.91000	-	131.8 Hz	
	FM	W3BMD	444.97500	+	110.9 Hz	WPRC
Blakeslee	DMR/BM	KC2IRV	449.82500	-	CC1	
	DMR/MARC	KG3I	447.27500	-	CC0	ARCC
Bloomsburg	FM	WB3DUC	53.13000	52.13000	131.8 Hz	ARCC
	FM	WB3DUC	147.12000	+	131.8 Hz	ARCC
	FM	WB3DUC	447.02500	-	91.5 Hz	
Blossburg, Bloss Mountain						
	FM	N3TJJ	442.40000	+		
Blue Knob, Ski Resort						
	FM	KB3KWD	147.15000	+	167.9 Hz	
Boalsburg	FM	W3YA	146.85000	-	146.2 Hz	
Booth's Corner	FM	W3KG	223.94000	-	88.5 Hz	ARCC
Boothwyn	FM	W3KG	446.77500	-	88.5 Hz	
Brackinridge	FM	WA3WOM	145.37000	-	131.8 Hz	
Bradford	DSTAR	W3VG B	446.70000			
	FM	KD3OH	147.24000	+	173.8 Hz	
Brentwood, Brentwood Fire Depa						
	FM	AB3PJ	145.33000	-	131.8 Hz	WPRC
Brentwood, Brentwood Fire Hall						
	FM	KW3LO	443.60000	+	131.8 Hz	
Bridgeville	FM	N3WX	51.94000	-	131.8 Hz	WPRC
	FM	KS3R	145.13000	-		
Briggsville	FM	WC3H-R	441.90000	441.30000		
Bryn Mawr	FM	WB3JOE	224.42000	-	131.8 Hz	ARCC
Buck	FM	AK3E	224.78000	-	151.4 Hz	
Bucktown	DSTAR	KB3SLR B	445.08125	-		
	DSTAR	KB3SLR A	1255.60000	+		
	DSTAR	KB3SLR D	1297.50000			
	FM	N3KZ	147.27000	+	77.0 Hz	
	FM	W3EOC	446.17500	-	100.0 Hz	ARCC
Burgettstown	FM	K3PSP	147.39000	+	131.8 Hz	
Butler, Alameda Park						
	FM	K3PSG	147.30000	+	131.8 Hz	
Butler, Center Township Water						
	FM	W3UDX	147.36000	+	131.8 Hz	
Butler, Sunnyview Long Term Ca						
	FM	K3PSG	443.90000	+	131.8 Hz	WPRC
California	FM	KA3FLU	145.11000	-		

Location	Mode	Call sign	Output	Input	Access	Coordinator
Camelback Mountain						
	FM	N3KZ	53.79000	52.79000	131.8 Hz	ARCC
Camelback Mtn.	DMR/MARC	WR3IRS	441.55000	+	CC1	
Canonsburg	FM	N3FB	443.65000	+	131.8 Hz	
	FUSION	KB3IJY	430.12500			
Carbondale	DMR/BM	K1NRA	440.05625	+	CC8	
	FUSION	K1NRA	145.11000	-		
Carnegie	FM	W3KWH	426.25000	439.25000		
Carnegie, Settlers Cabin Park						
	FM/YSF	W3KWH	444.45000	+	103.5 Hz	
Carnot-Moon	FM	KA3IRT-R	444.15000	+		
Carrick	FM	W3PGH	29.64000	-	131.8 Hz	
	FM	W3PGH	52.64000	51.64000	131.8 Hz	
	FM	W3PGH	146.61000	-	131.8 Hz	
	FM	W3PGH	444.95000	+	131.8 Hz	
Carroltown, NEXT TO WATER TOWE						
	FM	N3LAD	146.77500	-	123.0 Hz	WPRC
Castle Shannon	FM	K3CSF	440.60000	+	131.8 Hz	
Catasauqua	DMR/BM	KC2ABV	441.10000	+	CC1	
Catawissa	FM	KB3BJO	147.22500	+	85.4 Hz	ARCC
Centerville	FM	N3NQT	146.79000	-	123.0 Hz	
Central City	DMR/BM	KE3UC	443.57500	+	CC1	
	FM	WR3AJL	146.62500	-	123.0 Hz	
Central City, Statler Hill						
	FM	KE3UC	443.57500	+	123.0 Hz	
Chalfont	FM	W3DBZ	223.90000	-	107.2 Hz	ARCC
Chambersburg	DMR/MARC	WR3IRS	223.90000	-	CC1	
	DMR/MARC	WR3IRS	441.90000	+	CC1	ARCC
	FM	N3KZ	443.70000	+	131.8 Hz	
	FUSION	K3WVU	147.52500			
	FUSION	N1XGH	440.00000			
Chambersburg VHF						
	DMR/MARC	KA3LAO	146.41500	147.41500	CC1	WPRC
Charlestown	DMR/MARC	WR3IRS	440.20000	+	CC1	ARCC
Cherry Hill	FM	N8XUA	146.76000	-	186.2 Hz	
	FM	WA3USH	444.92500	+		
Cherry Valley	FM	KC8PHW	442.32500	+		
Chester	DMR/MARC	KM3W	443.92500	+	CC1	
	FM	KM3W	146.53500		131.8 Hz	
	FM	KM3W	444.70000	+	131.8 Hz	ARCC
Chester, Crozer Chester Medica						
	FM	KM3W	224.70000	-	131.8 Hz	ARCC
Clarion	FM	KE3EI	442.65000	+		
	FM	N3HZX	444.32500	+	110.9 Hz	
Clearfield, Rockton Mountain						
	FM	N5NWC	52.90000	-	173.8 Hz	
	FM	W3CPA	147.25500	+	173.8 Hz	
Clifford	FM	WR2M	224.86000	-		
	FM	WR2M	445.47500	-		
Clinton	FM	K3KEM	147.21000	+	100.0 Hz	
	FM	K3KEM	443.00000	+		
	FM	K3KEM	444.85000	+	131.8 Hz	
Coatesville	FM	W3EOC	441.95000	+	100.0 Hz	ARCC
Cochranville	FM	WB3LGG	449.67500	-	94.8 Hz	
Connellsville	FM	WB3JNP	145.17000	-	131.8 Hz	
	FM	W3NAV	146.89500	-	131.8 Hz	
	FM	N3LGY	444.82500	+	151.4 Hz	
Coopersburg	FM	W3LR	449.27500	-	151.4 Hz	ARCC
Cornwall	DMR/BM	W3AD	449.02500	-	CC1	
	FM	K3LV	147.31500	+	82.5 Hz	ARCC
	FM	N3TPL	224.82000	-	114.8 Hz	ARCC
	FM	KA3CNT	224.84000	-	131.8 Hz	ARCC

Location	Mode	Call sign	Output	Input	Access	Coordinator
Cornwall	FM	W3BXW	442.15000	+	131.8 Hz	ARCC
	FM	N3FYI	446.47500	-	114.8 Hz	
Cornwall Mountain						
	FM	N3TUQ	927.58750	902.58750	114.8 Hz	ARCC
Cornwall, Cornwall Mtn						
	FM	W3AD	145.39000	-	118.8 Hz	ARCC
Corry	DMR/BM	N3RSN	444.20000	+	CC1	
	FM	W3YXE	147.09000	+	186.2 Hz	
	FM	KE3PD	224.06000	-	186.2 Hz	
	FM	W3CCB	443.50000	+		
	FM	W3YXE	444.80000	+		
	FUSION	W3CCB	444.00000	+		
Coudersport	FM	N3PC	146.68500	-	173.8 Hz	WPRC
	FM	KB3EAR	443.30000	+		
Cowansville	FM	N1RS	146.50500	147.50500	131.8 Hz	WPRC
	FM	KA3HUK	224.18000	-		
	FM	N1RS	444.30000	+	131.8 Hz	
Cranberry Twp.	FUSION	KC3LGT	145.55500			
Cranesville	DMR/BM	KC3NRI	440.20000	+	CC1	
Crescent Lake		KB3EJM-R	146.86500			
Dallas	FM	W3LR	449.27500	-	151.4 Hz	
Darby	FM	KM3W	223.10000	-		
Darby, Mercy Fitzgerald Hospit						
	FM	W3UER	147.36000	+	131.8 Hz	ARCC
Delano	FM	W3SC	53.31000	52.31000		
	FM	W3SC	145.37000	-	123.0 Hz	ARCC
	FM	W3TWA	146.95500	-		
Delta	DMR/MARC	N3CNJ	147.16500	+	CC1	
Denison	FM	W3LWW-R	147.18000	+		
Derry	FM	W3CRC	145.15000	-	131.8 Hz	
	FM	N1RS	146.49000	147.49000	131.8 Hz	
	FM	KE3PO	442.27500	+	131.8 Hz	
Dingmans Ferry	FM	AA2HA	145.33000	-	141.3 Hz	ARCC
Dover	FM	WB3EPJ	442.70000	+	74.4 Hz	ARCC
Downington	DMR/MARC	N3JCS	448.05000	-	CC1	
Doylestown	FM	WA3EPA	145.35000	-	131.8 Hz	ARCC
Drexel Hill	DSTAR	N3AEC B	440.04375	+		
	DSTAR	N3AEC A	1255.52500	+		
	DSTAR	N3AEC A	1299.70000			
	DSTAR	N3AEC D	1299.70000			
Du Bois, Rockton Mountain						
	FM	N3QC	147.31500	+	173.8 Hz	WPRC
Dublin	FUSION	KB3ZWH	145.26000	+		
Duryea	FUSION	KC3MN	146.83500			
Eagel Stream	FM	AA3E-R	146.83500	-		ARCC
Eagle	DMR/MARC	WR3IRS	441.30000	+	CC1	
Eaglehurst	FM	W3GV-R	146.61000	-		
Eagles Peak	FM	N3KZ	442.40000	+	131.8 Hz	ARCC
Eagleville	DMR/BM	AA3E	449.28125	-	CC1	
	DSTAR	AA3E B	445.01875	-		
	DSTAR	AA3E A	1255.57500	+		
	DSTAR	AA3E D	1298.70000			
	FM	K3CX	449.92500	-	100.0 Hz	ARCC
Earlville	FM	N3KZ	53.87000	52.87000	131.8 Hz	ARCC
	FM	K3ZMC	147.21000	+	131.8 Hz	
	FM	K3ZMC	443.55000	+	131.8 Hz	
East Brady	FUSION	W3HRS	145.10000			
East Monongahela						
	FM	N3OVP	223.90000	-		
	FM	W3CSL	442.42500	+		
	FM	W3CDU	443.35000	+		
East Stroudsburg	DSTAR	KB3TEM C	144.92000			

Location	Mode	Call sign	Output	Input	Access	Coordinator
East Stroudsburg	DSTAR	KB3TEM C	146.55000	-		
	DSTAR	KB3TEM B	438.00000			
Easton	FM	N3LWY	51.82000	-	88.5 Hz	ARCC
	FM	KB3AJF	224.74000	-	100.0 Hz	ARCC
	FM	N2ZAV	1294.00000	1274.00000		ARCC
Easton, Braden Airport						
	FM	KB3VPK	145.27000	-	151.4 Hz	
Eau Claire	FM	W3ZIC	145.19000	-	186.2 Hz	
Edinboro, Franklin Township EO						
	FM	KB3PSL	146.98500	-	186.2 Hz	
Effort	DMR/BM	K4MTP	445.37500		CC1	ARCC
Elizabethville, Berry Mountain						
	FM	KB3VDL	147.24000	+	123.0 Hz	
Elk Mountain	FM	N3HPY	447.37500	-	131.8 Hz	ARCC
Elk Mountain Ski	FM	N3KZ	145.43000	-	77.0 Hz	
Ellendale	FM	KB3NIA	147.07500	+	123.0 Hz	ARCC
Ellwood City	FM	N3ZJM	443.62500	+		
Elverson	DMR/MARC	W3SJS	441.03500	+	CC1	
Emporium	FM	N3FYD	146.80500	-		
Ephrata	DMR/MARC	K3TUF	443.60000	+	CC1	
	FM	W3XP	145.45000	-	100.0 Hz	ARCC
	FM	W3XP	444.65000	+	131.8 Hz	ARCC
Erie	DMR/BM	N3APP	443.37500	+	CC1	
	FM	KB5ELV	442.15000	+	186.2 Hz	
Etters	FM	KB3DHG	445.35000	-	123.0 Hz	
Evans City	FM	KA3HUK	224.98000	-		
	FM	N3XCD	442.67500	+		
	FM	KB3LSM	443.70000	+	131.8 Hz	WPRC
Exeter		WK8X-R	440.00000			
		WK8X-L	445.90000			
Fairfield VHF	DMR/MARC	KA3LAO	146.47500	147.47500	CC1	ARCC
Fairless Hills	DMR/MARC	W3BXW	447.12500	-	CC1	
	FM	W3BXW	147.30000	+	131.8 Hz	ARCC
Fairview Township						
	DMR/MARC	N2JEH	444.05625	+	CC1	ARCC
Fairview Village	FM	N3CVJ	224.20000	-	88.5 Hz	ARCC
Falls Creek, KDUJ Airport						
	FM	N3QC	443.85000	+	173.8 Hz	WPRC
Feasterville	FM	N3SP	223.80000	-	131.8 Hz	ARCC
	FM	WB3BLG	224.98000	-		
Fernwood	FM	N3UXQ-R	449.97500	-	69.3 Hz	ARCC
Finleyville	FM	N3OVP	51.98000	-	141.3 Hz	WPRC
	FUSION	K3MI	439.50000			
Forkston	DMR/MARC	WR3IRS	440.10000	+	CC1	
	FM	N3KZ	442.00000	+	131.8 Hz	ARCC
Franklin	FM	W3ZIC	145.23000	-	186.2 Hz	
	FM	N3QCR	224.74000	-	186.2 Hz	
Freeland	FM	WC3H	53.59000	52.59000	77.0 Hz	
Freeland, Water Tower						
	FM	W3HZL	449.42500	-	103.5 Hz	
Galeton	FM	KB3EAR	147.34500	+	131.8 Hz	
Gatchellville	DMR/MARC	N3CNJ	447.72500	-	CC1	
Gayly	FM	W3KWH-R	147.03000	+		
Geiger		AK3J-R	443.25000			
Georgeville	FM	KB3CNS	442.85000	+		
Gettysburg	FM	W3KGN	145.35000	-	103.5 Hz	ARCC
	FUSION	KC3OJR	146.04000	+		
Gibsonia	DSTAR	W3PGH B	444.35000	+		
Girard, West Erie Co Emergency						
	FM	WE3OPS	146.95500	-	186.2 Hz	
Glades		W3HZU-R	146.58000			
Glen Mills	FM	W3LW	224.98000	-	94.8 Hz	ARCC

Location	Mode	Call sign	Output	Input	Access	Coordinator
Glen Mills	FM	W3LW	1295.80000	1280.80000	94.8 Hz	ARCC
Grand Valley	FM	W3GFD	443.05000	+		WPRC
Grantville	FM	AA3RG	448.22500	-	192.8 Hz	ARCC
Grantville, Blue Mtn						
	FM	K3LV	147.16500	+	82.5 Hz	
Gray	FUSION	K3VL	433.50000			
Green Lane	FM	AA3E	449.12500	-	88.5 Hz	ARCC
Greensburg	DMR/BM	WC3PS	145.44000	-	CC1	
	DMR/BM	WC3PS	442.15000	+	CC1	
	DSTAR	WC3PS C	145.44000	-		
	DSTAR	WC3PS B	442.15000	+		
	DSTAR	WC3PS D	1250.00000			
	DSTAR	WC3PS A	1250.00000			
	DSTAR	WC3PS	1286.00000	1266.00000		
	DSTAR	WC3PS A	1286.00000	-		
Greensburg, D.M.V. Center						
	FM	N3RSJ	444.80000	+	123.0 Hz	
Greentown	FM	WA2AHF	444.65000	+	114.8 Hz	ARCC
Greenville	DMR/BM	KE3JP	444.37500	+	CC8	WPRC
	DSTAR	K3WRB	145.43000	-		WPRC
Greenville, Western Union Towe						
	FM	KE3JP	443.42500	+	186.2 Hz	WPRC
Grove City, Grove City Medical						
	FM	W3LIF	146.68500	-		
Hanover Pa Pigeon Hills						
	DMR/MARC	KB3VVB	445.23125	-	CC1	
Hanover, Pigeon Hills						
	FM	W3MUM	147.33000	+	123.0 Hz	ARCC
Harleysville	FUSION	N3IIG	145.19000	-		
Harrisburg	FM	KA3TKW	145.21000	-	123.0 Hz	ARCC
	FM	W3UU	146.76000	-	100.0 Hz	ARCC
	FM	KA3RKW	224.18000	-	123.0 Hz	ARCC
	FM	W3ND	448.07500	-	123.0 Hz	ARCC
Harrisburg, Blue Mountain						
	FM	W3ND	145.29000	-	123.0 Hz	ARCC
	FM	W3ND	145.47000	-	123.0 Hz	ARCC
	FM	W3ND	444.45000	+	123.0 Hz	ARCC
Harrisburg, Ellendale Forge						
	FM	W3ND	145.11000	-	131.8 Hz	ARCC
Hatfield	FM	WA3RYQ	147.33000	+		ARCC
Havertown	FM	WA3ADI	147.43500		88.5 Hz	
	FM	KA3VEZ	446.02500	-	88.5 Hz	
	FUSION	KC3PTC	444.80000	+		
Haycock	DMR/BM	K2UWC	449.47500	-	CC1	
Hazelwood	FM	WA3PBD	145.47000	-	71.9 Hz	
	FM	KA3IDK	444.05000	+		
	FM	WA3PBD	444.10000	+		
	FM	WA3PBD	923.25000	910.25000		
Hazleton	FM	WC3H	53.59000	52.59000	77.0 Hz	ARCC
	FM	W3OHX	146.67000	-	103.5 Hz	ARCC
	FM	W3RC	224.60000	-	77.0 Hz	ARCC
	FM	W3RC	441.90000	+	114.8 Hz	ARCC
	FM	W3RC	927.32500	902.32500		ARCC
Hegins	DMR/BM	KB3VXB	147.39000	+	CC7	
Hellertown	FM	KH2EI	147.56500		88.5 Hz	
	FM	KH2EI	147.58000		100.0 Hz	
	FM	N3TKD	445.62500	-	100.0 Hz	
	FUSION	YY6HBO	441.67500			
Hermitage	FM	K3AWS	147.15000	+		
Hilltown	FM	W3HJ	145.33000	-	131.8 Hz	ARCC
	FM	W3HJ	147.39000	+	100.0 Hz	ARCC
	FM	W3CCX	224.58000	-		ARCC

Location	Mode	Call sign	Output	Input	Access	Coordinator
Hilltown	FM	W3HJ	442.90000	+	123.0 Hz	
	FM	K3DN	443.95000	+	131.8 Hz	ARCC
	FM	K3BUX	927.31250	902.31250		ARCC
Hollidaysburg	DMR/BM	NU3T	442.10000	+	CC1	
Holtwood	DMR/BM	KX3B	448.77500	-	CC1	
Homestead	FM	WA3PBD	29.62000	-	118.8 Hz	
	FM	WA3PBD	51.74000	-	100.0 Hz	
	FM	WA3PBD	146.73000	-	100.0 Hz	
	FM	WA3PBD	223.94000	-	118.8 Hz	
	FM	KA3IDK	224.14000	-		
Honey Brook	FM	K3CX	53.33000	52.33000	131.8 Hz	
Honeybrook	DMR/BM	N3TJJ	449.27500	-	CC1	
Hopwood	FM	W3PIE	443.75000	+	131.8 Hz	
Horsham	FM	K3JJO	147.16500	+	162.2 Hz	ARCC
	FM	WA3TSW	444.55000	+	100.0 Hz	ARCC
Hughestown	FM	KC3MN-R	146.83500	-		
Hummelstown	FUSION	W3MW	147.45000			
Hunlock Creek	FM	N3CSE	146.80500	-	82.5 Hz	ARCC
Huntersville, Long Ridge						
	FM	KB3DXU	145.45000	-	167.9 Hz	ARCC
Huntingdon	FM	W3WIV	145.31000	-		
	FM	WB3CJB	146.70000	-		
	FM	WO3T	442.60000	+	123.0 Hz	
Independence	FM	KA3IRT	145.45000	-		
Indiana	DMR/BM	W3BMD	444.97500	+	CC1	
	FM	W3BMD	29.66000	-	131.8 Hz	WPRC
Industry	FM	N3CYR	146.41500	147.41500		
Irwin	FM	W3OC	147.12000	+	131.8 Hz	WPRC
	FM	W3OC	442.25000	+	131.8 Hz	WPRC
	FUSION	N3JPP	146.53500			
Jamestown	DMR/BM	K3WRB	444.82500	+	CC8	
Jamison City		WE3WEE-L	145.00000			
Jeannette/Hempfield						
	FM	N3RSJ	444.22500	+	123.0 Hz	
Jennerstown, Laurel Mountain						
	FM	NJ3T	444.47500	+	123.0 Hz	
Jennersville	DMR/BM	K3ZED	447.87500	-	CC1	
Jennersville, Route 1 At Route						
	FM	N3SLC	145.25000	-	114.8 Hz	
Jim Thorpe	FM	W3HA	147.25500	+	162.2 Hz	ARCC
	FUSION	KC3MLI	445.00000			
Johnstown	DMR/BM	N3YFO	145.39000	-	CC1	WPRC
	DMR/BM	N3YFO	442.82500	+	CC1	WPRC
	DMR/BM	KE3UC	444.47500	+	CC1	
	FM	N3FQQ	51.80000	-		
	FM	WA3WGN	146.94000	-	123.0 Hz	
	FM	N3LZX	147.37500	+		
	FM	W3IW	224.26000	-		
	FM	K3WS	224.68000	-	123.0 Hz	
Joliet	DMR/MARC	W3SC	444.40625	+	CC1	
Joliett	FM	W3SC	147.34500	+	123.0 Hz	ARCC
Joliett, Keffers Fire Tower						
	FM	K4MTP	53.05000	52.05000	131.8 Hz	ARCC
	FM	K4MTP	223.82000	-		
Julian	FM	K3HOT	443.42500	+	107.2 Hz	
Kane	FM	WB3IGM	53.47000	52.47000	173.8 Hz	
	FM	WB3IGM	146.73000	-	173.8 Hz	WPRC
Keyser Valley	FM	N3EVW-R	448.82500	-	136.5 Hz	ARCC
Kilbuck	FM	WA3RSP	53.29000	52.29000		
Kintersville	FUSION	KC1FLU	145.01000			
Kittanning	FM	K3TTK	145.41000	-	173.8 Hz	

Location	Mode	Call sign	Output	Input	Access	Coordinator
Kittanning, Armstrong Co EOC						
	FM	K3QY	443.97500	+		WPRC
Kunkletown	DMR/BM	K2ESF	443.52500	+	CC1	
Kylertown	DSTAR	W3PHB C	146.25500	+		
	DSTAR	W3PHB C	147.25500	+		
Lake Harmony	FM	N3KZ	442.10000	+	131.8 Hz	ARCC
Lake Wallenpaupack						
	FM	WA2ZPX	442.35000	+		ARCC
Lancaster	DMR/BM	W3PC	448.57500	-	CC1	
	FM	KA3CNT	449.32500	-		ARCC
Lancaster, Gap Hill						
	FM	N3EDM	449.52500	-	114.8 Hz	
Lancaster, Lancaster General H						
	FM	W3RRR	147.01500	+	118.8 Hz	ARCC
	FM	W3RRR	449.57500	-	114.8 Hz	ARCC
Lancaster, Pennsylvania						
	FM	N3FYI	224.32000	-	114.8 Hz	
	FM	N3FYI	446.47500	-	114.8 Hz	ARCC
Landisburg	DMR/MARC	N3TWT	146.68500	-	CC1	ARCC
Laporte	FM	N3XXH	145.31000	-	167.9 Hz	ARCC
Larchmont	FM	WA3NNA-R	442.60000	+		ARCC
Latrobe	FUSION	KE3PO	146.49000	147.49000		
Lawrenceville, Childrens Hospi						
	FM	KF2CHP	443.40000	+	131.8 Hz	WPRC
Lebanon	FM	W3WAN	146.88000	-	74.4 Hz	
	FM	KE3RG	147.24000	+	82.5 Hz	ARCC
	P25	K3LV	447.67500	-	82.5 Hz	ARCC
Leechburg	FM	K3QY	147.33000	+	173.8 Hz	WPRC
Lehigh Valley	FUSION	W3LUX	147.50500			
Lehigh Valley-Easton, High Ato						
	FM	N3LWY	146.65500	-	136.5 Hz	ARCC
Levittown	DMR/BM	N3JHS	430.20000	+	CC1	
	FM	N3JHS	436.00000		100.0 Hz	
	FM	N3JHS	441.20000	+	100.0 Hz	
	FM	N3JHS	446.10000	-	88.5 Hz	
Lewisburg	FM	K3FLT	146.62500	-	110.9 Hz	ARCC
Lewistown	FM	K3DNA	146.91000	-	123.0 Hz	WPRC
Lewistown, Strodes Mills, Gran						
	FM	W3DBB	145.19000	-	123.0 Hz	
Liberty	FM	WA2JOC	145.29000	-	151.4 Hz	ARCC
Lima	DSTAR	W3AEC B	440.05625	+		
	DSTAR	W3AEC A	1255.55000	+		
	DSTAR	W3AEC A	1299.90000			
	DSTAR	W3AEC D	1299.90000			
Lima, Fair Acres	DSTAR	W3AEC	440.05625	+		ARCC
	DSTAR	W3AEC	1255.55000	1275.55000		ARCC
Lititz	FM	KA3CNT	224.44000	-	131.8 Hz	ARCC
	FM	KA3CNT	449.22500	-		ARCC
Little Offset	FM	KA2QEP	448.52500	-	131.8 Hz	ARCC
Lock Haven	DMR/BM	W3LHU	146.47500	147.47500	CC1	
Lock Haven, Swissdale						
	FM	NC3PA	147.36000	+	173.8 Hz	WPRC
Loganton	FM	N3XXH	224.38000	-	85.4 Hz	
Loganton, Riansares Mountain						
	FM	NC3PA	53.77000	52.77000	85.4 Hz	
Long Branch	FM	W3RON	443.12500	+		
Long Pond	FM	KB3WW	146.44500	147.44500	131.8 Hz	ARCC
	FM	KB3WW	224.34000	-	131.8 Hz	ARCC
	FM	K4MTP	224.92000	-	127.3 Hz	ARCC
	FM	N3BUB	448.27500	-	131.8 Hz	ARCC
	FM	N3VAE	448.47500	-	123.0 Hz	ARCC

Location	Mode	Call sign	Output	Input	Access	Coordinator
Long Pond, Near The Pocono Int						
	FM	KG3I	446.57500	-	151.4 Hz	ARCC
Lower Burrell	DMR/BM	KC3QWF	146.46000	147.46000	CC1	
Luzerne Co.	FM	K3YTL	145.45000	-	82.5 Hz	
Lykens	FM	KB3VDL	449.82500	-	123.0 Hz	
Macungie	DMR/BM	WA3PNY	447.87500	+	CC2	
	FUSION	W3PLG	447.62500	-		
Manchester Beach						
		N8AD-R	147.00000			
Manheim	FM	K3IR	145.23000	-	118.8 Hz	ARCC
	FM	K3IR	449.97500	-	114.8 Hz	ARCC
	FUSION	K3LV/R	447.92500	-		
Mansfield	DMR/MARC	N3FE	441.61250	+	CC1	
	DMR/MARC	N3FE	441.71250	+	CC1	
	DMR/MARC	N3FE	444.60000	+	CC1	
Mars	FM	K3RS	224.94000	-		WPRC
Meadowbrook	FM	WA3UTI	146.71500	-	131.8 Hz	ARCC
	FM	WA3UTI	443.15000	+	131.8 Hz	ARCC
Meadville	FM	W3MIE	147.21000	+	186.2 Hz	
	FM	W3MIE	444.07500	+	186.2 Hz	
Meadville, Crawford County Fai						
	FM	W3MIE	145.13000	-	186.2 Hz	
Mechanicsburg	FM	N3TWT	443.30000	+	67.0 Hz	ARCC
	FUSION	KC3MRX	147.52500			
Mechanicsburg, Three Square Ho						
	FM	N3TWT	146.46000	147.46000	67.0 Hz	ARCC
Media	FM	W3AWA	145.23000	-	131.8 Hz	ARCC
	FM	W3AEC	146.94000	-	131.8 Hz	ARCC
Mehoopany	FM	WA3PYI	53.35000	52.35000	131.8 Hz	ARCC
Mehoopany, Forkston Mountain						
	FM	N3KZ	147.21000	+	77.0 Hz	ARCC
Meyersdale	DMR/BM	W3DCW	444.37500	+	CC1	
	FM	KK3L	224.52000	-		
	FM	N3KZ	442.20000	+	131.8 Hz	
Meyersdale, Hays Mills Fire To						
	FM	KQ3M	145.27000	-	123.0 Hz	
Middleburg	FM	K3SNY	146.82000	-	100.0 Hz	
Milford	DMR/MARC	WS2E	440.95000	+	CC1	
Milton	DMR/BM	N3NCG	445.16875	-	CC1	
	FM	K3FLT	146.98500	-	110.9 Hz	ARCC
	FM	AB3CE	444.60000	+	151.4 Hz	
Mohrsville	FUSION	NQ3U	145.15000	-		
Monongahela	FM	KA3BFI	147.22500	+		
Monroeville	FM	WA3PBD	444.00000	+	131.8 Hz	
Montoursville	DMR/BM	KB3HLL	145.49000	-	CC1	
	DMR/BM	KC3FOW	447.06000	-	CC2	
	FM	KB3DXU	443.50000	+	167.9 Hz	ARCC
Montrose	FM	K3SQO	147.52000	+		
Montrose Fairgrounds						
	FM	N3KZ	147.37500	+	77.0 Hz	ARCC
Morrisville	DMR/BM	W2FUV	145.25000	-	CC1	
	DMR/BM	WB0YLE	444.95000	+	CC1	
	DMR/BM	W2FUV	927.65000	902.65000	CC1	
	FM	WB0YLE	224.54000	-	141.3 Hz	
	FM	WR3B	447.47500	-	103.5 Hz	ARCC
	FM	WB0YLE	927.65000	902.65000	141.3 Hz	ARCC
	FUSION	WB0YLE	145.25000	-		
Mount Holly Springs						
	FM	N3TWT-L	145.43000	146.43000		
	FM	W3TWT	444.30000	+	151.4 Hz	
Mount Lebanon	FM	N3SH	146.95500	-	131.8 Hz	WPRC
	FM	N3SH	442.55000	+	131.8 Hz	

Location	Mode	Call sign	Output	Input	Access	Coordinator
Mount Pleasant	FM	KA3JSD	51.96000	-	141.3 Hz	
	FM	KA3JSD	147.01500	+	127.3 Hz	WPRC
	FM	KA3JSD	444.87500	+		
Mount Rock	FM	N3TWT-R	145.43000	-	67.0 Hz	ARCC
Mt. Pleasant	FUSION	W3SDR	145.67000			
Murrysville	FM	W3GKE	443.50000	+		
Nazareth	DSTAR	W3OK C	145.11000	-		
	DSTAR	W3OK B	445.43125	-		
	FM	W3OK	51.76000	-	151.4 Hz	ARCC
	FM	W3OK	145.11000	-		ARCC
	FM	W3OK	146.70000	-	151.4 Hz	ARCC
	FM	KB3KKZ	443.45000	+	127.3 Hz	ARCC
	FM	W3OK	444.90000	+	151.4 Hz	ARCC
New Bethlehem	FM	N3TNA	442.72500	+		
	FM	N3TNA	444.42500	+	186.2 Hz	WPRC
New Castle	DMR/BM	KB3YBB	444.02500	+	CC8	
	DSTAR	KB3YBB	443.07500	+		
	DSTAR	KB3YBB B	443.07500	+		
	FM	KC3BDF	146.62500	-	131.8 Hz	WPRC
	FM	N3ETV	147.19500	+	131.8 Hz	
	FM	K3ACS	444.17500	+	131.8 Hz	
	FM	N3ETV	444.72500	+		
New Columbia		KB3KUM-L	145.29000			
New Cumberland Reesers Summit						
	DMR/MARC	KB3TWW	146.79000	-	CC1	ARCC
New Galilee	FM	KE3ED	51.72000	-		
New Germany	DMR/BM	KC3DVR	440.85000	+	CC1	
	DMR/BM	KE3UC	444.20000	+	CC1	
	FM	KC3DES	145.21000	-	123.0 Hz	
New Holand	FUSION	K3JV	145.61000			
New Holland	FUSION	N3IXP	433.20000			
New Kensington	DMR/MARC	W3PRL	146.46000	147.46000	CC1	
	FM	N1RS	146.49000	147.49000	131.8 Hz	
	FM	K3MJW	146.64000	-	131.8 Hz	WPRC
	FM	N1RS	442.80000	-	141.3 Hz	
	FM	K3MJW	444.52500	+	131.8 Hz	
New London	FM	KB3DRX	448.97500	-	107.2 Hz	ARCC
Newmanstown	FM	N3SWH	147.28500	+	131.8 Hz	ARCC
Newport	DMR/MARC	KA0JSW	147.30000	+	CC1	
	FM	W3ND	444.55000	+	123.0 Hz	
Newtown Square	DMR/BM	WR3IRS	441.20000	+	CC1	ARCC
	FM	WB3JOE	147.06000	+	131.8 Hz	
	FM	W3DI	147.19500	+	100.0 Hz	ARCC
	FM	W3DI	442.25000	+	131.8 Hz	ARCC
NOAA Allentown	WX	WXL39	162.40000			
NOAA Altoona	WX	WNG589	162.42500			
NOAA Clearfield	WX	WXL52	162.55000			
NOAA Coatesville	WX	WNG704	162.42500			
NOAA Coudersport						
	WX	WNG591	162.50000			
NOAA Erie	WX	KEC58	162.40000			
NOAA Harrisburg	WX	WXL40	162.55000			
NOAA Honesdale	WX	WNG705	162.45000			
NOAA Huntingdon						
	WX	WWG52	162.52500			
NOAA Johnstown	WX	WXM33	162.40000			
NOAA Meadville	WX	KZZ32	162.47500			
NOAA Parker	WX	WWG53	162.42500			
NOAA Philadelphia						
	WX	KIH28	162.47500			
NOAA Pittsburgh	WX	KIH35	162.55000			

Location	Mode	Call sign	Output	Input	Access	Coordinator
NOAA Punxsutawney						
	WX	KZZ42	162.50000			
NOAA State College						
	WX	WXM59	162.47500			
NOAA Towanda	WX	WXM95	162.52500			
NOAA Warren	WX	WWG51	162.45000			
NOAA Wellsboro	WX	WXM94	162.47500			
NOAA Wilkes-Barre						
	WX	WXL43	162.55000			
NOAA Williamsport						
	WX	WXL55	162.40000			
Norristown	FM	N3CDP	223.86000	-	131.8 Hz	ARCC
	FM	N3CB	448.67500	-	131.8 Hz	ARCC
	FUSION	K3PDR	447.47500	-		
Norrisville	FM	W3MIE	147.03000	+	186.2 Hz	
North Hills	FM	W3EXW	444.40000	+	88.5 Hz	
North Washington, North Washin						
	FM	K3PSG	442.90000	+	131.8 Hz	
Northern Cambria	FM	N3LAD	443.87500	+	167.9 Hz	
Oakland	FM	WA3YOA	443.55000	+		
Oil City	DMR/BM	W3ZIC	444.12500	+	CC1	WPRC
Orson, Mount Ararat						
	FM	K4MTP	53.05000	52.05000	131.8 Hz	ARCC
Oxford	FM	W3EOC	448.87500	-	100.0 Hz	ARCC
Palmerton	DMR/MARC	W3NTT	448.62500	-	CC0	
	FM	N3DVF	224.26000	-	94.8 Hz	ARCC
Palmerton, Blue Mountain						
	FM	W3EPE	449.37500	-	131.8 Hz	ARCC
Paoli	FM	WB3JOE	145.13000	-	131.8 Hz	
Paoli, Hospital	FM	WB3JOE	445.67500	-	131.8 Hz	ARCC
Parkesburg	FM	W3GMS	146.98500	-	100.0 Hz	ARCC
	FM	KJ6AL	442.00000	+	94.8 Hz	ARCC
Pecan Grove		WB5RF-L	147.54000			
Pennfield Manor	FM	N3RZL	442.35000	+		
Pennside		N3PVZ-L	445.95000			
Perkasie	DMR/MARC	K3BUX	441.84375	+	CC1	
	FM	W3AI	145.31000	-	131.8 Hz	ARCC
Philadelphia	DMR/BM	W3PVI	145.27000	-	CC2	
	DMR/BM	AB3LI	445.97500	-	CC1	
	DMR/BM	AB3LI	446.05000	-	CC1	
	DMR/MARC	WR3IRS	440.65000	+	CC1	ARCC
	DSTAR	K3PDR C	146.61000	-		
	DSTAR	K3PDR B	445.18125	-		
	DSTAR	K3PDR B	445.18130	-		
	FM	KD3WT	145.41000	-	127.3 Hz	ARCC
	FM	WB3EHB	224.06000	-	131.8 Hz	ARCC
	FM	K3TU	224.80000	-	131.8 Hz	ARCC
	FM	K3CX	440.15000	+	100.0 Hz	ARCC
	FM	K3TU	442.80000	+	131.8 Hz	ARCC
	FM	KD3WT	446.87500	-	131.8 Hz	ARCC
	FM	W3PHL	923.25000	910.25000		ARCC
	FUSION	K3REY	146.41500			
	FUSION	K3FZT	439.75000			
	FUSION	K3FZT	444.05000	+		
Philadelphia, Roxborough Tower						
	FM	W3SBE	442.55000	+	91.5 Hz	ARCC
Philadelphia, University Of Pe						
	FM	WM3PEN	146.68500	-	146.2 Hz	ARCC
Philipsburg	DSTAR	KC3BMB	444.75000	+		
Pine Grove	FM	AA3RG	145.17000	-	110.9 Hz	ARCC
	FM	AA3RG	146.64000	-	82.5 Hz	ARCC
Pine Grove Mills	FM	K3YV	444.85000	+	100.0 Hz	

Location	Mode	Call sign	Output	Input	Access	Coordinator
Pittsburgh	DSTAR	W3EXW C	146.82000	-		
	FM	KB3CNN	444.10000	+	71.9 Hz	
	FM	W3VC	444.65000	+	131.8 Hz	
	FUSION	KC3TOI	442.75000	+		
	FUSION	NU3S	446.12500			
Pittsburgh, Carnegie Mellon Un						
	FM	W3VC	145.19000	-	131.8 Hz	
Pittsburgh, WQED TV-13 Tower						
	DSTAR	W3EXW	146.82000	-		
	FM	W3EXW	146.88000	-	88.5 Hz	
Pittston	DMR/MARC	KB3TEM	445.10000	-	CC1	
	DMR/MARC	KB3TEM	446.05000	-	CC1	
	DMR/MARC	KB3TEM	446.20000	-	CC1	
	DMR/MARC	KB3TEM	446.50000	-	CC1	
	DMR/MARC	KB3TEM	447.80000	-	CC1	
Pittston, Suscon	FM	W3RC	147.03000	+	77.0 Hz	ARCC
	FM	N3FCK	443.60000	+	100.0 Hz	
Pleasant Mount	FM	K2KQZ	53.07000	52.07000	136.5 Hz	ARCC
Pleasant Township						
	FM	W3YZR	146.97000	-	186.2 Hz	
Pleasantville	FM	W3ZIC	147.12000	+	186.2 Hz	WPRC
Plumstead	FM	N3EXA	449.72500	-	136.5 Hz	ARCC
Plumsteadville	FM	KB3AJF	447.97500	-	131.8 Hz	ARCC
Pocopson	DSTAR	W3EOC C	146.49000	147.49000		
	DSTAR	W3EOC B	445.06875	-		
	DSTAR	W3EOC	445.06875	-		
	DSTAR	W3EOC B	445.06880	-		
	DSTAR	W3EOC A	1255.50000	+		
	DSTAR	W3EOC A	1299.40000			
	DSTAR	W3EOC D	1299.50000			
	FM	W3EOC	1255.50000	1275.50000		ARCC
Port Royal, Tuscarora Mountain						
	FM	K3TAR	147.04500	+	146.2 Hz	ARCC
Portable	DMR/MARC	N3OBL	442.00000	+	CC15	
Portable Repeater	DMR/MARC	KA3LAO	442.90000	+	CC1	
Pottstown	DMR/BM	N3QAM	445.82500	-	CC1	
	DMR/BM	K3EMG	449.26875	-	CC2	
	FM	K3ZMC	224.02000	-	131.8 Hz	ARCC
	FM	KI3I	442.75000	+	141.3 Hz	ARCC
Pottsville	DMR/BM	W3TWA	442.30000	+	CC5	
	DMR/MARC	W3SC	444.39375	+	CC1	
	FM	WX3N	443.00000	+	77.0 Hz	ARCC
Pottsville, Delano	FM	W3SC	444.95000	+	123.0 Hz	
Prospect	FM	N3HWW	224.24000	-		
Punxsutawney	FM	N5NWC	146.71500	-	173.8 Hz	
	FM	N3GPM	442.47500	+		
	FM	N5NWC	443.47500	+		
Quakertown	FM	WA3IPP	146.88000	-	131.8 Hz	ARCC
	FM	WA3KEY	443.20000	+	114.8 Hz	ARCC
Quarryville	FM	N3EIO	448.17500	-	94.8 Hz	ARCC
Ransom	FM	N3EVW	53.43000	52.43000	136.5 Hz	ARCC
Rawlinsville	DMR/BM	N3TPL	448.62500	-	CC1	
	FM	WA3WPA	224.32000	-	131.8 Hz	ARCC
Reading	DMR/MARC	WR3IRS	440.80000	+	CC1	
	DMR/MARC	K3TI	444.35000	+	CC0	ARCC
	DMR/MARC	KB3WLV	445.17500	-	CC1	
	FM	KA3KDL	29.64000	-		
	FM	K3TI	145.49000	-	114.8 Hz	
	FM	KA3KDL	146.62500	-		
	FM	W3BN	146.91000	-	131.8 Hz	ARCC
	FM	K3SJH	446.92500	-	156.7 Hz	
	FM	W3MEL	448.72500	-	146.2 Hz	ARCC

Location	Mode	Call sign	Output	Input	Access	Coordinator
Reading	FM	K3CX	449.62500	-	100.0 Hz	ARCC
Reading , Mt Penn						
	FM	KB3OUC	443.97500	+	114.8 Hz	
Reading, Mount Penn						
	FM	K3TI	224.64000	-	114.8 Hz	ARCC
	FUSION	K3TI	145.49000	-	114.8 Hz	ARCC
Reading, Mt Penn	FUSION	K3TI	145.15000	-		ARCC
Reading, Mt Penn Fire Tower						
	FM	K2SEH	147.18000	+	110.9 Hz	ARCC
Red Lion	DMR/MARC	N3CNJ	448.52500	-	CC1	
	FM	W3ZGD	146.86500	-	123.0 Hz	ARCC
	FM	KA3CNT	224.84000	-	131.8 Hz	ARCC
	FM	N3NRN	449.42500	-	123.0 Hz	ARCC
Red Rock	DMR/MARC	WR3IRS	441.30000	+	CC1	
	FM	N3VTH	147.00000	+	77.0 Hz	
Reesers Summit	FM	W3ND	446.42500	-	123.0 Hz	ARCC
Richboro		KE0AFZ-L	147.60000			
	FM	WA3DSP	53.03000	52.03000	131.8 Hz	
	FM	N3TS	146.79000	+	131.8 Hz	ARCC
Richfield, Shade Mountain						
	FM	K3SNY	146.82000	-	100.0 Hz	
Ridgway	DMR/BM	K3GVH	146.55000	146.49000	CC1	
	FM	N3NIA	147.00000	+	173.8 Hz	WPRC
	FM	N3NWL	147.28500	+		
	FM	N3RZL	442.20000	+		
	FM	N3NIA	443.80000	+		
Rochester Mills	FM	KB3CNS	224.90000	-		
Rockton	DMR/BM	N3QC	442.95000	+	CC1	WPRC
	FM	KE3DR	147.39000	+	173.8 Hz	
Rockton Mtn.	DMR/MARC	WR3IRS	443.00000	+	CC1	
Rockton Mtn. VHF						
	DMR/MARC	WR3IRS	147.16500	+	CC1	
Ron - Bensalem	FM	NY3J	446.12500	-	88.5 Hz	
Ross Township	FM	N3TXG	446.22500	-	131.8 Hz	
Rossiter	FM	KE3DR	146.65500	-		
	FM	N3FXN	444.57500	+		
Roxborough	FM	W3WAN	441.70000	+	74.4 Hz	ARCC
	FUSION	W3QV	444.80000	+		ARCC
Salem MT. Wayne Co.						
	FM	K1NRA	145.11000	-	94.8 Hz	
Sandy Lake	FM	WA3NSM	443.17500	+	186.2 Hz	WPRC
Sayre	FUSION	KA3EQU	443.80000	+		
Scandia, Kinzua Reservoir						
	FM	W3GFD	444.47500	+		WPRC
Scenery Hill	FM	K3PSP	147.28500	+	131.8 Hz	
Schaefferstown	FM	N3JOZ	448.92500	-	146.2 Hz	ARCC
Schahola	FM	K3TSA	145.35000	-	100.0 Hz	ARCC
Schnecksville	DSTAR	W3EPE B	445.22500	-		
	DSTAR	W3EPE B	445.22500	-		
Schnecksville, Lehigh Career &						
	FM	K3TE	443.10000	+	131.8 Hz	
Scranton	DMR/MARC	N3MBK	441.35000	+	CC2	
	FM	K3CSG	146.94000	-	127.3 Hz	ARCC
	FM	WB3FEQ	147.28500	+	136.5 Hz	
	FM	KC3MN	224.56000	-	136.5 Hz	
Scranton(Bald MT) Lackawanna						
	FM	N3MBK	146.71500	-	136.5 Hz	
Scranton, Top Of Morgan Highwa						
	FM	N3FCK	442.55000	+	100.0 Hz	ARCC
Selinsgrove, Selinsgrove Cente						
	FM	K3SNY	147.18000	+	100.0 Hz	ARCC
Sellersville	FM	W3AI	444.75000	+	103.5 Hz	ARCC

Location	Mode	Call sign	Output	Input	Access	Coordinator
Seneca	FM	W3ZIC	145.25000	-	123.0 Hz	
Seven Fields	FUSION	W3TXG	441.02500			
Seven Springs	DMR/MARC	W3WGX	146.83500	-	CC1	WPRC
	FM	KB9WCX	443.92500	+	123.0 Hz	
Shahola Pike Co.	FM	K3TSA	145.35000	-	100.0 Hz	
Sharon, Keel Ridge						
	FM	W3LIF	145.35000	-	186.2 Hz	
Sharpsville	FM	KB3GRF	444.37500	+	186.2 Hz	
Sheffield	FM	N3KZ	442.70000	+	186.2 Hz	
Shickshinny, PA, State Game La						
	FM	N3FCK	444.50000	+	100.0 Hz	ARCC
Shohola PA Pike Co.						
	FM	K3TSA	145.35000	-	100.0 Hz	
Shohola, Walker Lake						
	FM	WB1FXX	444.32500	+	107.2 Hz	
Shrewsbury	DMR/MARC	K3AE	449.72500	-	CC1	
Sigel	FM	N3JGT	147.10500	+	173.8 Hz	
	FM	N3GPM	443.27500	+	110.9 Hz	
Slippery Rock	FM	KA3HUK	224.84000	-		
Smethport	FM	NJ3K	147.30000	+	173.8 Hz	WPRC
Smithfield	FUSION	KC3QWL	144.70000			
Somerset	FM	K3SMT	147.19500	+	123.0 Hz	
	FM	N3VFG	443.95000	+	88.5 Hz	
Souderton	FM	N3ZA	145.19000	-		ARCC
Southampton	FM	W3SK	146.79000	-	131.8 Hz	
	FUSION	W3SK	448.22500	-	131.8 Hz	ARCC
Spring Garden	FM	WB0CPR-R	449.77500	-		ARCC
Spring Grove	FM	N3TVL	53.03000	52.03000	123.0 Hz	
	FM	KB3SNM	446.30000	-	88.5 Hz	
Spring Mount Summit						
	FM	AA3RE-R	51.94000	-		ARCC
Springboro		KB3NJY-L	146.52000			
	DMR/BM	KE3JP	442.60000	+	CC8	
	FM	KF8YF	146.46000	147.46000	100.0 Hz	
Springfield Pa.	FM	AA3VZ	445.92500	-	131.8 Hz	
Springtown	FM	W3BXW	442.95000	+	131.8 Hz	ARCC
St. Thomas	DMR/MARC	KB3UAG	145.25000	-	CC1	
Stanleys Corner		KB3KBR-L	446.45000			
State College	FM	K3CR	145.45000	-	146.2 Hz	
	FM	W3GA	146.76000	-	146.2 Hz	WPRC
	FM	K3CR	443.65000	+	146.2 Hz	WPRC
State College, Black Moshannon						
	FM	N3EB	444.70000	+	114.8 Hz	WPRC
Steelton	FM	N3NJB	147.30000	+	100.0 Hz	ARCC
Stowe	FM	KB3OZC	145.25000	-	100.0 Hz	ARCC
Strattanville	FM	N3HZV	444.22500	+		
Stroudsburg	P25	N3GRQ	448.22500	-	131.8 Hz	
	P25	N3GRQ	927.22500	902.22500	131.8 Hz	
Sugar Grove	FM	W3GFD	145.11000	-	186.2 Hz	WPRC
Summerdale	FM	N3KZ	442.20000	+	131.8 Hz	ARCC
Summerdale PA	DMR/MARC	W3BXW	442.45000	+	CC1	ARCC
Summit Station, Blue Mountain						
	FM	N3TJJ	224.14000	-	114.8 Hz	
Sunbury, Areffe Knob						
	FM	KC3FIT	146.65500	-	107.2 Hz	
Susquehanna	FM	WB2BQW	145.25000	-	100.0 Hz	ARCC
Tafton	FM	K3TSA	145.49000	-	82.5 Hz	
Tannersville	FM	W3WAN	145.23000	-	77.0 Hz	ARCC
	FM	WX3OES	146.86500	-	70.0 Hz	ARCC
	FUSION	KC3NIU	146.46000			
Tannersville, Camelback Mounta						
	FM	K4MTP	53.05000	52.05000	131.8 Hz	

Location	Mode	Call sign	Output	Input	Access	Coordinator
Test Repeater	DMR/MARC	KB3TWW	444.92500	+	CC1	
Texter Mtn	FM	N3SWH	449.07500	-	131.8 Hz	ARCC
Thompson	FM	N3DUG	147.04500	+	141.3 Hz	
Thorndale	FM	AA3VI	224.36000	-	123.0 Hz	ARCC
	FM	AA3VI	447.07500	-	123.0 Hz	ARCC
Tioga, Jackson Summit						
	FM	KB3EAR	146.62500	-	131.8 Hz	ARCC
Tirzah	FM	N3DUG-L	146.74500	-		ARCC
Titusville	FM	WB3KFO	51.82000	-	82.5 Hz	WPRC
Towanda	FM	K3ABC	147.28500	+	82.5 Hz	ARCC
	FM	KB3FHS	441.85000	+	85.4 Hz	
	FM	WA3GGS	444.25000	+	151.4 Hz	ARCC
	FUSION	KB3FHS	146.45000			
	FUSION	KB3FHS	147.04000			
Towanda, Kellogg Mountain						
	FM	N3XXH	224.24000	-	85.4 Hz	
	FM	N3XXH	441.85000	+	85.4 Hz	
Trevose	FUSION	W2SRH	445.95000			
Trout Run, Shrivers Ridge						
	FM	KB3DXU	145.15000	-	167.9 Hz	ARCC
Troy	FM	KB3DOL	444.05000	+	100.0 Hz	ARCC
Tunkhannock, Forkston						
	FM	N3FCK	441.15000	+	100.0 Hz	
Tuscarora Mtn.	FM	KI3D	147.04500	+	146.2 Hz	
Ulysses	FM	KB3HJC	145.43000	-	127.3 Hz	WPRC
Union City	DMR/BM	WA3UC	441.90000	+	CC1	
	FM	WA3UC	146.70000	-	186.2 Hz	
Union Dale, Elk Mountain						
	FM	N3DUG	448.77500	-	141.3 Hz	
Union Dale, Elk Mountain Ski R						
	FM	N3KZ	145.43000	-	77.0 Hz	ARCC
Uniondale, Elk Mountain						
	FM	N3SQ	449.40000	-	127.3 Hz	
Uniontown	FM	W3PIE	147.04500	+	131.8 Hz	
	FM	W3PIE	147.25500	+		
	FM	WA3UVV	442.02500	+	131.8 Hz	WPRC
	FUSION	W3PIE	443.75000	+		
University Park	DMR/BM	N4EVA	444.00000	+	CC1	
	DSTAR	K3CR C	145.37000	-		
University Park, Penn State Un						
	DSTAR	K3CR	145.37000	-		
Upper Darby	FM	N3UXQ	145.65000		100.0 Hz	
	FM	N3UXQ	446.00000	-	100.0 Hz	
Upper Darby, Delaware Co. Memo						
	DSTAR	N3AEC	440.04375	+		ARCC
	DSTAR	N3AEC	1255.52500	1275.52500		ARCC
Upper Potsgrove	FM	W3PS	445.82500	-	156.7 Hz	ARCC
Upper Strasburg	FM	W3ACH	147.12000	+	100.0 Hz	
Utica, Western Union Tower						
	FM	KE3JP	442.60000	+		WPRC
Valley Forge	DMR/BM	WR3IRS	441.75000	+	CC1	
	DMR/MARC	WN3A	441.30000	+	CC1	
	DMR/MARC	WR3IRS	441.75000	+	CC1	
	FM	W3PHL	53.41000	52.41000	131.8 Hz	ARCC
	FM	W3PHL	146.76000	-	131.8 Hz	ARCC
	FM	W3PHL	224.94000	-	131.8 Hz	ARCC
	FM	W3PHL	919.20000	894.20000	131.8 Hz	ARCC
	FM	W3PHL	1292.00000	1272.00000	131.8 Hz	ARCC
Valley Forge, Valley Forge Mou						
	FM	W3PHL	443.90000	+		ARCC
Vowinckel	FM	N3GPM	51.70000	-	186.2 Hz	WPRC
Vowinkel	FM	N3UOH	147.07500	+	110.9 Hz	WPRC

Location	Mode	Call sign	Output	Input	Access	Coordinator
Warminster	FM	K3MFI	53.37000	52.37000	131.8 Hz	ARCC
Warminster, Township Building						
	FM	K3DN	147.09000	+	131.8 Hz	ARCC
Warren	DMR/BM	W3KKC	147.37500	+	CC1	
	DMR/BM	W3KKC	442.00000	+	CC1	
	DMR/MARC	W3KKC	145.15000	-	CC1	WPRC
	DSTAR	KB3BSA B	442.22500	-		
	FM	KB3ORS	145.27000	-	173.8 Hz	WPRC
	FM	KB3KOP	146.76000	-	186.2 Hz	
	FM	N3MWD	443.90000	+		WPRC
Warren, Hearts Content						
	FM	W3GFD	147.01500	+		
Warren, Kinzua Dam						
	DSTAR	KB3BSA	442.22500	+		
Warrington	FM	WA3ZID	147.00000	+	131.8 Hz	ARCC
Washington	FM	W3CYO	145.49000	-		
	FM	K3PSP	146.79000	-		
	FM	W3PLP	147.34500	+	131.8 Hz	
	FM	W3CYO	224.40000	-		
	FM	W3PLP	442.12500	+	131.8 Hz	
	FM	W3CYO	443.30000	+	131.8 Hz	
	FUSION	WA8JAN	147.03000	+		
Washington Crossing						
	FUSION	N3OBY	145.56250			
Waterford	FM	KE3JP	145.43000	-		
	FM	W3GV	146.82000	-	186.2 Hz	
	FM	KF8YF	443.95000	+	100.0 Hz	
Waterville, Ramsey						
	FM	KB3DXU	145.35000	-	167.9 Hz	ARCC
Waynesburg	FM	N3GC	146.43000	147.43000	131.8 Hz	WPRC
	FM	K3PSP	147.31500	+	131.8 Hz	
Wellsboro	DMR/BM	NR3K	443.85000	+	CC1	
	DMR/BM	K3LSY	446.50000	-	CC1	
	FM	NR3K	145.27000	-	127.3 Hz	ARCC
Wellsboro, Dutch Hill						
	FM	NR3K	147.06000	+	127.3 Hz	
West Alexander	FM	K3PSP	145.25000	-	131.8 Hz	
West Bradford Township						
	FUSION	K3ZA	446.07500			
West Chester	FM	W3EOC	446.52500	-	100.0 Hz	ARCC
	FUSION	W3JJI	144.60000			
West Creek	FM	N3SNN-R	147.18000	+		
West Hazleton	FM	KB3LVC	927.40000	902.40000	100.0 Hz	
West Mifflin	FM	KA3IDK	444.50000	+		
	FM	KA3IDK	444.52500	+		
	FM	KA3IDK	444.55000	+		
	FM	KA3IDK	1285.00000	1265.00000		
West Newton	FM	N3OVP	442.70000	+		
Wexford, Large Tower Northeast						
	FM	K3SAL	147.24000	+		
Whitnyville	DMR/MARC	N3FE	146.91000	-	CC1	
	DMR/MARC	N3FE	442.85000	+	CC1	
	DMR/MARC	N3FE	444.61250	+	CC1	
Widnoon	FM	K3QY	145.41000	-	173.8 Hz	WPRC
Wilkes Barre, Bunker Hill						
	FM	K3YTL	145.45000	-	82.5 Hz	ARCC
Wilkes-Barre	DMR/MARC	WR3IRS	441.75000	+	CC1	
	FM	WB3FKQ	146.61000	-	82.5 Hz	ARCC
	FM	N3KZ	442.20000	+	131.8 Hz	ARCC
	FM	WB3FKQ	927.81250	902.81250	82.5 Hz	
Wilkes-Barre, Bear Creek						
	FM	N3FCK	146.46000	147.46000	100.0 Hz	ARCC

Location	Mode	Call sign	Output	Input	Access	Coordinator
Wilkes-Barre, Penobscot Knob						
	FM	N3DAP	224.42000	-	94.8 Hz	ARCC
Williamsburg	DMR/BM	WO3T	442.60000	+	CC1	
Williamsport	DMR/BM	KB3HLL	147.09000	+	CC1	
	DMR/BM	KB3HLL	443.05000	+	CC1	
	FM	KB3AWQ	29.66000	-	173.8 Hz	
	FM	KB3AWQ-L	52.49000		173.8 Hz	
	FM	W3AHS	147.30000	+	151.4 Hz	
	FM	N3XXH	224.28000	-	85.4 Hz	ARCC
	FM	KB3AWQ-R	444.90000	+	173.8 Hz	
	FM	N3SSL	927.03750	902.03750		
	FM	NC3PA	927.03750	902.03750		
Williamsport, Armstrong Mounta						
	FM	W3SC	53.31000	52.31000	123.0 Hz	
Williamsport, Bald Eagle Mount						
	FM	KB3DXU	145.33000	-	167.9 Hz	ARCC
	FM	WX3N	443.20000	+	77.0 Hz	ARCC
Willimsport	DMR/BM	W3AVK	444.00000	+	CC1	
Wind Gap	FM	N3MSK	53.29000	52.29000		ARCC
	FM	KA3HJW	443.70000	+	151.4 Hz	ARCC
	FM	W3BXW	447.57500	-	131.8 Hz	ARCC
	FM	KC2IRV	449.87500	-	131.8 Hz	
Windber	FM	N3LZV	443.15000	+	123.0 Hz	
Wooddale	FM	N3JNZ	448.37500	-	91.5 Hz	ARCC
Wyncote	FM	N3FSC	224.38000	-	107.2 Hz	ARCC
Wyndmoor	DMR/BM	K3PDR	447.62500	-	CC1	
	DSTAR	K3PDR	146.61000	-		
	DSTAR	K3PDR	445.18125	-		
	FM	K3PDR	447.47500	-		
Yardley	FUSION	KB3BB	146.48000			
Yeadon	DMR/BM	N3UXQ	440.35000	+	CC1	
York	DMR/BM	W3HZU	447.27500	-	CC1	
	DMR/MARC	WR3IRS	441.15000	+	CC1	
	FM	W3HZU	53.97000	52.97000	127.3 Hz	ARCC
	FM	N3KZ	442.05000	+	131.8 Hz	ARCC
	FM	W3SBA	444.25000	+	146.2 Hz	
	FM	KC3HOZ	446.10000	-		
York, Rocky Ridge County Park						
	FM	W3HZU	146.97000	-	123.0 Hz	ARCC
Youngsville	FM	N3MTX	146.43500			
	FM	W3GFD	442.07500	+	186.2 Hz	WPRC
PUERTO RICO						
Adjuntas	FM	KP4ST	147.35000	+	127.3 Hz	
Adjuntas, Cerro Cerca Del Ciel						
	FM	KP4NET	448.60000	-	123.0 Hz	WIRCI
Aguada	FM	KP4MPR	146.57000		100.0 Hz	
	FM	WP4S	147.03000	+		
Aguada, Atalaya	FM	WP3OF	449.02500	-		
Aguadilla	FM	KP4IP	146.45000		100.0 Hz	
	FM	WP4LHN	146.47000		100.0 Hz	
	FM	WP4DYV	146.57000		100.0 Hz	
	FM	KP4BAI	447.83750	-	77.0 Hz	WIRCI
Aguas Buenas	FM	WP4OCD	145.23000	-	77.0 Hz	
	FM	KP4RF	145.45000	-		
	FM	WP4JLH	146.73000	-	123.0 Hz	
	FM	KP4CK	146.85000	-	127.3 Hz	
	FM	WP4YF	447.17500	-	127.3 Hz	WIRCI
	FM	WP4YF	449.17500	-	127.3 Hz	WIRCI
	FM	WP4YF	449.90000	-		WIRCI
Aguas Buenas, Cerro Marquesa						
	FM	KP3BR	447.22500	-	77.0 Hz	WIRCI

Location	Mode	Call sign	Output	Input	Access	Coordinator
Aguas Buenas, La Mesa						
	FM	KP4RF	447.60000	-		WIRCI
Anasco	FM	WP4OYM	447.50000	-	100.0 Hz	
Arroyo	FM	KP4KGZ	447.15000	-	107.2 Hz	WIRCI
Bajadero	FM	KP3JD	449.21250	-	100.0 Hz	WIRCI
Barranquitas	FM	KP4RF	145.41000	-	127.3 Hz	
	FM	KP3AJ	147.33000	+	151.4 Hz	
	FM	KP4LP	224.08000	-		
	FM	KP4LP	447.25000	-		
	FM	WP4YF	447.65000	-	136.5 Hz	
	FM	NP3EF	448.77500	-	67.0 Hz	WIRCI
Bayamon	DMR/BM	KP3AJ	447.80000	-	CC0	WIRCI
	FM	WP3BM	51.62000	50.62000	136.5 Hz	
	FM	KP4ZZ	440.17500	+	141.3 Hz	
	FM	KP3ZZ	447.12500	-	94.8 Hz	
	FM	WP4O	448.07500	-		WIRCI
	FM	WP4F	448.22500	-		WIRCI
	FM	KP4CB	448.45000	-	88.5 Hz	WIRCI
	FM	KP3CB	448.47500	-	88.5 Hz	WIRCI
	FM	NP3A	448.68750	51.31250	100.0 Hz	WIRCI
	FM	KP4FHT	449.17500	-	123.7 Hz	WIRCI
	FM	WP4XI	449.60000	-	100.0 Hz	
	FM	WP4KMB	449.62500	-	250.3 Hz	WIRCI
	FM	WP4KMB	449.65000	-		
	FM	KP4XC	449.67500	-		
	FM	WP4MXY	449.90000	-		
Beatriz	FM	KP4LDR	449.22500	-		WIRCI
Boqueron	FM	KC2EMM	445.50000	-	100.0 Hz	
Botijas	FM	WP3OF	449.02500	-		WIRCI
Cabo Rojo	FM	WP4MVW	146.58000		100.0 Hz	
	FUSION	WP3PZ	146.56000			
Caguas	FM	KP3AB	145.19000	-	123.0 Hz	WIRCI
	FM	KP3AB	146.73000	-	123.0 Hz	WIRCI
	FM	KP3AB	223.98000	-	123.0 Hz	WIRCI
	FM	KP3AB	224.02000	-	123.0 Hz	WIRCI
	FM	KP4NB	224.10000	-		
	FM	NP4H	224.98000	-		
	FM	WP4FMX	447.90000	-		
	FM	KP3AB	927.10000	902.10000		
Camuy	FUSION	KP4VET	433.00000			
Camuy, Quebrada						
	FM	KP4EYT	449.30000	-	123.0 Hz	WIRCI
Canaovamas	FM	KP4HL	447.56250	-	100.0 Hz	WIRCI
Canovanas	FM	WP4JP	147.17000	+		
	FM	KP4LO	147.23000	+		
	FM	KP4IN	224.18000	-		
	FM	NP3FV	449.37500	-		
	FM	NP4HV	449.86250	-		WIRCI
	FM	WP3OF	449.91250	-		WIRCI
Carolina	FM	WP4BVS	224.06000	-		
	FM	NP4VG	224.16000	-		
	FM	WP4N	224.22000	-		
	FM	KP4PR	448.27500	-	127.3 Hz	
Cayey	FM	KP4ID	147.09000	+	127.3 Hz	
	FM	KP4GE	223.94000	-		
	FM	KP3AB	223.98000	-		
	FM	NP4H	224.86000	-		
	FM	WP4MXB	447.37500	-		WIRCI
	FM	KP4LST	448.57500	-	225.7 Hz	WIRCI
	FM	KP4LDR	449.22500	-	110.9 Hz	
	FM	KP4ZZ	449.30000	-	127.3 Hz	
	FM	KP3AB	449.97500	-		

Location	Mode	Call sign	Output	Input	Access	Coordinator
Cayey, Puerto Rico						
	DSTAR	WP4MXB	1293.00000	1273.00000		
Ceiba	FM	WP4DE	448.55000	-		
Ciales	FM	KP3AB	145.35000	-	123.0 Hz	
Cidra	FM	KP4QW	147.37000	+		WIRCI
Corozal	FM	KP3AV	29.66000	-		
	FM	WP3XH	146.61000	-	151.4 Hz	
	FM	NP4CB	224.30000	-		
	FM	KP4DH	224.46000	-		
	FM	KP4DH	447.35000	-	100.0 Hz	WIRCI
	FM	WP4AIX	447.50000	-		
	FM	KP3I	447.70000	-	151.4 Hz	
	FM	KP4AOB	447.95000	-		
	FM	WP4Q	448.47500	-	88.5 Hz	WIRCI
	FM	WPEOF	449.02500	-	100.0 Hz	WIRCI
Fajardo	FM	KP3AB	145.19000	-	100.0 Hz	
	FM	WP3CB	145.25000	-	88.5 Hz	
	FM	NP3CB	145.47000	-		
	FM	NP3H	146.69000	-		
	FM	KP4FGL	147.27000	146.77000	127.3 Hz	WIRCI
	FM	NP3H	224.24000	-		
	FM	KP4MTG	448.05000	-	127.3 Hz	WIRCI
	FM	NP3H	448.25000	-		
	FM	KP4GX	448.72500	-	151.4 Hz	
	FM	WP4MQZ	449.50000	5.00000		WIRCI
Guayama	FM	KP4QI	146.83000	-	136.5 Hz	WIRCI
	FM	KP4FRA	448.40000	-	123.0 Hz	WIRCI
	FM	KP4JMT	448.68750	51.31250		WIRCI
Guaynabo	FM	KP4GA	51.82000	-		WIRCI
	FM	KP4CE	147.27000	+		
	FM	KP4KA	224.58000	-		
	FM	KP4XK	449.82500	-		
	FUSION	KP4GA	447.85000	-		
Gurabo	FM	KP4FAK	145.31000	-		
	FM	WP4LXE	146.79000	-		
	FM	WP4B	146.95000	-	127.3 Hz	
	FM	WP4KAG	449.00000	-		
Hacienda Llanada	FM	KP3JD	448.26250	-	100.0 Hz	WIRCI
Hatillo	FUSION	WP4CRG	448.30000	-		
Humacao	FM	WP4GUL	224.52000	-		
	FM	NP3CP	448.78750	-		WIRCI
	FM	KP4BW	449.63750	-		WIRCI
Isabela	DSTAR	WP4QYG	447.50000	-		WIRCI
	FM	WP4MMR	447.40000	-	100.0 Hz	
	FM	KP4MSR	447.55000	-	127.3 Hz	
Jayuya	FM	NP4A	145.29000	-	136.5 Hz	WIRCI
	FM	KP4ILO	146.75000	-		
	FM	NP3H	146.99000	-		
	FM	WP4IFU	147.15000	+	100.0 Hz	
	FM	KP4IN	147.25000	+		
	FM	KP4IN	224.04000	-		
	FM	KP4PK	224.42000	-		
	FM	WP4AZT	447.05000	-	127.3 Hz	
	FM	KP4PK	447.17500	-		
	FM	WP4CBC	447.72500	-		
	FM	KP3AJ	447.80000	-	136.5 Hz	
	FM	WP4CRG	448.30000	-	100.0 Hz	
	FM	KP4SA	448.37500	-	123.0 Hz	WIRCI
	FM	WP4AZT	448.50000	-	127.3 Hz	
	FM	KP4IS	448.52500	-		
	FM	KP4CAR	449.80000	-		WIRCI
	FM	WP4MJP	449.85000	-		

Location	Mode	Call sign	Output	Input	Access	Coordinator
Juana Diaz	FM	WP4CBC	449.82500	-	100.0 Hz	WIRCI
	FM	KP4LRL	449.87500	-	110.9 Hz	
Juncos	FM	KP4IJ	224.38000	-		
	FM	KP4GX	447.47500	-		
Lajas, PR	FM	WP4FD	440.20000	+		WIRCI
Lares	FM	KP4ARN	146.79000	-	79.7 Hz	
	FM	NP3AB	447.87500	-	74.4 Hz	WIRCI
	FM	KP4EML	449.66250	-	199.0 Hz	WIRCI
Las Marias	FUSION	KP4UVA	449.10625			
Las Piedras	FM	WP4OCK	146.65000	-	114.8 Hz	WIRCI
	FM	KP4EGM	448.12500	-	123.0 Hz	WIRCI
	FM	WP4OCK	449.52500	-	114.8 Hz	WIRCI
Las Piedras Pr	FUSION	WP4PZL	434.00000			
Luquillo	FM	NP4ZB	51.72000	50.72000		
	FM	NP3EF	147.35000	+		
	FM	WP4NPX	447.02500	-	136.5 Hz	
	FM	WP3HY	447.90000	-	100.0 Hz	
Manati	FM	KP4PG	224.90000	-		
Maricao	FM	KP3AB	146.77000	-	123.0 Hz	WIRCI
	FM	KP4BKY	146.87000	-		
	FM	KP4FRA	146.93000	-	136.5 Hz	
	FM	WP4CPV	147.07000	+	146.2 Hz	
	FM	WP4CPV	147.23000	+	146.2 Hz	
	FM	KP3AB	224.92000	-		
	FM	KP4UK	447.55000	-		
	FM	KP4NIN	449.77500	-	123.0 Hz	WIRCI
Maricao, Monte Del Estado						
	FM	KP4SE	147.29000	+	127.3 Hz	
Maricao, Monte Del Estado, Pue						
	FM	KP4SE	448.97500	443.87500	136.5 Hz	
Mayaguez	FM	KP4AIC	146.69000	-	88.5 Hz	
	FM	WP3L	147.13000	+	100.0 Hz	WIRCI
	FM	WP3L	432.17500		100.0 Hz	
	FM	KP4RDL	445.45000	-	100.0 Hz	
	FM	WP4MPR	447.92500	-	107.2 Hz	
	FM	WP3L	448.65000	-	100.0 Hz	WIRCI
Mayaguez, Monte Del Estado						
	FM	KP4IP	147.13000	+	100.0 Hz	WIRCI
	FM	KP4IP	448.65000	-	100.0 Hz	WIRCI
Moca	FM	KP4KJI	145.17000	-	114.8 Hz	
	FM	KP4RS	447.63750	-	88.5 Hz	WIRCI
Moca, Cordillera Jaicoa Moca						
	FM	KP4JED	447.63750	-	88.5 Hz	
Morovis	FM	WP4KY	145.76000		100.0 Hz	
Naguabo	FM	KP4EMS	447.78750	-	136.5 Hz	WIRCI
Naranjito	FM	WP4FHR	147.01000	+		
	FM	WP4NPC	147.23000	+		
	FM	KP4FO	224.50000	-		
	FM	KP4AMV	448.80000	-	136.5 Hz	WIRCI
	FM	WP4FUI	449.92500	-	179.9 Hz	
Orocovis	FM	KP4OG	145.39000	-	94.8 Hz	
	FM	KP4DEU	146.71000	-	88.5 Hz	
	FM	KP4BCQ	147.39000	+		
	FM	NP4TX	447.32500	-	136.5 Hz	
	FM	KP4FRE	447.52500	-	136.5 Hz	
	FM	KP3JD	449.25000	-	100.0 Hz	
Patillas	FM	KP4KGZ	447.15000	-	107.2 Hz	
Penuelas	FM	WP4MXM	146.45000		88.5 Hz	
	FM	KP4EEC	147.42500		100.0 Hz	
Ponce	FM	KP4EGY	51.72000	-		WIRCI
	FM	NP3SE	147.29000	+	127.3 Hz	WIRCI
	FM	WP4JLQ	147.39000	+		

Location	Mode	Call sign	Output	Input	Access	Coordinator
Ponce	FM	KP4EGY	448.17500	-		WIRCI
	FM	KP4PSA	448.37500	-	123.0 Hz	WIRCI
	FM	WP4NQR	448.82500	-		WIRCI
	FM	NP3SE	448.97500	-	123.0 Hz	WIRCI
	FM	KP4GBF	449.10000	-		
	FM	KP4ASD	449.15000	-	110.9 Hz	WIRCI
	FM	KP4KC	449.35000	-	123.0 Hz	WIRCI
	FM	KP4ALT	449.58750	-	100.0 Hz	WIRCI
	FM	KP4EGY	449.70000	-		WIRCI
	FM	KP4KC	449.72500	-	123.0 Hz	WIRCI
	IDAS	NP3WP	449.55000	-	127.3 Hz	
	FUSION	WP4JOT	446.00000			
Quebradillas	FM	WP3OF	146.87000	-		
Rio Grande	FM	NP3CB	145.25000	-	88.5 Hz	WIRCI
	FM	KP4FRA	146.93000	-		
	FM	NP3H	146.99000	-		
	FM	NP4SB	147.03000	+	151.4 Hz	
	FM	NP3EF	147.31000	+	88.5 Hz	
	FM	NP3CB	224.70000	-		
	FM	KP4SQ	447.37500	-		
	FM	KB9EZX	448.15000	-	100.0 Hz	WIRCI
	FM	WP4FWN	449.27500	-		
	FM	NP3EF	449.75000	-	100.0 Hz	
Rio Piedras	FM	WP4MQQ	449.52500	-		
Roncador Utuado	FM	WP3OF	447.57500	-		WIRCI
Salinas	FM	WP4NVY	448.02500	-	173.8 Hz	
	FM	WP4NWR	448.85000	-	100.0 Hz	WIRCI
	FM	WP4NZE	449.32500	-	123.0 Hz	
San Antonio	FM	KP4PMD	448.83750	-	127.3 Hz	WIRCI
San German	FM	NP3WP	224.08000	-	136.5 Hz	WIRCI
	FM	WP4GAV	448.32500	-	100.0 Hz	
San Juan	FM	KP4FAK	147.39000	+		
	FM	WP4BFC	224.66000	-		
	FM	KP4ZZ	440.12500	+	127.3 Hz	
	FM	WP4GZO	447.35000	-		
	FM	WP4FAE	449.05000	-	127.3 Hz	WIRCI
	FM	WP4PO	449.07500	-	131.8 Hz	WIRCI
	FM	NP3A	449.17500	-		
	FM	WP4POX	449.58750	-		WIRCI
	FM	KP4AIC	449.72500	-		
	FM	N1TKK	449.95000	-		
	FUSION	KP4RMG	446.85000			
	FUSION	WP4X	448.42500	-		
San Juan, Cerro Collores						
	FM	KP4MCR	146.89000	-		WIRCI
San Lorenzo	FM	WP4LTR	147.03000	+		
	FM	KP4YS	447.55000	-	100.0 Hz	
	FM	WP4KZ	448.03750	-	123.0 Hz	WIRCI
	FM	WP4MHS	448.45000	-		
San Patricio	FM	WP4POX	449.95000	-	123.0 Hz	WIRCI
San Sebastian	FM	NP4LW	51.74000	-		WIRCI
	FM	WP4HVS	147.29000	+	123.0 Hz	
	FM	NP4LW	447.42500	-		WIRCI
	FM	WP4HVS	449.45000	-		
	FUSION	NP4PC	449.73750	-		
San Sebastian , Colinas Verdes						
	FM	NP4PC	449.73750	-	88.5 Hz	
Santa Isabel	FM	KP4VY	448.92500	-	91.5 Hz	WIRCI
Santo Domingo	FM	KP4IP	146.55000	-	100.0 Hz	
Toa Alta	FM	WP4MLC	224.30000	-	100.0 Hz	WIRCI
	FM	WP4BCK	224.34000	-		
	FM	WP4MLC	448.13750	-	100.0 Hz	WIRCI

Location	Mode	Call sign	Output	Input	Access	Coordinator
Toa Alta	FM	KP4KC	449.35000	-	123.0 Hz	
Toa Baja	FM	WP3ZQ	145.27000	-		
	FM	WP3TM	447.27500	-	100.0 Hz	
	FM	WP3DN	448.18750	-	136.5 Hz	WIRCI
Utuado	FM	KP4CD	145.43000	-	127.3 Hz	
	FM	NP4PS	449.40000	-	67.0 Hz	
Vega Alta	FM	KP3JD	146.71000	-	88.5 Hz	
	FM	KP3JD	448.26250	-	100.0 Hz	WIRCI
Vieques	FM	NP3MR	448.62500	-		
Villalba	FM	KP3AB	145.19000	-	136.5 Hz	
	FM	WP4IZI	146.41000	-		
	FM	NP4WI	146.97000	-	127.3 Hz	
	FM	WP4AZT	147.05000	+	127.3 Hz	
	FM	KP3AB	224.02000	-		
	FM	KP4FRA	448.40000	-	136.5 Hz	
	FM	KP4JDV	449.63750	-	123.0 Hz	WIRCI
Villlalba	FM	KP3AB	448.10000	-	123.0 Hz	WIRCI
Yabucoa	FM	WP4BV	145.33000	-		
	FM	KP4DMR	447.41250	-	123.0 Hz	WIRCI
	FM	KP4MCR	447.62500	-		
	FM	KP4DDF	447.67500	-	100.0 Hz	
	FM	KH2RU	447.82500	-		
	FM	WP4BV	448.35000	-		
Yauco	FM	NP4QH	147.07000	+		
	FM	KP3AB	147.35000	+		
Yauco, Monte Alto De La Bander						
	FM	KP4ILO	145.47000	-		WIRCI
	FM	KP4KJI	448.20000	-	100.0 Hz	WIRCI

RHODE ISLAND

Location	Mode	Call sign	Output	Input	Access	Coordinator
Barrington	FUSION	N1TOQ	437.00000			
Bristol	DMR/MARC	K1CW	145.33000	-	CC2	
	FM	K1CW	443.15000	+	94.8 Hz	
Coventry	FM	N1JBC	147.16500	+	67.0 Hz	
	FM	KA1ABI	223.90000	-		
Cranston	DSTAR	KB1TIA	145.40000	144.60000		
	FM	K1CR	146.70000	-		
	FM	N1NTP	147.28000	+	67.0 Hz	
Cumberland	DMR/BM	W1DMR	146.62500	-	CC0	
	FM	NB1RI	145.17000	-	67.0 Hz	
	FM	KR1RI	146.94000	-	67.0 Hz	
	FM	W1DMR	927.67500	902.07500		NESMC
	NXDN	KB1ISZ	146.44000	144.94000		
East Providence	FM	W1AQ	147.33000	+	173.8 Hz	
Exeter	FM	NB1RI	146.98500	-	67.0 Hz	
Foster	FM	NB1RI	146.91000	-	67.0 Hz	NESMC
	FM	KB1TUG	444.40000	+	67.0 Hz	
Fruit Hill	FM	N1JBC-R	449.22500	-		
Greenville	FM	N1MIX	53.87000	52.87000	85.4 Hz	
	FM	N1MIX	146.85000	-	67.0 Hz	
	FM	N1MIX	448.07500	-		
	FM	N1MIX	927.82500	902.82500		
Hope	FM	KR1RI-R	146.76000	-		
Johnston	DMR/MARC	W1OP	447.72500	-	CC2	
	FM	KB1TOT	146.83500	-		
	FM	W1OP	223.98000	-		
Kingston	DMR/MARC	KA1REO	446.52500	-	CC1	
Lime Rock		K1RSR-R	449.32500			
Lincoln	FM	NB1RI	146.46000	144.96000	67.0 Hz	
	FM	N1BS	224.62000	-	67.0 Hz	NESMC
	FM	K1RSR	447.77500	-	67.0 Hz	
Newport	FM	WC1R	146.88000	-	100.0 Hz	

Location	Mode	Call sign	Output	Input	Access	Coordinator
Newport	FM	KC2GDF	448.32500	-	67.0 Hz	
NOAA Providence	WX	WXJ39	162.40000			
North Providence	DMR/MARC	N1JBC	145.37000	-	CC2	
	FM	NB1RI	224.56000	-		
	FM	N1JBC	224.92000	-		
	FM	KA1EZH	927.76250	902.76250	67.0 Hz	
	FUSION	W1RAC	145.51000			
North Smithfield	FUSION	KC1PHW	444.05000			
Portsmouth	DSTAR	W1AAD C	145.30000	-		
	FM	NB1RI	53.17000	52.17000	67.0 Hz	
	FM	W1AAD	145.30000	-		NESMC
	FM	W1SYE	145.45000	-	100.0 Hz	NESMC
	FM	NB1RI	147.07500	+	67.0 Hz	
Providence	FM	N1BS	29.64000	-	67.0 Hz	NESMC
	FM	N1BS	145.35000	-	67.0 Hz	NESMC
	FM	N1RWX	147.12000	+	67.0 Hz	
	FM	N1RWX	444.20000	+	88.5 Hz	
	FM	N1MIX	446.77500	-	146.2 Hz	
	FM	K1CR	448.92500	-	88.5 Hz	
	FM	N1RWX	927.51250	902.51250	127.3 Hz	
Rumford	FUSION	KA1TNV	144.97500			
Saunderstown	FM	K1NQG	146.71500	-	67.0 Hz	
Scituate	FM	KB1NZZ	53.55000	52.55000	203.5 Hz	
	FM	K1KYI	223.76000	-		
Smithfield	DMR/MARC	KB1ISZ	446.42500	-	CC1	
Warwick		KA1MXL-L	145.00000			
	DMR/BM	KA1MXL	433.10000	432.10000	CC8	
	DMR/BM	KA1MXL	434.20000	+	CC4	
	DMR/BM	WA1OKB	442.55000	+	CC1	
	DMR/BM	KA1MXL	444.83750	+	CC1	
	DMR/MARC	KA1MXL	433.50000	+	CC2	
	DMR/MARC	KA1MXL	443.44500	441.44500	CC12	
	FM	KA1MXL	53.58000	52.58000	141.3 Hz	
	FM	KA1LMX	223.92000	-		
	FM	KA1MXL	446.20000	-	100.0 Hz	
	FM	WA1ABC	447.02500	-	67.0 Hz	
	FM	WA1ABC	927.75000	902.05000	67.0 Hz	
West Greenwich	DMR/BM	K1EWG	448.82500	-	CC2	
	FM	KA1RCI	449.32500	-	127.3 Hz	
	FM	W1WNS	449.93750	-		
West Warwick	DSTAR	W1HDN	147.04500	+		
	FM	W1RI	145.13000	-	77.0 Hz	
	FM	K1WYC	224.30000	-	100.0 Hz	
	FM	KA1SOO	224.76000	-		
	FUSION	N1GMB	145.70000			
West Warwick, Court House						
	FM	KC1DGM	446.72500	-	100.0 Hz	
Westerly	FM	N1LMA	147.24000	+	100.0 Hz	
	FM	W1WRI	147.31500	+	110.9 Hz	
	FM	NB1RI	147.39000	+	67.0 Hz	
	FM	N1LMA	224.98000	-	136.5 Hz	
	FM	N1LMA	449.67500	-	127.3 Hz	

SOUTH CAROLINA

Location	Mode	Call sign	Output	Input	Access	Coordinator
Abbeville	DMR/BM	N4VDE	443.97500	+	CC1	
Aiken	DMR/BM	N2ZZ	443.46250	+	CC1	SERA - SC
	DSTAR	KR4AIK C	145.16000	-		
	DSTAR	KR4AIK B	443.41250	+		
	FM	W4ZKM	145.45000	-	123.0 Hz	
	FM	N4ADM	147.28500	+	100.0 Hz	
	FM	WR4SC	441.52500	+	91.5 Hz	SERA - SC

Location	Mode	Call sign	Output	Input	Access	Coordinator
Aiken Regional Med Ctr						
	FM	N2ZZ-R	145.35000	-	156.7 Hz	
Aiken, Old Aiken Hospital						
	DSTAR	KR4AIK	145.16000	-		
	DSTAR	KR4AIK	443.41250	+		
Anderson	DMR/MARC	N4LRD	444.53750	+	CC1	
Anderson, Anderson Memorial Ho						
	FM	N4AW	146.97000	-		SERA - SC
Anderson, Anmed Hospital						
	FM	KB4JDH	442.82500	+	127.3 Hz	SERA - SC
Awendaw	DSTAR	KR4CHS C	145.12000	-		
Aynor	FM	WR4SC	146.71500	-	162.2 Hz	
	FM	NE4SC	147.09000	+	123.0 Hz	SERA - SC
	FM	WR4SC	441.67500	+	162.2 Hz	SERA - SC
Back Swamp	FM	W4APE-L	442.05000	+		SERA - SC
Bamberg	FM	WB4TGK	145.33000	-	156.7 Hz	
Barnwell	DMR/MARC	WR4SC	440.68750	+	CC1	SERA - SC
	FM	KK4BQ	147.03000	+	156.7 Hz	SERA - SC
	FM	WR4SC	442.00000	+	91.5 Hz	
	FM	KK4BQ	449.25000	-	156.7 Hz	
Barrell Landing		AI4HH-L	147.55000			
Beach Island	DMR/MARC	WR4SC	444.28750	+	CC1	SERA - SC
Beaufort	DMR/MARC	WR4SC	441.98750	+	CC1	
	DSTAR	KJ4LNJ C	145.48000	-		
	FM	W4BFT	145.13000	-	88.5 Hz	SERA - SC
Beaufort, Beaufort Memorial Ho						
	FM	W4BFT	443.85000	+	123.0 Hz	SERA - SC
Beaufort, WJWJ	FM	W4BFT	146.65500	-		SERA - SC
Beech Island	DSTAR	KM4LOD C	145.26000	-		
	DSTAR	KM4LOD B	440.55000	+		
	FM	WR4SC	147.34500	+	91.5 Hz	
	FM	WR4SC	443.12500	+	91.5 Hz	
Bennettsville	FM	KG4HIE	443.00000	+	123.0 Hz	
Blacksburg, Whitacker Mtn						
	FM	KF4SCG	442.62500	+	107.2 Hz	
Blacksburg, Whitaker Mountain						
	FM	W4NYR	146.88000	-		
	FM	W4NYR	444.32500	+		
Bluffton	FM	W4IAR	442.67500	+	100.0 Hz	
Bowman	FUSION	KM4GMG	145.56250			
Caesar's Head Mountain						
	FM	WR4SC	145.13000	-	123.0 Hz	
	FM	K4ECG	443.12500	+	123.0 Hz	
Caesars Head		WX4PG-R	442.40000			
Calhoun Falls	FM	KI4CCZ	444.00000	+	118.8 Hz	SERA - SC
	FM	KI4CCZ	444.57500	+	103.5 Hz	SERA - SC
Cayce	DMR/MARC	W4EAE	433.10000	+	CC1	
Chapin	FM	N3RAD	147.36000		100.0 Hz	
Charleston	DMR/MARC	WR4SC	443.03750	+	CC1	SERA - SC
	DMR/MARC	K4IUG	443.45000	+	CC1	
	DSTAR	KR4CHS	145.12000	-		
	DSTAR	W4HRS	145.16000	-		
	DSTAR	W4HRS C	145.16000	-		
	DSTAR	W4HRS	444.11250	+		
	DSTAR	W4HRS B	444.11250	+		
	FM	WR4SC	146.76000	-	123.0 Hz	
	FM	WR4SC	147.10500	+	123.0 Hz	
	FM	WR4SC	441.57500	+	123.0 Hz	
	FM	WR4SC	441.72500	+	123.0 Hz	
	FM	W4HRS	444.77500	+	123.0 Hz	
Charleston, Adams Run						
	FM	W4ANK	147.34500	+	123.0 Hz	

Location	Mode	Call sign	Output	Input	Access	Coordinator
Charleston, Rutledge Tower (MU						
	FM	W4HRS	145.45000	-	123.0 Hz	
	FM	W4HRS	444.82500	+	123.0 Hz	
Charleston, Tree Top						
	FM	K4IUG	443.37500	+	100.0 Hz	SERA - SC
Charleston, USS Yorktown						
	FM	WA4USN	146.79000	-	123.0 Hz	
Cheraw	FM	W4APE	145.49000	-	123.0 Hz	SERA - SC
	FM	K4CCC	147.13500	+	123.0 Hz	
	FM	KG4HIE	444.37500	+	91.5 Hz	
Chester	FM	W4CHR-R	145.31000	-	167.9 Hz	SERA - SC
	FM	KW4BET-R	442.47500	+	162.2 Hz	SERA - SC
Clemson	DMR/MARC	K4BAN	442.23750	+	CC1	
	DMR/MARC	K4BAN	444.62500	+	CC1	
	DSTAR	WD4EOG	444.22500	+		
	DSTAR	WD4EOG B	444.22500	+		
Clemson, Clemson University						
	FM	WD4EOG	145.45000	-		SERA - SC
	FM	WD4EOG	444.62500	+	156.7 Hz	SERA - SC
Clemson, Kite Hill - WSBF-FM						
	FM	WD4EOG	147.38250	+	123.0 Hz	
	FM	WD4EOG	444.38750	+		
Clover	FM	KC4KPJ	443.72500	+		SERA - SC
Colony Subdivision						
	FM	W4IPT	146.61000	-		SERA - SC
Columbia	DMR/MARC	WR4SC	440.61250	+	CC1	SERA - SC
	DMR/MARC	WR4SC	442.51250	+	CC1	
	DSTAR	KJ4FCS	145.38000	-		SERA - SC
	DSTAR	KJ4FCS C	145.38000	-		
	DSTAR	KJ4BWK C	145.40000	-		
	DSTAR	KJ4FCS	442.77500	+		
	DSTAR	KJ4FCS B	442.77500	+		
	DSTAR	KJ4BWK B	443.20000	+		
	DSTAR	W4CAE	443.20000	+		
	DSTAR	KJ4BWK D	1253.00000			
	DSTAR	KJ4FCS A	1284.00000	-		
	DSTAR	KJ4BWK A	1284.22500	+		
	DSTAR	W4CAE	1284.22500	1264.22500		
	FM	KJ4BWK	145.40000	144.60000		
	FM	WR4SC	146.71500	-	91.5 Hz	
	FM	W4CAE	147.33000	+	156.7 Hz	SERA - SC
	FM	K4HI	147.36000	+	100.0 Hz	SERA - SC
	FM	WR4SC	441.72500	+	91.5 Hz	
	FM	N7GZT	442.20000	+		
	FM	N5CWH	444.20000	+		
	FM	K9OH	444.87500	+	91.5 Hz	SERA - SC
	FM	N5CWH	927.63750	902.63750		
	FUSION	W4EAE	147.36000	+		
Conway	DMR/MARC	NE4SC	443.66250	+	CC1	
	DSTAR	NE4SC	144.98000	147.48000		
	DSTAR	NE4SC	442.78750	+		
	FM	W4GS	145.11000	-	85.4 Hz	
	FM	AA2UC	443.80000	+	141.3 Hz	
	FM	W4GS	444.67500	+	85.4 Hz	
	FUSION	KD2OJQ	147.52500			
Darlington	FM	KB4RRC	147.25500	+	162.2 Hz	SERA - SC
	FM	KJ4OEF	444.60000	+	162.2 Hz	
Darlington, Florence Darlingto						
	FM	KB4RRC	444.80000	+	91.5 Hz	SERA - SC
Dillion	DSTAR	W4PDE C	145.34000	-		
	DSTAR	W4PDE B	443.88750	+		
Dillon	DMR/MARC	WR4SC	443.16250	+	CC1	SERA - SC

Location	Mode	Call sign	Output	Input	Access	Coordinator
Dillon	FM	KJ4OEF	444.95000	+	162.2 Hz	
Dillon, WPDE News 15 Tower						
	DSTAR	W4PDE	145.34000	-		
	DSTAR	W4PDE	443.88750	+		
	FM	W4PDE	146.74500	-	82.5 Hz	SERA - SC
	FM	NE4SC	224.04000	-	123.0 Hz	SERA - SC
Dorchester	FM	W4HNK	147.18000	+	123.0 Hz	
	FM	W4HNK	443.80000	+	123.0 Hz	
Edgefield	FM	WR4EC	146.85000	-	91.5 Hz	SERA - SC
Elgin	FUSION	KI4IVP	146.56500			
	FUSION	KI4IVP	147.24000	+		
Florence	DMR/MARC	WR4SC	442.16250	+	CC1	SERA - SC
	DMR/MARC	WX4ARC	442.28750	+	CC1	
	FM	WR4SC	146.68500	-	91.5 Hz	SERA - SC
	FM	W4APE	147.19500	+	123.0 Hz	SERA - SC
	FM	WR4SC	441.57500	+	91.5 Hz	SERA - SC
Florence , MUSC Florence						
	FM	W4ULH	444.00000	+		
Florence, City County Complex						
	FM	W4GEY	146.97000	-	167.9 Hz	SERA - SC
Florence, ETV Tower						
	FM	W4ULH	146.85000	-		SERA - SC
Florence, McLeod Regional Medi						
	FM	KJ4OEF	444.85000	+	162.2 Hz	
Fork	FM	K4KNJ	146.52000		100.0 Hz	
Fort Jackson	FM	W4CAE	146.77500	-	156.7 Hz	
Fort Mill	FM	KT4TF	145.11000	-	110.9 Hz	
	FM	KT4TF	224.80000	-	110.9 Hz	
Gaffney	FM	KG4JIA	224.50000	-	123.0 Hz	
	FM	N6WOX	443.62500	+	162.2 Hz	
Gaffney, Draytonville Mtn						
	FM	KE4MDP	145.43000	-	162.2 Hz	
Georgetown	DMR/MARC	WR4SC	441.81250	+	CC1	
Georgetown, Memorial Hospital						
	FM	W4HRS	146.70000	-	123.0 Hz	
Goose Creek		KK4MA-L	147.30000			
Greeleyville	FM	KG4AQH	145.23000	-	123.0 Hz	SERA - SC
	FM	KG4AQH	444.75000	+	123.0 Hz	SERA - SC
Green Pond	DSTAR	KJ4LNJ	145.48000	-		SERA - SC
	DSTAR	KJ4LNJ	444.07500	+		
Greenville	DMR/MARC	WR4SC	443.11250	+	CC1	SERA - SC
	FM	WR4SC	145.37000	-	123.0 Hz	
	FM	W4IQQ	146.94000	-	107.2 Hz	
	FM	W4ILY	224.20000	-		
	FM	WR4SC	441.67500	+	91.5 Hz	
	FM	WA4MWC	1250.00000	1280.00000		
	FUSION	W4MBC	144.62000			
Greenville, Caesars Head Mount						
	ATV	N4VDE	421.25000	434.05000		SERA - SC
Greenville, Paris Mountain						
	FM	W4NYK	146.82000	-		
	FM	KB4PQA	442.25000	+		
Greenwood	DMR/MARC	WR4SC	443.83750	+	CC1	
	DSTAR	W4GWM C	145.42000	-		
	FM	WR4SC	441.62500	+	91.5 Hz	
	FM	W4GWD	443.90000	+	107.2 Hz	
Greenwood, Self Regional						
	DSTAR	W4GWM	145.42000	-		
Greenwood, Tower						
	FM	KK4SM	444.82500	+	162.2 Hz	SERA - SC
Greer	DMR/MARC	KO4MZ	145.43000	-	CC1	
Hardeeville	FM	KK4ONF	147.06000	+	123.0 Hz	

Location	Mode	Call sign	Output	Input	Access	Coordinator
Hartsville	DMR/MARC	KA3KDL	446.62500	-	CC1	
Hilton Head Island						
	DMR/BM	HHI	145.35000	-	CC1	
	DSTAR	W4IAR C	147.37500	+		
	FM	W4IAR	145.31000	-	100.0 Hz	
	FM	W4IAR	147.24000	+	100.0 Hz	
	FM	W4IAR	444.35000	+	123.0 Hz	
Honea Path	FM	KJ4VLT	443.77500	+	127.3 Hz	
Indian Land	FM	KB9HVQ	439.60000			
Indianland, Water Tank						
	FM	KT4TF	443.47500	+	110.9 Hz	
Inman, Greenville	FM	W4IQQ	443.35000	+		
Iva	FM	AI4JE	443.25000	+	123.0 Hz	
Jackson , SRS ?C? Road Near Ce						
	FM	W4ZKM	145.45000	-	123.0 Hz	
Jedburg	FM	W4ANK	147.27000	+	123.0 Hz	
Knightsville	FM	WA4USN	146.94000	-	123.0 Hz	
	FM	WA4USN	441.45000	+	123.0 Hz	
Ladson	FM	N2OBS	146.86500	-	123.0 Hz	
Lake City	DMR/MARC	WR4SC	440.63750	+	CC1	
Lake Wylie		W4WXL-R	444.70000			
Landrum, NEAR Lake Lanier At A						
	FM	N2PNE	444.92500	+		SERA - SC
Laurens	FM	KD4HLH	146.86500	-	107.2 Hz	
Leesville	DSTAR	KC4GYM C	146.65500	-		
	DSTAR	AK2H	146.65500	-		
	DSTAR	KC4GYM B	443.50000	+		
	DSTAR	AK2H	443.50000	+		
	FM	N5CWH	53.27000	52.27000	162.2 Hz	
	FM	W4RRC	147.25500	+	123.0 Hz	SERA - SC
	FM	N5CWH	224.56000	-	162.2 Hz	
	FM	N5CWH	443.32500	+	162.2 Hz	
Lexington	FM	KA4FEC	147.39000	+	156.7 Hz	
Lexington, South Carolina						
	P25	N4SCG	147.00000	+		
Liberty	FM	N4VDE	443.97500	+	103.5 Hz	SERA - SC
Little Mountain	DMR/MARC	WR4SC	443.53750	+	CC1	SERA - SC
	DSTAR	KJ4MKV	145.24000	+		
	DSTAR	KJ4MKV C	145.24000	+		
	DSTAR	KJ4MKV	443.32500	+		
	DSTAR	KJ4MKV B	443.32500	+		
	DSTAR	KJ4MKV A	1284.20000	-		
	FM	KJ4MKV	53.21000	52.21000	88.5 Hz	
	FM	K4AVU	147.21000	+	156.7 Hz	
	FM	N4UHF	444.65000	+		
Longs	FM	N2CUE	440.80000	+	179.9 Hz	
Loris	DMR/MARC	K2PJ	147.28500	+	CC1	
Lucknow	FM	W4APE	146.92500	-	123.0 Hz	SERA - SC
Lugoff	FM	KI4RAX	146.82000	-	91.5 Hz	
	FM	KI4RAX	441.80000	+	91.5 Hz	
Mailbu	DSTAR	KD4PAP B	445.85500	-		
Manning	FM	KM4ABW	145.15000	-	91.5 Hz	SERA - SC
Marietta, Caesars Head Mountai						
	FM	K9OH	145.47000	-	91.5 Hz	SERA - SC
Marion	FM	KO4L	147.00000	-	91.5 Hz	SERA - SC
Moncks Corner	FM	W4BRK	146.61000	-	123.0 Hz	SERA - SC
	FM	WD4NUN	147.15000	+	91.5 Hz	SERA - SC
Moncks Corner, EOC						
	FM	W4HRS	145.49000	-	103.5 Hz	
Monetta		KF4NQN-R	446.10000			
Mount Olive	FM	W4GWD-R	147.16500	+		SERA - SC
Mount Pleasant	FM	WA4USN	441.45000	+	123.0 Hz	

Location	Mode	Call sign	Output	Input	Access	Coordinator
Mountain Rest, Long Mtn						
	FM	KJ4YLP	147.03000	-	123.0 Hz	
	FM	N4LRD	442.77500	+	127.3 Hz	
Mountain Rest, Oconee State Pa						
	FM	KJ4YLO	442.20000	+	123.0 Hz	SERA - SC
Mt Allison	DSTAR	K6LRG B	444.68750	+		
	DSTAR	K6LRG A	1286.62500	-		
Mt. Pleasant, East Cooper Medi						
	FM	KK4ZBE	146.68500	-	162.2 Hz	SERA - SC
Mullins	FM	W4APE	145.47000	-	123.0 Hz	SERA - SC
Murrells Inlet	DMR/MARC	WR4SC	441.88750	+	CC1	SERA - SC
	FM	W4GS	146.80500	-	85.4 Hz	
Myrtle Beach	DMR/MARC	N3TX	431.40000	438.00000	CC1	
	DMR/MARC	WR4SC	441.91250	+	CC1	SERA - SC
	FM	NE4SC	53.05000	52.05000	123.0 Hz	
	FM	W4GS	147.12000	+	85.4 Hz	
	FM	NE4SC	444.90000	+	100.0 Hz	
	FM	NE4SC	444.97500	+	123.0 Hz	
Myrtle Beach / Conway						
	DSTAR	NE4SC C	144.98000	147.48000		
	DSTAR	NE4SC B	442.78750	+		
Myrtle Beach, Sheraton Myrtle						
	FM	W4GS	145.29000	-	85.4 Hz	
N Myrtle Bch	FUSION	K3SLS	145.56250			
	FUSION	K3SLS	446.50000			
NOAA Aiken	WX	WNG627	162.45000			
NOAA Aynor	WX	KEC95	162.40000			
NOAA Barnwell	WX	KHC29	162.50000			
NOAA Beaufort	WX	WXJ23	162.45000			
NOAA Charleston	WX	KHB29	162.55000			
NOAA Cheraw	WX	WXK90	162.45000			
NOAA Columbia	WX	WXJ20	162.40000			
NOAA Cross	WX	WXM93	162.47500			
NOAA Florence	WX	WXJ22	162.55000			
NOAA Georgetown						
	WX	WNG628	162.50000			
NOAA Greenville	WX	WXJ21	162.55000			
NOAA Jasper County						
	WX	KEC85	162.40000			
NOAA Kirksey	WX	KHC28	162.42500			
NOAA Orangeburg						
	WX	KHA35	162.52500			
NOAA Rock Hill	WX	KHC27	162.42500			
NOAA Sumter	WX	WWG77	162.42500			
North Augusta	FM	K4NAB	146.73000	-		
	FM	KE4RAP	444.80000	+	146.2 Hz	SERA - SC
	FM	KG4HIR	927.80000	902.80000		
North Charleston	DMR/MARC	WR4SC	442.46250	+	CC1	
North Charleston, Trident Hosp						
	FM	W4HRS	146.73000	-	123.0 Hz	
North Myrtle Beach						
	DMR/MARC	NE4SC	444.08750	+	CC1	SERA - SC
Northfall Acres		KB4RA-L	147.50000			
Orangeburg	DMR/MARC	WR4SC	440.58750	+	CC1	SERA - SC
	DSTAR	KX4DOR	145.28000	-		SERA - SC
	FM	KJ4QLH	146.80500	-	156.7 Hz	
	FM	WR4SC	146.88000	-	123.0 Hz	
	FM	KJ4QJH	147.09000	+	156.7 Hz	SERA - SC
	FM	KO4BR	224.78000	-		
	FM	WR4SC	441.75000	+	123.0 Hz	
	FM	AD4U	444.97500	+		
Pageland	FM	W4JMY	53.37000	52.37000	100.0 Hz	SERA - SC

Location	Mode	Call sign	Output	Input	Access	Coordinator
Pageland	FM	W4APE	146.89500	-	123.0 Hz	SERA - SC
Pickens		WX4PG-L	442.40000			
	DMR/BM	AA2C	444.75000	+	CC1	
	DMR/MARC	WX4PG	442.31250	+	CC1	
	DMR/MARC	KN4SWB	927.51250	902.51250	CC1	
	FM	AC4RZ	53.35000	52.35000	162.2 Hz	
	FM	WT4F	146.70000	-	107.2 Hz	
	FM	WB4LZT	927.51250	902.51250	100.0 Hz	SERA - SC
	FUSION	AA2C	145.09000			
Pickens, Caesars Head Mountain						
	FM	WR4XM	224.14000	-	131.8 Hz	
	FM	WR4XM	442.40000	+	127.3 Hz	
Pickens, Glassy Mountain						
	FM	WB4YXZ	147.00000	-	151.4 Hz	
	FM	WR4XM	224.40000	-	131.8 Hz	
	FM	AC4RZ	443.45000	+	110.9 Hz	SERA - SC
Pickens, Glassy Mtn						
	FM	WX4PG	147.19500	+	141.3 Hz	
	FM	KN4SWB	444.35000	+	127.3 Hz	
Pickens, Sassafras Mtn						
	FM	N4AW	224.32000	-	131.8 Hz	SERA - SC
Pickens, Sassafrass Mountain						
	FM	N4AW	146.79000	-		SERA - SC
Richburg	FM	KC4KPJ	444.72500	+	110.9 Hz	
Rock Hill	DMR/BM	KC4KPJ	444.72500	+	CC6	
	DMR/MARC	WR4SC	440.51250	+	CC1	
	FM	K4YTZ	147.03000	-	88.5 Hz	SERA - SC
	FM	KD4EOD	147.22500	+	110.9 Hz	
	FM	KB4GA	224.84000	-	123.0 Hz	
	FM	W3SPC	440.25000	+		
	FM	WR4SC	441.52500	+	162.2 Hz	
	FM	W4FTK	444.92500	+	91.5 Hz	
Russellville	FM	KK4B	147.30000	+	162.2 Hz	SERA - SC
Saint George	FM	K4ILT	147.04500	+	103.5 Hz	
Saluda, Water Tank						
	FM	W4DEW	146.91000	-	123.0 Hz	SERA - SC
Seabrook Island	FM	WA4USN	145.41000	-	123.0 Hz	
Shoals Junction	DMR/BM	WJ4X	442.60000	+	CC1	SERA - SC
Simpsonville	FM	WA4UKX	146.73000	-	100.0 Hz	
Six Mile	FM	W4TWX	441.80000	+	110.9 Hz	SERA - SC
Six Mile, Six Mile Mountain						
	FM	WA4SSJ	224.10000	-	131.8 Hz	SERA - SC
	FM	W4TWX	441.87500	+	110.9 Hz	SERA - SC
Six Mile, Six Mile Mountian						
	FM	W4TWX	145.17000	-	162.2 Hz	SERA - SC
Socastee	FM	W2SOC	443.00000	+	100.0 Hz	
South Charleston	DMR/MARC	WR4SC	442.38750	+	CC1	SERA - SC
Spartanburg	DMR/MARC	WR4SC	440.66250	+	CC1	SERA - SC
	FM	K4JLA	147.31500	+	123.0 Hz	SERA - SC
	FM	K4II	224.44000	-		SERA - SC
	FM	WR4SC	441.95000	+	162.2 Hz	SERA - SC
	FM	K4II	442.07500	+	123.0 Hz	SERA - SC
Spartanburg, Camp Croft						
	FM	WR4SC	147.09000	+	162.2 Hz	SERA - SC
Spartanburg, Spartanburg Downt						
	FM	K4CDN	444.07500	+	100.0 Hz	SERA - SC
Spartanburg, Spartanburg Regio						
	FM	KI4WVC	442.80000	+		
St George	DMR/MARC	WR4SC	440.65000	+	CC1	
St Matthews	FM	AD4U	146.67000	-	156.7 Hz	
Summerville	DSTAR	KX4DOR C	145.28000	-		
	DSTAR	KX4DOR B	442.83750	+		

Location	Mode	Call sign	Output	Input	Access	Coordinator
Summerville	FUSION	K9VYH	442.12500	+		
Summerville, Summerville Med.						
	FM	W1GRE	146.98500	-	123.0 Hz	
Sumter	DMR/MARC	WR4SC	442.31250	+	CC1	
	FM	W4GL	53.77000	52.77000		
	FM	W4GL	146.64000	-	156.7 Hz	
	FM	W4GL	147.01500	+	156.7 Hz	SERA - SC
	FM	W4GL	224.12000	-		
	FM	W4VFR	224.66000	-		
	FM	WR4SC	441.62500	+	162.2 Hz	
	FM	W4GL	444.15000	+	123.0 Hz	
Sumter Downtown						
	DMR/MARC	WR4SC	441.83750	+	CC1	SERA - SC
Travelers Rest	FM	AC4RZ	442.92500	+	162.2 Hz	
Trenton, SC	FM	W4DV	145.49000	-	71.9 Hz	SERA - SC
Union	FM	K4USC	145.15000	-		SERA - SC
	FM	K4USC	146.68500	-		
	FM	K4USC	442.10000	+		
Walhalla	DMR/MARC	KN4SWB	442.53750	+	CC1	
Walhalla, Long Mountain						
	FM	K4WD	145.29000	-	162.2 Hz	SERA - SC
Walhalla, Stumphouse Mtn						
	FM	KJ4YLO	443.70000	+	91.5 Hz	
Wallace	FM	W4APE	29.60000	-	136.5 Hz	
Walterboro	FM	KG4BZN	53.31000	52.31000	123.0 Hz	
	FM	KG4BZN	145.39000	-		
	FM	KG4BZN	147.13500	+		
	FM	KG4BZN	444.55000	+	123.0 Hz	
Walterboro, Colleton County Me						
	FM	W4HRS	444.85000	+	123.0 Hz	
Wedgefield	FM	WB4BZA	145.43000	-	156.7 Hz	
West Columbia	FUSION	K4HI	147.36000	+		
	FUSION	K4HI	441.15000			
White Hall	FM	WR4SC	146.71500	-	123.0 Hz	
	FM	WA4SJS	146.91000	-	156.7 Hz	
	FM	WR4SC	441.67500	+	123.0 Hz	
York	FM	W4PSC	443.37500	+	110.9 Hz	
	FUSION	W3SPC	443.45000			

SOUTH DAKOTA

Location	Mode	Call sign	Output	Input	Access	Coordinator
Aberdeen	FM	WB0TPF	147.03000	+	146.2 Hz	
Beresford	FM	KA0VHV	147.24000	+	141.3 Hz	
Bowdle	FM	N0AHL	147.12000	+	146.2 Hz	
Box Elder	FUSION	W0MTA	145.07500			
Brookings	FM	W0BXO	146.94000	-	110.9 Hz	
Bruce, Oakwood Lakes						
	FM	KC0FLK	444.25000	+	146.2 Hz	
Buffalo Chip		KE5GII-L	146.41000			
Canton	FUSION	KF7MT	440.00000			
Castlewood		AE5ED-L	146.58000			
	FM	W0WTN	443.10000	+	146.2 Hz	SouDak
Clear Lake	FM	W0GC	444.30000	+	136.5 Hz	SouDak
Colonial Pine Hills	FM	K0LGB	444.45000	+	146.2 Hz	
Crandell, Sweetwater Lake						
	FM	N0AHL	146.79000	-	146.2 Hz	
Custer, Bear Mountain						
	FM	KC0BXH	146.85000	-	146.2 Hz	
Custer, Mt Coolidge						
	FM	K0HS	147.12000	+	146.2 Hz	SouDak
Custer, Water Tank Hill						
	FM	WN6QJN	147.09000	+	146.2 Hz	SouDak
Fairview	FM	N0JPE	146.56000		67.0 Hz	

Location	Mode	Call sign	Output	Input	Access	Coordinator
Flandreau	FM	K0TGA	146.98500	-	146.2 Hz	
Hot Springs	FM	W0FUI	146.47500		146.2 Hz	
Hot Springs, Battle Mountain						
	FM	K0HS	146.70000	-	146.2 Hz	SouDak
Humboldt	FM	N0LCL	147.28500	+	103.5 Hz	
Huron	FM	K0OH	147.09000	+		
	FM	W0NOZ	443.85000	+		
Lead, Terry Peak	FM	KC0BXH	146.76000	-	146.2 Hz	
	FM	WB0JEK	147.03000	+	146.2 Hz	
Lead, Terry Peak Summit						
	FM	WB0JEK	443.65000	+		
Madison	DSTAR	WG0F B	442.75000	+		
	FM	KB0MRG	440.17500	+	131.8 Hz	
Miller	DMR/BM	WV8CW	145.39000	-	CC1	
	FM	WV8CW	144.15000		91.5 Hz	
	FM	KC0WNG	440.65000	+	241.8 Hz	
Mitchell	FM	W0ZSJ	146.64000	-	146.2 Hz	
Mobridge	FM	N3NTV	145.50500			
	FM	W0YMB	147.21000	+	146.2 Hz	
Murdo	FM	AA0CT	147.30000	+	146.2 Hz	
New Underwood	FM	KA1OTT	146.97000	-		
NOAA Aberdeen	WX	WXM25	162.47500			
NOAA Arlington	WX	KXI71	162.52500			
NOAA Faith	WX	WNG557	162.47500			
NOAA Firesteel	WX	WNG551	162.42500			
NOAA Hot Springs						
	WX	WXK64	162.42500			
NOAA Lead	WX	WXL23	162.52500			
NOAA Lowry	WX	WXM40	162.50000			
NOAA Mitchell	WX	WWH36	162.45000			
NOAA Philip	WX	KXI59	162.45000			
NOAA Pickstown	WX	KXI25	162.42500			
NOAA Pierre	WX	WXM26	162.40000			
NOAA Porcupine	WX	KZZ59	162.50000			
NOAA Rapid City	WX	WXM63	162.55000			
NOAA Reliance	WX	KZZ60	162.52500			
NOAA Sioux Falls	WX	WXM28	162.40000			
NOAA South Shore						
	WX	WXM41	162.42500			
NOAA Wessington						
	WX	WXM27	162.55000			
NOAA White River						
	WX	WNG558	162.55000			
North Spearfish		K7RE-L	147.55000			
Philip	FM	N0OMP	147.37500	+	146.2 Hz	
Pierpont	FM	W0JOZ	147.33000	+	146.2 Hz	
Pierre	FM	W0PIR	145.35000	-	146.2 Hz	
	FM	KD0S	146.54000			
	FM	KD0S	146.56500		146.2 Hz	
	FM	KD0S	146.73000	-	146.2 Hz	
Rapid City	DMR/BM	KE0QIB	444.70000	+	CC1	
	FM	W0BLK	146.94000	-	146.2 Hz	
	FM	K0VVY-L	147.50000			
	FM	WA0MFZ	147.57000		146.2 Hz	
	FM	W0RE	443.85000	+		
	FM	W0RE	444.20000	+	82.5 Hz	
	FM	W0BLK	444.57500	+	146.2 Hz	
Redfield	FM	WD0BIA	147.15000	+	146.2 Hz	
Reliance	FM	N0NPO	146.94000	-	146.2 Hz	
Salem	FM	W0SD	145.51000	-	146.2 Hz	
Sioux Falls	DMR/BM	WD0EXR	443.40000	+	CC1	
	DSTAR	W0ZWY B	442.75000	+		

Location	Mode	Call sign	Output	Input	Access	Coordinator
Sioux Falls	DSTAR	W0ZWY	442.75000	+		
	FM	W0ZWY	146.89500	-	146.2 Hz	
	FM	W0FSD	223.86000	-		
	FM	KB0WSW	443.77500	+	146.2 Hz	
	FM	W0ZWY	444.20000	+	82.5 Hz	
	FM	KD0ZP	444.82500	+	146.2 Hz	
	FM	KD0ZP-R	444.90000	+		
	FUSION	AF3O	147.60000			
Sisseton	FM	W0WM	146.88000	-		
Springfield, Norwegian Hill						
	FM	W0OJY	147.21000	+	146.2 Hz	
Tabor	FM	KC0TOW	147.31500	+		
Toronto	FM	KC0OVC	146.77500	-	146.2 Hz	
Turkey Ridge	FM	W0SD	444.97500	+	146.2 Hz	
Vermillion, Cement Plant						
	FM	W0OJY	147.37500	+	146.2 Hz	SouDak
Volga	FUSION	N0VEK	444.05000	+		
Watertown		KB0KBJ-L	146.52000			
	DMR/BM	KB0LCR	443.72500	+	CC1	
	FM	W0WTN	146.85000	-		
	FM	K0TY	442.00000	+	146.2 Hz	
Webster	FM	KC0MYX	442.10000	+	88.5 Hz	
	FM	N0PTW	443.92500	+		
Wessington Springs						
	FM	AA0F	147.34500	+	146.2 Hz	
Yankton	FM	W0OJY	146.85000	-	146.2 Hz	SouDak

TENNESSEE

Location	Mode	Call sign	Output	Input	Access	Coordinator
Adamsville		AG4KB-L	145.07000			
	FM	AG4NX	145.00000			
Alcoa	FM	K4BTL	442.00000	+		
Allegheny	FM	K4MFD-R	145.15000	-		SERA
Altamont	FM	KF4TNP	146.88000	+	167.9 Hz	SERA
Arlington	FM	W4TIP	145.49000	-	100.0 Hz	
Arrington	DMR/BM	N4ULM	441.90000	+	CC1	
Athens		W4HRC-L	146.49000			
	FM	KG4FZR	147.06000	-	141.3 Hz	SERA
	FM	KG4FZR	442.27500	+	141.3 Hz	
Bartlett	FM	N4GMT	1284.25000	1264.25000	107.2 Hz	SERA
Bean Station	FM	W2IQ	443.45000	+	156.7 Hz	SERA
Bean Station, Clinch Mtn						
	FM	W2IQ	147.03000	+	156.7 Hz	SERA
Beechwood	FM	K4EGC-R	146.70000	-		SERA
Benton	DSTAR	KM4MCN	144.98000	147.48000		
	DSTAR	KM4MCN C	144.98000	147.48000		
	DSTAR	KM4MCN D	1253.00000			
Benton, Chilhowee Mountain						
	FM	WD4DES	147.18000	+	118.8 Hz	SERA
	FM	WD4DES	442.25000	+	118.8 Hz	SERA
	FM	KA4ELN	444.80000	+	123.0 Hz	SERA
Bethpage, Mutton Hollow						
	FM	W4LKZ	145.39000	-	114.8 Hz	SERA
	FM	W4LKZ	443.30000	+	107.2 Hz	SERA
Blackman		WN9J-L	223.96000			
Blaine	DMR/MARC	N9BRG	444.87500	+	CC1	
Blountville	FM	W4CBX	147.00000	+		
Bon Aqua	FUSION	WM4Q	144.69000	+		
	FUSION	WM4Q	146.57000			
Bray (historical)	FM	KA7UEC-R	443.30000	+	107.2 Hz	SERA
Brentwood		AC5MR-R	146.94000			
	FM	WC4EOC	145.21000	-	173.8 Hz	
Brighton	FM	KE4ZBI	145.49000	-	100.0 Hz	

Location	Mode	Call sign	Output	Input	Access	Coordinator
Bristol	FM	W4UD	146.67000	-		SERA
	FM	KE4CCB	146.70000	-		SERA
	FUSION	KD4ODW	147.00000	+		
Bristol, Bristol Regional Hosp						
	FM	W4DOH	441.95000	+	146.2 Hz	SERA
Bristol, Holston Mountain						
	FM	KG4VBS	145.11000	-		SERA
	FM	W4CBX	224.20000	-		SERA
	FM	KE4CCB	442.20000	+	100.0 Hz	SERA
Brownsville, Brownsville-Haywo						
	FM	NA8X	444.52500	+	107.2 Hz	SERA
Burns	FUSION	W0ADD	446.62500			
Caryville		W4HKL-L	146.46000			
	DSTAR	KK4VQG	145.02000	+		
	FM	KB4PNG	444.55000	+	77.0 Hz	SERA
	FM	W4HKL	444.67500	+	100.0 Hz	
Caryville, Caryville Mountain						
	FM	KA4OAK	224.28000	-		SERA
Centerville	FM	KI4DAD	442.55000	+	123.0 Hz	SERA
	FM	N4XW	443.70000	+	123.0 Hz	SERA
Chattanooga	DMR/BM	W4PL	444.15000	+	CC1	SERA
	DMR/BM	N4LMC	444.72500	+	CC1	
	DSTAR	N4LMC C	145.16000	-		
	DSTAR	W4PL C	145.29000	-		
	DSTAR	W4PL B	443.15000	+		
	DSTAR	W4RRG B	444.72500	+		
	DSTAR	W4RRG	444.72500	+		SERA
	DSTAR	W4PL D	1251.00000			
	DSTAR	W4PL A	1291.00000	1271.00000		
	FM	K4VCM	53.35000	52.35000		SERA
	FM	K4CMY	145.13000	-		SERA
	FM	K4VCM-R	146.79000	-		SERA
	FM	K4VCM	224.78000	-		SERA
Chattanooga, Lookout Mountain						
	DSTAR	N4LMC	145.16000	-		SERA
	FM	N4LMC	224.12000	-	146.2 Hz	
	FM	W4AM	444.10000	+		SERA
Chattanooga, Signal Mountain						
	DSTAR	W4PL	145.29000	-		
	DSTAR	W4PL	443.15000	+		
	DSTAR	W4PL	1291.00000	1271.00000		
	FM	N4LMC	144.92000	147.42000		
	FM	W4AM	145.39000	-	107.2 Hz	SERA
	FM	W4AM	146.61000	-	107.2 Hz	
	FM	K4VCM	224.42000	-		SERA
Church Hill	FUSION	K4HPY	446.60000			
Clarksville	DMR/BM	W3DMJ	440.70000	+	CC1	
	DSTAR	WU5PIG B	442.60000	+		
	FM	NE4MA	442.62500	+	107.2 Hz	
Clarksville, Indian Mound						
	FM	AA4TA	146.92500	-	110.9 Hz	SERA
Cleveland	DMR/BM	WB4BSD	436.61000	-	CC1	
	DMR/BM	W4GZX	440.70000	+	CC1	
	DMR/MARC	WB4JGI	440.80000	+	CC1	
	DMR/MARC	WB4JGI	443.82500	+	CC1	
	DSTAR	KK4BXE C	145.48000	-		
	DSTAR	KK4BXE	145.48000	-		SERA
	DSTAR	KK4BXE	440.52500	+		
	DSTAR	KK4BXE B	440.52500	+		
	FM	KA4ELN	442.40000	+	123.0 Hz	SERA
	FM	W4OAR	442.92500	+	100.0 Hz	SERA
	FM	W4GZX	444.27500	+	114.8 Hz	SERA

Location	Mode	Call sign	Output	Input	Access	Coordinator
Cleveland	P25	KA4ELN	145.45000	147.95000		
	FUSION	WM4RB	145.31000	-		
Cleveland, CARC Clubhouse						
	FM	KA4ELN	224.10000	-	123.0 Hz	SERA
Clinton, I 75	FM	WX4RP	442.15000	+	100.0 Hz	
Collegedale, White Oak Mountai						
	FM	KA6UHV	147.00000	+	131.8 Hz	SERA
	FM	KA6UHV	443.57500	+	131.8 Hz	
Collierville	FM	KA7UEC	443.62500	+	107.2 Hz	SERA
	FM	KJ4FYA	444.12500	+	107.2 Hz	SERA
	FUSION	KB4CO	431.00000			
Columbia	FM	W4GGM	147.12000	+	127.3 Hz	
	FM	KG4LUY	442.72500	+		
	FM	W4GGM	443.17500	+	100.0 Hz	SERA
	FUSION	ND9W	145.50000			
Cookeville	DMR/BM	KK4TD	145.11000	-	CC1	
	FM	W4HPL	147.21000	+		SERA
	FM	W4EOC	444.60000	+	107.2 Hz	
Counce	DMR/BM	AB5OR	444.25000	+	CC1	
	FM	WV4P	444.80000	+	131.8 Hz	
Cross Plains	FM	N4RCA	147.34500	+	114.8 Hz	
	FM	NE4MA	443.90000	+	107.2 Hz	
Crossville	FM	W8EYU	146.86500	-	118.8 Hz	SERA
	FM	W4KEV	147.34500	+	118.8 Hz	SERA
	FM	W4KEV	443.87500	+	88.5 Hz	SERA
	FUSION	KG5BBM	145.55000			
	FUSION	KG5BBM	146.55000			
Crossville, Exit 320 I-40, Old						
	FM	W8EYU	146.89500	-	118.8 Hz	
Crossville, Fairfield Glade Re						
	FM	W8EYU	443.85000	+		
Crossville, Hinch Mountain						
	FM	W4KEV	53.93000	52.93000		
Cumberland Furnace						
	DMR/BM	N4GRW	441.81250	+	CC1	SERA
	FM	N4GRW	53.15000	52.15000	91.5 Hz	SERA
	FM	N4GRW	224.42000	-		SERA
	FM	N4GRW	927.52500	902.52500	107.2 Hz	SERA
Dandridge	FM	W4KEV	146.89500	-	100.0 Hz	SERA
	FM	KD4TUD	444.62500	+	173.8 Hz	
Dayton	DMR/BM	KK4GGK	442.07500	+	CC1	SERA
	FUSION	KE4IDF	446.12500			
Dayton, Evensville Mountain						
	FM	K4DPD	147.39000	+		
Decatur	FM	KG4FZR	145.15000	-	141.3 Hz	
	FM	KG4FZR	443.27500	+	100.0 Hz	
Decaturville	FM	KA4P	443.32500	+	131.8 Hz	
Dixie Homes		KK4IOH-L	145.45000			
Dresden	DMR/BM	KB4IBW	145.15000	-	CC1	
	DMR/BM	KA4BNI	442.15000	+	CC1	
	FM	KB4IBW	53.13000	52.13000	107.2 Hz	SERA
Dunlap	FM	KB4ACS	444.70000	+		
Dupont Springs, Green Top Mtn						
	FM	KD4CWB	444.00000	+	100.0 Hz	
Dupont Springs, Greentop						
	FM	W4KEV	147.00000	-	100.0 Hz	SERA
	FM	KD4CWB	224.86000	-	100.0 Hz	SERA
Eaton	FM	KI4OAS	147.27000	+		SERA
	FM	KJ4HRM	442.30000	+	100.0 Hz	
Elizabethton	FM	KN4E	53.89000	52.89000	88.5 Hz	SERA
	FM	K4LNS	224.88000	-		SERA
	FM	WM4T	441.80000	+		SERA

Location	Mode	Call sign	Output	Input	Access	Coordinator
Elizabethton	FM	KN4E	442.75000	+	88.5 Hz	SERA
	FUSION	KE4MVW	145.65000			
Elizabethton, Holston Mountain						
	FM	WR4CC	145.29000	-	103.5 Hz	
	FM	K4LNS	147.27000	+	88.5 Hz	SERA
Erwin	FM	WB4IXU	53.95000	52.95000		
	FM	KC4DSY	147.16500	+		SERA
	FM	WB4IXU	224.78000	-		
Estill Springs	DMR/MARC	AJ4YS	442.96250	+	CC1	
Etowah, Starr Mtn	FM	KG4FZR	441.80000	+	141.3 Hz	
Fairview	DMR/BM	N4ULM	442.32500	+	CC1	
Falling Water, Signal Mountain						
	FM	K4VCM	443.12500	+	103.5 Hz	SERA
Fayetteville	FM	W4BV	147.03000	+	114.8 Hz	SERA
Franklin	DMR/BM	WC4EOC	448.47500	447.87500	CC1	
	DMR/BM	WC4EOC	448.60000	448.00000	CC1	
	FM	WA4BGK	53.05000	52.05000	114.8 Hz	
	FM	W9WHF	147.77500			
	FM	NE4MA	443.47500	+	107.2 Hz	
Franklin, Cool Springs Mall						
	FM	W4SQE	146.79000	-		
Galbraith Springs	FM	KE4KQI-R	147.13500	+		SERA
Gallatin	DMR/MARC	K4OZE	442.91250	+	CC1	
	FM	W4CAT	444.45000	+	107.2 Hz	SERA
Gallatin, Mockingbird Hill						
	FM	W4LKZ	147.27000	+	114.8 Hz	
Gallatin, Music Mountain						
	FM	W4LKZ	146.88000	-		
	FM	W4CAT	147.30000	+		SERA
Gatlinburg, Glades Rd						
	FM	W4UO	147.42000			
Gatlinburg, Ski Mountain						
	FM	W4KEV	147.19500	+	100.0 Hz	SERA
	FM	W4KEV	444.90000	+	100.0 Hz	SERA
Georgetown	FM	WE4MB	442.02500	+	100.0 Hz	SERA
Germantown, Water Tower						
	FM	W4BS	146.62500	-	107.2 Hz	
Gleason	DMR/BM	KA4BNI	145.47000	-	CC1	
Gray	DMR/BM	WM4T	441.80000	+	CC7	
	FM	WM4T	145.25000	-		SERA
	FM	W4YSF	442.50000	+		SERA
Greenbrier	FUSION	N4AAN	145.41000	-		
Greeneville	DMR/MARC	N4FV	144.92000	147.42000	CC1	
	DMR/MARC	K4MFD	444.03750	+	CC1	SERA
	DMR/MARC	N4FV	444.35000	+	CC1	
	FM	W4WC	53.01000	52.01000	100.0 Hz	SERA
	FM	N4FV	147.06000	+	88.5 Hz	SERA
	FM	KI4OTR	441.85000	+	100.0 Hz	SERA
	FM	N4CAG	443.15000	+	100.0 Hz	
	FM	K4GNR	443.27500	+	100.0 Hz	
Greeneville, Bald Mtn						
	FM	W4KEV	145.41000	-	127.3 Hz	SERA
Greeneville, Camp Creek Bald M						
	FM	W4WC	145.39000	-	88.5 Hz	SERA
	FM	W4WC	443.20000	+	100.0 Hz	SERA
Greeneville, Round Knob Mounta						
	FUSION	K4ETN	444.75000	+		SERA
Greeneville, Viking Mountain						
	FM	K4MFD	29.64000	-	118.8 Hz	
	FM	K4MFD	224.44000	-	118.8 Hz	SERA
	FM	K4MFD	444.20000	+	118.8 Hz	SERA
	FM	K4MFD	927.05000	902.05000	118.8 Hz	

Location	Mode	Call sign	Output	Input	Access	Coordinator
Hartford	DMR/BM	KG4LDK	443.77500	+	CC1	
Henderson, City Fire Station #						
	FM	KU4RT	147.10500	+	156.7 Hz	SERA
Hendersonville	FM	AK4GS	442.42500	+	107.2 Hz	SERA
	FM	W4LKZ	444.00000	+	107.2 Hz	
	FUSION	K6QS	146.79000	-		
Heritage	FM	NE4MA	443.07500	+	156.7 Hz	
Hixson	FM	N4YH	442.90000	+	156.7 Hz	SERA
	FM	WJ9J	444.45000	+		
	FM	N4YH	444.87500	+	156.7 Hz	SERA
Hobbs Hill	FM	NQ4Y-R	145.41000	-		SERA
Hockley	FM	WA5SON	441.90000	+	88.5 Hz	
Hollow Rock	FM	KM4TFZ	146.71500	-		
Howardville	FM	K4TCH-L	145.52500			
	FM	W4CLM-L	146.91000	-		
Huntingdon	FM	KA4ZGK	146.83500	-	123.0 Hz	SERA
Jacksboro	FM	KC4SLE	445.86500	-	91.5 Hz	
	FM	KC4SLE	445.87500	-	91.5 Hz	
Jackson	DMR/BM	KA4BNI	443.71250	+	CC1	
	DSTAR	NT4MC	145.08000	146.48000		
	DSTAR	NT4MC C	145.08000	146.48000		
	FM	KF4SC	145.31000	-	107.2 Hz	
	FM	WF4Q	147.21000	+	107.2 Hz	
	FM	KA4BNI	224.24000	-	131.8 Hz	SERA
	FM	NE4MA	444.45000	+	123.0 Hz	SERA
	FM	KA4BNI	444.87500	+	131.8 Hz	SERA
	FUSION	KN4YOB	433.07500			
Jamestown, Round Mtn						
	FM	KC4MJN	443.62500	+		
Jamestown, Round Mtn Rd						
	FM	KI4KIL	147.09000	+		
Jasper	FM	KD4ATW	443.10000	+	88.5 Hz	SERA
Jefferson	FM	KB5YJC	443.72500	+	100.0 Hz	
Joelton	DMR/BM	KG4YFA	444.20000	+	CC5	
	FM	KC4PRD	146.98500	-		
	FM	KF4TNP	442.95000	+	167.9 Hz	SERA
Johnson City	FM	AE4BT	442.87500	+	100.0 Hz	SERA
	FM	W4YSF	443.95000	+	118.8 Hz	SERA
	FM	K4LNS	444.10000	+	103.5 Hz	SERA
	FM	W4YSF	444.28750	+		SERA
	FUSION	N4JFD	146.13750			
Johnson City, ETSU						
	FM	W4DOH	442.77500	+		
Johnson City, Franklin Woods C						
	FM	W4ABR	146.79000	-	131.8 Hz	SERA
Johnson City, Tennessee						
	FM	W4BUC	443.25000	+		SERA
Jonesborough	DMR/MARC	KK4WTI	442.58750	+	CC1	
	FM	K4ETN	443.10000	+		SERA
Kingsport	FM	W4TRC	146.97000	-	123.0 Hz	SERA
Kingsport, Bays Mountain						
	FM	K4DWQ	443.17500	+	100.0 Hz	
	FM	W4TRC	443.32500	+	123.0 Hz	SERA
	FM	W4YSF	443.56250	+		SERA
	FM	W4TRC	927.02500	902.02500	123.0 Hz	
Kinkaid Estates		K4LMP-R	146.82000			
Knoxville	DMR/BM	W4KEV	440.55000	+	CC1	
	DMR/BM	AA4UT	445.60000	-	CC1	
	DMR/MARC	K1LNX	443.56250	+	CC1	
	DMR/MARC	K1LNX	443.66250	+	CC1	
	DMR/MARC	KB4REC	444.17500	+	CC1	SERA
	DSTAR	K4HXD	144.94000	147.44000		

Location	Mode	Call sign	Output	Input	Access	Coordinator
Knoxville	DSTAR	K4HXD C	144.94000	147.44000		
	DSTAR	KN4EM C	145.10000	-		
	FM	KB4REC	53.47000	52.47000	100.0 Hz	SERA
	FM	N4OQJ	224.38000	-	100.0 Hz	SERA
	FM	AA4UT	443.00000	+		SERA
	FM	W4KEV	444.50000	+	100.0 Hz	SERA
Knoxville, Bays Mtn - WJBZ Tow						
	FM	WB4GBI	145.43000	-	118.8 Hz	SERA
Knoxville, Beaver Ridge						
	FM	KB4REC	444.52500	+	123.0 Hz	
Knoxville, Chilhowee Mountain						
	FM	W4BBB	53.77000	52.77000	100.0 Hz	
Knoxville, Cross Mountain						
	FM	WB4GBI	145.47000	-	118.8 Hz	SERA
Knoxville, McKinney Ridge						
	FM	WB4GBI	147.07500	+	118.8 Hz	SERA
Knoxville, Sharp's Ridge						
	FM	W4BBB	145.21000	-	100.0 Hz	
	FM	WA4FLH	443.25000	+	88.5 Hz	SERA
Knoxville, Sharps Ridge						
	DSTAR	W4KEV	145.10000	-		
	FM	W4KEV	29.68000	-	127.3 Hz	
	FM	W4KEV	146.88000	-		SERA
	FM	W4KEV	224.20000	-	100.0 Hz	
	FM	W4KEV	927.61250	902.61250	146.2 Hz	SERA
	P25	W4KEV	441.83750	+		SERA
Knoxville, View Park Hill						
	FM	WB4GBI	145.17000	-	118.8 Hz	SERA
Knoxville, WIMZ Tower						
	FM	W4KEV	53.25000	52.25000		
	FM	W4KEV	145.23000	-	103.5 Hz	SERA
Knoxville, WJXB Tower						
	FM	W4KEV	442.50000	+	100.0 Hz	SERA
La Vergne	FM	W4CAT	145.23000	-	114.8 Hz	SERA
LaFollette	DMR/BM	WB4CDK	444.85000	+	CC1	SERA
LaFollette, Cross Mountain						
	FM	KA4OAK	147.36000	+	100.0 Hz	SERA
LaFollette, Demory Community						
	FM	KA4OAK	145.13000	-	100.0 Hz	
Lawrenceburg	FM	KG4LUY	146.65500	-	100.0 Hz	
	FM	WD4RAT	147.39000	+		
	FM	NE4MA	443.40000	+		
Lebanon	DMR/BM	W4DMM	440.62500	+	CC1	
	FM	W4EAO	442.12500	+	100.0 Hz	
	FUSION	KT4EEE	440.00000			
Lebanon, Sparta Pike						
	FM	KM4GHM	444.95000	+		
Lebanon, WJFB-TV Tower						
	FM	WC4AR	147.10500	+	156.7 Hz	SERA
Lenoir City	FM	KF4DKW	444.25000	+	127.3 Hz	SERA
	FM	W4WVJ	444.60000	+		
	FUSION	K4MJF	146.58000			
Lenoir City, Greenback Communi						
	FM	W4WVJ	443.05000	+	100.0 Hz	SERA
Lewisburg	FM	N4MRS	146.62500	-	107.2 Hz	SERA
	FM	KF4TNP	442.10000	+	107.2 Hz	SERA
Linden, Top Of Hill West Of Li						
	FM	KJ4TVS	443.50000	+	100.0 Hz	
Lobelville	FM	WA4VVX	145.43000	-	114.8 Hz	
	FM	WA4VVX	442.85000	+	107.2 Hz	SERA
Loiusville	FM	W4KEV	927.03750	902.03750	100.0 Hz	SERA
Lookout Mtn.	FM	W4EDP-R	145.35000	+		SERA

Location	Mode	Call sign	Output	Input	Access	Coordinator
Louisville, Red Hill						
	FM	N4ABV	443.37500	+	100.0 Hz	
Lyles	FM	KI4DAD	443.85000	+	123.0 Hz	
Lynchburg	FM	KF4TNP	145.45000	-	127.3 Hz	SERA
Madison	DMR/MARC	KJ4RVN	145.44000	-	CC1	
Madison, Candelabra TV Towers						
	FM	K4SNG	444.62500	+	107.2 Hz	
Manchester	DMR/MARC	KF4TNP	441.88750	+	CC1	
	DMR/MARC	KF4TNP	442.86250	+	CC1	
	FM	KF4TNP	443.22500	+	127.3 Hz	
	FM	KF4TNP	444.07500	+	127.3 Hz	SERA
Martin	DMR/BM	KA4BNI	444.71250	+	CC1	
Martin, U T Martin	FM	W4UTM	146.62500	-	100.0 Hz	SERA
Maryville	DMR/BM	KK4XA	444.07500	+	CC1	
	FM	KK4DKW	145.27000	-	127.3 Hz	SERA
	FM	W1BEW	441.82500	+		SERA
	FM	N4ABV	442.62500	+	100.0 Hz	SERA
	FM	NE4MA	443.90000	+	100.0 Hz	
	FM	KK4DKW	444.77500	+	94.8 Hz	SERA
	FM	KE4FGW	444.82500	+	100.0 Hz	SERA
	FUSION	KF4QVF	145.56250			
	FUSION	KW4WX	438.50000			
	FUSION	W4OLB	443.07500	+	100.0 Hz	
Maryville, Reservoir Hill						
	FM	W4OLB	146.65500	-	100.0 Hz	SERA
McEwen, Water Tower						
	FM	NO4Q	147.22500	+	114.8 Hz	
McMinnville, Harrison Ferry Mo						
	FM	WD4MWQ	146.97000	-	151.4 Hz	
Medina	DMR/BM	NQ4U	442.81250	+	CC1	
	FM	WF4Q	146.77500	-	107.2 Hz	SERA
	FM	WT4WA	146.97000	-	107.2 Hz	
Memphis		KK4SZO-L	146.42000			
	DMR/BM	KK4BWF	441.88750	+	CC1	
	DMR/MARC	W4LET	443.01250	+	CC1	SERA
	DSTAR	WB4KOG C	144.94000	147.44000		
	DSTAR	W4LET	145.06000	146.46000		SERA
	DSTAR	W4LET C	145.06000	146.46000		
	DSTAR	WB4KOG B	442.03750	+		
	DSTAR	W4LET	443.98750	+		SERA
	DSTAR	W4LET B	443.98750	+		
	DSTAR	W4LET D	1297.30000			
	FM	WA4ADT-R	146.73000	-	107.2 Hz	
	FM	W4GMM	147.09000	+	107.2 Hz	SERA
	FM	W4BS	147.36000	+	107.2 Hz	SERA
	FM	W4BS	443.20000	+	107.2 Hz	SERA
	FM	NS4B	445.55000	-	107.2 Hz	
Memphis, East Memphis Hilton H						
	FM	WB4KOG	146.85000	-	107.2 Hz	SERA
Memphis, First Tennessee Bank						
	FM	WB4KOG	145.45000	-	107.2 Hz	
	FM	WB4KOG	444.77500	+	107.2 Hz	SERA
Memphis, Hilton East Memphis						
	DSTAR	WB4KOG	144.94000	147.44000		SERA
	DSTAR	WB4KOG	442.03750	+		SERA
	FM	WB4KOG	53.01000	52.01000	107.2 Hz	SERA
Memphis, Hilton Hotel						
	FM	WB4KOG	224.78000	-	107.2 Hz	SERA
Memphis, Methodist North Hospi						
	FM	W4BS	224.42000	-		SERA
Memphis, SCO	FM	WB4KOG	146.88000	-		SERA

Location	Mode	Call sign	Output	Input	Access	Coordinator
Memphis, WKNO Tower						
	FM	W4EM	927.61250	902.61250	146.2 Hz	
Memphis, WPTY Tower						
	FM	W4BS	146.82000	-	107.2 Hz	SERA
Middleburg		W4RSG-R	443.10000			
Milan	FM	KA4BNI	442.67500	+	131.8 Hz	SERA
Monteagle Mtn	DMR/BM	NQ4Y	146.88000	-	CC1	
	DMR/BM	NQ4Y	442.00000	+	CC1	
Mooresburg	FM	KE4KQI	927.61250	902.61250	114.8 Hz	SERA
Morristown	DMR/BM	W4LDG	442.38750	+	CC1	
	DMR/BM	W4LDG	443.38750	+	CC1	
	DMR/MARC	N4FNB	442.38750	+	CC1	
	DSTAR	W4LDG C	144.92000	147.42000		
	DSTAR	W4LDG	144.92000	+		SERA
	DSTAR	W4LDG B	444.47500	+		
	DSTAR	W4LDG	444.47500	+		SERA
	FM	KQ4E	145.45000	-	141.3 Hz	SERA
	FM	WB4OAH	147.22500	+	141.3 Hz	
	FM	KQ4E	147.39000	+		SERA
	FM	AK4EZ	442.95000	+		SERA
	FM	KG4GVX	444.60000	+	100.0 Hz	
	FM	KQ4E	444.97500	+		
Morristown TN	DMR/BM	W4LDG	442.38750	+	CC1	
Morristown, I-81 I-40 Split						
	FM	KM4UIP	443.42500	+		SERA
Moss	DMR/MARC	W4LSX	147.31500	+	CC1	
Mount Juliet	FUSION	KM4BNR	146.55000			
Mountain City		KJ4HB-R	224.28000			
	FM	W4MCT	145.47000	-	103.5 Hz	SERA
	FM	K4DHT	146.61000	-	103.5 Hz	SERA
	FM	K4DHT	224.28000	-	103.5 Hz	SERA
	FM	K4DHT	441.60000	+	151.4 Hz	SERA
Mountain City, Forge Mountain						
	FM	K4DHT	443.92500	+	103.5 Hz	SERA
Mountain City, Stone Mountain						
	FM	K4DHT	53.33000	52.33000	103.5 Hz	SERA
Murfreesboro	DMR/BM	W4DMM	145.12000	-	CC1	
	DMR/BM	W4DMM	444.30000	+	CC1	
	DMR/MARC	N2YCX	146.61000	-	CC4	
	FM	KU4B	145.17000	-	114.8 Hz	SERA
	FUSION	KM4CRC	146.50000			
	FUSION	WB9PJZ	146.79000	-		
Nashville	DMR/BM	NE4MA	441.92500	+	CC1	
	DMR/MARC	W4DER	440.52500	+	CC1	
	DMR/MARC	AK4GS	443.08750	+	CC4	
	DMR/MARC	WA4BGK	444.58750	+	CC1	
	DSTAR	K4CPO C	147.18000	+		
	DSTAR	KI4SDI C	147.18000	+		
	DSTAR	K4CPO	147.18000	+		
	DSTAR	W4JYV C	147.18000	+		
	FM	WA4BGK	53.01000	52.01000	107.2 Hz	
	FM	WA4PCD	146.76000	-		
	FM	W4CAT	146.95500	-	114.8 Hz	
	FM	WR3S	147.37000	+		
	FM	K1FB	224.18000	-	67.0 Hz	SERA
	FM	WA4RCW	442.75000	+	100.0 Hz	SERA
	FM	NE4MA	442.80000	+	107.2 Hz	SERA
	FM	WA4BGK	444.52500	+	107.2 Hz	
	FUSION	W4GHD	147.30000	+		
	FUSION	K4LRC	443.25000	+		
Nashville, East Nashville						
	FM	AF4TZ	146.64000	-	114.8 Hz	SERA

Location	Mode	Call sign	Output	Input	Access	Coordinator
Nashville, Lipscomb University						
	FM	K4LRC	443.25000	+		
Nashville, Sullivan's Ridge						
	FM	AF4TZ	146.67000	-	114.8 Hz	SERA
	FM	AF4TZ	147.01500	+	114.8 Hz	SERA
Nashville, Vanderbilt Universi						
	FM	AA4VU	443.80000	+	123.0 Hz	
Nashville, Wessex Towers						
	FM	AF4TZ	444.15000	+	107.2 Hz	SERA
New Market	FM	W4BWW	53.05000	52.05000	100.0 Hz	SERA
Newport	FM	KG4LHC	927.70000	902.70000	203.5 Hz	SERA
Newport / Dandridge						
	FM	KM4ULP	443.42500	+		
Newport, English Mountain						
	FM	WB4GBI	146.73000	-	118.8 Hz	SERA
Newport, Halls Top						
	FM	N2UGA	442.92500	+	103.5 Hz	SERA
NOAA Bristol	WX	WXK47	162.55000			
NOAA Centerville	WX	KWN53	162.45000			
NOAA Chattanooga						
	WX	WXK48	162.55000			
NOAA Clarksville	WX	WWH37	162.50000			
NOAA Clifton	WX	WZ2506	162.50000			
NOAA Cookeville	WX	WXK61	162.40000			
NOAA Dyersburg	WX	WWH30	162.50000			
NOAA Hickman	WX	WXN74	162.50000			
NOAA Jackson	WX	WXK60	162.55000			
NOAA Knoxville	WX	WXK46	162.47500			
NOAA La Follette	WX	WNG732	162.45000			
NOAA Lafayette	WX	WNG631	162.52500			
NOAA Lawrenceburg						
	WX	WWF84	162.42500			
NOAA Lobelville	WX	KWN52	162.52500			
NOAA Memphis	WX	WXK49	162.47500			
NOAA Nashville	WX	KIG79	162.55000			
NOAA Shelbyville	WX	WXK63	162.47500			
NOAA Spencer	WX	WNG629	162.45000			
NOAA Vale	WX	KHA46	162.45000			
NOAA Waverly	WX	WXK62	162.40000			
NOAA Winchester	WX	WNG554	162.52500			
Nolensville	FM	WD4JYD	145.35000	-		
	FM	KB5YJC	443.72500	+	107.2 Hz	
North Knoxville	FM	W4KEV-R	145.37000	-	100.0 Hz	SERA
Northport	FM	KG4LHC-R	147.09000	+		SERA
Nunnely	FM	KG4UHH	444.07500	+	100.0 Hz	SERA
Oak Ridge	FM	W4KEV	441.92500	+	100.0 Hz	SERA
Oak Ridge, Water Tower						
	FM	W4SKH	146.97000	-	88.5 Hz	SERA
Oakfield	DMR/BM	NQ4U	145.44000	-	CC1	
Oakfield, Jackson, TN Area						
	FM	WA4BJY	147.39000	+	162.2 Hz	SERA
Oakland, Water Tower						
	FM	WB4KOG	146.94000	-		SERA
Oliver Springs, Windrock Mount						
	FM	WB4GBI	147.15000	+	118.8 Hz	SERA
Oneida	DSTAR	W4BSF B	444.38750	+		
Oneida, Signal Mountain						
	FM	KB4PNG	145.35000	-	77.0 Hz	SERA
Ooltewah	DMR/BM	W4YI	444.90000	+	CC1	
Paris	FM	N4ZKR	147.33000	+	131.8 Hz	SERA
	FM	KJ4ISZ	147.36000	+		
Parsons	FM	W4LSR	147.19500	-	94.8 Hz	SERA

Location	Mode	Call sign	Output	Input	Access	Coordinator
Pasquo	FM	NE4MA	443.97500	+	107.2 Hz	
Petros, Frozen Head Mountain						
	FM	KJ4SI	147.25500	+	94.8 Hz	SERA
Peytona		KL7EZ-L	146.55000			
Pikeville	FM	KF4JPU	147.28500	+		
Pleasant View	FUSION	KO4KAJ	446.57500			
Portland	FM	KB4KDL	146.46000			
Portland, Music Mountain						
	FM	W4LKZ	147.24000	+	114.8 Hz	
	FM	W4LKZ	444.35000	+	107.2 Hz	
Pulaski	FM	KF4TNP	146.80500	-	114.8 Hz	SERA
	FM	KG4NVX	443.55000	+	100.0 Hz	
Reelfoot Lake Area						
	FM	W4NWT	147.04500	+	107.2 Hz	
	FM	W4NWT	442.50000	+	114.8 Hz	
Ripley	FM	KE4NTL	145.23000	-	100.0 Hz	SERA
Rockwood, Mt Roosevelt						
	DSTAR	KE4RX	441.81250	+		SERA
	DSTAR	KE4RX	1298.50000			SERA
	FM	KE4RX	443.97500	+	110.9 Hz	SERA
Rockwood, Mt. Roosevelt						
	FM	KE4RX	147.01500	+	110.9 Hz	SERA
	FM	K4APY	147.12000	+	82.5 Hz	SERA
Rogersville	DMR/BM	KN4EHX	440.56250	+	CC1	
Savannah	FM	KA4ESF	146.70000	-	123.0 Hz	
	FM	WV4P	442.80000	+	131.8 Hz	SERA
Savannah, Courthouse						
	FM	K4SDS	146.43500			
Selmer	DMR/BM	KN4TST	444.30000	+	CC1	
	FM	WB4MMI	146.80500	-	107.2 Hz	
Sevierville	DMR/BM	WB4GBI	440.57500	+	CC1	
	DMR/MARC	K4USD	145.04000	146.44000	CC1	SERA
	DMR/MARC	K4USD	443.50000	+	CC1	
Sevierville, Bluff Mountain						
	FM	WB4GBI	146.94000	-	118.8 Hz	SERA
	FM	WB4GBI	444.30000	+	118.8 Hz	SERA
	FM	WB4GBI	927.06250	902.06250	151.4 Hz	SERA
Sevierville, Bluff Mountain (G						
	FM	WB4GBI	146.85000	-	118.8 Hz	SERA
Seymour	DSTAR	AD4DS C	145.61000	144.41000		
	DSTAR	AD4DS B	444.47500	+		
	DSTAR	AD4DS D	1253.00000			
	DSTAR	AD4DS A	1293.00000	1273.00000		
Shelbyville	FM	KI4NJJ	147.06000	+	127.3 Hz	
	FM	KK4LFI	442.70000	+	100.0 Hz	
	FM	WA4AWI	443.35000	+	127.3 Hz	
Short Mountain	DMR/BM	W4DMM	440.70000	+	CC1	
	FM	NE4MA	444.65000	+	107.2 Hz	
Signal Mountain	FM	KB4ACS	444.70000	+		
Signal Mtn	FM	KG4OVQ	442.15000	+		SERA
Smithville	FUSION	AB4ZB	442.01250	+	107.2 Hz	
Sneedville	FM	KE4KQI	147.24000	+	114.8 Hz	
	FM	KE4KQI	442.45000	+	100.0 Hz	SERA
	FM	KE4WX	443.62500	+	114.8 Hz	SERA
Southport	FM	NE4MA	442.72500	+	100.0 Hz	
Sparta	DMR/BM	KR4BT	147.16500	+	CC1	
	FM	KD4WX	146.68500	-	114.8 Hz	
	FM	N9IWJ	442.62500	+	114.8 Hz	
	FM	K4TAX/R	442.97500	+	100.0 Hz	
	FM	KD4WX	444.37500	+	123.0 Hz	
Spring Hill	FM	N5AAA	442.65000	+	127.3 Hz	SERA
Springfield	DMR/BM	AD4RM	443.05000	+	CC1	

Location	Mode	Call sign	Output	Input	Access	Coordinator
Springfield	DMR/BM	AC4AM	444.32500	+	CC1	
	FM	N8ITF	29.68000	-	88.5 Hz	SERA
	FM	N8ITF	145.19000	-		
	FM	N8ITF	443.05000	+	88.5 Hz	
Stanton, Water Tower On Neblet						
	FM	NA8X	146.65500	-	156.7 Hz	SERA
Sulphur Springs	FM	K4DWQ	147.12000	+		SERA
	FM	K4DWQ	442.05000	+	100.0 Hz	SERA
Surgoinsville	FUSION	W4JEL	433.00000			
Sweetwater	FM	W4YJ	145.25000	-	100.0 Hz	SERA
	FM	W4YJ	444.12500	+		
Tellico Plains	FM	W3FCC	443.35000	+	141.3 Hz	
Tellico Plains, Waucheesi Moun						
	FM	K4EZK	146.82000	-	141.3 Hz	
Tellico Village	FM	WB4BSC	442.10000	+	100.0 Hz	SERA
Top Of The World Estates, Chil						
	FM	WB4GBI	146.62500	-	118.8 Hz	SERA
Tracy City	DSTAR	KN4WAN B	440.55000	+		
	FUSION	KT4QF	145.41000	-		
Trenton	FM	KN4KP	146.86500	-		
Tullahoma	FM	KB4JHU	147.06000	+	127.3 Hz	
Twin Oaks	FM	KA4ELN-R	147.37500	+		SERA
Unicoi	FM	WB4IXU	443.02500	+	210.7 Hz	
Union City	DMR/BM	W4NWT	147.01500	+	CC5	
	DMR/BM	K4JTM	442.35000		CC1	
	DMR/BM	K4JTM	443.50000	+	CC1	
	FM	WA4YGM	146.70000	-	100.0 Hz	
Walden	DSTAR	W4PL A	1291.00000	1271.00000		
Walland	FM	AC4JF	145.33000	-	100.0 Hz	SERA
Walland, Chilhowee Mountain						
	FM	WB4GBI	53.15000	52.15000	118.8 Hz	SERA
Walland, Chilhowee Mtn						
	FM	W4BBB	147.30000	+	100.0 Hz	SERA
	FM	N4OQJ	224.22000	-		
	FM	W4BBB	444.57500	+	100.0 Hz	
Wartrace	FUSION	N4VFB	144.40000			
	FUSION	N4VFB	147.55500			
Watertown	FM	W4LYR	146.83500	-	100.0 Hz	
Wayne Co.	FM	NE4MA	443.95000	+	100.0 Hz	
Waynesboro	FM	KF4TNP	443.10000	+	167.9 Hz	SERA
White Bluff	FM	KG4HDZ	147.37500	+	146.2 Hz	SERA
White House	FM	W4LKZ	443.40000	+	107.2 Hz	SERA
	FUSION	KK4OVW	145.41000	-		
	FUSION	KK4OVW	434.35000			
Whiteville	DSTAR	KM4GHK B	444.43750	+		
Williston	FM	WB4KOG	147.18000	+	107.2 Hz	SERA
	FM	WB4KOG	444.40000	+	107.2 Hz	SERA
Winchester	DMR/MARC	KF4TNP	444.95000	+	CC1	SERA
Winchester, Keith Spring Mtn						
	FM	W4UOT	146.82000	-	114.8 Hz	
Woodbury	FUSION	KD4WFE	432.20000			
Woodbury, Short Mountain						
	FM	W4YXA	146.91000	-	114.8 Hz	SERA
	FM	WR3S	147.36000	+	114.8 Hz	
Woodbury, Short Mtn						
	FUSION	KU4B	145.49000	-	100.0 Hz	SERA
Woodlawn	DMR/BM	K4VL	444.32500	+	CC4	
Yellow Creek	FM	WA4ROB-R	442.85000	+		SERA

TEXAS

Location	Mode	Call sign	Output	Input	Access	Coordinator
Abilene	DMR/BM	W5SLG	442.40000	+	CC4	
	DMR/BM	KF5JJK	443.96250	+	CC14	

Location	Mode	Call sign	Output	Input	Access	Coordinator
Abilene	DMR/BM	KF5JJK	444.17500	+	CC14	
	DMR/MARC	KF5JJK	443.66250	+	CC14	
	DMR/MARC	KA3IDN	444.53750	+	CC1	
	DSTAR	KG5MMT B	444.17500	+		
	DSTAR	KF5JJK B	444.50000	+		
	DSTAR	KG5MMU B	444.82500	+		
	FM	KC5PPI	145.35000	-	110.9 Hz	TVHFS
	FM	KI5ZS	145.49000	-	88.5 Hz	TVHFS
	FM	KC5OLO	146.76000	-	146.2 Hz	TVHFS
	FM	AI5TX	443.50000	+		TVHFS
	FM	KD5YCY	444.00000	+	167.9 Hz	TVHFS
	FM	WX5TX	444.17500	+	100.0 Hz	TVHFS
	FM	KB5GAR	444.75000	+	88.5 Hz	TVHFS
	FM	KE5OGP	444.87500	+	114.8 Hz	TVHFS
	FM	N5TEQ	927.03750	902.03750	141.3 Hz	TVHFS
	FUSION	W5SLG	441.13500			
Abilene, Cedar Gap Mountain						
	FM	KC5OLO	146.96000	-	146.2 Hz	TVHFS
Abilene, Near Lake Kirby						
	FM	K5CCG	444.42500	+	146.2 Hz	TVHFS
Addicks	FM	N5ZUA	145.35000	-	67.0 Hz	
	FM	N5ZUA	146.84000	-	151.4 Hz	
Adkins	DMR/MARC	W5ROS	442.00000	+	CC1	
	FM	KK5LA	444.77500	+	123.0 Hz	TVHFS
Albany	FM	N5TEQ	444.90000	+	114.8 Hz	TVHFS
Aldine	DMR/MARC	K5GJ	440.47500	+	CC9	
Aledo	FUSION	KJ5MA	441.15000			
Aledo, Lake Weatherford						
	FM	KA5HND	223.90000	-	110.9 Hz	TVHFS
	FM	KA5HND	443.20000	+	110.9 Hz	TVHFS
Alice	DMR/BM	KF5UPC	441.97500	+	CC1	
Allen		WA5RCL-L	446.45000			
	DSTAR	K5PRK B	441.57500	+		
	DSTAR	K5PRK	441.57500	+		TVHFS
	DSTAR	K5PRK D	1258.60000			
	DSTAR	K5PRK A	1293.50000	1273.50000		
	DSTAR	K5PRK	1295.00000	1315.00000		TVHFS
	FM	K5PRK	147.18000	+	107.2 Hz	TVHFS
	FM	N5UIG	441.30000	+	179.9 Hz	TVHFS
	FM	N5LTN	441.50000	+	110.9 Hz	TVHFS
	FM	AA5CT	442.55000	+		TVHFS
	FM	W5AIM	442.87500	+	162.2 Hz	
	FM	N5UIG	443.10000	+	110.9 Hz	
	FM	K5PRK	444.25000	+	79.7 Hz	TVHFS
	FUSION	KC5ADM	446.35000	-		
Alpine	FM	AD5BB	145.23000	-	146.2 Hz	TVHFS
	FM	K5FD	146.72000	-	146.2 Hz	TVHFS
	FM	WX5II	443.92500	+		TVHFS
	FM	K5FD	446.15000	-	146.2 Hz	
Alvarado	FM	K5AEC	147.22000	+	110.9 Hz	TVHFS
Alvery Junction	FM	KC5EZZ-R	441.75000	+		TVHFS
Alvin	DMR/MARC	KA5AXV	444.75000	+	CC7	TVHFS
	FM	KA5QDG	145.11000	-	123.0 Hz	TVHFS
	FM	KD5OQS	145.23000	-	107.2 Hz	TVHFS
	FM	KA5QDG	223.96000	-	123.0 Hz	TVHFS
	FM	KA5QDG	442.20000	+	103.5 Hz	TVHFS
Amarillo	DMR/MARC	KA3IDN	444.96250	+	CC14	
	FM	N5ZLU	146.74000	-	88.5 Hz	TVHFS
	FM	N5LTZ	146.92000	-		TVHFS
	FM	W5WX	147.34000	+		TVHFS
	FM	WR9B	441.37500	+	88.5 Hz	
	FM	N5LUL	441.65000	+	127.3 Hz	TVHFS

Location	Mode	Call sign	Output	Input	Access	Coordinator
Amarillo	FM	N5LTZ	443.50000	+		TVHFS
	FM	N5LTZ	444.20000	+	88.5 Hz	TVHFS
	FM	W5JTC	444.30000	+		
	FUSION	W5WX	444.47500	+		
Amarillo, KVII Tower (ABC 7)						
	FM	W5WX	146.94000	-		TVHFS
Anahuac	FM	KK5XQ	145.33000	-	123.0 Hz	TVHFS
	FM	KB5FLX	442.10000	+	103.5 Hz	TVHFS
Anderson Mill (historical)						
		W2DB-L	441.35000			
	FM	KC5WLF	146.84000	-		TVHFS
Angleton	DMR/MARC	K5BRZ	440.57500	+	CC5	
	FM	N9QXT	147.18000	+	141.3 Hz	TVHFS
	FM	KE5WFD-L	442.30000	+		TVHFS
Anna	DMR/MARC	WS5W	440.52500	+	CC1	
	DMR/MARC	WO5J	445.72500	-	CC1	
	FUSION	KA5ZTP	147.45000			
Annaville	FM	N5KOU-L	1294.50000			
Anthony	FM	N5ZRF	442.95000	+	67.0 Hz	TVHFS
Arlington	DMR/BM	KG5ZET	441.31250	+	CC1	
	DMR/BM	KF5UGN	441.33750	+	CC1	
	DMR/BM	NC7Q	442.25000	+	CC1	
	DMR/MARC	WD5DBB	443.40000	+	CC1	TVHFS
	FM	WD5DBB	146.86000	-	110.9 Hz	TVHFS
	FM	K5SLD	147.14000	+	110.9 Hz	TVHFS
	FM	K5SLD	224.80000	-	110.9 Hz	TVHFS
	FM	NR5E	441.35000	+		TVHFS
	FM	N4MSE	442.75000	+	127.3 Hz	
	FM	AI5TX	443.67500	+		TVHFS
	FM	WA5VHU	443.85000	+	110.9 Hz	TVHFS
	FM	K5SLD	444.20000	+		TVHFS
	FM	W5PSB	444.55000	+		TVHFS
	FUSION	WB5UGC	432.60000			
	FUSION	KF5CFW	446.47500			
Asherton	DMR/BM	AF5EK	440.72500	+	CC1	
Aspermont	FM	KC5ATZ	444.70000	+		
Atascocita, Atascocita Fire De						
	FM	W5SI	443.55000	+	103.5 Hz	TVHFS
Athens	FM	K5EPH	147.22000	+	136.5 Hz	TVHFS
	FM	W5ETX	442.85000	+	136.5 Hz	TVHFS
	FM	KF5WT	443.30000	+	100.0 Hz	TVHFS
	FM	AI5TX	443.70000	+		TVHFS
Atlanta	DMR/BM	WX5CSS	440.15000	+	CC5	
	DMR/MARC	KA5AHS	440.52500	+	CC9	
	FM	K5HCM	145.25000	-	100.0 Hz	TVHFS
	FM	WA5JYZ	147.26000	+	151.4 Hz	TVHFS
Atlanta, Caver Ranch						
	FM	K5HCM	146.98000	-	100.0 Hz	TVHFS
Atlanta, Christus St. Michaels						
	FM	K5HCM	443.30000	+	100.0 Hz	TVHFS
Atlanta, Springdale						
	FM	WX5FL	145.31000	-	100.0 Hz	TVHFS
Atlanta, Springdale Tower						
	FM	KB5SQL	444.55000	+	100.0 Hz	
Aubrey	DMR/MARC	K5RNB	443.45000	+	CC1	
	FM	K5RNB	145.23000	-	100.0 Hz	TVHFS
Austin	DMR/BM	KA5D	441.32500	+	CC1	
	DMR/BM	K5TRA	443.07500	+	CC1	
	DMR/BM	K5TRA	444.71250	+	CC1	
	DSTAR	W5KA C	146.78000	-		
	DSTAR	W5KA B	440.65000	+		
	DSTAR	K5SOC B	443.40000	+		

Location	Mode	Call sign	Output	Input	Access	Coordinator
Austin	DSTAR	W5KA D	1248.10000			
	DSTAR	W5KA A	1293.10000	1273.10000		
	DSTAR	K5SOC A	1293.40000	1273.40000		
	FM	WB5PCV	146.61000	-	103.5 Hz	TVHFS
	FM	WB5PCV	224.94000	-		TVHFS
	FM	K5LBJ	441.67500	+	131.8 Hz	TVHFS
	FM	N5OAK	441.77500	+		TVHFS
	FM	KA9LAY	441.97500	+	97.4 Hz	TVHFS
	FM	W5TRI	442.02500	+	114.8 Hz	TVHFS
	FM	K5AB	442.20000	+	100.0 Hz	TVHFS
	FM	WB5FNZ	442.50000	+	162.2 Hz	TVHFS
	FM	WA5VTV	443.80000	+	131.8 Hz	
	FM	AI5TX	443.95000	+		TVHFS
	FM	WB5PCV	444.00000	+	107.2 Hz	TVHFS
	FM	W5KA	444.10000	+	103.5 Hz	TVHFS
	FM	K5TRA	444.50000	+	110.9 Hz	
	FM	K5TRA	927.01250	902.01250	225.7 Hz	
	FM	K5TRA	927.11250	902.11250		TVHFS
	FM	KA5D	927.17500	902.17500	110.9 Hz	TVHFS
	P25	N0GSZ	146.86000	-	146.2 Hz	TVHFS
	FUSION	KI5MEF	145.37000	-		
	FUSION	W5KA	146.88000	-		
	FUSION	NI5B	147.50000			
	FUSION	AE5WW	441.07500			
	FUSION	KB5HTB	442.06250	+		
	FUSION	KA5C	442.15000	+		
	FUSION	KI5MEF	444.95000	+		
	FUSION	KI5MEF	446.10000			
Austin Texas	FUSION	KI5ESV	144.44000			
Austin, Buckman Mountain						
	FM	N5MHI	1292.40000	1272.40000	107.2 Hz	TVHFS
Austin, Buckman Mtn						
	FM	WA5VTV	147.36000	+	131.8 Hz	TVHFS
Austin, Oak Hill	FUSION	N5OAK	147.32000	+	114.8 Hz	TVHFS
Austin, Pickle Research Center						
	FUSION	W5KA	146.88000	-	107.2 Hz	TVHFS
Austin, South Austin Hospital						
	DSTAR	W5KA	440.65000	+		TVHFS
Austin, South Austin Med Ctr						
	DSTAR	W5KA	1293.10000	1273.10000		TVHFS
Austin, University Of Texas						
	FM	KA5D	441.32500	+	97.4 Hz	TVHFS
Austin, Water Tower						
	FM	AE5WW	444.85000	+	103.5 Hz	TVHFS
Austin, Westlake Hills						
	FM	N5ZUA	145.11000	-	103.5 Hz	TVHFS
Avinger, Lake-O-The Pines / Wa						
	FM	WX5FL	145.47000	-	136.5 Hz	
Avondale		KJ5RM-L	445.80000			
Axtell	FUSION	KG5AWL	147.24000	+		
	FUSION	KG5AWL	147.92000	-		
	FUSION	KG5AWL	441.35000	+		
Azle	FM	WB5IDM	147.16000	+	110.9 Hz	TVHFS
	FM	WB5IDM	223.94000	-	110.9 Hz	TVHFS
	FM	WB5IDM	442.15000	+	110.9 Hz	TVHFS
	FM	WB5IDM	927.01250	902.01250	110.9 Hz	TVHFS
	FUSION	KG5JBC	446.50000			
Bacon		W3TUA-L	445.50500			
Balcones Heights	FM	K5NNN-L	145.21000	-		TVHFS
Bandera	FM	W5MWI	145.31000	-		
	FM	W5MWI	443.30000	+		
Bangs	ATV	KB5ZVV	147.00000	+	94.8 Hz	TVHFS

Location	Mode	Call sign	Output	Input	Access	Coordinator
Bastrop	DMR/MARC	K5VXN	443.26250	+	CC1	
	FM	NA6M	147.34000	+	100.0 Hz	TVHFS
	FM	N5FRT	441.55000	+	114.8 Hz	
	FM	WB6ARE	441.95000	+		TVHFS
	FM	WB6ARE	442.72500	+	114.8 Hz	TVHFS
	FM	WB6ARE	443.17500	+	114.8 Hz	TVHFS
	FM	WB5UGT	444.30000	+	203.5 Hz	TVHFS
	FM	K5TRA	927.02500	902.02500		
Bay City	FM	W5WTM	146.72000	-	146.2 Hz	TVHFS
Bayou Vista	DMR/BM	N5FOG	433.27500	+	CC1	
Baytown	FM	NE5TX	145.31000	-	167.9 Hz	TVHFS
	FM	K5BAY	146.78000	-	100.0 Hz	TVHFS
	FM	K5BAY	443.80000	+	100.0 Hz	TVHFS
	FM	KB5IAM	443.87500	+	173.8 Hz	
	FUSION	KA5QDG	147.26000	+		
	FUSION	KI5GNL	147.86000	+		
	FUSION	KI5FQW	444.97500	-		
Beaumont	DMR/BM	WB5ITT	444.50000	+	CC1	
	DMR/MARC	N5YX	145.45000	-	CC1	
	FM	W5RIN-R	146.70000	-	107.2 Hz	TVHFS
	FM	W5RIN	146.76000	-	107.2 Hz	TVHFS
	FM	W5APX	146.94000	-	100.0 Hz	TVHFS
	FM	W5XOM	147.30000	+	103.5 Hz	TVHFS
	FM	KB5OVJ	147.34000	+	131.8 Hz	TVHFS
	FM	W5RIN	444.70000	-	107.2 Hz	TVHFS
Beckville	FM	KA5HSA	444.50000	+	151.4 Hz	
Bedford	FM	N5VAV	442.82500	+	110.9 Hz	TVHFS
Bee Cave	FM	AI5TX	443.62500	+		TVHFS
	FM	K5GJ	443.92500	+		TVHFS
	FM	K5TRA	927.08750	902.08750	151.4 Hz	
Beeville	DMR/BM	W6AUS	440.32500	+	CC1	
	DMR/MARC	W5DTW	444.70000	+	CC1	
	FM	KI5OEP	146.44000		225.7 Hz	
Bellaire	FM	KI5LIC	145.70000			
	FM	AK5G	441.82500	+		TVHFS
Bellville	DSTAR	W5SFA C	146.93000	-		
	DSTAR	W5SFA B	440.70000	+		
	FM	WR5AAA	146.88000	-	203.5 Hz	TVHFS
	FM	W5SFA	444.87500	+	103.5 Hz	TVHFS
Belton	DMR/BM	N5JLP	442.67500	+	CC10	
	FM	KE5CDE	446.10000	-	123.0 Hz	
	FM	WD4IFU	927.15000	902.15000	114.8 Hz	
	FUSION	WD5EMS	145.19000	-		
Belton, Belton High School						
	FM	KG5PIV	145.35000	-		
Benbrook	FUSION	KA5TWA	440.70000	+	136.5 Hz	TVHFS
Bethel	FM	W5MGM-L	146.44000			
Big Bend	FM	AD5BB	146.82000	-	146.2 Hz	TVHFS
Big Lake	FM	N5SOR	442.30000	+	162.2 Hz	TVHFS
Big Spring	DMR/BM	W5LND	443.22500	+	CC1	TVHFS
	DMR/BM	W5AW	443.50000	+	CC1	
	DMR/MARC	KE5PL	443.43750	+	CC14	
	DSTAR	W5AW	147.24000	+		
	DSTAR	W5AW C	147.24000	+		
	DSTAR	W5AW	440.68750	-		
	DSTAR	W5AW B	440.68750	+		
	DSTAR	W5AW D	1253.30000			
	DSTAR	W5AW A	1273.30000	1293.30000		
	FM	KE5PL	443.95000	+		TVHFS
Big Spring, Tower Ridge						
	FM	W5LND	147.04000	+	88.5 Hz	TVHFS
	FM	W5LND	442.10000	+	162.2 Hz	TVHFS

Location	Mode	Call sign	Output	Input	Access	Coordinator
Bivins	FM	N5YU	145.41000	-	100.0 Hz	
Black	FM	N5LTZ	444.42500	+		TVHFS
Blanco	FM	KF5KOI	145.28000	-	77.0 Hz	TVHFS
Blanket	FM	N5AG	224.72000	-	94.8 Hz	TVHFS
	FUSION	N5AG	432.50000			
Bluetown	DMR/MARC	KC5HWB	443.88750	+	CC9	
Boerne	FM	KB5TX	145.19000	-	88.5 Hz	
	FM	AB5UE	145.42000	-	123.0 Hz	
	FM	KB5TX	146.64000	-	88.5 Hz	
	FM	WB5CIT	441.65000	+	103.5 Hz	
	FM	AB5UE	443.27500	+	97.4 Hz	
	FM	AB5UE	443.60000	+	123.0 Hz	
	FM	W5VEO	444.75000	+	162.2 Hz	TVHFS
	FM	KB5TX	444.90000	+	88.5 Hz	TVHFS
	FUSION	KC6BAV	442.50000	+		
Bonham		K5FRC-R	145.47000			
Boonsville	FM	K5RHV	443.90000	+	100.0 Hz	TVHFS
Borger	DMR/BM	KD5ROK	146.13125	-	CC14	
	DMR/MARC	KE5CJ	441.33750	+	CC14	
	FM	W5WDR	147.00000	+	88.5 Hz	
Bowie	FM	K1RKH	145.39000	-	192.8 Hz	TVHFS
	FM	WX5ARC	147.32000	+	192.8 Hz	TVHFS
	FM	WX5ECT	441.77500	+		TVHFS
Boyd, Courthouse	FM	K5JEJ	146.98000	-	110.9 Hz	TVHFS
Brackettville	FM	AA5KC	146.88000	-	127.3 Hz	TVHFS
	FM	WB5TZJ	443.62500	+		TVHFS
	FM	AA5KC	443.72500	+	100.0 Hz	TVHFS
Brady	DMR/BM	WA5HOT	441.80000	+	CC1	
	DMR/BM	KG5YMG	443.57500	+	CC1	
	DSTAR	WA5HOT	444.87500	+	162.2 Hz	TVHFS
	FM	AA5JM	146.62000	-	114.8 Hz	TVHFS
	FM	KC5EZZ	146.90000	-	162.2 Hz	TVHFS
	FM	WO5OD	444.07500	+	110.9 Hz	
Brazos, Chestnut Mountain						
	FM	W5SUF	444.17500	+	114.8 Hz	TVHFS
Brenham	DMR/MARC	W5JWP	440.50000	+	CC3	
Brenham, Blinn College						
	FM	W5AUM	147.26000	+	103.5 Hz	TVHFS
Brenham, Brenham High School						
	FM	KF5ZRT	441.32500	+	103.5 Hz	
Brenham, Brenham National Bank						
	FM	W5AUM	145.39000	-	103.5 Hz	TVHFS
	FM	N5MBM	441.65000	+	110.9 Hz	TVHFS
Brenham, Kruse Village						
	FM	N5MBM	441.92500	+	123.0 Hz	TVHFS
Brenham, Police Dept Communica						
	FM	W5AUM	443.25000	+	103.5 Hz	TVHFS
Bridgeport	FM	N5WEB	927.12500	902.12500	100.0 Hz	TVHFS
Brownfield	FM	WA5OEO	147.34000	+	162.2 Hz	TVHFS
Brownsville	DMR/BM	KC5MOL	443.82500	+	CC1	
	DMR/BM	KC5MAH	444.37500	+	CC1	
	DMR/BM	KC5MOL	444.82500	+	CC1	
	DSTAR	KG5EUU B	445.50000			
	FM	K5MPH	145.52000			
	FM	W5RGV	147.04000	+	114.8 Hz	TVHFS
	FM	N5XWO	441.30000	+	151.4 Hz	TVHFS
	FM	N5RGV	444.17500	+	114.8 Hz	
	FM	W5RGV	444.40000	+	114.8 Hz	
Brownwood	FM	K5BWD	146.94000	-	94.8 Hz	TVHFS
	FM	AI5TX	443.92500	+		TVHFS
	FM	K5BWD	444.70000	+	94.8 Hz	TVHFS
	WX	W5CBT	146.82000	-	94.8 Hz	TVHFS

Location	Mode	Call sign	Output	Input	Access	Coordinator
Brownwood, Bangs Hill						
	FUSION	WD9ARW	443.90000	+	94.8 Hz	
Bruceville	DMR/BM	AA5RT	444.72500	+	CC1	
	DSTAR	W5HAT C	147.24000	+		
	DSTAR	W5HAT B	440.62500	+		
	DSTAR	W5NGU	440.62500	+		TVHFS
	FM	W5NCD	147.24000	+	97.4 Hz	TVHFS
	FM	W5NCD	444.47500	+		TVHFS
Brushy Creek		AD5TF-L	146.46000			
Bryan	DSTAR	W5AC B	443.40000	+		
	FM	KD5DLW	443.42500	+	127.3 Hz	TVHFS
Buffalo	FM	W5UOK-R	147.28000	+		TVHFS
Buffalo, Water Tower						
	FM	WD5EMS	444.25000	+		
Bullard	FM	KB9LFZ	443.20000	+	127.3 Hz	
Bulverde	FM	WA5KBQ	443.25000	+	103.5 Hz	TVHFS
	FM	W5DK	444.35000	+	151.4 Hz	TVHFS
Buna	FM	W5JAS	145.39000	-	118.8 Hz	TVHFS
	FM	W5JAS	442.42500	+	118.8 Hz	TVHFS
	P25	KB5OVJ	147.38000	+		TVHFS
Burkburnett	DMR/BM	KD5UBW	464.25000	+	CC4	
	FM	W5DAD	146.70000	-	192.8 Hz	TVHFS
	FM	KD5PWT	444.02500	+	192.8 Hz	TVHFS
	FM	KD5INN	444.30000	+		
Burleson	FM	WA5JRS	444.52500	+	167.9 Hz	
	FUSION	KI5CEY	439.20000			
	FUSION	KI5CEY	439.52500			
Burnet	FM	KB5YKJ	145.29000	-	114.8 Hz	TVHFS
	FM	K5HLA	147.02000	+	88.5 Hz	
Byers	FM	KF5DFD	146.82000	-	192.8 Hz	TVHFS
Bynum		W5GGH-L	145.50000			
		WB5UGC-L	145.73000			
Caddo	FM	KB5WB	444.72500	+	110.9 Hz	TVHFS
Caddo Mills	FUSION	KF5NXR	146.40000			
Cameron, McClaren Hill						
	FM	KE5URD	147.02000	+	123.0 Hz	TVHFS
Canyon	FM	N5LTZ	443.65000	+	88.5 Hz	TVHFS
Canyon Lake	FM	W5ERX	444.45000	+	114.8 Hz	TVHFS
	FM	K5TRA	927.03750	902.03750	141.3 Hz	
	FUSION	KJ5IK	441.32500			
	FUSION	KE5MQI	446.32500	-		
Carlton	FM	W5GKY	145.27000	-	110.9 Hz	TVHFS
	FM	W5GKY	147.30000	+	100.0 Hz	TVHFS
Carrizo Springs, Center Of Tow						
	FM	W5EVH	443.30000	+	100.0 Hz	TVHFS
Carrollton		KB5NFT-L	446.00000			
	DMR/MARC	N5GDL	440.45000	+	CC1	
	FM	KB5A	145.21000	-	110.9 Hz	TVHFS
	FM	K5ZYZ	146.82000	-	110.9 Hz	TVHFS
	FM	K5JG	441.62500	+	100.0 Hz	
	FM	K5GWF	441.82500	+		TVHFS
	FM	KB5A	442.65000	+	110.9 Hz	TVHFS
	FM	K5AB	444.45000	+	110.9 Hz	TVHFS
	FUSION	KI5X	146.46000			
	FUSION	N5VFX	147.32000	+		
Carrollton, Baylor Hospital						
	FM	N5KRG	927.17500	902.17500	110.9 Hz	TVHFS
Carthage	FM	KA5HSA	146.72000	-		TVHFS
	FM	KA5HSA	444.80000	+	151.4 Hz	TVHFS
Cason, Deaton Brothers Tower						
	FM	WA5OQR	146.88000	-	151.4 Hz	TVHFS
Castle Hills		AA5KG-L	147.56000			

Location	Mode	Call sign	Output	Input	Access	Coordinator
Castroville	FM	K5YDE	146.80000	-	162.2 Hz	TVHFS
	FM	KD5DX	147.20000	+	162.2 Hz	TVHFS
Cat Spring	FM	WB5UGT	444.07500	+	103.5 Hz	TVHFS
Cedar Creek	FM	WA5AP	444.05000	+	141.3 Hz	
Cedar Hil	DSTAR	N5DRP B	440.10000	+		
	DSTAR	N5DRP D	1258.60000			
Cedar Hill	FM	W5WB	147.06000	+	110.9 Hz	TVHFS
	FM	W5AHN	147.26000	+	85.4 Hz	TVHFS
	FM	AI5TX	224.10000	-		TVHFS
	FM	WB5YUV	442.40000	+	110.9 Hz	TVHFS
	FM	AI5TX	443.50000	+		TVHFS
	FM	N5UN	443.97500	+	156.7 Hz	TVHFS
	FM	W5AUY	444.50000	+		TVHFS
Cedar Park	DMR/BM	KC5AFM	441.32500	+	CC1	
	DMR/MARC	KC5AFM	441.35000	+	CC1	
	DMR/MARC	KE5ZW	442.65000	+	CC1	
	FM	W3MRC	146.90000	-	100.0 Hz	TVHFS
	FM	W2MN	146.98000	-	103.5 Hz	TVHFS
	FM	W2MN	147.12000	+	103.5 Hz	TVHFS
	FM	W3MRC	444.60000	+	100.0 Hz	TVHFS
	P25	KE5ZW	146.68000	-	123.0 Hz	TVHFS
	FUSION	KC5WLF	145.37000	-		
Celina	FM	N5MRG	224.24000	-	103.5 Hz	
	FM	KE5UT	444.51250	+	123.0 Hz	TVHFS
	FM	N5BCW	444.97500	+	103.5 Hz	
Centerville	DSTAR	KF5MQZ C	147.38000	+		
	FM	K3WIV	145.21000	-		TVHFS
	FM	K3WIV	145.45000	-	114.8 Hz	TVHFS
	FM	N5HLC	146.78000	-	103.5 Hz	TVHFS
	FM	KD0RW	147.30000	+	114.8 Hz	TVHFS
	FM	WA5GED	441.65000	+	103.5 Hz	
	FM	K3WIV	442.77500	+		TVHFS
	FM	K3WIV	442.97500	+		TVHFS
	FM	AI5TX	443.67500	+		TVHFS
Chalk Mountain	FM	K5AB	145.47000	-	110.9 Hz	TVHFS
	FM	W5DNT	147.02000	+	162.2 Hz	TVHFS
Channelview	FM	KC5TCT	441.60000	+	203.5 Hz	TVHFS
	FM	KE5CWO	446.10000	-	141.3 Hz	
Channelview, I-10 E & BW8 E						
	FM	K5CAP	443.18000	+	179.9 Hz	
Chappell Hill	DMR/MARC	N5MBM	145.15000	-	CC13	TVHFS
	FM	N5MBM	52.35000	51.35000		TVHFS
	FM	N5MBM	224.90000	-	103.5 Hz	TVHFS
	FM	N5MBM	441.62500	+	103.5 Hz	TVHFS
	FM	N5MBM	927.15000	902.15000	103.5 Hz	TVHFS
Childress	DMR/MARC	AA5LB	444.72500	+	CC1	
	FM	N5OX	146.96000	-		TVHFS
	FM	N5OX	442.40000	+	100.0 Hz	
China Spring	FUSION	K5KCL	441.37500	+		
Chita	FM	W5IOU	145.35000	-	131.8 Hz	TVHFS
Choate	FM	K5ZZT	443.65000	+		TVHFS
Christine	FM	W5DK	443.77500	+	141.3 Hz	TVHFS
Chub	FM	N5MXE-R	442.02500	+		TVHFS
Clarendon	FM	KE5NCA	444.27500	+	127.3 Hz	
Clarksville	FM	KI5DX	147.34000	+	100.0 Hz	
Clear Lake Shores						
	FM	KA5QDG	145.39000	-	123.0 Hz	TVHFS
Clear Lake Shores, Water Tower						
	FM	WA5LQR	442.37500	+	103.5 Hz	
Clear Lake, Boeing Building						
	FM	K5HOU	442.75000	+	103.5 Hz	TVHFS

Location	Mode	Call sign	Output	Input	Access	Coordinator
Clear Lake, Boeing Building 37						
	FM	K5HOU	146.86000	-	100.0 Hz	TVHFS
Cleburne	FM	KB5YBI	145.49000	-	88.5 Hz	TVHFS
	FM	W5JCR	224.76000	-	88.5 Hz	
	FM	KY5O-R	444.00000	+	136.5 Hz	TVHFS
	FUSION	KY5O/R	443.75000	+		
Cleveland	FM	N5AK	146.90000	-	100.0 Hz	TVHFS
	FM	N5AK	224.78000	-		TVHFS
	FUSION	N5BSB	145.28000	-		
	FUSION	N5AK	444.65000	+		
Clifton	FM	W5BCR	147.18000	+	123.0 Hz	
	FM	W5BCR	444.40000	+	123.0 Hz	TVHFS
Coldspring	FUSION	KO5K	146.55000			
	FUSION	WB5HZM	147.16000	+		
	FUSION	KO5K	443.02500	+		
College Station	DMR/BM	NU5D	441.31250	+	CC1	
	DMR/BM	KG5RKI	441.35000	+	CC1	
	DMR/BM	W5AC	441.36250	+	CC1	
	DMR/BM	K5ZY	444.12500	+	CC1	
	DMR/MARC	N1WP	444.55000	+	CC1	
	DSTAR	KC5QGY D	1254.00000			
	DSTAR	KC5QGY A	1293.00000	1313.00000		
	FM	K5ZY	147.16000	+	88.5 Hz	
College Station, Skyline Commu						
	FM	W5BCS	146.68000	-	88.5 Hz	TVHFS
College Station, Texas A&M Uni						
	FM	W5AC	146.82000	-	88.5 Hz	TVHFS
Colleyville	FM	W5RV	441.90000	+	110.9 Hz	TVHFS
Colorado City	FM	K5WTC	444.85000	+	162.2 Hz	TVHFS
Columbus	FM	W5SFA	147.14000	+	103.5 Hz	TVHFS
	FM	WB5UGT	442.75000	+	141.3 Hz	TVHFS
Comfort	FM	KD3VK	441.82500	+	82.5 Hz	TVHFS
Commerce	FM	WB5MQP	147.02000	+	167.9 Hz	TVHFS
	FM	W5AMC	444.52500	+	103.5 Hz	TVHFS
Conroe	DMR/BM	KB5RAB	441.37500	+	CC1	
	DMR/MARC	N5LUY	444.75000	+	CC3	
	FM	NE5TH	147.02000	+	136.5 Hz	TVHFS
	FM	N5KWN	147.14000	+	136.5 Hz	TVHFS
	FM	KF5RDE	441.30000	+	118.8 Hz	
	FM	KE5PTZ	441.75000	+	123.0 Hz	TVHFS
	FM	WB5DGR	442.25000	+	103.5 Hz	TVHFS
	FM	W5SAM	442.52500	+	127.3 Hz	TVHFS
	FM	WB5DGR	442.90000	+	151.4 Hz	TVHFS
	FM	AG5EG	444.57500	+	103.5 Hz	TVHFS
Coppell	FM	W5CPL	441.37500	+	103.5 Hz	
Coppell, Coppell High School						
	FM	KC5BY	444.27500	+	114.8 Hz	
Copperas Cove	DMR/BM	K5CRA	441.31250	+	CC1	
	FM	K5CRA	147.26000	+	88.5 Hz	TVHFS
	FM	K5CRA	443.32500	+	88.5 Hz	TVHFS
Cornudas	FM	WS5B	147.32000	+	110.9 Hz	TVHFS
Coronado Hills		AE5RJ-R	443.55000			
Corpus Christi	DMR/BM	W5QLD	441.35000	+	CC1	
	DMR/MARC	AD5CA	441.60000	+	CC1	
	DMR/MARC	KC5HWB	444.60000	+	CC9	
	FM	N5CRP	146.82000	-	107.2 Hz	TVHFS
	FM	N5CRP	146.88000	-	107.2 Hz	TVHFS
	FM	K5GGB	147.06000	+	107.2 Hz	TVHFS
Corsicana	DMR/MARC	KC5HWB	442.92500	+	CC9	TVHFS
	DSTAR	K5NEM C	147.34000	+		
	DSTAR	K5NEM	147.34000	+		TVHFS
	FM	N5ZUA	29.66000	-	192.8 Hz	

Location	Mode	Call sign	Output	Input	Access	Coordinator
Corsicana	FM	N5ZUA	444.77500	+	100.0 Hz	TVHFS
Cotulla	FM	WY5LL	146.79000	-	192.8 Hz	
Crockett	DMR/MARC	KG5OKB	440.35000	+	CC9	
	FM	W5DLC	145.31000	-	103.5 Hz	TVHFS
	FM	WA5EC	146.70000	-	123.0 Hz	TVHFS
	FM	WA5FCL	443.60000	+	100.0 Hz	TVHFS
	FM	WB5UGT	444.22500	+	123.0 Hz	TVHFS
Crosby	FM	KB5IJF	442.05000	+	103.5 Hz	TVHFS
	FM	AI5TX	443.70000	+		TVHFS
	FM	W5TWO	444.77500	+	103.5 Hz	TVHFS
Crosbyton	FM	WB5BRY	147.16000	+	179.9 Hz	TVHFS
	FM	KC5MVZ	442.27500	+	107.2 Hz	TVHFS
Cross Plains	FM	KA9DNO	444.65000	+	77.0 Hz	TVHFS
Cypress	DMR/MARC	N5LUY	444.47500	+	CC7	
	FM	N5LUY	442.65000	+	156.7 Hz	TVHFS
	FUSION	KG5QAP	433.73750			
Daingerfield	FM	NG5F	145.23000	-	151.4 Hz	TVHFS
Dale, Flag Hill	FM	KE5AMB	145.43000	-	114.8 Hz	
	FM	KE5AMB	443.00000	+	114.8 Hz	TVHFS
Dallas	DMR/BM	N4MSE	442.02500	+	CC1	
	DMR/MARC	AB5U	440.13750	+	CC1	
	DMR/MARC	W5EBQ	440.47500	+	CC1	
	DMR/MARC	W5EBQ	440.63750	+	CC1	
	DMR/MARC	W5EBQ	441.63750	+	CC1	
	DMR/MARC	WA5YST	444.35000	+	CC1	
	DMR/MARC	N4MSE	927.05000	902.05000	CC1	
	DSTAR	W5FC	145.13000	-		TVHFS
	DSTAR	W5FC C	145.13000	-		
	DSTAR	K5TIT	147.36000	+		TVHFS
	DSTAR	K5TIT C	147.36000	+		
	DSTAR	W5FC	440.57500	+		TVHFS
	DSTAR	W5FC B	440.57500	+		
	DSTAR	K5TIT	442.00000	+		TVHFS
	DSTAR	K5TIT B	442.00000	+		
	DSTAR	K5TIT D	1253.00000			
	DSTAR	W5FC D	1259.00000			
	DSTAR	K5TIT	1293.00000	1273.00000		TVHFS
	DSTAR	K5TIT A	1293.00000	1273.00000		
	DSTAR	W5FC	1295.00000	1275.00000		TVHFS
	DSTAR	W5FC A	1295.00000	1275.00000		
	FM	W5EBQ	52.59000	51.59000	110.9 Hz	TVHFS
	FM	KA5CTN	145.19000	-	110.9 Hz	TVHFS
	FM	K5AHT	146.64000	-	118.8 Hz	TVHFS
	FM	W5FC	146.88000	-	110.9 Hz	TVHFS
	FM	W5WRL-L	147.52000			
	FM	N4MSE	224.70000	-	127.3 Hz	TVHFS
	FM	W5FC	224.88000	-	110.9 Hz	TVHFS
	FM	KG5LL	441.55000	+	110.9 Hz	TVHFS
	FM	W5DCR	442.07500	+	110.9 Hz	TVHFS
	FM	N5ZW	442.27500	+		TVHFS
	FM	W5FC	442.42500	+	110.9 Hz	TVHFS
	FM	WO5E	442.47500	+		TVHFS
	FM	N5ARC	442.50000	+	110.9 Hz	TVHFS
	FM	N5DA	443.00000	+	110.9 Hz	TVHFS
	FM	K5TIT	443.47500	+	156.7 Hz	TVHFS
	FM	AI5TX	443.95000	+		TVHFS
	FM	K5TAO	444.15000	+	100.0 Hz	
	FM	N4MSE	444.65000	+	186.2 Hz	
	FM	N4MSE	927.06250	902.06250		
	FUSION	W5DCR	146.96000	-		
	FUSION	KB5A	444.07500	+	110.9 Hz	TVHFS
	FUSION	K5KOY	445.47500			

Location	Mode	Call sign	Output	Input	Access	Coordinator
Dallas Texas	FM	AA5NO	433.50000			
Dallas, Green Building						
	FM	W5EBQ	146.70000	-	110.9 Hz	TVHFS
Davilla, Davilla VFD						
	FM	KG5DUO	147.00000	+	123.0 Hz	
Davy	FM	WD5IEH	147.32000	+	141.3 Hz	TVHFS
Decatur	FM	W5KFC	146.78000	-	131.8 Hz	TVHFS
	FM	WQ5A	442.60000	+	131.8 Hz	TVHFS
	FM	N5ERS	443.22500	+	110.9 Hz	TVHFS
	FM	KE5WBO	444.40000	+	156.7 Hz	TVHFS
Del Rio	FM	KD5HAM	146.82000	-	127.3 Hz	TVHFS
	FM	K5CXR	147.30000	+		TVHFS
	FM	WB5TZJ	443.50000	+		TVHFS
Del Valle	FM	KB5HTB	145.17000	-	88.5 Hz	TVHFS
Denison	FM	W5DWH	145.33000	-	100.0 Hz	TVHFS
	FM	KD5HQF	441.35000	+	100.0 Hz	
	FUSION	W5CBT	441.05000			
Denton	DMR/MARC	W5NGU	146.92000	-	CC1	
	DMR/MARC	N5LS	440.66250	+	CC1	TVHFS
	DMR/MARC	N5LS	927.66250	902.66250	CC1	TVHFS
	DSTAR	W5NGU C	147.45000	146.45000		
	DSTAR	W5NGU B	442.92500	+		
	DSTAR	W5NGU D	1253.60000			
	DSTAR	W5NGU A	1293.40000	1273.40000		
	FM	W5NGU	441.32500	+	88.5 Hz	TVHFS
	FM	N5LS	927.41250	902.41250		
Denton, EOC	DSTAR	W5NGU	147.45000	146.45000		TVHFS
	DSTAR	W5NGU	442.92500	-		TVHFS
	FM	W5FKN	145.17000	-	110.9 Hz	TVHFS
	FM	W5NGU	927.61250	902.61250		TVHFS
Denton, Stark Hall	FM	AF5RS	224.92000	-	110.9 Hz	
Devers	FM	N5FJX	146.98000	-	103.5 Hz	TVHFS
	FM	KA5QDG	224.92000	-	123.0 Hz	TVHFS
	FM	N6LXX	444.85000	+	151.4 Hz	TVHFS
Devine	FM	WB5LJZ	146.61000	-		TVHFS
	FM	WB5LJZ	146.88000	-	141.3 Hz	TVHFS
Dickens	FM	WX5LBB	444.32500	+	162.2 Hz	TVHFS
Dimmitt	FM	KW5KW	444.70000	+	110.9 Hz	
Donna	FM	KC5YFP	146.74000	-	114.8 Hz	TVHFS
Doss	FM	W5RP	147.16000	+	162.2 Hz	TVHFS
	FM	W5RP	442.30000	+	162.2 Hz	TVHFS
Double Mountain	FM	AI5TX	443.70000	+		TVHFS
Doucette	FM	WD5TYL	147.22000	+	100.0 Hz	TVHFS
Driftwood	DMR/BM	KI5QYB	444.35000	+	CC1	
Dripping Springs	DMR/BM	N5OAK	441.30000	+	CC1	
	FM	W5MIX	146.74000	-	67.0 Hz	TVHFS
Dumas	DMR/MARC	KD5ROK	443.01250	+	CC14	
	FM	N5LTZ	444.35000	+	88.5 Hz	TVHFS
Duncanville	FM	KA5KEH	441.35000	+	114.8 Hz	TVHFS
	FUSION	K5BBZ	146.56000			
Eastland	FM	KB5WB	442.72500	+	114.8 Hz	TVHFS
Eastland, Lake Leon						
	FM	KB5WB	444.80000	+	156.7 Hz	TVHFS
Eddy	FM	W5BEC-R	147.14000	+	123.0 Hz	TVHFS
Eden	DMR/BM	KC5EZZ	444.12500	+	CC1	
	FM	AI5TX	443.97500	+		TVHFS
Edgewood	FM	W5EEY	444.20000	+	136.5 Hz	TVHFS
Edna	DMR/MARC	W5LCR	444.05000	+	CC7	
Edom	FM	W5ETX	146.62000	-	136.5 Hz	TVHFS
El Paso	DMR/MARC	N5RWZ	442.22500	+	CC1	
	DMR/MARC	N5RWZ	442.32500	+	CC1	
	DMR/MARC	AE5RJ	443.60000	+	CC1	

Location	Mode	Call sign	Output	Input	Access	Coordinator
El Paso	DMR/MARC	W5WIN	444.50000	+	CC1	
	DSTAR	K5WPH C	145.11000	-		
	DSTAR	W5ELP C	146.62000	-		
	DSTAR	KG5ZPX	440.65000	+		
	DSTAR	K5WPH B	443.22500	+		
	DSTAR	N6TOC	444.60000	+		
	FM	K5WPH	53.55000	52.55000		TVHFS
	FM	K5WPH	145.33000	-	67.0 Hz	TVHFS
	FM	WX5ELP	145.41000	-	88.5 Hz	TVHFS
	FM	N6TOC	146.34000	+		
	FM	K5ELP	146.70000	-	114.8 Hz	TVHFS
	FM	N6TOC	146.94000	-	123.0 Hz	
	FM	KJ5EO	147.06000	+		TVHFS
	FM	KJ5EO	147.10000	+		TVHFS
	FM	K5ELP	147.20000	+	67.0 Hz	TVHFS
	FM	K5WPH	147.24000	+	162.2 Hz	TVHFS
	FM	KD6CUB	147.28000	+	67.0 Hz	TVHFS
	FM	K5KKO	147.32000	+	162.2 Hz	TVHFS
	FM	KE5OIB	147.36000	+		TVHFS
	FM	KD6CUB	224.82000	-	100.0 Hz	TVHFS
	FM	N5ZFF	441.70000	+	100.0 Hz	TVHFS
	FM	WB5LJO	442.10000	+	123.0 Hz	TVHFS
	FM	N5FAZ	442.12500	+	103.5 Hz	TVHFS
	FM	K5WPH	442.25000	+	100.0 Hz	TVHFS
	FM	WB5LJO	442.55000	+	100.0 Hz	TVHFS
	FM	KJ5EO	442.60000	+		TVHFS
	FM	K5ELP	442.82500	+	100.0 Hz	TVHFS
	FM	KJ5EO	443.00000	+		TVHFS
	FM	N6TOC	443.37500	+	100.0 Hz	TVHFS
	FM	K5WPH	443.40000	+	100.0 Hz	TVHFS
	FM	W5DPD	443.65000	+		TVHFS
	FM	WB5LJO	443.70000	+		TVHFS
	FM	KB6JYF	443.85000	+	100.0 Hz	
	FM	KA5CDJ	443.92500	+		TVHFS
	FM	K5ELP	444.20000	+	100.0 Hz	TVHFS
	FUSION	KG5ZJV	444.40000	+		
	FUSION	KG5ZJV	444.62500	-		
	FUSION	WA5UFO	444.85000	+		
El Paso, Montana Vista						
	FM	W5HFN	444.32500	+	103.5 Hz	TVHFS
El Paso, North Mount Franklin						
	FM	K5ELP	146.88000	-	88.5 Hz	TVHFS
El Paso, North Park						
	FM	NM5ML	147.14000	+	67.0 Hz	TVHFS
Eldorado	DMR/MARC	WM5L	443.72500	+	CC14	
	DSTAR	N5QHO	443.82500	+		
	DSTAR	N5QHO B	443.82500	+		
Elgin	FM	KC5WXT	442.80000	+	114.8 Hz	TVHFS
Elmendorf	DMR/MARC	W5ROS	147.34000	+	CC1	
	FM	W5ROS	146.86000	-	123.0 Hz	TVHFS
Elmo	FM	W5EEY	421.25000	439.25000		TVHFS
Emory	FM	W5ENT	146.92000	-	88.5 Hz	TVHFS
	FM	W5ENT	443.62500	+	151.4 Hz	TVHFS
Enchanted Valley		K5DJN-L	145.62500			
		KD5U-L	446.22500			
Ennis	FM	WD5DDH	145.41000	-	131.8 Hz	
	FM	KB0BWG	444.82500	+	131.8 Hz	TVHFS
Euless		KG5CNA-L	445.97000			
	DMR/BM	W1ZOT	441.37500	+	CC1	
	FM	W5EUL	442.90000	+	110.9 Hz	TVHFS
Everman	FM	AB5XD	224.86000	-	110.9 Hz	TVHFS
	FM	AB5XD	441.52500	+	110.9 Hz	TVHFS

Location	Mode	Call sign	Output	Input	Access	Coordinator
Fabens	FM	W5PDC	147.98000	-	162.2 Hz	TVHFS
	FM	W5PDC	442.45000	+	203.5 Hz	TVHFS
Fairfield	FM	WB5YJL	145.11000	-	146.2 Hz	TVHFS
Fairview	DMR/MARC	N5ITU	441.33750	+	CC1	TVHFS
Farmersville	DMR/BM	N5SN	441.60000	+	CC1	
	DMR/MARC	WA5DKW	440.01250	+	CC1	TVHFS
	DSTAR	WA5DKW	440.61250	+		
	FM	N5MRG	147.08000	+	110.9 Hz	
	FM	N5MRG	224.64000	-	100.0 Hz	
	FM	N5MRG	443.27500	+	100.0 Hz	
	FM	W5GDC	927.07500	902.07500		TVHFS
Ferris	FUSION	NG5N	446.60000			
Flint	FUSION	KB5DMZ	146.55000			
Floresville	FM	WB5LOP	441.85000	+	179.9 Hz	TVHFS
Flower Mound	DMR/MARC	KM4NNO	448.05000	-	CC0	
	FUSION	W6PXE	435.00000			
Floydada	FM	WA5OEO	444.77500	+	162.2 Hz	TVHFS
Fort Davis, McDonald Observato						
	FM	K5FD	146.62000	-	146.2 Hz	TVHFS
Fort Davis, Mount McElroy						
	FM	KD5CCY	442.40000	+	146.2 Hz	TVHFS
	FM	N5HYD	443.95000	+		TVHFS
Fort Davis, Prude Ranch						
	FM	W5TSP	442.80000	+	110.9 Hz	
Fort Stockton	DSTAR	KG5OXR	147.60000	-		
	FM	KB5GLA	145.37000	-	88.5 Hz	TVHFS
	FM	N5SOR	146.68000	-	88.5 Hz	TVHFS
	FM	AD5BB	146.92000	-	146.2 Hz	TVHFS
	FM	KF5AEJ	147.24000	+	88.5 Hz	TVHFS
	FM	N5SOR	444.80000	+	162.2 Hz	TVHFS
Fort Worth	DMR/BM	K5TKR	441.30000	+	CC1	
	DMR/MARC	K5FTW	440.53750	+	CC1	
	DMR/MARC	AC5MG	440.60000	+	CC1	
	DMR/MARC	KG5EEL	442.00000	+	CC1	
	DMR/MARC	KB5ASY	444.03750	+	CC1	
	DSTAR	KB5DRP	440.55000	+		TVHFS
	DSTAR	KB5DRP B	440.55000	+		
	DSTAR	W5SH B	441.97500	+		
	DSTAR	KF5MMX B	444.03750	+		
	DSTAR	KF5YMQ B	444.97500	+		
	DSTAR	KB5DRP D	1259.60000			
	FM	W5DFW	29.66000	-	192.8 Hz	
	FM	K5FTW	145.11000	-	110.9 Hz	TVHFS
	FM	K5FTW	146.68000	-	110.9 Hz	TVHFS
	FM	K5FTW	146.76000	-		TVHFS
	FM	W5SH	146.84000	-	110.9 Hz	TVHFS
	FM	K5FTW	146.94000	-	110.9 Hz	TVHFS
	FM	K5COW	147.28000	+	110.9 Hz	TVHFS
	FM	K5MOT	147.32000	+	110.9 Hz	TVHFS
	FM	KF5LOG	147.54000		110.9 Hz	
	FM	W0BOD	224.68000	-	103.5 Hz	TVHFS
	FM	N5UN	224.78000	-	110.9 Hz	TVHFS
	FM	K5FTW	224.94000	-	110.9 Hz	TVHFS
	FM	N5UN	423.97500	+	156.7 Hz	TVHFS
	FM	W7YC	441.30000	+		TVHFS
	FM	W5FA	441.37500	+		
	FM	W5FWS	441.60000	+	162.2 Hz	
	FM	KA5GFH	442.12500	+	156.7 Hz	TVHFS
	FM	K5HIT	442.22500	447.32500	110.9 Hz	TVHFS
	FM	N5UA	442.97500	+	110.9 Hz	TVHFS
	FM	N5PMB	443.15000	+	110.9 Hz	TVHFS
	FM	N4MSE	443.45000	+	127.3 Hz	TVHFS

Location	Mode	Call sign	Output	Input	Access	Coordinator
Fort Worth	FM	K5SXK	443.92500	+		TVHFS
	FM	N5UN	443.97500	+	131.8 Hz	TVHFS
	FM	K5FTW	444.10000	+		TVHFS
	FM	W5FA	444.90000	+	110.9 Hz	TVHFS
	FM	K5TKR	446.10000	-	136.5 Hz	
	FUSION	KI5IXM	145.65000			
	FUSION	K3IH	147.50000			
	FUSION	K3IH	434.00000			
	FUSION	K5ZIA	441.30000			
Fort Worth, North Benbrook						
	FM	K5COW	224.42000	-	110.9 Hz	TVHFS
	FM	K5COW	442.20000	+	110.9 Hz	TVHFS
Fort Worth, North Fort Worth						
	FM	WX5ATX	444.77500	+	123.0 Hz	
Franklin	FM	W5KVN	146.96000	-	146.2 Hz	TVHFS
Fredericksburg	FM	AI5TX	443.70000	+		TVHFS
Fredericksburg, Hill Country M						
	FM	W5FBG	146.47000	-	162.2 Hz	TVHFS
Fredericksburg, N.E Gillespie						
	FM	W5FBG	145.47000	-	162.2 Hz	TVHFS
Freeport	FM	KA5VZM	147.38000	+	141.3 Hz	TVHFS
Freestone	FM	AK5G	441.82500	+	123.0 Hz	TVHFS
Fresno	DMR/MARC	K3JMC	440.68750	+	CC3	TVHFS
Friendswood	FM	KD5GR	147.12000	+		TVHFS
Ft Worth	FM	KB5WB	443.85000	+	110.9 Hz	
Gail	FM	KK5MV	443.75000	+	162.2 Hz	TVHFS
Gainesville	FM	K5AGG	145.29000	-	100.0 Hz	TVHFS
	FM	WB5FHI	147.34000	+	100.0 Hz	TVHFS
	FM	WB5FHI	442.77500	+	100.0 Hz	TVHFS
	FM	K5AGG	443.12500	+	100.0 Hz	TVHFS
Galveston	DMR/BM	KC5FOG	443.27500	+	CC1	
	FM	WB5BMB	146.68000	-	103.5 Hz	TVHFS
	FM	WB5BMB	147.04000	+		TVHFS
	FM	AI5TX	443.95000	+		TVHFS
Galveston, Moody Gardens						
	FM	KA5QDG	147.30000	+	123.0 Hz	TVHFS
	FM	KA5QDG	442.15000	+	123.0 Hz	TVHFS
Garden City	FM	KD5CCY	442.90000	+	91.5 Hz	TVHFS
Gardendale	DMR/MARC	KD4LXC	444.83750	+	CC14	
	FM	WD5MOT	442.15000	+		TVHFS
	FM	N5LTZ	444.40000	+	88.5 Hz	TVHFS
	FM	WR5FM	444.52500	+	146.2 Hz	TVHFS
	FM	WR5FM	927.06250	902.06250	203.5 Hz	TVHFS
Garland	DMR/BM	AB5U	441.95000	+	CC1	TVHFS
	FM	K5QHD	146.66000	-	110.9 Hz	TVHFS
	FM	K5QBM	147.24000	+	110.9 Hz	TVHFS
	FM	K5QHD	442.70000	+	110.9 Hz	TVHFS
Gatesville	DMR/BM	NU5D	441.72500	+	CC1	
	DMR/MARC	NU5D	441.33750	-	CC1	
	DMR/MARC	NU5D	441.36250	+	CC1	
	FM	W5AMK	146.96000	-	123.0 Hz	TVHFS
Geneva	FM	K5TBR	146.74000	-	118.8 Hz	TVHFS
George West	FM	KD5FVZ	443.67500	+	156.7 Hz	TVHFS
Georgetown	DMR/BM	NH7R	440.55000	+	CC1	
	DMR/MARC	NA6M	444.52500	+	CC1	TVHFS
	FM	N5TT	145.25000	-	162.2 Hz	
	FM	NA6M-R	147.08000	+		TVHFS
	FM	KC1ATT	147.47500			
	FM	N5KF	441.57500	+	100.0 Hz	TVHFS
	FM	K5SCT	441.62500	+	103.5 Hz	
	FM	K5TRA	927.06250	902.06250	203.5 Hz	TVHFS
	FUSION	KI5QWQ	145.65500			

Location	Mode	Call sign	Output	Input	Access	Coordinator
Georgetown	FUSION	NH7R-RPT	434.55000			
Giddings	FM	NE5DX	147.22000	+	114.8 Hz	TVHFS
	FM	KE5DX	442.57500	+	114.8 Hz	TVHFS
Gilmer	FM	K5UAR	146.94000	-	107.2 Hz	
Goldthwaite	FM	N5QBU	146.79000	-	94.8 Hz	
	FM	K5AB	147.10000	+	100.0 Hz	
	FM	K5AB	442.60000	+	100.0 Hz	
Goliad	FM	WB5MCT	146.74000	-	103.5 Hz	TVHFS
Gonzales	FM	WD5IEH	443.12500	+	141.3 Hz	TVHFS
Graham	FM	N5SMX	147.00000	+	110.9 Hz	TVHFS
	FM	K7KAB	147.34000	+		TVHFS
Granbury	DMR/MARC	WD5GIC	442.57500	+	CC1	
	DMR/MARC	NA5AA	443.90000	+	CC1	TVHFS
	DSTAR	N1DRP	440.65000	+		
	DSTAR	K1DRP B	440.65000	+		
	DSTAR	W5HCT B	441.35000	+		
	DSTAR	W5HCT	441.35000	+		
	DSTAR	K1DRP D	1258.80000			
	FM	KE5WEA	145.43000	-	162.2 Hz	
	FM	KE5WEA	146.74000	-	162.2 Hz	TVHFS
	FM	WD5GIC	147.08000	+	88.5 Hz	TVHFS
	FM	KE5WEA	147.24000	+	162.2 Hz	TVHFS
	FM	WD5GIC	224.34000	-	88.5 Hz	TVHFS
	FM	WD5GIC	442.02500	+	88.5 Hz	TVHFS
	FM	AI5TX	443.62500	+		TVHFS
Grand Bluff		W5CWT-L	438.87500			
Grapevine	DMR/MARC	N5EOC	440.50000	+	CC1	TVHFS
	FM	N5EOC	443.87500	+	110.9 Hz	TVHFS
	FM	N5ERS	444.85000	+	110.9 Hz	TVHFS
Greenville	DMR/BM	W5NNI	444.62500	+	CC1	
	DMR/MARC	K5VOM	441.97500	+	CC1	
	FM	K5VOM	224.90000	-	100.0 Hz	
	FM	K5VOM	441.80000	+	100.0 Hz	
	FM	N5SN	443.90000	+	71.9 Hz	TVHFS
Greenville, Hunt Regional Medi						
	FM	K5GVL	146.78000	-	114.8 Hz	TVHFS
Greenville, Majors Field Airpo						
	FM	W5NNI	147.16000	+	100.0 Hz	TVHFS
Gun Barrel City	FM	K8MKN	441.37500	+	136.5 Hz	
	FM	K5CCL	444.05000	+		
	FUSION	K8MKN	145.23000	-		
	FUSION	K5CCL-RPT	146.24000	+		
Gunter	DMR/BM	N5GI	444.37500	+	CC1	
Halletsville	FM	KD5RCH	147.08000	+	173.8 Hz	TVHFS
	FM	KC5RXW	444.75000	+	127.3 Hz	TVHFS
Hamilton	FM	K5AB	146.92000	-	100.0 Hz	TVHFS
	FM	AB5BX	147.20000	+	88.5 Hz	TVHFS
Happy	FUSION	N5HTX	442.10000			
Harlingen	DMR/BM	KD4FJ	443.87500	+	CC1	
	FM	K5VCG	145.39000	-	114.8 Hz	TVHFS
	FM	W5RGV	146.80000	-	114.8 Hz	TVHFS
	FM	W5RGV	147.10000	+	114.8 Hz	TVHFS
	FM	W5RGV	147.14000	+	114.8 Hz	TVHFS
	FM	W5STX	147.20000	+	114.8 Hz	
	FM	AK5Z	443.60000	+	114.8 Hz	TVHFS
	FM	K5RAV	444.50000	+	114.8 Hz	
	FUSION	WD5ADC	444.55000	+		
Haslet	FM	W5BYT	145.25000	-	100.0 Hz	TVHFS
Hawkins	FM	W5ETX	147.24000	+	136.5 Hz	TVHFS
Heath	FM	KK5PP	441.37500	+	141.3 Hz	TVHFS
Hebbronville	DMR/BM	KE5NL	443.00000	+	CC1	
Hempstead	FM	K5FLM	441.35000	+	110.9 Hz	

Location	Mode	Call sign	Output	Input	Access	Coordinator
Henderson	FM	NU5G	442.30000	+		TVHFS
Henderson, REA 410' Tower						
	FM	N5RCA	146.78000	-	131.8 Hz	TVHFS
Henderson, Rusk County Court H						
	FM	N5RCA	145.25000	-		
Henderson, UT Health-Henderson						
	FM	W5ETX	147.04000	+	136.5 Hz	TVHFS
Henrietta	FM	KF5DFD	146.68000	-	192.8 Hz	TVHFS
	FM	KA5WLR	146.80000	-	192.8 Hz	TVHFS
	FM	KF5DFD	146.86000	-	192.8 Hz	TVHFS
	FM	KF5DFD	444.72500	+	192.8 Hz	TVHFS
	FM	KA5WLR	444.85000	+	192.8 Hz	TVHFS
Hideaway	FUSION	W5MJF	144.61250			
Hideaway, Golf Course						
	FM	W5ETX	145.33000	-	136.5 Hz	
Hillsboro	DMR/MARC	KC5HWB	443.27500	+	CC9	
Hockley	DMR/MARC	KC5DAQ	439.95000	449.95000	CC1	
	DMR/MARC	KC5DAQ	441.52500	+	CC5	
	DMR/MARC	KC5DAQ	446.00000		CC1	
Hondo	FM	KD5DX	145.29000	-	162.2 Hz	TVHFS
	FM	KD5DX	443.35000	+	141.3 Hz	TVHFS
	FM	KA5IID	927.12500	902.12500	103.5 Hz	
	FUSION	KD5DX	443.35000	+		
Houston	DMR/BM	W5RPT	145.47000	-	CC3	
	DMR/BM	K5WH	441.00000	446.50000	CC1	
	DMR/BM	KA5PLE	441.17500	+	CC1	
	DMR/BM	KD5HKQ	443.37500	+	CC1	TVHFS
	DMR/MARC	KC5DAQ	441.10000	441.70000	CC1	
	DMR/MARC	AC5FD	441.35000	+	CC7	
	DMR/MARC	KD5DFB	441.77500	+	CC7	TVHFS
	DMR/MARC	W5ICF	441.87500	+	CC2	
	DMR/MARC	W5VOM	443.75000	+	CC9	
	DMR/MARC	KB5PBM	444.92500	+	CC1	
	DSTAR	KG5FAE	440.00000	+		
	FM	WB5ITT	29.65000	-	100.0 Hz	
	FM	KA5QDG	145.17000	-	123.0 Hz	TVHFS
	FM	W5INP	145.34000	-	88.5 Hz	
	FM	KD5HKQ	145.45000	-	103.5 Hz	TVHFS
	FM	KA5AKG	146.66000	-	100.0 Hz	TVHFS
	FM	WA5TWT	146.70000	-	103.5 Hz	TVHFS
	FM	K5GZR	146.82000	-	103.5 Hz	TVHFS
	FM	KF5GDR	146.84000	-	151.4 Hz	
	FM	WR5AAA	146.88000	-	146.2 Hz	
	FM	WB5UGT	146.92000	-	103.5 Hz	TVHFS
	FM	W5JUC	146.96000	-	103.5 Hz	TVHFS
	FM	WD5X	147.00000	+	103.5 Hz	TVHFS
	FM	W5ATP	147.08000	+	103.5 Hz	TVHFS
	FM	WA5QXE	147.32000	+	100.0 Hz	TVHFS
	FM	K5DX	147.36000	+	100.0 Hz	TVHFS
	FM	KG5FYV	147.53000			
	FM	WD5X	224.10000	-	103.5 Hz	TVHFS
	FM	WB5ITT	224.50000	-		
	FM	WD5X	224.80000	-	103.5 Hz	TVHFS
	FM	KB5ELT	441.30000	+	100.0 Hz	TVHFS
	FM	WA5F	442.50000	+	123.0 Hz	TVHFS
	FM	K5TRC	443.00000	+	88.5 Hz	
	FM	KC5AWF	443.07500	+	88.5 Hz	TVHFS
	FM	AD5OU	443.52500	+	136.5 Hz	TVHFS
	FM	N5TZ	443.65000	+		TVHFS
	FM	KB5TFE	443.72500	+	110.9 Hz	TVHFS
	FM	WB5UGT	443.82500	+	103.5 Hz	TVHFS
	FM	WD5X	444.22500	+	103.5 Hz	TVHFS

Location	Mode	Call sign	Output	Input	Access	Coordinator
Houston	FM	W5TMR	444.25000	+		TVHFS
	FM	W5NC	444.37500	+	103.5 Hz	TVHFS
	FUSION	KG5RPC	145.55500			
	FUSION	KB5AKO	147.52000			
	FUSION	AG5AA	430.00000			
	FUSION	AG5AA	433.83750			
	FUSION	WB5TUF	444.00000	+		
Houston, Astrodome						
	FM	KA5QDG	147.06000	+	123.0 Hz	TVHFS
Houston, BP Building						
	FM	W5BSA	145.19000	-	123.0 Hz	TVHFS
Houston, Ellington Field						
	FM	KA5QDG	444.80000	+	141.3 Hz	
Houston, Galleria Area						
	FM	K5ILS	224.96000	-	88.5 Hz	TVHFS
Houston, Houston NW Medical Ce						
	FM	KD0RW	147.30000	+	151.4 Hz	TVHFS
Houston, Houston Transtar						
	FM	N5TRS	145.37000	-	123.0 Hz	TVHFS
Houston, Missouri City Antenna						
	FM	KG5EEO	146.94000	-	167.9 Hz	TVHFS
Houston, San Felipe Building						
	FM	W5VOM	1292.10000	1272.10000		TVHFS
Houston, The Galleria						
	FM	N5ZUA	444.30000	+	123.0 Hz	TVHFS
Houston, TMC	DSTAR	W5HDR	440.60000	+		TVHFS
	DSTAR	W5HDR	1293.20000	1273.20000		TVHFS
Howe	DMR/MARC	KC5HWB	440.20000	+	CC9	
	FM	KD5HQF	224.16000	-	100.0 Hz	
	FM	KD5HQF	442.45000	+	100.0 Hz	
Hubbard	FUSION	WB5YFX	146.18000	+		
Huntsville	FM	WA5AM	146.64000	-	131.8 Hz	TVHFS
	FM	W5HVL	146.86000	-		TVHFS
	FM	WD5CFJ	442.15000	+	103.5 Hz	TVHFS
	FM	W5SAM	442.85000	+	127.3 Hz	TVHFS
	FM	AI5TX	443.97500	+		TVHFS
	FUSION	KG5TNK	445.73000			
Hurst	DMR/MARC	W5DMR	443.26250	+	CC1	TVHFS
	FM	W5HRC-R	147.10000	+	110.9 Hz	TVHFS
Hurst, Hurst North Water Tower						
	FM	W5HRC	442.85000	+	110.9 Hz	TVHFS
Idalou	FM	KC5MVZ	223.90000	-	123.0 Hz	TVHFS
	FM	N5TYI	443.00000	+	67.0 Hz	TVHFS
	FM	KC5MVZ	443.27500	+	107.2 Hz	TVHFS
Independence	FM	N5MBM	145.25000	-	103.5 Hz	
Independence, Rocky Hill Fire						
	FM	N5MBM	441.85000	+	123.0 Hz	TVHFS
Industry	FM	KF5KXL	441.67500	+	103.5 Hz	TVHFS
Ingleside	DSTAR	W5ICC B	444.90000	+		
	DSTAR	W5ICC	444.90000	+	151.4 Hz	
	FM	NZ5J	147.22000	+	173.8 Hz	TVHFS
Ingram	FM	KD5HNM	147.08000	+	151.4 Hz	
	FM	AI5TX	443.92500	+		TVHFS
Iola	FM	K5ZY	145.29000	-		
Iowa Park	FM	N5JRF	145.49000	-	192.8 Hz	TVHFS
Iraan	FM	AI5TX	443.95000	+		TVHFS
Irving	FM	N2DFW	145.45000	-	110.9 Hz	TVHFS
	FM	WA5CKF	224.40000	-	110.9 Hz	TVHFS
	FM	WA5CKF	442.67500	+	110.9 Hz	TVHFS
	FM	AL7HH	444.80000	+	110.9 Hz	TVHFS
	FUSION	N5VUJ	145.45000	-		
Italy	FM	KD5OXM-L	145.29000	-		

Location	Mode	Call sign	Output	Input	Access	Coordinator
Italy, Downtown Water Tower						
	FM	WD5DDH	442.52500	+	88.5 Hz	TVHFS
Jacksonville	FM	KR5Q	145.43000	-	136.5 Hz	TVHFS
	FM	K5JVL	146.80000	-	136.5 Hz	TVHFS
	FM	K5JVL	444.52500	+	136.5 Hz	TVHFS
Jamaica Beach	FM	KA5QDG	444.80000	+	103.5 Hz	TVHFS
Jasper	FM	W5JAS	147.00000	-	118.8 Hz	TVHFS
	FM	K5PFE	224.86000	-	118.8 Hz	TVHFS
	FM	W5JAS	442.20000	+	192.8 Hz	TVHFS
	FM	W5JAS	444.55000	+	118.8 Hz	TVHFS
Jentsch Acres		N5TAB-L	146.46000			
Jewett	FM	KC5SWI	145.23000	-	146.2 Hz	TVHFS
Jollyville	FM	KA9LAY	145.21000	-	97.4 Hz	TVHFS
Jourdanton	FM	N5XO	147.24000	+	82.5 Hz	TVHFS
Junction	FM	AI5TX	443.65000	+		TVHFS
Kamay	FM	N5AAJ	444.67500	+	192.8 Hz	TVHFS
Karnes City	FM	WA5S	224.46000	-	192.8 Hz	
	FM	WA5S	442.77500	+	192.8 Hz	
Katy	FM	KF5KHM	145.34000	-		
	FM	W5EMR	441.97500	+	123.0 Hz	TVHFS
	FM	WD8RZA	442.35000	+	131.8 Hz	TVHFS
	FM	N5TM	927.06250	902.06250	203.5 Hz	
Kaufman	DSTAR	KA5DRP D	1252.00000			
Keene	FM	KC5PWQ	443.12500	+	110.9 Hz	
	FUSION	KI5NLX	446.25000			
Keller	DMR/MARC	W5DFW	424.97500	+	CC1	
	DMR/MARC	W4BSB	442.58750	+	CC1	
	FM	KA5HND	147.20000	+	88.5 Hz	TVHFS
	FM	W5DFW	443.17500	+	100.0 Hz	TFCA
	FM	N5EOC	444.70000	+	110.9 Hz	TVHFS
	FUSION	K5LTG	145.02500			
Kempner	FUSION	N5YTT	434.00000			
Kenney	FM	WR5DC	146.64000	-	141.3 Hz	
Kent	FM	KE5PL	443.92500	+		TVHFS
Kentwood Manor	FM	N5MRM-R	145.39000	-		
Kerrville	DMR/BM	N6LKA	441.71250	+	CC10	
	FM	W3XO	146.79000	-	162.2 Hz	TVHFS
	FM	K5ZZT	443.62500	+		TVHFS
Kerrville, State Hospital						
	FM	K5KSH	441.31250	+	162.2 Hz	
Kilgore	DMR/BM	N5VGQ	147.30000	+	CC1	
	DMR/BM	N5VGQ	444.97500	+	CC1	
	DMR/MARC	N5YEY	443.95000	+	CC1	
	FM	WX5FL	145.45000	-	136.5 Hz	TVHFS
Killeen	DMR/BM	N5OU	444.65000	445.15000	CC7	
	FM	KK5AN-R	147.04000	+		TVHFS
	FUSION	KF5F	145.67000			
Kingsville	FM	KD5QWJ	146.62000	-	107.2 Hz	TVHFS
	FM	W5KCA	444.22500	+	107.2 Hz	
Kingsville, Dick Kleberg Park						
	FM	W5KCA	146.68000	-	107.2 Hz	TVHFS
Kingwood	FM	W5SI	145.43000	-		TVHFS
	FM	W5SI	147.28000	+	103.5 Hz	TVHFS
	FM	K5NX	147.56000		100.0 Hz	
	FM	W5SI	444.82500	+		TVHFS
	FUSION	K9NXS	145.56250			
Klein	DMR/MARC	K5MAP	440.30000	+	CC3	
Knollwood Estates						
	FM	KD5OQS-R	442.07500	+		TVHFS
Kress	FM	AB2NP-R	441.57500	+		
Kyle	FM	KE5LOT	147.05000	+	114.8 Hz	
La Feria	FM	W5RGV	146.70000	-	114.8 Hz	TVHFS

Location	Mode	Call sign	Output	Input	Access	Coordinator
La Grange	DMR/BM	NA5RC	441.55000	+	CC5	
	FM	KG5QMO	440.35000	+	103.5 Hz	
	FM	N5FRT	441.55000	+	114.8 Hz	TVHFS
	FM	AI5TX	443.70000	+		TVHFS
	FM	WB5UGT	444.72500	+	141.3 Hz	TVHFS
La Grange, Hostyn						
	FM	N5FRT	147.38000	+		TVHFS
	FM	N5FRT	441.30000	+	114.8 Hz	
	FM	K5TRA	927.16250	902.16250	151.4 Hz	
La Marque	FM	KA5QDG	146.90000	-	123.0 Hz	TVHFS
La Porte	DMR/MARC	N5LUY	442.85000	+	CC7	TVHFS
Lago Vista	FM	KC5WLF	224.84000	-	103.5 Hz	
Lake Jackson	FUSION	KD5HTK	146.42000			
Lakehills	FUSION	W5HEX	146.40000			
Lakeway	FM	WB5PCV	145.41000	-	103.5 Hz	
	FM	N5TXR	147.30000	+	131.8 Hz	TVHFS
	FM	WB5PCV	444.40000	+	103.5 Hz	TVHFS
Lamesa	FM	N5BNX	145.15000	-	100.0 Hz	TVHFS
	FM	N5BNX	146.86000	-	100.0 Hz	TVHFS
	FM	KD5CCY	442.70000	+	91.5 Hz	TVHFS
	FM	KE5PL	443.50000	+		TVHFS
	FM	K5WTC	444.75000	+	162.2 Hz	TVHFS
	FM	N5SVF	444.95000	+	100.0 Hz	TVHFS
Lampasas	FM	N5ZXJ	145.49000	-	123.0 Hz	
	FM	K5AB	147.06000	+	100.0 Hz	
	FM	KB5SXV	147.22000	+	88.5 Hz	TVHFS
	FM	K6STU	224.30000	-	88.5 Hz	
	FM	KE5ZW	443.65000	+		TVHFS
	FM	K6STU	444.42500	+	88.5 Hz	
	FM	WD5EMS	927.07500	902.07500	218.1 Hz	
Laredo	DMR/BM	W5LRD	442.17500	+	CC1	
	DSTAR	KE5WFB B	440.60000	+		
	FM	W5EVH	145.15000	-	100.0 Hz	TVHFS
	FM	W5LRD	146.62000	-	100.0 Hz	
	FM	W5EVH	147.12000	+	100.0 Hz	TVHFS
	FM	W5EVH	444.00000	+	100.0 Hz	TVHFS
Laredo, Airport	FM	W5EVH	146.94000	-	100.0 Hz	TVHFS
League City	FM	WR5GC	145.41000	-	131.8 Hz	TVHFS
	FM	WR5GC	442.22500	447.32500	131.8 Hz	TVHFS
	FUSION	K5BDH	444.00000	+		
Leander	FM	N5TT	146.64000	-	162.2 Hz	TVHFS
	FM	KE5RS	441.60000	+	100.0 Hz	TVHFS
Leonard	FM	KW5DX	145.41000	-	114.8 Hz	TVHFS
Levelland	DMR/BM	KC5TNB	442.90000	+	CC1	
	FM	WB5BRY	146.78000	-	179.9 Hz	TVHFS
	FM	N5SOU	147.12000	+	162.2 Hz	TVHFS
	FM	KC5TAF	443.15000	+	136.5 Hz	TVHFS
	FM	WA5OEO	444.37500	+	162.2 Hz	TVHFS
	FUSION	N5QNS	145.67000			
Lewisville	DMR/MARC	KK4JI	440.40000	+	CC1	TVHFS
Liberty Hill	DMR/MARC	AL5O	433.15000	+	CC1	
	DMR/MARC	AL5O	442.50000	-	CC1	
	DMR/MARC	AL5O	443.15000	-	CC1	
	DMR/MARC	AL5O	444.00000	+	CC1	
	DMR/MARC	AL5O	445.00000	+	CC1	
Lindale	FM	W5NFL	145.60000		146.2 Hz	
Little Elm	DMR/BM	WB8GRS	421.25000	439.25000	CC1	
	DMR/BM	WB8GRS	441.38750	+	CC1	
	FM	WB8GRS-L	145.76000		123.0 Hz	
	FM	WB8GRS	224.98000	-	123.0 Hz	TVHFS
	FM	WB8GRS	927.50000	902.50000	123.0 Hz	
	FM	WB8GRS	927.63750	902.63750	100.0 Hz	

Location	Mode	Call sign	Output	Input	Access	Coordinator
Little Elm	FUSION	K5VOP	443.30000	+		
Littlefield	FM	WB5BRY	146.64000	-	179.9 Hz	TVHFS
	FM	WA5OEO	444.85000	+	162.2 Hz	TVHFS
Live Oak	DMR/BM	K5NKK	444.02500	+	CC1	TVHFS
	FM	KE5HBB	145.37000	-	114.8 Hz	
	FM	KE5HBB	441.90000	+	103.5 Hz	TVHFS
Livingston	FM	WB5HZM	147.04000	+	136.5 Hz	TVHFS
	FM	WB5HZM	147.16000	+	103.5 Hz	TVHFS
	FM	WB5UGT	443.12500	+	103.5 Hz	TVHFS
	FUSION	KI5TLH	438.80000			
Llano	FM	AI5TX	443.50000	+		TVHFS
Lockhart	DMR/BM	W5LOS	440.72500	+	CC1	
	FM	AD5JT	145.15000	-	136.5 Hz	TVHFS
Longfellow	FM	N5BPJ	147.34000	+	88.5 Hz	TVHFS
	FM	WX5II	443.97500	+		TVHFS
Longview	DMR/BM	K5TKR	440.60000	+	CC1	
	DMR/MARC	K5JG	441.62500	+	CC1	
	DSTAR	K5LET C	147.06000	+		
	DSTAR	K5LET B	443.97500	+		
	DSTAR	KF5WEX B	444.99500	+		
	FM	K5TKR	147.16000	+	136.5 Hz	
	FM	K5JG	443.42500	+		TFCA
	FM	KD5UVB	444.72500	+	136.5 Hz	TVHFS
Longview, East Mountain						
	FM	K5LET	147.34000	+	136.5 Hz	TVHFS
Longview, East Mtn						
	FM	K5LET	146.64000	-	136.5 Hz	TVHFS
Longview, Lake Cherokee						
	FM	KB5MAR	145.30000	-	146.2 Hz	
Los Fresnos	DMR/BM	W5VDR	442.47500	+	CC1	
	DMR/BM	N5JLR	444.75000	+	CC2	TVHFS
Louise	DMR/MARC	N5TZV	442.27500	+	CC7	
Lubbock	DMR/BM	KC5CZX	441.70000	+	CC1	
	DMR/BM	WA5TBB	443.80000	+	CC1	
	DMR/BM	WB5BRY	444.00000	+	CC1	TVHFS
	DMR/BM	WA5TBB	444.80000	+	CC1	
	DMR/MARC	N5ZTL	444.30000	+	CC1	
	DMR/MARC	KA3IDN	444.68750	+	CC14	
	DSTAR	K5LIB	145.43000	-		TVHFS
	DSTAR	K5LIB C	145.43000	-		
	DSTAR	KB5KYJ	443.05000	+		
	DSTAR	KB5KYJ B	443.05000	+		
	FM	KC5CZX	146.56500		123.0 Hz	
	FM	K5LIB	146.84000	-	88.5 Hz	TVHFS
	FM	WB5BRY	146.94000	-	179.9 Hz	TVHFS
	FM	WB5BRY	147.00000	-	179.9 Hz	TVHFS
	FM	WA5OEO	147.20000	+	162.2 Hz	TVHFS
	FM	N5ZTL	147.30000	+	88.5 Hz	TVHFS
	FM	W5WAT	441.67500	+	97.4 Hz	TVHFS
	FM	W5WAT	441.97500	+	97.4 Hz	TVHFS
	FM	W5WAT	442.17500	+	97.4 Hz	TVHFS
	FM	K5WAT	442.47500	+	97.4 Hz	TVHFS
	FM	K5LIB	443.07500	+	88.5 Hz	TVHFS
	FM	AI5TX	443.92500	+		TVHFS
	FM	WR5FM	444.02500	+	146.2 Hz	TVHFS
	FM	K5TTU	444.10000	+	146.2 Hz	TVHFS
	FM	KZ5JOE	444.45000	+	114.8 Hz	TVHFS
	FM	WB5BRY	444.50000	+	118.8 Hz	TVHFS
	FM	KC5OBX	444.62500	+	118.8 Hz	TVHFS
	FM	N5UQF	444.87500	+	162.2 Hz	TVHFS
	FM	WA5OEO	444.97500	+	162.2 Hz	TVHFS
	FM	KA3IDN	927.01250	902.01250	225.7 Hz	TVHFS

Location	Mode	Call sign	Output	Input	Access	Coordinator
Lubbock, NTS Communications Bu						
	FM	WB5BRY	224.64000	-		
Lucas	DMR/BM	KE5FCO	441.35000	+	CC5	
	DMR/BM	K5LFD	442.21250	+	CC2	
Lufkin	DMR/BM	KE5CJE	440.72500	+	CC1	
	DMR/MARC	WD5EFY	440.00000	+	CC9	
	FM	KD5TD	53.71000	52.71000	100.0 Hz	TVHFS
	FM	KD5TD	145.37000	-	100.0 Hz	TVHFS
	FM	W5IRP	146.94000	-	141.3 Hz	TVHFS
	FM	K5RKJ	147.26000	+	141.3 Hz	TVHFS
	FM	KB5LS	147.36000	+	107.2 Hz	TVHFS
	FM	WB5UGT	444.42500	+	203.5 Hz	TVHFS
	FM	KB5LS	444.57500	+	107.2 Hz	TVHFS
	FM	KD5TD	444.90000	+	107.2 Hz	TVHFS
Lufkin, Courthouse						
	FM	W5IRP	444.97500	+	107.2 Hz	TVHFS
Luling	DMR/BM	W5LOS	440.72500	+	CC1	
Lumberton	FUSION	AB5WX	438.15000			
Mabank	DMR/BM	K5CCL	146.84000	-	CC1	
	FM	K5CCL-R	146.90000	-	136.5 Hz	TVHFS
	FM	K8MKN	441.37500	+	136.5 Hz	
	FUSION	K8MKN	144.63000			
Madisonville	FM	W5ZYX	441.35000	+		
Magnolia	DMR/MARC	W5JSC	144.52500	+	CC1	
	DMR/MARC	W5JSC	440.71250	+	CC7	
	FM	W5JON	442.95000	+	123.0 Hz	TVHFS
	FM	KB5FLX	443.02500	+	103.5 Hz	TVHFS
	FM	KD0RW	444.67500	+	192.8 Hz	TVHFS
Manor	FM	KI4MS	442.42500	+	100.0 Hz	TVHFS
Mansfield	FM	WA5FWC	145.39000	-	167.9 Hz	
	FM	WA5JRS	448.77500	-	167.9 Hz	TVHFS
Marathon	FM	AI5TX	443.50000	+		TVHFS
Marble Falls	DMR/BM	N5JFP	145.43000		CC1	TVHFS
	DMR/BM	N5JFP	440.60000	+	CC1	TVHFS
	DSTAR	N5JFP C	145.43000	-		
	DSTAR	N5JFP B	440.60000	+		
	FM	N5KUQ	442.85000	+	103.5 Hz	TVHFS
	FM	KB5YKJ	444.82500	+	114.8 Hz	
Marble Falls, Hidden Falls Adv						
	FM	N5KUQ	145.39000	-	103.5 Hz	TVHFS
Marietta, Cusetta Mountain						
	FM	WX5FL	146.84000	-	100.0 Hz	
Marietta, Cussetta Mountain						
	FM	WX5FL	52.37000	51.37000	136.5 Hz	
Marietta, Cussetta Mtn.						
	FM	WX5FL	145.19000	-	151.4 Hz	TVHFS
Markham	FM	WA5SNL	444.70000	+	146.2 Hz	TVHFS
Marshall	FM	KB5MAR	146.86000	-	146.2 Hz	TVHFS
	FM	K5HR	223.94000	-		TVHFS
	FM	KB5MAR	444.15000	+	146.2 Hz	
Maydelle	FM	KB5VQG	147.02000	+		TVHFS
Mayflower	FM	W5JAS	147.12000	+	203.5 Hz	TVHFS
McAllen	DMR/BM	KC5MOL	443.82500	+	CC1	
	DSTAR	ND5N	147.60000	-		
	DSTAR	ND5N C	147.60000	-		
	FM	N5SIM	145.23000	-	114.8 Hz	TVHFS
	FM	W5RGV	146.76000	-	114.8 Hz	TVHFS
	FM	W5RGV	444.60000	+	114.8 Hz	TVHFS
Mccamey	FM	KK5MV	443.47500	+		TVHFS
Mccamey, King Mountain						
	FM	N5SOR	444.70000	+	162.2 Hz	TVHFS
McDade	FM	N5KF	441.57500	+	100.0 Hz	

Location	Mode	Call sign	Output	Input	Access	Coordinator
McKinney		K5ECD-R	147.12000			
		KG5GKC-L	445.77500			
	DMR/BM	N5GI	145.35000	-	CC1	TVHFS
	DMR/BM	W9DXM	441.32500	+	CC1	
	DMR/BM	N5GI	442.57500	+	CC1	TVHFS
	FM	W5MRC-R	146.74000	-	110.9 Hz	TVHFS
	FM	KF5TU	442.35000	+	100.0 Hz	TVHFS
	FM	N4MSE	927.16250	902.16250		TVHFS
McKinney, Office Building						
	FM	KG5IAN	440.02500	+	110.9 Hz	
Melissa	FM	W5MRC	443.20000	+	100.0 Hz	TVHFS
Melody Hills		WX5FWD-R	441.02500			
		WX5FWD-L	446.47500			
	FM	K5MOT-R	444.30000	+		TVHFS
Mercedes	FM	KR4ZAN	441.60000	+	114.8 Hz	TVHFS
Merkel	FUSION	WB5VIH	145.58000			
Mesquite	DSTAR	NT5RN	145.15000	-		TVHFS
	DSTAR	NT5RN C	145.15000	-		
	DSTAR	NT5RN	443.02500	+		TVHFS
	DSTAR	NT5RN B	443.02500	+		
	DSTAR	NT5RN D	1253.80000			
	DSTAR	NT5RN A	1293.50000	1273.50000		
	FM	AK5DX	52.75000	51.75000	110.9 Hz	TVHFS
	FM	WJ5J	145.31000	-	110.9 Hz	TVHFS
	FM	AK5DX	147.04000	+	136.5 Hz	TVHFS
	FM	AK5DX	440.30000	+		TVHFS
	FM	AK5DX	442.62500	+	110.9 Hz	TVHFS
	FM	WJ5J	444.42500	+	156.7 Hz	TVHFS
Mexia	FM	W5NFL	145.39000	-	146.2 Hz	TVHFS
Miami	FM	KA5KQH	145.11000	-	88.5 Hz	TVHFS
	FM	N5LTZ	444.85000	+	88.5 Hz	TVHFS
Mico	FUSION	WA5FRF	443.35000	+		
Midland		KF5WDJ-R	443.27500			
	DMR/MARC	KE5PL	147.22000	+	CC7	
	DMR/MARC	KE5PL	444.36250	+	CC14	
	DSTAR	W5EOC	146.70000	-		
	DSTAR	WT5ARC	441.55000	+		
	FM	W5QGG	146.76000	-	88.5 Hz	TVHFS
	FM	N5XXO	146.90000	-	88.5 Hz	TVHFS
	FM	K5MSO	147.22000	+	88.5 Hz	TVHFS
	FM	W5QGG	147.30000	+	88.5 Hz	TVHFS
	FM	W5LNX	442.20000	+	162.2 Hz	TVHFS
	FM	K5PSA	442.97500	+	162.2 Hz	TVHFS
	FM	N5XXO	443.27500	+	162.2 Hz	TVHFS
	FM	W5WRL	443.30000	+	146.2 Hz	TVHFS
	FM	KD5CCY	443.40000	+		TVHFS
	FM	KE5PL	443.57500	+		TVHFS
	FM	KE5PL	443.65000	+		TVHFS
	FM	N5SOR	443.72500	+		TVHFS
	FM	KK5MV	443.80000	+	162.2 Hz	TVHFS
	FM	W5QGG	444.20000	+	162.2 Hz	TVHFS
	FM	KB5MBK	444.60000	+	146.2 Hz	TVHFS
	FM	W5UA	444.77500	+	88.5 Hz	TVHFS
	FM	KE5PL	927.05000	902.05000		TVHFS
Minden	FM	WB5WIA	145.25000	-	123.0 Hz	TVHFS
Mineral Wells	FM	W5ABF	146.64000	-	85.4 Hz	TVHFS
	FM	W5PPC	146.86000	-	156.7 Hz	
	FM	WB5TTS	442.70000	+	85.4 Hz	TVHFS
Mission	DMR/MARC	K5HYT	444.95000	+	CC1	
Missouri City	FM	KD5HKQ	145.25000	-	156.7 Hz	
Mobile Repeater	DMR/BM	N5GI	441.32500	+	CC1	
Mont Belvieu	FM	KK5XQ	441.80000	+	103.5 Hz	TVHFS

Location	Mode	Call sign	Output	Input	Access	Coordinator
Montgomery	DMR/BM	WA5AIR	443.90000	+	CC4	
	DMR/BM	WA5EOC	445.37500	-	CC7	
	DMR/MARC	KB5FLX	444.92500	+	CC7	
Moody	FM	W5ZDN	145.15000	-	123.0 Hz	TVHFS
	FM	AI5TX	443.92500	+		TVHFS
	FUSION	KD5ARN	442.30000	+	123.0 Hz	TVHFS
Moulton	FM	KC5RXW	444.47500	+	127.3 Hz	TVHFS
Mound Creek	FM	WD5IEH	441.92500	+		TVHFS
Mount Pleasant, Purley Tower E						
	FM	W5KNO	444.95000	+	151.4 Hz	TVHFS
Mount Vernon	FM	WA5YVL	147.32000	+	151.4 Hz	TVHFS
Murphy	FM	AA5BS	441.70000	+		TVHFS
Mustang Ridge, HWY 130/21 Inte						
	FM	AC5PS	441.56250	+		TVHFS
Nacogdoches	FM	W5NAC	147.32000	+	141.3 Hz	TVHFS
	FM	KE5EXX	441.35000	+	141.3 Hz	TVHFS
	FM	KE5EXX	444.00000	+		TVHFS
	FM	W5NAC	444.05000	+	141.3 Hz	TVHFS
Nassau Bay	FM	NB5F	145.15000	-		TVHFS
	FM	NB5F	442.47500	+		TVHFS
Navasota	FM	W5JSC	146.74000	-	156.7 Hz	
	FM	KG5JRA	441.87500	+	110.9 Hz	TVHFS
Nederland	DMR/MARC	KG5HFL	444.92500	+	CC3	
	DSTAR	W5SSV C	146.62000	-		
	DSTAR	W5SSV B	440.72500	+		
	FUSION	N5DWE	445.85000	-		
Nevada	FM	KA5HND	444.92500	+	110.9 Hz	TVHFS
New Boston	FM	KE5ZHF	147.20000	+	100.0 Hz	TVHFS
New Braunfels	FM	WB5LVI	147.00000	-	103.5 Hz	TVHFS
	FM	WB5LVI	147.22000	+	103.5 Hz	TVHFS
	FM	W5DK	443.50000	+	141.3 Hz	TVHFS
	FM	WB5LVI	443.85000	+	103.5 Hz	TVHFS
New Ulm	FUSION	N5CNB	446.12500			
New Ulm, Frelsburg						
	FM	N5CNB	927.13750	902.13750	131.8 Hz	
New Waverly	DMR/BM	WA5AIR	440.25000	+	CC4	
	FM	W5SAM	147.18000	+	136.5 Hz	TVHFS
	FM	N4UAV	441.02500	+	225.7 Hz	
	FM	NA5SA	442.27500	+		TVHFS
	FM	N5ZUA	442.72500	+	103.5 Hz	TVHFS
	FUSION	NR5US	147.55000			
Nipton	FM	N6LXX	53.86000	52.86000	107.2 Hz	
	FM	N6LXX	440.00000	+	110.9 Hz	
No Limits	DMR/MARC	KC5HWB	439.00000		CC1	
No Padre Is-Corpus						
	DMR/MARC	K1IMD	433.63750	+	CC1	
NOAA Alpine	WX	KJY69	162.55000			
NOAA Amarillo	WX	WXK38	162.55000			
NOAA Austin	WX	WXK27	162.40000			
NOAA Bay City	WX	WWG40	162.42500			
NOAA Beaumont	WX	WXK28	162.47500			
NOAA Big Spring	WX	WXK37	162.47500			
NOAA Borger	WX	KXI88	162.40000			
NOAA Brownsville						
	WX	WWG34	162.55000			
NOAA Bryan	WX	WXK30	162.55000			
NOAA Burkeville	WX	KXI54	162.42500			
NOAA Carrizo Springs						
	WX	WNG692	162.55000			
NOAA Center	WX	WNG650	162.52500			
NOAA Childress	WX	KJY97	162.52500			
NOAA Cisco	WX	WNG636	162.50000			

Location	Mode	Call sign	Output	Input	Access	Coordinator
NOAA Coleman	WX	WXN89	162.47500			
NOAA Corpus Christi						
	WX	KHB41	162.55000			
NOAA Corsicana	WX	KXI87	162.52500			
NOAA Crowley / Fort Worth						
	WX	KEC55	162.55000			
NOAA Cumby	WX	KWN31	162.50000			
NOAA D Hanis	WX	WNG600	162.52500			
NOAA Dallas	WX	KEC56	162.40000			
NOAA Del Rio	WX	WXJ98	162.40000			
NOAA Dickens	WX	WZ2507	162.50000			
NOAA Dilley	WX	WNG523	162.50000			
NOAA El Paso	WX	WXK25	162.47500			
NOAA El Paso Spanish						
	WX	WNG652	162.55000			
NOAA Gilmer	WX	KWN32	162.42500			
NOAA Gonzales	WX	KXI56	162.52500			
NOAA Guadalupe Peak						
	WX	WZ2503	162.52500			
NOAA Houston	WX	KGG68	162.40000			
NOAA Junction	WX	WWG93	162.47500			
NOAA Kerrville	WX	WWF90	162.45000			
NOAA La Grange	WX	WWG55	162.50000			
NOAA Laredo	WX	WXK26	162.55000			
NOAA Llano	WX	WWF91	162.42500			
NOAA Lubbock	WX	WXK79	162.40000			
NOAA Lufkin	WX	WXK23	162.55000			
NOAA Marietta	WX	WNG653	162.52500			
NOAA Miami	WX	WNG713	162.45000			
NOAA Midland / Odessa						
	WX	WXK32	162.40000			
NOAA Milano	WX	WNG649	162.52500			
NOAA Mineral Wells						
	WX	WNG651	162.52500			
NOAA Muenster	WX	KHA99	162.42500			
NOAA New Taiton						
	WX	KJY78	162.45000			
NOAA Onalaska	WX	KXI55	162.50000			
NOAA Ozona	WX	WXL44	162.50000			
NOAA Palestine	WX	KWN34	162.45000			
NOAA Paris	WX	WXK20	162.55000			
NOAA Pecos	WX	WNG695	162.45000			
NOAA Perryton	WX	KJY88	162.47500			
NOAA Pharr	WX	KHB33	162.40000			
NOAA Plainview	WX	WNG561	162.45000			
NOAA Port O Connor						
	WX	WXL26	162.47500			
NOAA Richland Springs						
	WX	WWG94	162.52500			
NOAA Rio Grande City						
	WX	WNG601	162.42500			
NOAA Riviera	WX	WNG609	162.52500			
NOAA San Angelo						
	WX	WXK33	162.55000			
NOAA San Antonio						
	WX	WXK67	162.55000			
NOAA Seguin	WX	WNG641	162.47500			
NOAA Seminole	WX	WNG562	162.42500			
NOAA Sherman	WX	WXK22	162.47500			
NOAA Stephenville						
	WX	KWN33	162.45000			

Location	Mode	Call sign	Output	Input	Access	Coordinator
NOAA Summerfield						
	WX	WNG657	162.50000			
NOAA Texarkana	WX	WXJ49	162.55000			
NOAA Three Rivers						
	WX	WNG696	162.45000			
NOAA Throckmorton						
	WX	WNG722	162.42500			
NOAA Tyler	WX	WXK36	162.47500			
NOAA Uvalde	WX	KWN51	162.42500			
NOAA Victoria	WX	WXK34	162.40000			
NOAA Waco	WX	WXK35	162.47500			
NOAA Wichita Falls						
	WX	WXK31	162.47500			
Nocona	FM	N5VAV	147.36000	+	123.0 Hz	TVHFS
Nolanville	FM	KX5DX	147.44000		100.0 Hz	
	FM	KX5DX	446.05000	+	100.0 Hz	
Norchester		K5WH-L	444.45000			
	FM	K5WH-R	146.76000	-		TVHFS
North Richland Hills						
	FM	AB5L	52.31000	51.31000		
	FM	K5NRH	441.75000	+	100.0 Hz	TVHFS
North Richland Hills, Water To						
	FM	K5NRH	145.37000	-	110.9 Hz	TVHFS
Notrees	DMR/MARC	K5MSO	443.88750	+	CC14	
	DSTAR	W5EOC C	146.70000	-		
	DSTAR	W5EOC B	442.35000	+		
	DSTAR	W5EOC	442.35000	+		
	FM	N5XXO	147.02000	+	88.5 Hz	TVHFS
	FM	AI5TX	443.70000	+		TVHFS
	FM	N5XXO	444.67500	+	162.2 Hz	TVHFS
Oak Hill		N5ADA-R	145.49000			
	FM	K5TRA-L	443.07500	+		TVHFS
	FM	K5TRA-R	927.11200	902.11200		TVHFS
Oak Ridge North	FM	KW5O	441.32500	+		TVHFS
Odem	FM	W5JYJ	443.50000	+		TVHFS
Odessa	DMR/BM	KG5YJT	440.72500	+	CC14	
	DMR/MARC	N5RGH	443.65000	+	CC1	
	DMR/MARC	KA3IDN	444.23750	+	CC14	
	FM	W5CDM	145.41000	-	88.5 Hz	TVHFS
	FM	KD5CCY	146.74000	-	91.5 Hz	TVHFS
	FM	KF5ZPM	441.70000	+	162.2 Hz	
	FM	N5MI	441.90000	+	173.8 Hz	TVHFS
	FM	KD5CCY	442.30000	+	91.5 Hz	TVHFS
	FM	WT5ARC	443.10000	+	162.2 Hz	TVHFS
	FM	KE5PL	443.62500	+		TVHFS
	FM	W5CDM	444.10000	+	162.2 Hz	TVHFS
	FM	KA3IDN	444.23500	+	71.9 Hz	TVHFS
	FM	WT5ARC	444.42500	+	162.2 Hz	TVHFS
	FM	K5PSA	444.97500	+	179.9 Hz	TVHFS
	FM	KA3IDN	927.07500	902.07500	82.5 Hz	TVHFS
Old Union	FM	N5EOC-R	145.40000	-		TVHFS
Olmito	FM	KC5WBG	147.18000	+	114.8 Hz	TVHFS
Olney	FM	W5IPN	147.24000	+		
Orange	FM	AA5P	147.06000	+	103.5 Hz	TVHFS
	FM	W5ND	147.18000	+	103.5 Hz	TVHFS
Ovalo	FM	KD5YCY	444.97500	+	103.5 Hz	TVHFS
Ovilla	FUSION	K5BSM	442.00000			
Ozona	FM	K5SPE	147.12000	+		
	FM	KE5PL	443.62500	+		TVHFS
Palestine	FM	KR5Q	145.49000	-	136.5 Hz	TVHFS
	FM	KR5Q	146.74000	-	136.5 Hz	TVHFS
	FM	W5DLC	147.08000	+	103.5 Hz	TVHFS

Location	Mode	Call sign	Output	Input	Access	Coordinator
Palestine	FM	W5DLC	147.14000	+	103.5 Hz	TVHFS
	FM	KR5Q	442.37500	+	136.5 Hz	TVHFS
Palestine, NALCOM Tower						
	FM	K5PAL	444.60000	+	103.5 Hz	TVHFS
Palo Pinto	DMR/MARC	W5PPC	145.19000	-	CC1	
	DMR/MARC	W5PPC	442.87500	+	CC1	
Pampa	FM	W5TSV	146.90000	-		TVHFS
	FM	N5LTZ	444.40000	+	88.5 Hz	TVHFS
Pandale	FM	N5UFV	443.92500	+		TVHFS
Paris	DMR/MARC	KC5HWB	440.58750	+	CC9	
	DSTAR	WN5ROC C	147.06000	+		
	DSTAR	WN5ROC	147.06000	444.26000		
	DSTAR	K5PTR B	442.12500	+		
	DSTAR	K5PTR	442.12500	+		
	DSTAR	WN5ROC B	444.27500	+		
	FM	KI5DX	145.13000	-	100.0 Hz	
	FM	N5JEP	145.39000	-	114.8 Hz	TVHFS
	FM	WB5RDD	146.76000	-	203.5 Hz	TVHFS
	FM	KC5OOS	147.04000	+	100.0 Hz	TVHFS
	FM	KA5RLK	147.34000	+	110.9 Hz	TVHFS
	FM	KI5DX	444.47500	+	100.0 Hz	TVHFS
	FM	WB5RDD	444.50000	+		TVHFS
	FUSION	N5YSQ	443.55000			
	FUSION	W5PTX	446.50000			
Pasadena	FM	KD5HKQ	145.25000	-	167.9 Hz	
	FM	W5PAS	145.29000	-	103.5 Hz	TVHFS
	FM	KD5HKQ	145.45000	-	127.3 Hz	
	FM	KD5QCZ	224.48000	-	156.7 Hz	
	FM	WB5ZMY	443.45000	+	114.8 Hz	TVHFS
	FM	KD5QCZ	443.77500	+		
	FM	W5PAS	444.27500	+	103.5 Hz	TVHFS
Pasadena, El Jardin						
	FM	W5PAS	145.27000	-	123.0 Hz	
Patricia	DMR/MARC	KA3IDN	443.18750	+	CC1	
Pattison		N5FRT-R	145.27000			
Payne Springs	FM	K5CCL	426.25000	1255.05000		TVHFS
Pearland	DMR/MARC	K3JMC	440.27500	+	CC8	
	DMR/MARC	N5KJN	441.92500	+	CC8	
	DMR/MARC	K5PLD	443.05000	+	CC3	TVHFS
	FM	K5PLD	147.16000	+	167.9 Hz	TVHFS
	FM	K5PLD	147.22000	+	167.9 Hz	TVHFS
	FM	N5KJN	443.40000	+	141.3 Hz	TVHFS
Peaster	FM	KB5WB	442.45000	+	156.7 Hz	TVHFS
Penwell	FM	N5SOR	443.67500	+		TVHFS
	FM	WR5FM	444.57500	+	146.2 Hz	TVHFS
	FM	WR5FM	927.11250	902.11250		TVHFS
Perryton	FM	K5IS	146.64000	-	88.5 Hz	TVHFS
Pflugerville	FM	KC5CFU	441.82500	+	114.8 Hz	TVHFS
Pine Springs	FM	N5SOR	444.05000	+		TVHFS
Pipe Creek	FM	WD5FWP	147.28000	+	156.7 Hz	TVHFS
Pipe Creek, Red Cross						
	FM	N5XO	147.12000	+	82.5 Hz	TVHFS
Plainview	DMR/MARC	KA3IDN	443.03750	+	CC1	
	FM	W5WV	146.72000	-	88.5 Hz	TVHFS
	FM	N5RNY	147.10000	+	88.5 Hz	TVHFS
	FM	AI5TX	443.95000	+		TVHFS
Plano	FM	K5CG	441.31250	+	110.9 Hz	
	FM	AI5TX	443.65000	+		TVHFS
	FM	W5SUF	444.17500	+	110.9 Hz	TVHFS
	FUSION	K5BSA	442.80000	+	110.9 Hz	TVHFS
	FUSION	W5DLA	446.32500	-		
Pleasant Valley	FM	N5LOC-R	145.25000	-		TVHFS

Location	Mode	Call sign	Output	Input	Access	Coordinator
Pleasanton	FM	KD5ZR	145.43000	-	162.2 Hz	TVHFS
	FM	KE6LGE	441.50000	+	100.0 Hz	
	FM	NU5P	443.97500	+		TVHFS
	FM	KG5EBI	450.30000	+	71.9 Hz	
Plum Grove	FM	WB5UGT	444.17500	+	103.5 Hz	TVHFS
Port Aransas	FM	KG5BZ	145.29000	-	110.9 Hz	TVHFS
Port Arthur	FM	KD5QDO	146.86000	-	103.5 Hz	TVHFS
Port Lavaca	DMR/BM	W5KTC	442.67500	+	CC1	TVHFS
	FM	W5KTC	147.02000	+	103.5 Hz	TVHFS
Port Neches	FM	KC5YSM-L	444.80000	+		
	FM	KC5YSM	446.05000	-	118.8 Hz	
Portable	DMR/MARC	KC5HWB	440.51250	+	CC9	
	DMR/MARC	KD5DFB	441.35000	+	CC7	
	DMR/MARC	KC5TGF	441.37500	+	CC5	
Porter	FUSION	N6AHB	146.52000			
Post	FM	WB5BRY	147.06000	+	179.9 Hz	TVHFS
Potosi	FM	KD5YCY	443.10000	+	88.5 Hz	TVHFS
Powderly	FUSION	KI5FDH	144.42000			
Presidio, Cibolo Creek Ranch						
	FM	K5FD	147.12000	+	146.2 Hz	TVHFS
Purves	FM	KD5HNM	147.34000	+	107.2 Hz	
Quanah	FM	KY7D	146.64000	-	173.8 Hz	
Quinlan, Lake Tawakoni						
	FM	K5VOM	224.96000	-		
Quitman	FM	WX5FL	147.10000	+	136.5 Hz	TVHFS
Ranger	FM	N5RMA	147.06000	+	131.8 Hz	TVHFS
	FM	AI5TX	443.67500	+		TVHFS
	FM	K6DBR	444.95000	+	88.5 Hz	TVHFS
Rankin	FM	KE5PL	443.92500	+		TVHFS
Raymondville	FM	W5RGV	146.90000	-	114.8 Hz	
	FM	W5RGV	444.90000	+	114.8 Hz	TVHFS
Refugio	FM	AD5TD	147.18000	+	136.5 Hz	TVHFS
	FM	AD5TD	443.87500	+	107.2 Hz	TVHFS
Rendon		KC5TIL-L	145.54000			
Rice	FM	W5TSM	145.47000	-	110.9 Hz	TVHFS
Richardson	DMR/MARC	K5RWK	440.37500	+	CC1	
	FM	N5CXX	441.87500	+	131.8 Hz	TVHFS
	FM	NT5NT	443.32500	+	110.9 Hz	TVHFS
	FM	WX5O	444.02500	+	110.9 Hz	TVHFS
	FM	N5UA-R	444.67500	+		TVHFS
Richardson, Palisades Central						
	FM	K5RWK	147.12000	+	110.9 Hz	TVHFS
	FM	K5RWK	443.37500	+	110.9 Hz	TVHFS
	FM	K5RWK	444.72500	+	110.9 Hz	TVHFS
Richardson, University Of Texa						
	FM	K5UTD	223.82000	-	110.9 Hz	
Richardson, UTD Campus						
	FM	K5UTD	145.43000	-	110.9 Hz	TVHFS
Richboro	FM	W5LEX-R	444.85000	+		TVHFS
Richland Hills	DMR/MARC	KC5HWB	440.08750	+	CC9	
Richmond	DMR/BM	WB5RF	441.32500	+	CC1	
	FM	KD5HAL	145.49000	-	123.0 Hz	TVHFS
	FM	WB4KTH	438.50000	+	100.0 Hz	
	FM	KD5HAL	444.52500	+	123.0 Hz	TVHFS
Rio Medina	FM	W5TSE	443.00000	+		TVHFS
Robert Lee	FM	KC5EZZ	147.34000	+	88.5 Hz	TVHFS
Rockdale	FM	KG5DUO	146.76000	-	123.0 Hz	
	FM	AF5C	147.28000	+	162.2 Hz	TVHFS
Rockport	FM	KM5WW	147.26000	+	103.5 Hz	TVHFS
Rockwall	DSTAR	W5MIJ C	144.67000	-		
	DSTAR	K5MIJ C	144.67000	+		
	DSTAR	W5MIJ B	440.67000	+		

Location	Mode	Call sign	Output	Input	Access	Coordinator
Rockwall	DSTAR	K5MIJ B	440.67000	+		
	DSTAR	W5MIJ D	1253.67000			
	DSTAR	K5MIJ D	1253.67000			
	DSTAR	W5MIJ A	1292.67000	1272.67000		
	DSTAR	K5MIJ A	1292.67000	1312.67000		
	FM	KK5PP	441.52500	+	141.3 Hz	TVHFS
	FM	NF2W	441.73750	+	107.2 Hz	
	FM	K5GCW	443.55000	+	162.2 Hz	TVHFS
Rosanky	FM	N5FRT	145.40000	-	114.8 Hz	
Rose Hill	FM	K5SOH	53.27000	52.27000	123.0 Hz	TVHFS
	FM	K5IHK	146.72000	-	123.0 Hz	TVHFS
	FM	K5SOH	223.84000	-	123.0 Hz	TVHFS
	FM	K5IHK	443.10000	+	123.0 Hz	TVHFS
	FM	KC5PCB	927.20000	902.20000	123.0 Hz	TVHFS
Rosston	DMR/MARC	W5NGU	440.68750	+	CC1	
	DSTAR	KE5YAP C	147.49000	146.49000		
	DSTAR	KE5YAP B	440.71250	+		
	DSTAR	KE5YAP	440.71250	+		
	DSTAR	KE5YAP D	1259.20000			
	DSTAR	KE5YAP	1293.20000	1273.20000		
	DSTAR	KE5YAP A	1293.20000	1273.20000		
	FM	WD5U	145.49000	-	85.4 Hz	TVHFS
	FM	N6LXX	443.73750	+	141.3 Hz	
	FM	W5FKN	927.05000	902.05000	110.9 Hz	
Round Rock	FM	N5MNW	146.70000	-	110.9 Hz	
	FM	KM5MQ	441.70000	+	110.9 Hz	TVHFS
	FM	AI5TX	443.67500	+		TVHFS
	FUSION	WD5EMS	444.87500	+		
Round Rock, St Davids Surgical						
	FM	WD5EMS	29.64000	-	110.9 Hz	
	FM	WD5EMS	52.95000	51.95000	100.0 Hz	
	FM	WD5EMS	224.36000	-	100.0 Hz	TVHFS
	FM	WD5EMS	927.05000	902.05000	110.9 Hz	TVHFS
	FUSION	WD5EMS	444.87500	+	100.0 Hz	TVHFS
Rowlett	FM	AB5U	147.39000	+	85.4 Hz	
	FM	K5DUR	441.72500	+	173.8 Hz	
Rowlett, Kirby Road Water Tank						
	FM	AB5U	441.32500	+	162.2 Hz	TVHFS
Royse City	DMR/BM	K5VOM	441.77500	+	CC1	
Runaway Bay	FM	K5JEJ	444.82500	+	110.9 Hz	TVHFS
Rusk	FM	W5ETX	146.92000	-	136.5 Hz	TVHFS
	FM	N5UYI	442.52500	+	118.8 Hz	
Sachse	FUSION	WB8ZWI	147.57000			
Saginaw	DMR/MARC	W5BYT	444.32500	+	CC1	TVHFS
	FM	K5SAG	441.37500	+	100.0 Hz	TVHFS
Saginaw- Haslet	FUSION	W5BYT	147.56000			
Saint Hedwig	FM	WA5FSR	444.07500	+	123.0 Hz	TVHFS
Saint Malo (historical)						
	FM	KB5UJM-R	442.35000	+		
Salt Flat	DMR/BM	WS5B	444.62500	+	CC1	
	FM	WS5B	432.47000		88.5 Hz	
San Angelo	DMR/BM	KC5EZZ	441.75000	+	CC1	
	DMR/BM	KB5GLC	444.93750	+	CC1	
	DMR/MARC	KG5NDK	434.62500	+	CC0	
	DMR/MARC	KD5TKR	441.30000	+	CC1	
	DMR/MARC	KC5HWB	443.75000	+	CC1	
	DMR/MARC	KC5EZZ	444.12500	+	CC1	
	DMR/MARC	KG5CNG	444.55000	+	CC1	
	DMR/MARC	KG5CNG	444.65000	+	CC1	
	DMR/MARC	KA3IDN	444.66250	+	CC1	
	DSTAR	KG5CNG B	444.55000	+		
	FM	N5SVK	53.63000	52.63000	88.5 Hz	TVHFS

Location	Mode	Call sign	Output	Input	Access	Coordinator
San Angelo	FM	W5QX	145.27000	-	88.5 Hz	TVHFS
	FM	K5CMW	146.88000	-	88.5 Hz	TVHFS
	FM	KC5EZZ	146.94000	-	103.5 Hz	TVHFS
	FM	N5DE	147.06000	+		TVHFS
	FM	N5SVK	147.30000	+	88.5 Hz	TVHFS
	FM	W5RP	442.25000	+	162.2 Hz	TVHFS
	FM	AI5TX	443.70000	+		TVHFS
	FM	KC5EZZ	444.22500	+	162.2 Hz	TVHFS
	FUSION	K7PTZ	145.60000			
San Angelo, Corp Of Engineers						
	FM	N5RV	444.35000	+	162.2 Hz	TVHFS
San Antonio		KC5AUO-L	147.54000			
	DMR/BM	AA5RO	147.32000	+	CC1	TVHFS
	DMR/BM	N5AMD	441.76250	+	CC1	TVHFS
	DMR/BM	AA5RO	443.87500	+	CC1	
	DSTAR	K5VPW	145.35000	-		TVHFS
	DSTAR	WD5STR C	146.49000	147.49000		
	DSTAR	WD5STR B	440.60000	+		
	DSTAR	WA5UNH	440.70000	+		TVHFS
	DSTAR	WA5UNH B	440.70000	+		
	DSTAR	NV5TX	442.10000	+		TVHFS
	DSTAR	WD5STR D	1253.30000			
	DSTAR	WD5STR A	1293.30000	1273.30000		
	FM	WA5KBQ	53.17000	52.17000	88.5 Hz	TVHFS
	FM	K5LT	53.21000	52.21000	141.3 Hz	TVHFS
	FM	W5DK	145.17000	-	141.3 Hz	TVHFS
	FM	KD5GSS	145.47000	-	110.9 Hz	TVHFS
	FM	W5STA	146.66000	-	110.9 Hz	TVHFS
	FM	NH7TR	146.72000	-	114.8 Hz	TVHFS
	FM	WA5FSR	146.82000	-	179.9 Hz	TVHFS
	FM	KF5FGL-R	146.84000	-		TVHFS
	FM	WB5LJZ	146.88000	-	141.3 Hz	TVHFS
	FM	WB5FWI	146.94000	-	179.9 Hz	TVHFS
	FM	WB5FNZ	146.96000	-	162.2 Hz	TVHFS
	FM	W5RRA	147.02000	+	88.5 Hz	TVHFS
	FM	KK5LA	147.04000	+	123.0 Hz	TVHFS
	FM	N5CSC	147.08000	+	162.2 Hz	TVHFS
	FM	K5EOC	147.18000	+	103.5 Hz	TVHFS
	FM	WD5FWP	147.28000	+	162.2 Hz	TVHFS
	FM	W5XW	147.30000	+	107.2 Hz	TVHFS
	FM	WA5UNH	147.36000	+	179.9 Hz	TVHFS
	FM	AA5RO	147.38000	+	162.2 Hz	TVHFS
	FM	N5WSU	147.53000		100.0 Hz	
	FM	K5VPW	147.56000			
	FM	K5VPW	147.59000		114.8 Hz	
	FM	WA5UNH	224.38000	-	179.9 Hz	
	FM	K5VPW	431.05000		136.5 Hz	
	FM	KD5GSS	442.12500	+	127.3 Hz	TVHFS
	FM	WD5FWP	442.37500	+	141.3 Hz	
	FM	WS5DRC	443.20000	+		TVHFS
	FM	KD5GAT	443.40000	+	88.5 Hz	TVHFS
	FM	WB5FNZ	443.47500	+	162.2 Hz	TVHFS
	FM	AI5TX	443.67500	+		TVHFS
	FM	WX5II	443.70000	+		TVHFS
	FM	WX5II	443.72500	+		TVHFS
	FM	WX5II	443.95000	+	146.3 Hz	TVHFS
	FM	WB5FWI	444.10000	+	179.9 Hz	TVHFS
	FM	WA5UNH	444.12500	+	179.9 Hz	TVHFS
	FM	KG5FEC	444.66250	+		TVHFS
	FM	AA5RO	444.85000	+	162.2 Hz	
	FM	WA5KBQ	444.95000	+	103.5 Hz	TVHFS
	FUSION	WS5DRC	146.78000	-	162.2 Hz	TVHFS

Location	Mode	Call sign	Output	Input	Access	Coordinator
San Antonio	FUSION	N8IQT	147.16000	+		
	FUSION	KB3FXA	438.00000			
	FUSION	N8IQT	440.27500	+		
	FUSION	N8IQT	442.75000	+		
	FUSION	WF3H	446.12500			
San Antonio, Near The Airport						
	FM	N5YBG	441.37500	+		TVHFS
San Antonio, Near The Medical						
	FM	WA5LNL	223.82000	-	141.3 Hz	TVHFS
San Antonio, Red Cross						
	FM	N5XO	443.02500	+	82.5 Hz	
San Antonio, Red Cross Center						
	FM	K5TRA	927.07500	902.07500	218.1 Hz	
San Antonio, University Hospit						
	FM	AA5RO	927.05000	902.05000	110.9 Hz	TVHFS
San Benito	DMR/BM	AE5JO	442.17500	+	CC1	
	FUSION	AE5JO	442.57500	+		
San Felipe	FM	W0FCM	442.02500	+	123.0 Hz	
San Marcos	FM	AI5TX	443.65000	+	114.8 Hz	
	FUSION	W5TAA-ND	145.56250			
	FUSION	K5MPS	446.15000			
San Marcos , Devils Backbone						
	FM	W5DK	146.92000	-	131.8 Hz	TVHFS
San Marcos, Texas State Univer						
	FM	KG5PVG	442.70000	+	123.0 Hz	
Sanctuary	DMR/BM	N0FTW	441.35000	+	CC1	
Sansom Park		K5AMM-R	441.67500			
Santa Anna	WX	KE5NYB	147.12000	147.97000	94.8 Hz	TVHFS
Santa Fe	FM	N5NWK	443.47500	+		TVHFS
Santa Maria	FM	W5RGV	444.27500	+	114.8 Hz	TVHFS
SE Houston	DMR/MARC	W5ICF	441.36000	+	CC2	
Seabrook	FM	KD5QCZ	53.03000	52.03000	156.7 Hz	TVHFS
Seabrook, City Hall						
	FM	W5SFD	147.26000	+	162.2 Hz	TVHFS
	FM	KE5VJH	443.25000	+	127.3 Hz	TVHFS
Sealy	FM	W0FCM	441.02500	+	103.5 Hz	
Seguin	DSTAR	KG5FJW C	145.49000	-		
	DSTAR	KG5FJW B	442.22500	+		
	FM	WA5AP	145.49000	-	141.3 Hz	
	FM	WA5GC	146.76000	-	141.3 Hz	TVHFS
	FUSION	KC5GPG	147.50000			
Selma	FUSION	N2MOO	440.50000	+		
	FUSION	K9ASS	445.50000	-		
Seminole	FM	N5SOR	145.45000	-	88.5 Hz	TVHFS
	FM	N5SOR	146.78000	-	88.5 Hz	TVHFS
Sheeks		KE5RAD-L	146.46000			
Sheffield	FM	N5SOR	443.50000	+		TVHFS
Shepp	FM	NZ5V	145.23000	-	88.5 Hz	TVHFS
Sherman	FM	W5RVT	147.00000	+	100.0 Hz	TVHFS
	FM	W5COP	147.28000	+	107.2 Hz	TVHFS
	FM	W5RVT	444.75000	+	100.0 Hz	TVHFS
Shiner	FM	KC5QLT	146.68000	-		TVHFS
	FM	W5CTX	147.12000	+	141.3 Hz	TVHFS
	FM	WD5IEH	443.77500	+	141.3 Hz	TVHFS
	FM	WA5PA	444.27500	+	141.3 Hz	TVHFS
Silsbee	DMR/MARC	KB5OVJ	442.40000	+	CC9	
	FUSION	KI5CDP	144.10000			
Sinton	FM	W5CRP	147.08000	+	107.2 Hz	TVHFS
Sisterdale	DMR/BM	KA5WJY	441.76250	+	CC1	
Slidell	DSTAR	W5FKN	442.92500	+		TVHFS
Smithville	FUSION	KE5FKS	145.35000	-	114.8 Hz	TVHFS
	FUSION	AC5RY	147.48000			

Location	Mode	Call sign	Output	Input	Access	Coordinator
Smyer	FM	KB5MBK	442.07500	+	146.2 Hz	TVHFS
Snyder	FM	K5SNY	146.92000	-	67.0 Hz	TVHFS
	FM	AI5TX	443.62500	+		TVHFS
Socorro	DSTAR	W5WIN	147.01000	+		
Sonora	FM	N5SOR	443.97500	+		TVHFS
South Padre Island						
	FM	W5RGV	147.12000	+	114.8 Hz	TVHFS
	FM	KE5KLY	147.24000	+	114.8 Hz	TVHFS
	FM	W5RGV	444.87500	+	114.8 Hz	
Southlake	DMR/BM	KI5BLU	446.31250	-	CC1	
	FM	N1OZ	442.17500	+	110.9 Hz	TVHFS
Sowers	FM	WA5CKF-R	146.72000	-		TVHFS
Speaks	FM	K5SOI	442.52500	+	103.5 Hz	TVHFS
Spearman	FM	N5DFQ	147.04000	+	88.5 Hz	TVHFS
	FM	N5DFQ	442.00000	+	88.5 Hz	TVHFS
	FM	KC5WBK	443.20000	+	88.5 Hz	
Splendora	FM	W5OMR	441.70000	+		TVHFS
Spring	DMR/BM	N5DBH	441.37500	+	CC1	
	DMR/MARC	N5LUY	440.65000	+	CC3	
	DSTAR	KF5KHM C	145.34000	-		
	DSTAR	KB2WF	147.58000			
	DSTAR	KF5KHM B	440.57500	+		
	DSTAR	KF5KHM D	1259.00000			
	DSTAR	KF5KHM A	1272.20000	1292.20000		
	FM	WB5UGT	442.70000	+	103.5 Hz	TVHFS
	FM	K5JLK	442.80000	+	146.2 Hz	
	FM	KA2EEU	444.35000	+	103.5 Hz	TVHFS
Spring Branch	DMR/BM	WB5BL	444.35000	+	CC1	
Springtown	DMR/MARC	N5GMJ	440.67500	+	CC1	
	DMR/MARC	N5GMJ	440.82500	+	CC1	
	DMR/MARC	N5GMJ	443.50000	+	CC1	
	FUSION	AC5V-L	145.25000	-	162.2 Hz	
Spur	FM	KC0FGJ	446.07500		88.5 Hz	
St Paul	FUSION	KG5EIU	442.42500	+		
Stagecoach	FM	W5NC	146.66000	-	100.0 Hz	TVHFS
Stephenville	DSTAR	K5IIY	147.36000	+	110.9 Hz	TVHFS
	FM	K5DDL	145.29000	-	110.9 Hz	TVHFS
	FM	KD5HNM	444.77500	+	88.5 Hz	TVHFS
Sterling City	FM	N5FTL	146.64000	-	88.5 Hz	TVHFS
	FM	WR5FM	441.57500	+	156.7 Hz	TVHFS
	FM	AI5TX	443.67500	+		TVHFS
Stinnett	DMR/MARC	KE5CJ	443.43750	+	CC14	
	FM	W5WDR	444.80000	+		
Sugar Land	FM	KD5HKQ	147.24000	+	127.3 Hz	TVHFS
	FM	KC5EVE	443.00000	+		TVHFS
Sulphur Springs	FM	WX5FL	145.11000	-	100.0 Hz	
	FM	K5SST	146.68000	-	151.4 Hz	TVHFS
	FM	K5SST	444.82500	+	151.4 Hz	TVHFS
	FM	WX5FL	444.90000	+		TVHFS
Summit Bechtel Reserve						
	DSTAR	WV8BSA B	441.81250	+		
Sundown	FM	KD5SHB	444.72500	+		TVHFS
Sweet Home	FM	KF5KOI	442.05000	+	77.0 Hz	TVHFS
	FM	WB5UGT	443.82500	+	203.5 Hz	TVHFS
Sweetwater	FM	KC5NOX-R	145.25000	-	162.2 Hz	TVHFS
	FM	KE4QFH	147.08000	+	162.2 Hz	TVHFS
	FM	AI5TX	443.65000	+		TVHFS
	FM	KC5NOX	927.11250	902.11250		TVHFS
	FUSION	KE5YF	146.68000	-		
Sweetwater, 9 Mile Hill						
	FM	KE5YF	444.77500	+	162.2 Hz	TVHFS

Location	Mode	Call sign	Output	Input	Access	Coordinator
Sweetwater, 9 Mile Hill (South						
	FM	W5NCA	146.68000	-	162.2 Hz	
Tabor	FM	KD5DLW	443.52500	+	127.3 Hz	TVHFS
Taft	FM	K5YZZ	444.80000	+	107.2 Hz	TVHFS
Talco	FM	N5REL	442.20000	+	151.4 Hz	TVHFS
Tarzan	FM	K5MSO	52.65000	51.65000	123.0 Hz	TVHFS
Taylor	FM	N5TT	145.45000	-	162.2 Hz	TVHFS
	FM	N3ERC	145.47000	-	114.8 Hz	TVHFS
Temple	DMR/BM	WB5TTY	440.20000	+	CC10	
	DMR/BM	WB5TTY	444.02500	+	CC10	
	DMR/BM	WB5TTY	444.12500	+	CC10	
	DSTAR	K5CTX	147.34000	+		
	DSTAR	K5CTX C	147.34000	+		
	DSTAR	K5CTX	440.52500	+		TVHFS
	DSTAR	K5CTX B	440.52500	+		
	DSTAR	K5CTX D	1253.00000			
	DSTAR	K5CTX	1292.10000	1272.10000		TVHFS
	DSTAR	K5CTX A	1292.10000	1272.10000		
	FM	KG5HFI	53.23000	52.23000	162.2 Hz	
	FM	W5LM	146.82000	-	123.0 Hz	
Terrell	FM	K5RCP	441.67500	+	110.9 Hz	TVHFS
Test	DMR/MARC	K1IMD	433.63750	+	CC1	
Texarkana	DMR/MARC	N5RGA	444.42500	+	CC9	
	DSTAR	KD5RCA	440.10000	+		
Texarkana, Barkman Creek						
	FM	WX5FL	145.39000	-	100.0 Hz	TVHFS
	FM	WX5FL	444.42500	+	100.0 Hz	
Texarkana, Christus St Michael						
	FM	KD5RCA	145.45000	-	100.0 Hz	
Texarkana, KTAL Tower						
	FM	KD5RCA	146.62000	-	100.0 Hz	TVHFS
Texas City	DMR/MARC	W5ZMV	440.62500	+	CC5	TVHFS
	FM	WR5TC	147.14000	+	167.9 Hz	TVHFS
	FM	K5BS	442.02500	+	103.5 Hz	TVHFS
The Colony	FM	K5LRK-R	147.38000	+	110.9 Hz	TVHFS
	FM	K5LRK	224.00000	-	110.9 Hz	
	FM	K5LRK	443.30000	+		
The Woodlands	DMR/MARC	W5ZM	440.57500	+	CC10	
	DMR/MARC	WB5TUF	442.55000	+	CC9	
	DMR/MARC	KB5FLX	442.67500	+	CC7	TVHFS
	FM	N5HOU	146.80000	-	103.5 Hz	
The Woodlands, Woodlands Fire						
	FM	W5WFD	444.10000	+	136.5 Hz	TVHFS
Timpson	FM	KK5XM	145.15000	-	107.2 Hz	TVHFS
	FM	KK5XM	444.67500	+	107.2 Hz	TVHFS
Tom Bean	FM	N5MRG	52.73000	51.73000		
	FM	N5MRG	223.84000	-		
	FM	N5MRG	441.65000	+	100.0 Hz	TVHFS
Tomball	DMR/MARC	W5ZMV	147.38000	+	CC5	TVHFS
	DMR/MARC	KB5FLX	441.60000	+	CC7	TVHFS
	DMR/MARC	W5ZMV	444.62500	+	CC5	
Topga	FUSION	WB5HVC	442.82500	+		
Trinity	FM	N5ESP	145.33000	-	103.5 Hz	TVHFS
Troy	DMR/BM	N5SIM	147.39000	+	CC10	
	DMR/BM	N5SIM	441.65000	+	CC10	
	DMR/MARC	KE5KLY	440.70000	+	CC10	
	DMR/MARC	N5SIM	442.65000	+	CC10	
	FM	WD5EMS	442.70000	+		TVHFS
	FM	WD5EMS	927.03750	902.03750	141.3 Hz	
Tuleta	FM	K5DJS	145.71500			
Tulia	FM	WU5Y	147.36000	+	88.5 Hz	TVHFS
Tuscola	FUSION	N5DUP	443.05000			

Location	Mode	Call sign	Output	Input	Access	Coordinator
Tuxedo	FM	KD5YCY	447.25000	-		
Tyler	DMR/MARC	KE5FGC	443.57500	+	CC1	
	DSTAR	KI4JLQ C	146.00000	+		
	DSTAR	W5ETX	147.12000	147.92000		TVHFS
	DSTAR	W5ETX C	147.12000	147.87000		
	DSTAR	KI4JLQ B	444.00000	+		
	DSTAR	W5ETX B	444.85000	+		
	DSTAR	W5ETX	444.85000	+		TVHFS
	FM	W5WVH	145.37000	-	136.5 Hz	TVHFS
	FM	K5TYR	146.96000	-	136.5 Hz	TVHFS
	FM	K5TYR	147.00000	+	136.5 Hz	TVHFS
	FM	W5ETX	224.20000	-	136.5 Hz	TVHFS
	FM	W5MCT	443.10000	+	136.5 Hz	
	FM	K5TYR	444.40000	+	136.5 Hz	TVHFS
Uncertian	DMR/BM	K5TKR	441.97500	+	CC9	
Utopia	FM	W5FN	53.15000	52.15000	127.3 Hz	
	FM	W5FN	147.10000	+	127.3 Hz	TVHFS
Uvalde	FM	W5FN	146.76000	-	127.3 Hz	TVHFS
	FM	N5RUI	146.90000	-	100.0 Hz	TVHFS
	FM	KN5S	147.24000	+	77.0 Hz	TVHFS
	FM	W5LBD	147.26000	+	100.0 Hz	TVHFS
	FM	AA5EK-R	147.57000	-		
	FM	K5DRT	443.65000	+		TVHFS
	FM	AB5JK	444.60000	+	162.2 Hz	TVHFS
Valley Mills	FUSION	AI5AI	147.24000	+		
	FUSION	AI5AI	446.07000			
Van Alstyne	FM	W5VAL	443.80000	+	103.5 Hz	TVHFS
	FM	WB4GHY	444.12500	+		TVHFS
Vanderpool	FM	N4MUJ	145.40000	144.60000		
Venus	DMR/MARC	KN5TX	441.72500	+	CC1	
	FM	WA5FWC	1292.98000	1272.98000		TVHFS
Vernon	FM	NC5Z	147.02000	+		TVHFS
	FM	N5LEZ	147.16000	+	192.8 Hz	TVHFS
	FM	WB5AFY	224.42000	-	192.8 Hz	
	FM	NC5Z	444.15000	+	192.8 Hz	TVHFS
Victoria	DMR/BM	K5COD	443.76000	+	CC1	
	DMR/MARC	W5VOM	443.75000	+	CC9	
	FM	W5DSC	145.13000	-	103.5 Hz	TVHFS
	FM	W5DSC	145.19000	-	103.5 Hz	TVHFS
	FM	W5DK	147.16000	+	141.3 Hz	TVHFS
	FM	WD5IEH	443.22500	+	141.3 Hz	TVHFS
	FM	WD5IEH	443.97500	+	103.5 Hz	TVHFS
	FM	K5SOI	444.65000	+	103.5 Hz	TVHFS
	FM	WB5MCT	444.67500	+	162.2 Hz	TVHFS
Victoria, Citizens Hospital						
	FM	K5VCT	146.70000	-	127.3 Hz	TVHFS
	FM	W5DSC	443.80000	+	103.5 Hz	TVHFS
Vidor	FM	KD5UNK	224.20000	-		
Vinson		K5HDM-L	446.51200			
Waco	DMR/BM	AE5CA	441.30000	+	CC10	
	DSTAR	W5ZDN	146.98000	-		TVHFS
	DSTAR	W5ZDN C	146.98000	-		
	FM	K5AB	146.66000	-	123.0 Hz	TVHFS
	FM	WA5BU	147.16000	+	123.0 Hz	TVHFS
	FM	W5ZDN	421.25000	439.25000		TVHFS
	FM	WA5BU	442.45000	+		TVHFS
	FM	K5AB	442.80000	+	123.0 Hz	TVHFS
	FM	W5ZDN	442.87500	+	123.0 Hz	TVHFS
	FM	KC5QIH	443.55000	+	123.0 Hz	TVHFS
	FM	AA5RT	444.15000	+	123.0 Hz	TVHFS
Walburg	DSTAR	KE5RCS	145.13000	-		TVHFS
	DSTAR	KE5RCS C	145.13000	-		

Location	Mode	Call sign	Output	Input	Access	Coordinator
Walburg	DSTAR	KE5RCS B	440.57500	+		
	DSTAR	KE5RCS	440.57500	+		TVHFS
	DSTAR	KE5RCS D	1259.20000			
	DSTAR	KE5RCS A	1293.20000	1273.20000		
	FM	K5AB	443.30000	+	88.5 Hz	TVHFS
	FM	KE5RCS	1293.20000	1273.20000		TVHFS
Waller	DMR/MARC	KC5DAQ	444.70000	+	CC5	
Waller, Monaville	FM	KF5GXZ	444.90000	+	100.0 Hz	TVHFS
Walnut Springs	FM	WC5WC	442.57500	+		
Watauga	FM	K0BRN	443.42500	+	100.0 Hz	TFCA
	FM	W7YC	444.57500	+	110.9 Hz	TVHFS
	FUSION	K0BRN	145.11000			
	FUSION	K0BRN/R	145.27000	-		
Waxahachie	DMR/BM	KI5LER	444.72500	445.32500	CC8	
	FM	WD5DDH	927.03750	902.03750	110.9 Hz	
Wayside	FM	N5LTZ	444.57500	+	88.5 Hz	TVHFS
Weatherford	DMR/MARC	KN5TX	440.35000	+	CC1	
	DMR/MARC	N5GMJ	441.97500	+	CC1	TVHFS
	FM	WB5IDM	147.04000	+	110.9 Hz	TVHFS
	FM	AI5TX	443.70000	+		TVHFS
	FM	W0BOE	444.27500	+	103.5 Hz	
Webster	FM	KA5QDG	146.74000	-	107.2 Hz	TVHFS
Wellington, DOT Tower						
	FM	N5OLP	147.24000	+		TVHFS
Weslaco	FM	KC5WBG	146.72000	-	114.8 Hz	TVHFS
	FM	WA5S	224.62000	-		TVHFS
	FM	KC5WBG	444.20000	+	114.8 Hz	TVHFS
	FUSION	NA5J	433.00000			
West Columbia	DMR/MARC	KN5D	443.66250	+	CC1	TVHFS
	FM	AI5TX	443.62500	+		TVHFS
West Tawakoni, Lake Tawakoni						
	FM	K5VOM	146.80000	-	141.3 Hz	
Wharton	DMR/BM	WJ1D	444.91250	+	CC1	
	DMR/MARC	WJ1D	441.75000	+	CC12	
	FM	W5DUQ	145.33000	-	167.9 Hz	TVHFS
	FM	W5DUQ	444.12500	+	167.9 Hz	TVHFS
Whitney	FM	NZ5T	146.62000	-	123.0 Hz	TVHFS
	FM	W5WK	442.20000	+	103.5 Hz	TVHFS
Wichita Falls	FM	WX5TWS	145.15000	-	192.8 Hz	TVHFS
	FM	K5WFT	146.66000	-	192.8 Hz	TVHFS
	FM	W5US	146.94000	-	192.8 Hz	TVHFS
	FM	W5GPO	147.06000	+	156.7 Hz	TVHFS
	FM	N5LEZ	147.12000	+	192.8 Hz	TVHFS
	FM	W5DAD	442.52500	+	192.8 Hz	TVHFS
	FM	WG5K	442.80000	+	192.8 Hz	TVHFS
	FM	N5WF	444.00000	+	192.8 Hz	TVHFS
	FM	WB5ALR	444.20000	+	118.8 Hz	TVHFS
	FM	K5WFT	444.32500	+	192.8 Hz	TVHFS
	FM	WX5TWS	444.52500	+	192.8 Hz	TVHFS
	FM	K5HRO	444.77500	+	173.8 Hz	TVHFS
	FM	N5AAJ	444.95000	+	192.8 Hz	TVHFS
	FM	N5LEZ	444.97500	+	192.8 Hz	TVHFS
Wichita Falls, American Red Cr						
	FM	N5WF	147.14000	+	192.8 Hz	TVHFS
Willis	FM	WA5EOC	224.24000	-	103.5 Hz	TVHFS
	FM	WA9JG	441.32500	+	82.5 Hz	
	FM	W5JSC	442.62500	+	88.5 Hz	TVHFS
Willis, Lake Conroe						
	FM	KB5ASW	441.67500	+	114.8 Hz	TVHFS
Wills Point	FM	K5RKW	145.27000	-	136.5 Hz	TVHFS
	FM	W5DLP	147.28000	+	136.5 Hz	
	FM	W5ETX	443.25000	+	136.5 Hz	TVHFS

Location	Mode	Call sign	Output	Input	Access	Coordinator
Wimberley	FM	WA5AP	147.10000	+	141.3 Hz	TVHFS
	FM	WA5PAX	444.15000	+	114.8 Hz	TVHFS
Windsor	FUSION	KI7CMV	144.50000			
Woodlands	DMR/BM	WA5AIR	443.22500	+	CC4	
Woodway	FUSION	N5LUB	442.30000	+		

U.S. VIRGIN ISLANDS

Location	Mode	Call sign	Output	Input	Access	Coordinator
St Croix	FM	NP2VI	147.11000	+	100.0 Hz	
St Croix, Mount Welcome						
	FM	NP2VI	147.25000	+	100.0 Hz	
St John	FM	KP2I	146.97000	-		
St John, Bordeaux Mountain						
	FM	KP2SJ	146.63000	-	100.0 Hz	
St Thomas	FM	KP2O	146.81000	-	100.0 Hz	
	FM	NP2GO	146.95000	-	67.0 Hz	
	FM	K9VV	448.17500	-		WIRCI

UTAH

Location	Mode	Call sign	Output	Input	Access	Coordinator
Alpine, Silver Lake Flat						
	FM	K7UVA	448.22500	-	100.0 Hz	
American Fork	DSTAR	NT3ST B	447.97500	-		UVHFS
American Fork, Utah Lake						
	FM	KA7EGC	449.17500	-	131.8 Hz	UVHFS
Antelope Island, Frary Peak						
	FM	K7DAV	147.04000	+	123.0 Hz	
	FM	K7DAV	447.20000	-	127.3 Hz	UVHFS
Bountiful, Golf Course						
	FM	K7DAV	449.92500	-	100.0 Hz	UVHFS
Brigham City	FM	K7UB	145.29000	-	123.0 Hz	UVHFS
Brighton	FM	W7SP	146.62000	-		UVHFS
Brighton, Scott's Peak						
	FM	K7JL	449.52500	-	131.8 Hz	UVHFS
Brighton, Scotts Peak						
	FM	K7JL	145.27000	-	100.0 Hz	UVHFS
Bryce Canyon	FM	W6DZL	145.35000	-	123.0 Hz	
Butterfield Peak	FM	WB7TSQ	145.45000	-	100.0 Hz	
Castle Dale	DMR/BM	WX7Y	145.17500	-	CC1	
	DMR/BM	WX7Y	447.62500	-	CC1	
Castle Dale, Cedar Mountain						
	FM	K7SDC	147.14000	+	88.5 Hz	UVHFS
	FM	K7YI	447.12500	-	100.0 Hz	UVHFS
	FM	K7SDC	448.55000	-	88.5 Hz	UVHFS
Castle Dale, Horn Mountain						
	FM	K7SDC	147.06000	+	88.5 Hz	UVHFS
	FM	K7YI	447.62500	-	100.0 Hz	UVHFS
	FM	WX7Y	447.70000	-	123.0 Hz	UVHFS
Castledale	FM	K7JL	147.12000	+	100.0 Hz	UVHFS
Cedar City	DSTAR	WR7AAA	145.15000	-		
	DSTAR	WR7AAA C	145.15000	-		
	DSTAR	KG7OOW B	446.05000	-		
	DSTAR	WR7AAA B	447.95000	-		
	DSTAR	WR7AAA	1299.25000	1279.25000		UVHFS
	FM	WV7H	145.47000	-		UVHFS
	FM	WA7GTU	447.57500	+		UVHFS
	FM	N7DZP	448.10000	-		UVHFS
	FM	WA7GTU	449.90000	-	100.0 Hz	UVHFS
Cedar City, Blowhard Mountain						
	FM	WV7H	146.80000	-	100.0 Hz	UVHFS
	FM	KB6BOB	448.65000	-		UVHFS
Cedar City, Hospital						
	FM	N7AKK	147.06000	+		UVHFS

Location	Mode	Call sign	Output	Input	Access	Coordinator
Cedar City, Iron Mountain						
	FM	K7JH	146.76000	-	123.0 Hz	UVHFS
	FM	N7KM	146.98000	-	100.0 Hz	UVHFS
	FM	K7JH	448.80000	-	100.0 Hz	UVHFS
	FM	WA7GTU	449.50000	-	100.0 Hz	UVHFS
Cedar Fort, Internet Mountain						
	FM	KO7R	449.70000	-	127.3 Hz	UVHFS
Cedar Hills	DMR/BM	NG6K	927.16250	902.16250	CC1	
Centerville	FUSION	K7UHP	449.87500	-		
Clearfield	FM	KR7K	447.15000	-	114.8 Hz	UVHFS
Clearfield, Civic Center						
	FM	NJ7J	449.95000	-	123.0 Hz	UVHFS
Coalville, Lewis Peak						
	FM	K7HEN	147.24000	+	136.5 Hz	UVHFS
	FM	WA7GIE	147.36000	+	100.0 Hz	UVHFS
	FM	WA7GIE	448.65000	-		UVHFS
	FM	WB7TSQ	448.90000	-		UVHFS
	FM	WA7GIE	449.55000	-	100.0 Hz	UVHFS
Delta, Notch Peak	FM	KB7WQD	147.38000	+	203.5 Hz	UVHFS
Draper	DMR/BM	KF7KGN	446.77500	-	CC1	
Draper, Fire Station						
	FM	KG7EGM	447.10000	-	100.0 Hz	
Draper, Lake Mountain						
	FM	WX7Y	147.08000	+	77.0 Hz	UVHFS
Draper, Point Of The Mountain						
	FM	N7IMF	224.90000	-	156.7 Hz	UVHFS
Duchense	FM	N7PQD	147.26000	+		UVHFS
Eagle Mountain	FM	W7SP-R	146.76000	-		UVHFS
	FM	WD7N	449.25000	-	110.9 Hz	UVHFS
East Of Holden	FM	WB7REL	449.30000	-	88.5 Hz	UVHFS
East Salina, Salina Canyon						
	FM	WB7REL	146.72000	-	100.0 Hz	UVHFS
Enterprise	FM	NR7K	146.74000	-	100.0 Hz	UVHFS
Enterprise, Black Hills						
	FM	KD7YK	449.72500	-		UVHFS
Ephraim, Horseshoe						
	FM	W7DHH	146.66000	-	100.0 Hz	UVHFS
	FM	N7IMF	224.64000	-		UVHFS
Eureka, Eureka Peak						
	FM	KC7KRY	447.87500	-		
Farmington	FM	WB7TSQ	146.96000	0.60000	100.0 Hz	
Farmington, Shepard Peak						
	FM	K7DAV	53.01000	52.01000	141.3 Hz	UVHFS
Garrison	FM	N7ELY	442.10000	+	114.8 Hz	
Glendale, Spencer Bench						
	FM	WB7REL	146.72000	-	100.0 Hz	UVHFS
Goshen, West Mountain						
	FM	WA7UAH	147.02000	+	100.0 Hz	UVHFS
	FM	K7UCS	147.34000	+	100.0 Hz	UVHFS
	FM	WA7FFM	448.95000	-		UVHFS
Gunnison, N7RVS QTH						
	FM	N7RVS	447.35000	-	88.5 Hz	UVHFS
Hanksville, Ellen Peak						
	FM	K7SDC	147.08000	+	136.5 Hz	UVHFS
Heist		AE7HY-R	146.64000			
Herriman	DMR/BM	N6SLY	449.46250	-	CC1	
	FUSION	KK7DLM	450.00000			
Herriman, High School						
	FM	N7HRC	449.25000	-	118.8 Hz	UVHFS
Holden, Beesting Peak						
	FM	N7GGN	147.10000	+	100.0 Hz	UVHFS

Location	Mode	Call sign	Output	Input	Access	Coordinator
Howell, Blue Springs Hill						
	FM	K7UB	145.43000	-	123.0 Hz	UVHFS
	FM	K7UB	448.30000	-	123.0 Hz	UVHFS
Huntington, Skyline Dr						
	FM	WX7Y	223.92000	-	88.5 Hz	UVHFS
Huntsville	FM	W7DBA	145.21000	-	123.0 Hz	UVHFS
	FM	W7DBA	448.02500	-	123.0 Hz	UVHFS
Hurricane	FM	KG7FOT	449.55000	-	100.0 Hz	
Hurricane, Hurricane Mesa						
	FM	K5JCA	449.27500	-		UVHFS
Indianola, Indianola Peak						
	FM	WB7REL	146.72000	-	100.0 Hz	UVHFS
Kanab, TV Site	FM	W7NRC	146.88000	-	123.0 Hz	UVHFS
Kearns	FM	K7LNP	447.57500	-	114.8 Hz	UVHFS
Lake Mountain	FM	WA7FFM	145.23000	-		
	FM	WB7TSQ	145.37000	-	100.0 Hz	
Laketown, Bear Lake						
	FM	K7OGM	147.02000	+	100.0 Hz	UVHFS
	FM	K7OGM	448.45000	-	131.8 Hz	UVHFS
	FM	K7OGM	448.97500	-		UVHFS
	FM	K7OGM	449.70000	-	100.0 Hz	UVHFS
Layton	DMR/BM	KR1P	447.05000	-	CC1	
Layton, Francis Peak						
	FM	K7MLA	146.96000	-	100.0 Hz	UVHFS
Layton, Shepard Peak						
	FM	K7DAV	449.87500	-		UVHFS
Lehi	DMR/BM	KI7MAT	446.50000		CC2	
	DMR/BM	KC7WST	447.05000	-	CC1	
	FM	KG7QWU	448.87500	-		
Lehi, City Offices	FM	KI7USB	448.92500	-	100.0 Hz	
Levan, Levan Peak						
	FM	K7JL	145.27000	-	103.5 Hz	UVHFS
Logan		WA7MXZ-L	146.68000			
	DMR/BM	WA7KMF	447.35000	-	CC1	
	DMR/MARC	NU7TS	447.00000	-	CC1	UVHFS
	DSTAR	AC7O C	145.15000	-		
	DSTAR	AC7O B	447.97500	-		
	DSTAR	AC7O D	1299.75000			
	FM	N7RRZ	147.24000	+	79.7 Hz	UVHFS
	FM	N7RRZ	449.32500	-	156.7 Hz	UVHFS
	FUSION	K5AGC	147.33500	+		
Logan, Mt Logan	DSTAR	AC7O	1299.75000	1279.75000		
	FM	WA7KMF	146.72000	-	103.5 Hz	UVHFS
	FM	AC7O	449.62500	-	103.5 Hz	UVHFS
Logan, Mt Pisgah	FM	AC7II	449.65000	-	100.0 Hz	UVHFS
Logan, WA7KMF QTH						
	DSTAR	AC7O	145.15000	-		UVHFS
	DSTAR	AC7O	447.97500	-		
Magna, Kessler Peak						
	FM	W7YDO	448.85000	-		
Manti	FM	N7YFZ	449.75000	-	131.8 Hz	UVHFS
Manti, Barton Peak						
	FM	KD7YE	448.27500	-	107.2 Hz	UVHFS
Mantua, Murrays Hill						
	FM	WA7KMF	449.80000	-	103.5 Hz	UVHFS
Mapleton	FM	N6EZO	146.80000	-	100.0 Hz	UVHFS
Mendon	FM	N7PKI	448.92500	-	100.0 Hz	UVHFS
Mexican Hat	FM	KD7HLL	449.90000	-	123.0 Hz	UVHFS
Midway	FM	N7ZOI	449.95000	-		UVHFS
Midway, Wilson Peak						
	FM	N7ZOI	147.20000	+	88.5 Hz	UVHFS

Location	Mode	Call sign	Output	Input	Access	Coordinator
Milford, Frisco Peak						
	FM	WR7AAA	146.94000	-		
	FM	K7JL	448.67500	-		UVHFS
Millcreek	FUSION	KZ9HMR	445.00000			
Moab	FM	K7QEQ	146.90000	-	88.5 Hz	UVHFS
	FUSION	NQ0A	430.00000			
	FUSION	KD0SBN	447.50000			
Moab, Bald Mesa	FM	K7QEQ	146.76000	-		
	FM	K7QEQ	449.10000	-	107.2 Hz	UVHFS
Monroe, Monroe Peak						
	FM	WA7HSW	146.64000	-	100.0 Hz	UVHFS
	FM	WB7REL	146.86000	-	100.0 Hz	UVHFS
	FM	W7DHH	447.45000	-	114.8 Hz	UVHFS
Monticello, Abajo Peak						
	FM	K7SDC	146.61000	-	88.5 Hz	UVHFS
	FM	K7QEQ	447.40000	-		UVHFS
Monticello, Abajo Pk						
	FM	K7QEQ	223.94000	-		UVHFS
Morgan	DSTAR	KM7ARC C	145.16250	-		
	DSTAR	KM7ARC B	447.96250	-		
	DSTAR	KM7ARC D	1297.75000			
Morgan, TV Site.	FM	KB7ZCL	147.10000	+	123.0 Hz	UVHFS
Murray	FM	NM7P	145.35000	-	100.0 Hz	UVHFS
	FM	N7HIW	448.12500	-	100.0 Hz	UVHFS
Murray, Intermountain Med Ctr						
	DSTAR	KO7SLC	145.15000	-		
	DSTAR	KO7SLC	447.95000	-		
	DSTAR	KO7SLC	1298.75000	1278.75000		
Murray, Intermountain Medical						
	FM	KE7LMG	447.25000	-	100.0 Hz	UVHFS
Myton, Flat Top	FM	W7BYU	145.49000	-	136.5 Hz	UVHFS
NOAA Bear Lake	WX	WXL63	162.50000			
NOAA Castle Dale						
	WX	WNG669	162.50000			
NOAA Coalville / Park City						
	WX	KJY60	162.47500			
NOAA Escalante	WX	KJY61	162.42500			
NOAA Lake Powell						
	WX	WXM89	162.55000			
NOAA Logan	WX	WXM22	162.40000			
NOAA Manti	WX	WNG594	162.42500			
NOAA Milford / Cedar City						
	WX	WXM24	162.40000			
NOAA Moab	WX	WNG556	162.47500			
NOAA Monticello	WX	WNG687	162.45000			
NOAA Salt Lake City						
	WX	KEC78	162.55000			
NOAA South Mountain						
	WX	WWF46	162.45000			
NOAA St. George	WX	WWF51	162.47500			
NOAA Tabiona	WX	KJY79	162.55000			
NOAA Vernal	WX	WXM23	162.40000			
NOAA Vernon Hills						
	WX	WWF47	162.52500			
NOAA Wendover	WX	KXI30	162.47500			
North Logan	DMR/BM	AC7JT	449.25000	-	CC1	
Oakcrest Estates		K7UHP-R	447.52500			
Ogden	DMR/BM	N7ADV	438.30000		CC1	
	FM	K7JL	145.49000	-	100.0 Hz	UVHFS
	FM	WB7TSQ	147.38000	+		UVHFS
	FM	KW7TES	449.07500	-		UVHFS
	FUSION	KW7TES	146.90000	-		

Location	Mode	Call sign	Output	Input	Access	Coordinator
Ogden, Downtown						
	FM	WB6CDN	224.50000	-	167.9 Hz	UVHFS
Ogden, Foothills	FM	WB7TSQ	145.41000	-	123.0 Hz	UVHFS
Ogden, Little Mountain						
	FM	W7SU	448.57500	-	100.0 Hz	UVHFS
	FUSION	W7SU	146.82000	-	123.0 Hz	UVHFS
Ogden, Mt Ogden	FUSION	KE7EGG	146.90000	-		UVHFS
	FUSION	KE7EGG	448.60000	-	123.0 Hz	UVHFS
Ogden, Powder Mountain						
	FUSION	KE7EGG	145.47000	-	123.0 Hz	UVHFS
	FUSION	KE7EGG	447.77500	-	123.0 Hz	UVHFS
Ogden, Promontory Pt						
	FM	K7JL	145.49000	-	100.0 Hz	UVHFS
	FM	AC7O	147.26000	+	103.5 Hz	UVHFS
Ogden, Sheriff's Office						
	DSTAR	KE7EGG	447.95000	-		UVHFS
	DSTAR	KE7EGG	1298.75000	1278.75000		UVHFS
Ogden, Weber State University						
	FM	KD7FDH	145.25000	-	123.0 Hz	UVHFS
Orem	FM	KD7BBC	146.78000	-	100.0 Hz	
	FM	N7IMF	224.88000	-	156.7 Hz	UVHFS
	FM	KD7BBC	448.20000	-	100.0 Hz	
	FM	K7WCS	448.32500	-	103.5 Hz	
Orem, Lake Mountain						
	FM	K7UVA	146.78000	-	100.0 Hz	UVHFS
	FM	K7UVA	224.56000	-	100.0 Hz	UVHFS
	FM	K7UVA	448.20000	-	100.0 Hz	UVHFS
Orem, Point Of The Mountain						
	FM	KD7RBR	447.60000	-	162.2 Hz	UVHFS
Orem, QTH AC7DM						
	FM	N7BSA	145.47000	-	100.0 Hz	UVHFS
Page (AZ), Navajo Mountain						
	FM	W7WAC	146.96000	-	100.0 Hz	UVHFS
	FM	NA7DB	448.75000	-	100.0 Hz	UVHFS
	FM	W7CWI	449.92500	-	100.0 Hz	UVHFS
Page, Navajo Mountain						
	FM	WA7VHF	448.60000	-	100.0 Hz	UVHFS
Panguitch, Mount Dutton						
	FM	N7NKK	147.16000	+	100.0 Hz	UVHFS
Paradise, AC7II QTH						
	DSTAR	KF7VJO	447.95000	-		UVHFS
Park City	FM	NZ6Z	145.23000	-	100.0 Hz	UVHFS
	FM	NZ6Z	447.50000	-		UVHFS
Park City, Murdock Peak						
	FM	KB7HAF	448.47500	-		UVHFS
Payson	FM	NV7V	447.00000	-	100.0 Hz	UVHFS
	FM	KB7M	448.02500	-	100.0 Hz	UVHFS
Pleasant Grove	FM	KB7YOT	223.88000	-	156.7 Hz	UVHFS
	FM	N7UEO	449.32500	-	114.8 Hz	UVHFS
	FM	K8BKT	449.77500	-		UVHFS
Portable	DMR/BM	KC7WSU	436.00000		CC1	
	DMR/BM	KC7WSU	449.25000	-	CC1	
Price	FUSION	NK7F	449.25000	-		
Price / Cedar Mtn	DSTAR	K7YI B	448.07500	-		
Price, Wood Hill	FM	W7CEU	145.43000	-	88.5 Hz	UVHFS
	FM	K7GX	147.20000	+	88.5 Hz	UVHFS
	FM	W7CEU	224.50000	-	88.5 Hz	UVHFS
	FM	W7CEU	448.30000	-	88.5 Hz	UVHFS
Promontory Point	FUSION	KE7EGG	146.92000	-	123.0 Hz	UVHFS
	FUSION	KE7EGG	448.77500	-	123.0 Hz	UVHFS
Provo	FM	N7BYU-R	145.33000	-		UVHFS
	FM	N7IMF	224.64000	-	156.7 Hz	UVHFS

Location	Mode	Call sign	Output	Input	Access	Coordinator
Provo, BYU	FM	N7BYU	449.07500	-	167.9 Hz	UVHFS
Provo, Lake Mountain						
	FM	K7UCS	145.23000	-	131.8 Hz	UVHFS
	FM	K7UCS	147.28000	+	141.3 Hz	UVHFS
	FM	W7WJC	224.42000	-	156.7 Hz	UVHFS
	FM	WA7GIE	449.47500	-	100.0 Hz	UVHFS
	FM	K7UCS	449.67500	-	173.8 Hz	UVHFS
	FM	K7UCS	449.97500	-	131.8 Hz	UVHFS
Provo, Sundance	FM	K7UVA	145.25000	-	100.0 Hz	UVHFS
Provo, UVRMC	FM	WA7FFM	449.85000	-	146.2 Hz	UVHFS
Red Spur	FM	WA7KMF	145.31000	-	103.5 Hz	UVHFS
Richfield, Monroe Peak						
	FM	WA7VHF	146.84000	-	100.0 Hz	UVHFS
River Heights	FM	W7BOZ-R	449.30000	-		UVHFS
Riverside	DSTAR	N7RDS	447.92500	-		UVHFS
	DSTAR	N7RDS B	447.92500	-		
	DSTAR	WA7KMF	449.57500	-		UVHFS
Robinson Place		AD7ZW-L	147.10000			
Roosevelt	FM	W7BYU	146.92000	-	136.5 Hz	UVHFS
Saint George	DMR/BM	W7CRC	447.35000	-	CC3	
	DMR/BM	N4NZA	448.05000	-	CC1	
	DSTAR	KF7YIX C	145.15000	-		
	DSTAR	KF7YIX B	447.95000	-		
Salina, Beesting Peak						
	FM	WB7REL	449.30000	-		
Salt Lake	DSTAR	WA7GIE C	147.38000	+		
	DSTAR	WA7GIE B	448.72500	-		
	WX	K2NWS	447.52500	-	107.2 Hz	UVHFS
Salt Lake City	DMR/MARC	N6DVZ	447.93750	-	CC1	UVHFS
	DSTAR	KF6RAL C	145.12500	-		
	DSTAR	KF6RAL B	448.07500	-		
	DSTAR	KF6RAL A	1287.00000	-		
	DSTAR	KF6RAL D	1299.25000			
	FM	KD0J	146.88000	-	88.5 Hz	UVHFS
	FM	W0HU	447.02500	-	100.0 Hz	UVHFS
	FM	W7SAR	447.17500	-		UVHFS
	FM	K7MRS	447.25000	-	100.0 Hz	UVHFS
	FM	WB7TSQ	448.42500	-	100.0 Hz	
	FM	KA7OEI	449.75000	-	151.4 Hz	UVHFS
	FM	W7XDX	927.58800	902.58800		UVHFS
	FUSION	K7TFT	438.80000			
Salt Lake City, Capitol						
	FM	AA7JR	145.21000	-		UVHFS
	FM	W7DES	448.00000	-	100.0 Hz	UVHFS
Salt Lake City, Ensign Peak						
	FM	KC7IIB	146.70000	-	100.0 Hz	UVHFS
	FM	WA7SNS	147.16000	+	127.3 Hz	UVHFS
	FM	KD7IMS	448.17500	-	203.5 Hz	UVHFS
	FM	KC7IIB	448.45000	-	100.0 Hz	UVHFS
	FM	K7XRD	448.52500	-		UVHFS
	FM	WA7VHF	449.27500	-	88.5 Hz	UVHFS
	FM	K7JL	449.40000	-	100.0 Hz	UVHFS
	FM	KD0J	449.90000	-	100.0 Hz	UVHFS
Salt Lake City, Farnsworth Pea						
	DSTAR	KF6RAL	145.12500	-		UVHFS
	DSTAR	KF6RAL	448.07500	-		UVHFS
	DSTAR	KF6RAL	1287.00000	1267.00000		UVHFS
	FM	KI7DX	53.15000	52.15000	146.2 Hz	UVHFS
	FM	W7SP	146.62000	-		UVHFS
	FM	WA7VHF	146.94000	-	88.5 Hz	UVHFS
	FM	K7JL	147.12000	+	100.0 Hz	UVHFS
	FM	KI7DX	448.15000	-	127.3 Hz	UVHFS

Location	Mode	Call sign	Output	Input	Access	Coordinator
Salt Lake City, Farnsworth Pea						
	FM	K7JL	449.15000	-	100.0 Hz	UVHFS
	FM	K7JL	449.50000	-	100.0 Hz	UVHFS
Salt Lake City, IHC						
	FM	W7IHC	448.55000	-	100.0 Hz	UVHFS
Salt Lake City, Intermountain						
	FM	W7IHC	448.40000	-		UVHFS
Salt Lake City, Jordan Vly Hos						
	FM	N7PCE	146.84000	-		UVHFS
	FM	KD0J	224.78000	-	100.0 Hz	UVHFS
Salt Lake City, LDS HQ						
	FM	WD7SL	448.42500	-	100.0 Hz	UVHFS
Salt Lake City, Meridian Peak						
	FM	WB6CDN	224.82000	-	167.9 Hz	UVHFS
Salt Lake City, Nelson Peak						
	FM	WA7GIE	433.60000	-	100.0 Hz	UVHFS
	FM	WA7GIE	448.72500	-		UVHFS
	FM	WA7GIE	449.00000	-		UVHFS
	FM	WA7GIE	449.42500	-	100.0 Hz	UVHFS
Salt Lake City, SLC						
	FM	K7CSW	448.05000	-	100.0 Hz	UVHFS
Salt Lake City, U Of U Hospita						
	FM	KD7NX	146.74000	-	114.8 Hz	UVHFS
	FM	KD7NX	448.10000	-	114.8 Hz	UVHFS
Salt Lake County	DSTAR	KO7SLC C	145.15000	-		
	DSTAR	KO7SLC B	447.95000	-		
	DSTAR	KO7SLC D	1298.75000			
Salt Lake, Carrigan Ridge						
	FM	KE7GHK	145.41000	-		UVHFS
Sandy	FM	KA7EGC	224.64000	-	156.7 Hz	
	FM	W7ROY	448.37500	-	100.0 Hz	UVHFS
	FUSION	K7TYL	437.95000			
Saratoga Springs	DMR/BM	KE7NHU	447.42500	-	CC1	
	FM	AC7DU	447.67500	-	100.0 Hz	UVHFS
Scofield, Boardinghouse Rdge						
	FM	WX7Y	224.98000	-	88.5 Hz	UVHFS
Scofield, Boardinghouse Ridge						
	FM	K7SDC	147.08000	+	88.5 Hz	UVHFS
Scofield, Ford Ridge						
	FM	K7SDC	145.31000	-	88.5 Hz	UVHFS
Snowbird, Hidden Peak						
	FM	K7JL	147.18000	+	100.0 Hz	UVHFS
South Jordan	DMR/BM	W7XDX	447.96250	-	CC1	
	FUSION	KJ7QMF	448.52500			
South Salt Lake City, Fire Sta						
	FM	KF7YXL	447.70000	-	100.0 Hz	UVHFS
Springville	FM	N7KYY	447.32500	-	114.8 Hz	UVHFS
	FM	WD7N	447.47500	-	186.2 Hz	UVHFS
St George	FM	N7ARR	145.37000	-		UVHFS
	FM	KA7STK	146.70000	-		UVHFS
	FM	NR7K	449.32500	-		UVHFS
	FM	KA7STK	449.42500	-		
St George, Scrub Peak						
	FM	WB6TNP	448.72500	-		UVHFS
St George, Seegmiller Peak						
	FM	NR7K	146.91000	-	100.0 Hz	UVHFS
St George, Utah Hill						
	FM	NR7K	146.82000	-	100.0 Hz	UVHFS
	FM	K7OET	449.35000	-	100.0 Hz	
	FM	W7AOR	449.75000	-	123.0 Hz	UVHFS
St George, Webb Hill						
	FM	W7DRC	146.64000	-	100.0 Hz	UVHFS

Location	Mode	Call sign	Output	Input	Access	Coordinator
St. George	DMR/BM	K6IB	447.80000	-	CC1	
	DMR/BM	K6IB	448.47500	-	CC1	
St. George, Webb Hill						
	FM	K7OET	927.55000	902.55000		
Starling, Sterling	FM	WB7REL	145.29000	-	131.8 Hz	UVHFS
Sterling	DSTAR	KB7BSK	145.15000	-		
	DSTAR	K7BSK C	145.15000	-		
	DSTAR	KB7BSK	447.95000	-		
	DSTAR	K7BSK B	447.95000	-		
	FM	WB7REL	447.85000	-	131.8 Hz	UVHFS
Sterling, Salina Canyon						
	FM	WB7REL	449.25000	-	131.8 Hz	UVHFS
Sunny Side, Bruin Peak						
	FM	WX7Y	145.17500	-		
Sunnyside, Bruin Point						
	FM	K7SDC	147.32000	+	88.5 Hz	UVHFS
	FM	K7SDC	449.05000	-	88.5 Hz	UVHFS
Thiokol	FM	K7UB	448.30000	-	123.0 Hz	UVHFS
Tooele	DMR/BM	N6DVZ	447.81250	-	CC1	
	FUSION	N6RBV	442.36250	+		
Tooele, Black Mountain						
	FM	K7HK	145.35000	-		UVHFS
	FM	W7EO	146.98000	-		UVHFS
Tooele, Home QTH						
	FM	N6RBV	447.36250	-		
Tooele, South Mountain						
	FM	W7EO	147.30000	+	100.0 Hz	UVHFS
	FM	W7EO	449.35000	-	100.0 Hz	UVHFS
Toquerville, Toquerville Hill						
	FM	W7DRC	145.45000	-	100.0 Hz	UVHFS
Torquerville, Hurricane Mesa						
	DSTAR	KF7YIX	145.15000	-		UVHFS
	DSTAR	KF7YIX	447.95000	-		UVHFS
	DSTAR	KF7YIX	1299.25000	1279.25000		UVHFS
Tremonton	DMR/MARC	NU7TS	447.12500	-	CC1	UVHFS
Vernal	FM	W7BYU	449.70000	-	136.5 Hz	UVHFS
	FUSION	W7BAR	449.90000	-		
Vernal, Blue Mountain						
	FM	W7BAR	147.10000	+	136.5 Hz	UVHFS
Vernal, Grizzly Ridge						
	FM	K7HEN	145.49000	-	136.5 Hz	UVHFS
	FM	W7BAR	147.04000	+	136.5 Hz	UVHFS
Vernal, Tabby Mountain						
	FM	KG7DSO	147.34000	+	136.5 Hz	UVHFS
Vernal, Uintah County EOC						
	FM	W7BAR	449.90000	-	136.5 Hz	
Vernon, Black Crook Peak						
	FM	W7EO	145.39000	-	100.0 Hz	UVHFS
Vernon, Vernon Hills						
	FM	W7EO	449.95000	-	100.0 Hz	UVHFS
Wellsville	DSTAR	NU7TS	449.57500	-		
	DSTAR	NU7TS B	449.57500	-		
	FM	AF7FH	927.51250	902.51250	103.5 Hz	UVHFS
Wendover, Wendover Peak						
	FM	W7EO	147.20000	+	100.0 Hz	UVHFS
	FM	WA7GIE	449.55000	-	123.0 Hz	UVHFS
West Bountiful	DSTAR	KF7ZNS C	145.13750	-		
	DSTAR	KF7ZNS B	447.97500	-		
	DSTAR	KF7ZNS D	1298.25000			
West Jordan	FM	K7LNP	447.57500	-	114.8 Hz	UVHFS
	FM	WD7P	447.75000	-	100.0 Hz	UVHFS
	FUSION	KC7CO	446.02500			

Location	Mode	Call sign	Output	Input	Access	Coordinator
West Jordan, Butterfield Peak						
	FM	K7MLA	147.14000	+	127.3 Hz	UVHFS
	FM	W7XDX	927.11250	902.11250		UVHFS
West Jordan, Butterfield Pk						
	FM	WB7TSQ	449.72500	-	151.4 Hz	UVHFS
West Kaysville, Sewer Plant						
	FM	K7DOU	449.70000	-	100.0 Hz	UVHFS
West Point, West Point City Bu						
	FM	W7WPC	447.07500	-		UVHFS
West Valley City, WVCFD Statio						
	FM	K2WVC	448.80000	448.30000	100.0 Hz	
Woodland Hills	DMR/BM	KC7WST	449.80000	-	CC1	
	FM	WB7RPF	447.30000	-	77.0 Hz	UVHFS
Woods Cross	DMR/BM	K7BBR	442.37500	+	CC1	
VERMONT						
Arlington	DMR/BM	W2FCC	145.60000	147.60000	CC1	
Athens	FM	K2KDA	441.65000	+	110.9 Hz	
Bellows Falls	FM	KB1NXN	447.57500	-		
Bolton	DMR/MARC	KI1P	445.07500	-	CC7	
Bouplon Corner	FM	K1SV-R	146.83500	-		VIRCC
Brandon	FM	AA1PR	52.49000	51.49000	131.8 Hz	
Brandon, Village Park						
	FM	AA1PR	146.47500		173.8 Hz	
Brattleboro	DMR/MARC	WR1VT	444.40000	+	CC1	NESMC
Brownsville, Mount Ascutney						
	FM	W1IMD	448.12500	-	110.9 Hz	VIRCC
Burke	FM	W1AAK	449.12500	-	110.9 Hz	
Burke Mtn	DMR/MARC	KI1P	448.57500	-	CC5	
Burlington	DMR/MARC	KI1P	446.47500	-	CC1	
	FM	W1KOO	146.61000	-	100.0 Hz	VIRCC
	FM	W1KOO	443.15000	+		
Cabot	FM	W1BD	146.82000	-	100.0 Hz	VIRCC
	FM	K1US	449.62500	-		
Coleman Corner		K1ZK-L	223.42000			
Corinth	DMR/MARC	KA1UAG	443.90000	+	CC8	VIRCC
East Barre	FM	N1IOE	147.39000	+	100.0 Hz	VIRCC
East Corinth	FM	KB1FDA	147.21000	+	100.0 Hz	VIRCC
Essex Junction	FM	KB1KJS	146.79000	-	100.0 Hz	VIRCC
Hartford	DMR/BM	N1CIV	145.13000	-	CC7	
	DMR/BM	WX1NH	444.00000	-	CC7	
Jay	DMR/MARC	KI1P	446.37500	-	CC7	
Jay, Jay Peak Ski Resort						
	FM	K1JAY	146.74500	-	100.0 Hz	
Jericho, Mt Mansfield						
	FM	W1KOO	146.94000	-	100.0 Hz	VIRCC
Lincoln Mobile Homes Court						
	FM	AA1PR-L	446.10000	-		
Manchester, Equinox Mountain						
	FM	WA1ZMS	145.39000	-	100.0 Hz	VIRCC
Manchester, Mount Equinox						
	FM	K1EQX	444.05000	+	100.0 Hz	
Marlboro, Hogback Mountain						
	FM	N1HWI	147.01500	+	100.0 Hz	VIRCC
Monkton	DMR/MARC	W1IMD	443.75000	+	CC7	
	FM	W1AAK	444.65000	+	110.9 Hz	VIRCC
Montpelier	FM	K1VIT	449.67500	-	103.5 Hz	
Mt Equinox	DMR/MARC	KB1VP	441.35000	+	CC7	
Mt. Ascutney	DMR/MARC	W1UWS	448.47500	-	CC5	VIRCC
Mt. Snow	DMR/MARC	KI1P	446.27500	-	CC6	
Newfane		KC1AAB-L	147.43000			
	FM	WA1KFX	147.09000	+	110.9 Hz	VIRCC

Location	Mode	Call sign	Output	Input	Access	Coordinator
Newfane	FM	WA1KFX	444.70000	+	110.9 Hz	
NOAA Burlington	WX	KIG60	162.40000			VIRCC
NOAA Castleton	WX	WNG671	162.50000			VIRCC
NOAA Marlboro	WX	WXM68	162.42500			VIRCC
NOAA St. Johnsbury						
	WX	WWG50	162.42500			VIRCC
NOAA Windsor	WX	WXM44	162.47500			VIRCC
Northfield	DMR/MARC	KI1P	449.47500	-	CC6	
Perkinsville	FUSION	AK1VT	443.27500			
Pico Peak	DMR/MARC	W1IMD	444.50000	+	CC1	
Poultney	DSTAR	KC2YXS	145.60000			
Proctorsville	FM	W1TAL	146.41500		123.0 Hz	
Rutland	FM	W1OOR	146.49000		123.0 Hz	
	FM	WA1ZMS	449.17500	-	100.0 Hz	
Rutland, Boardman Hill						
	FM	W1GMW	147.04500	-	100.0 Hz	VIRCC
Rutland, Killington Peak						
	FM	W1AAK	146.88000	-	110.9 Hz	VIRCC
	FM	W1ABI	444.55000	+	110.9 Hz	VIRCC
Rutland, Pico Peak						
	FM	W1IMD	444.40000	+		
Saint Albans	FM	N1STA	443.40000	+	162.2 Hz	
Saint Albans, French Hill						
	FM	N1STA	145.23000	-	100.0 Hz	VIRCC
Tunbridge	FM	K1MOQ	146.97000	-		
Underhill, Mount Mansfield						
	FM	W1IMD	447.17500	-	82.5 Hz	VIRCC
Warren	DMR/MARC	K1VIT	145.41000	-	CC1	
Warren, Lincoln Peak						
	FM	K1VIT	145.47000	-	100.0 Hz	VIRCC
Wells	FM	N1VT	224.96000	-		VIRCC
White River Jct	FM	N1DAS	444.00000	+		
Williamstown	DMR/MARC	W1IMD	448.87500	-	CC7	VIRCC
	FM	W1BD	146.62500	-	100.0 Hz	VIRCC
	FM	W1AAK	444.60000	+	110.9 Hz	
Windsor, Mt Ascutney						
	FM	W1UWS	146.76000	-	110.9 Hz	VIRCC
VIRGINIA						
Abingdon	FM	NM4L	147.34500	+	103.5 Hz	
	FUSION	K4MIN	146.48000			
Abingdon, Brummley Mtn						
	FM	KB8KSP	442.97500	+		
Accomac	FM	K4BW	147.25500	+	156.7 Hz	
	FM	K4BW	444.30000	+		
Alexandria	DMR/MARC	W4HFH	442.41250	+	CC1	T-MARC
	DMR/MARC	N3JLT	443.10000	+	CC1	T-MARC
	DSTAR	W4HFH C	145.38000	-		
	DSTAR	W4HFH B	442.06000	+		
	DSTAR	W4HFH D	1253.60000			
	DSTAR	W4HFH A	1284.60000	-		
	FM	W4HFH	53.13000	52.13000	107.2 Hz	
	FM	W4HFH	147.31500	+	107.2 Hz	
	FM	W4HFH	224.82000	-	107.2 Hz	T-MARC
	FM	W4HFH	444.60000	+	107.2 Hz	T-MARC
	FM	W4HFH	927.60000	902.60000	107.2 Hz	T-MARC
	FM	W4HFH	1282.60000	-	107.2 Hz	T-MARC
	FUSION	N4FKH	146.42000			
Alexandria, George Washington						
	FM	K4US	146.65500	-	141.3 Hz	T-MARC
Alexandria, Inova Alexandria H						
	DSTAR	W4HFH	1253.60000			T-MARC

Location	Mode	Call sign	Output	Input	Access	Coordinator
Alto		KB4JNK-R	224.58000			
Alton	DMR/BM	KB3CVS	147.36000	+	CC1	
Amherst	FM	K4CQ	145.49000	-	136.5 Hz	SERA-VA
	FUSION	WD4KQI	444.95000	+		
Antioch, Bull Run Mountain						
	FM	WA3KOK	447.77500	-	67.0 Hz	T-MARC
	FM	N3KL	1286.10000	1266.10000		T-MARC
Arlington	FM	WB4MJF	145.15000	-		T-MARC
	FM	W4WVP	145.47000	-	107.2 Hz	T-MARC
	FM	WB4MJF	224.06000	-		T-MARC
	FM	WB4MWF	224.62000	-		T-MARC
	FM	W4CIA	441.45000	+	110.9 Hz	
	FM	AB4YP	443.20000	+	114.8 Hz	T-MARC
	FM	K4AF	444.55000	+	88.5 Hz	T-MARC
	FM	W4AVA	448.62500	-	107.2 Hz	T-MARC
	FM	W4WVP	449.32500	-	151.4 Hz	T-MARC
Arlington, National Capitol Re						
	FM	W4AVA	146.62500	-	107.2 Hz	T-MARC
Ashburn	DMR/BM	KO4NCX	447.67500	-	CC1	
	DMR/MARC	WB6EFW	442.13750	+	CC1	T-MARC
	DMR/MARC	N3QEM	442.90000	+	CC1	T-MARC
	FM	NV4FM	53.61000	52.61000		T-MARC
	FM	WB6EFW	145.18500	-	103.5 Hz	
	FM	KI4AD	447.90000		100.0 Hz	
	FM	KI4AD	448.82500	-	77.0 Hz	T-MARC
Ashland	DMR/BM	KD4RJN	443.13750	+	CC1	
Auburn Chase		N4NQY-R	446.10000			
Banco, Fork Mountain						
	FM	K3HOT	443.25000	+	107.2 Hz	
Baskerville	FUSION	KI4SHC	432.50000			
Basye, Great North Mountain						
	FM	K4MRA	444.60000	+	131.8 Hz	T-MARC
Bath, Warm Springs Mountain						
	FM	W4COV	146.80500	-	107.2 Hz	
Beaverdam	DMR/MARC	WA4FC	444.61250	+	CC1	
Beaverdam, Ashland Berry Farm						
	FM	KD4RJN	147.06000	+	74.4 Hz	SERA-VA
Bedford	DMR/BM	WA1ZMS	443.80000	+	CC1	
	FM	K4LYL	53.01000	52.01000		
	FM	W1IE-R	145.19500	+		
Bedford, Apple Orchard Mtn						
	FM	WA1ZMS	146.68500	-	100.0 Hz	SERA-VA
	FM	WA1ZMS	442.65000	+	100.0 Hz	SERA-VA
Bedford, Thaxton Mountain						
	FM	K4LYL	53.15000	52.15000		SERA-VA
Bent Mountain	FUSION	AE4JA	442.20000	+		
Bent Mountain, Slings Gap						
	FM	W4KZK	442.92500	+	107.2 Hz	SERA-VA
Blacksburg, Brush Mountain						
	FM	W9KIC	146.71500	-		SERA-VA
	FM	N4NRV	444.65000	+	107.2 Hz	
Bland	FM	KD4LMZ	145.35000	-	103.5 Hz	SERA-VA
Blue Mountain	FM	KC4CK	224.16000	-		T-MARC
Bluefield	DMR/BM	W8MOP	444.45000	+	CC1	
	DMR/MARC	WZ8E	145.25000	-	CC1	
	DMR/MARC	WZ8E	443.62500	+	CC1	
Bluefield, Oneida Peak						
	FM	N8FWL	224.44000	+	123.0 Hz	T-MARC
Bluemont	DMR/MARC	N3JLT	449.92500	-	CC1	T-MARC
	FM	K8GP	53.37000	52.37000		
	FM	K8GP	224.34000	-	77.0 Hz	T-MARC

Location	Mode	Call sign	Output	Input	Access	Coordinator
Bluemont, Blue Ridge						
	FM	WA4TSC	147.30000	+	146.2 Hz	T-MARC
Bon Air, WCVE Tower						
	FM	W4RAT	146.88000	-	74.4 Hz	SERA-VA
	FM	W4RAT	442.55000	+	74.4 Hz	SERA-VA
Bristol	FUSION	KD4CCO	146.56000			
	FUSION	KD4CCO	444.50000			
Bristow	FUSION	KO4MBN	146.55000			
Buckingham	FM	WR4CV	224.40000	-	110.9 Hz	
	FM	WR4CV	444.95000	+	110.9 Hz	SERA-VA
Buckingham Co	DMR/MARC	KJ4PGD	147.00000	+	CC1	
Bull Run Mountain						
	FM	K8GP	448.32500	-	77.0 Hz	
Bumpass	FUSION	KG8F	146.52000			
Burke	FM	WA3TOL	448.67500	-	100.0 Hz	T-MARC
Chantilly	DMR/BM	KD4RTH	443.15000	+	CC1	
Chantilly, Dulles Airport						
	FM	KI4AD	145.31000	-	77.0 Hz	T-MARC
	FM	K4IAD	147.33000	+	203.5 Hz	T-MARC
	FM	K4IAD	444.75000	+	100.0 Hz	T-MARC
Charlottesville	DMR/MARC	WA4FC	444.91250	+	CC1	SERA-VA
	DMR/MARC	KF4UCI	444.98750	+	CC1	
	FM	KG4HOT	224.60000	-	151.4 Hz	SERA-VA
Charlottesville, Buck's Elbow						
	FM	WA4TFZ	224.76000	-	151.4 Hz	
Charlottesville, Carter's Moun						
	FM	KF4UCI	442.07500	+	151.4 Hz	SERA-VA
Charlottesville, Carters Mount						
	FM	K4DND	146.73000	-	151.4 Hz	
Charlottesville, Martha Jeffer						
	FM	WA4TFZ	146.92500	-	151.4 Hz	SERA-VA
	FM	WA4TFZ	444.25000	+	151.4 Hz	SERA-VA
Charlottesville, University Of						
	FM	W4UVA	443.00000	+	151.4 Hz	
Check	FM	N4MAV	147.55500			
Chesapeake	DMR/BM	WA3QWA	443.55000	+	CC1	
	DMR/BM	KE4NYV	444.27500	+	CC1	
	DMR/MARC	KK4WTI	442.58750	+	CC1	
	FM	K4AMG	145.15000	-	103.5 Hz	
	FUSION	W4CAR	444.00000	+		
Chesapeake, Bowers Hill						
	FM	W4CAR	146.61000	-	162.2 Hz	
Chesapeake, Greenbriar						
	FM	W4CAR	146.82000	-	162.2 Hz	
	FM	W4CAR	444.00000	+	162.2 Hz	
Chester	FM	KA4CBB	147.36000	+		
Chester, Carver Middle School						
	FM	KD4KWP	145.31000	-	127.3 Hz	
Chilhowie	FM	W4DWN	442.00000	+	103.5 Hz	
	FUSION	N4XRD	146.45000			
	FUSION	W4DWN	146.46000			
Christiansburg	DMR/MARC	KD4ADL	444.25000	+	CC1	
Christiansburg, Poor Mountain						
	FM	N4VL	145.41000	-	103.5 Hz	
Clifton Forge, Warm Springs Mo						
	FM	N4HRS	444.37500	+	167.9 Hz	SERA-VA
Clinchco	FM	KB4RFN	147.15000	+	88.5 Hz	SERA-VA
Columbia	FM	WA4FC	444.35000	+	74.4 Hz	
Country Club Estates						
	FM	KF4RGH-L	146.88000	-		SERA-VA
Covesville, Heard Mountain						
	FM	WA4TFZ	146.76000	-	151.4 Hz	SERA-VA

Location	Mode	Call sign	Output	Input	Access	Coordinator
Covesville, Heard Mountain						
	FM	WA4TFZ	224.76000	-	151.4 Hz	SERA-VA
Covington	FM	WA4PGI	442.25000	+	100.0 Hz	SERA-VA
Covington, Warm Springs Mounta						
	FM	KF4YLM	146.97000	-	91.5 Hz	
Craddockville	FM	N4TIK	147.21000	+		
Crozet, Bucks Elbow Mountain						
	FM	WA4TFZ	146.89500	-	151.4 Hz	SERA-VA
Culpeper	FM	KA4DCS	53.91000	52.91000	100.0 Hz	T-MARC
Dale City	FUSION	KK4TCE	444.45000	+		
Damascus, White Top Mountain						
	FM	KM4X	443.00000	+	103.5 Hz	SERA-VA
Danville	FUSION	KO4HMB	441.10000	+		
Dismal Peak	DMR/BM	KD4BNQ	147.13500	+	CC1	
	DMR/BM	KD4BNQ	444.97500	+	CC1	
Dunreath (historical)						
	FM	W4VA-R	147.16500	+	167.9 Hz	T-MARC
Eagle Oak	FM	K4EZ-R	146.77500	-		SERA-VA
Eastville	FM	KN4GE	147.34500	+	156.7 Hz	
Elk Creek, Iron Mtn						
	FM	N4MGQ	147.24000	+	107.2 Hz	SERA-VA
Everona	FM	W4CUL-R	147.12000	+		
Fairfax	DMR/BM	N3QEM	442.88750	+	CC13	
	DMR/BM	N3QEM	442.91250	+	CC13	
Fairfax, Fair Oaks Hospital						
	FM	K4XY	448.37500	-		T-MARC
Fairfax, Fairfax County Public						
	FM	NV4FM	146.79000	-		T-MARC
	FM	W4YHD	224.10000	-	77.0 Hz	T-MARC
Falls Church	FM	W4AVA	447.62500	-	107.2 Hz	T-MARC
Fancy Gap	DMR/BM	W4BAD	146.97000	-	CC1	
	DMR/BM	WX4F	444.15000	+	CC1	
	DMR/MARC	N4YR	440.66250	+	CC14	
	DMR/MARC	WX4F	443.93750	+	CC1	
	FM	KE4QQX	29.66000	-	88.5 Hz	
	FM	N4YR	53.63000	52.63000		
	FM	N4VRD	145.33000	-	77.0 Hz	
	FM	N4YR	442.22500	+		
	FM	KB4GHT	442.32500	+	100.0 Hz	
	FM	KF4OVA	442.42500	+	107.2 Hz	SERA-VA
	FM	WA4LOY	444.10000	+	136.5 Hz	SERA-VA
Fancy Gap, Pops Peak						
	FM	K4IL	442.57500	+	100.0 Hz	SERA-VA
Farmville, Leigh Mtn						
	FM	N4HRS	146.91000	-		
	FM	N4HRS	444.32500	+		
Farmville, Water Tower						
	FM	WR4CV	146.95500	-	136.5 Hz	SERA-VA
	FM	WR4CV	443.30000	+	136.5 Hz	SERA-VA
Floyd	FM	W4FCV	147.21000	+	114.8 Hz	SERA-VA
Floyd, Floyd School Admin Offi						
	FM	W4FCV	442.90000	+	114.8 Hz	SERA-VA
Floyd, NWS Doppler Radar Tower						
	FM	KG4MAV	443.35000	+	114.8 Hz	SERA-VA
Forest Lake Estates						
	FM	W4BRM-R	448.22500	-		T-MARC
Fork Mountain	FM	WA3KOK	443.25000	+	107.2 Hz	T-MARC
Fork Union	DMR/MARC	K4JK	444.53750	+	CC1	
Foxwood		KM4KOG-L	147.47500			
Franklin	FM	WT4FP	147.27000	+	131.8 Hz	SERA-VA
Fredericksburg	DMR/MARC	N8RAT	442.11250	+	CC1	
	FUSION	KN4LLQ	443.85000	+		

Location	Mode	Call sign	Output	Input	Access	Coordinator
Fredericksburg, Chancellor Lan						
	FM	K4TS	147.01500	+	79.7 Hz	T-MARC
	FM	K4TS	443.85000	+	79.7 Hz	
Fredericksburg, Four Mile Fork						
	FM	W1ZFB	927.03750	902.03750	91.5 Hz	T-MARC
Front Royal	FM	K4QJZ	51.94000	50.94000	141.3 Hz	T-MARC
Front Royal, High Knob Mountai						
	FM	K4QJZ	145.21000	-	141.3 Hz	T-MARC
	FM	NO4N	442.72500	+	107.2 Hz	T-MARC
Gainesville	FM	W4LAM	224.46000	-		T-MARC
Gate City	FM	K4GV	441.90000	+		
	FM	KF4VTM	444.70000	+	103.5 Hz	
Gate City, Clinch Mountain						
	FUSION	KF4VTM	146.82000	-	103.5 Hz	SERA-VA
Ghent	FM	W4VB-L	145.33000		131.8 Hz	
Gloucester Courthouse, Walter						
	FM	WN4HRT	145.21000	-	100.0 Hz	SERA-VA
	FM	W4HZL	145.37000	-	100.0 Hz	SERA-VA
Goochland	FM	WB4IKL	147.27000	+	203.5 Hz	SERA-VA
Gordonsville	FM	KF4UCI	444.40000	+	151.4 Hz	T-MARC
Gordonsville, Gibson Mountain						
	FM	K3VB	224.18000	-	146.2 Hz	T-MARC
	FM	W4CUL	443.80000	+	146.2 Hz	
Gore	FM	KM4OGQ	444.25000	+	100.0 Hz	T-MARC
Greenbush	DMR/MARC	K9AGR	440.67500	+	CC1	
	DMR/MARC	K9AGR	442.57500	+	CC1	
Greene, Flat Top Mountain						
	FM	AA4DH	145.47000	-	151.4 Hz	
Grundy	FM	K4NRR	147.31500	+		
Gum Spring	FM	KB4MIC	53.07000	52.07000	203.5 Hz	
Hampton	DMR/BM	KA4VXR	147.22500	+	CC1	SERA-VA
	DMR/MARC	W4HPT	443.50000	+	CC1	
	DSTAR	W4HPT C	145.20000	-		
	DSTAR	K4HPT B	443.50000	+		
	DSTAR	W4HPT B	444.21250	+		
	DSTAR	W4HPT D	1298.50000			
	FM	KE4UP	145.49000	-	100.0 Hz	
	FM	W4QR	146.73000	-	100.0 Hz	SERA-VA
	FM	K4TM	146.92500	-		SERA-VA
	FM	W4QR	444.55000	+	100.0 Hz	
	FUSION	KD4JJT	147.51000			
Hampton, City Hall						
	DSTAR	W4HPT	145.20000	-		SERA-VA
	DSTAR	W4HPT	444.21250	+		SERA-VA
	DSTAR	W4HPT	1298.50000			SERA-VA
Hampton, Sentara Careplex Hosp						
	DSTAR	K4HPT	443.50000	+	100.0 Hz	SERA-VA
Hampton, Sentera Care Plex						
	FM	WA4ZUA	145.17000	-	131.8 Hz	SERA-VA
Harrisonburg	DMR/MARC	K4JK	444.66250	+	CC1	
	FM	N4DSL	224.50000	-	131.8 Hz	T-MARC
Harrisonburg, EMU						
	FM	K4MRA	147.31500	+	131.8 Hz	T-MARC
Harrisonburg, Lairds Knob						
	FM	KC4GXI	443.15000	+	131.8 Hz	T-MARC
Harrisonburg, Little North Mou						
	FM	K4KLH	147.22500	+	131.8 Hz	T-MARC
Harrisonburg, Massanutten Peak						
	FM	K4MRA	145.13000	-	131.8 Hz	T-MARC
Haymarket	DMR/BM	W4BRM	448.32500	-	CC6	
	DMR/MARC	W4YP	444.16250	+	CC1	
	DMR/MARC	W4YP	448.97500	-	CC6	T-MARC

Location	Mode	Call sign	Output	Input	Access	Coordinator
Haymarket	DSTAR	N4USI C	145.45000	-		
	DSTAR	N4USI	442.41250	+		
	FM	N3KL	145.13000	-		
	FM	N3AUY	449.02500	-	156.7 Hz	T-MARC
	FUSION	W4BRM	448.22500	-		
Haymarket, Bull Run Mountain						
	FM	W4BRM	53.49000	52.49000	77.0 Hz	
	FM	W4BRM	224.40000	-	77.0 Hz	T-MARC
	FM	W4BRM	927.62500	902.62500	77.0 Hz	T-MARC
Haymarket, VA	DSTAR	W4BRM	145.45000	-		T-MARC
Heathsville	DMR/MARC	WX4EMC	442.70000	+	CC1	
	FM	W4NNK	147.33000	+	100.0 Hz	SERA
Henrico	FUSION	AE4TC	146.49000			
Herndon	DMR/MARC	N3QEM	145.16500	-	CC12	
	DMR/MARC	N3QEM	442.43750	+	CC1	
	DMR/MARC	N3QEM	442.86250	+	CC13	
	DMR/MARC	N3QEM	442.88750	+	CC13	
	DMR/MARC	N4CV	443.08750	+	CC1	
	DMR/MARC	N3QEM	927.66250	902.66250	CC1	
	FM	W4CIA	147.21000	+	110.9 Hz	T-MARC
Hillsville	DMR/BM	K4EZ	442.52500	+	CC1	
	FM	W4GHS	145.27000	-	103.5 Hz	SERA-VA
	FUSION	K4EZ	145.69000			
Hillsville, VA	FM	K4EZ	147.04500	+		SERA-VA
Honaker	FM	KD4JTK	145.37000	-	103.5 Hz	SERA-VA
	FM	KK4EH	146.83500	-		
	FM	KD4JTK	147.25500	+		
Honaker / Big A Mtn.						
	FM	KM4HDM	145.21000	-	103.5 Hz	SERA-VA
Honaker, Big A Mountain						
	FM	KM4HDM	442.10000	+	103.5 Hz	
Hopewell	FM	KG4DCX	147.09000	-		
Independence	DMR/MARC	WZ8E	443.71250	+	CC1	
	FM	W4TOW	443.37500	+	103.5 Hz	SERA-VA
Isle Of Wight	FM	WT4RA-R	147.19500	+		SERA-VA
Jarrett	FM	N4LLE	146.62500	-	100.0 Hz	SERA-VA
Jonesville	FM	AJ4G	442.57500	+	100.0 Hz	SERA-VA
Kilmarnock	FM	W4NNK	146.83500	-	100.0 Hz	SERA-VA
Kilmarnock, Fire Station						
	FM	W4GSF	145.45000	-		
King George	FM	K4GVA	448.47500	-	79.7 Hz	T-MARC
King George, Dahlgren Naval Su						
	FM	N3PZZ	145.17000	-	88.5 Hz	
King George, Dalhgren Naval Su						
	FM	N3PZZ	145.33000	-	88.5 Hz	
King George, Harry Nice Bridge						
	FM	W4KGC	146.74500	-	107.2 Hz	T-MARC
Leavells	FM	W1ZFB-R	51.86000	50.86000		T-MARC
Leesburg	DMR/BM	N3EV	145.17000	-	CC1	
	DMR/BM	N3EV	442.90000	+	CC1	
	DMR/BM	N3EV	447.72500	-	CC1	
	DMR/BM	N3EV	447.82500	-	CC1	
	DMR/BM	N3EV	447.87500	-	CC1	
	DMR/MARC	WR3D	443.90000	+	CC1	
	FM	WA4TXE	146.70000	-	77.0 Hz	T-MARC
	FM	WA4TXE	442.10000	+	77.0 Hz	T-MARC
Lexington	DMR/BM	W4DHW	442.05000	+	CC1	
	DMR/MARC	W4DHW	441.92500	+	CC1	
Lexington, Rocky Knob						
	FM	KG4HOT	224.58000	-	136.5 Hz	
Lexington, Rocky Mountain						
	FM	W4ROC	53.01000	52.01000		

Location	Mode	Call sign	Output	Input	Access	Coordinator
Lexington, Rocky Mountain						
	FM	W4ROC	147.33000	+		SERA-VA
	FM	W4ROC	444.15000	+		SERA-VA
	FM	WR4CV	927.46250	902.46250	151.4 Hz	SERA-VA
Linden	DMR/MARC	N8RAT	443.16250	+	CC1	T-MARC
	FM	N3UHD	444.15000	+	77.0 Hz	T-MARC
Linden, Atop Blue Mountain At						
	FM	N8RAT	224.28000	-	100.0 Hz	T-MARC
Linden, Blue Ridge Mountains						
	FM	N3UR	442.35000	+	123.0 Hz	T-MARC
Louisa	FM	KD4OUZ	442.22500	+	131.8 Hz	SERA-VA
Lynchburg	DMR/BM	WA4RTS	146.65500	-	CC1	
	FM	KC4RBA	145.37000	-	186.2 Hz	
Lynchburg, Candlers Mountain						
	FM	N3OG	146.61000	-	136.5 Hz	SERA-VA
	FM	N3OG	442.60000	+	136.5 Hz	SERA-VA
Lynchburg, Tobacco Row Mountai						
	FM	N4HRS	443.50000	+		
	FM	K4LBG	444.75000	+	136.5 Hz	SERA-VA
Lynchburg, Tobacco Row Mtn						
	FM	K4CQ	444.50000	+	136.5 Hz	SERA-VA
Lynnhaven		N6DLH-L	147.52500			
Machipongo	FUSION	WA4RX	446.05000			
Madison	DMR/BM	AE4ML	147.03000	+	CC1	
	DMR/BM	AE4ML	442.57500	+	CC1	
Manassas	DSTAR	W4OVH C	146.86500	-		
	DSTAR	W4OVH B	442.51250	+		
	FM	W4OVH	146.85000	-		
	FM	W4OVH	146.97000	-	100.0 Hz	T-MARC
	FM	W4OVH	224.66000	-	100.0 Hz	T-MARC
	FM	K4GVT	443.50000	+	110.9 Hz	T-MARC
	FUSION	KC4DV	146.46000			
	FUSION	W4OVH	442.20000	+		
Manassas, NOVEC Communications						
	DSTAR	W4OVH	146.86500	-		T-MARC
	FM	W4OVH	442.51250	+		T-MARC
Marion	FM	W4GHS	145.27000	-	103.5 Hz	
	FM	KM4X	146.64000	-	103.5 Hz	
Martinsville	DMR/MARC	N2TEK	441.85000	+	CC15	SERA-VA
	FM	K4MVA	147.12000	+	107.2 Hz	
	FM	N4HRS	444.87500	+		SERA-VA
Martinsville, Chestnut Knob						
	FM	K4MVA	147.28500	+	107.2 Hz	
	FM	KF4RMT	441.75000	+	77.0 Hz	
Maurertown	FM	N3UHD	442.47500	+	77.0 Hz	T-MARC
Max Meadows, Hamiltons Knob						
	FM	K4IJ	442.62500	+	103.5 Hz	SERA-VA
Meadowview	FUSION	KD4WMX	443.00000	+		
Middleburg	FM	KA4DCS	29.68000	-	146.2 Hz	T-MARC
Millwood	FM	K4IAD	444.75000	+	173.8 Hz	T-MARC
Montebello, Whetstone Ridge Ra						
	FM	WR4CV	145.45000	-	136.5 Hz	SERA-VA
Montross	FM	W4GMF	146.89500	-	146.2 Hz	T-MARC
	FM	KJ4PGD	442.00000	+	110.9 Hz	T-MARC
	FUSION	KT4MI	147.52500			
Mount Jackson	FM	KB6VAA	146.71500	-	146.2 Hz	T-MARC
Mountain Lake	DMR/BM	KD4BNQ	146.91000	-	CC1	SERA-VA
	DMR/BM	KD4BNQ	441.80000	+	CC1	
Muck Cross	FM	KB2AHZ-R	443.52500	+		SERA-VA
New Market	FM	KQ4D	443.35000	+		
New Market, Luray Caverns						
	FM	KQ4D	146.62500	-	131.8 Hz	T-MARC

Location	Mode	Call sign	Output	Input	Access	Coordinator
Newport New	FM	WN4HRT	147.42000		100.0 Hz	
Newport News	DSTAR	W4MT C	145.30000	-		
	DSTAR	W4MT B	441.81250	+		
	DSTAR	W4MT	441.81250	+		
	FM	W4MT	145.23000	-	100.0 Hz	SERA-VA
	FM	W4CM	147.16500	+	100.0 Hz	SERA-VA
	FUSION	AE4AN	145.70000			
Newport News, Riverside Region						
	FM	WN4HRT	147.00000	-	100.0 Hz	
NOAA Covesville	WX	KZZ28	162.45000			
NOAA Fredericksburg						
	WX	WZ2527	162.42500			
NOAA Halifax	WX	KJY86	162.52500			
NOAA Heathsville	WX	WXM57	162.40000			
NOAA Lynchburg	WX	WXL92	162.55000			
NOAA Manassas	WX	KHB36	162.55000			
NOAA Norfolk	WX	KHB37	162.55000			
NOAA Richmond	WX	WXK65	162.47500			
NOAA Roanoke	WX	WXL60	162.47500			
NOAA Sand Mountain						
	WX	WZ2500	162.45000			
Norfolk	DMR/BM	K4LCT	440.51250	+	CC7	SERA-VA
	DMR/BM	W2CID	445.51250	-	CC7	
	FM	W4VB	145.33000	-	131.8 Hz	
	FM	W4VB	147.37500	+	131.8 Hz	
Norfolk, Fire Station 10						
	FM	W4VB	444.47500	+	74.4 Hz	
Norfolk, Norfolk Waterfront						
	FM	KC2HTT	147.07500	+	100.0 Hz	
	FM	KC2HTT	442.45000	+	100.0 Hz	
Norton	FM	KM4OKT	444.07500	+	136.5 Hz	
Norton , High Knob Mt						
	FM	WD4GSM	224.42000	-		SERA-VA
Onancock	FM	WN4HRT	146.56500		156.7 Hz	
Palmyra	FM	K4MSR	145.17000	-	151.4 Hz	
	FUSION	N4PJL	144.44000			
Pearisburg, Bald Knob						
	FM	KD4BNQ	441.95000	+	107.2 Hz	SERA-VA
Pearisburg, Dismal Peak						
	FM	KE4JYN	53.47000	52.47000	107.2 Hz	
	FM	KQ4Q	224.86000	-	107.2 Hz	SERA-VA
	FM	N4HRS	444.67500	+		SERA-VA
Pearisburg, Giles County Court						
	FM	W4NRV	147.37500	+	100.0 Hz	SERA-VA
Pennington Gap	FM	KG4OXG	145.49000	-	131.8 Hz	
Petersburg	DMR/MARC	WA4FC	442.68750	+	CC1	SERA-VA
	FM	KE4SCS	146.98500	-		
	FM	KK4QAK	147.39000	+	74.4 Hz	
	FM	KK4QAK	444.97500	+	74.4 Hz	
	FUSION	KE4SCS	146.38500	+		
Portable	DMR/MARC	KV4VP	440.80000	+	CC1	
Portsmouth	FM	W4POX	53.89000	52.89000		SERA-VA
	FM	W4POX	443.80000	+		SERA-VA
Portsmouth, Maryview Hospital						
	FM	AA4AT	146.70000	-		
Portsmouth, Portsmouth Naval H						
	FM	W4POX	146.85000	-	100.0 Hz	SERA-VA
Powhatan	DMR/MARC	N4POW	443.35000	+	CC1	SERA-VA
	FUSION	WB4HOT	432.10000			
Powhatan, Powhatan Water Tower						
	FM	N4POW	147.31500	+	74.4 Hz	SERA-VA

Location	Mode	Call sign	Output	Input	Access	Coordinator
Prince George, South Point Bus						
	FM	KG4YJB	444.27500	+	103.5 Hz	
Pulaski, Peaks Knob						
	FM	K4XE	442.07500	+		SERA-VA
Pungoteague	DMR/MARC	N4TIK	147.21000	747.21000	CC1	
	FM	N4TIK	145.11000	-	156.7 Hz	
Quantico	FM	K3FBI	147.34500	+	167.9 Hz	T-MARC
	FM	K3FBI	443.55000	+		T-MARC
Radford	FM	KB4RU	147.00000	+	107.2 Hz	SERA-VA
Radford, Cloyd's Mountain						
	FM	N4NRV	147.18000	+	103.5 Hz	T-MARC
Reston	FM	N2LEE	443.00000	+	88.5 Hz	T-MARC
Richlands Big A Mtn						
	DMR/BM	KM4HDM	442.10000	+	CC1	
Richmond	DMR/BM	WA4FC	443.53750	+	CC1	
	DMR/BM	WA4ONG	449.95000	+	CC1	
	DMR/MARC	WA4FC	147.18000	+	CC1	
	DMR/MARC	W4RAT	443.58750	+	CC1	
	DMR/MARC	WA4FC	927.01250	902.01250	CC1	
	DSTAR	W4FJ C	147.25500	+		
	DSTAR	W4FJ B	443.71250	+		
	DSTAR	W4FJ A	1284.00000	1264.00000		
	DSTAR	W4FJ	1284.00000	1264.00000		
	FM	W4FJ	147.25500	+		
	FM	W4MEV-R	224.42000	-		SERA-VA
	FM	WA4FC	224.52000	-	74.4 Hz	
	FM	W4FJ	443.71250	+		SERA-VA
	FUSION	WA4MAS	145.11000	-		
	FUSION	W4MAF	444.65000	+		
Richmond, Downtown						
	FM	WA4FC	224.52000	-	74.4 Hz	SERA-VA
	FM	WA4FC	927.05000	902.05000		SERA-VA
	FM	WA4FC	1282.00000	1262.00000	88.5 Hz	SERA-VA
Richmond, James Monroe Buildin						
	FM	KN4SKI	146.94000	-	74.4 Hz	SERA-VA
Richmond, Southside Richmond						
	P25	WA4FC	927.07500	902.07500		SERA-VA
Richmond, WTVR-TV Tower						
	FM	KG4MRA	145.43000	-	74.4 Hz	
Ridgeway	FM	WS4W	224.38000	-	88.5 Hz	
Ripplemead	DMR/BM	KD4BNQ	440.80000	+	CC1	
Roanoke	DMR/BM	KK4WDG	441.82500	+	CC1	
	DMR/MARC	WB4EOT	440.80000	+	CC1	
	DMR/MARC	K4ITL	441.88750	+	CC1	
	DMR/MARC	W5CUI	444.77500	+	CC1	SERA-VA
	DSTAR	KO4DQA B	440.60000	+		
	FM	WB8BON	53.09000	52.09000	123.0 Hz	SERA-VA
	FM	W4KDN	146.94000	-	107.2 Hz	SERA-VA
	FM	K5JCT	442.30000	+	127.3 Hz	SERA-VA
	FM	KS4BO	443.67500	+	110.9 Hz	
	FUSION	KK4VA	442.20000	+		
Roanoke Co.	DMR/BM	KD4EG	440.70000	+	CC1	
Roanoke, Community Hospital						
	FM	N4HRS	444.27500	+	103.5 Hz	SERA-VA
Roanoke, Mill Mountain						
	FM	W4KZK	442.75000	+	107.2 Hz	SERA-VA
Roanoke, Poor Mountain						
	FM	W4CA	146.98500	-	107.2 Hz	SERA-VA
	FM	K4ARO	442.60000	+	114.8 Hz	
	FM	N4HRS	444.17500	+		SERA-VA
Roanoke, Poor Mtn						
	FM	K1GG	146.74500	-	107.2 Hz	SERA-VA

Location	Mode	Call sign	Output	Input	Access	Coordinator
Roanoke, Tinker Mountain						
	FM	N4HRS	444.47500	+		
Roanoke, Tinker Mtn						
	FM	WB8BON	444.92500	+	107.2 Hz	
Round Hill	FM	K0QBU	449.42500	-	100.0 Hz	
Ruckersville		KE4LWT-L	445.50000			
Salem, Ft Lewis Mtn						
	FM	WB8BON	444.92500	+	77.0 Hz	
Salem, Sugar Loaf Mountain						
	FM	W4KZK	444.85000	+	107.2 Hz	SERA-VA
Salem, VA Hospital						
	FM	W4KZK	443.75000	+	107.2 Hz	
Shenandoah	FM	N4PJI	146.67000	-	114.8 Hz	T-MARC
Smithfield, Isle Of Wight Cour						
	FM	WT4RA	442.82500	+	100.0 Hz	SERA-VA
South Boston	FM	W4HCH	145.35000	-		
	FM	KF4AGO	147.06000	-		
South Boston Va	DMR/MARC	K4DJQ	443.11250	+	CC1	
South Hill	DMR/MARC	K4MJO	444.78750	+	CC1	
	FM	W4CMH	145.47000	-	82.5 Hz	SERA-VA
	FM	KB2AHZ	147.00000	+	77.0 Hz	SERA-VA
Spotsylvania	DMR/BM	AE4ML	442.40000	+	CC1	T-MARC
	DMR/BM	AE4ML	442.85000	+	CC1	T-MARC
	DMR/BM	AE4ML	446.10000		CC1	
	DSTAR	WW4EMC C	145.24000	-		
	DSTAR	WW4EMC B	448.46000	-		
	DSTAR	WW4EMC D	1254.00000			
	DSTAR	WW4EMC A	1282.40000	-		
	FM	WW4EMC	224.26000	-		T-MARC
	FM	AE4ML	442.50000	+		
	FM	WW4EMC	442.70000	+	114.8 Hz	T-MARC
Springfield	FM	NO2F	445.50000	-	100.0 Hz	
Stafford	DSTAR	WS4VA C	145.32000	-		
	DSTAR	WU5MC	442.48750	+		
	DSTAR	WU5MC B	442.48750	+		
	DSTAR	WS4VA	447.27500	-		
	DSTAR	WS4VA B	447.27500	-		
	DSTAR	WS4VA	1282.20000	1262.20000		T-MARC
	DSTAR	WS4VA A	1282.20000	-		
	DSTAR	WS4VA D	1298.40000			
	FM	WS4VA	147.37500	+	79.7 Hz	T-MARC
	FM	WS4VA	444.45000	+	79.7 Hz	T-MARC
	FUSION	WS4VA	449.45000	-		
Standardsville, Snow Mountain						
	FM	KF4UCI	443.90000	+	151.4 Hz	SERA-VA
Staunton	FM	N4KYM	146.70000	-	131.8 Hz	
	FUSION	N4RLI	446.50000	-		
	FUSION	K3RFP	447.02500	-		
Staunton, Elliot Knob						
	FM	KG4HOT	224.30000	-	131.8 Hz	
	FM	KG4HOT	444.10000	+	131.8 Hz	
Staunton, Elliott Knob						
	FM	KG4HOT	147.04500	+	131.8 Hz	
Staunton, Hermitage						
	FM	WA4ZBP	146.85000	-	131.8 Hz	
Stephens City	DMR/BM	N2XIF	442.05000	+	CC1	
Sterling	DMR/MARC	N3QEM	442.87500	+	CC1	
Stuarts Draft	FUSION	K4UEK	446.03750			
Suffolk, Driver (WHRO Tower)						
	FM	N4SD	146.79000	-	100.0 Hz	
Surry	DMR/BM	K4JST	443.31250	-	CC1	
Tinker Mountain	FM	K4YDG	224.90000	-		

Location	Mode	Call sign	Output	Input	Access	Coordinator
Tysons Corner	DMR/BM	N9KET	441.65000	+	CC2	
	DMR/MARC	N9KET	441.33750	+	CC1	T-MARC
	DMR/MARC	N3QEM	443.06250	+	CC3	T-MARC
	DSTAR	NV4FM	145.34000	-		T-MARC
	DSTAR	NV4FM	448.03500	-		T-MARC
	DSTAR	NV4FM	1282.80000	1262.80000		T-MARC
	FM	NV4FM	146.91000	-	77.0 Hz	T-MARC
	FM	NV4FM	447.02500	-	77.0 Hz	T-MARC
Tysons Corner (Fairfax)						
	DSTAR	NV4FM C	145.34000	-		
	DSTAR	NV4FM B	448.03500	-		
	DSTAR	NV4FM D	1254.20000			
	DSTAR	NV4FM A	1282.80000	-		
Union	FM	K4LYL-R	147.10500	+		SERA-VA
Vesta	FM	NJ1K	145.11000	-	114.8 Hz	SERA-VA
Vesuvius, Whetstone Ridge						
	FM	K4DND	145.45000	-	110.9 Hz	SERA-VA
Vienna	DMR/MARC	N3QEM	145.17500	-	CC13	
	DMR/MARC	N9KET	442.87500	+	CC3	
	DMR/MARC	N3QEM	442.90000	+	CC1	
	DMR/MARC	N3QEM	927.67500	902.67500	CC1	
	DMR/MARC	N3QEM	927.70000	902.70000	CC1	
	FM	K4HTA	146.68500	-	110.9 Hz	T-MARC
	FM	W4CIA	147.21000	+	110.9 Hz	
Virginia Beach	DMR/BM	WB4JCX	442.23750	+	CC1	
	DMR/MARC	W4BSB	442.58750	+	CC1	
	DSTAR	W4BBR C	145.35000	-		
	DSTAR	W4BBR B	441.90000	+		
	DSTAR	W4BBR A	1284.60000	-		
	FM	KE4HGP	145.20000	-		
	FM	W4KXV	146.89500	-	141.3 Hz	
	FM	WN4HRT	147.30000	+	100.0 Hz	
Virginia Beach, Fire Station #						
	FM	W4KXV	146.97000	-	141.3 Hz	
Virginia Beach, Virginia Beach						
	FM	W4KXV	444.95000	+	141.3 Hz	
Walkerton	FM	W4TTL	146.71500	-		
Wallops Island	DMR/MARC	W4WFF	444.88000	+	CC1	
Warrenton	FM	W4VA	442.25000	+	167.9 Hz	T-MARC
	FUSION	KG4EHL	146.42000			
Waynesboro	FUSION	KC8MTV	145.29000	-		
Waynesboro , Bear Den Mountain						
	FM	W4PNT	147.07500	+	131.8 Hz	
Waynesboro, Afton Mountain						
	FM	NM9S	53.41000	52.41000		
Waynesboro, Bear Den Mountain						
	FM	KC8MTV	145.29000	-	131.8 Hz	SERA-VA
	FM	KF4UCI	444.77500	+	151.4 Hz	
Williamsburg	DMR/BM	N4ARI	145.41000	-	CC1	
	DMR/BM	N4ARI	444.70000	+	CC1	SERA-VA
	FM	KB4ZIN	146.76000	-	118.8 Hz	SERA-VA
	FM	KB4ZIN	147.10500	+	118.8 Hz	
	FM	KB4ZIN	444.10000	+		SERA-VA
Winchester	FM	W3IF	442.00000	+	146.2 Hz	T-MARC
	FUSION	KG4Y	444.55000	+		
Winchester North Mountain						
	FM	NM4CC	442.60000	+	141.3 Hz	T-MARC
Winchester, Great North Mounta						
	FM	W4RKC	146.82000	-	146.2 Hz	T-MARC
	FM	W4RKC	448.77500	-	146.2 Hz	T-MARC
Winchester, North Mountain						
	FM	K4USS	145.39000	-	146.2 Hz	T-MARC

Location	Mode	Call sign	Output	Input	Access	Coordinator
Winchester, North Mountain						
	FM	KG4Y	224.90000	-	146.2 Hz	T-MARC
	FM	KG4Y	444.55000	+		T-MARC
Wintergreen	DMR/BM	WR4CV	444.43750	+	CC1	
	DSTAR	WR4CV B	444.93750	+		
	DSTAR	WR4CV	444.93750	+	151.4 Hz	
	FM	WR4CV	146.82000	-	136.5 Hz	
Wintergreen, Wintergreen Resor						
	FM	WR4CV	224.40000	-	136.5 Hz	SERA-VA
	FM	WR4CV	444.55000	+	136.5 Hz	SERA-VA
Wirtz	DMR/BM	W4JWC	440.75000	+	CC1	
Wise	DMR/BM	KM4OKT	444.07500	+	CC15	
Woodbridge	DSTAR	WD4HRO D	1254.00000			
	DSTAR	WD4HRO	1293.00000	1273.00000		
	DSTAR	WD4HRO A	1293.00000	1273.00000		
	FM	W4IY	147.24000	+	107.2 Hz	T-MARC
	FM	W4IY	224.78000	-		T-MARC
	FM	W4IAD	447.87500	-		
	FUSION	W4IY	444.90000	+		
Woodbridge, Potomac Mills						
	FM	K4IAD	444.85000	+		
Wytheville	DMR/BM	W4VSP	146.89500	-	CC1	
	DMR/BM	W4VSP	441.97500	+	CC1	
	DMR/MARC	K4EZ	443.26250	+	CC1	SERA-VA
	FUSION	W4VSP	144.32500			
	FUSION	W4VSP	434.98000			
Wytheville, Walker Mountain						
	FM	K4YW	224.56000	-	77.0 Hz	SERA-VA
Yorktown	DMR/BM	KN4KV	444.60000	+	CC1	
WASHINGTON						
Aberdeen	FM	W7ZA	147.16000	+	88.5 Hz	
	FM	KA7DNK	444.60000	+	100.0 Hz	
	FM	N7UJK	444.82500	+	118.8 Hz	
Airway Heights	FM	W7TSC	443.32500	+		
Alder	FM	KB7CNN	145.45000	-	110.9 Hz	
Almira	FM	W7OHI	147.00000	+	100.0 Hz	
Anacortes	FM	KG7OCP	443.35000	+	100.0 Hz	
	FUSION	N6VIN	444.00000			
Anacortes, 29th St Water Tank						
	FM	KG7OCP	443.35000	+		
Anacortes, Mt Erie						
	FM	W7PSE	441.72500	+	103.5 Hz	
Ariel	DMR/MARC	WA7DMR	147.41250	146.41250	CC1	
Arlington	FM	N7XCG	440.40000	+	123.0 Hz	
	FM	N7NFY	443.22500	+	103.5 Hz	
	FUSION	K7HJK	145.70000			
Ashford	FM	K7DNR	53.39000	51.69000	100.0 Hz	
	FM	K7DNR	145.25000	-	186.2 Hz	
	FM	K7DNR	442.57500	+	141.3 Hz	
	FM	K7DNR	927.52500	902.52500	114.8 Hz	
Auburn	FM	K7SYE-R	147.24000	+		
	FUSION	AA9MQ	146.55000			
Bainbridge Island	DSTAR	W7NPC	444.56250	+		
	DSTAR	W7NPC B	444.56250	+		
	DSTAR	W7NPC	1290.50000	1270.50000		
	FM	W7NPC	53.43000	51.73000	100.0 Hz	
	FM	WA6PMX	224.42000	-	88.5 Hz	
	FM	K7LD	440.20000	+	103.5 Hz	
	FM	W7NPC	444.47500	+	103.5 Hz	
Baldi Mtn	FM	N7FSP	1292.30000	-	103.5 Hz	WWARA
Belfair	FM	NM7E	145.17000	-	103.5 Hz	

Location	Mode	Call sign	Output	Input	Access	Coordinator
Belfair	FM	KE7OYB	145.45000	-	100.0 Hz	
Bell Hill	FM	KO6I-R	442.05000	+		
Bellevue	DMR/MARC	N7ERP	441.28750	+	CC1	
	DMR/MARC	AE7WZ	445.00000	-	CC3	
	DSTAR	K7LWH	146.41250	147.41250		
	DSTAR	K7LWH C	146.41250	147.41250		
	DSTAR	K7LWH B	443.00000	+		
	DSTAR	K7LWH	443.06250	+		
	DSTAR	K7LWH D	1247.00000			
	DSTAR	K7LWH	1290.00000	1270.00000		
	DSTAR	K7LWH A	1290.00000	1270.00000		
	FM	KC7IYE	441.10000	+	156.7 Hz	
Bellevue, Cougar Mountain						
	ATV	WW7ATS	1253.25000	433.95000		
	FM	K7SLB	146.96000	-	103.5 Hz	
	FM	KE7GFZ	441.82500	+	103.5 Hz	
	FM	K7MMI	442.32500	+	151.4 Hz	
	FM	K7PP	443.40000	+	123.0 Hz	
	FM	K7OET	444.32500	+	100.0 Hz	
	FM	W7DME	444.85000	+	103.5 Hz	ORRC
Bellevue, Lincoln Square						
	FM	K7LWH	444.60000	+	103.5 Hz	
Bellingham	DMR/BM	W7BFD	442.30000	+	CC1	
	DMR/MARC	K7SKW	146.50000	+	CC1	
	DSTAR	WC7SO C	146.45000	147.45000		
	DSTAR	WC7SO B	440.47500	+		
	FM	N7FYU	441.92500	+	103.5 Hz	
Bellingham, King Mountain						
	FM	K7SKW	147.16000	+	103.5 Hz	
	FM	N7FYU	224.86000	-	103.5 Hz	
	FM	K7SKW	443.65000	+	103.5 Hz	
	FM	N7FYU	1290.95000	1270.95000	103.5 Hz	
Bellingham, Lookout Mountain						
	DSTAR	WC7SO	440.47500	+		
	FM	W7ECG	224.16000	-	156.7 Hz	
	FM	WA7ZWG	927.48750	902.48750	114.8 Hz	
Bellingham, Lookout Mtn						
	DSTAR	WC7SO	146.45000	147.45000		
Bellingham, Squalicum Mountain						
	FM	K7SKW	443.75000	+	103.5 Hz	
Blaine	FM	W7BPD	927.37500	902.37500	114.8 Hz	
	FUSION	KJ7VWR	444.55000	438.55000		
Bluecreek		KE7HTU-R	443.72500			
Blyn	FM	W7FEL-R	146.76000	-		
Blyn, Blyn Lookout						
	FM	WR7V	53.37000	51.67000	100.0 Hz	
Boistfort	DMR/MARC	WA7DMR	440.73750	+	CC1	
Boistfort, Baw Faw Peak						
	FM	W7WRG	224.08000	-	103.5 Hz	
Bothell	DSTAR	KF7UUY	441.26250	+		
	DSTAR	KF7UUY B	441.26250	+		
	FM	K7SLB	147.47500	146.47500	114.8 Hz	
	FM	WA7HJR	442.55000	+	103.5 Hz	
Boylston	FM	W7CCY-R	146.94000	-		
Bremerton	DMR/BM	WA7JH	145.20000	-	CC1	
	DMR/BM	WA7JH	441.17500	+	CC1	
	DMR/BM	WA7JH	443.00000	+	CC9	
	DMR/BM	KC7Z	444.07500	+	CC1	
	DMR/MARC	AF7PR	440.72500	+	CC1	
	FM	K7OET	442.25000	+	123.0 Hz	
	FM	K7OET	444.80000	+	100.0 Hz	

Location	Mode	Call sign	Output	Input	Access	Coordinator
Bremerton, Gold Mountain						
	FM	WW7RA	146.62000	-	103.5 Hz	
	FM	W7UFI	224.66000	-	103.5 Hz	
	FM	W7TWA	441.50000	+	100.0 Hz	
	FM	WW7RA	442.65000	+	103.5 Hz	
Bremerton, Green Mountain						
	FM	W7PSE	441.75000	+	103.5 Hz	
Brewster, Dyer Hill						
	FM	W7GSN	146.74000	-	110.9 Hz	IACC
Bridgeport	FM	WA7CUG	146.74000	-	110.9 Hz	
Brush Prairie	DMR/MARC	WA7HAA	444.11250	+	CC7	
Buck Mtn	FM	W7WRG	224.58000	-	103.5 Hz	WWARA
Buckley	FM	WA7LBS	443.02500	+	107.2 Hz	
Buckley, Three Sisters						
	FM	N7BUW	444.67500	+	136.5 Hz	
Buckley, Three Sisters Summit						
	FM	WB7DOB	147.30000	+	88.5 Hz	
	FM	WB7DOB	223.92000	-	103.5 Hz	
Burien	DMR/BM	KE0CO	442.80000	+	CC1	
	DMR/BM	W7BUR	443.70000	+	CC1	
	DSTAR	KF7CLD	147.50000	146.50000		
	DSTAR	KF7CLD C	147.50000	146.50000		
	DSTAR	KF7CLD	443.42500	+		
	DSTAR	KF7CLD B	443.42500	+		
Burlington	DMR/BM	KF7CFR	441.95000	+	CC1	
Camano Island	FM	W7PIG	147.36000	+	127.3 Hz	
	FM	W7PIG	223.88000	-	103.5 Hz	
	FM	W7PIG	441.05000	+	103.5 Hz	
Camas, Livingston Mountain						
	FM	W7AIA	147.24000	+	94.8 Hz	
	FM	W7AIA	224.36000	-	94.8 Hz	ORRC
	FM	W7AIA	443.92500	+	94.8 Hz	ORRC
Camas, Prune Hill	FM	KE7BK	444.52500	+	103.5 Hz	ORRC
Carnation	FM	KE7GFZ	145.59000			
	FM	W7PFB	223.90000	-	88.5 Hz	
Carson	FM	KB7APU	145.25000	-	186.2 Hz	
	FM	KB7APU	224.02000	-	136.5 Hz	ORRC
Carson--augs-or Sar						
	DMR/MARC	KB7APU	440.63750	+	CC1	
Cathlamet, KM Hill						
	FM	NM7R	147.02000	+	118.8 Hz	
Centralia	FM	K7CEM	146.86000	-	110.9 Hz	
Centralia, Cook's Hill Fire St						
	FM	K7CEM	145.49000	-	110.9 Hz	
	FM	K7CEM	442.05000	+	110.9 Hz	
Chehalis	DMR/MARC	AF7PR	440.73750	+	CC1	
	FM	WA7UHD	145.43000	-	110.9 Hz	
	FUSION	WA7PAG	446.08750			
Chehalis, Baw Faw Peak						
	FM	K7CH	52.93000	51.23000	100.0 Hz	
	FM	KD7HTE	444.45000	+	100.0 Hz	
	FM	K7CH	927.92500	902.92500	114.8 Hz	
Chehalis, Baw Faw Peak (Boistf						
	FM	WA7UHD	147.06000	+	110.9 Hz	
Chehalis, Crego Hill						
	FM	K7KFM	146.74000	-	110.9 Hz	
	FM	K7KFM	443.45000	+	110.9 Hz	
Chelan	DMR/MARC	KF7EEL	147.56000		CC7	
	FM	K7SRG	145.45000	-		IACC
Chelan / Wenatchee						
	FM	K7YR	53.45000	51.75000	100.0 Hz	IACC

Location	Mode	Call sign	Output	Input	Access	Coordinator
Chelan, McNeal Canyon						
	FM	K7SMX	147.10000	+		
	FM	K7SMX	444.52500	+	94.8 Hz	
Chelan/manson	FM	K7SRG	145.43000	-		IACC
Cheney	DMR/BM	WA7DRE	145.15000	-	CC1	
Chewelah	FM	N7WRR	147.36000	+	103.1 Hz	IACC
	FM	K7SRG	223.88000	-		IACC
	FM	AK2O	223.90000	-		IACC
Chewelah, Stensgar Mountain						
	FM	N7BFS	145.25000	-		IACC
Chinook, Megler Mountain						
	FM	NM7R	147.18000	+	82.5 Hz	
	FM	W7BU	440.92500	+	118.8 Hz	
	FM	NM7R	444.92500	+	82.5 Hz	
Clarkston	FM	NA5XX	223.48000		88.5 Hz	
Clarkston, Potter Hill						
	FM	KA7FAJ	145.39000	-		
Cle Elum	DSTAR	WR7KCR B	444.91250	+		
	FM	W7HNH	444.92500	+	131.8 Hz	IACC
Cle Elum, Sky Meadows						
	DSTAR	WR7KCR	444.91250	+		IACC
	FM	WR7KCR	147.36000	+	141.3 Hz	IACC
Clinton	DMR/MARC	N7ER	224.62000	-	CC1	
	DMR/MARC	N7ER	430.46250	439.46250	CC1	
	DMR/MARC	N7ER	440.72500	+	CC1	
Colfax, Kamiak Butte						
	FM	N7ZUF	53.75000	52.05000	100.0 Hz	IACC
	FM	W7HFI	146.74000	-		IACC
College Place	FM	KH6IHB	147.14000	+	94.8 Hz	IACC
Colville	FM	K7SRG	145.45000	-		IACC
Colville Indian Reservation, K						
	FM	KF7VSX	446.50000	-	100.0 Hz	
Colville, Monumental Mountain						
	FM	K7JAR	146.62000	-	77.0 Hz	IACC
Cosmopolis	FM	WA7ARC	444.37500	+	100.0 Hz	
Cosmopolis, Cosmopolis Hill						
	FM	W7EOC	145.39000	-	118.8 Hz	
Coupeville	FM	W7AVM	146.86000	-	127.3 Hz	
Coupleville	FM	WB7DBJ	146.50000		167.9 Hz	
Covington	FM	N7UIC	444.90000	+	103.5 Hz	
Cowiche, Cowiche Mtn						
	FM	N7YRC	442.72500	+	127.3 Hz	IACC
Darrington	FM	W7MB	442.67500	+	127.3 Hz	
	FM	W7UFI	443.87500	+	103.5 Hz	
Darrington, Barlow Pass						
	FM	KD7VMK	442.80000	+		
Davenport, Teel Hill						
	FM	W7OHI	147.04000	+		
Deer Park	FM	AD7QJ	442.75000	+		IACC
	FM	KG5AO	442.80000	+	100.0 Hz	IACC
Delphi	FM	K7CPR-R	145.47000	-		
Duvall	FM	N6TJQ	441.85000	+	203.5 Hz	
	FM	KE7GFZ	443.25000	+	103.5 Hz	
East Queen Anne	FM	WW7PSR-R	146.96000	-	103.5 Hz	
East Wenatchee	FM	KB7MVF	443.65000	+		IACC
	FM	K7TKR	444.87500	+	151.4 Hz	IACC
East Wenatchee, Badger Mountai						
	FM	N7RHT	444.75000	+	100.0 Hz	
Eastsound, Mt. Constitution, O						
	FM	W7MBY	53.21000	51.51000	100.0 Hz	
Eatonville	FM	W7PFR	53.41000	51.71000	100.0 Hz	
	FM	W7EAT	224.18000	-	103.5 Hz	

Location	Mode	Call sign	Output	Input	Access	Coordinator
Eatonville	FM	W7PFR	443.97500	+	103.5 Hz	
Eatonville, Pack Forest						
	FM	W7EAT	146.70000	-	103.5 Hz	
Edelweiss	DMR/MARC	NO7RF	438.38000	449.38000	CC3	
Edmonds	DSTAR	NW7DR	146.46250	147.46250		
	DSTAR	NW7DR C	146.46250	147.46250		
	DSTAR	NW7DR A	224.56000	-		
	DSTAR	NW7DR	444.72500	+	123.0 Hz	
	DSTAR	NW7DR B	444.72500	+		
	FM	W7RNB	29.68000	-		
	FM	WE7SCA	440.37500	+	103.5 Hz	
	FM	WE7SCA	444.02500	+	103.5 Hz	
Eldon	FM	WB7DVN	146.45000	+		
Electron	FM	W7UDI	444.25000	+	103.5 Hz	
Elk	FUSION	K6RRS	146.55000			
Ellensburg	DMR/MARC	K7RHT	440.92500	+	CC1	
	FM	W7HMT	145.21000	-	151.4 Hz	IACC
	FM	KI7DQG	147.19000	+		
	FM	WR7KCR	442.20000	+	131.8 Hz	IACC
	FM	K7RHT	444.45000	+	131.8 Hz	IACC
	FM	K7RMR	444.82500	+	100.0 Hz	
	FM	KI7DQH	447.42500	-		
Ellensburg, Table Mountain						
	FM	K7RHT	444.45000	-	131.8 Hz	
Elma, Minot Peak	FM	W7EOC	444.05000	+	118.8 Hz	
Elmer City, Keller Butte						
	FM	KF7VSX	146.50000		100.0 Hz	
Enumclaw	DMR/MARC	NF6C	441.35000	+	CC0	
	DMR/MARC	NO7RF	902.48750	927.48750	CC1	
	DSTAR	W7JD B	442.62500	+		
	FM	N7OEP	440.07500	+	103.5 Hz	
	FM	N7OEP	443.17500	+	107.2 Hz	
Enumclaw, Baldi	FM	W7WRG	224.88000	-	103.5 Hz	
Enumclaw, Baldi Mountain						
	FM	N7OEP	53.33000	51.63000	100.0 Hz	
	FM	K7MMI	146.98000	-	131.8 Hz	
	FM	WB7DOB	147.14000	+	123.0 Hz	
	FM	WB7DOB	224.76000	-	103.5 Hz	
	FM	W7TWA	441.62500	+	100.0 Hz	
	FM	W7PSE	441.70000	+	103.5 Hz	
	FM	WB7DOB	442.62500	+	103.5 Hz	
	FM	K7OET	444.80000	+	141.3 Hz	
	FM	N7FSP	1292.30000	1272.30000	103.5 Hz	
Enumclaw, Grass Mountain						
	FM	W7SIX	53.87000	52.17000	100.0 Hz	
	FM	W7AAO	145.37000	-	136.5 Hz	
Ephrata	DMR/MARC	WA7DMR	147.41250	146.41250	CC1	IACC
	FM	N7BHB	52.95000	51.25000	100.0 Hz	IACC
	FM	N7BHB	53.21000	51.51000	100.0 Hz	IACC
Ephrata, Beezly Hill						
	DSTAR	W7TT	443.90000	+		
	FM	W7TT	145.31000	-	100.0 Hz	
	FM	W7DTS	444.90000	+	103.5 Hz	
Evans	FUSION	N1JJB	145.45000	-		
Everett	DSTAR	NR7SS	440.35000	+		
	DSTAR	NR7SS B	440.35000	+		
	DSTAR	NR7SS A	1251.65000	1271.65000		
	FM	W2ZT	145.39000	-	123.0 Hz	
	FM	KH6VM	147.12000	+	103.5 Hz	
	FM	K7UID	224.06000	-	103.5 Hz	
	FUSION	KF7LAN	146.55000			
	FUSION	WA7LAW-R	147.18000	+	103.5 Hz	

Location	Mode	Call sign	Output	Input	Access	Coordinator
Everett	FUSION	WA7LAW	444.57500	+	103.5 Hz	
Everson	DMR/MARC	W7BPD	440.37500	+	CC1	
Fairchild AFB	FM	KC5GI	440.50000	+	100.0 Hz	
Federal Way	DSTAR	WA7FW C	146.84000	-		
	DSTAR	WA7FW	146.84000	-		
	DSTAR	WA7FW B	443.85000	+		
	DSTAR	WA7FW	443.85000	+		
	DSTAR	WA7FW D	1249.25000			
	DSTAR	WA7FW	1249.25000			
	DSTAR	WA7FW	1290.10000	1270.10000		
	DSTAR	WA7FW A	1290.10000	1310.10000		
	FM	WA7FW	146.76000	-	103.5 Hz	
	FM	WA7FW	147.04000	+	103.5 Hz	
	FM	WA7FW	442.92500	+		
	FM	WA7FW	442.95000	+	103.5 Hz	
	FM	KF7TCP	446.17500	-	110.9 Hz	
	FUSION	KF7OFL	144.52000			
Ferndale	DMR/BM	W7ECG	440.73750	+	CC1	
	FM	W7ECG	442.82500	+	156.7 Hz	
Forks, Mount Octupus						
	FM	K7PP	147.28000	+	123.0 Hz	
Forks, Police Department						
	FM	W7FEL	145.21000	-	100.0 Hz	
Friday Harbor	DSTAR	N7JN	145.25000	-		
	DSTAR	N7JN C	146.45000	147.45000		
	DSTAR	N7JN B	442.46250	+		
Friday Harbor, Hillview Terrac						
	DSTAR	N7JN	442.46250	+		
Gig Harbor	FM	W7TJL-R	224.20000	-	123.0 Hz	
	FM	KC5EMF	444.87500	+		
Gold Bar	FM	W7EAR	442.17500	+	103.5 Hz	
	FM	W7ERH	1293.00000	1273.00000	103.5 Hz	
Gold Bar, Haystack Mountain						
	FM	N7NFY	443.87500	+	127.3 Hz	
Goldendale	FM	KF7LN	443.35000	+	136.5 Hz	IACC
Goldendale, Juniper Point						
	FM	WC7EC	146.82000	-	103.5 Hz	IACC
Goldendale, Simcoe Mountains						
	FM	KC7UTD	146.92000	-	88.5 Hz	
Graham	DSTAR	KF7GVL B	441.42500	+		
	DSTAR	WA7DR B	442.92500	+		
	FM	N3KPU	145.23000	-	146.2 Hz	
Graham, Baldi Mtn						
	FM	N7BUW	444.67500	+	127.3 Hz	
Graham, Graham Hill						
	DSTAR	WA7DR	442.92500	+		
Grand Coulee, Grand Coulee Dam						
	FM	KE7NRA	146.86000	-	100.0 Hz	
Granger, Cherry Hill						
	FM	KB7CSP	147.04000	+	123.0 Hz	
Granite Falls	FM	WB7VYA	146.92000	-	123.0 Hz	
	FUSION	KI7ICO	145.52000			
Greenacres	FM	K7HRT	442.42500	+	100.0 Hz	
Greenwater, Crystal Mountain						
	FM	WB7DOB	145.41000	-	162.2 Hz	
Hartline	FM	KB7WPU	224.42000	-	103.5 Hz	
	FM	KB7WPU	444.45000	+	100.0 Hz	
Hazel Dell	FM	KC7QPD	443.80000	+	100.0 Hz	ORRC
Hemlock Valley		WA7HJR-R	444.65000			
Henrys		KF7BIG-R	442.12500			
High Point		K7LER-R	441.80000			
Highline	FM	N7IO	443.37500	+	103.5 Hz	

Location	Mode	Call sign	Output	Input	Access	Coordinator
Hobart, Rattlesnake Ridge						
	FM	KF7BJI	442.15000	+	103.5 Hz	
Hockinson	FM	K7BPR	147.08000	+	107.2 Hz	ORRC
	FM	K7BPR	444.72500	+	107.2 Hz	ORRC
Holtzinger	FM	AB7XQ-R	444.22500	+		
Issaquah	FM	N9VW	53.83000	52.13000	123.0 Hz	
	FM	N9VW	440.25000	+	123.0 Hz	
	FM	N9VW	442.30000	+	123.0 Hz	
	P25	K7TGU	146.42500	+		
Issaquah, East Tiger Mountain						
	FM	N7NW	223.98000	-	100.0 Hz	
	FM	K7LED	224.12000	-	103.5 Hz	
Issaquah, Squak Mountain						
	FM	N7KGJ	444.52500	+	103.5 Hz	
Issaquah, Tiger Mountain						
	FM	K7PF	146.88000	-		
	FM	W7WWI	147.08000	-	110.9 Hz	
Issaquah, Tiger Mountain East						
	DSTAR	WA7HJR	444.63750	+		
	FM	K7LED	146.82000	-	103.5 Hz	
	FM	KC7RAS	147.10000	+	123.0 Hz	
	FM	K7DNR	442.60000	+	127.3 Hz	
	FM	K7KG	443.30000	+	156.7 Hz	
	FM	N6OBY	443.32500	+	103.5 Hz	
	FM	KB7CNN	1292.20000	1272.20000	103.5 Hz	
Issaquah, West Tiger Mountain						
	FM	K7NWS	145.33000	-	179.9 Hz	
	FM	K7NWS	224.34000	-	110.9 Hz	
	FM	K7NWS	442.07500	+	110.9 Hz	
Kalama	FM	WB7DFV	442.82500	+	131.8 Hz	
Kalama, China Garden Rd						
	FM	K7CH	927.27500	902.27500	114.8 Hz	
Kendall, Sumas Mountain						
	FM	W7BPD	145.23000	-	103.5 Hz	
Kennewick		W7BSD-L	449.62500			
	DMR/MARC	WA7DMR	146.42500	147.42500	CC0	IACC
	FM	K7SRG	145.45000	-	156.7 Hz	IACC
	FM	WF7S	146.62000			
	FM	WB7JON	146.64000	-	100.0 Hz	
	FM	KI7KYL	224.52000	-	100.0 Hz	IACC
	FM	W7JWC	443.77500	+		
	FM	W7UPS	443.95000	+	123.0 Hz	
	FM	W7UPS	444.05000	+	100.0 Hz	IACC
	FUSION	K7CBJ	144.30000			
	FUSION	WB7JON/R	442.00000			
Kennewick, Johnson Butte						
	FM	W7AZ	146.64000	-	100.0 Hz	
	FM	N7LZM	147.22000	+		
Kennewick, Jump Off Joe						
	FM	N7LZM	145.41000	-	100.0 Hz	
	FM	KC7WFD	147.08000	+	94.8 Hz	
Kent	FM	K7CST	147.32000	+	103.5 Hz	
Kent, Emerald Park Elementary						
	FM	K7RFH	443.35000	+	103.5 Hz	
Kingston	FM	W7KWS	442.22500	447.32500	100.0 Hz	
Kirkland	DSTAR	N7IH	146.48750	147.48750		
	DSTAR	N7IH C	147.48750	146.48750		
	DSTAR	N7IH B	443.57500	+		
	DSTAR	N7IH	443.57500	+		
	DSTAR	N7IH D	1248.05000			
	DSTAR	N7IH	1290.20000	1270.20000		
	DSTAR	N7IH A	1290.20000	1270.20000		

Location	Mode	Call sign	Output	Input	Access	Coordinator
Kirkland	FM	K7LWH	441.07500	+	103.5 Hz	
Kirkland , Rose Hill						
	FM	K7LWH	53.17000	51.47000	100.0 Hz	
Kirkland, Rosehill	FM	K7LWH-R	145.49000	-	103.5 Hz	
La Center	FM	K7ABL	444.92500	+	94.8 Hz	ORRC
Lacey	FM	WC7I	146.80000	-	97.4 Hz	
	FM	W6TOZ	440.55000	+	103.5 Hz	
	FM	WC7I	442.47500	+	100.0 Hz	
Lake Forest Park	FM	WA7FUS	224.22000	-	103.5 Hz	
	FM	WE7SCA	442.00000	+	141.3 Hz	
Lakeland South		W7ILY-L	147.44500			
Langley, Whidbey Island						
	FM	W7AVM	147.22000	+	127.3 Hz	
Lebam, KO Peak	FM	N7XAC	224.04000	-	118.8 Hz	
	FM	N7XAC	441.67500	+	118.8 Hz	
Liberty Lake	FM	W7TRF	443.65000	+		
Liberty Lake, Agilent Bldg						
	FM	W7TRF	443.47500	+	88.5 Hz	
Lind, Lind Hill	FM	W7UPS	448.70000	-	123.0 Hz	
Long Beach, County Building						
	FM	NM7R	444.80000	+	118.8 Hz	
Longmire	DMR/BM	WW7CH	145.13000	-	CC1	
Longview	DMR/MARC	N3EG	441.70000	+	CC1	
	DMR/MARC	N3EG	444.98750	+	CC1	
	FM	W7DG	147.26000	+	114.8 Hz	
	FM	W7DG	224.14000	-	114.8 Hz	
	FM	AB7F	440.37500	+	123.0 Hz	ORRC
	FM	KJ6RA	443.52500	+	173.8 Hz	
	FM	W7DG	444.90000	+	114.8 Hz	
	FM	W6RJG	447.87250	-	100.0 Hz	
	FM	KB7ADO	927.97500	902.97500	114.8 Hz	
Longview, Columbia Heights						
	FM	N3EG	442.12500	+	114.8 Hz	
Longview--open Use 900						
	DMR/MARC	KB7APU	927.15000	902.15000	CC1	
Longview--OR SAR						
	DMR/MARC	KB7APU	444.23750	+	CC9	
Loon Lake	FM	WB7UCI	444.67500	+	114.8 Hz	
Lost River	DMR/MARC	NO7RF	438.38000	449.38000	CC0	
Lyman, Lyman Hill						
	FM	W7UMH	53.09000	51.39000	100.0 Hz	
	FM	N7GDE	145.19000	-	127.3 Hz	
	FM	W7MBY	223.86000	-	103.5 Hz	
	FM	N7RIG	224.78000	-	103.5 Hz	
	FM	W7UMH	442.40000	+	107.2 Hz	
	P25	WA7ZUS	444.50000	+	103.5 Hz	
Lynnwood	DMR/MARC	K7MLR	444.15000	+	CC1	WWARA
	FM	WA7DEM	146.78000	-	162.2 Hz	
	FM	N7NFY	146.80000	-	136.5 Hz	
	FM	N6CES	444.67500	+	173.8 Hz	
Mabton, Missouri Falls						
	FM	KB7CSP	443.82500	+	100.0 Hz	
Maple Valley	DSTAR	KF7NPL	442.67500	+		
Marrowstone	FM	AH6EZ-L	440.72500	+		
Marysville	FM	WA7DEM	224.38000	-	103.5 Hz	
Mazama	DMR/BM	NO7RF	440.71250	+	CC1	
	DMR/MARC	NO7RF	145.21000	147.99000	CC3	
	DMR/MARC	N07RF	147.41250	148.41250	CC3	
	DMR/MARC	NO7RF	433.15000	449.15000	CC0	
	FM	KB7SVP	147.16000	+	100.0 Hz	IACC
	FM	KB7SVP	442.15000	+	110.9 Hz	IACC
McGowan		WA7WIW-L	145.45000			

Location	Mode	Call sign	Output	Input	Access	Coordinator
Medical Lake	FM	WA7RVV	443.60000	+	100.0 Hz	
Meglar Mtn	FM	W7BU	440.92500	+	118.8 Hz	WWARA
Megler	FM	W7BU-R	145.45000	-		
Megler WA--OR SAR						
	DMR/MARC	KB7APU	444.23750	+	CC9	
Mercer Island	FM	W7MIR	147.16000	+	146.2 Hz	
	FM	W7MIR	440.15000	+	103.5 Hz	
Methow	DMR/MARC	NO7RF	440.71250	+	CC1	
Mill Creek	FM	WR7DS	442.72500	+		
	FM	N7IBF	444.92500	+	100.0 Hz	
Mineral	FM	K7HW	146.68000	-	103.5 Hz	
Monroe	FM	K7MJ	224.10000	-	123.0 Hz	
Monroe, Rattlesnake Mountain						
	FM	K7SLB	443.12500	+		
Morton, Rooster Rock						
	FM	KB7WVX	444.97500	+	110.9 Hz	
Moses Lake	DMR/MARC	WA7DMR	440.92500	+	CC1	
Mount Vernon	DMR/MARC	AF7PR	440.92500	-	CC1	
Mount Vernon, Cultus Mountain						
	FM	WE7T	53.59000	51.89000	100.0 Hz	
	FM	K7OET	444.35000	+	100.0 Hz	
	FM	N7CRA	444.62500	+	103.5 Hz	
	FM	K7OET	927.55000	902.55000	114.8 Hz	
Mountlake Terrace						
	FM	WA7DEM	443.72500	+	103.5 Hz	
Moxee City	FM	KC7WFD	147.12000	+		
Moxee City, Elephant Mountain						
	FM	W7AQ	146.84000	-	123.0 Hz	
	FM	WA7SAR	444.60000	+	123.0 Hz	
Mukilteo, Boeing	FM	W7FLY	443.92500	+	100.0 Hz	
Naches, Whites Pass						
	FM	KD7LZN	442.47500	+	210.7 Hz	
Naselle, Naselle Ridge						
	FM	NM7R	440.67500	+	118.8 Hz	
Neilton	FM	WA7ARC	146.96000	-	203.5 Hz	
Neilton Peak	FM	W7EOC	444.70000	+	118.8 Hz	WWARA
Neilton, Neilton Peak						
	FM	W7ZA	146.90000	-	88.5 Hz	
	FM	W7EOC	444.70000	+	118.8 Hz	
Newcastle	DSTAR	W7RNK	441.21250	+		
Newcastle, Cougar Mt						
	FM	KF7BJI	146.96000	-	103.5 Hz	
Newman Lake	FUSION	AE7RJ	444.50000	+		
Newport, Cooks Mountain						
	FM	KB7TBN	444.57500	+	100.0 Hz	
NOAA Astoria	WX	KEC91	162.40000			
NOAA Blaine	WX	KAD93	162.52500			
NOAA Cle Elum	WX	WXN21	162.40000			
NOAA Davis Peak						
	WX	WNG604	162.52500			
NOAA Dayton	WX	KZZ73	162.52500			
NOAA Forks	WX	KXI27	162.42500			
NOAA Neah Bay	WX	KIH36	162.55000			
NOAA Okanogan	WX	WWF49	162.52500			
NOAA Olympia	WX	WXM62	162.47500			
NOAA Plymouth	WX	WWH27	162.42500			
NOAA Puget Sound Marine						
	WX	WWG24	162.42500			
NOAA Randle	WX	WZ2502	162.42500			
NOAA Richland	WX	WWF56	162.45000			
NOAA Seattle	WX	KHB60	162.55000			
NOAA Spokane	WX	WXL86	162.40000			

Location	Mode	Call sign	Output	Input	Access	Coordinator
NOAA The Dalles	WX	WXM34	162.40000			
NOAA Wenatchee						
	WX	WXM48	162.47500			
NOAA Yakima	WX	KIG75	162.55000			
North Bend	DMR/MARC	WA7DMR	146.50000	147.50000	CC1	
	DMR/MARC	WA7VC	440.72500	+	CC1	
	FM	N9VW	53.85000	52.15000	100.0 Hz	
	FM	K7SLB	147.47500	146.47500	127.3 Hz	
	FM	W7EFR	442.72500	+	123.0 Hz	
North Bend, Green Mountain						
	FM	KD7VMK	146.92000	-	103.5 Hz	
North Bend, Rattlesnake Mounta						
	FM	KC7SAR	145.11000	-	127.3 Hz	
	FM	W7PSE	441.77500	+	103.5 Hz	
	FM	W7SRG	442.30000	+	123.0 Hz	
	FM	N7NFY	927.88750	902.88750	114.8 Hz	
North Bend, Rattlesnake Ridge						
	FM	N7NFY	441.65000	+	127.3 Hz	
North Cove	FM	NM7R	145.31000	-	118.8 Hz	
North Point	FM	N7QDY	146.66000	-	107.2 Hz	
Ocean Park	FM	K7EAN	441.77500	+	100.0 Hz	
Ocean Park, Fire Hall						
	FM	NM7R	145.17000	-	118.8 Hz	
Ocean Shores	DMR/MARC	WA7DMR	146.41250	147.41250	CC1	
Ocean Shores, City Shops						
	FM	WA7OS	441.12500	+	123.0 Hz	
Okanogan, Pitcher Mountain						
	FM	WA7MV	146.72000	-	100.0 Hz	
	FM	WA7MV	443.55000	+	100.0 Hz	
Olalla	FM	K7PAG	53.23000	51.53000	103.5 Hz	
	FM	W7ZLJ	145.35000	-	103.5 Hz	
	FM	WR7HE	440.22500	+	103.5 Hz	
	FM	KF7SOV	444.10000	+	103.5 Hz	
Olympia	DMR/MARC	KG7KPH	440.72500	-	CC1	
	DMR/MARC	AF7PR	440.92500	+	CC1	
	DMR/MARC	WA6VYL	441.32500	441.82500	CC1	
	FM	W7PSE	145.15000	-	103.5 Hz	
	FM	N7EBB	146.78000	-	156.7 Hz	
	FM	NT7H	440.72500	+		
	FM	KC7CKO	443.07500	+	103.5 Hz	
	FM	W7USJ	443.80000	+	146.2 Hz	
Olympia, Capitol Peak						
	FM	W7SIX	53.57000	51.87000	100.0 Hz	
	FM	W7WRG	224.08000	-	103.5 Hz	
	FM	W7WRG	440.50000	+	110.9 Hz	
	FM	N7UJK	444.95000	+	118.8 Hz	
	FM	W7SIX	927.30000	902.30000	114.8 Hz	
Olympia, Crawford Mountain						
	FM	NT7H	441.40000	+	103.5 Hz	
Olympia, Water Tower						
	FM	NT7H	147.36000	+	103.5 Hz	
Omak	FM	K7SRG	147.20000	+		IACC
Omak, Tunk Mountain						
	FM	WA7MV	53.11000	51.41000	100.0 Hz	IACC
	FM	WA7MV	147.32000	+	100.0 Hz	
Orcas Island, Mount Constituti						
	FM	N7JN	224.48000	-	103.5 Hz	
	FM	K7SKW	442.00000	+	110.9 Hz	
Orcas Island, Mt Constitution						
	FM	K7SKW	146.74000	-	103.5 Hz	
	FM	N7JN	146.90000	-	131.8 Hz	
	FM	WA6MPG	224.54000	-	67.0 Hz	

Location	Mode	Call sign	Output	Input	Access	Coordinator
Orcas Island, Mt Constitution						
	FM	N7JN	443.45000	+	103.5 Hz	
	FM	K7SKW	444.05000	+	103.5 Hz	
Oroville, Buckhorn Mountain						
	FM	WA7DJ	147.14000	+	103.5 Hz	
Orting	DMR/MARC	NF6C	441.32500	+	CC0	
Oso	DMR/MARC	K7MLR	443.90000	+	CC1	
Othello	FM	N7MHE	145.35000	-	100.0 Hz	IACC
	FM	KK7BIM	443.15000	+	123.0 Hz	
Otis Orchards	FM	NV2Z	442.92500	+	100.0 Hz	
Otis Orchards, Fox Hill						
	FM	AD7DD	147.14000	+	127.3 Hz	IACC
Packwood	FM	K7KFL	146.74000	-	131.8 Hz	
Paradise, Mt Rainier						
	FM	WW7CH	146.78000	-	103.5 Hz	
Pasco	FUSION	WF7S	146.62000	-	123.0 Hz	
	FUSION	K7EP	446.67500			
Phinney Ridge		K7MAQ-L	445.87500			
Plymouth	FM	AI7HO	147.02000	+	103.5 Hz	IACC
	FM	AI7HO	443.75000	+	103.5 Hz	IACC
Plymouth, Sillusi Butte						
	FM	KC7RWC	145.49000	-	67.0 Hz	
Point Roberts	FM	KJ1U	443.30000	+	100.0 Hz	
Port Angeles	DMR/BM	WA7EBH	147.06000	+	CC0	
	DMR/BM	WF7W	442.12500	+	CC1	
	DMR/BM	WA7EBH	443.70000	+	CC1	
	FM	WF7W	145.13000	-	100.0 Hz	
Port Ludlow	FM	N7PL	441.57500	+	103.5 Hz	
Port Ludlow, Mats Mats						
	FM	WR7V	442.52500	+	103.5 Hz	
Port Orchard	FM	N7IG	145.39000	-	88.5 Hz	
	FM	W6AV	441.57500	+	100.0 Hz	
	FM	K7BTZ	444.10000	+	100.0 Hz	
Port Townsend	DMR/BM	W7JCR	443.82500	+	CC1	
Port Townsend, Morgan Hill						
	FM	W7JCR	145.15000	-	114.8 Hz	
Potreros	DMR/MARC	WA7DMR	147.41250	146.41250	CC1	
Poulsbo	FM	W7LOR	441.27500	+	123.0 Hz	
	FM	WA6PMX	442.20000	+	103.5 Hz	
Prosser	FM	KA7SSB	147.18000	+	123.0 Hz	IACC
	FM	W7LYV	147.38000	+	123.0 Hz	IACC
	FM	WB7WHF	444.87500	+	141.3 Hz	
Pullman	DMR/MARC	K7LL	444.10000	+	CC1	
	DSTAR	W7YH B	443.16250	+		
	DSTAR	W7YH	443.16250	+		
	FM	KC7AUI	444.30000	+	103.5 Hz	
Pullman, SEL Campus						
	FM	K7SEL	147.10000	+	103.5 Hz	IACC
Puyallup		KG7QIN-L	147.54000			
	FM	KB7CNN	444.75000	+	103.5 Hz	
Quilcene, Buck Mountain						
	FM	W7FHZ	53.29000	51.59000	100.0 Hz	
	FM	K7PP	441.20000	+		
	FM	W2ZT	442.50000	+	123.0 Hz	
Quilcene, Buck Mtn						
	FM	K7MMI	147.20000	+	131.8 Hz	
	P25	K7SCN	440.95000	+	110.9 Hz	
Quilcene, Hood Canal						
	FM	WO7O	443.42500	+	103.5 Hz	
Ragnar		K7FZO-L	446.52500			
Randle	FM	AB7F	444.87500	+	100.0 Hz	
Rathdrum	FM	K7FVA	441.65000	+	156.7 Hz	IACC

Location	Mode	Call sign	Output	Input	Access	Coordinator
Rattlesnake Mtn	FM	N7NFY	441.65000	+	141.3 Hz	WWARA
Ravensdale	DSTAR	KF7NPL B	442.67500	+		
Raymond	FM	KB7IEU	442.15000	+	127.3 Hz	
Redmond	DMR/BM	N7QT	442.32500	+	CC1	
	DMR/MARC	KE7SFF	444.40000	+	CC1	
	FM	KC7IYE	145.31000	-	103.5 Hz	
	FM	N6OBY	440.67500	+	103.5 Hz	
Renton	DMR/MARC	KJ7OKL	442.45000	443.05000	CC1	
	FM	KC7IGT	441.45000	+	123.0 Hz	
	FM	K7FDF	443.60000	+	103.5 Hz	
Renton, Lake Youngs						
	FM	WB7DOB	441.37500	+	173.8 Hz	
Republic	FM	N7XAY	145.19000	-		
Richland	FM	WF7S	146.62000	-	123.0 Hz	
Richland , Rattlesnake Mtn						
	FM	W7VPA	146.76000	-	100.0 Hz	
Richland, Rattlesnake Mtn						
	FM	W7AZ	449.10000	-	100.0 Hz	
Ridgecrest Mobile Home Park						
	FM	W7GHJ-R	443.72500	+		IACC
Ritzville	DMR/MARC	WA7DMR	147.42750	148.42750	CC1	
	FM	WD7C	146.72000	-		
	FM	W7UPS	444.05000	+	100.0 Hz	
Roche Harbor	FM	W6QC	441.60000	+	131.8 Hz	
Roosevelt	FM	W7NEO	145.19000	-		
Roy	FM	KB7UXE	444.27500	+	203.5 Hz	
Saddle Mtn	FM	W7ZA	146.90000	-	88.5 Hz	WWARA
Salmon Creek	FM	K7KSN	440.27500	+	123.0 Hz	
Sammamish	DMR/MARC	KK7TR	442.05000	+	CC1	WWARA
	FM	W7SRG	440.25000	+	123.0 Hz	
	FM	KG7OI	442.12500	+	123.0 Hz	
SeaTac	DSTAR	KF7BFS B	440.27500	+		
	FM	NC7G	146.66000	-	103.5 Hz	
	FM	KE7WMH	443.10000	+	103.5 Hz	
SeaTac, Station 46						
	DSTAR	KF7BFS	440.27500	+		
Seattle	DMR/BM	W7AW	147.50000	146.50000	CC2	
	DMR/BM	N7IEI	440.90000	+	CC1	
	DMR/MARC	NO7RF	433.15000	449.65000	CC0	
	DMR/MARC	WW7PSR	440.77500	+	CC2	
	DMR/MARC	KF7BJI	440.92500	+	CC1	WWARA
	DMR/MARC	W7AW	440.97500	+	CC2	
	DMR/MARC	W7ACS	441.02500	+	CC2	
	DMR/MARC	K7SLB	441.32500	+	CC1	
	DMR/MARC	NF6C	441.35000	+	CC0	
	DMR/MARC	WW7PSR	441.77500	+	CC2	
	DMR/MARC	W7WWI	442.02500	+	CC1	
	DMR/MARC	K7NWS	442.07500	+	CC2	
	DMR/MARC	K7SLB	443.52500	+	CC1	
	DSTAR	W7ACS	440.76250	+		
	DSTAR	WA7HJR B	444.63750	+		
	FM	K7SLB	440.10000	+	110.9 Hz	
	FM	W7ACS	443.00000	+	156.7 Hz	
	FM	W7FED	443.35000	+	100.0 Hz	
	FM	W7ACS	443.47500	+	141.3 Hz	
	FM	K7SPG	444.00000	+	103.5 Hz	
	FM	KC7LFW	444.22500	+	123.0 Hz	
	FM	W7VTX	445.52500	-	103.5 Hz	
	FM	W7VTX	445.80000	-	103.5 Hz	
	FM	W7BMW	445.82500	-	100.0 Hz	
	FM	W7VTX	446.87500	-	100.0 Hz	
	P25	WA7LZO	442.90000	+	103.5 Hz	

Location	Mode	Call sign	Output	Input	Access	Coordinator
Seattle	FUSION	WD0TCH	145.25000	147.25000		
	FUSION	AE7G	444.42500	+		
Seattle, Beacon Hill						
	FM	W7SRZ	146.90000	-	103.5 Hz	
	FM	W7SRZ	224.68000	-	100.0 Hz	
	FM	W7ACS	440.52500	+		
	FM	W7SRZ	443.55000	+	103.5 Hz	
Seattle, Capitol Hill						
	FM	WA7UHF	442.87500	+		
	FM	AJ7JA	444.37500	+	88.5 Hz	
Seattle, High Point - Myrtle R						
	FM	W7AW	53.29000	51.59000	100.0 Hz	
Seattle, Highpoint	FM	W7AW	441.80000	+	141.3 Hz	
Seattle, KOMO TV Tower						
	FM	WW7SEA	444.42500	+	141.3 Hz	
Seattle, Maple Leaf						
	FM	W7DX	147.00000	-	103.5 Hz	
Seattle, Northwest Hospital						
	FM	W7SRZ	444.82500	+	103.5 Hz	
Seattle, Queen Anne Hill						
	FM	WW7SEA	444.70000	+	103.5 Hz	
Seattle, Roosevelt Hill						
	FM	W7ACS	443.65000	+	141.3 Hz	
Seattle, West Seattle						
	FM	W7AW	147.06000	+	107.2 Hz	
Sedro-Wooley, Lyman Hill						
	FM	KF7VUR	147.43750	146.43750		
Selah	FM	W7HAR	444.27500	+	110.9 Hz	
Selah, Yakima Canyon						
	FM	KC7VQR	147.24000	+	192.8 Hz	
Sequim	DMR/BM	K6MBY	440.75000	+	CC1	
	DMR/BM	KC7EQO	442.10000	+	CC1	
	DMR/MARC	WA7DMR	440.43750	+	CC1	
	FM	N7NFY	442.80000	+	123.0 Hz	WWARA
	FM	AF7DX	444.27500	+	100.0 Hz	
Sequim, Blyn Lookout						
	FM	KC7EQO	442.10000	+	100.0 Hz	
Sequim, Blyn Mountain						
	FM	N7NFY	442.80000	+	123.0 Hz	
Sequim, Maynard Peak						
	FM	WB0CZA	441.12500	+	123.0 Hz	
	FM	W7PSE	442.42500	+	103.5 Hz	
Shelton	DMR/MARC	N9VW	147.02000	+	CC2	
	FM	WB7OXJ	53.09000	51.39000	110.9 Hz	
	FM	N7SK	443.25000	+	100.0 Hz	
Shelton, South Mountain						
	FM	K7CH	145.27000	-	127.3 Hz	
	FM	K7CH	440.65000	+	100.0 Hz	
	FM	K7CH	441.92500	+	100.0 Hz	
	FM	K7CH	927.25000	902.25000	114.8 Hz	
Shelton, Water Tower						
	FM	N7SK	146.72000	-	103.5 Hz	
	FM	N7SK	927.41250	902.41250	114.8 Hz	
Shoreline	FM	KC7ONX	440.30000	+	103.5 Hz	
	FUSION	AH0Y	445.45000			
Shoreline, CRISTA						
	FM	W7AUX	442.82500	+	103.5 Hz	
Silverdale		KG7TAN-L	145.70000			
	FM	KD7WDG	145.43000	-	88.5 Hz	
	FM	AA7SS	445.92500	+	123.0 Hz	
Skokomish, South Mountain						
	FM	K7CH	53.03000	51.33000	100.0 Hz	

Location	Mode	Call sign	Output	Input	Access	Coordinator
Skykomish	FM	KC7SAR	145.11000	-	123.0 Hz	
Snohomish	DMR/MARC	K7LKA	444.23750	+	CC3	
	DSTAR	KG7QPU B	443.90000	+		
	DSTAR	KG7QPU	443.90000	+	151.4 Hz	
	FM	KG7QPU	441.15000	+		
	FUSION	K7IU	146.58000			
	FUSION	K7IU	443.92500	+		
Snohomish, Clearview						
	FM	WA7DEM	442.97500	+		
Snohomish, Mt Pilchuck						
	DSTAR	NR7SS	440.32500	+		
Snoqualmie	DMR/MARC	WA7DMR	440.73750	+	CC1	
	DSTAR	N7SNO B	442.70000	+		
	FM	N7SNO	444.92500	+	85.4 Hz	
Snoqualmie, Rattlesnake Ridge						
	DSTAR	N7SNO	442.70000	+		
South Bend, Holy Cross Mountai						
	FM	NM7R	147.34000	+	82.5 Hz	
	FM	NM7R	224.82000	-	82.5 Hz	
	FM	NM7R	442.67500	+	118.8 Hz	
South Cle Elum	FM	WR7UKC	147.16000	+	131.8 Hz	IACC
	FUSION	KG7HRU	146.55000			
Spanish Lakes Golf Village Mob						
		WD4KAV-L	146.48000			
Spokane	DMR/MARC	WA7DMR	147.41250	146.41250	CC1	
	DMR/MARC	KC7AAD	434.12500	+	CC1	
	DMR/MARC	WA7DMR	440.73750	+	CC1	
	DMR/MARC	KC7AAD	444.12500	+	CC1	
	DMR/MARC	KC7AAD	444.13750	+	CC1	
	DMR/MARC	KC7AAD	444.15000	+	CC1	IACC
	DSTAR	WA7DRE B	443.12500	+		
	DSTAR	WA7DRE D	1249.00000			
	DSTAR	WA7DRE	1293.30000	1313.30000		
	DSTAR	WA7DRE A	1293.30000	1273.30000		
	FM	N7FM	145.33000	-	88.5 Hz	IACC
	FM	N1NG	223.84000	-	192.8 Hz	IACC
	FM	N7FM	442.60000	+	100.0 Hz	
	FM	WA7DRE	443.52500	+		
	FM	KA7ENA	443.80000	+	123.0 Hz	IACC
	FM	KD7IKZ	443.85000	+	114.8 Hz	IACC
	FM	KG7SD	444.05000	+	123.0 Hz	IACC
	FM	N7FM	444.42500	+	100.0 Hz	IACC
	FM	K7SRG	444.70000	+		IACC
	FM	N7ISP	927.25000	902.25000	114.8 Hz	IACC
	FM/FUSION	K7EMF	444.50000	+	136.5 Hz	IACC
	FUSION	KI7FSG	147.28000	+		
	FUSION	AE7Z	147.50625			
Spokane Valley	DMR/MARC	WA7DMR	440.37500	+	CC1	
	FM	N7FM	146.66000	-		
	FM	W7TRF	223.65000	144.61000		IACC
	FM	W7TRF	223.67000	144.61000		IACC
Spokane Valley, Arbor Crest						
	FM	WR7VHF	444.90000	+	123.0 Hz	IACC
Spokane Valley, Liberty Lake						
	FM	K7MMA	145.17000	-	114.8 Hz	IACC
Spokane, Beacon Hill						
	DSTAR	WA7DRE	443.12500	+		
Spokane, Booth Hill						
	FM	KA7ENA	443.80000	+	123.0 Hz	
Spokane, Brownes Mountain						
	FM	W7GBU	147.30000	+	100.0 Hz	IACC

Location	Mode	Call sign	Output	Input	Access	Coordinator
Spokane, Downtown Spokane						
	FM	WR7VHF	147.34000	+	123.0 Hz	IACC
Spokane, Five Mile						
	FM	N7BFS	147.06000	+	77.0 Hz	IACC
	FM	N7BFS	444.17500	+		IACC
Spokane, Krell Hill						
	FM	WR7VHF	146.88000	-	123.0 Hz	IACC
Spokane, Liberty Lake						
	FM	K7MMA	224.40000	-	114.8 Hz	IACC
Spokane, Mica Peak						
	FM	WA7UOJ	53.29000	51.59000	100.0 Hz	IACC
	FM	WA7UOJ	145.11000	-	118.8 Hz	IACC
	FM	WA7HWD	147.24000	+	127.3 Hz	IACC
	FM	W7OE	147.38000	+	100.0 Hz	IACC
Spokane, Mt. Spokane						
	FM	WR7VHF	444.60000	+	123.0 Hz	IACC
Spokane, Paradise Rim						
	FM	KG7SD	147.10000	+	100.0 Hz	IACC
Spokane, South Hill						
	FM	K7EKM	147.16000	+	136.5 Hz	IACC
	FM	N1NG	444.35000	+	192.8 Hz	UVHFS
Spokane, South Valley						
	FM	W7TRF	145.21000	-	100.0 Hz	IACC
Spokane, Spokane Airport						
	FM	K7MMA	444.45000	+	77.0 Hz	IACC
Spokane, Tower Mountain						
	FM	KA7ENA	145.37000	-	141.3 Hz	IACC
Sprague	FM	W7OHI	145.19000	-		IACC
Stanwood	DMR/BM	K7BLA	444.17500	+	CC1	
	FUSION	NT7X	145.67000			
	FUSION	KJ7FGG	147.36000	+		
Stehekin / Chelan	FM	K7SMX	146.80000	-	103.5 Hz	IACC
Sudden Valley	FM	WA7SV-R	442.75000	+		
Sultan	FM	W7SKY	53.35000	51.65000	100.0 Hz	
	FM	W7SKY	444.12500	+	103.5 Hz	
Sultan, Haystack	FM	W7WRG	224.58000	-	103.5 Hz	
Sultan, Haystack Lookout						
	FM	W7UFI	224.24000	-	103.5 Hz	
Sultan, Haystack Mountain						
	FM	WC7T	441.87500	+	103.5 Hz	
	FM	W2ZT	444.97500	+	114.8 Hz	
Sumner, White River Junction						
	FM	W7PSE	443.62500	+	103.5 Hz	
Sunbeach		N7CPM-L	146.51000			
		KG7NFF-L	147.49500			
Tacoma	DMR/MARC	KI7WIR	440.85000	+	CC1	
	DMR/MARC	AF7PR	440.92500	+	CC1	
	DMR/MARC	KG7KPH	441.42500	441.92500	CC1	
	DMR/MARC	WA7DMR	927.48750	952.48750	CC1	
	FM	K7HW	53.19000	51.49000	100.0 Hz	
	FM	KB7CNN	146.64000	-	103.5 Hz	
	FM	K7HW	146.94000	-	103.5 Hz	
	FM	W7TED	147.02000	+	103.5 Hz	
	FM	W7DK	147.28000	+	103.5 Hz	
	FM	KD7LXL	147.30000	+	88.5 Hz	
	FM	N3KPU	147.45000	146.45000		
	FM	K7HW	224.52000	-	103.5 Hz	
	FM	W7DK	440.62500	+	103.5 Hz	
	FM	W7TED	442.45000	+	103.5 Hz	
	FM	WW7MST	443.67500	+	103.5 Hz	
	FM	NB7N	446.35000	-	103.5 Hz	
	FM	KB7CNN	1292.40000	1272.40000	103.5 Hz	

Location	Mode	Call sign	Output	Input	Access	Coordinator
Tacoma	FUSION	K7ORV	146.55000			
	FUSION	AF7PR	441.65000	+		
Tacoma WA	DMR/BM	WA7DMR	440.72500	+	CC1	
Tacoma, Ch 28 Tower						
	FM	W7DK	145.21000	-	141.3 Hz	
Tacoma, Dash Point						
	FM	N7QOR	443.95000	+	131.8 Hz	
Tacoma, Madigan Army Medical C						
	FM	KE7YYD	442.75000	+	146.2 Hz	
Tenino, Crawford Mountain						
	FM	W7DK	147.38000	+	103.5 Hz	
	FM	NT7H	224.46000	-	103.5 Hz	
Tieton	FM	N7YRC	53.93000	52.23000		IACC
Tonasket	FM	W7ORC	145.47000	-	173.8 Hz	IACC
Tri-Cities	DMR/MARC	WA7DMR	147.41250	146.41250	CC1	
Trout Lake	DMR/MARC	N7LF	443.25000	+	CC1	
Trout Lake, King Mountain						
	FM	WA7SAR	147.08000	+	123.0 Hz	
Tukwila	DSTAR	KF7BFT B	440.42500	+		
Tukwila, Station 52						
	DSTAR	KF7BFT	440.42500	+		
Tulalip	DMR/MARC	KJ7ICL	442.35000	+	CC1	
	DMR/MARC	KJ7ICL	444.10000	+	CC1	
Tumwater	FM	N7EHP	147.12000	+	173.8 Hz	
Tumwater, Bush Mountain						
	FM	KD7HTE	927.75000	902.75000	114.8 Hz	
Twin Spits	FM	N7MTC-L	443.05000	+		
Twisp	DMR/MARC	NO7RF	444.85000	+	CC3	IACC
Twisp, McClure Mountain						
	FM	WA7MV	147.22000	+	100.0 Hz	
	FM	WA7MV	444.80000	+	110.9 Hz	IACC
Underwood, Underwood Mountain						
	FM	KB7DRX	147.20000	+	100.0 Hz	
University Place	FM	K7NP	53.01000	51.31000	100.0 Hz	
	FM	K7NP	145.29000	-	114.8 Hz	
	FM	K7NP	442.37500	+	103.5 Hz	
	FM	N7EHP	443.15000	+	173.8 Hz	
	FM	K7NP	927.60000	902.60000	114.8 Hz	
Vancouver	DMR/BM	K7KSN	440.22500	+	CC5	
	DMR/MARC	AF7PR	147.15000	+	CC1	
	DMR/MARC	W7NCX	434.00000	+	CC1	
	DMR/MARC	W7NCX	440.22500	+	CC1	
	DSTAR	K7CLL B	440.01250	+		
	FM	KB7APU	53.13000	51.43000	107.2 Hz	ORRC
	FM	AB7F	224.64000	-	123.0 Hz	ORRC
	FM	KB7APU	224.72000	-	100.0 Hz	ORRC
	FM	KB7APU	440.77500	+		ORRC
	FM	K7GJT	442.10000	+		
	FM	W7AIA	443.82500	+	94.8 Hz	
	FM	KB7APU	443.97500	+		ORRC
	FM	N7XMT	444.55000	+	131.8 Hz	ORRC
	FM	W7AIA	1292.50000	1272.50000	94.8 Hz	ORRC
	FUSION	KB7RQQ	145.65500			
	FUSION	KE7DUX	432.25000			
Vancouver, Larch Mountain						
	DSTAR	K7CLL	440.01250	+		
	FM	W7LT	146.84000	-	123.0 Hz	ORRC
	FM	AB7F	442.37500	+	123.0 Hz	ORRC
	FM	KE7FUW	443.67500	+	107.2 Hz	
	FM	W7AIA	443.90000	+	94.8 Hz	ORRC
	FM	K5TRA	927.13750	902.13750	131.8 Hz	ORRC

Location	Mode	Call sign	Output	Input	Access	Coordinator
Vancouver, Livingston Mountain						
	FM	AB7F	145.37000	-	123.0 Hz	ORRC
Vancouver--220 Mix Mode						
	DMR/MARC	KB7APU	224.00000	-	CC1	
Vancouver-DOWNTOWN-OPEN USE						
	DMR/MARC	KB7APU	927.15000	902.15000	CC1	
Vancouver-LIVINGSTON						
	DMR/MARC	KB7APU	442.95000	+	CC1	
Vancouver-sw Med Ctr						
	DMR/MARC	KB7APU	146.73000	-	CC1	
Vancouver-YACOLT						
	DMR/BM	KB7APU	442.96250	+	CC1	ORRC
Vashon Island	FM	W7VMI	443.50000	+	103.5 Hz	
	FM	KG7CM	443.77500	+	103.5 Hz	
Vaughn	FM	KF7SOV	223.76000	-	100.0 Hz	
Walla Walla	DMR/BM	N7DMR	445.30000	-	CC1	
	FM	AL1Q	146.96000	-	74.4 Hz	
	FM	KH6IHB	147.14000	+	94.8 Hz	
	FM	AL1Q	443.45000	+	123.0 Hz	IACC
	FM	KL7NA	444.25000	+		
Walla Walla, Hertzer Peak						
	FM	AL1Q	146.96000	-	74.4 Hz	
	FM	AL1Q	443.45000	+	123.0 Hz	
Washington	DSTAR	W3AGB D	1248.50000			
	DSTAR	W3AGB A	1283.10000	-		
Wauconda	FM	KH6UG	442.55000	+		
Wenatchee	DMR/MARC	N7RHT	443.75000	+	CC1	IACC
	FM	N7RHT	146.78000	-	156.7 Hz	
	FM	K7SRG	147.20000	+		IACC
Wenatchee, Mission Ridge						
	FM	WR7ADX	146.90000	-	173.8 Hz	
	FM	WR7ADX	224.74000	-	179.9 Hz	
Wenatchee, Naneum Ridge						
	FM	KB7TYR	147.26000	+	156.7 Hz	
West Richland	FM	WA7BCA	442.87500	+	203.5 Hz	
White Salmon	FM	NB7M	443.17500	+	88.5 Hz	ORRC
White Salmon, Near LDS Church						
	FM	KB7DRX	147.00000	+	100.0 Hz	
White Swan, Fort Simcoe						
	FM	KA7IJU	146.72000	-	123.0 Hz	
Wilderness Village						
	FM	KF7NPL-R	147.26000	+		
Winthrop	DMR/MARC	NO7RF	145.12500	147.12500	CC1	
	DMR/MARC	NO7RF	145.21000	147.99000	CC3	
	DMR/MARC	NO7RF	439.39000	449.39000	CC3	
	DMR/MARC	NO7RF	440.92500	449.92500	CC3	
	FM	NO7RF	146.52000		100.0 Hz	
Woodinville	FM	K6RFK	147.34000	+	100.0 Hz	
	FM	WA7TZY	442.77500	+	100.0 Hz	
Woodland	FM	N7XAC	224.30000	-	103.5 Hz	
	FM	K7LJ	444.47500	+	100.0 Hz	
Woodland, Fire Station						
	FM	W7DG	147.30000	+	114.8 Hz	
Woodland, Oil Can Henrys						
	FM	W7BO	442.17500	+		
Yacolt	FM	W7RY	440.32500	+	100.0 Hz	ORRC
	FM	W7AIA	443.12500	+	94.8 Hz	ORRC
Yacolt Mtn--or Sar	DMR/MARC	KB7APU	442.98750	+	CC9	
Yacolt, Yacolt Mountain						
	FM	W7AIA	52.95000	51.25000	94.8 Hz	ORRC
	FM	K7CLL	224.42000	-	94.8 Hz	
	FM	KC7NQU	441.20000	+	107.2 Hz	ORRC

Location	Mode	Call sign	Output	Input	Access	Coordinator
Yakima	DMR/MARC	WA7SAR	147.12000	+	CC1	
	DMR/MARC	W7AQ	224.90000	-	CC1	
	FM	K7SRG	147.20000	+		IACC
	FUSION	N7AWM	146.55000			
Yakima, Bethel Ridge						
	FM	W7AQ	147.30000	+	123.0 Hz	
Yakima, Darland Mountain						
	FM	WA7SAR	146.86000	-	123.0 Hz	
Yakima, Eagle Peak						
	FM	W7AQ	146.66000	-	123.0 Hz	
Yakima, Lookout Point						
	FM	N7YRC	444.75000	+	131.8 Hz	IACC
Yakima, West Rattlesnake Peak						
	FM	KC7IDX	444.55000	+		
Yakima, Yakima Valley						
	FM	WA7SAR	147.06000	+	85.4 Hz	
Zindel (historical)	FM	WF7L-L	446.05000	-		

WASHINGTON DC
NOAA Washington D.C.

	Mode	Call sign	Output	Input	Access	Coordinator
	WX	WNG736	162.45000			
Washington	DSTAR	W3AGB	1283.10000	1263.10000		T-MARC
	FM	K3MRC	145.43000	-	114.8 Hz	
	FM	N3ADV	447.17500	-	156.7 Hz	T-MARC
	FM	KC3VO	448.87500	-		T-MARC
	FM	W3HAC	449.42500	-		T-MARC
	FM	WA3KOK	449.97500	-	107.2 Hz	T-MARC
	P25	W3DCA	147.27000	+	100.0 Hz	T-MARC
	FUSION	WA6MPR/1	147.42000			
Washington, Harry S. Truman Bu						
	FM	W3DOS	145.19000	-	151.4 Hz	T-MARC
Washington, Union Station						
	FM	K3WS	447.37500	-	123.0 Hz	T-MARC
Washington, Wilbur J. Cohen Bu						
	FM	K3VOA	147.04500	+	77.0 Hz	T-MARC
	FM	K3VOA	448.57500	-	77.0 Hz	T-MARC

WEST VIRGINIA

Location	Mode	Call sign	Output	Input	Access	Coordinator
Alderson	DMR/MARC	KC8AFH	442.87500	+	CC1	SERA
	FM	KE4QOX	53.23000	52.23000	123.0 Hz	
Alderson, Keeney Knob						
	FM	KD8BBO	146.76000	-	162.2 Hz	SERA
Ansted	DMR/BM	KC8OGK	444.27500	+	CC1	
Beckley	DMR/BM	K8DLT	440.51250	+	CC1	
	DSTAR	W8ARA C	145.23000	-		
	DSTAR	W8ARA B	444.80000	+		
	FM	N8FWL	147.36000	+		
	FM	N8FWL	443.05000	+		
	FM	W8VT-R	443.80000	+		SERA
Beckley, IVY Knob						
	FM	KC8AFH	444.85000	+		SERA
Belington	DMR/BM	KX8T	444.35000	+	CC1	
	FM	N8SCS	53.65000	52.65000	141.3 Hz	
	FM	KC8AJH	145.23000	-	103.5 Hz	SERA
	FM	N8SCS	444.90000	+	141.3 Hz	
Bellaire		K8JRG-L	146.76000			
Berkeley Springs	FM	WA3KOK	442.45000	+	107.2 Hz	T-MARC
	FM	KK3L	443.85000	+	123.0 Hz	
	FM	K7SOB	444.75000	+	127.3 Hz	SERA
Berkeley Springs, Cacapon Moun						
	FM	KK3L	146.74500	-	123.0 Hz	T-MARC
	FM	W3VLG	224.70000	-	123.0 Hz	

Location	Mode	Call sign	Output	Input	Access	Coordinator
Berkeley Springs/Romney						
	FM	N8RAT	444.95000	+	123.0 Hz	T-MARC
Birch River	FM	N8FMD	145.27000	-	103.5 Hz	SERA
Bluefield	FM	WZ8E	146.95500	-	100.0 Hz	
	FM	W8MOP	442.45000	+	103.5 Hz	SERA
Bluefield, East River Mountain						
	FM	W8MOP	145.49000	-	103.5 Hz	SERA
Bluefield, Windmill Gap						
	FM	W8MOP	147.06000	-	103.5 Hz	SERA
Bolt	DMR/MARC	W8LG	443.22500	+	CC1	
Bolt, Ivy Knob	FM	KC8AFH	145.17000	-	100.0 Hz	
Bridgeport	FM	W8SLH	147.12000	+	118.8 Hz	
Bruceton Mills	DMR/BM	KC8TAI	444.56250	+	CC1	
Buckhannon	DMR/BM	W8LD	442.67500	+	CC1	
	FM	N8ZAR	53.11000	52.11000	103.5 Hz	SERA
	FM	K8VE	146.85000	-		
	FM	N8ZAR	147.03000	+	103.5 Hz	SERA
	FM	K8VE	444.47500	+	146.2 Hz	
Buckhannon, West Virginia Wesl						
	FM	W8LD	145.41000	-	103.5 Hz	SERA
Cameron	FM	KC8FZH	146.91000	-	123.0 Hz	SERA
Charles Town	FM	WV8VRC	441.95000	+		T-MARC
	FM	W3VLG	442.65000	+	79.7 Hz	
	FM	N3EAQ	444.35000	+		T-MARC
	FUSION	W3VLG	145.48000	-		
	FUSION	W3VLG	145.56250			
Charleston	FM	W8GK	145.35000	-	91.5 Hz	
	FM	W8GK	444.20000	+	91.5 Hz	
	FM	WB8CQV	444.95000	+	203.5 Hz	
Charleston, Kanawha City						
	FM	WB8YST	444.35000	+	107.2 Hz	SERA
Charleston, Middle Ridge Of Da						
	FM	W8KTM	147.18000	+	91.5 Hz	
	FM	W8KTM	444.40000	+	91.5 Hz	
Charleston, Nitro	FM	WB8YST	224.36000	-	107.2 Hz	SERA
Chestnut Knob, Man Mountain						
	FM	N8LVE	444.12500	+	107.2 Hz	
Circleville, Spruce Knob						
	FM	N8HON	147.28500	+	103.5 Hz	
Clarksburg	FM	N8FMD	146.68500	-	103.5 Hz	SERA
	FM	WV8HC	147.16500	+		
	FM	N8FMD	147.21000	+		
	FM	N8FMD	444.17500	+		SERA
	FUSION	WB8P	145.60000			
	FUSION	K8DF	147.21000	+		
	FUSION	K1WVA	437.50000			
Cowen	FM	KC8ECX	146.83500	-	110.9 Hz	
Craigsville	FM	KC8LRN	224.48000	-	91.5 Hz	
Crawford, Union Hill						
	FM	W8OO	145.13000	-	103.5 Hz	SERA
	FM	W8OO	147.06000	+	103.5 Hz	SERA
Danese, Man Mountain, Chestnut						
	FM	WV8B	145.31000	-	100.0 Hz	
Danville, Drawdy Mountain						
	FM	W8NAM	147.12000	+	203.5 Hz	SERA
Danville, WZAC Tower						
	FM	W8NAM	146.68500	-	203.5 Hz	SERA
Davis	FM	KC8AJH	147.13500	+	103.5 Hz	SERA
Droop, Briary Knob NNW Of Droo						
	FM	N8KUK	147.39000	+	100.0 Hz	
Dry Fork	FM	WV8ZH	29.64000	-	162.2 Hz	
Eglon	FUSION	KE8UXX	147.54000			

Location	Mode	Call sign	Output	Input	Access	Coordinator
Elkins	FM	WV8ZH	53.03000	52.03000	162.2 Hz	
	FM	WV8ZH	145.21000	-	162.2 Hz	
	FM	K8VE	146.74500	-	103.5 Hz	
	FM	KB8BWZ	146.77500	-		
	FM	N8RLR	444.85000	+	162.2 Hz	SERA
Elkins, Rich Mountain						
	FM	KD8JCS	442.10000	+	162.2 Hz	
Fairmont	FM	W8SP	443.87500	+	103.5 Hz	
Fairmont, Valley Falls State P						
	FM	W8SP	145.35000	-	103.5 Hz	SERA
Fayetteville, Gauley Mountain						
	FM	KC8ZQZ	146.79000	-		SERA
Flat Top	FM	WV8B	224.12000	-	100.0 Hz	
	FM	WV8B	927.52500	902.52500		
Flat Top, Huff Knob						
	FM	WV8B	146.62500	-	100.0 Hz	
Franklin	FM	KC8FPC	147.34500	+		
Frost	FM	N8RV	145.11000	-	107.2 Hz	
Gilbert	DMR/MARC	KB8PCW	442.72500	+	CC1	
Glenmore		AD8T-L	146.55000			
Glenville	FM	WB8WV	145.29000	-	91.5 Hz	
	FM	KA8ZXP	444.32500	+		
Grafton	FM	W8SLH	147.37500	+	103.5 Hz	
	FM	W8SLH	444.75000	+	118.8 Hz	SERA
	FUSION	KE8QZZ	146.06500	+		
Green Bank	FM	KC8CSE	224.52000	-	123.0 Hz	
Hambleton	FUSION	AC8HQ	444.67500	+		
Hamlin	FM	N8IKT	443.95000	+	123.0 Hz	
Hernshaw	FM	WB8CQV	146.82000	-	203.5 Hz	
	FM	WB8CQV	444.70000	+	203.5 Hz	
Hillsboro	FM	KC8LRN	224.22000	-	91.5 Hz	
Hillsboro, Droop Mountain						
	FM	W3ATE	145.33000	-	136.5 Hz	
Hinton	FM	KC8CNL	147.25500	+	100.0 Hz	
	FM	KC8CNL	443.90000	+	100.0 Hz	
Horner	FM	WV8CW	145.75000			
	FM	WV8CW	145.90000	145.75000		
	FM	WV8CW	147.34000	+		
Horse Pen Mount	FM	KB8PCW	146.85000	-	100.0 Hz	SERA
Huntington	DMR/MARC	KB8TGK	443.55000	+	CC1	
Huntington, Barkers Ridge						
	FM	N8HZ	146.64000	-		
Huntington, Rotary Park						
	FM	W8VA	146.76000	-	131.8 Hz	
Huntington, Veterans Medical C						
	FM	N8OLC	146.98500	-	131.8 Hz	
Hurricane	FUSION	NY8S	431.50000	+		
Iaeger	FM	N8SNW	146.65500	-	100.0 Hz	SERA
Imperial Estates		AC8JA-L	146.55000			
Kanawha City, Kanawha City						
	FM	WB8YST	145.43000	-	107.2 Hz	SERA
Kenna, Kenna Water Tower						
	FM	WD8JNU	443.72500	+	127.3 Hz	SERA
Kenova	FM	KC8PFI	53.87000	52.87000	91.5 Hz	
Keyser	FM	WV8BS	444.12500	+	103.5 Hz	SERA
Lenore	FM	AI4UK	145.39000	-	100.0 Hz	
Letart, Missile Tree Hill						
	FM	KC8MNR	444.80000	+	100.0 Hz	SERA
Lewisburg	DMR/MARC	KE8DID	444.25000	+	CC1	
Lick Knob, Paint Mountain						
	FM	N8FWL	145.23000	-		
Little Rock	FM	N8ZAR-R	444.25000	+		

Location	Mode	Call sign	Output	Input	Access	Coordinator
Lobelia, Briery Knob						
	FM	KC8CSE	224.60000	-	123.0 Hz	
Logan	DMR/MARC	KB8PCW	444.43750	+	CC1	SERA
Logan, Ward Rock Mountain						
	FM	W8LOG	146.97000	-	100.0 Hz	
Madison, Workman's Knob						
	FM	WV8CCC	442.55000	+	100.0 Hz	SERA
Marietta	FM	W8JTW	223.50000	-		
Marlinton, Sharp Knob						
	FM	N8PKP	147.09000	+	162.2 Hz	
Martinsburg	FM	W8ORS	145.15000	-	179.9 Hz	T-MARC
	FM	WB8YZV	147.25500	+	123.0 Hz	T-MARC
	FM	K1LLS	442.70000	+		
Martinsburg, North Mountain						
	FM	N8RAT	442.85000	+	100.0 Hz	T-MARC
McCuetown		WV8CW-L	146.36000			
Middlebourne	FM	WV8TC	147.36000	+	110.9 Hz	
Millwood, Evergreen Hill						
	FM	KD8OOF	145.49000	-	123.0 Hz	SERA
	FM	KD8OOF	443.50000	+		SERA
Moorefield	FM	N8VAA	145.19000	-	118.8 Hz	T-MARC
	FM	K7SOB	442.40000	+	127.3 Hz	
Moorefield, Branch Mountain						
	FM	KD8IFP	146.98500	-	123.0 Hz	T-MARC
	FM	KD8AZC	447.32500	-	103.5 Hz	SERA
Moorefield, Brnach Mountain						
	FM	KD8IFP	444.40000	+	103.5 Hz	SERA
Moorefield, Nathanial Wildlife						
	FM	N8RAT	442.50000	+	123.0 Hz	T-MARC
Morgantown	DMR/BM	W8CUL	440.63750	+	CC1	SERA
	DMR/BM	KD8YNY	441.92500	+	CC1	SERA
	FM	W8MWA	145.43000	-		
	FM	AA8CC	146.42000			
	FM	AA8CC	146.92500	-	103.5 Hz	
	FM	KD8BMI	147.07500	+	103.5 Hz	
	FM	W8MWA	444.70000	+		
Morgantown, Chestnut Ridge						
	FM	K8MCR	442.60000	+		
Morgantown, WVU Engineering Sc						
	FM	W8CUL	146.76000	-	103.5 Hz	
	FM	W8CUL	444.80000	+	103.5 Hz	
Mossy	DMR/MARC	KC8AFH	443.87500	+	CC1	SERA
Moundsville	FUSION	KC8FZH	146.91000	-		
Moundsville, Grand Vue State P						
	FM	KC8FZH	146.71500	-	110.9 Hz	
	FM	KC8FZH	441.95000	+	123.0 Hz	
	FM	KC8FZH	444.07500	+	123.0 Hz	SERA
Mount Hope, Garden Grounds						
	DSTAR	WV8BSA	441.81250	+		
Mt Zion	FM	N8LGY	145.45000	-	107.2 Hz	
Mullens	FM	KC8IT	147.03000	+		
New Martinsville	FM	KF8LL	146.98500	-		
Newell	FM	W8LPN	442.30000	+	162.2 Hz	
NOAA Backbone Mountain						
	WX	KXI73	162.45000			
NOAA Beckley	WX	WXM71	162.55000			
NOAA Charleston	WX	WXJ84	162.40000			
NOAA Clarksburg	WX	WXJ85	162.55000			
NOAA Garfield	WX	WXM70	162.50000			
NOAA Gilbert	WX	WXM75	162.47500			
NOAA Greggs Knob						
	WX	KWN36	162.50000			

Location	Mode	Call sign	Output	Input	Access	Coordinator
NOAA Hinton	WX	WXM72	162.42500			
NOAA Monterville	WX	KXI74	162.52500			
NOAA Moorefield	WX	WXM73	162.40000			
NOAA Morgantown						
	WX	KWN35	162.47500			
NOAA Sutton	WX	WXM74	162.45000			
Old Fields	DMR/BM	KD8AZC	447.87500	-	CC1	
Parkersburg	FM	WD8CYV	147.39000	+	91.5 Hz	
Parkersburg, Sand Hill						
	FM	WC8EC	147.25500	+	131.8 Hz	SERA
	FM	WA8LLM	443.17500	+	146.2 Hz	SERA
Parsons	FM	KD8MIV	145.37000	-		SERA
	FM	KD8MIV	444.67500	+	103.5 Hz	SERA
Pennsboro	FM	WV8RAG	147.30000	+	107.2 Hz	
	FM	WB8NSL	442.85000	+	103.5 Hz	
Philippi	FM	K8VE	145.15000	-	103.5 Hz	
	FUSION	AD8DA	438.80000			
Poe	FM	W3ATE-R	147.31500	+		SERA
Pt. Pleasant, Water Tower On J						
	FM	KE8COT	442.40000	+	91.5 Hz	
Richwood	FM	WB8YST	53.71000	52.71000	107.2 Hz	
	FM	WA8YWO	53.83000	52.83000	100.0 Hz	SERA
	FM	WB8YJJ	145.19000	-	146.2 Hz	
	FM	KB8YDG	147.15000	+	100.0 Hz	
	FM	WB8YST	223.86000	-	107.2 Hz	
	FM	KC8SDN	443.37500	+	100.0 Hz	SERA
Richwood, Grasshopper Knob						
	FM	W8TFC	147.01500	+		SERA
Ripley, Ripley 911 Tower						
	FM	WD8JNU	146.67000	-	107.2 Hz	
Rock Branch, Nitro 1,000 AGL P						
	FM	AB8DY	444.50000	+	151.4 Hz	
Rockport	FM	KC8LTG	147.13500	+	123.0 Hz	SERA
Saint ALBANS	DMR/BM	N1DTA	146.71500	-	CC1	
	DMR/BM	N1DTA	444.57500	+	CC1	
Saint Joseph, German Settlemen						
	FM	KC8FZH	444.87500	+	123.0 Hz	
Salt Rock	FM	K8SA-R	145.11000	-		SERA
Scott Depot	FM	WV8AR	441.82500	+	123.0 Hz	SERA
Scott Depot, Coal Mountain						
	FM	WV8AR	147.27000	+		
Shirley	FM	KB8TJH	53.31000	52.31000		
	FM	KB8TJH	145.31000	-		
	FM	KB8TJH	444.42500	+		
Skyline	FM	K7SOB	147.36000	+	127.3 Hz	SERA
Snowshoe	FM	KC8CSE	53.33000	52.33000	156.7 Hz	SERA
South Charleston	FM	WB8CQV	146.88000	-		
	FUSION	W8XRW	440.85000			
	FUSION	KE8LSN	441.82500			
	FUSION	W8XRW	446.50000			
Stanaford	FM	KD8PIQ	443.40000	+	67.0 Hz	SERA
Stonewood	FM	KD8TC	443.27500	+	91.5 Hz	
Sugar Grove	FUSION	WV8MT	146.59000			
Sumerco	DMR/MARC	KB8PCW	440.52500	+	CC1	
Sumerco, Buck Knob						
	FM	KD8CVI	147.34500	+	100.0 Hz	
Summersville	DMR/MARC	KC8AFH	444.10000	+	CC1	
	FM	KE4QOX	29.66000	-	88.5 Hz	SERA
	FM	N8YHK	145.47000	-	100.0 Hz	
Sutton	FM	W8COX	224.40000	-	123.0 Hz	
Terra Alta	FM	KC8KCI	147.00000	+	103.5 Hz	
Thomas	FM	K7SOB	441.90000	+	103.5 Hz	

Location	Mode	Call sign	Output	Input	Access	Coordinator
Valley Head	FM	KC8AJH	146.67000	-	103.5 Hz	
Webster Springs	FM	KC8HFG	146.89500	-	123.0 Hz	
	FM	KC8CSE	224.66000	-	123.0 Hz	
Weirton	DMR/BM	KE8EOD	146.65500	-	CC1	
Weirton, Weirton Medical Cente						
	FUSION	W8CWO	146.94000	-	114.8 Hz	T-MARC
Welch	FM	WV8ED	145.45000	-	100.0 Hz	
	FM	KE8BRP	147.33000	+	100.0 Hz	
	FM	N8SNY	443.72500	+		
West Union	FM	K8DCA	146.95500	-	103.5 Hz	
Weston	FM	WD8EOM	145.39000	-		
	FM	N8MIN	443.97500	+	123.0 Hz	
Wharton, Pilot Knob, Bolt Mtn.						
	FM	WV8CCC	147.19500	+	100.0 Hz	
Wheeling	FM	KA8YEZ	145.19000	-	156.7 Hz	
	FM	W8ZQ	146.76000	-	67.0 Hz	SERA
	FM	KA8YEZ	443.02500	+	156.7 Hz	
	FM	N8EKT	444.97500	+		
	FUSION	KE8ICS	146.71500	-		
Wheeling, Mount Olivet						
	FM	W8MSD	444.57500	+	156.7 Hz	
Williamson, EKB Tower						
	FM	KB8QEU	145.33000	-	127.3 Hz	SERA
	FM	KB8QEU	224.14000	-	127.3 Hz	SERA
	FM	KB8QEU	443.20000	+	127.3 Hz	SERA
Winchester	FM	N8RAT	443.20000	+	123.0 Hz	T-MARC

WISCONSIN

Location	Mode	Call sign	Output	Input	Access	Coordinator
Adams	DSTAR	AC9AR	442.26875	+		WAR
	DSTAR	AC9AR B	442.26875	+		
	FM	AC9AR	147.03000	+	123.0 Hz	WAR
Allenton	DMR/MARC	W9RCG	442.03125	+	CC9	
	FM	N9GMT	442.35000	+	123.0 Hz	WAR
Amberg	FM	WI9WIN	443.70000	+	100.0 Hz	WAR
Antigo	FM	W9SM	145.31000	-	114.8 Hz	WAR
	FM	W9SM	147.25500	+	114.8 Hz	
	FM	N9TEV	147.31500	+	114.8 Hz	WAR
Appleton	DMR/BM	N9KRG	444.05000	+	CC6	WAR
	FM	K9STN	145.15000	-	100.0 Hz	WAR
	FM	KB9BYP	146.65500	-	100.0 Hz	WAR
	FM	W9ZL	146.76000	-	100.0 Hz	WAR
	FM	W9ZL	443.65000	+	100.0 Hz	WAR
	FM	N9KRG	445.92500		107.2 Hz	
	FUSION	W9ZL	145.33000	-		
	FUSION	KD9QHQ	145.51000			
	FUSION	WJ9K	442.17500	+		
Appleton, Darboy	FM	WJ9K	224.50000	-	100.0 Hz	WAR
Arlington	FM	KC9HEA	443.35000	+	123.0 Hz	WAR
Baldwin	DMR/BM	N9UPC	443.75000	+	CC4	
	FM	WE9COM	145.25000	-	110.9 Hz	WAR
	FM	N9UPC	442.22500	447.32500	110.9 Hz	WAR
	FUSION	N9UPC	147.49375			
	FUSION	N9UPC	443.22500	+		
Balsam Lake	FM	N9XH-R	147.19500	+		WAR
	FM	N9XH	443.72500	+	110.9 Hz	WAR
Baraboo	DMR/MARC	W9RCG	442.11875	+	CC9	
	DSTAR	WB9FDZ C	145.31500	-		
	FM	WR9ABE	146.88000	-	123.0 Hz	WAR
	FM	N9BDR	443.57500	+	123.0 Hz	WAR
	FM	WI9WIN	443.90000	+	77.0 Hz	WAR
	FM	N9GMT	444.50000	+	123.0 Hz	WAR

Location	Mode	Call sign	Output	Input	Access	Coordinator
Baraboo, Baraboo Bluffs						
	DSTAR	WB9FDZ	145.31500	-		WAR
	FM	WB9FDZ	147.31500	+	123.0 Hz	WAR
Baraboo, City EOC						
	FM	KC9MIO	443.82500	+	123.0 Hz	WAR
Barron	FM	KD9EJA	443.65000	+		WAR
Barronett	FM	N9PHS	147.04500	+	110.9 Hz	WAR
Bay City	DSTAR	KB9LUK	145.21000	-		
Bayfield	FM	N0BZZ	146.70000	-	103.5 Hz	WAR
	FM	N0BZZ	443.85000	+		WAR
Beetown	DMR/BM	KD9HAE	443.20000	+	CC2	
	FM	N0WLU	146.89500	-	114.8 Hz	
Beldenville	FM	W0MDT	147.22500	+		
Beloit	FM	WA9JTX	147.12000	+	123.0 Hz	WAR
Black River Falls	FM	KC9GEA	145.39000	-		
	FM	WI9WIN	443.55000	+	131.8 Hz	WAR
Bloomer	FM	W9EJH	145.47000	-	110.9 Hz	
	FM	W9EJH	433.20000		100.0 Hz	
	FM	W9EJH	445.95000	-	110.9 Hz	
Bloomer, Home Shop						
	FM	W9EJH	146.65500	-	110.9 Hz	WAR
Boscobel	FM	WI9WIN	444.45000	+	131.8 Hz	
Brooklyn	FM	K9QB	29.65000	-	123.0 Hz	
	FM	K9QB	145.17000	-	123.0 Hz	
	FM	K9QB	224.06000	-	123.0 Hz	WAR
	FM	K9QB	927.33750	902.33750	123.0 Hz	
Brothertown	DMR/BM	KC9HYC	444.51870	+	CC6	
Brussels	FM	WE9COM	146.80500	-	146.2 Hz	
	FM	W9DOR	444.00000	+	107.2 Hz	WAR
Burlington	DMR/MARC	WB9COW	442.84375	+	CC9	
	DMR/MARC	WB9COW	442.85000	+	CC9	WAR
Cambria	FM	KC9CZH	147.01500	+	123.0 Hz	WAR
Cedarburg	FM	W9CQO	146.97000	-	127.3 Hz	WAR
	FM	W9CQO	224.18000	-	127.3 Hz	WAR
	FM	K9QLP	442.10000	+	127.3 Hz	WAR
	FUSION	KC9ONY	442.77500	+		
	FUSION	W9DHI	444.97500	+		
Chaffey	FM	KC9EMI	147.10500	+	110.9 Hz	WAR
	FM	KC9AEG	444.95000	+	110.9 Hz	WAR
Chilton	DMR/BM	KC9HYC	442.77500	+	CC6	
	FM	KD9TZ	444.80000	+	107.2 Hz	WAR
	FUSION	K9ZIE	147.47000			
Chippewa Falls	DSTAR	KD9ICN C	146.94000	-		
	DSTAR	KD9ICN	146.94000	-		WAR
	FM	AA9JL	145.23000	-	110.9 Hz	WAR
	FM	W9CVA	147.37500	+	110.9 Hz	WAR
	FM	AA9JL	147.42000		110.9 Hz	
Clam Lake	FM	K9JWM-R	145.21000	-		WAR
Clinton	FM	WB9SHS	146.71500	-	123.0 Hz	WAR
	FM	W9MUP	224.48000	-	123.0 Hz	
	FM	WB9SHS	443.17500	+		WAR
Colfax	FM	W9RMA	444.35000	+	110.9 Hz	WAR
Coloma	DMR/MARC	W9RCG	442.23125	+	CC8	
	FM	W9LTA	146.70000	-	123.0 Hz	WAR
	FM	WE9COM	147.10500	-	123.0 Hz	WAR
	FM	W9LTA	442.67500	+	123.0 Hz	WAR
Cumberland		W9ABA-R	444.45000			
	DMR/BM	KD9EJA	443.50000	+	CC4	
	FM	KD9EJA	145.39000	-	110.9 Hz	
Dacada		K9KEA-R	927.61200			
Delafield	FM	K9ABC	146.82000	-	127.3 Hz	WAR
	FM	K9ABC	444.12500	+	127.3 Hz	WAR

Location	Mode	Call sign	Output	Input	Access	Coordinator
Delafield, HWY C And I-94						
	FM	N9GMT	440.30000	+	123.0 Hz	WAR
DePere	DMR/MARC	KC9UHI	442.83125	+	CC6	
Dodgeville	FM	WE9COM	145.23000	-	123.0 Hz	WAR
Dunnville	DSTAR	WW9RS C	146.88000	-		
	DSTAR	WW9RS	146.88000	-		WAR
Durand	FM	WB9NTO	145.35000	-	110.9 Hz	WAR
	FM	WW9RS	443.40000	+	110.9 Hz	WAR
East Farmington	FM	KC9NVV	144.39000			
East Troy	FM	N9WMN	440.77500	+	127.3 Hz	WAR
Eau Claire	FM	W9EAU	146.91000	-	110.9 Hz	WAR
	FM	WI9WIN	442.80000	+	110.9 Hz	WAR
	FM	KB9R	443.30000	+	110.9 Hz	WAR
	FM	N9QWH	927.60000	902.60000	110.9 Hz	WAR
Eau Galle	DMR/BM	WW9RS	442.62500	+	CC13	WAR
	FM	WW9RS	145.21000	-	173.8 Hz	WAR
Edgerton	FM	WI9WIN	442.30000	+	123.0 Hz	WAR
Egg Harbor	FM	W9AIQ	146.73000	-	107.2 Hz	WAR
Elcho	FUSION	KC9AOE	146.55000			
Elkhorn	FM	WI9ELK	146.86500	-	127.3 Hz	WAR
Elm Tree Corners		AL7RH-L	147.52500			
Evansville	FM	WB9RSQ	442.32500	+	123.0 Hz	WAR
Fitchburg	FM	KA9VDU	53.23000	51.53000	123.0 Hz	WAR
	FM	KA9VDU	444.00000	+	123.0 Hz	WAR
Fond Du Lac	DMR/MARC	KB9LQC	443.19375	+	CC12	
	DSTAR	KD9GXT	145.34500	-		
	DSTAR	KD9GXT C	145.34500	+		
	FM	K9FDL	145.43000	-		
	FM	K9DJB	147.09000	+	107.2 Hz	WAR
	FM	KC9RUE	147.18000	+	146.2 Hz	WAR
	FM	KC9RUE	223.90000	-	107.2 Hz	
	FM	WI9WIN	442.40000	+	100.0 Hz	WAR
	FM	N9WQ	443.87500	+		WAR
	FM	N9GMT	444.60000	+	123.0 Hz	WAR
Fontana	FM	N9ZXP	443.70000	+	123.0 Hz	WAR
Foxboro	DMR/BM	AB9AC	444.90000	+	CC4	
Franklin	DMR/MARC	N9OIG	443.43125	+	CC9	
	FUSION	AB9DW	445.55000			
Fremont	FUSION	N9AOT	445.75000			
Galesville	FM	N9TUU	147.00000	+	131.8 Hz	WAR
	FM	WI9WIN	442.50000	+	131.8 Hz	WAR
Germantown	FM	W9CQ	442.87500	+	127.3 Hz	WAR
	FM	WD9IEV-R	444.52500	+		WAR
Gillett, Jct 22-32	FM	W0LFE	444.22500	+	107.2 Hz	WAR
Gilmanton	FM	WE9COM	145.43000	-	131.8 Hz	WAR
Glenwood City	FM	N9LIE	145.27000	-	110.9 Hz	WAR
	FM	N9LIE	444.67500	+	110.9 Hz	WAR
Grafton	DSTAR	W9FRG	145.22500	-		
	DSTAR	W9FRG C	145.22500	-		
	DSTAR	W9FRG	442.81875	+		
	DSTAR	W9FRG B	442.81875	+		
	DSTAR	W9FRG A	1282.15000	-		
	DSTAR	W9FRG	1282.15000	1262.15000		
	DSTAR	W9FRG D	1297.50000			
Granite Quarry (historical)						
	FM	W9GAP-R	146.92500	-		WAR
	FM	N5IIA-R	444.90000	+		WAR
Granton	FM	N9RRF	146.77500	-	114.8 Hz	WAR
Green Bay	DMR/MARC	N9PAY	443.50000	+	CC6	
	DSTAR	K9EAM	444.20625	+		
	DSTAR	K9EAM B	444.20625	+		
	FM	KB9GKC	146.68500	-	107.2 Hz	

Location	Mode	Call sign	Output	Input	Access	Coordinator
Green Bay	FM	N9DKH	147.07500	+	107.2 Hz	
	FM	K9GB	147.12000	+	107.2 Hz	WAR
	FM	K9EAM	147.36000	+	100.0 Hz	WAR
	FM	K9JQE-R	223.94000	-		WAR
	FM	N9GMT	442.80000	+	123.0 Hz	
	FM	WI9WIN	443.40000	+	100.0 Hz	WAR
	FM	KB9AMM	443.50000	+	107.2 Hz	WAR
	FM	KB9GKC	444.55000	+	107.2 Hz	WAR
	FM	K9EAM	444.77500	+	107.2 Hz	WAR
	FUSION	N9BC	440.77500	+		
Greenville	FUSION	ND9DW	433.10000			
	FUSION	ND9DW	446.30000			
Hales Corners	FM	W9JOL	443.42500	+	127.3 Hz	WAR
Hancock	FM	WI9WIN	442.72500	+	123.0 Hz	WAR
Hayward	DMR/BM	N9UPC	443.75000	+	CC3	
	FM	N9UPC	147.25500	+	110.9 Hz	WAR
High Bridge	FM	KC9GSK	147.21000	+	110.9 Hz	WAR
Highland Shore	FM	KC9SDK-R	147.24000	+	100.0 Hz	
Holcombe	FM	N9LIE	52.81000	51.11000	110.9 Hz	WAR
	FM	N9LIE	145.47000	-	110.9 Hz	WAR
	FM	N9LIE	444.52500	+	110.9 Hz	WAR
Holcombe, Holcomb Hill						
	FM	AA9JL	147.34500	+	136.5 Hz	WAR
Hollandale	DSTAR	WI9WIN	147.28500	+		WAR
	DSTAR	WI9WIN C	147.28500	+		
	FM	WI9WIN	444.55000	+	123.0 Hz	WAR
Hudson	FM	N9UPC	145.13000	-	110.9 Hz	WAR
	FUSION	N9TOW	147.22500	+		
Irma	FM	KB9QJN	146.64000	-		WAR
	FM	WE9COM	146.89500	-	114.8 Hz	WAR
	FM	KC9NW	146.97000	-	71.9 Hz	WAR
	FM	KB9QJN	442.77500	+	114.8 Hz	WAR
Janesville	FM	WB9SHS	145.45000	-	123.0 Hz	
	FM	K9FRY	147.07500	+	123.0 Hz	WAR
	FM	K9TSU-R	147.34500	+		
	FM	KC9KUM	443.22500	+	123.0 Hz	WAR
	FUSION	K9GJN	146.71500	-		
	FUSION	KC9RLI	444.00000			
Jefferson	FM	W9MQB	145.49000	-	123.0 Hz	WAR
Juneau	FM	W9TCH	146.64000	-	123.0 Hz	WAR
Kaukauna	FM	ND9Z	444.45000	+	100.0 Hz	WAR
Kenosha	DMR/MARC	W2WAY	927.88750	902.88750	CC9	
Kewaskum	FM	N9NLU-R	146.79000	-		WAR
	FM	N9NLU	444.27500	+	127.3 Hz	WAR
Kimberly	FM	W9ZL-R	145.33000	-		WAR
Knapp/Menomonie						
	DMR/MARC	W8JWW	442.27500	+	CC1	
La Crosse	FM	AB9TS	444.47500	+	131.8 Hz	WAR
	FUSION	W9UP	146.97000	-		
La Crosse, Downtown						
	FM	N0EXE	444.75000	+	131.8 Hz	
La Pointe	P25	KB9QJN	146.82000	-		WAR
Lac Du Flambeau	FM	W9BTN	146.70000	-	114.8 Hz	WAR
LaCrosse	FM	N9ETD	147.09000	+	131.8 Hz	
Lake Geneva	DMR/MARC	KB9LTE	442.12500	+	CC9	WAR
	FM	N9GMT	441.52500	+	123.0 Hz	WAR
Lake Hallie		N9QWH-L	146.55000			
Lake Tomahawk	DSTAR	KC9ZJF	147.59000			
	DSTAR	KC9ZJF	446.42500	-		
Lampson	FM	N9PHS	146.97000	-	110.9 Hz	WAR
Land O Lakes	FUSION	W9VRC	145.39000	-		
Lisbon	FM	KC9HBO	444.22500	+	151.4 Hz	WAR

Location	Mode	Call sign	Output	Input	Access	Coordinator
Madison	DMR/BM	W9YT	443.60000	+	CC9	WAR
	DMR/MARC	W9RCG	442.57500	+	CC9	WAR
	DMR/MARC	KD8DRG	444.20000	+	CC7	
	DSTAR	W9HSY	145.30500	-		WAR
	DSTAR	W9HSY C	145.30500	-		
	FM	N9KAN	53.07000	51.37000	103.5 Hz	WAR
	FM	WD8DAS	53.15000	51.45000	123.0 Hz	WAR
	FM	KC9FNM	145.37000	-	123.0 Hz	WAR
	FM	W9YT	146.68500	-	123.0 Hz	WAR
	FM	WR9ABE	146.94000	-	123.0 Hz	WAR
	FM	W9HSY	147.15000	+	123.0 Hz	
	FM	WD8DAS	147.18000	+	107.2 Hz	WAR
	FM	WB9RSQ	224.16000	-	123.0 Hz	WAR
	FM	WD8DAS	224.18000	-		
	FM	WI9WIN	441.40000	+	123.0 Hz	WAR
	FM	N9KAN	443.40000	+	123.0 Hz	WAR
	FM	N9BDR	444.37500	+	123.0 Hz	WAR
	FM	KB9DRZ	444.57500	+	123.0 Hz	WAR
	FM	NG9V	444.77500	+	123.0 Hz	WAR
	FUSION	KC9TS	145.79000			
Madison, Beltline	FM	N9GMT	444.47500	+	123.0 Hz	WAR
Madison, Capital Square						
	FM	N9EM	442.55000	+		WAR
	IDAS	N9EM	145.15000	-	123.0 Hz	WAR
Madison, University Wisconsin						
	FM	WI9HF	443.77500	+	123.0 Hz	WAR
Madison, UW Hospital						
	FM	W9HSY	146.76000	-	123.0 Hz	WAR
Manitowish Waters						
	FM	KB9WCK	145.39000	-	114.8 Hz	WAR
Manitowoc	FM	W9DK	146.61000	-	107.2 Hz	WAR
	FM	W9RES	146.89500	-	146.2 Hz	
	FM	W9RES	443.15000	+	100.0 Hz	WAR
Marinette	FM	AB9PJ	444.50000	+	146.2 Hz	WAR
Markesan	FM	WB9RBC	146.95500	-	123.0 Hz	WAR
Marshfield	DSTAR	KD9FUR	147.04500	+		WAR
	DSTAR	KD9FUR C	147.04500	+		
	FM	AA9US	147.18000	+	114.8 Hz	WAR
	FM	WI9WIN	444.85000	+	114.8 Hz	WAR
Mauston	FM	KB9WQF	146.85000	-	123.0 Hz	WAR
Medford	DMR/BM	KA9WDX	443.97500	+	CC5	
	DSTAR	WI9WIN	444.15000	+		WAR
	FM	N9LIE	145.49000	-	114.8 Hz	WAR
	FM	KB9OBX	147.15000	+	114.8 Hz	WAR
	FM	KA9WDX/R	433.00000		88.5 Hz	
	FM	N9LIE	444.82500	+	114.8 Hz	WAR
	FUSION	KA9WDX/R	443.97500	+		
Menomonee Falls	DMR/MARC	W9RCG	442.01875	+	CC9	WAR
Menomonie	DMR/MARC	K4USD	442.17500	+	CC1	SERA
	FM	K9KGB	146.61000	-	110.9 Hz	
	FM	N9QKK	146.68500	-	110.9 Hz	WAR
Merton	FM	W9JPE	444.62500	+	127.3 Hz	WAR
Meteor	FM	WE9COM	147.07500	+	110.9 Hz	WAR
Meteor, Meteor Hill						
	FM	N9MMU	145.11000	-	110.9 Hz	
Milwaukee		AB9RH-L	147.52500			
	DMR/MARC	K9MAR	442.05000	+	CC11	
	DMR/MARC	KB9ZB	442.20625	+	CC9	
	DMR/MARC	N9PAY	444.53125	+	CC1	
	DSTAR	K9AES C	145.23500	-		
	DSTAR	KC9LKZ	145.24500	-		WAR
	DSTAR	KC9LKZ C	145.24500	-		

Location	Mode	Call sign	Output	Input	Access	Coordinator
Milwaukee	DSTAR	KC9LKZ	442.46875	+		
	DSTAR	KC9LKZ B	442.46875	+		
	DSTAR	KC9LKZ A	1290.05000	1270.05000		
	DSTAR	KC9LKZ	1290.05000	1270.05000		WAR
	DSTAR	KC9LKZ D	1298.00000			
	FM	W9DHI	53.03000	52.03000	103.5 Hz	WAR
	FM	N9LKH	145.13000	-	127.3 Hz	WAR
	FM	KA9WXN	145.25000	-		
	FM	W9HHX	145.27000	-	127.3 Hz	WAR
	FM	W9RH	145.39000	-	127.3 Hz	WAR
	FM	K9MAR	145.76000		100.0 Hz	
	FM	N9BMH	146.62500	-	127.3 Hz	WAR
	FM	N9PAY	146.94000	-		WAR
	FM	WB0AFB	147.04500	+	127.3 Hz	WAR
	FM	K9IFF	147.10500	+	127.3 Hz	WAR
	FM	W9WK	147.16500	+	127.3 Hz	WAR
	FM	N9UUR	442.42500	+	127.3 Hz	
	FM	W9HHX	443.02500	+	114.8 Hz	WAR
	FM	WI9WIN	443.27500	+	127.3 Hz	WAR
	FM	N9LKH	443.55000	+	127.3 Hz	WAR
	FM	W9EFJ	444.45000	+	114.8 Hz	WAR
	FM	WB9HKE	444.75000	+		
	FM	W9DHI	444.85000	+	127.3 Hz	WAR
	FM	WA9AZA	446.10000	-		
	FM	N9PAY	927.51250	952.51250	127.3 Hz	WAR
	FUSION	W9RH	144.79000	+		
	FUSION	KB9E	440.32500			
Mobile Repeater	DMR/MARC	N9OIG	442.93750	+	CC4	
Monroe	FM	W9MUP	52.97000	51.27000		WAR
	FM	KO9LR	145.11000	-	123.0 Hz	WAR
	FM	W9MUP	443.52500	+		WAR
Montello	FM	KC9ASQ	146.74500	-	123.0 Hz	WAR
Mount Sterling	FM	W9DMH	147.36000	+	131.8 Hz	WAR
Mukwonago		KB7QDI-L	145.50000			
Necedah	FM	KC9IPY	147.21000	+	123.0 Hz	WAR
	FM	K9UJH	444.12500	+	123.0 Hz	WAR
Neenah	FUSION	KA9GOU	145.00000			
	FUSION	KB9AIT	145.55000			
	FUSION	KB9AIT	145.70000			
Nekoosa	FUSION	KC9FLU	146.55000			
New Berlin	DMR/MARC	N9PAY	441.43750	+	CC1	WAR
	FM	W9DHI	53.03000	52.03000	127.3 Hz	
	FM	WI9MRC	146.91000	-	127.3 Hz	
	FM	KB9SIF	442.07500	+		WAR
	FM	WA9AOL	442.67500	+	127.3 Hz	WAR
	FM	W9LR	443.30000	+	127.3 Hz	WAR
	FM	W9DHI	444.85000	+	127.3 Hz	
	FM	KC9FTE	927.01250	902.01250		
New Holstein	FM	KA9OJN	147.30000	+	107.2 Hz	WAR
Niagara	FM	W9MB	223.82000	-	114.8 Hz	WAR
NOAA Ashland	WX	KZZ78	162.52500			
NOAA Baraboo	WX	KHA47	162.45000			
NOAA Black River Falls						
	WX	WNG564	162.50000			
NOAA Coloma	WX	WWF40	162.40000			
NOAA Crandon	WX	WWG88	162.45000			
NOAA Dubuque	WX	WXL64	162.40000			
NOAA Fond Du Lac						
	WX	WWG87	162.50000			
NOAA Green Bay	WX	KIG65	162.55000			
NOAA Janesville	WX	WWG90	162.42500			
NOAA Ladysmith	WX	WNG577	162.55000			

Location	Mode	Call sign	Output	Input	Access	Coordinator
NOAA Madison	WX	WXJ87	162.55000			
NOAA Menomonie						
	WX	WXJ88	162.40000			
NOAA Milwaukee	WX	KEC60	162.40000			
NOAA New London						
	WX	WNG552	162.52500			
NOAA Park Falls	WX	WXM91	162.50000			
NOAA Prairie Du Chien						
	WX	WWG86	162.50000			
NOAA Racine	WX	KZZ76	162.45000			
NOAA Rhinelander						
	WX	WNG565	162.40000			
NOAA Richland Center						
	WX	WWG89	162.47500			
NOAA Sheboygan						
	WX	WWG91	162.52500			
NOAA Sister Bay	WX	WXN69	162.42500			
NOAA Spooner	WX	KZZ79	162.47500			
NOAA Wausau	WX	WXJ89	162.47500			
NOAA Wausaukee						
	WX	WNG553	162.40000			
NOAA Winona	WX	KGG95	162.42500			
NOAA Withee	WX	KZZ77	162.42500			
North Freedom	FM	KD9UU	443.67500	+	123.0 Hz	WAR
Oconomowoc		N9UUP-L	146.48000			
Oconto Falls	FM	KB9DSV	146.83500	-	107.2 Hz	WAR
Ogema	FUSION	N0GMJ	147.69000	-		
Onalaska	FUSION	KD9GVS	144.97000			
Oostburg	FUSION	K9KMS	443.50000	+	146.2 Hz	
Oshkosh	DMR/BM	KC9LYF	444.47500	+	CC1	
	DMR/MARC	W9RCG	442.21875	+	CC6	
	FM	N9GDY	442.07500	+	107.2 Hz	WAR
	FM	N9GMT	443.62500	+	123.0 Hz	WAR
	FUSION	KD9CJL	145.60000			
Park Falls	DMR/MARC	W9PFP	145.34500	-	CC1	
	DMR/MARC	KD9IPR	146.71500	-	CC2	
	DMR/MARC	W9PFP	444.45000	+	CC1	
	DSTAR	W9PFP C	145.34500	-		
	DSTAR	W9PFP	442.48125	+		WAR
	DSTAR	W9PFP B	442.48125	+		
	FM	W9PFP-R	444.75000	+		WAR
Pewaukee	DMR/MARC	KB9ZB	442.38125	+	CC9	
Plat		AB9XI-L	446.25000			
Platteville	FM	WI9WIN	442.20000	+	123.0 Hz	
	FM	W9UWP	444.17500	+	131.8 Hz	
	FM	KC9KQ	444.32500	+	131.8 Hz	WAR
	FUSION	W9JFK	145.52000			
Pleasant Prairie, St. Catherin						
	FM	K9KEA	927.61250	902.61250	127.3 Hz	WAR
Plover	FM	W9SM	442.05000	+	114.8 Hz	WAR
Plymouth	FM	WE9COM	146.85000	-	100.0 Hz	WAR
	FM	WE9R	147.06000	+	107.2 Hz	WAR
	FM	KD9TZ	443.22500	+	107.2 Hz	WAR
	FM	WE9R	444.35000	+	114.8 Hz	WAR
Port Washington	FM	AC9CD	147.33000	+	127.3 Hz	WAR
	FM	AC9CD	443.52500	+	114.8 Hz	WAR
	FM	W9CQO	443.75000	+	127.3 Hz	WAR
Porterfield	FM	W4IJR	444.40000	+	100.0 Hz	WAR
Pound	FM	WI9WIN	442.00000	+	114.8 Hz	WAR
Preble	FM	W9OSL-R	444.75000	+	100.0 Hz	WAR
Racine	DMR/MARC	KR9RK	440.00625	+	CC9	
	DMR/MARC	W2WAY	927.98750	902.98750	CC9	

Location	Mode	Call sign	Output	Input	Access	Coordinator
Racine	DSTAR	WI9RAC B	441.81875	+		
	DSTAR	WI9RAC D	1298.00000			
	FM	KR9RK	147.27000	+	127.3 Hz	WAR
	FM	KC9QKJ	224.80000	-	127.3 Hz	WAR
	FM	KR9RK	442.00000	+	127.3 Hz	
	FM	KA9LOK	444.05000	+	114.8 Hz	WAR
Radisson	FM	N9UPC	444.22500	+		
Rhinelander	FM	KC9HBX	146.94000	-	114.8 Hz	WAR
Rice Lake	FM	WI9WIN	442.10000	+	110.9 Hz	WAR
	FM	KB9TYC	446.00000	-		
	P25	KD9EJA	444.45000	+		WAR
Richfield	DSTAR	K9PAQ C	146.85000	+		
	DSTAR	K9PAQ B	443.82500	+		
Richland Center	DSTAR	KC9WDW	147.19500	+		WAR
	DSTAR	KC9WDW B	442.48750	+		
	DSTAR	KC9WDW	442.48750	+		
	FM	WI9WIN	442.70000	+	131.8 Hz	WAR
Ripon	FM	N9GMT	444.95000	+	123.0 Hz	WAR
River Falls	FM	WI9WIN	443.02500	+	110.9 Hz	WAR
Roberts	FM	N9UPC	147.33000	+	110.9 Hz	WAR
Rosendale	FM	KB9YET	147.37500	+	107.2 Hz	
Rubicon	FM	WB9KPG	145.35000	-	123.0 Hz	WAR
Rudolph	FM	WD9GFY	444.32500	+	114.8 Hz	WAR
Sayner	DSTAR	KD9JHE C	147.36000	+		
	DSTAR	KD9JHE B	444.40000	+		
	DSTAR	KD9JHE	444.40000	+		WAR
	FM	WE9COM	145.13000	-	114.8 Hz	WAR
	FM	KD9JHE	147.36000	+		WAR
Shawano	FM	KA9NWY	145.35000	-	114.8 Hz	WAR
Sheboygan	DMR/BM	WB9X	443.12500	+	CC9	
	DMR/BM	WB9X	443.32500	+	CC9	
	DSTAR	KC9WUS C	146.98500	-		
	DSTAR	KC9WUS	146.98500	-		
	DSTAR	KC9SJY	147.25500	+		WAR
	DSTAR	KC9SJY C	147.25500	+		
	DSTAR	KC9SJY	442.48125	+		WAR
	DSTAR	KC9SJY B	442.48125	+		
	FM	KC9AXZ	443.45000	+	107.2 Hz	
	FM	WI9WIN	444.30000	+	146.2 Hz	
Sheboygan Falls	FM	KB5ZJU	224.94000	-	100.0 Hz	WAR
	FUSION	KB5ZJU	445.87500			
Siren	FM	N9PHS	146.62500	-	110.9 Hz	WAR
Sister Bay	FM	W9AIQ	147.18000	+	100.0 Hz	WAR
Slinger	FM	KC9PVD	147.21000	+	127.3 Hz	WAR
	FM	WB9BVB	442.65000	+	127.3 Hz	
	FM	KC9PVD	443.82500	+	127.3 Hz	WAR
Solon Springs	FM	AA9JL	145.49000	-	110.9 Hz	WAR
Spooner	FM	KB9OHN	147.30000	+	110.9 Hz	WAR
	FM	KB9OHN	443.50000	+	110.9 Hz	WAR
Spooner/Hertel	FM	KB9OHN	145.19000	-	110.9 Hz	WAR
St. Lawrence	FM	WB9BVB	146.73000	-	127.3 Hz	
Stevens Point	DSTAR	N9NMH	146.50000			
	FM	WB9QFW	146.67000	-	114.8 Hz	WAR
	FM	WB9QFW	146.98500	-	114.8 Hz	WAR
	FM	KC9NW	444.70000	+	114.8 Hz	WAR
Stockbridge	FUSION	AB9PM	146.50500			
Sturgeon Bay	FM	W9DOR	147.21000	+	107.2 Hz	WAR
Sturtevant	DMR/MARC	W2WAY	927.72500	902.72500	CC9	
Superior	FM	WA9KLM	145.17000	-		WAR
	FM	K9UWS	146.76000	-	110.9 Hz	WAR
Suring	FM	WE9COM	145.29000	-	114.8 Hz	WAR
	FM	AB9PJ	145.47000	-	114.8 Hz	WAR

Location	Mode	Call sign	Output	Input	Access	Coordinator
Suring	FM	AB9PJ	442.55000	+	146.2 Hz	WAR
Sussex	FM	W9CQ	147.39000	+	127.3 Hz	WAR
Three Lakes	FM	N9GHE	147.19500	+	114.8 Hz	WAR
	FM	N9GHE	224.54000	-	114.8 Hz	WAR
Tomah	FM	KC9KVE	146.80500	-	131.8 Hz	WAR
	FM	WI9WIN	444.80000	+	131.8 Hz	WAR
Tomahawk	FM	N9MEA	52.83000	51.13000	114.8 Hz	WAR
	FM	N9CLE	145.43000	-	114.8 Hz	WAR
	FM	N9CLE	223.76000	-	114.8 Hz	WAR
	FM	N9CLE	444.57500	+	114.8 Hz	WAR
Town Of Weston	FM	WW9RS	146.80500	-	110.9 Hz	WAR
Townsend	DMR/BM	AA9JR	443.95000	+	CC1	
Trevor	DMR/MARC	N9OIG	442.19375	+	CC9	
	FM	KA9VZD	442.60000	+	123.0 Hz	WAR
Tripoli	FM	KC9HBX	147.12000	+	114.8 Hz	WAR
Twinlakes	FM	KB9LPP	440.84380	+	127.3 Hz	
Union Grove	DMR/MARC	N9OIG	146.74500	-	CC9	
	DMR/MARC	N9OIG	442.24375	+	CC9	
	DMR/MARC	N9OIG	442.93750	+	CC9	
Unity, Brighton Tower						
	FM	W9BCC	145.41000	-	114.8 Hz	
Viroqua	FM	N9TUU	145.17000	-	131.8 Hz	WAR
Walworth	DMR/MARC	N9OIG	441.94375	+	CC9	
Washburn	FM	KB9JX	145.15000	-	103.5 Hz	WAR
Washington Island						
	FM	WI9DX	145.49000	-	100.0 Hz	
Waterford	DMR/MARC	N9OIG	440.76875	+	CC4	
Waterloo	FM	W9DRR	446.00000	-	136.5 Hz	
Watertown	DSTAR	W9TTN B	440.15000	+		
	DSTAR	W9TTN	440.15000	+		
	FM	K9LUK	145.19000	-	123.0 Hz	WAR
Waukesha	DMR/MARC	WE9COM	147.47000	+	CC1	
	FM	WE9COM	145.47000	-	127.3 Hz	WAR
	FM	W9RIX	224.82000	-	127.3 Hz	
	FM	WQ9A	444.20000	+	127.3 Hz	
	FM	KD9AMZ	449.15000		127.3 Hz	
Waupaca	FM	W9KL	147.39000	+	118.8 Hz	
	FM	WI9WIN	444.67500	+	114.8 Hz	WAR
Wausau	DMR/BM	W9KFD	442.12500	+	CC1	
	DMR/BM	W9BCC	443.75000	+	CC1	
	DMR/MARC	W9RCG	442.13125	+	CC9	
	DSTAR	W9BCC	145.24500	-		WAR
	DSTAR	W9BCC C	145.24500			
	DSTAR	W9BCC	442.46875	+		WAR
	DSTAR	W9BCC B	442.46875	+		
	DSTAR	W9BCC	1282.10000	1262.10000		WAR
	DSTAR	W9BCC A	1282.10000	-		
	DSTAR	W9BCC D	1298.00000			
	FM	W9SM	29.64000	-		WAR
	FM	W9MEA	52.89000	51.19000	114.8 Hz	WAR
	FM	KB9KST	145.37000	-	114.8 Hz	WAR
	FM	W9SM	146.86500	-	114.8 Hz	WAR
	FM	W9SM	147.13500	+	114.8 Hz	WAR
	FM	W9SM	224.64000	-	114.8 Hz	WAR
	FM	WI9WIN	442.20000	+	114.8 Hz	WAR
	FM	KA9HQE	443.32500	+	100.0 Hz	WAR
	FM	W9SM	443.52500	+	114.8 Hz	WAR
	FM	KC9NW	443.75000	+	71.9 Hz	WAR
	FM	W9SM	444.10000	+	114.8 Hz	WAR
	FM	W9BCC	444.30000	+	114.8 Hz	WAR
	FM	W9SM	444.42500	+	114.8 Hz	WAR

Location	Mode	Call sign	Output	Input	Access	Coordinator
Wausau, Rib Mountain						
	FM	W9BCC	146.73000	-		
	FM	W9BCC	146.82000	-	114.8 Hz	WAR
Wausaukee	FM	WA8WG	146.88000	-	136.5 Hz	WAR
Webster	DMR/BM	N0DZQ	443.15000	+	CC3	
West Allis	FM	KA9JCP	224.52000	-	127.3 Hz	WAR
	FM	N9MKX	444.42500	+	127.3 Hz	WAR
West Milwaukee	FM	N9FSE	147.13500	+	141.3 Hz	WAR
Willard	FM	N9UWX	147.27000	+	114.8 Hz	WAR
Wisconsin Rapids	FM	W9MRA	146.79000	-	114.8 Hz	WAR
	FM	W9MRA	147.33000	+	114.8 Hz	WAR
Wisconsin Rapids, East Side Wa						
	FM	W9MRA	442.42500	+	114.8 Hz	
Wonewoc	DSTAR	KD9BLN C	146.71500	-		
	DSTAR	KD9BLN	146.71500	-		WAR
	DSTAR	KD9BLN B	443.69375	+		
	DSTAR	KD9BLN	443.69375	+		WAR
Woodruff	DSTAR	KA9SRO	445.97500	-		
WYOMING						
Afton, The Narrows						
	FM	KD7LVE	146.97000	-	100.0 Hz	
Big Goose	FM	WY7SHR	147.25500	+	100.0 Hz	
Big Horn		KF7FCA-L	145.49000			
Big Piney	FM	KC7BJY	145.14500	-	100.0 Hz	WRCG
Big Piney, The Hogsback						
	FM	KC7BJY	146.88000	-	100.0 Hz	WRCG
Blairtown	FM	N7ABC-R	444.50000	+		
Boysen, Boysen Peak						
	DSTAR	N7HYF	147.06000	+		WRCG
Buffalo	DMR/BM	WY7BRK	449.85000	-	CC7	
	DMR/MARC	WY7EOC	445.05000	-	CC11	
	FM	WY7BRK	147.18000	+	110.9 Hz	WRCG
Buffalo, Windy Ridge						
	FM	NX7Z	146.88000	-	100.0 Hz	WRCG
Burlington, Tatman Mtn						
	DSTAR	KG7PRH	147.21000	+	123.0 Hz	WRCG
Casper	DMR/MARC	WY7EOC	449.98750	-	CC11	WRCG
	FM	W7VNJ	52.98000	-	131.8 Hz	WRCG
	FM	K7PLA	145.46000	-	110.9 Hz	WRCG
	FM	KD7AGA	146.64000	-	173.8 Hz	WRCG
	FM	W7VNJ	146.94000	-	123.0 Hz	WRCG
	FM	NG7T	449.10000	-		
	FM	W7VNJ	449.57500	-	173.8 Hz	WRCG
Casper, Casper Mountain						
	FM	W7VNJ	145.23500	-	100.0 Hz	
	FM	K7PLA	145.46000	-	110.9 Hz	WRCG
	FM	W7VNJ	146.94000	-	123.0 Hz	WRCG
	FUSION	N7RRB	449.90000	-		WRCG
Casper, Casper Mtn.						
	FM	NB7I	449.50000	-	100.0 Hz	
Casper, Wyoming Med Center						
	FM	W7VNJ	449.57500	-	173.8 Hz	WRCG
Cedar Mtn	FM	KE7UJB	444.77500	-	103.5 Hz	
Cheyenne	DMR/BM	N7JJY	448.87500	-	CC1	
	DMR/BM	KC7DHF	448.95000	-	CC15	WRCG
	DMR/MARC	K7PFJ	449.93750	-	CC7	WRCG
	DMR/MARC	WY7EOC	449.97500	-	CC11	WRCG
	DSTAR	KC7SNO B	447.22500	-		
	FM	KB7SWR	448.15000	-	100.0 Hz	WRCG
	FM	N7JJY	449.90000	-	100.0 Hz	
	FUSION	W3ORR	447.40000	-		

Location	Mode	Call sign	Output	Input	Access	Coordinator
Cheyenne	FUSION	W3ORR	449.20000	-		
Cheyenne, Chalk Bluffs						
	FM	N7JJY	449.30000	-		WRCG
Cheyenne, Denver Hill						
	FM	KC7SNO	146.77500	-	114.8 Hz	WRCG
Cheyenne, North Park						
	FM	KC7SNO	147.10500	+	91.5 Hz	WRCG
Cody	DMR/BM	KC7NP	146.94000	-	CC1	
	DMR/BM	KC7NP	448.35000	-	CC1	
	DMR/MARC	W7BEQ	447.32500	-	CC11	
	FM	KC7NP	29.68000	-		
	FM	KE7UJB	147.12000	+		WRCG
	FM	KE7UJB	444.50000	+	103.5 Hz	
Cody, Cedar Mtn	FM	KE7UJB	147.12000	+		WRCG
Cody, McCullough Peaks						
	FM	KI7W	146.85000	-	103.5 Hz	WRCG
Douglas	FM	KK7BA	147.15000	+		
Dubois	FM	KD7BN	146.82000	-	100.0 Hz	WRCG
Evanston	FM	K7JL	449.15000	-	100.0 Hz	UVHFS
Evanston, Medicine Butte						
	FM	K7JL	146.86000	-	100.0 Hz	WRCG
Gilette	FM	W7WBW	145.33000	-	123.0 Hz	
Gillette	DMR/BM	WY7VAF	446.55000	-	CC1	
	DMR/BM	WY7VAF	447.11250	-	CC11	
	DMR/BM	NE7WY	448.75000	-	CC11	
	DSTAR	NE7WY C	145.34000	-		
	DSTAR	NE7WY	146.96000	-		WRCG
Gillette, Antelope Butte						
	FM	NE7WY	147.36000	+	123.0 Hz	WRCG
Gillette, Bliss Ranch						
	FM	NE7WY	147.27000	+	123.0 Hz	WRCG
Green River, Green River High						
	FM	AD0BN	444.77500	+	123.0 Hz	WRCG
Jackson	DMR/MARC	WY7EOC	445.20000	-	CC11	
Jackson, Snow King Mountain						
	FM	W7TAR	146.91000	-		WRCG
	FM	W7TAR	447.70000	-	123.0 Hz	WRCG
Kaycee, Pack Saddle						
	FM	W7QQA	145.43000	-	110.9 Hz	WRCG
Kemmerer	FM	KA7SHX	449.82500	-	100.0 Hz	WRCG
Kemmerer, Dempsey Ridge						
	FM	KF7EHE	449.07500	-	123.0 Hz	
Kemmerer, Qualey Ridge						
	FM	N7ERH	449.30000	-	127.3 Hz	
Kemmerer, Quealy Peak						
	FM	KG7VVQ	147.09000	+	100.0 Hz	WRCG
	FM	KA7SHX	449.82500	-	100.0 Hz	WRCG
Lander	FM	N7HYF	53.03000	52.03000		WRCG
	FM	N7HYF	449.97500	-	100.0 Hz	WRCG
Lander, Airport	FM	KD7PPP	145.44500	-	110.9 Hz	WRCG
Lander, Limestone Mountain						
	FM	N7HYF	449.90000	-		WRCG
Laramie	DMR/MARC	WY7EOC	447.22500	-	CC11	WRCG
	FM	N7UW	146.61000	-		WRCG
	FM	N7UW	147.01500	+	146.2 Hz	WRCG
Laramie, Beacon Hill						
	FM	KC7SNO	146.82000	-	114.8 Hz	WRCG
Laramie, Jelm Mountain						
	FM	N7UW	147.01500	+	146.2 Hz	
Laramie, University						
	FM	N7UW	146.61000	-		WRCG
Lovell	DMR/MARC	W7BEQ	446.92500	-	CC11	

Location	Mode	Call sign	Output	Input	Access	Coordinator
Lovell, Medicine Mountain						
	FM	W7BEQ	147.16500	+	103.5 Hz	WRCG
Lusk, 77 Hill	FM	KG7OMT	147.33000	+	103.5 Hz	
Marbleton	FM	KC7BJY	145.14500	-	100.0 Hz	WRCG
Meeteetse, 3 Mile Hill						
	FM	KI7W	147.33000	+	103.5 Hz	WRCG
Mountain View, Hickey Mtn						
	FM	WY7BV	144.63500	+	100.0 Hz	
Newcastle, Mt Pisgah						
	FM	NE7WY	147.30000	+	162.2 Hz	WRCG
NOAA Afton	WX	WNG569	162.42500			
NOAA Casper	WX	WXM47	162.40000			
NOAA Cheyenne	WX	WXM37	162.55000			
NOAA Cody	WX	WNG563	162.40000			
NOAA Dubois	WX	WNG723	162.45000			
NOAA Elk Plaza	WX	WNG686	162.42500			
NOAA Evanston	WX	KXI85	162.45000			
NOAA Gillette	WX	WNG660	162.50000			
NOAA Glendo	WX	WNG571	162.45000			
NOAA Grant Village						
	WX	WNG667	162.45000			
NOAA Jackson	WX	KWN39	162.52500			
NOAA Kaycee	WX	WNG662	162.55000			
NOAA Kemmerer	WX	KJY75	162.52500			
NOAA Lander	WX	WXM61	162.47500			
NOAA Newcastle	WX	WNG661	162.47500			
NOAA Pinedale	WX	WNG679	162.50000			
NOAA Rawlins	WX	KXI37	162.42500			
NOAA Rock Springs						
	WX	KXI34	162.55000			
NOAA Sheridan	WX	WXM46	162.47500			
NOAA Thermopolis						
	WX	WNG573	162.50000			
NOAA Worland	WX	WNG568	162.52500			
North Rock Springs						
		K7DRA-R	444.70000			
Pinedale	FM	KC7BJY	448.10000	-	100.0 Hz	WRCG
Powell	DMR/BM	KG7PRH	444.72500	+	CC3	
	DMR/BM	W7BEQ	444.92500	+	CC1	
Rawlins	DMR/MARC	WY7EOC	445.05000	-	CC11	
	FM	N7RON	146.70000	-	162.2 Hz	WRCG
	FM	KC7OZU	146.76000	-	100.0 Hz	
	FM	N7GCR	147.24000	+	100.0 Hz	WRCG
	FM	KD7BN	147.39000	+	100.0 Hz	
Rawlins, Elk Mountain						
	FM	N7GCR	147.24000	+	100.0 Hz	WRCG
Riverton	DMR/BM	KA0NDS	147.94000	-	CC1	
	DMR/BM	KA0NDS	449.98750	-	CC10	
	DSTAR	N8CZI B	443.57500	+		
	FUSION	W0MUD	147.58000			
Riverton, Griffey Hill						
	FM	K0FOP	145.11500	-	100.0 Hz	WRCG
Riverton, Griffy Hill						
	DSTAR	N7DMO	441.67000	+		
	FM	N7HYF	449.97500	-	127.3 Hz	WRCG
Rock River	FM	K7UWR	53.03000	52.03000		
Rock Springs	DMR/BM	KE7UUJ	465.02500	+	CC11	
	DMR/MARC	KF7OBL	147.30000	+	CC1	
	DMR/MARC	K7DRA	447.11250	-	CC11	
	DMR/MARC	KF7OBL	448.87500	-	CC1	
	DSTAR	KI7BER C	145.15000	+		

Location	Mode	Call sign	Output	Input	Access	Coordinator
Rock Springs, Aspen Mountain						
	FM	KE7FGD	146.61000	-	100.0 Hz	WRCG
	FM	KE7UUJ	146.94000	-	100.0 Hz	WRCG
Rocky Point	FM	NE7WY	147.27000	+	123.0 Hz	WRCG
Saddlestring		KF7FCA-R	145.49000			
Sheridan	DMR/BM	K7VU	448.00000	-	CC1	
	DMR/BM	K7VU	449.97500	-	CC1	
	DMR/MARC	W7BEQ	446.72500	-	CC11	
	FUSION	K7VU	449.80000	-		
Sheridan, Big Horn Mountain						
	FM	W7GUX	449.70000	-	100.0 Hz	WRCG
Shoshoni	DMR/MARC	W7BEQ	446.82500	-	CC11	
Shoshoni, Copper Mtn						
	FM	W7BEQ	146.80500	-	100.0 Hz	WRCG
South Baxter	FM	KE7UUJ-R	146.65500	-		
Statewide	DMR/MARC	WY7EOC	445.01250	-	CC11	
Strouds		K7YE-L	146.58000			
Sundance, Warren Peak						
	FM	NE7WY	146.79000	-	100.0 Hz	WRCG
Ten Sleep	DMR/MARC	W7BEQ	446.62500	-	CC11	
	FM	W7BEQ	145.14500	-	103.5 Hz	WRCG
Ten Sleep, Meadowlark Mountain						
	FM	KG7KBJ	147.37500	+	110.9 Hz	
Teton Village, Rendezvous Moun						
	FM	W7TAR	146.73000	-	123.0 Hz	WRCG
Thayne	FUSION	N7MSM	433.45000			
	FUSION	KN6LL	448.20000	-		
Torrington	FM	KD7JNQ	448.32500	-	151.4 Hz	
Wheatland	DMR/BM	KD7YUW	449.47500	-	CC11	
	DMR/MARC	WY7EOC	445.05000	-	CC11	
	FM	WA7SNU	146.88000	-		
	FM	WA7SNU	449.62500	-	151.4 Hz	
Worland	DMR/BM	W7BEQ	444.92500	+	CC1	
	DMR/MARC	W7BEQ	445.01250	-	CC11	
	FM	W7BEQ	444.82500	-	103.5 Hz	
Wright	FM	NE7WY	147.06000	+	100.0 Hz	WRCG
Wright, Pumpkin Butte						
	FM	NX7Z	146.98500	-	100.0 Hz	WRCG
ALABAMA						
Calgary	FM	VA6TWO	53.39000	52.39000	131.8 Hz	
	FM	VE6ARA	145.15000	-	110.9 Hz	
	FM	VA6TWO	147.39000	+	100.0 Hz	
	FM	VA6TWO	442.20000	+	131.8 Hz	
	P25	VE6WRO	927.05000	902.05000	131.8 Hz	
	P25	VA6TRE	927.72500	902.72500	131.8 Hz	
ALBERTA						
Airdrie	FM	VE6AA	145.31000	-	100.0 Hz	ARLA
	FM	VE6JBJ	147.54000			
	FUSION	VA6SVT	430.80000			
Alberta	FM	VE6HUB	443.57500	+		
	FM	VE3KPT	444.55000	+	136.5 Hz	
Aldersyde	FM	VE6HRA	147.00000	+	110.9 Hz	ARLA
Aldersyde, Gladys Ridge						
	FM	VE6RPX	145.47000	-	100.0 Hz	
Alix	FM	VE6PAT	147.21000	+		ARLA
	FM	VE6PAT	448.97500	-		ARLA
Andrew	FM	VE6JET	146.70000	-		ARLA
Athabasca	FM	VE6BOX	146.73000	-		ARLA
Balzac	FM	VE6EDS	444.85000	+		ARLA
Banff	DSTAR	VE6WRO C	147.31500	+		

Location	Mode	Call sign	Output	Input	Access	Coordinator
Banff	FM	VE6FAA	147.57000		100.0 Hz	
	FM	VE6MPR	444.78750	+		ARLA
Banff National P	DSTAR	VE6WRO C	147.03000	+		
	DSTAR	VE6WRO B	444.82500	+		
Banff National Park						
	DSTAR	VE6WRO A	1248.50000			
Banff, Tunnel Mtn	FM	VE6BNF	146.67000	-	131.8 Hz	
Barons	FM	VE6CAM	146.88000	-		ARLA
Beaver Lodge	FM	VE6BL	146.85000	-		ARLA
Big Valley	FM	VE6UK	145.43000	-		ARLA
Bonneville	FM	VE6ADI	146.71500	-		ARLA
Borradaile	FM	VE6BDL	449.07500	-		ARLA
Bragg Creek	FM	VE6RAY	444.87500	+	110.9 Hz	ARLA
Brooks	FM	VE6HBR	145.35000	-		ARLA
	FM	VE6SPK-L	446.30000	-		
Burmis	FM	VE6HRP	145.39000	-		ARLA
Calgary	DMR/BM	VE6GCD	443.37500	+	CC1	
	DMR/MARC	VA6DRU	147.42000	146.42000	CC1	
	DMR/MARC	VE6GCD	443.37500	+	CC1	
	DMR/MARC	VE6GCD	443.37500	+	CC1	
	DMR/MARC	VE6GCD	443.37500	+	CC1	
	DMR/MARC	VE6RYC	444.00000	+	CC1	ARLA
	DMR/MARC	VA6EDN	445.00000	419.00000	CC1	
	DMR/MARC	VE6NHM	927.25000	902.25000	CC1	
	DMR/MARC	VE6CQM	927.95000	902.95000	CC0	
	DSTAR	VA6ACW C	145.65000			
	DSTAR	VE6WRN C	146.80500	145.60500		
	DSTAR	VE6GHZ C	147.09000	+		
	DSTAR	VE6IPG C	147.28500	+		
	DSTAR	VA6MEO B	433.87500	-		
	DSTAR	VE6WRE B	444.82500	+		
	DSTAR	VE6WRN B	444.92500	+		
	DSTAR	VE6GHZ B	444.95000	+		
	DSTAR	VE6IPG B	444.96250	+		
	DSTAR	VA6ACW B	445.85000	-		
	DSTAR	VA3URU B	448.65000	+		
	DSTAR	VE6WRN A	1247.50000			
	DSTAR	VE6IPG A	1248.05000			
	DSTAR	VE6IPG D	1248.05000			
	DSTAR	VE6GHZ A	1253.00000			
	DSTAR	VE6GHZ D	1253.00000			
	DSTAR	VE6IPG A	1275.95000	+		
	DSTAR	VE6WRN A	1287.50000	1267.50000		
	DSTAR	VE6GHZ A	1287.97500	1267.97500		
	FM	VE6RYC	53.03000	52.03000	110.9 Hz	ARLA
	FM	VE6ZV	145.23000	-	110.9 Hz	
	FM	VA6CTV	145.29000	-		ARLA
	FM	VE6RGB	145.39000	-	103.5 Hz	
	FM	VE6OIL	146.61000	-	114.8 Hz	ARLA
	FM	VE6CID	146.68500	-		ARLA
	FM	VE6MX	146.73000	-		ARLA
	FM	VE6RYC	146.85000	-	110.9 Hz	ARLA
	FM	VE6RPT	146.94000	-		ARLA
	FM	VE6REC	147.18000	+		ARLA
	FM	VE6RPC	147.21000	+	110.9 Hz	ARLA
	FM	VE6QCW	147.24000	+		ARLA
	FM	VE6RY	147.27000	+		ARLA
	FM	VE6RYC	224.85000	223.15000	110.9 Hz	ARLA
	FM	VE6OIL	442.90000	+	131.8 Hz	ARLA
	FM	VE6NZ	443.15000	+		ARLA
	FM	VE6ZV	444.27500	+	110.9 Hz	ARLA

Location	Mode	Call sign	Output	Input	Access	Coordinator
Calgary	FM	VE6EHX	444.35000	+	110.9 Hz	ARLA
	FM	VE6RY	444.57500	+	110.9 Hz	ARLA
	FM	VE6FIL	444.67500	+		ARLA
	FM	VE6DDC	444.80000	+		ARLA
	FM	VA6TRE	444.87500	+	131.8 Hz	
	FM	VA6TWO	927.01250	902.01250		ARLA
	FUSION	VA6QAS	144.00000			
	FUSION	VE6LIT	144.91000			
	FUSION	VA6DWF	147.55000			
	FUSION	VE6ANX	443.48750	+		
	FUSION	VA6QAS	448.85000	-		
Calgary Alberta	FM	VE6AZX	147.50000		100.0 Hz	
Camrose	FM	VE6UU	444.02500	+		ARLA
Canmore	FM	VE6RJZ	146.58000		100.0 Hz	
	FM	VE6XRP	147.30000	+		ARLA
	FM	VE6RMT	147.36000	+	110.9 Hz	ARLA
Carbon	FM	VE6RCB	146.71500	-	110.9 Hz	ARLA
Cheadle	FM	VE6GLR	147.01500	+		ARLA
Chipman	FM	VE6TNC	146.61000	-	100.0 Hz	ARLA
Claresholm	DMR/BM	VE6AAH	145.21000	-	CC1	
	DSTAR	VE6WRT C	147.39000	+		
	FM	VE6AAH	145.21000	-	103.5 Hz	ARLA
Claresholm, Burton Creek						
	FM	VE6HRK	145.43000	-	110.9 Hz	
Cochrane	FM	VE6PR	147.37500	+		ARLA
	FM	VE6PR	449.05000	-		ARLA
	P25	VE6RPT	444.90000	+		ARLA
	FUSION	VE6HG	434.40000			
Cold Lake	FM	VE6ADI	147.09000	+		ARLA
Coleman	FM	VE6FRC	145.49000	-		
College Heights	FM	VA6REB-L	146.42000	+		
Crossfield	FM	VE6TPA	147.13500	+		
	FM	VE6YXR	448.75000	-	107.2 Hz	ARLA
Crossfield, Moneys Mushrooms						
	FM	VE6HRF	145.35000	-	110.9 Hz	
Crowsnest Pass	FM	VE6CNP	145.49000	-		ARLA
Delia	FM	VE6GWR	444.42500	+	114.8 Hz	
	FM	VE6HB	448.12500	-		ARLA
Drayton Valley	FM	VE6HUB	442.90000	+	131.8 Hz	ARLA
Edmonton	DMR/BM	VE6AFP	147.21000	+	CC1	
	DMR/BM	VA6KGA	440.82500	+	CC1	
	DMR/BM	VE6EMS	442.25000	+	CC1	
	DMR/BM	VA6AFP	444.37500	+	CC1	
	DMR/BM	VA6PCC	444.77500	+	CC1	
	DMR/MARC	VE6AFP	147.21000	+	CC1	
	DMR/MARC	VE6VPR	440.80000	+	CC1	
	DMR/MARC	VE6AFP	444.37500	+	CC1	
	DSTAR	VE6KM C	145.47000	-		
	DSTAR	VE6KM C	145.47000	-		
	DSTAR	VA6XG C	145.71000			
	DSTAR	VA6XG C	147.42000			
	DSTAR	VE6BHX B	440.75000	+		
	DSTAR	VA6KGA B	440.80000	+		
	DSTAR	VE6KM B	444.90000	+		
	DSTAR	VE6KM B	444.90000	+		
	DSTAR	VA6XG B	446.47500	-		
	DSTAR	VE6KM D	1248.50000			
	DSTAR	VA6XG A	1282.00000	-		
	DSTAR	VE6KM A	1287.50000	-		
	FM	VA6WY	145.01000			
	FM	VE6RPA	145.19000	-		ARLA
	FM	VE6NHB	145.41000	-	114.8 Hz	ARLA

Location	Mode	Call sign	Output	Input	Access	Coordinator
Edmonton	FM	VE6QCR	146.64000	-	100.0 Hz	ARLA
	FM	VE6FDX	146.83500	-		
	FM	VE6OG	146.85000	-	100.0 Hz	ARLA
	FM	VE6HM	147.06000	+	100.0 Hz	ARLA
	FM	VE6EDM	147.12000	+	100.0 Hz	
	FM	VE6PAW	147.18000	+	100.0 Hz	ARLA
	FM	VE6UV	147.24000	+	100.0 Hz	ARLA
	FM	VE6TOP	147.30000	+	100.0 Hz	ARLA
	FM	VE6TOP	147.39000	+	100.0 Hz	
	FM	VA6XG	147.42000		110.9 Hz	
	FM	VA6RS	224.56000	-	123.0 Hz	ARLA
	FM	VE6DBD	444.02500	+	146.2 Hz	
	FM	VE6HM	444.10000	+	100.0 Hz	ARLA
	FM	VE6GPS	444.40000	+		ARLA
	FM	VE6EHR	444.67500	+		
	FM	VE6TOP	444.70000	+	123.0 Hz	ARLA
	FM	VE6EDM	444.75000	+	136.5 Hz	
	FM	VE6NHB	444.95000	+	114.8 Hz	ARLA
	FM	VE6FDX	449.02500	-	100.0 Hz	
	FUSION	VA6RV	443.15000	449.15000		
	FUSION	VE6SCA	444.72500	+	146.2 Hz	
	FUSION	VE6WXX	448.15000	-		
Edmonton, River Cree Casino						
	FM	VE6JN	147.33000	+	100.0 Hz	
Edmonton, Sherwood Park						
	FM	VE6HM	53.43000	52.43000	100.0 Hz	
Edmonton, South West						
	FM	VA6KGA	440.80000	+		
Edson	FM	VE6YFR	146.68500	-		
	FM	VE6RDF	147.37500	+		ARLA
	FM	VA6JAC	147.55500			
	FM	VE6MBX	444.62500	+	156.7 Hz	ARLA
Evanston	FM	VE6BUL-R	145.57000	+		
Falun	FM	VE6PLP	147.09000	+	100.0 Hz	ARLA
Fort McMurray	FM	VE6TBC	146.94000	-	100.0 Hz	
	FM	VE6TRC	147.00000	+	100.0 Hz	ARLA
	FM	VA6CYR	147.15000	+		
	FUSION	VE6YMM	449.60000	-		
Fortress Mountain	FM	VE6AQA	147.12000	+	110.9 Hz	ARLA
Ft. Saskatchewan	FM	VE6CWW	147.27000	+		ARLA
Furman	FM	VE6ARS-L	145.21000	-		
	FM	VE6ROT-R	146.79000	-		ARLA
Glendon	FM	VE6HOG	145.45000	-		ARLA
	FM	VE6COW	444.97500	+		ARLA
Grande Cache	FM	VE6YGR	147.39000	+		ARLA
Grande Prairie	FM	VE6OL	147.06000	+		ARLA
	FM	VE6XN	147.15000	+		ARLA
	FM	VE6AAV	444.77500	+	146.2 Hz	ARLA
	FM	VE6MDK	449.10000	-	100.0 Hz	ARLA
Grande Prairie EchoIRLP 61640						
	FM	VE6HIM	146.58000		146.2 Hz	
Grimshaw	FM	VE6AAA	448.51500	-		ARLA
Hailstone Butte	DSTAR	VE6WRT C	147.39000	+		
Hanna	FM	VE6HB	146.82000	-		ARLA
Hardisty	FM	VE6HDY	145.17000	-		ARLA
High Prairie	FM	VE6PRR	146.64000	-		ARLA
High River	FM	VE6HRB	145.17000	-		ARLA
	FM	VA6HRH	443.55000	+	110.9 Hz	ARLA
High River, Hospital						
	FM	VA6PF	146.70000	-	110.9 Hz	
Hinton	FM	VE6YAR	146.76000	-		ARLA
Holden	FM	VE6POE	145.49000	-		ARLA

Location	Mode	Call sign	Output	Input	Access	Coordinator
Innisfree	FM	VE6INN	147.34500	+		ARLA
Jasper	FM	VE6YPR	147.15000	+		
Kathyrn	FM	VE6OTR	145.39000	-		
Kingman	FM	VE6MTR	444.17500	+	123.0 Hz	ARLA
Kitscoty	FM	VE6YHB	444.22500	+	141.3 Hz	ARLA
Lake Eliza	FM	VE6BGB-R	146.67000	-		
Lake Louise	FM	VE6BNP	146.88000	-		ARLA
	FM	VE6HWY	147.33000	+		ARLA
Lethbridge	FM	VA6IRL	146.97000	-		
	FM	VE6UP	147.15000	+		ARLA
	FM	VE6DOK	442.07500	+	100.0 Hz	
	FM	VE6XA	444.85000	+		ARLA
	FM	VE6LRH	448.38000	-		
Lethbridge EchoIRLP 2722						
	FM	VE6COM	446.27500	-	131.8 Hz	
Lime Stone Mtn	FM	VE6MTR	145.27000	-	250.3 Hz	ARLA
Little Smoky	FM	VE6MBX	147.07500	+	156.7 Hz	ARLA
Lloydminster	FM	VE5FN-L	146.94000	-		
	FM	VE5YLL	444.72500	+	100.0 Hz	ARLA
Longview	FM	VE6HRL	145.37000	-		ARLA
	FM	VE6WRT	224.94000	-		ARLA
Medicine Hat	DSTAR	VE6MHD C	147.09000	+		
	DSTAR	VE6VOA B	433.10000			
	DSTAR	VA6SRG B	444.80000	+		
	DSTAR	VE6MHD B	445.90000	-		
	DSTAR	VE6MHD A	1287.50000	-		
	FM	VE6VVR	145.41000	-		
	FM	VE6HHO	146.70000	-	100.0 Hz	ARLA
	FM	VE6HAT	147.06000	+	100.0 Hz	ARLA
	FM	VE6RCM	147.57000		100.0 Hz	
	FM	VE6VOA	449.92500	-		
	FUSION	VE6MLD	145.56500			
Medicine Hat, Bowell						
	FM	VE6BWL	449.92500	-		
Meeting Creek	FM	VE6REP	449.17500	-	114.8 Hz	
Millarville	FM	VE6HRC	145.19000	-		ARLA
Morinville	FM	VA6CYR	146.55000			
	FM	VE6AEC-R	442.15000	+		ARLA
	FM	VE6TOP	447.75000	-	100.0 Hz	
Nanton	FM	VE6HRB	449.15000	-		ARLA
New Brigden	FM	VE6NBR	146.89500	-		
Nordegg	FM	VE6PZ	145.21000	-		ARLA
North Red Deer	FM	VE6YXR-R	449.55000	-		
Olds	FM	VE6OLS	145.49000	-		ARLA
	FM	VA6SVM	147.42500			
Peace River	FM	VE6AAA	145.49000	-		ARLA
	FM	VE6PRR	146.82000	-		ARLA
Pigeon Lake	FM	VE6SS	146.88000	-	100.0 Hz	ARLA
Pincher Creek	FM	VE6PAS	145.45000	-	110.9 Hz	ARLA
Pine Lake	FM	VE6REP	224.80000	-		ARLA
Raymond	FM	VE6EVY	146.67000	-		ARLA
Red Deer	FM	VE6REP	145.33000	-		ARLA
	FM	VE6QE	147.15000	+		ARLA
	FM	VE6QE	444.75000	+		ARLA
	WX	VBC336	162.55000			
	FUSION	VE6RNR	147.55500			
Red Deer County	DMR/BM	VA6DMR	145.79000	147.40500	CC7	
	DMR/BM	VA6DMR	443.66250	+	CC6	
Red Deer, Pine Lake						
	FM	VE6REP	443.57500	+		
Riverbend	FM	VE6RGB-L	144.97000	+		
Rocky Mtn Hse	FM	VE6VHF	146.91000	-		ARLA

Location	Mode	Call sign	Output	Input	Access	Coordinator
Sangudo	FM	VE6TOP	147.30000	+	100.0 Hz	
Sherwood Park	FM	VE6VPR	145.29000	-		ARLA
Slave Lake	FM	VE6SLR	147.03000	+		ARLA
Smoky Lake	FM	VE6TOP	146.68500	-	100.0 Hz	
	FM	VE6SSM	446.97500	-	114.8 Hz	ARLA
St. Albert	FM	VE6LAW-R	144.94000	-		
St. Paul	FM	VE6SB	146.67000	-		ARLA
St.Albert	DSTAR	VE6JKB B	444.25000	+		
Sturgeon County	FUSION	VE6HMG	442.12500	+		
Sundre	FM	VE6AMP	147.03000	+	131.8 Hz	ARLA
	FM	VE6GAB	147.07500	+	100.0 Hz	ARLA
	FM	VE6MTR	443.57500	+	114.8 Hz	ARLA
Swan Hills	FM	VE6SHR	145.35000	-		ARLA
Valley Ridge	FM	VE6CIZ	223.52000	-	88.5 Hz	
Valley View	FM	VE6YK	147.24000	+		ARLA
Vulcan	FM	VE6AAP	444.97500	+	114.8 Hz	ARLA
Wabamun	FM	VE6PLP	444.27500	+	446.0 Hz	ARLA
Wainwright	FUSION	VA6FP	433.30000			
Weatheradio-Bassano						
	WX	VFU885	162.52500			
Weatheradio-Brooks						
	WX	VDC816	162.40000			
Weatheradio-Burmis						
	WX	VBX254	162.55000			
Weatheradio-Calgary						
	WX	XLF339	162.40000			
Weatheradio-Cold Lake						
	WX	VFZ535	162.52500			
Weatheradio-Cooking Lake						
	WX	XOF962	162.47500			
Weatheradio-Drumheller						
	WX	VBX367	162.55000			
Weatheradio-Edmonton						
	WX	XLM572	162.40000			
Weatheradio-Edson						
	WX	VBU827	162.40000			
Weatheradio-Fort Chipewyan						
	WX	VFR368	162.55000			
Weatheradio-Grande Prairie						
	WX	VBA557	162.40000			
Weatheradio-Highvale						
	WX	VBU829	162.47500			
Weatheradio-Limestone Mountain						
	WX	VDA280	162.40000			
Weatheradio-Long Lake						
	WX	VFS310	162.55000			
Weatheradio-Medicine Hat						
	WX	VBK616	162.55000			
Weatheradio-Milk River						
	WX	XKA598	162.40000			
Weatheradio-Peace River						
	WX	VBU374	162.47500			
Weatheradio-Two Hills						
	WX	VXF723	162.52500			
Weatheradio-Whitecourt						
	WX	VBU828	162.55000			
Wetaskiwin	FM	VE6WCR	145.37000	-		ARLA
	FM	VE6MTR	449.32500	-	123.0 Hz	ARLA
White Court	FM	VE6PP	146.82000	-	100.0 Hz	ARLA
	FM	VE6MTR	449.30000	-	156.7 Hz	ARLA
Wild Cat Hills	FM	VE6AUY	147.06000	+	110.9 Hz	ARLA
Wimborne	FM	VE6BT	146.97000	-		ARLA

Location	Mode	Call sign	Output	Input	Access	Coordinator
BRITISH COLUMBIA						
100 Mile House	FM	VE7SCQ	146.74000	-		BCARCC
108 Mile Ranch	DMR/MARC	VA7KKW	145.45000	-	CC1	
	DMR/MARC	VA7KKW	443.10000	+	CC1	
Abbotsford	FM	VE7RVA	52.52500	51.52500		
	FM	VE7RVA	52.85000	51.15000	100.0 Hz	BCARCC
	FM	VE7PKV	145.03000	+		BCARCC
	FM	VE7RVA	146.61000	-	110.9 Hz	BCARCC
	FM	VE7ASM	147.28000	+	110.9 Hz	BCARCC
	FM	VE7RVA	442.02500	+	110.9 Hz	BCARCC
Anvil Island	FM	VE7QRO	52.91000	51.21000		BCARCC
Apex Mtn	FM	VE7OKN	146.92000	-		BCARCC
Atlin Mountain	FM	VA7ATN	146.34000	+		BCARCC
Atlin, Atlin Mountain						
	FM	VA7ATN	147.36000	+	100.0 Hz	
Barriere	FM	VE7RTN	147.24000	+		BCARCC
	FM	VE7RTN	147.30000	+		BCARCC
	FM	VA7RTN	442.65000	+		BCARCC
	FM	VE7RTN	442.87500	+		BCARCC
Barriere, Garrison Mtn						
	FM	VE7LMR	147.38000	+		
Bennett Lake	FM	VE7RFT	147.24000	+		BCARCC
Blackpool	FM	VE7RBP	146.90000	-	100.0 Hz	BCARCC
	FM	VE7RBP	444.00000	+		BCARCC
British Columbia	FM	VE7DJA	145.43000	-		
	FM	VE7RVA	146.60000	-	110.9 Hz	
	FM	VE7PQU	147.08000	+	141.3 Hz	
	FM	VE7RTN	147.32000	+		
	FM	VE7RSL	147.36000	+		
	FM	VE7PQE	442.52500	449.52500		
	FM	VE7RSL	443.77500	+		
	FM	VE7PQA	444.20000	+		
Burnaby	DMR/BM	VA7DIZ	145.02250	+	CC1	
	FM	VE7TEL	145.17000	-		BCARCC
	FM	VE7RBY	145.35000	-	127.3 Hz	BCARCC
	FM	VE7RBY	224.80000	-	127.3 Hz	BCARCC
	FM	VE7VYL	224.96000	-		BCARCC
	FM	VE7REM	442.05000	+	156.7 Hz	BCARCC
	FM	VA7LNK	442.20000	+	110.9 Hz	
	FM	VE7RBY	442.85000	+		BCARCC
	FM	VE7TEL	442.87500	+		BCARCC
	FM	VE7TEL	443.42500	+		
	FM	VE7CBN	443.67500	+	114.8 Hz	BCARCC
	FM	VE7ROX	444.75000	+	123.0 Hz	BCARCC
	FUSION	VE7YYO	446.20000			
Burnaby, TELUS	FM	VE7TEL	145.09000	+		
Burns Lake	FM	VE7LRB	146.94000	-	100.0 Hz	BCARCC
Campbell River	FM	VE7CRC	146.55000			
	FM	VE7XJR	146.76000	-		BCARCC
	FM	VE7RVR	146.82000	-	100.0 Hz	BCARCC
	FM	VE7CRC	146.96000	-		BCARCC
	FM	VE7NVI	442.45000	+		BCARCC
	FM	VE7CRC	443.65000	+	100.0 Hz	BCARCC
	FUSION	VA7GMI	144.00000			
Castlegar	FM	VE7FL	147.44000		100.0 Hz	
Charlie Lake	FUSION	VE7SST	147.27000	+		
Chemainus	FM	VE7RNA	146.68000	-	141.3 Hz	BCARCC
	FM	VE7RNA	224.94000	-	141.3 Hz	BCARCC
	FM	VE7RNA	442.60000	+	141.3 Hz	BCARCC
Chetwynd	FM	VA7XX	146.91000	-	100.0 Hz	
Chilliwack	DMR/BM	VA7CRC	443.00000	+	CC1	BCARCC

Location	Mode	Call sign	Output	Input	Access	Coordinator
Chilliwack	DSTAR	VE7RCK C	145.06000	+		
	DSTAR	VE7RCK B	444.62500	+		
	FM	VA7RSH	145.11000	-		BCARCC
	FM	VE7VCR	146.86000	-	88.5 Hz	BCARCC
	FM	VA7CRC	146.96000	-	110.9 Hz	BCARCC
	FM	VE7VCR	147.00000	+	88.5 Hz	
	FM	VE7RCK	147.10000	+	110.9 Hz	BCARCC
	FM	VE7VCR	147.22000	+	88.5 Hz	
	FM	VE7TMQ	147.52500			
	FM	VE7RVA	224.26000	-	110.9 Hz	BCARCC
	FM	VA7RSH	442.80000	+	110.9 Hz	BCARCC
	FM	VE7TPC	443.37500	+		
	FM	VE7RAD	444.70000	+		BCARCC
	FUSION	VE7RCK	145.06000	+		
	FUSION	VE7TDT	430.12500			
Clearwater	FM	VE7RWG	146.92000	-		BCARCC
Clinton	FM	VE7RKL	146.68000	-		BCARCC
	FM	VE7LMR	147.36000	+		BCARCC
	FM	VE7LMR	442.65000	+		BCARCC
	FM	VE7LMR	442.82500	+		BCARCC
Clinton Village	FM	VA7MWR	446.20000	-	67.0 Hz	
Cobble Hill	FM	VE7BH-L	144.68000	+		
Comox	DSTAR	VE7RAP B	444.50000	+		
	FUSION	VA7CV	441.00000			
Comox Valley	FM	VE7RCV	146.78000	-	141.3 Hz	BCARCC
	FM	VE7RAP	447.57500	-		BCARCC
Copper Creek	FM	VE7JMN-L	146.46000	+		
	FM	VE7EHP-L	147.55500	+		
Coquihalla	FM	VE7TYN	146.98000	-	123.0 Hz	BCARCC
	FM	VE7LGN	147.10000	+		BCARCC
Coquitlam	DSTAR	VE7NZD A	1290.50000	1270.50000		
	FM	VE7MFS	145.31000	-	127.3 Hz	BCARCC
	FM	VE7NZ	223.42000	-	156.7 Hz	
	FM	VE7VFB	223.92000	-		BCARCC
	FM	VE7MFS	224.92000	-		BCARCC
	FM	VE7MFS	224.94000	-		
	FM	VE7KHZ	443.60000	+	100.0 Hz	
	FUSION	VE7ROF	144.44000			
Courtenay	DMR/MARC	VE7RAP	442.57500	+	CC1	
	FM	VE7NIR	146.62000	-	141.3 Hz	BCARCC
	FM	VE7RAP	146.91000	-	141.3 Hz	BCARCC
	FM	VE7NIR	443.70000	+	141.3 Hz	BCARCC
Cowichan Valley	FM	VE7RNA	224.90000	-	141.3 Hz	BCARCC
Cranbrook	FM	VE7CAP	146.94000	-		BCARCC
	FM	VE7CAP	443.62500	+		BCARCC
Creston	FM	VE7RCA	146.80000	-		BCARCC
Dawson Creek	FM	VE7RMS	146.76000	-	100.0 Hz	BCARCC
	FM	VE7RDC	146.94000	-		BCARCC
Delta	DMR/BM	VE7SUN	440.72500	+	CC1	
	DSTAR	VE7SUN B	440.72500	+		
	DSTAR	VA7GQ B	445.77500	+		
	FM	VE7SUN	147.34000	+	107.2 Hz	BCARCC
	FM	VE7EPP	442.35000	+		BCARCC
	FM	VE7EPP	443.35000	+	127.3 Hz	BCARCC
	FM	VA7RPA	443.55000	+		BCARCC
	FUSION	VA7PI	448.55000	-		
Duncan	FM	VE7RVC	145.47000	-	127.3 Hz	BCARCC
	FM	VA7CDH	442.15000	+	141.3 Hz	BCARCC
East Richmond	DSTAR	VA7REF C	145.10000			
East Sooke, Mount Matheson						
	FM	VE7RAH	145.43000	-	100.0 Hz	

Location	Mode	Call sign	Output	Input	Access	Coordinator
Edgewood/Nakusp						
	FM	VE7SMT	449.25000	-		BCARCC
Esquimalt / Victoria						
	FM	VE7RRU	446.02500	-	123.0 Hz	
FairmontHotSpring						
	FM	VE7RIN	146.85000	-		BCARCC
Fishpot - Nazko	FM	VE7MBM	147.15000	+		BCARCC
Fort Nelson	FM	VE7VFN	146.94000	-		BCARCC
Fort St. James	FM	VE7RFF	147.24000	+	100.0 Hz	BCARCC
	FM	VE7DPG	147.33000	+	100.0 Hz	BCARCC
Fort St. John	FM	VA7XX	146.64000	-	100.0 Hz	
	FM	VE7RUC	147.21000	+	100.0 Hz	BCARCC
	FUSION	VE7TRW	146.50000			
Fraser Lake	FM	VE7RES	146.84000	-	100.0 Hz	BCARCC
Fraser Mountain	FM	VE7RFT	146.94000	-		BCARCC
Gabriola Island	FM	VE7GEC	443.00000	+	141.3 Hz	BCARCC
Grand Forks	FM	VE7RGF	146.94000	-	100.0 Hz	BCARCC
	FM	VE7RGF	147.28000	+		BCARCC
	FM	VE7KGF	147.33000	+	67.0 Hz	
	FM	VA7KT	147.52500		67.0 Hz	
Granisle	FUSION	VA7JRC	146.54500			
Granite Peak	FM	VE7RNH	146.76000	-		BCARCC
Haney	FM	VE7HNY	443.07500	+		
Hazelton	FM	VE7RHD	146.80000	-	100.0 Hz	BCARCC
Hope	DMR/BM	VA7ILR	145.43000	-	CC1	
	FM	VE7UVR	146.70000	-	77.0 Hz	BCARCC
	FM	VE7RVB	147.08000	+	110.9 Hz	BCARCC
Horsefly	FM	VE7WLP	147.18000	+	162.2 Hz	BCARCC
Houston	FM	VE7RHN	147.06000	+	100.0 Hz	BCARCC
Houston B.C.	FM	VE7CUP	147.31000	+	100.0 Hz	
Hudson's Hope	FM	VA7RHH	146.88000	-	100.0 Hz	BCARCC
Hudsons Hope	FM	VA7RHH	146.54000		100.0 Hz	
ICOM Canada	DSTAR	VA7ICM AD	1293.15000	-		
Kamloops	DMR/MARC	VE7RLO	442.65000	+	CC1	
	FM	VE7DUF	146.94000	-		BCARCC
	FM	VE7TSI	146.96000	-		
	FM	VE7RLD	147.00000	+		
	FM	VE7KEG	147.18000	+		BCARCC
	FM	VE7RLO	147.32000	+		BCARCC
	FM	VE7CRW	442.05000	+	103.5 Hz	BCARCC
	FM	VE7RLO	442.12500	+		
	FM	VE7RLO	442.15000	147.95000		BCARCC
	FM	VE7RLO	442.17500	147.87500		BCARCC
	FM	VE7TPK	442.55000	+		
	FM	VE7WM	443.16000			
	FM	VE7JFB	446.27500	-		
	FM	VE7RXD	447.50000	-	146.2 Hz	
	FM	VE7RLO	449.25000	-		BCARCC
	FM	VE7RHM	449.30000	-		BCARCC
	FM	VE7KIG	449.50000	-		BCARCC
	FUSION	VE7LTW	145.50000			
	FUSION	VE7WM	439.15000			
	FUSION	VE7WM	443.12000			
	FUSION	VE7UT	448.52500	-		
Kelowna	DMR/BM	VE7KTV	146.60000	-	CC1	
	DMR/BM	VA7JPL	146.70000	-	CC1	
	DMR/BM	VA7CNN	146.84000	-	CC1	
	DMR/BM	VA7NBC	147.10000	+	CC1	
	DMR/BM	VE7ATT	442.60000	+	CC1	
	DMR/BM	VA7CNN	444.00000	+	CC1	
	DMR/BM	VE7EQN	444.17500	+	CC1	
	DMR/BM	VA7NBC	444.80000	+	CC1	

Location	Mode	Call sign	Output	Input	Access	Coordinator
Kelowna	DMR/BM	VA7UN	449.90000	-	CC1	
	DSTAR	VA7DIG C	145.03000	+		
	DSTAR	VA7DIG B	440.95000	+		
	DSTAR	VA7DIG A	1247.00000	+		
	DSTAR	VA7DIG D	1293.15000			
	FM	VE7HWY	145.49000	-	88.5 Hz	BCARCC
	FM	VE7OGO	146.62000	-		
	FM	VE7OGO	146.68000	-		BCARCC
	FM	VE7EJP	146.72000	-		BCARCC
	FM	VE7SFX	146.78000	-	88.5 Hz	BCARCC
	FM	VE7ROC	146.82000	-		BCARCC
	FM	VE7RBG	146.86000	-	88.5 Hz	BCARCC
	FM	VE7OGO	147.00000	+	88.5 Hz	
	FM	VE7VTC	147.14000	+		BCARCC
	FM	VE7RIM	147.24000	+		BCARCC
	FM	VE7KTV	147.30000	+		BCARCC
	FM	VA7JPL	147.36000	+	88.5 Hz	BCARCC
	FM	VA7YLW	147.42000			
	FM	VE7OGO	147.57000		100.0 Hz	
	FM	VA7SPY	147.60000	-		
	FM	VA7JPL	444.00000	5444.00000	88.5 Hz	
	FM	VA7KRG	444.10000	+		
	FM	VE7KTV	444.30000	+		BCARCC
	FM	VA7JPL	444.50000	5444.50000	88.5 Hz	
	FM	VA7UN	444.70000	1044.70000	88.5 Hz	
	FM	VA7KEL	444.82500	+	88.5 Hz	
	FM	VA7UN	447.30000	-	88.5 Hz	BCARCC
	FM	VE7KEL	447.77500	-		BCARCC
	FUSION	VE7KEL	145.09000	+		
	FUSION	VE7RBJ	145.49000	-		
Kelowna, Mount Dilworth						
	FM	VA7OGO	146.68000	-	88.5 Hz	
Kelowna, Mount Last						
	FM	VA7KEL	449.12500	-		
Kimberley	DMR/BM	VE7DCX	443.75000	+	CC1	
	FM	VE7REK	145.19000	-		
Kitimat	FM	VA7TF	146.46000	+	100.0 Hz	
	FUSION	VA7TF	146.46000	+		
	FUSION	VE7SNO	146.82000	-	100.0 Hz	BCARCC
	FUSION	VE7RAF	147.06000	+	100.0 Hz	BCARCC
	FUSION	VA7LM	446.02500			
Kootenay Nat. Park						
	FM	VE7KNP	146.70000	-	131.8 Hz	BCARCC
Ladysmith	FM	VA7DXH	224.04000	-	141.3 Hz	BCARCC
	FM	VE7RNX	444.80000	+	156.7 Hz	BCARCC
Langford BC	FM	VE7LEP	442.72500	+	123.0 Hz	
Langley	FM	VE7LGY	146.78000	-		BCARCC
	FM	VA7OAC	147.00000	-	110.9 Hz	
	FM	VE7RMH	441.37500	+		BCARCC
	FM	VE7RLY	443.97500	+		BCARCC
	FM	VE7NPN	444.12500	+	127.3 Hz	BCARCC
	FM	VE7ICA	446.75000	-		
	FUSION	VA7OAC	146.40000	+		
	FUSION	VE7HUR	147.00000	-		
	FUSION	VE7RXE	433.00000			
Langley East	FM	VE7RLY	147.38000	+	203.5 Hz	BCARCC
Lillooett	FM	VE7TJS	147.38000	+		
Logan Lake	FM	VE7CPQ	146.58000			
Lone Butte	FM	VA7AZQ	147.22000	+	88.5 Hz	BCARCC
Loos	FM	VE7RES	146.88000	-	100.0 Hz	BCARCC
Lumby	FM	VE7HSP	144.50000			
	FUSION	VE7WEA	145.50000			

Location	Mode	Call sign	Output	Input	Access	Coordinator
Lund	FM	VA7LND	147.00000	+	100.0 Hz	BCARCC
	FM	VA7LND	444.35000	+	100.0 Hz	BCARCC
Lytton	FM	VE7HGR	147.06000	+		BCARCC
Mackenzie	FM	VE7MKR	146.82000	-	100.0 Hz	
Malahat	FM	VE7XMR	146.98000	-	123.0 Hz	BCARCC
	FM	VA7XMR	443.02500	+		
Maple Ridge	FM	VE7RMR	146.80000	-	156.7 Hz	BCARCC
	FM	VE7RMR	224.88000	-		BCARCC
	FM	VE7RMR	443.62500	+	156.7 Hz	BCARCC
McBride	FM	VE7RMB	146.76000	-	100.0 Hz	BCARCC
McLeod Lake	FM	VE7ZBK-R	147.33000	+		BCARCC
Merritt	FM	VE7IRN	146.66000	-		BCARCC
	FM	VE7RIZ	147.08000	+	110.9 Hz	BCARCC
Mill Bay	FUSION	VE7RGT	146.54000			
Millstream	FM	VE7US-L	145.13000	-		BCARCC
Monashee Pass	FM	VE7SMT	146.74000	-	123.0 Hz	BCARCC
Mt Seymour	DSTAR	VE7RAG C	147.02000	+		
	DSTAR	VE7RAG B	443.40000	+		
	DSTAR	VE7RAG A	1271.94000			
	DSTAR	VE7RAG A	1291.94000	1271.94000		
Mt. Avola	FM	VE7RBP	145.35000	-		BCARCC
Nakusp	FM	VE7EDA	146.94000	-		
Nanaimo	DMR/MARC	VE7NHR	440.82500	+	CC1	
	FM	VA7ANI	146.98000	-	141.3 Hz	BCARCC
	FM	VE7RBB	147.18000	+	100.0 Hz	BCARCC
	FM	VE7RXZ	147.22000	+	100.0 Hz	BCARCC
	FM	VA7SZU	442.52500	+		
	FM	VE7ITS	444.72500	+	141.3 Hz	BCARCC
	FM	VA7ZSU	444.80000	+		
Nanoose Bay	FM	VA7LPG	444.30000	+	141.3 Hz	BCARCC
Nelson	DMR/MARC	VE7BDY	147.04000	+	CC1	
	DMR/MARC	VE7BTU	147.06000	+	CC1	BCARCC
	FM	VE7RCT	146.64000	-		BCARCC
	FM	VE7RCT	444.55000	+		BCARCC
New Denver	FM	VE7FL-R	146.56000	+		
New Westminster	DMR/MARC	VE7NWR	444.60000	+	CC1	BCARCC
	FM	VE7WCC	145.15000	-	123.0 Hz	
	FM	VE7NWR	145.39000	-	100.0 Hz	BCARCC
	FM	VA7HPS	442.37500	+	110.9 Hz	BCARCC
Nimpo Lake	FM	VA7SPY	444.82500	+	88.5 Hz	BCARCC
North Campbell River						
	FM	VA7UW-L	147.57000	+		
North Vancouver	DMR/MARC	VE7RAG	443.40000	+	CC1	
	FUSION	VE7LTV	444.65000	+		
North Vancouver, Mount Seymour						
	FM	VE7LAN	145.07000	+		
Oak Bay	FM	VE7XIC	146.84000	-	107.2 Hz	BCARCC
Okanagan Falls	FM	VE7DTT	144.56000	+	123.0 Hz	
	FM	VE7DTT	147.33000	+	100.0 Hz	
	FM	VE7DTT	147.56000		123.0 Hz	
Okanagan/Shuswap						
	FM	VE7RNR	147.06000	+		BCARCC
Oliver	FM	VE7RBD	147.16000	+		BCARCC
	FM	VE7ROR	147.38000	+		BCARCC
	FM	VE7RSO	444.60000	+	100.0 Hz	
Osoyoos	FM	VE7OSY	145.27000	-	107.2 Hz	BCARCC
	FM	VE7EHF	145.29000	-	107.2 Hz	BCARCC
	FM	VE7OSY	146.66000	-	156.7 Hz	
	FM	VE7STA	146.94000	-		BCARCC
	FM	VE7OJP	147.18000	+	88.5 Hz	BCARCC
	FM	VE7OSY	222.60000	+	156.7 Hz	BCARCC

Location	Mode	Call sign	Output	Input	Access	Coordinator
Osoyoos, Mount Kobau						
	FM	VE7EHF	147.34000	+	107.2 Hz	
Parksville	FM	VE7RPQ	145.37000	-	100.0 Hz	BCARCC
	FM	VA7RFR	147.08000	+	141.3 Hz	BCARCC
	FM	VE7PQA	147.28000	+	141.3 Hz	BCARCC
	FM	VE7MIR	147.34000	+	141.3 Hz	
	FM	VE7MIR	440.85000	+	100.0 Hz	
	FM	VE7JPS	442.27500	+	136.5 Hz	
	FM	VE7PQD	444.20000	+		BCARCC
Peachland	FM	VA7OKV	447.22500	-	88.5 Hz	BCARCC
Pemberton	FM	VE7PVR	146.98000	-		BCARCC
Penticton	DMR/BM	VA7PTV	449.70000	-	CC1	
	FM	VE7PEN	146.58000		123.0 Hz	
	FM	VE7RCP	146.64000	-	131.8 Hz	BCARCC
	FM	VE7RPC	147.12000	+		BCARCC
	FM	VE7RPC	444.50000	+		BCARCC
	FM	VE7RCP	444.77500	+	136.5 Hz	
Pine Pass	FM	VE7RES	146.64000	-	100.0 Hz	BCARCC
Pitt Meadows	FM	VE7MTY	443.62500	+		
Port Alberni	DMR/MARC	VE7CIM	444.25000	+	CC1	
	FM	VE7RPA	147.15000	+	141.3 Hz	BCARCC
	FM	VE7KU	147.24000	+	141.3 Hz	BCARCC
	FM	VE7KU	444.45000	+		BCARCC
Port Alberni, Mount Cokely						
	FM	VE7RTU	444.75000	+	100.0 Hz	
Port Coquitlam	FM	VA7RPC	145.49000	-	94.8 Hz	BCARCC
	FM	VE7UDX	443.10000	+	94.8 Hz	BCARCC
	FM	VE7VDU	443.15000	+	127.3 Hz	
	FUSION	VE7VDU	446.10000			
Port McNeil	FM	VA7RNI	146.92000	-		BCARCC
	FM	VE7RNI	146.94000	-		BCARCC
Port McNeill	FM	VE7KJA	146.44500			
Port Moody	DMR/BM	VA7HIZ	145.01000	+	CC1	
	DMR/BM	VA7DIZ	145.62250	-	CC1	
	DMR/BM	VA7FIZ	440.13125	+	CC1	
Pouce Coupe	FM	VE7AGJ	146.25000	+		BCARCC
Powell River	FM	VE7PRR	147.20000	+	141.3 Hz	BCARCC
	FM	VE7PRR	444.50000	+		BCARCC
Prince George	DSTAR	VE7RES C	147.02000	+		
	DSTAR	VE7RES B	442.10000	+		
	DSTAR	VE7RES A	1291.94000	1271.94000		
	FM	VE7RES	145.43000	-	100.0 Hz	BCARCC
	FM	VE7RWT	146.91000	-	100.0 Hz	BCARCC
	FM	VE7RPM	146.94000	-	100.0 Hz	BCARCC
	FM	VE7RES	147.30000	+	100.0 Hz	BCARCC
	FM	VE7RQU	442.86200	+		
	FM	VE7RUN	444.00000	+		
	FUSION	VE7TSW	145.43000	-		
Prince George, Tabor Mountain						
	FM	VE7FFF	146.70000	-	100.0 Hz	
	FM	VE7RUN	147.00000	+		
Prince Rupert	FM	VE7RPR	146.88000	-		BCARCC
	FM	VE7RKI	146.94000	-		BCARCC
	FM	VE7RMM	147.28000	+		BCARCC
	FM	VE7DQC	147.33000	+		
Qualicum Beach	DMR/BM	VE7EVS	440.85000	+	CC1	
	FM	VE7RPQ	442.25000	144.75000	141.3 Hz	BCARCC
	FM	VE7RQR	445.00000	144.80000		BCARCC
Queen Charlotte	FM	VE7RQI	146.68000	-		BCARCC
Quesnel	FM	VE7RQL	147.06000	+		BCARCC
	FM	VE7RES	147.21000	+	100.0 Hz	BCARCC
	FM	VE7RQM	444.30000	+		

Location	Mode	Call sign	Output	Input	Access	Coordinator
Quesnel, Airport	FM	VE7YQZ	146.97000	-		
Radium, Mount Sinclair						
	FM	VE7PNR	146.88000	-	131.8 Hz	
Revelstoke	FM	VA7AZG	146.72000	-		BCARCC
	FM	VE7RJP	147.20000	+		BCARCC
Richmond	DSTAR	VA7REF C	144.93000			
	FM	VE7RMD	147.14000	+	79.7 Hz	BCARCC
	FM	VE7BAS	147.51000		156.7 Hz	
	FM	VE7RMD	442.37500	+	203.5 Hz	BCARCC
	FUSION	VA7REF	442.50000	+		
River Springs	FM	VE7SVG-L	445.55000	-		
Saanich	FM	VE7SER	145.29000	-	167.9 Hz	BCARCC
	FM	VA7XMR	443.07500	+		BCARCC
	FM	VE7SLC	449.45000	-	100.0 Hz	BCARCC
Salmo	FM	VE7KNL-L	144.39000	+		
Salmon Arm	FM	VE7CAL	146.16000	+		BCARCC
	FM	VE7RAM	146.64000	-		BCARCC
	FM	VE7RSA	147.02000	+		BCARCC
	FM	VE7RAM	442.45000	+		BCARCC
Salt Spring Is	FM	VA7VIC	146.66000	-	100.0 Hz	
Salt Spring Isl	DSTAR	VE7MDN B	440.95000	+		
Salt Spring Island	DSTAR	VE7XNR B	444.85000	+		
	FM	VE7GDH	147.57000		100.0 Hz	
	FUSION	VE7RGP	444.55000	+		
Saltspring Is	FM	VE7RSI	147.32000	+	88.5 Hz	BCARCC
Santa Rosa, Christina Lake						
	FM	VE7RCL	146.70000	-		
Saturna Island	FM	VA7RMI	444.55000	+	97.4 Hz	
Sayward	FM	VE7RNC	146.70000	-		BCARCC
	FM	VE7RNC	224.62000	-		BCARCC
	FM	VE7RNC	443.70000	+		BCARCC
Sechelt	FM	VE7SSC	444.62500	+		
Sherwood Park	DSTAR	VE6DXH B	444.30000	+		
Shirley/Jordon River						
	FM	VE7RSK	147.22000	+	123.0 Hz	BCARCC
Shirley/Otter Point	FM	VE7RYF	145.41000	-	100.0 Hz	BCARCC
Shuswap	FM	VE7LIM	147.08000	+		BCARCC
Sicamous	FM	VE7QMR	145.47000	-		BCARCC
	FM	VE7BYN	147.54000			
	FM	VE7BYN	147.57000			
Silver Star	FM	VE7RHW	146.90000	-	123.0 Hz	BCARCC
Smithers	FM	VE7RBH	146.88000	-	100.0 Hz	BCARCC
	FM	VE7RBH	147.33000	+	100.0 Hz	
	FUSION	VE7RBH	146.48000			
Sooke	DMR/MARC	VA7PRR	146.12000	+	CC1	
	FM	VE7RWS	145.41000	-	103.5 Hz	
	FM	VE7XSK	146.84000	-	123.0 Hz	BCARCC
	FUSION	VE7RYF	444.80000	+		
Sorrento	FM	VE7RXX	146.64000	-		BCARCC
	FM	VA7AHR	147.14000	+		BCARCC
	FM	VE7SPG	444.10000	+		BCARCC
South Okanagan	FM	VE7RSO	147.34000	+	107.2 Hz	BCARCC
Sparwood	FM	VE7RSQ	147.30000	+	100.0 Hz	BCARCC
Squamish	DMR/MARC	VA7WRP	443.85000	+	CC3	
	FM	VE7SQR	147.00000	+	77.0 Hz	BCARCC
Squilax	FM	VE7FPG	442.52500	+		
Summerland	FM	VE7NUT	145.35000	-		
Sunshine Coast	FM	VE7RXZ	442.65000	+	123.0 Hz	BCARCC
Sunshine Hills	FM	VA7DEP-R	444.42500	+		
Surrey	DMR/MARC	VE7CNC	440.60000	+	CC1	
	FM	VE7DQ	53.53000	52.53000		
	FM	VE7RSC	147.36000	+	110.9 Hz	BCARCC

Location	Mode	Call sign	Output	Input	Access	Coordinator
Surrey	FM	VE7IKB	223.40000	-		
	FM	VE7MAN	441.07500	+		
	FM	VE7MAN	443.60000	+		BCARCC
	FM	VE7RSC	443.77500	+	110.9 Hz	BCARCC
Survey Mountain	FM	VE7RYF	444.92500	+	100.0 Hz	BCARCC
Tappen	FM	VE7RAM	146.48500			
Tatlayoko Lake	FM	VE7SML	146.82000	-		
Tatlayoko Valley	FM	VA7TKR	147.28000	+	162.2 Hz	BCARCC
Terrace	FM	VE7RTK	146.60000	-	100.0 Hz	
	FM	VE7FFU	146.80000	-		BCARCC
	FM	VE7RDD	146.94000	-		BCARCC
	FM	VE7FFU	147.33000	+		
	FM	VE7RDD	444.97500	+		BCARCC
	FUSION	VA7WLR	146.28000	+		
Texada Island	FM	VE7TIR	444.02500	+	141.3 Hz	BCARCC
Tofino	FM	VE7TOF	146.88000	-	141.3 Hz	BCARCC
Triangle Mtn	FM	VE7RMT	146.84000	-	131.8 Hz	BCARCC
Tumbler Ridge	FM	VE7RTR	147.27000	+	100.0 Hz	
Ucluelet	FM	VE7RWC	147.00000	+	100.0 Hz	BCARCC
Valemont	FM	VE7YCR	146.60000	-		BCARCC
	FM	VE7RES	147.00000	+	100.0 Hz	BCARCC
Vancouver	DMR/BM	VE7KEY	440.02500	+	CC1	
	DMR/BM	VE7RHS	442.45000	+	CC1	
	DMR/BM	VE7AAU	442.95000	+	CC1	
	DMR/BM	VE7ZIT	447.57500	-	CC1	
	DMR/MARC	VE7RYS	442.17500	+	CC1	
	DMR/MARC	VA7XPR	443.50000	+	CC1	
	DSTAR	VA7ICM C	145.04000	+		
	DSTAR	VE7RAG C	147.02000	+		
	DSTAR	VA7ICM B	442.00000	+		
	DSTAR	VA7ICM A	1247.00000	+		
	DSTAR	VE7RAG D	1251.94000			
	DSTAR	VE7RAG A	1291.94000	1271.94000		
	DSTAR	VA7ICM A	1293.15000	-		
	DSTAR	VA7ICM D	1293.15000			
	FM	VE7HCP	52.89000	51.19000		BCARCC
	FM	VE7ROX	145.15000	-	123.0 Hz	BCARCC
	FM	VE7RTY	145.21000	-		BCARCC
	FM	VE7RHS	145.27000	-	100.0 Hz	BCARCC
	FM	VA7IP	145.29000	-	100.0 Hz	BCARCC
	FM	VE7RBI	146.72000	-		BCARCC
	FM	VE7RPT	146.94000	-		BCARCC
	FM	VE7RCH	147.04000	+		BCARCC
	FM	VE7VAN	147.12000	+	156.7 Hz	BCARCC
	FM	VE7RNS	147.26000	+		BCARCC
	FM	VE7RDX	147.30000	+		BCARCC
	FM	VE7RPT	224.30000	-		BCARCC
	FM	VE7NYE	224.60000	-	127.3 Hz	BCARCC
	FM	VE7RVK	224.64000	-		BCARCC
	FM	VE7RHS	224.70000	-		BCARCC
	FM	VE7RHS	441.97500	+		BCARCC
	FM	VE7RPS	442.22500	+	88.5 Hz	BCARCC
	FM	VE7VHF	442.32500	+	100.0 Hz	BCARCC
	FM	VE7UBC	442.45000	+		
	FM	VE7ZIT	442.57500	+	114.8 Hz	BCARCC
	FM	VE7AAU	442.95000	+	114.8 Hz	BCARCC
	FM	VE7YV	443.05000	+	110.9 Hz	BCARCC
	FM	VE7NSR	443.20000	+		BCARCC
	FM	VE7RCH	443.25000	+		BCARCC
	FM	VE7RCI	443.27500	+		BCARCC
	FM	VE7RPT	443.52500	+		BCARCC
	FM	VE7UHF	443.80000	+	100.0 Hz	BCARCC

Location	Mode	Call sign	Output	Input	Access	Coordinator
Vancouver	FM	VE7URG	444.00000	+	156.7 Hz	BCARCC
	FM	VE7TOK	444.07500	+		BCARCC
	FM	VE7ROY	444.10000	+	100.0 Hz	BCARCC
	FM	VE7RIO	444.17500	+	156.7 Hz	BCARCC
	FM	VE7PRA	444.47500	+		BCARCC
	FM	VA7DTR	444.65000	+	156.7 Hz	
	FM	VE7VYL	444.82500	+	156.7 Hz	BCARCC
	FM	VE7WAR	444.92500	+		
	FM	VE7RNV	444.95000	+		BCARCC
	FM	VE7SKY	444.97500	+		BCARCC
	NXDN	VE7NYE	443.15000	+	127.3 Hz	BCARCC
	FUSION	VA7CAB	442.30000	+		
	FUSION	VA7DTR	444.65000	+		
Vancouver WIN System Affiliate						
	FM	VA7SCA	444.40000	+	100.0 Hz	
Vancouver, Anvil Island						
	FM	VE7QRO	444.40000	+	100.0 Hz	
Vancouver, Seymour Mtn						
	FM	VE7RVF	145.45000	-	100.0 Hz	
Vanderhoof	FM	VE7RSM	146.80000	-	100.0 Hz	BCARCC
	FM	VE7RON	146.88000	-		BCARCC
Vanway	FM	VE7CKZ-L	446.10000	-		
Verdun	FM	VE7LRB	146.76000	-	100.0 Hz	BCARCC
Vernon	DMR/BM	VA7VTV	449.60000	-	CC1	
	DMR/MARC	VE7KHZ	145.05000	+	CC1	
	FM	VA7VMR	52.01000	-	110.9 Hz	BCARCC
	FM	VE7EGO	145.45000	-		
	FM	VE7KI-L	146.56500	+		
	FM	VE7EGO	146.80000	-		BCARCC
	FM	VE7RSS	146.88000	-		BCARCC
	FM	VE7RIP	147.04000	+		BCARCC
	FM	VA7VMR	147.22000	+		BCARCC
	FM	VE7DIR	147.49500		151.4 Hz	
	FM	VA7NWS	441.15000	147.55000		BCARCC
	FM	VE7PE	442.42500	+		
	FM	VE7RFM	444.35000	+	100.0 Hz	BCARCC
	FM	VE7RVP	447.42500	-		
	FM	VE7RVP	447.50000	-		
	FUSION	VE7EGO	147.38000	+		
	FUSION	VE7AM	440.12500			
Vernon, Silver Star Mtn						
	FM	VE7RVN	444.27500	+	110.9 Hz	
Victoria	DMR/MARC	VE7VIC	146.66000	453.34000	CC7	
	DMR/MARC	VE7VIC	443.95000	+	CC1	
	DSTAR	VE7VIC C	145.08000	+		
	DSTAR	VE7VIC A	1291.50000	-		
	DSTAR	VE7VIC D	1291.50000			
	FM	VE7DAT	51.27000	-		
	FM	VE7RSX	52.83000	51.13000	100.0 Hz	BCARCC
	FM	VE7RFR	52.97000	51.27000		BCARCC
	FM	VE7VIC	146.84000	-	100.0 Hz	BCARCC
	FM	VE7RYF	146.98000	-	103.5 Hz	BCARCC
	FM	VE7RBA	147.12000	+	100.0 Hz	BCARCC
	FM	VE7RFR	147.24000	+		BCARCC
	FM	VE7VIC	224.14000	-	100.0 Hz	BCARCC
	FM	VE7RGP	224.50000	-		BCARCC
	FM	VE7OVY	441.50000	+	100.0 Hz	
	FM	VE7RFR	442.70000	+		BCARCC
	FM	VA7CRT	442.77500	+		BCARCC
	FM	VE7RYF	443.02500	+	100.0 Hz	BCARCC
	FM	VE7RAA	443.57500	+		BCARCC
	FM	VE7VOP	443.82500	+	100.0 Hz	BCARCC

Location	Mode	Call sign	Output	Input	Access	Coordinator
Victoria	FM	VE7RFR	443.90000	+	141.3 Hz	BCARCC
	FM	VE7US	444.15000	+	103.5 Hz	BCARCC
	FM	VE7FNI	444.25000	+		
	FM	VE7SLC	444.45000	+	100.0 Hz	
	FM	VE7XIC	449.87500	146.27500		BCARCC
	FUSION	VE7IGN	145.56250			
	FUSION	VE7OVY	444.55000	+		
Victoria, BC, Canada						
	DSTAR	VE7VIC B	447.00000	+		
	DSTAR	VE7VIC AD	1261.75000			
Victoria, Fire Hall 1						
	FM	VE7GHO	443.82500	+	100.0 Hz	
Victoria, Mount McDonald						
	FM	VE7BEL	224.90000	-		
	FM	VE7USA	444.87500	+	107.2 Hz	
Weatheradio-Alert Bay						
	WX	VAF	162.55000			
Weatheradio-Barry Inlet						
	WX	XLK897	162.40000			
Weatheradio-Bowen Island						
	WX	XLK672	162.47500			
Weatheradio-Calvert Island						
	WX	VGL24	162.40000			
Weatheradio-Castlegar						
	WX	XMD482	162.55000			
Weatheradio-Chilliwack						
	WX	VFV785	162.40000			
Weatheradio-Cranbrook						
	WX	VBI853	162.40000			
Weatheradio-Crawford Bay						
	WX	VFD904	162.42500			
Weatheradio-Cumshewa						
	WX	XLK894	162.47500			
Weatheradio-Eliza Dome						
	WX	VGI57	162.55000			
Weatheradio-Estevan Point						
	WX	XLA840	162.47500			
Weatheradio-Fort Nelson						
	WX	VXB567	162.55000			
Weatheradio-Fort St John						
	WX	VXL336	162.47500			
Weatheradio-Kelowna						
	WX	XMD480	162.55000			
Weatheradio-Klemtu						
	WX	XLK899	162.55000			
Weatheradio-Mount Gil						
	WX	XLK898	162.40000			
Weatheradio-Mount Helmcken-Vic						
	WX	XLA726	162.47500			
Weatheradio-Naden Harbour						
	WX	XLK895	162.47500			
Weatheradio-Nootka						
	WX	VGZ36	162.40000			
Weatheradio-Penticton						
	WX	XMD481	162.47500			
Weatheradio-Port Alberni						
	WX	XLA823	162.40000			
	WX	VFM825	162.52500			
Weatheradio-Port Hardy						
	WX	VBH444	162.47500			
	WX	VFM839	162.52500			

Location	Mode	Call sign	Output	Input	Access	Coordinator
Weatheradio-Prince George						
	WX	VGB723	162.40000			
Weatheradio-Prince Rupert						
	WX	VXB571	162.42500			
Weatheradio-Texada Island						
	WX	VBG969	162.55000			
Weatheradio-Van Inlet						
	WX	XLK896	162.55000			
Weatheradio-Vancouver						
	WX	VXL665	162.55000			
Weatheradio-Vernon						
	WX	VFM608	162.47500			
Weatheradio-Victoria						
	WX	XKK506	162.40000			
Wells/Barkerville	FM	VE7RLS	147.38000	+	100.0 Hz	BCARCC
West Vancouver	DMR/MARC	VE7SLV	443.85000	+	CC1	BCARCC
Westbank	FM	VE7CJU	147.20000	+		
Westview	FM	VA7UQ-L	146.56500	+		
Whistler	DMR/MARC	VE7WRP	443.85000	+	CC2	
	DSTAR	VA7WHI C	146.22000	+		
	FM	VE7WHR	147.06000	+		BCARCC
White Rock	FM	VE7RWR	146.90000	-	91.5 Hz	BCARCC
Williams Lake	DMR/MARC	VE7PW	444.10000	+	CC1	
	DMR/MARC	VE7ZIG	449.10000	+	CC1	
	FM	VE7RTI	146.62000	-	100.0 Hz	BCARCC
	FM	VE7RWL	147.12000	+	100.0 Hz	BCARCC
	FM	VE7ZIG	444.10000	+		BCARCC
Woss Lake	FM	VE7RWV	146.88000	-		BCARCC
Yennadon	FM	VE7NLY-L	146.50000	+		
MANITOBA						
Adam Lake	FM	VE4IHF	146.25000	+		NDFC
	FM	VE4IHF	146.85000	-	127.3 Hz	NDFC
Austin	FM	VE4MTR	146.91000	-	127.3 Hz	MARCC
	FM	VE4MTR	444.27500	+		MARCC
Baldy Mountain	FM	VE4BMR	147.03000	+		MARCC
	FM	VE4BMR	448.40000	-		
Basswood	FM	VE4BAS	145.15000	-	127.3 Hz	MARCC
Beausejour	FM	VE4BRC	147.54000			MARCC
Brandon	FM	VE4CTY	146.64000	-	127.3 Hz	MARCC
	FM	VE4TED	146.73000	-		MARCC
	FM	VE4BDN	146.94000	-		MARCC
	FM	VE4CTY	443.70000	+	127.3 Hz	MARCC
Bruxelles	FM	VE4MRS	145.31000	-		MARCC
	FM	VE4HS	146.88000	-		MARCC
Channing	FM	VA4BG-L	145.00000	+		
Chatfield	FM	VE4TGN	443.80000	+		
East Selkirk	FM	VE4SLK	146.73000	-	127.3 Hz	MARCC
Elie	FM	VE4RAG	147.24000	+	127.3 Hz	MARCC
Falcon Lake	DMR/BM	VA4DMR	444.43750	+	CC4	
	FM	VE4FAL	146.64000	-		MARCC
	FUSION	VE4YSF	147.52500			
Flin Flon	DMR/BM	VE4FFR	147.88500	147.82500	CC1	
	FM	VA4BOB	145.00000		100.0 Hz	
	FM	VE4FFR	146.94000	-		MARCC
	FM	VA4BOB	147.00000	+	100.0 Hz	
Flin Flon, Smoke Stack						
	FM	VE5ROD	146.94000	-		
Gimli	FM	VE4GIM	146.85000	-		MARCC
Hadashville	FM	VE4EMB	147.36000	+		MARCC
Headingley	FM	VE4AGA	444.50000	+	127.3 Hz	MARCC
Killarney	FM	VE4KIL	444.50000	+	123.0 Hz	MARCC

Location	Mode	Call sign	Output	Input	Access	Coordinator
Lundar	FM	VE4LDR	146.97000	-		MARCC
Milner Ridge	FM	VE4MIL	145.21000	-		MARCC
Morris	FM	VE4CDN	145.27000	-		MARCC
Notre Dame	FM	VE4HJ	444.32500	+		MARCC
Pinawa	FM	VE4PIN	146.49000			MARCC
Portage	FM	VE4PLP	147.16500	+		MARCC
Portage La Prairie	DMR/BM	VE4DMP	444.80000	+	CC4	
Rice Creek	FM	VE4JAR	147.36000	+		MARCC
Russell	FM	VE4BVR	147.24000	+		MARCC
Selkirk	DMR/BM	VE4DMS	443.72500	+	CC4	
	DMR/MARC	VE4SLK	444.15000	+	CC1	MARCC
Spearhill	FM	VE4SHR	146.70000	-	127.3 Hz	MARCC
St Pierre-Jolys	FUSION	VE4SCU	449.72500	-		
St. Andrews	FUSION	VE4COR	146.82000	-		
Starbuck	FM	VE4MAN	146.61000	-		MARCC
Steinbach	DMR/BM	VE4UHF	444.65000	+	CC4	
Swan River	FM	VE4SRR	146.94000	-		MARCC
	FM	VE4SRR	443.40000	+		MARCC
Teulon	FM	VE4TEU	145.41000	-		MARCC
The Pas	FM	VE4PAS	145.35000	-		MARCC
	FM	VE4PAS	145.40000	-	127.3 Hz	
	FUSION	VE4REM	146.55000			
Thompson	FM	VE4TPN	146.94000	-		MARCC
Weatheradio-Altona						
	WX	VFN684	162.42500			
Weatheradio-Brandon						
	WX	VAO302	162.55000			
Weatheradio-Dauphin						
	WX	VBA814	162.55000			
Weatheradio-Falcon Lake						
	WX	VXE212	162.42500			
Weatheradio-Haywood						
	WX	VBL854	162.40000			
Weatheradio-Long Point						
	WX	VCI386	162.55000			
Weatheradio-Pointe Du Bois						
	WX	VXG567	162.45000			
Weatheradio-Reston						
	WX	VXK206	162.42500			
Weatheradio-Riverton						
	WX	XLF471	162.40000			
Weatheradio-Steinbach						
	WX	VFN683	162.47500			
Weatheradio-Thompson						
	WX	VXI858	162.40000			
Weatheradio-Winnipeg						
	WX	XLM538	162.55000			
Windy Hill	FM	VE4WHR	145.45000	-		MARCC
Winkler	FM	VE4VRG	145.19000	-		MARCC
	FM	VE4BBS	146.91000	-		
	FM	VE4TOM	147.33000	+	127.3 Hz	
Winnipeg	ATV	VE4EDU	1289.25000	914.95000		MARCC
	DMR/BM	VE4DMR	443.67500	+	CC4	
	DMR/MARC	VE4DHR	442.00000	+	CC1	
	DSTAR	VE4WDR C	145.49000	-		
	DSTAR	VE4UMR B	443.27500	+		
	DSTAR	VE4WDR B	444.57500	+		
	DSTAR	VE4WDR D	1248.30000			
	FM	VE4PAR	145.17000	-	141.3 Hz	MARCC
	FM	VE4ARC	145.23000	-	127.3 Hz	MARCC
	FM	VE4ARS	145.35000	-	127.3 Hz	MARCC
	FM	VE4PNO	146.46000		100.0 Hz	MARCC

Location	Mode	Call sign	Output	Input	Access	Coordinator
Winnipeg	FM	VE4JRA	146.67000	-		MARCC
	FM	VE4UMR	147.27000	+	127.3 Hz	MARCC
	FM	VE4EDU	147.30000	+		MARCC
	FM	VE4WPG	147.39000	+	127.3 Hz	MARCC
	FM	VE4WSC	147.57000			MARCC
	FM	VA4ARS	443.22500	+	127.3 Hz	MARCC
	FM	VE4VJ	443.50000	+	127.3 Hz	MARCC
	FM	VE4UHF	444.00000	+		MARCC
	FM	VA4ART	444.10000	+		MARCC
	FM	VA4UHF	444.75000	+		MARCC
	FM	VE4KEY	444.93750	+	88.5 Hz	
	P25	VE4KEY	147.01500	+	127.3 Hz	MARCC
	P25	VE4KEY	927.01250	902.01250		MARCC
	FUSION	VE4UMR	147.27000	+		
	FUSION	VE4PAR	443.02500	+		
	FUSION	VA4JF	443.50000	+		
	FUSION	VE4RNP	449.10000	-		
Woodlands	FM	VE4SIX	145.43000	-	127.3 Hz	MARCC

NEW BRUNSWICK

Location	Mode	Call sign	Output	Input	Access	Coordinator
Acadieville	FM	VE9ACD	145.43000	-		
Amherst, Nova Scotia Provincia						
	FM	VE1WRC	147.28500	+		
Antigonish	DSTAR	VE1JSR B	441.80000	+		
Bathurst	FM	VE1BRD	147.31500	+		
	FUSION	VE9BAT	147.24000			
	FUSION	VE9TEK	147.54000			
Bridgewater	DSTAR	VE1DSR C	145.29000	-		
Campbellton	FM	VE1CTN	146.65500	-		
	FM	VE9SMR	146.95500	-		
	FM	VE1LES	147.00000	+		
	FUSION	VE9ARM	145.52000			
	FUSION	VE9ARM/3	145.79000			
Campbellton, Seven Mile Ridge						
	FM	VE9VDR	147.39000	+		
Charlottetown	DSTAR	VE1UHF C	146.71500	-		
	DSTAR	VE1UHF B	443.30000	+		
Chipman, Bronson						
	FM	VE9GLA	145.19000	-	123.0 Hz	
Crabbe Mountain	DMR/MARC	VE9ACP	147.25500	+	CC1	
	FM	VE1PD	146.76000	-		
Dalhousie	FM	VE9DNB	145.49000	-		
	FUSION	VE9DEN	146.82000	-		
	FUSION	VE2RPG	147.18000	+		
Dalhousie NB	FM	VE9DEN	146.82000	+		
	FUSION	VE9DEN	147.57000			
Doaktown	FM	VE1XI	146.91000	-		
Dsl De Drummond						
	FUSION	VE9GFY	147.79500	-		
Edmunston	FM	VE9RCV	145.13000	-		
Elmtree	FM	VE9ELM	145.41000	-		
Fairfield	FM	VE9SKV	145.23000	-		
Fredericton	DMR/MARC	VE9FTN	147.16500	+	CC1	
	FM	VE1BM	147.12000	+		
	FM	VE9FNB	147.30000	+		
	FM	VE9FTN	927.68750	902.68750	100.0 Hz	
	FUSION	VE9HAM	145.39000	-		
	FUSION	VE9AI	445.90000			
Fredericton, CBC Fredericton S						
	FM	VE9ARZ	448.70000	-	141.3 Hz	
Fredericton, Nashwaaksis						
	FM	VE9CWM	146.65500	-	123.0 Hz	

Location	Mode	Call sign	Output	Input	Access	Coordinator
Fredericton, Nashwaaksis						
	FM	VE9HAM	147.25500	+	123.0 Hz	
Fundy National Park						
	FM	VE9TCF	145.17000	-		
Grand Falls	DMR/MARC	VE9ARZ	145.29000	-	CC12	
	FM	VE9GFL	146.94000	-		
Grand Manan Island						
	FM	VE9GMI	146.95500	-		
Hartland	FM	VE9DKS-L	147.18000	+		
Irishtown	FUSION	VE9MTV	446.60000			
Kedgwick	FUSION	VE9MIK	146.82000			
Maces Bay	FM	VE9MBY	444.87500	+		
Mckendrick	FM	VE9LRC	146.95500	140.95500		
Miramichi	FM	VE9MIR	147.15000	+		
Moncton	DMR/MARC	VE9DMR	146.92500	-	CC1	
	FM	VE9TCR	147.34500	+		
	FM	VE9SHM	449.32500	-		
	FUSION	VE9GUS	446.50000			
Moncton, Indian Mountain						
	FM	VE1MTN	147.09000	+		
Moncton, Lutz Mountain						
	FM	VE1RPT	146.88000	-		
NBDMR Test Rptr	DMR/MARC	VE9ARZ	145.29000	-	CC1	
New Harbour	FM	VE1HMY-L	146.55000	+		
Notre-Dame	FUSION	VE9JEC	445.80000			
Oromocto	FM	VE9OPH	145.31000	-		
	FM	VE1BAS	145.74000			
Perth-Andover, Kintore Mountai						
	FM	VE9KMT	147.06000	+		
Pleasant Ridge	FM	VE1BI	146.70000	-		
Quispamsis	FUSION	VE1OL	441.75000			
Sackville	FUSION	VE9DWJ	434.27500			
Saint George, Poor House Hill						
	FM	VE9STG	147.22500	+		
Saint John	DMR/MARC	VE9SJN	145.49000	-	CC1	
	DSTAR	VE9SJN C	145.29000	-		
	FM	VE9STJ	146.82000	-		
	FM	VE9SJW	146.89500	-		
	FM	VE9SJW	443.60000	+		
Saint John, Baxters Mountain						
	FM	VE9PSA	147.39000	+		
Saint John, Dickie Mountain						
	FM	VE9HPN	145.13000	-		
Saint John, Grove Hill						
	FM	VE9STM	145.33000	-		
Saint Leonard	FM	VE9STL	145.35000	-		
Saint Quentin	FM	VE9SQN	145.23000	-		
Sandy Point Road	FM	VE9SJN-R	147.27000	+		
Skiff Lake, Canterbury						
	FM	VE9IRG	145.37000	-		
Sormany	FUSION	VE9RDJ	147.57000			
St-Basile	FUSION	VE9TMR	147.30000	+		
St. Stephen	FM	VE1IE	146.64000	-		
Stanley	FM	VE9NRV	147.03000	+		
Stilesville	FUSION	VE9MFR	146.62500			
Sussex	FUSION	VE9SUX	146.98500	-		
Sussex, Scotch Mountain						
	FM	VE9SMT	146.61000	-		
Tracadie	FM	VE9SID	146.70000	-		
	FM	VE1AZU	147.03000	+		
Tracadie, Academie Ste Famili						
	FM	VE9CR	145.47000	-		

Location	Mode	Call sign	Output	Input	Access	Coordinator
Weatheradio-Dalhousie						
	WX	XLK418	162.55000			
Weatheradio-Eskimo Point						
	WX	CKO583	162.40000			
Weatheradio-Fort McMurray						
	WX	CFA340	162.40000			
Weatheradio-Fredericton						
	WX	VCF757	162.47500			
Weatheradio-Hay River						
	WX	CIE211	162.55000			
Weatheradio-Holden						
	WX	CFB635	162.55000			
Weatheradio-Kamloops						
	WX	CIT768	162.40000			
Weatheradio-La Ronge						
	WX	CFJ262	162.40000			
Weatheradio-Lougheed						
	WX	CFB636	162.40000			
Weatheradio-Millville						
	WX	XLM404	162.55000			
Weatheradio-Miscou Island						
	WX	XMQ533	162.55000			
Weatheradio-Moncton						
	WX	XLM467	162.55000			
Weatheradio-Perth-Andover						
	WX	VFH526	162.50000			
Weatheradio-Revelstoke						
	WX	CIT386	162.40000			
Weatheradio-Saint-Isidore						
	WX	XLK417	162.40000			
Weatheradio-Scotch Mountain						
	WX	XLM403	162.40000			
Weatheradio-Sicamous						
	WX	CIQ882	162.40000			
Weatheradio-St Margarets						
	WX	VFQ820	162.45000			
Weatheradio-St Paul						
	WX	CIM235	162.40000			
Weatheradio-St Stephen						
	WX	XLM490	162.47500			
Weatheradio-Tagish						
	WX	VFS369	162.55000			
Weatheradio-Temagami						
	WX	CFE261	162.40000			
Weatheradio-Ucluelet						
	WX	CIZ319	162.52500			
Weatheradio-Whitehorse						
	WX	CIY270	162.40000			

NEWFOUNDLAND

Location	Mode	Call sign	Output	Input	Access	Coordinator
Grand Falls-Windsor						
	DMR/BM	VO1GFR	444.00000	+	CC5	
	DMR/BM	VO1JY	444.25000	+	CC5	
Labrador City	DMR/BM	VO2ETC	444.00000	+	CC5	
Portugal Cove	DMR/BM	VO1ICE	444.40000	+	CC5	
St. John	DMR/BM	VO1UHF	443.40000	+	CC5	

NEWFOUNDLAND AND LABRADOR

Location	Mode	Call sign	Output	Input	Access	Coordinator
Argentia	FM	VO1ARG	146.82000	-		
Bay De Verde	FM	VO1TBR	147.30000	+		
Big Pond	FM	VO1ISR-L	147.22000	+		
Botwood	FM	VO1BOT	147.38500	+		

Location	Mode	Call sign	Output	Input	Access	Coordinator
Cape Norman	FM	VO1STA-R	147.96500	-		
Cape Pine	FM	VO1CPR	147.12000	+		
Carbonear, Freshwater Ridge						
	FM	VO1FRR	147.39000	+		
	FM	VO1FRR	444.97500	+		
Coley's South Point						
	FM	VO1IC	146.73000	-	94.8 Hz	
Corner Brook	FM	VO1MO	147.36000	+		
Ferryland	FM	VO1CQD	147.28000	+		
Gander	FM	VO1ADE-R	146.88000	-		
	FM	VO1GLR	147.18000	+		
Goose Bay	FM	VO2GB	146.34000	+		
Grand Falls, Red Cliff						
	FM	VO1GFR	146.91000	-		
Grand Falls-Windsor, Water Tow						
	FM	VO1JY	146.76000	-		
Grand-Falls Windsor, Hodges Hi						
	FM	VO1HHR	146.60000	-		
Holyrood, Hawke Hill						
	FM	VO1BT	146.76000	-		
Hopedale	FM	MB7IPT-L	145.21200	-		
Jersey Side	FM	VO1PFR	147.01000	+		
Labrador City, Round Hill						
	FM	VO2LMC	146.76000	-		
Lewisporte	FM	VO1LJR	147.32000	+		
Marystown	FM	VO1MST	146.85000	-		
	FM	VO1AWR	147.22000	+		
New Harbour NL Canada						
	FM	VO1PCR	147.09000	+		
Placentia	FM	VO1SEP	447.12500	-		
Portugal Cove South						
	FM	VO1ILR	147.03000	+		
Ramea	FM	VO1RIR	147.28000	+		
Shearstown	FM	VO1EHC	447.50000	-		
Shoal Harbour	FM	VO1SHR	146.66000	-		
St Johns	DSTAR	VO1TZ C	145.09000	+		
	DSTAR	VO1TZ B	443.40000	+		
	DSTAR	VO1TZ D	1251.94000			
St. Alban's	FM	VO1BDR	147.38000	+		
St. Anthony	FM	VO1GNP	147.96500	-		
St. John S NL	FM	VO1RCR	147.34500	+	100.0 Hz	
St. John's	FM	VO1GT	146.94000	-		
	FM	VO1EHC	147.57000			
St. John's, NTV / OZFM Tower						
	FM	VO1NTV	147.06000	+		
St. Lawrence	FM	VO1AIR	147.19000	+		
Swift Current	FM	VO1PBR	147.22000	+		
Torbay	FM	VO1ZA	147.00000	+		
Weatheradio-Birchy Lake						
	WX	XLM665	162.40000			
Weatheradio-Brent S Cove						
	WX	XLW297	162.40000			
Weatheradio-Codroy Pond						
	WX	XLW201	162.40000			
Weatheradio-Conche						
	WX	XLW296	162.55000			
Weatheradio-Corner Brook						
	WX	XLW200	162.55000			
Weatheradio-Gander						
	WX	XLM616	162.40000			
Weatheradio-Grand Falls						
	WX	XLM664	162.55000			

Location	Mode	Call sign	Output	Input	Access	Coordinator
Weatheradio-Hermitage						
	WX	XLW204	162.55000			
Weatheradio-Marystown						
	WX	XLM663	162.40000			
Weatheradio-Mount St Margaret						
	WX	XLW295	162.55000			
Weatheradio-Port Rexton						
	WX	XLM615	162.55000			
Weatheradio-Portland Creek						
	WX	XLW298	162.40000			
Weatheradio-Ramea						
	WX	XLW203	162.40000			
Weatheradio-Red Rocks						
	WX	XLW202	162.55000			
Weatheradio-St Anthony						
	WX	XLW299	162.40000			
Weatheradio-St John S						
	WX	XLM614	162.40000			
Weatheradio-Trepassey						
	WX	XLM662	162.55000			

NORTHWEST TERRITORIES

Location	Mode	Call sign	Output	Input	Access	Coordinator
Northwest Territories						
	FM	VE3KRG	146.97000	-	118.8 Hz	
Weatheradio-Inner Whaleback Ro						
	WX	XKI403	162.55000			
Weatheradio-Inuvik						
	WX	VBU996	162.40000			
Weatheradio-Pine Point						
	WX	XJS786	162.47500			
Weatheradio-Yellowknife						
	WX	VBC200	162.40000			
Yellowknife, Jackfish Lake						
	FM	VE8YK	146.94000	-	100.0 Hz	

NOVA SCOTIA

Location	Mode	Call sign	Output	Input	Access	Coordinator
Antigonish	DMR/BM	VE1JSR	145.67000		CC1	
	DMR/BM	VE1JSR	441.80000	+	CC1	
	DMR/BM	VE1JSR	442.72500	+	CC1	
	FM	VE1RTI	146.82000	-		
	FUSION	VE1JCS	446.80000	-		
Antigonish NS	DSTAR	VE1JSR C	145.67000			
	DSTAR	VE1JSR D	445.67000	-		
Barrington	FM	VE1OPK	147.25500	+		
	FM	VE1KDE	443.80000	+		
Barrington Passage						
	FM	VE1JNR	146.88000	-		
Biblehill	DSTAR	VE1DNR C	144.95000	+		
Boisdale	FM	VE1HAM	146.88000	-		
Bridgetown	FM	VE1BO	147.06000	+		
Bridgewater	FM	VE1KIN	147.12000	+		
	FUSION	VE1CYP	446.50000			
Brooklyn	DMR/MARC	VE1RQM	146.92500	-	CC1	
Cape Smokey	FM	VE1CBI	147.24000	+		
Chester	FM	VE1LUN	147.33000	+		
Church Lake, Lun Co.						
	DSTAR	VE1DSR C	145.29000	-		
Dartmouth	FM	VE1DAR	147.15000	+		
	FM	VE1DAR	444.60000	+		
	FUSION	VE1EJM	145.70000			
	FUSION	VE1ZC	434.30000			
Digby	FM	VE1AAR	147.01500	+		

Location	Mode	Call sign	Output	Input	Access	Coordinator
East Kemptville	FM	VE1EKV	147.10500	147.75000		
Fall River	FUSION	VE1PYE	442.97500	+		
Fletchers Lake	FUSION	VE1DXC	147.52500			
Glace Bay	FUSION	VE1PRB	146.47500			
Glenmont	FUSION	VE1AEH	145.37000	-		
Gore	FM	VE1OM	51.62000	-		
	FM	VE1OM	146.64000	-		
Granite Village	FM	VE1BBY	147.36000	+		
Greenwood	FM	VE1WN	147.24000	+		
Halifax	FM	VE1PSR	53.55000	52.55000	151.4 Hz	
	FM	VE1HNS	146.94000	-	82.5 Hz	
	FM	VE1PSR	147.27000	+		
	FM	VE1CDN	444.00000	+		
	FM	VE1PSR	444.35000	+		
	FM	VE1PS	449.25000	-		
	FUSION	VE1HPR	145.49000	-		
	FUSION	VE1DFG	146.41500			
Halifax, Upper Sackville						
	FM	VE1CDN	146.97000	-		
Hammonds Plains	FM	VE1PKT	146.68500	-		
Hebron	FUSION	VE1LN	146.86500	-		
Italy Cross	FM	VE1VL	147.09000	+		
Kejimkujik National Park						
	FM	VE1KEJ	147.19500	+		
Kentville	FM	VE1WRG-L	144.43000	+		
	FUSION	VE1WRG	145.67000			
Kiltarlity	FM	VE1KIL	146.73000	-		
Kingston, Stronach Mountain						
	FM	VE1VLY	444.05000	+		
Liverpool	FM	VE1QW	147.06000	+		
	FM	VE1VO	147.30000	+		
Lower Sackville	FM	VA1AA	147.58500			
Lundy	FM	VE1GYS	146.70000	-		
Middlefield	FM	VE1AVA	147.39000	+		
New Glasgow	FM	VE1HR	146.76000	-		
New Minas	FUSION	VE1CSE	145.95000			
North Kingston	FUSION	VE1CFY	145.21000	-		
	FUSION	VE1JW	146.62500	-		
Oban	FM	VE1OBN	147.10500	+		
Parrsboro	FM	VE1PAR	145.47000	-		
	FM	VE1NET	146.74500	-		
Parrsboto	FUSION	VE1USR	444.82500	+		
Plympton Station	FM	VE1JSO-L	147.01500	+		
Sand River	FM	VE1SDR	145.27000	-		
Shelburne	FM	VE1SCR	146.61000	-		
Sherbrooke	FM	VE1SAB	145.39000	-		
Southampton	FUSION	VE1BFB	146.77500	-		
Southampton, Nova Scotia Provi						
	FM	VE1EWS	443.45000	+		
Springfield	FM	VE1LCA	146.83500	-		
Springhill	DMR/MARC	VE1XPR	145.29000	-	CC1	
	FM	VE1SPR	444.20000	+		
Springhill, All Saints Hospita						
	FM	VE1SPH	146.80500	-		
Springhill, Lynn Mountain						
	FM	VE1SPR	147.00000	+		
Stronach Mountain						
	FM	VE1VAL	145.21000	-		
	FM	VE1VLY	449.05000	-		
Sydney	FM	VE1HK	146.94000	-		
Timberlea	FUSION	VE1TXL	144.00000			
Truro	DMR/MARC	VA1DIG	442.65000	+	CC1	

Location	Mode	Call sign	Output	Input	Access	Coordinator
Truro	FM	VE1XK	146.79000	-		
	FM	VE1HAR	147.13500	+		
	FUSION	VE1XK	146.79000	-		
	FUSION	VE1AO	146.98500	-		
Truro, Nuttby Mountain						
	FM	VE1TRO	147.21000	+		
Valley	FUSION	VE1LV	433.60000			
Weatheradio-Aspen						
	WX	XLK499	162.40000			
Weatheradio-Bay St Lawrence						
	WX	XLM667	162.55000			
Weatheradio-Ben Eoin						
	WX	XLW262	162.47500			
Weatheradio-Bridgewater						
	WX	XLK409	162.40000			
Weatheradio-Cheticamp						
	WX	XLW263	162.47500			
Weatheradio-Halifax						
	WX	XLK473	162.55000			
Weatheradio-Middleton						
	WX	XLK497	162.55000			
Weatheradio-New Tusket						
	WX	XLK496	162.55000			
Weatheradio-Oak Park						
	WX	XLW502	162.47500			
Weatheradio-River Denys						
	WX	XLK445	162.55000			
Weatheradio-Shelburne						
	WX	XLK410	162.55000			
Weatheradio-Sydney						
	WX	XLK444	162.40000			
Weatheradio-Truro						
	WX	XLK498	162.40000			
Weatheradio-Yarmouth						
	WX	XLW573	162.47500			
West Chezzetcook						
	FM	VE1ESC-R	147.03000	+		
West Leicester	FUSION	VE1AMH	145.19000	-		
Western Shore	DMR/BM	VA1LUN	430.42000		CC1	
Windsor	FM	VE1HCA	146.91000	-		
Yarmouth	FM	VE1YAR	146.73000	-		

NUNAVUT

Location	Mode	Call sign	Output	Input	Access	Coordinator
Baker Lake	FM	VY0MBK-R	146.76000	-		
Iqaluit	FM	VY0SNO	146.94000	-		
Resolute	FM	VY0FG-L	448.92500	-		
Weatheradio-Cape Dorset						
	WX	XJS717	162.55000			
Weatheradio-Iqaluit						
	WX	VEV284	162.55000			
Weatheradio-Rankin Inlet						
	WX	XJS716	162.40000			

ONTARIO

Location	Mode	Call sign	Output	Input	Access	Coordinator
Acton	FM	VE3RSS	147.03000	+		
	FM	VE3PAQ	442.12500	+	131.8 Hz	
	FM	VA3GTU	442.82500	+	103.5 Hz	
Agincourt	FM	VE3WOO	29.64000	-		
Ajax	DMR/BM	VE3SBX	443.53750	+	CC3	
	FM	VE3SPA	147.37500	+	103.5 Hz	
	FM	VE3DAX	444.60000	+	103.5 Hz	
Alban	FM	VE3BLZ	146.70000	-	100.0 Hz	

Location	Mode	Call sign	Output	Input	Access	Coordinator
Alfred	FM	VA3TLO	443.50000	+	110.9 Hz	
Almonte	DMR/BM	VA3AAR	145.55000	-	CC1	
	DSTAR	VA3AAR C	145.55000	-		
	DSTAR	VA3AAR B	444.10000	+		
	DSTAR	VA3AAR A	1281.00000	-		
	DSTAR	VA3AAR D	1299.30000			
	FM	VA3AAR	147.27000	+		
Almonte, Almonte Fire Hall						
	FM	VA3AAR	444.30000	+	100.0 Hz	
Almonte, Union Hall						
	FM	VA3ARE	147.24000	+	100.0 Hz	
	FM	VA3ARE	444.10000	+		
Ancaster	FM	VE3RDM	145.27000	-	136.5 Hz	
	FM	VE3RTJ-R	442.50000	+		
	FM	VE3DJ-L	446.43700	-		
Armbro Heights	FM	VA3AGC-L	144.00000	+		
Arnprior	DSTAR	VA3JJA C	145.63000			
	DSTAR	VA3JJA B	445.84000	-		
	DSTAR	VA3JJA A	1286.00000	-		
Arnprior, Police / Fire Bldg						
	FM	VE3YYX	443.20000	+	114.8 Hz	
Atikokan	FM	VE3RIB	147.12000	+		
	FUSION	VE3FYN	433.50000			
Aurora	DMR/BM	VE3YRA	444.51250	+	CC1	
	FM	VE3YRA	145.35000	-	103.5 Hz	
	FM	VE3YRC	147.22500	+	103.5 Hz	
	FM	VE3ULR	224.88000	-		
	FUSION	VE3YRC	147.22500	+		
Aylmer	DMR/BM	VE3XXL	443.22500	+	CC1	
Baden, Baden Sand Hill						
	FM	VE3KSR	146.97000	-	131.8 Hz	
Ballantrae	DMR/BM	VE3RPT	443.22500	+	CC1	
	DMR/BM	VE3URU	444.46250	+	CC1	
	DMR/BM	VA3BAL	444.98750	+	CC1	
	FM	VE3ULR	145.47000	-	103.5 Hz	
	FM	VA3BAL	147.33000	147.83000	103.5 Hz	
	FM	VE3ULR	442.02500	+	103.5 Hz	
	FM	VA3URU	442.47500	+	103.5 Hz	
	FM	VE3SNM	442.85000	+	136.5 Hz	
	FM	VA3BAL	443.70000	+	103.5 Hz	
Ballinafad	FM	VA3LNK-R	443.42500	+		
Balsam Lake	DSTAR	VE3NYY B	444.58750	+		
	FM	VE3NY	441.00000	+	100.0 Hz	
Bancroft	FM	VE3BNI	146.61000	-	100.0 Hz	
Banks	FM	VA3ROG	145.37000	-	156.7 Hz	
Barrie	DMR/MARC	VE3CQI	443.83750	+	CC1	
	DSTAR	VE3RIG B	442.05000	+		
	FM	VE3RAG	147.00000	+	156.7 Hz	
Barrys Bay	FM	VE3RKA	146.97000	-		
Belleville	FM	VE3OR	146.47500	+		
	FM	VE3QAR	146.98500	-	118.8 Hz	
	FM	VE3ALC	147.51000	-		
	FM	VE3QAR	444.47500	+	118.8 Hz	
	FUSION	VE3CDC	146.42000			
	FUSION	VE3UR	146.56500	-		
	FUSION	VE3OR	147.00000	+		
Berkeley	FM	VA3CAX	145.29000	-	156.7 Hz	
Birkendale	FM	VE3MUS-R	146.77500	-		
Black Hawk	FM	VE3RBK	147.04500	+		
Blenheim	DSTAR	VA3IBA C	145.79000			
Bolton	FM	VA3EDE	146.43000		67.0 Hz	
	FM	VA3OPG	146.83500	-	103.5 Hz	

Location	Mode	Call sign	Output	Input	Access	Coordinator
Bolton	FM	VA3OPR	444.95000	+	103.5 Hz	
Bowmanville	DMR/BM	VA3DBJ	442.00000	+	CC1	
Bradford	FM	VE3ZXN	224.48000	-		
	FM	VE3ZXN	927.90000	902.90000		
	FUSION	VE3RQB	446.00000			
Brampton	DSTAR	VE3UMG C	146.40000	+		
	FM	VE3PRC	146.88000	-	103.5 Hz	
	FM	VE3WSA	224.24000	-		
	FM	VE3PRC	443.55000	+	103.5 Hz	
	FUSION	VA3AGZ	146.54000			
Brantford	DMR/BM	VA3JCV	145.59000	534.41000	CC1	
	DMR/BM	VA3JCD	442.36250	+	CC1	
	DMR/BM	VA3JCV	443.36250	+	CC1	
	DMR/BM	VA3JCD	444.36250	+	CC1	
	DMR/BM	VE3MEI	444.91250	+	CC1	
	FM	VE3MBX	145.27000	-	131.8 Hz	
	FM	VE3TCR	147.15000	+	131.8 Hz	
	FM	VE3TCR	443.02500	+	131.8 Hz	
	FM	VE3DTE	921.00000	-		
Bridgenorth	FM	VE3BTE	147.30000	+		
Brockville	DMR/BM	VA3BDR	442.10000	+	CC1	
	FM	VE3IWJ-R	146.82000	-		
Buckhorn	FM	VE3KLR	443.15000	+	103.5 Hz	
Burks Falls	FM	VA3BFR	145.17000	-	156.7 Hz	
Burlington	DMR/BM	VE3RSB	442.03750	+	CC1	
	DSTAR	VE3OBP B	443.20000	+		
	FM	VE3DUO	53.59000	52.59000	131.8 Hz	
	FM	VE3WIK	224.96000	-	131.8 Hz	
	FM	VE3BUR	443.15000	+		
	FM	VE3RSB	444.82500	+	131.8 Hz	
	FUSION	VE3ZLG	147.22500	+		
Cachet	FM	VA3CTR-R	442.27500	+		
Caledon	FM	VE3SKV	146.89500	-		
	FM	VE3UPR	443.60000	+		
	FM	VE3WOO	444.17500	+	103.5 Hz	
Cambridge	FM	VE3SWR	146.79000	-		
Campbellford	FM	VE3KFR	145.33000	-	162.2 Hz	
Campbellville	FM	VE3RJS	446.95000	-		
Campden	FM	VE3ALS	443.57500	+	107.2 Hz	
Cannington	FM	VA3TVE	444.45000	+		
	FM	VA3TVE	1288.00000	-		
Carlisle	FM	VE3WIK	53.11000	52.11000	131.8 Hz	
	FM	VE3WIK	146.71500	-	131.8 Hz	
	FM	VE3WIK	443.67500	+	131.8 Hz	
Carp	FM	VA3WJC	444.05000	+	123.0 Hz	
	FM	VE3IEV	445.07500	-	100.0 Hz	
	FUSION	VA3HOA	147.27000	+		
Carson Grove	FM	VE3JGL-L	444.50000	+		
Chatham	DMR/MARC	VA3XLT	443.98750	+	CC7	
	FM	VE3KCR	144.39000	+		
	FM	VE3COZ	145.19000	-	100.0 Hz	
	FM	VE3CRC	146.68000	-	100.0 Hz	
	FM	VE3KCR	147.12000	+	100.0 Hz	
	FM	VE3CBS	224.12000	-	131.8 Hz	
	FM	VE3MGK	442.20000	+		
	FM	VE3COZ	444.32500	+	250.3 Hz	
Cn Tower Toronto	DMR/BM	VA3RCI	444.80000	+	CC1	
Cobourg	DMR/BM	VE3RWN	444.97500	+	CC1	
Cobourg / Peterborough						
	DSTAR	VE3RTR C	146.89500	-		
Cobourg, Rice Lake						
	FM	VE3RTR	145.15000	-	162.2 Hz	

Location	Mode	Call sign	Output	Input	Access	Coordinator
Cobourg, Rice Lake						
	FM	VE3MXR	444.97500	+	162.2 Hz	
Colemans	FM	VE3NUU-L	446.80000	-		
Collingwood	DMR/BM	VA3ROG	146.79000	-	CC29	
	DMR/MARC	VA3BMR	442.38750	+	CC1	
	FM	VE3RMT	53.15000	52.15000	156.7 Hz	
	FM	VE3BMR	146.79000	-	156.7 Hz	
	FM	VE3BMR	442.60000	+	156.7 Hz	
	FM	VE3QCR	443.27500	+		
	FM	VE3RMT	921.50000	-	156.7 Hz	
Cookstown	FM	VA3TWO	444.68750	+	156.7 Hz	
Cornwall	DMR/BM	VA3EDG	442.10000	+	CC1	
	DSTAR	VA3SDG C	145.57000	-		
	DSTAR	VA3SDG B	444.45000	+		
	FM	VE3YGM	145.17000	-		
	FM	VE3XID-L	146.47500	+		
	FM	VE3PGC	443.00000	+	110.9 Hz	
	FM	VE3MTA	443.65000	+	110.9 Hz	
Cornwall, Hotel Dieu Hosp						
	FM	VE3SVC	147.18000	+	110.9 Hz	
Courtland	DMR/BM	VE3DPL	146.65500	-	CC1	
	DMR/BM	VA3PPO	442.87500	+	CC1	
Coventry	FM	VA3JMF-L	146.83500	-		
Creemore	FUSION	VA3AZV	447.00000	-		
Cumberland	FM	VA3RCB	444.35000	+	100.0 Hz	
Delhi	DMR/BM	VA3JCD	442.91250	+	CC1	
Devlin	FM	VE3BIK	146.57000		123.0 Hz	
Distillery District	FM	VE3BGD-R	147.27000	+		
Dorchester	FM	VE3NDT	147.24000	+		
Dryden	FM	VE3TBO	145.78000			
	FM	VE3DRY	147.25500	+		
	FM	VA3ANE	147.34500	+	123.0 Hz	
	FM	VA3DIS	147.37500	+		
	FM	VE3YDN	147.52500			
	FUSION	VA3EOD	144.82500	+		
	FUSION	VE3YDN	145.42500	-		
	FUSION	VE3YHD	146.94000	-	123.0 Hz	
Dundalk	FM	VA3WWM	442.92500	+	131.8 Hz	
Dunnville	FM	VE3HNR	147.07500	+	123.0 Hz	
	FM	VE3KYO	444.70000	+		
	FUSION	VA3HET	448.78750	-		
Dutton	FM	VE3ISR	147.36000	+	114.8 Hz	
Dwight	FM	VE3MUS	146.82000	-	156.7 Hz	
Dysart	FM	VA3LTX	147.10500	+		
Eagle Lake	FM	VA3HAL	442.00000	+	162.2 Hz	
	FM	VA3HAL	444.80000	+	162.2 Hz	
Edgar	DMR/BM	VA3IMB	147.28500	+	CC29	
	DMR/MARC	VE3UHF	442.88750	+	CC1	
	DSTAR	VE3LSR AD	1248.50000			
	FM	VE3LSR	146.85000	-	156.7 Hz	
	FM	VE3KES	147.15000	+	156.7 Hz	
	FM	VA3IMB	147.28500	+	156.7 Hz	
	FM	VE3LSR	147.31500	+	156.7 Hz	
	FM	VE3LSR	442.57500	+	103.5 Hz	
	FM	VA3BNI	444.27500	+	103.5 Hz	
Egypt	FUSION	VE3BNI	146.07000	+		
Eldorado	FM	VA3SDR	145.41000	-	118.8 Hz	
Elizabeth Park	FM	VE3RIX-R	145.45000	-		
Elliot Lake	FM	VE3TOP	147.00000	+		
	FUSION	VA3EMX	447.00000	-		
Embrun	FM	VE3EYV	147.19500	+	110.9 Hz	
Englehart	FM	VE3TAR	146.97000	-		

Location	Mode	Call sign	Output	Input	Access	Coordinator
ERA System Southern Ontario						
	FM	VA3ERA	443.67500	+	131.8 Hz	
Essex	FM	VE3SMR	53.03000	52.03000	118.8 Hz	
Essex County	DMR/MARC	VA3LLL	444.71250	+	CC7	
Essonville	FM	VE3TBF	224.84000	-		
Etobicoke	FM	VA3GTU	442.77500	+	103.5 Hz	
	FM	VA3GTU	442.80000	+	103.5 Hz	
Exeter	FM	VE3JEZ-L	146.76000	-		
Fauquier	FM	VA3FOK	443.80000	+	156.7 Hz	
Fergus	FM	VA3EHI-L	146.56500	+		
Fisherville	FM	VA3WJO-L	444.70000	+		
Fonthill	DMR/MARC	VA3XPR	442.71250	+	CC1	
	DSTAR	VE3PLF B	444.72500	+		
	FM	VE3PLF	53.29000	52.29000	107.2 Hz	
	FM	VE3WCD	147.30000	+	107.2 Hz	
	FM	VE3UCS	224.58000	-	107.2 Hz	
	FM	VE3EI	224.80000	-	107.2 Hz	
	FM	VE3EI	444.72500	+	107.2 Hz	
Fonthill, Lookout Village						
	FM	VE3RNR	443.17500	+	107.2 Hz	
Fonthill- ON	DSTAR	VE3PLF B	444.72500	+		
Forest Hill	FM	VE3NOR-R	443.65000	+	103.0 Hz	
Fort Frances	FM	VE3RLC	146.82000	-		
	FM	VE3BVC	147.52500		123.0 Hz	
	FUSION	VE3BVC	145.11000	-		
Foxboro	FUSION	VE3OR	146.48000			
Foymount	FM	VE3UCR	145.43000	-	114.8 Hz	
Frankford	FM	VE3TRR	147.01500	+		
Franktown	FM	VE3WCC	444.30000	+	100.0 Hz	
Frontenac County	FM	VE3FRG	146.20500	+	151.4 Hz	
Gatineau	FM	VA2XAD	430.05000	434.95000		
Glasgow	FM	VA3TE-L	146.43000			
	FM	VA3OPG-L	444.95000	+		
Goderich	DMR/MARC	VE3OBC	442.07500	+	CC1	
	FM	VE3OBC	146.91000	-	123.0 Hz	
Goodwood	FM	VE3GTU	442.07500	+	103.5 Hz	
Grand Bend	FM	VE3SRT	442.05000	+	114.8 Hz	
	FM	VE3SRT	442.07500	+	114.8 Hz	
Grasshill	FM	VE3LNZ-R	147.19500	+		
Grassie	FM	VE3BQQ	442.72500	+	131.8 Hz	
Grassmere	FM	VA3BFR-R	145.27000	-		
	FM	VE3RAK-R	444.70000	-		
Grimsby	FM	VE3IUW	1283.60000	-		
Guelph	DMR/BM	VE3BNF	438.80000	-	CC1	
	FM	VE3ZMG	145.21000	-	131.8 Hz	
	FM	VE3OVQ	147.54000		131.8 Hz	
Guelph Ontario	FM	VA3SLD	147.36000	+	131.8 Hz	
Guelph, Guelph General Hospita						
	FM	VE3GEG	147.00000	+	131.8 Hz	
Haliburton	FM	VE3SRU	53.05000	52.05000		
Haliburton County	FM	VE3ZHR	146.65500	-	162.2 Hz	
Hamilton	DMR/BM	VA3UEC	442.75000	-	CC15	
	DMR/MARC	VE3LOW	443.83750	+	CC1	
	DMR/MARC	VE3UHM	444.03750	+	CC1	
	DSTAR	VE3WIK C	145.33000	-		
	DSTAR	VA3FS C	145.51000	-		
	DSTAR	VE3WIK C	146.71500	-		
	DSTAR	VE3WIK B	443.63750	+		
	DSTAR	VA3FS B	445.82500	-		
	DSTAR	VA3FS A	1286.00000	-		
	FM	VA3TVW	146.58000			
	FM	VE3NCF	146.76000	-	131.8 Hz	

Location	Mode	Call sign	Output	Input	Access	Coordinator
Hamilton	FM	VE3ISX	147.58500		136.5 Hz	
	FM	VE3UHM	442.52500	+	103.5 Hz	
	FM	VE3NCF	444.07500	+	131.8 Hz	
	FM	VE3TTO	446.57500	-	131.8 Hz	
	FUSION	VE3RGU	438.88000			
Hamilton ON	FM	VE3TTO	146.46000		131.8 Hz	
Hamilton, Gore Park						
	FM	VE3ESM	442.55000	+	131.8 Hz	
Hammond	DMR/BM	VA3PRA	442.75000	+	CC1	
	DMR/BM	VE3PRV	442.85000	+	CC1	
	DMR/BM	WB3ISP	446.00000		CC1	
	DMR/MARC	VE3PRV	442.85000	+	CC1	
Hammond, ON, CA						
	FM	VE3PRV	147.33000	+	110.9 Hz	
Hampton Heights	FM	VE3RFI-R	443.25000	442.65000		
Hearst	DMR/BM	VA3YVL	442.87500	+	CC3	
Hillsburgh	DMR/BM	VE3DDW	444.68750	+	CC1	
	FM	VE3ZAP	443.87500	+	88.5 Hz	
Holland Landing	FUSION	VE3URG	449.99500			
Horton	FM	VE3ZRR	146.91000	-		
Huntsville	FM	VE3URU	146.95500	-	100.0 Hz	
Ignace, Ignace School						
	FM	VA3IGN	147.18000	+	123.0 Hz	
Ingersoll	FM	VE3NRJ-L	145.14000	-		
	FM	VA3PLL	145.17000	-	114.8 Hz	
	FM	VE3OHR	147.27000	+	114.8 Hz	
	FM	VE3OHR	443.45000	+	114.8 Hz	
Inverary	FUSION	VE3KJN	146.55000			
	FUSION	VE3KJN	146.94000	-		
Ipperwash Beach	FM	VE3TCB	146.94000	-	114.8 Hz	
Iroquois	FM	VE3IRO-R	145.29000	-		
Kagawong	FM	VE3LTR	146.67000	-		
Kanata	FUSION	VE3KMN	144.10000			
Kanata-Katimavik	DSTAR	VA3AIT C	145.51000	-		
	DSTAR	VA3AIT B	445.90000	-		
	DSTAR	VA3AIT A	1283.50000	-		
Kapuskasing	DMR/BM	VA3MCK	442.47500	+	CC3	
	FM	VE3YYU	442.00000	+		
Kemptville	FUSION	VE3NGR	444.22500	+		
	FUSION	VE3KAE	446.80000			
Kenora	FM	VE3YQK	146.56000		123.0 Hz	
	FM	VE3LWR	147.03000	+		
	FUSION	VE3XTI	146.91000	-		
Keswick	FM	VA3PTX	147.28500	+	156.7 Hz	
Kincardine	FM	VE3TIV	146.61000	-		
King City	FM	VE3GSR	145.31000	-	103.5 Hz	
	FM	VE3WAS	146.61000	-	103.5 Hz	
	FM	VE3UKC	444.30000	+	103.5 Hz	
King Township	DMR/MARC	VE3TSU	442.16250	+	CC1	
Kingston	P25	VE3KTO	443.30000	+		
Kingston, Kingston ARC						
	FM	VE3KBR	146.94000	-	151.4 Hz	
Kirkfield	DMR/BM	VE3NYY	444.58750	+	CC1	
Kitchener	DMR/MARC	VE3DWI	444.53750	+	CC7	
	FM	VE3SED	53.37000	52.37000	131.8 Hz	
	FM	VA3XTO	146.58000			
	FM	VE3RCK	146.86500	-	131.8 Hz	
	FM	VE3IXY	224.34000	-	131.8 Hz	
	FM	VE3SED	442.20000	+	131.8 Hz	
	FM	VE3BAY	442.35000	447.37000	131.8 Hz	
Lanark	DSTAR	VE3ENH B	442.00000	+		
	DSTAR	VE3ENH A	1282.50000	-		

Location	Mode	Call sign	Output	Input	Access	Coordinator
Lancaster	FM	VE2REH	147.52500	145.67000	131.8 Hz	
Lansdowne	FM	VA3LGA	146.62500	-	100.0 Hz	
Lavant	FM	VE3KJG	146.64000	-		
Lavant Station, Mountain Top						
	FM	VA3LGP	53.23000	52.23000	141.3 Hz	
Leamington	DMR/MARC	VE3TOM	443.26250	+	CC7	
	DSTAR	VE3LNK C	145.69000			
	FM	VE3TOM	146.97000	+	118.8 Hz	
	FM	VE3ZZZ	147.10000	+	118.8 Hz	
	FM	VA3XFD	147.33000	+	118.8 Hz	
	FM	VA3LLL	442.05000	+	118.8 Hz	
	FUSION	VE3ZZZ	147.10000	+		
Lindsay	FM	VE3RWN	145.11000	-	118.8 Hz	
Lindsay, City Of Kawartha Lake						
	FM	VE3CKL	145.45000	-	162.2 Hz	
	FM	VE3CKL	444.65000	+	162.2 Hz	
Lionshead	FM	VE3CAX	146.71500	-	156.7 Hz	
Listowel	FM	VA3LIS	147.12000	+	114.8 Hz	
Little Current	DMR/BM	VE3RXR	442.05000	+	CC1	
	DSTAR	VE3RXR C	145.31000	-		
	DSTAR	VE3RXR B	442.05000	+		
	FM	VE3RQQ	146.55000		156.7 Hz	
	FM	VE3RMI	147.27000	+		
	FM	VE3RQQ	444.30000	+	100.0 Hz	
London	DMR/BM	VE3TTT	434.45000	+	CC1	
	DMR/MARC	VE3RGM	444.61250	+	CC7	
	DSTAR	VE3TTT B	442.30000	+		
	DSTAR	VE3TTT A	1285.50000	-		
	FM	VE3GYQ	145.35000	-	114.8 Hz	
	FM	VA3MGI	145.39000	-	114.8 Hz	
	FM	VE3OME	145.45000	-	114.8 Hz	
	FM	VE3OES	146.49000		114.8 Hz	
	FM	VA3LON	147.06000	+	114.8 Hz	
	FM	VA3FEZ	444.10000	+	114.8 Hz	
	FM	VE3SUE	444.40000	+	114.8 Hz	
	FM	VE3LSG-L	446.15000	-		
	FM	VA3PFL	446.50000	-	77.0 Hz	
	FM	VA3CCC	922.00000	-	114.8 Hz	
London, Ontario	DSTAR	VE3TTT A	1285.50000	-		
Mactier	FM	VA3XY	147.48000			
Mallorytown	FM	VE3IGE	146.97000	-		
	FM	VE3IGE	443.90000	+		
Manitowaning	FM	VE3RII	444.17500	+	156.7 Hz	
Maple	DMR/BM	VA3ITL	442.21250	+	CC1	
	DSTAR	VE3LEO C	144.30000			
	DSTAR	VA3ITL B	442.21250	+		
	DSTAR	VE3LEO B	446.00000	-		
	DSTAR	VE3LEO A	1282.50000	-		
	FM	VE3RSB-R	147.21000	+		
	FM	VA3ITL	442.41250	-		
Marathon	FUSION	VE3JTD	147.21000	+		
Marina Veilleux	FM	VA3YHF-R	146.70000	-		
Markham	DMR/BM	VE3CBC	444.10000	+	CC1	
Marmora	FM	VE3OUR	443.47500	+		
Mattawa	FM	VE3NBR	147.15000	+		
Maynooth	FM	VE3WPR	147.00000	+		
Mcarthur Mills	FM	VA3PLA	147.18000	+		
McGregor	FM	VE3KUC	145.39000	-	118.8 Hz	
	FM	VE3RRR	145.47000	-	118.8 Hz	
	FM	VE3RRR	224.70000	-	118.8 Hz	
	FM	VE3SOT	1282.50000	-		
Midland	DMR/MARC	VE3UGB	443.88750	+	CC1	

Location	Mode	Call sign	Output	Input	Access	Coordinator
Midland	FM	VE3UGB	146.91000	-		
Milton	FM	VE3HAL	442.30000	+	131.8 Hz	
	FM	VE3ADT	444.12500	+	131.8 Hz	
	FUSION	VA3AKI	442.03750			
Milton ON	DSTAR	VE3ELF B	446.07500	-		
Milverton	DSTAR	VE3NMN C	147.16500	+		
	DSTAR	VE3NMN C	147.41500			
	DSTAR	VE3NMN B	438.10000			
	DSTAR	VE3NMN A	1282.45000	-		
	FM	VE3NMN-R	444.92500	+		
Mindemoya	FM	VE3WVU	444.45000	+	156.7 Hz	
Minden	FM	VE3VHH	147.07500	+	162.2 Hz	
Mississauga	DMR/BM	VE3RSD	443.81250	+	CC1	
	DMR/BM	VA3PMO	444.25000	+	CC1	
	DSTAR	W8ORG C	146.50000			
	DSTAR	VE3RSD C	147.54000			
	DSTAR	VE2YUU B	442.05000	+		
	DSTAR	VA3URU B	443.81250	+		
	DSTAR	VA3PMO B	444.25000	+		
	FM	VE3MIS	145.43000	-	103.5 Hz	
	FM	VA3PMO	224.24000	-	103.5 Hz	
	FM	VE3RSD	224.62000	-	103.5 Hz	
	FM	VE3RSD	224.72000	-	103.5 Hz	
	FM	VE3MIS	444.57500	+		
Mitchell	FM	VE3XMM	147.28500	+	114.8 Hz	
Monkland	FM	VE2NUU	445.92500	-		
	FM	VE2NUU	445.97500	-		
Moose Creek	DMR/BM	VE3OJE	145.37000	-	CC1	
	DMR/BM	VE3TYF	443.05000	+	CC1	
	FM	VE3OJE	145.37000	-		
	FM	VE3TYF	443.05000	+	151.4 Hz	
Moosonee	FM	VE3CIJ	446.25000	-	103.5 Hz	
Morrisburg	DMR/BM	VE3SVR	146.76000	-	CC1	
	DMR/BM	VA3ESD	443.15000	+	CC1	
Mount Forest	FM	VA3CRV	147.16500	+	156.7 Hz	
Mt.St. Patrick	DSTAR	VE3STP C	147.54000			
	DSTAR	VE3STP B	443.60000	+		
	DSTAR	VE3STP B	443.81250	+		
	DSTAR	VE3STP A	1282.45000	-		
Nestor Falls	FUSION	VE3JJA	146.71500	-		
New Dundee	FM	VE3RND	145.33000	-	131.8 Hz	
New Liskeard	FM	VE3CIJ	145.19000	-		
Newmarket	DSTAR	VE3YRK C	147.18000	+		
	DSTAR	VE3YRK B	444.51250	+		
	FM	VA3NMK	444.20000	+	103.5 Hz	
	FUSION	VE3ORE	439.75000			
Niagara Falls	DSTAR	VA3WAJ B	442.42500	+		
	FM	VE3JOY	144.91000			
	FM	VE3WAJ	224.18000	-	107.2 Hz	
	FM	VA3WAJ	442.42500	+	107.2 Hz	
	FM	VE3GRW	442.90000	+	107.2 Hz	
	FUSION	VE3JOY	144.91000			
Niagara On The Lake						
	DSTAR	VA3YYZ C	144.93000	+		
	DSTAR	VA3YYZ B	442.68750	+		
	DSTAR	VA3YYZ A	1282.50000	-		
	DSTAR	VA3YYZ D	1299.15000			
Norfolk	DSTAR	VE3HJ B	444.55000	+		
North Bay	FM	VE3NFM	147.30000	+	107.2 Hz	
North York	FM	VE3TNC	147.27000	+	103.5 Hz	
	FM	VA3OBN	442.75000	+	103.5 Hz	
Oak Ridges	FM	VE3MPI-L	146.49000	+		

Location	Mode	Call sign	Output	Input	Access	Coordinator
Oakville	DMR/BM	VA3NEG	444.42500	+	CC1	
	DSTAR	VE3OBP B	445.01250	-		
	FM	VE3MIJ	147.01500	+	131.8 Hz	
	FM	VE3OKR	442.45000	+		
	FM	VE3OAK	444.32500	+	131.8 Hz	
	FM	VE3XCN	445.17500	-	131.8 Hz	
Oakville ON	FM	VA3WIK	438.17500		131.8 Hz	
Omemee	FM	VA3OME	147.09000	+	162.2 Hz	
	FM	VA3MME	444.90000	+		
Ontario	FM	VE3NFM	145.11000	-		
	FM	VE3OBC	146.31000	+	97.4 Hz	
	FM	VA3YOS	146.64000	-	156.7 Hz	
	FM	VE3DPL	146.66500	-	131.8 Hz	
	FM	VE3BIC	147.22500	+	131.8 Hz	
	FM	VE3KAR	147.69000	-	131.8 Hz	
	FM	VA3JFD	442.07500	+	123.0 Hz	
	FM	VE3BGA	442.82500	+	100.0 Hz	
	FM	VE3OBN	443.90000	+	127.3 Hz	
	FM	VE3AA	444.90000	+		
	FM	VA3JFD	447.07500	-	123.0 Hz	
	FM	VA3DJJ	448.07500	-	123.0 Hz	
	FUSION	VE3TVV	447.85000			
Orangeville	FM	VA3FYI	145.23000	-		
	FM	VE3ORX	444.02500	+	156.7 Hz	
	FM	VA3FYI	444.62500	+		
Orchard	FM	VA3MFD-L	446.12500	-		
Orillia	DMR/BM	VE3ORC	444.56250	+	CC1	
	DMR/MARC	VA3URU	444.68250	+	CC1	
	FM	VE3SYY	146.50500		156.7 Hz	
	FM	VE3URG	146.56500		156.7 Hz	
	FM	VA3OPS	146.65500	-		
	FM	VE3ORR	147.21000	+	156.7 Hz	
Orleans	DMR/BM	VE3RAM	443.70000	+	CC1	
Oshawa	DMR/BM	VE3OBI	442.13750	+	CC1	
	DMR/BM	VE3OUR	442.87500	+	CC1	
	FM	VE3OSH	147.12000	+	156.7 Hz	
	FM	VE3NAA	443.00000	+	136.5 Hz	
Ottawa	DMR/BM	VE3HOZ	442.30000	+	CC1	
	DMR/BM	VA3ODG	444.85000	+	CC1	
	DMR/MARC	VA3RFT	444.47500	+	CC1	
	DSTAR	VA3ODG C	145.53000	-		
	DSTAR	VA3ODG B	444.85000	+		
	DSTAR	VE3FSR B	445.86000	-		
	DSTAR	VA3ODG A	1282.00000	-		
	DSTAR	VA3ODG A	1299.20000			
	DSTAR	VA3ODG D	1299.20000			
	FM	VE3TST	29.62000	-	136.5 Hz	
	FM	VE3RVI	53.03000	52.03000		
	FM	VE3TST	53.09000	52.09000	136.5 Hz	
	FM	VE3OTW	145.19000	-	136.5 Hz	
	FM	VA3OFS	146.67000	-	136.5 Hz	
	FM	VE3TST	146.70000	-	136.5 Hz	
	FM	VA3LCC	146.79000	-		
	FM	VE3ORF	146.85000	-	136.5 Hz	
	FM	VE3OCE	146.88000	-	136.5 Hz	
	FM	VA3EMV	146.98500	-	100.0 Hz	
	FM	VE3TWO	147.30000	+	100.0 Hz	
	FM	VE3DRE	147.43500		100.0 Hz	
	FM	VE3PNO	147.57000		103.5 Hz	
	FM	VA3OTW	224.68000	-		
	FM	VE3ORF	224.72000	-		
	FM	VE3OCE	443.80000	+	136.5 Hz	

Location	Mode	Call sign	Output	Input	Access	Coordinator
Ottawa	FM	VE3TST	444.12500	+	136.5 Hz	
	FM	VE3TWO	444.20000	+	110.9 Hz	
	FM	VE3ORF	444.55000	+	136.5 Hz	
	FM	VA3DSP	444.82500	+		
	FM	VA3OFS	444.95000	+	136.5 Hz	
	FM	VA3OFS	449.95000	-	136.5 Hz	
	FUSION	VE3SXY	144.00000			
	FUSION	VE3IGN	145.45000	-		
	FUSION	VE3PD	146.40000			
	FUSION	VE3DRE	147.43500			
	FUSION	VE3ORF	444.55000	+		
Oungah	FM	VE3UGG	443.00000	442.40000		
Owen Sound	FM	VE3OSR-R	146.94000	-		
	FM	VE3OSR	442.35000	+	156.7 Hz	
Paisley	FM	VE3RTE	146.73000	-	156.7 Hz	
Pakenham	FM	VE2REH	145.33000	-	110.9 Hz	
Paris	FM	VE3DIB	145.49000	-	131.8 Hz	
Parry Sound	DMR/BM	VE3UPS	444.80000	+	CC1	
	FM	VE3RPL	145.49000	-		
	FM	VE3RPL	443.57500	+		
Parry Sound, McKellar						
	FM	VE3AAY	53.11000	52.11000		
Pefferlaw	FM	VA3PTX	53.09000	52.09000		
Pembroke	FM	VE3KKO-L	144.50000	+		
	FM	VE3NRR	146.76000	-	100.0 Hz	
	FM	VE3NRR	448.02500	-	100.0 Hz	
Penetang	FM	VE3SGB	146.76000	-	156.7 Hz	
Perth	DSTAR	VA3RDD C	147.24000	+		
	DSTAR	VA3RDD B	444.80000	+		
	FM	VE3LCA	146.95500	-		
Perth, Christie Lake						
	FM	VA3TEL	145.23000	-		
Perth, Otty Lake	FM	VE3IEV	444.45000	+	100.0 Hz	
Petawawa	FM	VA3AUL	446.00000			
Peterborough	DMR/MARC	VE3BTE	443.13750	+	CC1	
	DSTAR	VE3SSF C	147.36000	+		
	FM	VE3BUY	146.37000	+	162.2 Hz	
	FM	VE3ACD	146.62500	-		
	FM	VA3RZS	147.30000	+	162.2 Hz	
	FM	VE3SSF	443.37500	+	162.2 Hz	
	FUSION	VE3BUY	146.37000	+		
	FUSION	VA3PBO	449.57500	-		
Peterborough, Kawarthas						
	FM	VE3PBO	146.62500	-	162.2 Hz	
Phelpston	DMR/BM	VE3RIG	442.05000	+	CC1	
Picton	FM	VE3TJU	146.73000	-	118.8 Hz	
Pine Grove	FM	VE3VTG-L	147.51000	+		
Point Alexander, Laurentian Hi						
	FM	VA3RBW	146.79000	-	114.8 Hz	
Port Crewe	FM	AC8LR-L	146.44000	+		
Port Elgin	FM	VE3PER	146.82000	-		
Port Perry	FUSION	VA3PPI	444.86250	+		
	FUSION	VA3NSC	446.50000			
Pottageville	FM	VA3ATL-R	444.77500	+		
Powassan, Powassan Hill						
	FM	VE3ERX	147.03000	+		
Queenswood Village						
	FM	VE3MPC-R	147.15000	+	100.0 Hz	
Raglan	DMR/BM	VE3LBN	443.98750	+	CC3	
	DMR/MARC	VA3BMI	442.13750	+	CC0	
	FM	VE3OSH	53.27000	52.27000		
	FM	VE3OBI	444.52500	+	103.5 Hz	

Location	Mode	Call sign	Output	Input	Access	Coordinator
Ramsayville	FM	VE3YRR	224.94000	-		
Red Lake	FM	VE3RLD	147.00000	+		
Renfrew	DMR/BM	VE3STP	147.06000	-	CC1	
	DMR/BM	VE3STP	443.60000	+	CC1	
Richmond Hill	FM	VE3YRC	53.49000	52.49000		
	FM	VE3YRC	444.22500	+		
Rideau Ferry, Bell Tower						
	FM	VE3REX	442.20000	+		
Ridgeway	FM	VE3RAC	147.16500	+	107.2 Hz	
Roslin	FUSION	VE3SJA	147.42000			
Sarnia	FM	VE3WHO	146.95500	-		
	FM	VE3WHO	442.35000	+		
	FM	VA3SAR	444.55000	+	123.0 Hz	
Sarnia, BlueWater Health Hospi						
	FM	VE3SAR	145.37000	-	123.0 Hz	
Sarnia-Oil Springs	WX	XJV492	162.40000			
Sault Ste Marie	DMR/MARC	VE3MHL	444.45000	+	CC1	
Sault Ste. Marie	DSTAR	VA3SNR C	145.21000	-		
	FM	VE3SSM	146.94000	-	107.2 Hz	
	FM	VE3MHL	147.06000	+		
	FM	VE3SSM	442.65000	+		
Sault Ste. Marie, ON						
	DSTAR	VA3SNR C	145.21000	-		
Sault Ste.Marie	DMR/BM	VA3OTL	442.85000	+	CC1	
Scarborough	DMR/BM	VE3BRA	144.32500	-	CC1	
	DMR/BM	VE3XLX	443.38750	+	CC1	
	DSTAR	VE3VXZ C	147.54000			
	DSTAR	VE3VXZ B	443.14000	+		
	DSTAR	VE3VXZ A	1282.50000	-		
	FM	VE3CTV	145.37000	-		
	FM	VE3HJL	147.40500		100.0 Hz	
	FM	VE3RAL	224.78000	-		
	FM	VE3RTC	443.35000	+	131.8 Hz	
	FM	VA3GTU	443.75000	+	103.5 Hz	
Scotland	FM	VE3PPO	53.23000	52.23000		
	FM	VE3PPO	224.44000	-		
Shedden	DMR/BM	VE3MMX	443.66250	+	CC1	
Shelburne	FM	VE3ZAP	146.68500	-	88.5 Hz	
Simcoe	FM	VE3TCO	147.50000		131.8 Hz	
Simcoe County	DMR/MARC	VE3LSR	443.56250	+	CC1	
	DSTAR	VE3LSR C	145.19000	-		
	DSTAR	VE3LSR B	444.35000	+		
Singhampton	FM	VA3WIK	444.90000	+	156.7 Hz	
Sioux Lookout	FM	VA3SLT	147.31500	+	127.3 Hz	
	FUSION	VA3SLT	147.19500	+		
	FUSION	VA3ADI	147.31500	+		
Sioux Lookout, Sioux Mountain						
	FM	VE3YXL	146.85000	-		
Sioux Narrows	FM	VE3RSN	145.17000	-		
	FM	VE3JJA	146.58000		123.0 Hz	
	FUSION	VE3JJA	147.33000	+		
Smiths Falls	FM	VA3WDP	444.75000	+	136.5 Hz	
	FUSION	VE3RLR	447.75000	-		
Smooth Rock Falls						
	DMR/BM	VA3SRF	442.67500	+	CC3	
	FM	VA3UHY	147.36000	+		
South Frontenac	FM	VE3FRG	146.80500	-	203.5 Hz	
	FM	VE3FRG	445.13750	-	203.5 Hz	
South River	FM	VA3URU	146.97000	-	100.0 Hz	
Southampton	FM	VA3ITG	445.20000	-	103.5 Hz	
St Catharines	DSTAR	VE3NUU B	443.83750	+		
St Thomas	FM	VE3STR	147.33000	+	114.8 Hz	

Location	Mode	Call sign	Output	Input	Access	Coordinator
St Thomas	FM	VE3STR	224.78000	-	114.8 Hz	
	FM	VE3STR	443.82500	+		
St. Catharines	FUSION	VE3RNR	443.17500	+		
St. Marys	FM	VA3SMX	444.37500	+	114.8 Hz	
Stayner	DMR/BM	VE3XF	442.00000	+	CC1	
Stewartville	DSTAR	VE3BFH C	145.64000			
	DSTAR	VE3BFH B	442.00000	+		
	DSTAR	VE3BFH B	445.83000	-		
	DSTAR	VE3BFH A	1282.50000	-		
Stittsville	DSTAR	VA3HOA C	145.51000	-		
	DSTAR	VA3HOA B	443.60000	+		
	DSTAR	VA3HOA B	445.84000	+		
	DSTAR	VA3HOA A	1286.00000	-		
Stoney Creek	FM	VE3OBP	147.34000	+	131.8 Hz	
Stratford	FM	VE3RFC	145.15000	-	114.8 Hz	
	FM	VE3FCG	444.97500	+	114.8 Hz	
	FUSION	VE3AAZ	446.95000			
Stratford, Ont.CA.	DSTAR	VE3FCD C	145.65000			
Sudbury	DMR/BM	VE3GOB	444.85000	+	CC1	
	DSTAR	VA3SRG C	147.09000	+		
	FM	VE3YGR	146.92500	-	156.7 Hz	
	FM	VE3SRG	147.06000	+	100.0 Hz	
	FM	VE3RVE	147.21000	+	100.0 Hz	
	FM	VE3RKN	147.39000	+		
	FM	VE3VLY	433.80000		156.7 Hz	
	FM	VE3YGR	444.20000	+	100.0 Hz	
	FM	VE3FKR	447.00000	-	156.7 Hz	
	FUSION	VE3FKR	147.12000	+		
	FUSION	VE3VLY	433.80000			
	FUSION	VE3AC	449.80000			
Tarts / Era	DSTAR	VE3YYZ AD	1250.00000			
Tavistock	DSTAR	VE3DSL B	441.00000	+		
Thornhill	DSTAR	VE3EBX B	444.00000	+		
Thornill	DSTAR	VE3QSB B	442.00000	+		
	DSTAR	VE3QSB A	1282.50000	-		
Thorold	FM	VE3RAF	145.19000	-	107.2 Hz	
	FM	VE3NRS	147.24000	+	107.2 Hz	
	FM	VA3RFM	443.72500	+	107.2 Hz	
Thunder Bay	FM	VA3LU	145.45000	-	123.0 Hz	
	FM	VA3LU	146.82000	-	107.2 Hz	
	FM	VE3WNJ	146.94000	-	100.0 Hz	
	FM	VE3FW	147.06000	+		
	FM	VA3OJ	147.52500		123.0 Hz	
Tillsonburg	DMR/BM	VE3PPO	146.36250		CC1	
	DMR/BM	VE3WHR	443.92500	+	CC1	
	DMR/BM	VE3PPO	444.57500	+	CC1	
Timmins	DSTAR	VE3YTS C	145.67000	-		
	DSTAR	VE3TIR C	147.21000	+		
	DSTAR	VE3KKA B	443.92500	+		
	DSTAR	VE3YTS B	444.40000	+		
	FM	VE3OPO	146.61000	-	110.9 Hz	
Timmins On. Canada						
	FM	VE3AA	147.06000	+	156.7 Hz	
Tiny	FUSION	VA3KBW	147.52500			
Toledo	FM	VE3HTN	146.86500	-		
Toronto	DMR/BM	VE3XLX	146.65500	-	CC1	
	DMR/BM	VE3CYW	442.00000	+	CC1	
	DMR/BM	VA3SLU	442.14500	+	CC1	
	DMR/BM	VE3WOO	442.17500	+	CC1	
	DMR/BM	VE3YCX	442.75000	+	CC1	
	DMR/BM	VA3WIK	443.36250	+	CC4	
	DMR/BM	VE3NUS	444.28750	+	CC1	

Location	Mode	Call sign	Output	Input	Access	Coordinator
Toronto	DMR/BM	VA3DVN	444.73750	+	CC1	
	DMR/MARC	VA3XFT	441.95000	+	CC1	
	DMR/MARC	VA3XPR	442.33750	+	CC1	
	DMR/MARC	VA3RVU	444.50000	+	CC1	
	DMR/MARC	VE3CQI	444.92500	+	CC1	
	DSTAR	VA3MCU C	144.91000			
	DSTAR	VE3YYZ C	144.93000	+		
	DSTAR	VE3YYZ C	144.94000	+		
	DSTAR	VA3SLU B	442.41250	+		
	DSTAR	VE3YYZ B	442.70000	+		
	DSTAR	VE3CBC B	444.10000	+		
	DSTAR	VE3NUS B	444.28750	+		
	DSTAR	VA3DVN B	444.73750	+		
	DSTAR	VA3MCU B	446.65000	+		
	DSTAR	VE3YYZ A	1250.00000			
	DSTAR	VE3YYZ D	1250.00000			
	DSTAR	VE3YYZ A	1287.50000	-		
	FM	VA3GTU	53.35000	52.35000	103.5 Hz	
	FM	VA3ECT	53.39000	52.39000		
	FM	VE3WOO	145.11000	-	77.0 Hz	
	FM	VE3OBN	145.23000	-	103.5 Hz	
	FM	VE3YYZ	147.18000	+		
	FM	VA3WHQ	224.30000	-	103.5 Hz	
	FM	VE3KRC	224.40000	-	103.5 Hz	
	FM	VA3GTU	442.37500	+	103.5 Hz	
	FM	VE3URU	442.47500	+	103.5 Hz	
	FM	VE3CAY	442.60000	+	103.5 Hz	
	FM	VA3GTU	442.65000	+	100.0 Hz	
	FM	VA3SF-R	442.75000	+	103.5 Hz	
	FM	VA3GTU	442.97500	+	103.5 Hz	
	FM	VA3SCR	443.02500	+	103.5 Hz	
	FM	VE3YYZ	443.05000	+	156.7 Hz	
	FM	VE3SKI	443.10000	+		
	FM	VE3RAK	443.12500	+	103.5 Hz	
	FM	VE3VOP	443.32500	+	103.5 Hz	
	FM	VA3SLU	443.40000	+	103.5 Hz	
	FM	VA3BMI	444.45000	+	103.5 Hz	
	FM	VE3URU	444.47500	+	103.5 Hz	
	FM	VE3UKW	444.85000	+	136.5 Hz	
	FM	VA3NCO	444.90000	+		
	FM	VA3DHJ	444.92500	+	100.0 Hz	
	FM	VA3IHX	445.95000	-		
	FM	VE3YYZ	1250.00000			
	FM	VA3GTU	1284.00000	-	103.5 Hz	
	FUSION	VE3SKY	146.98500	-		
	FUSION	VA3NCO	444.90000	+		
	FUSION	VE3WOO/R	447.33750	-		
Toronto (Uxbridge)						
	DSTAR	VE3RPT C	145.25000	-		
	DSTAR	VE3RPT B	443.22500	+		
Toronto, 1st Canadian Pl						
	FM	VE3NIB	443.50000	+	103.5 Hz	
Toronto, Canada	DSTAR	VA3SLU C	145.53500			
Toronto, CN Tower						
	FM	VE3TWR	145.41000	-	103.5 Hz	
Toronto, First Canadian Pl						
	FM	VE3WOO	443.90000	+	127.3 Hz	
Toronto, St. James Town						
	FM	VA3XPR	462.57500	+		
Tottenham	FM	VE3VGA	1285.00000	-		
Tweed	FM	VE3RNU	145.37000	-		
Unionville	FM	VE3OC	444.10000	+	103.5 Hz	

Location	Mode	Call sign	Output	Input	Access	Coordinator
Upsala	FM	VE3UPP	145.47000	-		
Uxbridge	DMR/BM	VE3YRK	147.18000	747.18000	CC1	
	DSTAR	VE3RPT C	145.25000	-		
	DSTAR	VE3RPT B	443.22500	+		
	FM	VE3TFM	29.62000	-	103.5 Hz	
	FM	VE3PIC	146.67000	-	67.0 Hz	
	FM	VE3RPT	224.86000	-	103.5 Hz	
Uxbridge, Skyloft	FM	VE3SIX	53.03000	52.03000	103.5 Hz	
	FM	VE3RPT	147.06000	+	103.5 Hz	
	FM	VE3RPT	442.10000	+	103.5 Hz	
	FM	VE3RPT	1286.00000	-	103.5 Hz	
Val Albert	FM	VA3NKP-R	146.93000	-		
Val Caron	FUSION	VE3KWN	447.50000	-		
Vinemount	FM	VE3VSC	444.65000	+	131.8 Hz	
	FM	VE3VSC	1283.50000	-	131.8 Hz	
Walker Lk Huntsville						
	FM	VE3KR	446.55000	-	103.5 Hz	
Wallaceburg	DMR/BM	VE3FDW	146.90000	-	CC7	
	DMR/BM	VE3FDW	444.90000	+	CC7	
	DMR/MARC	VA3YFU	147.27000	+	CC5	
	FM	VE3OEN	446.10000	-		
Wasaga Beach	DSTAR	VE3UHF B	444.82500	+		
Waterloo	DMR/BM	VA3KWC	443.30000	+	CC1	
	FM	VE3WFM	147.09000	+	131.8 Hz	
Weatheradio-Algonquin Park						
	WX	VEF956	162.40000			
Weatheradio-Atikokan						
	WX	VFI331	162.40000			
Weatheradio-Barry S Bay						
	WX	VFK722	162.52500			
Weatheradio-Beardmore						
	WX	XLJ892	162.47500			
Weatheradio-Belleville						
	WX	VFK720	162.42500			
Weatheradio-Britt	WX	VFJ213	162.47500			
Weatheradio-Brockville						
	WX	VFK721	162.42500			
Weatheradio-Collingwood						
	WX	XMJ316	162.47500			
Weatheradio-Fort Frances						
	WX	VDB224	162.40000			
Weatheradio-Goderich						
	WX	XLT839	162.40000			
Weatheradio-Greater Sudbury						
	WX	XLJ898	162.40000			
Weatheradio-Kawartha Lakes						
	WX	VAW217	162.40000			
Weatheradio-Kenora						
	WX	XLJ890	162.47500			
Weatheradio-Kingston						
	WX	XJV363	162.40000			
Weatheradio-Kitchener						
	WX	XMJ330	162.55000			
Weatheradio-Lavant						
	WX	VBE716	162.55000			
Weatheradio-Little Current						
	WX	XMJ375	162.47500			
Weatheradio-London						
	WX	XLN470	162.47500			
Weatheradio-Marathon						
	WX	VAT341	162.55000			

Location	Mode	Call sign	Output	Input	Access	Coordinator
Weatheradio-Montreal River						
	WX	VAT404	162.47500			
Weatheradio-Moose Creek						
	WX	VBE718	162.45000			
Weatheradio-Mount Forest						
	WX	XLN600	162.40000			
Weatheradio-Nipigon						
	WX	XLJ891	162.55000			
Weatheradio-Normandale						
	WX	VFI621	162.45000			
Weatheradio-North Bay						
	WX	XLJ893	162.47500			
Weatheradio-Orillia						
	WX	VBV562	162.40000			
Weatheradio-Ottawa-Gatineau						
	WX	VBE719	162.55000			
Weatheradio-Paisley						
	WX	XMJ320	162.55000			
Weatheradio-Pembroke						
	WX	VAV559	162.47500			
Weatheradio-Peterborough						
	WX	VEU671	162.55000			
Weatheradio-Ramore						
	WX	VDB885	162.40000			
Weatheradio-Renfrew						
	WX	VEA549	162.42500			
Weatheradio-Rosseau						
	WX	VBT629	162.55000			
Weatheradio-Sault Ste Marie						
	WX	XMJ373	162.40000			
Weatheradio-Shelburne						
	WX	VXB212	162.52500			
Weatheradio-St Catharines						
	WX	VAD320	162.47500			
Weatheradio-Thunder Bay						
	WX	XMJ374	162.47500			
Weatheradio-Timmins						
	WX	VDB886	162.47500			
Weatheradio-Toronto						
	WX	XMJ225	162.40000			
Weatheradio-Windsor						
	WX	VAZ533	162.47500			
Whitby	DMR/BM	VE3WOM	443.47500	+	CC3	
	FM	VA3UYP	224.66000	-	103.5 Hz	
	FM	VE3WOQ	444.37500	+	103.5 Hz	
Whitechurch	DMR/MARC	VE3WWD	443.07500	+	CC1	
	DSTAR	VE3WWD C	147.19500	+		
Wilberforce	FM	VE3BDJ	147.24000	+		
Winchester	FM	VA3NDC	146.97000	-	100.0 Hz	
Windsor	DMR/MARC	VE3RRR	444.30000	+	CC7	
	DMR/MARC	VE3UUU	444.40000	+	CC7	
	DSTAR	VA3WDG C	145.61000			
	DSTAR	VE3ZIN C	147.42000			
	DSTAR	VA3WDG B	445.82500	-		
	DSTAR	VA3WDG A	1282.00000	-		
	FM	VE3RRR	53.05000	52.05000	118.8 Hz	
	FM	VE3SXC	145.39000	-		
	FM	VE3EOW	145.41000	-	118.8 Hz	
	FM	VE3WHT	146.88000	-	118.8 Hz	
	FM	VE3WIN	147.00000	+	118.8 Hz	
	FM	VE3III	147.06000	+	118.8 Hz	
	FM	VA3BBB	147.39000	+	118.8 Hz	

Location	Mode	Call sign	Output	Input	Access	Coordinator
Windsor	FM	VE3OOO	224.66000	-		
	FM	VA3ARK	444.11250	+	118.8 Hz	
	FM	VE3III	444.50000	+	118.8 Hz	
	FM	VE3WIN	444.60000	+	118.8 Hz	
	FUSION	VA3ROC	145.54000			
	FUSION	VE3GQG	147.42000			
Windsor Downtown						
	DMR/MARC	VE3WIN	442.06250	+	CC7	
Wingham	DMR/BM	VA3EMT	430.87500	446.87500	CC7	
Woodstock	FM	VA3OHR	442.87500	+	131.8 Hz	
York Region	DSTAR	VE3YRK C	147.18000	+		
	DSTAR	VE3YRK B	444.51250	+		

PRINCE EDWARD ISLAND

Location	Mode	Call sign	Output	Input	Access	Coordinator
Bloomfield	FUSION	VY2JOE	147.37500	+		
Bucktown	DSTAR	W4IHS A	1297.80000			
Charlottetown	DMR/BM	VE1CRA	442.65000	+	CC1	
	FM	VE1CRA	146.67000	-		
	FM	VY2CS	147.39000	+		
	FM	VE1CRA	444.40000	+		
	FM	VY2UHF	448.35000	-		
Cornwall	DMR/MARC	VE1UHF	443.30000	+	CC1	
	FUSION	VE1AIC	147.25500	+		
	FUSION	VE1AIC	446.50000			
Glen Valley	FM	VY2SIX	53.59000	52.59000		
Glenfinnan	FM	VY2WU-L	147.57000	+		
Hazel Grove, Fredricton PEI						
	FM	VE1HI	146.94000	-	77.0 Hz	
Kensington	DMR/BM	VY2CFB	147.31500	+	CC1	
O'Leary, Aliant Cellular Tower						
	FM	VY2CFB	147.12000	+		
Weatheradio-Charlottetown						
	WX	XLM647	162.40000			
Weatheradio-O Leary						
	WX	XLK645	162.47500			
Weatheradio-Souris						
	WX	XLK644	162.40000			

QUEBEC

Location	Mode	Call sign	Output	Input	Access	Coordinator
Acton Vale	FM	VE2RBY	443.95000	+	110.9 Hz	
Albanel	FM	VA2TFL	147.37500	147.98000		
Alma	DMR/BM	VE2LPO	147.36000	+	CC12	
	DSTAR	VE2RVI B	442.65000	+		
	FM	VE2RYK	53.25000	52.25000		
	FM	VE2RKY	145.00000			
	FM	VE2RVI	146.00000	+		
	FM	VE2RCA	146.67000	-	131.8 Hz	
	FM	VE2CVT	147.00000	+		
	FM	VA2RIT	147.04500	147.65000		
	FM	VE2RVX	147.27000	+		
	FM	VE2RPJ	147.28500	147.89000		
	FM	VE2LPO	147.36000	+	123.0 Hz	
	FM	VE2RIU	449.42500	444.43000		
	FM	VA2RIU	449.62500	444.63000		
Alma, Saint-Nazaire						
	DSTAR	VE2RVI B	442.65000	+		
Amos	FUSION	VE2MBT	147.15000	+		
Anjou	FM	VA2GGR	440.44000	+		
Arthabaska	FM	VE2RBF	147.14000	+		
Baie-Comeau	FM	VA2RRB	145.23000	-		
	FM	VA2RSP	146.82000	-		
	FM	VE2RMH	146.97000	-		

Location	Mode	Call sign	Output	Input	Access	Coordinator
Baie-Comeau	FM	VA2LMH	147.04500	147.65000		
	FM	VA2RGV	147.16500	147.77000	151.4 Hz	
	FM	VE2RBC	147.30000	+		
	FM	VE2RUJ	147.39000	+	88.5 Hz	
	FM	VE2RBG	442.35000	+	131.8 Hz	
	FM	VE2RUU	442.62500	447.63000		
	FM	VE2RMH	443.85000	+		
	FM	VA2RLP	444.00000	+	123.0 Hz	
	FM	VE2RBC	447.62500	442.63000		
	FM	VE2RBD	449.60000	-		
Baie-Johan-Beetz	FM	VE2RJI	146.94000	-		
Baie-Trinite	FM	VA2RBT	145.47000	-		
Beaconsfield	FM	VE2RNC	224.60000	-	100.0 Hz	
	FM	VE2RNC	224.80000	-	100.0 Hz	
Becancour	DMR/BM	VE2RPB	442.25000	+	CC1	
	FM	VE2KKO	147.72000		110.9 Hz	
Becancour G9H2S8						
	DMR/BM	VA2YRP	146.83500	-	CC1	
Beloeil	FM	VE2RGB	147.16500	147.77000		
Blainville	DMR/MARC	VE2YUU	442.05000	+	CC1	
	DSTAR	VE2YUU C	144.00000			
	DSTAR	VE2YUU B	442.00000	+		
	DSTAR	VE2YUU B	443.55000	+		
	DSTAR	VE2YUU A	1282.50000	-		
	FM	VE2RNO	53.31000	52.31000		
	FM	VE2THE	146.82000	-	136.5 Hz	
	FM	VE2RVV	449.72500	444.73000	103.5 Hz	
	FUSION	VE2YU	146.50000			
	FUSION	VE2RZY	443.55000	+		
Bois-Franc	FM	VA2REH	145.17000	-	100.0 Hz	
Boucherville	FM	VE2MRQ	53.13000	52.31000	103.5 Hz	
	FM	VE2MRQ	145.25000	-	103.5 Hz	
	FM	VE2MRQ	449.82500	444.83000	103.5 Hz	
Brossard	FUSION	VE2CLM	442.40000	+		
Cantley	FM	VA2CMB	444.70000	+	123.0 Hz	
Cantons De Melbourne -UHF						
	DMR/MARC	VE2RHK	443.60000	+	CC1	
Cantons De Melbourne -VHF						
	DMR/MARC	VE2RHK	147.25500	-	CC1	
Cap-a-L'aigle	FM	VA2RKT	145.29000	-		
Cap-de-la-Madeleine						
	FM	VE2RBN	145.74500		136.5 Hz	
Carleton	FM	VE2RXT	147.06000	+		
Causapscal	FM	VE2RTF	145.13000	-		
Chambord	FM	VE2RVP	146.64000	-		
Chandler	FM	VE2CGR	146.85000	-		
Charlesbourg	FM	VA2UX	147.18000	+	100.0 Hz	
Charny	FM	VE2RDB	444.60000	+		
Chelsea	FM	VE2KPG	147.36000	+	203.5 Hz	
Chibougamau-Chapais						
	FM	VA2RRC	147.39000	+		
Chicoutimi	DMR/BM	VA2RFI	147.24000	+	CC7	
	DMR/BM	VE2RRY	448.12500	-	CC2	
	DMR/BM	VE2RRV	448.92500	-	CC2	
	FM	VE2RHS	145.23000	-	127.3 Hz	
	FM	VE2RMI	145.43000	-	85.4 Hz	
	FM	VE2RCI	147.07500	+	127.3 Hz	
	FM	VE2RCC	147.12000	+	127.3 Hz	
	FM	VE2RPA	147.30000	+		
	FM	VE2RKA	449.02500	444.03000		
	FM	VE2RDH	449.70000	-	100.0 Hz	
Chisasibi	DMR/MARC	VA2RJB	448.62500	-	CC7	

Location	Mode	Call sign	Output	Input	Access	Coordinator
Chute-Des-Passes						
	FM	VE2RFN	147.27000	+		
Coaticook	FM	VE2RDM	147.36000	+	118.8 Hz	
	FM	VE2RJV	449.27500	444.28000	118.8 Hz	
	FUSION	VE2RDM	147.36000	+		
Collines Poudrier	FM	VE2GPA	449.72500	444.73000	100.0 Hz	
Contrecoeur	FM	VE2CKC	145.35000	-	141.3 Hz	
Contrecouer	FM	VE2CKC	443.65000	+	141.3 Hz	
Coupe Du Ciel	FM	VE2RKJ	147.03000	+	127.3 Hz	
Covey Hill	DMR/BM	VE2REX	441.75000	+	CC1	
	DMR/MARC	VE2REX	448.52500	-	CC1	
	DSTAR	VE2REX C	145.59000	-		
	DSTAR	VA2REX B	448.32500	-		
	DSTAR	VA2REX A	1248.50000			
	DSTAR	VA2REX A	1266.30000	1246.30000		
	DSTAR	VA2REX A	1283.50000			
	DSTAR	VA2REX D	1297.37500			
	FM	VE2REX	146.68500	-	100.0 Hz	
	FM	VA2CYH	444.82500	+		
	FM	VA2REX	448.52500	-	100.0 Hz	
Cowansville	FM	VE2RCZ	447.67500	442.68000	118.8 Hz	
Crabtree	DSTAR	VA2RIU C	145.00000			
	DSTAR	VA2RIU B	446.30000	-		
	DSTAR	VA2RIU A	1283.50000	-		
Davidson Corner	FM	VA2LOJ-L	446.12500	-		
Delson	FM	VE2LHF	442.15000	+		
DMRplus Gateway						
	DMR/MARC	VA2XPR	439.81250	430.41250	CC0	
Dolbeau	FM	VE2RCD	146.70000	-		
Donnacona	FM	VE2RBJ	145.33000	-	100.0 Hz	
Dorval	FUSION	VE2WTH	147.48000			
Drummondville	DMR/BM	VA2RPO	145.61000	-	CC1	
	DSTAR	VA2XNY C	145.55000	-		
	FM	VE2ROC	53.27000	52.27000		
	FM	VA2RCQ	146.83500	146.24000	110.9 Hz	
	FM	VE2RDV	147.09000	+	110.9 Hz	
	FM	VE2RBU	442.95000	+	110.9 Hz	
	FM	VE2RDL	444.15000	449.10000	110.9 Hz	
	FUSION	VE2PYO	144.00000			
Drummondvlle	FM	VE2RBZ	444.05000	+	110.9 Hz	
Dstar-rptr(B)	DSTAR	VE3AZX B	445.85000	-		
Eastmain	FM	VE2LRE	147.53500		85.4 Hz	
	FM	VE2LRE	147.55500		85.4 Hz	
Eastman, Mont-Orford						
	FM	VA2CAV	448.37500	-	123.0 Hz	
Faribault	FM	VA2RSJ	147.09000	+		
Farnham	FM	VE2RDH	224.84000	-	103.5 Hz	
Fermont	FM	VE2RGA	146.82000	-		
Fire Lake	FM	VE2RGF	147.06000	+		
Fleurimont	FM	VA2LGX	146.86500	146.30000		
	FM	VE2RLX	442.92500	447.93000		
Forestville	FM	VE2RLI	146.70000	-	151.4 Hz	
	FM	VE2RFG	146.91000	-	151.4 Hz	
	FM	VE2REE	147.25500	+	100.0 Hz	
	FM	VE2REJ	147.28500	147.89000		
Frampton	FM	VA2III	145.31000	-		
Gagnon	FM	VE2RGH	146.69000	-		
Gaspe	FM	VE2OK-L	146.55000	+		
	FM	VE2RLE	146.86500	146.30000		
	FM	VE2RLE	146.89500	146.30000		
Gatineau	DMR/BM	VE2RAO	441.95000	+	CC1	
	DMR/BM	VE2REH	442.65000	+	CC1	

Location	Mode	Call sign	Output	Input	Access	Coordinator
Gatineau	DSTAR	VE2REG C	147.18000	+		
	DSTAR	VE2REG B	442.65000	+		
	FM	VE2REH	29.68000	-	173.8 Hz	
	FM	VE2REH	53.11000	52.11000	110.9 Hz	
	FM	VA2XAD	145.35000	-	162.2 Hz	
	FM	VE2REH	145.49000	-	110.9 Hz	
	FM	VE2REH	224.76000	-	110.9 Hz	
	FM	VA2XAD	444.90000	+	162.2 Hz	
	FM	VE2NTM	445.17500	-	110.9 Hz	
Gore	DMR/BM	VE2REO	446.87500	-	CC1	
Granby	FM	VE2RVM	146.79000	-		
	FM	VE2RTA	147.18000	+	118.8 Hz	
	FM	VE2RGJ	448.62500	443.63000	118.8 Hz	
Granby, Mont Yamaska						
	FM	VA2RMY	442.35000	+	103.5 Hz	
Grand Fonds, Mont-Noir						
	FM	VE2CTT	147.00000	+		
Grand-mere	DMR/MARC	VE2KBS	438.33500	-	CC1	
	DSTAR	VE2SKG C	145.55000			
	DSTAR	VE2SKG B	442.00000	+		
	DSTAR	VE2SKG A	1282.50000	-		
	FM	VA2RTI	53.11000	52.11000	141.3 Hz	
	FM	VE2RLM	449.52500	444.53000		
	FM	VE2RGM	449.67500	444.68000	110.9 Hz	
	FM	VA2RTI	449.92500	444.93000		
	FM	VA2RDX	449.97500	-	110.9 Hz	
Grand-Mere, Mauricie						
	FM	VE2RGM	146.92500	146.33000	110.9 Hz	
Grande-Anse	FM	VE2RLT	147.00000	+		
Grande-Rivi	FM	VE2RDI	145.17000	-		
Grenville	FM	VE2RCS	53.01000	52.01000		
	FM	VE2RCS	146.71500	-	123.0 Hz	
Grnade-Riviere	FM	VE2RBM	146.73000	-		
Grosses-Roches	FM	VA2RLJ	145.37000	-		
Hatley	DMR/MARC	VE2RWJ	449.95000	-	CC1	
Havelock	DMR/MARC	VA2CYH	443.52500	+	CC1	
	DMR/MARC	VE2OCZ	449.95000	-	CC1	
	FUSION	VA2CLM	449.07500	-		
	FUSION	VA2SPB	449.72500	-		
Havre-Saint-Pierre						
	FM	VE2TIO	145.49000	-		
	FM	VE2RFD	146.97000	-		
Henrysburg	FM	VA2IPX-L	440.00000	+		
Herbertville	FM	VE2RCV	146.79000	-	127.3 Hz	
Hull	FM	VE2CRA	443.30000	+	100.0 Hz	
Iberville	FM	VE2RJE	449.75000	-	103.5 Hz	
Joliette	FM	VE2RHO	147.03000	+	103.5 Hz	
	FM	VE2RLJ	147.30000	+		
	FM	VA2ATV	439.25000	910.00000		
	FM	VE2RLJ	444.62500	449.63000	103.5 Hz	
	FM	VE2RIA	444.80000	+	103.5 Hz	
	FM	VE2RHO	449.12500	444.13000		
Jonquiere	DMR/BM	VA2RFQ	147.15000	+	CC7	
	DMR/BM	VE2RCB	147.25500	+	CC1	
	DMR/BM	VA2RFQ	448.92500	-	CC7	
	FM	VE2REY	146.41500		100.0 Hz	
	FM	VE2VP	146.82000	-		
	FM	VE2DHC	147.06000	+		
	FM	VE2RVG	147.24000	+		
	FM	VE2RLG	147.39000	+	100.0 Hz	
	FM	VE2RNU	444.07500	+		
	FM	VE2RPA	449.00000	-		

Location	Mode	Call sign	Output	Input	Access	Coordinator
Jonquiere	FM	VE2RFL	449.10000	-		
Jonquiere-nord	DMR/BM	VA2NA	147.06000	+	CC7	
L'Aanse Saint-Jean						
	FM	VA2RUA	146.77500	-	85.4 Hz	
L'Aascension	FM	VA2RGP	147.51000			
L'anse-Saint-Jean	FM	VE2RME	449.90000	-		
L'Anse-St-Jean	FM	VE2RME	145.15000	-		
L'Avevenir	FM	VA2RHP	147.25500	147.86000	123.0 Hz	
La Baie	DMR/BM	VE2RRX	145.41000	-	CC7	
	DMR/MARC	VA2RUR	442.60000	+	CC7	
	FM	VE2RCZ	145.27000	-	127.3 Hz	
	FM	VE2RCX	146.61000	-	85.4 Hz	
	FM	VE2RCE	146.73000	-	179.9 Hz	
	FM	VE2RCX	444.95000	+		
	FM	VE2RRZ-R	448.12500	-		
La Pocatiere	FM	VE2RDJ	146.62500	146.03000	151.4 Hz	
	FM	VE2RDJ	147.36000	+	100.0 Hz	
	FM	VE2RIP	448.97500	443.98000		
La Sarre	FM	VE2RSL	146.70000	-		
La Tuque	DMR/BM	VE2RKK	146.65500	-	CC7	
	FM	VE2RTL	146.79000	-		
	FM	VA2RVD	146.83500	146.24000		
	FM	VE2RLF	146.94000	-		
Labrieville	FM	VE2ROA	147.10500	147.71000		
Lac Aux Sables	FM	VE2RSA	147.21000	+		
Lac Brassard	FM	VE2RIT	145.21000	-		
Lac Canot Mont-Valin						
	FM	VE2RGU	145.45000	-		
Lac Castor	FM	VA2RLC	145.39000	-		
	FM	VE2RUR	444.95000	+		
Lac Daran	FM	VE2RLD	145.29000	-		
	FM	VE2RLD	442.10000	447.00000		
Lac Des Commissaires						
	FM	VE2RHC	146.97000	-		
Lac Edouard	FM	VE2RCL	147.22500	147.83000		
Lac Etchemin	FM	VE2RKM	147.24000	+	100.0 Hz	
Lac Ha! Ha!	FM	VE2RCK	147.33000	+	127.3 Hz	
Lac Larouche	FM	VE2RPV	449.62500	444.63000		
Lac Larouche, Parc De La Veren						
	FM	VE2RPV	145.49000	-		
Lac Ouachishmana						
	FM	VA2RLL	147.09000	+		
Lac P	FM	VA2JAC	146.85000	-	127.3 Hz	
Lac Pail	FM	VA2ZGB	147.19500	+	103.5 Hz	
Lac Paul	FM	VA2RHS	147.69000	-	127.3 Hz	
Lac St-Arnault	FM	VA2ZGB	147.24000	+	103.5 Hz	
Lac-Castor	FM	VA2RUR	146.68500	-	85.4 Hz	
Lac-des-Commissaires						
	FM	VE2RHC	146.73000	-		
Lac-Echo	DSTAR	VA2RMP C	145.51000	-		
	DSTAR	VA2RMP B	443.55000	+		
	DSTAR	VA2RMP B	448.62500	+		
	DSTAR	VA2RMP A	1286.00000	-		
Lac-Jacques-Cartier						
	FM	VE2RPL	145.49000	-		
Lac-Sainte-Marie	FM	VE2REH	53.21000	52.21000	136.5 Hz	
	FM	VE2REH	146.61000	-	110.9 Hz	
Lachute	FM	VE2RCS	224.58000	-		
	FM	VE2RCS	443.85000	+	123.0 Hz	
LAnge-Gardien	DMR/BM	VE2REH	442.55000	+	CC1	
Laterriere	FM	VE2RGT	146.76000	-	85.4 Hz	
Lauzon	FM	VE2RYC	145.11000	-	100.0 Hz	

Location	Mode	Call sign	Output	Input	Access	Coordinator
Laval	DMR/BM	VA2YYQ	433.82500		CC1	
	DMR/BM	VE2RVL	443.10000	+	CC1	
	DMR/BM	VE2RVL	447.42500	-	CC1	
	DSTAR	VE2CSA B	449.97500	-		
	FM	VA2RTO	146.76000	146.19000		
	FM	VE2REZ	442.90000	+	103.5 Hz	
	FM	VE2JKA	448.17500	443.18000	107.2 Hz	
	FM	VE2CSA	449.97500	-	74.4 Hz	
Lavenir	DMR/MARC	VA2RHP	443.75000	+	CC1	
Le Bic	FM	VE2BQA	147.19500	147.80000		
Le Gardeur	FM	VE2CZX	442.30000	+	103.5 Hz	
Les Coteaux	FM	VA2BDL	443.35000	+	103.5 Hz	
Les Escoumins	FM	VE2REB	146.67000	-		
Les M	FM	VE2RNM	147.27000	+		
Levis-Lauzon	FM	VE2RCT	147.15000	+	100.0 Hz	
Longueuil	DSTAR	VE2QE C	147.54000			
	DSTAR	VE2QE B	446.25000	-		
	DSTAR	VE2QE A	1241.00000	1261.00000		
	FM	VE2RSM	145.39000	-	103.5 Hz	
	FM	VE2RVC	146.73000	-	100.0 Hz	
	FM	VE2RXN	146.83500	146.24000	100.0 Hz	
	FM	VE2RSM	445.22500	-		
Longueuil, Hospital Pierre-Bou						
	FM	VE2HPB	442.40000	+	103.5 Hz	
Maliotenam	FM	VA2RUM	147.18000	+	104.5 Hz	
Mascouche	FM	VE2RHL	147.34500	147.95000	103.5 Hz	
	FM	VE2RHL	443.80000	+	141.3 Hz	
Maskinonge	DMR/BM	VE2RRJ	442.20000	+	CC3	
	FM	VA2MLP	147.09000	+		
Matagami	FM	VE2RBO	146.91000	-		
Matane	FM	VA2RAM-R	146.88000	-		
	FM	VE2RAS	147.12000	+		
Mercier	FM	VE2RTF	442.10000	447.00000		
	FM	VE2RTS	444.50000	+		
Mille-Isles	FM	VA2RJZ	447.72500	-	103.5 Hz	
Milles-Isles	DMR/MARC	VA2RDG	443.12500	+	CC1	
Mont Rougemont	FM	VE2RAW	144.39000			
	FM	VE2RAW	444.32500	-	103.5 Hz	
	FM	VA2RDG	444.90000	+	107.2 Hz	
Mont Saint-Bruno	FM	VE2RST	449.10000	-		
Mont St-Gregoire	DSTAR	VA2RKA C	145.53000	-		
	DSTAR	VA2RKA B	446.15000	-		
	DSTAR	VA2RKA A	1266.20000	1246.20000		
	FM	VE2RKL	147.39000	+	100.0 Hz	
Mont Ste-Marie	FM	VA2REH	146.61000	-	110.9 Hz	
Mont Sutton	FM	VE2RTC	442.20000	447.50000		
Mont Tremblant	FM	VE2RNF	145.43000	-	136.5 Hz	
Mont Victor Trembley						
	FM	VE2RTV	147.34500	147.95000		
Mont Yamaska	FM	VA2WDH	449.85000	-	100.0 Hz	
Mont-Apica	FM	VE2RHX	145.35000	-		
	FM	VE2RCP	146.91000	-	127.3 Hz	
Mont-Ate-Anne	FM	VE2RAA	447.37500	442.38000	110.9 Hz	
Mont-Belair	FM	VE2OM	146.00000	+	100.0 Hz	
Mont-Carmel	FM	VE2RIR	447.07500	442.08000	110.9 Hz	
	FM	VA2RES	447.67500	-	100.0 Hz	
Mont-Cosmos	FM	VA2III	449.87500	444.88000	156.7 Hz	
Mont-Fournier	FM	VE2RMQ	147.27000	+		
Mont-gladys	FM	VE2RMG	442.40000	+		
Mont-Laurier	DMR/BM	VE2REH	444.15000	+	CC1	
	FM	VE2REH	147.10500	+	131.8 Hz	

Location	Mode	Call sign	Output	Input	Access	Coordinator
Mont-Laurier, Mont Sir Wilfrid						
	FM	VE2RMC	146.97000	-		
Mont-Laurier, Montagne Du Diab						
	FM	VE2RMC	444.62500	449.63000		
Mont-ONeil	DSTAR	VE2RMF A	1283.00000	1263.00000		
	FM	VE2RMF	147.39000	+		
Mont-Orford	DMR/MARC	VA2CAV	443.25000	+	CC11	
	DSTAR	VE2RTO B	442.00000	+		
	DSTAR	VE2RTO A	1266.10000	1246.10000		
	DSTAR	VE2RTO D	1297.07500			
	FM	VE2RTO	145.27000	-	103.5 Hz	
Mont-Saint-Grego	DSTAR	VE2RVR B	444.20000	+		
Mont-Saint-Gregoire						
	DSTAR	VA2RKA C	145.53000	-		
	DSTAR	VA2RKA B	446.15000	-		
	DSTAR	VE2RVR A	1247.00000			
	DSTAR	VA2RKA D	1248.00000			
	DSTAR	VA2RKA A	1286.00000	-		
	FM	VE2RKL	145.51000			
	FM	VE2RKL	147.39000	+	100.0 Hz	
	FM	VE2RKL	444.00000	+		
Mont-Saint-Hilaire	FM	VE2RMR	147.19500	+	103.5 Hz	
Mont-Sainte-Anne	FM	VE2RAA	146.82000	-	100.0 Hz	
Mont-Sainte-Marguerite						
	FM	VE2LRE	146.85000	-		
Mont-Tanguay - Dixville						
	DMR/MARC	VE2RWE	448.12500	-	CC1	
Mont-Valin	FM	VE2RES	146.88000	-		
Mont-Wright	FM	VE2RGW	145.13000	-	77.0 Hz	
Mont-Yamaska - UHF						
	DMR/MARC	VE2RAU	444.52500	+	CC1	
Mont-Yamaska - VHF						
	DMR/MARC	VE2RAU	146.77500	-	CC1	
Montmagny	FM	VE2RAB	146.97000	-		
Montreal	DMR/BM	VA2RXO	927.18750	902.18750	CC1	
	DMR/MARC	VE2RJN	442.80000	+	CC1	
	DMR/MARC	VE2SUS	443.42500	+	CC1	
	DMR/MARC	VE2RCM	447.62500	-	CC1	
	DMR/MARC	VA2RMP	448.62500	-	CC1	
	DSTAR	VA2RKA C	144.91000	+		
	DSTAR	VE2RIO C	144.95000	-		
	DSTAR	VE2RHH C	147.54000			
	DSTAR	VE2VPS B	440.00000	+		
	DSTAR	VE2PUK B	443.81250	+		
	DSTAR	VE2MRC B	448.47500	-		
	DSTAR	VA2RMP B	448.62500	-		
	DSTAR	VE2RIO B	449.92500	-		
	DSTAR	VE2VPS A	1240.00000	1260.00000		
	DSTAR	VE2RHH A	1247.00000	+		
	DSTAR	VE2RIO A	1248.00000			
	DSTAR	VE2RIO A	1266.40000	1246.40000		
	DSTAR	VE2RIO A	1283.00000	-		
	DSTAR	VE2RIO D	1297.47500			
	FM	VE2PSL	146.67000	-	103.5 Hz	
	FM	VE2RMP	146.76000	-	103.5 Hz	
	FM	VE2BG	147.06000	+		
	FM	VE2RED	147.27000	+	103.5 Hz	
	FM	VA2OZ	147.37500	147.98000	107.2 Hz	
	FM	VE2RXM	442.25000	+	141.3 Hz	
	FM	VE2MRC	442.45000	+	103.5 Hz	
	FM	VE2RNO	442.60000	+	103.5 Hz	
	FM	VE2ETS	442.65000	+	103.5 Hz	

Location	Mode	Call sign	Output	Input	Access	Coordinator
Montreal	FM	VE2JGA	442.80000	+		
	FM	VE2RVL	443.10000	+	141.3 Hz	
	FM	VA2KWG	443.20000	+	127.3 Hz	
	FM	VA2KWG	444.05000	+	127.3 Hz	
	FM	K3SL/VE2	444.15000	+	103.5 Hz	
	FM	VE2RVH	444.25000	+	88.5 Hz	
	FM	VE2REM	444.40000	+		
	FM	VE2REH	444.60000	+	114.8 Hz	
	FM	VE2RJX	447.02500	442.03000	103.5 Hz	
	FM	VA2RTO	447.37500	442.38000	107.2 Hz	
	FM	VE2TLM	447.77500	-	141.3 Hz	
	FM	VA2RJX	447.97500	442.98000	103.5 Hz	
	FM	VA2US	448.17500	443.18000	107.2 Hz	
	FM	VA2CME	448.72500	443.73000	103.5 Hz	
	FM	VE2AIF	449.30000	-		
	FM	VE2RGN	449.42500	444.43000	103.5 Hz	
	FM	VE2WM	449.47500	444.48000		
	FM	VE2TLM	449.77500	444.78000	103.5 Hz	
	FM	VE2RJS	449.97500	444.98000	77.0 Hz	
	FUSION	VE2RMP	146.76000	-		
	FUSION	VA2AIZ	433.22500			
	FUSION	VE2MRC	442.45000	+		
	FUSION	VE2RXM	443.27500			
	FUSION	VA2AIZ	445.56250			
Montreal West	DSTAR	VE1FKB B	442.25000	+		
Montreal, Ecole Polytechnique						
	FM	VE2RHH	224.90000	-	100.0 Hz	
Montreal, Mont-Royal						
	FM	VE2RWI	146.91000	-	88.5 Hz	
	FM	VE2RVL	147.07500	+	103.5 Hz	
	FM	VE2RWI	443.05000	+	141.3 Hz	
Montreal, Pineridge						
	FM	VE2RMP	146.76000	-	103.5 Hz	
Montreal-Nord	FM	VE2RPT	448.65000	-		
Montreal-PVM	DMR/MARC	VA2OZ	442.37500	+	CC1	
Mount Rigaud	FM	VE2RM	224.98000	-		
Mt Rougemont	DSTAR	VE2RIO AD	1297.47500			
Mt-Oorford	FM	VE2DCR	446.50000	-	71.9 Hz	
Mt-Shefford	FM	VE2RWQ	443.00000	+		
Mt-St-Gregoire	DSTAR	VA2RKA AD	1248.00000			
	DSTAR	VA2RKA A	1286.00000	-		
New Richmond	FM	VE2RPG	147.00000	+		
	FM	VE2RPG	147.18000	+		
Notre Dame De L'ile Perrot						
	FM	VE2USL	443.50000	+	97.4 Hz	
Notre-Dame-d-Mont-Carmel						
	FM	VA2LX	145.10000	-	110.9 Hz	
Old Chelsea, Camp Fortune						
	FM	VE2CRA	146.94000	-	100.0 Hz	
Orford	FUSION	VA2RWL-RPT	449.25000	-		
Ottawa/gatineau	DMR/BM	VE2CRA	444.44000	+	CC1	
Parc Chibougamau						
	FM	VE2RTG	147.03000	+		
Parc De Chibougamau						
	FM	VA2RRH	145.11000	-		
Parc Des Laurentides						
	FM	VE2RPE	147.15000	+	127.3 Hz	
Parc Des Laurentides, Mont-Gla						
	FM	VE2RMG	147.09000	+		
Parent	FM	VE2RPC	145.19000	-		
	FM	VE2LVJ	444.00000	+		

Location	Mode	Call sign	Output	Input	Access	Coordinator
Passes Dangereuses						
	FM	VA2ADW	145.25000	-		
Perce	FM	VE2RLC	146.79000	-		
Petite-Rivi	FM	VA2RAT	147.39000	+		
Pierrefonds	DMR/MARC	VE2JKA	448.37500	-	CC1	
	FM	VE2RKE	145.49000	-		
Pohenegamook	FM	VE2CKN-L	145.17000	-		
Pointe-Claire	DMR/MARC	VE2ROR	443.17500	+	CC1	
	FM	VE2RHI	448.65000	-		
Princeville	DMR/MARC	VE2TXD	443.45000	+	CC2	
	FM	VA2AD-L	146.58000	+		
	FUSION	VA2UF	442.45000	+		
Projet-Laplante	FM	VE2DPF-L	53.21000	52.21000		
	FM	VE2RBV-R	147.21000	+		
Provincewide	DMR/MARC	VA2XPR	439.37500	431.77500	CC1	
Quebec	DMR/BM	VA2LF	442.00000	+	CC1	
	DMR/BM	VE2RVJ	442.66250	+	CC1	
	DMR/BM	VE2XCX	442.80000	+	CC1	
	DMR/BM	VE2RRS	447.65000	-	CC1	
	DMR/BM	VA2RSL	448.12500	-	CC7	
	DMR/BM	VE2RIX	448.62500	-	CC7	
	DMR/BM	VE2REO	449.97500	-	CC1	
	DMR/MARC	VE2UCD	448.62500	-	CC7	
	DSTAR	VE2RQT C	144.95000	-		
	DSTAR	VE2RQT B	449.92500	-		
	DSTAR	VE2RMF A	1243.00000			
	DSTAR	VE2RMF D	1243.00000			
	DSTAR	VE2RMF A	1283.00000	1263.00000		
	FM	VE2RXD	144.81000	+		
	FM	VE2RHT	145.17000	-	100.0 Hz	
QuÃ©bec	FM	VA2HMC-R	145.47000	-		
Quebec	FM	VE2RQR	146.61000	-	100.0 Hz	
	FM	VE3CRA	146.94000	-	100.0 Hz	
	FM	VE2RUK	147.01500	147.62000		
	FM	VA2PRC	147.10500	+	100.0 Hz	
	FM	VE2RXD	441.17000	+		
	FM	VE2CWT	442.75000	+		
	FM	VE2RHD	444.10000	+		
	FM	VE2REA	444.50000	+	100.0 Hz	
	FM	VE2YUD	446.50000			
	FUSION	VE2TBQ	146.58000			
	FUSION	VE2RFU	147.12000	+		
	FUSION	VE2FU	147.55500			
	FUSION	VE2FTA	433.42500			
	FUSION	VE2CWT	442.75000	+		
	FUSION	VE2MSW	446.15000			
	FUSION	VE2YUD	446.50000			
Quebec Centre Ville, Hotel Des						
	FM	VE2RRS	145.35000	-	85.4 Hz	
Quebec City	DSTAR	VE2RQT C	144.95000	-		
	DSTAR	VE2RQT B	449.92500	-		
	FM	VE2RAX	146.79000	-	100.0 Hz	
	FM	VE2RUR	147.01500	147.62000	100.0 Hz	
	FM	VA2SHO	147.10500	147.71000	100.0 Hz	
	FM	VE2RCQ	147.30000	+	100.0 Hz	
	FM	VE2RXR	444.30000	+		
	FM	VE2RTB	444.50000	+	100.0 Hz	
	FM	VA2MD	445.10000	-	100.0 Hz	
Quebec City, CEGEP Limoilou						
	FM	VE2RQE	147.25500	+	100.0 Hz	
Quebec City, Mont-Belair						
	FM	VA2TEL	147.07500	147.68000	100.0 Hz	

Location	Mode	Call sign	Output	Input	Access	Coordinator
Quebec City, Mont-Belair						
	FM	VE2RAJ	147.43500	147.74000		
	FM	VE2RAX	444.20000	+		
	FM	VA2TEL	444.90000	+	100.0 Hz	
Quebec City, Parc Des Laurenti						
	FM	VE2RMG	442.37500	447.38000	110.9 Hz	
	FM	VE2RMG	442.50000	+		
Quebec, Mont St-Castin						
	FM	VE2UCD	146.65500	146.06000	100.0 Hz	
Rapide Blanc	FM	VE2RRB	146.61000	-		
Repentigny	DMR/MARC	VE2MRC	448.47500	442.47500	CC1	
	DSTAR	VE2PUK B	449.82500	-		
Rigaud	DMR/MARC	VE2SXE	443.07500	+	CC1	
	FM	VA2OZ	145.21000	-	110.9 Hz	
	FM	VA2OZ	146.76000	146.19000	107.2 Hz	
	FM	VE2RM	442.65000	+	103.5 Hz	
	FM	VE2PCQ	443.45000	+	103.5 Hz	
Rigaud Mountain	DSTAR	VE2RM B	442.25000	+		
Rigaud, Mount Rigaud						
	FM	VE2RM	147.00000	+	103.5 Hz	
Rimouski	DMR/BM	VE2PDS	442.10000	+	CC5	
	DSTAR	VE2RKI C	144.95000	+		
	DSTAR	VE2RKI C	145.31000	-		
	DSTAR	VE2RKI B	442.95000	+		
	FM	VE2RNJ	145.17000	-	141.3 Hz	
	FM	VE2RKI	145.31000	-		
	FM	VE2LAM-L	146.58000	+		
	FM	VE2RWM-R	146.61000	-		
	FM	VE2RIM	147.34000	+	141.3 Hz	
	FM	VE2ROE	147.36000	+		
	FM	VE2MYC	147.55500		97.4 Hz	
	FM	VE2RWM	442.62500	447.63000	123.0 Hz	
	FUSION	VE2MYC	144.81000			
	FUSION	VE2RNI	147.55500			
	FUSION	VE2EBR	444.90000	+		
	FUSION	VA2PKK	449.90000	-		
Rimouski, College De Rimouski						
	FM	VE2RXA	147.24000	+		
Rimouski, QC, Canada						
	DSTAR	VA2BQ C	147.53500			
	DSTAR	VA2BQ B	445.85000	-		
Ripon	FM	VE2REH	53.31000	52.31000	123.0 Hz	
	FM	VE2RBH	145.41000	-	123.0 Hz	
	FM	VE2REH	147.39000	+	146.2 Hz	
Riviere-au-Tonnerre						
	FM	VE2RET	147.03000	+		
Riviere-des-Prairies						
	FM	VE2RMK	146.82000	-	103.5 Hz	
	FM	VE2FXD	448.22500	443.23000	107.2 Hz	
Riviere-du-Loup	FM	VE2RAY	147.15000	+	107.2 Hz	
	FM	VE2RYE	444.40000	+	103.5 Hz	
	FUSION	VE2GL	434.22500			
Roberval	DMR/BM	VE2RFV	147.15000	+	CC7	
	FM	VA2RRE	145.49000	-		
	FM	VA2NA	145.53000	-	100.0 Hz	
	FM	VE2RRE	146.74500	146.15000	136.5 Hz	
	FM	VE2RSF	147.01500	147.62000	136.5 Hz	
Rosemere	FM	VE2RXZ	445.15000	-		
Rougemont	DSTAR	VE2RIO C	145.53000	-		
	DSTAR	VE2RIO B	449.92500	-		
	DSTAR	VE2RIO A	1266.40000	1246.40000		
	FM	VE2RXW-R	146.70000	-		

Location	Mode	Call sign	Output	Input	Access	Coordinator
Rougemont, Mont Rougemont						
	FM	VE2RAW	145.31000	-	103.5 Hz	
Rouyn-Noranda	FM	VE2RNR	146.64000	-		
	FM	VE2RON	146.82000	-		
	FM	VE2RYN	147.09000	+		
	FM	VE2RUI	442.00000	+		
	FUSION	VA2RC	145.75000			
Roxboro	DMR/BM	VE2RRC	443.50000	+	CC1	
Saguenay	FM	VE2ADW	147.09000	+	100.0 Hz	
	FM	VA2SYD	147.16500	147.77000	127.3 Hz	
	FM	VA2RUR	444.95000	+		
	FM	VE2XEN-L	446.12500	-		
	FM	VE2XEN-R	448.02500	-		
	FM	VE2XZM-R	448.22500	-		
	FM	VA2RU	448.52500	443.53000	85.4 Hz	
Saguenay-Centre	DMR/BM	VA2RPE	147.18000	+	CC7	
Sagunay, Monts-Valin						
	FM	VE2RJZ	147.21000	+	127.3 Hz	
Saint Francois D'Assise						
	FM	VA2RDP	146.62000	-		
Saint Raymond	DMR/BM	VE2CTI	450.01220	+	CC5	
Saint-ad	FM	VE2PCQ	444.98800	449.99000		
Saint-Adolphe D'Howard						
	FM	VE2RUN	146.89500	146.30000	141.3 Hz	
Saint-Adolphe-d'Howard						
	FM	VE2RYV	146.65500	-		
Saint-Aime	FM	VE2RJO	147.13500	147.74000		
Saint-Armand	FM	VE2RSN	443.80000	+	103.5 Hz	
Saint-Calixte	DSTAR	VA2RKB C	144.91000	+		
	DSTAR	VA2RKB C	145.51000	-		
	FM	VE2RVK	53.07000	52.07000	141.3 Hz	
	FM	VE2PCQ	146.73000	-	103.5 Hz	
	FM	VE2REM	147.01500	147.62000	103.5 Hz	
	FM	VA2RLD	442.60000	+	103.5 Hz	
	FM	VA2RLD	442.72500	447.73000	103.5 Hz	
	FM	VE2RVK	443.60000	+	141.3 Hz	
	FM	VA2RLD	444.00000	+	103.5 Hz	
	FM	VE2PCQ	449.98800	444.99000		
	FM	VE2RVK	1283.60000	1263.60000	141.3 Hz	
Saint-Calixte, North Of Montre						
	FM	VA2RLD	145.19000	-	141.3 Hz	
Saint-Calixte-Nord						
	FM	VE2PCQ-R	447.12500	-		
Saint-Charles-de-Bourget						
	FM	VE2RCR	146.94000	-	127.3 Hz	
	FM	VE2RCR	444.20000	+		
Saint-Constant	FM	VA2RSC	442.10000	447.00000		
	FM	VE2APO	442.20000	+		
	FUSION	VE2BTZ	433.47500			
Saint-Damien	FM	VE2RGC	145.29000	-	103.5 Hz	
Saint-Denis-sur-Richelieu						
	FM	VE2RSO	447.12500	442.13000		
Saint-Donat	FM	VA2RIA	147.00000	+	103.5 Hz	
	FM	VE2RRA	147.09000	+	103.5 Hz	
	FM	VE2RRA	444.60000	+	103.5 Hz	
	FM	VA2RIA	444.80000	+	103.5 Hz	
Saint-Donat De Rimouski						
	FM	VE2RAC	146.73000	-	123.0 Hz	
Saint-Donat-de-Montcalm						
	FM	VA2RSD	147.37500	147.98000	141.3 Hz	
Saint-Eleuthere	FM	VE2NY	442.37500	447.38000	110.9 Hz	
	FM	VE2NY	442.62500	447.63000	123.0 Hz	

Location	Mode	Call sign	Output	Input	Access	Coordinator
Saint-Elzear De Beauce						
	FM	VE2RVD	146.76000	-	100.0 Hz	
Saint-Etienne-des-Gres						
	FM	VE2RZX	147.19000	+		
Saint-Fracois-De-Sales						
	FM	VE2RRR	145.47000	-		
Saint-Frederic	FM	VE2LFO	147.24000	+	136.5 Hz	
Saint-Georges	FM	VE2RSG	147.28500	147.89000		
Saint-Honore	FM	VA2RCH	145.33000	-		
	FM	VA2RCH	145.39000	-		
	FM	VE2RKT	147.18000	+		
	FM	VA2RMV	147.22500	147.83000		
	FM	VA2RCH	147.48000			
	FM	VA2RCR	442.60000	+	127.3 Hz	
Saint-Hubert	FM	VA2CSA	147.30000	+		
	FM	VA2ASC	449.02500	444.03000		
Saint-Jean De Matha						
	FM	VE2RMM	145.41000	-	103.5 Hz	
Saint-Jean-de-Matha, Montagne						
	FM	VE2RHR	447.82500	442.83000	103.5 Hz	
Saint-Jean-Port-Joli						
	FM	VA2RWW	147.31500	+	100.0 Hz	
Saint-Jean-sur-Richelieu						
	DMR/BM	VA2DGR	449.22500	-	CC2	
	DSTAR	VE2RVR B	444.20000	+		
	FM	VE2RVR	442.85000	+	141.3 Hz	
Saint-Jerome	FM	VE2RVS	146.85000	-		
Saint-Jogues	FM	VE2RIN	146.82000	-		
Saint-Joseph Du Lac						
	FM	VA2RSD	145.33000	-	141.3 Hz	
Saint-Joseph-de-Beauce						
	FM	VE2RSJ	146.98500	146.39000	100.0 Hz	
	FM	VE2RSJ	445.05000	-		
Saint-Joseph-de-Sorel						
	FM	VE2CBS	446.25200	144.77000	103.5 Hz	
Saint-Joseph-du-Lac						
	FM	VE2RST	53.05000	52.05000		
	FM	VE2REL	147.31500	+		
	FM	VE2RST	449.87500	-	103.5 Hz	
Saint-Jospeh-du-Lac						
	FM	VE2RST	29.68000	-		
Saint-Laurent, College Saint-M						
	FM	VE2RVQ	439.25000	910.00000		
	FM	VE2RMS	444.70000	+	103.5 Hz	
	FM	VE2RVQ	923.25000	439.25000		
Saint-Lin-Laurentides						
	DMR/MARC	VE2BFK	444.70000	-	CC1	
	FM	VE2RFO	147.09000	+	103.5 Hz	
	FM	VE2RFO	147.36000	+	103.5 Hz	
	FM	VE2RFO	439.25000	1255.00000		
	FM	VE2RFO	444.65000	+	103.5 Hz	
Saint-Marguerite	FM	VE2RIX	53.09000	52.09000		
Saint-Michel-des-Saints						
	FM	VE2RLP-R	145.33000	-		
	FM	VE2ESN	443.85000	+	103.5 Hz	
Saint-Michel-des-Saints, Mont-						
	FM	VA2HMC	444.55000	+	103.5 Hz	
Saint-Nazaire	FM	VE2DCR	145.15000	-	136.5 Hz	
	FM	VA2RAU	145.19000	-		
	FM	VE2DCR	145.29000	-	136.5 Hz	
	FM	VE2RUB	145.37000	-	85.4 Hz	
	FM	VE2DCR	145.49000	-	136.5 Hz	

Location	Mode	Call sign	Output	Input	Access	Coordinator
Saint-Onesime	FM	VE2RAF	147.21000	+		
Saint-Pacome	FM	VE2RAK	146.70000	-		
Saint-Pascal	FM	VE2RGP	147.06000	+		
	FUSION	VE2MEL	449.57500	-		
Saint-Paul-d'Abbotsford, Mont						
	FM	VE2RMV	224.30000	-	103.5 Hz	
	FM	VE2RMV	443.30000	+	103.5 Hz	
SAINT-Philippe	FM	VA2RMS	145.37000	-	100.0 Hz	
Saint-Pie - Monteregie						
	DMR/MARC	VE2RAU	146.77500	-	CC2	
Saint-Raymond	FM	VE2RCJ	147.28500	147.89000	100.0 Hz	
Saint-Simon-les-Mines						
	FM	VE2RSG	146.64000	-		
	FM	VE2RSG	449.97500	444.98000	100.0 Hz	
Saint-Sophie D'Halifax						
	FM	VE2CTM	146.73000	-		
Saint-Therese	FM	VE2RWW	448.42500	443.43000	103.5 Hz	
Saint-Tite	FM	VE2RJA	147.04500	147.65000		
Saint-Tite-des-Caps						
	FM	VE2RTI	145.47000	-		
	FM	VA2RSL	147.04500	147.65000	100.0 Hz	
	FM	VE2RHM	147.34500	147.95000		
	FM	VA2RSL	147.37000	150.37000		
	FM	VE2RSB	447.20000	-		
SAINT-Ubalde	FM	VE2RBT	145.39000	-	100.0 Hz	
	FM	VE2RZT	442.30000	+		
Saint-Urbain	FM	VE2RAT	146.91000	-		
Sainte-Apolline-de-Patton						
	FM	VE2RIX	147.24000	+	127.3 Hz	
Sainte-Foy	FM	VE2SRC	147.12000	+		
	FM	VE2RCH	442.70000	+		
	FM	VE2RSX	444.70000	+		
	FM	VA2ROY	444.80000	+		
Sainte-Foy-Sillery-Cap-Rouge						
	FM	VE2RQR	146.61000	-	100.0 Hz	
Sainte-Marie	FM	VA2ABA-R	147.49500	+		
Sainte-Sophie D'Halifax						
	FM	VE2RNB	448.92500	443.93000		
Sainte-Vlictoire De Sorel						
	FM	VE2RBS	446.50000	144.77000	103.5 Hz	
Salaberry-de-Valleyfield						
	FM	VE2RVF	449.67500	-		
Saquenay	DSTAR	VE2RVI C	145.21000	-		
Scotstown, Mont Megantic						
	FM	VE2RJC	147.10500	147.71000	118.8 Hz	
Scott	FUSION	VE2MTK	439.95000			
Senneterre	FM	VE2RSZ	145.11000	-		
Sept-Iles	FM	VE2RDO	145.19000	-	88.5 Hz	
	FM	VE2RNN	146.64000	-	88.5 Hz	
	FM	VE2RRU	146.79000	-	88.5 Hz	
	FM	VA2RCJ	146.88000	-		
	FM	VE2RSI	146.94000	-	88.5 Hz	
Shawinigan	DMR/BM	VE2RPE	449.27500	-	CC1	
	FM	VE2REY	53.39000	52.39000	103.5 Hz	
	FM	VE2RTR-R	146.67000	-	110.0 Hz	
	FUSION	VE2KAH	146.50000			
Sherbrooke	DMR/BM	VE2RVO	442.50000	+	CC7	
	DMR/MARC	VE2RFX	440.50000	-	CC1	
	DMR/MARC	VA2RQF	442.20000	+	CC2	
	DMR/MARC	VE2BLT	442.55000	+	CC1	
	DMR/MARC	VE2RFX	447.52500	-	CC1	
	DSTAR	VE2RQF C	147.06000	+		

Location	Mode	Call sign	Output	Input	Access	Coordinator
Sherbrooke	DSTAR	VA2RNJ B	447.27500	-		
	DSTAR	VE2RQF A	1248.00000			
	DSTAR	VE2RQF A	1266.50000	1246.50000		
	DSTAR	VE2RQF D	1297.57500			
	FM	VE2RCO	29.63000	-		
	FM	VE2PAK	144.99000			
	FM	VE2RGX	145.23000	-	123.0 Hz	
	FM	VE2PAK	145.51000			
	FM	VE2PAK	145.61000			
	FM	VE2RSH	146.97000	-	118.8 Hz	
	FM	VE2RQM	444.75000	+		
Sherbrooke - Belvedere						
	DMR/MARC	VE2RHE	448.37500	-	CC7	
Sorel	DMR/BM	VE2CBS	927.40000	922.40000	CC1	
	DSTAR	VE2CST C	146.98500	-		
	DSTAR	VE2FCT B	446.25000	-		
	DSTAR	VE2CST A	1241.00000	1261.00000		
	FM	VE2FCT	146.61000	-	103.5 Hz	
	FM	VE2CBS	446.25000	-	103.5 Hz	
Sorel-Tracy	DSTAR	VE2FCT C	146.61000	-		
	DSTAR	VE2CST C	146.98500	-		
	DSTAR	VE2FCT B	446.25000	-		
	DSTAR	VE2CST A	1241.00000	1261.00000		
	DSTAR	VE2FCT A	1249.00000			
	DSTAR	VE2CST D	1299.00000			
	FUSION	VE2RBS	145.37000	-		
St Charles BorromÃƒÂ©e						
	DMR/BM	VA2RIU	442.55000	+	CC2	
St Fidele	DMR/BM	VE2RFJ	145.53000	-	CC7	
St Sauveur	DMR/BM	VE2RYM	449.97500	-	CC1	
St-Ambroise	FM	VE2HOM	144.99000			
St-Calixte	DMR/BM	VA2SIM	446.17500	-	CC1	
	FM	VA2RLD	145.43000	-	103.5 Hz	
St-Casimir	FM	VE2PMG	442.30000	+		
	FUSION	VE2PMG	442.30000	+		
St-Celestin	DMR/BM	VA2HRP	442.00000	+	CC1	
St-Felix-de-Valo	DSTAR	VA2RVB B	446.27500	-		
St-Felix-de-Valois	DMR/BM	VA2RVB	442.80000	+	CC2	
St-Hippolite	DMR/MARC	VE2RST	145.13000	-	CC1	
St-Hyacinthe	FM	VE2RBE	146.95500	146.36000		
St-j	FM	VE2RFR	145.29000	-	141.3 Hz	
	FM	VE2RFR	146.82000	-	103.5 Hz	
St-Jean De Matha	DMR/BM	VA2DWE	447.07500	-	CC2	
St-Jean-Richelieu	DMR/BM	VA2DGR1	439.77500	-	CC1	
St-Joseph Du Lac	DMR/BM	VE2RCW	442.50000	+	CC1	
St-Medard	FM	VE2RWO	147.14000	+	107.2 Hz	
St-Medard EQC	FM	VA2RXY	147.03000	+	141.3 Hz	
St-Tite	DMR/MARC	VE2RYZ	443.12500	+	CC7	
St-Ubalde	FM	VE2RPW	146.85000	-	100.0 Hz	
St-Ursule Louiseville						
	DMR/BM	VE2TOJ	449.57500	-	CC1	
St-z	FM	VA2KIK	147.36000	+	103.5 Hz	
St. Calixte	DMR/MARC	VA2RLD	443.15000	+	CC2	
St. Jerome	FM	VA2RMP	449.97500	-	74.4 Hz	
Ste Sophie D'Halifax						
	FUSION	VE2NBE	448.92500	-		
Stornoway	FUSION	VA2SQC	440.00000			
Sully	FM	VE2RXY-R	145.45000	-		
Sutton	FM	VE2RTC	146.64000	-		
Tach	FM	VE2RTX	449.02500	444.03000		
Tadossac	FM	VE2REY	444.55000	+	103.5 Hz	
Tadoussac	FM	VE2RSB	145.35000	-		

Location	Mode	Call sign	Output	Input	Access	Coordinator
Talon	FM	VE2RVR-R	147.24000	+		
Thetford Mines	FM	VE2RVA	145.13000	-	100.0 Hz	
	FM	VE2RDT	147.16500	147.77000		
	FM	VE2CVA	448.17500	443.18000		
Thetford Mines, Pontbriand						
	FM	VE2RSQ	147.37500	147.98000		
Tour-Val-Marie	FM	VE2RNI	147.07500	147.68000	141.3 Hz	
Tracy Sorel	DMR/MARC	VE2RBS	448.87500	-	CC2	
Trois Pistoles	DMR/BM	VE2RTJ	147.35000	+	CC7	
	FM	VE2SLJ-R	147.10500	+		
Trois Rivieres	DMR/BM	VA2LX	448.67500	-	CC1	
Trois-Rivieres	DMR/BM	VE2RRF	442.75000	+	CC1	
	DMR/BM	VE2NT	444.40000	+	CC1	
	DMR/BM	VA2DK	448.02500	-	CC1	
	DMR/BM	VE2TRQ	449.07500	-	CC1	
	DSTAR	VA2LX B	448.67500	-		
	DSTAR	VE2LKL B	449.17500	-		
	DSTAR	VE2LKL A	1246.00000			
	FM	VE2ROX	146.98500	146.39000	110.9 Hz	
	FM	VE2CTR	147.06000	+		
	FM	VE2LKL	147.27000	+		
	FM	VE2REY	442.50000	+	103.5 Hz	
	FM	VE2VIP	442.75000	+		
	FM	VE2RBN	448.67500	443.68000	136.5 Hz	
	FM	VE2RTZ	449.17500	444.18000	110.9 Hz	
Universite De Sherbrooke						
	FM	VE2PAK	441.14500	441.74500		
Vad-D'Irene	FM	VE2RDD	147.37500	147.98000		
Val Cartier	DMR/BM	VE2RAG	447.65000	-	CC1	
Val-Alain	DMR/MARC	VE2DXI	447.47500	-	CC1	
Val-Belair	DMR/BM	VE2RAG	442.65000	+	CC1	
	FM	VE2RGG	447.62500	442.63000		
Val-Brillant	FM	VE2ROL	147.00000	+		
Val-d'Or	FM	VE2RYL	146.76000	-	114.8 Hz	
Val-des-Monts	FM	VE2GFV	444.02500	+		
Valcartier-Village, Mont Triqu						
	FM	VE2RAG	145.45000	-		
Varennes	FM	VE2REQ	145.17000	-		
	FM	VE2REQ	448.27500	443.28000		
Variable	FM	VE2VK	447.52500	-	141.3 Hz	
Victoriarille	DSTAR	VA2RVO C	145.57000	-		
	DSTAR	VA2RVO C	147.39000	+		
	DSTAR	VA2RVO B	443.35000	+		
Victoriaville	DMR/BM	VE2RXX	444.65000	+	CC1	
	DMR/MARC	VA2RHP	447.52500	-	CC1	
	DSTAR	VA2RVO C	145.57000	-		
	FM	VE2RMD	144.81000	+	88.5 Hz	
	FM	VE2RMD	442.85000	+		
	FM	VE2RQC	443.00000	+		
	FM	VE2RQC	443.35000	+	103.5 Hz	
	FM	VE2RBF	443.50000	+		
	FM	VE2RHY	444.60000	+	110.9 Hz	
	FM	VE2RMD	448.82500	443.83000	97.4 Hz	
Ville De Saguenay, Holiday Inn						
	FM	VE2RKA	145.41000	-	100.0 Hz	
Ville-Marie	FM	VE2RTE	146.73000	-		
Waterloo	FM	VE2ESM	443.90000	+		
Weatheradio-Baie-TrinitÃ©						
	WX	VDD596	162.47500			
Weatheradio-Carleton-sur-Mer						
	WX	VDD598	162.50000			

Location	Mode	Call sign	Output	Input	Access	Coordinator
Weatheradio-Dégelis						
	WX	VDD225	162.55000			
Weatheradio-Gaspé						
	WX	VDD597	162.55000			
Weatheradio-La Tuque						
	WX	VBB499	162.47500			
Weatheradio-Longue-Pointe-de-M						
	WX	VOR669	162.40000			
Weatheradio-Magdalen Islands						
	WX	VOR668	162.55000			
Weatheradio-Mont-Fournier						
	WX	VDD464	162.40000			
Weatheradio-Mont-Tremblant						
	WX	VAF367	162.47500			
Weatheradio-Montreal						
	WX	XLM300	162.55000			
Weatheradio-Quebec						
	WX	XLM369	162.55000			
Weatheradio-Saint-Félicien						
	WX	VBS906	162.47500			
Wendake	FM	VA2RZ-L	147.57000	+		
Wentworth North	DMR/BM	VA2AE	440.00000	+	CC1	
Westmount	DMR/BM	VE2XDF	927.13750	902.13750	CC1	
	DMR/BM	VE2ZDF	927.15000	902.15000	CC1	
	DMR/BM	VE2XDF	927.16250	902.16250	CC1	
	DMR/BM	VE2XDF	927.17500	902.17500	CC1	
Zec Du Gros Brochet						
	FM	VA2ZGB	147.39000	+	103.5 Hz	
	FM	VA2ZGB	442.27500	+	103.5 Hz	

SASKATCHEWAN

Location	Mode	Call sign	Output	Input	Access	Coordinator
Arcola, Moose Mountain						
	FM	VE5MMR	146.82000	-		
Asquith	DSTAR	VE5KEV B	449.95000	-		
	FM	VE5KEV	146.70000	-	100.0 Hz	
Avonlea	FM	VE5ARG	147.06000	+		
	FM	VE5ARG	444.15000	+		
Battleford	FM	VE5BRC	147.24000	+		
Cactus Lake	FM	VE5IPL	146.91000	-		
Canora	FM	VE5RJM-R	147.30000	+		
	FM	VE5RJM	445.57500	-		
Christopher Lake	FM	VE5LAK	146.61000	-		
Davidson	FM	VE5RPD	145.19000	-		
Deschambault Lake						
	FM	VA5DES	145.30000	-		
Emma Lake	FM	VE5QU	145.35000	-		
Endeavour	FM	VA5INV	147.08000	+		
Engelfeld	FM	VE5NJR	146.73000	-		
Estevan	FM	VA5EST	147.03000	+		
	FM	VE5EST	147.18000	+		
	FM	VA5EST	224.70000	-		
	FM	VA5EST	444.80000	+		
Eyebrow	FM	VE5YMJ	147.36000	+		
Kindersley	FUSION	VE5TXP	146.50000			
La Ronge	FM	VE5LAR	146.97000	-		
Leroy	FM	VE5HVR	146.91000	-		
	FM	VE5HVR	445.57500	-		
Little Bear Lake	FM	VE5NLR	146.85000	-		
Lizard Lake	FM	VA5LLR	145.39000	-		
Lucky Lake	FM	VE5XW	146.73000	-		
Martensville	DSTAR	VE5MBX C	146.44000	-		
	DSTAR	VE5MBX B	449.50000	-		

Location	Mode	Call sign	Output	Input	Access	Coordinator
Martensville	DSTAR	VE5MBX	449.50000	-		
	FUSION	VE5MBX	446.25000			
Meadow Lake	FM	VE5MLR	147.33000	+		
Melfort	FM	VE5MFT	146.88000	-		
Melville Sk. Canada						
	FM	VE5MDM	147.00000	+		
Minatinas Hills	FM	VE5RPA	147.15000	+		
Moose Jaw	FM	VE5CI	146.94000	-		
	FM	VE5PSC	147.52500	-	100.0 Hz	
Moosomin Sk Canada						
	FM	VE5MRC	146.79000	-		
Nipawin	FM	VE5NIR	443.75000	+		
North Battleford	DSTAR	VE5RAD C	147.12000	+		
	FM	VE5BRC	146.88000	-		
Preeceville	FM	VE5SS-R	146.61000	-		
	FM	VE5SEE	147.39000	+		
	FUSION	VE5SS	147.38000	+		
Prince Albert	FM	VE5PA	147.06000	+		
Regina	FM	VE5REC	146.64000	-		
	FM	VE5WM	146.88000	-	103.5 Hz	
	FM	VE5YQR	147.12000	+	100.0 Hz	
	FM	VE5UHF	444.25000	+		
	FM	VE5EIS	446.25000	+	100.0 Hz	
	FUSION	VE5BBZ	447.25000	-		
Rocanville	FM	VE5LCM-R	146.31000	+		
Saskatoon	DMR/BM	VA5DMR	449.75000	-	CC1	
	DSTAR	VA5DR B	448.12500	-		
	FM	VA5SV	145.33000	-	100.0 Hz	
	FM	VE5SK	146.64000	-	100.0 Hz	
	FM	VE5CC	146.97000	-	100.0 Hz	
	FM	VE5HRF	147.39000	+		
	FM	VE5FUN	441.65000	+	100.0 Hz	
	FM	VE5CC	449.97500	449.97000		
	FUSION	VA5YXE	442.00000	+		
	FUSION	VE5RH	442.00000	+		
Saskatoon WIN System Affiliate						
	FM	VE5FUN	147.52500		100.0 Hz	
Snowden	FM	VE5NDR	147.09000	+		
Strasbourg, Last Mountain						
	FM	VE5AT	146.85000	-		
Swift Current	DMR/MARC	VE5DMR	443.00000	+	CC1	
	FM	VE5SCR	146.79000	-		
	FM	VE5SCC	146.88000	-		
Tisdale	FM	VE5FXR	146.70000	-		
Turtle Lake	DSTAR	VE5TLK C	145.45000	-		
	FM	VE5TLK	145.45000	-		
Unity	FM	VE5URC	147.00000	+		
Walsh Acres		VA5EIS	146.40000			
	DSTAR	VA5EIS C	144.95000	+		
Watrous	FM	VE5IM	146.70000	-		
Weatheradio-Broadview						
	WX	VCB462	162.47500			
Weatheradio-Elbow						
	WX	VBP687	162.47500			
Weatheradio-Estevan						
	WX	VAM595	162.40000			
Weatheradio-Lanigan						
	WX	VBU746	162.40000			
Weatheradio-North Battleford						
	WX	VAR552	162.47500			
Weatheradio-Prince Albert						
	WX	VAR551	162.40000			

Location	Mode	Call sign	Output	Input	Access	Coordinator
Weatheradio-Regina						
	WX	XLM537	162.55000			
Weatheradio-Regina Beach						
	WX	VBC936	162.40000			
Weatheradio-Saskatoon						
	WX	XLF322	162.55000			
Weatheradio-Stranraer						
	WX	VAR554	162.40000			
Weatheradio-Swift Current						
	WX	XLF524	162.55000			
Weatheradio-Waseca						
	WX	VDI204	162.40000			
Weatheradio-Yorkton						
	WX	VAM594	162.55000			
Weyburn	FM	VE5WEY	146.70000	-		
Wolseley	FM	VE5WRG	146.67000	-		
Yellow Creek	FM	VE5AG	147.18000	+		

YUKON TERRITORIES

Location	Mode	Call sign	Output	Input	Access	Coordinator
Carmacks	FM	VY1RMB	146.82000	-		BCARCC
Dezedeash, Klukshu Mountain						
	FM	VY1RDP	147.06000	+	100.0 Hz	
Faro	FM	VY1RRH	147.06000	+		BCARCC
Faro, Rose Hill	FM	VY1RRH	146.82000	-	100.0 Hz	
Haines Junction	FM	VY1RHJ	146.82000	-		BCARCC
	FM	VY1RPM	146.88000	-		BCARCC
Hayes Peak	FM	VY1RHP	147.06000	+		BCARCC
Keno	FM	VY1RBT	146.94000	-		BCARCC
Lindell Beach		VY1SK-L	902.28700			
Stewart Crosng	FM	VY1RFH	147.06000	+		BCARCC
Stewart Crossing, Ferry Hill						
	FM	VY1RFH	146.82000	-	100.0 Hz	
Upper Laberge	FM	VY1RM-R	147.28000	+		BCARCC
Whitehorse	DSTAR	VY1RDS C	146.84000	-		
	DSTAR	VY1RDS B	443.97500	+		
	DSTAR	VY1RDS A	1247.00000	1267.00000		
	DSTAR	VY1RDS D	1299.15000			
	FM	VY1IRL	146.88000	-	100.0 Hz	BCARCC
	FM	VY1RPT	146.94000	-		BCARCC
	FM	VY1RM	147.18000	+		BCARCC
Whitehorse, 6m Beacon						
	FM	VY1DX	50.03000	-		
Whitehorse, Haeckel Hill						
	FM	VY1IRL	444.25000	+	100.0 Hz